TREASURES OF THE BIBLE

"Scripture adapted from the *Bible in Basic English*.

ISBN: 0 - 7651 - 9186 - 5

Adapted from the French edition of:
La Bible est un Trésor
Tardy - Diffusion catéchistique - Lyon

Distibutor in the USA: SMITHMARK Publishers Inc.
115 West 18th Street, New York, NY 10011
Distributor in Canada: Prologue Inc.
1650 Bd Lionel Bertrand, Boisbriand, Québec J7H4N7

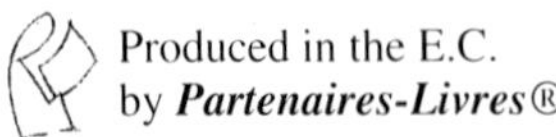
Produced in the E.C.
by ***Partenaires-Livres***®

TREASURES OF THE BIBLE

FLEURUS

Authors
The commentaries, notes and prayers were written
by team of Bible specialists
under the direction of:
Jean-Claude BRUNETTI
English translation and adaptation:
Janie BLOUGH
Linda CLEMENT
Owen LEEMING
Mark RUSSELL
Dominique PIERRE
Jacques BUCCHOLD

Artistic direction and layout:
Bruno LE SOURD and Monique BRUANT

More than 3,000 years ago, a people came out of the desert and settled in the land of Canaan. Around the fires at night, the elders unpacked the treasures of their memory.
They told stories about a certain Abraham,
the forefather of all the tribes.
This man had all his life been tuned to a mysterious divinity,
a God whose voice he had heard deep inside himself.
This God was different from the bloodthirsty idols worshipped
by the peoples in the lands around.
Abraham loyally put his trust in Him.
All through the severest hardships,
Abraham lived in an alliance, a covenant, with his God.

The elders also told how Moses in his turn heard
the message of God. Moses had gathered together the descendants of Abraham. He had delivered them from the slavery of Egypt
and led them into the Promised Land.
Moses had handed down the Ten Commandments
— kept in an ark of gold —
so that the people could live in The Covenant of God.

The most devout believers came to the Ark of the Covenant
— the chest containing The Law — to seek the enlightenment of God.
They pondered the great questions that have troubled
humankind from the beginning.
What is our purpose in the universe?
Why is there so much wickedness, so many wars and disasters?
The elders answered by telling stories
full of wisdom or reciting richly imaginative poems.
They recounted the difficulties people had in trusting God,
their refusal of The Covenant and their tendency
to rush to their doom, caring little for the life God
never stopped offering them.

The people let themselves be lulled into a humdrum form of religion.
Until along came the prophets, all outrage and reproach.

Their words stung the ears of the complacent ones.
"How can you sink into routine when you have the luck,
the privilege, of knowing the One True God,
who loves His people as parents love their children
or as a good husband loves his wife?"

Next it was the turn of the scribes. * *With their engraving tools and*
reed pens they took the colorful stories of the old sayers,
the outbursts of the prophets, and wrote them down in orderly lines
of characters on tablets and parchments.

The Story became a book, the Bible.
Still a treasurehouse, but one which had to be entered
into by praying for help from the Divine Spirit.
It alone could change the written words into cries, laughter and calls
to action, into the spoken word of God.
But this was not enough in God's eyes. He sent his Son.

Jesus came: "The Word was made flesh." He opened the book
and drew from it as from a treasure chest.
The old words spoke again.
Like jewels, they lent beauty to those who heard them.
Jesus added new gems to the Bible,
so brilliant that all the words that had gone before,
the words from olden times,
shone with new meaning.
He did not close the book. Rather he left it permanently open.

Today this treasure is in our hands, within heart's reach.
It is a treasure to be shared joyfully
with Christians and non-Christians alike.

May every reader of the words in this book
discover the gladness of hearing the Lord
and allowing His message to change her or his life.

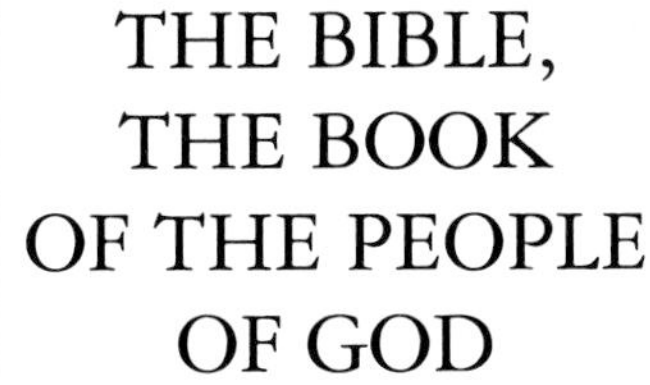

THE BIBLE, THE BOOK OF THE PEOPLE OF GOD

THE BIBLE A LIBRARY IN ITSELF

The English word "Bible" comes from a Greek word meaning "books." Opening the Bible is like walking into a library. It is full of all sorts of books — history, parables, law, codes of behavior, prayers, sermons, letters, poetry. They were written at different periods over a space of a thousand years or more. The final version of some of the books was arrived at only after several decades, or even centuries.*

THE JEWISH BIBLE

The Bible was initially the book of the people of Israel. At various times in history, these people were named Hebrews, and Jews.* Forced to move from Egypt to Babylon, across the former country of Canaan — the Promised Land, they received the revelation of a single deity, the creator of the universe, who wished to establish a covenant with all mankind.*

The memory of this revelation was recorded in various writings. Beginning in the 5th century BC these were read and explained in the synagogues. In 90 AD, a conclave of learned men was held in Jamnia.[1] It approved a list of the books written till that day as being divinely inspired.* That list made up the Jewish Bible. The Christians called this Bible the Old Testament.* Testament was another name for covenant.*

[1] Near the modern city of Tel Aviv.

THE CHRISTIAN BIBLE

The Christians added new books to the Jewish Bible, the Old Testament. These books were written during the 1st century AD. They recount the New Covenant proposed to mankind by Jesus, Son of God. Taken together, they make up the New Testament.

It has become customary to divide the Christian Bible into the Old and the New Testament. But there is a drawback. Speaking of the Old Testament or Covenant can give the impression that it is outdated and irrelevant. The fact is that this old Covenant is still very much alive. Jesus himself, in proposing a New Covenant,[1] *said that he had come not to destroy but to fulfil,*[2] *in other words, complete the Covenant applying to the people of old. It would be more appropriate to speak of the First Covenant, or First Testament. This would better convey that everything revealed before Jesus formed the source of the Gospel*[3] *and the bedrock of the Christian faith.*

THE BIBLE, A LONG TIME IN THE WRITING

The development of the Biblical texts was a long, drawn-out process. Many authors took part in it. It has been held that the books were written at the dictation of the Holy Spirit. It is not the Holy Spirit's way to use men as robots. The way of the Holy Spirit is to appeal to the hearts and minds of those who will let themselves be guided. It is to help them understand the meaning of things — birth, slavery, war, famine, plentiful harvests — so that they will discover the nature of God and his appeal to mankind.

Many authors, especially those of the Old Testament, are anonymous. The four books of 1 and 2 Samuel and 1 and 2 Kings, for example, were written by several scribes. They assembled the chronicles of the kings of Israel and other writings. Enlightened by the Holy Spirit, they sought to find a meaning to the history of the First Covenant people and tried to explain how God was at work. No wonder the writing process spread over so many years.*

[1] Luke 22:20, page 366.
[2] Matthew 5:17, page 261.
[3] Matthew 13:52, page 277.

All the authors of the Old and New Testaments, driven by the Holy Spirit, showed great respect for the message handed down by their forbears as well as wide freedom in developing it. They knew full well that the Word of God could not be boiled down to sets of ancient phrases. Their goal was to provide their contemporaries and descendants with what they saw to be a priceless treasure: the Word of God revealed through the history of His people. And, more particularly, the history of the one who was himself the Word of God, the living Word, Jesus Christ.

Turn to pages 10 and 11 to see in pictures the long and complex process by which the Bible came into being.

THE BIBLE, A BOOK FOR TODAY'S WORLD

Christians also turn to the Bible to learn what God has to say to the women and men of today. The Holy Spirit helps them to understand the deeper meaning of the texts and give life to the words contained in them. They are not just words written on paper. They are the message of the living God. The words, verses and chapters are like a road leading Christians to their meeting with God.

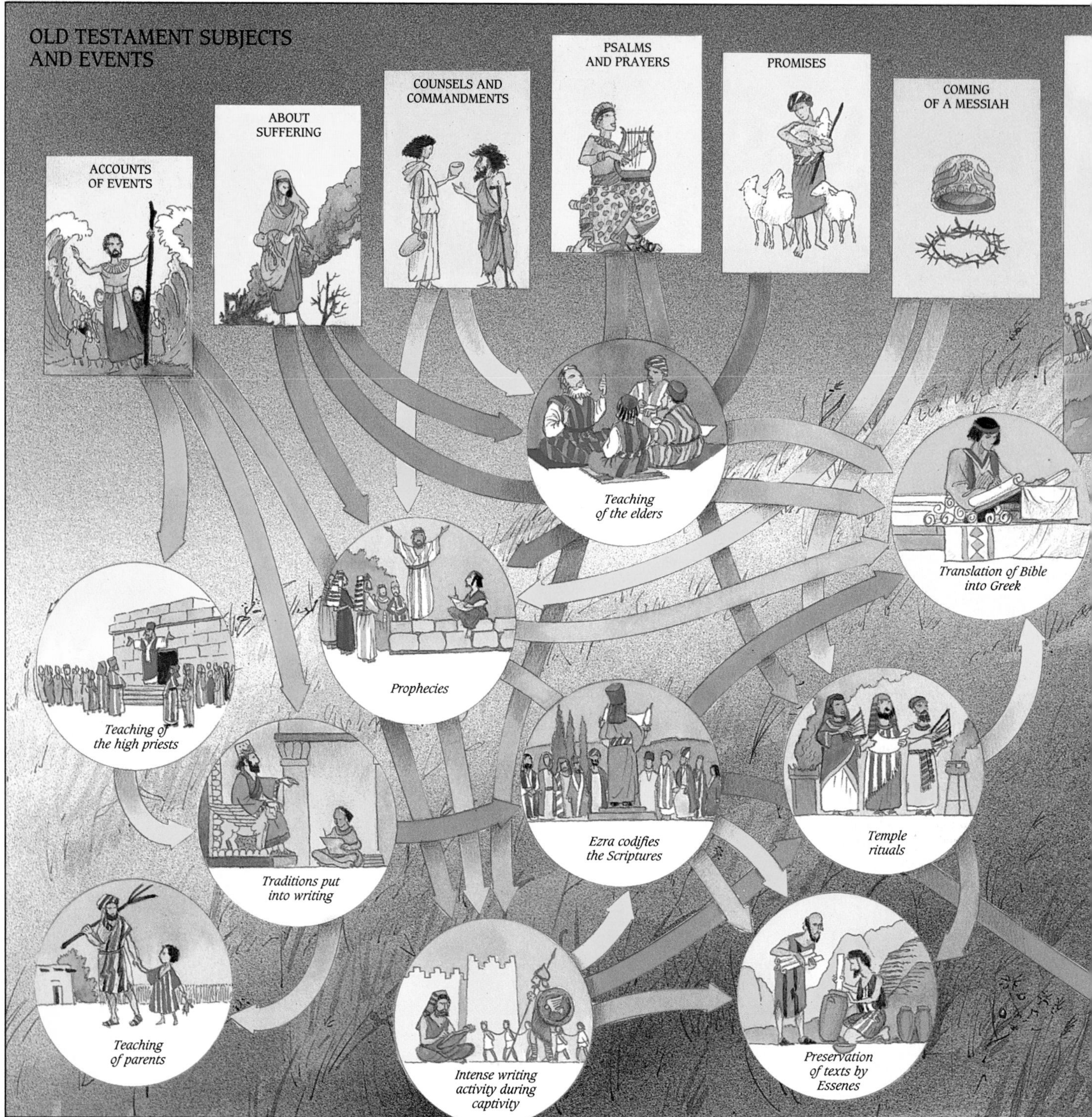

STAGES IN WRITING THE BIBLE

In the boxes along the top of the page, the illustrator shows some of the subjects that interested the writers of the Old and New Testaments. The road to the texts as we know them was long.

For example, the story of the crossing of the Red Sea was related orally, especially during pilgrimages to the Ark of the Covenant. It began to be written down during the reign of the Kings.

Parents told it to their children. The high priests exiled in Babylon wrote a new version of it. Ezra played a part in giving the narrative its final form. It was translated into Greek in the 3rd century BC.

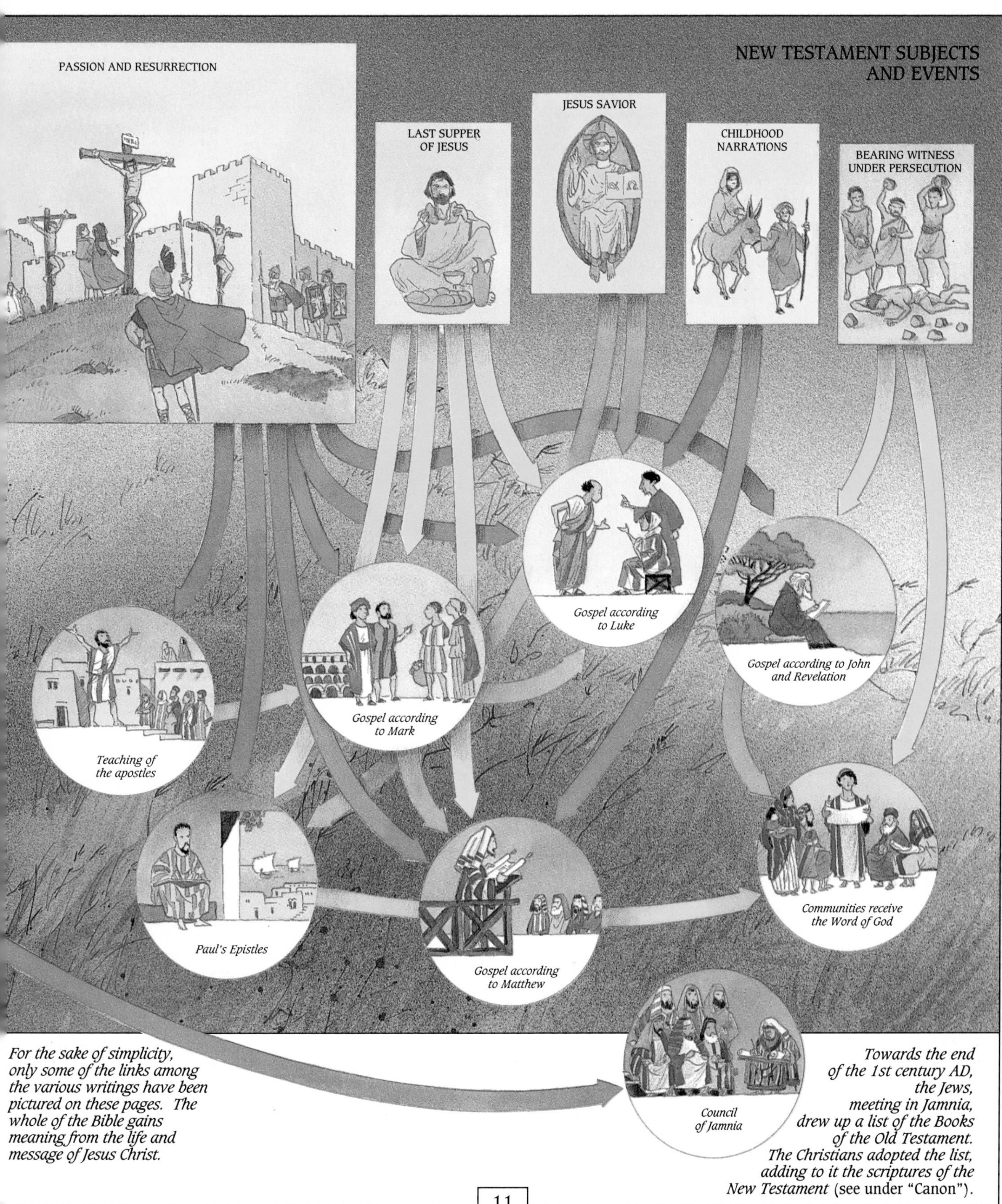

For the sake of simplicity, only some of the links among the various writings have been pictured on these pages. The whole of the Bible gains meaning from the life and message of Jesus Christ.

Towards the end of the 1st century AD, the Jews, meeting in Jamnia, drew up a list of the Books of the Old Testament. The Christians adopted the list, adding to it the scriptures of the New Testament (see under "Canon").

HOW TO USE "TREASURES OF THE BIBLE "

• *"Treasures of the Bible" offers a selection of Biblical writings. They are indexed on page 16. Some of them are also indexed according to their subject (pages 559 to 561).*

- *An adaptation of the* ***Bible in Basic English*** *has been used, as well as added passages of the Deuterocanonical books translated from the French* ***Crampon's Bible.***
- *The name of the book in the Bible from which the extracts are taken appears at the top of the page, e.g. JEREMIAH.*
- *For ease of reading, subtitles have been added. Passages in italics sum up, where necessary, the contents of the passages not quoted.*
- *The books of the Bible are divided into numbered chapters, which are themselves divided into numbered sentences or groups of sentences — called verses. A passage from the Bible is identified by naming the book, the chapter number and the verse number, in that order. For example, the passage telling the story of the Tower of Babel is Genesis 11:1-9 (see p.31).*

• *In this edition, each page of text is set inside an illustrated frame. The frame expresses the context of that part of the Bible as interpreted by artists from the present and the past. Notes on each frame may be found on pages 567 to 573.*

• *As an aid to understanding the pages of the Bible, various texts have been added in the illustrated frame:*
- *Meditations, printed on a white background like the pages of the Bible, but in italics and smaller characters. They give present meaning to the message of God.*
- *Comments, usually placed in the left of the illustrated frame. They are either introductions to a book or section of a book, or explanations of a particular passage. An index of the main comments can be found on pages 562 to 564.*
- *Notes, usually in the right of the frame, give historical and geographical information or cross-references to other passages of the Bible. Unfamiliar words are marked with an asterisk (*). They may be looked up in the glossary at the back of the book, pages 473 to 558. Most proper nouns have an entry in the glossary.*

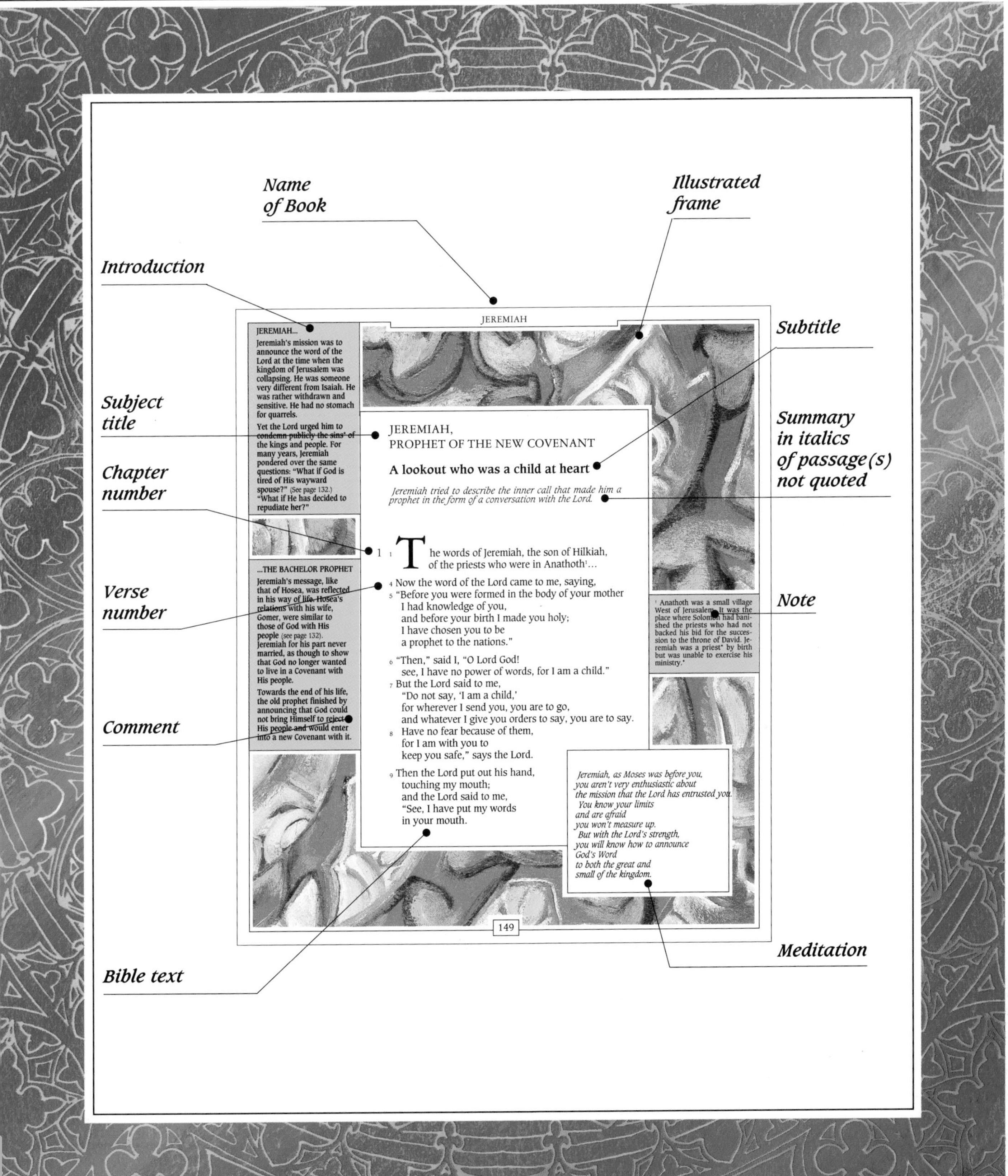

Name of Book
Illustrated frame
Introduction
Subtitle
Subject title
Summary in italics of passage(s) not quoted
Chapter number
Verse number
Note
Comment
Bible text
Meditation
JEREMIAH
JEREMIAH...
Jeremiah's mission was to announce the word of the Lord at the time when the kingdom of Jerusalem was collapsing. He was someone very different from Isaiah. He was rather withdrawn and sensitive. He had no stomach for quarrels.
Yet the Lord urged him to condemn publicly the sins* of the kings and people. For many years, Jeremiah pondered over the same questions: "What if God is tired of His wayward spouse?" (See page 132.) "What if He has decided to repudiate her?"
...THE BACHELOR PROPHET
Jeremiah's message, like that of Hosea, was reflected in his way of life. Hosea's relations with his wife, Gomer, were similar to those of God with His people (see page 132).
Jeremiah for his part never married, as though to show that God no longer wanted to live in a Covenant with His people.
Towards the end of his life, the old prophet finished by announcing that God could not bring Himself to reject His people and would enter into a new Covenant with it.
JEREMIAH,
PROPHET OF THE NEW COVENANT
A lookout who was a child at heart
Jeremiah tried to describe the inner call that made him a prophet in the form of a conversation with the Lord.
1 1 The words of Jeremiah, the son of Hilkiah,
of the priests who were in Anathoth[1]...
4 Now the word of the Lord came to me, saying,
5 "Before you were formed in the body of your mother
I had knowledge of you,
and before your birth I made you holy;
I have chosen you to be
a prophet to the nations."
6 "Then," said I, "O Lord God!
see, I have no power of words, for I am a child."
7 But the Lord said to me,
"Do not say, 'I am a child,'
for wherever I send you, you are to go,
and whatever I give you orders to say, you are to say.
8 Have no fear because of them,
for I am with you to
keep you safe," says the Lord.
9 Then the Lord put out his hand,
touching my mouth;
and the Lord said to me,
"See, I have put my words
in your mouth.
[1] Anathoth was a small village West of Jerusalem. It was the place where Solomon had banished the priests who had not backed his bid for the succession to the throne of David. Jeremiah was a priest* by birth but was unable to exercise his ministry.*
Jeremiah, as Moses was before you,
you aren't very enthusiastic about
the mission that the Lord has entrusted you.
You know your limits
and are afraid
you won't measure up.
But with the Lord's strength,
you will know how to announce
God's Word
to both the great and
small of the kingdom.
149

OLD TESTAMENT

These are the books recounting The Covenant between God and the people of Israel. Excerpts from these books are set out in the first three parts of this volume.*

1. The Torah (pages 17 to 89)

The first five books — Genesis, Exodus, Leviticus, Numbers and Deuteronomy — are the most important ones in the Jewish Bible. Jews group them under the name Torah.* In them, God reveals His wish to establish an alliance, or covenant.*

2. The Life of the People of Israel (pages 91 to 205)

This part contains narrations, the sayings of the prophets and proverbs. It covers the period stretching from the founding of the Kingdom of Israel until a few years before the birth of Jesus. The people of Israel continued their discovery of God through the events of everyday life.

3. The Prayer of the People of God (pages 207 to 227)

In this part are grouped the Psalms, which are the prayers of the people of God. Today as in the past, the Psalms bring Israel into contact with God. They have become prayers for Christians as well.

NEW TESTAMENT

These are the books recounting The "New and Everlasting" Covenant established with the whole of humanity by Jesus, Son of God. Excerpts from these Books are set out in parts four and five of this volume.*

4. The Gospels (pages 229 to 395)

This part is made up of four accounts of the life of Jesus, Son of God made man. They end with the Passion and apparitions of the risen Christ.

5. The Early Christians (pages 397 to 455)

This Part concerns some of the events that occurred after the Resurrection of Jesus. His disciples dispersed to spread word of the Gospel throughout the world. Part five contains excerpts from the Acts of the Apostles, the Epistles and Revelation.

6. Christian Prayers and Creeds (pages 457 to 471)

Some of the best-known Christian prayers, from the Catholic and the Protestant traditions and the texts called Creeds which stated the essentials of Christian belief.*

7. Glossary (pages 473 to 558)

Definitions and illustrations to explain the words followed by an asterisk (*) that appear all through the book.

The book also contains a number of double-page pictures. These are aimed at giving a fuller understanding of the Biblical writings and the life of the people of God. An index of these illustrations may be found on page 564.

INDEX OF BIBLE EXTRACTS

OLD TESTAMENT

NEW TESTAMENT

*These books belong to The Catholic Old Testament Canon but are considered as apocryphal by the Protestant Tradition. They have great historical value.

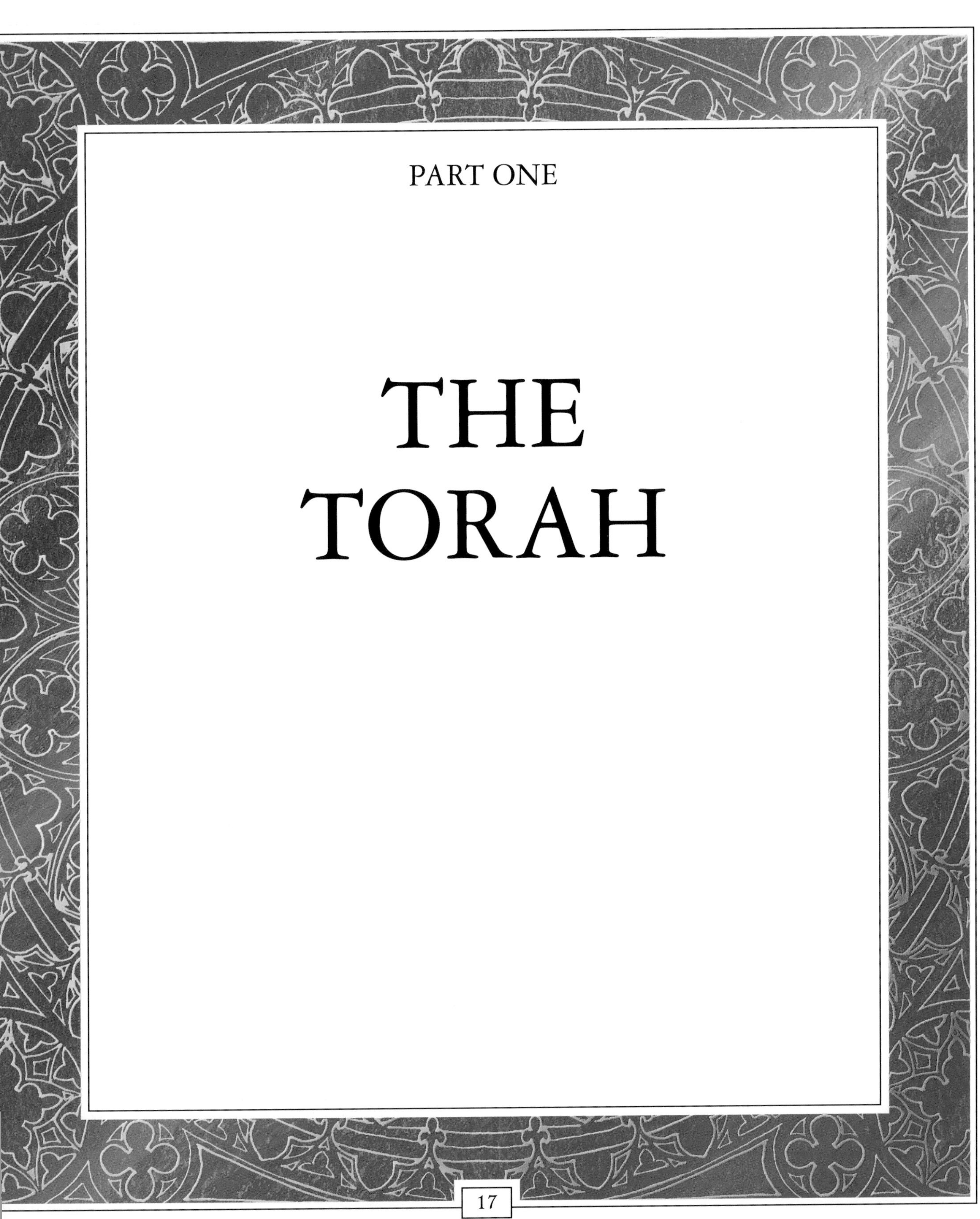

PART ONE

THE TORAH

In Jewish eyes, the most important books in the Bible are the first five: Genesis, Exodus, Leviticus, Numbers and Deuteronomy.

In Jesus' time, the Sadducees, who were the high priests* of the Temple, and their school held that the Word of God was communicated through those five books only. It is true that the creation narratives and the stories of Abraham and Moses contain the basic elements of The Covenant* willed by God for mankind.*

Genesis reveals that God created the world and everything in it in order to share His life with humankind. He chose Abraham to found a people. Through this people, God wished to make Himself known to all nations. The following books tell the story of Moses, who handed down God's Commandments* to the offspring of Abraham. They are rules of conduct meant to make mankind more humane and able to live in harmony. They were meant also to make the people more like God.*

In Hebrew,[1] the word TORAH*[2] is used to signify all the commandments, precepts and rules transmitted by God to His people. This is the name given to the five books.*

In Greek, they are called the Pentateuch, which means the "five scrolls," in reference to the parchment or papyrus on which they were presented.

Moses is held by the Scriptures to be the author of the five books and many people maintain this claim. Others think that these books were written over a long period of time by different authors, at various moments in the history of the people of God.

The Torah may be divided into three main sections:

[1] The original language of most of the Old Testament* Books. Some were written in Greek (most of the Deutero-canonical books) or Aramaic.

[2] Usually translated in English as "Law."

I

MAN AND THE WORLD

All the peoples of the Middle East have stories of how the world and, especially, the human race were created. The children of Israel had their own account of the beginning. But what interested them more than the actual creation was the question of why humans inhabited the world. Did their life, which was not always easy, have a meaning? The Israelites supplied an answer to this question which was very different from the ones believed in by the other peoples in the region. They held that the world and all it contains was the work of a single deity.*

God did not create us so as to have slaves at His beck and call. He wished to establish a loving relationship with the people created in His image. He created because He wanted to live in a covenant with humankind.*[1] *He entrusted the world to its care.*

The question then arises, "Where do natural disasters, wars, and the wickedness and envy in people's hearts come from?"

The Bible's answer is that humans have always refused to put their trust in God. They have hardened their hearts by sin. Sin, by breaking the pact between God and mankind, deforms the relations among people and the relations of people with nature.*

[1] Jesus said to his disciples, "Come ... take your inheritance, the kingdom prepared for you since the creation of the world." Matthew 25:34, page 295.

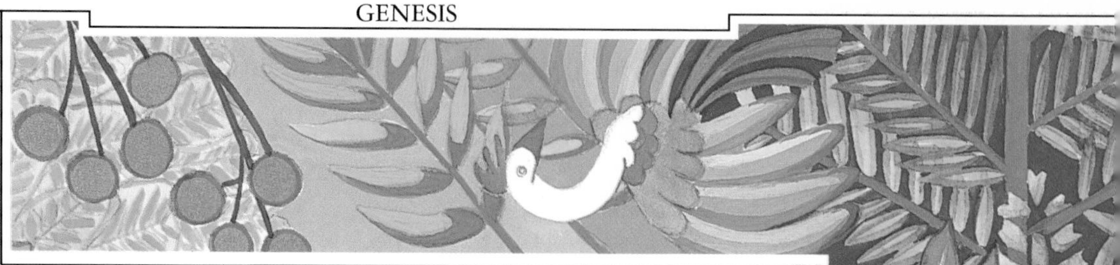

HUMANKIND, GOD'S MASTERPIECE

The Bible begins with this hymn to the seven days of God's labor of creation. It is not a scientific report. It is a deeply thought out poem stating the certainties of the children of Israel:

- All which exists comes from God.
- The stars, which some of the neighboring peoples worshipped as divinities, are no more than created objects.
- God's preferred creature, to whom He entrusts the whole of creation, is man.
- Created in the likeness of God, man is not a solitary being but a couple, a woman and a man who love each other, propagate and protect the life around them.
- Man, through his labor during six days of the week, shares in the creative work of God. On the seventh day he rests. His heart full of thanksgiving,* he takes stock of his real place in the universe. He is not the Creator, but receives the creation as a gift from God. His task is to complete it by responding ever more closely to the Creator's will.

The Poem of Creation

1 1 In the beginning, God made the heaven and the
3 earth.... | And God said, "Let there be light," and
4 there was light. | And God, looking on the light, saw that
it was good. God made a division between the light and
5 the dark, | naming the light, "Day," and the dark,
"Night." And there was evening and there was morning,
the first day.

6 And God said, "Let there be a solid arch stretching over
7 the waters, parting the waters from the waters." | And God
made the arch for a division between the waters which
were under the arch and those which were over it.[1] And it
8 was so. | God gave the arch the name of "Heaven." And
there was evening and there was morning, the second day.

9 And God said, "Let the waters under the heaven come
together in one place, and let the dry land be seen." And it
10 was so. | God gave the dry land the name of "Earth," and
the waters together in their place were named "Seas." And
God saw that it was good.

11 And God said, "Let grass come up on the earth, and
plants producing seed, and fruit trees giving fruit, in
which is their seed, after their sort." And it was so.
12-13 |....and God saw that it was good. | And there was
evening and there was morning, the third day.

14 And God said, "Let there be lights in the arch of heaven,
for a division between the day and the night, and let
them be for signs, and for marking the changes of the
15 year, and for days and for years." | ...And it was so.
16 | And God made the two great lights, the greater lights,
the greater light to be the ruler of the day, and the

[1] To see the ancient authors' view of the cosmos, go to pages 32 and 33.

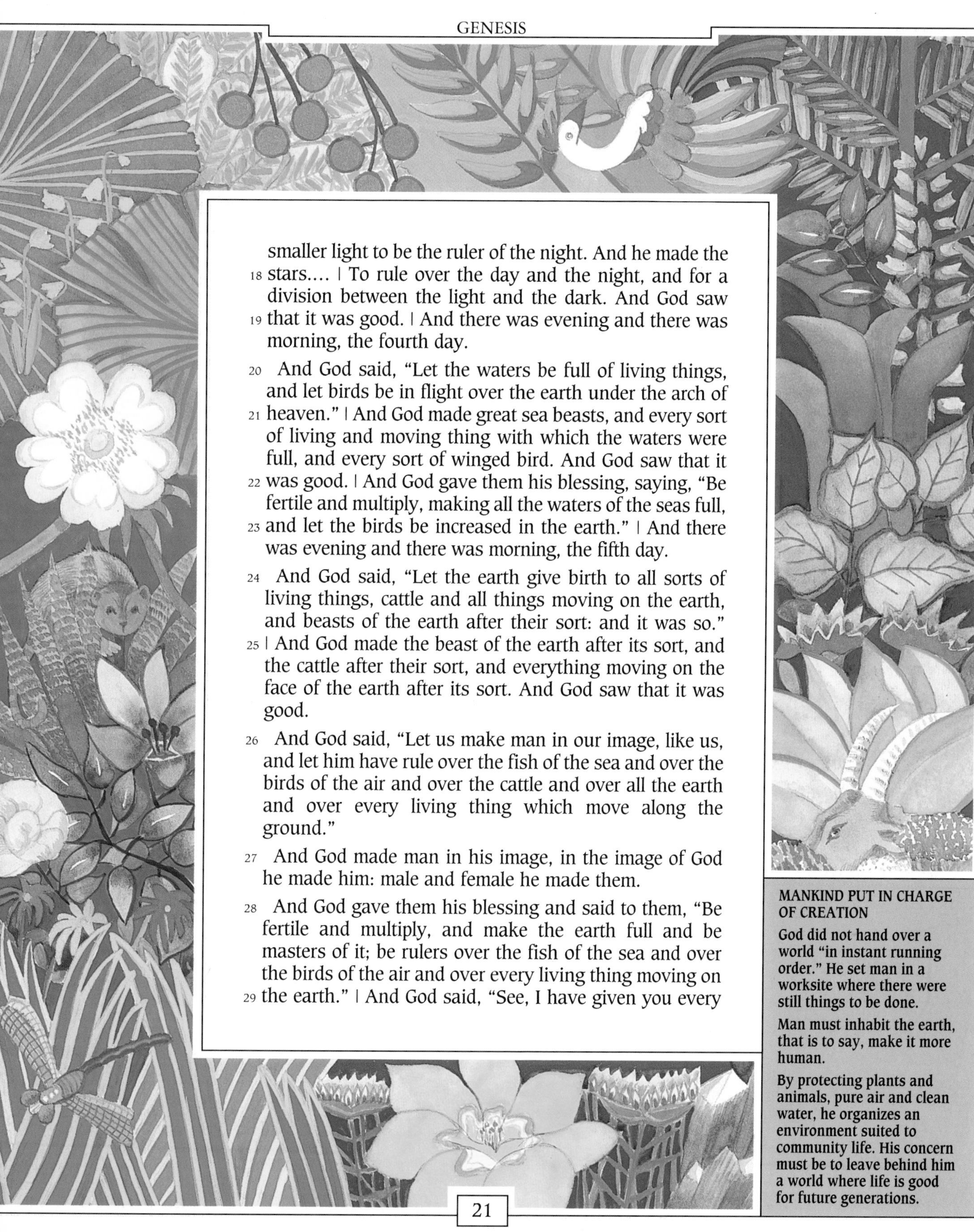

smaller light to be the ruler of the night. And he made the
18 stars.... | To rule over the day and the night, and for a
division between the light and the dark. And God saw
19 that it was good. | And there was evening and there was
morning, the fourth day.

20 And God said, "Let the waters be full of living things,
and let birds be in flight over the earth under the arch of
21 heaven." | And God made great sea beasts, and every sort
of living and moving thing with which the waters were
full, and every sort of winged bird. And God saw that it
22 was good. | And God gave them his blessing, saying, "Be
fertile and multiply, making all the waters of the seas full,
23 and let the birds be increased in the earth." | And there
was evening and there was morning, the fifth day.

24 And God said, "Let the earth give birth to all sorts of
living things, cattle and all things moving on the earth,
and beasts of the earth after their sort: and it was so."
25 | And God made the beast of the earth after its sort, and
the cattle after their sort, and everything moving on the
face of the earth after its sort. And God saw that it was
good.

26 And God said, "Let us make man in our image, like us,
and let him have rule over the fish of the sea and over the
birds of the air and over the cattle and over all the earth
and over every living thing which move along the
ground."

27 And God made man in his image, in the image of God
he made him: male and female he made them.

28 And God gave them his blessing and said to them, "Be
fertile and multiply, and make the earth full and be
masters of it; be rulers over the fish of the sea and over
the birds of the air and over every living thing moving on
29 the earth." | And God said, "See, I have given you every

MANKIND PUT IN CHARGE OF CREATION

God did not hand over a world "in instant running order." He set man in a worksite where there were still things to be done.

Man must inhabit the earth, that is to say, make it more human.

By protecting plants and animals, pure air and clean water, he organizes an environment suited to community life. His concern must be to leave behind him a world where life is good for future generations.

THE STORY OF THE GARDEN

**After the beautiful poem recounting the creation, comes the story of the Garden of Eden.
This story is very old, older even than the poem of the creation. The men told it in the evening in their encampments. The women would listen from the doorway of their tents, behind the circle of men** (see Genesis 18:10, page 41)**. Much later, this story was set down in writing.**

1 plant producing seed, on the face of all the earth, and
every tree which has fruit producing seed. They will be
30 for your food. | And to every beast of the earth and to
every bird of the air and every living thing moving on the
face of the earth I have given every green plant for food."
31 And it was so. | And God saw everything which he had
made and it was very good. And there was evening and
there was morning, the sixth day.

2 1 And the heaven and the earth and all things in them
2 were complete. | And on the seventh day God came to the
end of all his work; and on the seventh day he took his
3 rest from all the work which he had done. | God gave his
blessing to the seventh day and made it holy,[1] because on
that day he took his rest from all the work which he had
4 made and done. | These are the generations of the heaven
and the earth when they were made.

The Garden of Eden

In a beautiful tree-filled garden where two trees were especially magnificent, God fashioned a "he-person" into whom he breathed His own life. It is a way of showing that, among all His creatures, He accorded a special place to man.

But the "he-person" was lonely. So God shaped a "she-person" of the same kind as the "he-person".[2] There was joy in their meeting and speaking together. Man made in the image of God is not a "loner", but a couple.

2 5 When the Lord God made earth and heaven...
7 | the Lord God made man from the dust of the
earth, breathing into him the breath of life, and man
8 became a living soul. | And the Lord God made a garden
in the east, in Eden. There he put the man whom he had
9 made. | And out of the earth the Lord made every tree to

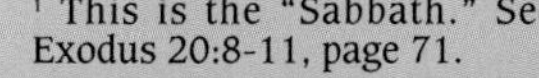

[1] This is the "Sabbath." See Exodus 20:8-11, page 71.

[2] The story, to show women's equality with men, says that the woman was made from the same human substance (the same "flesh"*) as the man. This emphasis was necessary in an age when women were often considered as being inferior to men.

:HOOSING LIFE OVER
)EATH

Vhy can man not eat the
ruit of the tree of the
:nowledge of good and evil
/ithout dying?

)oes God want to keep him in
state of ignorance?

)uite the opposite, say the
uthors of this story. God
ees man as a responsible
eing. He asks him to choose.
)oes he wish to live in a
'ovenant* with God, or does
e prefer to lead his life
lone, at the risk of
erishing?

'he double choice is
epresented metaphorically
y the two trees and their
ruit.

'o eat the fruit of the tree of
ife is choosing to live with
;od, and receive the gift of
ife.

'o eat the fruit of the tree of
:nowledge of good and evil
s, on the contrary, choosing
o do without God and decide
lone what is good and what
s evil. It is choosing
leliberately to cut loose from
he Creator, the source of life.

t is a choice of death: man
vill destroy himself.

grow, delighting the eye and good for food; and in the
middle of the garden, the tree of life and the tree of the
knowledge of good and evil.

15 And the Lord God took the man and put him in the
16 garden of Eden to do work in it and take care of it. | And
the Lord God gave the man orders, saying, "You may
17 freely eat the fruit of every tree of the garden, | but of the
fruit of the tree of the knowledge of good and evil you
may not eat. On the day when you eat it, death will
certainly come to you."

18 And the Lord God said, "It is not good for the man to be
by himself. I will make one like himself to be a helpmate
19 to him." | And from the earth the Lord God made every
beast of the field and every bird of the air, and took them
to the man to see what names he would give them.
Whatever name he gave to any living thing, that was its
name.

20-21 ...But Adam had no one like himself as a help. | And the
Lord God sent a deep sleep on the man, and took one of
the bones from his side while he was sleeping, joining up
22 the flesh again in its place. | And the bone which the Lord
God had taken from the man he made into a woman, and
23 took her to the man. | And the man said, "This is now
bone of my bone and flesh of my flesh. Let her name be
Woman because she was taken out of
Man."

24 For this reason will a man leave his
father and his mother and be joined to
his wife; and they will be one flesh.[1]

[1] See Matthew 19:5, page 285.

Lord, you have told us who you are
in the very first pages of the Bible.

When you made humanity in your likeness,
it was not to live in solitude
but as beings who find joy
in dialogue with others,
a couple living in communion.

Lord,
you are dialogue and communion.

We already have an idea
of what Jesus came to fully disclose:
the love of the Father, Son
and Holy Spirit.

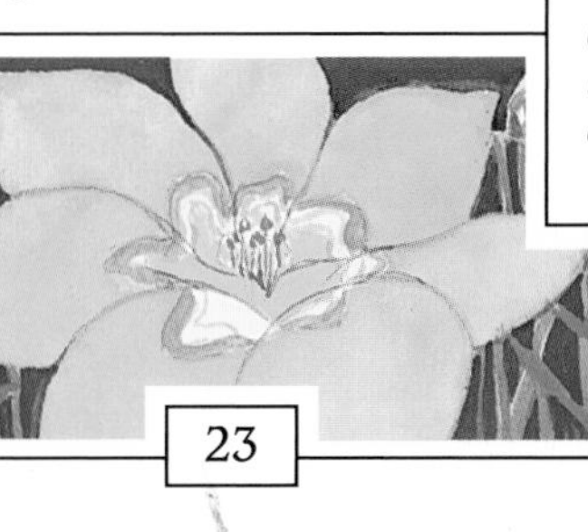

SIN

The man and the woman rejected the invitation to live with God.

They wished to "be like God," to choose independently what was right and wrong, not understanding that they would ruin their own lives .

In a flash of clear-sightedness, they saw themselves as they were: naked, vulnerable, deprived of the protection of God's love.

Sin enters the scene

3 1 Now the snake* was wiser than any beast of the
field which the Lord God had made. And he said
to the woman, "Has God truly said that you may not eat
2 the fruit of any tree in the garden?" | And the woman said,
3 "We may eat the fruit of the trees in the garden, | but of the
fruit of the tree in the middle of the garden, God has said,
'If you eat it or put your hands on it, death will come to
4 you.'" | And the snake said, "Death will not certainly come
5 to you: | for God sees that on the day when you take of its
fruit, your eyes will be open, and you will be as gods,
having knowledge of good and evil."

6 And when the woman saw that the tree was good for
food, and a delight to the eyes, and to be desired to make
one wise, she took of its fruit, and gave it to her husband.
7 | And their eyes were open and they were conscious that
they had no clothing. They made themselves coats of
leaves stitched together.

8 And there came to them the sound of the Lord God
walking in the garden in the evening wind: and the man
and his wife went to a secret place among the trees of the
9 garden, away from the eyes of the Lord God. | And the
voice of the Lord God came to the man, saying, "Where are
10 you?" | And he said, "Hearing your voice in the garden I
was full of fear, because I was without clothing: and I kept
11 myself from your eyes." | And he said, "Who gave you the
knowledge that you were unclothed? Have you eaten of
12 the fruit of the tree which I said you were not to eat?" | And
the man said, "The woman whom you gave to be with me,
13 she gave me the fruit of the tree and I ate it." | And the Lord

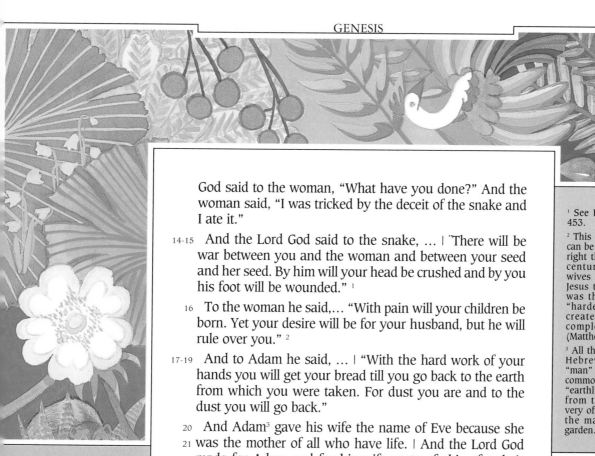

God said to the woman, "What have you done?" And the
woman said, "I was tricked by the deceit of the snake and
I ate it."

14-15 And the Lord God said to the snake, ... | "There will be
war between you and the woman and between your seed
and her seed. By him will your head be crushed and by you
his foot will be wounded." [1]

16 To the woman he said,... "With pain will your children be
born. Yet your desire will be for your husband, but he will
rule over you." [2]

17-19 And to Adam he said, ... | "With the hard work of your
hands you will get your bread till you go back to the earth
from which you were taken. For dust you are and to the
dust you will go back."

20 And Adam[3] gave his wife the name of Eve because she
21 was the mother of all who have life. | And the Lord God
made for Adam and for his wife coats of skins for their
23 clothing.... | So the Lord God sent him out of the Garden of
Eden to be a worker on the earth from which he was taken.
24 | So he sent the man out; and at the east of the Garden of
Eden he put a cherubim* and a flaming
sword flashing in every direction to
guard the way to the tree of life.

[1] See Revelation 12:1-6, page 453.

[2] This rule of men over women can be seen, for example, in the right they gave themselves for centuries to repudiate their wives so as to marry another. Jesus taught that this practice was the result of sin, of the "hardening of hearts." God created a pair of equal complementary persons. (Matthew 19:3-9, page 285).

[3] All through this narrative, the Hebrew word translated as "man" is Adam. It is, in fact, a common noun meaning simply "earthling," one who is drawn from the earth. The word is very often used as the name of the man in the story of the garden.

MAN CLOTHED IN MERCY*

The man and the woman were afraid of God. Yet, like a caring father, he protected their vulnerability with garments. Humans would later understand that God's wish is to clothe them "with power from on high" (Luke 24:49, page 392) and so enable them to crush the deceitful serpent, he who turns them aside from the paths of life.

Lord, when humanity
turns away from you,
living in communion is forgotten.
One of the first consequences of sin
is the break down of harmony
in a marriage.
Each one only thinks of himself
or herself and puts the blame on the other.
What should be dialogue
becomes conflict
because confidence no longer exists.

Lord, your only dream is to find
a way to revive this confidence
between fellow creatures
and between humanity and yourself.
Jesus, crush this divisive force
so that your dream becomes reality.

MORE STORIES

The story of paradise lost is continued in other narratives: Cain and Abel, Noah, the tower of Babel. While appearing to recount the origins of man, they describe the difficulties that have always faced humanity.

GOD LOOKS AT THE HEART

The book's author does not explain why God did not look with favor on Cain's offering. He merely suggests that Abel was better disposed towards God. He offered parts of the firstborn of his flock. He selected what was best. Cain offered some fruits of the soil. It is certain that God did not act on a whim. God does not look at what humans look at; He looks at the human heart (1 Samuel 16:1-7, page 99).

Cain and Abel

4 1 And the man has connection with Eve his wife,
and she became with child and gave birth to Cain,
2 and said, "I have conceived a man from the Lord." | Then
again she became pregnant and gave birth to Abel, his
brother. And Abel was a shepherd, but Cain was a
farmer.

3 And after a time, Cain gave to the Lord an offering of
4 the fruits of the earth. | And Abel gave an offering of the
young lambs of his flock and of their fat. And the Lord
5 was pleased with Abel's offering; | but in Cain and his
offering he had no pleasure. And Cain was angry and his
face became sad.

6 The Lord said to Cain, "Why are you angry? Why is
7 your face sad? | If you do well, will you not have honor?
If you do wrong, sin* is waiting at the door, desiring to
have you, but do not let it be your master."

8 And Cain said to his brother, "Let us go into the field."
When they were in the field, Cain made an attack on his
brother Abel and put him to death.

9 And the Lord said to Cain, "Where is your brother
Abel?" And he said, "I have no idea. Am I my brother's
10 keeper?" | And he said, "What have you done? The voice
of your brother's blood is crying to me from the earth. |
11 And now you are cursed from the earth, whose mouth is
12 open to take your brother's blood from your hand. | No
longer will the earth give you her fruit as the reward of
your work; you will be a wanderer in flight over the
13 earth." | And Cain said, "My punishment is greater than
14 my strength. | You have sent me out this day from the

GOD LOVES CAIN

To say that God did not look with favor on Cain's offering does not mean that God did not love him.

He showed trust in Cain: "You must master the jealousy which is eating at your heart. You can master it."

After the murder of Abel, God answered Cain's prayer and protected him by placing a mark on him.

God does not wish the death of the sinner; He wants him to change his ways and live (Ezekiel 18:23, page 162).

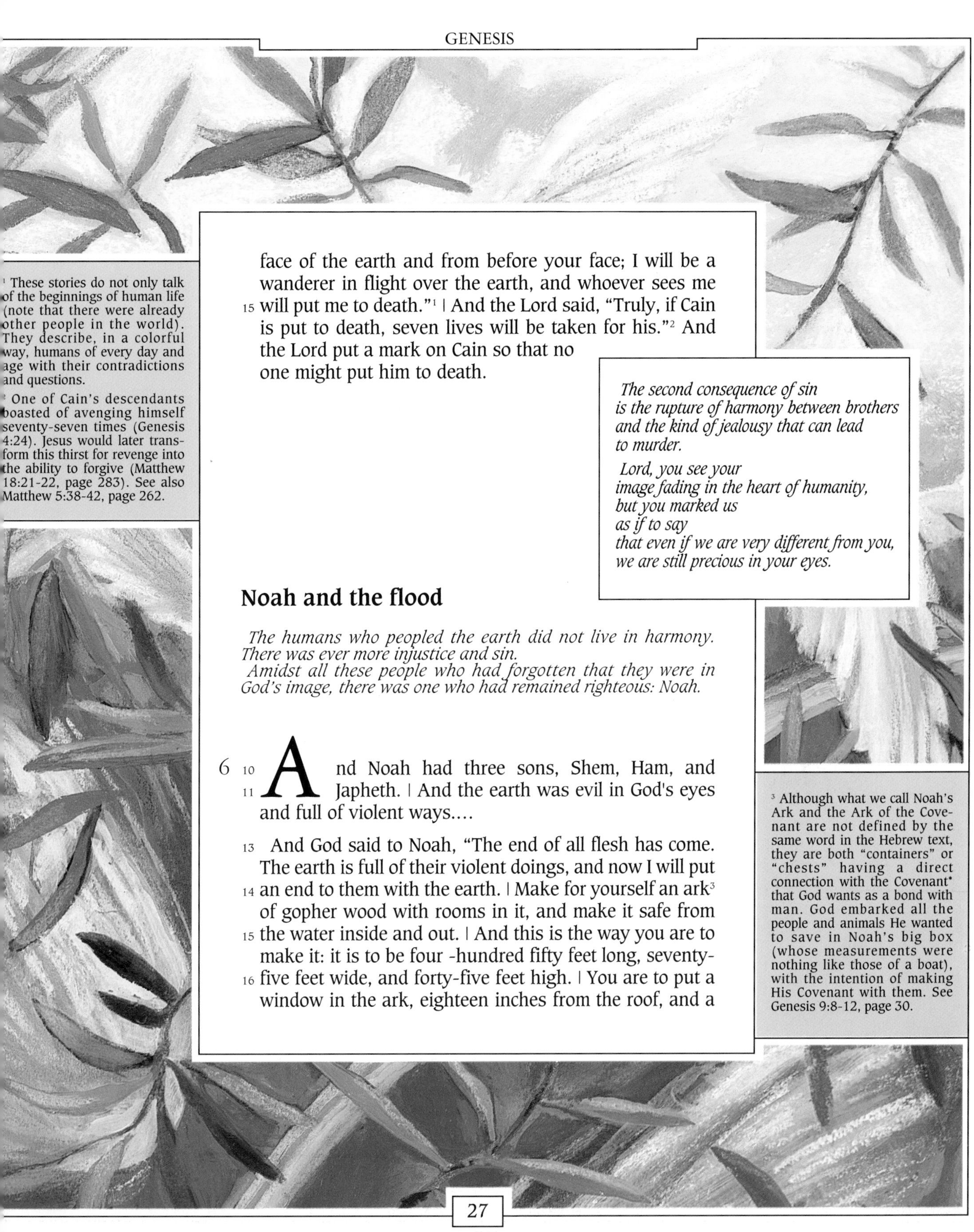

face of the earth and from before your face; I will be a
wanderer in flight over the earth, and whoever sees me
15 will put me to death."[1] | And the Lord said, "Truly, if Cain
is put to death, seven lives will be taken for his."[2] And
the Lord put a mark on Cain so that no
one might put him to death.

The second consequence of sin is the rupture of harmony between brothers and the kind of jealousy that can lead to murder.

Lord, you see your
image fading in the heart of humanity,
but you marked us
as if to say
that even if we are very different from you,
we are still precious in your eyes.

[1] These stories do not only talk of the beginnings of human life (note that there were already other people in the world). They describe, in a colorful way, humans of every day and age with their contradictions and questions.

[2] One of Cain's descendants boasted of avenging himself seventy-seven times (Genesis 4:24). Jesus would later transform this thirst for revenge into the ability to forgive (Matthew 18:21-22, page 283). See also Matthew 5:38-42, page 262.

Noah and the flood

The humans who peopled the earth did not live in harmony. There was ever more injustice and sin.
Amidst all these people who had forgotten that they were in God's image, there was one who had remained righteous: Noah.

6 10 And Noah had three sons, Shem, Ham, and
11 Japheth. | And the earth was evil in God's eyes
and full of violent ways....

13 And God said to Noah, "The end of all flesh has come.
The earth is full of their violent doings, and now I will put
14 an end to them with the earth. | Make for yourself an ark[3]
of gopher wood with rooms in it, and make it safe from
15 the water inside and out. | And this is the way you are to
make it: it is to be four -hundred fifty feet long, seventy-
16 five feet wide, and forty-five feet high. | You are to put a
window in the ark, eighteen inches from the roof, and a

[3] Although what we call Noah's Ark and the Ark of the Covenant are not defined by the same word in the Hebrew text, they are both "containers" or "chests" having a direct connection with the Covenant* that God wants as a bond with man. God embarked all the people and animals He wanted to save in Noah's big box (whose measurements were nothing like those of a boat), with the intention of making His Covenant with them. See Genesis 9:8-12, page 30.

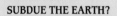

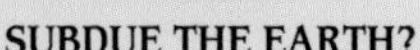

SUBDUE THE EARTH?

Humans no longer knew how to master the earth.

Nature was not only the Garden of Eden; it was also a hostile environment that generated catastrophes — earthquakes, tidal waves, eruptions. Noah, since he walked in the presence of God, received the gift of intelligence. He learned how to cope with life and, thanks to his labor, was saved from the flood.

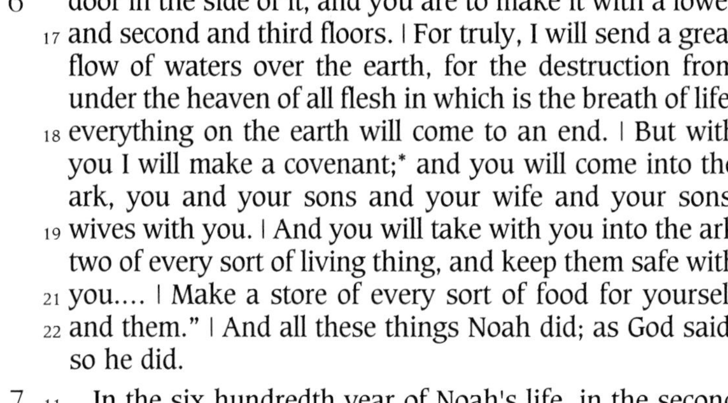

6 door in the side of it, and you are to make it with a lower
17 and second and third floors. | For truly, I will send a great
flow of waters over the earth, for the destruction from
under the heaven of all flesh in which is the breath of life;
18 everything on the earth will come to an end. | But with
you I will make a covenant;* and you will come into the
ark, you and your sons and your wife and your sons'
19 wives with you. | And you will take with you into the ark
two of every sort of living thing, and keep them safe with
21 you.... | Make a store of every sort of food for yourself
22 and them." | And all these things Noah did; as God said,
so he did.

7 11 In the six hundredth year of Noah's life, in the second
month, on the seventeenth day of the month, all the
fountains of the great deep came bursting through, and
12 the windows of heaven were open.[1] | And rain came
down on the earth for forty days and forty nights.

13 On the same day Noah, with Shem, Ham, and Japheth,
his sons, and his wife and his sons' wives, went into the
14 ark, | and with them, every sort of beast and cattle, and
every sort of thing which crawls on the earth, and every
15 sort of bird. | They went with Noah into the ark, two and
16 two of all flesh in which is the breath of life. | Male and
female of all flesh went in, as God had said, and the ark
was shut by the Lord.

[1] See how the ancient authors pictured the universe in the double-page illustration on pages 32 and 33.

The waters of the flood mounted higher than the highest mountains. Every living thing on the earth perished. The ark and its occupants floated on the water.

Ever since there was a separation
between the Creator and sinful humanity
we have become outsiders to creation.
The third consequence of sin
is the rupture of harmony between
humanity and nature.

Lord, you sent the animals
to Noah for protection
as if to remind us that in spite
of everything, we remain responsible
for creation.

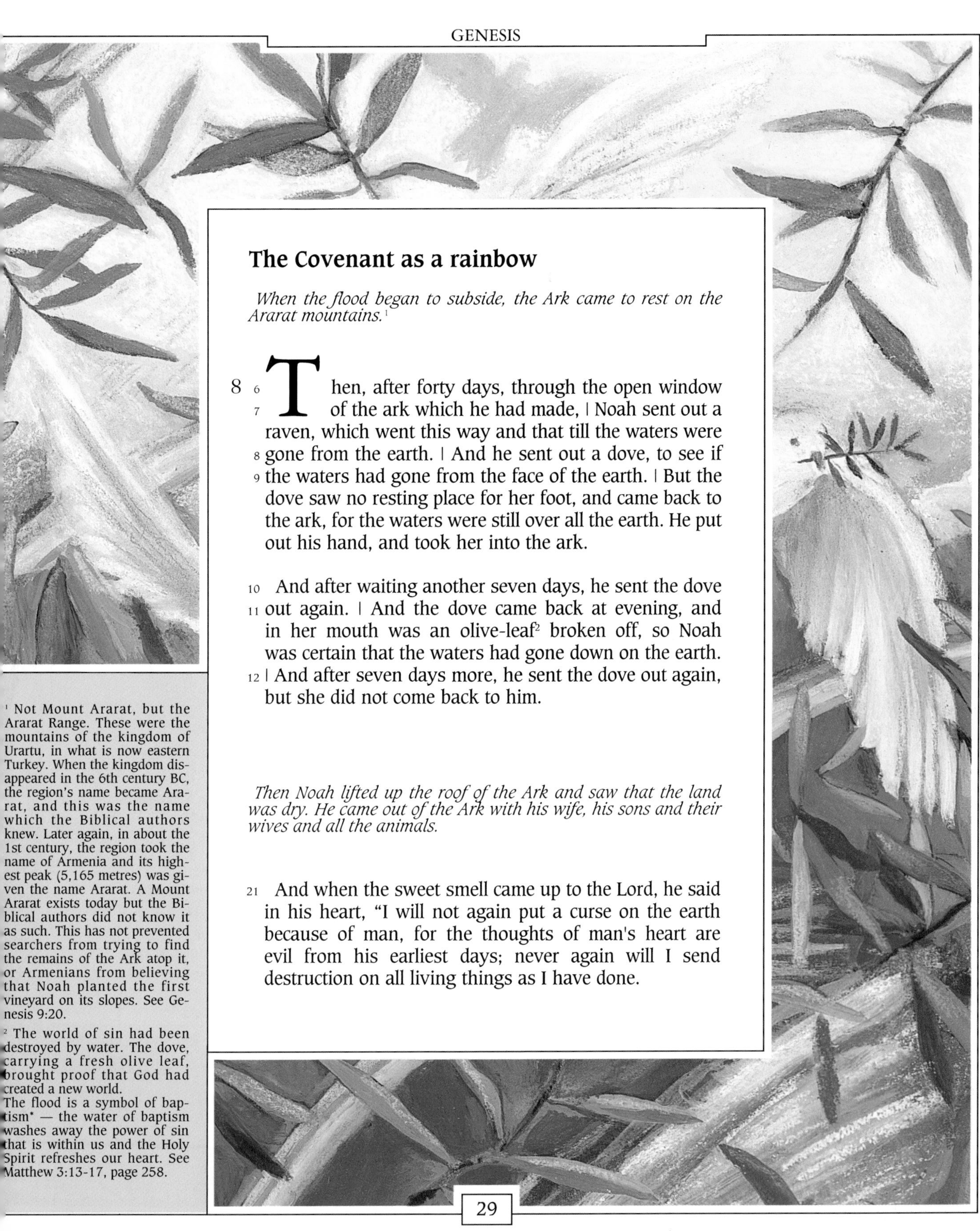

The Covenant as a rainbow

When the flood began to subside, the Ark came to rest on the Ararat mountains.[1]

8 6 Then, after forty days, through the open window
7 of the ark which he had made, | Noah sent out a
raven, which went this way and that till the waters were
8 gone from the earth. | And he sent out a dove, to see if
9 the waters had gone from the face of the earth. | But the
dove saw no resting place for her foot, and came back to
the ark, for the waters were still over all the earth. He put
out his hand, and took her into the ark.

10 And after waiting another seven days, he sent the dove
11 out again. | And the dove came back at evening, and
in her mouth was an olive-leaf[2] broken off, so Noah
was certain that the waters had gone down on the earth.
12 | And after seven days more, he sent the dove out again,
but she did not come back to him.

Then Noah lifted up the roof of the Ark and saw that the land was dry. He came out of the Ark with his wife, his sons and their wives and all the animals.

21 And when the sweet smell came up to the Lord, he said
in his heart, "I will not again put a curse on the earth
because of man, for the thoughts of man's heart are
evil from his earliest days; never again will I send
destruction on all living things as I have done.

[1] Not Mount Ararat, but the Ararat Range. These were the mountains of the kingdom of Urartu, in what is now eastern Turkey. When the kingdom disappeared in the 6th century BC, the region's name became Ararat, and this was the name which the Biblical authors knew. Later again, in about the 1st century, the region took the name of Armenia and its highest peak (5,165 metres) was given the name Ararat. A Mount Ararat exists today but the Biblical authors did not know it as such. This has not prevented searchers from trying to find the remains of the Ark atop it, or Armenians from believing that Noah planted the first vineyard on its slopes. See Genesis 9:20.

[2] The world of sin had been destroyed by water. The dove, carrying a fresh olive leaf, brought proof that God had created a new world.
The flood is a symbol of baptism* — the water of baptism washes away the power of sin that is within us and the Holy Spirit refreshes our heart. See Matthew 3:13-17, page 258.

THE GOD OF LIFE

The great story of Noah raises a question that is to be found in other parts of the Bible. "What if God one day gets sick of mankind and decides to destroy it because it is so bad?"

In some places, the biblical writers pictured God as being so angry against sinners that He caused disasters like the flood or the destruction of Sodom (see page 42).

But each time God was shown as not completing His destruction. He let a family live, because God loves life.

It was understood that even if God had to judge sin because of His holiness, His aim was to save people, and Peter would explain that God wanted to save even those who revolted against Him in the days of Noah (1 Peter 3:19-20, page 446).

To speak of God's anger* is a way of saying that God cannot remain indifferent when men turn their back on Him and rush to their doom. He cries out to call them back, so that they will return to Him and live with Him.

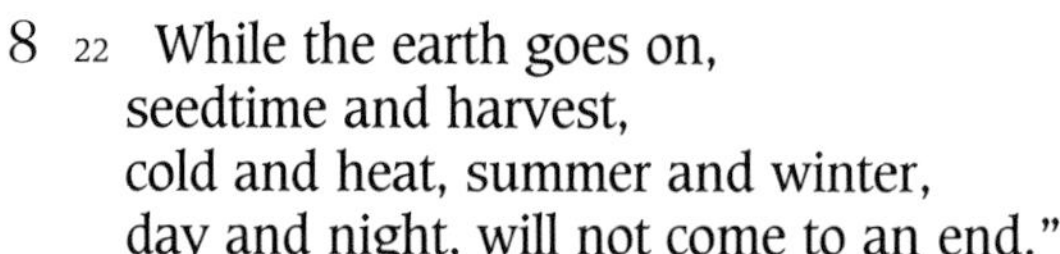

8 22 While the earth goes on,
seedtime and harvest,
cold and heat, summer and winter,
day and night, will not come to an end."

9 8-9 And God said to Noah and to his sons, | "Truly, I will
make my covenant with you and with your descendants
10 after you, | and with every living thing with you, all birds
and cattle and every beast of the earth which comes out
11 of the ark with you. | And I will make my covenant with
you; never again will all flesh be cut off by the waters;
never again will the waters come over all the earth for its
12 destruction." | And God said, "This is the sign of the
covenant which I make between me and you and every
13 living thing with you, for all future generations: | I will set
my rainbow in the clouds and it will be for a sign of the
14 covenant between me and the earth. | And whenever I
make a cloud come over the earth, the
15 rainbow will be seen in the cloud. | And
I will remember the covenant between
me and you and every living thing; and
never again will there be a great flow of
waters causing destruction to all flesh."

The rainbow!
This arch of light and color
joins
God's heavens
to humanity on earth!

Lord, the rainbow
is a sign of your desire to connect us to you.
You want each of us with
our distinctive qualities
and characteristics
to dance in your light
like the harmonious combination
of colors of the rainbow.

This rainbow is a sign
of your desire to make a covenant
with all humanity.

SMASHING THE IDOLS*

The people in the countries around Israel believed in gods jealously attached to their powers who divided men the better to rule over them. There is something of this in the story of the tower of Babel.

It was a long time before men would allow themselves to be purified,* abandoning images of God that reflected their own fears, selfishness and ignorance.

God would finally reveal His gentle and loving face by sending His Son to live with mankind.

The tower of Babel

11 1 And all the earth spoke one language and one
2 tongue. | And it came about that in their
wandering from the east, they came to a stretch of flat
3 country in the land of Shinar, and there they settled. | And
they said one to another, "Come, let us make bricks, burning
them well." And they had bricks for stone, putting them
4 together with sticky earth. | And they said, "Come, let us
make a town, and a tower whose top will go up as high as
heaven; and let us make a great name for ourselves, so that
5 we may not be wanderers over the face of the earth." | And
the Lord came down to see the town and the tower which
6 the children of men were building. | And the Lord said, "See,
they are all one people and have all one language; and this
is only the start of what they may do. Now it will not be
7 possible to keep them from any purpose of theirs. | Come, let
us go down and take away the sense of their language, so
that they will not be able to make themselves clear to one
8 another." | So the Lord God scattered them into every part of
9 the earth, and they gave up building their town. | So it was
named Babel, because there the Lord took away the sense of
all languages, and from there the Lord scattered them over
all the face of the earth.

LUST FOR POWER

It is pride which scatters people — their illusion that they can reach the skies, the very dwelling-place of God. It is the same old temptation, "You will be like God" (Genesis 3:5, page 24). In the race for power, it is hard to stay together — someone always wants to rise higher and be mightier than the others — and the bonds of understanding dissolve. Jesus, Son of the All-Powerful, ended the race for power by "descending from Heaven" to become the servant of mankind (John 6:38, page 344; Mark 10:35-45, page 248). On the day of Pentecost, the Holy Spirit showed men that they could rise above Babel and understand one another once more (Acts 2:7-11, page 401).

The fourth consequence of sin is the rupture of harmony between peoples. "Other people are different so they must be dangerous!" Sinful humanity moves farther and farther away from the communion so much desired by God.

Lord, you are already thinking about the time when your Spirit will compose the song of universal fraternity in harmony with all languages.

THE UNIVERSE OF GENESIS

1. The serpent tempts Adam and Eve in the Garden of Eden. God stations cherubim* to deny access to the tree of life (Genesis 3:1-24, page 24).*

2. Cain, the tiller of the soil, and 3. Abel, the herdsman (Genesis 4:1-5, page 26).

4. The Lord makes a Covenant with Noah (Genesis 6:10 to 9:15, pages 27-30). The symbol of this Covenant is the rainbow.

5. The heavens are thought of as a solid vault (Genesis 1:6-8, page 20). The "waters above" pour on the earth as rain when the "floodgates of the heavens" are opened (Genesis 7:11, page 28). The stars are set in the heavens (Genesis 1:14-19, page 20).

6. The "waters below" form the seas (Genesis 1:9-10, page 20). God fixed limits for them (Job 38:8-11, page 196). The seas are dangerous. Monsters like Leviathan are imagined as living in them (see also page 241).

7. Story of the tower of Babel (Genesis 11:1-9, page 31).

8. Under the earth is the realm of the dead, sheol.*

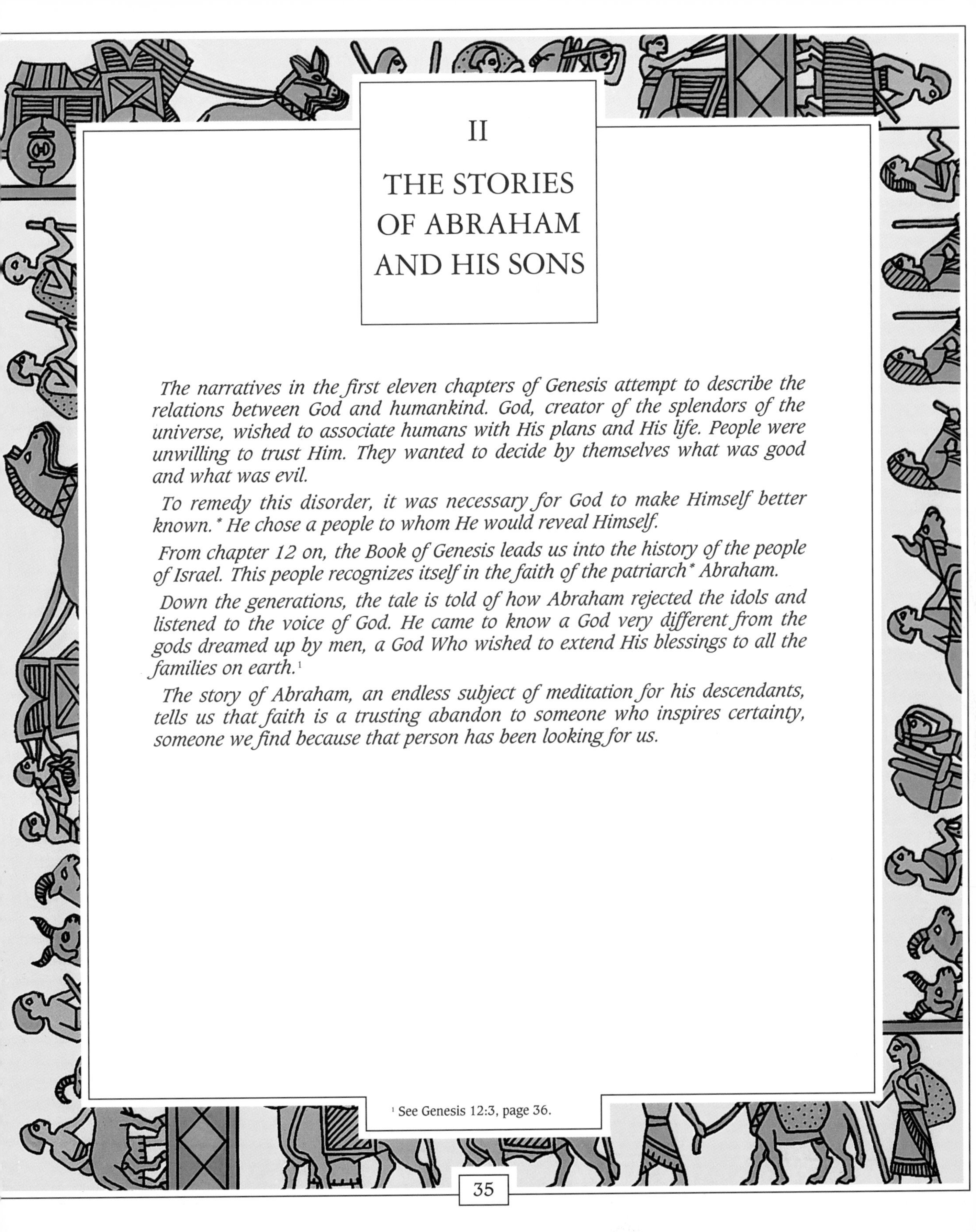

II

THE STORIES OF ABRAHAM AND HIS SONS

The narratives in the first eleven chapters of Genesis attempt to describe the relations between God and humankind. God, creator of the splendors of the universe, wished to associate humans with His plans and His life. People were unwilling to trust Him. They wanted to decide by themselves what was good and what was evil.

To remedy this disorder, it was necessary for God to make Himself better known. He chose a people to whom He would reveal Himself.*

From chapter 12 on, the Book of Genesis leads us into the history of the people of Israel. This people recognizes itself in the faith of the patriarch Abraham.*

Down the generations, the tale is told of how Abraham rejected the idols and listened to the voice of God. He came to know a God very different from the gods dreamed up by men, a God Who wished to extend His blessings to all the families on earth.[1]

The story of Abraham, an endless subject of meditation for his descendants, tells us that faith is a trusting abandon to someone who inspires certainty, someone we find because that person has been looking for us.

[1] See Genesis 12:3, page 36.

REVELATION

God wants men to know Him and discover the immensity of His love and fidelity.

He chose Abram, a man already mature and without child. He promised Abram that he would make of him a great people.

This people's task would be to share with all the families on earth the joy and happiness of knowing* God.

See "All peoples on earth will be blessed through you," page 474.

THE PROMISE OF A PEOPLE

Among the tribes of Israel, the story was told of Terah and his sons. Terah, the descendant of Shem (Noah's eldest son), lived in Ur in Chaldea. He had three sons, Abram, Nahor and Haran.

Abram married Sarai[1] but they had no children, since Sarai was sterile. Haran also married, and had a son, Lot, but died soon after. Terah left Ur, taking Abram and Sarai and Lot his grandson with him, intending to go to the land of Canaan. Before reaching Canaan, they settled in the city of Haran, where Terah died.*

12 1 Now the Lord said to Abram, "Leave your country
and your family and your father's house, into the
2 land to which I will be your guide. | I will make of you a great
nation, blessing you and making your name great; and you
3 will be a blessing: | To them who are good to you will I give
blessing, and on him who does you wrong will I put my
curse; You will become a name of blessing to all the families
of the earth."

4 So Abram went as the Lord had said to him, and Lot went
with him. Abram was seventy-five years old[2] when he left
5 Haran. | And Abram took Sarai, his wife, and Lot, his
brother's son, and all their goods and the servants which
they had got in Haran, and they went out to go to the land
6 of Canaan. | And Abram went through the land till he came
to Shechem, to the holy tree of Moreh. At that time, the
7 Canaanites were still living in the land. | And the Lord came
to Abram, and said, "I will give all this land to your
descendants." Then Abram made an altar* there to the Lord
8 who had let himself be seen by him. | And moving on from
there to the mountain on the east of Beth-el, he put up his
tent, having Beth-el on the west and Ai on the east. Tthere
he made an altar and gave worship to the name of the Lord.
9 | And he went on, journeying still to the South.

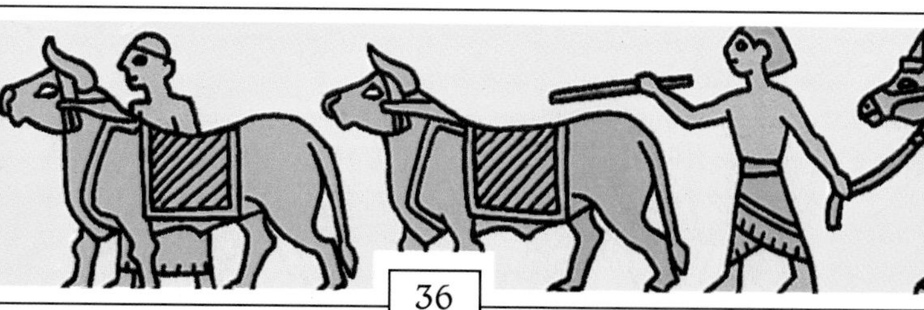

[1] God later changed the names of Abram and Sarai to mark the fact that He was entrusting them with a responsibility which would alter their lives. They would found a new people for God. See pages 39-40.

[2] It comes as a surprise to some that Abram was 75 and became Isaac's father at the age of 100. Numbers had a looser meaning in those days than now. The story's author was less concerned with the passage of time than with expressing his admiration for Abram. Abram was no longer a young man; he was at the ripe age when you think more of settling down than setting out on an adventure. Yet set out he did!

BETWEEN BROTHERS

Was this the story of Cain and Abel repeating itself?

No. Abram did not want to break with Lot. He gave up his privileges as the older man (his right of seniority, as it were) and let Lot have the land he wanted. Lot chose the fertile plain near Sodom and left Abram with the parched hillside.

Separating to avoid strife

13 2 Now Abram had great wealth of cattle and silver
5 and gold. | Lot, who went with him, had flocks
6 and herds and tents, | so that the land was not wide
enough for the two of them. Their property was so great
7 that there was not room for them together. | And there
was an argument between the keepers of Abram's cattle
and the keepers of Lot's cattle, at that time the
Canaanites and Perizzites were still living in the land.
8 | Then Abram said to Lot, "Let there be no argument
between me and you, and between my herdmen and your
9 herdmen, for we are brothers.[1] | Is not all the land before
you? Then let us go our separate ways. If you go to the
left, I will go to the right; or if you take the right, I will go
10 to the left." | And Lot, lifting up his eyes and
looking an the valley of Jordan, saw that it was well
watered everywhere. Before the Lord had sent
destruction on Sodom and Gomorrah, it was like the
garden of the Lord, like the land of Egypt, on the way to
11 Zoar. | So Lot took for himself all the valley of Jordan, and
went to the east, and they were parted from one another.
12 | Abram went on living in the land of Canaan, and Lot
went to the lowland towns, moving his tent as far as
13 Sodom. | Now the men of Sodom were evil, and great
sinners before the Lord.

The wealth of Sodom attracted plunderers. Lot was captured by brigands and Abram set out on a mission to rescue him.

The riches of Sodom corrupted the hearts of its citizens. They were great sinners. Abram interceded with the Lord to spare Lot from the punishment that would be inflicted on the city.[2]

[1] Lot was Abram's nephew, yet they called each other "brothers." The Bible uses the word in a much broader sense than that of brothers and sisters. It applies to any relation felt to be close, like an uncle, cousin or brother-in-law. See page 240.

[2] See page 42.

A PROMISED LAND

13 14 And the Lord had said to Abram, after Lot was
parted from him, "From this place where you are
take a look to the north and to the south, to the east and
15 to the west. | For all the land which you see I will give to
16 you and to your descendants for ever. | I will make your
children like the dust of the earth, so that if the dust of
the earth may be numbered, then will your children be
17 numbered. | Come, go through all the land from one end
18 to the other for I will give it to you." | Abram, moving his
tent, went to live by the holy tree of Mamre, which is in
Hebron, and made an altar* there to the Lord.

FROM LAND TO KINGDOM

People need a land to live in. God therefore promised a land to the man He said would become "a great nation."

But a land has to be conquered. The land of Canaan* would be conquered only after terrible battles.

Christians would later understand that the land promised us by Jesus can be conquered only by battling the violence that is within us. This land is not a territory on earth. It is the Kingdom* of God (John 18:33-38, page 374).

"Blessed are the meek, for they will inherit the earth."
Matthew 5:5, page 260.

Father of the faithful

Abram was now an old man, still childless. How could God's promise, "I will make you into a great nation," come true?

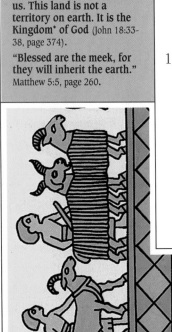

15 1 After these things, the word of the Lord came
to Abram in a vision, saying,
"Have no fear, Abram: I will keep you
safe, and great will be your reward."
2 | And Abram said, "What will you give
3 me? For I have no child.... | And Abram
said, "You have given me no child, and
a servant in my house will get the
heritage."

Abram, you are growing old.
Sometimes you wonder if this mysterious
God whose word you heard deep
in your heart isn't simply
a figment of your imagination,
a dream
or an illusion.
But you quickly
rid yourself of any doubts.
You believe that God and His Word are one.
God does what He says.
Your confidence remains in spite
of your advanced age.

4 Then said the Lord, "This man will not get the heritage,
but a son of your body will have your property after you."
5 | He took him out into the open air, and said to him, "Let
your eyes be lifted to heaven, and see if the stars may be
numbered; even so will your descendants."
6 | And he had faith in the Lord, and it was credited to him
as righteousness.*

THE PROMISE OF A SON

Abraham laughs

·Sarah was an intelligent woman. She admired the faith of her husband, who expected to have a son, but knew she was too old for childbearing. So she sent him her Egyptian servant, Hagar.

A child was born, Ishmael, but it was not the child of the promise.

LAUGHTER FOR ISAAC

The son of the promise was Isaac. The Bible gives us two accounts of the announcement of his birth. In one, Abraham laughs. In the other, it is Sarah who laughs.

The embarrassed laughter of two old people reacting to the preposterousness of this announcement, laughter tinged with doubt, which God would change into joy when Isaac came into the world.

17 1 When Abram was ninety-nine years old, the
the Lord came to him, and said, "I am God,
Ruler of all; walk before me[1] and be upright in all things, |
2 And I will make a covenant* between you and me, and
3 your offspring will be greatly increased." | And Abram
went down on his face on the earth, and the Lord God went
4 on talking with him, and said, | "As for me, my
covenant is made with you, and you will be the father of
5 nations without end. | No longer will your name be Abram,
but Abraham, for I have made you the father of a number
7 of nations.... | And I will make between me and you and
your seed after you through all generations, an eternal
8 covenant.... | And to you and to your descendants after
you, I will give the land in which you are living, all the land
of Canaan* for an eternal heritage; and I will be their God."
17 9 | And God said to Abraham, "On your side, you are to
keep the covenant, you and your descendants after you
10 through all generations. | And this is the covenant which

[1] See Micah 6:8, page 145.

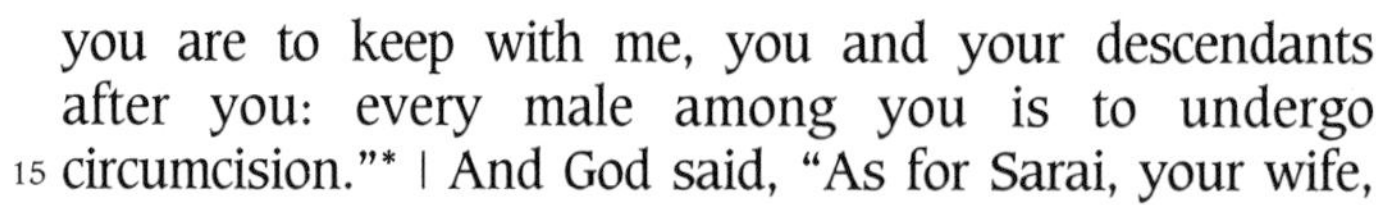

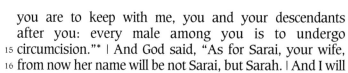

you are to keep with me, you and your descendants
after you: every male among you is to undergo
15 circumcision."* | And God said, "As for Sarai, your wife,
16 from now her name will be not Sarai, but Sarah. | And I will
give her a blessing so that you will have a son by her: truly
my blessing will be on her, and she will be the mother of
17 nations. Kings of peoples will be her offspring." | Then
Abraham went down on his face, and laughing, said in his
heart, "Can a man a hundred years old have a child? Will
18 Sarah, at ninety years old,[1] give birth?" | And Abraham
said to God, "If only Ishmael's life might
19 be so blessed!" | And God said, "Not so.
But Sarah, your wife, will have a son,
and you will name him Isaac, and I will
make my covenant with him forever
20 and with his seed after him. | As for
Ishmael, I have heard your prayer: truly
I have given him my blessing and I will
make him fertile and give him great
increase. He will be the father of twelve
chiefs, and I will make him a great
nation."[2]

*Abram, the Lord has changed your name.
He has acknowledged your confidence
during these long years
spent in His presence in spite
of unfulfilled promises.
Because of your faithfulness you
have become
Abraham which means
"father of the nations."
You are to become the first father
of those who are called to discover
that they have but one Father
who knows each one by name.*

The laughter of Sarah

18 1 Now the Lord came to him by the holy tree of
Mamre, when he was seated in the doorway of
2 his tent in the middle of the day. | And lifting up his eyes,
he saw three men before him; and seeing them, he went
quickly to them from the door of the tent, and went down

[1] See note 2, page 36.

[2] Ishmael was the son of Abraham and Hagar, Sarah's servant. Although not the son of the promise, Ishmael was blessed of God. He would have twelve sons, forebears of the Arab tribes — "a great nation," says the Bible.

3 on his face to the earth. | He said, "My Lord, if now I have
grace in your eyes, do not go away from your servant. |
4 Let me get water for washing your feet, and take your
5 rest under the tree. | And let me get a bit of bread to keep
up your strength, and after that you may go on your way,
for this is why you have come to your servant." And they
said, "Let it be so."

6 Then Abraham went quickly into the tent, and said to
Sarah, "Get three measures of meal immediately and
7 make cakes." | And running to the herd, he took a young
ox, soft and fat, and gave it to the servant and he quickly
8 made it ready. | And he took butter and milk and the
young ox which he had made ready and put it before
them, waiting by them under the tree while they ate. |
9 And they said to him, "Where is Sarah your wife?"
10 And he said, "She is in the tent." | And he said, "I will
certainly come back to you in the spring, and Sarah your
wife will have a son." And his words came to the ears of
11 Sarah who was at the back of the tent-door. | Now
Abraham and Sarah were very old, and Sarah was past
12 the time for giving birth. | And Sarah, laughing to herself,
said, "Now that I am used up am I still to have pleasure,
13 my husband himself being old?" | And the Lord[1] said,
"Why was Sarah laughing and saying,
'Is it possible for me, being old, to give
14 birth to a child?' | Is there any wonder
which the Lord is not able to do? At the
time I said, in the spring, I will come
back to you, and Sarah will have a
child."

[1] The story telling of the three travellers switches constantly from the plural to the singular. It is clearly the Lord God Whom is meant. The narrative afterwards distinguishes between the Lord and two men (Genesis 18:22, page 42) or possibly two angels. In this strange visit, Abraham recognizes the presence of God. Christians see this passage as a prefiguration of the Holy Trinity.*

Lord, you have come to meet us
in a surprising way.
We were expecting prodigies,
and you only sent three ordinary travellers.

Long before Jesus told us,
Abraham had already understood that God's
signs were often revealed through others.

Three travellers sitting in the shade
of an oak tree,
a child in a manger in Bethlehem,
a gardener near a tomb...
Lord, you are so near us yet so different
from what we had imagined you to be.

The intercession* of Abraham

18 16 And the men went on from there in the direction
of Sodom; and Abraham went with them on
17 their way. | And the Lord said, "Am I to keep back from
18 Abraham the knowledge of what I do, | seeing that
Abraham will certainly become a great and strong nation,
and his name will be used by all the nations of the earth
20 as a blessing?"... | And the Lord said, "Because the
outcry against Sodom and Gomorrah is very great, and
21 their sin is very evil, | I will go down now, and see if their
acts are as bad as they seem from the outcry which has
come to me; and if they are not, I will see."

22 And the men, turning from that place, went on to
Sodom, but Abraham was still waiting before the Lord.
23 | And Abraham came near, and said, "Will you let
24 destruction befall the upright with the sinners? | If by
chance there are fifty upright men in the town, will you
give the place to destruction and not have mercy on it
25 because of the fifty upright men? | Let such a thing be far
from you, to put the upright to death with the sinner: will
26 not the judge of all the earth do right?" | And the Lord
said, "If there are fifty upright men in the town, I will
27 have mercy on it because of them." | And Abraham
answering said, "Truly, I who am only dust, have
28 undertaken to put my thoughts before the Lord: | If by
chance there are five less than fifty upright men, will you
give up all the town to destruction because of these five?
And he said, I will not give it to destruction if there are
29 forty-five." | And again he said to him, "By chance there
may be forty there. And he said, I will not do it if there
30 are forty." | And he said, "Let not the Lord be angry with
me if I say, What if there are thirty there?" And he said,

THE SIN OF SODOM

The citizens of Sodom were filled with their scorn for others. When they saw a stranger, they asked themselves, "What can I get out of him? How can I use him?"
They did not try to relate to him as a person, but saw him as an object. They had debased the likeness of God in themselves. They were unable to produce good fruit. They were sterile like salty soil. This is what the two visitors found when they arrived there. They could not find ten righteous men in the city. Only Lot and his two daughters would escape from this place of death.

31 "I will not do it if there are thirty." | And he said, "See
now, I have boldly spoken my thoughts before the Lord:
what if there are twenty there?" And he said, "I will have
32 mercy because of the twenty." | And he said, "O let not
the Lord be angry and I will say only one word more: by
chance there may be ten there." And he said, "I will have
mercy because of the ten."

33 And the Lord went on his way when his talk with
Abraham was ended, and Abraham went back to his
place.

The laughter of God

"May God laugh" is what the name Isaac means. The child of the promise showed that God mocks all obstacles. He even made life spring from what was dead.[1]

[1] Sarah's chances of having a child were nil, or dead.
[2] Circumcision* is a mark in the flesh, a sign of the Covenant with God.

21 1 And the Lord came to Sarah as he had said and
2 did to her as he had proposed. | And Sarah
became with child, and gave Abraham a son when he
3 was old, at the time named by God. | And Abraham
gave to his son, to whom Sarah had given birth, the
4 name Isaac. | And when his son Isaac was eight days
old, Abraham made him undergo
circumcision,[2] as God had said to him....
6 And Sarah said, "God has given me
cause for laughing, and everyone who
has news of it will be laughing with
7 me." | And she said, "Who would have
said to Abraham that Sarah would have
a child at her breast? See, I have
given him a son now when he is old."

Lord, you cheered up Sarah in her old age.
Because of you, Elizabeth,
Mary, and all those who welcomed you
leaped for joy.
You wipe away the tears of those who cry
and teach them to laugh again.
You want all people
to enter into the joy of eternal life.
Thank you Lord because when you look
at me it is always with
a smile of love.

JOURNEY OF THE PATRIARCHS

1. Terah leaves Ur with Abram, Sarai and Lot (see page 36).

2. Abram leaves Haran with his wife and nephew in search of the land which God will show him (Genesis 12:1, page 36).

3. At Shechem, Abram builds an altar to the Lord (12:6-7, page 36).

4. Abraham welcomes three visitors at Mamre. Sarah listens at the entrance of the tent (Genesis 18:1-14, page 40).

5. Lot leaves Sodom with his two daughters (see Genesis 18:16-33, page 42).

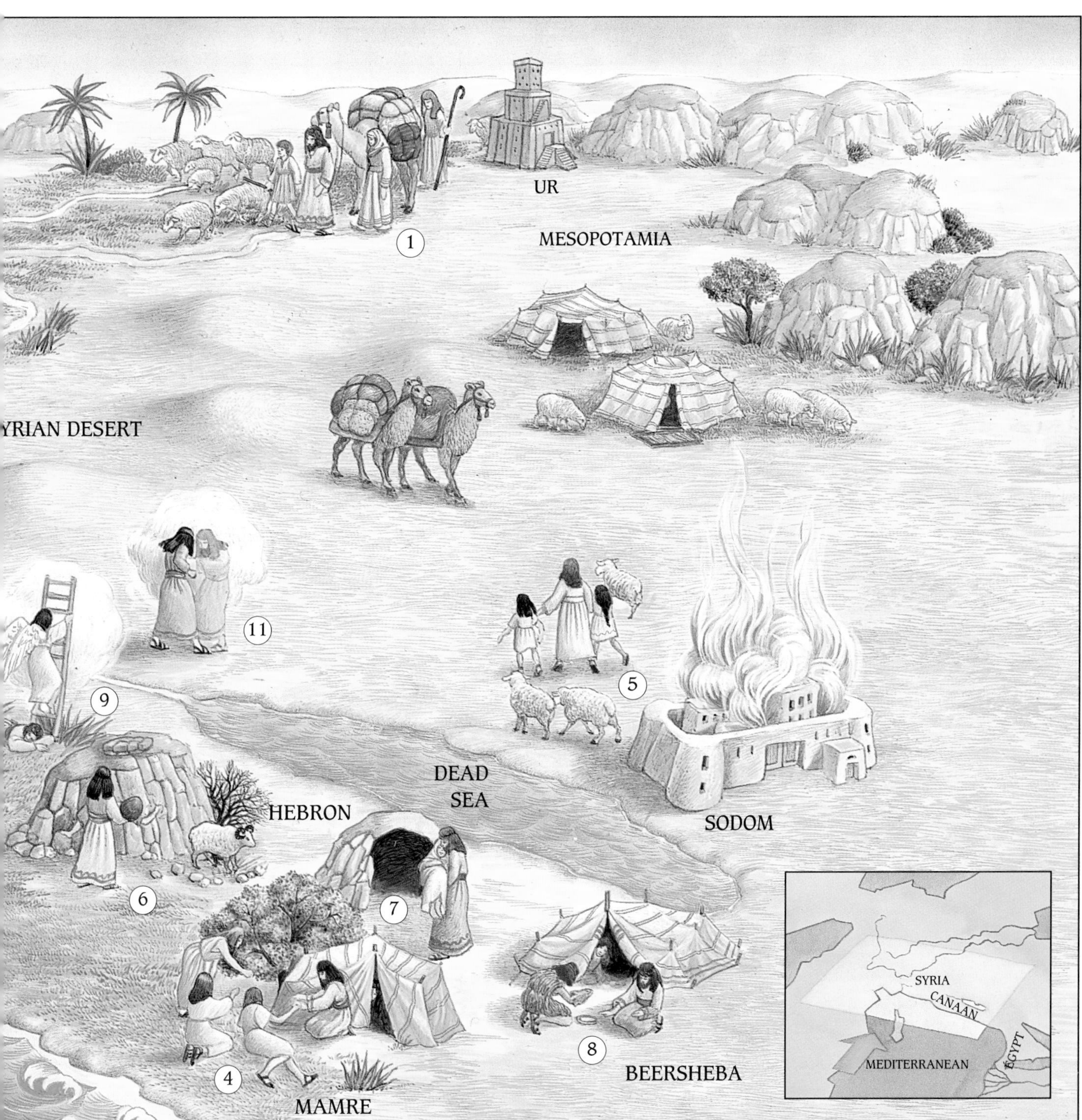

6. Abraham sacrifices a ram in place of Isaac (Genesis 22:1-13, page 46). The tradition will have it that this scene occurred in Jerusalem on the hill where the Temple would later be built.

7. Abraham buys a cave in Hebron as the burial place for Sarah (see page 47).

8. Jacob, urged on by Rebekah, deceives Isaac so as to receive his blessing (Genesis 27:1-29, page 47).

9. Jacob dreams of a ladder between earth and heaven (Genesis 28:10-21, page 49).

10. Jacob leaves Haran for the Promised Land, taking with him his two wives, Leah and Rachel. their serving-maids and his eleven children (see page 50).

11. Before entering the Promised Land, Jacob wrestles with a mysterious opponent who gives him a new name: Israel (Genesis 32:23-32, page 50).

12. Joseph is sold by his brothers (Genesis 37:21-28, page 52).

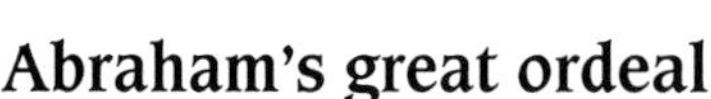

SACRIFICE OF THE FIRSTBORN

Abraham did not live in isolation. He was immersed in the life of the people of his time. Several stories show him on friendly terms with the Canaanites (people of Canaan) among whom he lived. They were a very religious people, which appeased their gods' demands with rituals we now see as barbarous, such as the sacrifice of firstborn children.

Abraham's ordeal has to be understood in this context. The story of Abraham's sacrifice was very important, since long after Abraham the children of Israel continued to ask themselves, "Should we not offer what is dearest to us, to show our faithfulness to God?" (See Micah 6:6-8, page 145.)

Abraham prepared for the sacrifice of Isaac. Despite his anguish, his heart remained confident and he was able to hear the word of God, "I do not want human sacrifices." God on high was different from the blood-lusting idols.

Abraham's great ordeal

22 1 Now after these things, God put Abraham to
the test, and said to him, "Abraham!" He said,
2 "Here am I." | And God said to him, "Take your son, your
dearly loved only son Isaac, and go to the land of Moriah
and give him as a burnt offering on one of the mountains
about which I will tell you."

3 And Abraham got up early in the morning, and made ready
his donkey, and took with him two of his young men and
Isaac, his son, and after the wood for the burnt offering had
been cut, he went on his way to the place of which God had
4 given him word. | And on the third day, Abraham, lifting up
5 his eyes, saw the place a long way off. | Then he said to his
young men, "Stay here with the donkey; I and the boy will
6 go on and give worship and come back again to you." | And
Abraham put the wood for the burnt offering on his son's
back, and he himself took the fire and the knife in his hand,
7 and the two of them went on together. | Then Isaac said to
Abraham, "My father?" He said, "Here am I, my son." And
he said, "We have wood and fire here, but
where is the lamb for the burnt offering?"
8 | And Abraham said, "God himself will
give the lamb for the burnt offering."* So
they went on together.

9 And they came to the place about which
God had spoken, and there Abraham
made the altar and put the wood in place
on it. Having made tight the bands round
Isaac his son, he put him on the wood on
the altar.*

10 And stretching out his hand, Abraham
took the knife to put his son to death. |

Abraham, all is darkness
within your heart.
Does the God of the Covenant want
the child of the promise to die?
Is God's laughter being transformed
into a cruel sneer?
But the stubborn little flame of
hope continues to burn.
"God well knows
where to find the sacrificial lamb."
Abraham, you remain confident
to the very end because you truly believe
that God is in favor of life and against
human sacrifice, and rightly so!
Later on God will say to the prophet Jeremiah,
"I never commanded
nor would have ever imagined such acts."
Those who thought
they were pleasing the Lord
by offering up their children in sacrifice
were sorely mistaken.

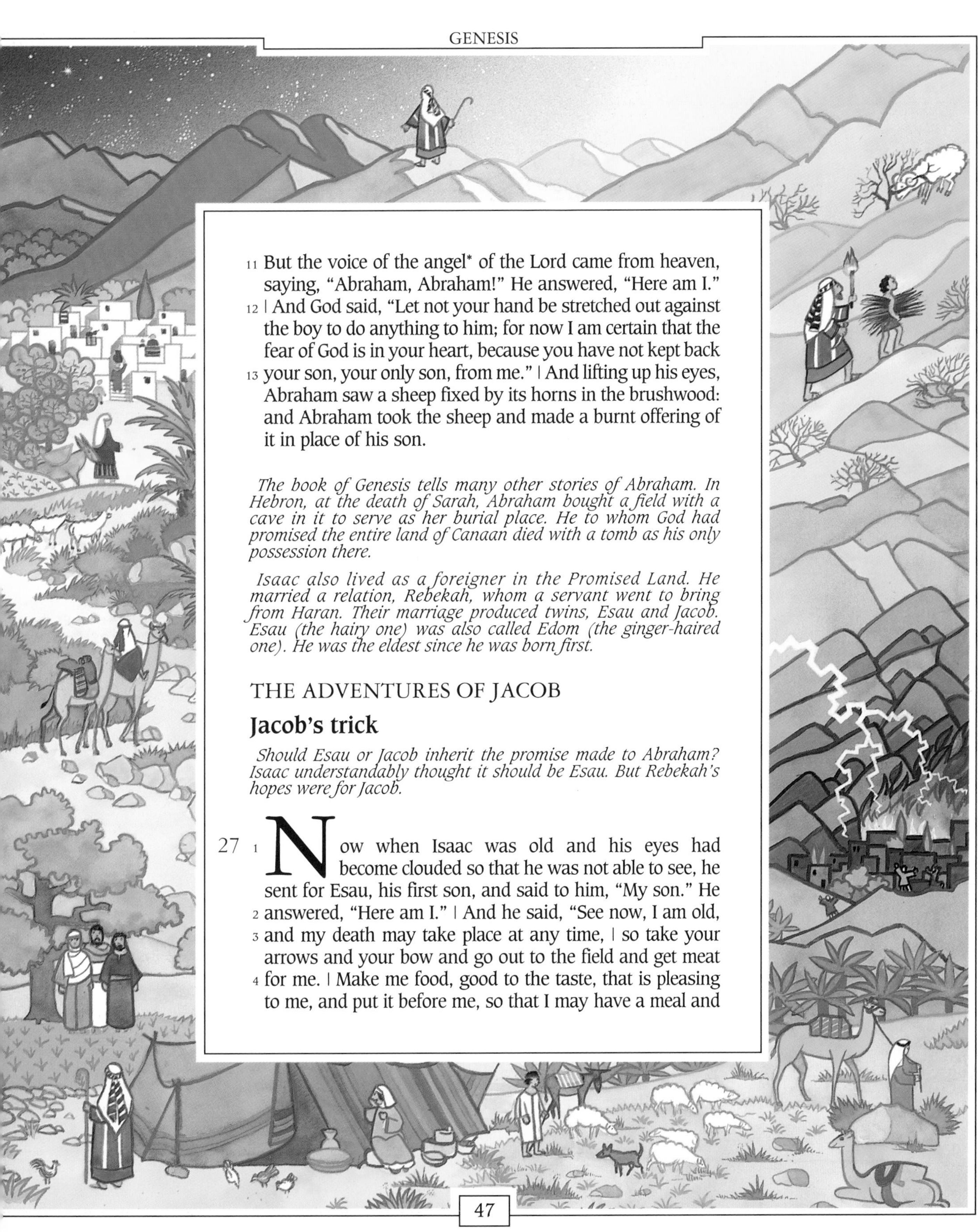

11 But the voice of the angel* of the Lord came from heaven,
saying, "Abraham, Abraham!" He answered, "Here am I."
12 | And God said, "Let not your hand be stretched out against
the boy to do anything to him; for now I am certain that the
fear of God is in your heart, because you have not kept back
13 your son, your only son, from me." | And lifting up his eyes,
Abraham saw a sheep fixed by its horns in the brushwood:
and Abraham took the sheep and made a burnt offering of
it in place of his son.

The book of Genesis tells many other stories of Abraham. In Hebron, at the death of Sarah, Abraham bought a field with a cave in it to serve as her burial place. He to whom God had promised the entire land of Canaan died with a tomb as his only possession there.

Isaac also lived as a foreigner in the Promised Land. He married a relation, Rebekah, whom a servant went to bring from Haran. Their marriage produced twins, Esau and Jacob. Esau (the hairy one) was also called Edom (the ginger-haired one). He was the eldest since he was born first.

THE ADVENTURES OF JACOB

Jacob's trick

Should Esau or Jacob inherit the promise made to Abraham? Isaac understandably thought it should be Esau. But Rebekah's hopes were for Jacob.

27 1 Now when Isaac was old and his eyes had
become clouded so that he was not able to see, he
sent for Esau, his first son, and said to him, "My son." He
2 answered, "Here am I." | And he said, "See now, I am old,
3 and my death may take place at any time, | so take your
arrows and your bow and go out to the field and get meat
4 for me. | Make me food, good to the taste, that is pleasing
to me, and put it before me, so that I may have a meal and

THE ROAD TO CONVERSION

Rebekah and Jacob lived in a society imbued with magic. The blessing for them was a sort of lucky charm. It did not matter that it was intended for Esau. Once it had been bestowed on Jacob, he was God's protégé.

God would help Jacob in his conversion.* Jacob would discover that God is Life and that you do not steal his blessing (see pages 50-51).

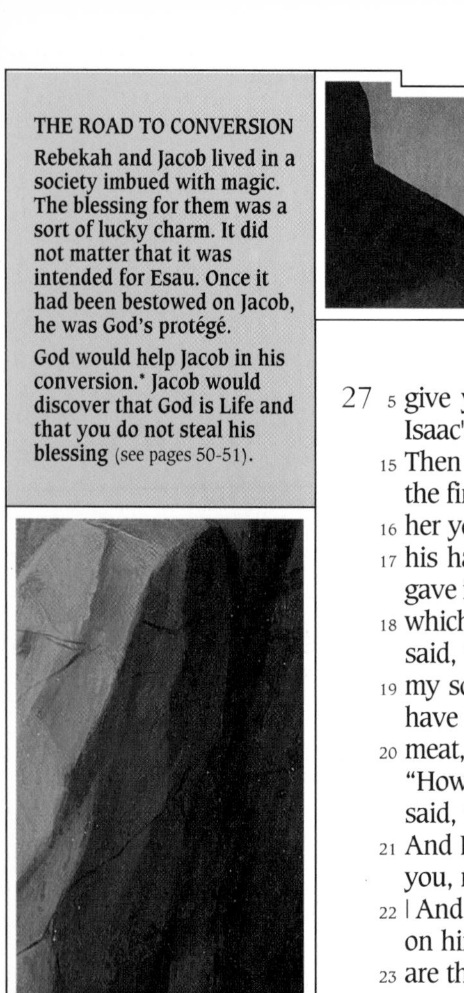

27 5 give you my blessing before death comes to me." | Now
Isaac's words to his son were said in Rebekah's hearing.
15 Then Esau went out to get the meat.... | And Rebekah took
the finest robes of her oldest son.... and put them on Jacob,
16 her younger son. | She put the skins of the young goats on
17 his hands and on the smooth part of his neck.[1] | And she
gave into the hand of Jacob, her son, the meat and the bread
18 which she had made ready. | And he came to his father, and
said, "My father." He answered, "Here am I. Who are you,
19 my son?" | And Jacob said, "I am Esau, your oldest son; I
have done as you said. Come now, be seated and eat my
20 meat, so that you may give me a blessing." | And Isaac said,
"How is it that you have got it so quickly, my son?" And he
said, "Because the Lord your God made it come my way." |
21 And Isaac said, "Come near so that I may put my hand on
you, my son, and see if you are truly my son Esau or not."
22 | And Jacob went near his father Isaac, and he put his hands
on him. He said, "The voice is Jacob's voice, but the hands
23 are the hands of Esau." | And he did not make out who he
was, because his hands were covered with hair like his
24 brother Esau's hands: so he gave him a blessing. | And he
said, "Are you truly my son Esau?" And he said, "I am." |
25 And he said, "Put it before me and I will eat my son's meat,
so that I may give you a blessing." And he put it before him
and he ate it; and he gave him wine, and he had a drink. |
26 And his father Isaac said to him, "Come near now, my son,
27 and give me a kiss." | And he came near
and gave him a kiss. Smelling the smell of
his clothing, he gave him a blessing, and
said, "See, the smell of my son is like the
smell of a field on which the blessing of the
28 Lord has come: | May God give you... all the
good things of the earth....

[1] Esau was a "hairy man," which is the meaning of his name.

Lord, what patience!
To shape the hearts
of people that know you,
you accept them as they are.
Jacob is so sure of himself.
He is much more interested
in success than meeting you,
so you come to him instead.
You help him understand
that you aren't some kind of magical
power that can be harnessed with formulas
or rituals.
You are the Living One
who walks along with us.

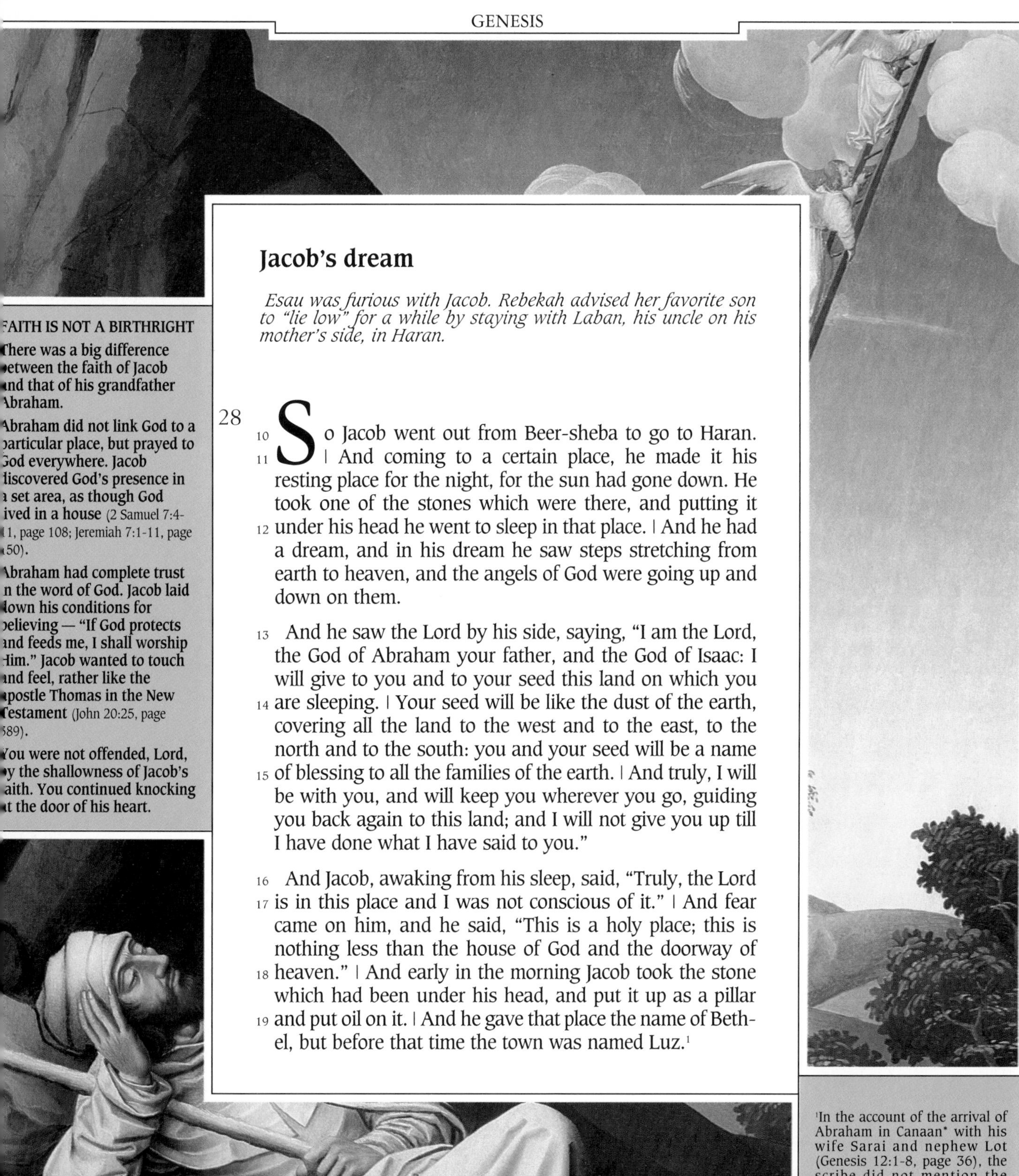

FAITH IS NOT A BIRTHRIGHT

There was a big difference between the faith of Jacob and that of his grandfather Abraham.

Abraham did not link God to a particular place, but prayed to God everywhere. Jacob discovered God's presence in a set area, as though God lived in a house (2 Samuel 7:4-11, page 108; Jeremiah 7:1-11, page 450).

Abraham had complete trust in the word of God. Jacob laid down his conditions for believing — "If God protects and feeds me, I shall worship Him." Jacob wanted to touch and feel, rather like the apostle Thomas in the New Testament (John 20:25, page 589).

You were not offended, Lord, by the shallowness of Jacob's faith. You continued knocking at the door of his heart.

Jacob's dream

Esau was furious with Jacob. Rebekah advised her favorite son to "lie low" for a while by staying with Laban, his uncle on his mother's side, in Haran.

28
10 So Jacob went out from Beer-sheba to go to Haran.
11 | And coming to a certain place, he made it his
resting place for the night, for the sun had gone down. He
took one of the stones which were there, and putting it
12 under his head he went to sleep in that place. | And he had
a dream, and in his dream he saw steps stretching from
earth to heaven, and the angels of God were going up and
down on them.

13 And he saw the Lord by his side, saying, "I am the Lord,
the God of Abraham your father, and the God of Isaac: I
will give to you and to your seed this land on which you
14 are sleeping. | Your seed will be like the dust of the earth,
covering all the land to the west and to the east, to the
north and to the south: you and your seed will be a name
15 of blessing to all the families of the earth. | And truly, I will
be with you, and will keep you wherever you go, guiding
you back again to this land; and I will not give you up till
I have done what I have said to you."

16 And Jacob, awaking from his sleep, said, "Truly, the Lord
17 is in this place and I was not conscious of it." | And fear
came on him, and he said, "This is a holy place; this is
nothing less than the house of God and the doorway of
18 heaven." | And early in the morning Jacob took the stone
which had been under his head, and put it up as a pillar
19 and put oil on it. | And he gave that place the name of Beth-
el, but before that time the town was named Luz.[1]

[1]In the account of the arrival of Abraham in Canaan* with his wife Sarai and nephew Lot (Genesis 12:1-8, page 36), the scribe did not mention the name Luz, but called it Bethel, which was the name invented for it by Jacob.

28 20 Then Jacob took an oath, and said, "If God will be with
me, and keep me safe on my journey, and give me food
21 and clothing to put on, | so that I come again to my
father's house in peace, then I will take the Lord to be my
God."

In Haran, Jacob fell madly in love with Laban's younger daughter, Rachel. But Laban made him marry Leah, his elder daughter, first. Polygamy being common at the time, Jacob was later able to marry Rachel also.

Jacob became the father of eleven sons during his stay in Haran. Having become very wealthy, he decided to return to the Promised Land with his wives, children and flocks.

The struggle of Jacob/Israel

32 23 He took them and sent them over the stream
24 with all he had. | Then Jacob was by himself; and
25 a man was fighting with him till dawn. | But when the man
saw that he was not able to overcome Jacob, he gave him
a blow in the hollow part of his leg, so
26 that his leg was damaged. | And he said
to him, "Let me go now, for the dawn is
near." But Jacob said, "I will not let you
go till you have given me your
27 blessing." | Then he said, "What is your
28 name?" And he said, "Jacob." | And he
said, "Your name will no longer be
Jacob, but Israel: for in your fight with
God and with men you have overcome."
29 | Then Jacob said, "What is your name?"
And he said, "What is my name to
you?" Then he gave him a blessing.

THE SPIRITUAL FIGHT

Jacob wrestled with a mysterious opponent and came out of the fight limping, off-balance yet stronger, at peace and reconciled with God. This very ancient story has been read and meditated upon down the ages by all the great mystics.[1] They see it as a metaphor of the spiritual struggle which every Christian must wage. It is a struggle against our certainties and our fears. It is also a battle against our refusals and false notions of God.

[1] The great mystics are those who devoted their lives to prayer and have become guides for many followers on the road that leads to God.

Jacob,
it wasn't Esau who came to you
as an enemy.
It was God himself who
you tried to deceive with
your crude disguise.
You were so sure of yourself but have
now become conscious of your weaknesses
Now you are asking
for the stolen benediction.
"I won't let go of you Lord.
Even if you don't want me,
I will keep hanging on to you.
From now on only you can help me
toe the line."
Israel, in the past you were strongly
opposed to this God who acted
as if He was abandoning you.
You have now become God's partner forever.

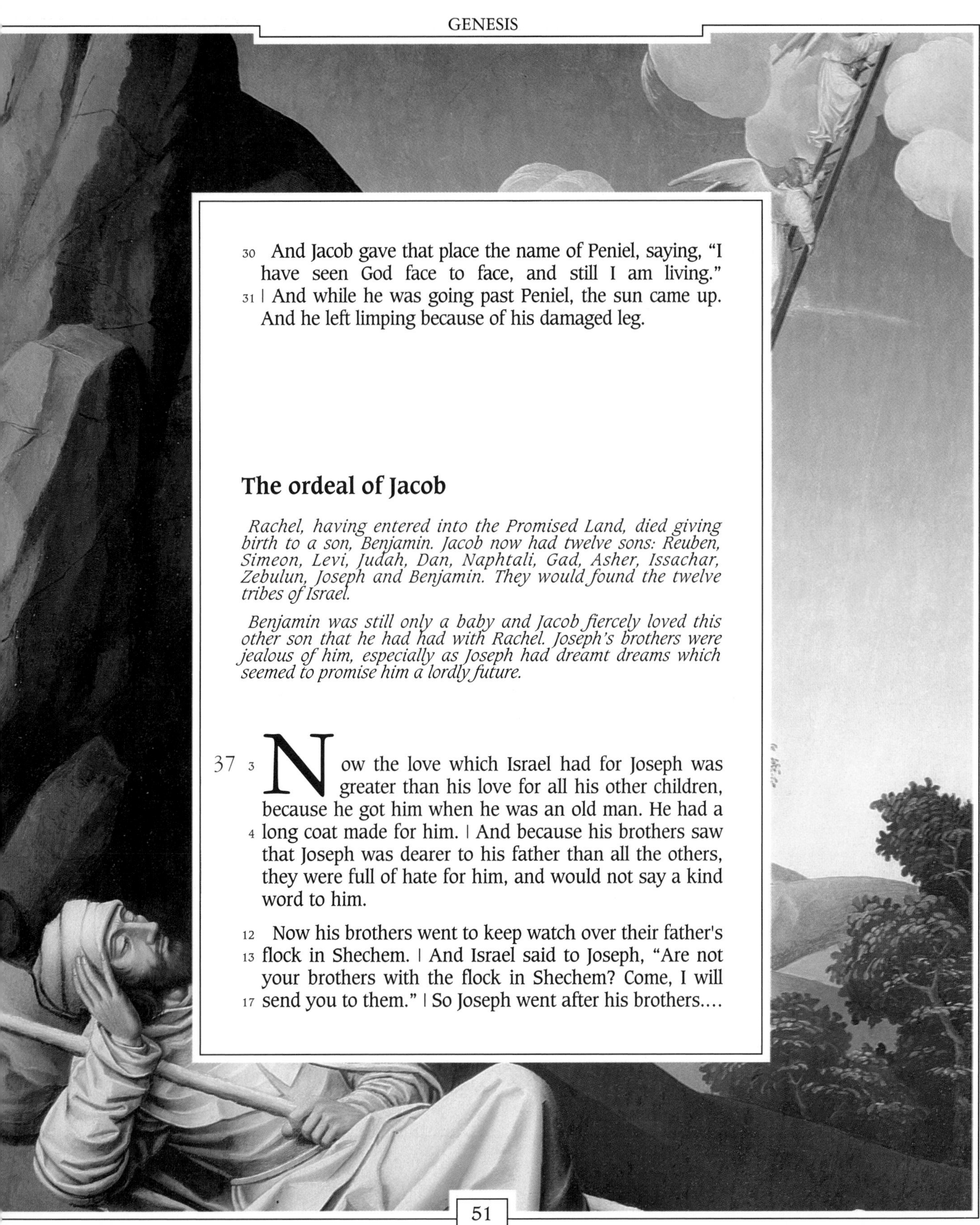

30 And Jacob gave that place the name of Peniel, saying, "I
have seen God face to face, and still I am living."
31 | And while he was going past Peniel, the sun came up.
And he left limping because of his damaged leg.

The ordeal of Jacob

Rachel, having entered into the Promised Land, died giving birth to a son, Benjamin. Jacob now had twelve sons: Reuben, Simeon, Levi, Judah, Dan, Naphtali, Gad, Asher, Issachar, Zebulun, Joseph and Benjamin. They would found the twelve tribes of Israel.

Benjamin was still only a baby and Jacob fiercely loved this other son that he had had with Rachel. Joseph's brothers were jealous of him, especially as Joseph had dreamt dreams which seemed to promise him a lordly future.

37 3 Now the love which Israel had for Joseph was
greater than his love for all his other children,
because he got him when he was an old man. He had a
4 long coat made for him. | And because his brothers saw
that Joseph was dearer to his father than all the others,
they were full of hate for him, and would not say a kind
word to him.

12 Now his brothers went to keep watch over their father's
13 flock in Shechem. | And Israel said to Joseph, "Are not
your brothers with the flock in Shechem? Come, I will
17 send you to them." | So Joseph went after his brothers....

37 18 | But they saw him when he was a long way off, and
before he came near them they made a secret plot against
19 him to put him to death, | saying to one another, "Here
20 comes this dreamer. | Let us now put him to death and
put his body into one of these holes. We will say, 'An evil
beast has put him to death.' Then we will see what
becomes of his dreams."

21 But Reuben, hearing this, saved him, saying, "Let us not
22 take his life. | Do not kill him violently, but put him in one
of the holes." He said this to keep him safe from their
hands, purposing to take him back to his father.

23 So when Joseph came to his brothers, they took off his
24 long coat which he had on, | and they took him and put
25 him in the hole. Now the hole had no water in it. | Then
seating themselves, they ate their meal, and looking up,
they saw a travelling band of Ishmaelites,* coming from
Gilead on their way to Egypt, with spices and perfumes on
26 their camels. | And Judah said to his brothers, "What
profit is there in putting our brother to death and covering
27 up his blood? | Let us give him to these Ishmaelites for a
price, and let us not be violent to him, for he is our brother,
28 our flesh." And his brothers listened to him. | And some
traders from Midian went by. So pulling Joseph up out of
the hole, they gave him to the Ishmaelites for twenty bits of
silver, and they took him to Egypt.

Joseph, sold as a slave in Egypt, became a minister to the Pharaoh, Egypt's ruler. His task was to build up food reserves and distribute them. He married Asenath, an Egyptian, daughter of an Egyptian priest. She bore him two sons, Manasseh and Ephraim.[1]

Joseph forgave his brothers and had them come to Egypt along with his aged father, Jacob/Israel. The tribes of Israel settled in the land of Goshen, where they carried on their pastoral life.

[1] These two sons are included in the list of the tribes of Israel. It is usual to speak, not of the tribe of Joseph, but of the tribes of Manasseh and of Ephraim. This makes thirteen tribes. When, later, each tribe took up residence in the Promised Land, there were only twelve territories for them. The tribe of Levi (the priests) were given ownership of the towns located on the territories of the twelve other tribes.

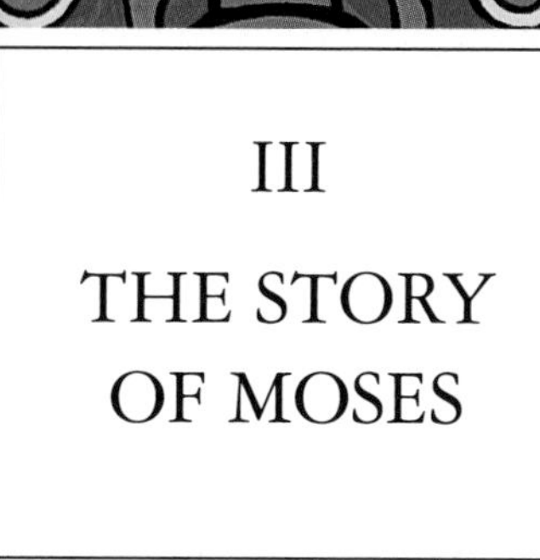

III

THE STORY OF MOSES

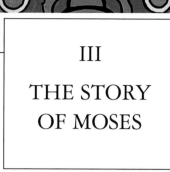

The Book of Genesis told, in the stories of Abraham, Isaac and Jacob/Israel, how the Creator began to make Himself known to the members of a family. He proposed that they live in a Covenant with Him.*

The four other books of the Pentateuch (Exodus, Leviticus, Numbers and Deuteronomy) collect the writings in which the family has multiplied into a whole people. The people lived in Egypt, where it had been reduced to slavery.

Moses was sent to the children of Israel. He revealed to them that God was close to them, conscious of their tribulations and willing to set them free.

He was a Savior God Who would release them from their chains of bondage. He was a dependable God Who had made a Covenant with them and would lead them back to their forefather's Promised Land.

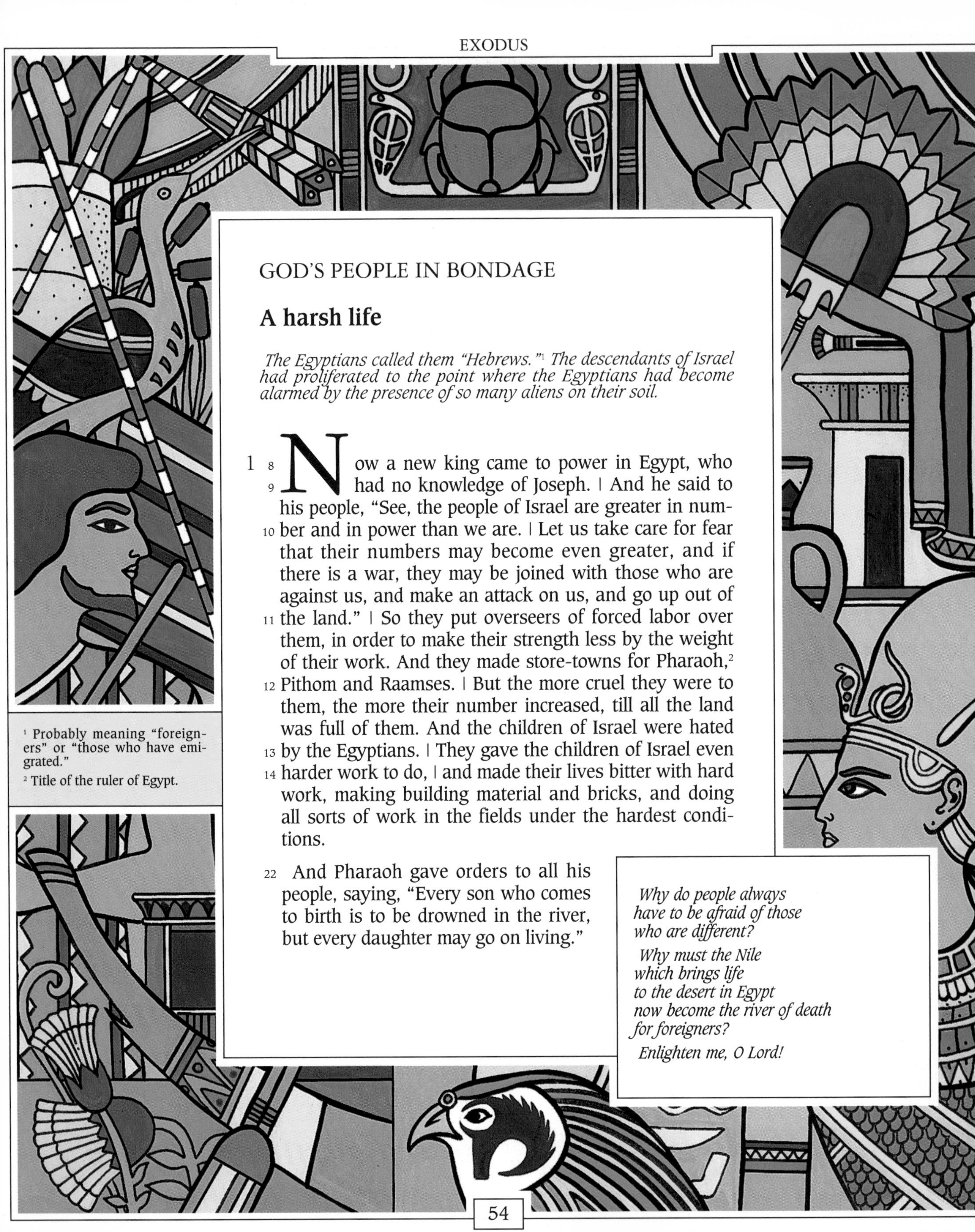

GOD'S PEOPLE IN BONDAGE

A harsh life

The Egyptians called them "Hebrews."[1] The descendants of Israel had proliferated to the point where the Egyptians had become alarmed by the presence of so many aliens on their soil.

1 8 Now a new king came to power in Egypt, who
9 had no knowledge of Joseph. | And he said to
his people, "See, the people of Israel are greater in num-
10 ber and in power than we are. | Let us take care for fear
that their numbers may become even greater, and if
there is a war, they may be joined with those who are
against us, and make an attack on us, and go up out of
11 the land." | So they put overseers of forced labor over
them, in order to make their strength less by the weight
of their work. And they made store-towns for Pharaoh,[2]
12 Pithom and Raamses. | But the more cruel they were to
them, the more their number increased, till all the land
was full of them. And the children of Israel were hated
13 by the Egyptians. | They gave the children of Israel even
14 harder work to do, | and made their lives bitter with hard
work, making building material and bricks, and doing
all sorts of work in the fields under the hardest conditions.

22 And Pharaoh gave orders to all his
people, saying, "Every son who comes
to birth is to be drowned in the river,
but every daughter may go on living."

Why do people always
have to be afraid of those
who are different?
Why must the Nile
which brings life
to the desert in Egypt
now become the river of death
for foreigners?
Enlighten me, O Lord!

[1] Probably meaning "foreigners" or "those who have emigrated."

[2] Title of the ruler of Egypt.

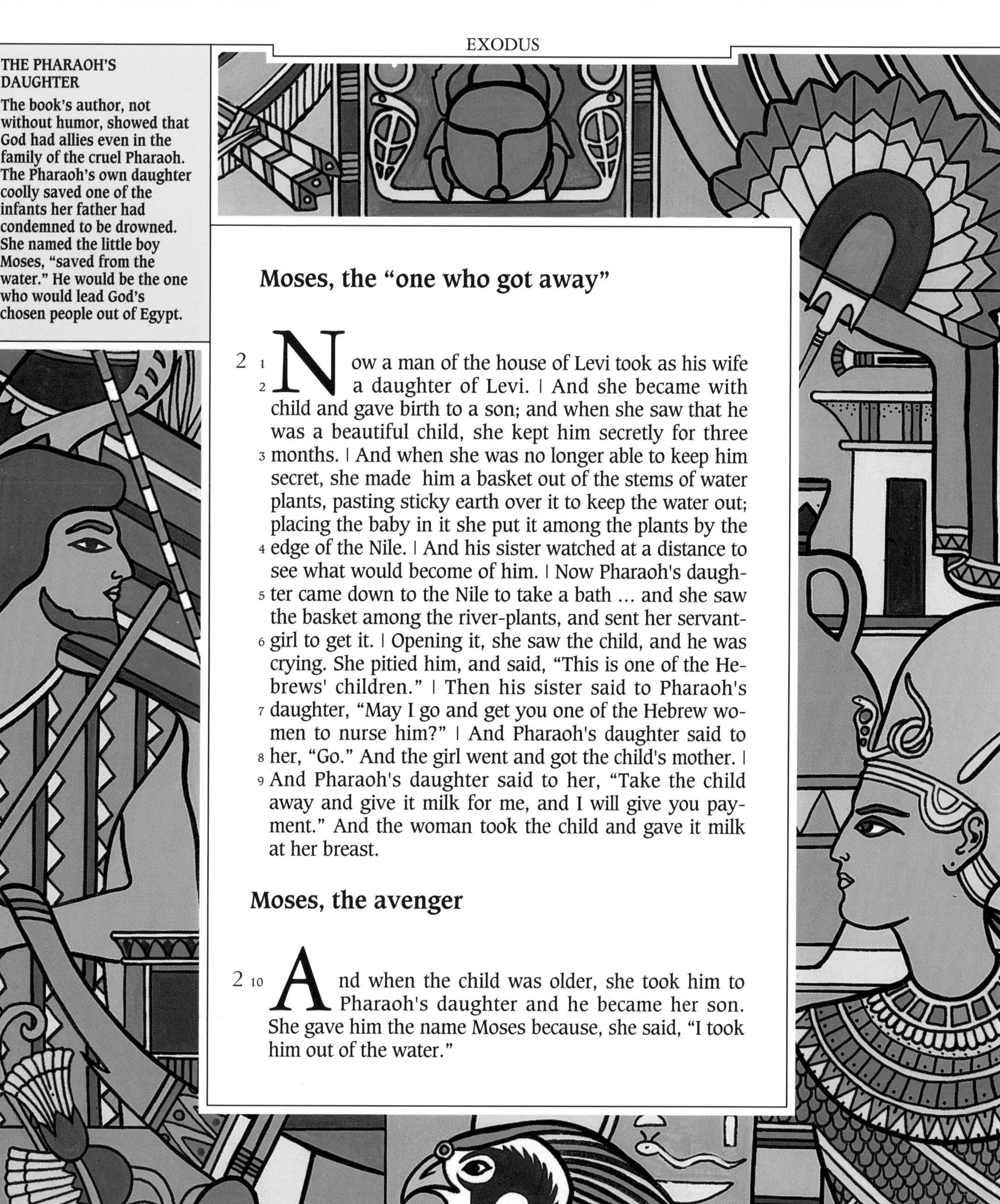

THE PHARAOH'S DAUGHTER

The book's author, not without humor, showed that God had allies even in the family of the cruel Pharaoh. The Pharaoh's own daughter coolly saved one of the infants her father had condemned to be drowned. She named the little boy Moses, "saved from the water." He would be the one who would lead God's chosen people out of Egypt.

Moses, the "one who got away"

2 1 Now a man of the house of Levi took as his wife
2 a daughter of Levi. | And she became with
child and gave birth to a son; and when she saw that he
was a beautiful child, she kept him secretly for three
3 months. | And when she was no longer able to keep him
secret, she made him a basket out of the stems of water
plants, pasting sticky earth over it to keep the water out;
placing the baby in it she put it among the plants by the
4 edge of the Nile. | And his sister watched at a distance to
see what would become of him. | Now Pharaoh's daugh-
5 ter came down to the Nile to take a bath ... and she saw
the basket among the river-plants, and sent her servant-
6 girl to get it. | Opening it, she saw the child, and he was
crying. She pitied him, and said, "This is one of the He-
brews' children." | Then his sister said to Pharaoh's
7 daughter, "May I go and get you one of the Hebrew wo-
men to nurse him?" | And Pharaoh's daughter said to
8 her, "Go." And the girl went and got the child's mother. |
9 And Pharaoh's daughter said to her, "Take the child
away and give it milk for me, and I will give you payment." And the woman took the child and gave it milk
at her breast.

Moses, the avenger

2 10 And when the child was older, she took him to
Pharaoh's daughter and he became her son.
She gave him the name Moses because, she said, "I took
him out of the water."

2 11 Now when Moses had become a man, one day he went
out to his people and saw how hard their work was; and
he saw an Egyptian beating a Hebrew, one of his people.
12 | And turning this way and that, and seeing no one, he
killed the Egyptian, covering his body with sand. | And
13 he went out the day after and saw two of the Hebrews
fighting. He said to him who was in the wrong, "Why
are you fighting your brother?" | And
14 he said, "Who made you a ruler and a
judge over us? are you going to put
me to death as you did the Egyptian?"
And Moses was in fear, and said, "It is
clear that the thing has come to light."
15 | Now when Pharaoh had news of this,
he would have put Moses to death.
But Moses escaped from Pharaoh into
the land of Midian,[1] and he took his
seat by a well.

Moses, you are outraged by the injustices that weigh down your brothers and sisters. You think you are capable of restoring justice through the use of violence. However, your brutality only produces mistrust within the hearts of those you want to help. Now your only choice left is to go through the desert.

After having lost your arrogance, you will now be able to return and put into place a new justice: God's.

Moses and the Lord Savior

In the land of Midian, Moses met a wise man named Jethro and married Zipporah, one of his daughters.

3 1 Now Moses was looking after the flock of Jethro,
his father-in-law, the priest of Midian. He took
the flock to the far side of the desert and came to Horeb,[2]
2 the mountain of God. | And the angel of the Lord was
seen by him in a flame of fire coming out of a bush.[3] He
saw that the bush was on fire, but it was not burned up.
3 | And Moses said, "I will go and see this strange thing,
why the bush is not burned up,"

[1] Midian, the ancestor of the Midianites (for whom the country of Midian was named), was a descendant of Abraham. A story in Genesis tells how Abraham, after the death of Sarah, married Keturah who bore him several children including Midian. See "All peoples on earth will be blessed through you," page 474.

[2] In other stories, this mountain is called Sinai.

[3] This bush has come to be known as "the burning bush."

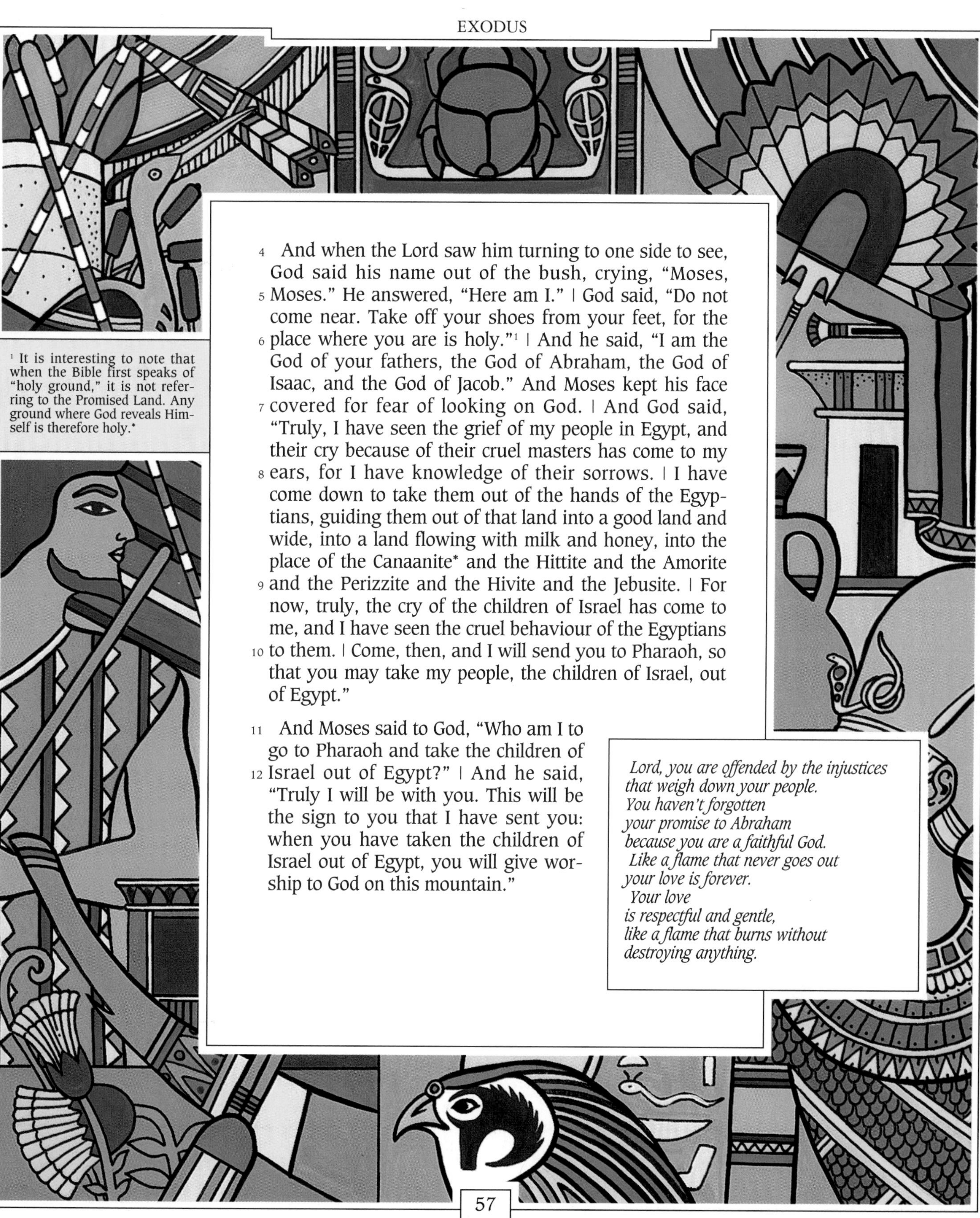

4 And when the Lord saw him turning to one side to see,
God said his name out of the bush, crying, "Moses,
5 Moses." He answered, "Here am I." | God said, "Do not
come near. Take off your shoes from your feet, for the
6 place where you are is holy."[1] | And he said, "I am the
God of your fathers, the God of Abraham, the God of
Isaac, and the God of Jacob." And Moses kept his face
7 covered for fear of looking on God. | And God said,
"Truly, I have seen the grief of my people in Egypt, and
their cry because of their cruel masters has come to my
8 ears, for I have knowledge of their sorrows. | I have
come down to take them out of the hands of the Egyptians, guiding them out of that land into a good land and
wide, into a land flowing with milk and honey, into the
place of the Canaanite* and the Hittite and the Amorite
9 and the Perizzite and the Hivite and the Jebusite. | For
now, truly, the cry of the children of Israel has come to
me, and I have seen the cruel behaviour of the Egyptians
10 to them. | Come, then, and I will send you to Pharaoh, so
that you may take my people, the children of Israel, out
of Egypt."

11 And Moses said to God, "Who am I to
go to Pharaoh and take the children of
12 Israel out of Egypt?" | And he said,
"Truly I will be with you. This will be
the sign to you that I have sent you:
when you have taken the children of
Israel out of Egypt, you will give worship to God on this mountain."

Lord, you are offended by the injustices
that weigh down your people.
You haven't forgotten
your promise to Abraham
because you are a faithful God.
Like a flame that never goes out
your love is forever.
Your love
is respectful and gentle,
like a flame that burns without
destroying anything.

[1] It is interesting to note that when the Bible first speaks of "holy ground," it is not referring to the Promised Land. Any ground where God reveals Himself is therefore holy.*

"THE NAME"*

Out of respect, the Hebrews* decided early on not to pronounce the name revealed by God to Moses.

In public readings, they replaced it by "Adonai," which means "The Lord." In private conversation, they referred only to "The Name." It was a way of saying that the beauty and goodness of God could not be expressed by any human word.

In translations from the Hebrew, The Name is usually expressed as "The LORD."*

I AM

Written Hebrew uses consonants only. The name revealed to Moses was made up of four consonants, which our alphabet transcribes as Y or J, H, W or V, and H. The four consonants of the name are sometimes referred to by the Greek word "tetragrammaton." Many Christian scholars in the 19th century thought that the missing vowels were e, o and a, whence the name JeHoVaH. This came to be viewed as a mistake since the word Jehovah, unlike every other Hebrew name, did not have any meaning of its own. It is now believed that the name's pronunciation was YaHWeH. This was a way of representing the name that God used twice for Himself in verse 14: "I am."

(See John 8:58, page 349.)

The Name of the Lord

3 13 And Moses said to God, "When I come to the children of Israel and say to them, 'The God of your
fathers has sent me to you,' and they say to me, 'What
14 is his name?' what am I to say to them?" | And God said
to him, "I AM WHAT I AM." He said, "Say to the chil-
15 dren of Israel, I AM has sent me to you." | And God
went on to say to Moses, "Say to the children of Israel,
'The Lord, the God of your fathers, the God of Abraham,
of Isaac, and of Jacob, has sent me to you.'This is my
16 name for ever,... | Go and get together the chiefs of the
children of Israel, and say to them, 'The Lord, the God of
your fathers, the God of Abraham, of Isaac, and of Jacob,
has been seen by me, and has said, Truly I have taken
up your cause, because of what is done to you in
Egypt.'...

18 And they will listen to your voice. You, with the chiefs
of Israel, will go to Pharaoh, the king of Egypt, and say
to him, 'The Lord, the God of the Hebrews, has come to
us. Let us then go three days' journey into the desert to
make an offering to the Lord our God.' | And I am cer-
19 tain that the king of Egypt will not let
you go without being forced. | But I
20 will put out my hand and overcome
Egypt with all the wonders which I will
do among them. After that he will let
you go."

Lord, over against the nothingness of idols,
you exist.
You are close to your people.
You are Yahweh.
But one name is not sufficient to express
all that you are.
You are our Father,
with a merciful heart,
the liberator and rock of Israel.
You are the shepherd, the friend, the
protector,
the God who is bigger than our hearts,
the God who is too big
to be imprisoned by our words.
Hallowed be your name!

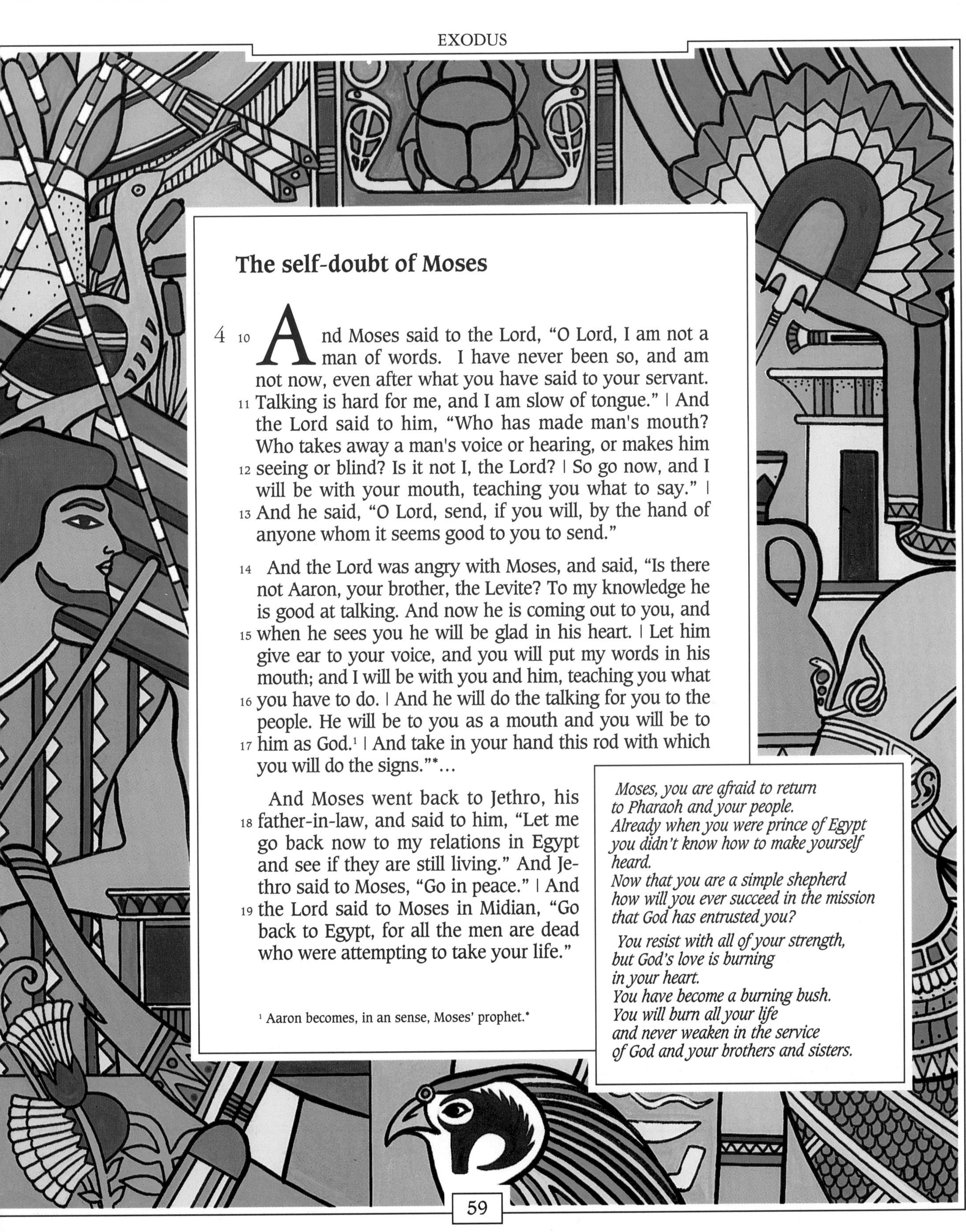

The self-doubt of Moses

4 10 And Moses said to the Lord, "O Lord, I am not a
man of words. I have never been so, and am
not now, even after what you have said to your servant.
11 Talking is hard for me, and I am slow of tongue." | And
the Lord said to him, "Who has made man's mouth?
Who takes away a man's voice or hearing, or makes him
12 seeing or blind? Is it not I, the Lord? | So go now, and I
will be with your mouth, teaching you what to say." |
13 And he said, "O Lord, send, if you will, by the hand of
anyone whom it seems good to you to send."

14 And the Lord was angry with Moses, and said, "Is there
not Aaron, your brother, the Levite? To my knowledge he
is good at talking. And now he is coming out to you, and
15 when he sees you he will be glad in his heart. | Let him
give ear to your voice, and you will put my words in his
mouth; and I will be with you and him, teaching you what
16 you have to do. | And he will do the talking for you to the
people. He will be to you as a mouth and you will be to
17 him as God.[1] | And take in your hand this rod with which
you will do the signs."*...

And Moses went back to Jethro, his
18 father-in-law, and said to him, "Let me
go back now to my relations in Egypt
and see if they are still living." And Je-
thro said to Moses, "Go in peace." | And
19 the Lord said to Moses in Midian, "Go
back to Egypt, for all the men are dead
who were attempting to take your life."

[1] Aaron becomes, in an sense, Moses' prophet.*

Moses, you are afraid to return
to Pharaoh and your people.
Already when you were prince of Egypt
you didn't know how to make yourself
heard.
Now that you are a simple shepherd
how will you ever succeed in the mission
that God has entrusted you?

You resist with all of your strength,
but God's love is burning
in your heart.
You have become a burning bush.
You will burn all your life
and never weaken in the service
of God and your brothers and sisters.

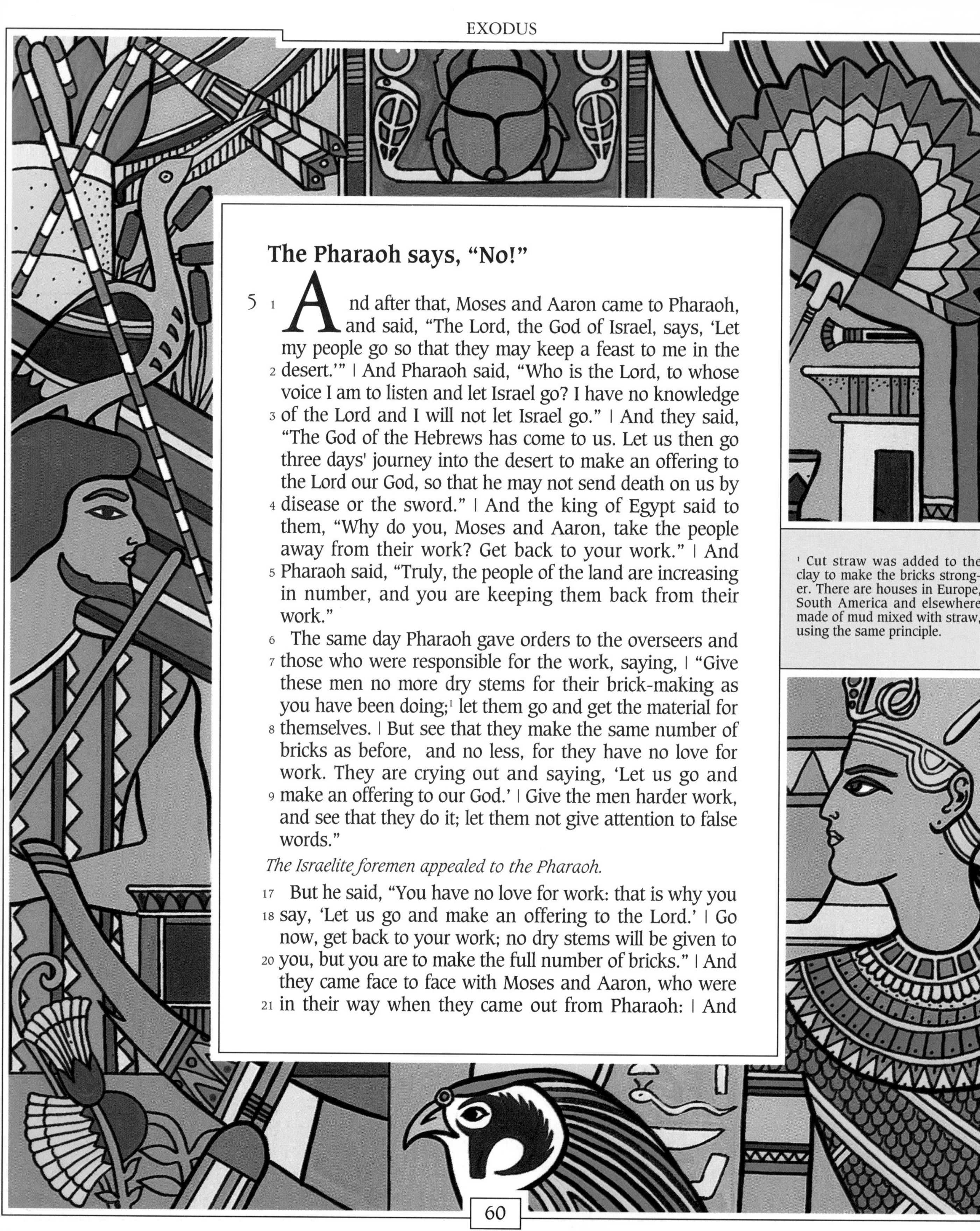

The Pharaoh says, "No!"

5 1 And after that, Moses and Aaron came to Pharaoh,
and said, "The Lord, the God of Israel, says, 'Let
my people go so that they may keep a feast to me in the
2 desert.'" | And Pharaoh said, "Who is the Lord, to whose
voice I am to listen and let Israel go? I have no knowledge
3 of the Lord and I will not let Israel go." | And they said,
"The God of the Hebrews has come to us. Let us then go
three days' journey into the desert to make an offering to
the Lord our God, so that he may not send death on us by
4 disease or the sword." | And the king of Egypt said to
them, "Why do you, Moses and Aaron, take the people
away from their work? Get back to your work." | And
5 Pharaoh said, "Truly, the people of the land are increasing
in number, and you are keeping them back from their
work."

6 The same day Pharaoh gave orders to the overseers and
7 those who were responsible for the work, saying, | "Give
these men no more dry stems for their brick-making as
you have been doing;[1] let them go and get the material for
8 themselves. | But see that they make the same number of
bricks as before, and no less, for they have no love for
work. They are crying out and saying, 'Let us go and
9 make an offering to our God.' | Give the men harder work,
and see that they do it; let them not give attention to false
words."

The Israelite foremen appealed to the Pharaoh.

17 But he said, "You have no love for work: that is why you
18 say, 'Let us go and make an offering to the Lord.' | Go
now, get back to your work; no dry stems will be given to
20 you, but you are to make the full number of bricks." | And
they came face to face with Moses and Aaron, who were
21 in their way when they came out from Pharaoh: | And

[1] Cut straw was added to the clay to make the bricks stronger. There are houses in Europe, South America and elsewhere made of mud mixed with straw, using the same principle.

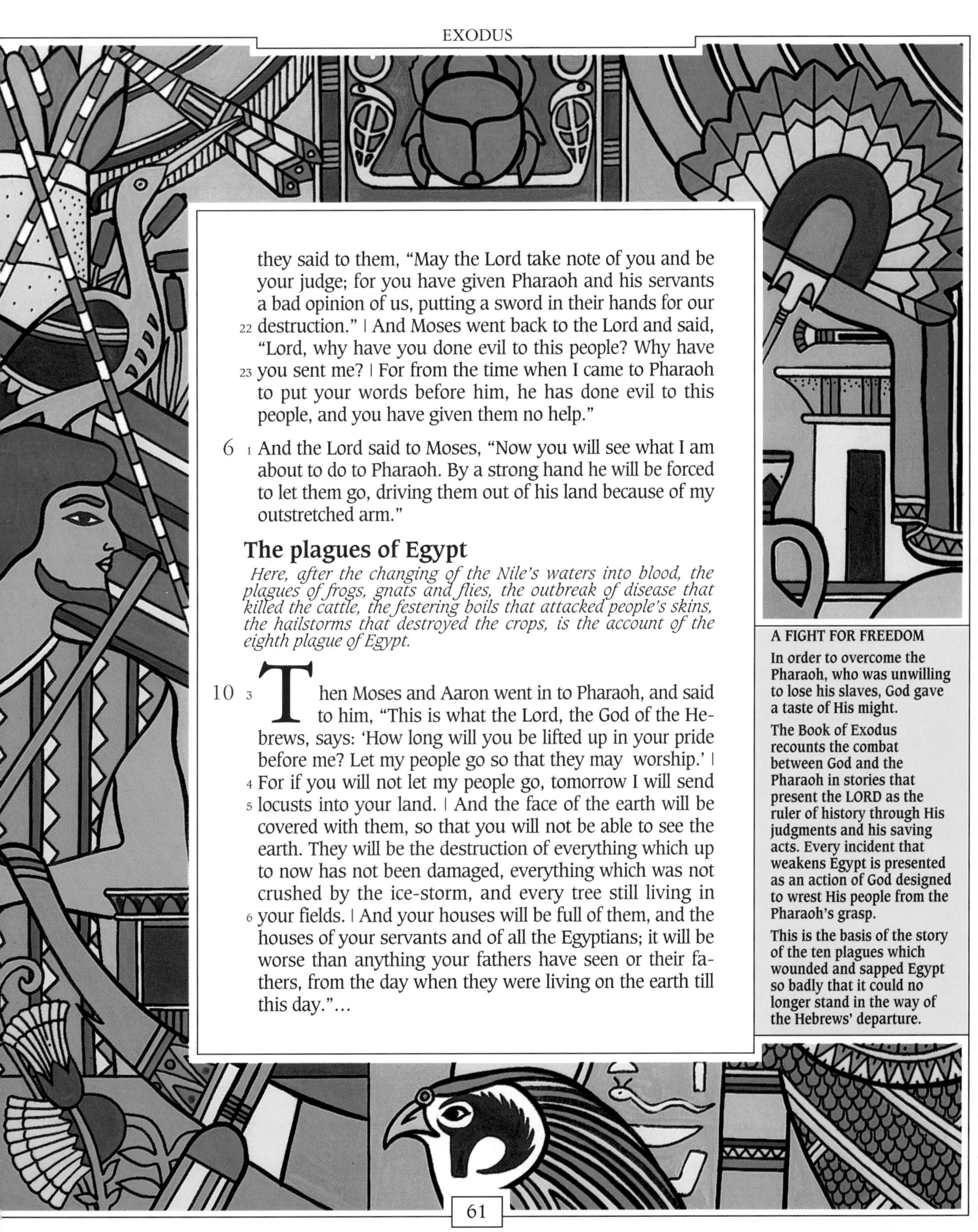

they said to them, "May the Lord take note of you and be
your judge; for you have given Pharaoh and his servants
a bad opinion of us, putting a sword in their hands for our
22 destruction." | And Moses went back to the Lord and said,
"Lord, why have you done evil to this people? Why have
23 you sent me? | For from the time when I came to Pharaoh
to put your words before him, he has done evil to this
people, and you have given them no help."

6 1 And the Lord said to Moses, "Now you will see what I am
about to do to Pharaoh. By a strong hand he will be forced
to let them go, driving them out of his land because of my
outstretched arm."

The plagues of Egypt

Here, after the changing of the Nile's waters into blood, the plagues of frogs, gnats and flies, the outbreak of disease that killed the cattle, the festering boils that attacked people's skins, the hailstorms that destroyed the crops, is the account of the eighth plague of Egypt.

10 3 Then Moses and Aaron went in to Pharaoh, and said
to him, "This is what the Lord, the God of the Hebrews, says: 'How long will you be lifted up in your pride
before me? Let my people go so that they may worship.' |
4 For if you will not let my people go, tomorrow I will send
5 locusts into your land. | And the face of the earth will be
covered with them, so that you will not be able to see the
earth. They will be the destruction of everything which up
to now has not been damaged, everything which was not
crushed by the ice-storm, and every tree still living in
6 your fields. | And your houses will be full of them, and the
houses of your servants and of all the Egyptians; it will be
worse than anything your fathers have seen or their fathers, from the day when they were living on the earth till
this day."...

A FIGHT FOR FREEDOM

In order to overcome the Pharaoh, who was unwilling to lose his slaves, God gave a taste of His might.

The Book of Exodus recounts the combat between God and the Pharaoh in stories that present the LORD as the ruler of history through His judgments and his saving acts. Every incident that weakens Egypt is presented as an action of God designed to wrest His people from the Pharaoh's grasp.

This is the basis of the story of the ten plagues which wounded and sapped Egypt so badly that it could no longer stand in the way of the Hebrews' departure.

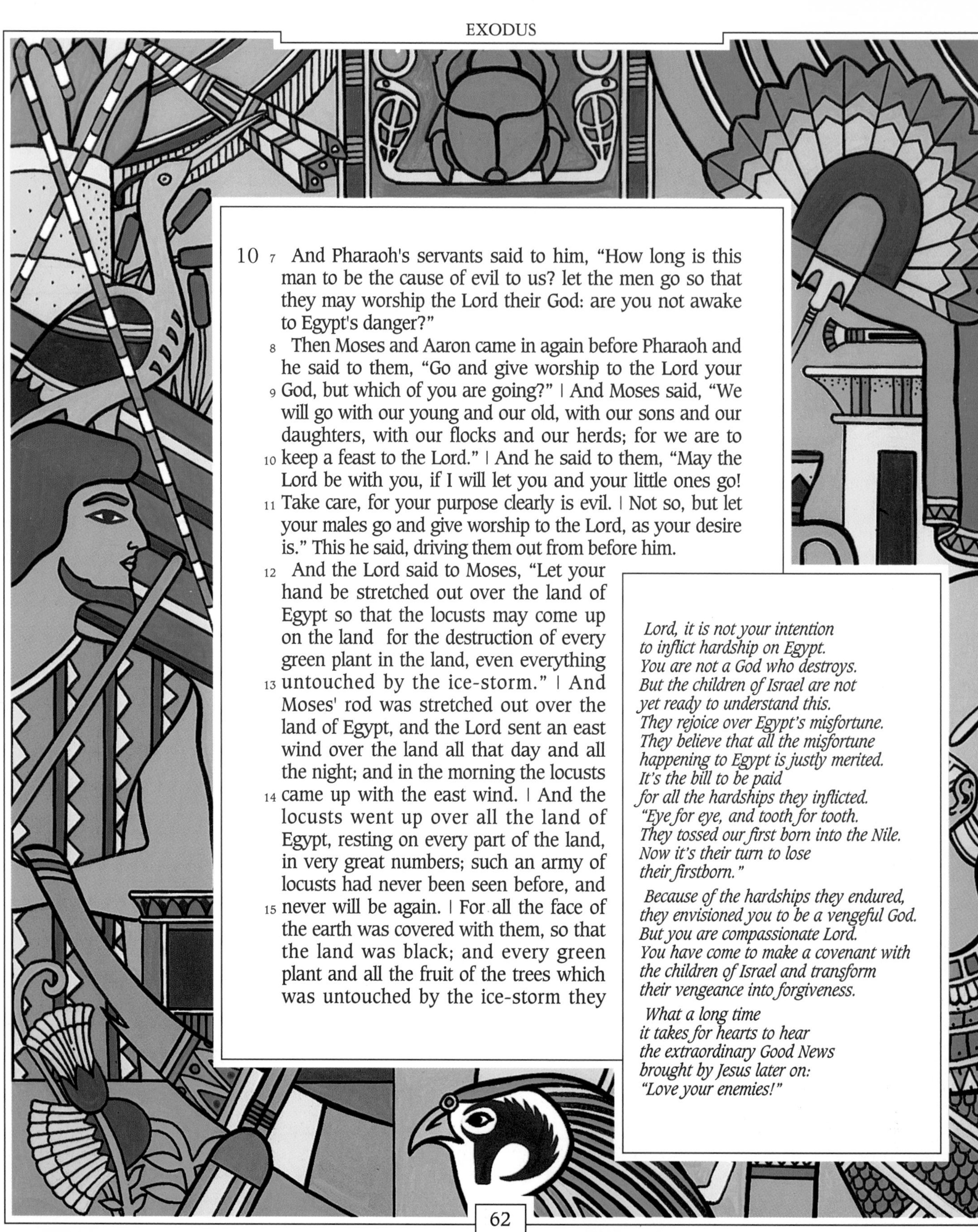

10 7 And Pharaoh's servants said to him, "How long is this
man to be the cause of evil to us? let the men go so that
they may worship the Lord their God: are you not awake
to Egypt's danger?"
8 Then Moses and Aaron came in again before Pharaoh and
he said to them, "Go and give worship to the Lord your
9 God, but which of you are going?" | And Moses said, "We
will go with our young and our old, with our sons and our
daughters, with our flocks and our herds; for we are to
10 keep a feast to the Lord." | And he said to them, "May the
Lord be with you, if I will let you and your little ones go!
11 Take care, for your purpose clearly is evil. | Not so, but let
your males go and give worship to the Lord, as your desire
is." This he said, driving them out from before him.
12 And the Lord said to Moses, "Let your
hand be stretched out over the land of
Egypt so that the locusts may come up
on the land for the destruction of every
green plant in the land, even everything
13 untouched by the ice-storm." | And
Moses' rod was stretched out over the
land of Egypt, and the Lord sent an east
wind over the land all that day and all
the night; and in the morning the locusts
14 came up with the east wind. | And the
locusts went up over all the land of
Egypt, resting on every part of the land,
in very great numbers; such an army of
locusts had never been seen before, and
15 never will be again. | For all the face of
the earth was covered with them, so that
the land was black; and every green
plant and all the fruit of the trees which
was untouched by the ice-storm they

Lord, it is not your intention
to inflict hardship on Egypt.
You are not a God who destroys.
But the children of Israel are not
yet ready to understand this.
They rejoice over Egypt's misfortune.
They believe that all the misfortune
happening to Egypt is justly merited.
It's the bill to be paid
for all the hardships they inflicted.
"Eye for eye, and tooth for tooth.
They tossed our first born into the Nile.
Now it's their turn to lose
their firstborn."

Because of the hardships they endured,
they envisioned you to be a vengeful God.
But you are compassionate Lord.
You have come to make a covenant with
the children of Israel and transform
their vengeance into forgiveness.

What a long time
it takes for hearts to hear
the extraordinary Good News
brought by Jesus later on:
"Love your enemies!"

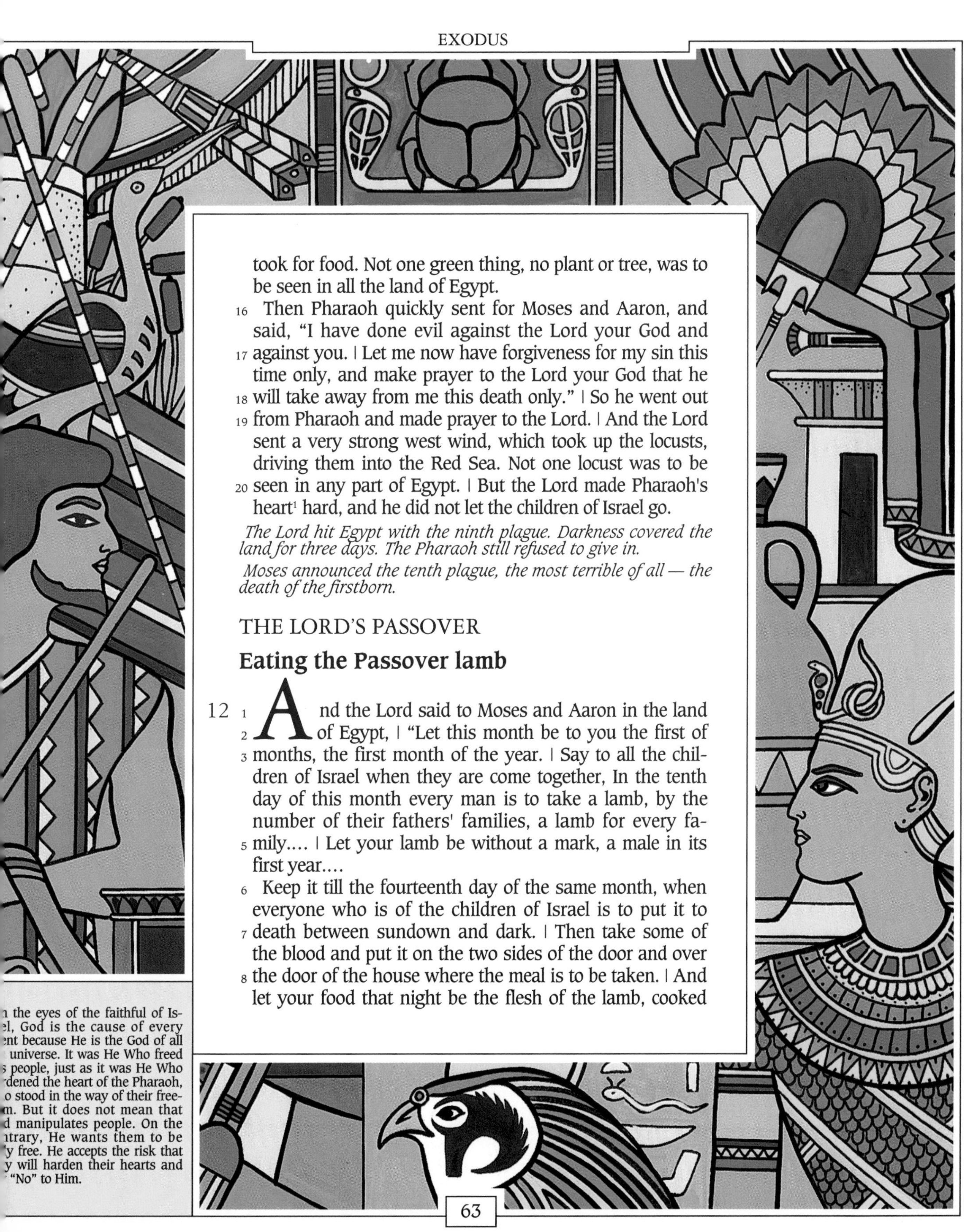

took for food. Not one green thing, no plant or tree, was to
be seen in all the land of Egypt.
16 Then Pharaoh quickly sent for Moses and Aaron, and
said, "I have done evil against the Lord your God and
17 against you. | Let me now have forgiveness for my sin this
time only, and make prayer to the Lord your God that he
18 will take away from me this death only." | So he went out
19 from Pharaoh and made prayer to the Lord. | And the Lord
sent a very strong west wind, which took up the locusts,
driving them into the Red Sea. Not one locust was to be
20 seen in any part of Egypt. | But the Lord made Pharaoh's
heart[1] hard, and he did not let the children of Israel go.

The Lord hit Egypt with the ninth plague. Darkness covered the land for three days. The Pharaoh still refused to give in.

Moses announced the tenth plague, the most terrible of all — the death of the firstborn.

THE LORD'S PASSOVER

Eating the Passover lamb

12 1 And the Lord said to Moses and Aaron in the land
2 of Egypt, | "Let this month be to you the first of
3 months, the first month of the year. | Say to all the chil-
dren of Israel when they are come together, In the tenth
day of this month every man is to take a lamb, by the
number of their fathers' families, a lamb for every fa-
5 mily.... | Let your lamb be without a mark, a male in its
first year....
6 Keep it till the fourteenth day of the same month, when
everyone who is of the children of Israel is to put it to
7 death between sundown and dark. | Then take some of
the blood and put it on the two sides of the door and over
8 the door of the house where the meal is to be taken. | And
let your food that night be the flesh of the lamb, cooked

n the eyes of the faithful of Is-
el, God is the cause of every
ent because He is the God of all
universe. It was He Who freed
s people, just as it was He Who
rdened the heart of the Pharaoh,
o stood in the way of their free-
m. But it does not mean that
d manipulates people. On the
ntrary, He wants them to be
y free. He accepts the risk that
y will harden their hearts and
"No" to Him.

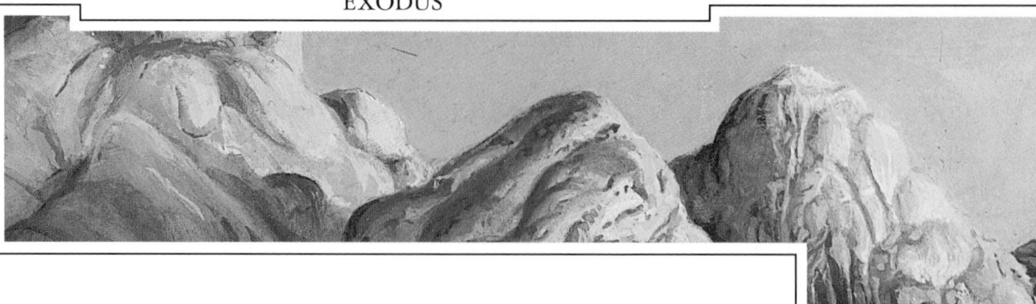

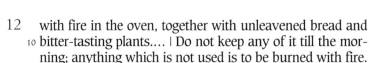

THE JEWISH PASSOVER

The Passover,* or Pasch, was, and still is, the great feast of the Jews.* In memory of the first Passover, in Egypt, they sacrificed a lamb like the one whose blood was smeared on the house doorposts.

Since the destruction of the Temple of Jerusalem in 70 AD, the Jews no longer sacrifice lambs. They evoke the sacrifice symbolically during the Passover meal.

Jew is the name given to the descendants of the Hebrews, children of Israel.

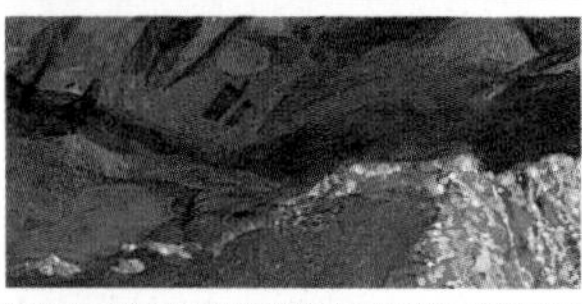

THE PASCHAL LAMB

The lamb of the Passover is the sign that God wishes to make free, to save, to let live.

Later, God sent his Son, Jesus. Jesus loves all people. He tears them away from the death* of sin.* He gave his own life so that humans can partake in the very life of God. This is why he is sometimes called the Lamb of God (John 1:36, page 334).

12 with fire in the oven, together with unleavened bread and
10 bitter-tasting plants.... | Do not keep any of it till the mor-
ning; anything which is not used is to be burned with fire.
11 | And eat your meal dressed as if for a journey, with your
shoes on your feet and your sticks in your hands. Eat it
12 quickly: it is the Lord's Passover.[1] | For on that night I will
go through the land of Egypt, sending
death on every first male child, of man
and of beast, and judging all the gods of
13 Egypt. I am the Lord. | And the blood will
be a sign on the houses where you are;
When I see the blood I will go over you,
and no evil will come on you for your
destruction, when my hand is on the
land of Egypt.
14 And this day is to commemorate:[2] you
are to keep it as a feast to the Lord
through all your generations, as an order
for ever."

The blood of a lamb was put on the sides
and tops of the doorframes and the doors
of the houses were closed.
Death passed over and God came
in to make a covenant.
The blood of a man
on the wood of a cross
cried out for forgiveness for his executioners
and the doors to hearts were opened.

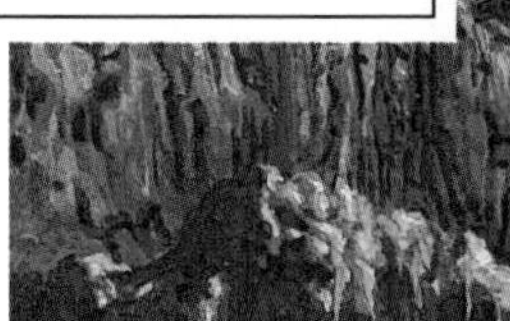

Crossing the sea on dry land

With the tenth plague, the Pharaoh gave in, and the Hebrews left in haste. They took bread with them in the form of flat loaves, since they did not have time to let the bread rise.[3]

14 5 And word came to Pharaoh of the flight of the
peopl. The feeling of Pharaoh and of his servants about the people was changed, and they said,
"Why have we let Israel go, so that they will do no more
6 work for us?" | So he had his chariot made ready and
7 took his people with him. | He took six hundred chariots,
all the chariots of Egypt, and captains over all of them....
9 | But the Egyptians went after them, ... and overtook
them in their tents by the sea.[4]...

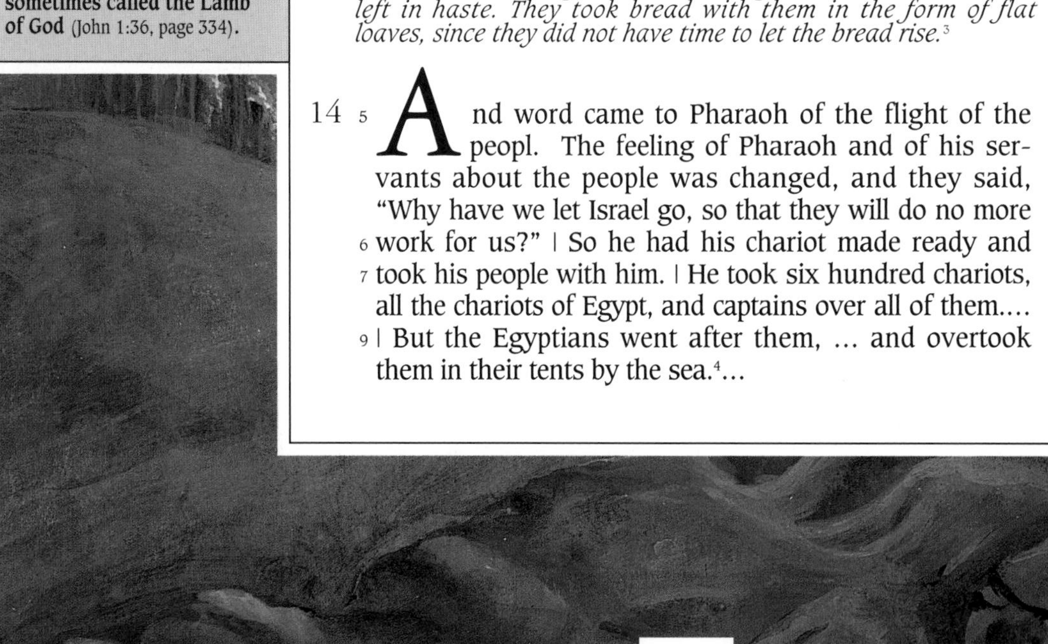

[1] The origin of the wor "Pasch" is obscure. It is usual said to mean the "passin over" by the Lord.

[2] A commemoration is not ju a remembrance; it is also a "enactment" of a past even God is doing today what He d in the past. He is freeing u from every kind of bondag and always will. When Jesu asked his apostles to re-ena his supper "in remembranc of him (1 Corinthians 11:2 26, page 434), he was origina ing a commemoration.

[3] This unleavened bread, i. bread without yeast, remair an important part of the Jewis Passover meal.

[4] To the Hebrews, the sea w Evil,* the great hostile forc before which humans we powerless. See the double-pa spread, pages 32-33, Mar 4:35-41 and Matthew 14:2 23.

10 When Pharaoh came near, the children of Israel, lifting
up their eyes, saw the Egyptians coming after them, and
11 were full of fear; and their cry went up to God. | And they
said to Moses, "Was there no resting place for the dead in
Egypt, that you have taken us away to come to our death
in the desert? Why have you taken us out of Egypt?"... |
13 But Moses said, "Stay where you are and have no fear.
Now you will see the salvation of the Lord which he will
give you today, for the Egyptians whom you see today
14 you will never see again. | The Lord will make war for
you, you have only to keep quiet."
15-16 And the Lord said to Moses, | "Let your rod be lifted up
and your hand stretched out over the sea, and it will be
parted in two. The children of Israel will go through on
17 dry land. | I will make the heart of the Egyptians hard, and
they will go in after them: and I will be honoured over
Pharaoh and over his army, his war-carriages, and his
18 horsemen. | And the Egyptians will see that I am the Lord,
when I get honour over Pharaoh and his chariots and his
horsemen."
21 And when Moses' hand was stretched out over the sea,
the Lord with a strong east wind made the sea go back all
night, and the waters were parted in two and the sea be-
22 came dry land.[1] | The children of Israel went through the
sea on dry land. The waters were a wall on their right side
23 and on their left. | Then the Egyptians went after them
24 into the middle of the sea.... | And in the morning watch,
the Lord, looking out on the armies of the Egyptians from
the pillar of fire and cloud, sent trouble on the army of the
25 Egyptians. | He made the wheels of their chariots stiff, so
that they had hard work driving them. The Egyptians
said, "Let us escape from Israel, for the Lord is fighting
for them against the Egyptians." | And the Lord said to
26 Moses, "Let your hand be stretched out over the sea, and

In Genesis 1:1-31, God divi-
ed the waters and let the dry
and appear on which He crea-
ed man. It is similar here. God
ivides the waters to create His
eople.

"THE WATERS WERE DIVIDED"

One undersands quite well why this outstanding event will be recalled by many writers of the other books of the Old Testament, in the Psalms and numerous passages of the prophets. It is not hard to see why film-makers have tried to reimagine this scene. Moses holds up his rod, and lo! the sea parts. The Hebrew column advances between the two walls of water. Moses, who himself was saved from the waters, leads his people through the sea to freedom. This is a magnificent vision, whose meaning it is important to understand.

The authors' intention was also to tell us how the event was interpreted by the children of Israel. It was the first time that the Hebrews as a people discovered God. God was the liberator, the God of life. He created a passage on dry land for the people whose road was blocked by the sea. Whatever the obstacle facing us, help will always come from God to surmount it. The slaves were henceforth out of the Pharaoh's reach. God lifted them out of bondage to freedom, from degrading servitude to satisfying service. He had already begun murmuring in their hearts, "I no longer call you servants; instead, I call you friends." (John 15:15, page 360.)

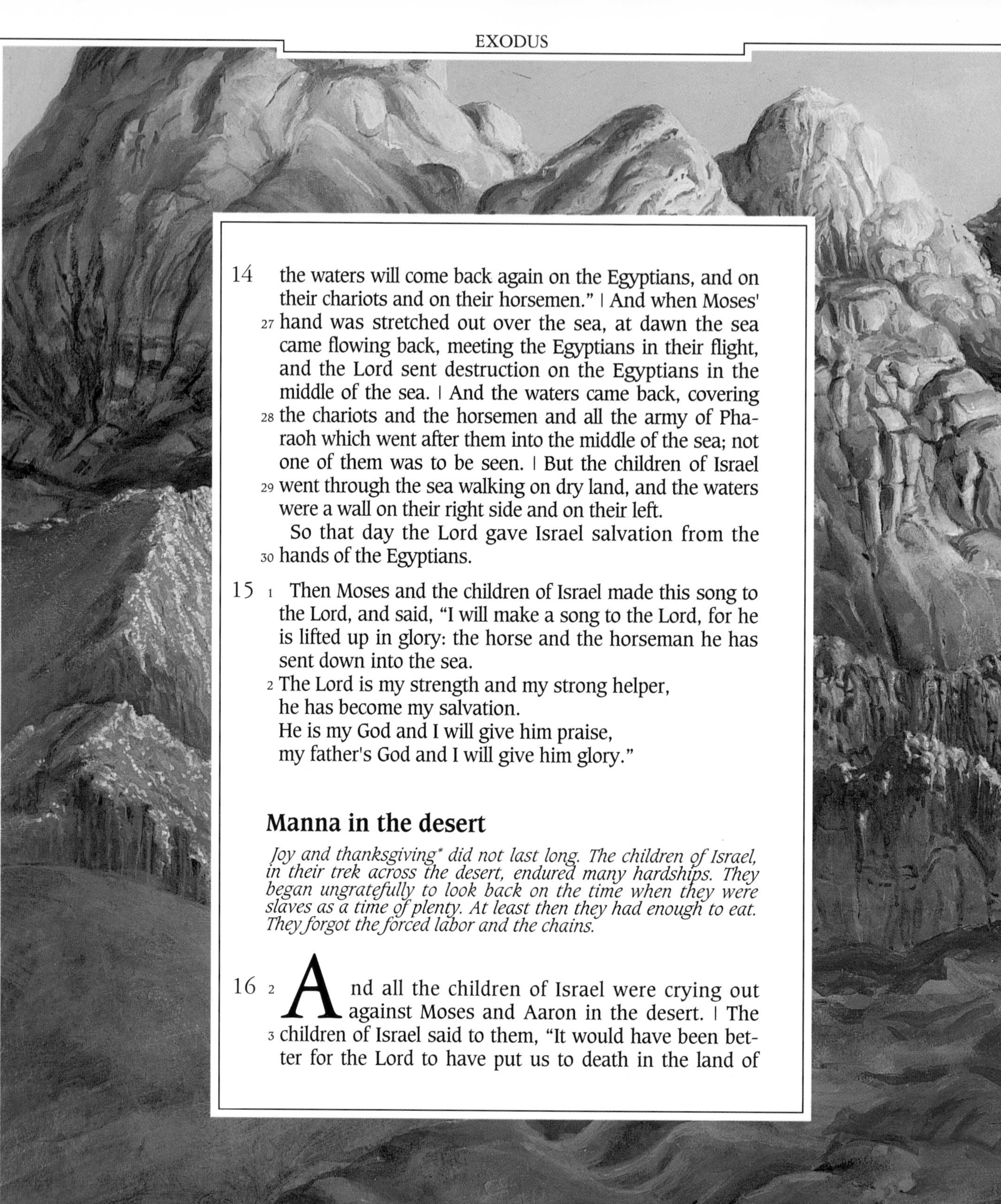

14 the waters will come back again on the Egyptians, and on
their chariots and on their horsemen." | And when Moses'
27 hand was stretched out over the sea, at dawn the sea
came flowing back, meeting the Egyptians in their flight,
and the Lord sent destruction on the Egyptians in the
middle of the sea. | And the waters came back, covering
28 the chariots and the horsemen and all the army of Pharaoh which went after them into the middle of the sea; not
one of them was to be seen. | But the children of Israel
29 went through the sea walking on dry land, and the waters
were a wall on their right side and on their left.
So that day the Lord gave Israel salvation from the
30 hands of the Egyptians.

15 1 Then Moses and the children of Israel made this song to the Lord, and said, "I will make a song to the Lord, for he is lifted up in glory: the horse and the horseman he has sent down into the sea.

2 The Lord is my strength and my strong helper,
he has become my salvation.
He is my God and I will give him praise,
my father's God and I will give him glory."

Manna in the desert

Joy and thanksgiving did not last long. The children of Israel, in their trek across the desert, endured many hardships. They began ungratefully to look back on the time when they were slaves as a time of plenty. At least then they had enough to eat. They forgot the forced labor and the chains.*

16 2 And all the children of Israel were crying out
against Moses and Aaron in the desert. | The
3 children of Israel said to them, "It would have been better for the Lord to have put us to death in the land of

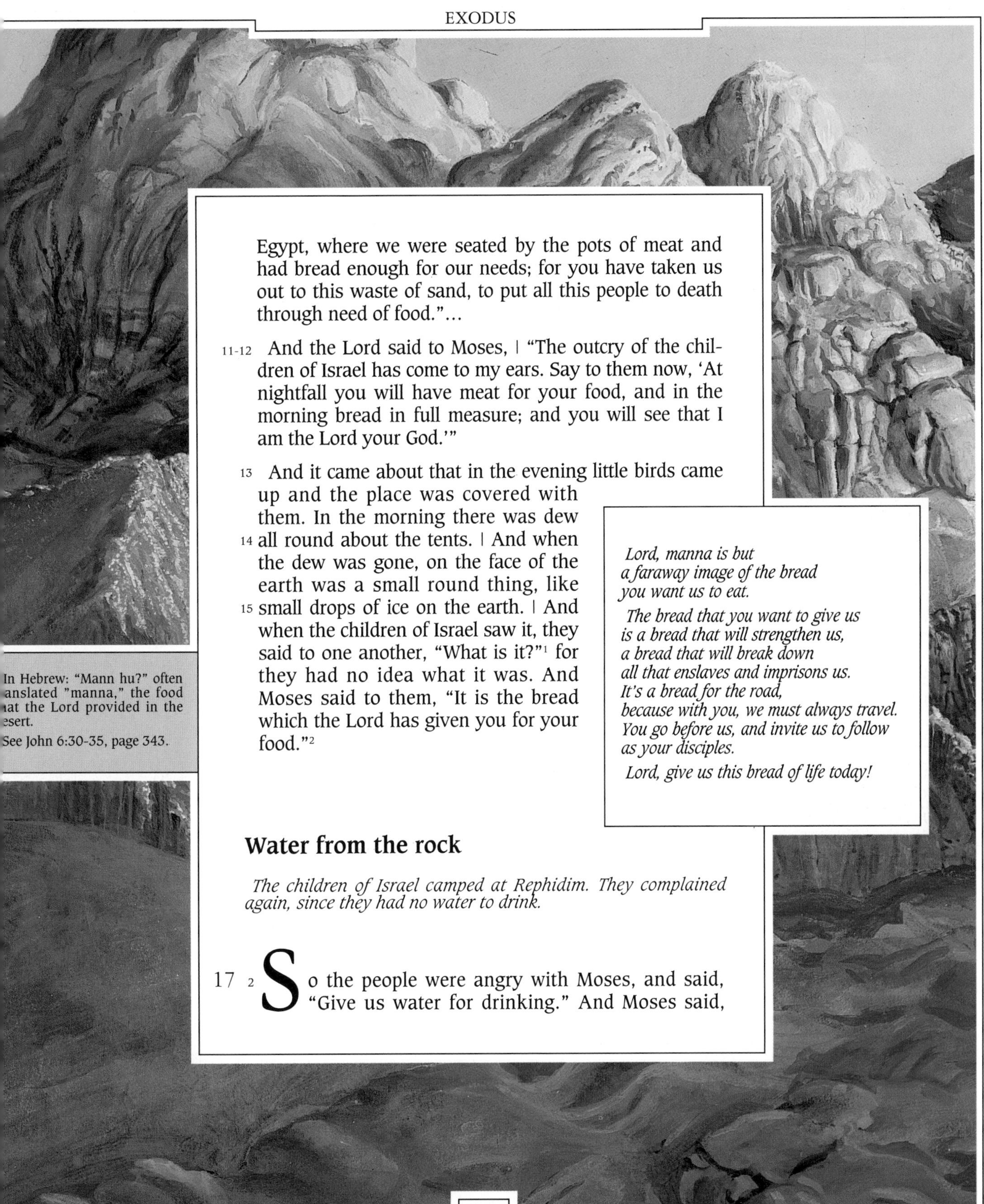

Egypt, where we were seated by the pots of meat and
had bread enough for our needs; for you have taken us
out to this waste of sand, to put all this people to death
through need of food."...

11-12 And the Lord said to Moses, | "The outcry of the chil-
dren of Israel has come to my ears. Say to them now, 'At
nightfall you will have meat for your food, and in the
morning bread in full measure; and you will see that I
am the Lord your God.'"

13 And it came about that in the evening little birds came
up and the place was covered with
them. In the morning there was dew
14 all round about the tents. | And when
the dew was gone, on the face of the
earth was a small round thing, like
15 small drops of ice on the earth. | And
when the children of Israel saw it, they
said to one another, "What is it?"[1] for
they had no idea what it was. And
Moses said to them, "It is the bread
which the Lord has given you for your
food."[2]

Lord, manna is but
a faraway image of the bread
you want us to eat.

The bread that you want to give us
is a bread that will strengthen us,
a bread that will break down
all that enslaves and imprisons us.
It's a bread for the road,
because with you, we must always travel.
You go before us, and invite us to follow
as your disciples.

Lord, give us this bread of life today!

In Hebrew: "Mann hu?" often
anslated "manna," the food
at the Lord provided in the
esert.

See John 6:30-35, page 343.

Water from the rock

The children of Israel camped at Rephidim. They complained again, since they had no water to drink.

17 2 So the people were angry with Moses, and said,
"Give us water for drinking." And Moses said,

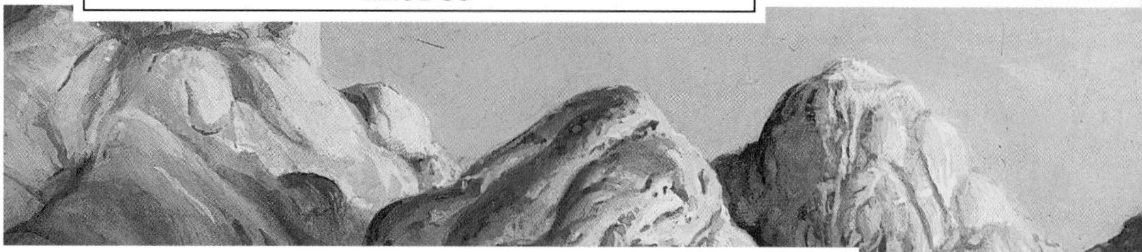

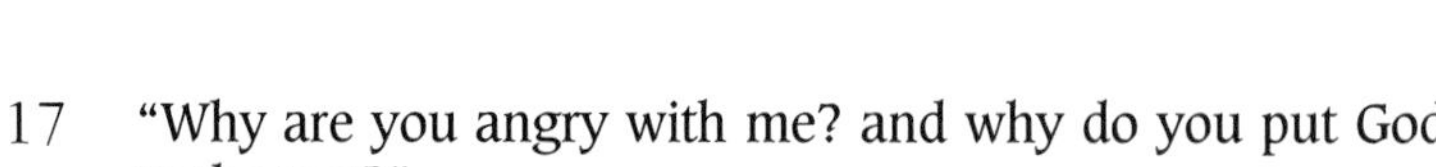

ROCK

Rock is solid and therefore secure. A house built on rock survives all storms. Hidden among the rocks, you are safe from your enemies. "Rock" thus became one of the names for God (see page 58). [1]

The rock produced water, that is to say, life for the marchers in the desert. This completes the image of God. The protector gives life — his own life — to those in His care. He is the fountain of life.

[1] Later, Jesus gave the name "rock" to one of his disciples, Simon son of Jonah, calling him "Kepha" (rock). (Matthew 16:18, page 281.)

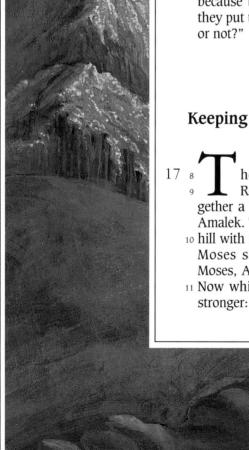

17 "Why are you angry with me? and why do you put God
to the test?"...

4 And Moses, crying out to the Lord, said, "What am I to
do to this people? They are almost ready to put me to
5 death by stoning."* | And the Lord said to Moses, "Go
on before the people, and take some of the elders* of Israel with you, and take in your hand the rod which was
stretched out over the Nile,[1] and go.

6 See, I will take my place before you on the rock in Horeb; and when you give the rock[2] a blow, water will
come out of it, and the people will have drink." And
Moses did so before the eyes of the chiefs of Israel.

7 And he gave that place the name Massah and Meribah,
because the children of Israel were angry, and because
they put the Lord to the test, saying, "Is the Lord with us
or not?"

Keeping his arms raised

17 8 Then Amalek came and made war on Israel in
9 Rephidim. | And Moses said to Joshua,[3] "Get to-
gether a band of men for us and go out, make war on
Amalek. Tomorrow I will take my place on the top of the
10 hill with the rod of God in my hand." | So Joshua did as
Moses said to him, and went to war with Amalek.
Moses, Aaron, and Hur[4] went up to the top of the hill. |
11 Now while Moses' hand was lifted up, Israel was the
stronger: but when he let his hand go down, Amalek be-

[1] An allusion to the first plagu of Egypt, when Moses struc the Nile with his rod and th waters turned into blood.

[2] For a different story concer ning the rock, see Number 20:1-12, page 80, where Mose struck the rock again instead o speaking to it.

[3] The name Joshua has th same meaning as the name Je sus: The Lord saves.

[4] A shadowy figure, very clos to Moses. He vanishes from th Exodus stories after the epi sode of the Golden Calf. Se page 74.

'RAYER AND ACTION

'he children of Israel, in
rder to escape from the
'iolence of the Amalekites,
ad need of the action of
oshua and the prayer of
loses.

'he person dear to God's
eart is one who accepts
esponsibilities, acts, invents
nd converses with his
laker.

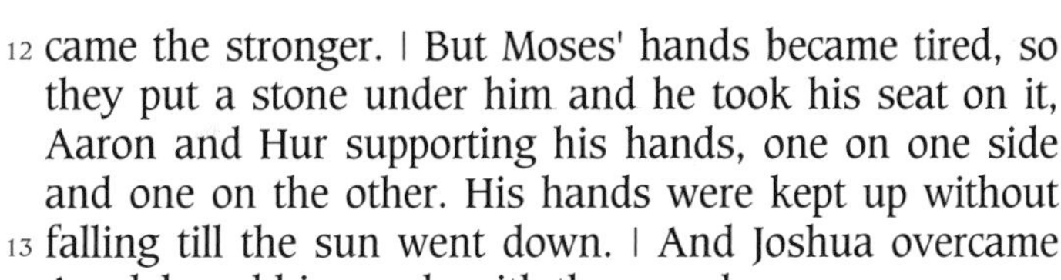

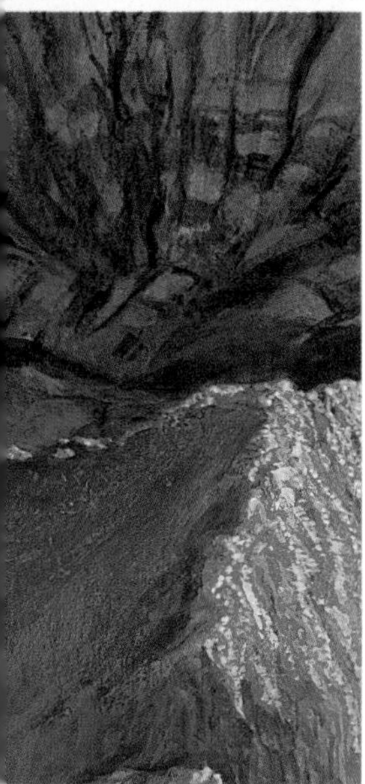

12 came the stronger. | But Moses' hands became tired, so
they put a stone under him and he took his seat on it,
Aaron and Hur supporting his hands, one on one side
and one on the other. His hands were kept up without
13 falling till the sun went down. | And Joshua overcame
Amalek and his people with the sword.

Lord, prayer
is not asking you
to do what we are afraid of doing
or what we don't feel like doing.

Prayer, Lord,
is receiving the strength
"to do with you"
because you love us too much
to do it for us.

THE COVENANT

The meeting with God

19 1 In the third month after the children of Israel went
out from Egypt, on the same day, they came into the
2 desert of Sinai. | And when they had gone away from
Rephidim and had come into the desert of Sinai, they
put up their tents in the desert before the mountain:
there Israel put up its tents.

3 And Moses went up to God, and the voice of the Lord
came to him from the mountain, saying, "Say to the fa-
mily of Jacob, and give word to the children of Israel: |
4 'You have seen what I did to the Egyptians, and how I
5 took you, as on eagles' wings, guiding you to myself. | If
now you will truly listen to my voice and keep my covenant,* you will be my special property out of all the
6 peoples: for all the earth is mine. | You will be a kingdom
of priests to me, and a holy nation.' These are the words
which you are to say to the children of Israel."...

'HE FIRST COVENANT

;od wished to seal a pact with
he people of the children of
braham so strong that
othing could undo it.

'his people, still under the
pell of idolatry,* was
ertainly the same in nature
s all other peoples. But God
vished to make them His
eople, His friends and allies
or all time.

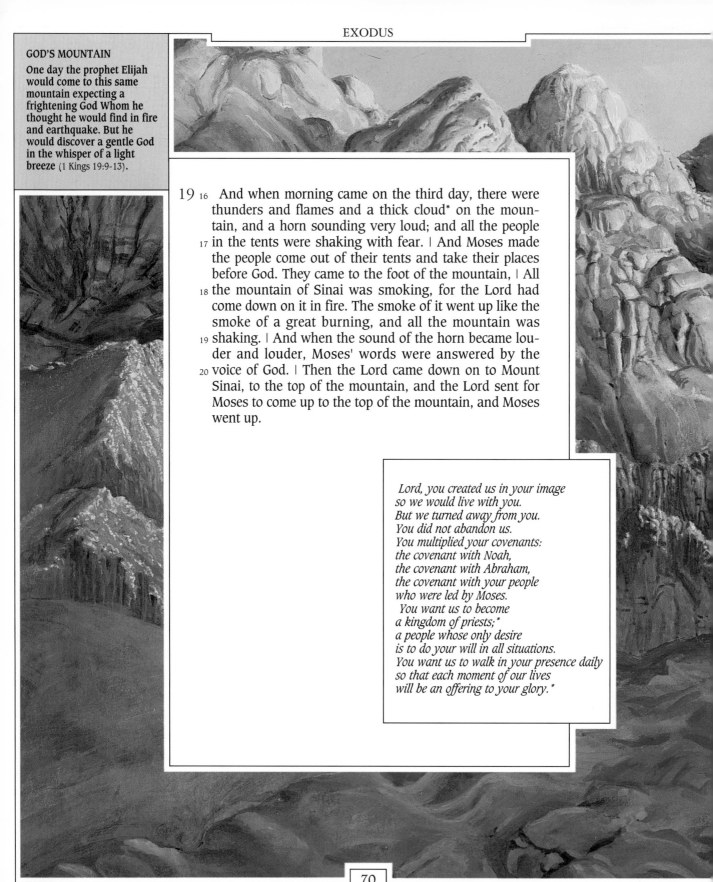

GOD'S MOUNTAIN

One day the prophet Elijah would come to this same mountain expecting a frightening God Whom he thought he would find in fire and earthquake. But he would discover a gentle God in the whisper of a light breeze (1 Kings 19:9-13).

19 16 And when morning came on the third day, there were
thunders and flames and a thick cloud* on the mountain, and a horn sounding very loud; and all the people
17 in the tents were shaking with fear. | And Moses made
the people come out of their tents and take their places
before God. They came to the foot of the mountain, | All
18 the mountain of Sinai was smoking, for the Lord had
come down on it in fire. The smoke of it went up like the
smoke of a great burning, and all the mountain was
19 shaking. | And when the sound of the horn became lou-
der and louder, Moses' words were answered by the
20 voice of God. | Then the Lord came down on to Mount
Sinai, to the top of the mountain, and the Lord sent for
Moses to come up to the top of the mountain, and Moses
went up.

Lord, you created us in your image
so we would live with you.
But we turned away from you.
You did not abandon us.
You multiplied your covenants:
the covenant with Noah,
the covenant with Abraham,
the covenant with your people
who were led by Moses.
You want us to become
*a kingdom of priests;**
a people whose only desire
is to do your will in all situations.
You want us to walk in your presence daily
so that each moment of our lives
*will be an offering to your glory.**

The ten statements of life

20 1 And God said all these words: | "I am the Lord
2 your God who took you out of the land of Egypt,
out of the land of slavery.
3 "You are to have no other gods but me.[1]
4 "You are not to make an idol* or picture of anything in
heaven or on the earth or in the waters under the earth. |
5 You may not go down on your faces before them or give
them worship....
7 "You are not to make use of the name of the Lord your
God for an evil purpose; whoever takes the Lord's name
on his lips for an evil purpose will be judged a sinner by
8 the Lord.[2] | Remember the Sabbath* and keep it a holy
9-10 day. | On six days do all your work, | but the seventh
day is a Sabbath to the Lord your God. On that day you
are to do no work, you or your son or your daughter,
your manservant or your womanservant, your cattle or
the foreigner who is living among you. | For in six days
11 the Lord made heaven and earth, and the sea, and everything in them, and he took his rest on the seventh
day: for this reason the Lord has given his blessing to
the seventh day and made it holy.
12 "Honor your father and your mother, so that your life
may be long in the land which the Lord your God is giving you.
13 "Do not murder.
14 "Do not commit adultery.
15 "Do not steal.
16 "Do not give false witness against your neighbour.*
17 "Do not covet your neighbor's house, or his wife or his
manservant or his womanservant or his ox or his donkey
or anything which is his."

THE WAY OF LIFE

God, in delivering His people from slavery in Egypt, did not lead them straight into another country. He made them come to Him. It is by meeting God that humans become completely free and alive.

The Ten Commandments* are statements of life. Like signposts, they mark the way leading to the meeting with God. Following this way is to choose happiness and life; straying from it is to choose unhappiness and death. (Deuteronomy 30:10-20, page 84-85.)

[1] See Luke 16:13, page 324.

[2] Misusing the name of the Lord is to make Him witness to a lie. It is also wanting the Lord to do harm to someone (see curse),* like James and John asking for fire from heaven to destroy a Samaritan* village which did not welcome them (Luke 9:52-56, page 315).

GOD AND OTHERS

Humans have a chronic tendency to exploit God so as to succeed in life in their own way. The decalogue* starts by reminding us that we do not exploit God, we respect Him. [1]

- **God is one. We shall not serve other Gods (money, power, pleasure).**
- **We shall not make images of God, since they would reduce Him to the scale of men.**
- **We shall honor the name of God by not uttering it right, left and center.**
- **By not working on the Sabbath Day, we may remember that the world is the property of God, not of men.**

The fifth statement is a bridge between respect for God and respect for others. Speaking of father and mother, it suggests God revealing Himself to men with the authority of a father and the tenderness of a mother. At the same time, it directs our thoughts to human parents.

The last five statements preclude everything which could interfere with loving relations with our neighbor.* These relations are described in great detail in other parts of the Torah.* It is a matter of respecting others, and especially the humble, those who are not strong enough to defend their own rights.

[1] The Bible uses another word for respect for God, which is fear* of God, not to be confused with terror.

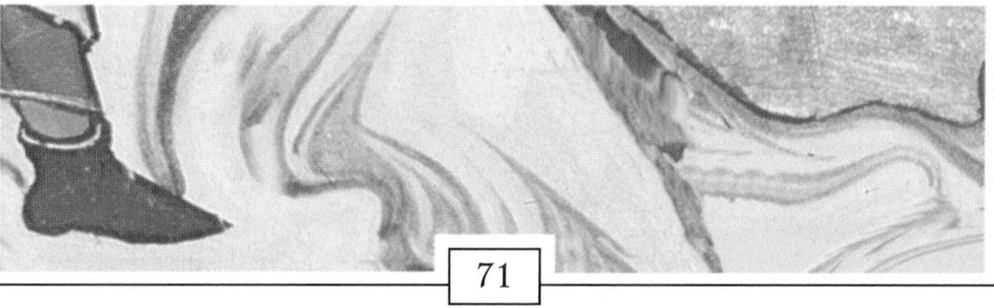

Respect for the downtrodden

The following extracts, taken from several books in the Pentateuch, illustrate the mindfulness of the Torah* towards the humble. A people "allied" with God must pay heed to those whose misfortune touches God's heart. From Mount Sinai, Moses gave the people the words of the LORD:*

22 21 "Do no wrong to a man from a foreign land,
and do not be hard on him; for you yourselves
were living in a foreign country, in the land of Egypt. |
22 "Do no wrong to a widow, or to a child whose father is
23 dead. | If you are cruel to them in any way, and their cry
24 comes up to me, I will certainly listen.[1] | And in the heat of
my wrath I will put you to death with the sword, so that
your wives will be widows and your children without fathers....
25 If ever you take your neighbor's clothing in exchange for
the use of your money, let him have it back before the
26 sun goes down: | For it is the only thing he has for cove-
ring his skin. What is he to go to sleep in? When his cry
comes up to me, I will listen, for my mercy is great."

LEVITICUS

19 1-2 And the Lord said to Moses, | "Say to all the people of Is-
rael, 'You are to be holy, for I, the Lord your God, am
13 holy.'*... | "Do not be cruel to your neighbor* or take what
is his; do not keep back a servant's payment from him all
14 night till the morning.[2] | "Do not put a curse on those who
have no hearing, or put a stumbling block in the way of
the blind, but keep the fear of your God before you. I am
the Lord.

[1] God had heard the cry of the Israelites when they were being mistreated in Egypt. See Exodus 3:7, page 57.

[2] A hired man was one who was taken on for a day's work. See Matthew 20:2, page 286.

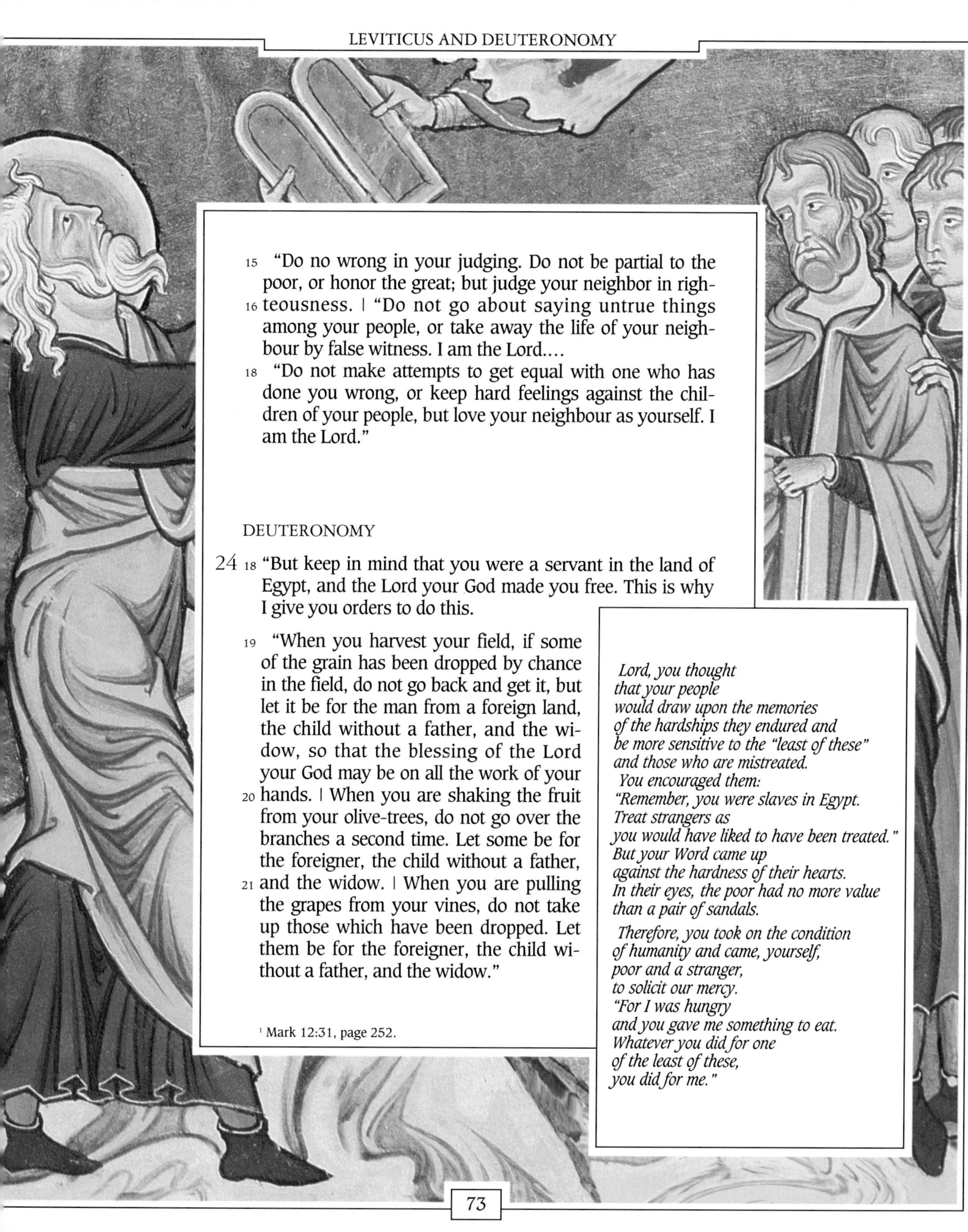

15 “Do no wrong in your judging. Do not be partial to the
poor, or honor the great; but judge your neighbor in righ-
16 teousness. | “Do not go about saying untrue things
among your people, or take away the life of your neighbour by false witness. I am the Lord....
18 “Do not make attempts to get equal with one who has
done you wrong, or keep hard feelings against the children of your people, but love your neighbour as yourself. I
am the Lord.”

DEUTERONOMY

24 18 “But keep in mind that you were a servant in the land of
Egypt, and the Lord your God made you free. This is why
I give you orders to do this.

19 “When you harvest your field, if some
of the grain has been dropped by chance
in the field, do not go back and get it, but
let it be for the man from a foreign land,
the child without a father, and the widow, so that the blessing of the Lord
your God may be on all the work of your
20 hands. | When you are shaking the fruit
from your olive-trees, do not go over the
branches a second time. Let some be for
the foreigner, the child without a father,
21 and the widow. | When you are pulling
the grapes from your vines, do not take
up those which have been dropped. Let
them be for the foreigner, the child without a father, and the widow.”

[1] Mark 12:31, page 252.

Lord, you thought
that your people
would draw upon the memories
of the hardships they endured and
be more sensitive to the “least of these”
and those who are mistreated.
You encouraged them:
“Remember, you were slaves in Egypt.
Treat strangers as
you would have liked to have been treated.”
But your Word came up
against the hardness of their hearts.
In their eyes, the poor had no more value
than a pair of sandals.

Therefore, you took on the condition
of humanity and came, yourself,
poor and a stranger,
to solicit our mercy.
“For I was hungry
and you gave me something to eat.
Whatever you did for one
of the least of these,
you did for me.”

Celebration of the Covenant

24 3 Then Moses came and put before the people all the
words of the Lord and his laws: and all the
people, answering with one voice, said, "Whatever the
Lord has said we will do."

4 Then Moses put down in writing all the words of the
Lord, and he got up early in the morning and made an
altar at the foot of the mountain, with twelve pillars for
5 the twelve tribes of Israel. | And he sent some of the
young men of Israel to make burnt offerings and peace-
6 offerings of oxen to the Lord. | And Moses took half the
blood and put it in basins, draining out half of the blood
7 over the altar. | And he took the book of the Covenant,
reading it to the people. They said, "Everything which
the Lord has said we will do, and we will keep his laws."

8 Then Moses took the blood and sprinkled it on the
people, and said, "This blood is the sign of the covenant
which the Lord has made with you in these words."

The Golden Calf

Moses climbed Sinai to receive the Ten Commandments, graven on tablets of stone, the Tables of the Law. He took Joshua with him, leaving the people in the care of Aaron and Hur. Forty days went by, and the people thought they had been abandoned. They forced Aaron to melt down a statue representing God. He used it to sculpt a golden calf.

Other stories, not included in the Bible,[1] *tell that Aaron obeyed the people so as not to meet the fate of Hur, who was murdered for refusing to make the idol.*

THE BLOOD OF THE COVENANT

Blood, when it circulates through the body, suffuses it with life. This is why, among some peoples, two friends pledging allegiance and willing to give their lives for one another will make a cut in their hands and press the cuts against each other to mingle their blood. "Now your blood flows in my veins. We share the same life-force for always."

Moses adapted this custom to show that a pledge of eternal friendship existed between God and His people. He took blood and sprinkled some on the altar and the rest on the people. It was as though, from then on, God and His people shared the same blood, the same life-force.

This was the blood of the Covenant.

See Mark 14:24, page 366.

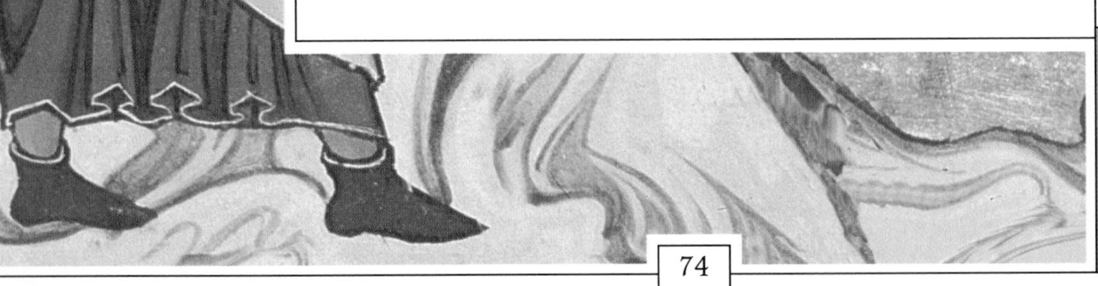

[1] Alongside the written Law, the people of Israel remembered the histories which made up the spoken Law. The most important ones and the commentaries on them were set down in writing from the 2nd century AD. They make up the Talmud, which is the second holy book of the Jews.

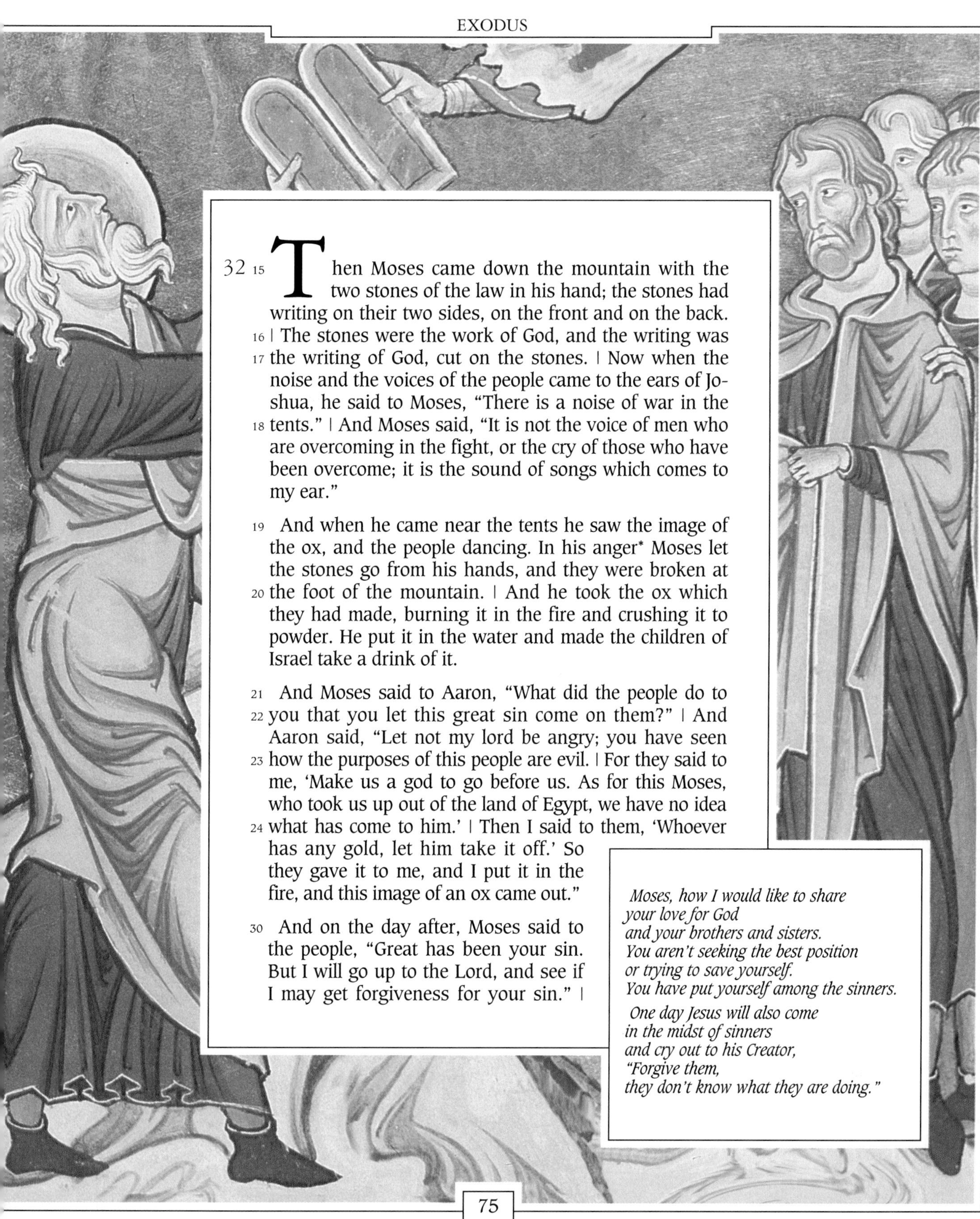

32 15 Then Moses came down the mountain with the
two stones of the law in his hand; the stones had
writing on their two sides, on the front and on the back.
16 | The stones were the work of God, and the writing was
17 the writing of God, cut on the stones. | Now when the
noise and the voices of the people came to the ears of Joshua, he said to Moses, "There is a noise of war in the
18 tents." | And Moses said, "It is not the voice of men who
are overcoming in the fight, or the cry of those who have
been overcome; it is the sound of songs which comes to
my ear."

19 And when he came near the tents he saw the image of
the ox, and the people dancing. In his anger* Moses let
the stones go from his hands, and they were broken at
20 the foot of the mountain. | And he took the ox which
they had made, burning it in the fire and crushing it to
powder. He put it in the water and made the children of
Israel take a drink of it.

21 And Moses said to Aaron, "What did the people do to
22 you that you let this great sin come on them?" | And
Aaron said, "Let not my lord be angry; you have seen
23 how the purposes of this people are evil. | For they said to
me, 'Make us a god to go before us. As for this Moses,
who took us up out of the land of Egypt, we have no idea
24 what has come to him.' | Then I said to them, 'Whoever
has any gold, let him take it off.' So
they gave it to me, and I put it in the
fire, and this image of an ox came out."

30 And on the day after, Moses said to
the people, "Great has been your sin.
But I will go up to the Lord, and see if
I may get forgiveness for your sin." |

Moses, how I would like to share
your love for God
and your brothers and sisters.
You aren't seeking the best position
or trying to save yourself.
You have put yourself among the sinners.

One day Jesus will also come
in the midst of sinners
and cry out to his Creator,
"Forgive them,
they don't know what they are doing."

32 31 Then Moses went back to the Lord and said, "This people
has done a great sin, making themselves a god of gold. |
32 But now, if you will give them forgiveness—but if not, let
33 my name be taken out of your book." | And the Lord said
to Moses, "Whoever has done evil against me will be ta-
34 ken out of my book. | But now, go, take the people into
that place of which I have given you word. See, my angel
will go before you: but when the time of my judging has
come, I will send punishment on them for their sin."

The back of God

33 18 And Moses said, "O Lord, let me see your glory."*
19 | And he said, "I will make all the light of my
being come before you, and will make clear to you what
I am. I will be kind to those to whom I will be kind, and
20 have mercy on those on whom I will have mercy. | But it
is not possible for you to see my face, for no man may
21 see me and still go on living."[1] | And the Lord said, "See,
there is a place near me, and you may take your place
22 on the rock. | And when my glory goes by, I will put you
in a hole in the rock, covering you with my hand till I
23 have gone past: | Then I will take away my hand, and
you will see my back, but my face is not to be seen."...

34 5 And the Lord came down in the cloud* and took his
place by the side of Moses, and Moses gave worship to
6 the name of the Lord. | And the Lord went past before
his eyes, saying, "The Lord, the Lord, a God full of pity
and grace,* slow to wrath and great in mercy and faith; |
7 having mercy on thousands, overlooking evil and
wrongdoing and sin; he will not let wrongdoers go free,
but will send punishment on children for the sins of

[1] During our earthly life, we know God only in the "half-light" of faith.* We shall see Him as He is when, through death, we enter into the fullness of His presence.

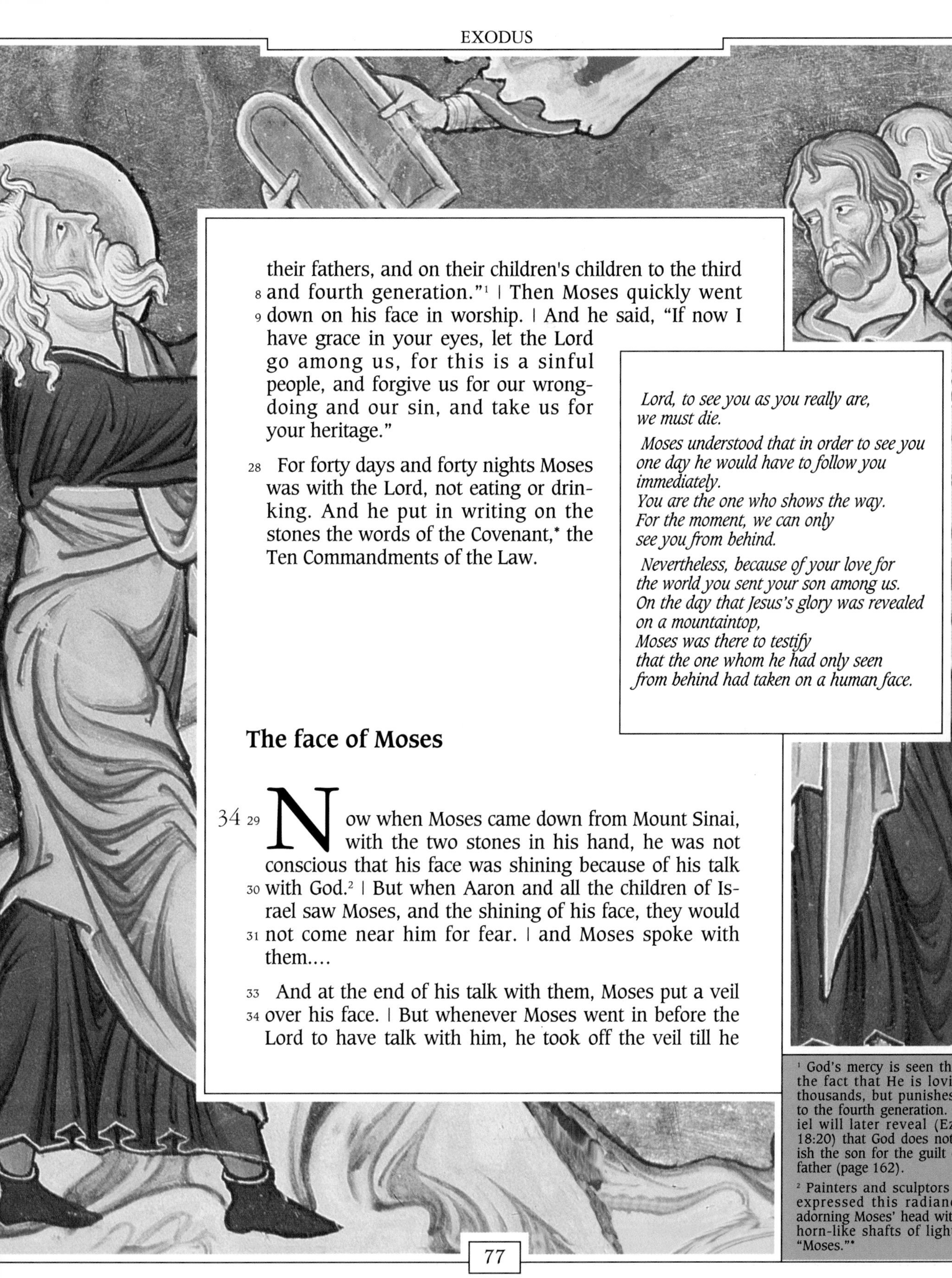

their fathers, and on their children's children to the third
8 and fourth generation."[1] | Then Moses quickly went
9 down on his face in worship. | And he said, "If now I
have grace in your eyes, let the Lord go among us, for this is a sinful people, and forgive us for our wrongdoing and our sin, and take us for your heritage."

28 For forty days and forty nights Moses was with the Lord, not eating or drinking. And he put in writing on the stones the words of the Covenant,* the Ten Commandments of the Law.

Lord, to see you as you really are,
we must die.

Moses understood that in order to see you
one day he would have to follow you
immediately.
You are the one who shows the way.
For the moment, we can only
see you from behind.

Nevertheless, because of your love for
the world you sent your son among us.
On the day that Jesus's glory was revealed
on a mountaintop,
Moses was there to testify
that the one whom he had only seen
from behind had taken on a human face.

The face of Moses

34 29 Now when Moses came down from Mount Sinai,
with the two stones in his hand, he was not
conscious that his face was shining because of his talk
30 with God.[2] | But when Aaron and all the children of Is-
rael saw Moses, and the shining of his face, they would
31 not come near him for fear. | and Moses spoke with
them....

33 And at the end of his talk with them, Moses put a veil
34 over his face. | But whenever Moses went in before the
Lord to have talk with him, he took off the veil till he

[1] God's mercy is seen through the fact that He is loving to thousands, but punishes only to the fourth generation. Ezekiel will later reveal (Ezekiel 18:20) that God does not punish the son for the guilt of the father (page 162).

[2] Painters and sculptors often expressed this radiance by adorning Moses' head with two horn-like shafts of light. See "Moses."*

34 came out. And whenever he came out he said to the
35 children of Israel what he had been ordered to say; | And
the children of Israel saw that the face of Moses was shining: so Moses put the veil over his face again till he
went to the Lord.

The tent and the Ark of the Covenant

Moses had again received the Tables of the Law. He deposited them, with some manna,[1] in a chest of precious wood, the Ark of the Covenant.*

*To house the Ark, Moses had a "tent"[2] erected. It would be the model for the Temple built by Solomon.**

40 16 And Moses did this as the Lord commanded,
17 so he did. | On the first day of the first month in
18 the second year the tabernacle was put up. | Moses put
up the tabernacle; placing its bases in position and lifting up its uprights, putting in the rods and planting the
19 pillars in their places, | stretching the outer tent over it,
20 and covering it, as the Lord had given him orders. | And
he took the law and put it inside the ark, and put the
21 rods at its side and the atonement cover* over it. | And
he took the ark into the tabernacle, hanging up the veil
before it as the Lord had given him orders.

[1] The Ark of the Covenant is usually considered as containing only the Tables of the Law. Some texts in the Bible, referred to in the Epistle to the Hebrews 9:4, mention also a jar of manna and Aaron's rod which had flowered (Numbers 17:8).

[2] The Latin word for tent is "tabernaculum." from which comes the word "tabernacle".*

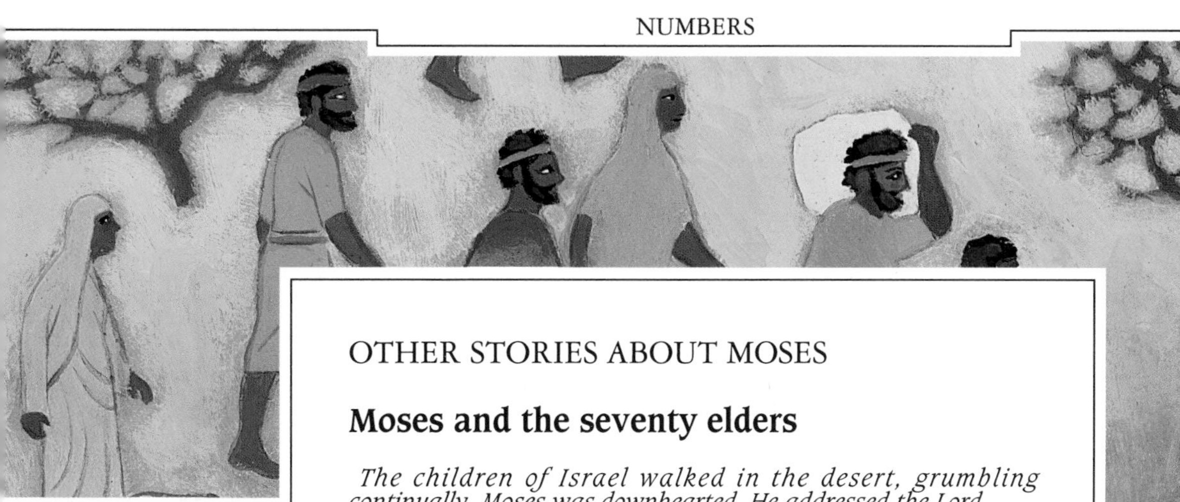

OTHER STORIES ABOUT MOSES

Moses and the seventy elders

The children of Israel walked in the desert, grumbling continually. Moses was downhearted. He addressed the Lord.

11 11 And Moses said to the Lord, "Why have you done
me this evil? Why have I not favor in your eyes,
that you have burdened me with the care of all this
12 people? | Am I the father of all this people? have I given
them birth, that you say to me, 'Take them in your
arms, like a child at the breast, to the land which you
13 gave by an oath to their fathers?' | Where am I to get
meat to give to all this people? For they are weeping to
14 me and saying, Give us flesh for our food. | I am not able
by myself to take the weight of all this people, for it is
15 more than my strength. | If this is to be my fate, put me
to death now in answer to my prayer, if I have grace in
your eyes; and let me not see my shame."

16 The Lord said to Moses, "Send for seventy of the elders* of Israel.... make them come to the Tent of meeting
17 and be there with you. | And I will come down and have
talk with you there. I will take some of the spirit which
is on you and put it on them, and they will take part of
the weight of the people off you, so that you do not have
to take it by yourself."

24 And Moses... took seventy of the responsible men of
the people, placing them round the Tent.

25 Then the Lord... put on the seventy men some of the
spirit which was on him. Now when the spirit came to
rest on them, they were like prophets, but only at that
time.

NUMBERS AND DEUTERONOMY

Moses was a figure so important that in addition to Genesis and Exodus, the Book of Numbers also tells of his life and experiences with God. Deuteronomy (Second Law) is more given over to commentaries, in the form of speeches, on the Ten Commandments.

THE ELDERS [1]

They were the moving forces of the community. They were prophets* assembling the people around the Word of God rather than around their own words.

They were also the visible sign of God's maternal love for each one of his people. They provided each person with the care due to a nurseling.

See Isaiah 49:15, page 169, where God compares Himself to a mother.

[1] The term from the Greek is "presbyters", which gives the words "priest" and "Presbyterian."

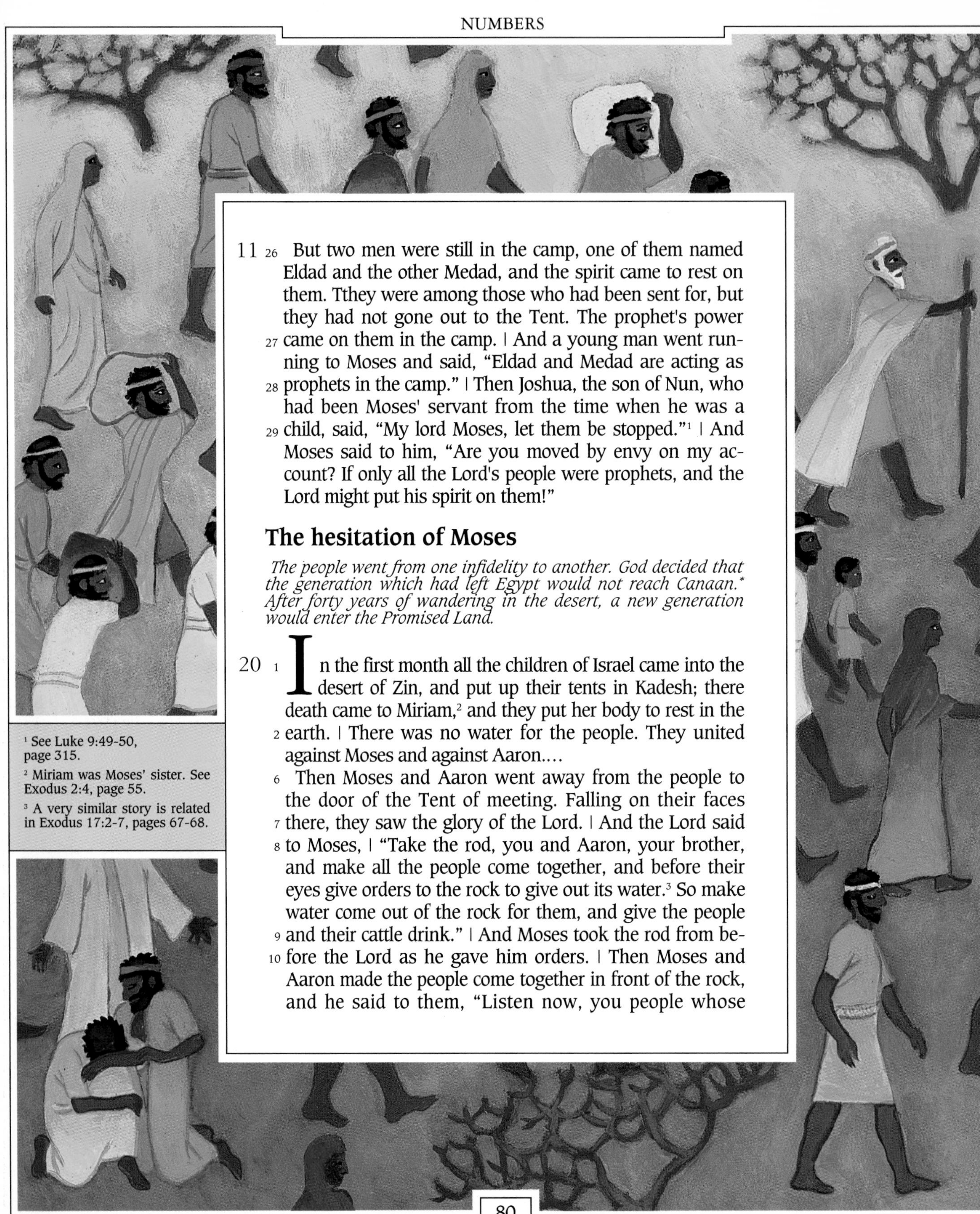

11 26 But two men were still in the camp, one of them named
Eldad and the other Medad, and the spirit came to rest on
them. Tthey were among those who had been sent for, but
they had not gone out to the Tent. The prophet's power
27 came on them in the camp. | And a young man went run-
ning to Moses and said, "Eldad and Medad are acting as
28 prophets in the camp." | Then Joshua, the son of Nun, who
had been Moses' servant from the time when he was a
29 child, said, "My lord Moses, let them be stopped."[1] | And
Moses said to him, "Are you moved by envy on my account? If only all the Lord's people were prophets, and the
Lord might put his spirit on them!"

The hesitation of Moses

The people went from one infidelity to another. God decided that the generation which had left Egypt would not reach Canaan. After forty years of wandering in the desert, a new generation would enter the Promised Land.*

20 1 In the first month all the children of Israel came into the
desert of Zin, and put up their tents in Kadesh; there
death came to Miriam,[2] and they put her body to rest in the
2 earth. | There was no water for the people. They united
against Moses and against Aaron....
6 Then Moses and Aaron went away from the people to
the door of the Tent of meeting. Falling on their faces
7 there, they saw the glory of the Lord. | And the Lord said
8 to Moses, | "Take the rod, you and Aaron, your brother,
and make all the people come together, and before their
eyes give orders to the rock to give out its water.[3] So make
water come out of the rock for them, and give the people
9 and their cattle drink." | And Moses took the rod from be-
10 fore the Lord as he gave him orders. | Then Moses and
Aaron made the people come together in front of the rock,
and he said to them, "Listen now, you people whose

[1] See Luke 9:49-50, page 315.

[2] Miriam was Moses' sister. See Exodus 2:4, page 55.

[3] A very similar story is related in Exodus 17:2-7, pages 67-68.

MOSES DOUBTS

One may ask himself why Moses, who had guided his people ever since Egypt, did not lead them as far as the Promised Land.

The answer lies in this story of the rock. Moses had given way to a moment of dejection and doubt.

On this account, Moses, while still a man filled with radiant faith (see Exodus 34:29, page 77), **in some way seems closer to us. Even for him, it was difficult to maintain his trust in the Lord.**

Once he had overcome his doubt, Moses resumed his journey without asking for any reward other than following Him Whose back he had seen.
See Exodus 33:18-23, page 76.

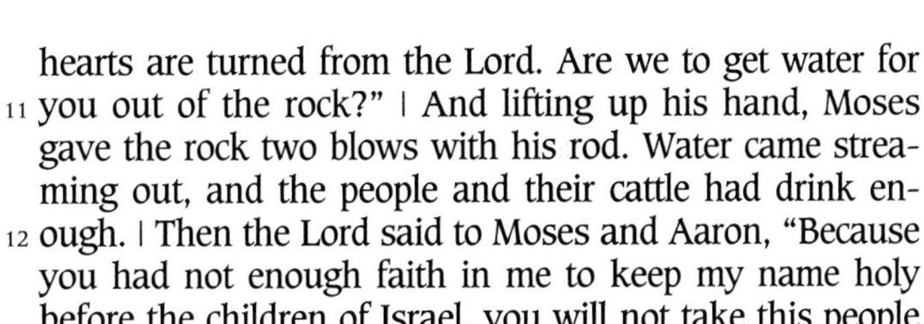

hearts are turned from the Lord. Are we to get water for
11 you out of the rock?" | And lifting up his hand, Moses
gave the rock two blows with his rod. Water came strea-
ming out, and the people and their cattle had drink en-
12 ough. | Then the Lord said to Moses and Aaron, "Because
you had not enough faith in me to keep my name holy
before the children of Israel, you will not take this people
into the land which I have given them."

Balaam's donkey

The people led by Moses were approaching the Promised Land. They had to cross the plains of Moab[1] but King Balak denied them passage. Feeling some anxiety, he sent for Balaam, a magician.[2]

22 4-5 Balak, was king of Moab.... | He sent men to Balaam,
son of Beor, at Pethor by the River in the land of the
children of his people, saying to him, "See, a people has
come out of Egypt, covering all the face of the earth, and
6 they have put up their tents opposite to me. | Come now, in
answer to my prayer, and put a curse on this people, for
they are greater than I. Then I may be strong enough to
overcome them and send them out of the land. It is clear that
good comes to him who has your blessing, but he on whom
you put your curse is cursed."

In response to the King of Moab's summons, Balaam saddled his donkey[3] and took to the road. God decided to interrupt his journey.

22 But God was angry because he went. The angel of the
Lord took up a position in the road to keep him from his
purpose. Now he was seated on his donkey, and his two
23 servants were with him. | And the donkey saw the angel
of the Lord waiting in the road with his sword in his
hand. Turning from the road, the donkey went into the
field. Balaam gave the ass blows, to get her back on to the
24 road. | Then the angel of the Lord took up his position in a

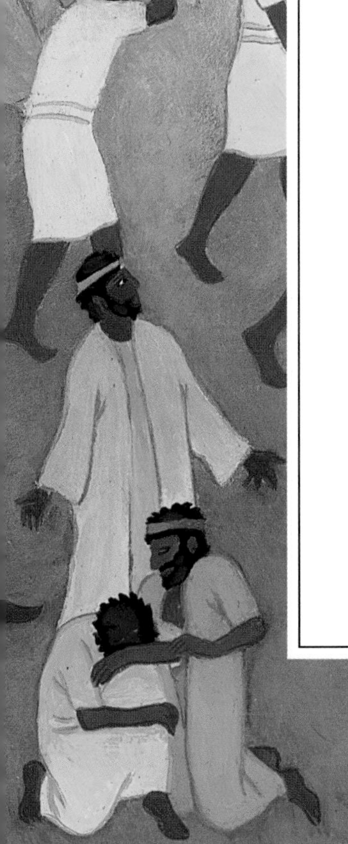

[1] The Moabites* were descended from Lot, Abraham's nephew. Their land was located to the North-West of the Dead Sea.

[2] The whimsical little story of Balaam, the magician,* offers us an interesting glimpse of how people were governed at the time. Before going into battle, kings would obtain the help of magicians who, by their curses,* would ensure the defeat of the enemy.

[3] See animal.*

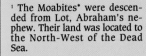

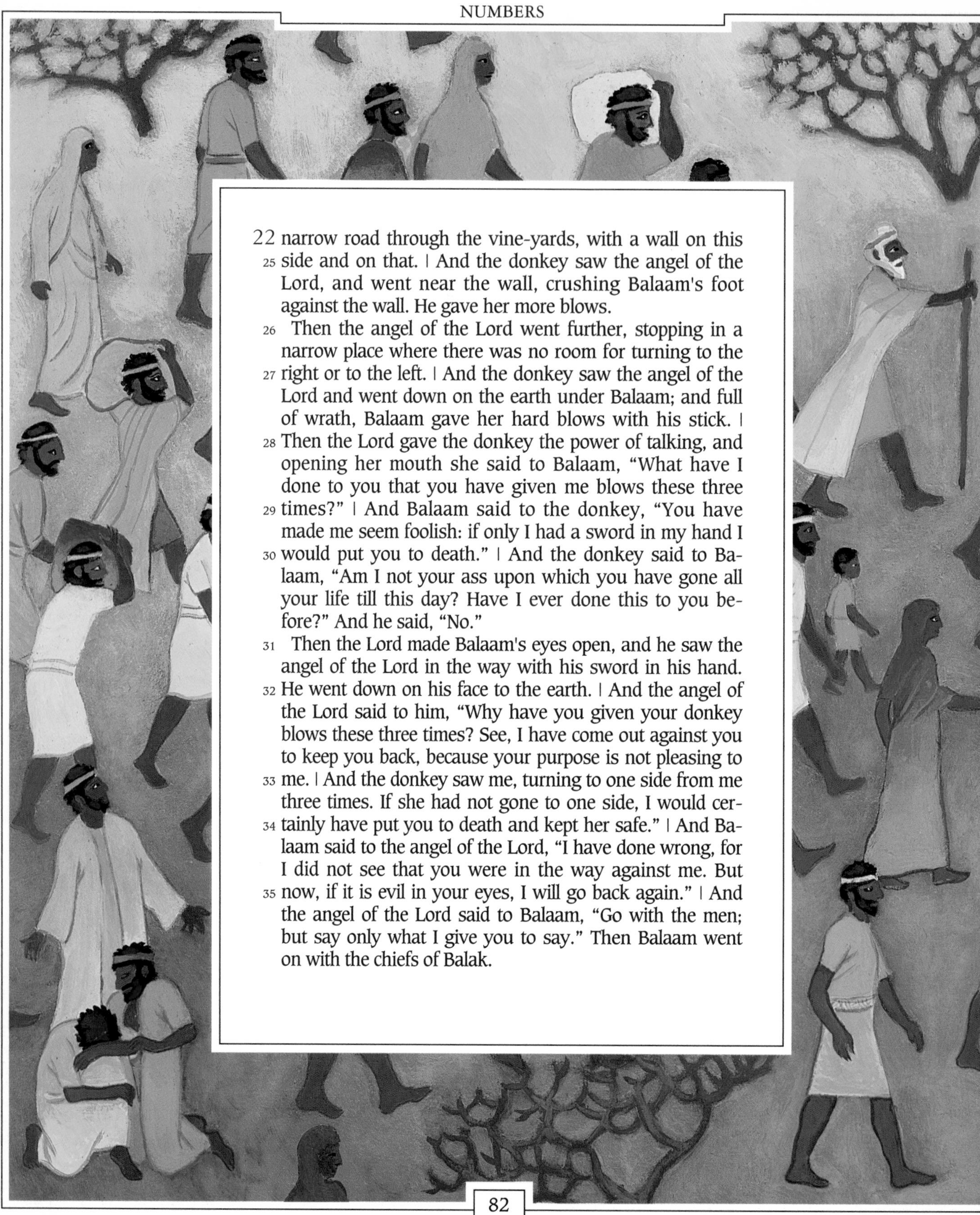

22 narrow road through the vine-yards, with a wall on this
25 side and on that. | And the donkey saw the angel of the
Lord, and went near the wall, crushing Balaam's foot
against the wall. He gave her more blows.
26 Then the angel of the Lord went further, stopping in a
narrow place where there was no room for turning to the
27 right or to the left. | And the donkey saw the angel of the
Lord and went down on the earth under Balaam; and full
of wrath, Balaam gave her hard blows with his stick. |
28 Then the Lord gave the donkey the power of talking, and
opening her mouth she said to Balaam, "What have I
done to you that you have given me blows these three
29 times?" | And Balaam said to the donkey, "You have
made me seem foolish: if only I had a sword in my hand I
30 would put you to death." | And the donkey said to Ba-
laam, "Am I not your ass upon which you have gone all
your life till this day? Have I ever done this to you before?" And he said, "No."
31 Then the Lord made Balaam's eyes open, and he saw the
angel of the Lord in the way with his sword in his hand.
32 He went down on his face to the earth. | And the angel of
the Lord said to him, "Why have you given your donkey
blows these three times? See, I have come out against you
to keep you back, because your purpose is not pleasing to
33 me. | And the donkey saw me, turning to one side from me
three times. If she had not gone to one side, I would cer-
34 tainly have put you to death and kept her safe." | And Ba-
laam said to the angel of the Lord, "I have done wrong, for
I did not see that you were in the way against me. But
35 now, if it is evil in your eyes, I will go back again." | And
the angel of the Lord said to Balaam, "Go with the men;
but say only what I give you to say." Then Balaam went
on with the chiefs of Balak.

BALAAM, MAN OF GOD

Balaam is an important figure in the memory of the people of Israel. He is a reminder that God breathes His spirit not only into the members of His people (Numbers 11:25, page 79) **but also into persons, like Balaam, who are complete foreigners. God is the only God. He loves all mankind, and wishes to bless* all nations** (Genesis 12:3, page 36).

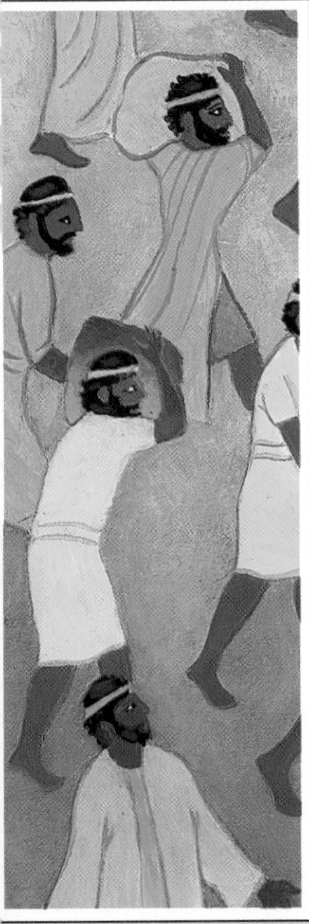

Balaam's blessing

Balaam went on his way and was led to the King of Moab. But, instead of cursing Israel, Balaam blessed it.

24 2 And lifting up his eyes, he saw Israel there, with
their tents in the order of their tribes. The spirit of
3 God came on him. | And moved by the spirit, he said,
"These are the words of Balaam, son of Beor,
the words of the man whose eyes are open.
4 He says, whose ears are open to the words of God,
who has seen the vision of the Ruler of all,
falling down, but having his eyes open.
5 How fair are your tents, O Jacob,
your houses, O Israel!
6 They are stretched out like valleys, like gardens by the
riverside, like flowering trees planted by the Lord,
like cedar trees by the waters.

7 Peoples will be in fear before his strength,
his arm will be on great nations,
his king will be higher than Agag,[1]
and his kingdom made great in honor."

15 Then he went on with his story and said, "These are the
words of Balaam, the son of Beor, the words of him
whose eyes are open:"

17 "I see him, but not now. looking on him, but not near: a
star will come out of Jacob,
and a rod of authority out of Israel."[2]...

A STAR RISES

Echoing the prophecy of Balaam, Zechariah, the father of John the Baptist, would speak of the birth of Jesus in these terms: "The rising sun will come to us from heaven to shine on those living in darkness and in the shadow of death to guide our feet into the path of peace." (Luke 1:78-79.)

Jesus would describe himself as the light of the world (John 9:5, page 349).

These two passages from the Scriptures guided the early Christians in their choice of the date of Christmas. From the 3rd century on, the Christians, who had till then kept a very low profile owing to persecution, were able to practice their religion openly. They decided to celebrate each year the birth of Jesus. Since they did not have any exact information on the date, they chose a symbolic one, that of the winter solstice when the days started to grow longer. Light began to triumph over darkness. The date of the birth was therefore set as 25th December.

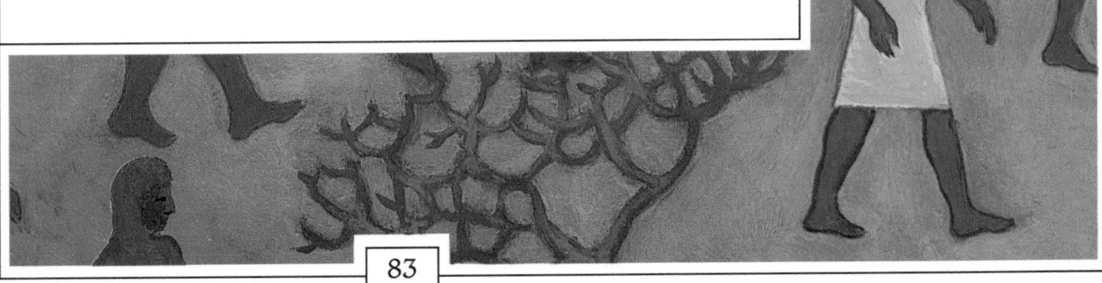

[1] The name Gog recurs several times in the Bible, always to indicate a barbarian conqueror opposed to the people of God. Some scholars believe that the historical model for Gog was Agag, an ancient ruler of Amalek.

[2] The Evangelist Matthew tells how this prophecy of Balaam was accomplished. Wise men* from the East came to Jerusalem because they had seen a star rise which announced the birth of a king. They came to pay homage to him. (Matthew 2:1-12, page 255.)

SHEMA ISRAEL

This text, beginning with the Hebrew words "Shema Israel" (Hear, O Israel), is recited several times a day in Jewish prayers.

Jesus quotes it, adding on the commandment to love your neighbor* as yourself (Mark 12:28-34, page 252). For him, the text summed up the whole of the Old Testament.*

Devout Jews put this text and some others in small boxes which, at prayer time, they tie round their foreheads and arms with leather thongs. They are called tefellin, or phylacteries.* A small case, the "mezouza," containing the same texts is fastened to the doorpost. It is respectfully touched or kissed on entering or leaving the house.

The testament of Moses

*The book of Deuteronomy contains three great speeches in which Moses expounded to the people the main points of the Covenant.**

6 4 Give ear, O Israel, the Lord our God is one Lord. |
5 And the Lord your God is to be loved with all
your heart and with all your soul and with all your
6 strength. | Keep these words, which I say to you this
7 day, deep in your hearts, | teaching them to your chil-
dren with all care, talking of them when you are at rest
in your house or walking by the way, when you go to
8 sleep and when you get up. | Let them be fixed as a sign
on your hand, and marked on your brow.

7 7 The Lord did not give you his love or take you for
himself because you were more in number than
any other people. For you were the smallest of the na-
8 tions. | But because of his love for you, and in order to
keep his oath to your fathers, the Lord took you out with
the strength of his hand, making you free from slavery
and from the hand of Pharaoh, king of Egypt.

30 10 If you give ear to the voice of the Lord your God,
keeping his orders and his laws which are recorded
in this book of the law,* and turning to the Lord your
11 God with all your heart and with all your soul. | For
these orders which I have given you today are not
12 strange and secret, and are not far away. | They are not

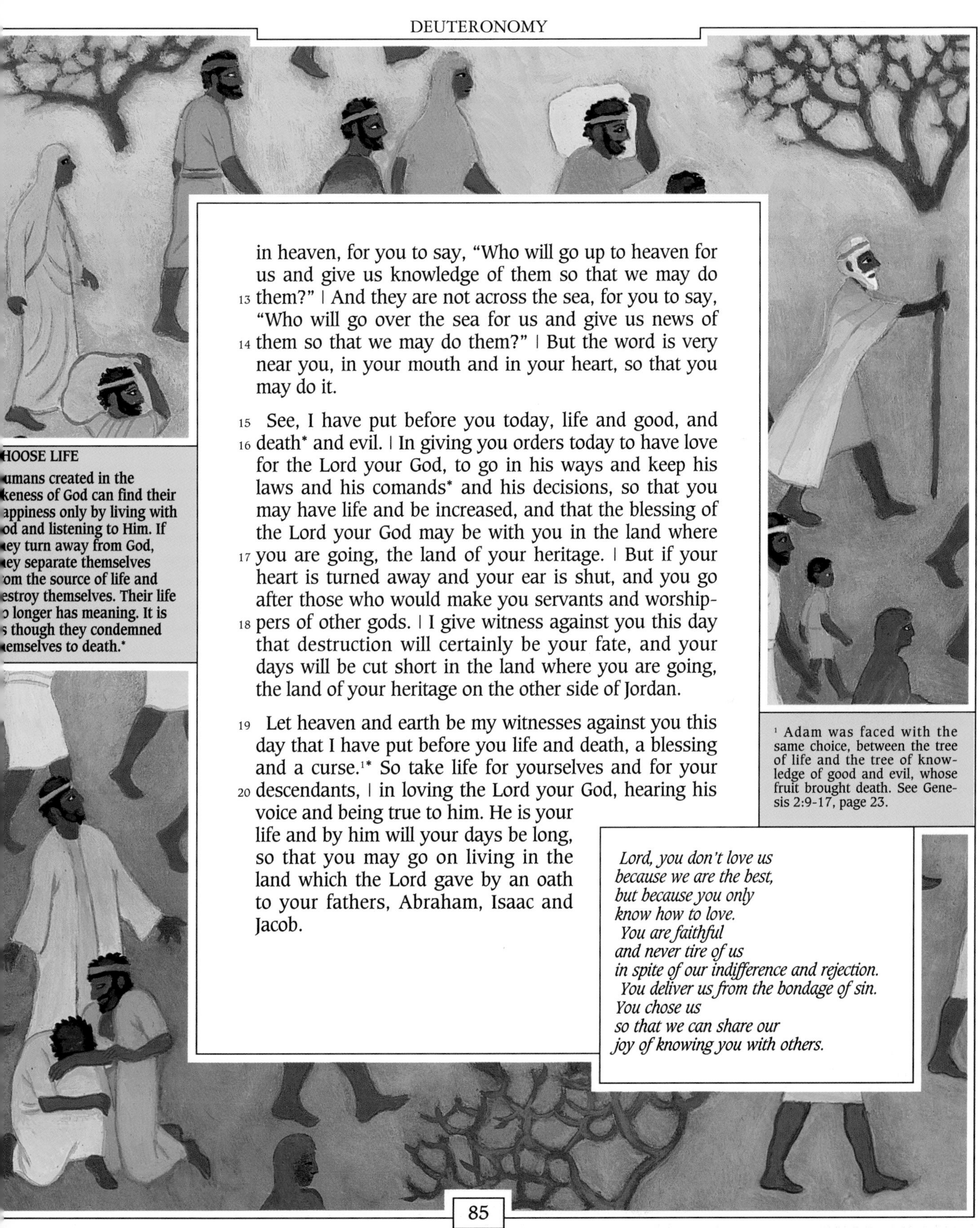

in heaven, for you to say, "Who will go up to heaven for
us and give us knowledge of them so that we may do
13 them?" | And they are not across the sea, for you to say,
"Who will go over the sea for us and give us news of
14 them so that we may do them?" | But the word is very
near you, in your mouth and in your heart, so that you
may do it.

15 See, I have put before you today, life and good, and
16 death* and evil. | In giving you orders today to have love
for the Lord your God, to go in his ways and keep his
laws and his comands* and his decisions, so that you
may have life and be increased, and that the blessing of
the Lord your God may be with you in the land where
17 you are going, the land of your heritage. | But if your
heart is turned away and your ear is shut, and you go
after those who would make you servants and worship-
18 pers of other gods. | I give witness against you this day
that destruction will certainly be your fate, and your
days will be cut short in the land where you are going,
the land of your heritage on the other side of Jordan.

19 Let heaven and earth be my witnesses against you this
day that I have put before you life and death, a blessing
and a curse.[1]* So take life for yourselves and for your
20 descendants, | in loving the Lord your God, hearing his
voice and being true to him. He is your
life and by him will your days be long,
so that you may go on living in the
land which the Lord gave by an oath
to your fathers, Abraham, Isaac and
Jacob.

HOOSE LIFE

umans created in the keness of God can find their appiness only by living with od and listening to Him. If ey turn away from God, ey separate themselves om the source of life and estroy themselves. Their life o longer has meaning. It is s though they condemned emselves to death.*

[1] Adam was faced with the same choice, between the tree of life and the tree of knowledge of good and evil, whose fruit brought death. See Genesis 2:9-17, page 23.

Lord, you don't love us
because we are the best,
but because you only
know how to love.
You are faithful
and never tire of us
in spite of our indifference and rejection.
You deliver us from the bondage of sin.
You chose us
so that we can share our
joy of knowing you with others.

THE HISTORY OF MOSES

1. The Hebrews, forced into slavery, make bricks (Exodus 1:8-14, page 54).

2. The Pharaoh's daughter saves a baby from the river. He is Moses (Exodus 2:1-9, page 55).

3. Moses kills an Egyptian slave-driver (Exodus 2:11-15, page 56).

4. On Mount Horeb, God calls to Moses from the burning bush (Exodus 3:1-12, page 56).

5. Moses and Aaron ask the Pharaoh to free their people (Exodus 5:1-9, page 60).

6. The Hebrews prepare the Passover meal. They are ready to flee Egypt (Exodus 12:1-14, page 63).

7. The Pharaoh's army pursues the Hebrews who, under Moses' leadership, cross the Red Sea (Exodus 14:5-30, page 64).

8. The people are fed with manna (Exodus 16:2-15, page 66).

9. The people's thirst is slaked with water from the rock (Exodus 17:2-7, page 67).

10. At Rephidim, Joshua fights the Amalekites while Moses prays on the mountain (Exodus 17:8-13, page 68).

11. Moses receives the Tables of the Law (see page 74).

12. Moses discovers that his people are worshipping idols. Aaron has fashioned a golden calf (Exodus 32:15-24, page 75).

13. The people resume their march towards the Promised Land, carrying with them the Ark of the Covenant (see pages 79 and after).

14. Moses puts a bronze serpent on a pole to protect the people from poisonous snakes (see John 3:14-15, page 338).

15. Moses dies on Mount Nebo, overlooking Jericho and the Promised Land (Deuteronomy 34:1-10, page 89).

The canticle of Moses

Moses hymns the greatness of God's love for His people.

32 1 Give ear, O heavens, to my voice;
let the earth take note of the words of my mouth:
2 My teaching is dropping like rain,
coming down like dew on the fields....
3 For I will give honour to the name of the Lord:
let our God be named great.
4 He is the Rock,[1] complete is his work;
for all his ways are righteousness:
a God without evil who keeps faith,
true and upright is he.
5 They have become false, they are not his children,
the mark of sin is on them;
they are an evil and hard-hearted generation.
6 Is this your answer to the Lord,
O foolish people and unwise?
Is he not your father, your creator?[2]
He has made you and given you your place.

God has chosen the people of Israel from among all the peoples on earth.

9 For the Lord's wealth is his people;
Jacob is the land of his heritage.
10 He came to him in the waste land,
in the unpeopled waste of sand:
putting his arms round him and caring for him,
he kept him as the light of his eye.
11 As an eagle, teaching her young
to make their flight,
with her wings outstretched over them,
takes them up on her strong feathers.
12 So the Lord only was his guide,
no other god was with him.

[1] See page 68.

[2] God willed that, of all his creatures, humans should be in His likeness. This wish of God creates a special relationship between humans and Himself like those binding a father to his children.

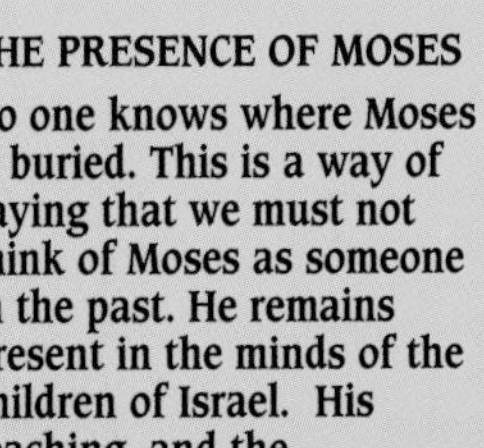

HE PRESENCE OF MOSES

o one knows where Moses s buried. This is a way of aying that we must not hink of Moses as someone n the past. He remains resent in the minds of the hildren of Israel. His eaching, and the ommandments which he lelivered, meditated upon nd explained, are the code f behavior of a whole eople.

The death of Moses

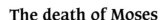

Moses has reached the end of his journey. With authority and compassion,[1] he had persuaded his people to take the Covenant with God seriously. He had led them to the edge of the Promised Land. He charged his most trusty disciple,* Joshua, with settling them there. He passed away, alone on the mountain, in communion with the God he had so fervently served.*

34 1 And Moses went up from the table-lands of Moab
to Mount Nebo, to the top of Pisgah which is fa-
cing Jericho. And the Lord let him see all the land.... |
4 And the Lord said to him, "This is the land about which
I made an oath to Abraham, Isaac, and Jacob, saying, 'I
will give it to your descendants.' Now I have let you see
it with your eyes, but you will not go in there."[2]

5 So death came to Moses, the servant of the Lord, there
6 in the land of Moab, as the Lord had said. | And the
Lord put him to rest in the valley in the land of Moab
opposite Beth-peor, but no man has knowledge of his
7 resting-place to this day. | And Moses at his death was a
hundred and twenty years old. His eye had not become
8 clouded, or his natural force become feeble. | For thirty
days the children of Israel were weeping for Moses in
the plains of Moab, till the days of weeping and sorrow
9 for Moses were ended. | And Joshua, the son of Nun,
was full of the spirit of wisdom; for Moses had put his
hands on him.[3] Tthe children of Israel listened to him,
and did as the Lord had given orders to Moses.

10 There has never been another prophet in Israel like
Moses, whom the Lord had knowledge of face to face....

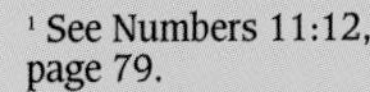

[1] See Numbers 11:12, page 79.

[2] Moses showed lack of faith by the waters of Meribah (see Numbers 20:12, page 81). He therefore shared the lot of most of the people who had fled Egypt with him. They would merely glimpse the glory of the land* in which their descendants would settle.

[3] Joshua was an exception. He was one of the few among those who had escaped from Egypt to enter the Promised Land.

PART TWO

THE LIFE OF THE PEOPLE OF ISRAEL

Part Two of "Treasures of the Bible" contains the Books which recount the life of the people of God from their entry into the Promised Land until the birth of Jesus. Through meditation on their history and with the help of the elders, prophets* and wise men, the people deepened their knowledge* of God. This long period of about a thousand years may be conveniently divided into three ages.*

THE AGE OF THE KINGS AND PROPHETS pages 93 to 145

Under the guidance of Joshua, the children of Israel settled with some difficulty among the peoples of Canaan. They were sometimes tempted to forget the God of the Covenant.[1] But when conflicts arose with the earlier inhabitants, they turned back to the Lord to express their anxieties. The Lord then sent them leaders, known as Judges,* to help them rid themselves of their oppressors. The most notable of the Judges were Gideon, Jephthah, Samson and a woman, Deborah.*

The elders realized that the people could not survive unless all the tribes united under the rule of a king. Saul, David and Solomon were kings who reigned over the twelve tribes. Later, the people separated into two kingdoms: a larger one in the North, the kingdom of Israel, and a smaller one in the South, the kingdom of Judah.

THE CAPTIVITY pages 148 to 172

After a period of prosperity, the kingdom of Israel was completely destroyed by the Assyrians. The population was deported and its place taken by foreigners. The kingdom of Judah was spared for a time but, a hundred years later, it fell to the Babylonians. This was the age of captivity, a time of suffering when understanding of God became even deeper. God does not protect His people against other peoples. He is the God of all. He wishes, through His people, to reveal Himself to the other nations.

AFTER THE CAPTIVITY pages 173 to 205

King Cyrus made it possible for the captives to return to their land. A number of them, now called Jews, rebuilt Jerusalem and the Temple from their ruins. They no longer had a king, but were dependent on Persian governors. Later, they passed under Greek and then Roman rule. A strong desire for a liberator made itself felt. But what sort of liberator? A mighty warrior or a humble messenger of peace?*

[1] At that time, only some biblical writings existed.

I

THE AGE OF THE KINGS AND PROPHETS

The tribes settled in the land of Canaan.* They had a difficult life. Other peoples were already living there. Yet more, like the Philistines,* were keen to move in. It was a time of endless combats.*

Joshua, whose authority was recognized by all the tribes, was succeeded by the Judges. Their authority extended to some of the tribes, or sometimes one of them only. The need to assemble all the tribes under a single leader became clear. In that way they would have more strength to deal with adversity. The people asked the last Judge, Samuel, to give them a king.*

Saul, followed by David, were the first kings of Israel. They were enthroned after being anointed with oil and thereby becoming "messiahs."[1] Their primary task was to listen to the Lord so as to lead the people well. Alas, many of the succeeding kings were poor guides, bad shepherds and unworthy messiahs. God then sent the prophets.*[2] Although not anointed, they received the spirit of the Lord and acted as the people's true shepherds. They corrected the mistakes of the kings and tirelessly reminded the people that they were the people of God.*

[1] Messiah means "anointed," the one who has received the unction. The spirit of God breathes in him, if he lets himself be guided by it, and gives him the wisdom to keep the people close to the Covenant.*

[2] It sometimes happened that a prophet lived at the same time as a good king, but in general the great prophets were called by God to make up for the shortcomings of the messiah-kings. See messiah.*

UNION OF THE TRIBES

The tribes of Israel took some time before uniting to form a kingdom. They did not find it easy to live together. There were divisions and disputes among them. Each one guarded its independence.

In a book written much later, Joshua is described as having assembled the representatives of the twelve tribes in Shechem immediately after settling in the Promised Land.

Very astutely, he challenged the tribes to continue to live as allies of God. The tribes accepted the challenge and solemnly pledged to live according to the Covenant.

Faith* in the same God was the bond of union among the tribes. They gradually gained awareness that they made up a single people. They would one day ask to be ruled by a king.

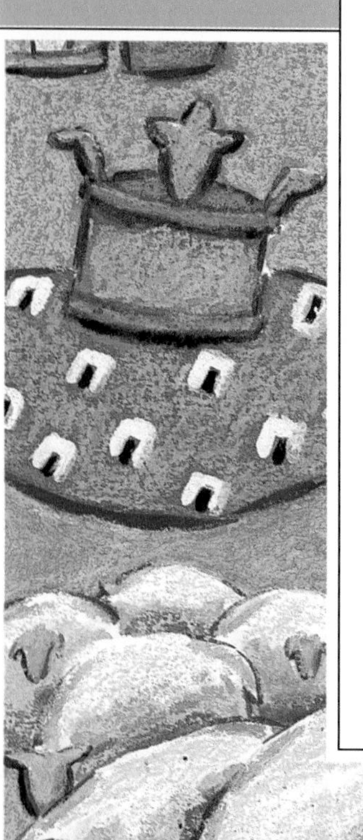

TOWARDS A KINGDOM

The pact of Shechem

24 1 Then Joshua got all the tribes of Israel together at Shechem.[1]

Joshua made a long speech in which he reminded the people of all the signs of love which God had shown them. Joshua, in a sense, lets God speak through his mouth: "I chose Abraham, son of Terah,[2] to whom I gave Isaac. I freed you from Egypt."

13 "I gave you a land on which you had done no work, and towns which you had not built, and you are now living in them. Your food comes from vineyards and olive groves which you had not planted."

Joshua continued his speech, speaking for himself. He confronted the people with a choice. Whom did they wish to serve? The gods of Terah, the gods of the Amorites[3] or the Lord God of Abraham and Moses?

15 "And if it seems evil to you to be the servants of the Lord, make the decision this day whose servants you will be, of the gods whose servants your fathers were across the River, or of the gods of the Amorites in whose land you are living. But I and my house will be the servants of the Lord."

16 Then the people answered, "Never will we give up the
17 Lord to be the servants of other gods; | for it is the Lord
our God who has taken us and our fathers out of the
land of Egypt, out of slavery, and who did all those

[1] Shechem was the first town i which Abraham lived in Ca naan. He built an altar there the Lord. See Genesis 12: page 36.

[2] See page 36.

[3] The Amorites were one of th peoples living in Canaan befo the Hebrews arrived. They live in the hills, whereas the Cana nites lived on the plain.

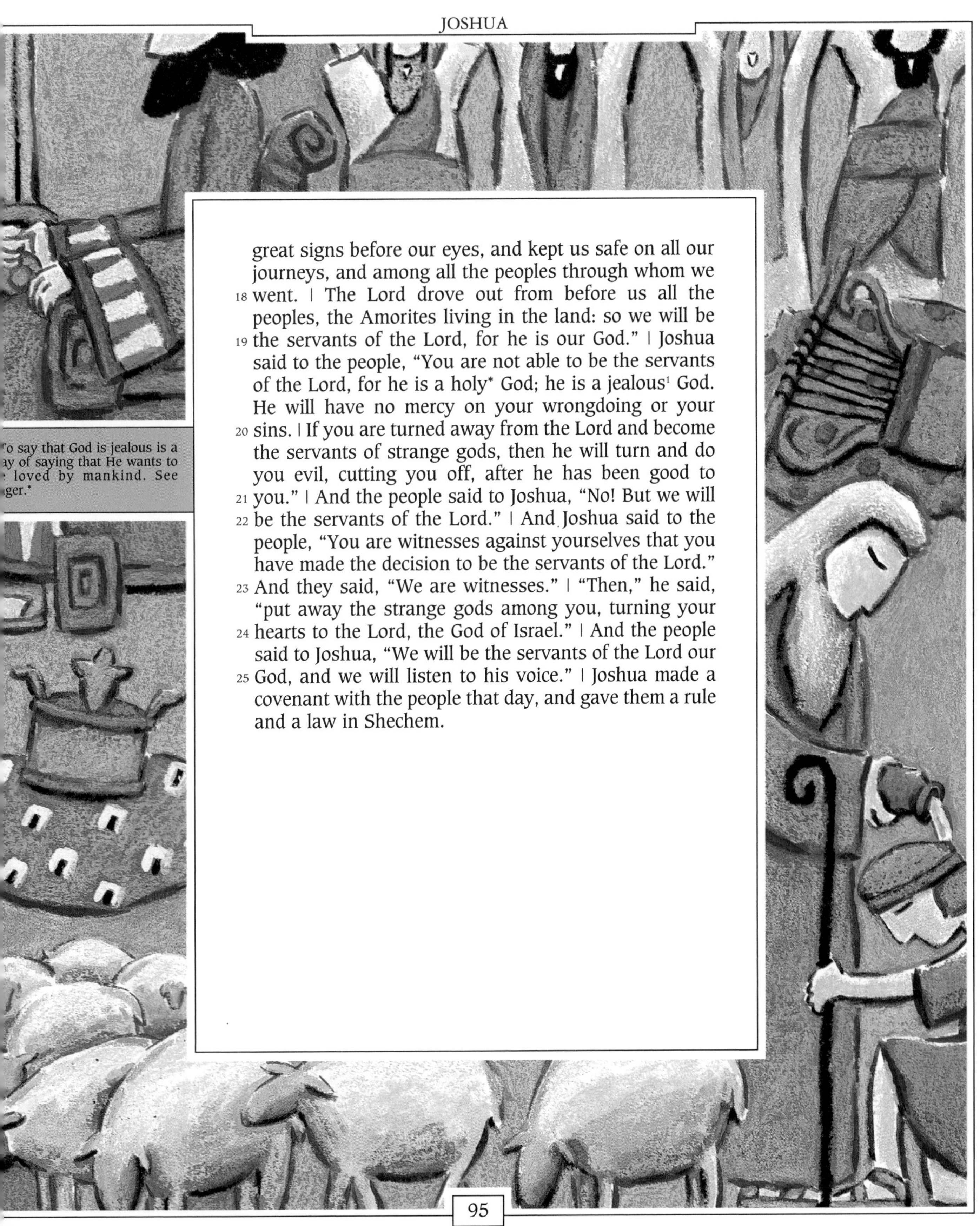

great signs before our eyes, and kept us safe on all our
journeys, and among all the peoples through whom we
18 went. | The Lord drove out from before us all the
peoples, the Amorites living in the land: so we will be
19 the servants of the Lord, for he is our God." | Joshua
said to the people, "You are not able to be the servants
of the Lord, for he is a holy* God; he is a jealous[1] God.
He will have no mercy on your wrongdoing or your
20 sins. | If you are turned away from the Lord and become
the servants of strange gods, then he will turn and do
you evil, cutting you off, after he has been good to
21 you." | And the people said to Joshua, "No! But we will
22 be the servants of the Lord." | And Joshua said to the
people, "You are witnesses against yourselves that you
have made the decision to be the servants of the Lord."
23 And they said, "We are witnesses." | "Then," he said,
"put away the strange gods among you, turning your
24 hearts to the Lord, the God of Israel." | And the people
said to Joshua, "We will be the servants of the Lord our
25 God, and we will listen to his voice." | Joshua made a
covenant with the people that day, and gave them a rule
and a law in Shechem.

'o say that God is jealous is a ay of saying that He wants to loved by mankind. See ger.*

[1] See 1 Kings 5:2-18, page 118.

[2] Samuel certainly knew a great deal about the Lord, the Ark of the Covenant and its history. He had many good ideas about God, but had not experienced Him as a living being.

The last of the Judges* is called

The Ark of the Covenant, a memento of the exodus, was venerated in a small hillside temple in Shiloh. In this rural shrine, very different from the one which Solomon would build in Jerusalem,[1] the Ark was visible to all. Samuel, who had been in the Lord's service since he was a small boy, slept next to it.

3 1 Now the young Samuel was the servant of the
Lord before Eli. In those days the Lord kept
his word secret from men; there were few visions.
2 And at that time, when Eli was resting in his usual
3 place.... | and the light of God was still burning, while
Samuel was sleeping in the Temple of the Lord where
4 the ark of God was, | the voice of the Lord said Samuel's
5 name; and he said, "Here am I." | And running to Eli he
said, "Here am I, for you said my name." And Eli said,
"I did not say your name; go to your rest again. So he
6 went back to his bed." | And again the Lord said,
"Samuel." And Samuel got up and went to Eli and said,
"Here am I; for you certainly said my name." But he
answered, "I said nothing, my son; go to your rest
7 again." | Now at that time Samuel had no knowledge[2] of
the Lord, and the revelation of the word of the Lord had
not come to him.
8 And for the third time the Lord said Samuel's name.
And he got up and went to Eli and said,
"Here am I; for you certainly said my
name." Then it was clear to Eli that the
voice which had said the child's name
9 was the Lord's. | So Eli said to Samuel,
"Go back. If the voice comes again, let
your answer be, 'Speak, Lord; for the
ears of your servant are open.'" So
10 Samuel went back to his bed. | Then the

"Hear, O Israel"
Listening is the believer's attitude.
Lord, I'm quietly listening.
I'm trying
to think only of you.
Even though I can't see you with my eyes
I know you are present.
I know that you are alive.
You know my name
just like you knew Samuel's.
You call me,
and I am filled with joy.

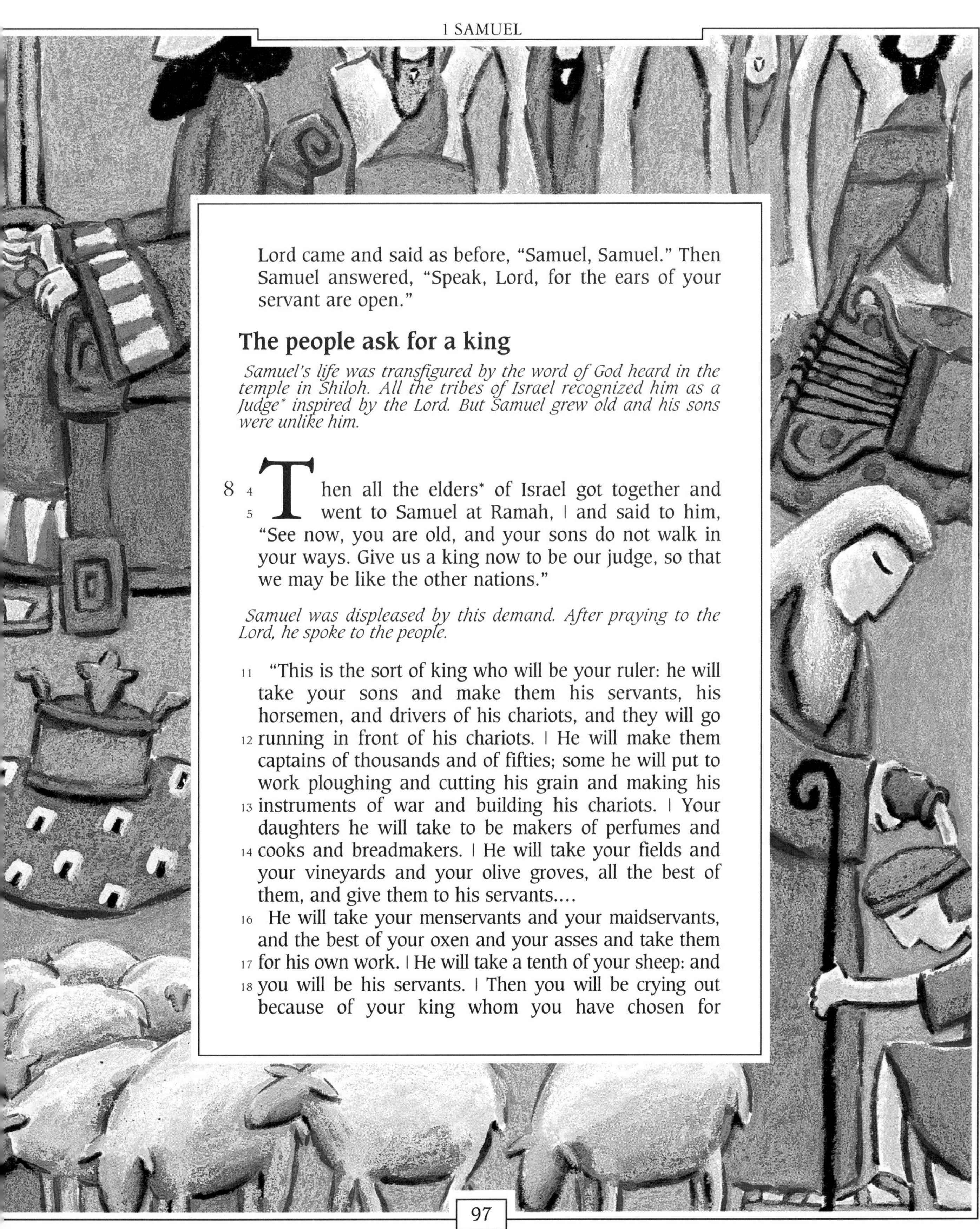

Lord came and said as before, "Samuel, Samuel." Then
Samuel answered, "Speak, Lord, for the ears of your
servant are open."

The people ask for a king

Samuel's life was transfigured by the word of God heard in the temple in Shiloh. All the tribes of Israel recognized him as a Judge inspired by the Lord. But Samuel grew old and his sons were unlike him.*

8 4 Then all the elders* of Israel got together and
5 went to Samuel at Ramah, | and said to him,
"See now, you are old, and your sons do not walk in
your ways. Give us a king now to be our judge, so that
we may be like the other nations."

Samuel was displeased by this demand. After praying to the Lord, he spoke to the people.

11 "This is the sort of king who will be your ruler: he will
take your sons and make them his servants, his
horsemen, and drivers of his chariots, and they will go
12 running in front of his chariots. | He will make them
captains of thousands and of fifties; some he will put to
work ploughing and cutting his grain and making his
13 instruments of war and building his chariots. | Your
daughters he will take to be makers of perfumes and
14 cooks and breadmakers. | He will take your fields and
your vineyards and your olive groves, all the best of
them, and give them to his servants....
16 He will take your menservants and your maidservants,
and the best of your oxen and your asses and take them
17 for his own work. | He will take a tenth of your sheep: and
18 you will be his servants. | Then you will be crying out
because of your king whom you have chosen for

8 yourselves; but the Lord will not give you an answer in
that day."
19 But the people paid no attention to the voice of Samuel;
20 They said, "No, but we will have a king over us, | so that
we may be like the other nations, and so that our king
21 may be our judge and lead us to war." | Then Samuel,
after hearing all the people had to say,
22 went and recounted it to the Lord. | And
the Lord said to Samuel, "Listen to them
and make a king for them."...

"We want to be like everyone else."
O God,
your people don't understand
your expectations.
You purposely chose them so they wouldn't
be like "the other nations."
You ask your people to love as you love,
to be holy as you are holy.
You want your people
to give other peoples
the desire to resemble
them and to know you.

KING SAUL

A tall king is chosen

Samuel summoned the people before the Lord at Mizpah to name the king.

10 20 So Samuel called all the tribes of
Israel together,and the tribe of
21 Benjamin was chosen. | Then he called forward the tribe
of Benjamin by families. The family of the Matrites was
chosen, and from them, Saul, the son of Kish, was
chosen. But when they went in search of him he was
22 nowhere to be seen. | So they put another question[1] to
the Lord, "Is the man present here?" And the answer of
the Lord was, "He is keeping himself from view among
23 the goods." | So they went quickly and made him come
out; and when he took his place among the people, he
24 was taller by a head than any of the people. | And
Samuel said to all the people, "Do you see the man of
the Lord's selection, how there is no other like him
among all the people?" And all the people with loud
cries said, "Long life to the king!"

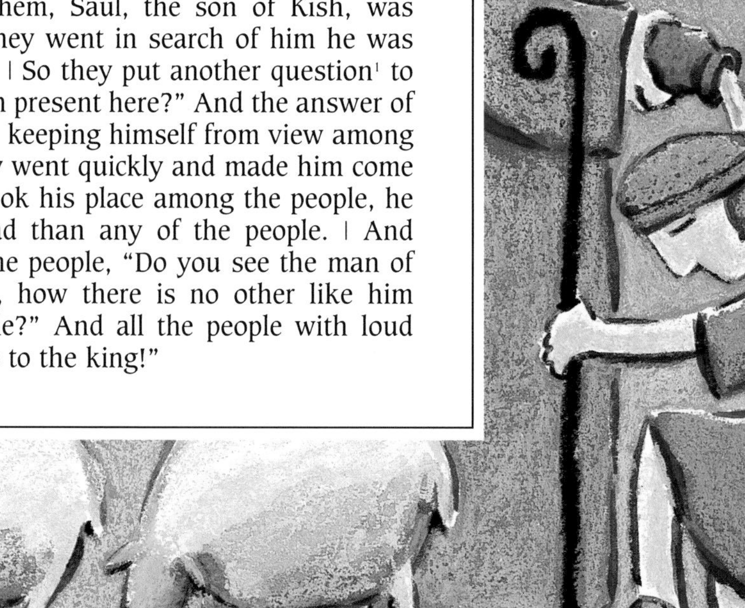

[1] Some of the methods used in those days for consulting the Lord were the same as the ones practiced by the other peoples of the region. Specialists, called seers, proclaimed the Lord's answers by means of odd rituals. They would sometimes use beads and counters of different shapes and colors. When one of these was drawn by chance, they would interpret its meaning. Later, this rather pagan custom would be abandoned and the prophets would announce the Lord's wishes directly.

Choosing a great king

David left such a big impression in the people's minds that it was said that God had chosen him to succeed Saul well before Saul died.

16 1 And the Lord said to Samuel, ... "Take oil in your
horn and go; I will send you to Jesse, the
Bethlehemite: for I have got a king for myself among his
2 sons." | And Samuel said, "How is it possible for me to go?
If Saul gets news of it he will put me to death." And the
Lord said, "Take a young cow with you and say, 'I have
3 come to make an offering to the Lord.' | And send for Jesse
to be present at the sacrifice, and I will make clear to you
what you are to do: and you are to anoint him whose name
I give you."
4 And Samuel did as the Lord said and came to Bethlehem. And the responsible men of the town came out to
5 him in fear and said, "Do you come in peace?" | And he
said, "In peace, I have come to make an offering to the
Lord. Consecrate* yourselves and come with me to make
the offering." And he consecrated Jesse and his sons, and
sent for them to be present at the offering.
6 Now when they came, looking at Eliab, he said, "Clearly
7 the man of the Lord's selection is before him." | But the
Lord said to Samuel, "Do not take note of his face or how
tall he is, because I will reject him, for the Lord's view is
not man's. Man takes note of the outer form, but the Lord
8 sees the heart." | Then Jesse sent for Abinadab and made
him come before Samuel. And he said,
"The Lord has not taken this one."...
10 And Jesse made his seven sons come
before Samuel. And Samuel said to
Jesse, "The Lord has not chosen any of
11 these." | Then Samuel said to Jesse, "Are

FROM SAUL TO DAVID

Saul was by all accounts a good and courageous man. Yet he did not succeed as a king. He and all his family were wiped out in the disastrous battle of Gilboa (2 Samuel 1:11-27, page 105). **David, his son-in-law, succeeded him to the throne. David was the great king the people had been waiting for. He unified the twelve tribes around a new capital, Jerusalem.**

Samuel, you are not being serious.
You are letting yourself be impressed
by Saul's broad shoulders.
You are being taken
in once again by
Eliab's stature.
Remember the Lord's primary interest
is the heart.
Once again the Lord will choose
the youngest and the smallest,
the one to whom no one paid attention.

16 all your children here?" And he said, "There is still the
youngest, and he is looking after the sheep." And Samuel
said to Jesse, "Send and make him come here: for we will
12 not take our seats till he is here." | So he sent and made
him come in. Now he had red hair and beautiful eyes and
pleasing looks. And the Lord said, "Come, put the oil on
13 him, for this is he." | Then Samuel took the bottle of oil,
and anoint him there among his brothers: and from that
day the spirit of the Lord came on David with power.[1] So
Samuel went back to Ramah.

[1] Oil sinks in and softens. It is the symbol of the divine spirit which wants to sink into us and soften our heart, making it more prepared to accept the will of God. The person anointed with oil, the messiah,* receives the strength of the divine spirit to lead his people as a shepherd leads his flock.

The shepherd boy versus the warrior giant

David the shepherd met Saul on the occasion of an extraordinary feat of arms. The armies of Israel were at war with the powerful people called the Philistines who lived near the Mediterranean coast. Among the Philistines was a giant named Goliath who had issued a challenge to the Israelites. "Let one of you fight against me. The winner will gain victory for his people." No soldier of Israel dared accept the challenge.*

David arrived at Saul's camp, bringing food for his brothers.

17 32 And David said to Saul, "Let no man's heart become feeble because of him; I, your servant, will
33 go out and have a fight with this Philistine." | And Saul
said to David, "You are not able to go out against this
Philistine and have a fight with him. You are only a boy,
and he has been a man of war from his earliest days...."
37 | And David said, "The Lord, who kept me safe from the
grip of the lion and the bear, will be my savior from the
hands of this Philistine." And Saul said to David, "Go! and
may the Lord be with you."...
40 Then he took his stick in his hand, and got five smooth
stones from the bed of the stream and put them in a bag

THE FAITH OF DAVID

David did not become king at once. His duel with Goliath represents one of the hidden stages of his accession to the throne.

The story is there mostly to illustrate the faith of David and induce the people to imitate him. David does not try to be a soldier like the others. He believes that God has chosen Israel to be His witness* before the nations. Thus God Himself ensures his people's safety.

This is a message which the prophets* will repeat again and again.

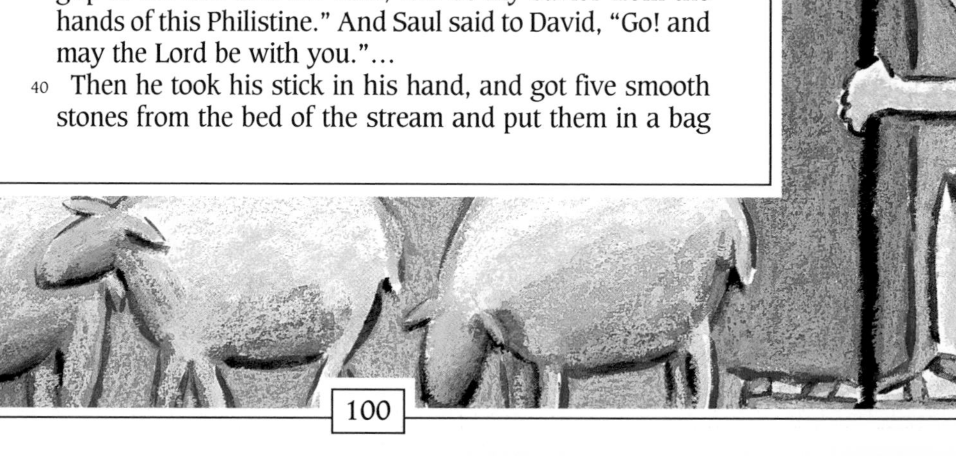

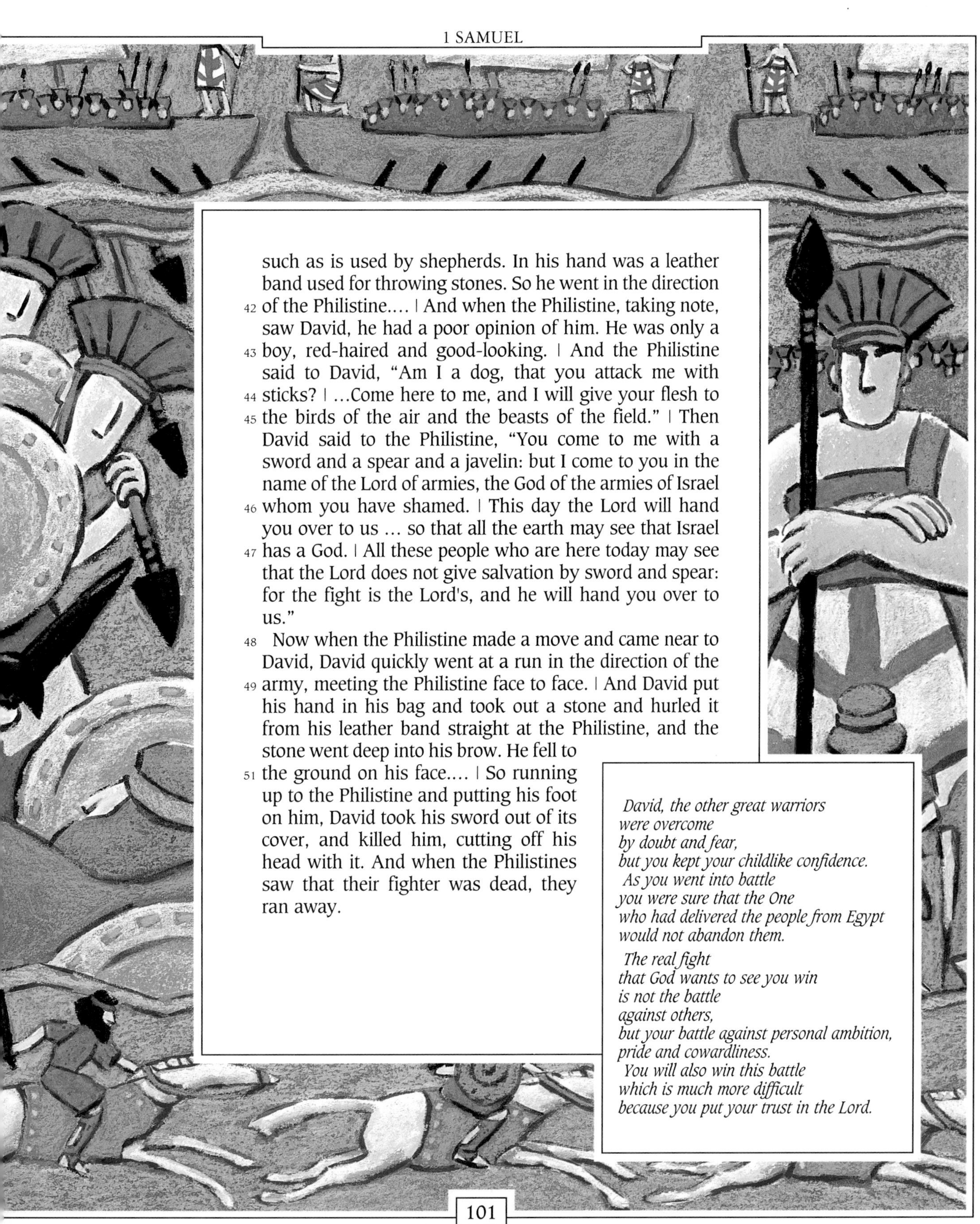

such as is used by shepherds. In his hand was a leather
band used for throwing stones. So he went in the direction
42 of the Philistine.... | And when the Philistine, taking note,
saw David, he had a poor opinion of him. He was only a
43 boy, red-haired and good-looking. | And the Philistine
said to David, "Am I a dog, that you attack me with
44 sticks? | ...Come here to me, and I will give your flesh to
45 the birds of the air and the beasts of the field." | Then
David said to the Philistine, "You come to me with a
sword and a spear and a javelin: but I come to you in the
name of the Lord of armies, the God of the armies of Israel
46 whom you have shamed. | This day the Lord will hand
you over to us ... so that all the earth may see that Israel
47 has a God. | All these people who are here today may see
that the Lord does not give salvation by sword and spear:
for the fight is the Lord's, and he will hand you over to
us."

48 Now when the Philistine made a move and came near to
David, David quickly went at a run in the direction of the
49 army, meeting the Philistine face to face. | And David put
his hand in his bag and took out a stone and hurled it
from his leather band straight at the Philistine, and the
stone went deep into his brow. He fell to
51 the ground on his face.... | So running
up to the Philistine and putting his foot
on him, David took his sword out of its
cover, and killed him, cutting off his
head with it. And when the Philistines
saw that their fighter was dead, they
ran away.

David, the other great warriors
were overcome
by doubt and fear,
but you kept your childlike confidence.
As you went into battle
you were sure that the One
who had delivered the people from Egypt
would not abandon them.

The real fight
that God wants to see you win
is not the battle
against others,
but your battle against personal ambition,
pride and cowardliness.
You will also win this battle
which is much more difficult
because you put your trust in the Lord.

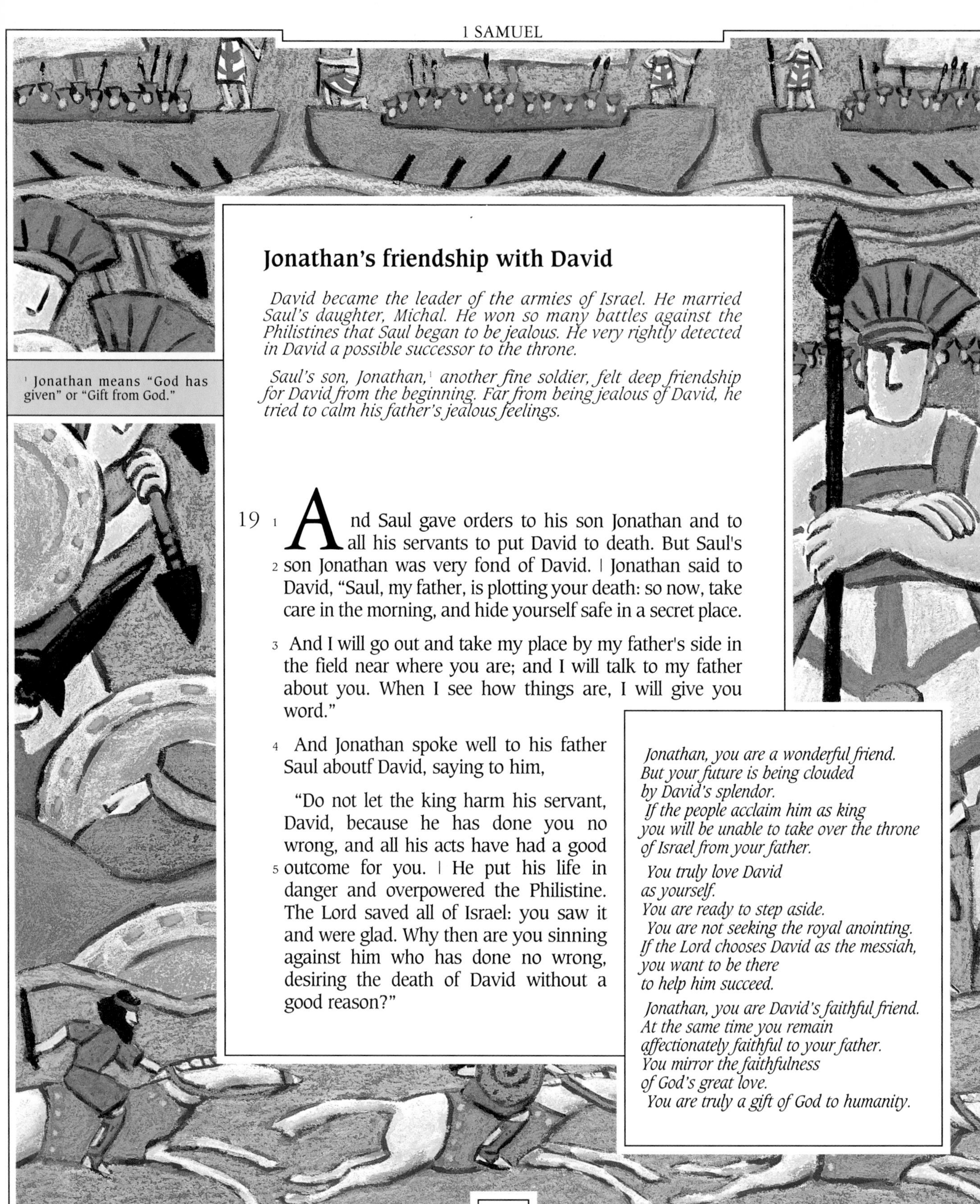

Jonathan's friendship with David

David became the leader of the armies of Israel. He married Saul's daughter, Michal. He won so many battles against the Philistines that Saul began to be jealous. He very rightly detected in David a possible successor to the throne.

Saul's son, Jonathan,[1] *another fine soldier, felt deep friendship for David from the beginning. Far from being jealous of David, he tried to calm his father's jealous feelings.*

[1] Jonathan means "God has given" or "Gift from God."

19 1 And Saul gave orders to his son Jonathan and to
all his servants to put David to death. But Saul's
2 son Jonathan was very fond of David. | Jonathan said to
David, "Saul, my father, is plotting your death: so now, take
care in the morning, and hide yourself safe in a secret place.

3 And I will go out and take my place by my father's side in
the field near where you are; and I will talk to my father
about you. When I see how things are, I will give you
word."

4 And Jonathan spoke well to his father
Saul aboutf David, saying to him,

"Do not let the king harm his servant,
David, because he has done you no
wrong, and all his acts have had a good
5 outcome for you. | He put his life in
danger and overpowered the Philistine.
The Lord saved all of Israel: you saw it
and were glad. Why then are you sinning
against him who has done no wrong,
desiring the death of David without a
good reason?"

Jonathan, you are a wonderful friend.
But your future is being clouded
by David's splendor.
If the people acclaim him as king
you will be unable to take over the throne
of Israel from your father.

You truly love David
as yourself.
You are ready to step aside.
You are not seeking the royal anointing.
If the Lord chooses David as the messiah,
you want to be there
to help him succeed.

Jonathan, you are David's faithful friend.
At the same time you remain
affectionately faithful to your father.
You mirror the faithfulness
of God's great love.
You are truly a gift of God to humanity.

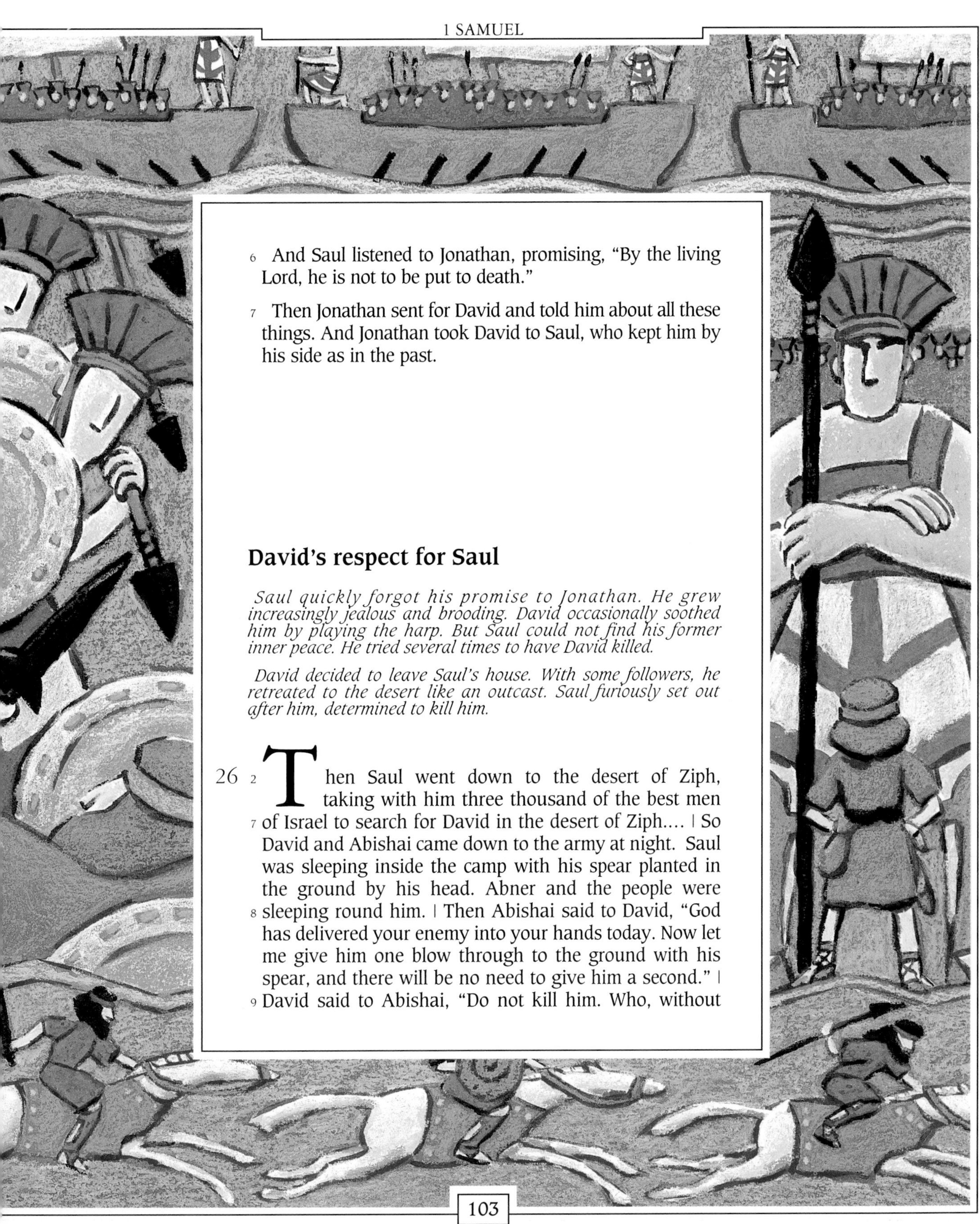

6 And Saul listened to Jonathan, promising, "By the living
Lord, he is not to be put to death."

7 Then Jonathan sent for David and told him about all these
things. And Jonathan took David to Saul, who kept him by
his side as in the past.

David's respect for Saul

Saul quickly forgot his promise to Jonathan. He grew increasingly jealous and brooding. David occasionally soothed him by playing the harp. But Saul could not find his former inner peace. He tried several times to have David killed.

David decided to leave Saul's house. With some followers, he retreated to the desert like an outcast. Saul furiously set out after him, determined to kill him.

26 2 Then Saul went down to the desert of Ziph,
taking with him three thousand of the best men
7 of Israel to search for David in the desert of Ziph.... | So
David and Abishai came down to the army at night. Saul
was sleeping inside the camp with his spear planted in
the ground by his head. Abner and the people were
8 sleeping round him. | Then Abishai said to David, "God
has delivered your enemy into your hands today. Now let
me give him one blow through to the ground with his
spear, and there will be no need to give him a second." |
9 David said to Abishai, "Do not kill him. Who, without

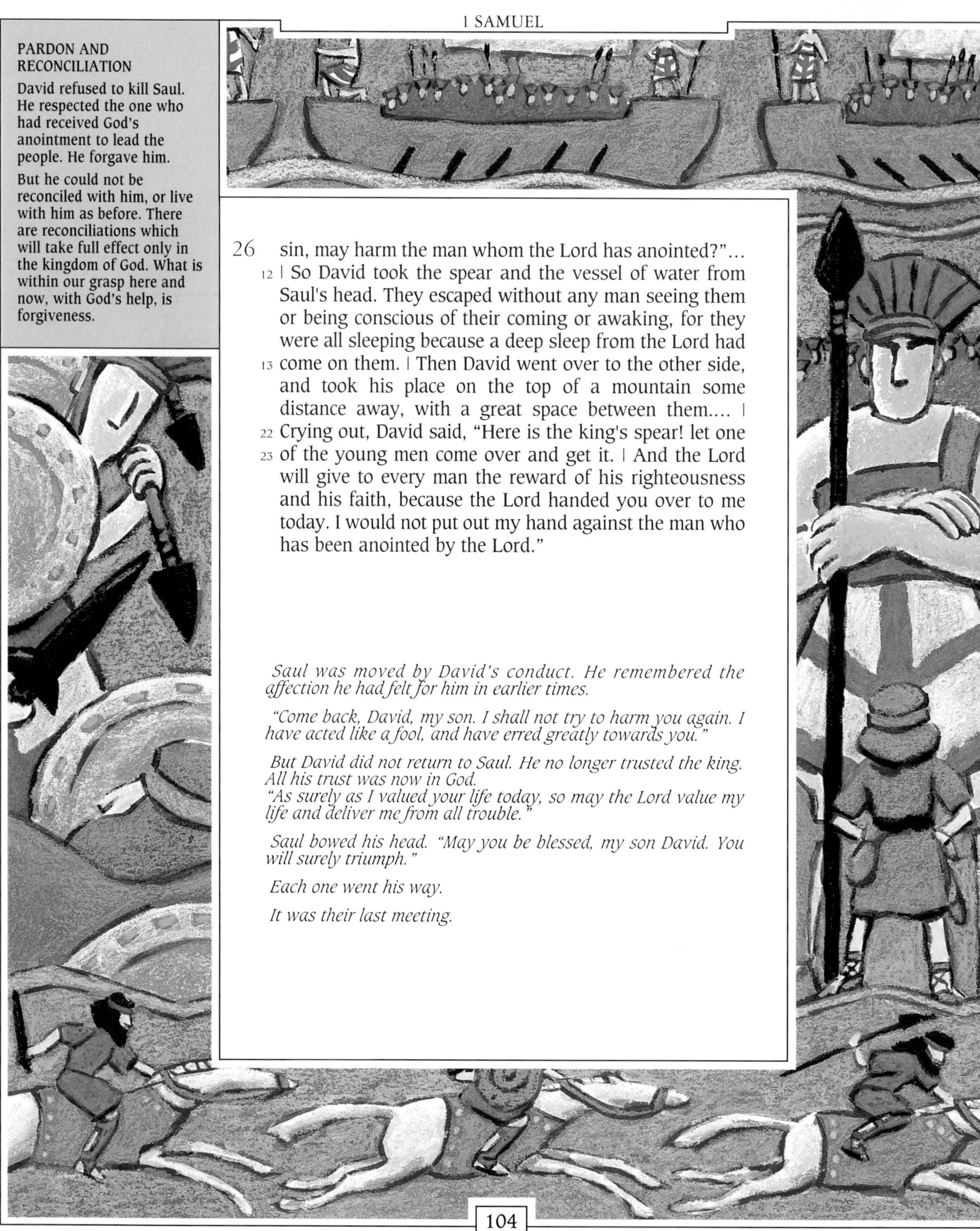

PARDON AND RECONCILIATION

David refused to kill Saul. He respected the one who had received God's anointment to lead the people. He forgave him.

But he could not be reconciled with him, or live with him as before. There are reconciliations which will take full effect only in the kingdom of God. What is within our grasp here and now, with God's help, is forgiveness.

26 sin, may harm the man whom the Lord has anointed?"...
12 | So David took the spear and the vessel of water from
Saul's head. They escaped without any man seeing them
or being conscious of their coming or awaking, for they
were all sleeping because a deep sleep from the Lord had
13 come on them. | Then David went over to the other side,
and took his place on the top of a mountain some
distance away, with a great space between them.... |
22 Crying out, David said, "Here is the king's spear! let one
23 of the young men come over and get it. | And the Lord
will give to every man the reward of his righteousness
and his faith, because the Lord handed you over to me
today. I would not put out my hand against the man who
has been anointed by the Lord."

Saul was moved by David's conduct. He remembered the affection he had felt for him in earlier times.

"Come back, David, my son. I shall not try to harm you again. I have acted like a fool, and have erred greatly towards you."

But David did not return to Saul. He no longer trusted the king. All his trust was now in God.
"As surely as I valued your life today, so may the Lord value my life and deliver me from all trouble."

Saul bowed his head. "May you be blessed, my son David. You will surely triumph."

Each one went his way.

It was their last meeting.

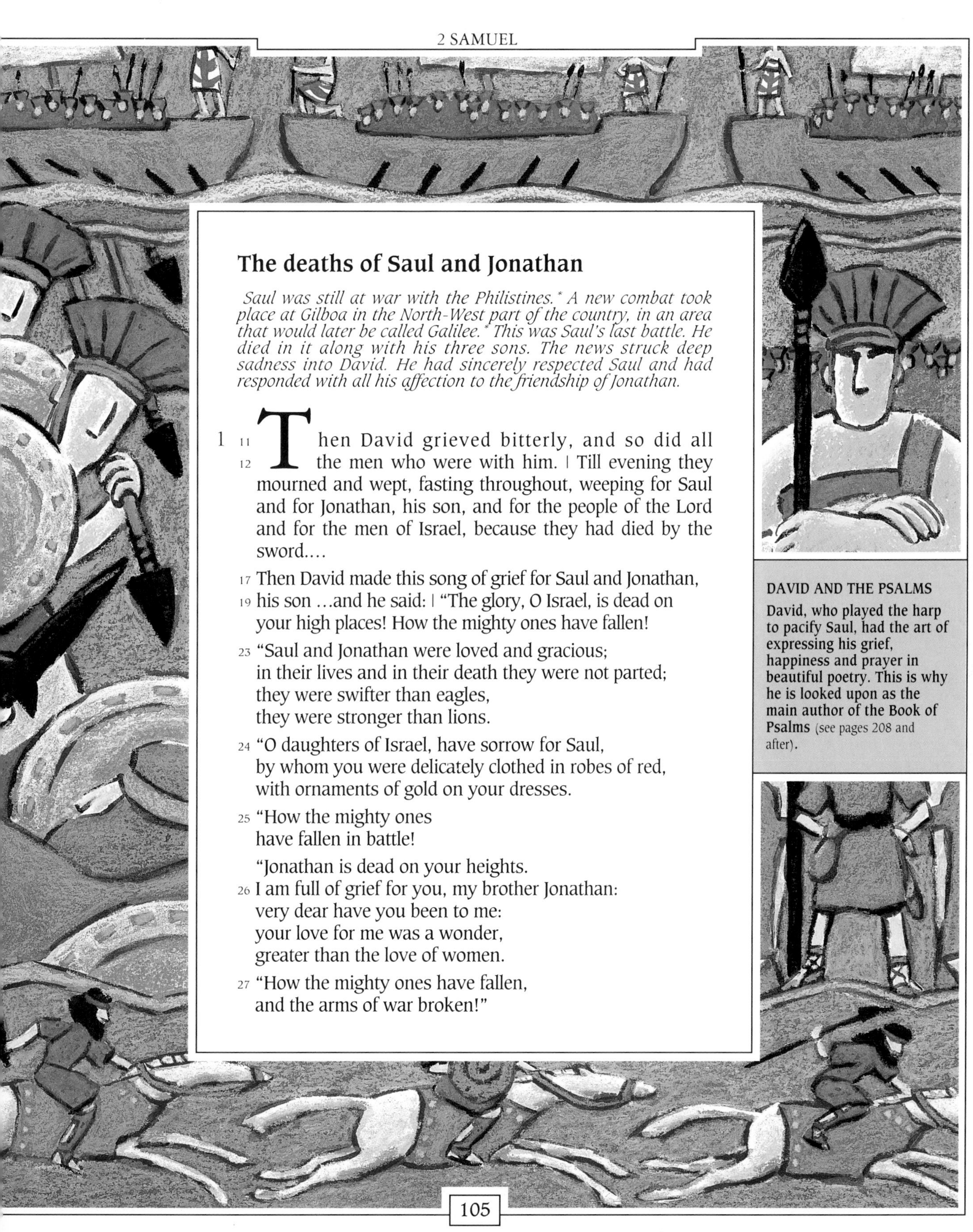

The deaths of Saul and Jonathan

Saul was still at war with the Philistines. A new combat took place at Gilboa in the North-West part of the country, in an area that would later be called Galilee.* This was Saul's last battle. He died in it along with his three sons. The news struck deep sadness into David. He had sincerely respected Saul and had responded with all his affection to the friendship of Jonathan.*

1 11 Then David grieved bitterly, and so did all
12 the men who were with him. | Till evening they
mourned and wept, fasting throughout, weeping for Saul
and for Jonathan, his son, and for the people of the Lord
and for the men of Israel, because they had died by the
sword....

17 Then David made this song of grief for Saul and Jonathan,
19 his son ...and he said: | "The glory, O Israel, is dead on
your high places! How the mighty ones have fallen!

23 "Saul and Jonathan were loved and gracious;
in their lives and in their death they were not parted;
they were swifter than eagles,
they were stronger than lions.

24 "O daughters of Israel, have sorrow for Saul,
by whom you were delicately clothed in robes of red,
with ornaments of gold on your dresses.

25 "How the mighty ones
have fallen in battle!

"Jonathan is dead on your heights.
26 I am full of grief for you, my brother Jonathan:
very dear have you been to me:
your love for me was a wonder,
greater than the love of women.

27 "How the mighty ones have fallen,
and the arms of war broken!"

DAVID AND THE PSALMS

David, who played the harp to pacify Saul, had the art of expressing his grief, happiness and prayer in beautiful poetry. This is why he is looked upon as the main author of the Book of Psalms (see pages 208 and after).

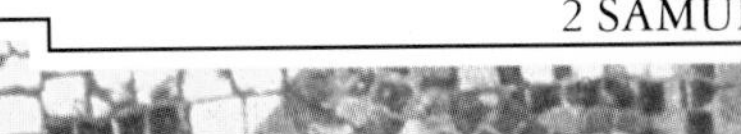

KING OF THE TWELVE TRIBES

After the death of Saul, the union of the twelve tribes fell apart. The tribe of Judah acknowledged David as king. David made his home in Hebron near the tomb of the patriarchs.* Seven years later, this was where the twelve tribes came to ask him to be king of the whole people. To achieve the unification of the twelve tribes, David looked for a new capital — a town which did not belong to any of the twelve tribes, where everyone could come to see the king without feeling like a stranger in someone else's land and where the king could be judge for the twelve tribes without being under obligation to any particular one (see Psalm 122, page 221).

Jerusalem, in the middle of the country, had not yet been conquered by the Israelites. It was ideal for David's purpose.

KING DAVID

Choice of a capital

5 1 Then all the tribes of Israel[1] came to David in
Hebron and said, "Truly, we are your flesh and
2 blood. | In the past when Saul was king over us, it was you
who led Israel when they went out or came in. The Lord
said to you, 'You are to be the shepherd of my people Israel
and their ruler.'"

3 So all the elders* of Israel came to the king at Hebron; and
King David made a covenant with them in Hebron before
the Lord. They anointed David and made him king over
4 Israel. | David was thirty years old when he became king,
and he was king for forty years..

6 The king and his men went to Jerusalem to attack the
Jebusites, the people of the land. They said to David, "You
will not enter here, but the blind and the lame will keep
you out." They said, "David will not be able to enter here."
7 | But David took the fortress of Zion,[2]* which is the town
of David.

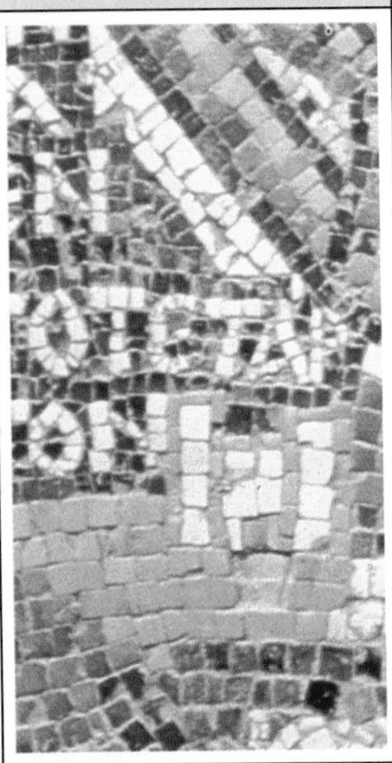

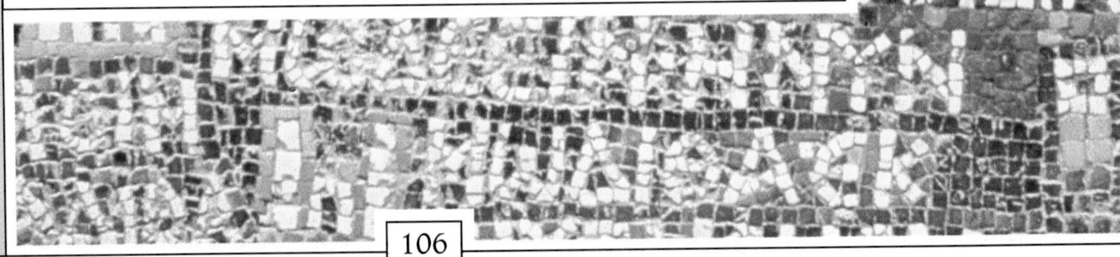

[1] It is usual to call the tribes of the North the "tribes of Israel" as distinct from the tribe of Judah in the South. They will later form the kingdom of Samaria (see pages 120-121).

[2] Zion was the Canaanite name for the citadel of Jerusalem. It is the name which would be given to the mount of the Temple.* Later Zion signified the whole city. To speak of Zion or Jerusalem was one and the same thing. It was as though the whole city was symbolized by the one holy place.

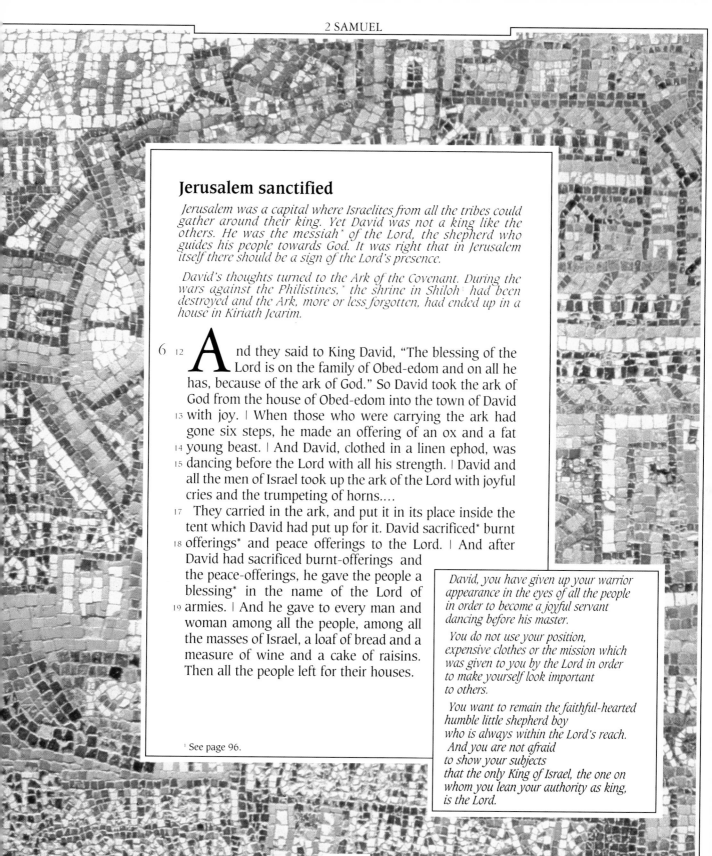

Jerusalem sanctified

Jerusalem was a capital where Israelites from all the tribes could gather around their king. Yet David was not a king like the others. He was the messiah of the Lord, the shepherd who guides his people towards God. It was right that in Jerusalem itself there should be a sign of the Lord's presence.*

David's thoughts turned to the Ark of the Covenant. During the wars against the Philistines, the shrine in Shiloh[1] had been destroyed and the Ark, more or less forgotten, had ended up in a house in Kiriath Jearim.*

6 12 And they said to King David, "The blessing of the
Lord is on the family of Obed-edom and on all he
has, because of the ark of God." So David took the ark of
God from the house of Obed-edom into the town of David
13 with joy. | When those who were carrying the ark had
gone six steps, he made an offering of an ox and a fat
14 young beast. | And David, clothed in a linen ephod, was
15 dancing before the Lord with all his strength. | David and
all the men of Israel took up the ark of the Lord with joyful
cries and the trumpeting of horns....
17 They carried in the ark, and put it in its place inside the
tent which David had put up for it. David sacrificed* burnt
18 offerings* and peace offerings to the Lord. | And after
David had sacrificed burnt-offerings and
the peace-offerings, he gave the people a
blessing* in the name of the Lord of
19 armies. | And he gave to every man and
woman among all the people, among all
the masses of Israel, a loaf of bread and a
measure of wine and a cake of raisins.
Then all the people left for their houses.

David, you have given up your warrior appearance in the eyes of all the people in order to become a joyful servant dancing before his master.

You do not use your position, expensive clothes or the mission which was given to you by the Lord in order to make yourself look important to others.

You want to remain the faithful-hearted humble little shepherd boy who is always within the Lord's reach. And you are not afraid to show your subjects that the only King of Israel, the one on whom you lean your authority as king, is the Lord.

[1] See page 96.

GOD THE NOMAD

The Ark found its old place under a tent* as it had in the desert. David, during all the time he had avoided Saul, had lived like a nomad. It seemed quite natural to him to pray to God under a tent.

But as David settled in, building himself a palace, setting up an administration and an army, he wanted to give another image of God. No more tents and wandering about. God would be housed in a fine temple,* like a king.

God refused at first. But later the Temple would be built, pleasing the crowds with the splendor of its rituals.*

God would pitch His tent without fuss among men. This is how the Evangelist John presents the coming of the Son of God among mankind (John 1:14, page 334).

He would take up His life as a nomad again, going from village to village, looking for the lost sheep, knocking at doors and waiting for someone to open them.

And the Temple would be deserted.

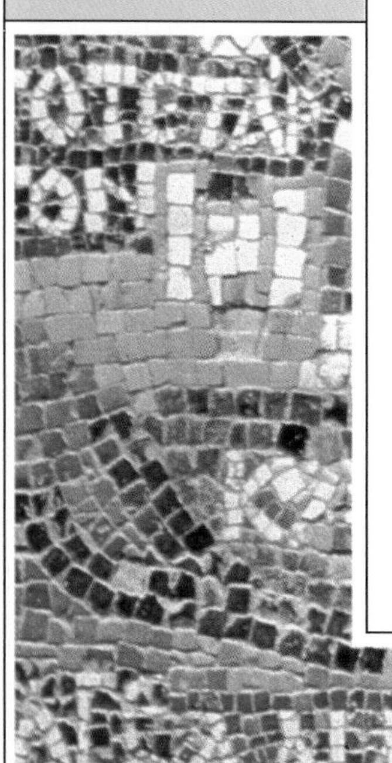

God's great promise

7 1 Now when the king was living in his palace, and the
Lord had given him rest from war all around him.
2 | The king said to Nathan the prophet, "See now, I am living
in a palace of cedar, but the ark of God is housed inside the
3 curtains of a tent." | And Nathan said to the king, "Go and
do whatever is in your heart, for the Lord is with you."
4 Now that night the word of the Lord came to Nathan,
5 saying, | "Go and say to my servant David, 'The Lord says,
Are you to be the builder of a house, a living-place for me?
6 | For from the day when I took the children of Israel up out
of Egypt till this day, I have had no house, but have gone
from place to place in a tent.
7 In all the places where I went with all the children of
Israel, did I ever say to any of the judges of Israel, to whom
I entrusted my people Israel, Why have you not made me a
house of cedar?'" | "Then say these words
8 to my servant David, 'The Lord of armies
says, I took you from the fields, from
keeping the sheep, so that you might be a
ruler over my people, over my people
9 Israel. | I have been with you wherever
you went, cutting off before you all those
who were against you; and I will make
your name great, like the name of the
greatest ones of the earth....
11 "'And the Lord says to you that he will
12 make you a house.[1] | And when the time
comes for you to go to rest with your
fathers, I will raise up in your place your
seed after you, the offspring of your body,
and I will make his kingdom strong.'...

Lord, why does humanity
always try to confine you
to a name or temple?
Is it so that you will be on hand
when needed?
Is it to know where to find you
if the path suddenly
becomes uncertain?

Lord,
you can't be fossilized
in words or a work of art.
You are alive,
and the only temple you want
to call home is the human heart.

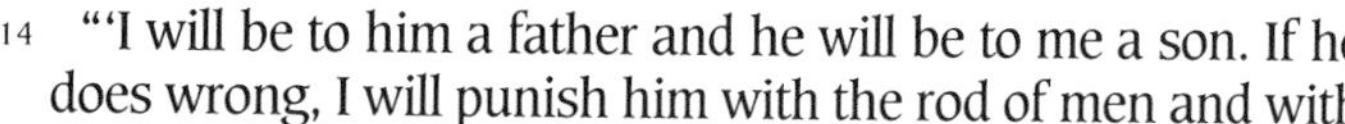

[1] Nathan makes a play upon words. "House" means dwelling but also those who live in it, family and kin. The house promised by God to David was a dynasty. From then on, the messiah* would always be a descendant of David.

[2] Isaiah helps us to understand the meaning of this promise (see page 141). God did not promise that the dynasty of David would last forever. It would end with Zedekiah in 587 BC (page 148). The promise referred to the coming of a "king" who would show men the path to the Kingdom of God. The promise would come true with the birth of Jesus (see Luke 1:32-33, page 300).

14 "'I will be to him a father and he will be to me a son. If he
does wrong, I will punish him with the rod of men and with
15 the blows of the children of men, | but my mercy* will not
be taken away from him, as I took it from him who was
16 before you. | 'And your family and your kingdom will
endure forever: your throne will never be overturned.'"[2]
17 So Nathan gave David an account of all these words and
this vision.

David sins

David was not perfect. He sometimes forgot that he had been the little servant dancing with joy before his God. He acted as a ruler indulging his whims with cruelty. But David was able to admit his sin.

11 1 Now in the spring, at the time when kings go
out to war, David sent Joab and his servants and
all Israel with him. They destroyed the land of the children
of Ammon, and beseiged Rabbah, shutting it in. But David
2 was still at Jerusalem. | Now one evening, David got up
from his bed, and while he was walking on the roof of the
king's house, he saw from there a woman bathing; and the
3 woman was very beautiful. | And David sent to get
knowledge who the woman was. And one said, "Is this not
Bath-sheba, the daughter of Eliam and wife of Uriah the
4 Hittite?"[3] | And David sent and took her; and she came to
5 him, and he slept with her.... | And the woman conceived;
and she sent word to David that she was with child.
6 And David sent to Joab saying, "Send Uriah the Hittite to
7 me. And Joab sent Uriah to David. | And when Uriah came
to him, David asked him about how Joab and the people
8 were, and how the war was going. | And David said to

[3] Uriah is a name which suggests Urartu, the land where the Ark came to rest (see note 1, page 29). It was the country inhabited by the Hittites, a people from central Anatolia in what is now Turkey. See Matthew 1:6, page 254.

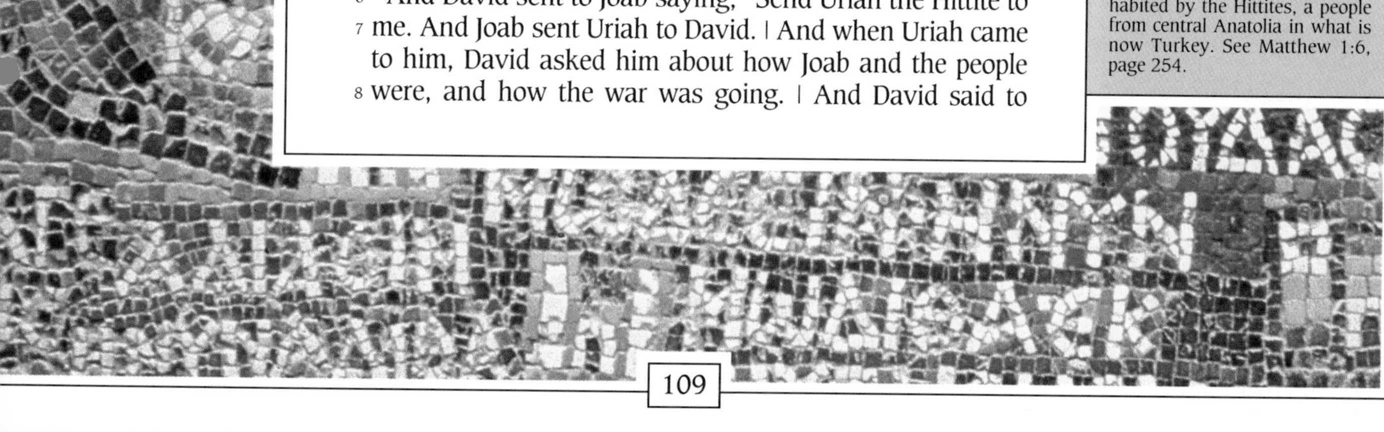

ADMITTING SIN

David was scared of what people would say. He wanted Uriah to be thought of as the father of Bathsheba's baby. When his strategem misfired, he had no qualms about having Uriah killed. He married the widow and the baby was born in secrecy in the palace. The great king had acted with cowardice and horrid cruelty. But when Nathan came and pointed out his sin, David did not try to hide the fact.

In that way he showed his true courage: admitting what he would have preferred to hide.

With childlike trust, David offered himself as he was into God's hands.

Psalm 51 (page 215) gives a good idea of how David prayed in these circumstances.

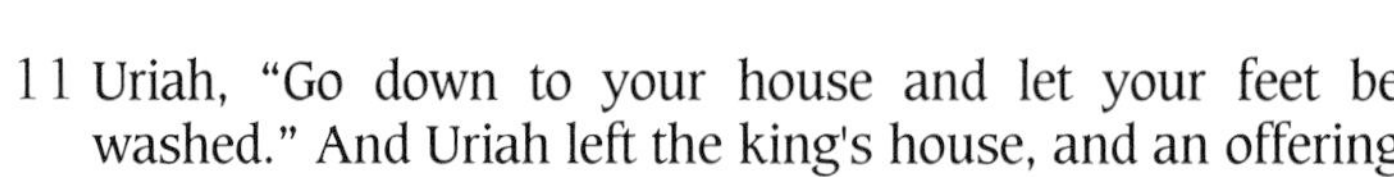

11 Uriah, "Go down to your house and let your feet be
washed." And Uriah left the king's house, and an offering
9 from the king was sent after him. | But Uriah rested at the
door of the king's house, with all the servants of his lord,
13 and did not go down to his house.[1]... | And when David
sent for him, he took meat and drink with him, and David
made him drunk. When evening came, he went to rest on
his bed with the servants of his lord, but he did not go
14 down to his house. | Now in the morning, David gave Uriah
15 a letter to take to Joab.[2] | And in the letter he said, "Take
care to put Uriah in the very front of the line, where the
fighting is most violent, and leave him, so that he may be
overcome and killed."

16 So while Joab was watching the town, he put Uriah in the
place where it was clear to him the best fighters were. |
17 ...and Uriah the Hittite was killed in battle.

God's forgiveness

12 1 And the Lord sent Nathan to David. And Nathan
came to him and said, "There were two men in the
2 same town: one man was wealthy, and the other poor. | The
3 wealthy man had great numbers of flocks and herds; | but
the poor man had only one little ewe lamb, which he had got
and taken care of. From its birth it had been with him like
one of his children. His meat was its food, and it drqnk from
his cup, resting in his arms. It was like a daughter to him. |
4 Now a traveller came to the house of the man of wealth, but
he would not take anything from his flock or his herd to
make a meal for the traveller who had come to him, but he
took the poor man's lamb and prepqred for the man who
had come."[3]

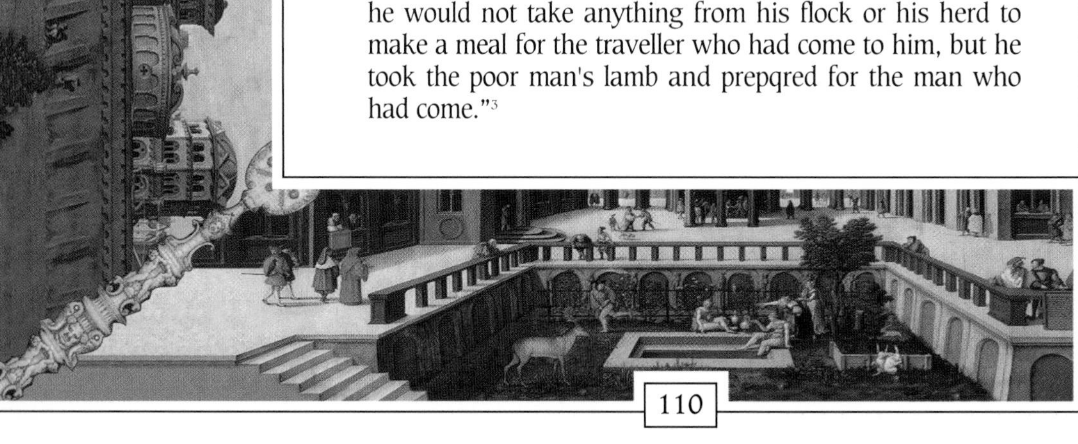

[1] In time of battle, warriors abstained from relations with their wives. Uriah did not want to take advantage of David's summons, which brought him close to his home, to break the rule being kept by his comrades fighting at Rabbah.

[2] Joab, David's nephew, was at the head of the army. He was a violent character. He fell into disgrace after the murder of Absalom (see page 112). Solomon had him put to death.

[3] Nathan was reciting a parable.*

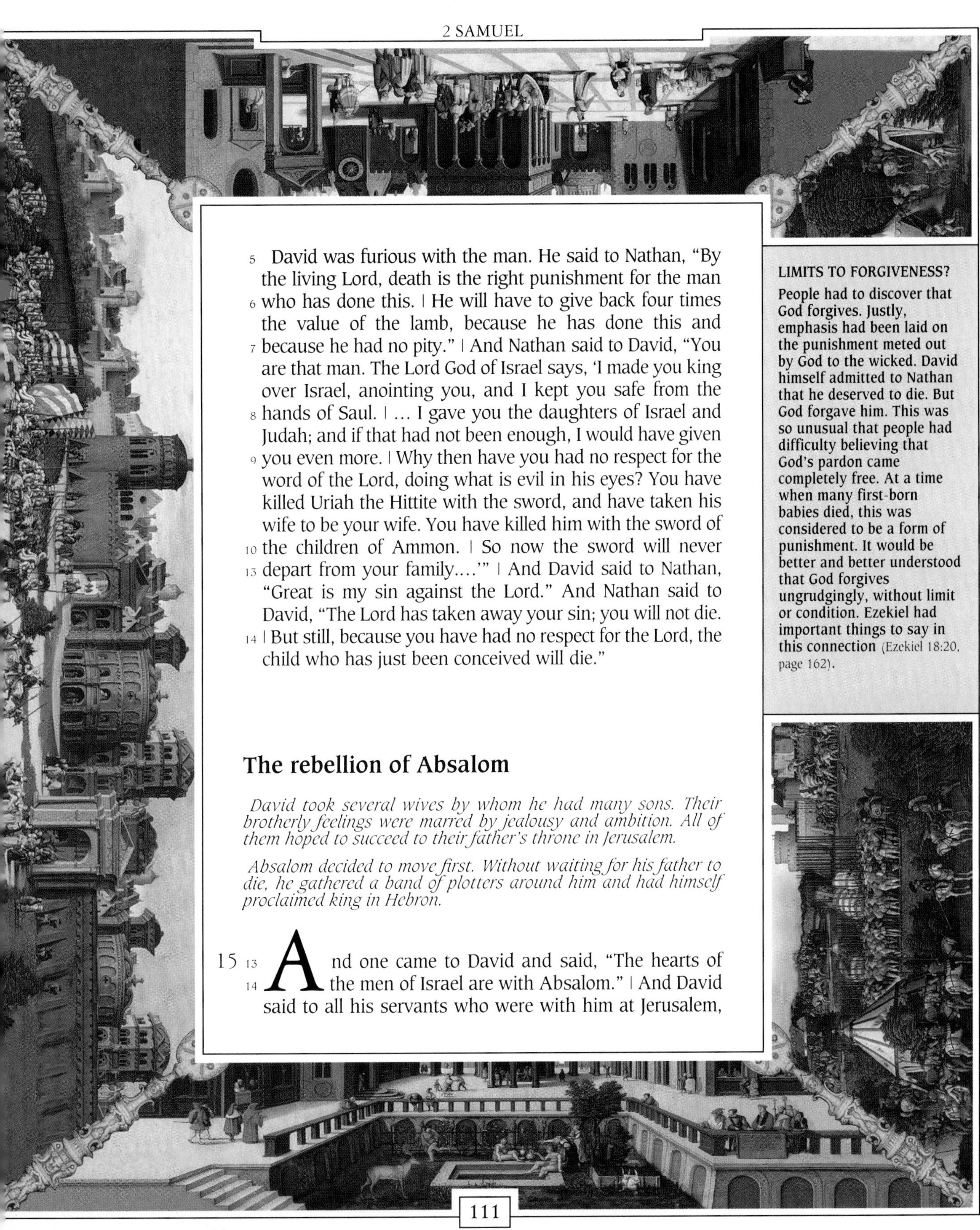

5 David was furious with the man. He said to Nathan, "By
the living Lord, death is the right punishment for the man
6 who has done this. | He will have to give back four times
the value of the lamb, because he has done this and
7 because he had no pity." | And Nathan said to David, "You
are that man. The Lord God of Israel says, 'I made you king
over Israel, anointing you, and I kept you safe from the
8 hands of Saul. | ... I gave you the daughters of Israel and
Judah; and if that had not been enough, I would have given
9 you even more. | Why then have you had no respect for the
word of the Lord, doing what is evil in his eyes? You have
killed Uriah the Hittite with the sword, and have taken his
wife to be your wife. You have killed him with the sword of
10 the children of Ammon. | So now the sword will never
13 depart from your family....'" | And David said to Nathan,
"Great is my sin against the Lord." And Nathan said to
David, "The Lord has taken away your sin; you will not die.
14 | But still, because you have had no respect for the Lord, the
child who has just been conceived will die."

LIMITS TO FORGIVENESS?

People had to discover that God forgives. Justly, emphasis had been laid on the punishment meted out by God to the wicked. David himself admitted to Nathan that he deserved to die. But God forgave him. This was so unusual that people had difficulty believing that God's pardon came completely free. At a time when many first-born babies died, this was considered to be a form of punishment. It would be better and better understood that God forgives ungrudgingly, without limit or condition. Ezekiel had important things to say in this connection (Ezekiel 18:20, page 162)**.**

The rebellion of Absalom

David took several wives by whom he had many sons. Their brotherly feelings were marred by jealousy and ambition. All of them hoped to succeed to their father's throne in Jerusalem.

Absalom decided to move first. Without waiting for his father to die, he gathered a band of plotters around him and had himself proclaimed king in Hebron.

15 13 And one came to David and said, "The hearts of
14 the men of Israel are with Absalom." | And David
said to all his servants who were with him at Jerusalem,

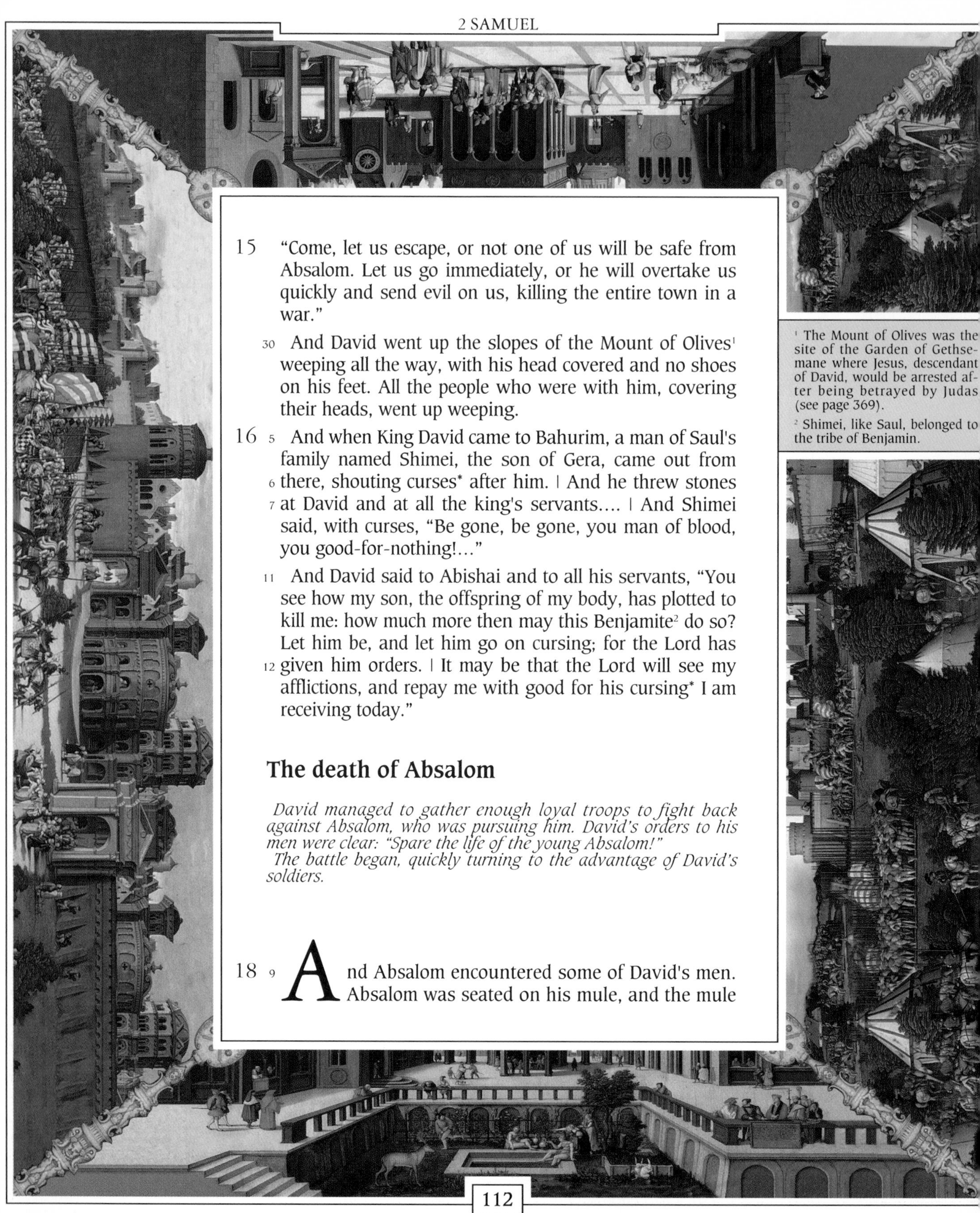

15 "Come, let us escape, or not one of us will be safe from
Absalom. Let us go immediately, or he will overtake us
quickly and send evil on us, killing the entire town in a
war."

30 And David went up the slopes of the Mount of Olives[1]
weeping all the way, with his head covered and no shoes
on his feet. All the people who were with him, covering
their heads, went up weeping.

16 5 And when King David came to Bahurim, a man of Saul's
family named Shimei, the son of Gera, came out from
6 there, shouting curses* after him. | And he threw stones
7 at David and at all the king's servants.... | And Shimei
said, with curses, "Be gone, be gone, you man of blood,
you good-for-nothing!..."

11 And David said to Abishai and to all his servants, "You
see how my son, the offspring of my body, has plotted to
kill me: how much more then may this Benjamite[2] do so?
Let him be, and let him go on cursing; for the Lord has
12 given him orders. | It may be that the Lord will see my
afflictions, and repay me with good for his cursing* I am
receiving today."

[1] The Mount of Olives was the site of the Garden of Gethsemane where Jesus, descendant of David, would be arrested after being betrayed by Judas (see page 369).

[2] Shimei, like Saul, belonged to the tribe of Benjamin.

The death of Absalom

David managed to gather enough loyal troops to fight back against Absalom, who was pursuing him. David's orders to his men were clear: "Spare the life of the young Absalom!"

The battle began, quickly turning to the advantage of David's soldiers.

18 9 And Absalom encountered some of David's men.
Absalom was seated on his mule, and the mule

WHY SO MUCH VIOLENCE IN THE BIBLE?

The Bible repeatedly points out that men want to have God on their side. In time of war, for example, they call on Him to crush their enemies. But the further the children of Israel went in understanding God, the more they realized that He did not approve of human violence. They had discovered God as their deliverer when they came out of Egypt. But they would also experience His presence during the Captivity* and the occupation of their land by foreign powers. They would come to see that God was not the God of Armies but was an "unarmed" God (Micah 4:3-4, page 144). His only weapon is love.

went under the thick branches of a great tree. His head
got stuck in the tree, lifitng him and suspending him
10 mid-air, while his mule walked on. | A
certain man saw it and said to Joab, "I
saw Absalom hanging in a tree." |
14 Joab took three spears in his hand,
and stabbed them through Absalom's
heart, while he was still alive in the
branches of the tree.

Joab, you will never be able to understand
David's compassion for Absalom because
you have too much blood on your hands.
You planned Uriah's murder,
among other terrible things,
while serving David.
You thought you were serving him
when you went against his orders
and put the rebel Absalom to death.

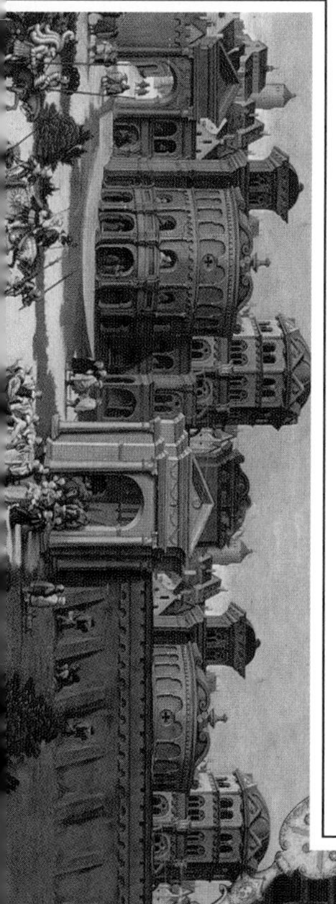

David learns of the death of Absalom

18 33 Then the king was greatly shaken, and went up
into the room over the door, weeping, and
saying, "O my son Absalom, my son, my son Absalom!
if only my life might have been given
for yours, O Absalom, my son, my
son!"

19 1 Word was given to Joab that the king
was weeping and sorrowing for
2 Absalom. | And the salvation of that
day was changed to sorrow for all the
people: for it was said to the people,
"The king is in bitter grief for his
3 son." | And the people made their way
back to the town quietly and secretly,
as those who are shamed go secretly
when they escape from the war.

David, your fatherly heart is broken.
God put you in charge of leading His people
like a shepherd leads his sheep
to good pastures. But you couldn't
even lead your own children.
They fought between themselves
like a pack of wolves.
Absalom rose up against you, but
instead of feeling resentment,
you only wanted to forgive.
Alas, all of Samuel's pessimistic predictions
are coming true
in your descendants.
They were unable
to reconcile within their hearts
the authority of the messiah
with the humility of the little shepherd boy
dancing before his Lord.

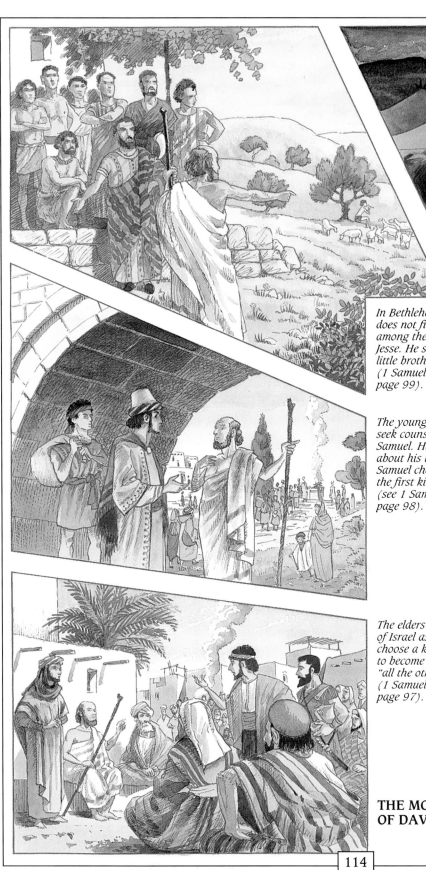

In Bethlehem, Samuel does not find a king among the seven sons of Jesse. He sends for their little brother, David (1 Samuel 16:1-13, page 99).

Saul was the first to have been anointed to rule over Israel. David respects the man who was the Lord's choice. He spares his life (1 Samuel 26:2-23, page 103).

The young Saul comes to seek counsel from Samuel. He wants advice about his lost donkeys. Samuel chooses Saul to be the first king of Israel (see 1 Samuel 10:20-24, page 98).

The elders of the tribes of Israel ask Samuel to choose a king. They wish to become a nation like "all the other nations" (1 Samuel 8:4-22, page 97).*

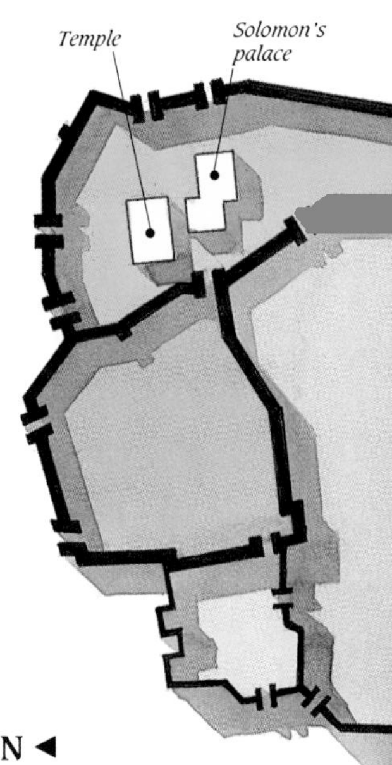

THE MONARCHY IN THE TIME OF DAVID AND SOLOMON

A fugitive brings David the crown and armband of Saul, killed at the battle of Gilboa. David tears his garments and voices his grief (see 2 Samuel 1:11-27, page 105).

David, in order to reign with justice over all Israel, wants to dwell in a town that does not belong to any of the tribes. He conquers Jerusalem by (probably) infiltrating the city's underground water system (see 2 Samuel 5:6-7, page 106).

David brings the Ark of the Covenant to Jerusalem. He installs it under a tent, as in the time of the exodus. In this way he signifies his wish to lead the people in the sight of God (see 2 Samuel 6:12-19, page 107).

Solomon supervises the building of the Temple of Jerusalem with Hiram, the chief architect (see note 1, page 118).

KING SOLOMON

David was dead. He was succeeded by Solomon, the second son of Bathsheba. In his youth, Solomon was a great messiah-king, full of wisdom.

A receptive heart

3 4 And the king went to Gibeon to make an offering
there, because that was the chief high place: it
was Solomon's custom to make a thousand burnt
offerings* on that altar.

5 In Gibeon, Solomon had a vision of the Lord in a
dream at night; and God said to him, "Tell me what I am
6 to give you." | And Solomon said, "Great was your
mercy to David my father, as his life was faithful to you
and his heart was true to you; and you have kept for
him this greatest mercy, a son to take his place this day.
7 | And now, O Lord my God, you have made your servant
king in the place of David my father; and I am only a
young boy, with no knowledge of how to carry out my
8 duties. | And your servant has round him the people of
your selection, a people so great that
they may not be numbered, and no
account of them may be given.

9 "Give your servant, then, a wise
heart for judging your people, able to
see what is good and what evil.[1] For
who is able to be the judge of this
great people?"

An attentive heart is one that listens.
Solomon understood this.
Listening
characterizes the people of God.
O Lord, give me
a heart which truly listens to
what you are saying to me so that along
with the others in your church enlightened
by the Holy Spirit, I can understand
and live my life as it pleases you.

[1] Unlike Adam (see page 24), Solomon made no attempt to acquire knowledge of good and evil. He made himself listen to what God might teach him.

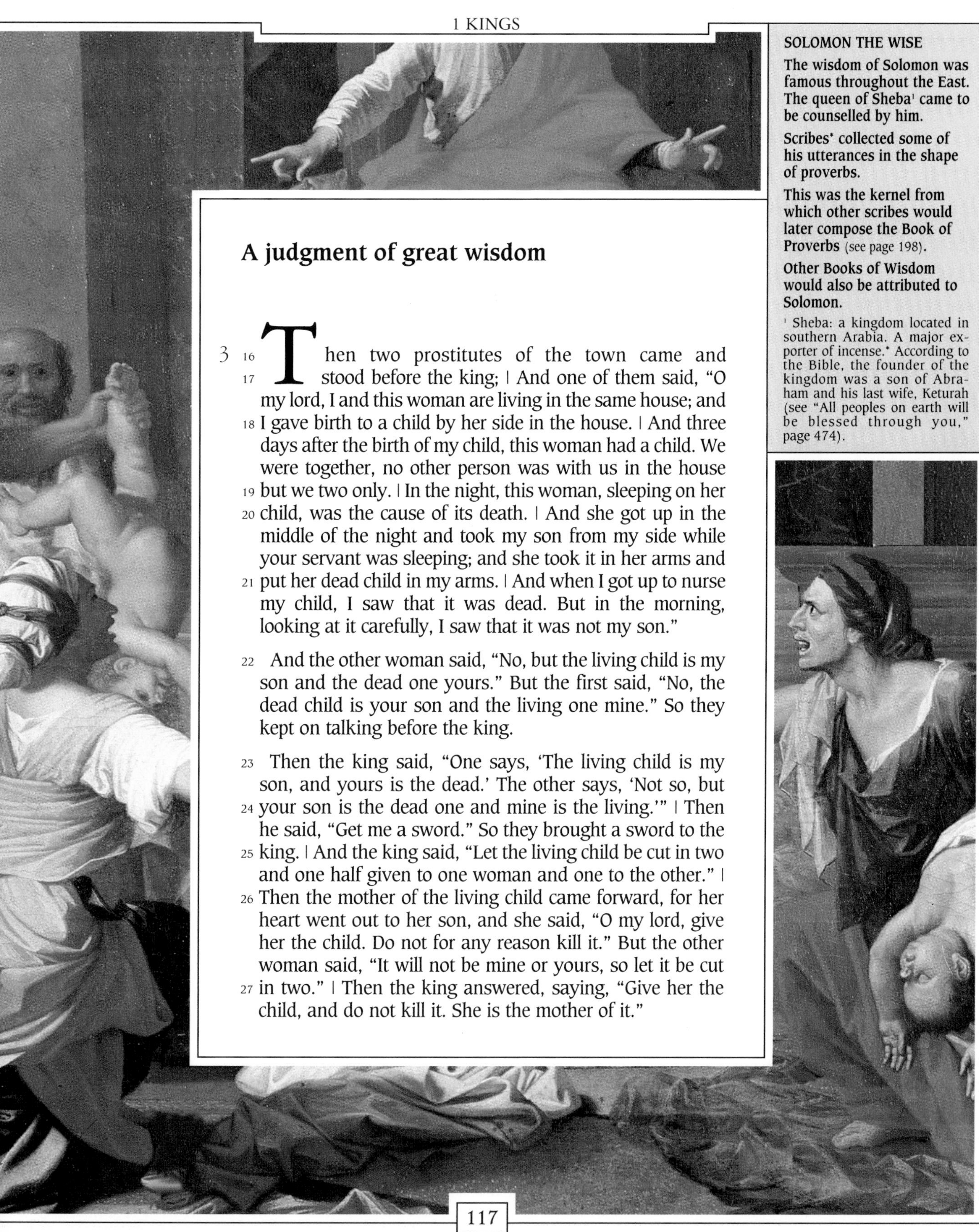

SOLOMON THE WISE

The wisdom of Solomon was famous throughout the East. The queen of Sheba[1] came to be counselled by him.

Scribes* collected some of his utterances in the shape of proverbs.

This was the kernel from which other scribes would later compose the Book of Proverbs (see page 198)**.**

Other Books of Wisdom would also be attributed to Solomon.

[1] Sheba: a kingdom located in southern Arabia. A major exporter of incense.* According to the Bible, the founder of the kingdom was a son of Abraham and his last wife, Keturah (see "All peoples on earth will be blessed through you," page 474).

A judgment of great wisdom

3 16 Then two prostitutes of the town came and
17 stood before the king; | And one of them said, "O
my lord, I and this woman are living in the same house; and
18 I gave birth to a child by her side in the house. | And three
days after the birth of my child, this woman had a child. We
were together, no other person was with us in the house
19 but we two only. | In the night, this woman, sleeping on her
20 child, was the cause of its death. | And she got up in the
middle of the night and took my son from my side while
your servant was sleeping; and she took it in her arms and
21 put her dead child in my arms. | And when I got up to nurse
my child, I saw that it was dead. But in the morning,
looking at it carefully, I saw that it was not my son."

22 And the other woman said, "No, but the living child is my
son and the dead one yours." But the first said, "No, the
dead child is your son and the living one mine." So they
kept on talking before the king.

23 Then the king said, "One says, 'The living child is my
son, and yours is the dead.' The other says, 'Not so, but
24 your son is the dead one and mine is the living.'" | Then
he said, "Get me a sword." So they brought a sword to the
25 king. | And the king said, "Let the living child be cut in two
and one half given to one woman and one to the other." |
26 Then the mother of the living child came forward, for her
heart went out to her son, and she said, "O my lord, give
her the child. Do not for any reason kill it." But the other
woman said, "It will not be mine or yours, so let it be cut
27 in two." | Then the king answered, saying, "Give her the
child, and do not kill it. She is the mother of it."

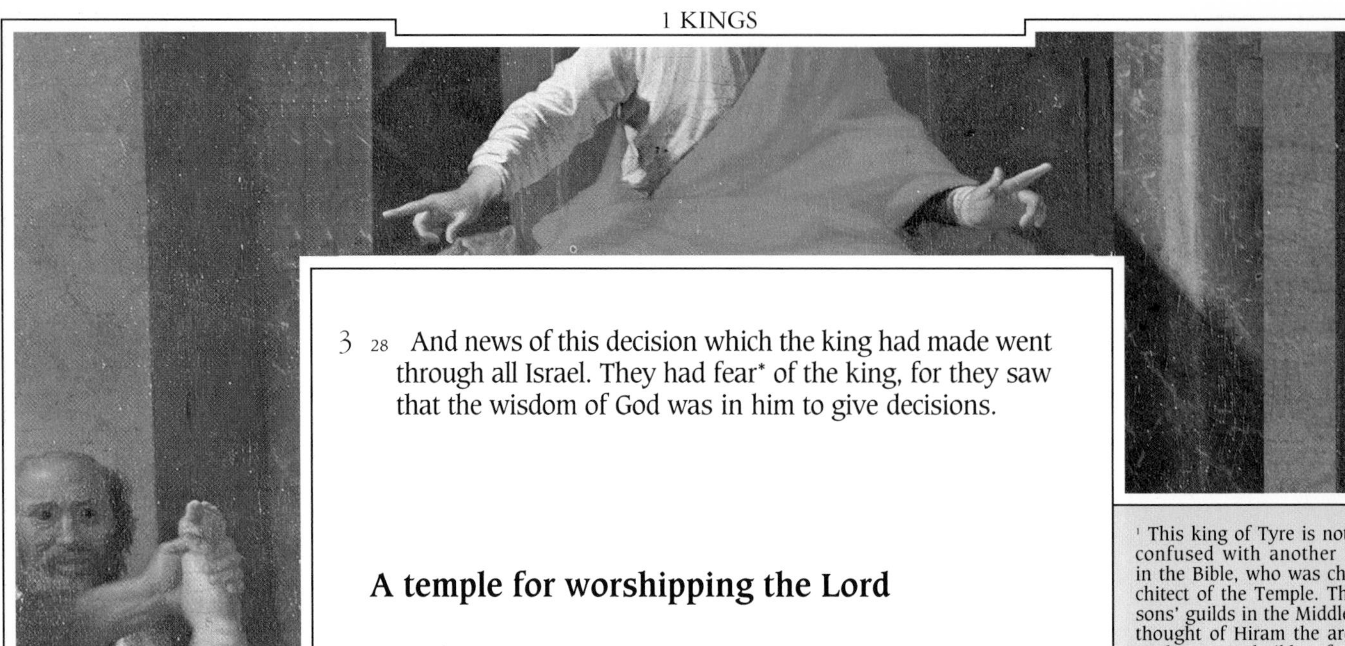

3 28 And news of this decision which the king had made went
through all Israel. They had fear* of the king, for they saw
that the wisdom of God was in him to give decisions.

A temple for worshipping the Lord

5 2 And Solomon sent word to Hiram,[1] saying,
3 | "You know that David, my father, was not able
to make a temple for the name* of the Lord his God,
because of the wars which surrounded him on every
side, till the Lord put all those who were against him
4 under his feet. | But now the Lord my God has given me
rest on every side; no one is making trouble, and no evil
5 is taking place. | And so it is my purpose to make a
temple for the name of the Lord my God, as he said to
David my father, 'Your son, whom I will make king in
your place, will be the builder of a temple for my name.'
6 | So now, will you have cedar-trees from Lebanon cut
down for me, and my servants will be with your
servants. I will give you payment for your servants at
whatever rate you say, for it is common knowledge that
we have no such wood-cutters among us as the men of
Zidon."...

17 By the king's orders, great stones, costly stones of
great quality, were cut out, so that the base of the
18 temple might be made of squared stone. | Solomon's
builders and Hiram's builders did the work of cutting
them, and put edges on them, and got the wood and the
stone ready for the building of the temple.

[1] This king of Tyre is not to be confused with another Hiram in the Bible, who was chief architect of the Temple. The masons' guilds in the Middle Ages thought of Hiram the architect as the master builder of all time and he was a character in many legends.

SOLOMON THE BUILDER

Solomon did a lot of major construction work — palaces, forts, cavalry stables, storehouses. The most impressive was the Temple* in Jerusalem.

Solomon used the same procedures as the other kings of his day. He made foreign laborers do the hard work (see Exodus 1:11-14, page 54, and 22:20, page 72). **Eventually, he pressed the men of the tribes of the North into performing some of the thankless tasks. This strained the unity of the twelve tribes that had been achieved by David** (see page 106).

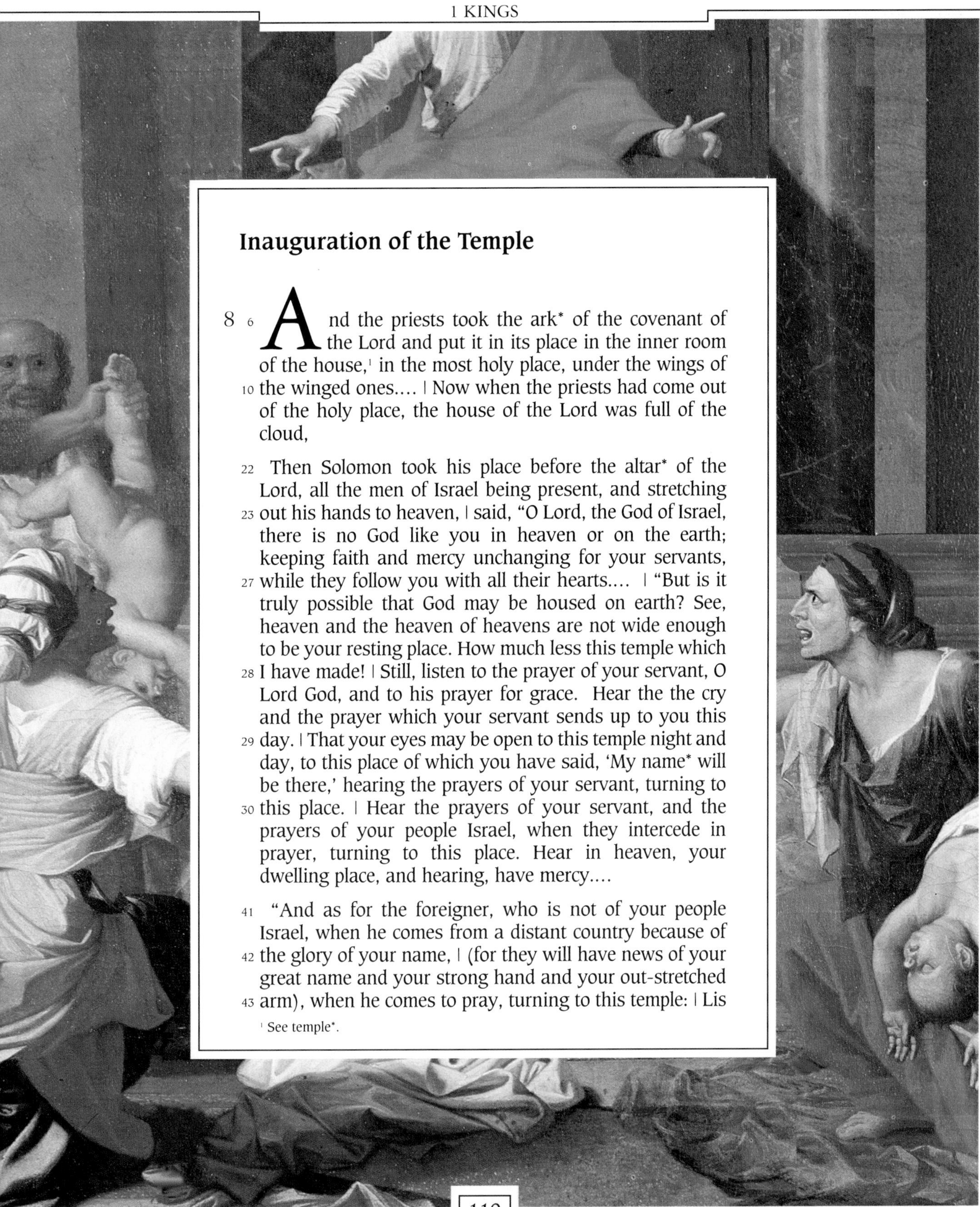

Inauguration of the Temple

8 6 And the priests took the ark* of the covenant of
the Lord and put it in its place in the inner room
of the house,[1] in the most holy place, under the wings of
10 the winged ones.... | Now when the priests had come out
of the holy place, the house of the Lord was full of the
cloud,

22 Then Solomon took his place before the altar* of the
Lord, all the men of Israel being present, and stretching
23 out his hands to heaven, | said, "O Lord, the God of Israel,
there is no God like you in heaven or on the earth;
keeping faith and mercy unchanging for your servants,
27 while they follow you with all their hearts.... | "But is it
truly possible that God may be housed on earth? See,
heaven and the heaven of heavens are not wide enough
to be your resting place. How much less this temple which
28 I have made! | Still, listen to the prayer of your servant, O
Lord God, and to his prayer for grace. Hear the the cry
and the prayer which your servant sends up to you this
29 day. | That your eyes may be open to this temple night and
day, to this place of which you have said, 'My name* will
be there,' hearing the prayers of your servant, turning to
30 this place. | Hear the prayers of your servant, and the
prayers of your people Israel, when they intercede in
prayer, turning to this place. Hear in heaven, your
dwelling place, and hearing, have mercy....

41 "And as for the foreigner, who is not of your people
Israel, when he comes from a distant country because of
42 the glory of your name, | (for they will have news of your
great name and your strong hand and your out-stretched
43 arm), when he comes to pray, turning to this temple: | Lis

[1] See temple*.

8 in heaven your dwelling place, and give him his desire,
whatever it may be, so that all the peoples of the earth
may have knowledge of your name, worshipping you as
do your people Israel, and that they may see that this
temple which I have built truly bears your name."

The end of Solomon's reign was inglorious and sad. The king filled his harem with wives and concubines brought back from neighboring lands. These women came carrying their idols and Solomon was soft enough to let them build shrines for these false gods and even to pray to them.*

The people were crushed under the weight of taxes and heavy labor. Rebellion was in the air.

THE REVOLT OF THE NORTHERN TRIBES

David had succeeded in preserving the unity of the twelve tribes. Solomon, towards the end of his reign, had neglected the tribes in the North in favor of the tribes of Judah and Benjamin whose lands were closer to Jerusalem. As soon as he had died and his son, Rehoboam, had ascended the throne, the grievances of the Northern tribes became more insistent.

THE KINGDOM TORN APART

The king who was no messiah*

Rehoboam went to Shechem to be hailed as king by the tribes of the North.

Using Jeroboam, of the tribe of Ephraim, as their spokesman, the people of the North complained to him.

12 4 "Your father put a heavy yoke on us. If you will
make the conditions under which your father
oppresses less cruel, and the weight of the yoke he put
5 on lighter, then we will be your servants." | And he said

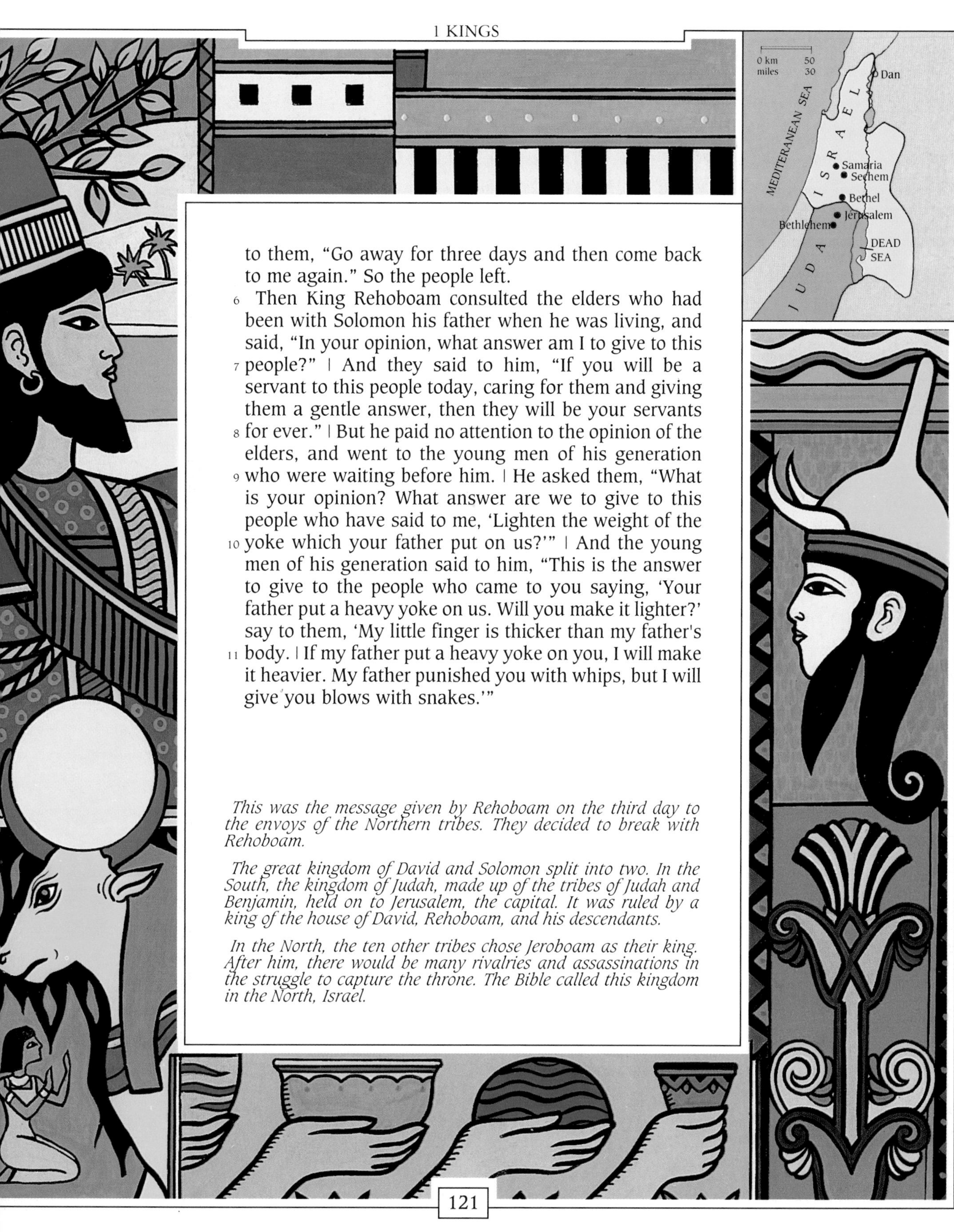

to them, "Go away for three days and then come back
to me again." So the people left.
6 Then King Rehoboam consulted the elders who had
been with Solomon his father when he was living, and
said, "In your opinion, what answer am I to give to this
7 people?" | And they said to him, "If you will be a
servant to this people today, caring for them and giving
them a gentle answer, then they will be your servants
8 for ever." | But he paid no attention to the opinion of the
elders, and went to the young men of his generation
9 who were waiting before him. | He asked them, "What
is your opinion? What answer are we to give to this
people who have said to me, 'Lighten the weight of the
10 yoke which your father put on us?'" | And the young
men of his generation said to him, "This is the answer
to give to the people who came to you saying, 'Your
father put a heavy yoke on us. Will you make it lighter?'
say to them, 'My little finger is thicker than my father's
11 body. | If my father put a heavy yoke on you, I will make
it heavier. My father punished you with whips, but I will
give you blows with snakes.'"

This was the message given by Rehoboam on the third day to the envoys of the Northern tribes. They decided to break with Rehoboam.

The great kingdom of David and Solomon split into two. In the South, the kingdom of Judah, made up of the tribes of Judah and Benjamin, held on to Jerusalem, the capital. It was ruled by a king of the house of David, Rehoboam, and his descendants.

In the North, the ten other tribes chose Jeroboam as their king. After him, there would be many rivalries and assassinations in the struggle to capture the throne. The Bible called this kingdom in the North, Israel.

LIKE A YOUNG BULL

"You shall not make for yourself an idol" (Exodus 20:4, page 71). **Jeroboam seemed unaware of the commandment shut away in the Ark of the Covenant in Jerusalem. To illustrate the presence of God among His people, he portrayed God in the form of a young bull, symbol of strength and fertility. This image, which may seem absurd to us today, was intended to honor the power of an eternally young God. But comparing God's strength to that of an animal was to exclude the revelation of God's gentleness and boundless love for mankind. It was to confuse him with the gods of the neighboring peoples.**

The return of the Golden Calves

12 26 And Jeroboam said in his heart, "Now the king-
27 dom will go back to the family of David: | If the
people go up to make offerings in the house of the Lord at
Jerusalem, their heart will return to their lord, to
Rehoboam, king of Judah They will kill me and go back to
28 Rehoboam, king of Judah." | So after seeking advice the
king made two golden calves; and he said to the people,
"You have been going up to Jerusalem long enough; see!
these are your gods, O Israel, who took you out of the land
29 of Egypt." | And he put one in Beth-el and the other in
Dan.

THE PROPHETS ELIJAH AND ELISHA

From 874 to 853 BC,[1] *Ahab reigned in Samaria, capital of the kingdom of Israel.*

He brought his wife, Jezebel, daughter of the king of Sidon, to live there. She was an adept of the cult of the god Baal. She soon persuaded her husband to give up worship of the Lord and adore Baal*[2] *instead.*

It was then that the prophet Elijah rose up. He said that there would be no more rain or dew. His meaning seemed to be, "Since you have put your trust in Baal, pray to him for rain. We shall see who has the stronger powers, Baal or the Lord."

Ahab hunted Elijah everywhere to have him put to death. So Elijah took refuge in Zarephath in Sidon, the kingdom which Jezebel had left. He was given lodging by a widow.

17 17 Now after this, the son of the woman of the
house became ill, so ill that he was no longer
18 breathing. | She said to Elijah, "What have you against
me, O man of God? Have you come to remind God of my
19 sin, and to kill my son?" | And he said to her, "Give your

GOD LOVES HIS PEOPLE, EVEN DIVIDED

Even divided into two kingdoms, the people remained for God His one chosen people.

He did not favour Jerusalen over Samaria. He sent prophets* to both the kingdom of Judah and the kingdom of Israel.

[1] The birth of Jesus is our ref rence point for counting t years. For us who live after J sus, every year takes us furth away from his birth. The ye we die will have a number bi ger than that of the year wh we were born. For the peop who lived before Jesus, it w just the opposite. Every ye brought them closer to the bir of Jesus.

[2] Baal was the god of rai storm and harvests. He was c ten shown wearing a horn helmet. Ahab did not really s much difference between th "bull" from Sidon and the on in Bethel and Dan.

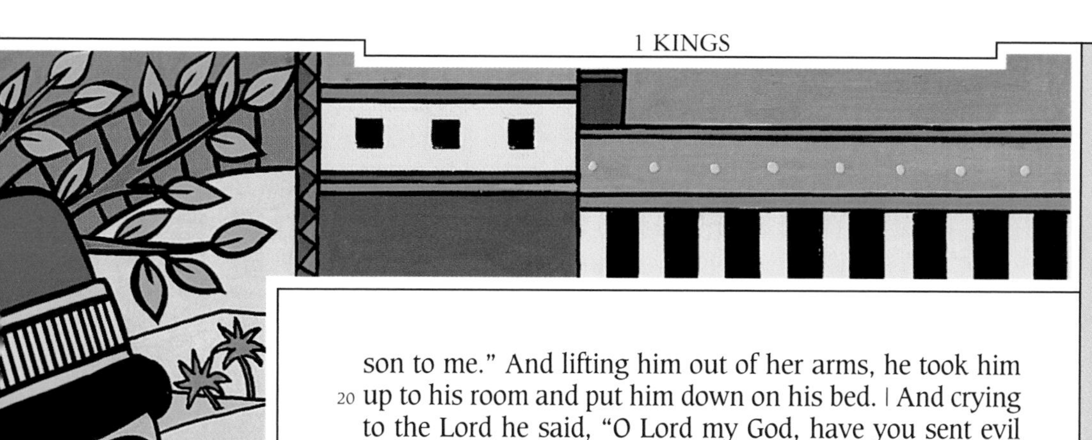

son to me." And lifting him out of her arms, he took him
20 up to his room and put him down on his bed. | And crying
to the Lord he said, "O Lord my God, have you sent evil
even on the widow whose guest I am, by causing her
21 son's death?" | And stretching himself out on the child
three times, he cried to the Lord, saying, "O Lord my God,
22 let this child's life return to him again." | And the Lord
litened to the voice of Elijah, and the child's spirit came
23 into him again, and he came back to life. | And Elijah took
the child down from his room into the house and gave
him to his mother and said to her, "See, your son is
24 living." | Then the woman said to Elijah, "Now I am
certain that you are a man of God, and that the word of
the Lord in your mouth is true."

The God of fire?

God sent Elijah back to Israel to announce the end of the drought. When Elijah arrived, he proposed a showdown between himself and the prophets of Baal brought from Sidon by Jezebel.*

Two sacrificial altars were erected on top of Mount Carmel. Elijah addressed the crowed,

18 23 "Now, let them give us two oxen. Let them
take one for themselves, and have it cut up, and
put it on the wood, but put no fire under it. I will get the
other ox ready, and put it on the wood, and put no fire
24 under it. | And you call on the name of your god, and I will
make a prayer to the Lord: and it will be clear that the one
who gives an answer by fire is God." And all the people in
25 answer said, "It is well said." | Then Elijah said to the
prophets of Baal, "Take one ox for yourselves and get it
26 ready first, for there are more of you...." | So they took the
ox which was given them, and prepared it, crying out to

GOD MIGHTIER THAN DEATH

This story of the dead boy who relives is one of the first accounts of God's power over death.

In Elijah's day, the Hebrews did not discern clearly what would happen at death. They knew that they sank down into a dark place, sheol,* where they did not remember anything of what was happening on earth.

Beginning with stories like this one, the idea took hold that God was stronger than death and His faithfulness continued beyond death. It would be asserted later that God would extract from sheol all who had been loyal to Him. They would live with Him forever.

See Resurrection*.

18 Baal from morning till the middle of the day, and saying,
"O Baal, hear us." But there was no voice and no answer.
And they were jumping up and down before the altar they
27 had made. | And in the middle of the day, Elijah taunted
them, saying, "Cry louder, for he is a god. He may be deep
in thought, or he may have gone away for some purpose,
or he may be on a journey, or by chance he is sleeping and
28 has to be awakened." | So they gave loud cries, cutting
themselves with knives and swords, as was their way, till
29 the blood came streaming out all over them. | And from
the middle of the day they went on with their prayers till
the time of the offering; but there was no voice, or any
answer, or any who gave attention to them....
36 At the time of the offering, Elijah the prophet stepped
forward and said, "O Lord, the God of Abraham, of Isaac,
and of Israel, let it be seen this day that you are God in
Israel, and that I am your servant, and that I have done all
37 these things by your order. | Give me an answer, O Lord,
give me an answer, so that this people may see that you
are God, and that you have made their hearts come back
again."
38 Then the fire of the Lord descended, burning up the
offering the wood, the stones and the
dust, and drinking up the water in the
39 drain. | And when the people saw it, they
all fell down on their faces in worship,
saying, "The Lord, he is God, the Lord,
he is God."

Elijah had won. He had demonstrated the Lord's superiority over Baal. The Lord was almighty.

The crowd put all the prophets of Baal to death in the sight of Ahab, and Elijah announced, at long last, the end of the drought.

Lord, I no longer understand you.
Who are you?
Are you the God who forgives David?
Are you a vindictive God who massacres unbelievers?
Are you the God of the Crusades and religious wars?
Are you a God who can be loving and gentle at times and violent and cruel at others?

"Follow Elijah's story through
to the very end.
At one point Elijah thought he knew me
so very well that he quit listening
to what I was saying deep within his heart.
Only when he stops trying
to defend me
will he realize that I am
a tender and loving God."

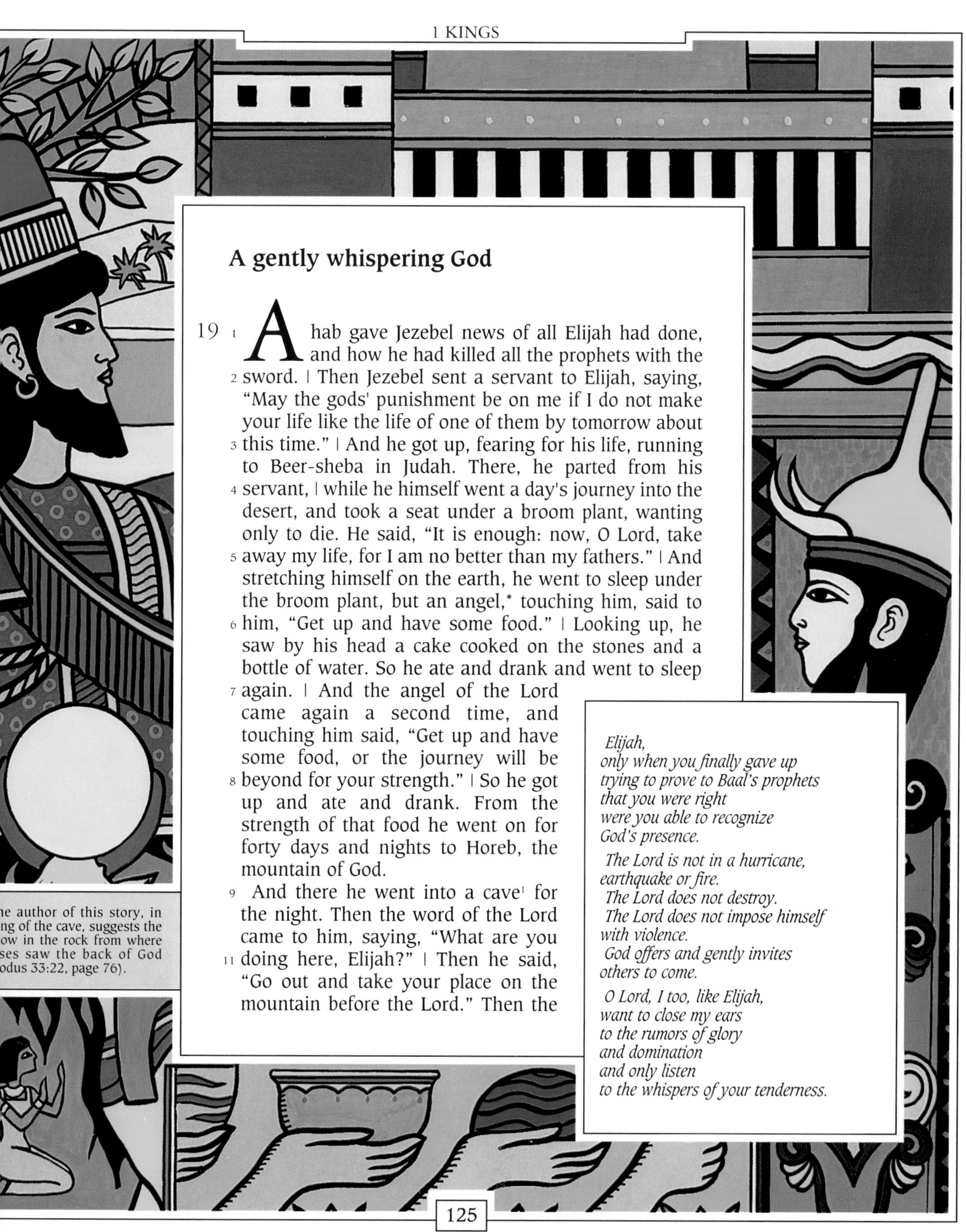

A gently whispering God

19 1 Ahab gave Jezebel news of all Elijah had done,
and how he had killed all the prophets with the
2 sword. | Then Jezebel sent a servant to Elijah, saying,
"May the gods' punishment be on me if I do not make
your life like the life of one of them by tomorrow about
3 this time." | And he got up, fearing for his life, running
to Beer-sheba in Judah. There, he parted from his
4 servant, | while he himself went a day's journey into the
desert, and took a seat under a broom plant, wanting
only to die. He said, "It is enough: now, O Lord, take
5 away my life, for I am no better than my fathers." | And
stretching himself on the earth, he went to sleep under
the broom plant, but an angel,* touching him, said to
6 him, "Get up and have some food." | Looking up, he
saw by his head a cake cooked on the stones and a
bottle of water. So he ate and drank and went to sleep
7 again. | And the angel of the Lord
came again a second time, and
touching him said, "Get up and have
some food, or the journey will be
8 beyond for your strength." | So he got
up and ate and drank. From the
strength of that food he went on for
forty days and nights to Horeb, the
mountain of God.
9 And there he went into a cave[1] for
the night. Then the word of the Lord
came to him, saying, "What are you
11 doing here, Elijah?" | Then he said,
"Go out and take your place on the
mountain before the Lord." Then the

Elijah,
only when you finally gave up
trying to prove to Baal's prophets
that you were right
were you able to recognize
God's presence.

The Lord is not in a hurricane,
earthquake or fire.
The Lord does not destroy.
The Lord does not impose himself
with violence.
God offers and gently invites
others to come.

O Lord, I too, like Elijah,
want to close my ears
to the rumors of glory
and domination
and only listen
to the whispers of your tenderness.

ne author of this story, in
ng of the cave, suggests the
ow in the rock from where
ses saw the back of God
odus 33:22, page 76).

19 Lord passed by, and mountains were parted by the force
of a great wind, rocks were broken before the Lord. But
the Lord was not in the wind. After the wind there was
an earthquake, but the Lord was not in the earthquake.
12 | And after the earthquake, a fire, but the Lord was not
in the fire. And after the fire, the sound of a soft breath.
13 | And Elijah, hearing it, went out, covering his face with
his robe, and took his place at the mouth of the cave.[1]...

[1] Like Moses, Elijah glimpse
little of God's glory on the sa
mountain. He would theref
be present with Moses on
mountain of the transfigurati
to show that Jesus was inde
the complete revelation, in h
man form, of God's beauty.
Mark 9:2-10, page 246.

A God without frontiers

2 KINGS
5 1 Now Naaman, chief of the army of the king of
Aram, was a man of high position with his
master... but he was a leper.

2 Now the Aramaeans had gone out in bands, and taken
prisoner from Israel a little girl, who became servant to
3 Naaman's wife. | And she said to her master's wife, "If
only my lord would go to the prophet in Samaria, he
would make him well."

The King of Syria, having been told, sent Naaman to Samaria bearing gifts and a letter.

6 He took the letter to the king of Israel,[2] in which the
king of Aram had said, "See, I have sent my servant
7 Naaman to you to be made well, for he is a leper." | But
the king of Israel, after reading the letter, was greatly
troubled and said, "Am I God, to give death and life?
why does this man send a leper to me to be made well?
is it not clear that he is looking for a reason to fight?" |

NAAMAN, THE SYRIAN

Elisha was a disciple* of Elijah. The story of Naaman[1] is a fine example of God's love for all mankind. Naaman, an enemy general, was cured of his leprosy and converted* to worship of the Lord. Elisha did not ask him to stay in Israel. He even allowed him to go with the king of Damascus to the temple of the Syrian god to perform the duties attached to his rank. What was important was for his heart to be completely at the service of the one true God.

[1] Jesus refers to the story of Naaman in Luke 4:27, page 308.

[2] In fact, the king of Sama
The usual name of the ki
dom of the North was Israel.

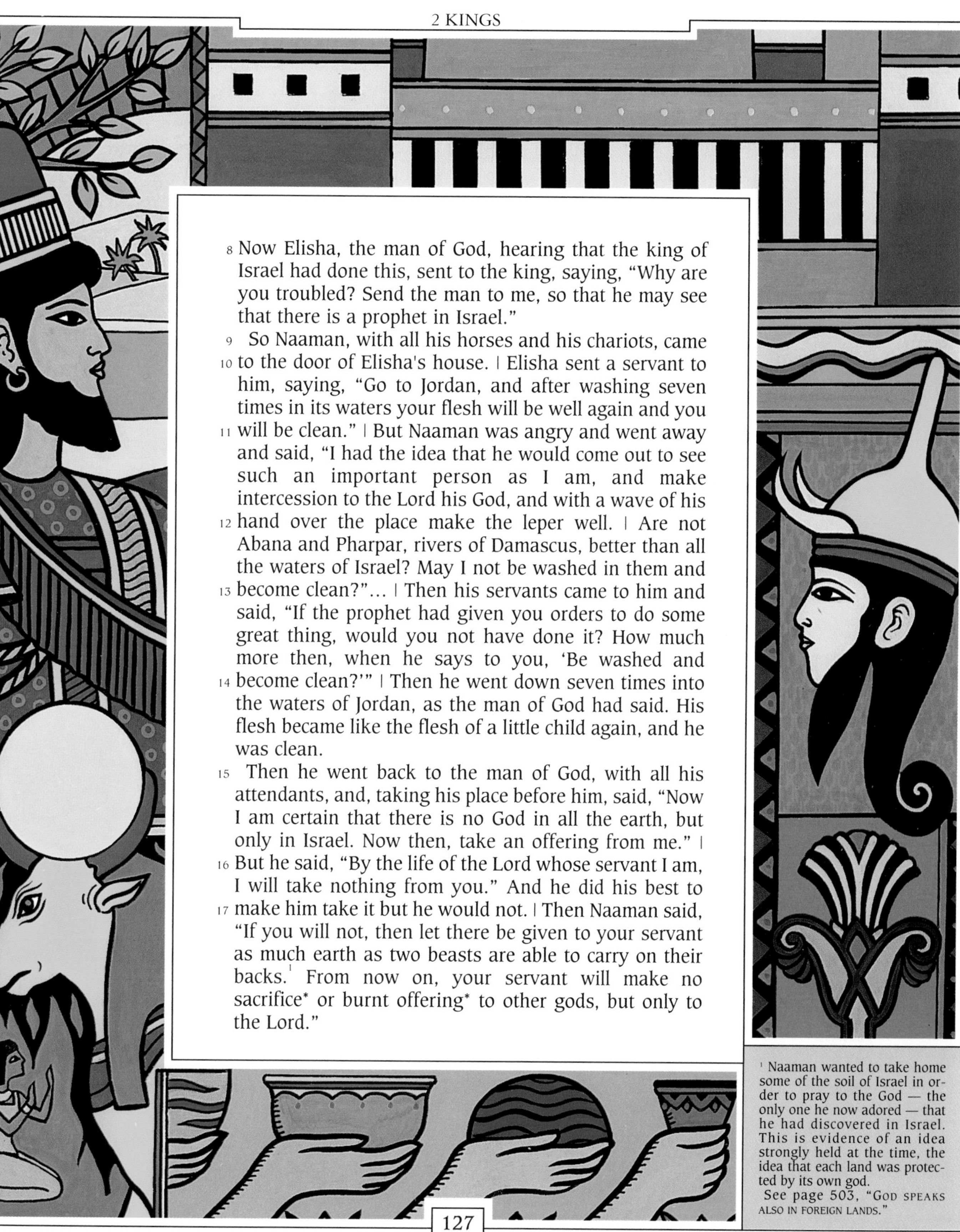

8 Now Elisha, the man of God, hearing that the king of
Israel had done this, sent to the king, saying, "Why are
you troubled? Send the man to me, so that he may see
that there is a prophet in Israel."
9 So Naaman, with all his horses and his chariots, came
10 to the door of Elisha's house. | Elisha sent a servant to
him, saying, "Go to Jordan, and after washing seven
times in its waters your flesh will be well again and you
11 will be clean." | But Naaman was angry and went away
and said, "I had the idea that he would come out to see
such an important person as I am, and make
intercession to the Lord his God, and with a wave of his
12 hand over the place make the leper well. | Are not
Abana and Pharpar, rivers of Damascus, better than all
the waters of Israel? May I not be washed in them and
13 become clean?"... | Then his servants came to him and
said, "If the prophet had given you orders to do some
great thing, would you not have done it? How much
more then, when he says to you, 'Be washed and
14 become clean?'" | Then he went down seven times into
the waters of Jordan, as the man of God had said. His
flesh became like the flesh of a little child again, and he
was clean.
15 Then he went back to the man of God, with all his
attendants, and, taking his place before him, said, "Now
I am certain that there is no God in all the earth, but
only in Israel. Now then, take an offering from me." |
16 But he said, "By the life of the Lord whose servant I am,
I will take nothing from you." And he did his best to
17 make him take it but he would not. | Then Naaman said,
"If you will not, then let there be given to your servant
as much earth as two beasts are able to carry on their
backs.[1] From now on, your servant will make no
sacrifice* or burnt offering* to other gods, but only to
the Lord."

[1] Naaman wanted to take home some of the soil of Israel in order to pray to the God — the only one he now adored — that he had discovered in Israel. This is evidence of an idea strongly held at the time, the idea that each land was protected by its own god.

See page 503, "God speaks also in foreign lands."

THE WRITER PROPHETS

The prophets* were usually orators, not writers. The words "prophet" and "writer" do not go well together. What are called "writer prophets" are the ones whose sayings, sometimes recorded by their disciples,* have been preserved in the books named after these prophets (see Glossary.)

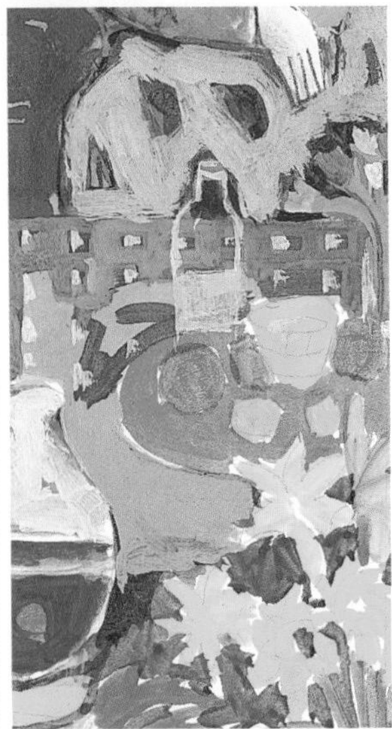

AMOS

He was the first of the writer prophets. He was born in Tekoa, not far from Bethlehem. Yet God chose him to be His messenger in the kingdom of the North. For God, the people split into two kingdoms was still a single people.

The kingdom of the North was wealthy and prosperous. King Jeroboam II (783-743 BC) kept peace with his neighbors and promoted trade. Fine houses were built. Looked at superficially, this material success was everything. The eye of God penetrated more deeply and saw the iniquity of the rich and the wretchedness of the poor. The scandal was all the greater in that overlords and underlings were fellow-countrymen, members of the people of the Covenant.

AMOS, PROPHET OF BROTHERLY LOVE

Prayer is not enough

3 1 Give ear to this word which the Lord has said
against you, O children of Israel, against all the
family which I took up out of the land of Egypt, saying,

2 "You only of all the families of the earth
have I taken care of: for this reason
I will send punishment on you for all your sins."

5 14 "Go after good and not evil,
so that life may be yours:
and so the Lord, the God of armies,
will be with you, as you say.
15 Be haters of evil and lovers of good,
and let right be done in the public
place:
it may be that the Lord,
the God of armies,
will have mercy
on the rest of Joseph.

21 "Your feasts are disgusting to me,
I will have nothing to do with them;
I will take no delight in
your holy meetings.
22 Even if you give me
your burnt offerings*
and your meal offerings,
I will not take pleasure in them:
I will have nothing to do
with the peace offerings
of your fat beasts.

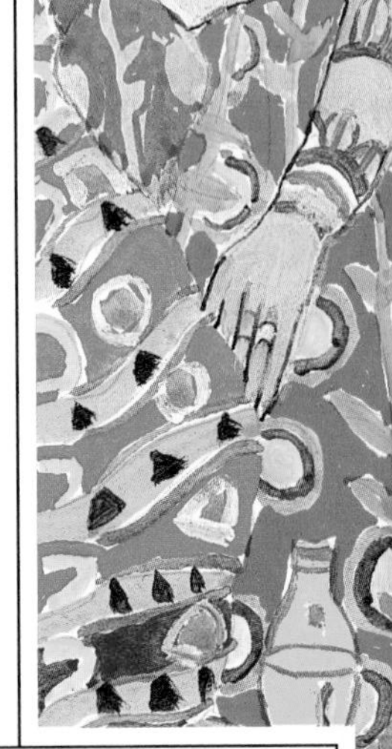

The inhabitants of Samaria
had good consciences.
They gave the appearance
of being honest citizens, and regularly
prayed in the temple at Bethel.
They paid no attention to the cost involved
in sacrificing fattened animals,
of having a multitude of musicians
or using a great amount of incense.

They were not concerned
with justice or righteousness.
They were not interested
in the right of the poor
to live like everyone else,
to be paid an honest salary,
to be judged fairly,
or to be helped in times of distress.

The people began to look out
only for themselves.
The most cunning would go to the temple
to celebrate their success
at arriving at the top.

And God cried out in pain
like a parent who has been deceived
by ungrateful children.

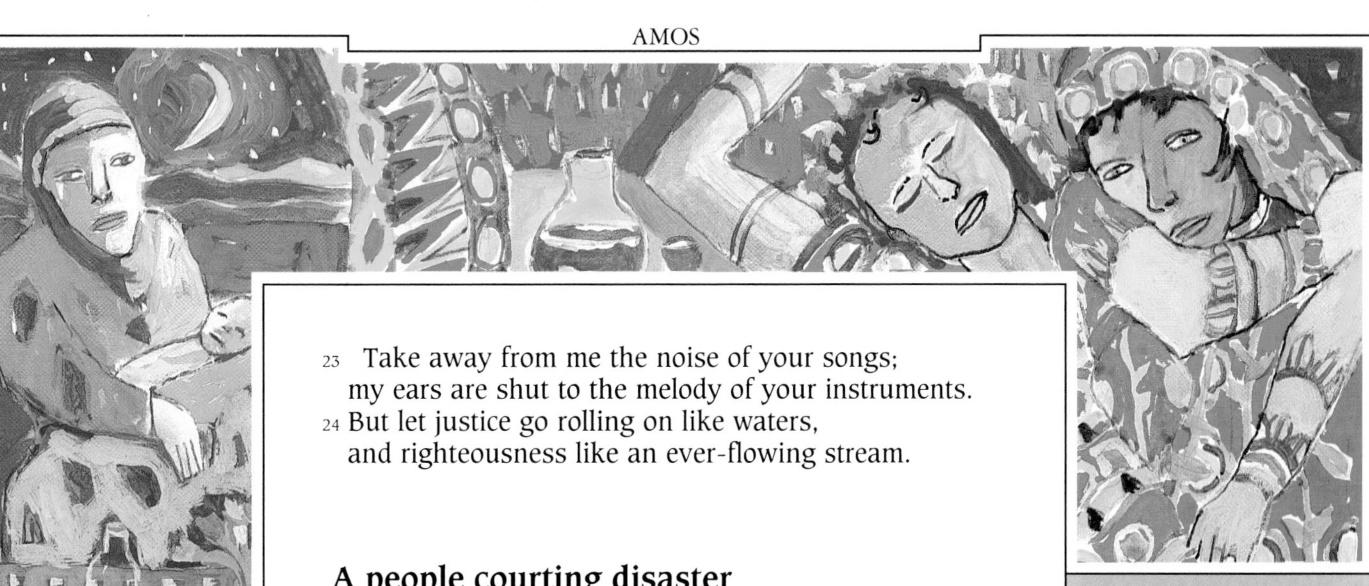

23 Take away from me the noise of your songs;
my ears are shut to the melody of your instruments.
24 But let justice go rolling on like waters,
and righteousness like an ever-flowing stream.

A people courting disaster

6 1 Sorrow to those who are resting in comfort in
Zion, and to those who have no fear of danger
in the mountain of Samaria![1]...

4 Who are resting on beds of ivory,
stretched out on soft seats,
feasting on lambs from the flock
and young oxen from the cattle-house;
5 Making foolish songs to the sound
of corded instruments,
and designing for themselves instruments
of music, like David;
6 Drinking wine in basins,
rubbing themselves with the best oils;
but they have no grief for the destruction of Joseph.

7 So now they will go into exile
with the first of those who are made prisoners,
and the loud cry of those who were stretched out
will come to an end.

8 4 Listen to this, you who are crushing the poor,
and whose purpose is to put an end to
those who are in need in the land,
5 Saying,

ımos was not a prophet from e "good" kingdom (that of ıvid's descendants) come to each to the "bad" kingdom ıat of Samaria). The whole ople, in Jerusalem as much in Samaria, had to change ways.

GOD IS MINDFUL OF THE POOR

Amos called on his fellow people to open their eyes. Behind the good life of the rich, the poor nursed their resentment in silence. But a people which has forgotten the bonds of solidarity cannot stand up to its enemies.[1] Its riches are a source of envy and its divisions rob it of the power of resistance.

1 Jesus said that a kingdom divided against itself cannot stand (Mark 3:24, page 240).

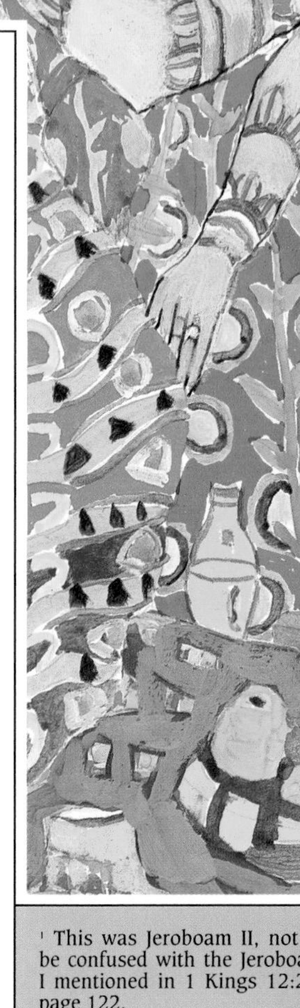

8 "When will the new moon be gone,
so that we may do trade in grain?
and the Sabbath,* so that we may
sellt in the market the produce of our fields?
making the measure small
and the price great,
and trading falsely with scales of deceit;

6 Buying the poor with silver,
and him who is in need for the price of two shoes,
and taking a price
for the waste parts of the grain.

7 The Lord has taken an oath by the pride of Jacob,
Truly I will never forget all their works."

Shepherd and prophet?

7 10 Then Amaziah, the priest of Beth-el, sent to
Jeroboam,[1] king of Israel, saying, "Amos has
conspired against you among the people of Israel: the land
11 is troubled by his words. | For Amos has said, 'Jeroboam
will die by the sword, and Israel will certainly be taken
away as a prisoner out of his land.'"

12 And Amaziah said to Amos, "O seer,
flee the land of Judah, and there earn
your living by working as a prophet. |
13 But be a prophet no longer at Beth-el,
for it is the holy place of the king, and
the king's house."

[1] This was Jeroboam II, not be confused with the Jeroboa I mentioned in 1 Kings 12:2 page 122.

Amaziah, you are not listening to God.
You do not recognize
the echo of God's Word
in the disturbing language of Amos.
You are a servant of the king.
You only want to hear
compliments and flattery.
Any call to conversion irritates you.
So you stalk the prophet
who transmits the Word of God.

CALLED BY GOD

Amos was a shepherd. In Bethel, his rough language did not win him friends.

He had the gall to call the rich wives of Samaria "cows of Bashan"[1]! Amaziah the priest and guardian of the Temple reported this to the king and had Amos expelled. Amaziah thought that being a prophet was a hereditary "profession," like the priesthood. The priesthood was transmitted from father to son. Amos retorted vigorously that God had called him and that he had given up his job in response to this call. He had come to convert* all those who deluded themselves that they were honoring God in the Temple while despising their fellow-men.

[1] Bashan was an especially fertile area on the other bank of the Jordan. Its cows were undoubtedly well-fed!

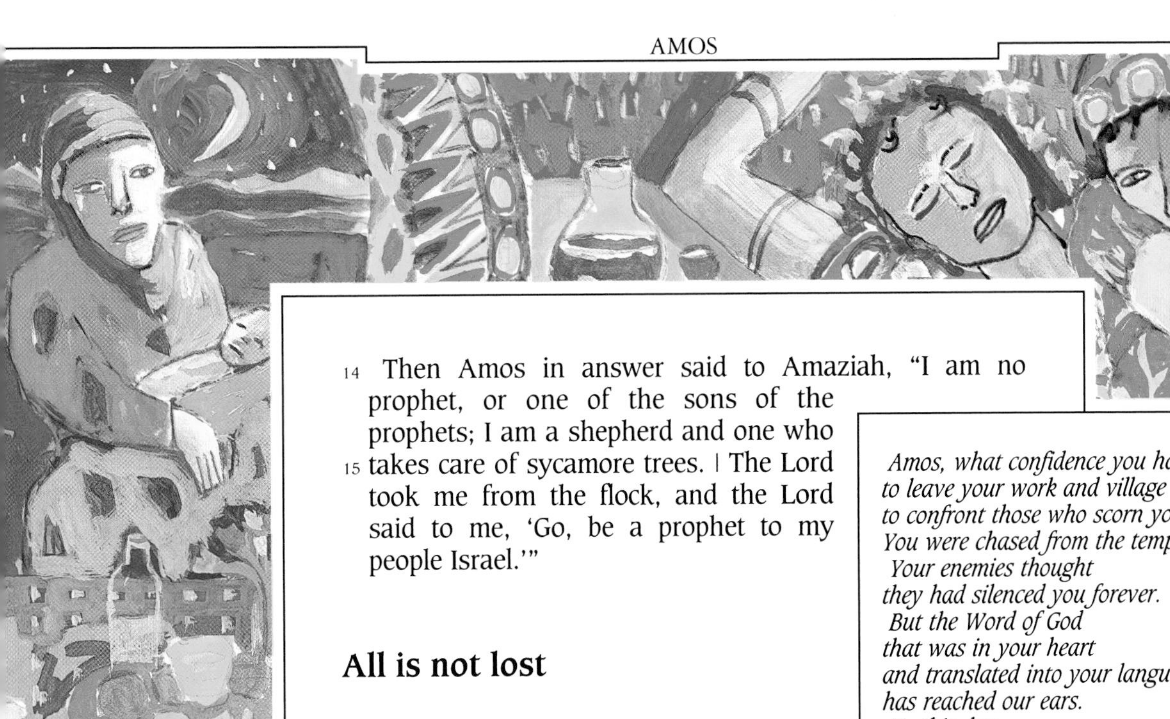

14 Then Amos in answer said to Amaziah, "I am no
prophet, or one of the sons of the
prophets; I am a shepherd and one who
15 takes care of sycamore trees. | The Lord
took me from the flock, and the Lord
said to me, 'Go, be a prophet to my
people Israel.'"

Amos, what confidence you had in God
to leave your work and village
to confront those who scorn you!
You were chased from the temple.
Your enemies thought
they had silenced you forever.
But the Word of God
that was in your heart
and translated into your language
has reached our ears.
To this day,
it still invites us to conversion.

All is not lost

9 11 "In that day I will put up the tent of David
which has come down,
and make good its broken places;
and I will put up again his damaged walls,
building it up as in the past;
12 So that the rest of Edom* may be their heritage, and
all the nations who bear my name,"
says the Lord, who is doing this.

13 "See, the days will come," says the Lord,
"when the ploughman will overtake him who
is cutting the grain, and the crusher of the grapes
him who is planting seed;
and sweet wine will be dropping from the mountains,
and the hills will be turned into streams of wine.

14 And I will let the fate of my people Israel be changed,
and they will be building up again the ruined towns
and living in them.
They will again be planting vineyards
and having wine to drink.
They will plant gardens and eat the fruit of them."

GOD IS LOYAL

Even when the people were disloyal, God remained loyal. The Book of Amos ends with this joyous promise — God will unite His people around a descendant of David and give them everything they need to live.

HOSEA

The prophet Hosea proclaimed the Word of God in Samaria, not long after Amos. He detected signs of Israel's weakness in face of the predatory designs of the Assyrians.[1] It was urgent to change and return to God.

Hosea, in speaking of God, used two comparisons which he developed into unforgettable images. God loves his people like a faithful husband, and like a merciful father.

[1] The Assyrians were subjugating all the peoples of the Middle East. The Assyrian sovereigns often changed their capital; for the Jews, the most famous of them was Nineveh. The Assyrians would capture Samaria and deport the population of the kingdom of the North. Before they could do the same thing to Jerusalem, they were conquered by the Babylonians. See pages 142-143.

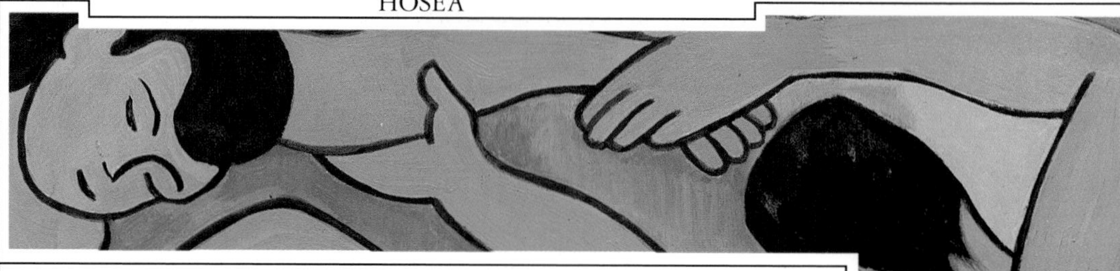

HOSEA, PROPHET
OF GOD'S GREAT LOVE

God, faithful spouse

2 14 "For this cause
I will allure her into the desert
and will say words of comfort to her.
15 I will give her back her vineyards[1] from there...
and she will give her answer there
as in the days when she was young,
and as in the time when she came up out of the land of Egypt.

16 "And in that day," says the Lord,
"you will say to me, 'my husband';
and you will never again give me
the name of 'my master';
17 For I will take away the names of the Baals out of her
mouth, and never again will she say their names....

19 "And I will take you as my bride forever.
Truly, I will take you as my bride
in righteousness and in justice,
in love and in mercies.

20 "I will take you as my bride in good faith,
and you will acknowledge the Lord."

[1] The image of the wife is linked to that of the vineyard. "Your wife will be like a fruitful vine in your house," says Psalm 128. The prophet Isaiah notes that the vine, bride of God, gives bad grapes and bad wine only because of its unfaithfulness (Isaiah 5:1-7, page 135). Only the Lord can enable His people to be faithful. "I shall bring you faithfulness and you will know the Lord."

GOD'S NUPTIALS

Hosea continued to love his wife, Gomer, even though she was unfaithful. "You are unfaithful towards God," he told the people. "Yet you will never, whatever your indifference or denial discourage God's love. God is faithful. He will make you faithful in your turn."

God had made a Covenant with Israel, not unlike a marriage. He considered Himself to be the spouse of His people. He offered to live with all the members of the house of Israel, women and men alike. It was not a matter of sparing a thought for Him from time to time but of building a life together, as a woman and man do in marriage.

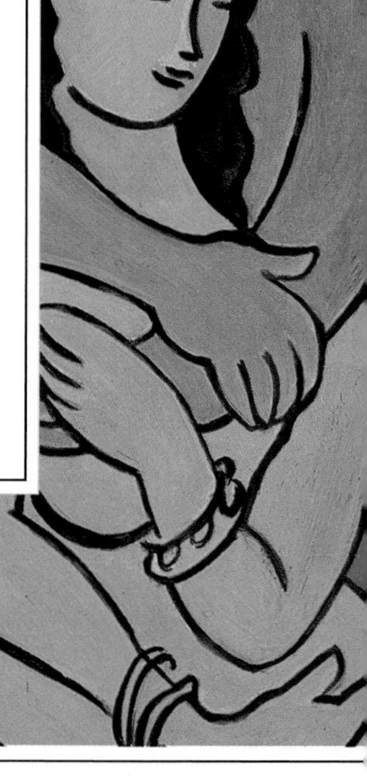

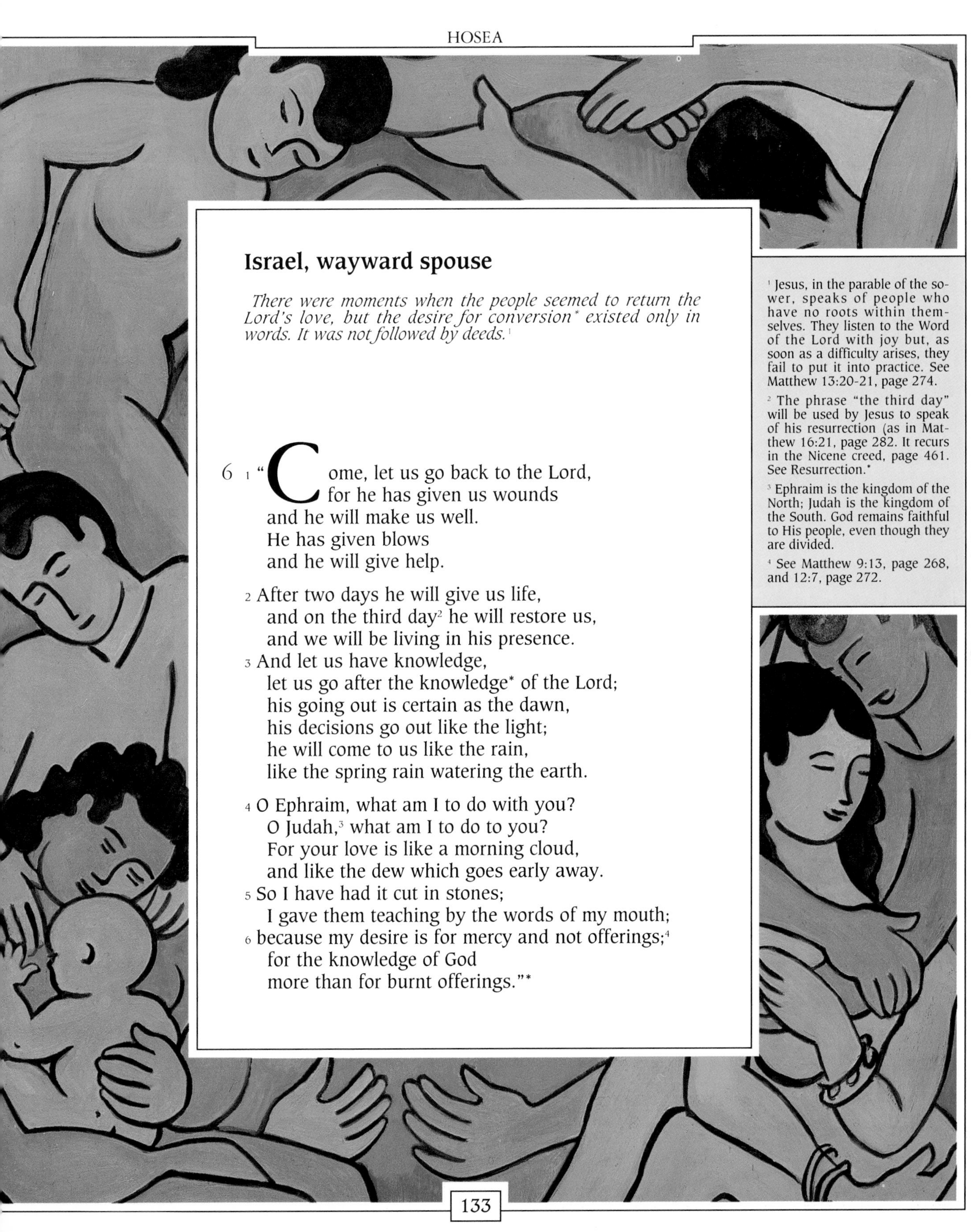

Israel, wayward spouse

There were moments when the people seemed to return the Lord's love, but the desire for conversion existed only in words. It was not followed by deeds.*[1]

6 1 "Come, let us go back to the Lord,
for he has given us wounds
and he will make us well.
He has given blows
and he will give help.

2 After two days he will give us life,
and on the third day[2] he will restore us,
and we will be living in his presence.
3 And let us have knowledge,
let us go after the knowledge* of the Lord;
his going out is certain as the dawn,
his decisions go out like the light;
he will come to us like the rain,
like the spring rain watering the earth.

4 O Ephraim, what am I to do with you?
O Judah,[3] what am I to do to you?
For your love is like a morning cloud,
and like the dew which goes early away.
5 So I have had it cut in stones;
I gave them teaching by the words of my mouth;
6 because my desire is for mercy and not offerings;[4]
for the knowledge of God
more than for burnt offerings."*

[1] Jesus, in the parable of the sower, speaks of people who have no roots within themselves. They listen to the Word of the Lord with joy but, as soon as a difficulty arises, they fail to put it into practice. See Matthew 13:20-21, page 274.

[2] The phrase "the third day" will be used by Jesus to speak of his resurrection (as in Matthew 16:21, page 282. It recurs in the Nicene creed, page 461. See Resurrection.*

[3] Ephraim is the kingdom of the North; Judah is the kingdom of the South. God remains faithful to His people, even though they are divided.

[4] See Matthew 9:13, page 268, and 12:7, page 272.

God, a father with a mother's heart

11 1 "When Israel was a child he was dear to me;
and I took my son out of Egypt....
3 But I was guiding Ephraim's footsteps;
I took them up in my arms,
but they were not conscious
that I was ready to make them well.
4 I made them come after me with the cords of man,
with the bands of love;
I was to them as one who took the yoke from off
their mouths, putting meat before them.
5 He will go back to the land of Egypt
and the Assyrian will be his king,
because they would not come back to me.

8 ...My heart changed in me,
it is soft with pity.
9 I will not put into effect the heat of my wrath;
I will not again send destruction on Ephraim;
for I am God and not man,
the Holy One* among you;
I will not put an end to you."

THE END OF THE KINGDOM OF THE NORTH

The kingdom of Israel could no longer withstand the onslaught of the Assyrians.[1] *In 721 BC, Samaria, after a long siege, fell to the armies of Sargon II.*

Large numbers of the population were massacred. The rest were carried off into captivity, never to return. In the ravaged country they left behind, the Assyrians settled people from other regions they had conquered. These heathens learned of the Lord from the few Israelites who had escaped deportation. They were the forebears of the people known as Samaritans in Jesus' day.*

Assyria then tried to overcome the kingdom of Jerusalem, but internal strife prevented them from taking the city.[2]

GOD'S MOTHERLY LOVE

To whom does Hosea compare God?

The glib answer is "to a father".

God is indeed often compared to a father in the Bible and Jesus would later teach us to call Him "Our Father" (Matthew 6:9-13, page 264).

If we examine carefully the images used by Hosea, we notice that they suggest rather a mother teaching her baby how to walk or leaning over to breast-feed it. There are other places in the Bible where God is explicitly compared to a mother (Isaiah 49:14-16, page 169, Ecclesiasticus 4:10, page 199). **Whenever God is called merciful, God's motherly love is being referred to. Mercy* is a mother's love for the child she has reared.**

[1] See page 132, "Hosea."

[2] See page 142 for the account of the aborted siege of Jerusalem.

ISAIAH

Isaiah takes us back in time to the kingdom of the South, a few years before the fall of Samaria. Isaiah was an important member of the royal court.

God appointed him to be His messenger, especially under the reign of Ahaz (736-716 BC) [1] and of Hezekiah (716-687 BC). See next page.

For a while, Isaiah thought perhaps Hezekiah was the Messiah* ordained by God. Hezekiah was a devout and kindly man, but the prophet soon realized that he was also a sinner with shortcomings. Isaiah then prophesied that the unblemished Messiah would appear later.

1 Not to be confused with Ahab of Samaria, who reigned at the time of the prophet Elijah (page 122).

ISAIAH, PROPHET OF THE MESSIAH

The vine and the bad grapes

5 1 Let me make a song about my loved one,
a song of love for his vineyard.
My loved one had a vineyard
on a fertile hill:
2 And after working the earth of it with a spade,
he took away its stones,
and put in it a very special vine;
and he put up a watchtower in the middle of it,
hollowing out in the rock a place
for the grape-crushing;
and he was hoping that it would give the best grapes,
but it gave common grapes.
3 "And now, you people of Jerusalem
and you men of Judah,
be the judges between me and my vineyard.

4 Is there anything which might have been done
for my vineyard which I have not done?
Why then, when I was hoping for the best grapes
did it give me common grapes?

5 And now, this is what I will do to my vineyard:
I will take away the circle of thorns round it,
and it will be burned up;
its wall will be broken down
and the beasts of the field will go through it.

6 And I will make it waste;
its branches will not be touched with the knife,
or the earth worked with the spade.
But blackberries and thorns will come up in it,

BEARING GOOD FRUIT

Isaiah had bad news for God, his friend — his beloved vine was producing nothing but bad grapes.

The vine was the people of Israel (kingdom of the North) and of Judah (kingdom of the South). Despite their separation they formed one people, one vine, before God.

Poorly ruled by inept and sinning messiahs,[*] the people no longer recognized God's love for them and slid into infidelity. They produced bad fruit.

Had God been a man, He would have uprooted his vine and thrown it away. But God is not a man (see Hosea 11:9, page 134).

5 and I will give orders to the clouds
not to send rain on it.

7 For the vineyard of the Lord
of armies
is the people of Israel,
and the men of Judah
are the plant of his delight.
He was looking for justice,
and there was blood;
for righteousness,
and there was a cry for help."

No,
God will not abandon His vineyard
to the thorns and brambles.
God loves it too much.
God loves His people too much.
Therefore, He will come
among his people.
He will become
one of David's descendants.
He will become a part of the vineyard.
And as a vigorous vine,
Jesus, the Son of God,
will bring new life to the branches
and they will bear good fruit.

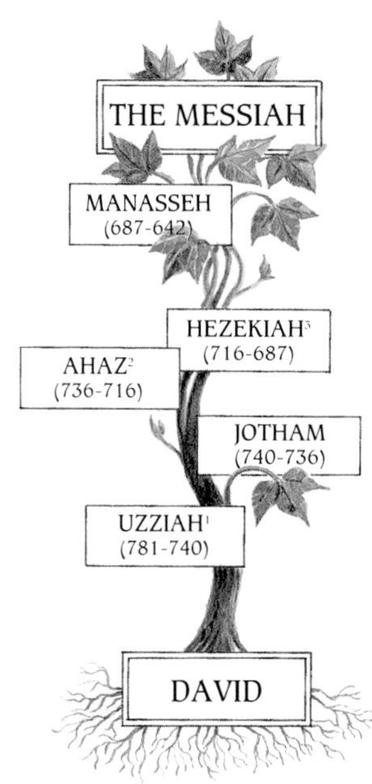

[1] Isaiah received his mission as prophet the year Uzziah died (Isaiah 6:1, page 137).

[2] It was to Ahaz that Isaiah foretold the coming of "Immanuel" (see page 138).

[3] See pages 140-143.

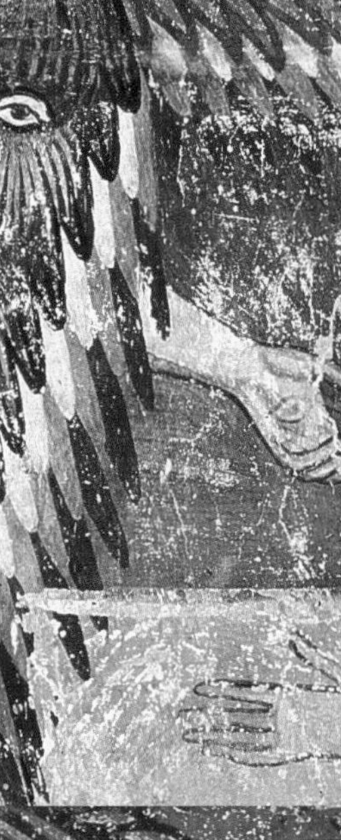

Messenger of the Lord of the universe

Uzziah, king of Jerusalem, died in 740 BC. He was succeeded by his son, Jotham, who reigned for sixteen years. They were good kings, but they failed to wean their people from idolatry.

6 1 In the year of King Uzziah's death I saw the Lord seated in his place, high and lifted up, and the Temple
2 was full of the wide skirts of his robe. | Over him were the
seraphs.* Each had six wings; two for covering his face,
3 two for covering his feed, and two for flight. | And one
said in a loud voice to another, "Holy,* holy, holy, is the
4 Lord of armies. All the earth is full of his glory." | And the
bases of the door pillars were shaking at the sound of his
5 cry, and the house was full of smoke. | "Then" I said, "The
curse is on me. My fate is destruction, because I am a man
of unclean lips, living among a people of unclean lips. My
6 eyes have seen the King, the Lord of armies." | Then a
seraph came to me with a burning coal in his hand, which
7 he had taken from off the altar with tongs. | And after
touching my mouth with it, he said,
"See, your lips have been touched with
this; your evil is removed, and you are
made clean from sin."
8 And the voice of the Lord came to my
ears, saying, "Whom am I to send, and
who will go for us?" "Then," I said,
"Here am I, send me."

Holy, holy, holy
Lord God of the universe.
The heavens where the seraphim fly
and the earth where your temple
stands are filled with your glory.

You who reign
above all
send messengers,
messiahs and prophets
with clean and unclean lips.
But one day
your son will descend from his throne
and proclaim the Good News
of your love in a language
that will be understandable to all.
Blessed is he who comes
in the name of the Lord!

KINGS AND PROPHETS

The task of the messiah-kings was to direct the people towards serving the one real King of Israel, the Lord.

The people began serving their idols and the kings were unable to stop them doing so. The King then chose other messengers, the prophets.*

The prophets, although lacking the kings' regal trappings,[1] reminded the people of the demands imposed under its Covenant with God. They did not replace the kings; they made up for the kings' inadequacies.

[1] The kings reigned with the help of their officials and the army. The pomp of their ceremonies inspired fear and admiration. Jesus would be a Messiah in the manner of the prophets, not of the kings.

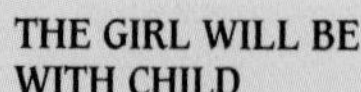

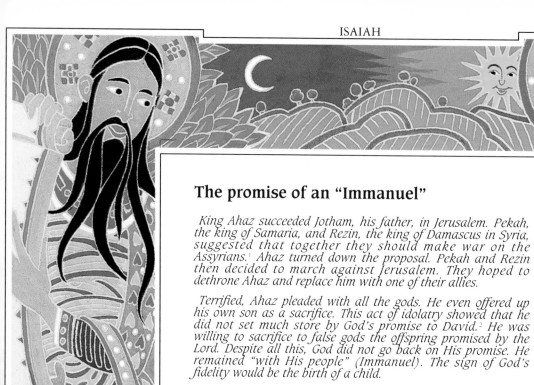

The promise of an "Immanuel"

King Ahaz succeeded Jotham, his father, in Jerusalem. Pekah, the king of Samaria, and Rezin, the king of Damascus in Syria, suggested that together they should make war on the Assyrians.[1] Ahaz turned down the proposal. Pekah and Rezin then decided to march against Jerusalem. They hoped to dethrone Ahaz and replace him with one of their allies.

Terrified, Ahaz pleaded with all the gods. He even offered up his own son as a sacrifice. This act of idolatry showed that he did not set much store by God's promise to David.[2] He was willing to sacrifice to false gods the offspring promised by the Lord. Despite all this, God did not go back on His promise. He remained "with His people" (Immanuel). The sign of God's fidelity would be the birth of a child.

7 1 Now it came about in the days of Ahaz, the son of
Jotham, the son of Uzziah, king of Judah, that
Rezin, the king of Aram, and Pekah, the son of Remaliah,
the king of Israel, came up to Jerusalem to make war
2 against it, but were not able to conquer it. | And word came
to the family of David that Aram had put up its tents in
Ephraim.[3] And the king's heart, and the hearts of his
people, were moved, like the trees of the wood shaking in
the wind.

The Lord sent the prophet Isaiah with a message for king Ahaz.

3-4 ..."Go out now, ... and you will come across Ahaz... | and
say to him,
'Take care and be quiet;
have no fear, and do not let your heart be feeble,
because of these two ends of smoking fire wood,
because of the bitter wrath of Rezin and Aram,
and of the son of Remaliah.
5 Because Aram has plotted against you,
saying,

THE GIRL WILL BE WITH CHILD

Isaiah perhaps had the king's young wife in mind. The birth would make up for the death of the son sacrificed to the idols and signify that God was with His people (Immanuel) and had not forgotten His promise. He would give Ahaz, the idolater, a son who would lead the people back to God. This son was Hezekiah. Later on, Isaiah would come to realize that Hezekiah, despite his good points, was not the perfect guide willed by God. The true Immanuel would be born at another time. The people would wait for his coming.

In the Greek translation dating from the 2nd or 3rd century BC, it was written that Immanuel would be born not of a girl, but of a virgin. The implication was that God would play a special role in the child's conception and that the child would in that way be especially attentive to his Father's will. (See Matthew 1:20-23, page 255.)

[1] Pekah was the next-to-last king of Samaria. He did everything he could to escape from the grip of the Assyrians. This was about ten years before Samaria finally fell (see page 134).

[2] 2 Samuel 7:11-16, page 109.

[3] Ephraim was one of the tribes of the North. The king of Syria had come to join forces with his ally, the king of Samaria. Their armies united to march on Jerusalem.

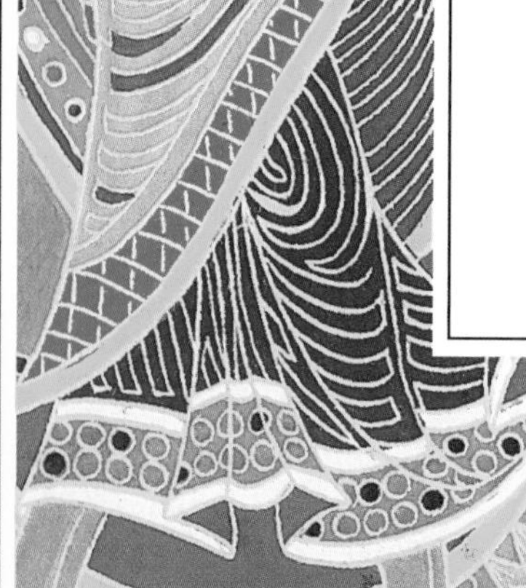

6 Let us go up against Judah, troubling her,
and forcing our way into her,
and let us put up a king in her,
even the son of Tabeel.'"
7 This is the word of the Lord God:
"This plot will not come about or be enacted."...

10 And Isaiah said again to Ahaz,
11 "Make a request to the Lord your God for a sign,
a sign in the deep places of the underworld,
or in the high heavens."
12 But Ahaz said, "I will not put the Lord to the test[1]
by making such a request."
13 And he said,
"Hear now, O family of David:
is it not enough that you are driving men to disgust?
will you do the same to my God?
14 For this reason the Lord himself will give you a sign.
A young woman is now with child,
and she will give birth to a son,
and she will give him the name Immanuel....

16 For before the child is old enough
to make a decision between evil and good,
the land whose two kings you are now fearing
will have become waste."

[1] Ahaz appeared to be someone who respected the Law.* He claimed not to want to put God to the test of showing His presence. (See Exodus 17:7, page 68.) Isaiah understood that Ahaz, in his idol-worshipping mind, sought protection from other gods.

UNTO US A CHILD IS BORN

Isaiah proclaims his joy, either at the birth of Hezekiah, son of Ahaz, or at his anointment, often likened to a rebirth. Psalm 2, used at royal anointings, quotes God as saying to the new messiah,* "You are my son; today I have become your Father." (See page 209.)

Hezekiah, with all his virtues, was only a pale copy of the Prince of Peace whom the Lord would one day send. The prophecy of Isaiah would be fulfilled by the birth of Jesus.

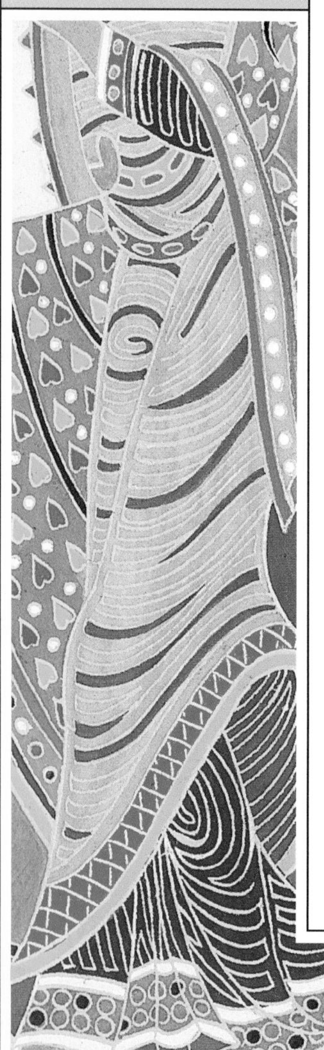

The promise fulfilled?

9 2 The people who went in the dark
have seen a great light,
and for those who were living in the land
of the deepest night, the light is shining.
3 You have made them very glad,
increasing their joy.
They are glad before you
as men are glad in the time of harvest,
or when they divide the goods taken in war.
4 For by your hand the yoke on his neck
and the rod on his back,
even the rod of his cruel master,
have been broken, as in the day of Midian.[1]
5 For every boot of the man of war
with his sounding step,
and the clothing rolled in blood,
will be for burning, food for the fire.
6 For to us a child has come,
to us a son is given;
and the government has been placed in his hands;
and he has been named Wise Guide,
Strong God, Father forever, Prince of Peace.
7 Of the increase of his rule and of peace
there will be no end,
on the seat of David, and in his kingdom;
to make it strong,
supporting it with wise decision and righteousness,
now and forever.

By the fixed purpose of the Lord of armies
this will be done.

[1] Midian was the name of a people related to the Israelites (see "All peoples on earth will be blessed through you," page 474). The relations between the two were sometimes good. Moses was received by the Midianites when fleeing from the Pharaoh (see page 56). But at other times they were very bad. The Judge* Gideon routed them decisively.

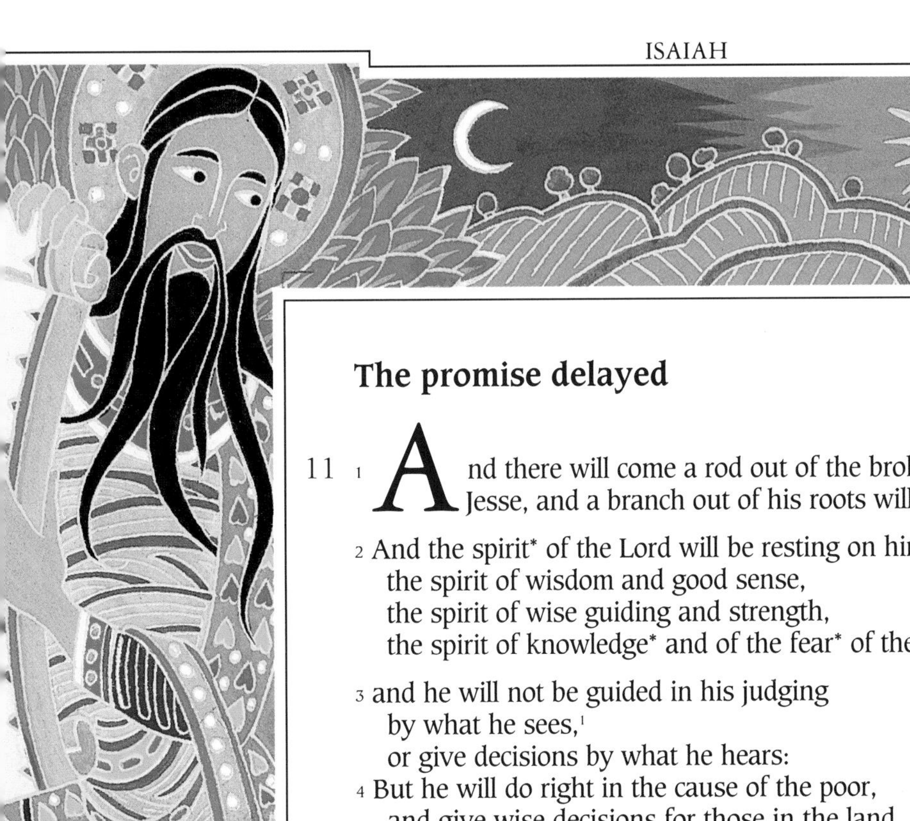

The promise delayed

11 1 And there will come a rod out of the broken tree of
Jesse, and a branch out of his roots will give fruit.

2 And the spirit* of the Lord will be resting on him,
the spirit of wisdom and good sense,
the spirit of wise guiding and strength,
the spirit of knowledge* and of the fear* of the Lord;

3 and he will not be guided in his judging
by what he sees,[1]
or give decisions by what he hears:
4 But he will do right in the cause of the poor,
and give wise decisions for those in the land
who are in need;
and the rod of his mouth will come down on the cruel,
and with the breath of his lips
he will put an end to the evil-doer.
5 And righteousness will be the cord of his robe,
and good faith the band round his breast.

6 And the wolf will be living with the lamb;
the leopard will take his rest with the young goat;
the lion will take grass for food like the ox;
the young lion will go with the young ones of the herd;
and a little child will be their guide.
7 And the cow and the bear will be friends
while their young ones are sleeping together.
8 And the child nursing will be playing
by the hole of the snake,
and the older child will put his hand
on the bright eye of the poison snake.[2]
9 There will be no cause of pain or destruction
in all my holy mountain,

UNDERSTANDING THE WORD OF GOD

When God passed on His word to a prophet,* He did not dictate messages ready to serve. He enlightened the prophet's mind, and it was the prophet who passed on what he had understood. Through prayer, meditation and thinking things over, the prophet was able to gain a deeper understanding of the message he had received. This was the case with Isaiah. He realized more and more clearly that Hezekiah was not the perfect messiah. God would send such a one at a later time. Under that messiah's guidance, all nations would learn to live in peace. And it would be possible for all humans to know God.

[1] This is a characteristic of God. See 1 Samuel 16:7, page 99.

[2] Animals which became tame were a symbol of mankind's reconciliation with God. A number of Biblical authors believed that the wildness of animals was a consequence of human sin. Once mankind returned to God, animals would recover their original docility. See animal.*

11 for the earth will be full of the knowledge of the Lord
as the sea is covered by the waters.
10 And in that day, the eyes of the nations
will be turned to the root of Jesse
which will be lifted up as the flag of the peoples;
and his resting place will be glory.

Setback for the Assyrians

The Assyrian king, after destroying Samaria,[1] attacked Jerusalem. After all his victories, he was convinced that an invincible god protected him. He derided all the other gods who were powerless to save their followers.

The faith with which Hezekiah reacted was remarkable. Unlike Ahaz, his father, he did not try to woo the favors of strange gods.[2] He knew that God was the only true God. He placed his trust in Him. Isaiah told him that the city would be preserved.*

37 9 And when news came to him that Tirhakah, king of
Ethiopia, had made an attack on him, ...And he
sent representatives to Hezekiah, king of Judah, saying, |
10 "This is what you are to say to Hezekiah, king of Judah:
Let not your God, in whom is your faith, give you a false
hope, saying, 'Jerusalem will not be delivered into the
11 hands of the king of Assyria.' | No doubt the story has
come to you of what the kings of Assyria have done to all
lands, destroying them. Will you be kept safe from their
fate?"
14 And Hezekiah took the letter from the hands of those
who had come with it. After reading it, Hezekiah went up
to the house of the Lord, opening the letter there before the
15-16 Lord. | He prayed to the Lord, saying, | "O Lord of armies,
the God of Israel, seated between the cherubim,* you only
are the God of all the kingdoms of the earth. You have
17 made heaven and earth. | Let your ear be turned to us, O
Lord. Let your eyes be open, O Lord, and see. Take note of

[1] See page 134. [2] See page 138.

ISAIAH AND THE EXPECTATION OF A MESSIAI

Before Isaiah, the people did not clearly await the coming of the messiah.* When a messiah-king died, one of his sons succeeded him. Isaiah realized that the messiah-kings were only rarely the sor of guide wished for by God. H revealed that God would send the Messiah of His heart's desire. From then on, the people looked forward to the coming of this Messiah as a savior.* The disappearance of the monarchy at the time of the captivity* (see page 148) **did not weaken this expectation. The people cried to the Lord t send the Messiah who would save them. For some, he woul be a mighty king. For others, he would be more like a prophet than a king** (see Zechariah, page 193).

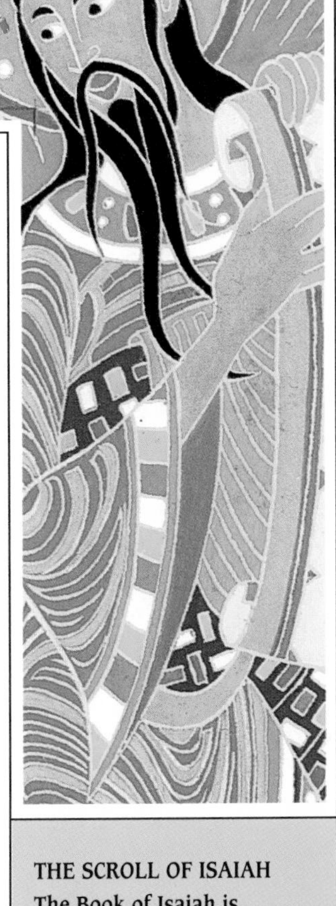

all the words of Sennacherib who has sent men to say evil
18 against the living God. | Truly, O Lord, the kings of Assyria
19 have laid waste all the nations and their lands, | and have
given their gods to the fire. For they were no gods, but
wood and stone, the work of men's hands, so they have
20 given them to destruction. | But now, O Lord our God, give
us salvation from his hand, so that it may be clear to all the
kingdoms of the earth that you, and you only, are the
Lord."

21 Then Isaiah, the son of Amoz, sent to Hezekiah, saying,
"The Lord, the God of Israel, says, 'The prayer you have
made to me against Sennacherib, king of Assyria, has
22 come to my ears.' | This is the word which the Lord has
said about him:

"In the eyes of the virgin daughter of Zion*
you are shamed and laughed at;
the daughter of Jerusalem
has mocked you."

33 "For this cause the Lord says about the king of Assyria,
'He will not come into this town,
or send an arrow against it;
he will not come before it with arms,
or put up an earthwork against it.
34 By the way he came he will go back,
and he will not get into this town.
35 For I will keep this town safe, for my honor,
and for the honor of my servant David.'"

36 And the angel of the Lord went out and killed a hundred
and eighty-five thousand men in the army of Assyrians.
When the people got up early in the morning, there was
37 nothing to be seen but dead bodies. | Sennacherib, king of
Assyria, went back to his place at Nineveh.[1]

Egyptian and Assyrian historical records, speaking of this event, mention an epidemic which killed off many of the Assyrian troops. Sennacherib was assassinated shortly afterwards. This marked the decline of the Assyrian empire, which would soon be supplanted by the Babylonians.

THE SCROLL OF ISAIAH

The Book of Isaiah is impressively long — 66 Chapters. Nowadays, nearly everyone agrees that the prophet's sayings* and main events in his life are set out in the first 39 Chapters.

The 27 other chapters may also contain the saying of Isaiah himself. But many think that they were uttered by other prophets. Their names are not known but, like Isaiah, they would have presented God as the Holy One of Israel. This would explain why their prophecies were copied on the same scroll.

Reference is sometimes made to the "second Isaiah" who prophesied in Babylon during the captivity (see pages 167-172) and the "third Isaiah" who spoke in Jerusalem at the end of the captivity (see pages 184-187).

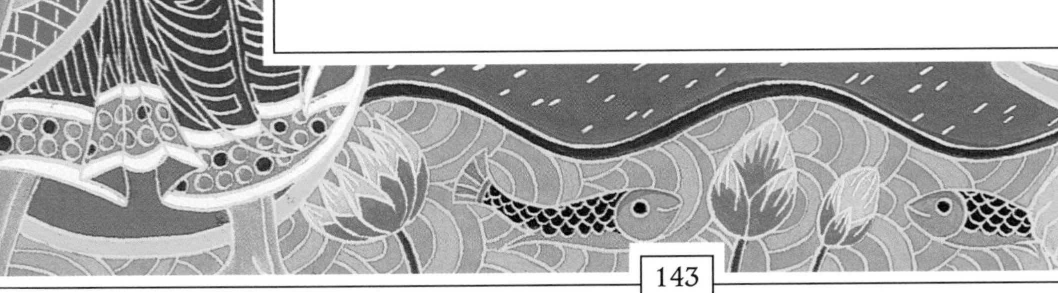

MICAH

Micah lived at the same time as Isaiah but was not a member of the royal court in Jerusalem.

At a time when the countryside was ravaged by war parties, Micah voiced the hopes of the humble, who were waiting for God to send a savior.

AN UNARMED GOD

The Lord was different from the cruel gods of the Assyrians. He did not give His people the power with which to subdue other peoples (see Isaiah 37:17-19, page 142). On the contrary, He invited all nations to find a friendly way of living together. The swords which pierced soldiers' bodies to kill them were to become ploughshares for digging into the soil and making it generate life.

This prophecy is also to be found in the Book of Isaiah 2:2-4.

MICAH, PROPHET OF PEACE

No more war

4 1 But in the last days
it will come about that the mountain
of the Lord's house
will be placed on the top of the mountains,
and be lifted up over the hills;
and peoples will be flowing to it.
2 And a number of nations* will go and say,
"Come, and let us go up to the mountain of the Lord,
and to the house of the God of Jacob;
and he will give us knowledge of his ways
and we will be guided by his word,"
for from Zion the law* will go out,
and the word of the Lord from Jerusalem.

3 And he will be judge between great peoples,
and strong nations far away will be ruled
by his decisions;
their swords will be hammered into ploughshares
and their spears into pruning hooks:
nations will no longer be lifting up their swords
against one another,
and knowledge of war will have gone forever.

4 But every man will be seated
under his vine and under his fig tree,
and no one will be a cause of fear to them:
for the mouth of the Lord of armies has said it.

Peaceful shepherd

Micah was distrustful of everything that went on in Jerusalem. The savior would be born far from the political intrigues of the court.

5 2 "And you, Beth-lehem Ephrathah,
the least among the families of Judah,
out of you one will come to me
who is to be ruler in Israel...."
3 For this cause he will give them up till the time
when she who is with child has given birth....
4 And he will take his place
and give food to his flock in the strength of the Lord....
and their resting place will be safe,
for now he will be great to the ends of the earth.
5 And this will be our peace....

Love is worth more than any sacrificial offering

The man who enters the Temple asks this question:

6 6 With what am I to come before the Lord
and go with bent head before the high God?
Am I to come before him with burnt offerings,
with young oxen a year old?
7 Will the Lord be pleased with thousands of sheep
or with ten thousand rivers of oil?
Am I to give my first child for my wrongdoing,
the fruit of my body for the sin of my soul?
8 He has made clear to you,
O man, what is good;
and what is desired from you by the Lord;
only doing what is right, and loving mercy,*
and walking without pride before your God.[1]

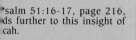

PLEASING THE LORD

Ahaz had killed his son as a sacrifice (see page 138)**. The question that Abraham himself had had to face was still being debated. Did the Lord want human sacrifice?** (See page 46.)

Micah's reply was perfectly clear. What the Lord wanted was for people to be righteous, merciful and allied with God.

*salm 51:16-17, page 216, ds further to this insight of cah.

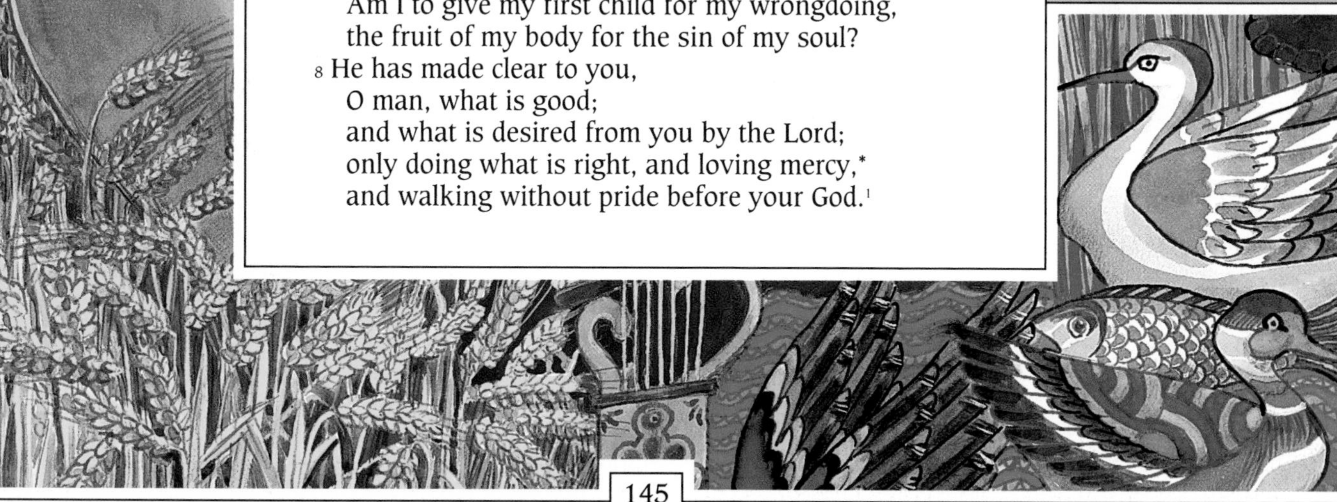

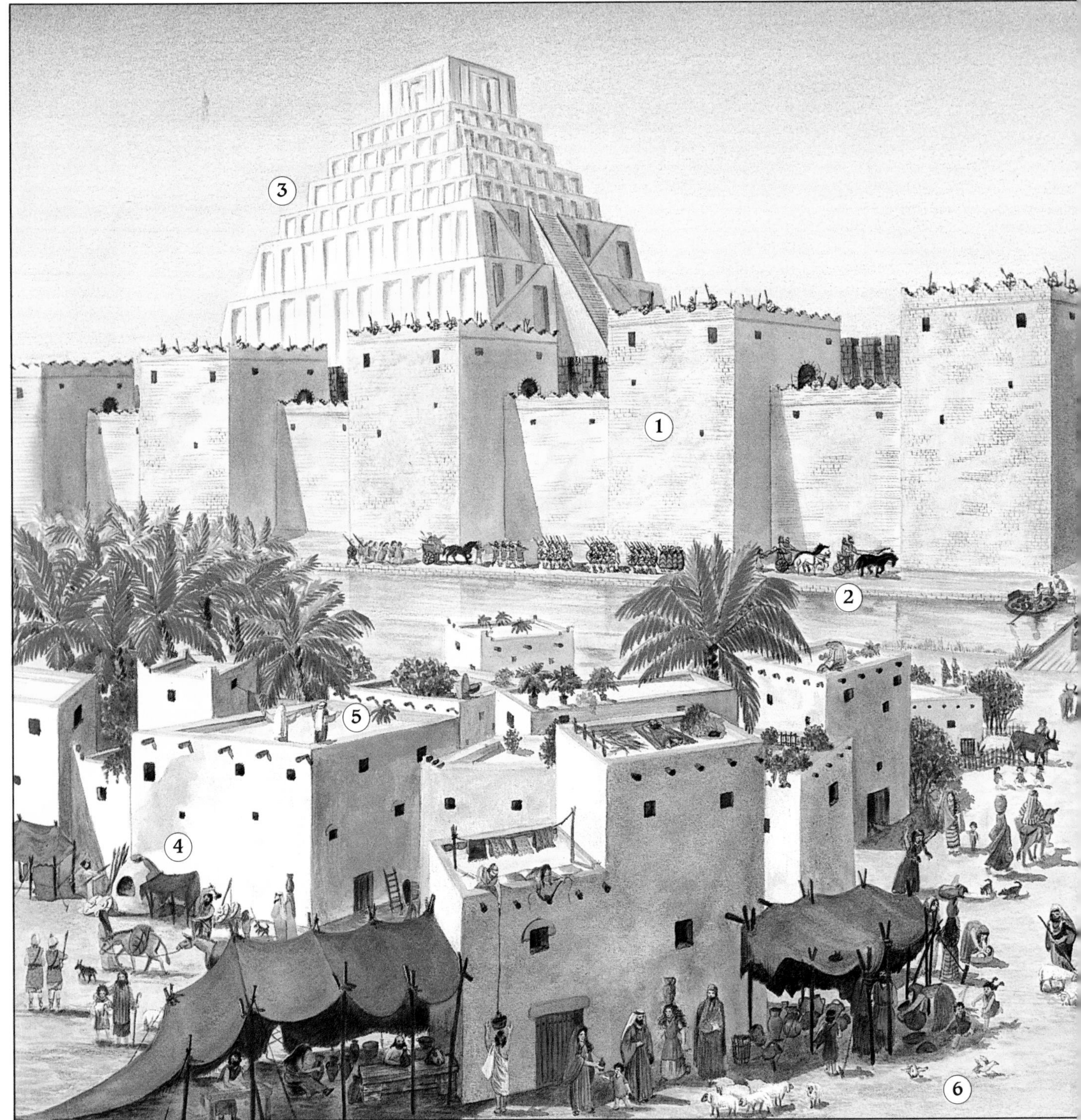

CAPTIVITY IN BABYLON

1. Babylon, with its fifty-three temples, royal palace and famous hanging gardens, was protected by a double row of walls eighteen kilometers long.

2. Nebuchadnezzar returning as the conqueror of Jerusalem (587 BC). King Zedekiah follows behind, in chains, his eyes put out. At the rear of the procession comes the treasure of the Temple carried off to Babylon (see "THE END OF THE KINGDOM", page 157).

3. The Ziggurat of Babylon, which was the model for the story of the Tower of Babel (Genesis 11:1-9, page 31). It was a temple made of brick, in the shape of a stepped tower.

4. At the time of the first captivity in 598 BC, Nebuchadnezzar had deported all the metalsmiths (see page 148). The captives, following the instructions of Jeremiah, settled in Babylon and toiled for the country's prosperity (Jeremiah 29:4-14, page 156).

5. The anonymous prophet known as the second Isaiah at prayer. He understood that the people would be freed by a servant (see page 167).

6. The captives founded families and had children (Jeremiah 29:6, page 156).

7. Ezekiel condemning the bad shepherds of Israel (Ezekiel 34:1-16, page 163).

8. People gathering to listen to the word of God and pray. This was the origin of the synagogues (see "The Religion of the Book", page 176).*

9. Scribes writing down the Bible stories. Ezra was one of the scribes in Babylon.*

10. Some exiles bitterly remembered Jerusalem. They hung their harps on the trees by the riverside. They refused to sing for their captors (Psalm 137, page 225).

11. The Euphrates.

II

THE CAPTIVITY

Josiah *reigned in Jerusalem from 640 to 609 BC. He tried to serve the Lord with all his might. With the help of his secretary, Shaphan,*[1] *he undertook major religious reforms.*[1] *But in 609 BC, when trying to prevent the pharaoh Neco from crossing his territory, he was killed at Megiddo.*[2]

The pharaoh Neco from that time on thought of himself as the "protector" of the kingdom of Judah. He appointed one of Josiah's sons to rule over Jerusalem, and gave him the name of ***Jehoiakim*** *(609-598 BC). Soon the power of Egypt was overshadowed by that of the new master of the Middle East,* ***Nebuchadnezzar****, king of Babylon. He demanded that Jerusalem pay tribute. Oddly enough, Jehoiakim preferred to remain loyal to the pharaoh who had killed his father rather than submit to the king of Babylon. Nebuchadnezzar accordingly laid siege to Jerusalem.*

After the death of Jehoiakim, his son, ***Jehoiachin*** *— whose short-lived reign lasted only three months — let Nebuchadnezzar's troops into Jerusalem. They did not destroy the city or the Temple. The king's life was spared but he was led away to exile in Babylon along with part of the population, including the locksmiths, metalsmiths*[3] *and the leaders of the people — in short, all those who could foment rebellion against Babylon. Among this first wave of captives was a priest called Ezekiel.*

Nebuchadnezzar appointed a new king for Jerusalem. He would be its last. ***Zedekiah*** *(598-587 BC) also nursed the illusion of escaping from the clutches of Babylon by allying himself with Egypt. He closed his ears to* ***Jeremiah****, the prophet, who told the people to put their trust in the Lord or suffer terrible consequences.*

Ezekiel was spreading much the same message in Babylon.

Nebuchadnezzar, angered by the rebelliousness of Zedekiah, sacked Jerusalem in 587 BC and destroyed the Temple. From this time on, Jeremiah and Ezekiel preached the hope of a new Covenant between God and His people, finally purified of its sins.*

According to many scholars, shortly after, an unknown prophet — often called the "second Isaiah"[4]*— revealed to the Jews* in exile that God did not want a people of conquering dominators but an obedient people which would help other nations to discover the one and only Lord.*

[1] Josiah purged the Temple of the idols that had been set up there, and had a heathen altar in Ben Hinnom valley demolished. See page 153.

[2] In the Book of Revelation, God was to stage the final battle against the forces of evil at Mount Megiddo (Armageddon).

[3] It was important to remove locksmiths and metalsmiths from Jerusalem, since they were capable of making weapons.

[4] See pages 143 and 167.

EREMIAH...

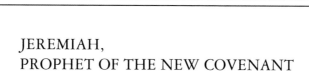

eremiah's mission was to
announce the Word of the
ord at the time when the
ingdom of Jerusalem was
ollapsing. He was someone
ery different from Isaiah. He
vas rather withdrawn and
ensitive. He had no stomach
or quarrels.

'et the Lord urged him to
ondemn publicly the sins* of
he kings and people. For
nany years, Jeremiah
ondered over the same
uestions: "What if God is
ired of His wayward
pouse?" (See page 132.)
What if He has decided to
epudiate her?"

**.THE BACHELOR
ROPHET**

eremiah's message, like
hat of Hosea, was reflected
n his way of life. Hosea's
elations with his wife,
omer, were similar to those
f God with His people (see
age 132). Jeremiah for his
art never married, as
hough to show that God no
onger wanted to live in a
ovenant with His people.

owards the end of his life,
he old prophet finished by
announcing that God could
ot bring Himself to reject
lis people and would enter
nto a new Covenant with it.

JEREMIAH,
PROPHET OF THE NEW COVENANT

A lookout who was a child at heart

Jeremiah tried to describe the inner call that made him a prophet in the form of a conversation with the Lord.

1 1 The words of Jeremiah, the son of Hilkiah,
of the priests who were in Anathoth[1]...

4 Now the word of the Lord came to me, saying,
5 "Before you were formed in the body of your mother
I had knowledge of you,
and before your birth I made you holy;
I have chosen you to be
a prophet to the nations."

6 "Then," said I, "O Lord God!
see, I have no power of words, for I am a child."
7 But the Lord said to me,
"Do not say, 'I am a child,'
for wherever I send you, you are to go,
and whatever I give you orders to say, you are to say.
8 Have no fear because of them,
for I am with you to
keep you safe," says the Lord.

9 Then the Lord put out his hand,
touching my mouth;
and the Lord said to me,
"See, I have put my words
in your mouth.

[1] Anathoth was a small village West of Jerusalem. It was the place where Solomon had banished the priests who had not backed his bid for the succession to the throne of David. Jeremiah was a priest* by birth but was unable to exercise his ministry.*

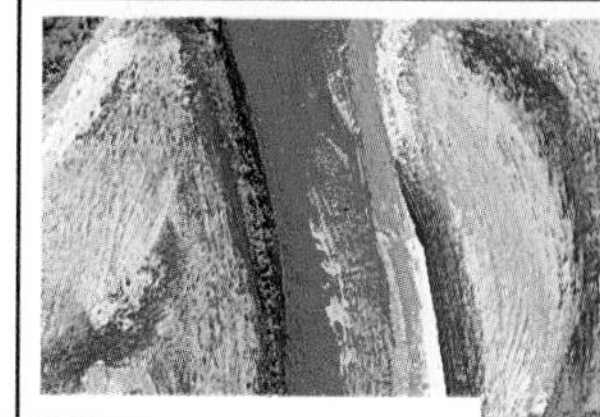

*Jeremiah, as Moses was before you,
you aren't very enthusiastic about
the mission that the Lord has entrusted you.
You know your limits
and are afraid
you won't measure up.
But with the Lord's strength,
you will know how to announce
God's Word
to both the great and
small of the kingdom.*

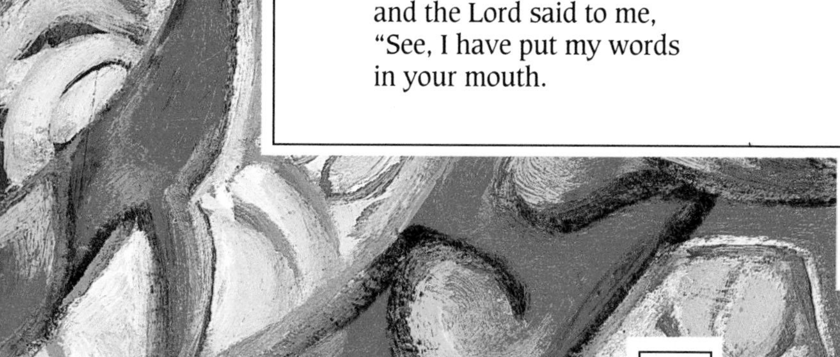

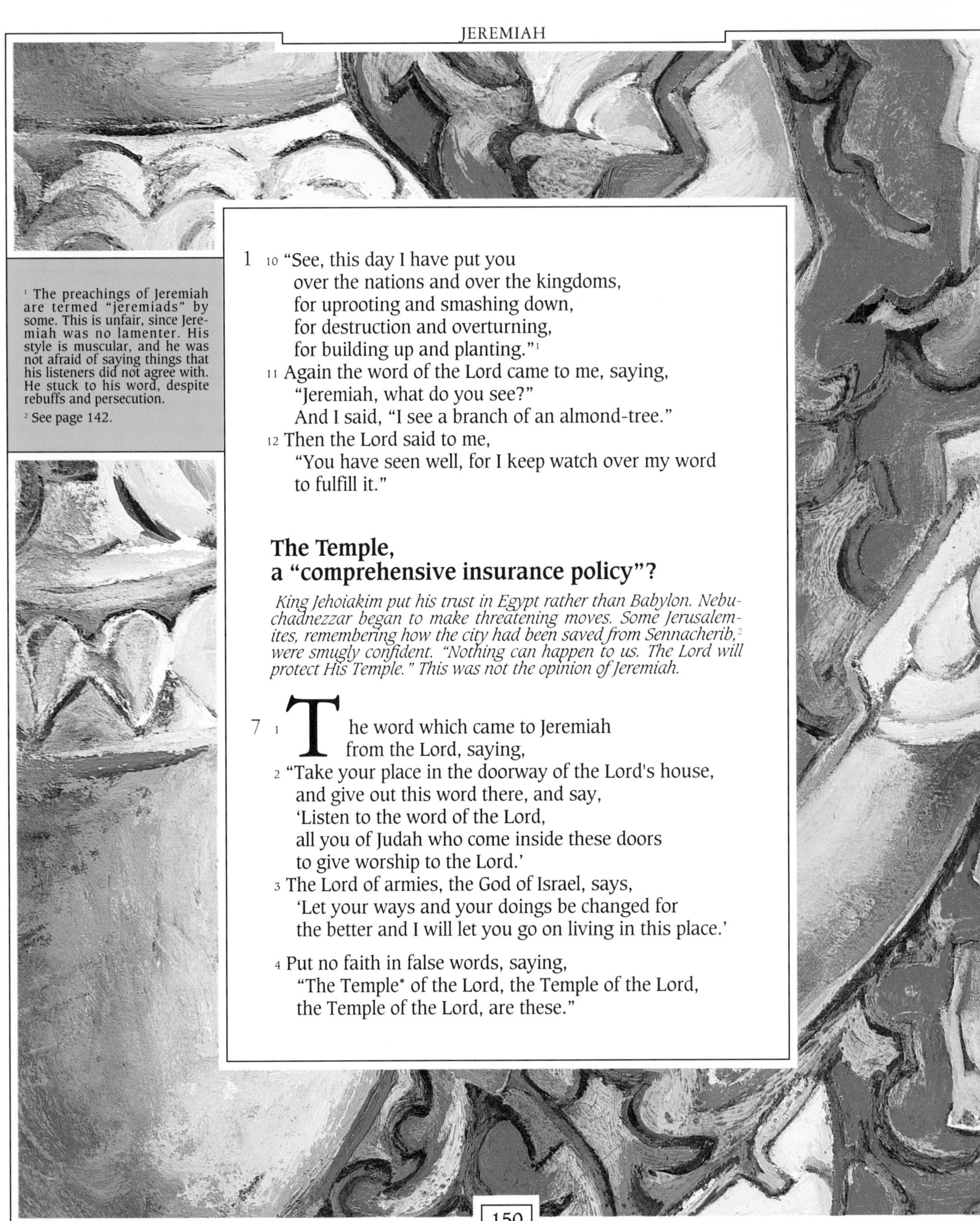

1 10 "See, this day I have put you
over the nations and over the kingdoms,
for uprooting and smashing down,
for destruction and overturning,
for building up and planting."[1]
11 Again the word of the Lord came to me, saying,
"Jeremiah, what do you see?"
And I said, "I see a branch of an almond-tree."
12 Then the Lord said to me,
"You have seen well, for I keep watch over my word
to fulfill it."

The Temple, a "comprehensive insurance policy"?

King Jehoiakim put his trust in Egypt rather than Babylon. Nebuchadnezzar began to make threatening moves. Some Jerusalemites, remembering how the city had been saved from Sennacherib,[2] were smugly confident. "Nothing can happen to us. The Lord will protect His Temple." This was not the opinion of Jeremiah.

7 1 The word which came to Jeremiah
from the Lord, saying,
2 "Take your place in the doorway of the Lord's house,
and give out this word there, and say,
'Listen to the word of the Lord,
all you of Judah who come inside these doors
to give worship to the Lord.'
3 The Lord of armies, the God of Israel, says,
'Let your ways and your doings be changed for
the better and I will let you go on living in this place.'

4 Put no faith in false words, saying,
"The Temple* of the Lord, the Temple of the Lord,
the Temple of the Lord, are these."

[1] The preachings of Jeremiah are termed "jeremiads" by some. This is unfair, since Jeremiah was no lamenter. His style is muscular, and he was not afraid of saying things that his listeners did not agree with. He stuck to his word, despite rebuffs and persecution.

[2] See page 142.

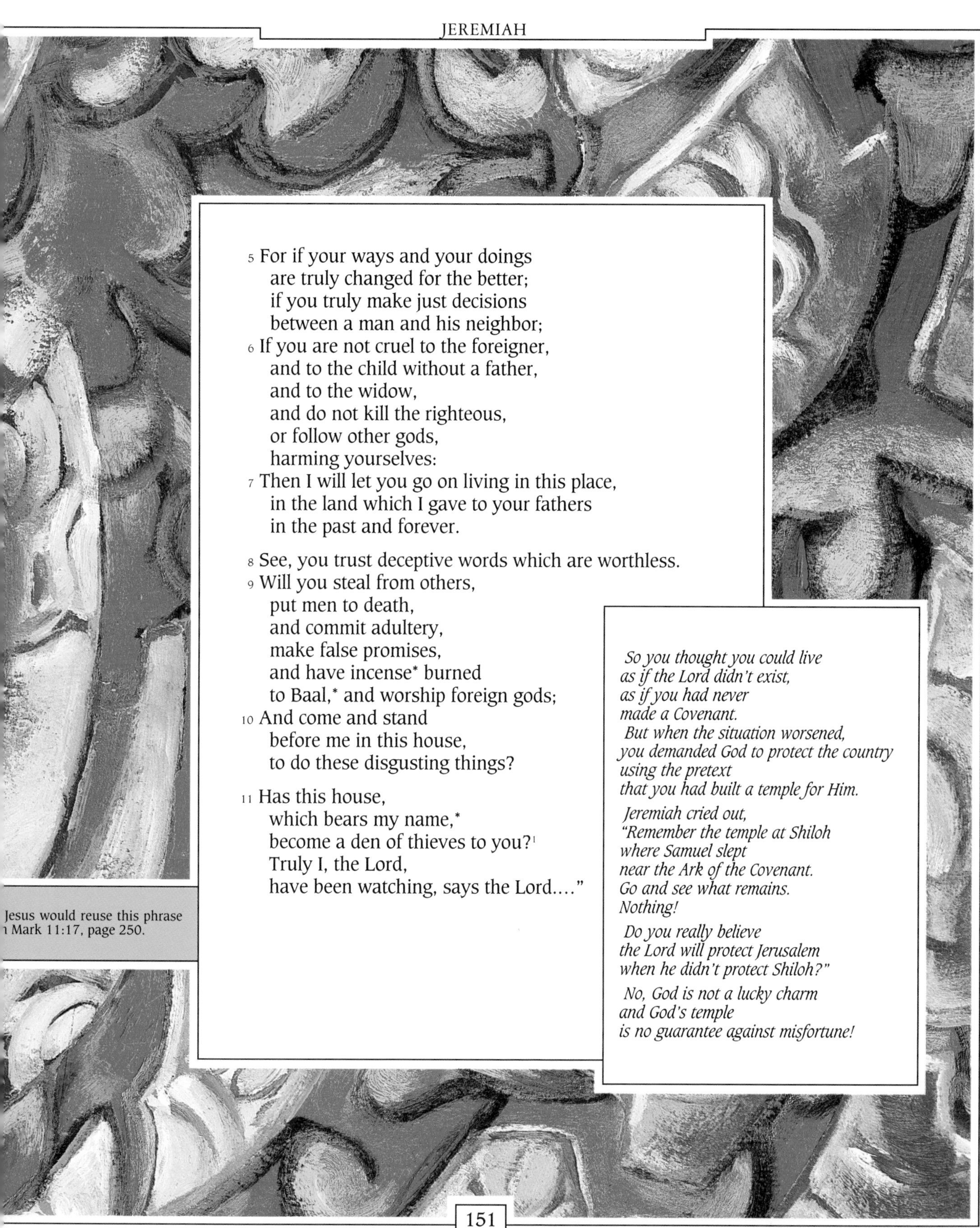

5 For if your ways and your doings
are truly changed for the better;
if you truly make just decisions
between a man and his neighbor;
6 If you are not cruel to the foreigner,
and to the child without a father,
and to the widow,
and do not kill the righteous,
or follow other gods,
harming yourselves:
7 Then I will let you go on living in this place,
in the land which I gave to your fathers
in the past and forever.

8 See, you trust deceptive words which are worthless.
9 Will you steal from others,
put men to death,
and commit adultery,
make false promises,
and have incense* burned
to Baal,* and worship foreign gods;
10 And come and stand
before me in this house,
to do these disgusting things?

11 Has this house,
which bears my name,*
become a den of thieves to you?[1]
Truly I, the Lord,
have been watching, says the Lord...."

So you thought you could live
as if the Lord didn't exist,
as if you had never
made a Covenant.
But when the situation worsened,
you demanded God to protect the country
using the pretext
that you had built a temple for Him.

Jeremiah cried out,
"Remember the temple at Shiloh
where Samuel slept
near the Ark of the Covenant.
Go and see what remains.
Nothing!

Do you really believe
the Lord will protect Jerusalem
when he didn't protect Shiloh?"

No, God is not a lucky charm
and God's temple
is no guarantee against misfortune!

[1] Jesus would reuse this phrase
in Mark 11:17, page 250.

The reshaped pot

18 1 The word which came to Jeremiah
from the Lord, saying,
2 "Go down to the potter's house,
and there I will lgive you a message."

3 Then I went down to the potter's house,
where he was doing his work on the stones.
4 And when the pot, which he was forming out of clay,
was damaged in his hands,
he made it again into another pot,
reshaping it as it seemed right to the potter.
5 Then the Lord spoke to me, saying,

6 "O Israel, am I not able to do with you
as this potter does?" says the Lord.
"See, like clay in the potter's hand
are you in my hands, O Israel.

7 Whenever I say anything about uprooting a nation or a
kingdom, smashing it and sending destruction on it;
8 If, at that time, that nation
repents* from its evil,*
the destruction I had planned for them will be changed.

9 And whenever I say anything
about building up a nation
or a kingdom, and planting it;
10 If, in that time,
it does evil in my eyes,
disobeying my orders,
then my blessing,
which I said I would bring,
will be changed."

CAN GOD REJECT THE PEOPLE HE HAS CHOSEN?

When a pot is malformed, the potter can make another one. The Lord, if He so wished, could reject Israel and fashion another "God's people" which would satisfy Him.

Lord, no matter
how hard you try,
your people refuse like resistant
clay to be molded
by your fatherly hands.

What if you grow weary of it?
What if you looked elsewhere
for hearts that are more open to your Word?

Faithful God,
do not abandon us.
Patiently pick up your work again.
Recreate us in your image.

OD'S ANGER

ike most of the prophets, eremiah spoke harshly. He ttered threats, since he was evealing God's anger* at the ins of the people of the ovenant.

he anger of God bears only remote resemblance to uman anger. God is not nraged by mankind's efusal. He is "upset" ecause He loves mankind nd knows that, when it urns away from Him, it is eading for its doom. This is vhy He shouts so loudly.

e never made the cruel emands that other religions ictated as being the gods' vishes. He wanted nothing ut the happiness of His eople. Was it so terribly ard to trust in Him?

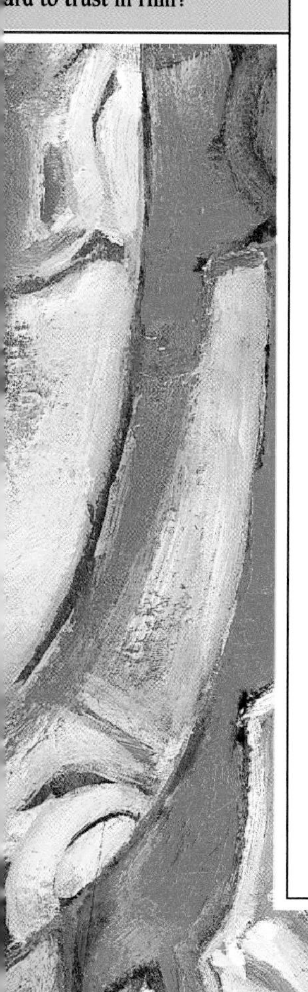

The broken jar

19 1 This is what the Lord says: "Go and buy
a clay jar, and take with you some of the el-
2 ders* of the people and of the priests. | Go to the Valley
of Ben Hinnom,[1] near the entrance of the Potsherd
Gate, and there announce in a loud voice my message:
3 | 'Listen to the word of the Lord, O kings of Judah and
people of Jerusalem. The Lord of armies, the God of Israel, has said, I will bring disaster to this place which
will be frightening news to anyone listening.

4 Because they have forsaken me, and made this place a
place of foreign gods, burning sacrifices in it to them,
of whom they and their fathers and the kings of Judah
did not know. They have made this place full of the
5 blood of those who have done no wrong; | and they
have put up the high places of the Baal,* burning their
sons in the fire; a thing which was not ordered by me,
6 and it was never in my mind.[2] | For this reason, a time
is coming, says the Lord, when this place will no longer be named Topheth, or, the Valley of Ben Hinnom,
but, the Valley of Death.

10 "Then let the potter's jar be broken before the eyes of
11 the men who go with you. | Say to them, 'This is what
the Lord Almighty has said: Even so will this people
and this town be destroyed by me, as a potter's jar is
broken and may not be put together again....'"

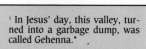

[1] In Jesus' day, this valley, turned into a garbage dump, was called Gehenna.*

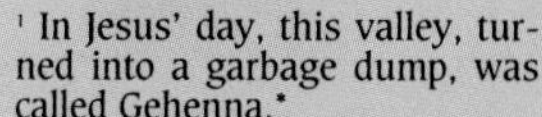

[2] It is worth rereading the account of Abraham's great ordeal (page 46) in the light of this unequivocal statement, "It is something I did not command or mention, nor did it enter My mind."

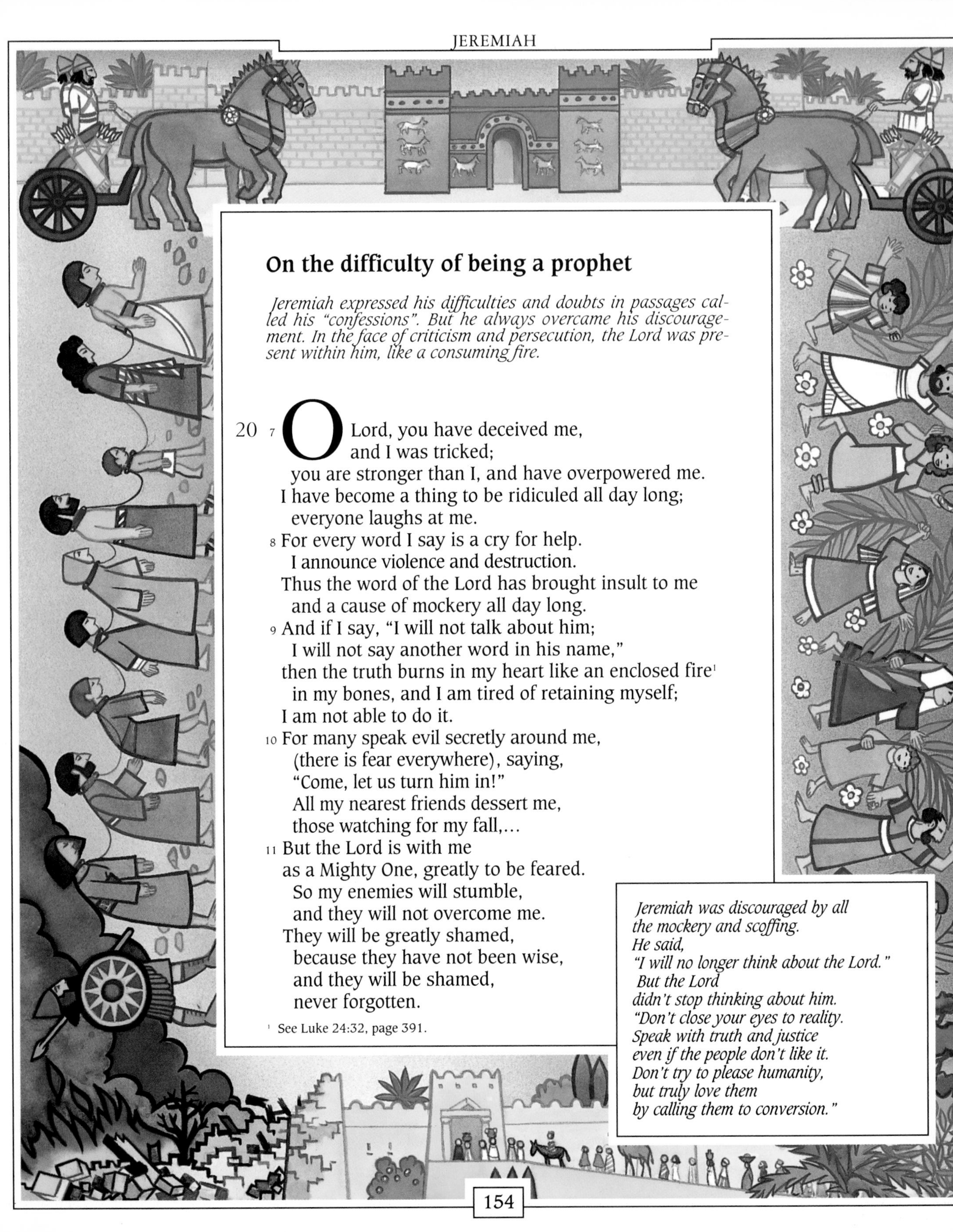

On the difficulty of being a prophet

Jeremiah expressed his difficulties and doubts in passages called his "confessions". But he always overcame his discouragement. In the face of criticism and persecution, the Lord was present within him, like a consuming fire.

20 7 O Lord, you have deceived me,
and I was tricked;
you are stronger than I, and have overpowered me.
I have become a thing to be ridiculed all day long;
everyone laughs at me.
8 For every word I say is a cry for help.
I announce violence and destruction.
Thus the word of the Lord has brought insult to me
and a cause of mockery all day long.
9 And if I say, "I will not talk about him;
I will not say another word in his name,"
then the truth burns in my heart like an enclosed fire[1]
in my bones, and I am tired of retaining myself;
I am not able to do it.
10 For many speak evil secretly around me,
(there is fear everywhere), saying,
"Come, let us turn him in!"
All my nearest friends dessert me,
those watching for my fall,...
11 But the Lord is with me
as a Mighty One, greatly to be feared.
So my enemies will stumble,
and they will not overcome me.
They will be greatly shamed,
because they have not been wise,
and they will be shamed,
never forgotten.

[1] See Luke 24:32, page 391.

Jeremiah was discouraged by all
the mockery and scoffing.
He said,
"I will no longer think about the Lord."
But the Lord
didn't stop thinking about him.
"Don't close your eyes to reality.
Speak with truth and justice
even if the people don't like it.
Don't try to please humanity,
but truly love them
by calling them to conversion."

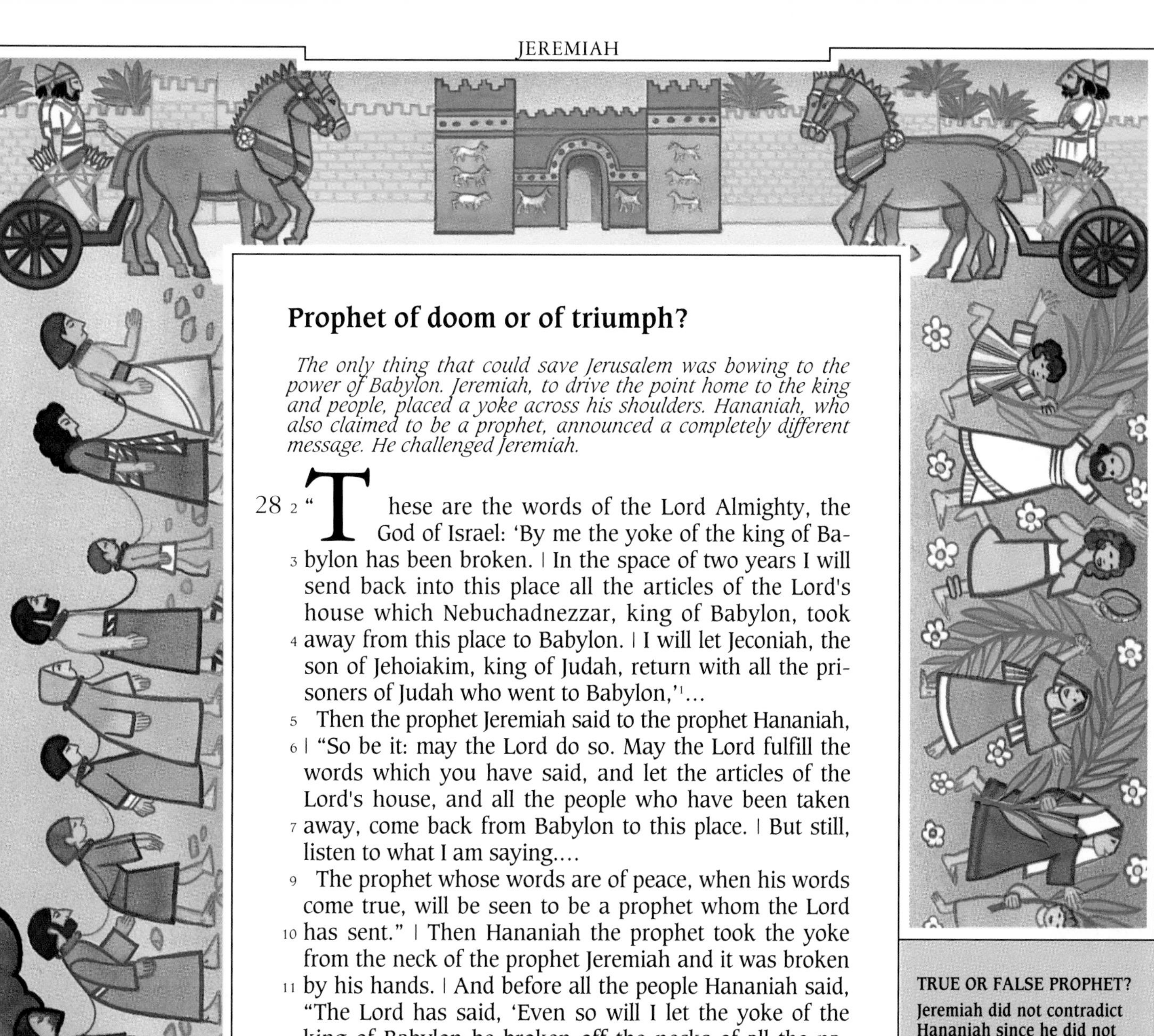

Prophet of doom or of triumph?

The only thing that could save Jerusalem was bowing to the power of Babylon. Jeremiah, to drive the point home to the king and people, placed a yoke across his shoulders. Hananiah, who also claimed to be a prophet, announced a completely different message. He challenged Jeremiah.

28 2 "These are the words of the Lord Almighty, the
God of Israel: 'By me the yoke of the king of Ba-
3 bylon has been broken. | In the space of two years I will
send back into this place all the articles of the Lord's
house which Nebuchadnezzar, king of Babylon, took
4 away from this place to Babylon. | I will let Jeconiah, the
son of Jehoiakim, king of Judah, return with all the prisoners of Judah who went to Babylon,'[1]...
5 Then the prophet Jeremiah said to the prophet Hananiah,
6 | "So be it: may the Lord do so. May the Lord fulfill the
words which you have said, and let the articles of the
Lord's house, and all the people who have been taken
7 away, come back from Babylon to this place. | But still,
listen to what I am saying....
9 The prophet whose words are of peace, when his words
come true, will be seen to be a prophet whom the Lord
10 has sent." | Then Hananiah the prophet took the yoke
from the neck of the prophet Jeremiah and it was broken
11 by his hands. | And before all the people Hananiah said,
"The Lord has said, 'Even so will I let the yoke of the
king of Babylon be broken off the necks of all the nations in the space of two years.'" Then the prophet Jeremiah went away.

The Lord let Jeremiah know that Hananiah was a false prophet. The yoke of Nebuchadnezzar would not be broken. Quite the contrary, it would weigh heavier than before.

[1] See page 148.

TRUE OR FALSE PROPHET?

Jeremiah did not contradict Hananiah since he did not have anything to say for the moment.

Hananiah was announcing good news. Why should Jeremiah have only bad news to offer? And what if he was wrong? The Lord comforted him. "Good news may be only lies. They are reassuring, but when misfortune strikes nobody is ready to cope with it. You must teach the people to face up squarely to the fate awaiting it. You must banish the people's illusions so that it will not be submerged by despair when the tempest arrives."

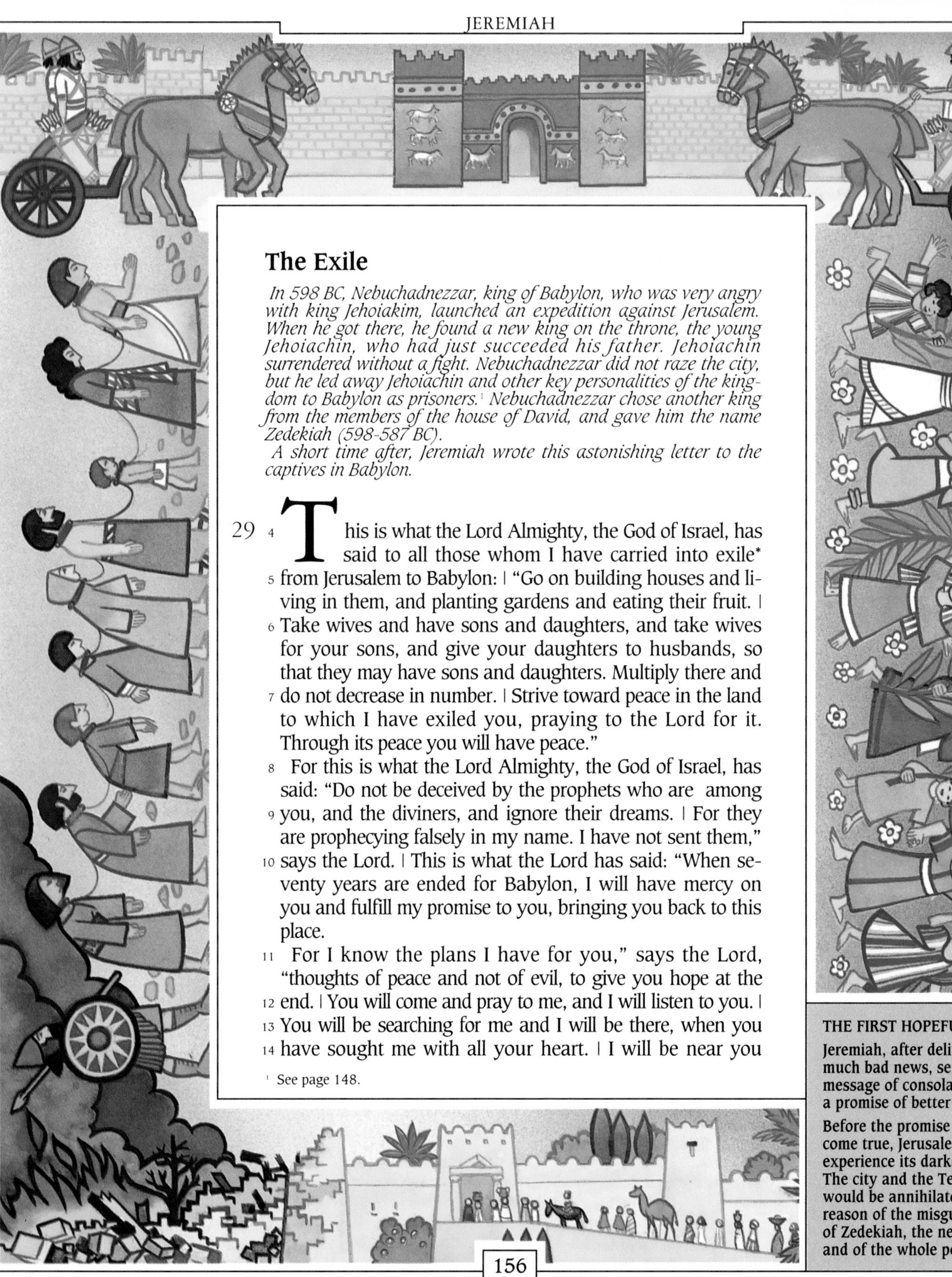

The Exile

In 598 BC, Nebuchadnezzar, king of Babylon, who was very angry with king Jehoiakim, launched an expedition against Jerusalem. When he got there, he found a new king on the throne, the young Jehoiachin, who had just succeeded his father. Jehoiachin surrendered without a fight. Nebuchadnezzar did not raze the city, but he led away Jehoiachin and other key personalities of the kingdom to Babylon as prisoners.[1] *Nebuchadnezzar chose another king from the members of the house of David, and gave him the name Zedekiah (598-587 BC).*

A short time after, Jeremiah wrote this astonishing letter to the captives in Babylon.

29 4 This is what the Lord Almighty, the God of Israel, has
said to all those whom I have carried into exile*
5 from Jerusalem to Babylon: | "Go on building houses and li-
ving in them, and planting gardens and eating their fruit. |
6 Take wives and have sons and daughters, and take wives
for your sons, and give your daughters to husbands, so
that they may have sons and daughters. Multiply there and
7 do not decrease in number. | Strive toward peace in the land
to which I have exiled you, praying to the Lord for it.
Through its peace you will have peace."
8 For this is what the Lord Almighty, the God of Israel, has
said: "Do not be deceived by the prophets who are among
9 you, and the diviners, and ignore their dreams. | For they
are prophecying falsely in my name. I have not sent them,"
10 says the Lord. | This is what the Lord has said: "When se-
venty years are ended for Babylon, I will have mercy on
you and fulfill my promise to you, bringing you back to this
place.
11 For I know the plans I have for you," says the Lord,
"thoughts of peace and not of evil, to give you hope at the
12 end. | You will come and pray to me, and I will listen to you. |
13 You will be searching for me and I will be there, when you
14 have sought me with all your heart. | I will be near you

[1] See page 148.

THE FIRST HOPEFUL NEWS

Jeremiah, after delivering so much bad news, sent a message of consolation and a promise of better things.

Before the promise could come true, Jerusalem would experience its darkest hour. The city and the Temple would be annihilated by reason of the misguidedness of Zedekiah, the new king, and of the whole people.

THE END OF THE KINGDOM OF JERUSALEM

Zedekiah ignored the advice of Jeremiah. Although placed upon the throne by Nebuchadnezzar, he persisted in trying to ally himself with Egypt against Babylon. Nebuchadnezzar laid siege to Jerusalem. The outcome was horrifying — the city was sacked and the Temple demolished. Zedekiah's eyes were put out after he had witnessed the execution of all his sons. He was led off in chains to Babylon.

All of God's promises seemed to have come to nothing. The people were torn from the Promised Land and deported to Babylon. There were no more kings. The lineage of David was exterminated, as though the promise made to Nathan (see 2 Samuel 7:11-16, page 108) had never existed. The Temple, where the Covenant had been celebrated, was gone. The Ark* itself was lost forever in the disaster.

In the midst of these ruins, when all hope seemed to be doomed, Jeremiah suddenly opened up new vistas.

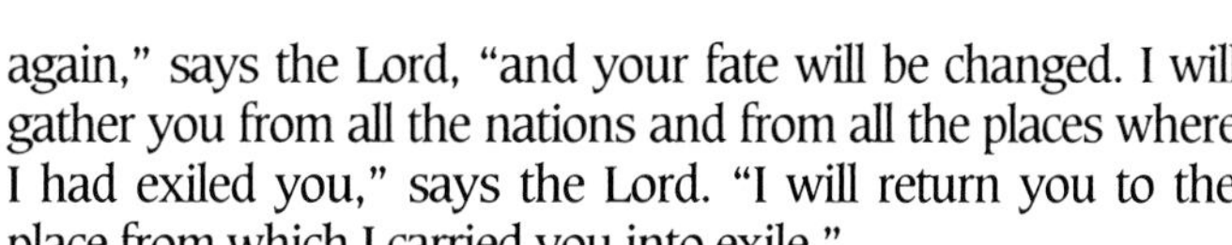

again," says the Lord, "and your fate will be changed. I will gather you from all the nations and from all the places where I had exiled you," says the Lord. "I will return you to the place from which I carried you into exile."

The new Covenant

31 31 "See, the days are coming," says the Lord, "when I
will make a new Covenant with the people of Israel
32 and with the people of Judah,[1] | not like the Covenant
which I made with their fathers, on the day when I took
them by the hand to be their guide out of the land of
Egypt. This Covenant was broken by them, and I gave
them up," says the Lord.
33 "But this is the Covenant which I will make with the
people of Israel since that time," says the Lord. "I will put
my law in their minds, writing it in their hearts. I will be
34 their God, and they will be my people. | And no longer will
they their neighbors and or a man his brother, saying,
'Know the Lord,' for they will all know me, from the least
of them to the greatest," says the Lord. "I
will forgive for their wickedness, and I
will forget their sin* forever."

[1] The disciples of Jeremiah who compiled his prophecies in this book were less interested than we are by the order of events. The promise of Jeremiah was almost certainly made after the destruction of Jerusalem (587 BC), whereas the following chapters — particularly the account of the purchase of the field at Anathoth — refer to an earlier time.

The people of the future

32 8 "So my cousin Hanamel came to
me ... in the courtyard of the
guard, saying, 'Buy my property which

The Ark of the Covenant and the tablets of the Testimony which were the visible signs of the Covenant that God had made with His people have disappeared forever. What sadness and desolation!

"No," said Jeremiah speaking in the name of the Lord.
"My law which was written on stone has yet to penetrate the hearts of humanity.
Some have quoted my law,
but have hearts of stone.
Now that the tablets are broken,
I'm going to write my law in their hearts.
This will be a new Covenant.
The people will love my Word
and put it into practice."

A STRANGE DEED OF SALE

Jerusalem was under siege and not an atom of hope seemed to be left. One of Jeremiah's cousins offered to sell him a field at Anathoth. Occupied as it was by the Babylonian troops, the field was worthless. Yet Jeremiah bought it without haggling over the price. He did this publicly, so signalling that all was not lost. There would be a return to this land in Israel and the devastated fields would be tilled again. God, ever faithful, would renew the Covenant with His people.

is in Anathoth in the land of Benjamin, for you have the
right to inherit it. Buy it for yourself. I knew that this was
the word of the Lord.'
9 So I bought the property in Anathoth from Hanamel,
the son of my father's brother, and gave him the money,
10 seventeen shekels of silver. | I put it in writing, stamping
it with my stamp. In front of witnesses, I put the money
12 into the scales.... | Then I gave the deed to Baruch, the
son of Neriah, the son of Mahseiah, in the presence of
Hanamel, the son of my father's brother, and of the witnesses who hadsigned the deed, and before all the Jews
13 who were seated in the courtyard. | I gave orders to Ba-
14 ruch in their presence, saying, | 'This is what the Lord Al-
mighty, the God of Israel, has said: Take this deed, the
proof of the purchase, the one which is rolled up and
stamped, and the one which is open. Put them in a clay
15 jar so that they may endure a long time. | For the Lord
Almighty, the God of Israel, has said, There will again be
trading in houses and fields and vineyards in this land.'
16 Now after I had given the deed to Baruch, the son of
24 Neriah, I prayed to the Lord, saying.... | "See, they have
built seige ramps around the town to take it. The town is
being handed over to the Chaldaeans who are fighting
against it, because of the sword, famine qnd plague.
What you predicted has taken place, and truly you see it.
25 | You have said to me, 'Give the money to buy a property,
and have the transaction witnessed, even though the
town is handed over to the Chaldaeans.'"
26 And the word of the Lord came to Jeremiah, saying, |
27 "See, I am the Lord, the God of all mankihd. Is there any-
28 thing so difficult that I am unable to do it? | So this is what
the Lord has said: See, I am giving this town into the
hands of the Chaldaeans and into the hands of Nebucha-
37 drezzar, the king of Babylon, and he will take it.... | See,

[1] See Genesis 18:14, page 41, and Luke 1:37, page 300.

PROPHETIC ACTS

Jeremiah preached not only by words but also by deeds which struck the imagination of his fellow-citizens: wearing a yoke on his neck (page 155) or buying a field under enemy rule (see at left). Prophetic acts of this kind were frequent in the preaching of Ezekiel. Jesus, too, would perform a few, like expelling the merchants from the Temple (page 336) or shrivelling the fig-tree (page 288).

GOD'S STEADFASTNESS

This utterance of Jeremiah, placed at the end of the book, is a rephrasing of the beautiful promise in chapter 31. It may be read as the farewell message of the old prophet who now knew that, whatever happened, God would never repudiate his Covenant with humankind.

THE PROPHET'S LAST YEARS

Nebuchadnezzar, after dethroning Zedekiah, appointed a governor over Judah. He was Gedaliah, son of Shaphan, the former secretary to Josiah (see page 148). Gedaliah paid close attention to the advice of Jeremiah. He was willing, in order to spare the people further misfortune, to co-operate uncomplainingly with the Babylonians. This attitude so infuriated the supporters of Egypt that they murdered him. The officers of Gedaliah, fearing the wrath of Nebuchadnezzar, fled in the direction of Egypt, bearing Jeremiah off with them.

the people will be dispersed. But I will gather them together from all the countries where I have exiled them in my
wrath and in my furious anger.* I will let them return to
38 this place where they may rest safely. | And they will be
39 my people, and I will be their God. | I will give them one
heart and one action, so that they may worship me forever,
40 for their own good and the good of their children. | And I
will make an eternal Covenant with them...."

The captivity will end

50 4 "In those days and in that time," says the Lord, "the
children of Israel will come, they and the children of
Judah together; they will go on their way weeping and
praying to the Lord their God.
5 They will be asking about the way to Zion,* with their
faces turned in its direction, saying, 'Come, and be united
to the Lord in an eternal Covenant which will be remembered forever.'
6 My people have been wandering sheep: their keepers
have led them astray, turning them loose on the mountains. They have wandered from mountain to hill, forgetting their resting place.[1]
19 And I will make Israel return to his own
pasture, and he will graze on Carmel and
Bashan,[2] and have his desire in full measure on the hills of Ephraim and in Gilead.
20 In those days and in that time, says the
Lord, when the guilt of Israel is sought,
there will be nothing; and in Judah no sins
will be seen, for I will forgive those whom
I will keep safe."

Jeremiah, you were
a prophet of doom
during a period when everyone
felt secure
in their guarded city.
Now you are a prophet of happiness
in a devastated city
with an uncertain future.
The people didn't know how to listen
to your call to conversion.
In the future, will they know how to be
open to the power of God's forgiveness ?

[1] The shepherds who had led the people astray were the kings. Jeremiah foretold that God would Himself come and take care of His flock. He would be His people's good shepherd. This was something that Ezekiel (page 163) and Psalm 23 (page 214) would announce even more explicitly.

[2] The pastures of Bashan and Mount Carmel, in the North of Israel, are mentioned on pages 130 and 123 respectively.

EZEKIEL

Ezekiel was a priest in the Temple in Jerusalem. He was among the first wave of captives carried into exile with king Jehoiachin in 598 BC (see page 148).

He received his calling as prophet* in Babylon. God also made His word known in foreign lands (see Glossary, page 503). **Ezekiel began prophesying in Babylon while Jeremiah was prophesying in Jerusalem. Their messages were similar in tone, although their styles were different. Until the destruction of Jerusalem and the Temple, Ezekiel's preaching, like Jeremiah's, was very bleak. He spoke of God's great weariness with His people. There was a period during which Ezekiel fell silent, showing that God had nothing further to say and was breaking off the conversation with His people.**

After the downfall of the Temple in Jerusalem, Ezekiel regained his voice. His preaching became full of hope.

EZEKIEL, PROPHET
OF THE REBORN PEOPLE

The vision of God's glory

1 2 On the fifth day of the month, in the fifth year
3 of the exile of King Jehoiachin, | the word of the
Lord came to me, Ezekiel the priest, the son of Buzi, in
the land of the Chaldaeans by the river Chebar; and the
hand of the Lord was on me there.

4 And, looking, I saw a windstorm coming out of the
north, a great cloud with flames of fire coming after
one another, and a bright light shining round about it
and in the heart of it was something like glowing me-
5 tal. | In the heart of it were the forms of four living
beings. This was what they were like: They had the
6 form of a man, | and each one had four faces, and each
8 had four wings.... | They had the hands of a man under
their wings; the four of them had faces on their four
sides.

10 As for the form of their faces, they had the face of a man,
and the four of them had the face of a lion on the right
side, and the four of them had the face of an ox on the left
12 side, and the four of them had the face of an eagle.[1] | Every
one of them went straight forward. Wherever the spirit
was to go they went, without turning.

13 And between the living beings it was like burning
coals of fire, as if flames were going one after the other
between the living beings. The fire was bright, and out
of the fire went flashes of lightning.

22 And over the heads of the living beings there was the
form of an arch, looking like ice, stretched out over
their heads on high.

[1] See "Symbols of the Four Evangelists," page 502.

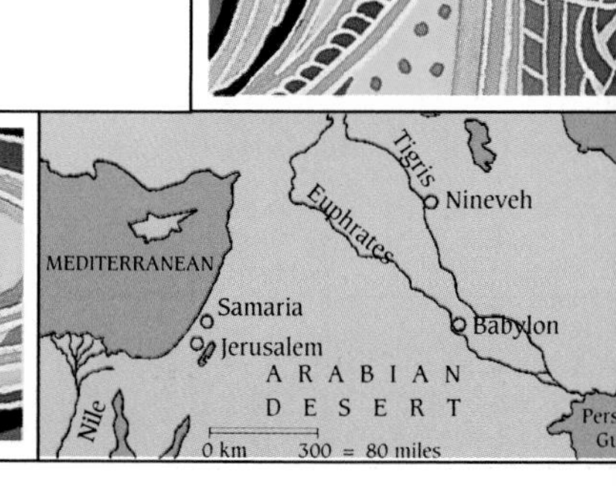

ANOTHER STYLE

Ezekiel's mission was like Isaiah's (Isaiah 6:1-8, page 137), but with important differences:

- The glory of God shines forth, not in the Temple in Jerusalem, but in Babylon. God is truly the God of the universe.
- Ezekiel's style is dense and his imagery astounding. There are all number of precious stones and metals, fire, smoke, rainbows, and wheels with eyes in them. Sometimes they perform impossible-seeming actions. The four living creatures bearing the throne of God all go straight ahead in four different directions!

These fantastic images ushered in a new kind of writer — the visionaries who would write the apocalypses* in the coming centuries. Ezekiel, despite his original style, was still very much a prophet. He wanted to help his fellow people to renew their Covenant with God through the events of history, whereas the apocalypses invited their readers to wait for the end of world.

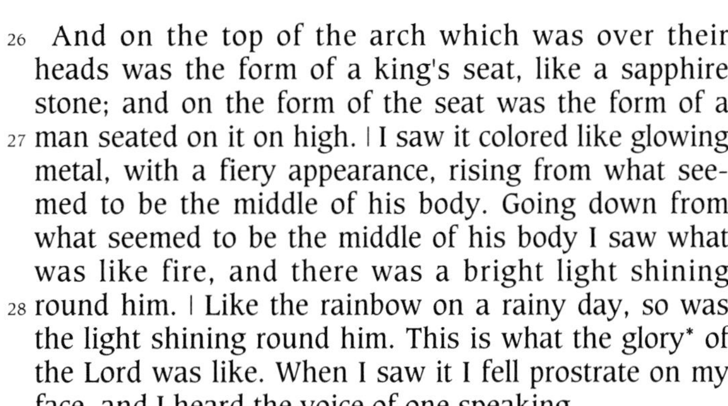

26 And on the top of the arch which was over their
heads was the form of a king's seat, like a sapphire
stone; and on the form of the seat was the form of a
27 man seated on it on high. | I saw it colored like glowing
metal, with a fiery appearance, rising from what seemed to be the middle of his body. Going down from
what seemed to be the middle of his body I saw what
was like fire, and there was a bright light shining
28 round him. | Like the rainbow on a rainy day, so was
the light shining round him. This is what the glory* of
the Lord was like. When I saw it I fell prostrate on my
face, and I heard the voice of one speaking.

Man does not live by bread alone

2 2 And at his words the spirit came into me and put me
3 on my feet; his voice came to my ears.[1] | He said to
me, "Son of man, I am sending you to the children of Israel,
to an uncontrolled nation which has rebelled against me:
they and their fathers have been sinners against me even to
8 this very day. | But you, son of man, listen to what I say to
you, and do not be rebellious like that people: let your
9 mouth be open and receive what I give you." | Looking, I
saw a hand stretched out to me, and I saw a scroll in it |
10 which he opened before me. It had writing on the front and
on the back; words of grief and sorrow and trouble were recorded.[2]
3 1 He said to me, "Son of man, eat this scroll for your food,
2 and go and speak my words to the children of Israel." | On
my opening my mouth, he made me eat the scroll as food
3-4 | ...and it was sweet as honey in my mouth. | He said to
me, "Son of man, go now to the children of Israel, and
speak my words to them."

[1] God does not speak to persons prostrate on the ground. He lifted Ezekiel to his feet and spoke to him as to a partner, not a slave.

[2] The words on which Ezekiel had to feed were full of doom and denunciation. This marked the first part of his ministry. Later, his words would emphasize hopefulness.

A PEOPLE OF RESPONSIBLE INDIVIDUALS

The people of Israel lived in groups — families, clans, tribes.* This style of living had bred a strong sense of solidarity among the members of these groups. Everyone was concerned by what happened to the others. The negative side of this was that not enough value was placed on personal responsibility. The family or the clan decided what work its members would do and whom they would marry.[1] When a member performed an act of valor or committed an evil deed, his whole family was covered in glory or in shame.

Ezekiel forcefully preached the notion of individual responsibility.

[1] See Jesus' relations with his family, as in Mark 3:20-55, page 240.

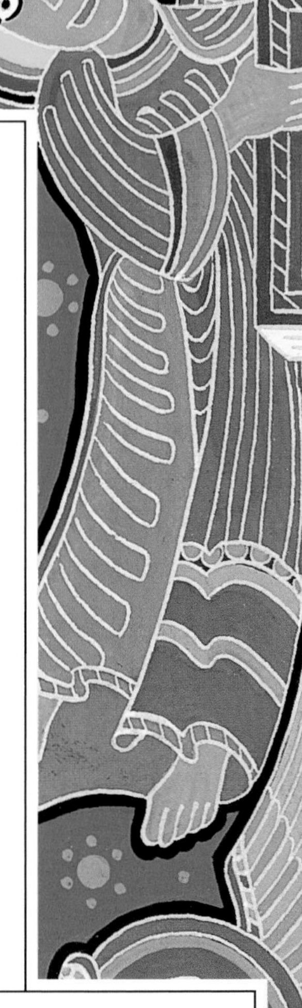

Every person is responsible for his actions

18 1 The word of the Lord came to me again, saying, |
2 "Why do you quote the proverb about the land
of Israel, 'The fathers have been tasting bitter grapes
3 and the children's teeth are on edge?' | As surely as I
live," says the Lord, "you will no longer quote this in
Israel."

20 The soul which does sin will be put to death. The son
will not be made responsible for the wickedness of the
father,[1] or the father for the wickedness of the son; the
righteousness* of the righteous* will be credited to
himself, and the wickedness of the wicked to himself.

21 "But if the wicked, turning away from all the sins
which he has done, keeps my rules and does what is
ordered and right, he will live; death will not be his
22 fate. | Not one of the sins which he has done will be
kept in memory against him: in the righteousness
23 which he has done he will have life. | Have I any plea-
sure in the death of the wicked? says the Lord. Am I
not pleased if he is turned from his way so that he may
24 have life?[2] | But when the righteous man, turning away
from his righteousness, does evil, like
all the disgusting things which the
evil man does, will he have life? Not
one of his righteous acts will be kept
in memory. In the wrong which he
has done and in his sin, death will
overtake him.

25 "But you say, 'The way of the Lord
is not just.' Listen, now, O children of
Israel; is my way not just? Are not
26 your ways unjust? | When the righ-

Lord,
do you think it's easy
to change behavior
when everything
is pressuring us to be
like everyone else?
Help us to hear your invitation!
Help us to support each other
and invent new paths to friendship,
respect and freedom.
You want us to be responsible.
Give us your Spirit so that we are capable
of changing our way of living.

[1] This was something that Nathan had not understood. This was why he viewed the death of David's child as a punishment for the parents' sins (see 2 Samuel 12:14, page 111). Even the apostles of Jesus did not understand. See John 9:1-2, page 349.

[2] See Deuteronomy 30:19, page 85.

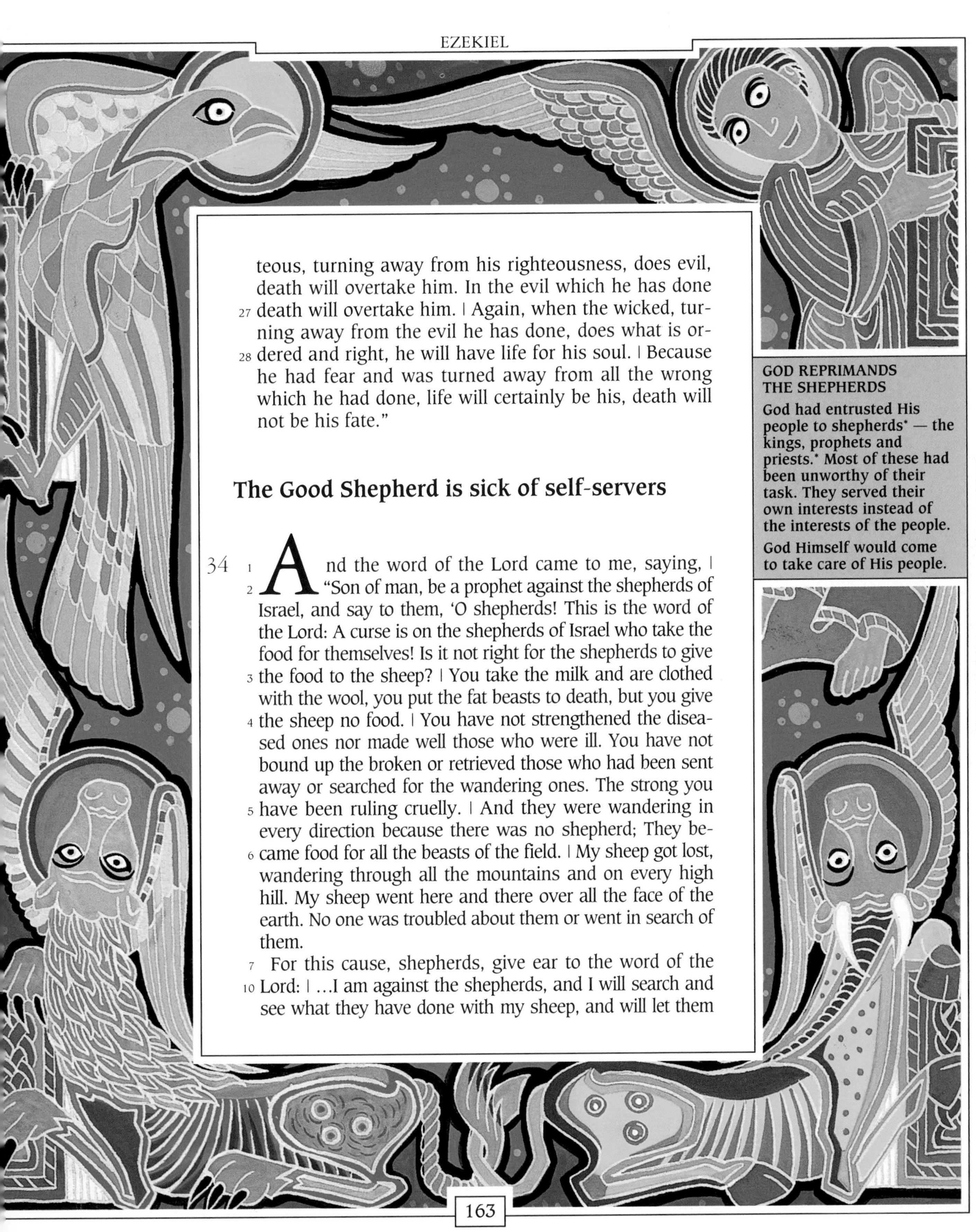

teous, turning away from his righteousness, does evil,
death will overtake him. In the evil which he has done
27 death will overtake him. | Again, when the wicked, tur-
ning away from the evil he has done, does what is or-
28 dered and right, he will have life for his soul. | Because
he had fear and was turned away from all the wrong
which he had done, life will certainly be his, death will
not be his fate."

The Good Shepherd is sick of self-servers

34 1 And the word of the Lord came to me, saying, |
2 "Son of man, be a prophet against the shepherds of
Israel, and say to them, 'O shepherds! This is the word of
the Lord: A curse is on the shepherds of Israel who take the
food for themselves! Is it not right for the shepherds to give
3 the food to the sheep? | You take the milk and are clothed
with the wool, you put the fat beasts to death, but you give
4 the sheep no food. | You have not strengthened the disea-
sed ones nor made well those who were ill. You have not
bound up the broken or retrieved those who had been sent
away or searched for the wandering ones. The strong you
5 have been ruling cruelly. | And they were wandering in
every direction because there was no shepherd; They be-
6 came food for all the beasts of the field. | My sheep got lost,
wandering through all the mountains and on every high
hill. My sheep went here and there over all the face of the
earth. No one was troubled about them or went in search of
them.

7 For this cause, shepherds, give ear to the word of the
10 Lord: | ...I am against the shepherds, and I will search and
see what they have done with my sheep, and will let them

GOD REPRIMANDS THE SHEPHERDS

God had entrusted His people to shepherds* — the kings, prophets and priests.* Most of these had been unworthy of their task. They served their own interests instead of the interests of the people.

God Himself would come to take care of His people.

[1] Jeremiah had already used the image of the good shepherd (see Jeremiah 50:6-19, page159). When Jesus said he was the Good Shepherd, after talking of hired sheep-minders (see John 10:11, page 352), he was portraying himself as God.

[2] The Holy Land,* which was where God revealed Himself, had been desecrated. The people, by putting up idols, had shown their refusal to know* the true God.

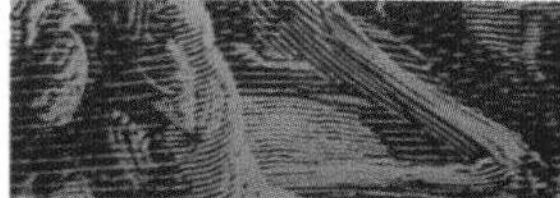

GOD'S "VENGEANCE"

No matter how often the people were unfaithful and rejected the Covenant, they did not wear God down. After periods of silence during which He seemed to lose interest in the fate of those who took His name in vain, He returned. He took the first step. He offered His forgiveness unconditionally. God's response to human infidelity was to be ever more loyal and to strengthen His Covenant with mankind.

be shepherds no longer; and the shepherds will no longer
get food for themselves. I will take my sheep out of their
11 mouths so that they may not be food for them. | For this is
what the Lord has said: Truly, I, even I, will go searching
12 and looking for my sheep. | As the shepherd goes looking
for his flock when he is among his wandering sheep, so I
will go looking for my sheep, and will get them safely out of
all the places where they have been sent
wandering in the day of clouds and dark-
16 ness.* | I will go in search of that which
had gone wandering from the way, and
will get back that which had been sent in
flight, and will put bands on that which
was broken, and give strength to that
which was ill. But the fat and the strong I
will give up to destruction. I will give
them for their food the punishment which is theirs by
right.'"

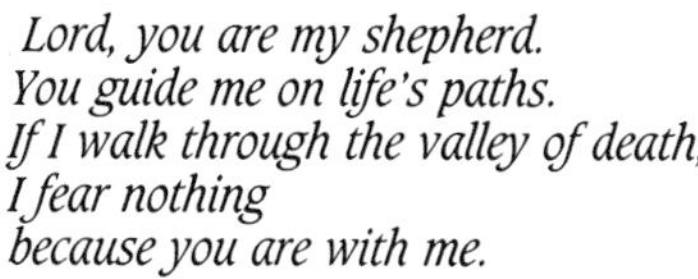

Lord, you are my shepherd.
You guide me on life's paths.
If I walk through the valley of death,
I fear nothing
because you are with me.

God renews His Covenant

36 16 Then the word of the Lord came to me, saying, |
17 "Son of man, when the children of Israel were
living in their land, they made it unclean by their way
18 and their acts... | So I let loose my wrath on them be-
cause of those whom they had violently put to death in
the land, and because they had defiled* it with their
19 idols:*[2] | I dispersed them among the nations to wander
through the countries. I was their judge, rewarding
them for their way and their acts.

20 And when they came among the nations, wherever
22 they went, they made my holy name* unclean,... | "For
this reason say to the children of Israel, 'This is what

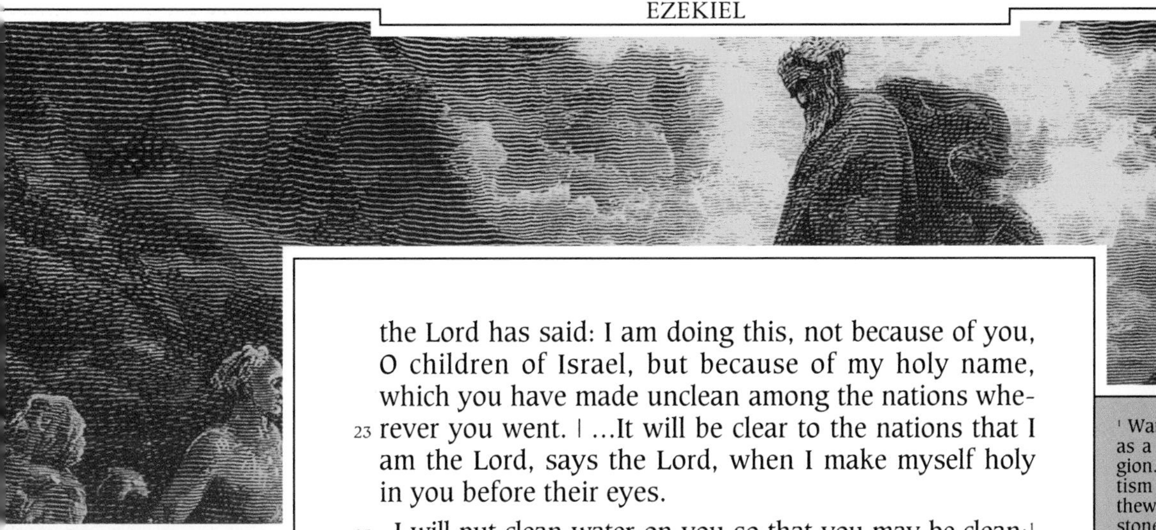

the Lord has said: I am doing this, not because of you,
O children of Israel, but because of my holy name,
which you have made unclean among the nations whe-
23 rever you went. | ...It will be clear to the nations that I
am the Lord, says the Lord, when I make myself holy
in you before their eyes.

25 I will put clean water on you so that you may be clean:[1]
from all your unclean ways and from all your images I
26 will make you clean. | I will give you a new heart and put
a new spirit in you. I will take away the heart of stone
from your flesh, and give you a heart of
27 flesh. | And I will put my spirit in you,
causing you to be guided by my rules,
and you will keep my laws* and do
28 them. | So that you may go on living in
the land which I gave to your fathers.
You will be my people, and I will be your
God.'"[2]

[1] Water would play a major role as a purifier in the Jewish religion. See, for example, the baptism of John the Baptist (Matthew 3:11-12, page 258) or the stone jars for ritual washing in Cana (John 2:6, page 336). See also "pure."*

[2] Reread verses 25-28 and compare them with Jeremiah 31:33-34, page 157.

Have pity on me, O God.
In your unfailing love, wash me of all my sins.
Create in me a pure heart.
Do not cast me from your presence.
Restore my joy of salvation.

God "resurrects" His people

37 1 The hand of the Lord had been on me, and he
took me out in the spirit of the Lord and put me
down in the middle of the valley; and it was full of
2 bones. | He made me go past them round about: and I
saw that there was a very great number of them on the
3 face of the wide valley, and they were very dry. | He
said to me, "Son of man, is it possible for these bones
to come to life?" And I answered, "It is for you to say,
4 O Lord." | And again he said to me, "Be a prophet to
these bones, and say to them, 'O you dry bones, give

CAN BONES LIVE AGAIN?

The people in exile were a "dead" people. They had no king. They had no Temple. They had no country. The ruins of Jerusalem were occupied by Babylonians. Edomites [1] had confiscated the property of the captives. Like so many other defeated races, the people would be assimilated by its conquerors and disappear.[2] They were like dry bones scattered in the desert sand. Had bones ever been known to live again? Likewise, the people scattered in a foreign land were doomed to ultimate destruction. "No," shouted Ezekiel, "the people which is seemingly dead will live again, for that is the will of God. To God nothing is impossible." (See Genesis 18:14, page 41, and Luke 1:37, page 300.)

[1] The Edomites* were the descendants of Edom (Esau), the brother of Jacob/Israel. At first settled in the far South of what is now Jordan, they later occupied the Negev around the town of Arad. They would later be called Idumeans.

[2] This is what happened to the ten tribes of the kingdom of Israel (Samaria). Those who were deported by the Assyrians (see page 134) did not return. They blended in with the populations among which they had been scattered. The members of the ten tribes who escaped this "death" were the ones who managed to flee to the kingdom of Jerusalem. From then on they shared their history with that of the tribe of Judah.

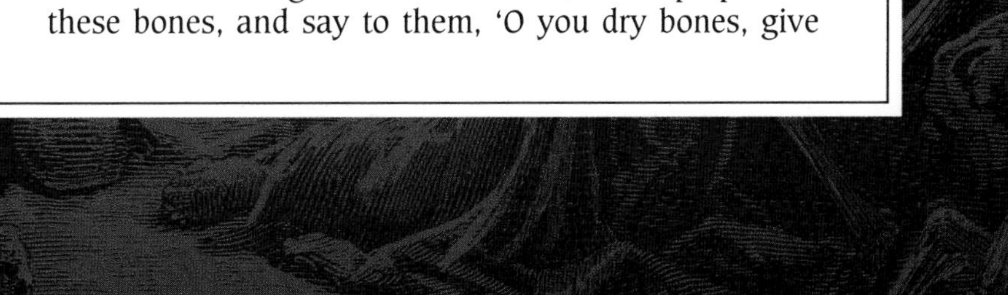

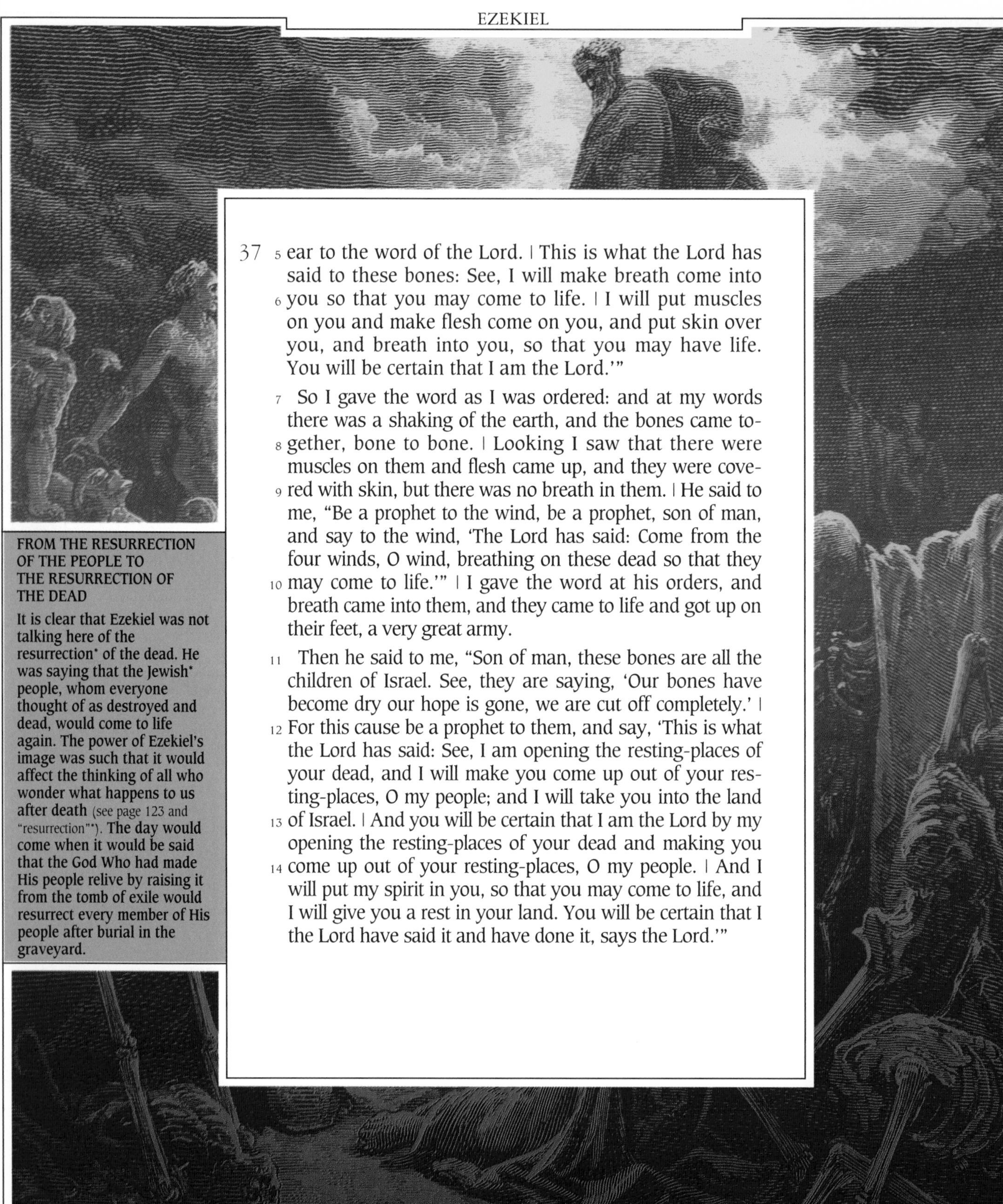

37 5 ear to the word of the Lord. | This is what the Lord has
said to these bones: See, I will make breath come into
6 you so that you may come to life. | I will put muscles
on you and make flesh come on you, and put skin over
you, and breath into you, so that you may have life.
You will be certain that I am the Lord.'"

7 So I gave the word as I was ordered: and at my words
there was a shaking of the earth, and the bones came to-
8 gether, bone to bone. | Looking I saw that there were
muscles on them and flesh came up, and they were cove-
9 red with skin, but there was no breath in them. | He said to
me, "Be a prophet to the wind, be a prophet, son of man,
and say to the wind, 'The Lord has said: Come from the
four winds, O wind, breathing on these dead so that they
10 may come to life.'" | I gave the word at his orders, and
breath came into them, and they came to life and got up on
their feet, a very great army.

11 Then he said to me, "Son of man, these bones are all the
children of Israel. See, they are saying, 'Our bones have
become dry our hope is gone, we are cut off completely.' |
12 For this cause be a prophet to them, and say, 'This is what
the Lord has said: See, I am opening the resting-places of
your dead, and I will make you come up out of your resting-places, O my people; and I will take you into the land
13 of Israel. | And you will be certain that I am the Lord by my
opening the resting-places of your dead and making you
14 come up out of your resting-places, O my people. | And I
will put my spirit in you, so that you may come to life, and
I will give you a rest in your land. You will be certain that I
the Lord have said it and have done it, says the Lord.'"

FROM THE RESURRECTION OF THE PEOPLE TO THE RESURRECTION OF THE DEAD

It is clear that Ezekiel was not talking here of the resurrection* of the dead. He was saying that the Jewish* people, whom everyone thought of as destroyed and dead, would come to life again. The power of Ezekiel's image was such that it would affect the thinking of all who wonder what happens to us after death (see page 123 and "resurrection"*). The day would come when it would be said that the God Who had made His people relive by raising it from the tomb of exile would resurrect every member of His people after burial in the graveyard.

'HE SECOND ISAIAH

'he Jews* had been living in
:xile in Babylon for thirty or
o years. In about 550 BC,
he king of a land bordering
abylon, King Cyrus of
'ersia, launched a war of
:onquest aimed at building a
/ast empire.

\ prophet, whose sayings*
were added to those of
saiah,[1] immediately foretold
he return of the people of
God to its lands. Cyrus, he
said, would be the liberator.
le even gave this heathen
:mperor the titles of
shepherd* and messiah.* Yet
ow could such a military
/ictor be the envoy of a
gentle God?

'he prophet's thinking
natured. He realized that
God could not bring freedom
hrough violence. More than
hat, God, in line with His
promises, would free all
nations along with Israel (see
Genesis 12:3, page 36).

This liberation by God would
be much greater than the
one performed by Cyrus.[2] It
would be the work of a
servant.

The prophet drew the
portrait of this "servant" in
'our poems which are called
he "Songs of the Servant."

See page143. This anonymous
prophet of the end of the captivity is generally admitted to be
he author of chapters 40-55 of
he Book of Isaiah. Other scho-
ars maintain that Isaiah himself wrote these chapters.

Cyrus, who defeated the king
of Babylon in 539 BC, allowed
all the peoples deported by Nebuchadnezzar to return to their
home countries.

SONGS OF A SERVANT

Trust in God the Creator

40 25 "Who then seems to you to be my equal?"
says the Holy One.
26 Let your eyes be lifted up on high, and see:
who has made these?
He who sends out their numbered army,
who has knowledge of all their names,
by whose great strength, because he is strong in power,
all of them are in their places.

27 Why do you say, O Jacob,
such words as these, O Israel,
"The Lord's eyes are not on my way,
and my God gives no attention to my cause?"

28 Have you no knowledge of it?
Has it not come to your ears?
The eternal God, the Lord,
the Maker of the ends of the earth,
is never feeble or tired;
there is no searching out of his wisdom.

29 He gives power to the feeble,
increasing the strength of him who has no force.

30 Even the young men will become feeble and tired, and
the best of them will come to the end of his strength;
31 But those who are waiting for the Lord
will have new strength;
they will get wings like eagles:
running, they will not be tired,
and walking, they will have no weariness.

GOD OF ALL

The author known as the second Isaiah (see page 143) left more than the Songs of the Servant. In many other places, he professes his faith in God the creator of the universe. The poem now set at the beginning of the Book of Genesis (page 20) was probably composed during the captivity. The prophet, in complete harmony with this poem, forcefully asserted that there was only one Creator.* This was why the salvation of all nations was so dear to His heart.

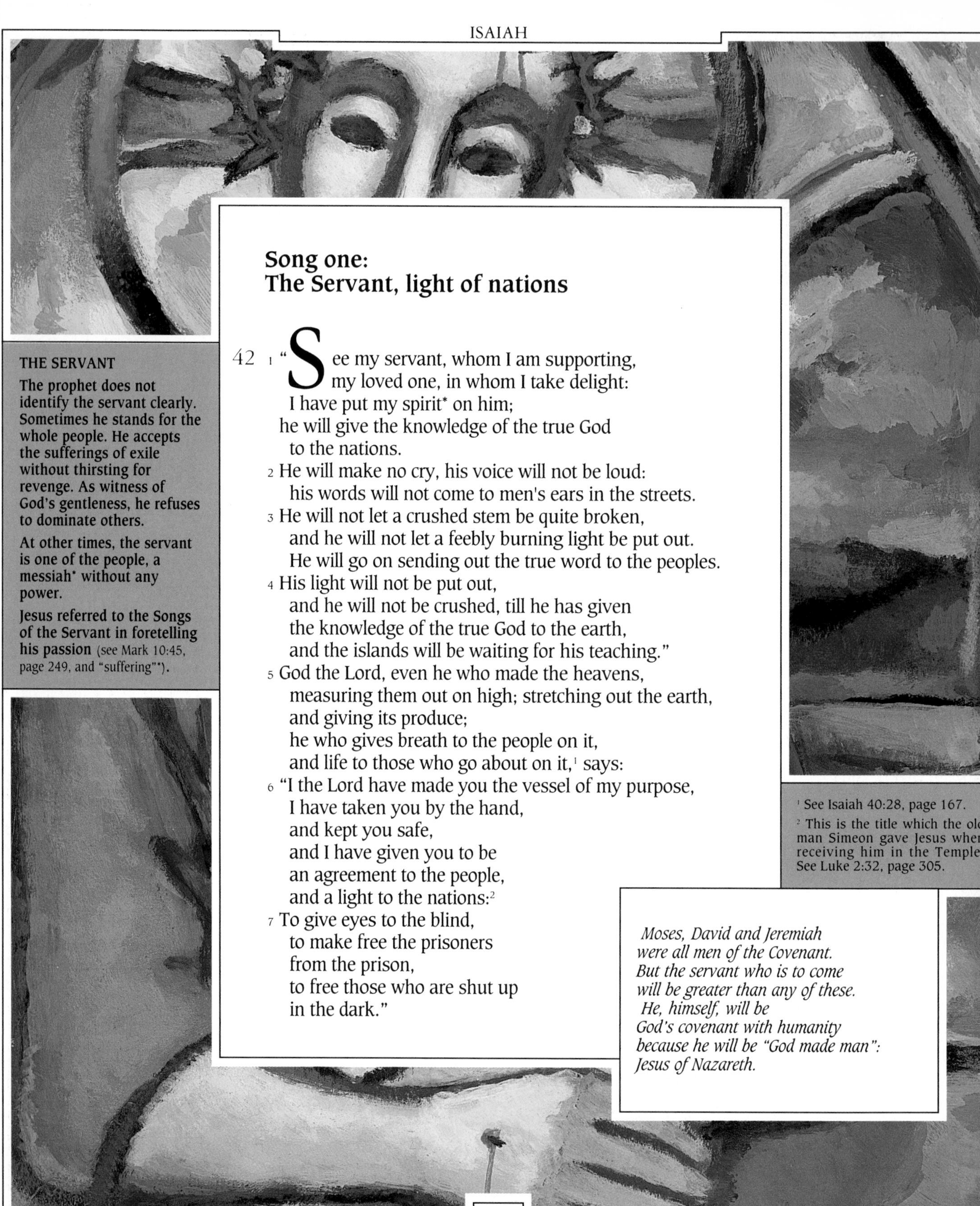

Song one: The Servant, light of nations

42 1 "See my servant, whom I am supporting,
my loved one, in whom I take delight:
I have put my spirit* on him;
he will give the knowledge of the true God
to the nations.
2 He will make no cry, his voice will not be loud:
his words will not come to men's ears in the streets.
3 He will not let a crushed stem be quite broken,
and he will not let a feebly burning light be put out.
He will go on sending out the true word to the peoples.
4 His light will not be put out,
and he will not be crushed, till he has given
the knowledge of the true God to the earth,
and the islands will be waiting for his teaching."
5 God the Lord, even he who made the heavens,
measuring them out on high; stretching out the earth,
and giving its produce;
he who gives breath to the people on it,
and life to those who go about on it,[1] says:
6 "I the Lord have made you the vessel of my purpose,
I have taken you by the hand,
and kept you safe,
and I have given you to be
an agreement to the people,
and a light to the nations:[2]
7 To give eyes to the blind,
to make free the prisoners
from the prison,
to free those who are shut up
in the dark."

THE SERVANT

The prophet does not identify the servant clearly. Sometimes he stands for the whole people. He accepts the sufferings of exile without thirsting for revenge. As witness of God's gentleness, he refuses to dominate others.

At other times, the servant is one of the people, a messiah* without any power.

Jesus referred to the Songs of the Servant in foretelling his passion (see Mark 10:45, page 249, and "suffering"*).

[1] See Isaiah 40:28, page 167.

[2] This is the title which the old man Simeon gave Jesus when receiving him in the Temple. See Luke 2:32, page 305.

Moses, David and Jeremiah were all men of the Covenant. But the servant who is to come will be greater than any of these. He, himself, will be God's covenant with humanity because he will be "God made man": Jesus of Nazareth.

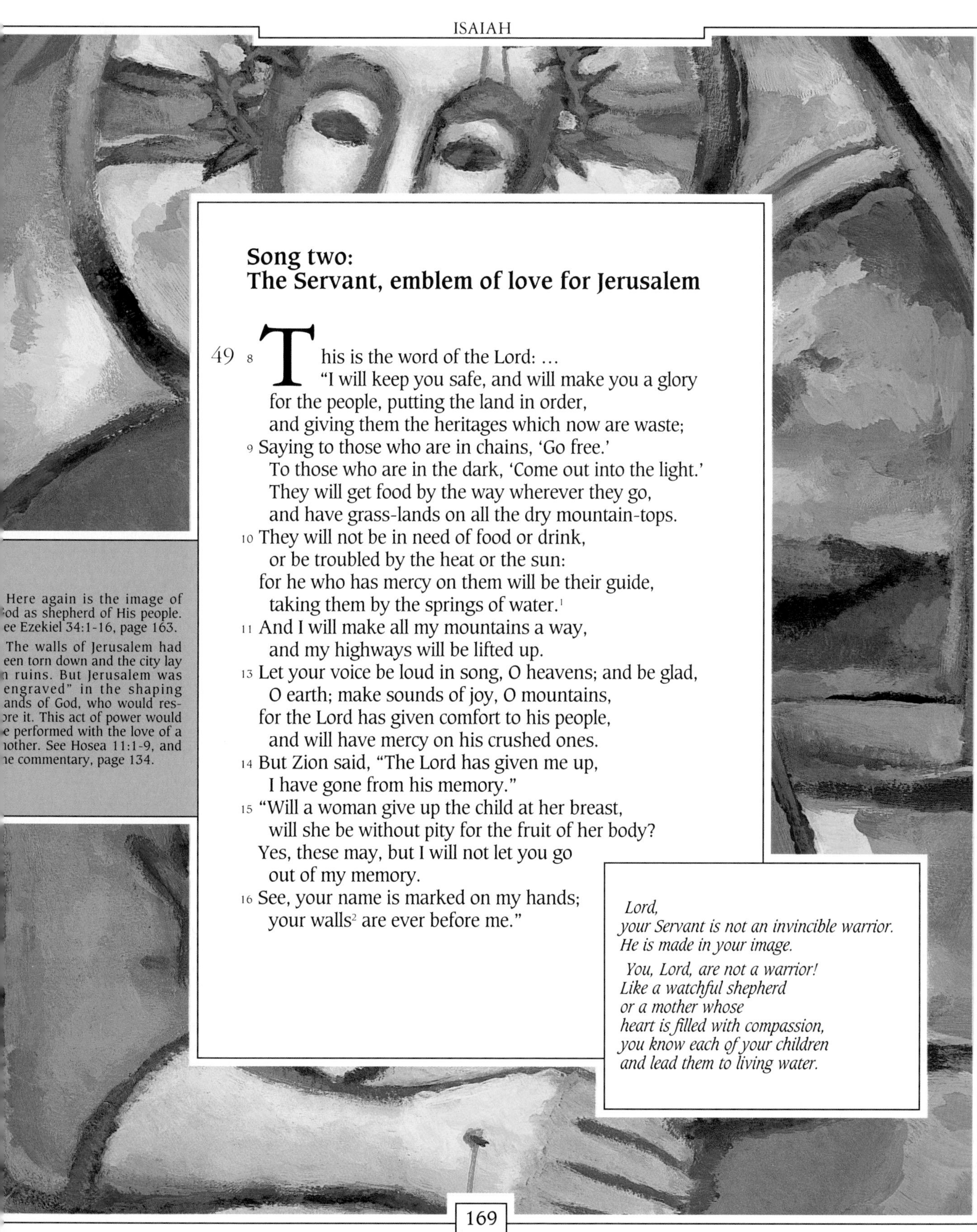

Song two: The Servant, emblem of love for Jerusalem

49 8 This is the word of the Lord: …
"I will keep you safe, and will make you a glory
for the people, putting the land in order,
and giving them the heritages which now are waste;
9 Saying to those who are in chains, 'Go free.'
To those who are in the dark, 'Come out into the light.'
They will get food by the way wherever they go,
and have grass-lands on all the dry mountain-tops.
10 They will not be in need of food or drink,
or be troubled by the heat or the sun:
for he who has mercy on them will be their guide,
taking them by the springs of water.[1]
11 And I will make all my mountains a way,
and my highways will be lifted up.
13 Let your voice be loud in song, O heavens; and be glad,
O earth; make sounds of joy, O mountains,
for the Lord has given comfort to his people,
and will have mercy on his crushed ones.
14 But Zion said, "The Lord has given me up,
I have gone from his memory."
15 "Will a woman give up the child at her breast,
will she be without pity for the fruit of her body?
Yes, these may, but I will not let you go
out of my memory.
16 See, your name is marked on my hands;
your walls[2] are ever before me."

Here again is the image of
od as shepherd of His people.
ee Ezekiel 34:1-16, page 163.

The walls of Jerusalem had
een torn down and the city lay
n ruins. But Jerusalem was
engraved" in the shaping
ands of God, who would res-
ore it. This act of power would
e performed with the love of a
nother. See Hosea 11:1-9, and
ne commentary, page 134.

Lord,
your Servant is not an invincible warrior.
He is made in your image.
You, Lord, are not a warrior!
Like a watchful shepherd
or a mother whose
heart is filled with compassion,
you know each of your children
and lead them to living water.

GENTLENESS AND STRENGTH

The Servant of God, because he would not cry out or break the bruised reed, was delivered into the hands of his enemies.

Since they did not want to hear his message, they decided to silence him once and for all.

The Servant found the strength to endure persecution, certain that the Lord would not abandon him.

Song three: The oppressed Servant places his trust in God

50 4 The Lord God has given me
the tongue of those who are experienced,
so that I may be able to give the word
a special sense for the feeble:
every morning my ear is open to his teaching,
like those who are experienced:
5 And I have not put myself against him,
or let my heart be turned back from him.
6 I was offering my back to those who gave me blows,
and my face to those who were pulling out my hair:[1]
I did not keep my face covered
from marks of shame.
7 For the Lord God is my helper;
I will not be put to shame:
so I have made my face like a rock,[2]
and I am certain that he will give me my right.
8 He who takes up my cause is near;
who will go to law with me?
let us come together before the judge.
Who is against me?
Let him come near to me.
9 See, the Lord God is my helper;
who will give a decision against me?...

HOW GOD PROTECTS HIS SERVANTS

This Chapter 50 reminds us of Jeremiah who was often rebuked, persecuted, humiliated and thrown in ja[il] yet who persevered with his mission.

God's protection does not provide miraculous shelter from oppression. It is an inner strength that enables [a] person to go on bearing witness despite persecution. (Matthew 10:16-23, page 270.)

It is the certainty that God's love is stronger than death. This is the message of song four of the Servant. (See facin[g] page.)

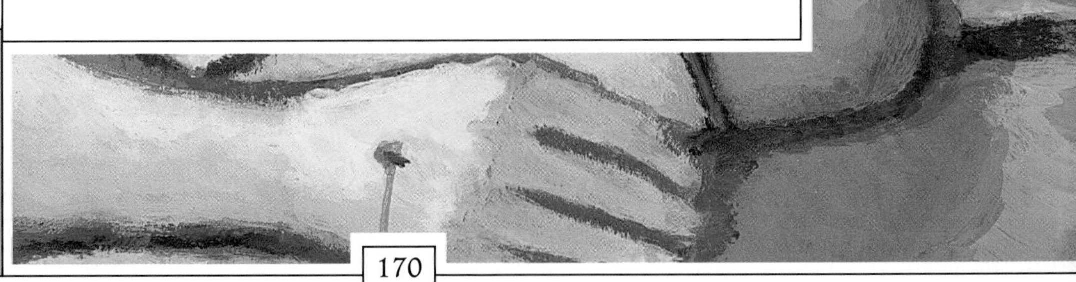

[1] See Matthew 5:39, page 262.

[2] See page 68, the paragraph on the rock. Under persecution, God imparts to His servant part of His own solidity. The face hard as stone suggests the rock on which storms break without ever dislodging it.

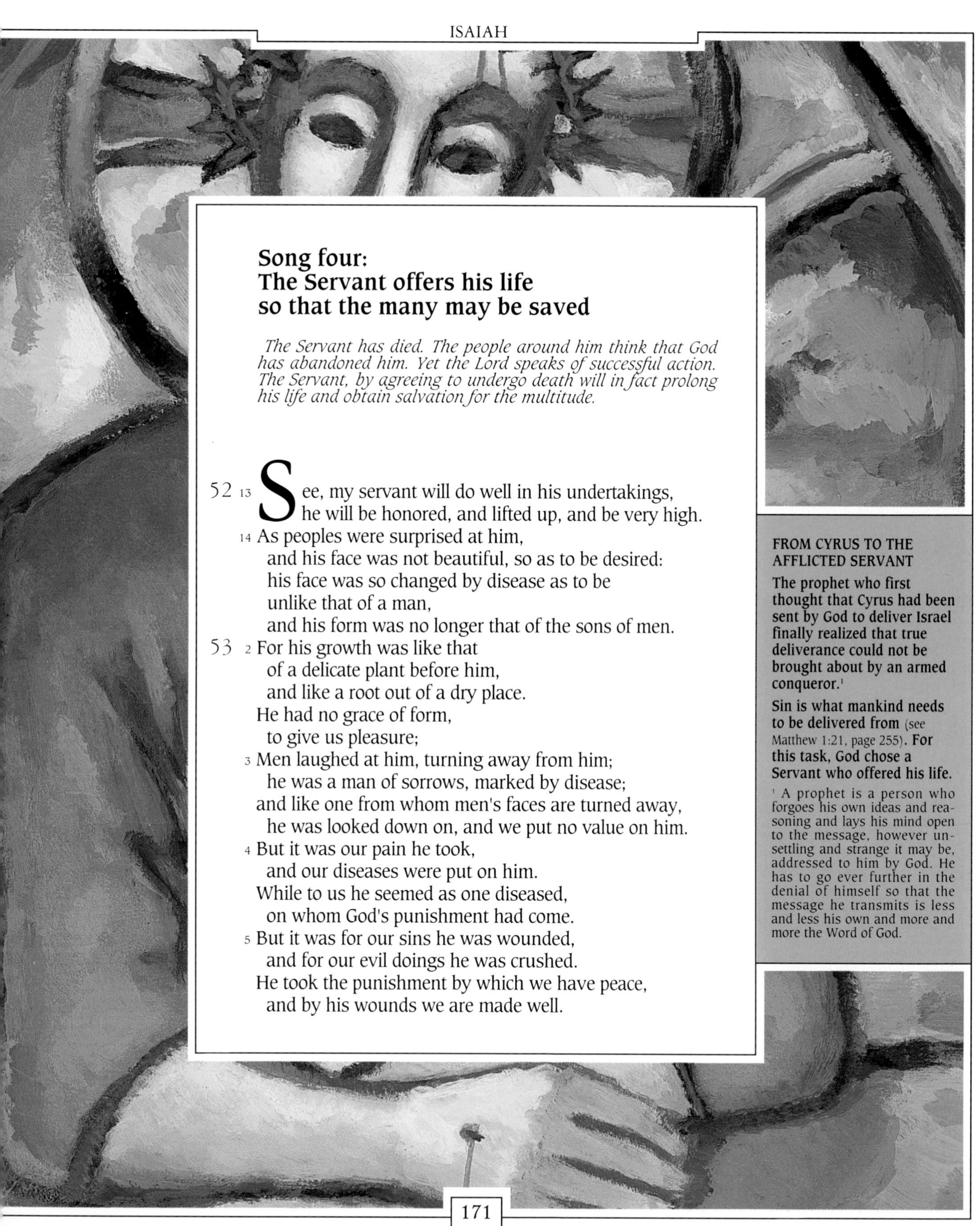

Song four: The Servant offers his life so that the many may be saved

The Servant has died. The people around him think that God has abandoned him. Yet the Lord speaks of successful action. The Servant, by agreeing to undergo death will in fact prolong his life and obtain salvation for the multitude.

52 13 See, my servant will do well in his undertakings,
he will be honored, and lifted up, and be very high.
14 As peoples were surprised at him,
and his face was not beautiful, so as to be desired:
his face was so changed by disease as to be
unlike that of a man,
and his form was no longer that of the sons of men.
53 2 For his growth was like that
of a delicate plant before him,
and like a root out of a dry place.
He had no grace of form,
to give us pleasure;
3 Men laughed at him, turning away from him;
he was a man of sorrows, marked by disease;
and like one from whom men's faces are turned away,
he was looked down on, and we put no value on him.
4 But it was our pain he took,
and our diseases were put on him.
While to us he seemed as one diseased,
on whom God's punishment had come.
5 But it was for our sins he was wounded,
and for our evil doings he was crushed.
He took the punishment by which we have peace,
and by his wounds we are made well.

FROM CYRUS TO THE AFFLICTED SERVANT

The prophet who first thought that Cyrus had been sent by God to deliver Israel finally realized that true deliverance could not be brought about by an armed conqueror.[1]

Sin is what mankind needs to be delivered from (see Matthew 1:21, page 255). **For this task, God chose a Servant who offered his life.**

[1] A prophet is a person who forgoes his own ideas and reasoning and lays his mind open to the message, however unsettling and strange it may be, addressed to him by God. He has to go ever further in the denial of himself so that the message he transmits is less and less his own and more and more the Word of God.

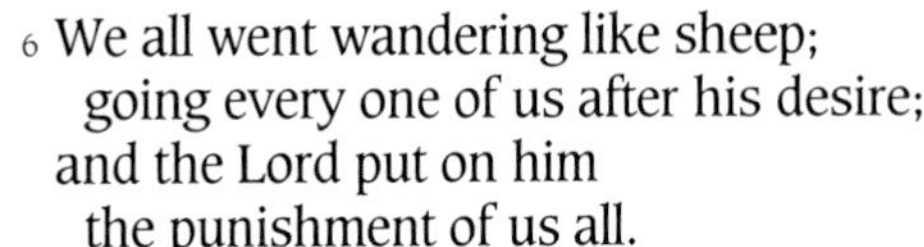

6 We all went wandering like sheep;
going every one of us after his desire;
and the Lord put on him
the punishment of us all.
7 Men were cruel to him, but he was gentle and quiet;
as a lamb taken to its death,
and as a sheep before those
who take her wool makes no sound,
so he said not a word.
8 They took away from him help and right,
and who gave a thought to his fate?
For he was cut off from the land of the living:
he came to his death for the sin of my people.
9 And they put his body into the earth with sinners,
and his last resting place was with the wicked,
though he had done no wrong,
and no deceit was in his mouth.
10 ...he will see his offspring, and grant him long life,[1]
...the will of the Lord will prosper in his hand....
11 After his suffering ...
he will be satisfied ... and many will be justified....
12 For this cause he will have
a heritage with the great,
and he will have a part
in the goods of war with the strong,
because he gave up his life,[2]
and was numbered with the evil-doers;
taking on himself the sins
of the people,
and making intercession for the transgressors.

There is a word missing in this text.
It is not written
down but permeates each line.
Why does the Servant accept humiliation, suffering and death if not for love?

The Servant gladly takes in
the love of God.
Far from leading him away from God,
his suffering permits him to discover
the suffering God
experiences when rejected by humanity.
The Servant's heart is filled
with God's desire—
that all be saved!

[1] How can someone who has been "assigned a grave with the wicked" prolong his days? The certainty becomes ever stronger that death is not the conclusive end to life (see page 123 and "resurrection"*).

[2] See "suffering."*

[3] Paul used very similar expressions in Philippians 2:1-11, page 440.

III
AFTER THE CAPTIVITY

The captivity of the Jews ended in 538 BC. Cyrus, the new master of Babylon, allowed all the people deported by Nebuchadnezzar to go home to their own countries. He gave them back the religious objects removed as booty and encouraged them to rebuild their temples so that each people could intercede with its god or gods.*

A number of Jews decided to return to Jerusalem.[1] *With much difficulty, they made a place for themselves among the Samaritans* and Edomites.**[2] *They remade the Temple.**[3] *They learned to live under the authority of the Persian governors. Later, they passed under Greek and then Roman rule.*

They found comfort in reading the Scriptures. They meditated on them. New books were written, which continued to proclaim God's fidelity towards His people.*

In very different styles, we find:

- books recounting episodes of the history of the people living under foreign domination, pages 174 to 183,

- books of prophecy, pages 184 to 193,

- meditation upon suffering, proverbs and wise counsels, pages 194 to 203,

- strange visions, in the Book of Daniel, pages 204-205.

[1] Many remained behind in Babylon. See "land."*

[2] Samaritans and Edomites were two peoples which settled on the territory of Israel. See pages 134.

[3] Historians speak of the second Temple, which king Herod would extend and embellish. See page 183 and Glossary, page 552.

PERSIANS, GREEKS AND ROMANS

The Jews who had resettled in Jerusalem lived under Persian administration for about two hundred years. They were under the authority of the "satrap," the governor of Transeuphratena, one of the Persian empire's 127 provinces.

In 333 BC, when Alexander the Great overcame the Persians, Judea became a Greek possession. Antiochus IV, a successor of Alexander, imposed worship of the Greek god Zeus on all the peoples in his empire. This abuse of power triggered the revolt of the Maccabeans* (see page 178). The Jews won several victories against the Greeks. Beginning in 106 BC, they managed to rebuild a kingdom, under the Hasmonean* dynasty (see page 183). In order to be more independent of the Greeks, the Jews entered into an alliance with Rome. The Romans gradually took over the country. It was Rome which nominated the last of the Hasmonean kings. Herod the Great, a Roman puppet, occupied the throne as king of the Jews when Jesus was born . See Matthew 2:1, page 255.

HISTORY

The expulsion of the foreign wives

The Jews had settled back in Jerusalem. Ezra, a priest who was also a scribe, arrived from Babylon. He noticed that many men returning from exile had married Babylonian women whose faith was unsure.*

He feared that, as previously under the reigns of Solomon[1] or Ahab,[2] these foreign wives might inveigle their husbands into practicing idolatry. Ezra prayed to the Lord.

9 7 "From the days of our fathers till this day we have
8 been great sinners.... | And now for a little time
grace has come to us from the Lord our God, to let a remnant of us get free and to give us a place in his holy place,
so that our God may give light to our eyes and a measure
of new life in our bondage....

10 "And now, O our God, what are we to say after this? For
11 we have not kept your laws, | Which you gave to your
12 servants the prophets, saying.... | 'Do not give your
daughters to their sons or take their daughters for your
sons or do anything for their peace or well-being forever,
so that you may be strong....'

15 O Lord God of Israel, righteousness is yours. We are only
a remnant which has been kept from death this day. See,
we are before you in our sin, for no one may his stay in
your presence because of this."

10 1 Now while Ezra was making his prayer and his statement of wrongdoing, weeping and falling down before the
house of God, a very great number of men and women
and children out of Israel came together round him. The

[1] See page 120. [2] See page 122.

GOD AND FOREIGNERS

Association with foreign women had not always had fortunate results, with some notable exceptions (see "foreign women"*).

The expulsion of the foreign women and their children was an exceptionally harsh measure. It gave rise to various reactions, including those in the Book of Jonah, which issued a vibrant reminder that God loves foreigners (see page 190).

OW GOD REVEALS
IMSELF

person can understand
›mething of God by
ımself. But not all.

zra was right in thinking
ıat the faith of the Jewish
eople should be preserved
om heathen influence. But
e was wrong in expelling
ıe foreign wives. The
eople of God could not live
ı isolation. Its task, on the
›ntrary, was to share its
ıith with the heathens.*

zra's decision gave rise to
ebate and protest. The
ook of Jonah was a
:minder that God loves all
ıankind. There are other
ooks praising the example
f foreign women such as
amar-Rahab and Ruth (see
ıge 504).

his helps us to understand
ıat God often reveals
imself through the
›mparison — or sometimes
ıe contradiction — between
vo inspired* authors.

2 people were weeping bitterly. | And Shecaniah, the son of
Jehiel, one of the sons of Elam, answering, said to Ezra,
"We have done evil against our God, and have taken as
our wives foreign women of the peoples of the land. But
3 still there is hope for Israel in this question. | Let us now
make a covenant with our God to aboandon all the wives
and all their children, if it seems right to my lord and to
those who fear the words of our God. Let it be done in
keeping with the law."

Back to bad habits

It was like stepping back to the time of Amos.[1] Once more, the wealthiest members of the community were exploiting the poor. Nehemiah[2] protested vigorously. He succeeded in converting the profiteers.

NEHEMIAH

5 1 Then there was a great outcry from the people and
2 their wives against their countrymen the Jews. | For
there were some who said, "We, our sons and our
daughters, are a great number. Let us get grain, so that we
4 may have food for our needs."… | And there were others
who said, "We have given up our fields and our vineyards
5 to get money for the king's taxes.[3] | But our flesh is the same
as the flesh of our countrymen, and our children as their
children. Now we are giving our sons and daughters into the
hands of others, to be their servants, and some of our
daughters are servants even now. We have no power to put
a stop to it; for other men have our fields and our
vineyards."

6 And on hearing their outcry and what they said I was
7 very angry. | And after turning it over in my mind, I made
a protest to the chiefs and the rulers, and said to them,

[1] See Amos 8:4-7, pages 129-130.

[2] Nehemiah was a Jew from Babylon. He was "cup-bearer" to king Artaxerxes. The cup-bearer was the steward responsible for the quality of the wine served at the royal table, as well as often being an adviser or special envoy of the king. Nehemiah had obtained letters of recommendation from Artaxerxes to help his compatriots to reorganize and to rebuild the walls of Jerusalem.

[3] This was the tax levied by the satrap of Transeuphratena on behalf of the king of Persia. See facing page, "Persians, Greeks, Romans."

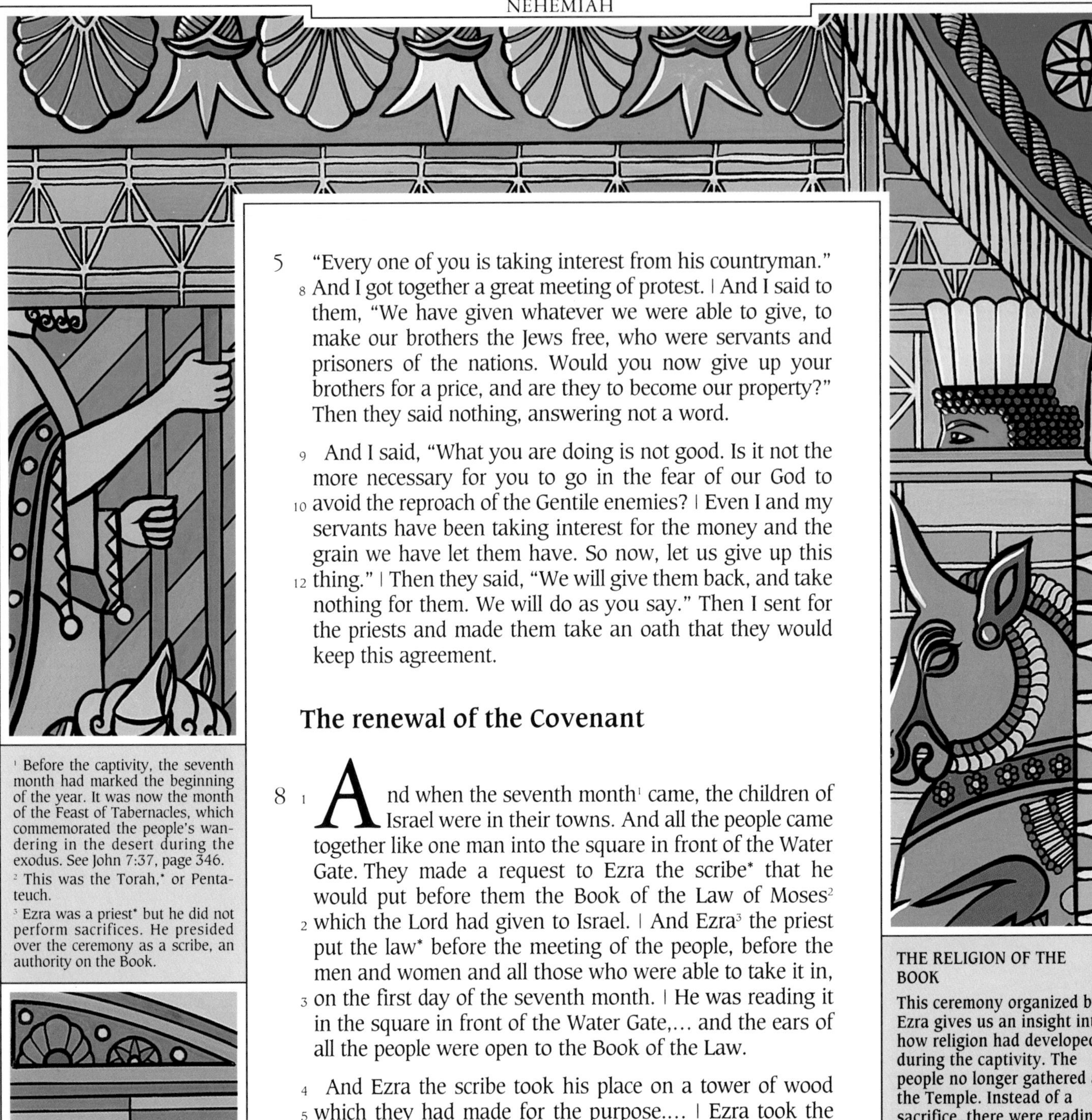

5 "Every one of you is taking interest from his countryman."
8 And I got together a great meeting of protest. | And I said to
them, "We have given whatever we were able to give, to
make our brothers the Jews free, who were servants and
prisoners of the nations. Would you now give up your
brothers for a price, and are they to become our property?"
Then they said nothing, answering not a word.

9 And I said, "What you are doing is not good. Is it not the
more necessary for you to go in the fear of our God to
10 avoid the reproach of the Gentile enemies? | Even I and my
servants have been taking interest for the money and the
grain we have let them have. So now, let us give up this
12 thing." | Then they said, "We will give them back, and take
nothing for them. We will do as you say." Then I sent for
the priests and made them take an oath that they would
keep this agreement.

The renewal of the Covenant

8 1 And when the seventh month[1] came, the children of
Israel were in their towns. And all the people came
together like one man into the square in front of the Water
Gate. They made a request to Ezra the scribe* that he
would put before them the Book of the Law of Moses[2]
2 which the Lord had given to Israel. | And Ezra[3] the priest
put the law* before the meeting of the people, before the
men and women and all those who were able to take it in,
3 on the first day of the seventh month. | He was reading it
in the square in front of the Water Gate,... and the ears of
all the people were open to the Book of the Law.

4 And Ezra the scribe took his place on a tower of wood
5 which they had made for the purpose.... | Ezra took the

[1] Before the captivity, the seventh month had marked the beginning of the year. It was now the month of the Feast of Tabernacles, which commemorated the people's wandering in the desert during the exodus. See John 7:37, page 346.

[2] This was the Torah,* or Pentateuch.

[3] Ezra was a priest* but he did not perform sacrifices. He presided over the ceremony as a scribe, an authority on the Book.

THE RELIGION OF THE BOOK

This ceremony organized by Ezra gives us an insight int how religion had developed during the captivity. The people no longer gathered a the Temple. Instead of a sacrifice, there were reading from the Book of God's Wor (compare with 1 Kings 8:6-30, pa 119). It was, in fact, the typ of service held in a synagogue.* The Book was now the center of the faith* of Israel. The whole people was invited, as the prophet Ezekiel had been (Ezekiel 2:2 3:4, page 161), to take its nourishment from the Book

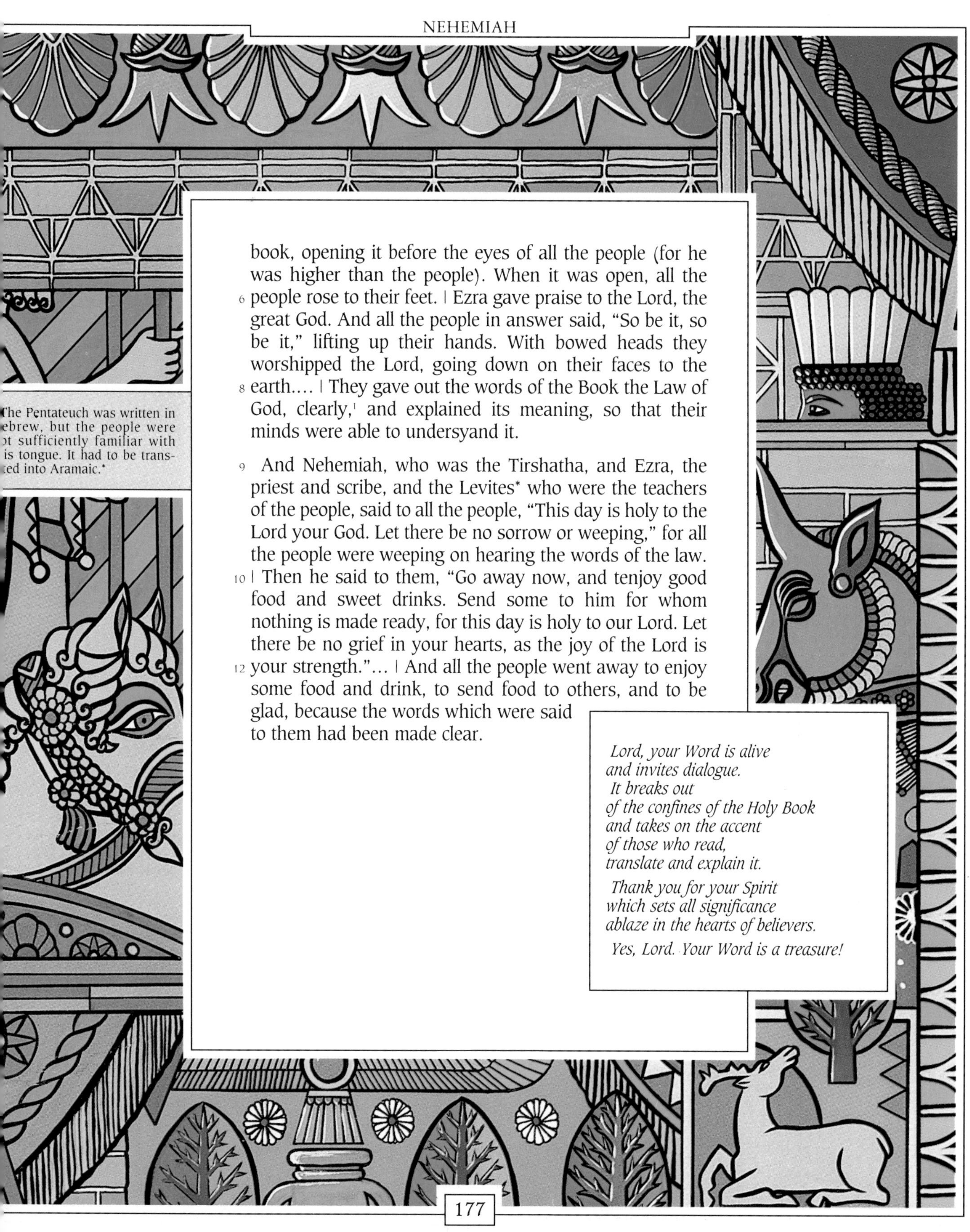

book, opening it before the eyes of all the people (for he
was higher than the people). When it was open, all the
6 people rose to their feet. | Ezra gave praise to the Lord, the
great God. And all the people in answer said, "So be it, so
be it," lifting up their hands. With bowed heads they
worshipped the Lord, going down on their faces to the
8 earth.... | They gave out the words of the Book the Law of
God, clearly,[1] and explained its meaning, so that their
minds were able to undersyand it.

9 And Nehemiah, who was the Tirshatha, and Ezra, the
priest and scribe, and the Levites* who were the teachers
of the people, said to all the people, "This day is holy to the
Lord your God. Let there be no sorrow or weeping," for all
the people were weeping on hearing the words of the law.
10 | Then he said to them, "Go away now, and tenjoy good
food and sweet drinks. Send some to him for whom
nothing is made ready, for this day is holy to our Lord. Let
there be no grief in your hearts, as the joy of the Lord is
12 your strength."... | And all the people went away to enjoy
some food and drink, to send food to others, and to be
glad, because the words which were said
to them had been made clear.

¹The Pentateuch was written in Hebrew, but the people were not sufficiently familiar with this tongue. It had to be translated into Aramaic.*

Lord, your Word is alive
and invites dialogue.
It breaks out
of the confines of the Holy Book
and takes on the accent
of those who read,
translate and explain it.

Thank you for your Spirit
which sets all significance
ablaze in the hearts of believers.

Yes, Lord. Your Word is a treasure!

THE GREEK OCCUPATION

In 333 BC, the Persians were overthrown by Alexander the Great. The Jews had to accept the Greeks as their new masters.

In 175 BC, Antiochus IV began his reign. He bore the title of Epiphanes, since he claimed to the epiphany* of Zeus.[1] He decreed that all the people under his authority must pay homage to him as a god.

A large part of the population of Judea, hoping to avoid persecution, gave up practicing the Jewish religion. Throughout the country, and in the Temple itself, altars were erected for offering sacrifices to the God-king. Circumcision* was abandoned. The dietary laws forbidding the eating of pork, among other rules, were ignored. The Greek lifestyle was in!

[1] called Jupiter by the Romans.

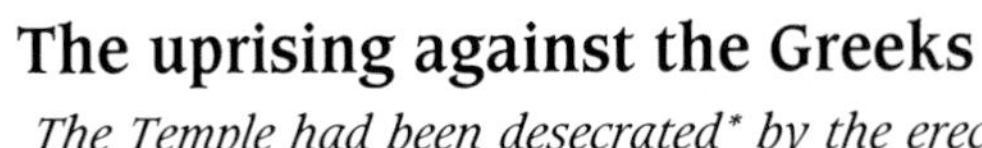

The uprising against the Greeks

The Temple had been desecrated by the erection of an altar to Zeus. Many priests had fled from Jerusalem. One of them was Mattathias, the father of Judas Maccabeus.*
(Note: Most protestant denominations consider 1 Maccabees as apocryphal.)*

2 15 The officers sent by the king to force the Jews to
apostasy* arrived in the town of Modine to
16 organize the sacrifices. | Many Israelites went over to
them, and Mattathias and his sons came to the meeting. |
17 The king's officers spoke to Mattathias: "You are a
powerful and honored leader in this town, supported by
18 sons and brothers. | You be the first to obey the orders of
the king, just as the other nations have done. Then you
and your sons will be friends of the king. You and your
sons will receive much silver and gold, as well as many
19 other gifts." | Mattathias replied with a strong voice: "All
the nations belonging to the king may obey him by
rejecting the religion of their fathers, and submitting to his
20 commands; | but I, my sons, and my brothers will follow
21 the covenant* of our fathers. | God keep us from ever
22 abandoning the law* and its statutes! | We will not obey
the commands of the king. We will not deviate from our
religion, neither to the left nor to the right."

23 As soon as he had finished speaking, a Jew came
forward, there at the altar of Modine to offer the sacrifice
24 commanded by the king. | When Mattathias saw this, he
was filled with indignation and shook with fury. A
righteous anger overcame him, and he ran after the man
25 and slaughtered him there on the altar. | Then Mattathias
killed the officer of the king sent to enforce the sacrifice,
and pulled down the altar.

THE REACTION OF THE FAITHFUL

There were Jews who determinedly resisted the excesses of Antiochus Epiphanes. Some stood up to their oppressors, preferring to die rather than disown the Covenant. They were the "martyrs of Israel." Others went underground and organized an armed resistance movement for fighting the Greeks and obtaining the purification* of the Temple. The movement was spearheaded by a family called the Maccabees,* from the nickname of one of its members.

HE BOOKS
F THE MACCABEES

he main episodes from the
esistance to Greek
aganism are related in two
ooks, called 1 and 2
laccabees, even though the
econd does not follow on
rom the first. They are
ndependent of one another
nd written by different
uthors.

27 Mattathias began to shout loudly throughout the town:
"All who are inflamed with passion for the law and who
28 keep the covenant, come out and follow me." | He escaped
with his sons to the mountains, leaving all their belon-
29 gings in the town. | Also, many others who sought justice
and followed the law went to live in the desert.

The purification* of the Temple

Judas Maccabeus became the leader of the rebellion after the death of his father, Mattathias. Despite being heavily outnumbered, he inflicted several stinging defeats on the Greeks, obliging them to negotiate.

The Temple of Jerusalem was reopened to worship of the Lord. The altar sullied by the sacrifices to Zeus was torn down and replaced by a new one.*

4 36 Judas Maccabaeus and his brothers declared: "Now
that our enemies have been crushed, let us go up
37 and purify* the temple." | The whole army was
52 assembled and they went up to Mount Zion.* | Early in the
53 morning on the twenty-fifth day of the ninth month, | the
priests offered the sacrifice required by the law on the
newly constructed altar of burnt offerings.*

54 The altar was dedicated with hymns sung to the sound
of lutes and harps and cymbals. It was exactly the anniversary of the date that the Gentiles had profaned* the
55 altar. | All the people prostrated themselves with their

4 faces to the ground to worship* and thank Heaven[1] for the
56 success of their effort. | For eight days they celebrated the
dedication of the temple, offering with joy the burnt
offerings, and the sacrifices of peace offerings and thank-
57 offerings. | They decorated the front of the temple with
golden wreaths and shields, and repaired the gates and
58 the rooms, and replaced the doors. | There was great joy
among the people, and the humiliation inflicted by the
pagans was removed.

59 Judas Maccabaeus, with his brothers and the whole
assembly of Israel, decided that the anniversary of the
dedication of the altar should be celebrated for eight days
each year with joy and happiness.[2]

To die with the hope of resurrection

7 1 Seven brothers were arrested with their mother.
With lashes of the whip and thong, the king
Antiochus tried to force them to eat pork, which was
2 unlawful for them. | One of them, speaking for all, said:
"We are ready to die rather than transgress the laws of
our fathers."

9 The second brother, with his last breath, said to him:
"You are a scoundrel, you who are taking us from this
present life, but because we die for his laws, the King of
the world will raise us up to a life eternal."

14 The fourth brother, on the point of death, spoke: "Better
to die by the hand of men, when we wait for the
resurrection promised by God. But for you, you will not
know the resurrection to a life eternal."[3]

[1] "...praised Heaven" instead o "...praised YHVH."* The Jews showed increasing reluctance to pronounce the name of God. They replaced it by expressions suggesting God. See page 58.

[2] This feast, still celebrated by Jews today, is called the Feast of Dedication (see John 10:22, page 353) or Hanukkah, meaning feast of lights. The story is told that, in the desecrated Temple, Judas Maccabeus found a small vial of oil bearing the seal of the high priest — hardly enough to keep the menorah, the seven-branched candelabrum, alight for a day. In fact, the oil burned for eight days. This explains the length of the feast and the shape of the lamp which each family lights during it. It is a candlestick with nine branches. One of them, different from the others is lit at the start of the feast in remembrance of the vial of oil found by Judas Maccabeus. The other eight branches are lit one by one on the following days of the feast. The candlestick is called hanukkiah.

[3] In the mind of the Maccabeans, resurrection was reserved for the "righteous." People who had tried in the course of their history to live with God would rise again. Those who had lived only for themselves would vanish forever in death. The Book of Daniel introduced the idea of resurrection for all. See page 205.

THE SECOND BOOK OF MACCABEES

While the first book of Maccabees recounted for the most part the rebellion of the Maccabees, the second, written by a different author, is concerned mostly with the history of ordinary people. Some preferred to die rather than break the Law.*

This book was written around 120 BC. It may be noted that at this period belief in resurrection* was gaining ground.

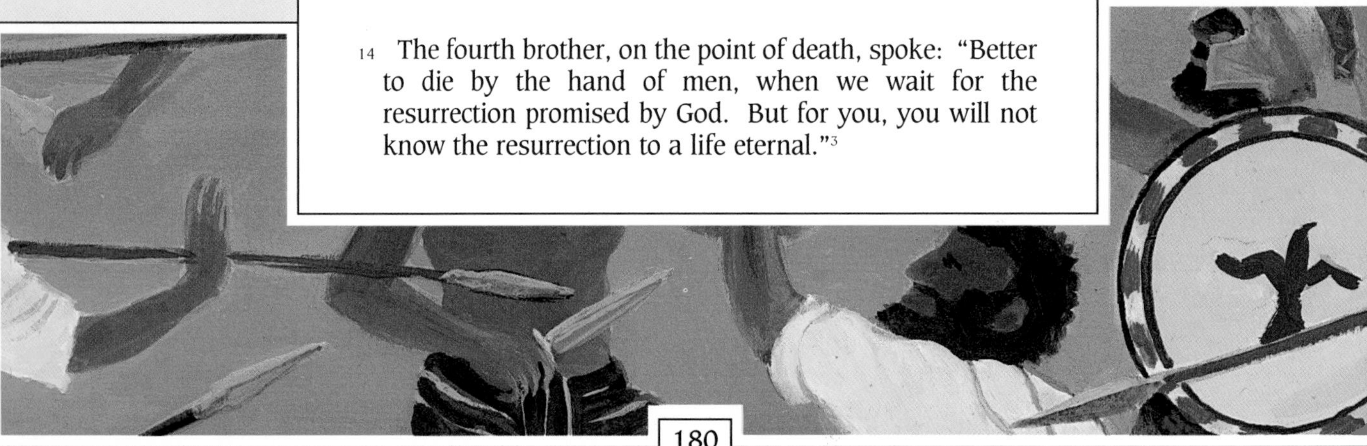

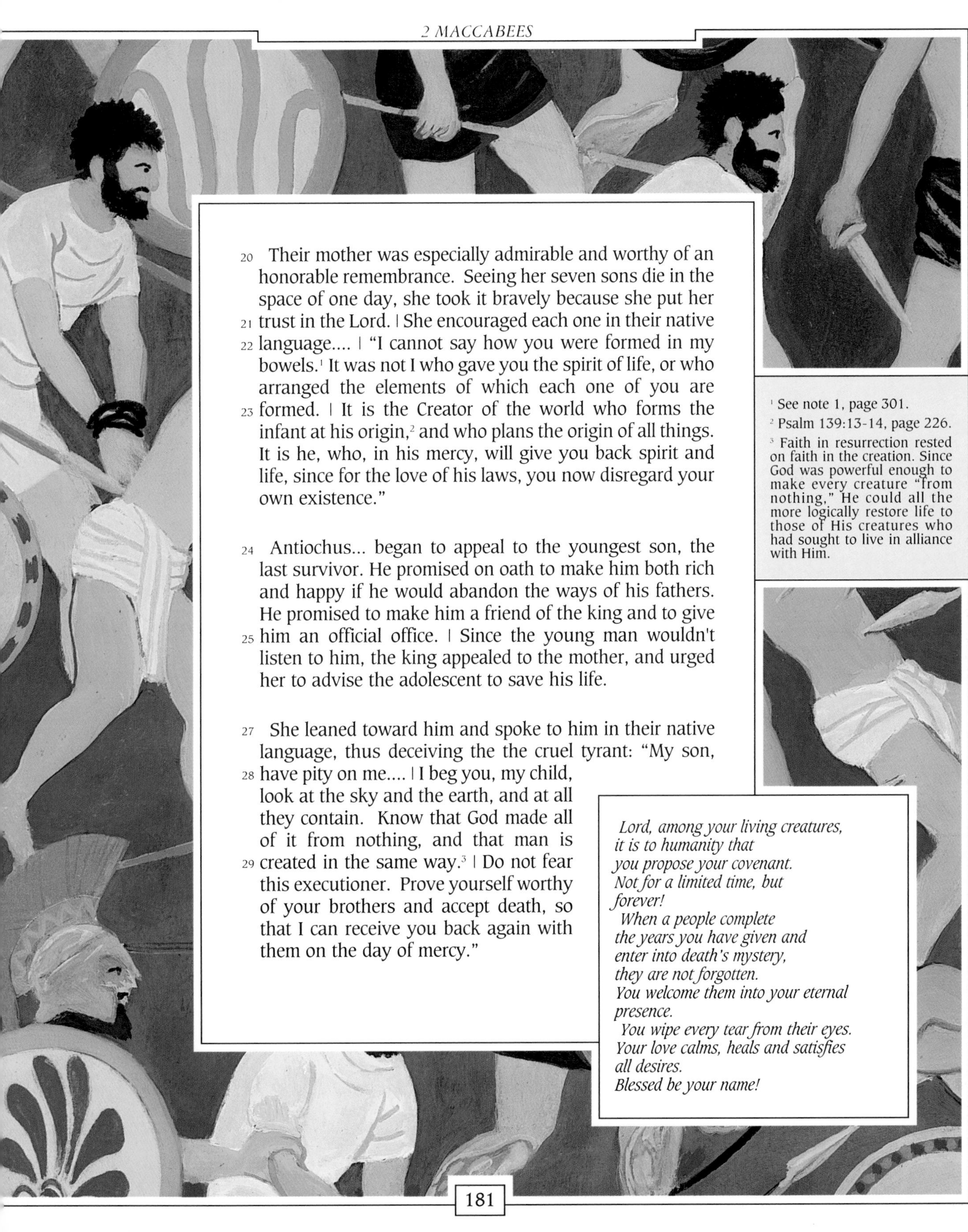

20 Their mother was especially admirable and worthy of an
honorable remembrance. Seeing her seven sons die in the
space of one day, she took it bravely because she put her
21 trust in the Lord. | She encouraged each one in their native
22 language.... | "I cannot say how you were formed in my
bowels.[1] It was not I who gave you the spirit of life, or who
arranged the elements of which each one of you are
23 formed. | It is the Creator of the world who forms the
infant at his origin,[2] and who plans the origin of all things.
It is he, who, in his mercy, will give you back spirit and
life, since for the love of his laws, you now disregard your
own existence."

24 Antiochus... began to appeal to the youngest son, the
last survivor. He promised on oath to make him both rich
and happy if he would abandon the ways of his fathers.
He promised to make him a friend of the king and to give
25 him an official office. | Since the young man wouldn't
listen to him, the king appealed to the mother, and urged
her to advise the adolescent to save his life.

27 She leaned toward him and spoke to him in their native
language, thus deceiving the the cruel tyrant: "My son,
28 have pity on me.... | I beg you, my child,
look at the sky and the earth, and at all
they contain. Know that God made all
of it from nothing, and that man is
29 created in the same way.[3] | Do not fear
this executioner. Prove yourself worthy
of your brothers and accept death, so
that I can receive you back again with
them on the day of mercy."

[1] See note 1, page 301.

[2] Psalm 139:13-14, page 226.

[3] Faith in resurrection rested on faith in the creation. Since God was powerful enough to make every creature "from nothing," He could all the more logically restore life to those of His creatures who had sought to live in alliance with Him.

Lord, among your living creatures,
it is to humanity that
you propose your covenant.
Not for a limited time, but
forever!
When a people complete
the years you have given and
enter into death's mystery,
they are not forgotten.
You welcome them into your eternal
presence.
You wipe every tear from their eyes.
Your love calms, heals and satisfies
all desires.
Blessed be your name!

7 30 When she finished speaking, the young man said: "What are you waiting for? I will not obey the command of the king, but I will obey the commands of the law given to our fathers by Moses."

Praying for the dead

During a battle against the Greeks, the Jews suffered losses. Judas Maccabeus, while burying the corpses of the slain, found on some of them charms dedicated to idols. He thereupon decided to offer sacrifices so that the sins of the dead might be pardoned.*

12 43 Judas, the leader of Israel, organized a collection of
contributions and sent two thousand pieces of silver
to Jerusalem for a sin-offering. It was a noble and
proper gesture, inspired by the thought of the
44 resurrection. | For if he had not expected that the fallen
would be resurrected, the prayer for the dead would have
45 been absurd and vain. | But since he believed that there
was a wonderful reward reserved for those who die in the
faith, it was an idea both pious and holy.
46 That is why he offered the sacrifice of atonement, so that
the dead would be delivered from their sin.[1]

[1] For many centuries, this chapter of 2 Maccabees was recited at Catholic funeral services.

Under the sway of Rome

The successors to Judas Maccabeus carried on the struggle against the Greeks. Whether through armed action or negotiation they strove to keep the Jewish people relatively independent.

They obtained recognition for the office of high priest[1] and then of king, so founding the Hasmonean[2] dynasty in about 100 BC.

They also tried to find allies who would help them in their struggle against the Greeks. Already under Judas they had approached the Romans for support.

Beginning in 63 BC, Rome, which had already extended its hold over all of the Middle East, took a direct hand in the affairs of its Jewish "ally". It was with Rome's backing that Herod the Great became king of the Jews in 37 BC.*

Herod was not Jewish. He was an Idumean. He married a Hasmonean, but this still did not give him the right to officiate as high priest. He entrusted this function to the Sadducees,* while keeping them under tight control. The priesthood was no longer for life, nor could it be transmitted from father to son. The king appointed the high priest and could dismiss him at will.[3]*

Herod, to win the good opinion of his Jewish subjects, had sumptuous religious edifices built in Hebron above the tomb of the patriarchs[4] and in Mamre, in remembrance of Abraham's encounter with the three visitors.[5] He had the Temple in Jerusalem[6] enlarged and redecorated. But he built his capital on the coast, calling it Caesarea in honor of the Roman emperor and filled it with pagan monuments, including a temple dedicated to Rome and Augustus.[7]

The Bible does not tell us much about this period. We know of it largely through historians, especially Flavius Josephus, a Jewish writer living in the second half of the 1st century AD.

[1] Since the end of the captivity, the high priests in charge of the Temple had always been chosen from the same family, that of Onias of the tribe of Levi.* Jonathan, the brother of Judas Maccabeus, who had obtained this office in about 150 BC was from the tribe of Levi but his family had never risen so high in the priesthood. His nomination excited a good deal of protest. This was probably when a dissident group went to live by the Dead Sea, at Qumran, refusing to set foot in the Temple again. For them it had been sullied by the presence of this "impious" priest. These breakaways were called the Essenes.*

[2] Hasmonean* meant descending from Hasmon. Hasmon was the name of the grandfather of Mattathias.

[3] Later the Roman governor would have the same power. See note 1, page 306.

[4] See page 47.

[5] Genesis 18:1-14, page 40.

[6] Sacrifices were offered in the Temple of Jerusalem for the emperor. But the Romans never forced the Jews to offer sacrifices to the deified emperor, the reason being that the Romans had never "vanquished" the Jews. The Romans had "moved into" Judea under the terms of the alliance concluded with Judas Maccabeus.

[7] Augustus Caesar, the emperor who ruled from 29 BC to 14 AD. See Luke 2:1, page 302.

"THE THIRD ISAIAH", JONAH, ZECHARIAH

After the captivity, there were fewer prophets. There were still some, however, who rose up to urge the people to keep trusting in the promises of the Lord.

The prophecies* of one them were added to the scroll of Isaiah (see page 143). He assured the people, discouraged by the difficulties of settling down again in the Promised Land, that God would make Jerusalem the religious capital towards which the whole world would converge (pages 184 to 187).

Another prophet wrote the Book of Jonah. He asserted that the mission of the people was to go before the nations and bear witness to the mercifulness* of God (pages 190 to 192).

Zechariah, at last, foretold — in sometimes veiled terms — that the Messiah* sent by God would be meek and peace-loving (page 193).

PROPHETS

Jerusalem, house of prayer for all people

During the first years after the return from the captivity, the prophet sometimes known as "the third Isaiah"[1] (see page 143) described the rebuilt temple in Jerusalem as a house of prayer for all people. Eastern hyperbole? Not at all. This prophecy would soon come true. The Jews dispersed in the diaspora spoke of God to the foreigners they met. Many of these heathens, wishing to know more about the God of the Jews, made the pilgrimage to Jerusalem.*[2]

56 1 The Lord says, "Let your way of life be upright,
and let your behavior be rightly ordered:
for my salvation is near,
and my righteousness will quickly be seen....

3 And let not the man from a foreign country,
who has been joined to the Lord, say,
"The Lord will certainly put a division
between me and his people."...

6 And as for those from a foreign country,
who are joined to the Lord,
to give worship to him and honor to his name,
to be his servants, even everyone who keeps
the Sabbath holy,
and keeps his Covenant with me:

7 I will make them come to my holy mountain,
and will give them joy in my house of prayer;
I will take pleasure
in the burnt offerings
which they make on my altar:
for my house will be named
a house of prayer for all peoples."[3]

*Lord, your people
are not a closed family circle.
It is not limited to the direct
descent of one ancestor.*

*Your people are those who believe
in you regardless of language or color.
Even though they aren't
of Abraham's direct lineage they are
all his children because they have
the same heart: a heart filled with
confidence and faithfulness.*

[2] The heathens* attracted by Judaism were admitted to a section of the outercourt of the Temple,* known as the Court of the Gentiles.* They were forbidden, under pain of death, to approach the place of sacrifice and the sanctuary at the center. From where they were, they could glimpse the smoke of the sacrifice rising from the altar and hear the psalms and canticles. Under the porticos bordering the outercourt, they were able to meet with scholars who explained the Word of God to them.

[3] See 1 Kings 8:42-43, page 119.

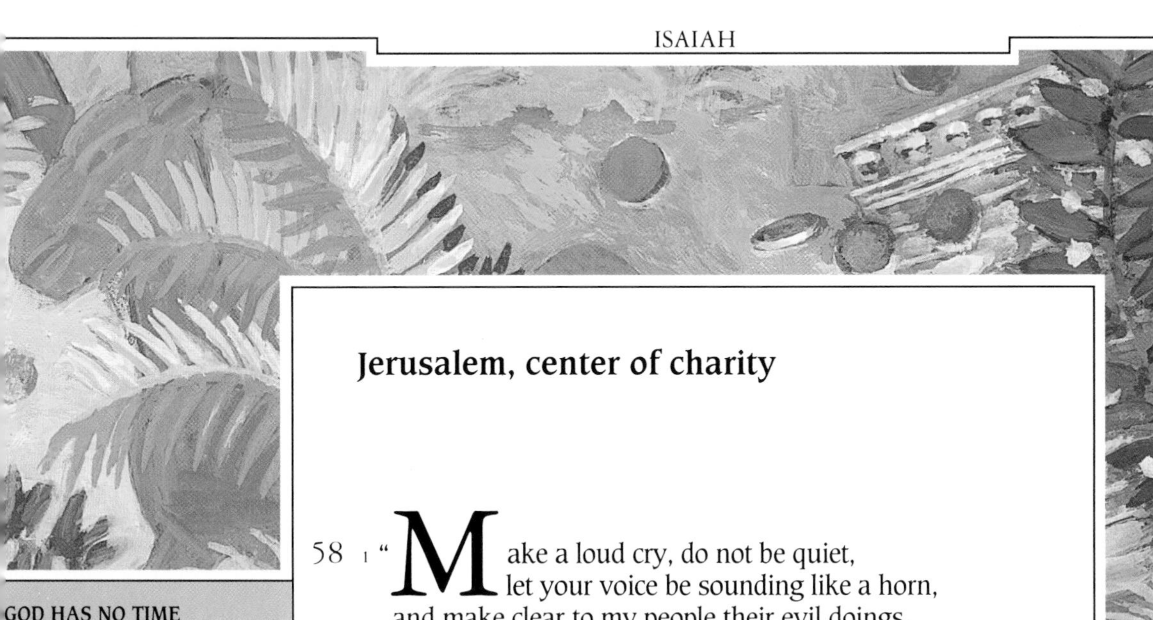

Jerusalem, center of charity

58 1 "Make a loud cry, do not be quiet,
let your voice be sounding like a horn,
and make clear to my people their evil doings,
and to the family of Jacob their sins.

2 Though they pray to me every day,
and take pleasure in the knowledge of my ways....
it is their delight to come near to God.

3 They say, 'Why have we fasted,
and you do not see it? why have we humbled ourselves,
and you take no note of it?'
If, in the days when you fast, you do as you please,
and take advantage of youyr workers;

4 If fasting makes you quickly angry,
ready for fighting and giving blows with evil hands;
your holy days will not be honored by God on high....

6 Is not this the holy day for which I have given orders:
to free those who have wrongly been made prisoners,
to undo the cords of the yoke,
and to let the oppressed go free,
and every yoke be broken?

7 Is it not to give your bread to those in need,
and to let the poor who have no resting-place
come into your house?
to put a robe on the unclothed one when you see him, and
not hide from your own flesh and blood?

GOD HAS NO TIME FOR HYPOCRITES

The prophet was castigating a state of affairs that Nehemiah had condemned differently (see page 175). **People in high places had slipped back into their old bad self-serving habits. They were hard with those who worked under them. This did not stop them from putting on a show of being holy, and fasting from time to time.**

The prophet used the same tone as Amos (see Amos 5:21-24, page 128) **to denounce their hypocrisy.**

FASTING PLEASING TO GOD

The prophet, in his indignation, seemed to be saying that fasting in terms of giving up food was worthless. It was only the person who gave up ill-gotten gains who was pleasing in the sight of God.

Jesus also placed justice and mercy higher than self-denial, but he attached meaning to fasting in terms of food. See Matthew 9:14-15, page 268.

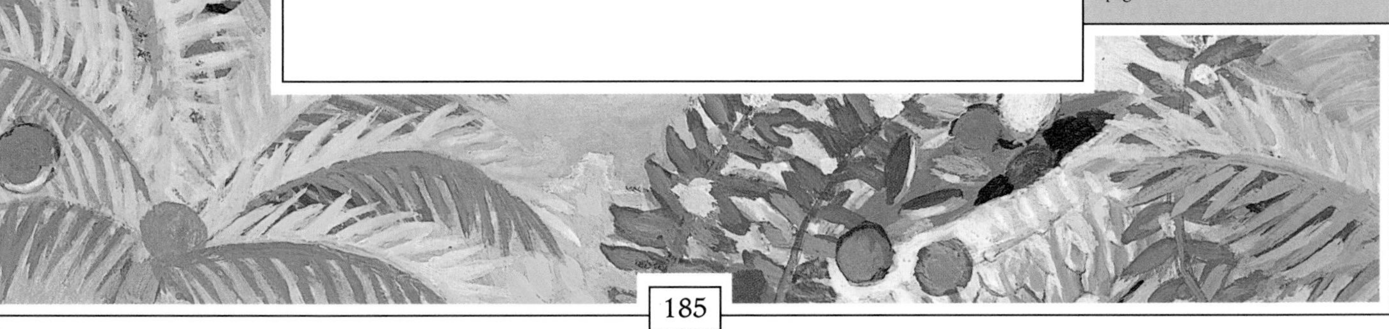

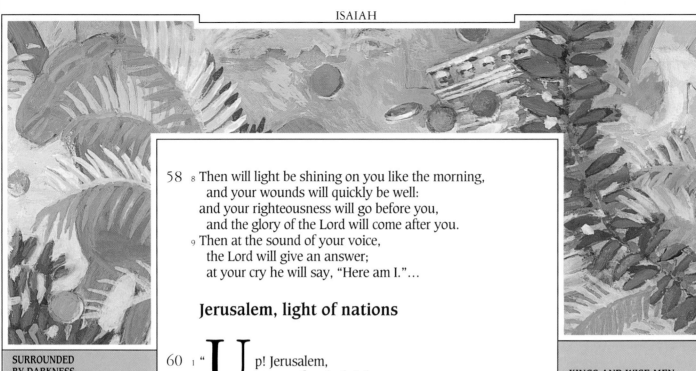

58 8 Then will light be shining on you like the morning,
and your wounds will quickly be well:
and your righteousness will go before you,
and the glory of the Lord will come after you.
9 Then at the sound of your voice,
the Lord will give an answer;
at your cry he will say, "Here am I."...

Jerusalem, light of nations

60 1 "Up! Jerusalem,
let your face be bright,
for your light has come,
and the glory of the Lord is shining on you.
2 For truly, the earth will be dark,
and the peoples veiled in blackest night;
but the Lord will be shining on you,
and his glory will be seen among you.
3 And nations will come to your light,
and kings to your bright dawn.
4 Let your eyes be lifted up, and see:
they are all coming together to you;
your sons will come from far,
and your daughters taken with loving care.
5 Then you will see, and be bright with joy,
and your heart will be overflowing with joy:
for the produce of the sea will be turned to you,
the wealth of the nations will come to you.
6 Your land will be full of herds of camels,
even the young camels of Midian and Ephah;
all from Sheba[1] will come,
with gold and spices,
proclaiming the great acts of the Lord."

[1] See "Solomon the wise", page 117.

SURROUNDED BY DARKNESS

The prophet once again says in no uncertain terms that Jerusalem will become a magnet for the heathens. The city that had been humbled would draw towards it its former oppressors. Like servants, they would come carrying the most precious gifts. The triumph of the people of the Covenant would be resplendent.

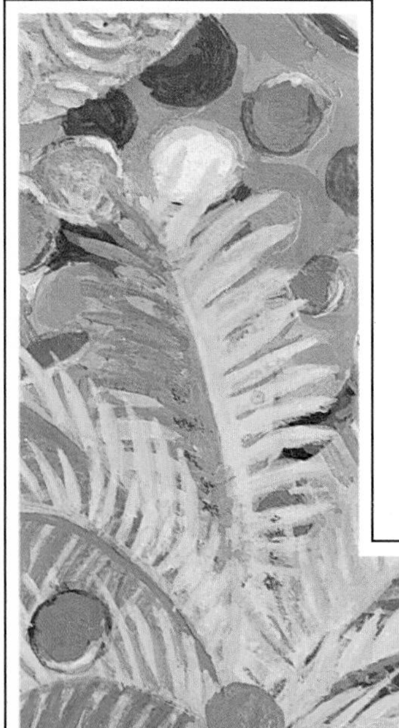

KINGS AND WISE MEN

Chapter 60 is sometimes read on the Day of the Epiphany* (or Twelfth Night). The "kings" foretold by Isaiah are paralleled by the wise men in the gospel of Matthew (see Matthew 2:1-12, page 255). For this reason, people often think of the wise men as kings. The kings in the prophecy bear gold and incense. The wise men in Matthew bring also myrrh, a mysterious perfume associated with death. The "king" sent by God therefore does not want to lord it over the nations or submit them to his power. He comes not to take but to give — to give his own life to save the many.

PROPHET AND MESSIAH

Certain prophets, like Isaiah or Jeremiah, had been called by God to correct the mistakes of the kings.

In this text, a prophet receives the messianic anointment. He becomes a messiah* but not a king. He remains a prophet inviting mankind as an equal to accept God's gifts.

See page 93 and messiah*-prophet.

Jerusalem, place of solace

61 1 The spirit* of the Lord is on me,
because I am anointed by him
to give good news to the poor;
he has sent me to make the broken-hearted well,
to say that the prisoners will be made free,
and that those in chains will see the light again;
2 To give knowledge that the year
of the Lord's good pleasure has come,
and the day of vengeance[1] from our God;
to give comfort to all who are sad;
3 To give them a crown of beauty in place of ashes,
the oil of joy in place of the clothing of grief,
praise in place of sorrow;
so that they may be named trees of righteousness,
the planting of the Lord, and so that he may have glory.
6 But you will be named the priests of the Lord,
the servants of our God:
you will have the wealth of the nations for your food,
and you will be clothed with their glory....
8 For I, the Lord, take pleasure in justice; I will not put up
with the robbery and iniquity; and I will certainly give
them their reward, and I will make an
eternal Covenant with them....
11 For as the earth puts out buds,
and as the garden gives growth
to the seeds which are planted in it,
so the Lord will make righteousness
and praise to be flowering before
all the nations.

[1] See "God's 'vengeance'", page 164.

HOW JESUS FULFILLED THIS PROPHECY

Jesus, after reciting the first part of this prophecy,* said in the synagogue of Nazareth, "Today this scripture is fulfilled in your hearing." See Luke 4:14-22.

Jesus interrupted his reading in the middle of verse 2. He did not want to read anything that smacked of vengeance. He did not intend to be a messiah like the kings. He was not guiding his people so that they could "feed on the wealth of nations". On the contrary, he had come to serve mankind and he invited his disciples to become servants like himself. See Mark 10:35-45, page 248.

Lord, living in covenant with you
doesn't mean dominating others.
You are not a God who forces yourself
on others.
You are gentle and patient.
Lord, living in covenant with you
means allowing your Holy Spirit
to enter our lives to soften
and break our hearts of stone.
It means to imitate your example of love
and forgiveness.
It means that you are the source
of our lives,
and that we look for no other reward
than your daily and eternal presence.

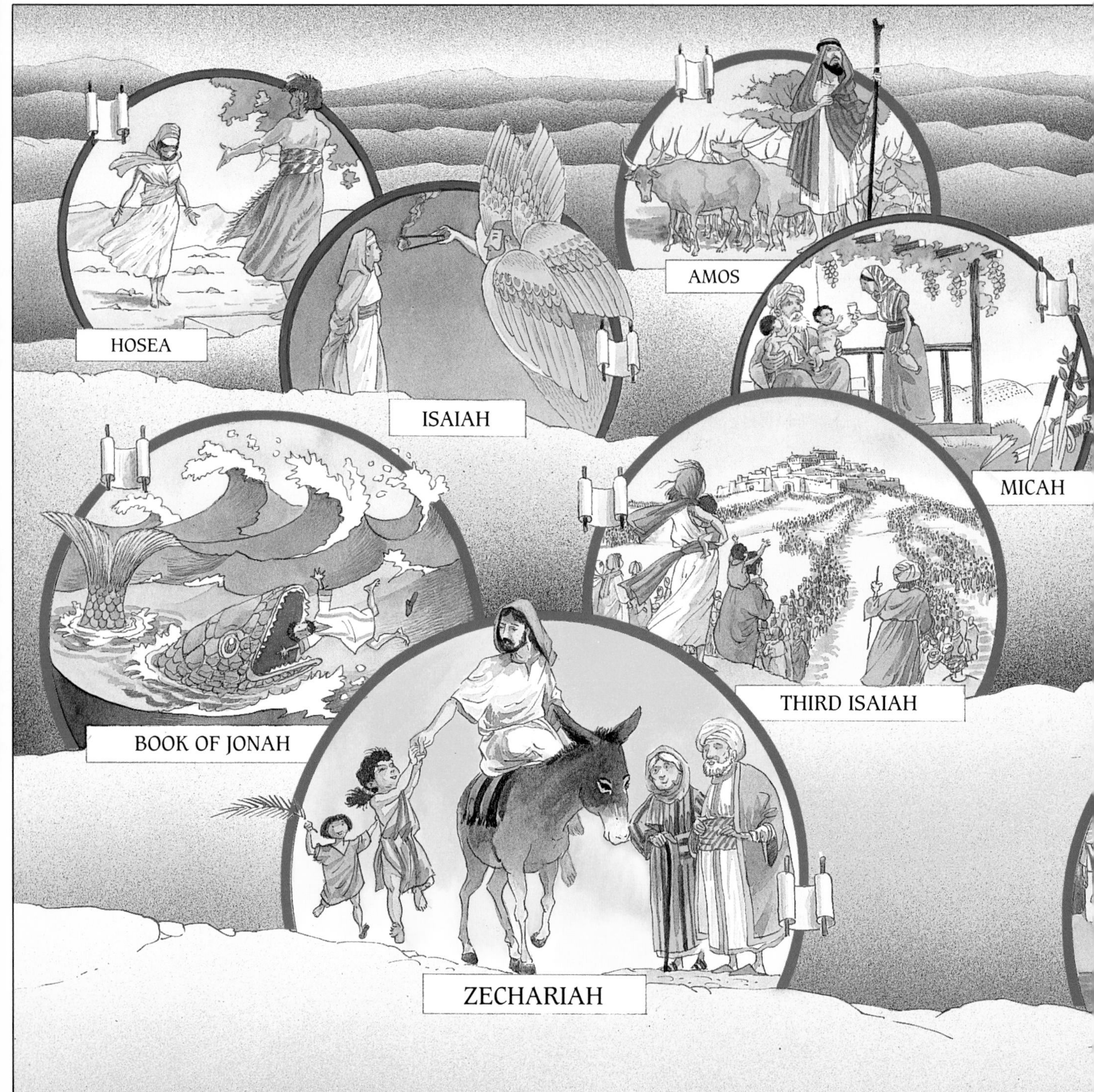

THE PROPHETS BLAZED HIS TRAIL

NATHAN *promised David that God would build him a "house" (2 Samuel 7:11-16, page 109 — Luke 1:30-33, page 300).*

ELIJAH *discovered God's presence in the sighing of a gentle wind (1 Kings 19:8-13, page 125 — see Mark 9:2-10, page 246).*

ELISHA *obtained the cure of Naaman the Syrian (2 Kings 5:9-17, page 109 — Luke 4:27, page 308).*

AMOS, *the herdsman, was sent to Bethel. He criticized the injustice of the mighty (pages 128-131 — see Mark 10:42-44, page 248).*

HOSEA *forgave his unfaithful wife. He revealed that God wished to celebrate His union with His people (pages 132-134 — Matthew 9:13, page 268).*

A seraph purified the lips of ***ISAIAH*** *so that he could be the messenger of God and announce the coming of the Messiah (Isaiah 6:1-8, page 137).*

MICAH *foretold an age of peace and plenty when God sent His shepherd (pages 144-145).*

JEREMIAH *advised the people to accept the yoke of Nebuchadnezzar (Jeremiah 28:2-11, page 155 — see Matthew 22:15-22, page 289).*

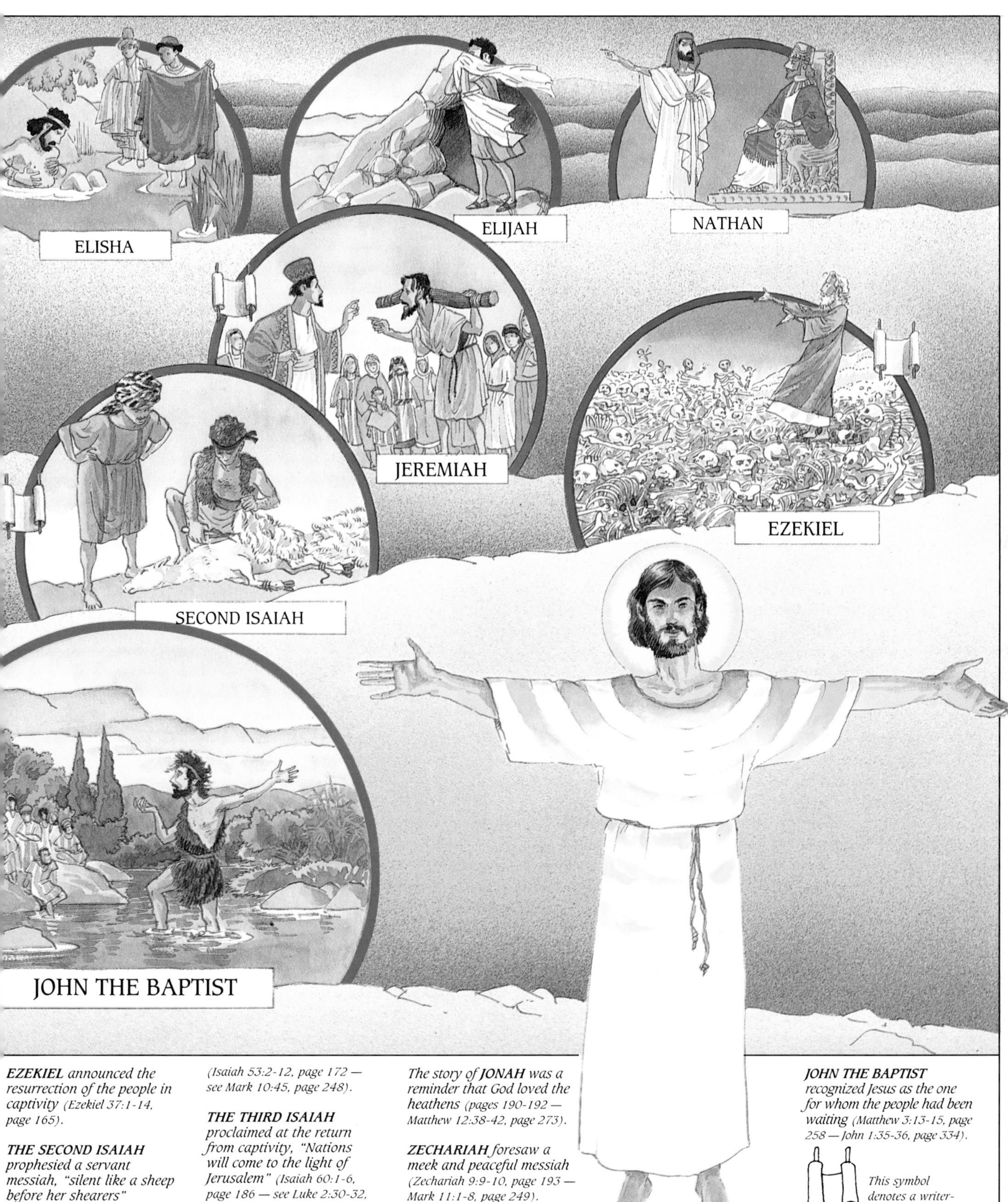

EZEKIEL *announced the resurrection of the people in captivity (Ezekiel 37:1-14, page 165).*

THE SECOND ISAIAH *prophesied a servant messiah, "silent like a sheep before her shearers" (Isaiah 53:2-12, page 172 — see Mark 10:45, page 248).*

THE THIRD ISAIAH *proclaimed at the return from captivity, "Nations will come to the light of Jerusalem" (Isaiah 60:1-6, page 186 — see Luke 2:30-32, page 305).*

The story of ***JONAH*** *was a reminder that God loved the heathens (pages 190-192 — Matthew 12:38-42, page 273).*

ZECHARIAH *foresaw a meek and peaceful messiah (Zechariah 9:9-10, page 193 — Mark 11:1-8, page 249).*

JOHN THE BAPTIST *recognized Jesus as the one for whom the people had been waiting (Matthew 3:13-15, page 258 — John 1:35-36, page 334).*

This symbol denotes a writer-prophet.*

THE STORY OF JONAH

The book is quite unlike the other prophets' books. It tells a story full of humor. The hero's name is Jonah and he is presented as a prophet. The real prophet is the author of the story. He was trying to answer a question being asked by the people of Israel, "How should we treat foreigners?" Ezra's advice was to have nothing to do with them (see page 174). **The "third Isaiah" thought that the foreigners would yield to Israel, and could in that way share in its faith (see pages 184 and 186).**

The author of the Book of Jonah denounces the spirit of superiority of the chosen people. His teaching is that God loves foreigners as much as Israel. See "How God reveals Himself," page 175.

The adventures of a balky prophet

The Lord sent Jonah to Nineveh, carrying a message of wrath. Jonah well knew that the anger of God expressed more a wish to forgive than to punish. Since Jonah loathed the Ninevites, he refused the mission and tried to escape from God's reach.*

1 1 And the word of the Lord came to Jonah, the son of
2 Amittai, saying, | "Up! go to Nineveh,[1] that great
town, and preach against it; for their wickedness has come
3 up before me."[2] | And Jonah ran away to Tarshish, away
from the Lord. He went down to Joppa, and saw there a ship
going to Tarshish, so he gave them the price of the journey
and headed to Tarshish, away from the Lord.
4 And the Lord sent out a great wind on to the sea and there
was a violent storm in the sea, so that the ship seemed in
5 danger of being broken. | Then the sailors were full of fear,
every man crying to his god; and the goods in the ship were
dropped out into the sea to make the weight less. But Jonah
had gone down into the inmost part of the ship where he
6 was stretched out in a deep sleep. | And the ship's captain
came to him and said to him, "What are you doing
sleeping? Get up! Pray to your God, if by chance God cares
7 about us, so that we may not come to destruction." | And
they said to one another, "Come, let us cast lots to see why
this evil has come on us." So they did so, and Jonah was
seen to be the cause.

The sailors asked Jonah what they should do to calm the waves.

12 And he said to them, "Take me up and put me into the
sea, and the sea will become calm for you: for I am certain
that because of me this great storm has come on you."
13 And the men were working hard to get back to the land,
but they were not able to do so. The sea got rougher and

JESUS AND JONAH

The gospels show that Jesus was very familiar with the story of Jonah. On several occasions, he told people who asked him for a sign, "I shall give you none but the sign of Jonah" (Matthew 12:38-42, page 273).

[1] In the eyes of the Jews, Nineveh was the perfect example of a godless city. The Ninevites were viewed as terrible sinners. They had ruthlessly wiped out the kingdom of Samaria for all time. See page 134.

[2] See Genesis 18:20-21, page 42.

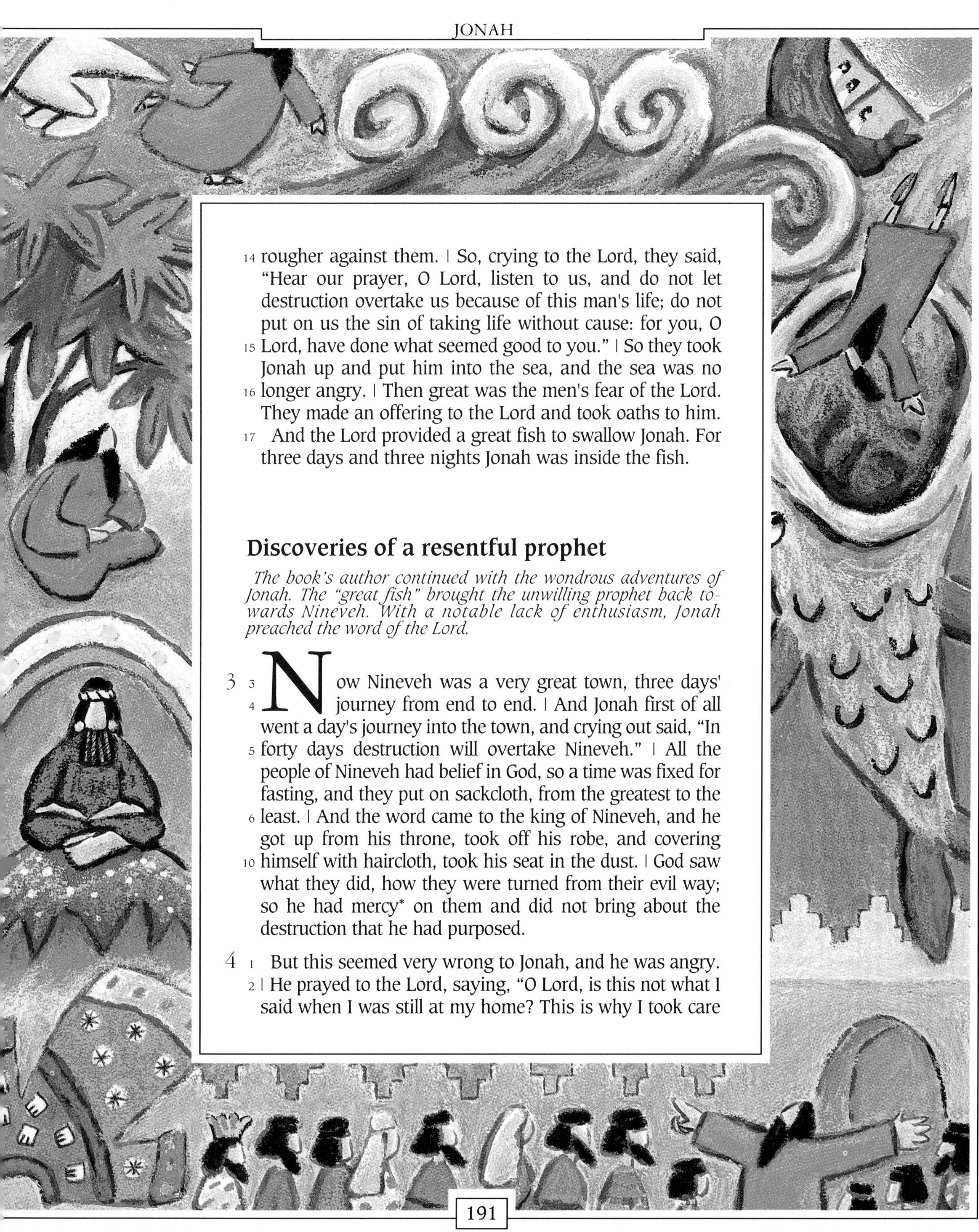

14 rougher against them. | So, crying to the Lord, they said,
"Hear our prayer, O Lord, listen to us, and do not let
destruction overtake us because of this man's life; do not
put on us the sin of taking life without cause: for you, O
15 Lord, have done what seemed good to you." | So they took
Jonah up and put him into the sea, and the sea was no
16 longer angry. | Then great was the men's fear of the Lord.
They made an offering to the Lord and took oaths to him.
17 And the Lord provided a great fish to swallow Jonah. For
three days and three nights Jonah was inside the fish.

Discoveries of a resentful prophet

The book's author continued with the wondrous adventures of Jonah. The "great fish" brought the unwilling prophet back towards Nineveh. With a notable lack of enthusiasm, Jonah preached the word of the Lord.

3 3 Now Nineveh was a very great town, three days'
4 journey from end to end. | And Jonah first of all
went a day's journey into the town, and crying out said, "In
5 forty days destruction will overtake Nineveh." | All the
people of Nineveh had belief in God, so a time was fixed for
fasting, and they put on sackcloth, from the greatest to the
6 least. | And the word came to the king of Nineveh, and he
got up from his throne, took off his robe, and covering
10 himself with haircloth, took his seat in the dust. | God saw
what they did, how they were turned from their evil way;
so he had mercy* on them and did not bring about the
destruction that he had purposed.

4 1 But this seemed very wrong to Jonah, and he was angry.
2 | He prayed to the Lord, saying, "O Lord, is this not what I
said when I was still at my home? This is why I took care

4 to escape to Tarshish: for I was certain that you were a
loving God, full of compassion, slow to be angry and great
3 in mercy, and ready to relent your plan of destruction. | So
now, O Lord, hear my prayer and take my life from me, for
4 death is better for me than life." | And the Lord said, "Have
you any right to be angry?"
5 Then Jonah went out of the town, took his seat on the
east side of the town and made himself a roof of branches.
He satt under its shade till he saw what would become of
6 the town. | And the Lord God made a vine come up over
Jonah to give him shade over his head. And Jonah was
7 very glad because of the vine. | But early on the morning
after, God provided a worm to destroy the vine, and it
8 became dry and dead. | Then when the sun came up, God
sent a burning east wind: and so great was the heat of the
sun on his head that Jonah was faint, and, requesting
death for himself, said, "Death is better for me than life."
9 And the Lord said to Jonah, "Have you any right to be
angry about the vine?" And he said, "I have a right to be
10 truly angry." | And the Lord said, "You had pity on the
vine,[1] for which you did no work and for the growth of
which you were not responsible. It grew in a night and died
11 in a night; | And am I not to have mercy on Nineveh, that
great town, in which there are more than
a hundred and twenty thousand persons
without the ability to judge between the
right and left, as well as much cattle?"

[1] God pretended to believe that Jonah's bad temper was due to concern for the plant. It was a way of showing that His divine anger always has its source in concern for a people or persons headed for disaster. There is no need to fear the anger of God. It is the shout of a father, saying "Come back!"

Lord, you love all humanity.
Long before Jonah appeared
you had already been at work in the hearts
of the people of Nineveh.
You gave them the desire to know you,
to be converted.
A number of people
in this pagan city already belonged to you.
But now you need Jonah's
harsh words so that the people's
vague ideas will be transformed
into concrete choices!

Conversion is not a series of wonderful ideas.
It's a new way of living!

A PEACEFUL AND MISUNDERSTOOD MESSIAH

The final prophecies of Zechariah* foresaw a messiah* without pomp. The Jews, humiliated by foreign occupation, were hoping for a king who would perform triumphant deeds. How would they respond to a lowly king riding on a donkey?

Zechariah sees a portent of tragedy in the life of the "pierced" messiah.

Zechariah and the king of peace

9 9 Be full of joy, O daughter of Zion;
give a glad cry, O daughter of Jerusalem:
See, your king comes to you:
he is righteous and has overcome;
gentle and seated on a donkey, on a young donkey.[1]

10 And he will have the chariot taken away from Ephraim,[2]
and the horse from Jerusalem,
and the bow of war will be cut off.
He will proclaim peace to the nations,
and his rule will be from sea to sea,
and from the River to the ends of the earth.

Zechariah and the "pierced" king

12 9 "On that day...
10 I will send down on the family
of David and on the people of Jerusalem
the spirit of grace and of supplication;
and their eyes will be turned to the one
who was wounded[3] by their hands.
They will be weeping for him as for an
only son, and their grief for him will be
bitter, like the grief of one sorrowing for
11 his oldest son. | In that day there will be
a great weeping in Jerusalem."...

They will beat
their swords into plowshares.
Abandoning his battle horse,
He will enter Jerusalem
riding on a peasant's mount.
He will not force peace on them,
but will proclaim it with
a loving impassioned heart.

Who will listen to Him?
Hate is rumbling
beneath the joyful cries.
The only Son will be pierced
because those of his household
refuse to believe in Him.

[1] Jesus fulfilled this prophecy on Palm Sunday (Mark 11:1-8, page 249).

[2] Ephraim was the main tribe in the kingdom of the North. Associating Ephraim with Jerusalem was a way of suggesting the lands of all twelve tribes.

[3] See John 19:37, page 381.

THE SAGES

The prophets* were interested in the people and its history. The sages were concerned with the problems facing people in everyday life.

— The Book of Job (pages 194-197) **treats of the questions mankind asks about suffering. Is it a punishment from God? How can suffering be endured?**

— The Book of Proverbs (page 198) **is a collection of easy-to-remember maxims, and simple rules of life. Some of the proverbs probably go back to the days of Solomon.**

— The Book of Ecclesiasticus (pages 199-201) **contains the teaching of a sage from Jerusalem in the 2nd century BC**

— The Book of Wisdom (pages 202-203) **was written in Egypt just a few years before the birth of Jesus.**

The latter two books are considered by protestants as apocryphal.*

WISE ADVICE

Why suffering?

3 1 Then, opening his mouth, and cursing the day
2 of his birth, | Job said,

3 "May the day of my birth be destroyed,
and the night on which it was said,
'A boy has been born.'...

11 "Why did death not take me when I came
out of my mother's body,
why did I not, when I came out, breathe my last breath?
13 For then I might have gone to my rest in quiet,
and in sleep have been in peace,
14 With kings and the counselors of the earth,
who built great houses for themselves.
16 Or as a child dead at birth
I might never have come into existence;
like young children who have not seen the light.

17 There the passions of the evil are over, and
those whose strength has come to an end have rest.[1]...

20 Why does he give light to him who is in trouble,
and life to the bitter in soul;
21 To those whose desire is for death, but it comes not;
who are searching for it more than for hidden treasure;

[1] Job is describing the abode of the dead, sheol* — a place of slumber and oblivion — as it was imagined by those who did not believe in resurrection.

JOB, A MAN IN REVOLT

Job's story is one of the best known in the Bible. It tells of a rich and contented man who becomes the victim of hideous afflictions. His crops are destroyed, and his herds stolen. His house topples down, killing his children. He is attacked by a skin disease which disfigures him.

Job is left alone and wretched in the company of his wife whom these reverses have soured. She prompts Job to deny the God Who has so badly rewarded his faithfulness.

Four of Job's friends come to comfort him. They all think that, if the God of justice has allowed such things to happen, it is to give Job the opportunity to atone for his sins. But Job refuses to be considered as a sinner. He turns to God and demands a reckoning.

Many people today
are crying out in distress.
Why is there so much injustice,
cruelty and hate?
Why are there so many innocent suffering?
How can God allow this to happen?
Why does He remain silent
when faced with so many dreadful things?
Now Job didn't bother to ask himself
these questions when he was rich,
when he could have shared or helped
to re-establish justice.
He left everything to God.
He thought that since everything was going well for him,
it must be going well for others.

22 Who are glad with great joy,
and full of delight
when they come
to their last resting place;
23 To a man whose way is hidden,
and who is cornered by God?"

Why does God keep a watch on us?

THE EYE OF GOD

Job, in the days when he was still a happy man, thought of the gaze of God as benevolent. Now, in his misery, Job sees it as "Big Brother," on the alert for faults and failings that will allow God to inflict His catalogue of punishments. This eternal snooping is intolerable.

A psalmist used almost the same terms to sing of the gaze of God constantly watching him. But he did not feel it as a constraint. It was rather the loving gaze of a friend always trying to guide the other on the road to eternity. See Psalm 139, page 226.

7 17 "What is man,
that you have made him great,
and that your attention is fixed on him,
18 And that your hand is on him every morning,
and that you are testing him every minute?
19 How long will it be before your eyes
are turned away from me,
so that I may have some time to breath?
20 If I have done wrong, what have I done to you,
O keeper of men? Why have you made me
a target for your punishment,
so that I am a burden to myself?
21 And why do you not pardon my offenses,
and let my sin be forgiven?
For now I go down to the dust,
and you will be searching for me everywhere,
but I will be gone."

God of the living

From time to time, Job stopped crying out in despair. It was then that hope could take root in his heart. He realized that he was journeying towards death. He even yearned for death. But was death the end of all contact with God? Job glimpsed the possibility of an encounter after death. God would shake him free of the dust of sheol.**

19 23 "If only my words might be recorded!
if they might be written in a book!
24 And with an iron pen, written on lead
be engraved into the rock forever!
25 But I am certain that my Redeemer is living,
and that in time to come he will stand on the earth;
26 And...without my flesh I will see God;
I will see[1] him on my side,
27 and not as a stranger to me.
My heart is broken with desire."

[1] These verses from Job were a stepping-stone in the slow development of the people's thinking as regards personal resurrection. See "resurrection."*

God replies to Job

The author makes God answer Job with sarcasm. Since Job was so good at criticizing his creator, he must be smarter than the almighty. Why could he not come and give advice or, better still, take the creator's place?*

38 1 And the Lord made answer to Job out of the
2 windstorm, saying, | "Who is this who makes the
counsel of God dark by words without knowledge?
3 Brace yourself like a man of war;
I will put questions to you,
and you will give me the answers.
8 Or where were you when the sea came to birth,
pushing out from its secret place;

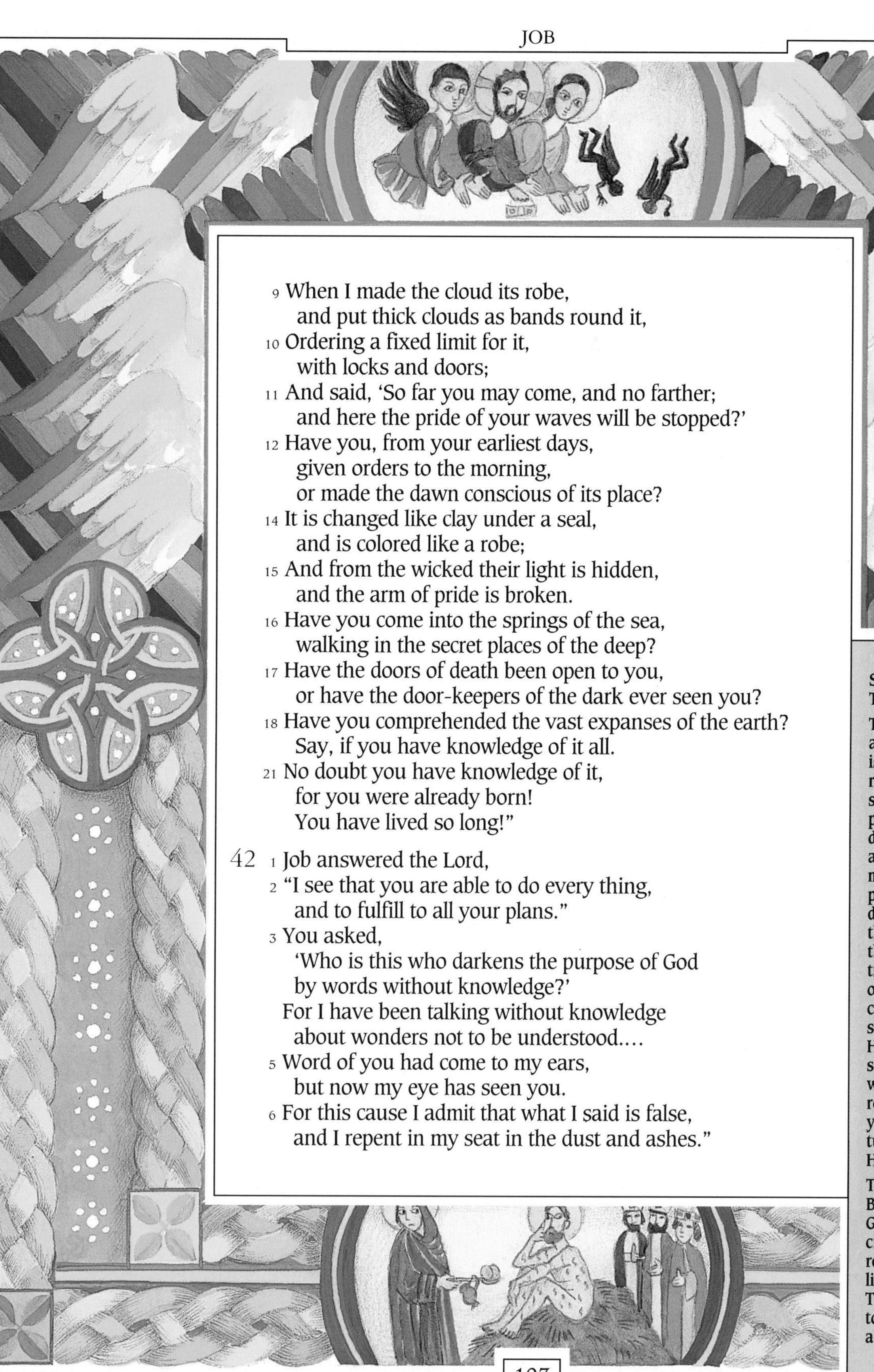

9 When I made the cloud its robe,
and put thick clouds as bands round it,
10 Ordering a fixed limit for it,
with locks and doors;
11 And said, 'So far you may come, and no farther;
and here the pride of your waves will be stopped?'
12 Have you, from your earliest days,
given orders to the morning,
or made the dawn conscious of its place?
14 It is changed like clay under a seal,
and is colored like a robe;
15 And from the wicked their light is hidden,
and the arm of pride is broken.
16 Have you come into the springs of the sea,
walking in the secret places of the deep?
17 Have the doors of death been open to you,
or have the door-keepers of the dark ever seen you?
18 Have you comprehended the vast expanses of the earth?
Say, if you have knowledge of it all.
21 No doubt you have knowledge of it,
for you were already born!
You have lived so long!"

42 1 Job answered the Lord,
2 "I see that you are able to do every thing,
and to fulfill to all your plans."
3 You asked,
'Who is this who darkens the purpose of God
by words without knowledge?'
For I have been talking without knowledge
about wonders not to be understood....
5 Word of you had come to my ears,
but now my eye has seen you.
6 For this cause I admit that what I said is false,
and I repent in my seat in the dust and ashes."

SUFFERING, A PATHWAY TO LIFE

The Book of Job only partly answers the question, "Why is there suffering?" It does rule out the idea that suffering is sent by God as a punishment for sin. God does not reward or punish act by act. He beckons to mankind via events, be they pleasant or painful, to deepen His Covenant* with them. When Job considered that he had been unjustly treated, he had a false idea of God. He felt entitled to a comfortable existence and summoned God to explain Himself. He was wrong. Yet since he had stayed in touch with God, he was able to realize the fact. He did not yield to the temptation to turn from God. And God let Himself be known.*

That was the message of the Book — to preserve trust in God whatever the circumstances; not to try to reshape the world in the light of our own "wisdom." The wisdom of God leads us to life through every trial and difficulty.

THE BOOK OF PROVERBS

Friendship, marriage, parent-child relations, concern for the poor and outcasts, laziness, pride in one's work — all these subjects had been endlessly mulled over by the sages.

They distrusted purely human wisdom, gained by the light of intelligence alone. They sought the wisdom that God, the only real "sage", grants to those who let themselves be enlightened by Him.

The thoughts of the sages were often compressed into "proverbs" — short, striking and easy to remember. After the captivity, sages compiled proverbs dating from different periods in the Book of Proverbs.

Wisdom for all

Solomon had always been regarded as a very wise man (see page 117). Some of the proverbs probably go back to his time.

14 31 He who oppresses the poor puts shame
on his Maker; but he who has mercy
on those who are in need gives him honor.

15 8 The offering of the wicked is disgusting to the Lord,
but the prayer of the righteous man is his delight.

16 9 A man may plan his course,
but the Lord is the guide of his steps.

16 How much better it is to get wisdom than gold! and
to get understanding[1] is more to be desired than silver.

27 9 Incense* and perfume gladden the heart,[2]
and the wise suggestion of a friend is sweet to the soul.

17 Iron makes iron sharp;
so a man sharpens his friend.

The wise person's prayer

30 7 "I have made request to you for two things;
do not keep them from me before my death:
8 Put far from me all false and foolish things:
do not give me great wealth or let me be in need,[3]
but give me only enough food.
9 I fear that if I am full, I may be false to you and say,
'Who is the Lord?' or if I am poor, I may become a thief,
using the name of my God wrongly."

[1] Not the sort of intelligence which piles up college degrees, but the intelligence capable of discerning God's presence in what happens around us.

[2] Perfume is here represented as the symbol of friendship. In Catholic ritual, the person anointed with chrism, a perfumed oil, is symbolically impelled by the Holy Spirit to seek friendship with others and share with them the good tidings of the gospel.*

[3] As the rest makes clear, the sage wishes to escape from misery. There is a distinction to be made between misery and poverty. Poverty, understood as a complete detachment from wealth, is a necessary condition for meeting with God. See Luke 16:1-13, page 323.

CCLESIASTICUS
en* Sirac (author of this
ook) was a citizen of
rusalem. He no doubt held
igh office and so had occasion
travel. He spent his life in an
ager quest for wisdom, which
e passed on to the young
eople of Jerusalem.
ate in life, in about 190 BC, he
ecided to set down his
achings in writing so that
very person "willing to learn
uld discover how to live
etter in accordance with the
aw."
he Book is regarded as
pocryphal by Protestants.

Give ear to the poor man

4 1 My son, do not take from the poor man
that which he needs to live,
and do not keep the beggar waiting.

2 Do not make a hungry man suffer,
nor aggravate a man in need.

3 Do not add trouble to a disturbed heart,
nor hold back your alms to a person in need.
4 Do not turn away from the one who appeals in his distress,
nor turn your back on the poor.

5 Do not look away from the needy,
nor give him reason to curse you.
6 If he curses you from the bitterness of his soul,
his maker will hear his prayer.[1]

8 Lend your ear to the poor man,
and reply with gentleness to his greeting.
9 Deliver the oppressed from the power of the oppressor,
and be firm in giving justice.

10 Be as a father to the orphans,
and as a husband to their mother.
Then you will be as a son to the Most High,
and he will love you even more than your own mother.[2]

[1] On the same subject, see the precepts of the Pentateuch,* page 72.

[2] Once again we find the image of God as mother. See Hosea 11:1-9, page 134, and Isaiah 49:14-16, page 169.

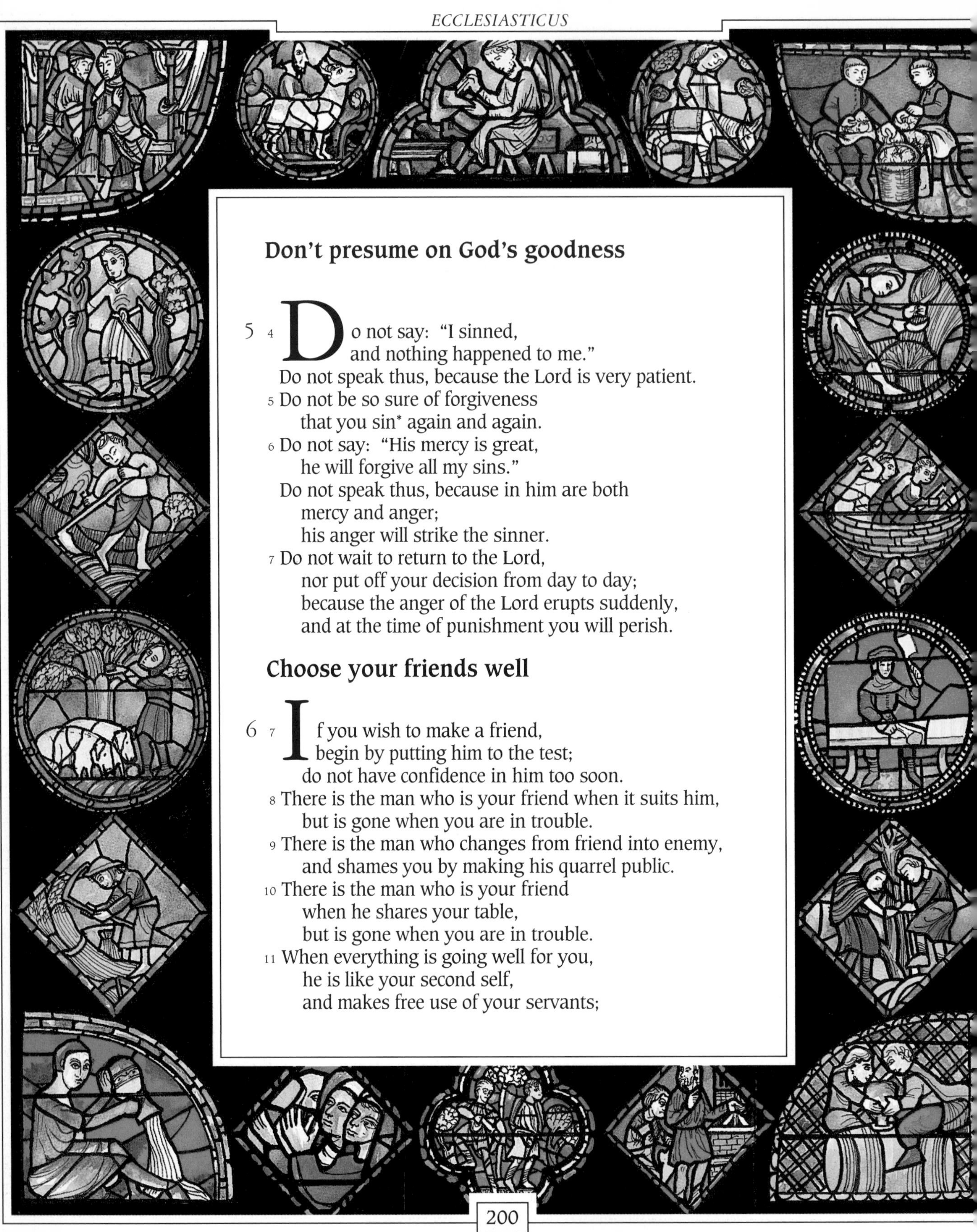

Don't presume on God's goodness

5 4 Do not say: "I sinned,
and nothing happened to me."
Do not speak thus, because the Lord is very patient.
5 Do not be so sure of forgiveness
that you sin* again and again.
6 Do not say: "His mercy is great,
he will forgive all my sins."
Do not speak thus, because in him are both
mercy and anger;
his anger will strike the sinner.
7 Do not wait to return to the Lord,
nor put off your decision from day to day;
because the anger of the Lord erupts suddenly,
and at the time of punishment you will perish.

Choose your friends well

6 7 If you wish to make a friend,
begin by putting him to the test;
do not have confidence in him too soon.
8 There is the man who is your friend when it suits him,
but is gone when you are in trouble.
9 There is the man who changes from friend into enemy,
and shames you by making his quarrel public.
10 There is the man who is your friend
when he shares your table,
but is gone when you are in trouble.
11 When everything is going well for you,
he is like your second self,
and makes free use of your servants;

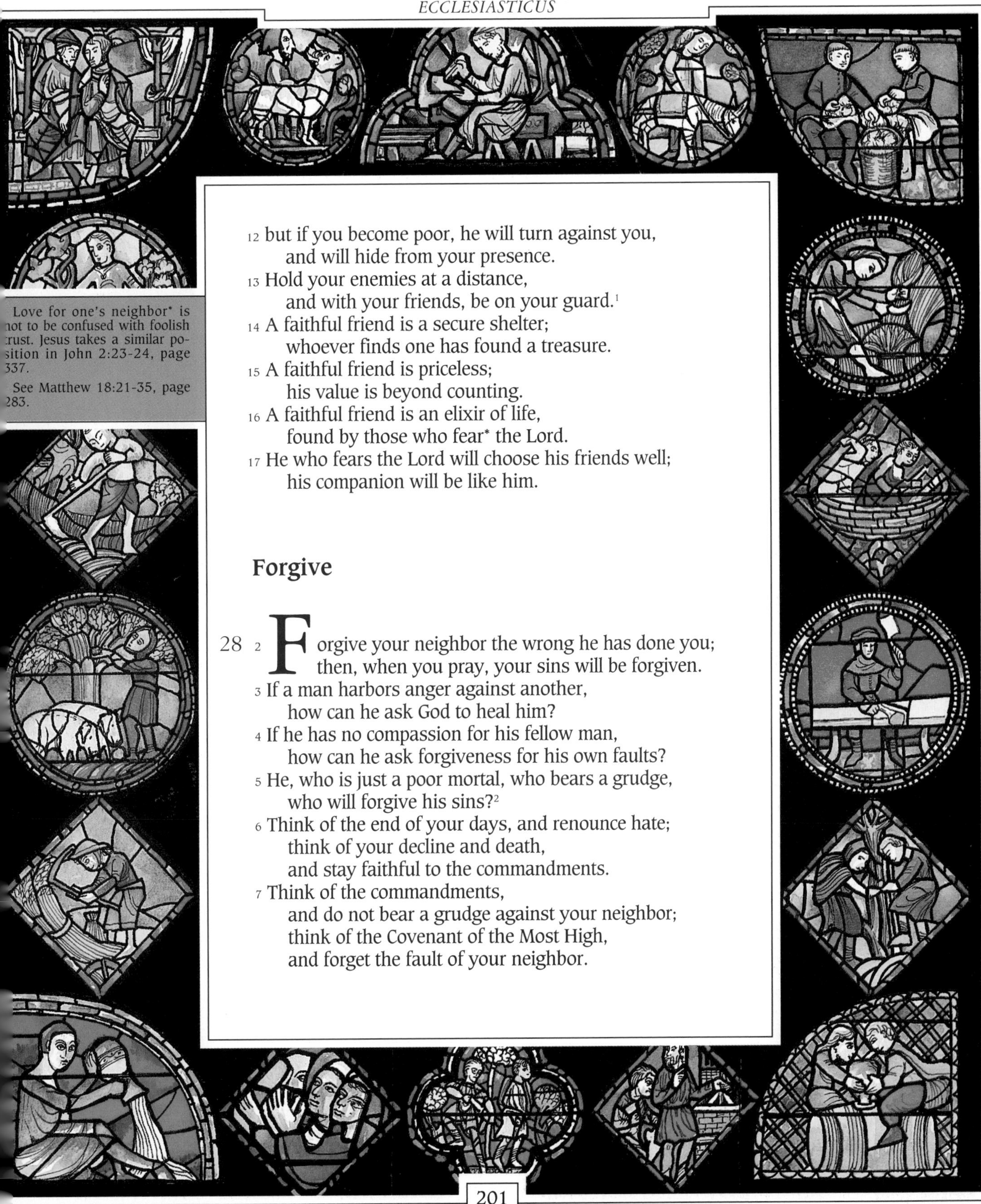

12 but if you become poor, he will turn against you,
and will hide from your presence.
13 Hold your enemies at a distance,
and with your friends, be on your guard.[1]
14 A faithful friend is a secure shelter;
whoever finds one has found a treasure.
15 A faithful friend is priceless;
his value is beyond counting.
16 A faithful friend is an elixir of life,
found by those who fear* the Lord.
17 He who fears the Lord will choose his friends well;
his companion will be like him.

Forgive

28 2 Forgive your neighbor the wrong he has done you;
then, when you pray, your sins will be forgiven.
3 If a man harbors anger against another,
how can he ask God to heal him?
4 If he has no compassion for his fellow man,
how can he ask forgiveness for his own faults?
5 He, who is just a poor mortal, who bears a grudge,
who will forgive his sins?[2]
6 Think of the end of your days, and renounce hate;
think of your decline and death,
and stay faithful to the commandments.
7 Think of the commandments,
and do not bear a grudge against your neighbor;
think of the Covenant of the Most High,
and forget the fault of your neighbor.

Love for one's neighbor* is not to be confused with foolish trust. Jesus takes a similar position in John 2:23-24, page 337.

See Matthew 18:21-35, page 283.

BOOK OF WISDOM

This book was written in Greek in the Egyptian city of Alexandria during the century before the birth of Jesus.

The Jews of the diaspora,* settled for generations past in the cities around the Mediterranean, no longer understood Hebrew. From the 3rd century BC on, Greek translations of the books of the Torah* and the prophets began to appear. Later, authors began writing books straight into Greek (see Canon).* These authors are considered by Catholics to be inspired.* In the Catholic view, they mark an important step in the history of God's revelation to mankind, since they showed that God was not Hebrew but universal. He wished to approach people of every tongue and culture. He made Himself present in different customs and ways of thinking in order to disclose His nature. To know Him, there was no need to change nationality or learn other languages. He came to greet people wherever they lived.

Most Protestant churches recognize only the Old Testament books written in Hebrew and treat the Greek books as apocryphal.*

Wisdom of God, folly of humans

2 12 "Let us lead the just man into a trap because he is
against us, and is opposed to our conduct;
he reproaches us for not obeying God's laws,
and accuses us of abandoning our traditions.*
13 He claims to possess knowledge* of God,
and calls himself son of the Lord.[1]
14 He is a condemnation of our ideas; and just his presence
15 weighs against us, | because his way of life is different
from other people's, and his conduct also.
16 He regards us as suspect, and avoids our paths as if
afraid of becoming unclean. He proclaims the final
outcome of the just to be happy, and boasts that God is
17 his father. | Let us see if his words are true; let us see
what will happen to him in the end.
18 If the just man is the son of God, God will help him, and
19 deliver him from his enemies. | Let us try him with
outrage and torment. We will see of what good is his
20 mildness; we will put his patience to the test. | Let us
condemn him to a shameful death, since he claims that
21 someone is watching over him." | That is how those
people reasoned, but they were misguided; their
22 wickedness had blinded them. | They did not know the
secrets of God. They never expected that holiness would
be rewarded; that a faultless soul* would be glorified.
23 But God created man for immortality,
making him the image of what is in himself.
24 It was by the jealousy of the devil
that death entered the world, and the experience
of it is for those who take his side.

[1] The true sage acknowledges that God loves her or him like a parent. This is the reason why the sage can claim to be the child of God. See John 1:12-13, page 333.

ACCEPTING WISDOM

The author returned to the theme of the difference between human and divine wisdom. Humans are constantly tempted to throw out God's wisdom, which their short-sighted reasoning views as insane (see what Paul has to say in 1 Corinthians 1:11-25, page 432). Did not Solomon himself, the wisest man in Israel, ask for a heart which could distinguish between good and evil and stay tuned to the messages sent by the Lord? And did he not let that heart harden to the point of bowing down before idols?* (See pages 116 and 120.)

The patience and mercifulness of God's wisdom

11 23 Lord, you have mercy for all men,
because you can do all things.
You close your eyes to their sins,
so that they will be converted.*

24 You love everything that exists.
You are not repelled by any of your creation,
because you would not have created
any being that you hated.

25 And how could any being exist
if you had not willed it?
How could it continue to exist
if you had not called it into being?

26 You spare all beings because they are yours,
master, who loves all life;
12 1 for it is your undying breath that gives life
to all things.

2 Those who fall, you pick back up
little by little,
warning them, and reminding them
how they sinned,
so that they will turn from evil,*
and believe in you, Lord.

13 There is no other God but you,
Lord;
you, who care for all things,
thus showing that your judgments
are not unjust.

THE GREEK BIBLE

The most famous Greek translation of the Old Testament books is called the "Septuagint" (from the Latin word for "seventy"). Tradition has it that seventy translators, all working separately, produced an identical translation. The legend is evidence that this translation carried great weight with the Jews. The disciples of Jesus quoted from the Septuagint in their preaching and letters.

Lord, you love all creation,
the sky and the stars,
the trees and the flowers,
the rivers, prairies, mountains
and animals.

You love all humankind;
not only the good and the perfect,
those who succeed in whatever they do,
but also the clumsy
and those who are hurting
in body and mind.
You love sinners,
those who are selfish or proud.
You want to save everyone
from sin because you know they are capable
of being like you.

Lord, I truly want to love
those whom you love!

A TIME OF APOCALYPSES

The years go by but there is no sign of improvement in human history. Wars, treachery and atrocities follow one another. Will not God tire of sending messengers whom nobody wants to hear? Will the Messiah* ever come? In answer to these questions, a number of books were written in the last three centuries before Christ. Rich in visionary images and esoteric language, they are called apocalypses.* They announce that the Messiah will come to usher in the end of the world. God will sort those who have tried to be loyal to Him from the rest. It is important for people to be ready and to keep their faith.*

The Old Testament retains only a small selection of these writings. They are found in the Book of Daniel, compiled during the persecutions of Antiochus Epiphanes (see page 178). Some scholars consider the book of Daniel to have been written in the sixth century.

FANTASTIC VISIONS

The beasts and the Son of Man

Human history is full of monstrous tyrants. Daniel portrays them as beasts. God sends a messenger, "like a son of man," to vanquish their barbarity. He will, humanely, found the reign of God, and the righteous will be filled with joy.*

7 2 Daniel said: "I had a vision at night, and saw the
four winds of heaven violently moving the great
3 sea. | And four great beasts came up from the sea, different
4 one from another.[1] | The first was like a lion and had eagle's
wings. While I was watching, its wings were pulled off, and
it was lifted up from the earth and placed on two feet like a
5 man, and a man's heart was given to it. | And I saw another
beast, like a bear, and it was lifted up on one side. Tthree
ribss were in its mouth, between its teeth, and they said to
6 it, 'Get up! Eat your fill of flesh.' | After this I saw another
beast, like a leopard, which had on its back four wings like
those of a bird. The beast had four heads, and the authority
7 to rule was given to it. | After this, in my vision of the
night, I saw a fourth beast, a fearful thing and very
troubling, full of power and strength. It had great iron teeth
with which it took its food, crushing some of it to bits and
stamping down the rest with its feet. It was different from
all the beasts before it. It had ten horns....
9 I went on looking till the seats of kings were placed, and
one like a very old man took his seat. His clothing was
white as snow,[2] and the hair of his head was like clean
wool; his seat was flames of fire and its wheels burning
10 fire. | A stream of fire was flowing and coming out from
before him: thousands upon thousands were his servants,
and ten thousand times ten thousand were in their places
before him. The judge was seated and the books were open.

[1] The author describes four "beasts", that are a monstrous combination of several animals created by God. They represent the four empires that have attacked Judah. The first is Babylon, the second the Medes, the third the Persians and the fourth the Greeks. They emerge from the sea, since the sea is the home of the powers of evil.* See pages 241-242.

[2] White is the color for God. See the account of the transfiguration, Mark 9:3, page 246.

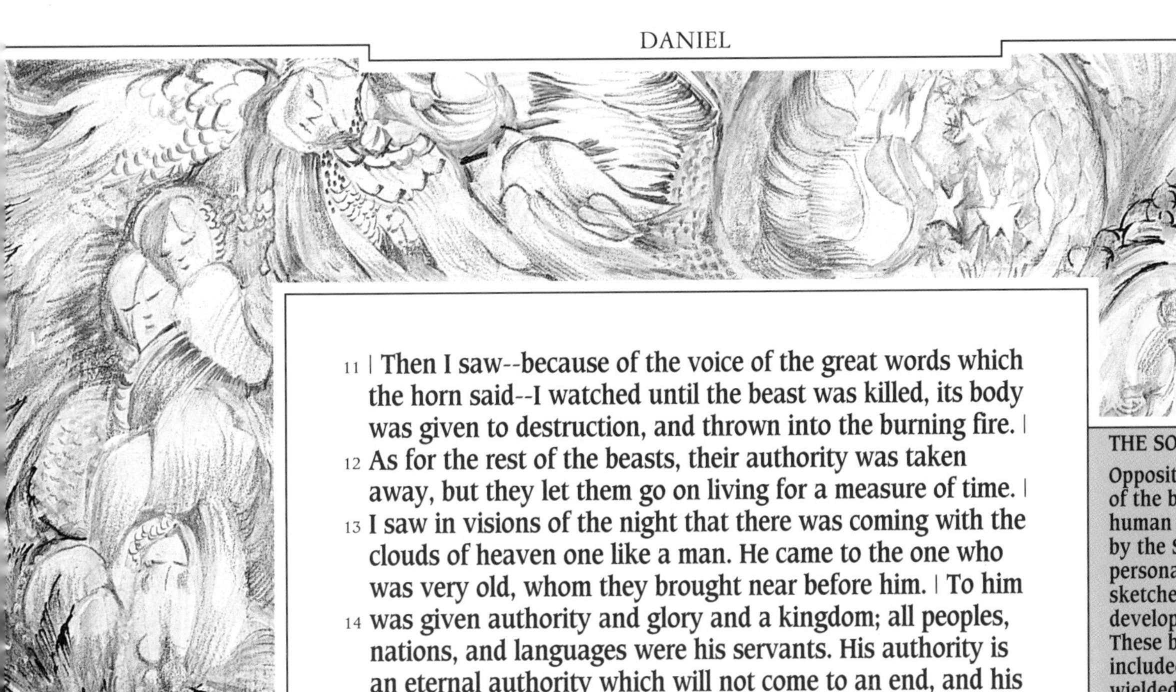

11 | Then I saw--because of the voice of the great words which
the horn said--I watched until the beast was killed, its body
was given to destruction, and thrown into the burning fire. |
12 As for the rest of the beasts, their authority was taken
away, but they let them go on living for a measure of time. |
13 I saw in visions of the night that there was coming with the
clouds of heaven one like a man. He came to the one who
was very old, whom they brought near before him. | To him
14 was given authority and glory and a kingdom; all peoples,
nations, and languages were his servants. His authority is
an eternal authority which will not come to an end, and his
kingdom is one which will never be destroyed."

THE SON OF MAN

Opposite the ghastly regime of the beasts, God sets a human government founded by the Son of Man. This persona, only lightly sketched by Daniel, is developed in other books. These books, although not included in the Bible, wielded a great deal of influence. The apocalypse of Henok, for example, presents the Son of Man as the messiah of the end of time. Jesus would often refer to himself by this title, as though to emphasize his heavenly origin.

The chief angel and resurrection for all

ENERAL RESURRECTION

The second Book of Maccabees clearly spoke of esurrection, but restricted it o the righteous (see page 80). **Daniel proclaimed esurrection for everyone. Some would receive an eternal reward; others would e doomed to eternal "downfall." In the view of the apocalypses, esurrection would occur after a period of terrible distress. In order to establish the reign of God, the angels would need to battle against a world corrupted by sin.**

12 1 "And at that time Michael,[1] will arise, the great
prince, who protects your people. There will be
a time of trouble,[2] such as there never was from the
beginning of nations until then. At that time your people
will be kept safe, everyone who is recorded in the book. |
2 A number of those who are sleeping in the dust of the
earth will come out of their sleep, some to eternal life and
some to eternal shame.[3]
3 And those who are wise will be shining like the
brightness of the heavens; and those who led many to
righteousness will be like the stars for ever and ever."

[1] There is much talk of angels in the apocalypses. Since the world was so badly perverted by sin, God could take action only through other beings.

[2] The apocalypses insisted so much on the final cataclysm (preceding the victory of God) that, in ordinary speech, the word apocalypse has become a synonym for disaster. Earthquakes and wars are often described as apocalyptic.

[3] This is the first mention of what came to be called Hell.* Not be confused with the nether world of sheol.*

MOYSES
SALOMON REX
DAVID REX
IEREMIAS
MICHEAS
IONAS
IOEL
MALACHIAS
ESDRAS
DANIEL
ISAAC
PAVLVS
IOHANNES
PETRVS
MARCVS
IVDAS
LVCAS
IACOBVS
INPRINCIPIO ERAT VERBVM

PART THREE

THE PRAYER OF THE PEOPLE OF GOD

THE BOOK OF PSALMS

Abraham, Moses, Isaiah and Jeremiah all made much use of prayer. They conversed with God as friend to friend.[1] *They listened to Him*[2] *and spoke to Him.*

In the minds of the people, it was David who was most remembered in connection with prayer. It was said that he invented musical instruments[3] *so as to sing to God of his grief, joy and repentance. He was the supposed author of the most beautiful prayers recited by the people in the Temple or the synagogues** (see page 105). *The compilation of these prayers is the Book of Psalms.**

The Psalms teach us that praying is going before God as we are, our hearts brimming with joy and gratitude in moments of happiness, or our heads bursting with screams and tears in times of misery. To go before God, there is no need to wear a mask, trying to look composed and amiable when we are boiling with anger or resentment. No, we must "let it all hang out" in front of God, the best and worst of ourselves. The Lord hears the person who approaches Him with trust. He makes Himself better known* to that person. He heals, and helps that person to change.*

[1] See Genesis 18:22-32, page 42; Deuteronomy 34:10, page 89; Isaiah 6:1-8, page 137; Jeremiah 20:7-11, page 154.

[2] The essential act of a believer is listening. See Deuteronomy 6:4-5, page 84; Luke 10:38-42, page 318.

[3] See Amos 6:5, page 129.

PSALM 2

The messiah, son of God

1 Why do the nations conspire so, and
why are the thoughts of the people so foolish?
2 The kings of the earth have taken their stand,
and the rulers stand together
against the Lord,
and against the king of his Anointed One, saying,
3 "Let their chains be broken,
and their cords taken from off us."[1]

4 Then he whose throne is in the heavens will be laughing:
the Lord will laugh at them.
5 Then will they hear his angry words,
and by his wrath they will be troubled:
6 "But I have put my king
on my holy hill of Zion."[2]

7 I will make clear the Lord's decision.
He has said to me, "You are my son,*
this day have I have become your father.[3]
8 Make your request to me, and
I will give you the nations for your heritage, and
the farthest limits of the earth will be under your hand.
9 They will be ruled by you with a rod of iron;[4]
they will be broken like a potter's jar."

[1] This psalm speaks of a victorious, overlording messiah. Jesus will profoundly alter this view. His authority rests entirely on love.

[2] This psalm was sung at royal coronations. It was still sung after the monarchy had disappeared. It was a way of asking God to send the promised Messiah.

[3] The anointing of the king made him a messiah. This was neither a reward nor a distinction placing him on a higher footing than anybody else. It signified the mission* entrusted to him by God. God called the king His "son." He "begot" him, that is to say, He gave him His spirit, so that the king would hold the people to the Covenant.*

[4] See Isaiah 11:4, page 141, and Revelation 12:5, page 453.

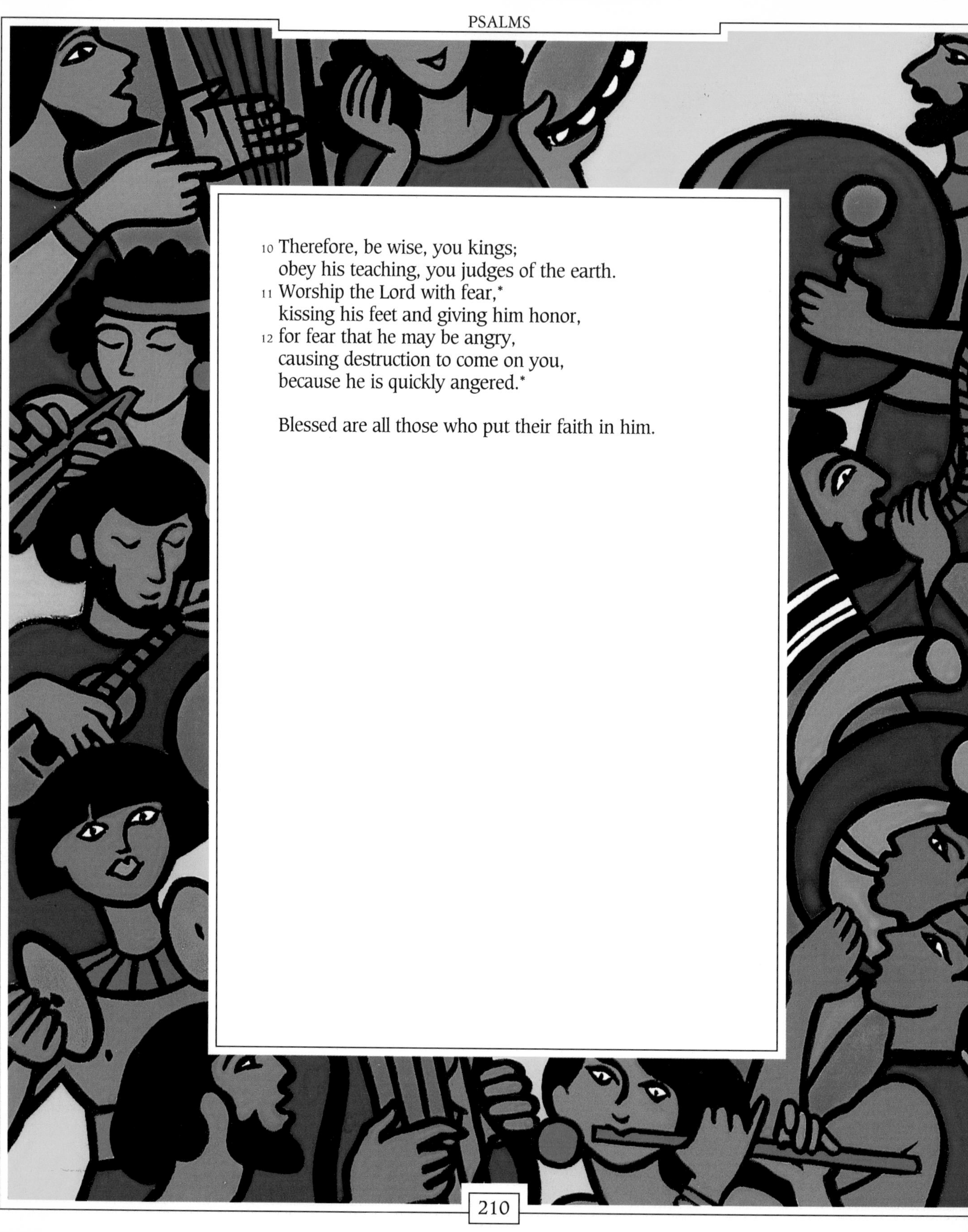

10 Therefore, be wise, you kings;
obey his teaching, you judges of the earth.
11 Worship the Lord with fear,*
kissing his feet and giving him honor,
12 for fear that he may be angry,
causing destruction to come on you,
because he is quickly angered.*

Blessed are all those who put their faith in him.

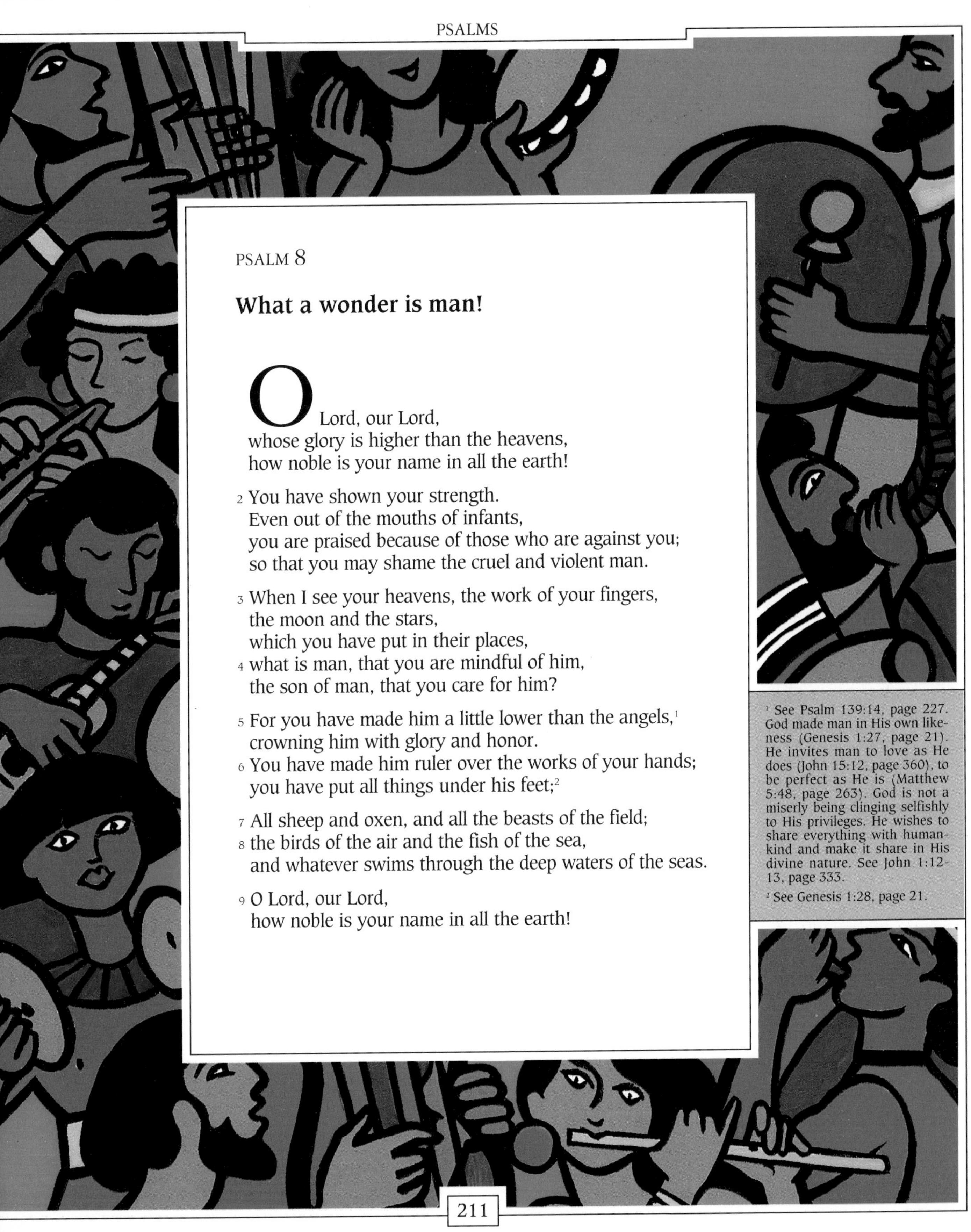

PSALM 8

What a wonder is man!

O Lord, our Lord,
whose glory is higher than the heavens,
how noble is your name in all the earth!

2 You have shown your strength.
Even out of the mouths of infants,
you are praised because of those who are against you;
so that you may shame the cruel and violent man.

3 When I see your heavens, the work of your fingers,
the moon and the stars,
which you have put in their places,
4 what is man, that you are mindful of him,
the son of man, that you care for him?

5 For you have made him a little lower than the angels,[1]
crowning him with glory and honor.
6 You have made him ruler over the works of your hands;
you have put all things under his feet;[2]

7 All sheep and oxen, and all the beasts of the field;
8 the birds of the air and the fish of the sea,
and whatever swims through the deep waters of the seas.

9 O Lord, our Lord,
how noble is your name in all the earth!

[1] See Psalm 139:14, page 227. God made man in His own likeness (Genesis 1:27, page 21). He invites man to love as He does (John 15:12, page 360), to be perfect as He is (Matthew 5:48, page 263). God is not a miserly being clinging selfishly to His privileges. He wishes to share everything with humankind and make it share in His divine nature. See John 1:12-13, page 333.

[2] See Genesis 1:28, page 21.

PSALM 22 OR 21 [1]

Lord, deliver me from fear!

My God, my God,
why have you forsaken me?[2]
why are you so far from helping me,
and from the words of my crying?
2 O my God, I cry out during the day,
and you give no answer;
and in the night, and have no rest....

4 Our fathers had faith in you:
they had faith and you were their savior.
5 They sent up their cry to you and were made free.
They put their faith in you and were not put to shame.

6 But I am a worm and not a man,
cursed by men, and looked down on by the people.
7 I am laughed at by all those who see me,
hurling insults and shaking their heads, they say,
8 "He put his faith in the Lord; let the Lord rescue him now.
Let the Lord be his savior, since he had delight in him."[3]

9 But it was you who cared for me from birth:

10 you gave me faith even from my mother's breasts.
I was in your hands even before my birth;
you are my God from the time
when I was in my mother's body.[4]

11 Be not far from me, for trouble is near;
there is no one to help me.
12 A great herd of oxen is round me:
I am shut in by the strong oxen of Bashan.[5]

[1] There are two numberings o the Psalms, the Hebrew and th Greek. In the Greek translatic of the Bible (see page 203 two Psalms were run togethe so producing a number les The Greek numbering, used i Catholic prayerbooks, is show in smaller characters. The He- brew numbering is given firs since it is the one found i Bibles.

[2] Jesus on the cross cried o this Psalm in anguish to hi Father (Matthew 27:4 page 380). It is the cry of on who firmly believes that God close by but does not feel th presence.

[3] This is the same as the argument in Wisdom 2:17-20, page 202.

[4] See Jeremiah 1:5, page 149.

[5] Amos introduced us to the region of Bashan. See page 130, "Called by God."

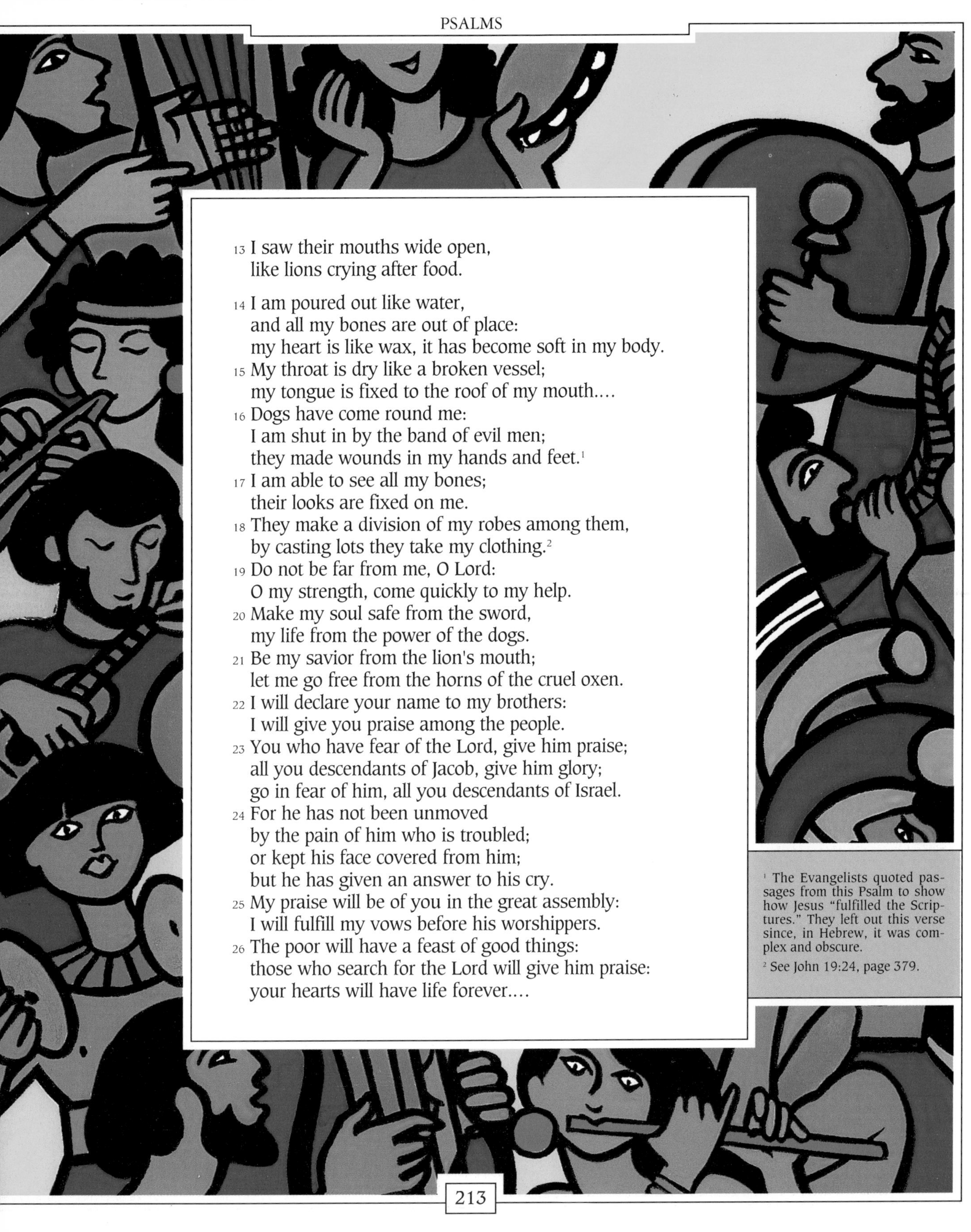

13 I saw their mouths wide open,
like lions crying after food.

14 I am poured out like water,
and all my bones are out of place:
my heart is like wax, it has become soft in my body.
15 My throat is dry like a broken vessel;
my tongue is fixed to the roof of my mouth....
16 Dogs have come round me:
I am shut in by the band of evil men;
they made wounds in my hands and feet.[1]
17 I am able to see all my bones;
their looks are fixed on me.
18 They make a division of my robes among them,
by casting lots they take my clothing.[2]
19 Do not be far from me, O Lord:
O my strength, come quickly to my help.
20 Make my soul safe from the sword,
my life from the power of the dogs.
21 Be my savior from the lion's mouth;
let me go free from the horns of the cruel oxen.
22 I will declare your name to my brothers:
I will give you praise among the people.
23 You who have fear of the Lord, give him praise;
all you descendants of Jacob, give him glory;
go in fear of him, all you descendants of Israel.
24 For he has not been unmoved
by the pain of him who is troubled;
or kept his face covered from him;
but he has given an answer to his cry.
25 My praise will be of you in the great assembly:
I will fulfill my vows before his worshippers.
26 The poor will have a feast of good things:
those who search for the Lord will give him praise:
your hearts will have life forever....

[1] The Evangelists quoted passages from this Psalm to show how Jesus "fulfilled the Scriptures." They left out this verse since, in Hebrew, it was complex and obscure.

[2] See John 19:24, page 379.

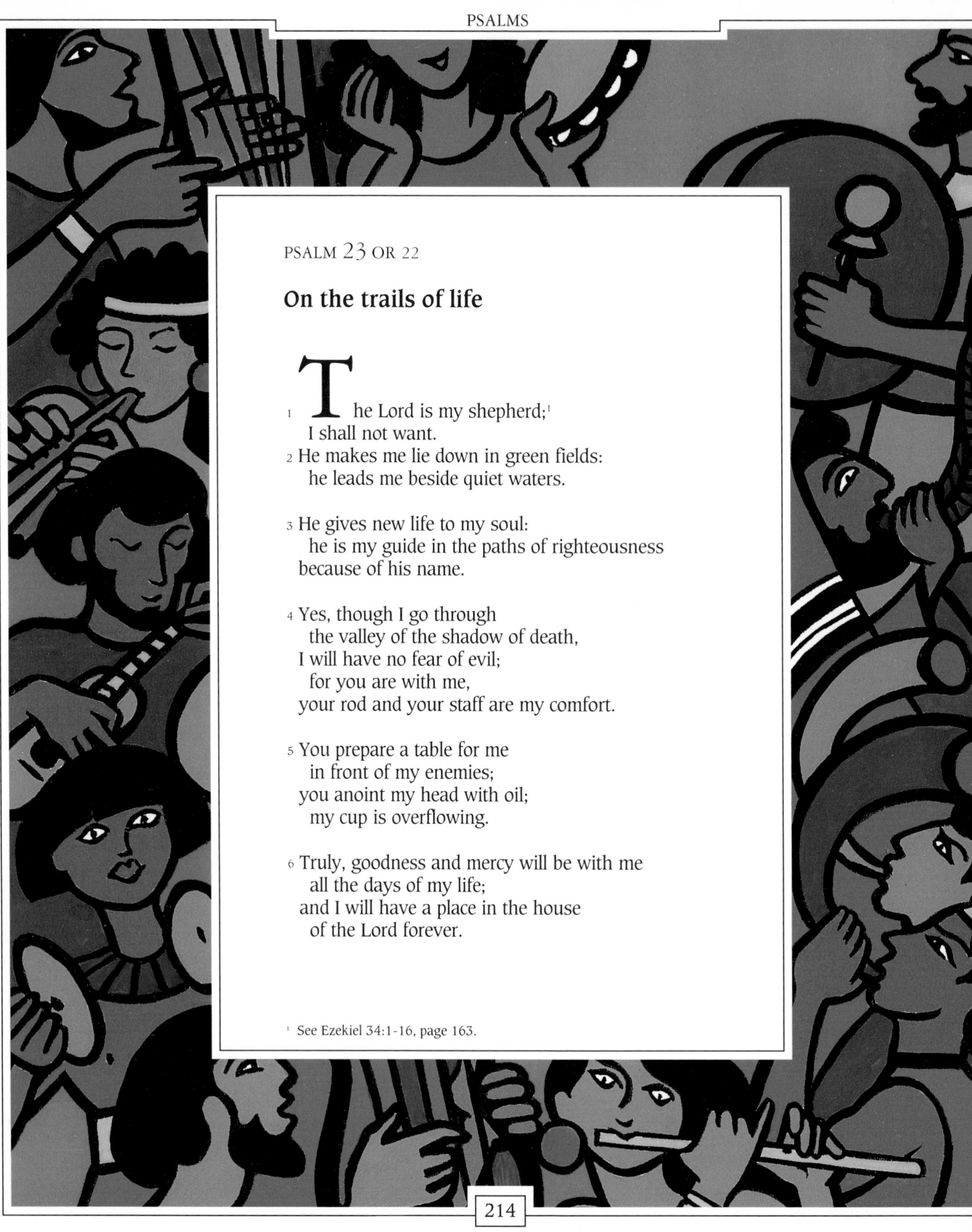

PSALM 23 OR 22

On the trails of life

1 The Lord is my shepherd;[1]
I shall not want.
2 He makes me lie down in green fields:
he leads me beside quiet waters.

3 He gives new life to my soul:
he is my guide in the paths of righteousness
because of his name.

4 Yes, though I go through
the valley of the shadow of death,
I will have no fear of evil;
for you are with me,
your rod and your staff are my comfort.

5 You prepare a table for me
in front of my enemies;
you anoint my head with oil;
my cup is overflowing.

6 Truly, goodness and mercy will be with me
all the days of my life;
and I will have a place in the house
of the Lord forever.

[1] See Ezekiel 34:1-16, page 163.

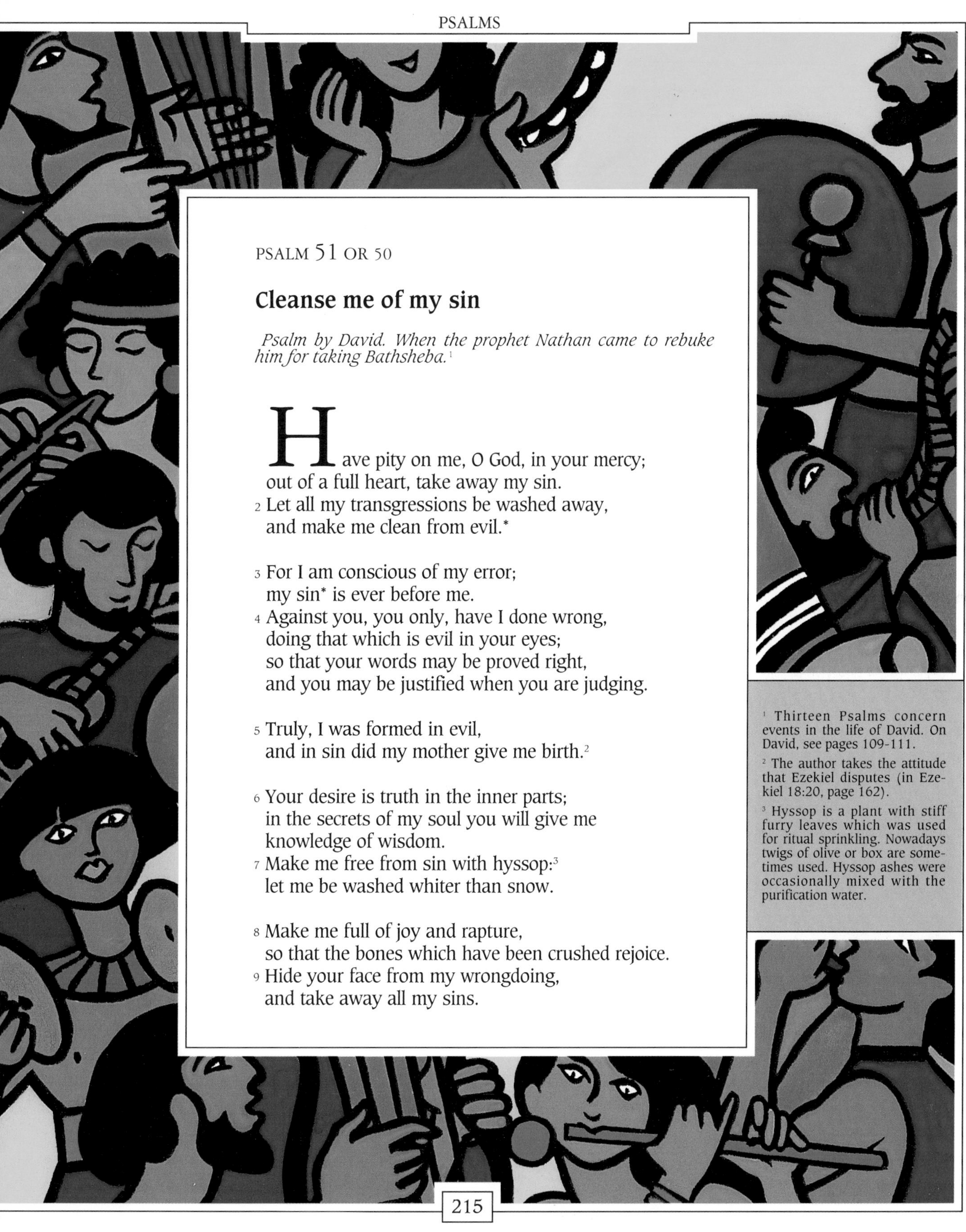

PSALM 51 OR 50

Cleanse me of my sin

Psalm by David. When the prophet Nathan came to rebuke him for taking Bathsheba.[1]

Have pity on me, O God, in your mercy;
out of a full heart, take away my sin.
2 Let all my transgressions be washed away,
and make me clean from evil.*

3 For I am conscious of my error;
my sin* is ever before me.
4 Against you, you only, have I done wrong,
doing that which is evil in your eyes;
so that your words may be proved right,
and you may be justified when you are judging.

5 Truly, I was formed in evil,
and in sin did my mother give me birth.[2]

6 Your desire is truth in the inner parts;
in the secrets of my soul you will give me
knowledge of wisdom.
7 Make me free from sin with hyssop:[3]
let me be washed whiter than snow.

8 Make me full of joy and rapture,
so that the bones which have been crushed rejoice.
9 Hide your face from my wrongdoing,
and take away all my sins.

[1] Thirteen Psalms concern events in the life of David. On David, see pages 109-111.

[2] The author takes the attitude that Ezekiel disputes (in Ezekiel 18:20, page 162).

[3] Hyssop is a plant with stiff furry leaves which was used for ritual sprinkling. Nowadays twigs of olive or box are sometimes used. Hyssop ashes were occasionally mixed with the purification water.

10 Make a clean heart in me, O God;
give me a right spirit again.
11 Do not send me out of your presence,
or take your holy spirit from me.

12 Give me back the joy of your salvation;
let a free spirit be my support.
13 Then will I make your ways clear to wrongdoers;
and sinners will be turned to you.

14 Be my savior from violent death, O God,
the God of my salvation;
and my tongue will give praise to your righteousness.
15 O Lord, let my lips be open,
so that my mouth may declare your praise.

16 You have no desire for a sacrifice or I would give it;
you have no delight in burnt offerings.*
17 The sacrifices of God
are a broken spirit;
a broken[1] and sorrowing heart,
O God, you will not despise....

[1] The sacrifice pleasing to God is the crushing of personal pride and the confession of being not a righteous person but a sinner who needs to be saved.
After the return from captivity in Babylon, another verse was added to this psalm. It spoke of the rebuilding of the Temple and the resumption of animal sacrifices.

PSALM 63 OR 62

My soul thirsts for you

Psalm by David. When he was in the desert of Judah..[1]

O God, you are my God;
earnestly will I search for you.
My soul is thirsts for you;
my flesh[2] longs for you,
as a dry and burning land where there is no water,
2 to see your power and your glory,
as I have seen you in the holy place.
3 Because your mercy is better than life,
my lips will praise you.

4 So will I go on blessing you all my life,
lifting up my hands in your name.
5 My soul will be comforted, as with good food;
and I will praise* you with songs of joy.

6 In bed I will remember you;
I will think of you at night.
7 Because you have been my help,
I will have joy in the shade of your wings.[3]

8 My soul keeps ever near you:
your right hand is my support.
9 But those who desire to destroy my soul
will go down to the depths of the earth.
10 They will be cut off by the sword;
they will be food for foxes.[4] ...

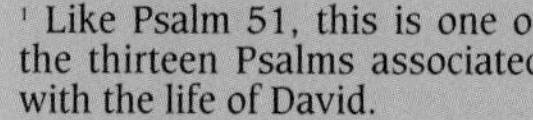

[1] Like Psalm 51, this is one of the thirteen Psalms associated with the life of David.

[2] In Jewish thinking, the "soul" and the "body" were two ways of denoting the human person. "My soul" and "my body" stood for the author of the Psalm. Verse 1 could be translated as "I thirst for you; I long for you." The soul refers to the person's desire to live with God, whereas the body suggests human frailty. A person relying on his own strength finds difficulty in living with God.

At the top of the Ark* of the 'ovenant were two cherubim* vho spread their wings over he cover known as the propi-iatory.* To sit under the wings vas to ensure God's benevo-ence. Gradually, the wings vere taken to be attributes of iod in everyday language.

Verses 10 and 11 express the salmist's vengeful feelings. It vas important to be able to ad-nit them to God. Otherwise, iod could not expunge the poi-on of hatred. See page 208, ast paragraph.

PSALM 100 OR 99

All the earth, praise God!

Make a glad sound to the Lord, all the earth.
2 Worship the Lord with joy;
come before him with a song.

3 Know* that the Lord is God;
it is he who has made us, and we are his;
we are his people, and the sheep of his pasture.[1]

4 Enter his gates with joy,
and his house with praise;
give him honor, blessing his name.

5 For the Lord is good,
and his love is never-ending;
his faithfulness is unchanging through all generations.

[1] See Ezekiel 34:1-16, page 163, and Psalm 23, page 214.

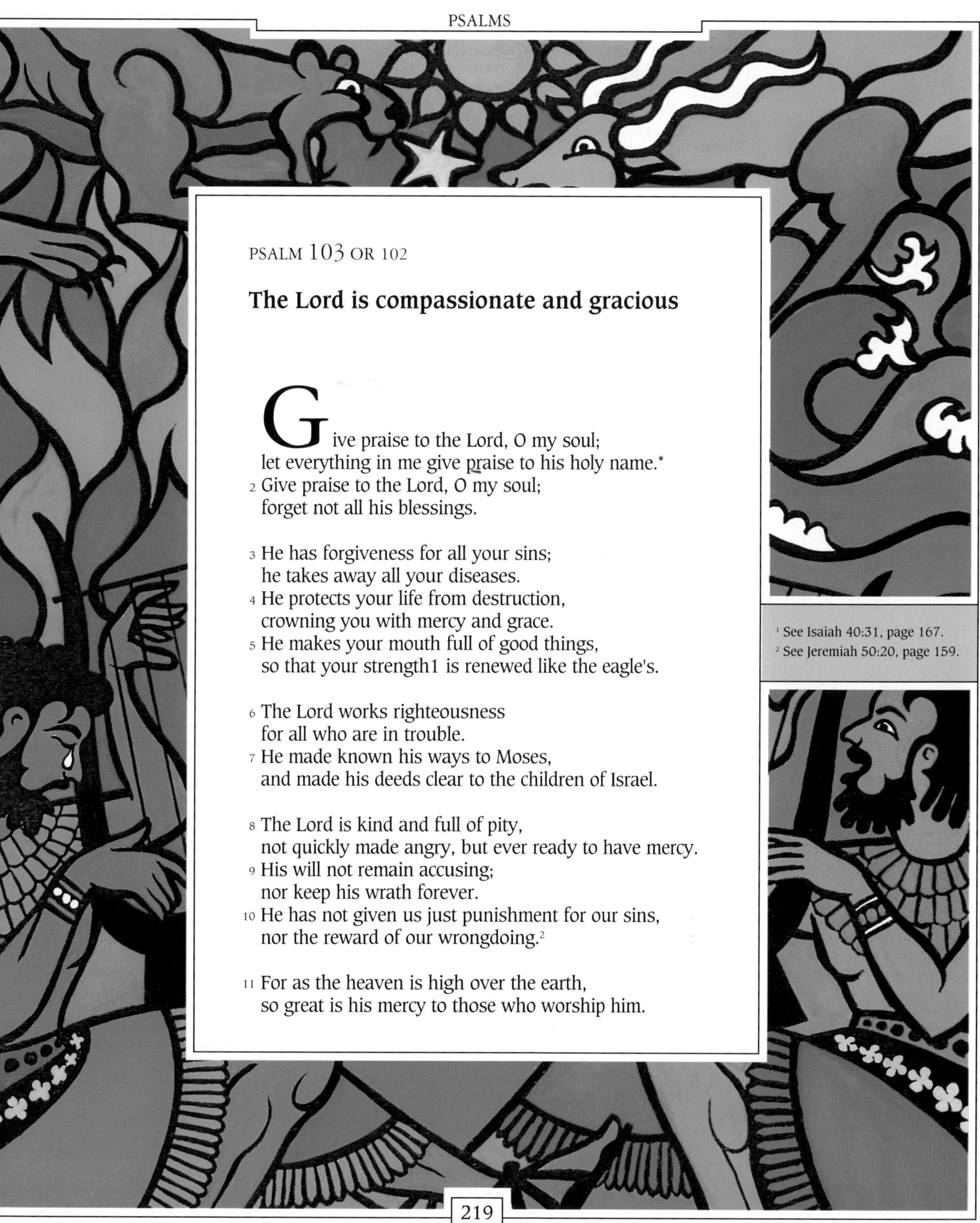

PSALM 103 OR 102

The Lord is compassionate and gracious

Give praise to the Lord, O my soul;
let everything in me give praise to his holy name.*
2 Give praise to the Lord, O my soul;
forget not all his blessings.

3 He has forgiveness for all your sins;
he takes away all your diseases.
4 He protects your life from destruction,
crowning you with mercy and grace.
5 He makes your mouth full of good things,
so that your strength1 is renewed like the eagle's.

6 The Lord works righteousness
for all who are in trouble.
7 He made known his ways to Moses,
and made his deeds clear to the children of Israel.

8 The Lord is kind and full of pity,
not quickly made angry, but ever ready to have mercy.
9 His will not remain accusing;
nor keep his wrath forever.
10 He has not given us just punishment for our sins,
nor the reward of our wrongdoing.[2]

11 For as the heaven is high over the earth,
so great is his mercy to those who worship him.

[1] See Isaiah 40:31, page 167.
[2] See Jeremiah 50:20, page 159.

12 As far as the east is from the west,
so far has he removed our sins from us.
13 As a father has pity on his children,
so the Lord has pity on those who fear* him.

14 For he has knowledge of how we are formed;
he sees that we are only dust.
15 As for man, his days are as grass:
his beautiful growth is like the flower of the field.
16 The wind goes over it and it is gone;
and its place sees it no longer.

17 But the mercy of the Lord is eternal
for those who fear him,
and their children's children
will see his righteousness;*
18 If they keep his Covenant,*
and obey his laws....

PSALM 122 OR 121

Peace to Jerusalem

I was glad because they said to me,
"We will go into the house of the Lord."
2 At last our feet were inside your doors,
O Jerusalem.
3 O Jerusalem, you are like a town
which is closely joined together;

4 To which the tribes went up,
even the tribes of the Lord,
for a witness to Israel,
to praise the name of the Lord.
5 There thrones for the judges were placed,
even the thrones of the house of David.

6 O pray for the peace of Jerusalem;[1]
may they whose love is given to you be secure.
7 May peace be inside your walls,
and wealth in your noble houses.

8 Because of my brothers and friends,
I will now say, "Let peace be with you."
9 Because of the house of the Lord our God,
I will be working for your good.

[1] Psalm 122, like Psalms 126, 130 and 131, forms part of the "psalms (or canticles) of the ascent" sung by pilgrims going up to Jerusalem for the great feasts.* The Hebrew word translated here as peace is shalom, which means not only harmony but also everything contributing to people's well-being (health, material and spiritual prosperity).

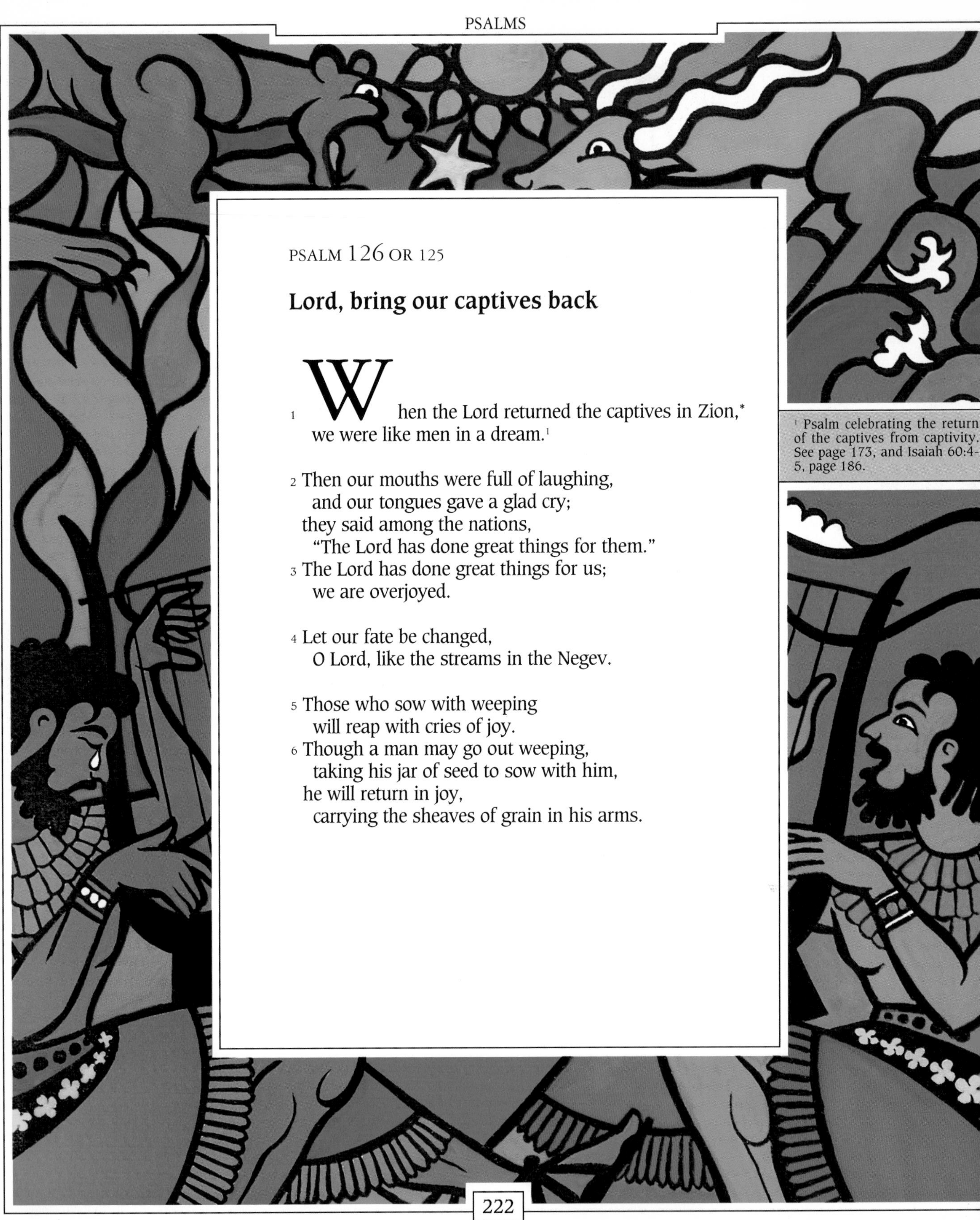

PSALM 126 OR 125

Lord, bring our captives back

1 When the Lord returned the captives in Zion,*
we were like men in a dream.[1]

2 Then our mouths were full of laughing,
and our tongues gave a glad cry;
they said among the nations,
"The Lord has done great things for them."
3 The Lord has done great things for us;
we are overjoyed.

4 Let our fate be changed,
O Lord, like the streams in the Negev.

5 Those who sow with weeping
will reap with cries of joy.
6 Though a man may go out weeping,
taking his jar of seed to sow with him,
he will return in joy,
carrying the sheaves of grain in his arms.

[1] Psalm celebrating the return of the captives from captivity. See page 173, and Isaiah 60:4-5, page 186.

PSALM 130 OR 129

With You lies pardon

Out of the depths have I sent up my cry to you,
O Lord.
2 Lord, let my voice come before you:
let your ears be awake
to the voice of my prayer.

3 O Lord, if you took note of every sin,
who would go free?
4 But there is forgiveness with you,
so that you may be feared.*

5 I am waiting for the Lord;
my soul is waiting for him, and my hope is in his word.

6 My soul is watching for the Lord
more than those who watch for the morning;
yes, more than the watchmen for the morning.

7 O Israel, have hope in the Lord;
for with the Lord is mercy and full salvation.
8 He will make Israel free from all their sins.

[1] Sin turns people into slaves. They are no longer free, blinded by pride and fettered by their passions. The Lord delivers slaves. Whence the image of emancipation — from servitude to service.

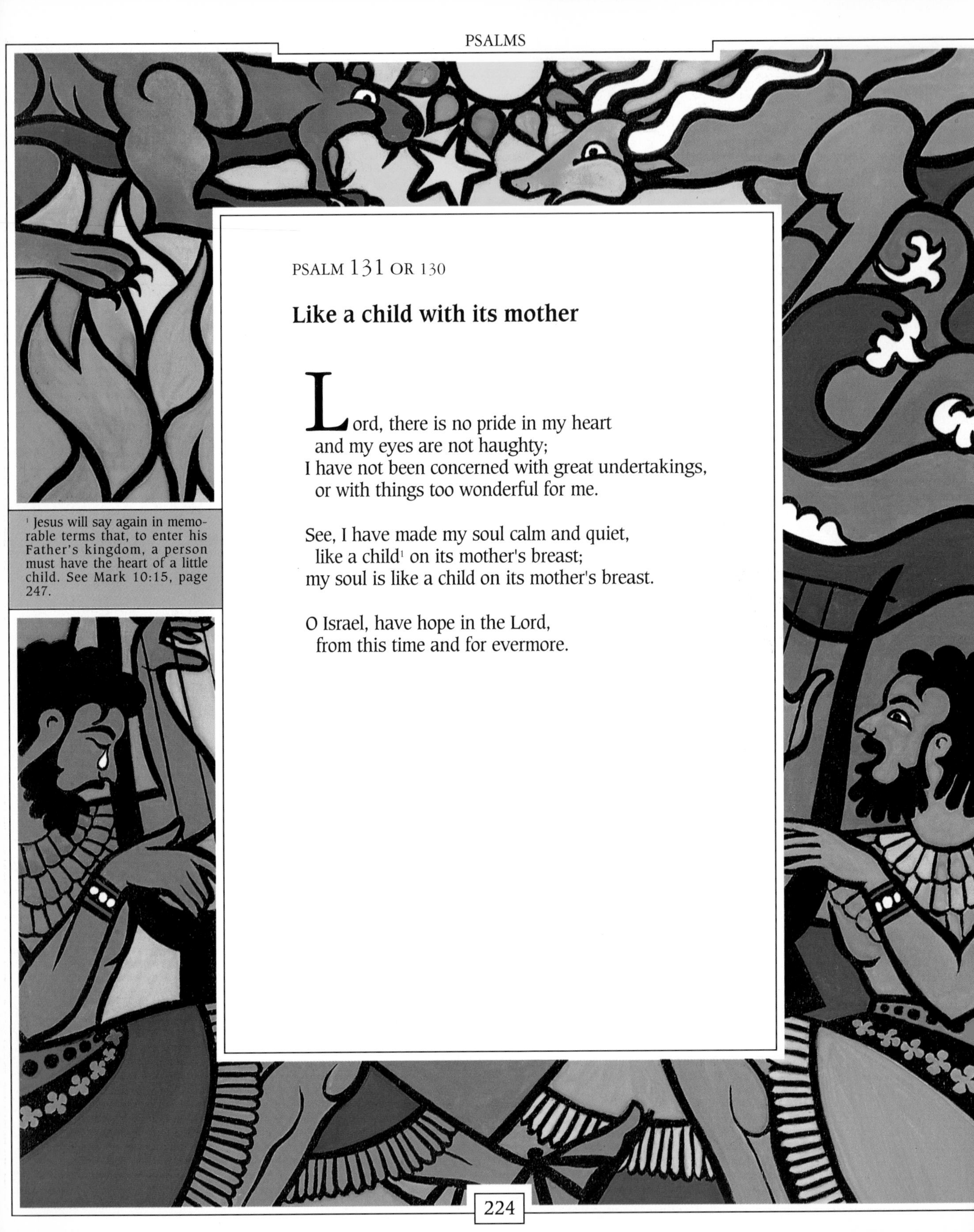

PSALM 131 OR 130

Like a child with its mother

Lord, there is no pride in my heart
and my eyes are not haughty;
I have not been concerned with great undertakings,
or with things too wonderful for me.

See, I have made my soul calm and quiet,
like a child[1] on its mother's breast;
my soul is like a child on its mother's breast.

O Israel, have hope in the Lord,
from this time and for evermore.

[1] Jesus will say again in memorable terms that, to enter his Father's kingdom, a person must have the heart of a little child. See Mark 10:15, page 247.

PSALM 137 OR 136

Lament of the captive in exile

1 By the rivers of Babylon we were seated,
weeping at the memory of Zion,
2 Hanging our instruments of music
on the trees by the waterside.

3 For there those who had taken us prisoners
asked us for a song;
and those who had taken away all we had
gave us orders to be glad,
saying, "Give us one of the songs of Zion."

4 How may we give the Lord's song
in a foreign land?
5 If I forget you, O Jerusalem,
let not my right hand remember its skill.

6 If I let you slip from my thoughts,
and if I do not consider Jerusalem
my greatest joy,
then let my tongue cling
to the roof of my mouth....

[1] A Psalm written in captivity.* The psalmist expresses his homesickness. He resents his "tormentors," and is heavy with sadness at being so far from Jerusalem. Since he shows himself to the Lord as he is, without pretence, the Lord will be able to console him. The people will sing psalms in this foreign land, having understood that the Lord's presence is not restricted to Jerusalem. See page 503, "God speaks also in foreign lands."

PSALM 139 OR 138

Lord, You know me through and through

O Lord, you know me so well,
searching out all my secrets.
2 You know when I am seated and when I get up;
you perceive my thoughts from far away.

3 You keep watch over my steps and my sleep,
and are familiar with all my ways.
4 For there is not a word I speak
which you do not understand, O Lord.

5 I am closed in by you on every side,
and you have put your hand on me.
6 Such knowledge is a wonder greater than my powers;
it is so high that I may not come near it.

7 Where can I hide from your spirit?
How might I escape you?
8 If I go up to heaven, you are there;
or if I make my bed in the underworld, you are there.[1]...

11 If I say, "The darkness will hide me

12 and the light about me become night;
even the dark is not dark to you.
The night is as bright as the day:
for dark and light are the same to you.

[1] The psalmist understood that God was not absent from the nether world (the abode of the dead), as used to be believed. The righteous awaited the resurrection. For an idea of how this "abode" was imagined, see the parable of Lazarus and the rich man (Luke 16:19-31, page 324). See also sheol.*

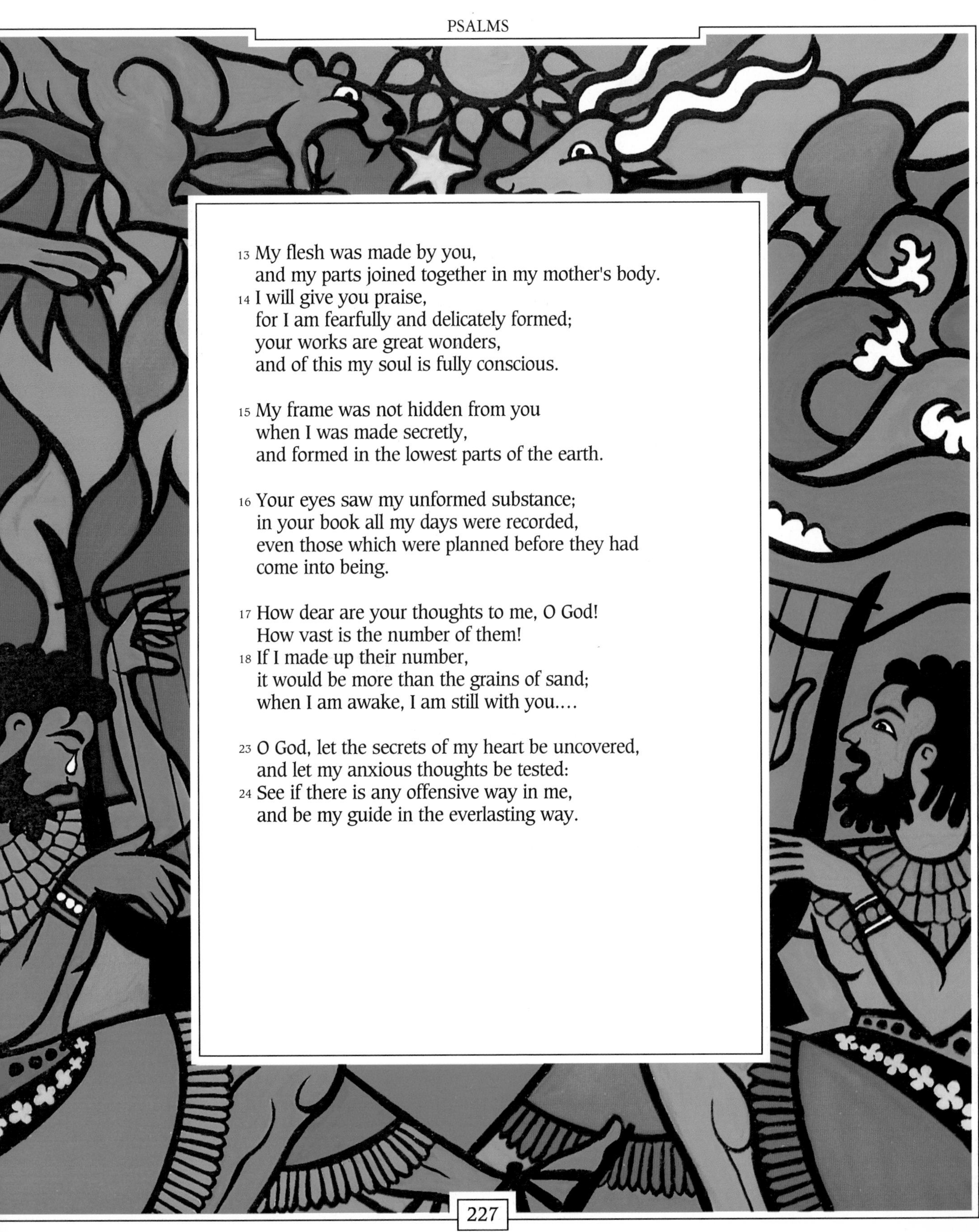

13 My flesh was made by you,
and my parts joined together in my mother's body.
14 I will give you praise,
for I am fearfully and delicately formed;
your works are great wonders,
and of this my soul is fully conscious.

15 My frame was not hidden from you
when I was made secretly,
and formed in the lowest parts of the earth.

16 Your eyes saw my unformed substance;
in your book all my days were recorded,
even those which were planned before they had
come into being.

17 How dear are your thoughts to me, O God!
How vast is the number of them!
18 If I made up their number,
it would be more than the grains of sand;
when I am awake, I am still with you....

23 O God, let the secrets of my heart be uncovered,
and let my anxious thoughts be tested:
24 See if there is any offensive way in me,
and be my guide in the everlasting way.

PART FOUR

THE GOSPEL

GOSPEL = GOOD TIDINGS

The word gospel comes from the Old English "godspell," meaning good story. Jesus' news was good. God loves all mankind. Their disloyalties and sins do not discourage Him. He wishes to save all people[1] by making an eternal Covenant with them.*

GODSPELL AND GOSPELS

Jesus' good tidings are contained in the four Gospels.

In order to understand the nature of the Gospels, two questions have to be answered.: Why were they written? and How were they written?

Why?

Jesus did not tell his apostles, "Go and write the Gospels!" He sent them to spread the good news. To begin with, the disciples did as Jesus had done and proclaimed their faith in the synagogues* or in the outer court of the Temple.*

They tried to explain to their listeners what they themselves had difficulty in understanding — the death of the Messiah on the cross and the founding of a spiritual kingdom. The Holy Spirit enlightened their minds, helping them to remember certain sayings of Jesus whose meaning they had not fully grasped. He prodded them into finding solutions to new situations and problems.[2]*

As time went by, preachers replaced the disciples. As a help to them, the most important sayings of Jesus, his most meaningful acts and the discoveries made under the guidance of the Holy Spirit were set down in writing. These were not really books—they were more like notes to jog their memories.

At length, the early witnesses grew old and were unable to tour all the communities springing up around the Mediterranean basin. It was decided to gather their recollections in fuller form so that the faith of the newly converted would have a solid base to rest on. This was the reason for writing the Gospels.

How?

Matthew, Mark, Luke and John, known as the four Evangelists, did not try to write an exhaustive biography of Jesus. They were not just telling the story of someone in the past.

1 1 Timothy 2:4, page 442.

2 Jesus had promised, "He will remind you of everything I have said to you.... He will guide you into all truth."

They were bearing witness to the fact that Jesus was living. They chose from among the words and deeds of Jesus the ones that would nourish the faith of the Christians for whom they were writing. To do this, they drew from earlier writings, from their own memories or from those of their community. They were sometimes able to question eyewitnesses.

Each Evangelist presented the message of Jesus for his own community. The Christian communities were different from one another. Some were made up mostly of Jews, others of gentiles who had become Christians. They lived in different places — Jerusalem, Antioch, Ephesus, Rome. They did not have the same problems. This partly explains the differences among the Gospels.

Far from being troubling, it is very enriching to have four accounts which add to each other. Each one makes its own contribution in revealing the living presence of Jesus amidst his people.

THE ORDER OF THE GOSPELS

In the Bible, the Gospels are usually arranged in the following order: Matthew, Mark, Luke and John. This order is based on certain accounts saying that Matthew was the first to have written a gospel, in Aramaic. Unfortunately, this work has not survived.

Most scholars think that the oldest of the existing Gospels is that of Mark, written in about 70-80 AD. Then, in 80-90 AD, were written that of Luke and that of Matthew, as we know it. The "new" Matthew, written in Greek,[1] *was probably a greatly expanded version of the Aramaic original. Lastly, towards the end of the first century AD, John produced a fourth Gospel, very different in presentation from the other three. (A few scholars think that the Gospels were written earlier.)*

"Treasures of the Bible" sets out several excerpts from each Gospel, from the earliest to the latest:
I. The Gospel according to Mark, pages 235 to 252.
II. The Gospel according to Matthew, pages 253-296.
III. The Gospel according to Luke, pages 297-330.
IV. The Gospel according to John, pages 331-362.
*V. The main passages of the four Gospels recounting the Passion and Resurrection are brought together on pages 363-396. The idea is less to reconstitute the final days of Jesus than to compare the texts and have a better idea of what each Evangelist had to say. It is also perhaps a better way of understanding some of the most important moments in the whole Christian revelation.**

[1] As are all the writings in the New Testament.

THE "SYNOPTIC" GOSPELS

Three of the four Gospels follow a fairly similar pattern which, simply stated, runs as follows: Jesus and John the Baptist; the ministry of Jesus in Galilee; his move to Jerusalem; his ministry in Jerusalem; his passion and resurrection. Mark seems to have been the first to adopt this order of presenting the message he wanted to convey. Matthew and Luke followed the same "storyline," while introducing their own personal notorial. These three Gospels were sometimes printed in three columns on the same page. This made it possible, in the same glance,[1] to see which passages were common to all three Evangelists and which ones were peculiar to one or two of them. It also made it easy to spot any differences in treatment of the same event or same teaching.*

THE JEWISH PEOPLE IN THE FIRST CENTURY AD

Jesus addressed his good news to the Jewish people in the first instance. It is therefore worth describing the geographical and historical situation of the Jews in those days.*

A people territorially scattered

The Jews living in Israel were outnumbered by those of the diaspora, that is, those who were living in foreign towns and other lands.*

The Jews of the Holy Land: *There were differences to be noted between the citizens of Jerusalem and the Galileans.*

In Jerusalem, almost the whole population was Jewish. The life of the city was focused on the Temple. Sacrifices marked the different hours of the day.[2] The times of year were signaled by pilgrimages, which drew immense crowds. There were numerous schools of scribes. Eminent teachers dispensed their learning in the synagogues or in the outer court of the Temple.*

In Galilee, on the other hand, the Jews lived side by side with heathen peoples. The towns of the "Decapolis"[3] were full of theatres and pagan temples containing idols. Greek was the language spoken. The Jerusalem Jews tended to regard their Galilean brethren as lukewarm believers, dissipated by their contact with the heathens.

1 The literal meaning of "synoptic."

2 For example, Acts of the Apostles 3:1, page 403.

3 The Decapolis was a group of about ten cities Hellenized at the time of Antiochus Epiphanes (see page 178). Jesus visited them several times. See Mark 5:1-20, page 242.

Samaria, between Jerusalem and Galilee, was inhabited by the Samaritans, descendants of foreign peoples settled there by the Assyrians.[1] *They considered their religion to be the same as that of the Jews, but the Jews did not accept this claim. They had built a temple on Mount Garizim. The shrine was in ruins in Jesus' day, but the Samaritans still gathered there to offer sacrifices. Relations between the Jews and the Samaritans were often strained, and the Jews avoided having to cross Samaria.*

The Jews of the Diaspora. *Many Jews never returned after the captivity.*[2] *They remained in Babylon. Others left to live in Alexandria in Egypt, or in the cities of the Roman Empire. Allowed by the Romans to practice their religion, the diaspora Jews erected synagogues.* Hardly any of them understood Hebrew. They used Greek translations of the Biblical Books. The best-known of these translations was the Septuagint.*[3] *They explained their faith to the heathens they mixed with, some of whom showed great interest in the Jewish Scriptures. There were even a few who became converted, had themselves circumcised and observed all the Jewish laws. They were called "proselytes." Others were wary of joining a religion which would cut them off from their society,*[4] *although they attended meetings in the synagogue and studied the Bible. They occasionally went up to the Temple in Jerusalem, where a large area of the outer court was set aside for them.*[5] *They were commonly known as "God-fearers" or "God-worshippers."*

A people spiritually divided

The Jews were split into different schools of thought. The two main ones were the Sadducees and the Pharisees.

The Sadducees* *were few but influential. They formed the Jerusalem "establishment," and included priestly families from among whom the high priests* were chosen. They were in charge of the Temple and were members of the Sanhedrin,* the court which tried religious offenses and crimes. The Sadducees recognized only the Torah* as Scripture truly inspired by God. They did not consider other sources of revelation as important. They believed neither in the resurrection of the dead nor in angels.*

The Pharisees* *were the descendants of the common people who had resisted under the persecutions of Aniochus Epiphanes on behalf of their faith.*[6] *They accepted not only the Torah as inspired writings but also the writings of the prophets and sages.*

[1] See page 134, "The end of the kingdom of the North."

[2] See page 503, "God speaks also in foreign lands?"

[3] See page 203.

[4] Jews were not allowed to enter a heathen's house, or eat at the same table. They were obliged to observe the Sabbath, etc.

[5] This was the Court of the Gentiles.*

[6] See page 178.

The Pharisees believed in scrupulously observing the Commandments. They believed in the resurrection of the dead. Pharisees sat in the Sanhedrin alongside the Sadducees.

Other coexisting movements at the time of the Gospels:

The Herodians were supporters of the House of Herod. King Herod* the Great was not a Jew but an Idumean.* Despite his efforts to win favor in the eyes of the Jews, he behaved as a heathen. Herod Antipas, his son and governor of Galilee, was closer to Judaism. He was affected by the preaching of John the Baptist [1] and went up to Jerusalem for the Passover.[2] The Herodians of his entourage were therefore Jews who tried to reconcile the practice of their religion with the exercise of power under the close watch of the Romans.*

The Essenes are not mentioned in the Bible. They were a kind of sect located in Qumran near the Dead Sea in a sort of monastery. They believed they were the sons of light as opposed to the sons of darkness. Their influence extended well beyond the area where they were settled. Certain archeologists think that there was an Essene neighborhood in Jerusalem.*

The Zealots first appeared as an organized movement in about 60 AD. Its earlier history is poorly documented. Its seeds probably existed in the minds of all who were opposed to Roman rule. They hoped for the coming of a warrior messiah who would restore Israel to the glory it had known under King David and King Solomon.*

A people under occupation

Since 63 BC, the Romans, with whom the Jews had formed an alliance, had become the masters of Judea. In 37 BC, they acknowledged the Idumean, Herod, as king of the Jews.*

After the death of Herod the Great, the kingdom was divided among his sons. Archelaus obtained Judea and Herod Antipas was given Galilee. Other sons, such as Philip, received territories further north, in the direction of what are now Syria and Lebanon. None had their father's title of king. They were governor princes.

In 6 AD, Archelaus was deposed and a Roman governor took over the administration of Judea. His seat was in Caesarea Maritima, but he went up to Jerusalem during the seasons of pilgrimage. Thus he could keep an eye on the crowds, among which the slightest spark was liable to touch off a full-scale rebellion. From 26 to 36 AD, the governor was a Roman named Pontius Pilate.

[1] Mark 6:20, page 243.

[2] Luke 23:7, page 376.

I
THE GOSPEL ACCORDING TO MARK

Who was Mark?

The Book of the Acts of the Apostles mentions a young John Mark[1] *whose mother, Mary, owned a large house in Jerusalem. The disciples* of Jesus liked to gather there to pray. Peter went there often.*[2]

Mary and John Mark had a relation, Barnabas, who held important responsibilities in the early Christian communities. When Barnabas was sent with Paul to evangelize the island of Cyprus, he suggested taking John Mark along. Possibly because he did not get on well with Paul, John Mark returned to Jerusalem before the end of the mission.

On a later occasion, Paul and Barnabas decided to go on another journey. Barnabas again wanted to take John Mark with them, but this time it was Paul who refused and they chose another companion.[3] *After the death of Barnabas, John Mark went to join Peter in Rome. He dropped his Jewish name, John. Probably after Peter's death, he compiled the gist of the teaching of the leader of the Twelve* in the booklet we know as the Gospel according to Mark.*

Since his Gospel starts with the preaching of John the Baptist in the desert, Mark is traditionally symbolized as a lion,[4] *a beast of the desert.*

It has also been said that Mark evangelized Alexandria in Egypt, and that he died a martyr.

For whom did Mark write his Gospel?

Tradition has it that Mark wrote in Rome for the Romans. His readers were probably unfamiliar with Jewish customs. Mark explained to them that the Jews had many purification* rites and complex dietary laws. The community for which he was writing therefore probably included heathens who had become Christians without encountering Judaism. Mark revealed to them that Jesus was not only a messenger from God — the Messiah* awaited by the Jews — but also the Son of God.*

[1] This was not a "double-barreled" name but two names, one Jewish the other Roman: John, meaning "God is merciful," and Mark, meaning "hard hitter."

[2] Acts of the Apostles 12:12, page 418.

[3] The relations between Paul and Mark did not stop there. Paul would later admit that Barnabas had been right in recommending Mark. Mark became a remarkable missionary (2 Timothy 4:11).

[4] Each Evangelist is represented by a symbolic creature. See page 502.

JOHN THE BAPTIST

Mark did not mention the childhood of Jesus.

He began his Gospel with a comparison between John the Baptist, whose way of life was out-of-the-ordinary, and Jesus whom nothing outwardly distinguished him from other men.

John the Baptist (or John the baptizer) drew crowds since his speaking manner was as rough-hewn as that of the Old Testament prophets. His clothing and eating habits made a strong impression on people's minds.

He invited people to change their ways, to renounce their selfishness and sin and adopt a life which was more generous and open to the presence of God.

He announced that someone would come who was greater than he. This someone would baptize with the Holy Spirit, that is to say, he would immerse those willing to follow him in the Spirit of God. That Spirit would wash through them.

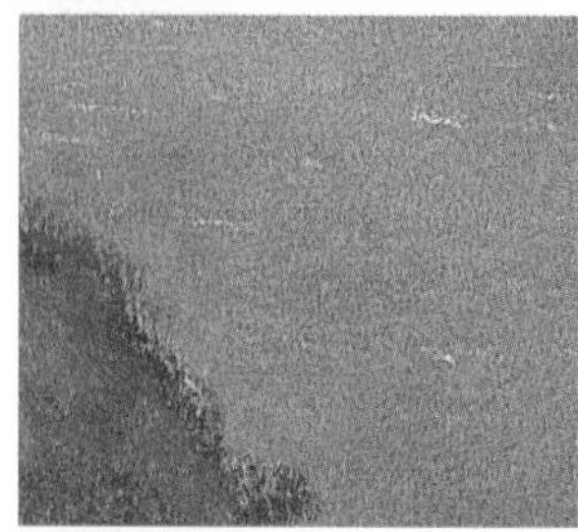

JESUS, SON OF GOD

1 1 The beginning of the gospel of Jesus Christ, the Son of God.
2 Even as it is said in the book of Isaiah the prophet,
"See, I send my servant ahead of you,
who will prepare your way;
3 *The voice of one crying in the desert,*
'Prepare the way of the Lord, make his roads straight;'"[1]

4 John came, and baptised in the desert, preaching baptism
as a sign of forgiveness of sin for those whose hearts were
changed.
5 All the people of Judaea came to him, and all those of
Jerusalem. They were baptised by him in the river Jordan,
6 confessing that they were sinners. | John was clothed in
camel's hair, with a leather band about him; his food was
7 locusts and honey. | He said to them all, "There is one
coming after me who is greater than I,[2] whose shoes I am
8 not good enough to untie. | I have baptised you with water,
but he will baptise you with the Holy Spirit."[3]

9 It came about in those days, that Jesus came from
Nazareth of Galilee, and was baptised by John in the
10 Jordan. | Immediiately, coming up out of
the water, he saw the heavens broken
open and the Spirit coming down on him
11 as a dove.[4] | A voice came out of heaven,
"You are my dearly loved Son, with
whom I am well pleased."

John the Baptist,
you are so different
from other men!
You choose to live
in heroic, radical poverty.
The crowds admire you and say,
"The Lord is with him."

Yet, in the midst of the crowd,
there is a stranger.
He is dressed like everyone else.
But, this stranger is greater than you.
He is the Son of God.

[1] A quotation from two prophets: verse 2 comes from Malachi 3:1; verse 3 is from Isaiah 40:3.

[2] See John 1:15, page 334.

[3] See John 3:1-8, page 338, where Jesus spoke of being reborn of water and the Spirit.

[4] See the corresponding passage in Matthew 3:13-17, page 258, and particularly note 4.

\PERNAUM

fter being baptized by John
.e Baptist, Jesus returned
Galilee. He stayed in
pernaum beside the lake
illed the "Sea of Galilee"
ith two fishermen, Simon
id Andrew.

ie brothers' home town
as Bethsaida, another
keside village. But Simon
as married to a Capernaum
oman and had come to live
ith her, in his mother-in-
w's house. His brother
ndrew had followed him.
iis was the house (or
ther group of houses
ound a courtyard) in
hich Jesus was lodged.

pernaum was a little town
pulated by peasants and
shermen, traders and
ficials. It lay on the border
etween the territory of
erod Antipas, prince of
alilee, and that of his
other, Philip. This explains
hy there was a customs
fice there (see Matthew 9:9,
ge 268) and a Roman
irrison under the command
a centurion (Matthew 8:5-
, page 267).

JESUS, SAVIOR OF ALL PEOPLE

In the synagogue

1 21 Jesus and his disciples came to Capernaum. On the
Sabbath* he went into the Synagogue* and taught.
22 And they were amazed by his teaching, because he
gave it as one having authority, and not like the scribes.* |
23 And there was in their Synagogue a man possessed by an
24 evil spirit. He cried out, | saying, "What have we to do with
you, Jesus of Nazareth? Have you come to put an end to
25 us? I see well who you are, the Holy One of God." | And
Jesus said to him sharply, "Be quiet, and come out of him."
26 | And the unclean spirit, shaking him violently, and crying
27 with a loud voice, left him. | They were all greatly
surprised, so that they put questions to one another,
saying, "What is this, a new teaching? With authority he
orders even the evil spirits, and they do what he says." |
28 News of him went out quickly everywhere into all parts of
Galilee.

In the country, early in the morning

1 35 And in the morning, a long time before daylight, he
got up and went out to a quiet place, and there he
36 gave himself up to prayer. | And Simon and those who
37 were with him came after him. | And when they came up
with him, they said to him, "Everyone is looking for you."

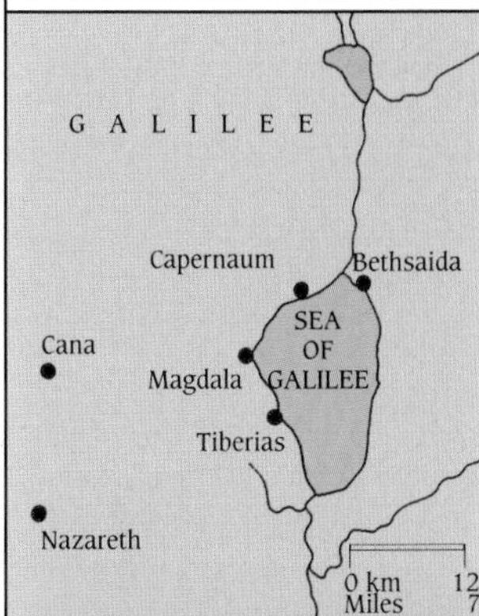

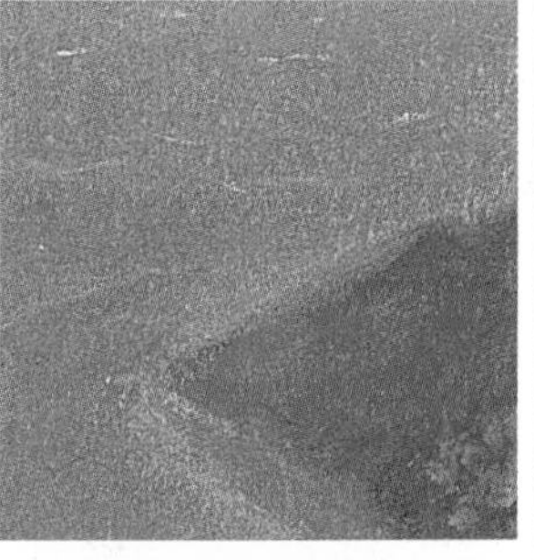

"HE GIVES ORDERS TO EVIL SPIRITS"

In the Capernaum synagogue, a man bluntly questioned Jesus. "Have you come to destroy us?" He was echoing the great doubt that Satan had sown in mankind since the beginning (see Genesis 3:5, page 24). God was suspected of being the one who prevented humans from growing up and wanted to keep them in a state of dependence. He wanted to "destroy" them. Jesus delivered this man from the evil spirit which possessed him. The man realized that Jesus had come to destroy what stopped people from living. Jesus was in favor of life; he wanted humans to have an abundance of life (John 10:10, page 352, and Luke 19:10, page 330). See "possessed."*

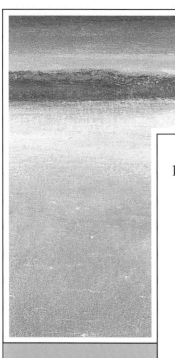

1 38 | And he said to them, "Let us go to other parts into the
nearest towns, so that I may teach, because for this
purpose I came."

39 He went into their synagogues in every
part of Galilee, preaching and driving
out evil spirits.

Jesus,
you are not going to stay in Capernaum
where everyone would like to keep you,
because everyone
has a right to hear the Good News.
Everyone needs to know
how much God loves them,
and calls them to share His life.

WHO CAN FORGIVE SINS?

The scribes were very honorable and serious people. They spent long hours copying the Bible and studying it in minute detail. They were quite right in saying that only God could forgive sins,* since sins were offenses against God. To obtain forgiveness, it was necessary to offer sacrifices in the Temple* in Jerusalem. Never had a mere man been heard to say, "I forgive you your sins."

Jesus helped them in their thinking. They taught that sickness and death had come into the world because of human sin. If Jesus could cure the sick, could he not also therefore forgive sins?

The scribes were perplexed. They were extremely troubled to see Jesus speaking and acting as though he were God.

2 1 And when he came into Capernaum again after
a time, the news traveled that he was in the house.
2 | A great number had gathered, so that there was no longer
room for them, not even outside the door. And Jesus
3 preached the word to them. | Four men came to him with
4 one on a bed who was paralyzed. | When they were unable
to get get him close to Jesus because of all the people, they
opened the roof[1] where he was. When it was opened, they
5 lowered the bed on which the man was. | Jesus, seeing
their faith, said to him, "Son, you have forgiveness for
your sins."

6 But there were certain scribes* seated there, reasoning in
7 their hearts, | "How can this man say such things? It is
blasphemy:* From whom does forgiveness come but from
8 God only?" | Jesus, having knowledge in his spirit of their
thoughts, said to them, "Why are you reasoning about
9 these things in your hearts? | Which is simpler, to say to a
man who is ill, 'You have forgiveness for your sins', or, 'Get
10 up, take up your bed, and go'? | But so that you may see
that the Son* of man has authority for the forgiveness of

[1] The houses in Capernau were only one floor high. Th were covered with branch and a thin mud stucco. Yo could climb on to the roof by a outside stone staircase. Th roofs were not exactly patio They were mostly used f drying fish and fruit. Arche logists have dug and found P ter's house in Capernaum.

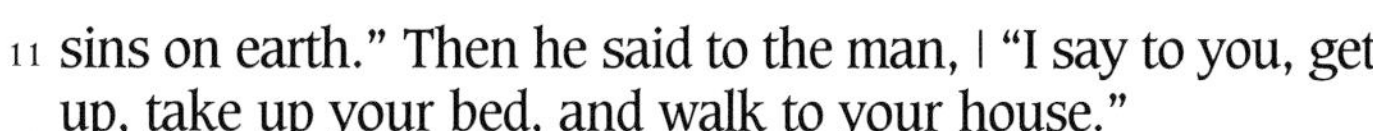

11 sins on earth." Then he said to the man, | "I say to you, get
up, take up your bed, and walk to your house."

12 And he got up, and immediately took
up the bed and went out ahead of them
all, so that they were all full of wonder,
and gave glory to God, saying, "We
have never seen anything like this."

Lord Jesus,
you didn't come to be a healer.

You came to save humanity from sin,
to release people from the paralysis
that keeps them away from God,
to put them all on the way
that leads to the waiting Father.

Jesus, Son of God,
only you can accomplish this miracle.

I need you to tell me
to get up and walk!

HE TWELVE*

'hether we call them
postles* or disciples,* it is
nportant to remember that
sus chose twelve men —
e Twelve.

'hen Moses climbed the
ountain to make a
ovenant* with God, the
ebrew people were made
of twelve tribes.* By
oosing twelve
mpanions, Jesus showed
at he had come to prepare
e people to enter into a
w Covenant with God.

e function of the Twelve
as to accompany Jesus and
his helpers in announcing
e gospel.

JESUS ASKS TO BE FOLLOWED

The choice of the Twelve

3 13 And he went up into the mountain, and sent for
those whom it was his pleasure to have with him.[1]
14 and they joined him. | He took twelve to be with him, so
15 that he might send them out as preachers, | and gave them
the power of driving out evil spirits:

16 To Simon he gave the second name of
17 Peter; | to James, the son of Zebedee,
and John, the brother of James, he gave
the second name of Boanerges, which
18 means, Sons of Thunder; | to Andrew,
and Philip, and Bartholomew, and
Matthew, and Thomas, and James, the
son of Alphaeus, and Thaddaeus, and
19 Simon the Zealot; | And Judas Iscariot,
who betrayed him.

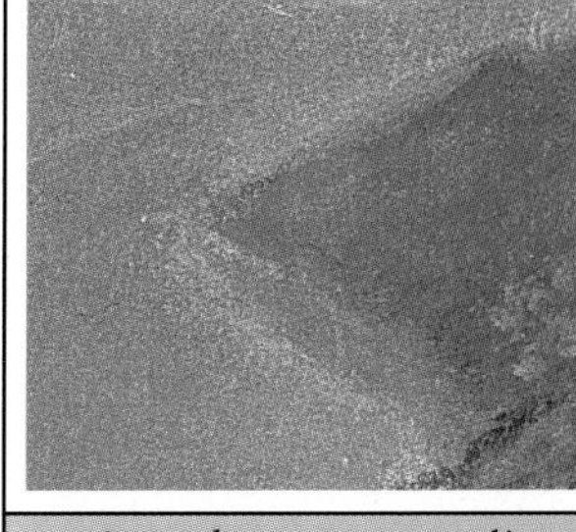

[1] See the corresponding account in Luke 6:12-16, page 309.

Lord, I want to be with you
in fatigue
looking for sinners on the byways,
in joyfulness,
when the poor
open up their hearts to you,
in prayer,
when fighting against temptation,
in suffering,
loving to the very end.

I want to be with you
in the joy of the Kingdom,
Forever!

THE MOTHER AND BROTHERS OF JESUS

In those days, young couples stayed near their parents after marrying. They lived in adjoining houses around the same courtyard. The children were raised together, like brothers and sisters (see Genesis 13:8 and page 37, note 1). **So the "brothers" of Jesus, according to Catholics, were close relations belonging to the same generation. Most Protestants think that Mary had other children after Jesus birth.**

They were annoyed with Jesus. They had heard the remarks of the scribes and wanted to get him back home before things turned nasty. It was then that Jesus introduced them to his new family — all those who had trust in him.

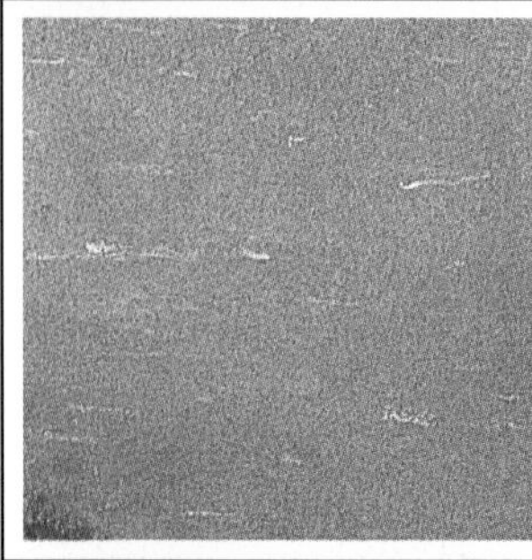

A new family

3 20 And he went into a house, where the people came
together again, so that they were not even able to
21 take bread. | When his friends had news of it, they went
out to get him, saying, "He is out of his mind."
22 The scribes who came down from Jerusalem, said, "He is
possessed by Beelzebub,"* and, "By the ruler of evil spirits
23 he sends evil spirits out of men." | Turning to them, he told
this parable. "How is it possible for Satan* to cast out
24 Satan? | If there is division in a kingdom, that kingdom will
25 come to destruction. | If there is division in a house, that
26 house will come to destruction. | If Satan is at war with
himself, and there is division in him, he will not remain on
27 his throne but will come to an end. | But no one is able to
go into the house of the strong man and take his goods,
without first binding the strong man before stealing his
28 possessions. | Truly, I say to you, the sons of men will have
forgiveness for all their sins and for all the evil words they
29 say. | But whoever blasphemes* against the Holy Spirit[1]
will never have forgiveness, but the evil he has done will
30 be with him forever." | Because they said, "He is possessed
by an evil spirit."
31 His mother and brothers came and were outside, and sent
32 for him, requesting to see him. | A great number were
seated round him, saying, "Look, your mother and your
33 brothers are outside looking for you." | He answered,
34 "Who are my mother and my brothers?" | And looking at
those who were seated around him, he said, "Look, here
35 are my mother and my brothers! | Whoever does God's
pleasure is my brother, and sister, and mother."

[1] To blaspheme against the Holy Spirit is to refuse to allow oneself to be guided by the Holy Spirit. It is preferring darkness to light. It is to claim that we need neither forgiveness nor conversion.* Persisting in this attitude produces a hardening of the heart which leaves no place for God's mercy.

BEELZEBUB

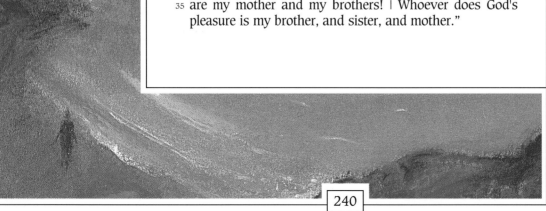

Jesus performed unexplaine cures while continuing to live like an ordinary person The scribes thought that, if God had chosen to act through a man, He would have chosen someone riche and more powerful.

If Jesus had not been sent b God, his power to heal coul come only from God's enemy, Satan, here given th name of Beelzebub, an old heathen god.

ESUS AND THE DEMONS

he scribes taught that all lness was a consequence of in. People pictured each lness as having a demon,* n evil spirit, behind it. So r them, when Jesus cured n illness, he was casting ut its demon.

he scribes had made a very erious accusation against esus. "He casts out devils to eceive us. He wants to gain ur trust, so as to draw us way from God. He is on the ide of the forces of evil."

HE SEA—"ABODE" F DEMONS

or the Jews, the sea* was ne demons' dwelling-place. ake Tiberias, also called ne Sea of Galilee, was in a ense, their "lair." Jesus was howing the Twelve and a ew other witnesses that he as the one who confined ne forces of evil to their ir.

JESUS, STRONGER THAN BEELZEBUB

Jesus makes the sea obey

4 35 And on that day, when the evening had come, he
said to them, "Let us go over to the other side."[1] |
36 And leaving the people, they took him with them, as he
37 was, in the boat. Other boats were also with him. | A great
storm of wind came up, spilling waves into the boat, so
38 that the boat was now becoming full. | He himself was in
the back of the boat, sleeping on the cushion. They,
awaking him, said, "Master, do you not care that we are in
39 danger of destruction?" | Jesus awoke, and commanded
the sea, "Peace, be at rest." The wind died down, and there
40 was a great calm. | He said to them, "Why are you full of
41 fear? Have you still no faith?" | Their fear was great, and
they said one to another, "Who then is this, that even the
wind and the sea obey his orders?"[2]

[1] The far bank was a region called the Decapolis (meaning "ten cities") populated by heathens only (which is why pigs, considered as impure by the Jews, could be found there). The inhabitants, of Greek origin, worshipped gods like Zeus and Artemis. Jesus proclaimed the gospel there also.

[2] Compare with Mark 1:25-28, page 237. Jesus addressed the sea as though it were an evil spirit. The witnesses all had the same reaction. Saint Mark clearly paints the sea as the "lair" of evil spirits. This idea existed in the old accounts of the creation, where God was described as setting limits to the sea (see Job 38:8-11, pages 196 and 197) and keeping His eye on it since it was home to monsters like Leviathan. See the double-page illustration, pages 32-33.

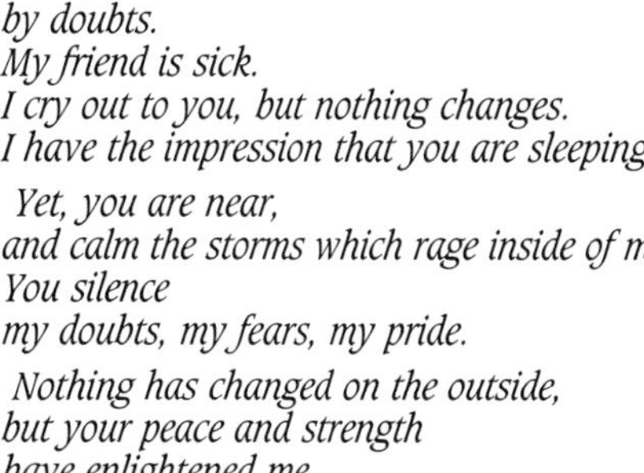

Lord, I am bewildered and overcome
by doubts.
My friend is sick.
I cry out to you, but nothing changes.
I have the impression that you are sleeping.

Yet, you are near,
and calm the storms which rage inside of me.
You silence
my doubts, my fears, my pride.

Nothing has changed on the outside,
but your peace and strength
have enlightened me.
I can walk with you once again!

JESUS AND THE SEA

The evil spirits, forced by Jesus to leave the man they possessed, sought shelter in a place from which nobody would chase them. They asked to go into the pigs.

But the pigs threw themselves into the sea.* That meant that the demons had to leave where they wanted to be and return to the "lair" of the forces of evil.

Jesus could now proclaim the gospel. But the people were afraid that the gospel would deprive them of much more than their pigs. It would oblige them to change their whole way of life. So they asked Jesus to go away.

Once again, Jesus would show that he was more powerful than all the forces of evil. He would walk on the waters (Matthew 14:25-33, page 279).

Later, in Revelation, John would imagine the new world which God wanted to give us. "I saw a new heaven and a new earth ... and there was no longer any sea." (Revelation 21:1, page 454).

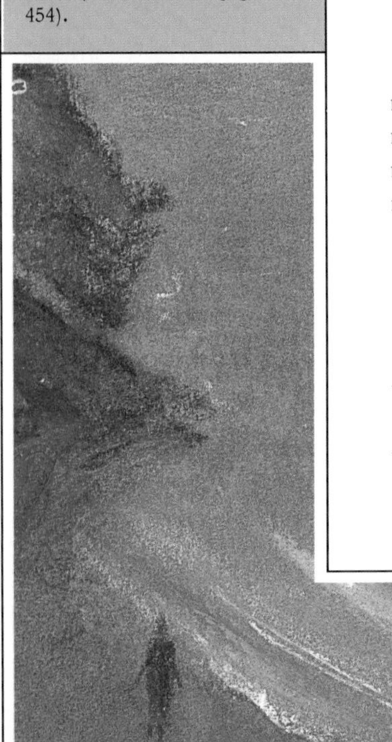

Jesus opens up the land of the heathens to the gospel

5 1 And they came to the other side of the sea, into the
2 country of the Gerasenes.[1] | And when he had got
out of the boat, immediately a man with an evil spirit arrived
3 from the tombs. | He was living in the tombs and no man
4 was able to refrain him, not with a chain. | He had frequently
been bound in chains and iron bands, but the chains had
been parted and the bands broken by him. No man was
5 strong enough to quiet him. | All day and all night, in the
tombs and in the mountains, he cried out, cutting himself
with stones.[2]

6 When he saw Jesus at a distance, he ran to him and
7 worshipped him. | Crying out with a loud voice he said,
"What have I to do with you, Jesus, Son of the Most High
8 God? In God's name, do not be cruel to me." | For Jesus had
9 said to him, "Depart from this man, you evil spirit." | Jesus
asked, "What is your name?" And he answered, "My
name is Legion, because there are a great number of us." |
10 He begged him not to send them away out of the country.
11 | Now on the mountain side there was a great herd of pigs
12 eating. | And Legion said to Jesus, "Send us into the pigs,
13 so that we may go into them." | And he let them do it. The
evil spirits left the man and entered the pigs. The herd
went rushing down a sharp slope into the sea, about two
thousand of them. There, in the sea they came to their
death.

14 And those tending them ran to tell everyone in the town
and the country. People came to see what had taken place.
15 | They came to see the man in whom had been the evil
spirits. He was seated, clothed and with full use of his

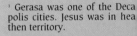

[1] Gerasa was one of the Deca
polis cities. Jesus was in hea
then territory.

[2] The demon-possessed ma
who lived in a graveyard was
for Mark, a concrete way o
showing that being separate
from God was to die. Sin* wa
true death.*

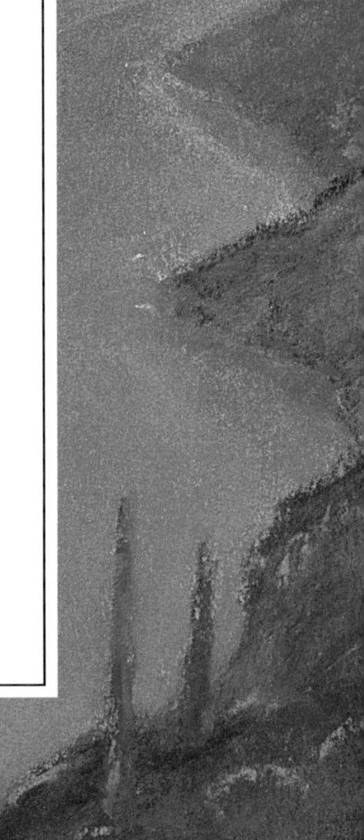

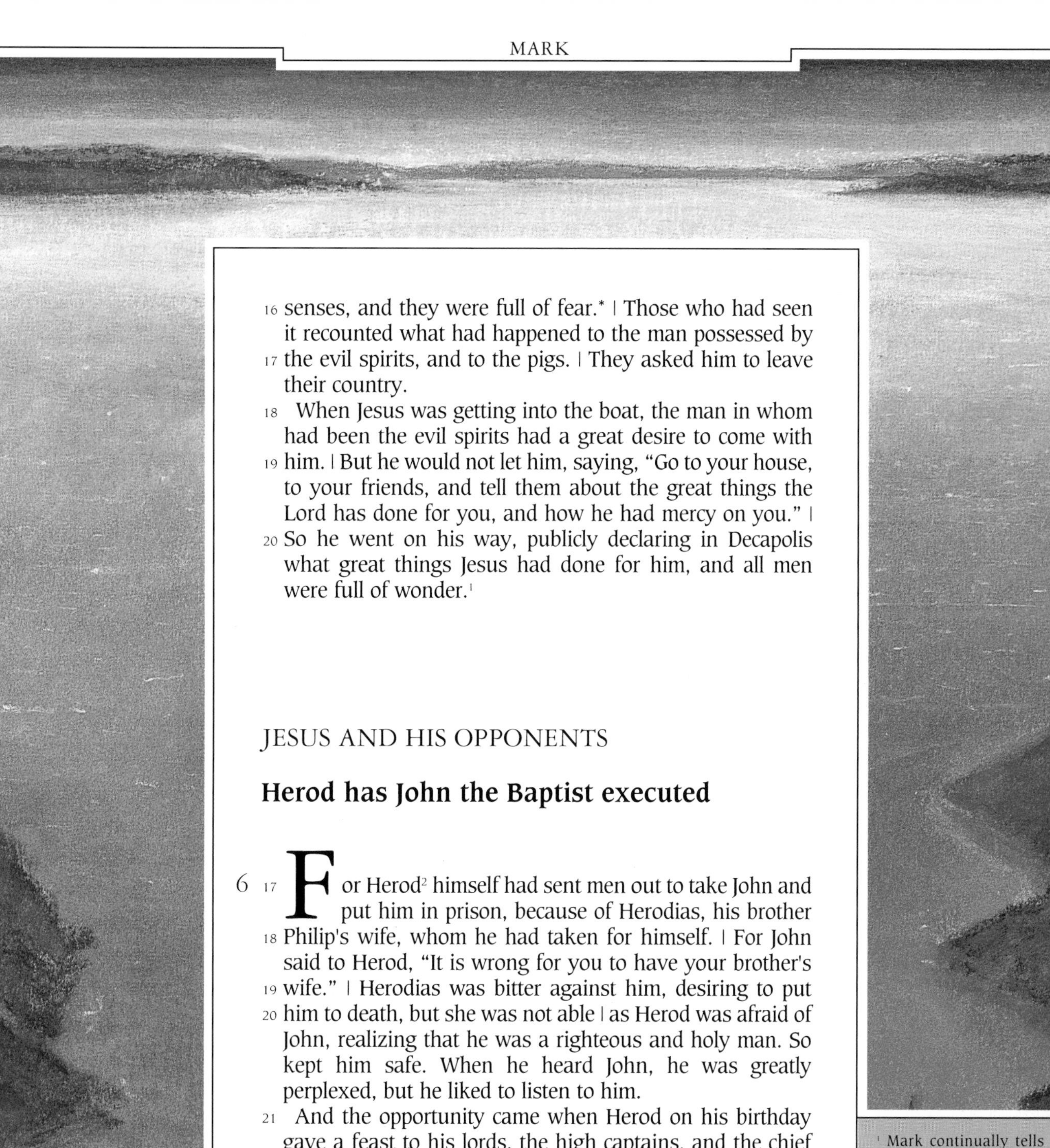

16 senses, and they were full of fear.* | Those who had seen
it recounted what had happened to the man possessed by
17 the evil spirits, and to the pigs. | They asked him to leave
their country.
18 When Jesus was getting into the boat, the man in whom
had been the evil spirits had a great desire to come with
19 him. | But he would not let him, saying, "Go to your house,
to your friends, and tell them about the great things the
Lord has done for you, and how he had mercy on you." |
20 So he went on his way, publicly declaring in Decapolis
what great things Jesus had done for him, and all men
were full of wonder.[1]

JESUS AND HIS OPPONENTS

Herod has John the Baptist executed

6 17 For Herod[2] himself had sent men out to take John and
put him in prison, because of Herodias, his brother
18 Philip's wife, whom he had taken for himself. | For John
said to Herod, "It is wrong for you to have your brother's
19 wife." | Herodias was bitter against him, desiring to put
20 him to death, but she was not able | as Herod was afraid of
John, realizing that he was a righteous and holy man. So
kept him safe. When he heard John, he was greatly
perplexed, but he liked to listen to him.
21 And the opportunity came when Herod on his birthday
gave a feast to his lords, the high captains, and the chief
22 men of Galilee.[1] | When the daughter of Herodias herself

[1] Mark continually tells us of the crowd's amazement and admiration for Jesus. He thereby leads his readers to ask themselves, "Who is Jesus?" He gives his own answer at the start of his Gospel and repeats it at the end, "Surely, this man was the Son of God." (Mark 15:39.)

[2] This was Herod* Antipas, the son of Herod the Great. He was governor of Galilee. Jesus would be summoned before him during the Passion (Luke 23:8-12, page 376).

6 came in and performed a dance, Herod and those who
were at the table with him were pleased with her. The king
said to the girl, "Make a request for anything and I will
23 give it you." | He vowed, saying to her, "Whatever is your
24 desire I will give it to you, even half of my kingdom." | So
she went out and said to her mother, "What is my request
25 to be?" She replied, "The head of John the Baptist." | She
quickly said to the king, "My desire is that you give me
26 immediately on a plate the head of John the Baptist." | The
king was very sad, but because of his vow, and those who
were with him at the table, he could not say "No" to her. |
27 Immediately the king sent out one of his armed men, and
ordered him to come back with the head. So he left to cut
28 off John's head in prison, | When he returned with the head
on a plate, he gave it to the girl who gave it to her mother.
29 When his disciples heard the news, they came to retrieve
John's body to bury it.

¹ The Jewish historian, Flaviu Josephus,* tells us that thi scene took place in the fortres of Macheronta. It was a build ing that overlooked the Dea Sea in what is now Jordan.

The Pharisees locked in human rules

7 1 And there gathered around Jesus the Pharisees* and
certain of the scribes* who had come from
2 Jerusalem. | They saw that some of his disciples ate with
3 unclean, that is to say, unwashed, hands. | Now the
Pharisees and the Jews never eat without ceremoniously
washing their hands, observing the tradition* of the
4 elders. | (When they come from the marketplace, they do
not eat until their hands are washed; a number of other
orders exist, which have been handed down to them to

BLESSED ARE THE PURE OF HEART

The Pharisees were well aware that only the pure* (unsullied) of heart would see God (see Matthew 5:8, page 260). **But the love of God keeps getting sullied with other appetites — for money, revenge, esteem. There is a constant need for purification. This is why the Pharisees observed so many rites of cleansing. By washing their hands, they reminded themselves that they had to wash their hearts.**

Little by little, the Pharisees became victim to ritualism. It sufficed to wash the outside to be pure inside.

Jesus objected, "Who can purify hearts?"

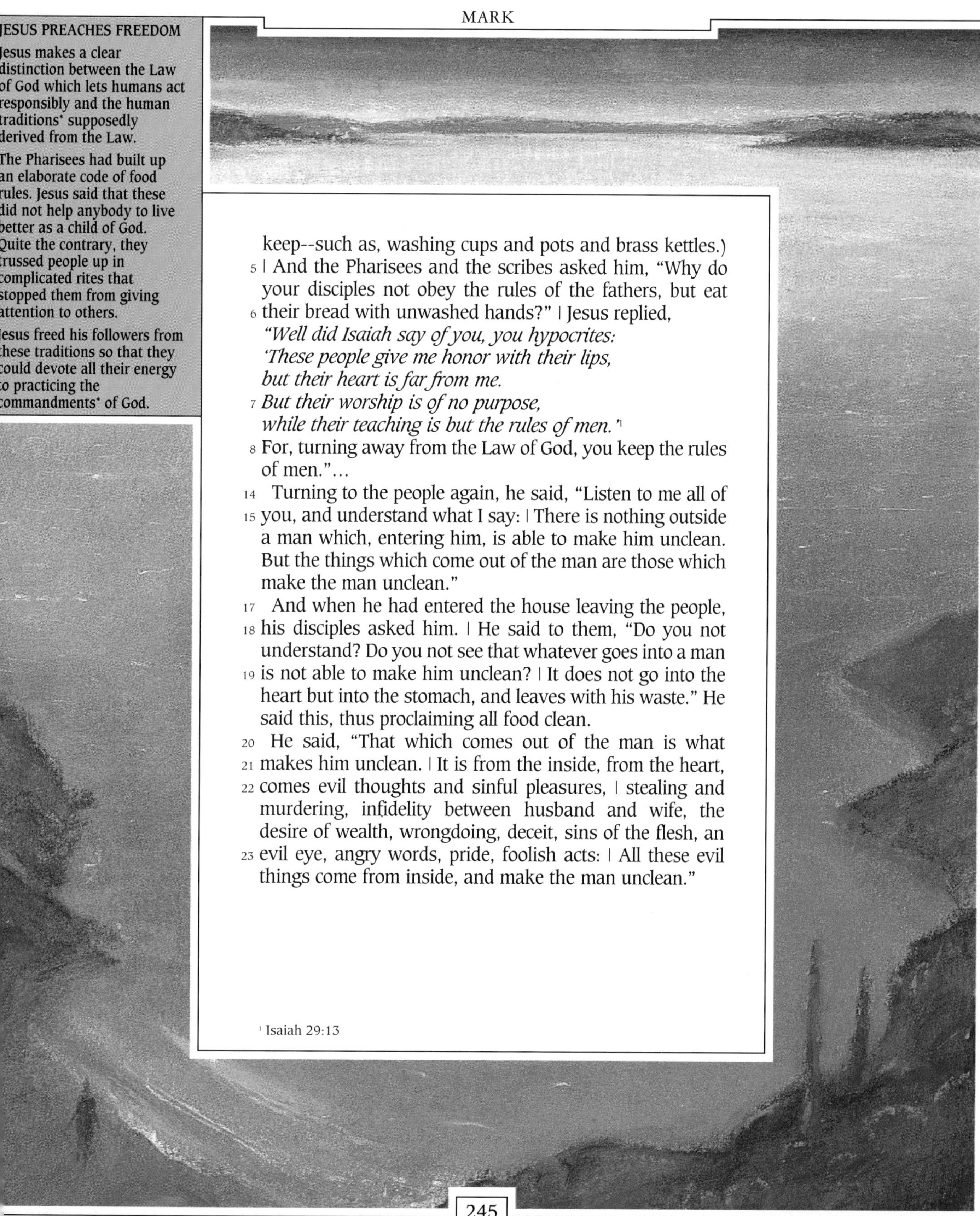

JESUS PREACHES FREEDOM

Jesus makes a clear distinction between the Law of God which lets humans act responsibly and the human traditions* supposedly derived from the Law.

The Pharisees had built up an elaborate code of food rules. Jesus said that these did not help anybody to live better as a child of God. Quite the contrary, they trussed people up in complicated rites that stopped them from giving attention to others.

Jesus freed his followers from these traditions so that they could devote all their energy to practicing the commandments* of God.

keep--such as, washing cups and pots and brass kettles.)
5 | And the Pharisees and the scribes asked him, "Why do
your disciples not obey the rules of the fathers, but eat
6 their bread with unwashed hands?" | Jesus replied,
"Well did Isaiah say of you, you hypocrites:
'These people give me honor with their lips,
but their heart is far from me.
7 *But their worship is of no purpose,*
while their teaching is but the rules of men.'[1]
8 For, turning away from the Law of God, you keep the rules
of men."...
14 Turning to the people again, he said, "Listen to me all of
15 you, and understand what I say: | There is nothing outside
a man which, entering him, is able to make him unclean.
But the things which come out of the man are those which
make the man unclean."
17 And when he had entered the house leaving the people,
18 his disciples asked him. | He said to them, "Do you not
understand? Do you not see that whatever goes into a man
19 is not able to make him unclean? | It does not go into the
heart but into the stomach, and leaves with his waste." He
said this, thus proclaiming all food clean.
20 He said, "That which comes out of the man is what
21 makes him unclean. | It is from the inside, from the heart,
22 comes evil thoughts and sinful pleasures, | stealing and
murdering, infidelity between husband and wife, the
desire of wealth, wrongdoing, deceit, sins of the flesh, an
23 evil eye, angry words, pride, foolish acts: | All these evil
things come from inside, and make the man unclean."

[1] Isaiah 29:13

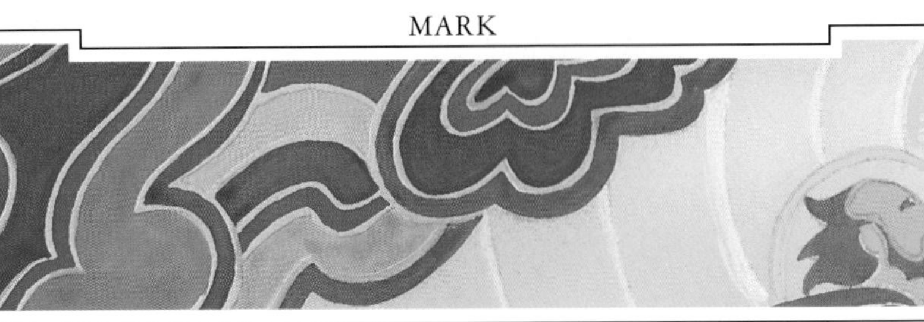

SELF-RENUNCIATION SO AS TO TRULY LIVE

Self-renunciation is realizing that, since we are made "in the image of God" (see Genesis 1:26-27, page 21), **we cannot build our lives around our own ego. Venturing into conversation, relationships with others, and .with God especially, is the only way to become truly human.**

HIGH ON A MOUNTAIN

Jesus, in order to prepare his friends for the great ordeal of his death on Calvary, revealed for an instant the glory of his divinity. The whiteness of his garment[1] was evidence of his closeness to the Father. He was the Eternal One Who had spoken with Moses and Elijah.

[1] White was the color for God. See Daniel 7:9, page 204.

JESUS SAVES THROUGH LOVE

To lose is to gain

8 34 And turning to the mass of people with his disciples,
he said to them, "If any man has
the desire to follow me, let him give up all
other desires, and take up his cross and
35 follow me. | Whoever has a desire to keep
his life, will lose it; whoever gives up his
life because of me and the gospel, will
keep it.

36 What profit has a man if he gains the
37 world but loses his life? | What would a
man give in exchange for his life? |
38 Whoever is ashamed because of me and
my words in this hypocritical and evil
generation, the Son* of Man will be
ashamed because of him, when he comes
in his Father's glory with the holy
angels."

Losing! Giving up!
These words frighten us.
But the Lord has given these words
a ring of victory.
He "lost" thirty years
in the obscurity of Nazareth;
thirty years of work
and everyday encounters,
just to learn how to live out his humanity.
Yes, Lord, you gave up
riches and success.
You handed over your life
as if you were giving away bread.
You held nothing back for yourself.
But, on Easter morning,
you showed that by losing yourself,
life was victorious over all the forces
of death which harden the heart.

At the pathway's end, transfiguration

9 2 And after six days Jesus took with him Peter and
James and John, and led them up with him into a
high mountain by themselves: where he was transfigured
3 before them. | His clothing shone a bright white, beyond
4 any white seen on earth. | There came before them Elijah
5 with Moses, who were talking with Jesus. | Peter said to

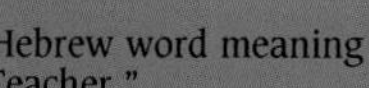

Hebrew word meaning
Teacher."

Compare with Matthew 18:1-
0, page 282.

BBA*

sus is the model for those ho accept the kingdom of od like children. In relation his Father, he is a child hose heart is full of trust nd admiration. He does not ecome the son who accuses is father (like the older son in e parable in Luke 15:28-30). If e wish to be disciples of sus, we must follow him in is childlike love for his ather and, with the help of e Holy Spirit, relearn how say "Abba" (see Romans 15, page 431).

Jesus, "Rabbi,* it is so wonderful here. Let us make three
6 tents, one for you, one for Moses, and one for Elijah." | He
7 was not certain what to say, for they were so afraid. | A
cloud* passed over them, and a voice came out of the
cloud, saying, "This is my dearly loved Son, listen to him."
8 | Suddenly looking around, they saw no one any longer,
other than Jesus with themselves.
9 And while they were descending the
mountain, he ordered them not to tell
any man of the things they had seen until
the Son of man had risen from the dead.
10 | They kept what had happened to
themselves, discussing only among
themselves what "rising from the dead"
might be.

Lord, Moses was with you
on the mountain during the Exodus,
but he only had a glimpse of you from behind.
Later on, Elijah recognized your presence
in the whisper of a gentle breeze.

On the Mount of Galilee,
Moses and Elijah were bursting with joy,
gazing upon the transfigured Jesus.
"He, whom we only saw from a distance,
is now close to you, wearing a human face."

I can no longer see your face
today, Lord,
but all humanity, your brothers and sisters,
make me think of you.

Like little children

10 13 And they took to him little children, so that he might
put his hands on them. The disciples rebuked
14 them. | When Jesus saw it, he was angry, saying, "Let the
little children come to me, and do not keep
them away, for of such[2] is the kingdom*
15 of God. | Truly I say to you, whoever does
not approach the Kingdom of God like a
16 little child, will not enter it at all." | Then
he took them in his arms, and blessed
the,, putting his hands on them.

A child's heart is filled with wonder,
and never doubting:
"When I ask my father for bread,
he doesn't give me a stone.
If, one day, he refuses
to give me something that I fervently desire,
it is in order to protect me from a danger
which my child-like eyes could not see."

Abba, teach me to always love your will,
since you always will what is best
for your children.

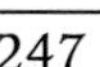

POWER AND AUTHORITY

In religion, there is no question of seizing power to force ideas on others or to be served.

On the contrary, it is a matter of helping one another to know* and love the Lord better.

Religious leaders are given one task, which is to allow each person to live according to the gospel while making full use of that person's talents.

Authority, while it may be stern, is not meant to crush. It is aimed at removing obstacles to brotherly love and the service of God.

For a fine example of evangelical authority, see 1 Corinthians 11:17-33, page 434.

To serve

10 35 And there came to him James and John, the sons of
Zebedee, saying to him, "Master, will you give us
36 whatever may be our request?" | Jesus replied, "What
37 would you have me do for you?" | They answered, "Let us
be seated, one at your right hand and one at your left, in
38 your glory." | But Jesus said to them, "You do not know
what you are saying. Are you able to drink of my cup?[1] Or
39 to endure the baptism* which I am to endure?"[2] | They
replied, "We are able." Thus, Jesus said, "You will drink of
the cup from which I drink; and the baptism which I am
40 about to endure you will endure. | But to be seated at my
right hand or at my left is not for me to promise. It is for
those for whom it has been prepared."
41 Hearing this, the ten became very angry with James and
42 John. | Jesus called them together, saying, "You see that
those who are made rulers over the Gentiles are lords over
43 them, and their rulers have authority over them. | But it is
not so among you. Whoever has a desire to become great
44 among you, let him be your servant, | and whoever has a
45 desire to be first among you, let him be servant of all. | For
truly the Son* of man did not come to have servants, but
to be a servant, and to give his life for the salvation of
men."

[1] See Mark 14:36, page 369.

[2] Like the cup to be drunk, baptism suggests the Passion. Jesus will be immersed in a bath of hatred and pain.*

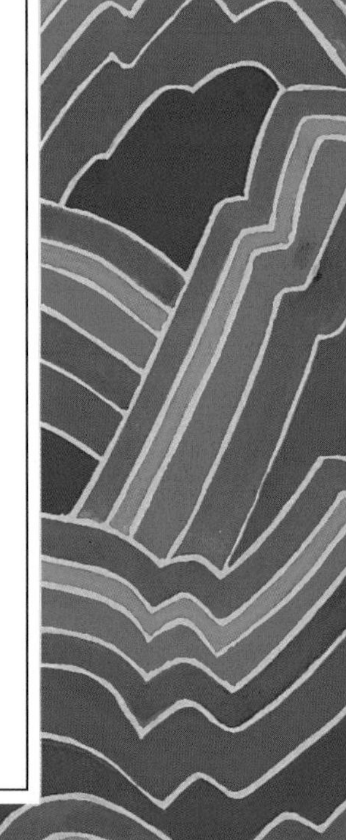

Long live the son of David!

10 46 And they came to Jericho. As he was going
out of Jericho, with his disciples* and a great
number of people, the son of Timaeus, Bartimaeus, a blind
47 man, was seated by the road, begging for money. | And

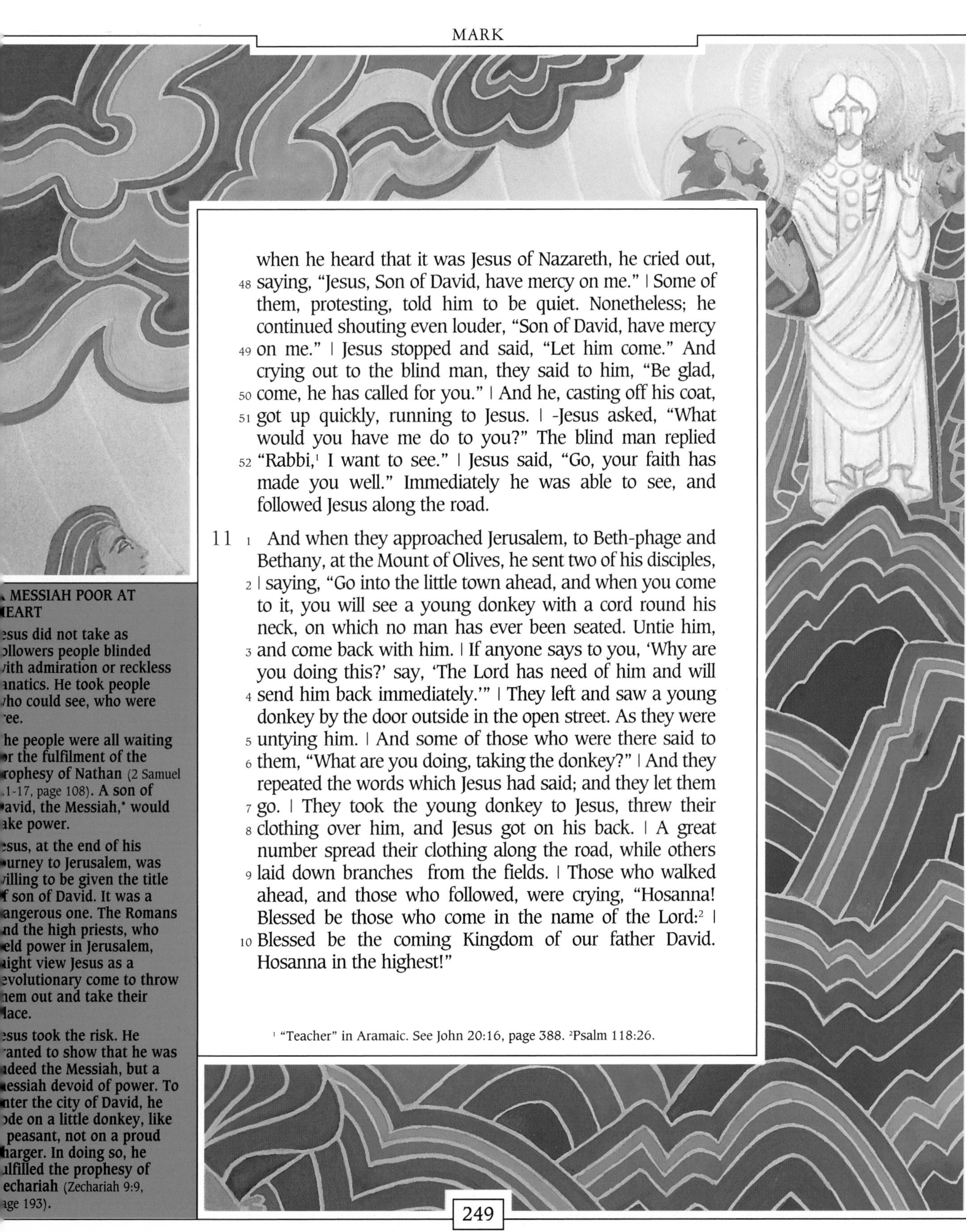

when he heard that it was Jesus of Nazareth, he cried out,
48 saying, "Jesus, Son of David, have mercy on me." | Some of
them, protesting, told him to be quiet. Nonetheless; he
continued shouting even louder, "Son of David, have mercy
49 on me." | Jesus stopped and said, "Let him come." And
crying out to the blind man, they said to him, "Be glad,
50 come, he has called for you." | And he, casting off his coat,
51 got up quickly, running to Jesus. | -Jesus asked, "What
would you have me do to you?" The blind man replied
52 "Rabbi,[1] I want to see." | Jesus said, "Go, your faith has
made you well." Immediately he was able to see, and
followed Jesus along the road.

11 1 And when they approached Jerusalem, to Beth-phage and
Bethany, at the Mount of Olives, he sent two of his disciples,
2 | saying, "Go into the little town ahead, and when you come
to it, you will see a young donkey with a cord round his
neck, on which no man has ever been seated. Untie him,
3 and come back with him. | If anyone says to you, 'Why are
you doing this?' say, 'The Lord has need of him and will
4 send him back immediately.'" | They left and saw a young
donkey by the door outside in the open street. As they were
5 untying him. | And some of those who were there said to
6 them, "What are you doing, taking the donkey?" | And they
repeated the words which Jesus had said; and they let them
7 go. | They took the young donkey to Jesus, threw their
8 clothing over him, and Jesus got on his back. | A great
number spread their clothing along the road, while others
9 laid down branches from the fields. | Those who walked
ahead, and those who followed, were crying, "Hosanna!
Blessed be those who come in the name of the Lord:[2] |
10 Blessed be the coming Kingdom of our father David.
Hosanna in the highest!"

[1] "Teacher" in Aramaic. See John 20:16, page 388. [2]Psalm 118:26.

**. MESSIAH POOR AT
IEART**

**esus did not take as
ollowers people blinded
vith admiration or reckless
anatics. He took people
vho could see, who were
ree.**

**he people were all waiting
or the fulfilment of the
rophesy of Nathan** (2 Samuel
.1-17, page 108). **A son of
avid, the Messiah,* would
ake power.**

**esus, at the end of his
ourney to Jerusalem, was
villing to be given the title
f son of David. It was a
angerous one. The Romans
nd the high priests, who
eld power in Jerusalem,
aight view Jesus as a
evolutionary come to throw
hem out and take their
lace.**

**esus took the risk. He
vanted to show that he was
ndeed the Messiah, but a
essiah devoid of power. To
nter the city of David, he
ode on a little donkey, like
peasant, not on a proud
harger. In doing so, he
ulfilled the prophesy of
echariah** (Zechariah 9:9,
age 193).

SACRIFICES IN THE TEMPLE

During the captivity* in Babylon, the Jews had understood that the sacrifice which really pleased God was to place the whole of one's life under His gaze (see Psalm 51:18-19, page 216). **After the captivity, the Temple had been rebuilt and animal sacrifices had resumed** (see, for example, 1 Maccabees 4:36-59, page 179). **To cater to the pilgrims wanting to offer a sacrifice, the Sadducees* had organized an animal market on the outercourt of the Temple. Since Roman coins bearing the portrait of the Emperor were forbidden in the Temple, the Sadducees had also introduced money-changers who supplied worshippers with traditional Jewish coins.**

No trading in the Temple!

11 15 And they came to Jerusalem where Jesus entered the
Temple.* He drove out those who were trading
there, overturning the tables of the money-changers and
16 the seats of those who were offering doves for money. | He
would not let any man takemerchandise through the
17 Temple. | He preached, saying, "Is it not written, 'My house
is a house of prayer for all the nations?[1] But you have
18 made it a den of thieves.'"[2] | When the chief priests and
scribes heard of this, they began scheming how they might
put him to death. They were afraid of him, because all the
19 people were amazed by his teaching. | When evening came,
he left the town.[3]

[1] See Isaiah 56:7, page 184.

[2] See Jeremiah 7:11, page 151.

[3] Compare the whole of this pa sage with John 2:13-22, pag 336.

[4] See Isaiah 5:1-7, page 135.

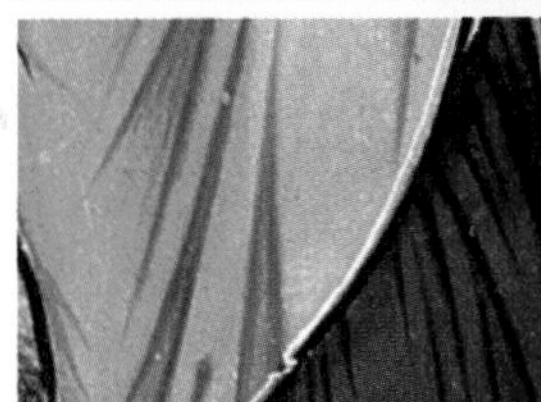

Throw him out and the vineyard will be ours

12 1 And he preached to them in parables.* "A man
had a vineyard planted, and put a wall about it. He
made a place for the winepress, and put up a tower.[4] He
rented it to some farmers, and left for another country.
2 And when the time came, he sent a servant to get from
3 the farmers some of the fruit of the garden. | Instead, they
siezed him and beat him, sending him away with nothing.
4 | So he sent another servant, whom they beat on the head,
5 and to whom they were very cruel. | He sent another whom
they killed, as well as many others, whipping some, and
6 killing others. | He still had one, a dearly loved son whom
he sent last to them, saying, 'They will have respect for my
7 son.' | But the farmers said among themselves, 'This is he
who will one day be the owner of the property. Come, let

PARABLES

Jesus, like Nathan (see 2 Samuel 12:1-4, page 110) **and the other prophets, often used parables when teaching. In these little stories, he presented God as a vintner or a forgiving father. He condemned behavior that pretended to be religious whereas it was, in fact, a denial of God. He pointed out the hard-heartedness of those who were ready to kill the prophets or even the son* rather than hear calls to conversion.***

"Treasures of the Bible" quotes most of Jesus' parables in the Gospels according to Matthew (see page 274 and following) **and according to Luke** (pages 317 328).

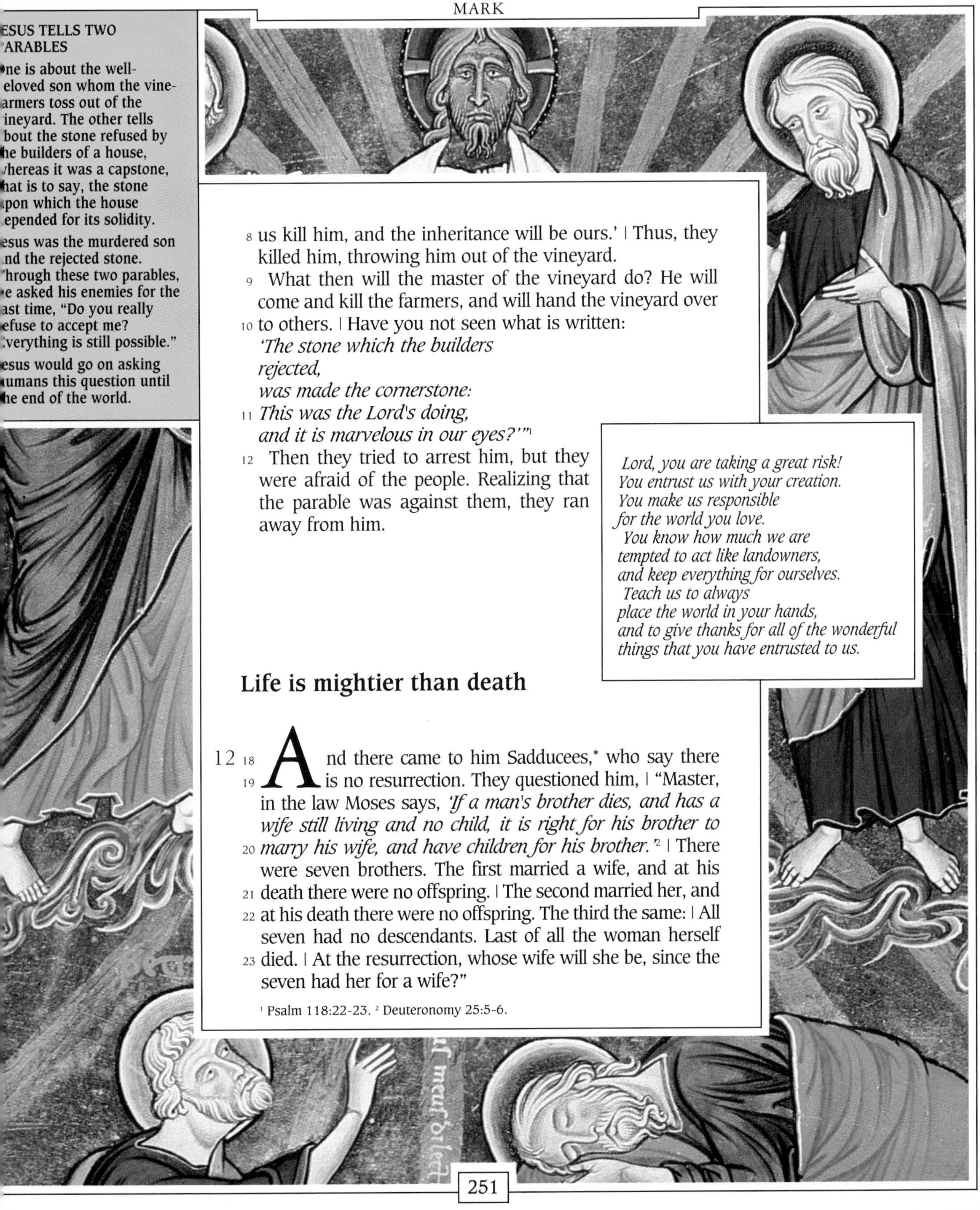

ESUS TELLS TWO 'ARABLES

ne is about the well-eloved son whom the vine-armers toss out of the ineyard. The other tells bout the stone refused by he builders of a house, /hereas it was a capstone, hat is to say, the stone ıpon which the house .epended for its solidity.

esus was the murdered son .nd the rejected stone. 'hrough these two parables, e asked his enemies for the ast time, "Do you really efuse to accept me? :verything is still possible."

esus would go on asking ıumans this question until he end of the world.

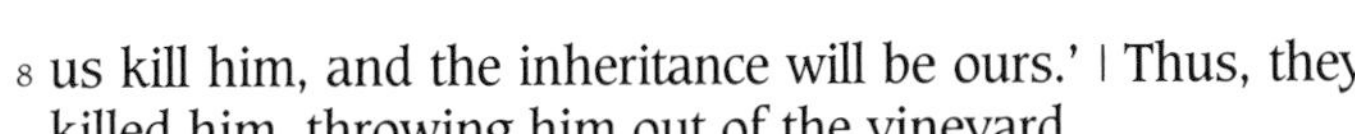

8 us kill him, and the inheritance will be ours.' | Thus, they
killed him, throwing him out of the vineyard.
9 What then will the master of the vineyard do? He will
come and kill the farmers, and will hand the vineyard over
10 to others. | Have you not seen what is written:
'The stone which the builders
rejected,
was made the cornerstone:
11 *This was the Lord's doing,*
and it is marvelous in our eyes?'"[1]
12 Then they tried to arrest him, but they
were afraid of the people. Realizing that
the parable was against them, they ran
away from him.

Lord, you are taking a great risk!
You entrust us with your creation.
You make us responsible
for the world you love.
You know how much we are
tempted to act like landowners,
and keep everything for ourselves.
Teach us to always
place the world in your hands,
and to give thanks for all of the wonderful
things that you have entrusted to us.

Life is mightier than death

12 18 And there came to him Sadducees,* who say there
19 is no resurrection. They questioned him, | "Master,
in the law Moses says, *'If a man's brother dies, and has a*
wife still living and no child, it is right for his brother to
20 *marry his wife, and have children for his brother.'*[2] | There
were seven brothers. The first married a wife, and at his
21 death there were no offspring. | The second married her, and
22 at his death there were no offspring. The third the same: | All
seven had no descendants. Last of all the woman herself
23 died. | At the resurrection, whose wife will she be, since the
seven had her for a wife?"

[1] Psalm 118:22-23. [2] Deuteronomy 25:5-6.

RESURRECTION*

The Pharisees* believed that one day God would resurrect the dead. The Sadducees* on the other hand thought that God rewarded the righteous and punished the unrighteous in this life. After death, there was nothing.

They made fun of Jesus. "This idea of life after death is ridiculous. With whom will people who have married several times have to live?"

Jests of this kind can still be heard today.

Jesus taught that rising again was not to live as before death. It was not returning to the past. While remaining ourselves, we would live in a different manner, since "like the angels in heaven" we would see forever the face of the Father (Matthew 18:10, page 283).

12 24 Jesus replied, "Are you not in error, because you have no
25 knowledge of the Scriptures* or of the power of God? | When
the dead rise, they do not marry, but are like the angels in
26 heaven. | Concerning the dead rising, have you not seen in
the book of Moses, about the burning bush, how God said
to him, *'I am the God of Abraham, and the God of Isaac, and*
27 *the God of Jacob?'*[1] | He is not the God of the dead, but of the
living. You are greatly mistaken."

The first commandment

12 28 And one of the scribes came, and hearing their
argument, and seeing that he had given them a
good answer, asked him, "Which law is the most
29 important?" | Jesus answered, "The first is, 'Listen, O
30 Israel: The Lord our God is one Lord. | You are to love the
Lord your God with all your heart, and with all your soul,
31 and with all your mind, and with all your strength.'[2] | The
second is this, 'Love your neighbor[3] as yourself.'[4] There is
32 no other law greater than these." | And the scribe said to
him, "Truly, Master, you are right in saying thar there is
33 no other but the Lord. | And to love him with all the heart,
and with all the mind, and with all the strength, and to
have the same love for his neighbor as for himself. This is
much more than all forms of offerings." |
34 And when Jesus saw that the scribe
responded wisely, Jesus said to him, "You
are not far from the kingdom* of God."

[1] See Exodus 3:6, page 57.

[2] Deuteronomy 6:4-5, page 84.

[3] The neighbor is not only the person who is close to us or like us. Jesus insists on loving the person who is different who bothers us. See Matthew 5:43-48, page 262, Matthew 25:31-46, page 295, and Luke 10:29-37, page 317.

[4] Leviticus 19:18, page 73.

Lord, we greatly desire
to love you and others.
But, this desire often remains
only a good intention,
or just words.
Actions don't follow
because we don't know how to love.
Only you, Lord,
can put our fears to rest,
make up for our blunders,
and help us to give of ourselves
because you are love.

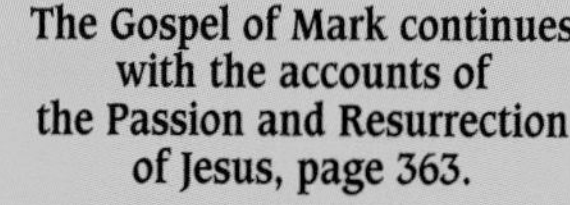
The Gospel of Mark continues with the accounts of the Passion and Resurrection of Jesus, page 363.

II
THE GOSPEL ACCORDING TO MATTHEW

Who was Matthew?

A 2nd century tradition has it that Matthew, one of the Twelve Apostles, "put in order the sayings of Jesus in the Hebrew tongue." There is no trace of this first book, called "The Aramaic Gospel of Matthew." Later, around 80 AD, the same Matthew or another author wrote the Gospel as we now know it in Greek, taking the Aramaic version as model.*

The name Matthew means "gift of the Lord." He was a "publican," or excise tax collector, in Capernaum. He is sometimes called Levi. Little is known of his life after the Resurrection of Jesus. Some traditions claim that he evangelized Persia and then Ethiopia, where he died a martyr.[1]

Since his Gospel begins with the family tree of Jesus, Matthew has traditionally been symbolized by the "man."[2]

For whom did Matthew write this Gospel?

Matthew was writing for Christians who had been converted from Judaism. He was concerned to show them that Jesus was indeed the one who had been foretold by the prophets.[3] *He presented Jesus as a new Moses, come to establish a new Covenant between God and His people.*

This people was no longer limited to Israel. Matthew showed how Jesus, faced with rejection by official Judaism,[4] *enlarged the people of the Covenant. Without going back on any of the promises made to Israel, he accepted heathens and so gave birth to a religion.*

Matthew was anxious to remind this religion of the rules needed for living in togetherness. He wanted to provide it with a sound catechesis by writing five great "discourses" in which he put the words of Jesus in order.*

[1] There is a fine set of pillar capitals in Nazareth, carved at the time of the Crusades, relating the story of Matthew in Ethiopia.

[2] See page 502.

[3] Matthew refers a hundred and thirty times, by allusion or direct quotation, to the Old Testament.*

[4] Large numbers of the people of Israel accepted Jesus and formed the first Christian communities. But, at the time of the writing of Matthew's Gospel, Pharisee* leaders were beginning to expel Jews who recognized Jesus as Messiah from the synagogues.

GOSPEL OF THE CHILDHOOD

The first two Chapters of Matthew merged several narratives of the birth and childhood of Jesus. The Evangelist's goal was not primarily to give biographical information about the early years of Jesus. In these two chapters, he set out the general message which he was to develop in the rest of the book. These chapters are often named the "Gospel of the Childhood" since, in the stories about the infant Jesus, the entire meaning of Jesus Christ's life was expressed.

Matthew showed that Jesus was the one who fulfilled the Old Testament prophecies. He was Balaam's star, the Messiah*, the descendant of David, Immanuel and more. He was above all a second Moses come to renew the Covenant.*

All these Old Testament images were only a dim foreshadow of Jesus, the presence of God among men.

Luke also wrote a "Gospel of the Childhood." See page 298.

JOSEPH'S ANNUNCIATION

Joseph was not dragged into an adventure that was past his understanding. He received the mission* to form, with Mary, a family circle in which Jesus could grow up. Joseph was not involved in the conception of Jesus. But even before Jesus was born he was a caring husband to Mary. Afterwards, he showed affectionate authority towards the young boy. "Your father and I have been anxiously searching for you," said Mary one day. Jesus, without belittling the fatherhood of Joseph, said that he had another Father who had first claim on him. (Luke 2:47-50, page 306.)

THE CHILDHOOD OF JESUS

Jesus, son of David

1 1 The record of the geneology of Jesus Christ,*
the son of David, the son of Abraham.
2 The son of Abraham was Isaac;
the son of Isaac was Jacob;
the sons of Jacob were Judah and his brothers;
3 the sons of Judah were Perez and Zerah by Tamar;
the son of Perez was Hezron;
the son of Hezron was Ram;
4 the son of Ram was Amminadab;
the son of Amminadab was Nahshon;
the son of Nahshon was Salmon;
5 the son of Salmon by Rahab was Boaz;
the son of Boaz by Ruth was Obed;
6 the son of Obed was Jesse; | the son of Jesse was David the
king; the son of David was Solomon
whose mother had been the wife of Uriah....

16 And the son of Jacob was Joseph the husband of Mary,
who gave birth to Jesus, whose name is Christ.
17 So there were fourteen generations from Abraham to
David are;
from David to the exile to Babylon,
fourteen generations;
and from theexile to Babylon to the coming of Christ, fourteen
generations.

Jesus, Immanuel

1 18 Now the birth of Jesus Christ was in this way:
When his mother Mary was going to be married
to Joseph, before they came together the discovery was

WOMEN FOREBEARS OF JESUS

In addition to Mary, four women are included in this recital of men's names: Tamar, the Canaanite, Rahab from Jericho and Ruth the Moabite (see page 504, "Foreign Women"). The fourth is calle the "wife of Uriah,*" who was a Hittite.* These four women, associated with foreign peoples, give a universal dimension to the ancestry of Jesus. The Son of God became a Jew, but he had ties of kinship with the heathen peoples.

[1] In Hebrew, numbers are writ-ten with letters of the alphabe (as in Latin). The figure 14 an the word David are written i exactly the same way. Matthew listed the ancestors of Jesus i three groups of 14 names. I was a way of drawing attentio to the name of David. He wa proving that Jesus was the des-cendant of David, the one fore-told by the prophets, for whon everyone was waiting.

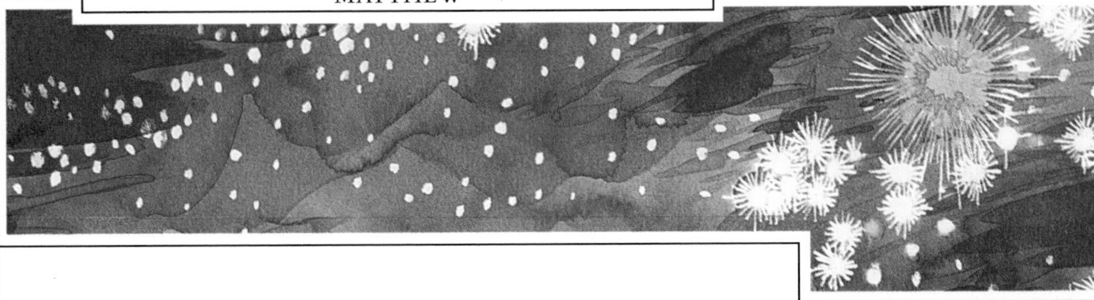

THE FEAR OF GOD

'ear* was a normal human eaction in the presence of ;od. If Joseph demurred at aking Mary into his home, t was because he suspected hat what was growing in er came from God.

Ie did not want to impose imself on God—exploit the hild so as to play a part in he history of God's people. Ie wanted to give Mary her reedom, out of respect for what God was ccomplishing in her.

oseph was truly a ighteous* man.

HEATHENS FILLED WITH FAITH

Balaam had said, "I see him, but not now. A star will come out of Jacob. A scepter will rise out of Israel." (Numbers 24:17, page 83.) The Wise Men traveling towards the "star" and "the one who has been born king" signaled the fulfilment of this prophecy.

The scribes* and priests,* quite secure in their knowledge, put the Wise Men on the right road but did not bother to go with them. In their haughtiness, they could not imagine the birth of the Messiah* being revealed to them by heathens.

19 made that she was with child by the Holy Spirit. | And
Joseph, her husband, being a righteous man, and not
desiring to make her a public disgrace, had a mind to
20 divorce her privately. | But when he was giving thought to
these things, an angel of the Lord came to him in a dream,
saying, "Joseph, son of David, have no fear of taking Mary
as your wife, because that which is in her body is of the
21 Holy Spirit. | She will give birth to a son whom you will
name Jesus, for he will give his people salvation from their
sins."
22 Now all this took place so that the word of the Lord
through the prophet might come true: |
23 *"See, the virgin will be with child, and*
will give birth to a son. They will give
him the name Immanuel, that is, God*
with us."[1]
24 Joseph did as the angel of the Lord had
said to him, and took her as his wife. |
25 He had no sexual union with her till she
bore the son whom he named Jesus.

[1] See Isaiah 7:14, page 139. Matthew used the Greek translation of the prophecy. The "young girl" was rendered as "virgin" to signify that the long-awaited Messiah had, more than any other, been formed by God, "knitted together in his mother's womb" (Psalm 138:13, page 226). He would so be in total harmony with God.

Joseph,
the Son of God needs you
to make his Father
known to humanity.
He needs to know what the word "father"
means in human language.

By confidently putting
his hand in yours,
and discovering
how good and righteous you are,
he can tell humanity
that their Father in heaven is like this,
and much more so!

Jesus, Balaam's star

2 1 Now when the birth of Jesus took place in Bethlehem
of Judaea, in the days of Herod* the king, there
2 came magi* from the east to Jerusalem, | Saying, "Where is
the King of the Jews whose birth has now taken place? We
have seen his star in the east and have come to worship
3 him." | When Herod the king heard this, he was troubled,

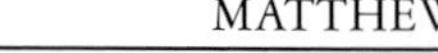

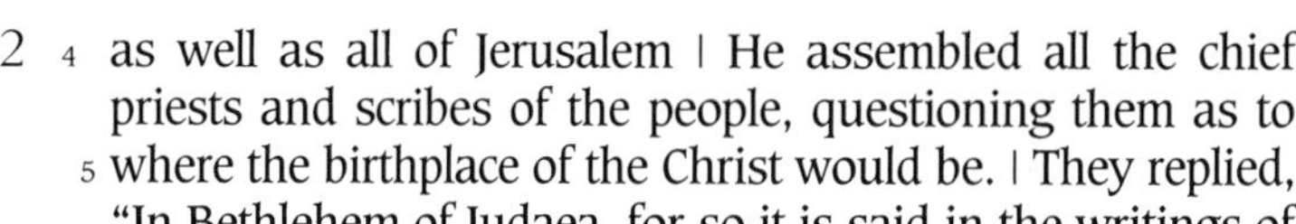

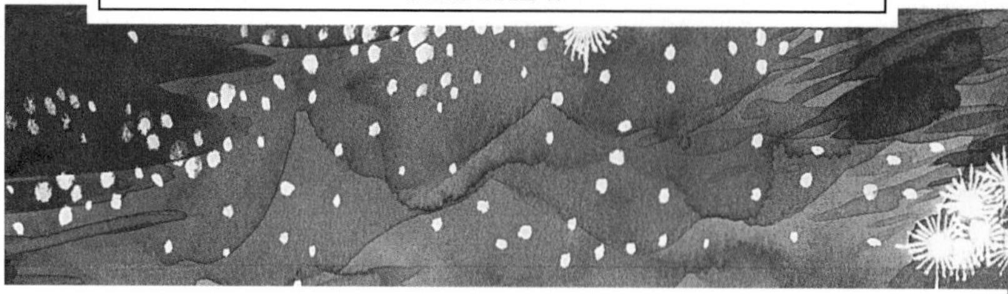

WISE MEN AND KINGS?

The Gospel does not tell us how many Wise Men came to kneel before Jesus. Since three presents are named, the conclusion is that there were three.

Matthew, in naming these presents, had in mind a prophecy from Isaiah (Isaiah 60:1-6, page 186), in which the nations led by their kings would come to Jerusalem to praise the Lord. These first heathens paying homage to Jesus were precursors of all those who would "come from the East and the West and take their places ... in the kingdom of heaven." (Matthew 8:11, page 267.)

In Christmas nativity scenes, it is fair therefore that the Wise Men should be shown as kings from Africa, Asia or Europe. It was the "Epiphany,"* the revelation of the Son of God to the whole world.

TOWARDS A NEW COVENANT

Jesus was taken into exile in Egypt, from where he would one day return in answer to God's call. Innocent children were slaughtered by a power-crazy and superstitious king. These events remind us of the life of Moses (see Exodus, Chapters 1 and 2, pages 54-56). Jesus was a second Moses, but much greater than Moses. He would build a new Covenant* between God and His people.

2 4 as well as all of Jerusalem | He assembled all the chief
priests and scribes of the people, questioning them as to
5 where the birthplace of the Christ would be. | They replied,
"In Bethlehem of Judaea, for so it is said in the writings of
6 the prophet, | *'You Bethlehem, in the land of Judah, are not
the least among the chiefs of Judah. Out of you will come
a ruler, who will be the shepherd of my people Israel.'"*[1] |
7 Then Herod sent for the magi privately, and questioned
8 them about what time the star had been seen. | He sent
them to Bethlehem saying, "Go and make certain where
the young child is. When you have seen him, let me know,
9 so that I may come and worship him." | And after listening
to the king, they went on their way. The star which they
saw in the east went before them, till it came to rest over
the place where the young child was.

10-11 When they saw the star they were full of joy. | They
entered the house, and seeing the young child with Mary,
his mother, they bowed down and worshipped him. Then
they opened their treasures, giving him offerings of gold,
incense and myrrh.[2]

12 Having been warned by God in a dream that they were
not to go back to Herod, they returned to their country by
another way.

Jesus, a second Moses

2 13 And when they had gone, an angel of the Lord came
to Joseph in a dream, saying, "Get up and take the
young child and his mother into Egypt. Do not go leave

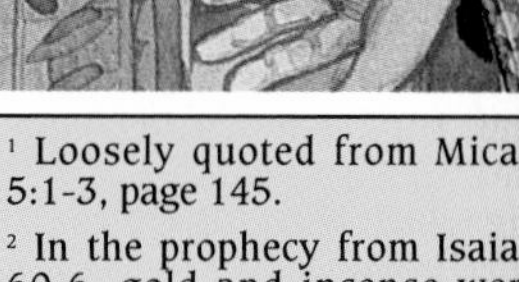

[1] Loosely quoted from Micah 5:1-3, page 145.

[2] In the prophecy from Isaiah 60:6, gold and incense were mentioned. Matthew added myrrh, an Eastern perfume often used in burials (see John 19:39, page 384). The three presents were a kind of description of the one to whom they were offered: a king (gold and incense) but mortal (myrrh) someone who took nothing who did not reign by violence but gave everything, including his own life.

there till I give you word, for Herod will be searching for
14 the young child to kill him." | So he took the young child
15 and his mother by night, and went into Egypt. | They
stayed there until Herod died, so that the word of the Lord
spoken through the prophet might come
true, *"Out of Egypt have I sent for my son."*[1]

16 Then Herod, when he realized that he
had been tricked by the magi, was
furious. He ordered the death of all the
male children from two years old and
under in Bethlehem and in all its
vicinity, according to the time which he
had been told by the magi.

The one designated by the prophets
as the Prince of Peace,
has come into the world,
but nothing has changed;
the evil still kill, and the poor are still crushed.

Lord, you don't force yourself on anyone.
You don't limit anyone's freedom.
You want to teach them
to use their freedom;
not for creating evil,
but for creating a loving response
in each circumstance.
Patiently, you invite each one
of us to convert.

THE CHILDREN OF ABRAHAM

Some believed that to be saved it was enough to belong to the people of Abraham. John the Baptist scotched that idea. God could make children of Abraham out of paving-stones.

This was a way of saying that the children of Abraham to whom he was talking had hearts of stone and were in need of conversion.

THE START OF JESUS' MINISTRY

The preaching of John the Baptist

3 1 And in those days John the Baptist came preaching
2 in the Desert of Judaea, | saying, "Repent* from
7 sin, for the kingdom[2] of heaven is near."... | But when he
saw a number of the Pharisees and Sadducees coming to
his baptism, he said to them, "Offspring of snakes, who
8 warned you to flee from the wrath* to come? | Let your
9 change of heart be seen in your works. | Do not say to
yourselves, 'We have Abraham for our father;' because I
say to you that God is able from these stones to make
10 children for Abraham. | Even now the axe is put to the root

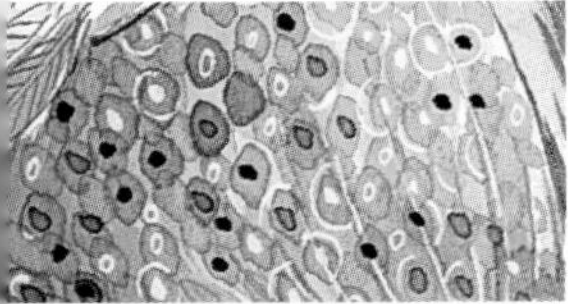

A MESSIAH-JUDGE

John preached conversion, since the one who would "come after" him would be a stern Messiah.* He would have an ax or a winnowing fork in his hand. He would separate the good from the wicked. To John's puzzlement, Jesus did not quite match this portrait (see Matthew 3:14).

[1] See Hosea 11:1, page 134.

[2] Matthew spoke of the Kingdom of Heaven, while the other Evangelists preferred "Kingdom of God." For the Jews, "the heavens" clearly evokes their God (who is in heaven). It is one of the expressions used to avoid pronouncing the name* of God. See page 58.

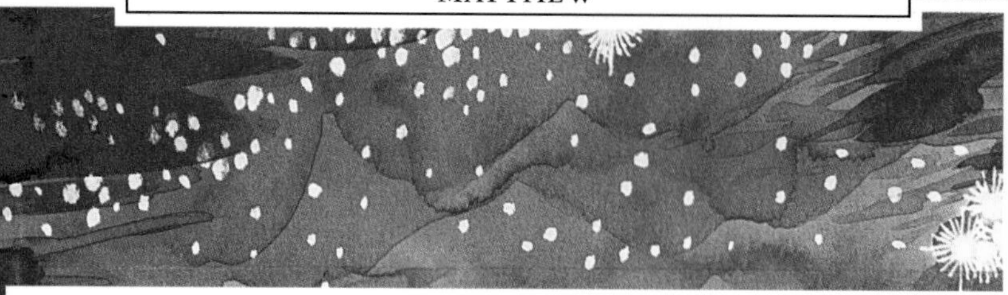

3 of the trees; every tree then which does not give good fruit
is cut down, and put into the fire.

11 Truly, I baptise with water those of you whose hearts are
changed, but he who comes after me is greater than I,
whose shoes I am not good enough to take up. He will
12 baptise you with the Holy Spirit and with fire:[1] | His
winnowing fork is in his hand and he will clear his
treshing floor[2], gathering his wheat into the barn and
burning the chaff with unquenchable fire."

Jesus is baptized

3 13 Then Jesus came from Galilee to John at the Jordan,
14 to bebaptised by him.[3] | But John tried to stop him,
saying, "It is I who have need of baptism from you, yet you
15 come to me?" | But Jesus replied, "Let it be so now, because
it is right for us to fulfill all righteousness." Then he
baptised him.

16 And Jesus, having been baptised,
immediately rose from the water. The
heavens opened, and he saw the Spirit
of God descending on him as a dove;[4] |
17 A voice came out of heaven, saying,
"This is my dearly loved Son, with
whom I am well pleased."

WHO WAS JESUS?

What a remarkable epiphany* for Jesus' first public appearance as a grown man: Son of God! This narrative tells us both what Jesus seemed to be and who he really was.

He came in the guise of a sinner. He did not put himself on a pedestal. From the start, it was clear that Jesus would not distance himself from sinners but would go all the way to meet them.

He was without sin, the beloved son of God, in communion with the Holy Spirit. This account introduces us to the mystery* of the Trinity.* God was not a solitary being but a "communion of love" of Father, Son and Spirit. The Son was made man to enable humans to share in the life of the Trinity (see John 17:24-26, page 362).

John the Baptist couldn't get over it!
The one whom he had announced
as "the one coming to clean up"
was standing in the middle of sinners,
and looked just like them!
In this way,
he will accomplish righteousness.
Is God's justice
so different from humanity's?
Jesus didn't come
to condemn sinners.
He came to live in their midst
in order to save them.
God's justice is to make us just!

[1] See Matthew 3:16.

[2] The winnowing fork was an instrument for separating the grain from the chaff. The ears were first spread on a hard surface, sometimes made of stone. Different methods (flails, wheels) were used to extract the grain from the husk. Then the winnowing fork was used to throw it all in the air. The chaff flew away and the grain fell to the ground at the winnower's feet.

[3] See the corresponding passage in Mark 1:9-11, page 236.

[4] Using the baptism of Jesus as an example, the Evangelists tried to reveal the meaning of Christian baptism.* The Holy Spirit, who took the form of a dove, was a reminder of the flood (page 29). Once the world of sin had perished beneath the water, the dove brought back an olive twig showing that God had created a new world. In baptism the Christian is immersed (baptized) in water as a sign of death. The Lord wishes to drown in that person everything that is sin, or attachment to evil. After the immersion, the Holy Spirit can create a new heart able to recognize the Father who says: "You are my beloved child."

ESUS AS SERVANT

:an the Son of God go on
iving like an ordinary man?
Will he not use his divine
power to feed himself and
eed the crowds? ¹ To draw
people to him, will he not do
niraculous and uncalled-for
hings to win admiration
and inspire awe? To subject
people to his authority, will
he not become king?

The Son of God would
become like the Emperor of
Rome, keeping nations in
obedience by giving them
bread and circuses.

esus would be tempted to
choose power, not only
during the forty days in the
desert but all through his
ife. He would bravely
refuse.

He had come not to impose
but to propose, like a
servant.*

When Jesus multiplied the loaves,
the crowd did not understand the
sign he was giving them. It trailed
after him so as to have more bread
(John 6:26, page 343).

The temptations in the desert

4 1 Then Jesus was sent by the Spirit into the desert
2 to be tested by the Devil.* | And after going without
3 food for forty days and forty nights, he was hungry. | The
tempter[1] came and said to him, "If you are the Son of God,
4 command these stones to become bread." | But he replied,
"It is written,

'Bread is not man's only need, but every word which comes out of the mouth of God.'"[2]

5 Then the Tempter took him to the holy town where he put
6 him on the highest point[3] of the Temple saying, | "If you are
the Son of God, jump, for it is written,

'He will command his angels;' and, 'In their hands they will lift you up, so that your foot may not be crushed against a stone.'"[4]

7 Jesus said to him, "Again it is written,

'You may not put the Lord your God to the test.'"[5]

8 Again, the tempter took him up to a very high mountain,
showing him all the kingdoms of the world and their glory.
9 | He said, "All these things I will give you, if you will bow
10 down and worship me." | Jesus replied, "Go away, Satan:*
for it is written,

'Worship the Lord your God and be his servant only.'"[6]

11 Then the tempter left him, and angels came and took care
of him.

[1] The tempter, that is to say, Satan or the Devil, can tempt a person internally or externally. Within, he can suggest thoughts that will distance a person from God. From the outside, he exerts pressure through friends or acquaintances. Jesus calls Peter Satan in Matthew 16:23, page 282, and Judas is called a devil in John 6:70, page 346.

[2] Deuteronomy 8:3.

[3] The highest point of the Temple overlooked the valley of Cedron.

[4] The tempter made use of Psalm 91:11-12. The Holy Scriptures inspired by the Holy Spirit can be read mischievously, in a way that deflects the reader from understanding God's word.

[5] Deuteronomy 6:16. In the desert, the people had often put God to the test. See Exodus 17:2-7, pages 67-68.

[6] Deuteronomy 6:13.

THE LAW OF THE NEW COVENANT

When God proposed the first Covenant to the people of Israel, he had given his Laws to Moses on the mountain (see Exodus 19:20, page 70, and the ten "statements of life," page 71).

Jesus, on a mount in Galilee, announced the laws of the new Covenant. He did not abolish any of the Old Testament* rules, but showed that all laws can be summed up in a single one: love God and your neighbor (Matthew 5:43-48, page 262).

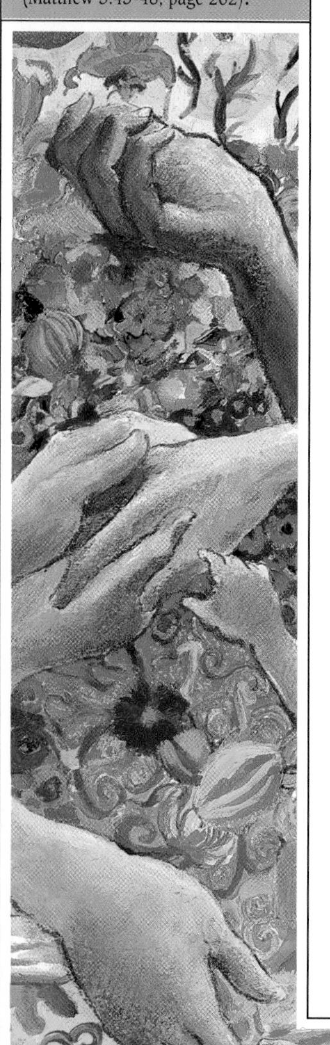

THE SERMON ON THE MOUNT

Life-giving words

5 1 And seeing great masses of people he went up into
the mountain. When he was seated, his disciples
2 came to him. | With these words he preached, saying,
3 " Blessed are the poor in spirit,
for the kingdom of heaven is theirs.
4 Blessed are those who are sad,
for they will be comforted.
5 Blessed are the gentle,
for they will inherit the earth.
6 Blessed are those whose heart's desire is
for righteousness,*
for they will have their desire.
7 Blessed are those who have mercy,*
for they will be given mercy.
8 Blessed are the pure* in heart,
for they will see God.
9 Blessed are the peacemakers,
for they will be named Sons of God.
10 Blessed are those who are attacked
because of righteousness,
for the kingdom of heaven
will be theirs.
11 Blessed are you when men insult you and
are cruel to you, saying all evil things
against you because of me.
12 Be glad and full of joy; for great is your
reward in heaven. For so were the
prophets* attacked who lived before you."

Lord,
you lead us from one surprise to another.
We discover that wealth can't make us happy,
but only disregard for material goods.
Happiness can't be found in violence,
but in meekness,
not in vengence, but in forgiveness;
not even in peace, but in the quest for peace.

You are not satisfied with just saying this.
You live it.
In you, Jesus,
we see what it really means to be poor,
to be meek, to be pure in heart,
without compromise,
completely oriented towards God,
your Father's vision.
Your happiness spreads
like Good News
in the hearts of those who follow you.

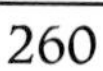

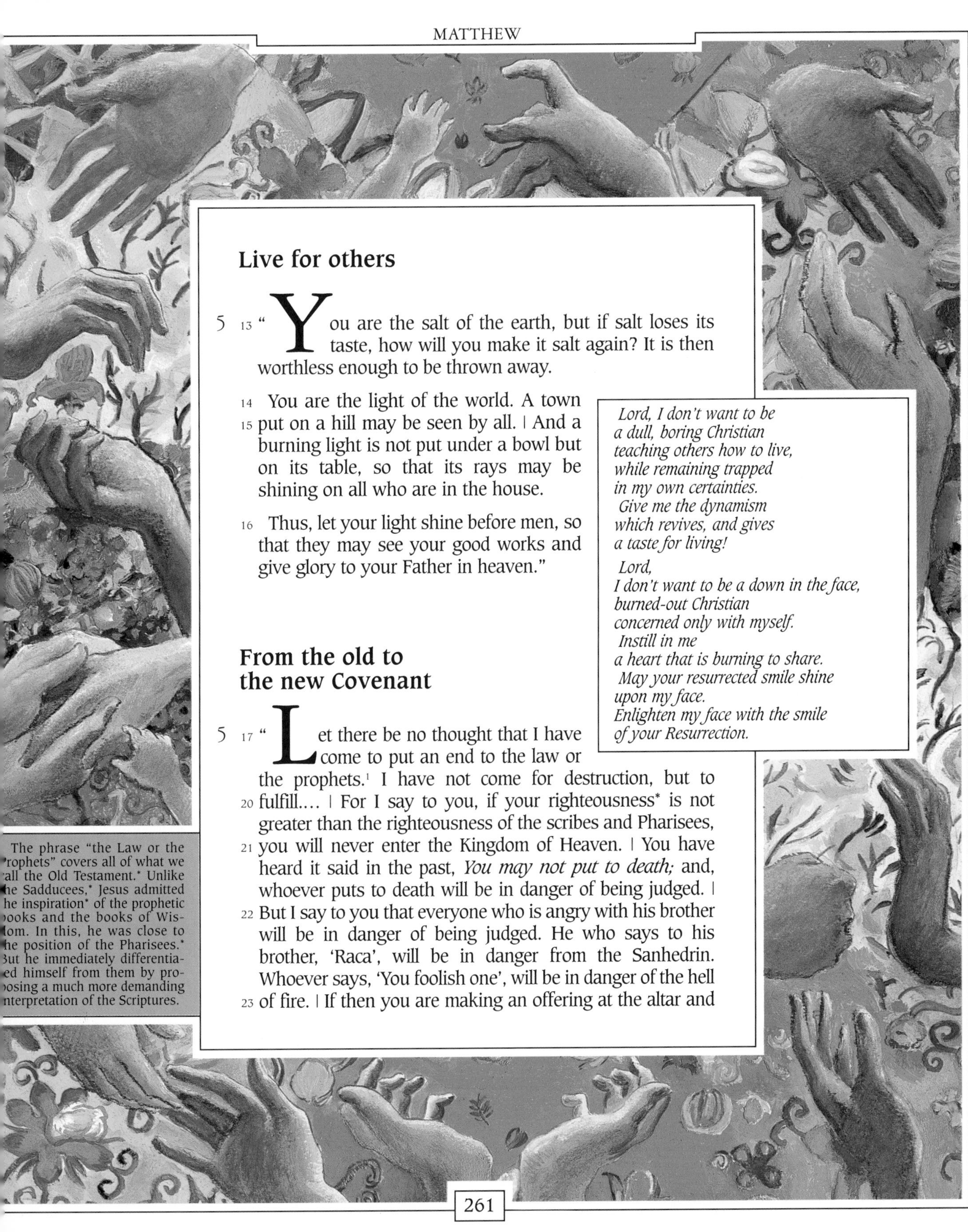

Live for others

5 13 "You are the salt of the earth, but if salt loses its
taste, how will you make it salt again? It is then
worthless enough to be thrown away.

14 You are the light of the world. A town
15 put on a hill may be seen by all. | And a
burning light is not put under a bowl but
on its table, so that its rays may be
shining on all who are in the house.

16 Thus, let your light shine before men, so
that they may see your good works and
give glory to your Father in heaven."

Lord, I don't want to be
a dull, boring Christian
teaching others how to live,
while remaining trapped
in my own certainties.
Give me the dynamism
which revives, and gives
a taste for living!
Lord,
I don't want to be a down in the face,
burned-out Christian
concerned only with myself.
Instill in me
a heart that is burning to share.
May your resurrected smile shine
upon my face.
Enlighten my face with the smile
of your Resurrection.

From the old to the new Covenant

5 17 "Let there be no thought that I have
come to put an end to the law or
the prophets.[1] I have not come for destruction, but to
20 fulfill.... | For I say to you, if your righteousness* is not
greater than the righteousness of the scribes and Pharisees,
21 you will never enter the Kingdom of Heaven. | You have
heard it said in the past, *You may not put to death;* and,
whoever puts to death will be in danger of being judged. |
22 But I say to you that everyone who is angry with his brother
will be in danger of being judged. He who says to his
brother, 'Raca', will be in danger from the Sanhedrin.
Whoever says, 'You foolish one', will be in danger of the hell
23 of fire. | If then you are making an offering at the altar and

The phrase "the Law or the Prophets" covers all of what we call the Old Testament.* Unlike the Sadducees,* Jesus admitted the inspiration* of the prophetic books and the books of Wisdom. In this, he was close to the position of the Pharisees.* But he immediately differentiated himself from them by proposing a much more demanding interpretation of the Scriptures.

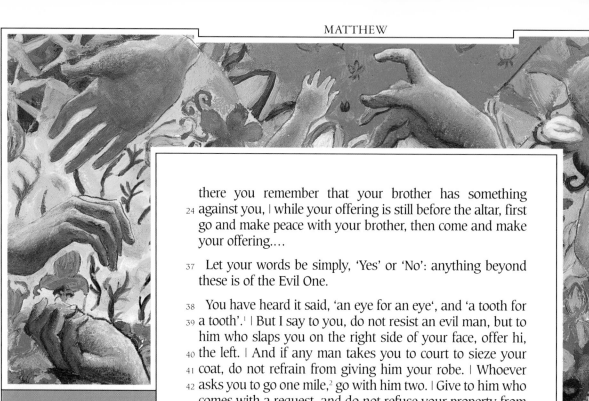

there you remember that your brother has something
24 against you, | while your offering is still before the altar, first
go and make peace with your brother, then come and make
your offering....

37 Let your words be simply, 'Yes' or 'No': anything beyond
these is of the Evil One.

38 You have heard it said, 'an eye for an eye', and 'a tooth for
39 a tooth'.[1] | But I say to you, do not resist an evil man, but to
him who slaps you on the right side of your face, offer hi,
40 the left. | And if any man takes you to court to sieze your
41 coat, do not refrain from giving him your robe. | Whoever
42 asks you to go one mile,[2] go with him two. | Give to him who
comes with a request, and do not refuse your property from
him who needs to borrow it.

43 You have heard it said, *'Love your neighbor,* and hate your
44 enemy.'[3] | But I say to you, love your enemy, and pray for
45 those who persecute you, | so that you may be the sons of
your Father in heaven; for his light shines
on the evil and the good, and he sends
rain on the righteous man as well as the
46 sinner. | For if you love those who love
you, what credit is it to you? Do not the tax
47 collectors the same? | If you say, 'Good
day', to your brothers only, what do you
do more than others? Do not even the
48 pagans* do the same? | Be then fully
righteousness, even as your Father in
heaven is fully righteous."

"I won't weigh you down with the burden of new commandments,"
says the Lord.
"I invite you
to fully live out the old ones."

"Do not kill in any way, shape or form!»
Lies, slander, and mockery
can destroy
as easily as a weapon.

"Love you neighbor."
Don't forget
that your enemy is also
your neighbor!

"Do not seek vengence."
By using patience and skilfulness,
you defuse the anger
of the one who is trying to hurt you.
Seek his good
with your whole heart.

[1] "An eye for an eye, a tooth for a tooth" was a principle that had enabled human justice to take a great step forward. Instead of blind revenge, redress should match the damage caused. Jesus here went one step further.

[2] Roman soldiers in the occupied lands had the right to commandeer labor for such tasks as portering. See Mark 15:21, page 376.

[3] It must be remembered that the Aramaic language spoken by Jesus was not rich in shades of meaning. "Hating" one's enemy really meant "You are not compelled to love your enemy."

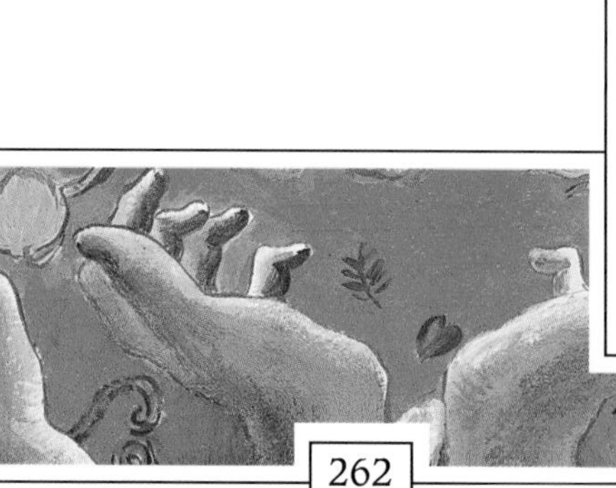

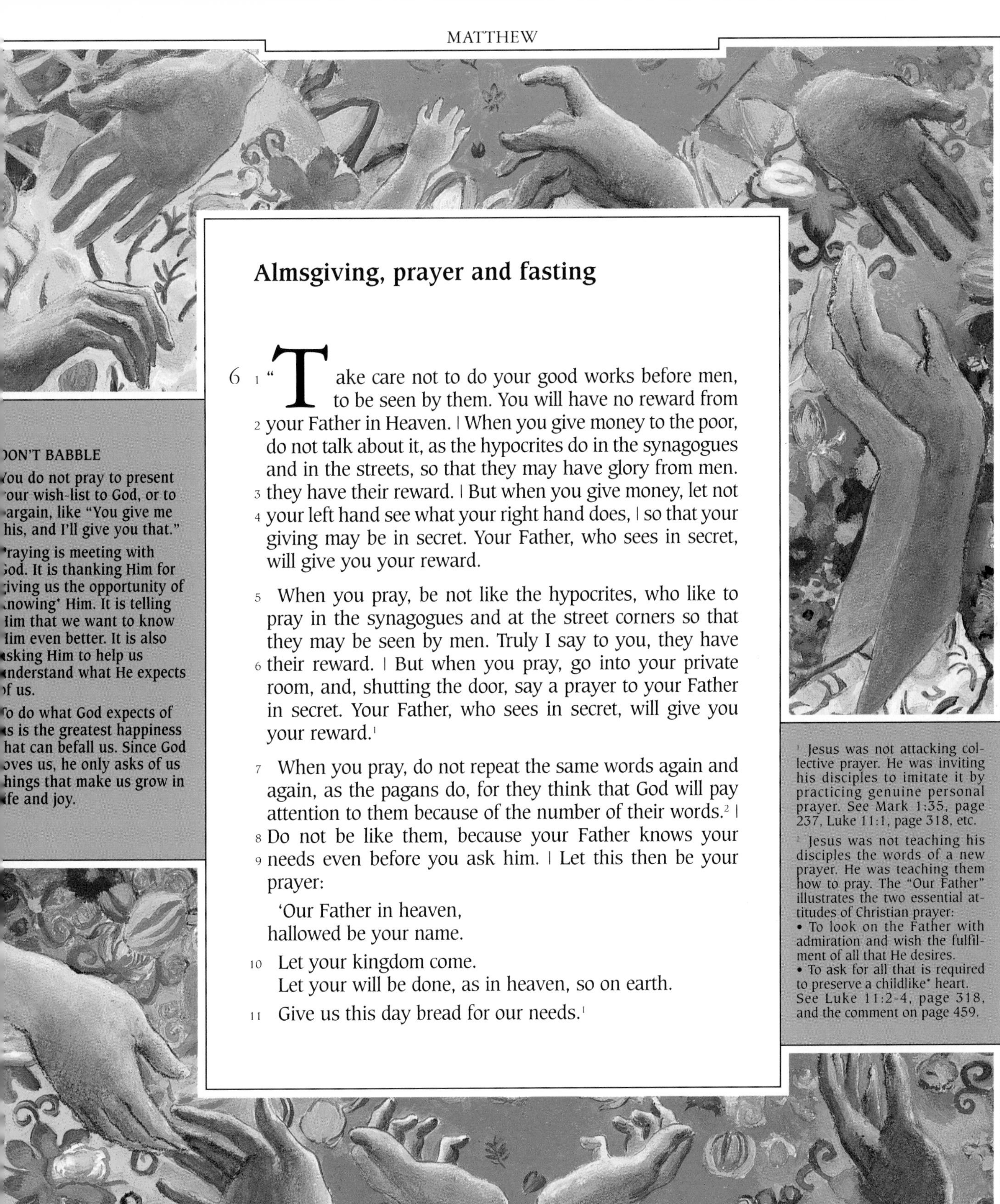

Almsgiving, prayer and fasting

6 1 "Take care not to do your good works before men,
to be seen by them. You will have no reward from
2 your Father in Heaven. | When you give money to the poor,
do not talk about it, as the hypocrites do in the synagogues
and in the streets, so that they may have glory from men.
3 they have their reward. | But when you give money, let not
4 your left hand see what your right hand does, | so that your
giving may be in secret. Your Father, who sees in secret,
will give you your reward.

5 When you pray, be not like the hypocrites, who like to
pray in the synagogues and at the street corners so that
they may be seen by men. Truly I say to you, they have
6 their reward. | But when you pray, go into your private
room, and, shutting the door, say a prayer to your Father
in secret. Your Father, who sees in secret, will give you
your reward.[1]

7 When you pray, do not repeat the same words again and
again, as the pagans do, for they think that God will pay
attention to them because of the number of their words.[2] |
8 Do not be like them, because your Father knows your
9 needs even before you ask him. | Let this then be your
prayer:

'Our Father in heaven,
hallowed be your name.

10 Let your kingdom come.
Let your will be done, as in heaven, so on earth.

11 Give us this day bread for our needs.[1]

DON'T BABBLE

You do not pray to present your wish-list to God, or to bargain, like "You give me this, and I'll give you that."

Praying is meeting with God. It is thanking Him for giving us the opportunity of knowing* Him. It is telling Him that we want to know Him even better. It is also asking Him to help us understand what He expects of us.

To do what God expects of us is the greatest happiness that can befall us. Since God loves us, he only asks of us things that make us grow in life and joy.

[1] Jesus was not attacking collective prayer. He was inviting his disciples to imitate it by practicing genuine personal prayer. See Mark 1:35, page 237, Luke 11:1, page 318, etc.

[2] Jesus was not teaching his disciples the words of a new prayer. He was teaching them how to pray. The "Our Father" illustrates the two essential attitudes of Christian prayer:
• To look on the Father with admiration and wish the fulfilment of all that He desires.
• To ask for all that is required to preserve a childlike* heart.
See Luke 11:2-4, page 318, and the comment on page 459.

6 12 And make us free of our debts,
as we have freed those who are in debt to us.

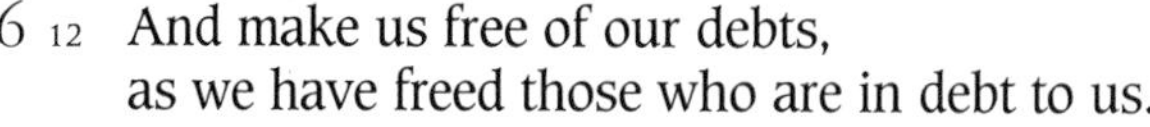

13 And lead us not into temptation[2],
but keep us safe from the Evil One.[3]

14 For if you forgive others for their sins, you will have
15 forgiveness from your Father in Heaven. | But if you do not
forgive others for their sins, you will not have forgiveness
from your Father for your sins.'[4]

16 And when you fast, do not be mournful as the hypocrites
are. For they disfigure themselves, so that men may see
that they are fasting. Truly I say to you, they have their
17 reward. | But when you fast, put oil on your head and
18 make your face clean, | so that no one may see that you are
fasting except your Father in secret. Your Father who sees
in secret, will give you your reward."

[1] See John 6:31-35, page 343.

[2] Temptation comes, not from God, but from the devil (see Matthew 4:1-3, page 259). As God is Almighty, we can ask Him to step in and protect us from seemingly irresistible temptations.

[3] Evil is the action of the Evil One who seeks to destroy trust in God in people's hearts.

[4] See Matthew 18:23-35, page 284.

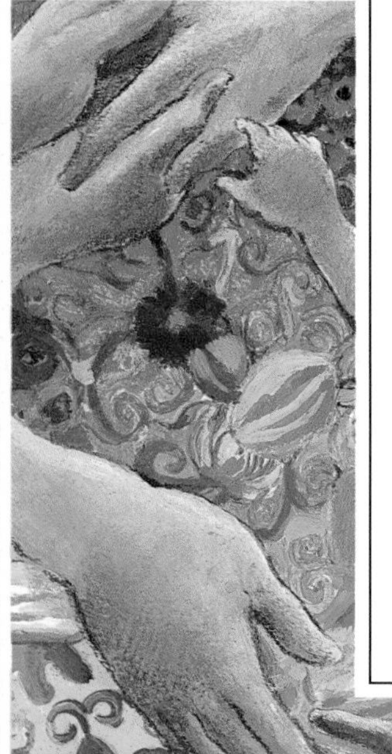

When you share what you have
with someone,
what are you looking to get out of it?

Are you really trying to help the person,
to be a friend?

Or, are you trying to be seen by others,
and be complimented for your generosity?

If you are only thinking of yourself,
don't be surprised
if you never meet Jesus.

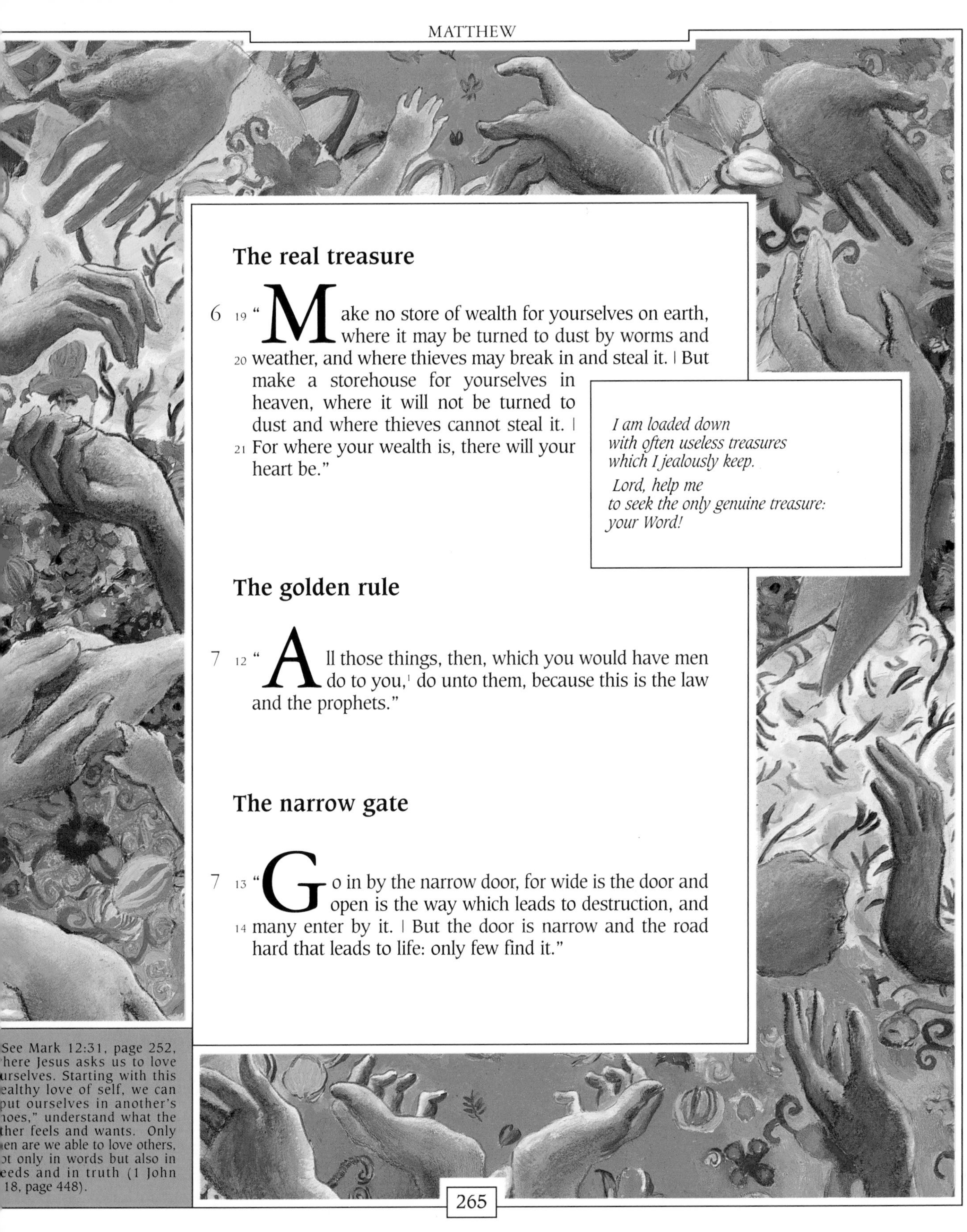

The real treasure

6 19 "Make no store of wealth for yourselves on earth,
where it may be turned to dust by worms and
20 weather, and where thieves may break in and steal it. | But
make a storehouse for yourselves in
heaven, where it will not be turned to
dust and where thieves cannot steal it. |
21 For where your wealth is, there will your
heart be."

I am loaded down
with often useless treasures
which I jealously keep.
Lord, help me
to seek the only genuine treasure:
your Word!

The golden rule

7 12 "All those things, then, which you would have men
do to you,[1] do unto them, because this is the law
and the prophets."

The narrow gate

7 13 "Go in by the narrow door, for wide is the door and
open is the way which leads to destruction, and
14 many enter by it. | But the door is narrow and the road
hard that leads to life: only few find it."

[1] See Mark 12:31, page 252, where Jesus asks us to love ourselves. Starting with this healthy love of self, we can "put ourselves in another's shoes," understand what the other feels and wants. Only then are we able to love others, not only in words but also in deeds and in truth (1 John 3:18, page 448).

Fond illusions

7 21 "Not everyone who says to me, 'Lord, Lord,' will
enter the Kingdom of Heaven, only those who
22 do the will of my Father in Heaven. | Many will say to me
on that day, 'Lord, Lord, were we not prophets in your
name, and did we not by your name cast
out evil spirits, and by your name do
23 works of power?' | And then will I say to
them, I never knew you. Depart from me,
you workers of evil."

People can continually have
God on their lips
and not know God;
claim to know all about God
without ever thinking
of becoming God's friend.

The solidly based house

7 24 "Everyone, then, who hears my words and who
does them, will be like a wise man who made his
25 house on a rock. | The rain fell, there was a rush of waters
and the winds were driving against that house, but it was
not moved, because it was founded on the rock.

26 Everyone who hears my words and does
not do them, will be like a foolish man
27 who built his house on sand. | The rain
fell, there was a rush of waters and the
winds were driving against that house,
and it collapsed and great was its fall."

Lord, teach me to listen to you.
Help me to empty my heart of my ideas
and desires
so that I will be able to understand
what you expect of me.

In this way,
solidly built on the rock of your Word,
I will open my home to all
who have never heard of you.

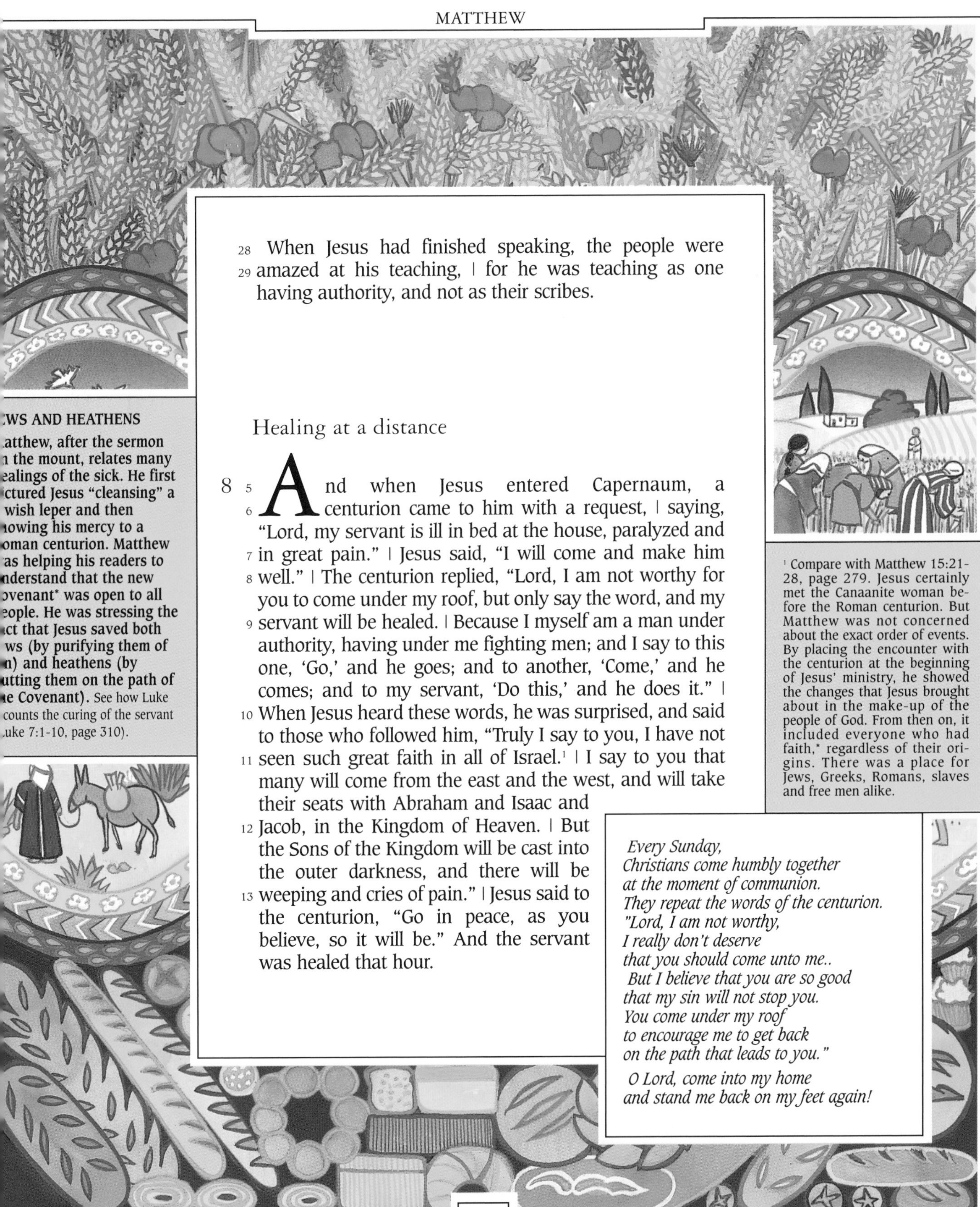

28 When Jesus had finished speaking, the people were
29 amazed at his teaching, | for he was teaching as one
having authority, and not as their scribes.

Healing at a distance

8 5 And when Jesus entered Capernaum, a
6 centurion came to him with a request, | saying,
"Lord, my servant is ill in bed at the house, paralyzed and
7 in great pain." | Jesus said, "I will come and make him
8 well." | The centurion replied, "Lord, I am not worthy for
you to come under my roof, but only say the word, and my
9 servant will be healed. | Because I myself am a man under
authority, having under me fighting men; and I say to this
one, 'Go,' and he goes; and to another, 'Come,' and he
comes; and to my servant, 'Do this,' and he does it." |
10 When Jesus heard these words, he was surprised, and said
to those who followed him, "Truly I say to you, I have not
11 seen such great faith in all of Israel.[1] | I say to you that
many will come from the east and the west, and will take
their seats with Abraham and Isaac and
12 Jacob, in the Kingdom of Heaven. | But
the Sons of the Kingdom will be cast into
the outer darkness, and there will be
13 weeping and cries of pain." | Jesus said to
the centurion, "Go in peace, as you
believe, so it will be." And the servant
was healed that hour.

:WS AND HEATHENS

**.atthew, after the sermon
ı the mount, relates many
ealings of the sick. He first
ictured Jesus "cleansing" a
wish leper and then
ıowing his mercy to a
oman centurion. Matthew
'as helping his readers to
nderstand that the new
ovenant* was open to all
eople. He was stressing the
ıct that Jesus saved both
ws (by purifying them of
n) and heathens (by
utting them on the path of
ıe Covenant).** See how Luke
counts the curing of the servant
.uke 7:1-10, page 310).

[1] Compare with Matthew 15:21-28, page 279. Jesus certainly met the Canaanite woman before the Roman centurion. But Matthew was not concerned about the exact order of events. By placing the encounter with the centurion at the beginning of Jesus' ministry, he showed the changes that Jesus brought about in the make-up of the people of God. From then on, it included everyone who had faith,* regardless of their origins. There was a place for Jews, Greeks, Romans, slaves and free men alike.

*Every Sunday,
Christians come humbly together
at the moment of communion.
They repeat the words of the centurion.
"Lord, I am not worthy,
I really don't deserve
that you should come unto me..
But I believe that you are so good
that my sin will not stop you.
You come under my roof
to encourage me to get back
on the path that leads to you."
O Lord, come into my home
and stand me back on my feet again!*

JESUS, INSTRUCTOR OF THE APOSTLES

Jesus was very careful about the training of the Twelve he had chosen to "be with him" (see Mark 3:14), since he wished to make them leaders of his people.

He did not give them vague general lessons. Through the events of everyday life, he led them to discover the freedom of the children of God whom no human tradition can imprison.

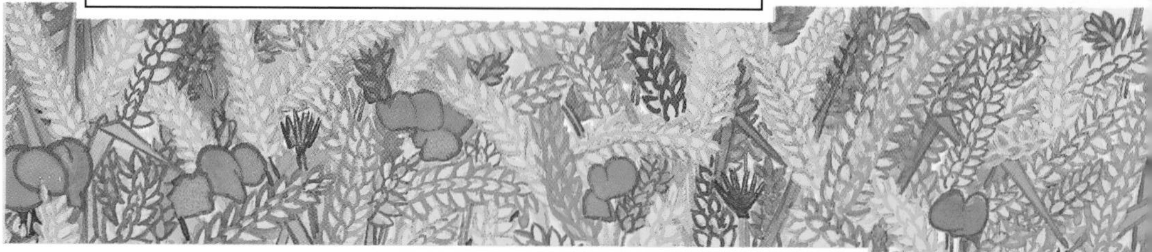

TO HUNGER AFTER THE WORD OF GOD

The Pharisees* and followers of John the Baptist fasted to show that they were hungry for the Word of God.

Jesus explained that fasting would have no meaning for his disciples. They were plentifully fed by his teaching, since he himself was the Word of God (see John 6:68, page 346). They could not complain that they were hungry.

They would fast later, when Jesus was no longer physically with them and they no longer heard his voice. Fasting would be like a prayer: "Lord, I wish to feed myself on your words. Teach me to hear your message through the words of the Scriptures.* Teach me to recognize it among all the other words that I hear. Feed my heart which is hungry for you."

JESUS AND THE TWELVE APOSTLES

Debate about meals: at table with all and sundry?

9 9 And when Jesus was leaving, he saw a
man whose name was Matthew, seated at the
place where taxes[1] were taken. He said to him, "Follow
me." And he got up and followed him.

10 While Jesus was in the house eating, a number of tax
collectors and sinners came and took their places with
11 Jesus and his disciples. | When the Pharisees* saw it, they
said to his disciples,* "Why does your Master eat with tax
12 collectors and sinners?"[2] | But hearing this he said, "Those
who are well have no need of a doctor, only those who are
13 ill. | But go and learn what these words mean: My desire is
for mercy, not offerings.[3] I have not come to save the
righteous, but sinners."[4]

To fast?

9 14 Then the disciples of John came to him, saying,
"Why do we and the Pharisees frequently fast, but
15 your disciples do not?" | Jesus replied, "Will the friends of
the bridegroom[5] be sad while he is with them? But the
days will come when he will be taken away from them, and
16 then they will fast. | No man patches new cloth onto an old
coat, for by pulling away from the old, it makes a worse

[1] Capernaum was at the bord between the territories of Herc Antipas and his brother, Phili Matthew levied duties on th goods which traveled from on to the other. He ran the cus toms office located at the ci gates.

[2] See Luke 7:31-35, page 311.

[3] Hosea 6:6, page 133. Thi quotation is repeated in Ma thew 12:7, page 272.

[4] Jesus invited all mankind t share his table. But those wh believed in their own righ teousness already had their re ward. They had no use for th friendship of Jesus. See Ma thew 6:2, 5 and 16, page 263.

[5] Jesus took the part of th spouse proclaimed by the prc phets (see page 132). See als John 2:1-12, page 336, wher Jesus acted in the place of th bridegroom in Cana by replen shing the supply of wine.

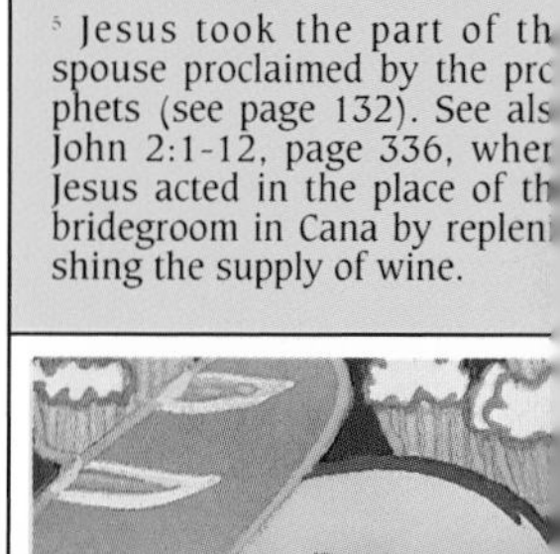

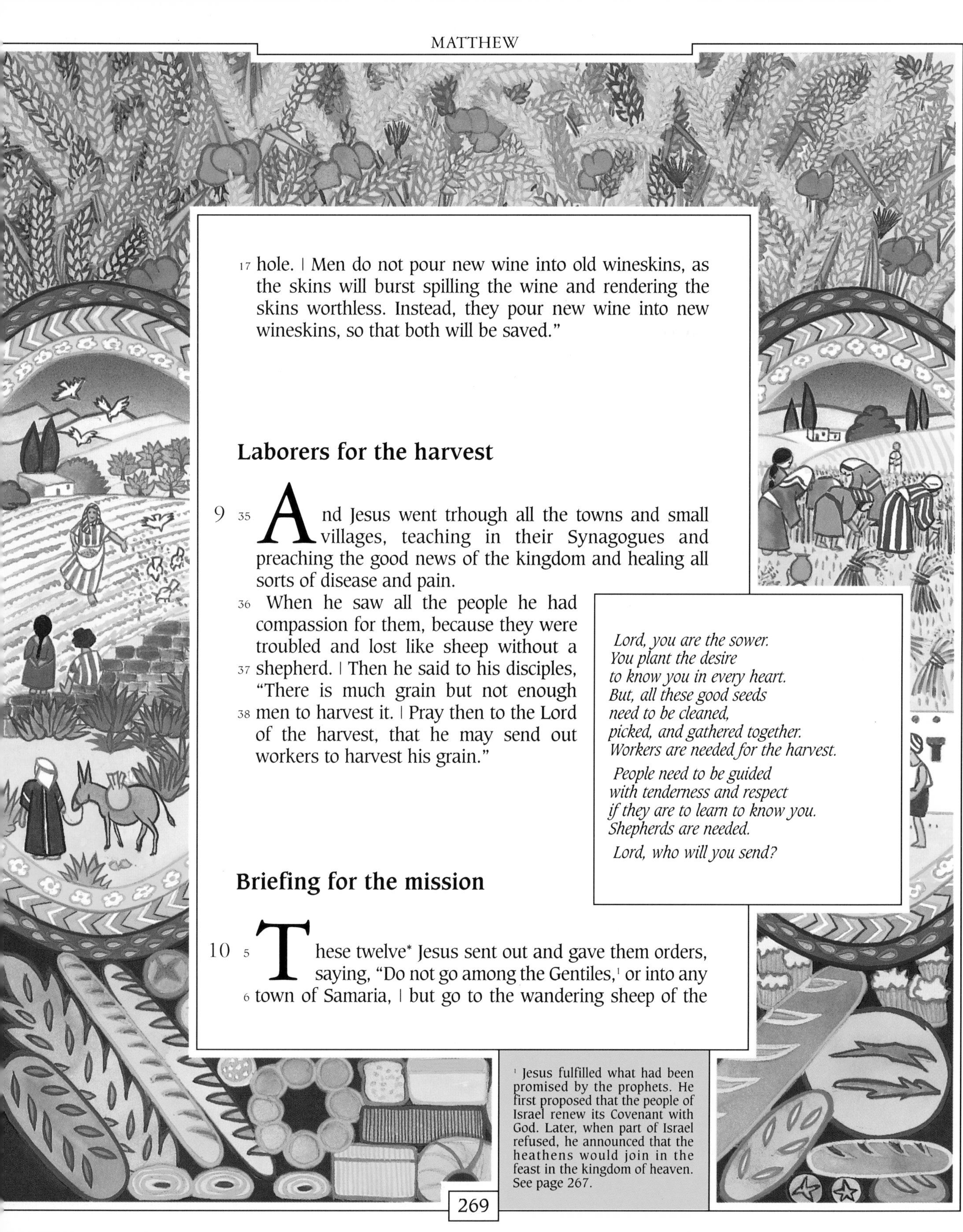

17 hole. | Men do not pour new wine into old wineskins, as
the skins will burst spilling the wine and rendering the
skins worthless. Instead, they pour new wine into new
wineskins, so that both will be saved."

Laborers for the harvest

9 35 And Jesus went trhough all the towns and small
villages, teaching in their Synagogues and
preaching the good news of the kingdom and healing all
sorts of disease and pain.
36 When he saw all the people he had
compassion for them, because they were
troubled and lost like sheep without a
37 shepherd. | Then he said to his disciples,
"There is much grain but not enough
38 men to harvest it. | Pray then to the Lord
of the harvest, that he may send out
workers to harvest his grain."

Lord, you are the sower.
You plant the desire
to know you in every heart.
But, all these good seeds
need to be cleaned,
picked, and gathered together.
Workers are needed for the harvest.

People need to be guided
with tenderness and respect
if they are to learn to know you.
Shepherds are needed.

Lord, who will you send?

Briefing for the mission

10 5 These twelve* Jesus sent out and gave them orders,
saying, "Do not go among the Gentiles,[1] or into any
6 town of Samaria, | but go to the wandering sheep of the

[1] Jesus fulfilled what had been promised by the prophets. He first proposed that the people of Israel renew its Covenant with God. Later, when part of Israel refused, he announced that the heathens would join in the feast in the kingdom of heaven. See page 267.

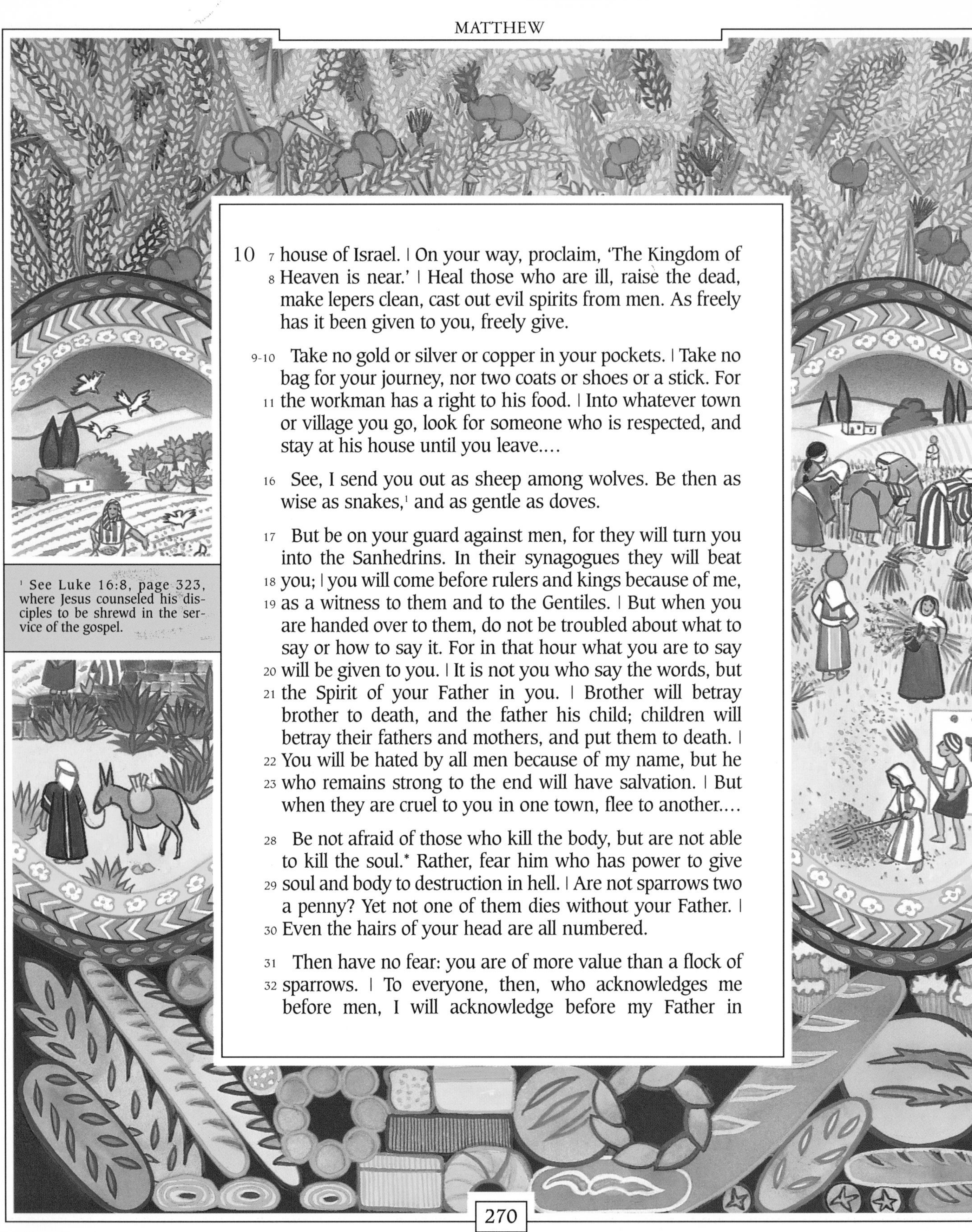

10 7 house of Israel. | On your way, proclaim, 'The Kingdom of
8 Heaven is near.' | Heal those who are ill, raise the dead,
make lepers clean, cast out evil spirits from men. As freely
has it been given to you, freely give.

9-10 Take no gold or silver or copper in your pockets. | Take no
bag for your journey, nor two coats or shoes or a stick. For
11 the workman has a right to his food. | Into whatever town
or village you go, look for someone who is respected, and
stay at his house until you leave....

16 See, I send you out as sheep among wolves. Be then as
wise as snakes,[1] and as gentle as doves.

17 But be on your guard against men, for they will turn you
into the Sanhedrins. In their synagogues they will beat
18 you; | you will come before rulers and kings because of me,
19 as a witness to them and to the Gentiles. | But when you
are handed over to them, do not be troubled about what to
say or how to say it. For in that hour what you are to say
20 will be given to you. | It is not you who say the words, but
21 the Spirit of your Father in you. | Brother will betray
brother to death, and the father his child; children will
betray their fathers and mothers, and put them to death. |
22 You will be hated by all men because of my name, but he
23 who remains strong to the end will have salvation. | But
when they are cruel to you in one town, flee to another....

28 Be not afraid of those who kill the body, but are not able
to kill the soul.* Rather, fear him who has power to give
29 soul and body to destruction in hell. | Are not sparrows two
a penny? Yet not one of them dies without your Father. |
30 Even the hairs of your head are all numbered.

31 Then have no fear: you are of more value than a flock of
32 sparrows. | To everyone, then, who acknowledges me
before men, I will acknowledge before my Father in

[1] See Luke 16:8, page 323, where Jesus counseled his disciples to be shrewd in the service of the gospel.

33 Heaven. | But if anyone does not acknowledge me in the
presence of other men, I will not acknowledge him in the
presence of my Father in Heaven."

Lord,
if you send us out like sheep,
it's not so that we will be
devoured by wolves!
Your heart's desire is that the wolves
will allow themselves to be tamed
by the sheep.
We must be as wise as serpents,
not deceitfully cunning,
but innocent as doves.

The burden of Jesus

11 28 "Come to me, all you who are troubled and heavily-
burdened,[1] and I will give you
29 rest. | Take my yoke on you and become
like me, for I am gentle and humble, and
30 you will have rest for your souls. | For my
yoke is easy, and my burden is light."

Someone once asked a little girl
carrying a baby
if he was too heavy.
She smiled and said,
"He isn't heavy, he's my brother."
Lord, you ask us
to love everyone like brothers and sisters.
It's demanding and, sometimes, difficult,
but never overwhelming,
because you are there.
You teach us the joy to be found
in the love that gives itself up for others.

The burden is the set of rules and obligations that a disciple must accept to follow the master. Jesus said that his burden was light. Jesus — unlike the Pharisees who had countless rules and placed on people's shoulders heavy loads that they themselves would not lift a finger to touch (Matthew 23:4, page 290) — summed up the whole of the Law* in one rule: do unto others as you would have them do unto you (Matthew 7:12, page 265).

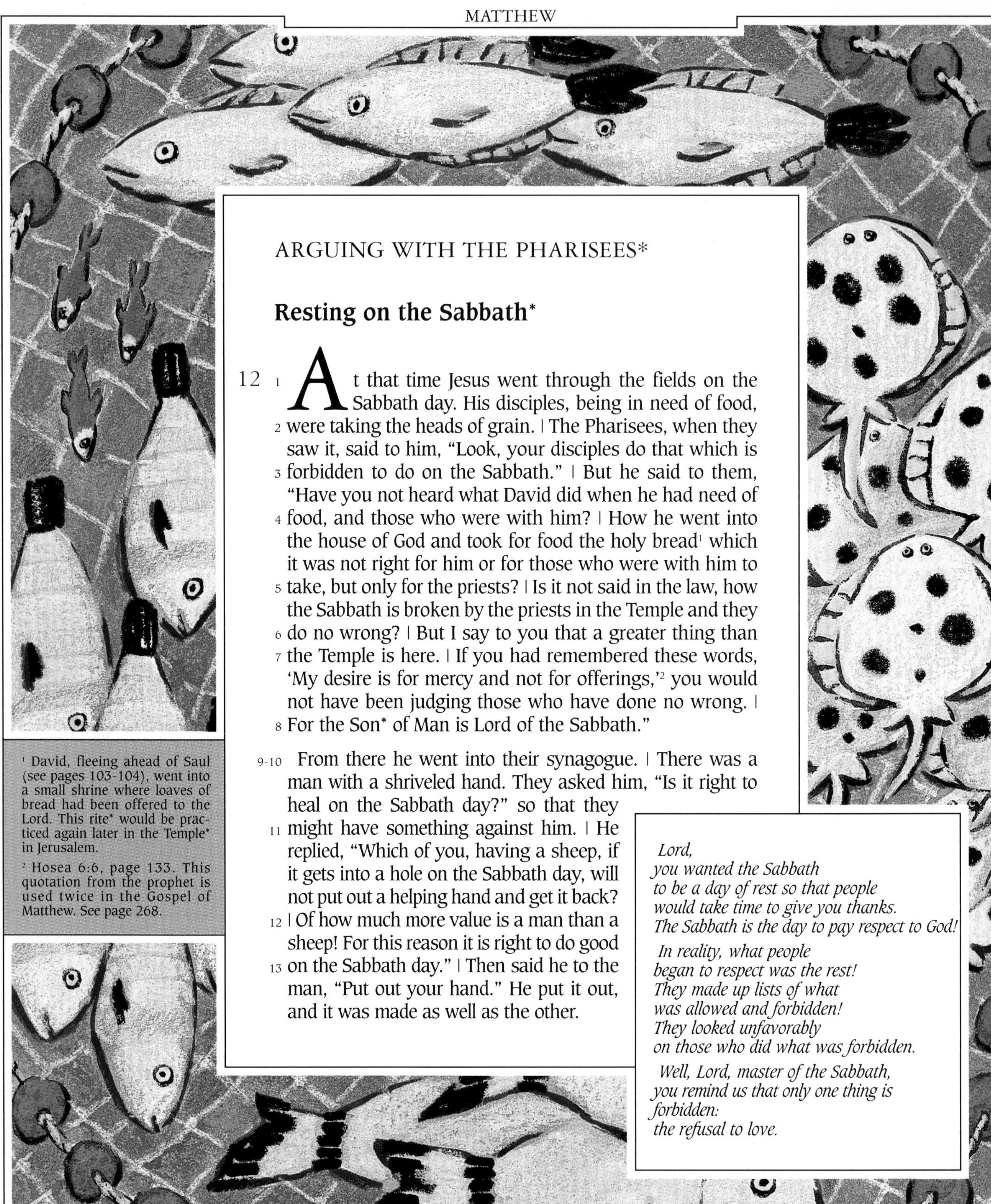

ARGUING WITH THE PHARISEES*

Resting on the Sabbath*

12 1 At that time Jesus went through the fields on the
Sabbath day. His disciples, being in need of food,
2 were taking the heads of grain. | The Pharisees, when they
saw it, said to him, "Look, your disciples do that which is
3 forbidden to do on the Sabbath." | But he said to them,
"Have you not heard what David did when he had need of
4 food, and those who were with him? | How he went into
the house of God and took for food the holy bread[1] which
it was not right for him or for those who were with him to
5 take, but only for the priests? | Is it not said in the law, how
the Sabbath is broken by the priests in the Temple and they
6 do no wrong? | But I say to you that a greater thing than
7 the Temple is here. | If you had remembered these words,
'My desire is for mercy and not for offerings,'[2] you would
not have been judging those who have done no wrong. |
8 For the Son* of Man is Lord of the Sabbath."

9-10 From there he went into their synagogue. | There was a
man with a shriveled hand. They asked him, "Is it right to
heal on the Sabbath day?" so that they
11 might have something against him. | He
replied, "Which of you, having a sheep, if
it gets into a hole on the Sabbath day, will
not put out a helping hand and get it back?
12 | Of how much more value is a man than a
sheep! For this reason it is right to do good
13 on the Sabbath day." | Then said he to the
man, "Put out your hand." He put it out,
and it was made as well as the other.

Lord,
you wanted the Sabbath
to be a day of rest so that people
would take time to give you thanks.
The Sabbath is the day to pay respect to God!

In reality, what people
began to respect was the rest!
They made up lists of what
was allowed and forbidden!
They looked unfavorably
on those who did what was forbidden.

Well, Lord, master of the Sabbath,
you remind us that only one thing is
forbidden:
the refusal to love.

[1] David, fleeing ahead of Saul (see pages 103-104), went into a small shrine where loaves of bread had been offered to the Lord. This rite* would be practiced again later in the Temple* in Jerusalem.

[2] Hosea 6:6, page 133. This quotation from the prophet is used twice in the Gospel of Matthew. See page 268.

14 But the Pharisees left, plotting how they might put him to
death.

The sign of Jonah

12 38 Then some of the scribes* and Pharisees,* hearing
this, said to him, "Master, we are looking for a sign
39 from you." | But he, answering, said to them, "An evil and
false generation is looking for a sign. No sign will be given
40 to it but the sign of the prophet Jonah. | For as Jonah spent
three days and three nights in the stomach of the great
fish, so will the Son* of Man be three days and three nights
41 in the heart of the earth. | The men of Nineveh will come at
the judgment to condemn this generation. They repented
from their sins at the preaching of Jonah. Now one greater
42 than Jonah is here. | The queen of Sheba[1] will come at the
judgment and condemn this generation, for she came from
the ends of the earth to listen to the wisdom of Solomon.
Now one greater than Solomon is here."

)NAH, THE FISH AND THE INEVITES

he Pharisees asked for a iraculous sign in order to elieve in Jesus. The healings f the sick or Jesus' concern r even the least of mortals iled to convince them. They anted more. Jesus refused to e a miracle-worker (see atthew 4:5-7, page 259). He ould give them the sign of nah and no more (see pages 90 to 192).

his was a twofold sign. nah had borne witness to od's mercifulness among the eathens of Nineveh, and he ad passed three days in the elly of the fish.

sus would send his apostles mong the heathens, who ould become members of od's people, and after being ead and buried, he would se again on the third day.

[1] The wisdom of Solomon was so renowned that all the East knew of it. The queen of Sheba, a kingdom in South Arabia, made the voyage to Jerusalem to seek his counsel (see page 117).

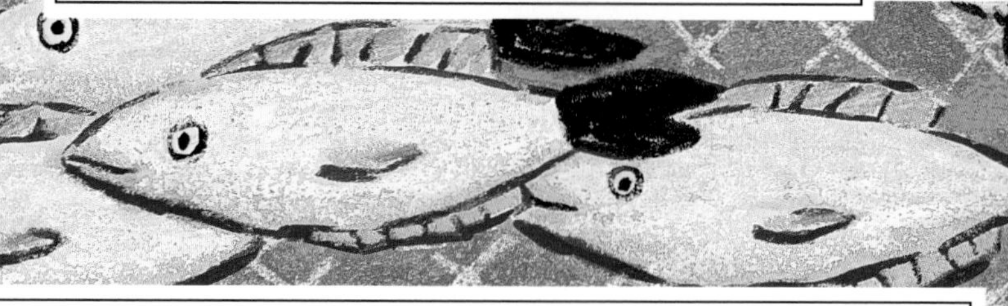

THE KINGDOM OF HEAVEN

Many people were awaiting a Messiah* who, like another David, would restore the kingdom of Israel. Jesus spoke of a kingdom but it was the "kingdom* of heaven." This was neither a place nor a future event. It was a way of life. It meant doing everything to make God reign in our lives. We may take Jesus as a model, since Jesus sought always to do his Father's will (see Mark 14:36, page 369). **We must make room in ourselves for this kingdom of heaven, let it grow and uplift us. It is a source of strength given by God to lead us forward, from today until the moment when we shall be with Him fully and for always.**

THE PARABLES OF THE KINGDOM

The sower

13 1 On that day Jesus went out of the house and was
2 seated by the lake. | A great crowd of people
gathered around him, so he got into a boat while the
3 people listened to him on the shore. | He taught them many
things in parables,* saying, "A man went out to sow seed
4 in the earth. | While he did so, some seeds were dropped
by the wayside, and the birds came and ate them for food.
5 | Some of the seed fell among the stones, where it had not
much soil, and immediately it grew because the earth was
6 not deep. | But when the sun was high, it was burned.
7 Since it had no root, it dried up and died. | Some seeds fell
among thorns. The thorns grew, but they had no room to
8 grow. | Others, falling on good soil, bore fruit, some a
9 hundred, some sixty, some thirty times as much. | He who
has ears, let him hear....

18 Listen,[1] then, to the story of the man who sowed the seed
19 in the soil. | When the news of the Kingdom is preached to
someone, and he does not understand,
the Evil One[2] comes to quickly steal that
which was put in his heart. He is the
20 seed dropped by the wayside. | The seed
which fell on the stones is he who,
hearing the word, immediately receives
21 it with joy. | But having no root in
himself, he lasts only for a time. When
trouble or pain comes because of the
word, he quickly becomes full of doubts.
22 | That which was dropped among the

Lord, I have the impression
of being everything at the same time.
I am the path, when my hardened heart
doesn't want to listen to your Word.
I am the rocky place,
when I am the person
that makes the most fun of you,
because I am afraid
to say that you are my friend.
I am the thorns, when
I only think about what makes me happy.
But, sometimes, I am also
good soil
in which your Word takes root.
Be the sower, Lord!
Help me to become, totally, good soil!

[1] Jesus explained the meaning of the parable to his disciples.

[2] Namely Satan.* See also "evil."*

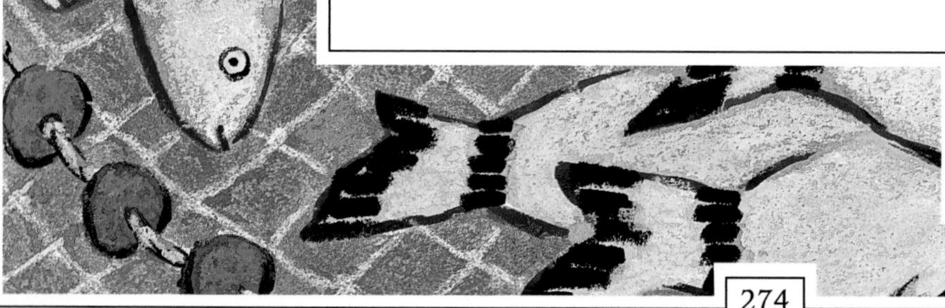

thorns is he who has the word, but the cares of this life,
and the deceits of wealth, stunt the growth of the word and
23 it bears no fruit. | The seed which was sown in good soil is
he who hears the word and understands it. He bears fruit,
some a hundred, some sixty, some thirty times as much."

The weeds

13 24 And he told them another parable, saying, "The
Kingdom of Heaven is like a man who planted
25 good seed in his field. | But while men were sleeping, his
26 enemy planted weeds[1] among the grain. | But when the
green stem came up and bore fruit, the weeds were seen at
27 the same time. | The servants of the master of the house
say, 'Sir, did you not put good seed in your field? How
28 then has it weeds?' | He replies, 'Someone has done this in
hate.' The servants say, 'Is it your pleasure that we go and
29 take them up?' | But he says, 'No,' for fear that by mistake
while you pull up the weeds, you may be rooting up the
30 grain with them. | Let them grow together until the harvest;
then I will say to the workers, 'Pull up first the weeds, and
gather them for burning. But put the grain into my
barn."...

36 Then he left the people and went into the house. His
disciples came to him, saying, "Explain the parable of the
37 weeds in the field." | He answered, "He who sows the good
38 seed in the earth is the Son of Man. | The field is the world;

[1] The weed was probably darnel, which looks like a food grain. When milled with wheat, it produces a flour with toxic properties.

esus explained the parable
f the weeds to his disciples
s he had done with the
arable of the sower. But,
etween the parable and its
xplanation, the Gospel
nserted the parables of the
nustard-seed and the yeast.

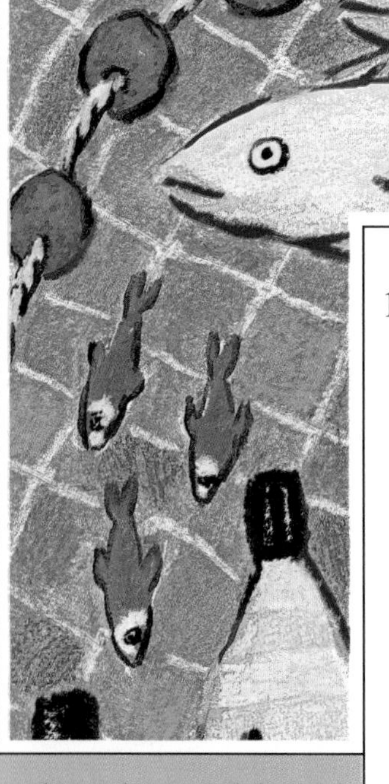

13
39 the good seed is the Sons of the Kingdom. The weeds are
the Sons of the Evil One. | He who planted them in the
earth is Satan,[1] and the harvest of the grain is the end of
40 the world. Those who harvest it in are the angels. | Just as
the weeds are gathered for burning, so will it be in the end
41 of the world. | The Son of Man will send out his angels, and
they will remove from his Kingdom everything which is a
42 cause of sin, and all those who do wrong. | He will put
them into the fire, and there will be weeping and cries of
43 sorrow.[2] | Then will the righteous be shining as the sun in
the Kingdom of their Father. He who has ears, let him
hear."

[1] The Greek text used the word "demon."

[2] In these images, Jesus was saying how important life in the present was. The kingdom must be accepted in the present. We must let ourselves be burned by the fire of love here and now, in order not to be devoured by despair later. See "hell."*

The mustard seed

13 31 He offered them another parable, saying, "The
Kingdom of Heaven is like a grain of mustard
32 seed which a man took and planted in his field. | It is the
smallest of all seeds, but when it grows it is greater than the
plants, and becomes a tree, so that the birds of Heaven
come and make their nests in its branches."

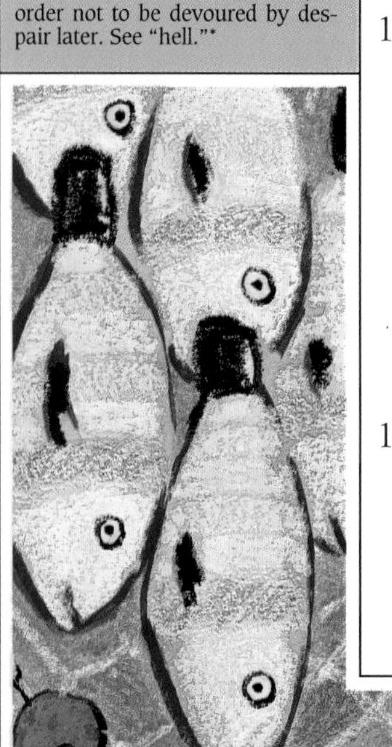

The yeast

13 33 Another parable he told them:
"The Kingdom of Heaven is like
leaven, which a woman took, and put in
three measures of meal, until it was all
leavened."

A tiny little seed
becomes a tree.
A pinch of yeast
makes the dough rise!
Lord, when your kingdom comes
into our lives, it is always very discreet!
But, if we open our hearts,
a force grows inside us
that helps us to live like you.
Your kingdom is a gift
that you place inside us
so that we become saints.

Lord, I want to resemble you.
I want to open myself to your kingdom.

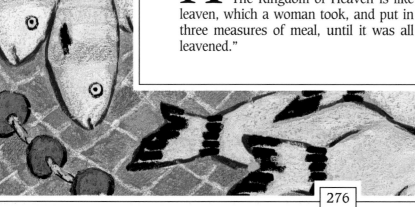

The treasure and the pearl

13 44 "The Kingdom of Heaven is like a treasuref
hidden in a field, which a man found and hid
again. In his joy he sells all he has to buy that field.

45 Again, the Kingdom of Heaven is like a trader searching
46 for beautiful jewels. | Finding one jewel of great price, he
sold all he had in exchange for it."

In understanding the parable f the net, it must be remembe-ed that, for the people in Jesus' ay, the sea was the home of ne powers of evil (see pages 41-242). When Jesus told Si-non that from henceforth he vould be a fisher of men (see uke 5:4-11, page 309), he was ssigning him the mission of catching" men so as to drag nem from the clutches of evil. he net was not a trap but an nstrument of deliverance.

Only Matthew quoted this aying, which signified that the ld and New Testaments* for-ned a whole and completed one nother. The scribe* was so-neone who had a thorough nowledge of the Scriptures. In unning his house, namely the ommunity under his care, he vould choose what was most pt from the message of the rophets and that of Jesus.

The net

13 47 "Again, the Kingdom of Heaven is like a net,[1] which
was cast into the sea and caught every sort of fish.
48 | When it was full, they took it to the shore, and seated
there they put the good into baskets, but the bad they
49 threw away. | So will it be in the end of the world. The
angels will come and separate the bad from the good, |
50 casting them into the fire. There will be weeping and cries
of sorrow.

51 "Are all these things now clear to you?" They replied,
52 "Yes." | He said to them, "For this reason every scribe who
has become a disciple of the Kingdom of Heaven is like the
owner of a house, who distributes from his storeroom
things new and old."[2]

Jesus used other, longer, parables about the kingdom. They are to found further on in the Gospel of Matthew, beginning in Chapter 18. See page 282 and after.

SIGNS FOR THE NEW COVENANT

When God concluded the first Covenant* with his people on Mount Sinai, He chose Moses as mediator, the intermediary between Himself and the people. He gave Moses the power to accomplish "signs," such as crossing the Red Sea or providing manna (see pages 64 to 67). **The people waiting for the renewal of the Covenant** (see Jeremiah 31:31) **hoped that the new mediator would accomplish other signs like those of Moses.**

A NEW COVENANT

The first multiplication of the loaves

14 13 Now when Jesus heard what had happened, he left
by boat to a solitary place by himself. The people, hearing
14 of it, followed him on foot from the towns. | When he came
out and saw a great number of people and he had
15 compassion for them, healing those who were ill. | When
evening had come, the disciples came to him, saying, "This
place is remote, and the time is now past. Send the people
away so that they may go into the towns and get
16 themselves food." | But Jesus said to them, "There is no
need for them to go away. Give them food yourselves." |
17 But they said, "We have here only five cakes of bread and
18-19 two fishes." | Jesus said, "Give them to me." | He asked the
people to be seated on the grass, and taking the five cakes
of bread and the two fishes, he looked up to heaven, giving
thanks, and divided the food. He gave it to the disciples,[1]
20 and the disciples gave it to the people. | They all took of the
food and had enough. They took up twelve baskets full of
21 broken bits which were not used.[2] | Those who had food
were about five thousand men, in addition to women and
children.

[1] Compare with Matthew 26:26, or Mark 14:22, page 366.

[2] See how John related the sequel to the multiplication of the loaves, pages 342 to 346.

COMMUNION IN GOD'S FIDELITY

The bread distributed in a barren place was a renewal of the sign of the manna, as well as being an anticipation of the bread of the last supper.

The people had not been faithful to the first Covenant. God had promised that there would be a new Covenant. He would give the people "singleness of heart and action" so that they would not turn away from Him again (see Jeremiah 32:39, page 158).

Jesus, Son of God, instituted a new meal of the Covenant. He gave himself as food to those who ate the bread of this meal and so partook of God's own fidelity. They would thereby remain steadfast within the Covenant.

Walking on the water

14 22 And immediately he made the disciples get into the
boat and go ahead of him to the other side, until
23 he had dismissed the people. | After he had dismissed the

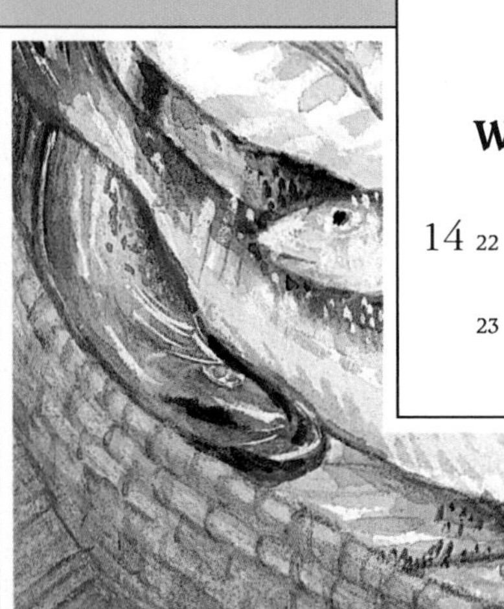

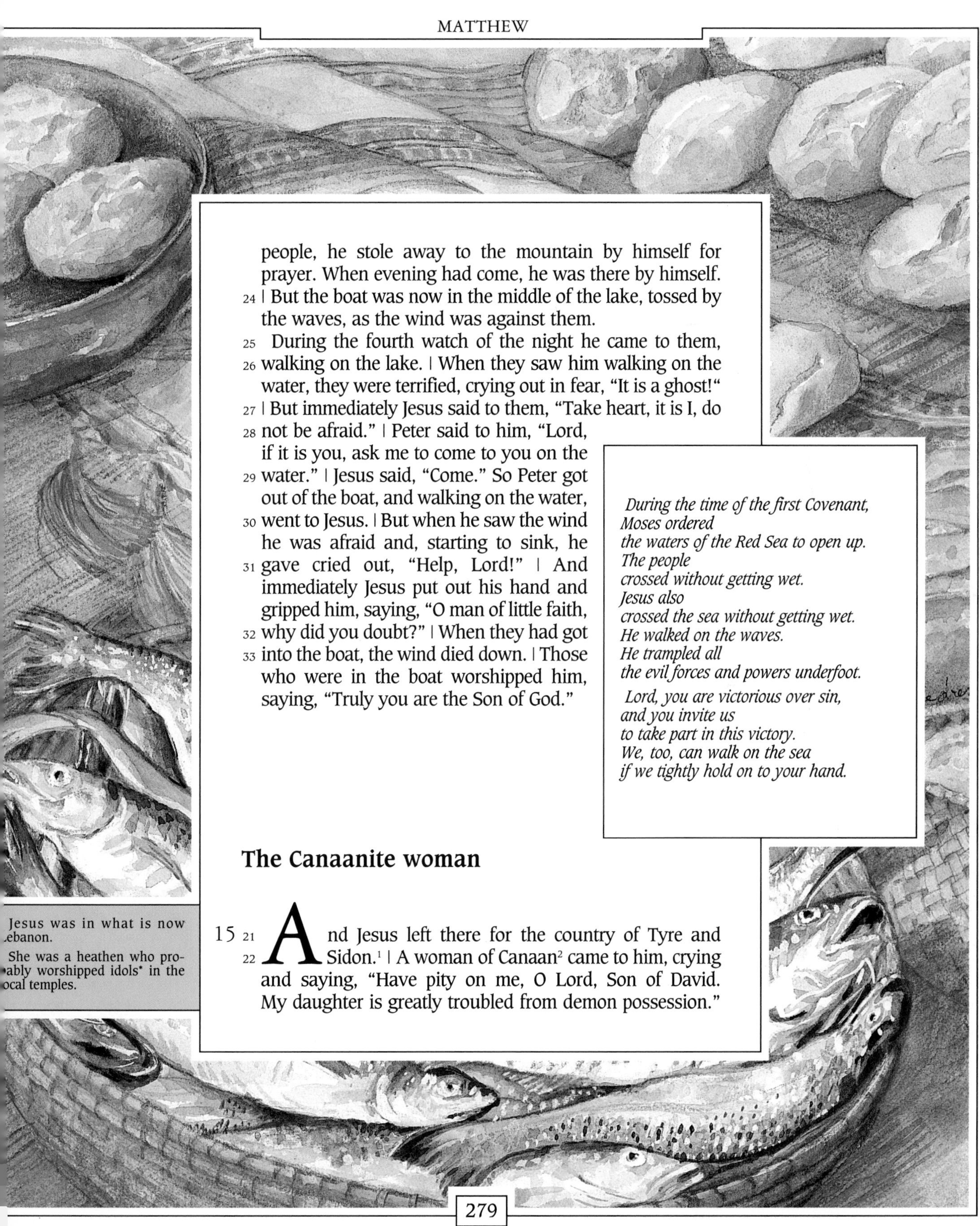

people, he stole away to the mountain by himself for
prayer. When evening had come, he was there by himself.
24 | But the boat was now in the middle of the lake, tossed by
the waves, as the wind was against them.
25 During the fourth watch of the night he came to them,
26 walking on the lake. | When they saw him walking on the
water, they were terrified, crying out in fear, "It is a ghost!"
27 | But immediately Jesus said to them, "Take heart, it is I, do
28 not be afraid." | Peter said to him, "Lord,
if it is you, ask me to come to you on the
29 water." | Jesus said, "Come." So Peter got
out of the boat, and walking on the water,
30 went to Jesus. | But when he saw the wind
he was afraid and, starting to sink, he
31 gave cried out, "Help, Lord!" | And
immediately Jesus put out his hand and
gripped him, saying, "O man of little faith,
32 why did you doubt?" | When they had got
33 into the boat, the wind died down. | Those
who were in the boat worshipped him,
saying, "Truly you are the Son of God."

During the time of the first Covenant,
Moses ordered
the waters of the Red Sea to open up.
The people
crossed without getting wet.
Jesus also
crossed the sea without getting wet.
He walked on the waves.
He trampled all
the evil forces and powers underfoot.
Lord, you are victorious over sin,
and you invite us
to take part in this victory.
We, too, can walk on the sea
if we tightly hold on to your hand.

The Canaanite woman

15 21 And Jesus left there for the country of Tyre and
22 Sidon.[1] | A woman of Canaan[2] came to him, crying
and saying, "Have pity on me, O Lord, Son of David.
My daughter is greatly troubled from demon possession."

Jesus was in what is now ebanon.

She was a heathen who pro-ably worshipped idols* in the ocal temples.

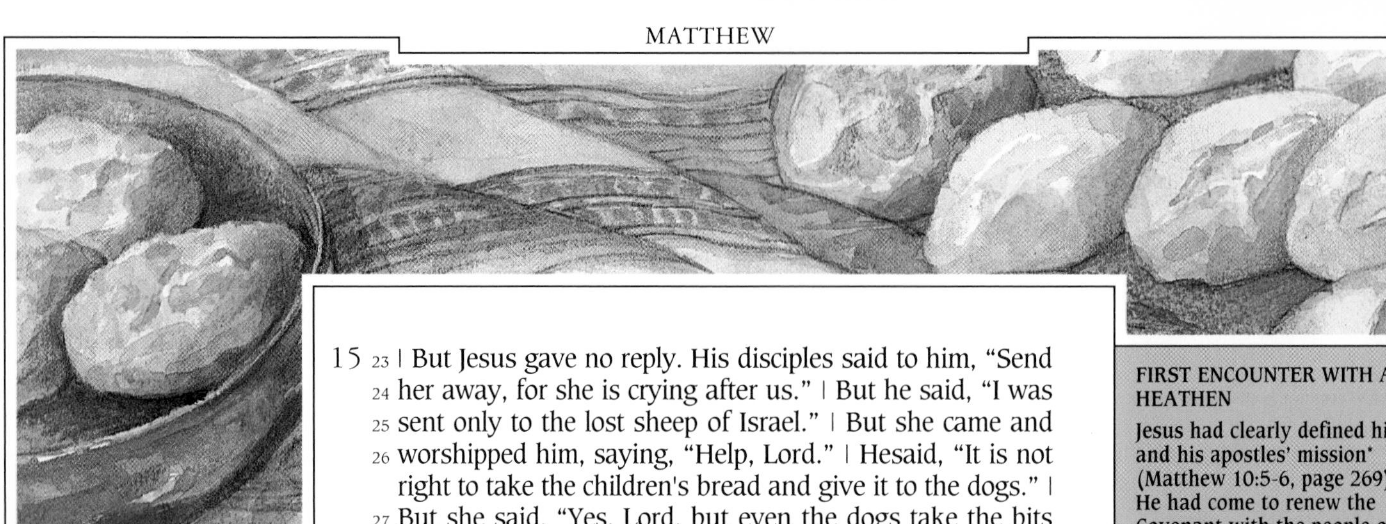

15 23 | But Jesus gave no reply. His disciples said to him, "Send
24 her away, for she is crying after us." | But he said, "I was
25 sent only to the lost sheep of Israel." | But she came and
26 worshipped him, saying, "Help, Lord." | Hesaid, "It is not
right to take the children's bread and give it to the dogs." |
27 But she said, "Yes, Lord, but even the dogs take the bits
28 from under their masters' table." | Then Jesus, answering,
said to her, "O woman, great is your faith. Let your desire
be done." And her daughter was healed from that hour.

FIRST ENCOUNTER WITH A HEATHEN

Jesus had clearly defined his and his apostles' mission* (Matthew 10:5-6, page 269). He had come to renew the Covenant with the people of Israel. This chosen people was to be God's witness among the nations.* He was not sent first to the heathens. This was what he told the Canaanite woman, rather bluntly. She was probably the first heathen he had met (see Matthew 8:5-13, page 267).

Jesus remarked that she had faith.* She had a strong desire to feed on the Word of God, but only crumbs came her way. From then on, Jesus would make room around the table of the kingdom for all believers, be they from East or West (Matthew 8:11, page 267, and 15:32-39, facing page).

The second multiplication of the loaves

15 32 And Jesus got his disciples together and said, "I
have compassion for the people, because they
have now been with me three days and have no food, and
I will not send them away without food, or they will have
33 no strength for the journey." | The disciples said to him,
"How can we get enough bread in such a remote place to
34 give food to so many people?" | Jesus replied, "How much
bread have you?" They said, "Seven cakes, and some
35 small fishes." | Then he gave an order to the people to be
36 seated on the ground. | He took the seven cakes of bread
and the fishes, and giving thanks, he gave the broken
bread to the disciples, and the disciples gave it to the
37 people. | They all ate and had enough. They gathered the
38 broken bits, seven baskets full. | There were four thousand
39 men who ate, together with women and children. | When
he had sent the people away, he got into the boat, and
entered the country of Magadan.

TWELVE AND SEVEN

The first multiplication of the loaves took place on Jewish territory. After the meal, twelve baskets of scraps had been gathered. Twelve was the number of tribes of Israel (Matthew 14:20, page 278).

The second multiplication of the loaves was performed in heathen country. Seven baskets of scraps were gathered. To the Jews, seven was a number associated with the heathen nations (see Acts 6:1-7, page 408). **Jesus showed that the table of the kingdom was open to all, the children of Abraham as well as people from East and West.**

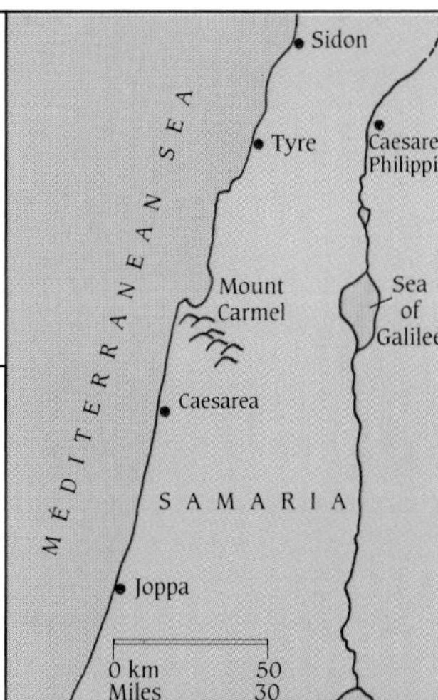

Caesarea Philippi was a Greco-
oman town at the foot of
lount Hermon on the road bet-
een Tyre and Damascus. It
as a district controled by Phi-
p, one of the sons of Herod the
reat. Jesus, by choosing this
lace to speak for the first time
f founding his church, was gi-
ing a clear hint that it would
ot be bound by territorial or
thnic limits. It would be uni-
ersal.

Since Simon had let himself be
nwardly instructed by the
ather, Jesus chose him for the
nission of outwardly demons-
rating one of God's qualities.
e was endowed with the soli-
ity of rock (see comment, page
8) in order to ensure the stabi-
ty of the church which Jesus
ished to build.

A PEOPLE RENEWED

A church built on rock

16 13 Now when Jesus entered the region of
Caesarea Philippi,[1] he questioned his disciples,
14 "Who do men say that the Son of man is?" | They said,
"Some say, 'John the Baptist.' Some, 'Elijah.' Others,
15 'Jeremiah, or one of the prophets.'" | He said to them, "But
16 who do you say that I am?" | And Simon Peter answered ,
You are the Christ,* the Son of the living God."
17 Jesus said to him, "Blessed are you, Simon son of Jonah
because this knowledge has not come to you from man,
18 but from my Father in heaven. | And I say to you that you
are Peter,[2] and on this rock will my Church be based, and
19 the doors of hell will not overcome it. | I will give to you the
keys of the kingdom of heaven: whatever is bound by you
on earth will be bound in heaven. Whatever you make free
on earth will be freed in heaven."
20 Then he gave orders to the disciples to tell no one that he
was the Christ.

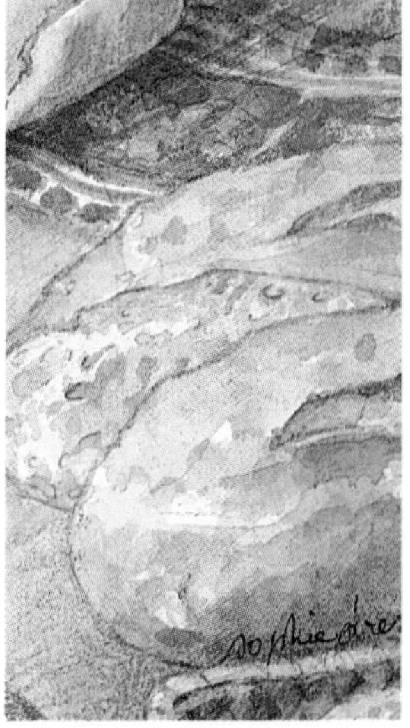

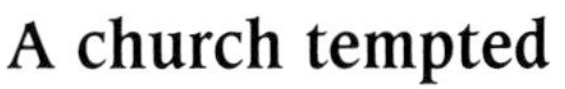

A church tempted

16 21 From that time Jesus began to explain to his
disciples how he would have to go up to Jerusalem,
and suffer at the hands of the elders* and the chief priests*

A TRUE DISCIPLE

Jesus, in Caesarea Philippi, saw that Simon Peter had received a revelation from the Father. Peter, seeming to think he had been raised to the status of prophet,* began offering advice to Jesus.

Confusing God's will with his own feelings, he tried to turn Jesus from the path of the Passion. In Peter's eyes, a Messiah had to be a figure of glory and victory.

Jesus called him Satan, a tempter. Peter, in trying to go before Jesus and show him the way, became a stumbling block. A disciple's place is behind. He follows his beloved master and seeks to understand him.

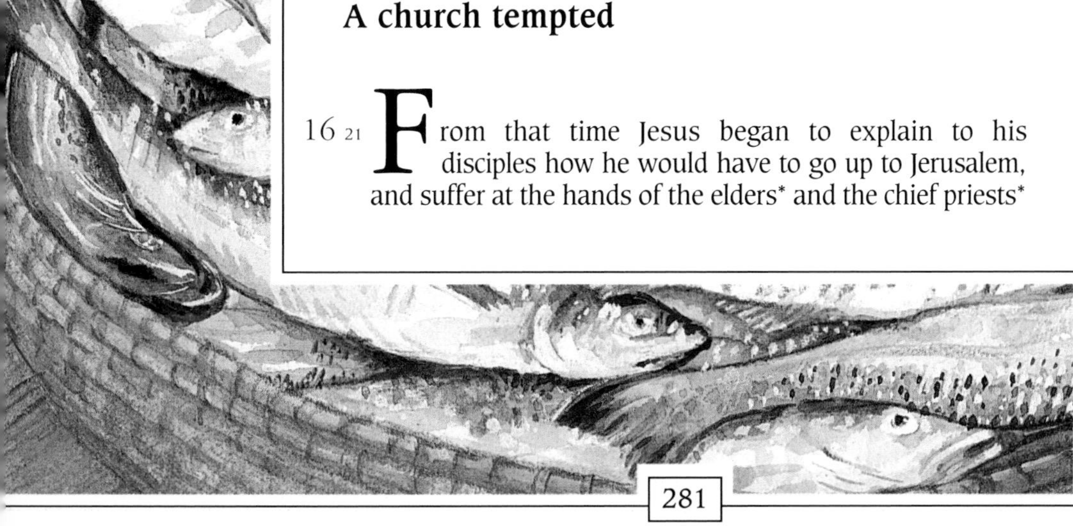

16 and scribes,* and be put to death, and the third day[1] be
raised.
22 But Peter, protesting, said to him, "Be
it far from you, Lord; it is impossible
23 that this will come about." | But he,
turning to Peter, said, "Get out of my
way,[2] Satan: you are a danger to me
because your mind is not on the things
of God, but on the things of men."

Why did Jesus
have to suffer so much and die?
Couldn't God protect
His son?

Jesus didn't come to live
among us as a privileged person.
He came to show us
that God really loves us,
even when we don't love Him;
even when we forget Him;
even when we reject Him.
He had to accept the death
that humanity prepared for him,
in order to proclaim that none of our refusals
will ever keep God from loving us.

A church of little children

18 1 In that hour the disciples came to Jesus, saying, "Who
2 is greatest in the Kingdom of Heaven?" | And he took
a little child, and put him in the middle of
3 them. | And he said, "Truly, I say to you,
if you do not have a change of heart and
become like little children, you will not
4 enter the Kingdom of Heaven. | Whoever,
then, will make himself as low as this
little child, he is the greatest in the
5 Kingdom of Heaven.[3] | And whoever
welcomes one such little child in my
name, welcomes to me.

6 But whoever is a cause of sin to one of
these little ones who have faith in me, it

Humble us before your face,
O Lord.
"My heart is not proud,
and my eyes are not haughty.
My soul is like a child's."
With your whole fatherly heart,
you want your children to grow up
and become responsible.
But, they break your heart
when they compete with one another,
crushing each other
in order to be the greatest.
Keep in me a childlike heart,
a heart like Jesus'.
He relinquished all powers,
to witness in our midst,
the joy that is felt in being a child of God.

[1] The third day was an expression taken from Hosea 6:2, page 133. See "resurrection."*

[2] The phrase "Get behind me" could be rendered as "Become my follower (or disciple) again." A disciple follows his master.

[3] Compare with Mark 10:13-16, page 247.

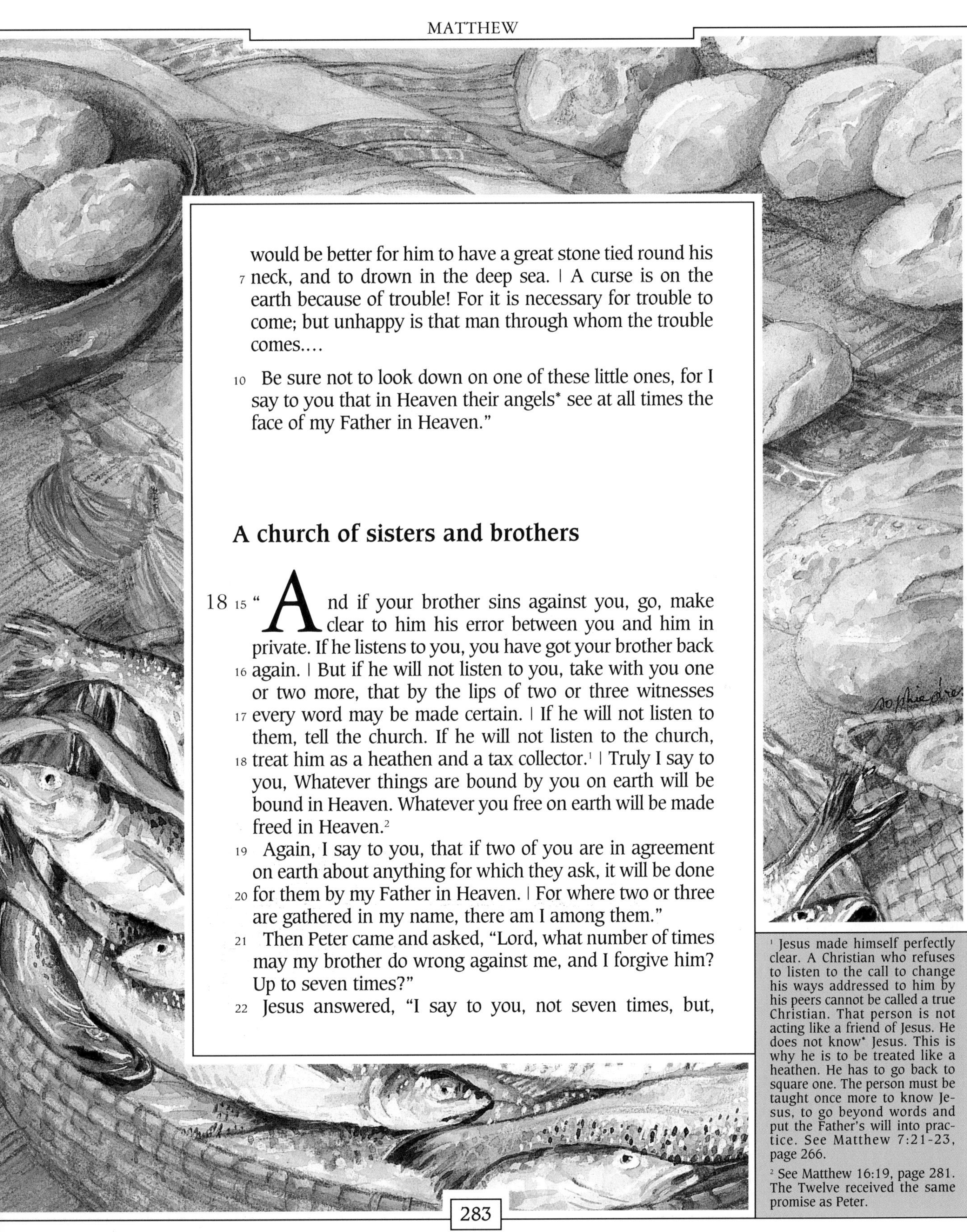

would be better for him to have a great stone tied round his
7 neck, and to drown in the deep sea. | A curse is on the
earth because of trouble! For it is necessary for trouble to
come; but unhappy is that man through whom the trouble
comes....

10 Be sure not to look down on one of these little ones, for I
say to you that in Heaven their angels* see at all times the
face of my Father in Heaven."

A church of sisters and brothers

18 15 "And if your brother sins against you, go, make
clear to him his error between you and him in
private. If he listens to you, you have got your brother back
16 again. | But if he will not listen to you, take with you one
or two more, that by the lips of two or three witnesses
17 every word may be made certain. | If he will not listen to
them, tell the church. If he will not listen to the church,
18 treat him as a heathen and a tax collector.[1] | Truly I say to
you, Whatever things are bound by you on earth will be
bound in Heaven. Whatever you free on earth will be made
freed in Heaven.[2]
19 Again, I say to you, that if two of you are in agreement
on earth about anything for which they ask, it will be done
20 for them by my Father in Heaven. | For where two or three
are gathered in my name, there am I among them."
21 Then Peter came and asked, "Lord, what number of times
may my brother do wrong against me, and I forgive him?
Up to seven times?"
22 Jesus answered, "I say to you, not seven times, but,

[1] Jesus made himself perfectly clear. A Christian who refuses to listen to the call to change his ways addressed to him by his peers cannot be called a true Christian. That person is not acting like a friend of Jesus. He does not know* Jesus. This is why he is to be treated like a heathen. He has to go back to square one. The person must be taught once more to know Jesus, to go beyond words and put the Father's will into practice. See Matthew 7:21-23, page 266.

[2] See Matthew 16:19, page 281. The Twelve received the same promise as Peter.

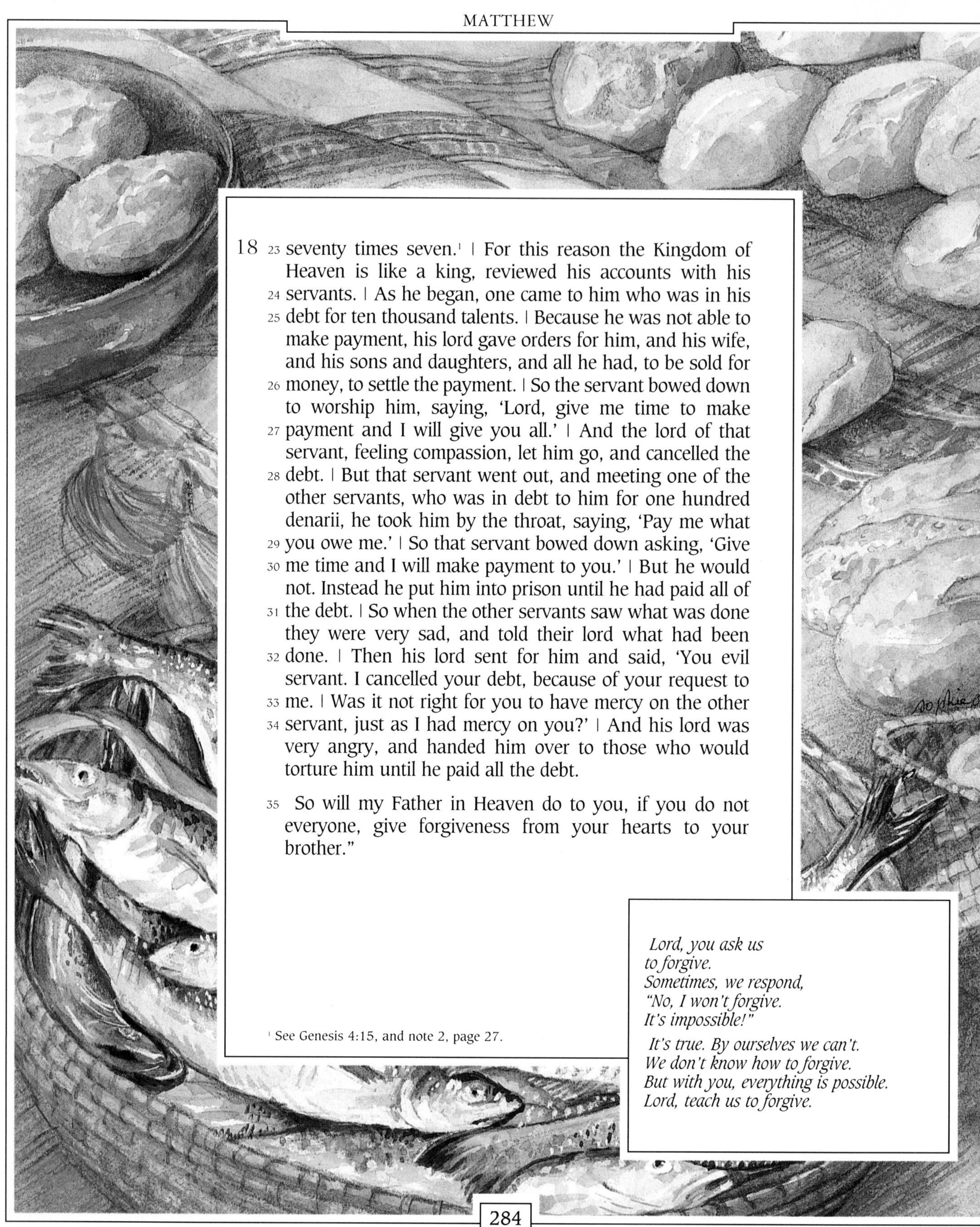

18 23 seventy times seven.[1] | For this reason the Kingdom of
Heaven is like a king, reviewed his accounts with his
24 servants. | As he began, one came to him who was in his
25 debt for ten thousand talents. | Because he was not able to
make payment, his lord gave orders for him, and his wife,
and his sons and daughters, and all he had, to be sold for
26 money, to settle the payment. | So the servant bowed down
to worship him, saying, 'Lord, give me time to make
27 payment and I will give you all.' | And the lord of that
servant, feeling compassion, let him go, and cancelled the
28 debt. | But that servant went out, and meeting one of the
other servants, who was in debt to him for one hundred
denarii, he took him by the throat, saying, 'Pay me what
29 you owe me.' | So that servant bowed down asking, 'Give
30 me time and I will make payment to you.' | But he would
not. Instead he put him into prison until he had paid all of
31 the debt. | So when the other servants saw what was done
they were very sad, and told their lord what had been
32 done. | Then his lord sent for him and said, 'You evil
servant. I cancelled your debt, because of your request to
33 me. | Was it not right for you to have mercy on the other
34 servant, just as I had mercy on you?' | And his lord was
very angry, and handed him over to those who would
torture him until he paid all the debt.

35 So will my Father in Heaven do to you, if you do not
everyone, give forgiveness from your hearts to your
brother."

[1] See Genesis 4:15, and note 2, page 27.

Lord, you ask us
to forgive.
Sometimes, we respond,
"No, I won't forgive.
It's impossible!"

It's true. By ourselves we can't.
We don't know how to forgive.
But with you, everything is possible.
Lord, teach us to forgive.

MARRIAGE AND CELIBACY

Humans: a couple

19 3 And certain Pharisees came to him, testing him,
saying, "Is it lawful for a man to divorce his wife
for every reason?"

4 And he replied,
"Have you not read,

that he who made them at the first made them male and
5 *female,* and said, | *'For this cause will a man go away from*
his father and mother, and be joined to his wife; and the
two will become one flesh?'[1]

6 So that they are no longer two, but one flesh. Then let not
that which has been joined by God be separated by man."

7 They asked him,
"Why then did Moses give orders that a husband might
give her a certificate of divorce and be free from her?"

8 He replied,
"Moses, because of your hard hearts, let you divorce your
9 wives, but it has not been so from the first. | I say to you,
whoever divorces his wife for any other reason except
marital infidelity, and marries another, is a false husband.
He who takes her as his wife when she is divorced, is no
true husband to her."

[1] Jesus quoted Genesis 1:27, page 21, and 2:24, page 25, in that order.

MARRIAGE

The Pharisees did not bother to ask themselves, "Is it lawful to repudiate one's wife?" They were sure of the answer.[1] They asked for Jesus' opinion on the reasons for doing so. In those days, two schools of thought existed. The followers of Shammai held that a serious reason, like adultery, was needed. But the followers of Hillel believed that lesser reasons (like talkativeness, telling lies, mistakes in the preparation of meals) were enough for repudiation. Jesus told the Pharisees that a wife could not be repudiated for any reason. God had wanted humans, alone of all His creatures, to be in His image, capable of love, forgiveness and fidelity. This was why humans, in the image of God, were not solitary beings. Woman and man were a couple. (See Genesis 1:27, page 21.)

When a woman and man decide to get married, they both give up self-centredness. "The two become one flesh." Instead of living this union as a burden, they find personal fulfilment in it. This was why Jesus invited his disciples to have a deep respect for marriage.

[1]The wife had no redress against her husband's decision. Jesus, by rejecting this unjust law of repudiation, continued his action of restoring full dignity to women (see page 347; note 1).

EMBLEM OF THE KINGDOM

Just after praising marriage, which was the normal condition of humans on this earth, Jesus invited some among his disciples* to live the single life. Life was not limited to the years between birth and death. After death, humans were summoned to enter into the fullness of the kingdom. Jesus was saying that, in that everlasting life, they would love each other better than they had on earth, since they would be immersed in the love of God Himself. This love would be completely spiritual. (See Mark 12:25, page 252.)

The person who chose celibacy would, from then on, be an emblem of the love to which all were destined.

Chosen for celibacy

19 10 The disciples said to him, "If this is the situation
between a man and his wife, it is better not to be
11 married." | But he replied, "Not all men are able to accept
12 this saying, but only those to whom it is given. | For there
are men who, from birth, were eunuchs. There are some
who were made so by men. There are others who have
made themselves so for the Kingdom of Heaven. He who
is able to accept it, let him accept it."

LAST TEACHINGS OF JESUS

The hands hired at the eleventh hour

20 1 "For the Kingdom* of Heaven is like the master of a
house, who went out early in the morning to hire
2 workers for his vineyard.[1] | And when he had made an
agreement with the workmen for a denarius a day, he sent
3 them into his vineyard. | And he went out about the third
hour, and saw others in the marketplace doing nothing." |
4 He said to them, "Go into the vineyard with the others, and
whatever is right I will pay you." And they went to work.

[1] The vineyard was the peop of God. See Isaiah 5:1-7, pag 135. Going to the vineyard re sembled going to the harves See Matthew 9:35-38, pag 269.

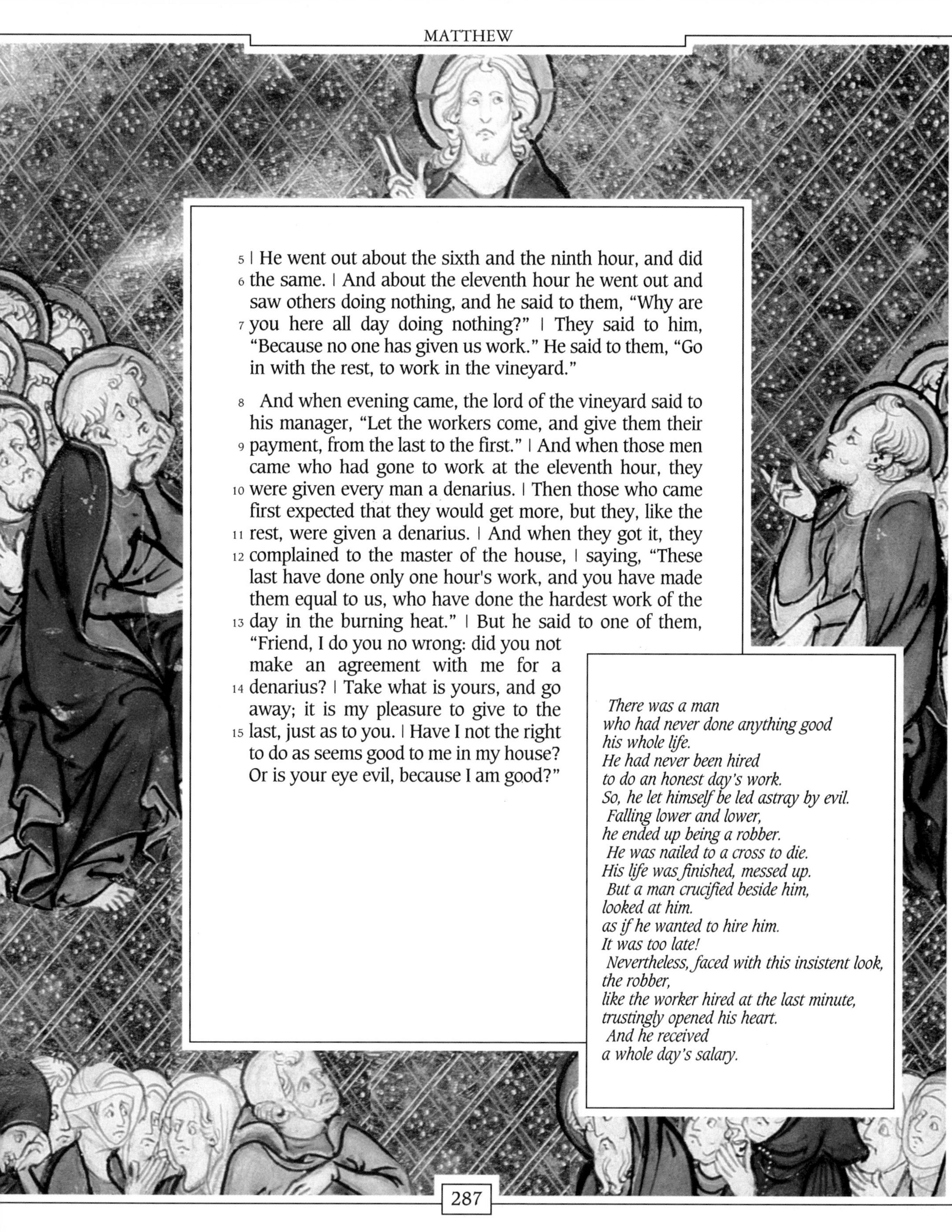

5 | He went out about the sixth and the ninth hour, and did
6 the same. | And about the eleventh hour he went out and
saw others doing nothing, and he said to them, "Why are
7 you here all day doing nothing?" | They said to him,
"Because no one has given us work." He said to them, "Go
in with the rest, to work in the vineyard."

8 And when evening came, the lord of the vineyard said to
his manager, "Let the workers come, and give them their
9 payment, from the last to the first." | And when those men
came who had gone to work at the eleventh hour, they
10 were given every man a denarius. | Then those who came
first expected that they would get more, but they, like the
11 rest, were given a denarius. | And when they got it, they
12 complained to the master of the house, | saying, "These
last have done only one hour's work, and you have made
them equal to us, who have done the hardest work of the
13 day in the burning heat." | But he said to one of them,
"Friend, I do you no wrong: did you not
make an agreement with me for a
14 denarius? | Take what is yours, and go
away; it is my pleasure to give to the
15 last, just as to you. | Have I not the right
to do as seems good to me in my house?
Or is your eye evil, because I am good?"

There was a man
who had never done anything good
his whole life.
He had never been hired
to do an honest day's work.
So, he let himself be led astray by evil.
Falling lower and lower,
he ended up being a robber.
He was nailed to a cross to die.
His life was finished, messed up.
But a man crucified beside him,
looked at him.
as if he wanted to hire him.
It was too late!
Nevertheless, faced with this insistent look,
the robber,
like the worker hired at the last minute,
trustingly opened his heart.
And he received
a whole day's salary.

A PARABLE IN ACTION

Jesus, like the prophets, did surprising things, always very instructive. Why did he dry up the fig-tree with its beautiful leaves but no fruit? The fig-tree is often associated with study of the Word of God (see John 1:48, page 335)**. By shriveling it up, Jesus was conveying a visual message, namely that his people were unable to gather fruit from their reading of the Scriptures.* They were unable to recognize the one whose coming God had promised. Luke, in a similar anecdote** (Luke 13:6-9, page 319)**, wrote of God's patience in giving the fig-tree another chance to bear fruit. Nothing is beyond redemption. Faith can move mountains and bring fruit to dried-up fig-trees.**

The withered fig tree

21 18 Now in the morning when he was coming back to
19 the town, he was hungry. | And seeing a fig tree
by the road, he came to it, but seeing nothing on it but
leaves, he said to it, "Let there be no fruit from you from
this time forward forever." And immediately the fig tree
20 shriveled up and died. | When the disciples saw it they
were surprised, saying, "How did the fig tree become dry
21 in so short a time?" | Jesus said to them, "Truly I say to
you, if you have faith, not only may you do what has been
done to the fig tree, you will say to this mountain, 'Go and
22 be cast into the sea,' and it will be done. | And all things,
whatever you ask request for in prayer, having faith, you
will get."

The wedding guests

22 1 And Jesus, talking to them again in parables,* said:
2 | "The kingdom of heaven is like a certain king,
3 who, making a feast when his son was married,[1] | sent out
his servants to call in the guests to the feast, but they
4 would not come. | Again he sent out other servants, with
orders to say to the guests, 'See, I have prepared my feast.
My oxen and my fat beasts have been put to death, and all
5 things are ready. Come to the feast.' | But they paid no
attention, and went about their business, one to his farm,
6 another to his trade. | The rest seized his servants, did evil
7 to them, and put them to death. | But the king was angry;
he sent his armies, and destroyed those who had put his
servants to death, burning their town.

[1] The important image of th wedding is used again (se Matthew 9:14-15, page 268). this parable, the people of Go are shown, not as the bride (a in Hosea 2:16, page 132), b as the guests.

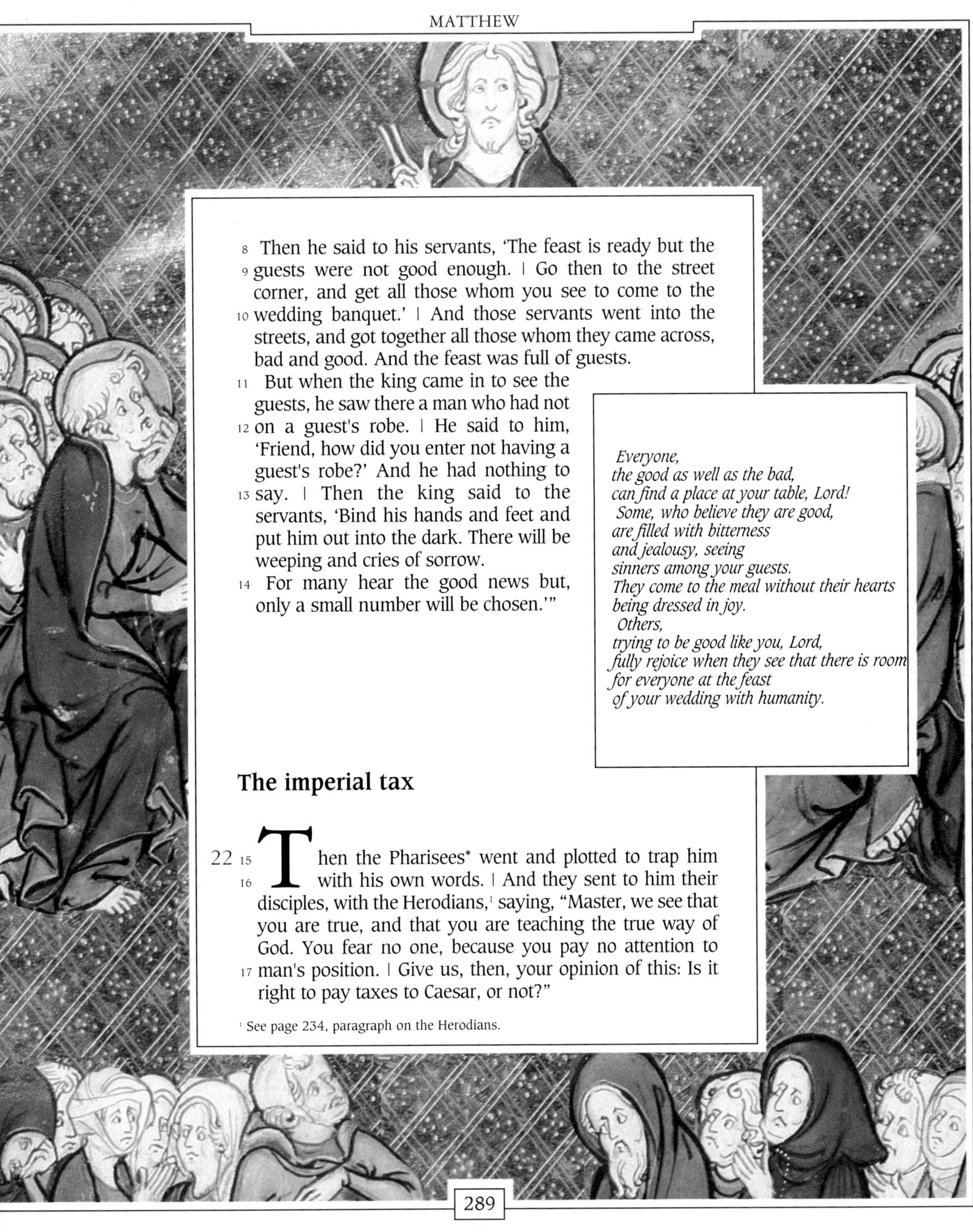

8 Then he said to his servants, 'The feast is ready but the
9 guests were not good enough. | Go then to the street
corner, and get all those whom you see to come to the
10 wedding banquet.' | And those servants went into the
streets, and got together all those whom they came across,
bad and good. And the feast was full of guests.
11 But when the king came in to see the
guests, he saw there a man who had not
12 on a guest's robe. | He said to him,
'Friend, how did you enter not having a
guest's robe?' And he had nothing to
13 say. | Then the king said to the
servants, 'Bind his hands and feet and
put him out into the dark. There will be
weeping and cries of sorrow.
14 For many hear the good news but,
only a small number will be chosen.'"

Everyone,
the good as well as the bad,
can find a place at your table, Lord!
Some, who believe they are good,
are filled with bitterness
and jealousy, seeing
sinners among your guests.
They come to the meal without their hearts
being dressed in joy.
Others,
trying to be good like you, Lord,
fully rejoice when they see that there is room
for everyone at the feast
of your wedding with humanity.

The imperial tax

22 15 Then the Pharisees* went and plotted to trap him
16 with his own words. | And they sent to him their
disciples, with the Herodians,[1] saying, "Master, we see that
you are true, and that you are teaching the true way of
God. You fear no one, because you pay no attention to
17 man's position. | Give us, then, your opinion of this: Is it
right to pay taxes to Caesar, or not?"

[1] See page 234, paragraph on the Herodians.

GIVE UNTO CAESAR

Submission to heathen rulers was considered intolerable by most Jews. They hoped that the Messiah* would deliver them from foreign occupation. Once they had regained their independence, they would subjugate other nations and lead them to recognize the one true God (see Isaiah 60:1-6, page 186)**.**

Jesus did not share this point of view. While admitting (unpretentiously) that he was the Messiah, he carefully avoided confusing his mission with that of an earthly king (see John 6:15, page 343, and page 259, "Jesus as servant")**. He made a clear distinction between what was due to the Roman emperor and what was due to God.**

Paul would faithfully repeat Christ's lesson by asking the first Christians to be loyal citizens of the Roman empire (Romans 13:1-7)**.**

22 18 But Jesus saw their trick and said, "Oh hypocrites, why are
19 you attempting to trap me? | Let me see the tax money."
20 And they gave him a denarius. | He said to them, "Whose
21 image and name is this?" | They replied, "Caesar's."[1] Then
he said, "Give to Caesar the things which are Caesar's, and
to God the things which are God's."
22 Hearing it, they were full of wonder, and left him.

Self-important religious leaders

23 1 Then Jesus said to the people and to his disciples:
2 | "The scribes and the Pharisees have the authority
3 of Moses.[2] | All things, then, which they give you orders to
do, do these and obey, but do not take their works as your
4 example, for they do not do as they say. | They make hard
laws and put great weights[3] on men's backs, but they
5 themselves will not lift a finger to move them. | But all their
works they do so as to be seen by men, for they make wide
6 their phylacteries, and the edges of their robes. | The things
desired by them are the first places at feasts, the chief seats
7 in the synagogues, | words of respect in the marketplaces,
8 and to be called by men, 'Teacher.' | But you may not be
called 'Teacher': for only one is your teacher, and you are
9 all brothers.[4] | Give no man the name of father on earth:
10 because only one is your Father, who is in Heaven.[5] | And
you may not be named guides, because you have only one
11 Guide, the Christ. | Let the greatest among you be your

[1] The emperor at the time wa[s] Tiberius* (see Luke 3:1, pag[e] 306). All the emperors bore th[e] title Caesar.

[2] The pulpit was the raise[d] structure from which an authority lectured his audience. Although Moses was not know[n] to have used one, all who explained the Law* were regarde[d] as his successors. Jesus depicted them as occupying the pulpit of Moses.

[3] See page 271, note 1.

[4] This recommendation by Jesu[s] updated the prophecy of Jeremiah (Jeremiah 31:34, pag[e] 157), which said that th[e] people of God would no longe[r] have to learn from one anothe[r] since all would know God. Jesus said that from now on the[y] would have only one teacher. Although the teacher was no[t] named, it could be none othe[r] than the Holy Spirit (see Joh[n] 16:13, page 360). Verses 8 t[o] 10 could be read as referring t[o] the Trinity,* since its three persons are named: Teacher, Father, Christ.

[5] Jesus was criticizing thos[e] who, by claiming the title o[f] "father," so enslaved their followers that they could no longer discover the fathership o[f] God. This was not the positio[n] of Paul who asked to be calle[d] "father" by the Corinthians (1 Corinthians 4:15), but only s[o] as to help them discover th[e] love of the Father.

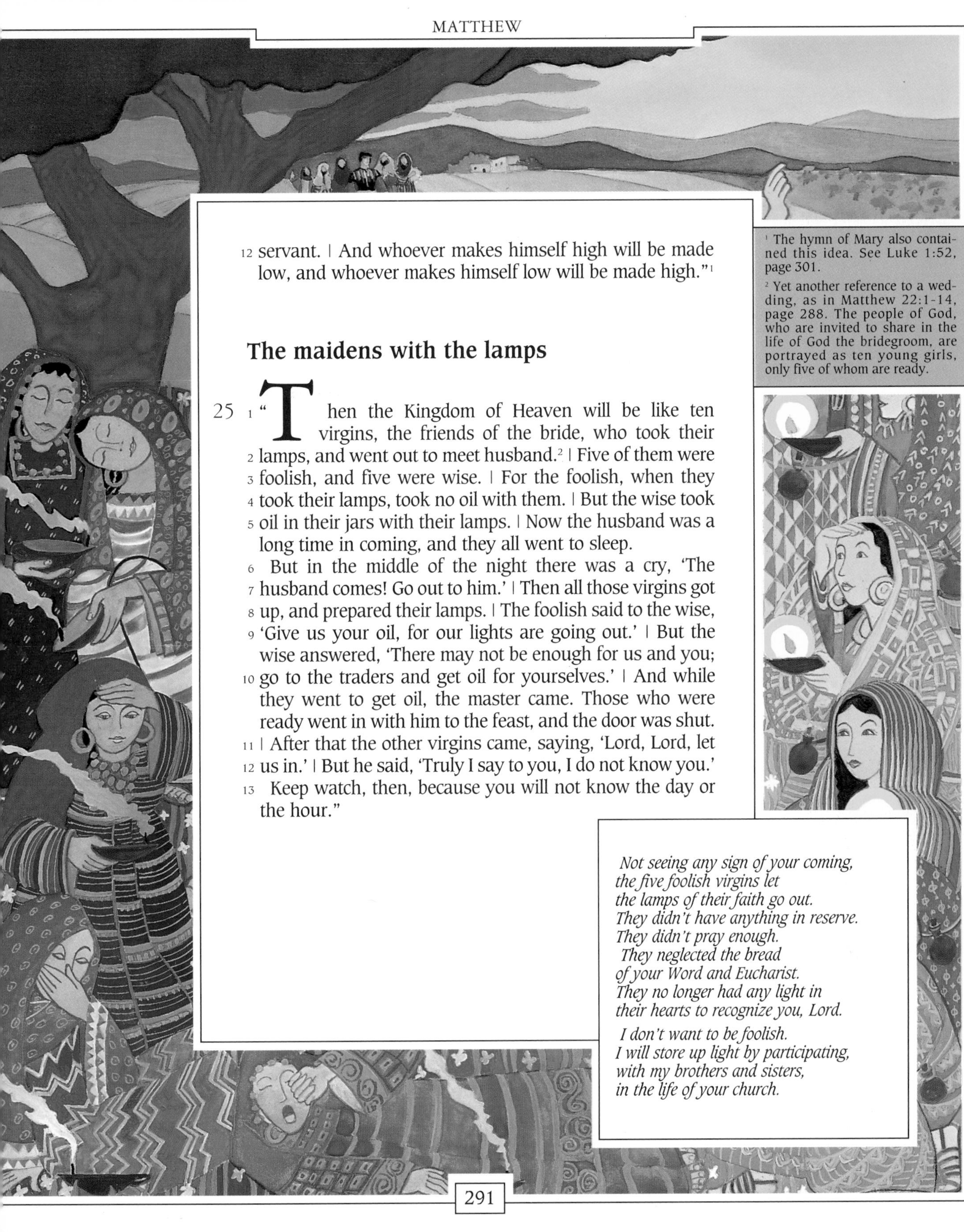

12 servant. | And whoever makes himself high will be made
low, and whoever makes himself low will be made high."[1]

The maidens with the lamps

25 1 "Then the Kingdom of Heaven will be like ten
virgins, the friends of the bride, who took their
2 lamps, and went out to meet husband.[2] | Five of them were
3 foolish, and five were wise. | For the foolish, when they
4 took their lamps, took no oil with them. | But the wise took
5 oil in their jars with their lamps. | Now the husband was a
long time in coming, and they all went to sleep.
6 But in the middle of the night there was a cry, 'The
7 husband comes! Go out to him.' | Then all those virgins got
8 up, and prepared their lamps. | The foolish said to the wise,
9 'Give us your oil, for our lights are going out.' | But the
wise answered, 'There may not be enough for us and you;
10 go to the traders and get oil for yourselves.' | And while
they went to get oil, the master came. Those who were
ready went in with him to the feast, and the door was shut.
11 | After that the other virgins came, saying, 'Lord, Lord, let
12 us in.' | But he said, 'Truly I say to you, I do not know you.'
13 Keep watch, then, because you will not know the day or
the hour."

[1] The hymn of Mary also contained this idea. See Luke 1:52, page 301.

[2] Yet another reference to a wedding, as in Matthew 22:1-14, page 288. The people of God, who are invited to share in the life of God the bridegroom, are portrayed as ten young girls, only five of whom are ready.

Not seeing any sign of your coming,
the five foolish virgins let
the lamps of their faith go out.
They didn't have anything in reserve.
They didn't pray enough.
They neglected the bread
of your Word and Eucharist.
They no longer had any light in
their hearts to recognize you, Lord.

I don't want to be foolish.
I will store up light by participating,
with my brothers and sisters,
in the life of your church.

ENCOUNTERS BY JESUS

1. Blessed are the poor in spirit (Matthew 5:1 to 7:29, pages 260 to 267).

2. Even the dogs eat the crumbs... (Matthew 15:21-28, page 279).

3. Say but the word (Luke 7:1-10, page 310).

4. Follow me (Matthew 9/9, page 268).

5. Is this not Joseph's son? (Luke 4:14-30, page 307).

6. I shall make you fishers of men (see page 237, "Capernaum," and Luke 5:1-11, page 308).

7. Jesus heals ten lepers (see Luke 17:11-19).

8. Young man, get up! (Luke 7:11-17, page 311).

9. You still lack one thing (Luke 18:18-30, page 328).

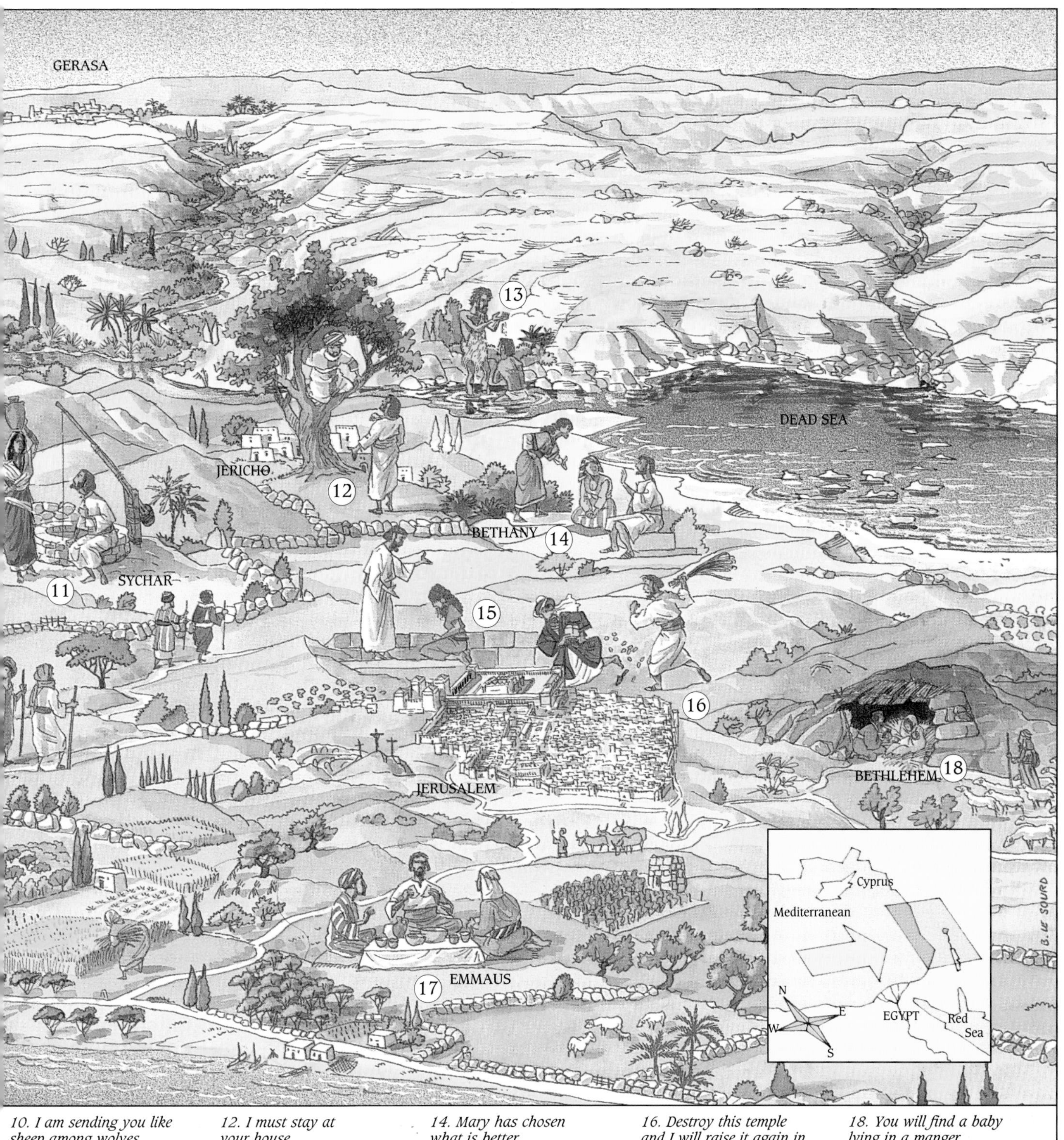

10. I am sending you like sheep among wolves (Matthew 10:5-33, page 269).

11. I shall give you living water (John 4:6-30, page 339).

12. I must stay at your house (Luke 19:1-10, page 329).

13. This is my beloved son (Matthew 3:13-17, page 258).

14. Mary has chosen what is better (Luke 10:38-42, page 318).

15. Go and sin no more (John 8:1-11, page 347).

16. Destroy this temple and I will raise it again in three days (John 2:13-22, page 336).

17. How slow of heart you are to believe! (Luke 24:13-35, page 390).

18. You will find a baby lying in a manger (Luke 2:1-20, page 302).

The talents

25 14 "For it is like a man, about to take a journey, when he
got his servants together, and gave them his
15 property.[1] | To one he gave five talents, to another two, to
another one,[2] to everyone as he was able. Then he went on
16 his journey. | Immediately he who had been given the five
17 talents traded with them, and made five more. | In the
same way he who had been given the two got two more. |
18 But he who was given the one went away and put it in a
hole in the earth, keeping his lord's money in a secret
place.
19 Now after a long time the lord of those servants came and
20 settled his account with them. | And he who had the five
talents came with his other five talents, saying, 'Lord, you
entrusted me with five talents. Look, I have got five more.'
21 | His lord said to him, 'Well done, good and true servant:
you have been true in a small thing, I will give you control
22 over great things. Come share your Lord's joy.' | And he
who had the two talents came and said, 'Lord, you
entrusted me with two talents. Look, I have got two more.'
23 | His lord said to him, 'Well done, good and true servant:
you have been true in a small thing, I will give you control
24 over great things.Come share your Lord's joy.' | And he
who had had the one talent came and
said, 'Lord, I knew that you are a hard
man, harvesting grain where you have
not planted seed, and making profits for
25 which you have done no work. | And I
was afraid, and went away, and put
your talent in the earth. Here is what is
26 yours.' | But his lord said to him, 'You

[1] Still referring to the kingdor of heaven mentioned in vers 1, page 291.

[2] A "talent" was a large sum c money, equal to about 5 pounds of silver. Even one ta lent was quite a treasure.

Lord, the kingdom is
like a treasure that you entrust to us.
It's not only for us.
It will become ours
if we learn how to share it,
each one according to his or her capacities.
The one who is gifted with words will teach.
Another will encourage dialogue
order to build unity.
Still another, with an attentive
(sensitive) heart,
will comfort his brothers and sisters,
and all will enter into the joy of Jesus.

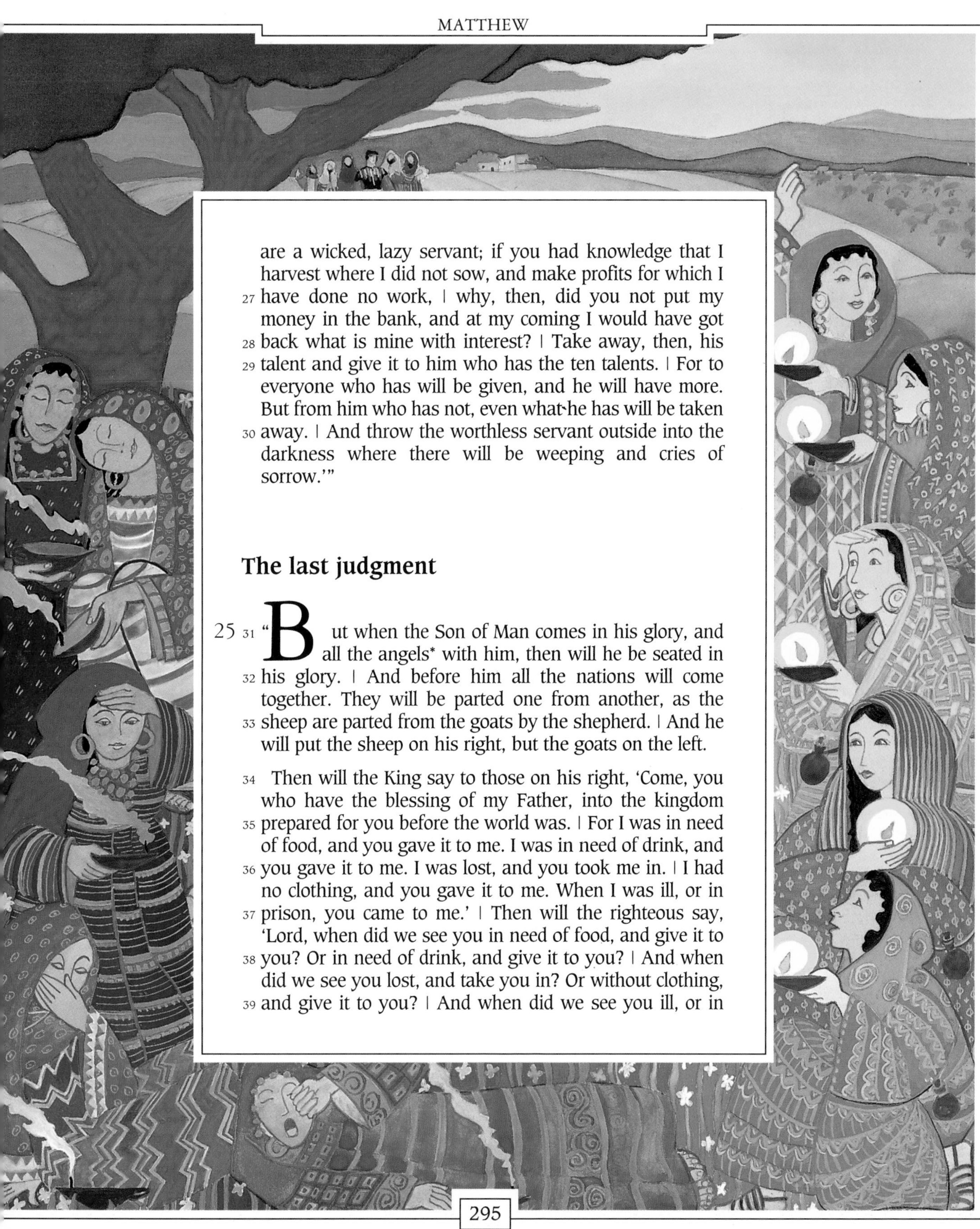

are a wicked, lazy servant; if you had knowledge that I
harvest where I did not sow, and make profits for which I
27 have done no work, | why, then, did you not put my
money in the bank, and at my coming I would have got
28 back what is mine with interest? | Take away, then, his
29 talent and give it to him who has the ten talents. | For to
everyone who has will be given, and he will have more.
But from him who has not, even what he has will be taken
30 away. | And throw the worthless servant outside into the
darkness where there will be weeping and cries of
sorrow.'"

The last judgment

25 31 "But when the Son of Man comes in his glory, and
all the angels* with him, then will he be seated in
32 his glory. | And before him all the nations will come
together. They will be parted one from another, as the
33 sheep are parted from the goats by the shepherd. | And he
will put the sheep on his right, but the goats on the left.

34 Then will the King say to those on his right, 'Come, you
who have the blessing of my Father, into the kingdom
35 prepared for you before the world was. | For I was in need
of food, and you gave it to me. I was in need of drink, and
36 you gave it to me. I was lost, and you took me in. | I had
no clothing, and you gave it to me. When I was ill, or in
37 prison, you came to me.' | Then will the righteous say,
'Lord, when did we see you in need of food, and give it to
38 you? Or in need of drink, and give it to you? | And when
did we see you lost, and take you in? Or without clothing,
39 and give it to you? | And when did we see you ill, or in

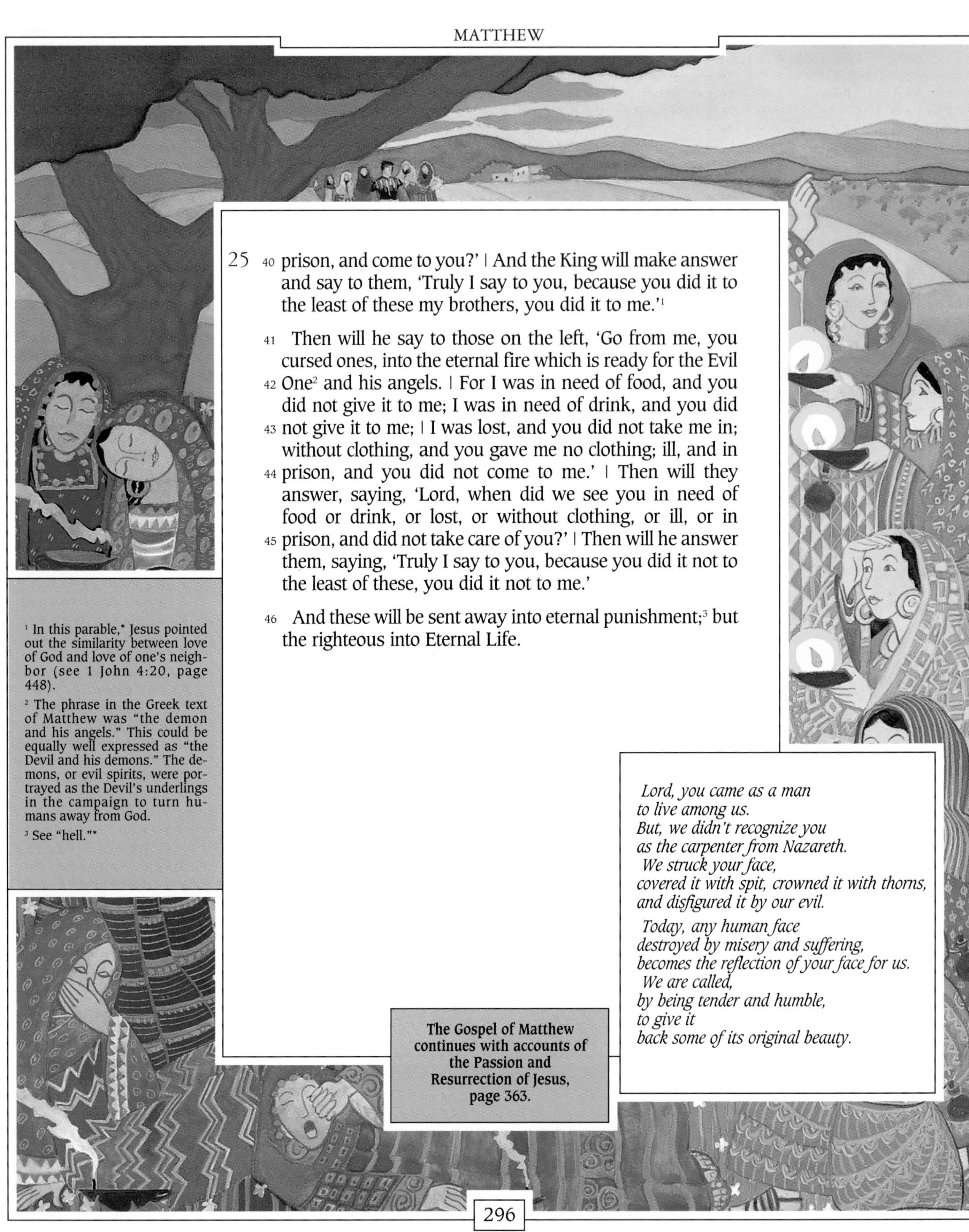

25 40 prison, and come to you?' | And the King will make answer
and say to them, 'Truly I say to you, because you did it to
the least of these my brothers, you did it to me.'[1]

41 Then will he say to those on the left, 'Go from me, you
cursed ones, into the eternal fire which is ready for the Evil
42 One[2] and his angels. | For I was in need of food, and you
did not give it to me; I was in need of drink, and you did
43 not give it to me; | I was lost, and you did not take me in;
without clothing, and you gave me no clothing; ill, and in
44 prison, and you did not come to me.' | Then will they
answer, saying, 'Lord, when did we see you in need of
food or drink, or lost, or without clothing, or ill, or in
45 prison, and did not take care of you?' | Then will he answer
them, saying, 'Truly I say to you, because you did it not to
the least of these, you did it not to me.'

46 And these will be sent away into eternal punishment;[3] but
the righteous into Eternal Life.

[1] In this parable,* Jesus pointed out the similarity between love of God and love of one's neighbor (see 1 John 4:20, page 448).

[2] The phrase in the Greek text of Matthew was "the demon and his angels." This could be equally well expressed as "the Devil and his demons." The demons, or evil spirits, were portrayed as the Devil's underlings in the campaign to turn humans away from God.

[3] See "hell."*

Lord, you came as a man
to live among us.
But, we didn't recognize you
as the carpenter from Nazareth.
We struck your face,
covered it with spit, crowned it with thorns,
and disfigured it by our evil.

Today, any human face
destroyed by misery and suffering,
becomes the reflection of your face for us.
We are called,
by being tender and humble,
to give it
back some of its original beauty.

The Gospel of Matthew continues with accounts of the Passion and Resurrection of Jesus, page 363.

III THE GOSPEL ACCORDING TO LUKE

Who was Luke?

Luke was a Greco-Latin name meaning "light." Paul spoke of him as a colleague, a doctor by profession.[1] *The early Christian writers (Irenaeus, Eusebius, Jerome) added that he was of heathen origin. He wrote the Gospel that bears his name and the Acts of the Apostles probably in Antioch in Syria around 80-90 AD. Several passages of the Acts were written in the first person plural, such as Chapter 16, verse 11, "We put out to sea.."*[2] *It is thought that they are the personal recollections of Luke. We learn that he was with Paul when Paul was arrested in Jerusalem and later imprisoned in Caesarea around 55-60 AD. Luke could then, while remaining in touch with his master, have completed the "investigation" he writes about at the beginning of his Gospel.*[3] *He possibly met Mary or people who had known her. He is the evangelist who tells us the most about her.*

He traveled to Rome with Paul[4] *in 60-61 AD. An ancient tradition has it that he was martyred with Andrew in Patrae in Greece at the age of 84.*

Since his Gospel begins in the Temple in Jerusalem where bulls were sacrificed, he is symbolically represented by a bull.[5]

For whom did Luke write his Gospel?

Luke wrote for a certain Theophilus. This name, which in Greek means "friend of God," might have stood for someone Luke knew or, much more probably, for communities of heathens converted to Christianity. It was a convention enabling Luke to tell each reader of his Gospel, "You also are invited to become a friend of God."

Luke gave special attention to the role of the Holy Spirit which inspires faith in human minds. He was particularly sensitive to the mercifulness* of Jesus. He gave women a more prominent place than any other evangelist.*

[1] See Colossians 4:14, and Philemon 24.

[2] See page 423.

[3] Luke 1:3, page 298.

[4] See Acts 28:11-31, page 427.

[5] See page 502.

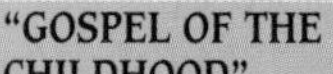

"GOSPEL OF THE CHILDHOOD"

Luke, like Matthew (see page 254), devoted the two first chapters of his Gospel to anecdotes concerning the birth and childhood of Jesus. Mary was given an especially important role. But Luke was doing more than collecting stories. His aim was to introduce Jesus to his readers. He emphasized his greatness and the novelty of his message by comparing him with John the Baptist.

John the Baptist was the last major figure of the Old Testament*:

- Like Isaac, he was born of a mother supposed to be barren (Genesis 18:9-14, page 41).
- He was filled with the spirit of the prophet Elijah* (see verse 17).
- His mission* was directed at the children of Israel whom he would "bring back to the Lord."

Jesus ushered in the age of the New Testament (the new Covenant):

- He was born of a young girl (virgin).
- He was not simply a prophet, but the Son of God.
- He would be "a light for the Gentiles" (Luke 2:32, page 305).

FOREWORD

1 1 As a number of attempts have been made to put
together an account of those events which took
2 place among us, | as they were handed down to us by the
3 first eyewitnesses who were servants of the word, | it
seemed good to me, having carefully investigated
everything from the beginning, to record the facts in
4 writing for you, most noble Theophilus;[1] | so that you may
know the certainty of those things of which you had been
taught.

CHILDHOOD OF JESUS

The birth of John the Baptist foretold

1 5 In the days of Herod,* king of Judaea, there was a
certain priest, named Zachariah, of the order of Abijah.
He had a wife from the family of Aaron whose name was
6 Elizabeth. | They were righteous in the eyes of God, obeying
all the commandments and regulations of God, and doing
7 no wrong. | They had no children because Elizabeth was
barren. At that time, they were very old.

8 Now it happened that Zachariah was acting as priest
9 before God. | As was required of the priests, he had to go
into the Temple to perform the burning of incense*....

11 There he saw an angel* of the Lord in his place on the right
12 side of the altar. | Zachariah was startled when he saw him,
13 and fear* seized him. | But the angel said, "Have no fear,

[1] See page 297, "For whom did Luke write his Gospel?"

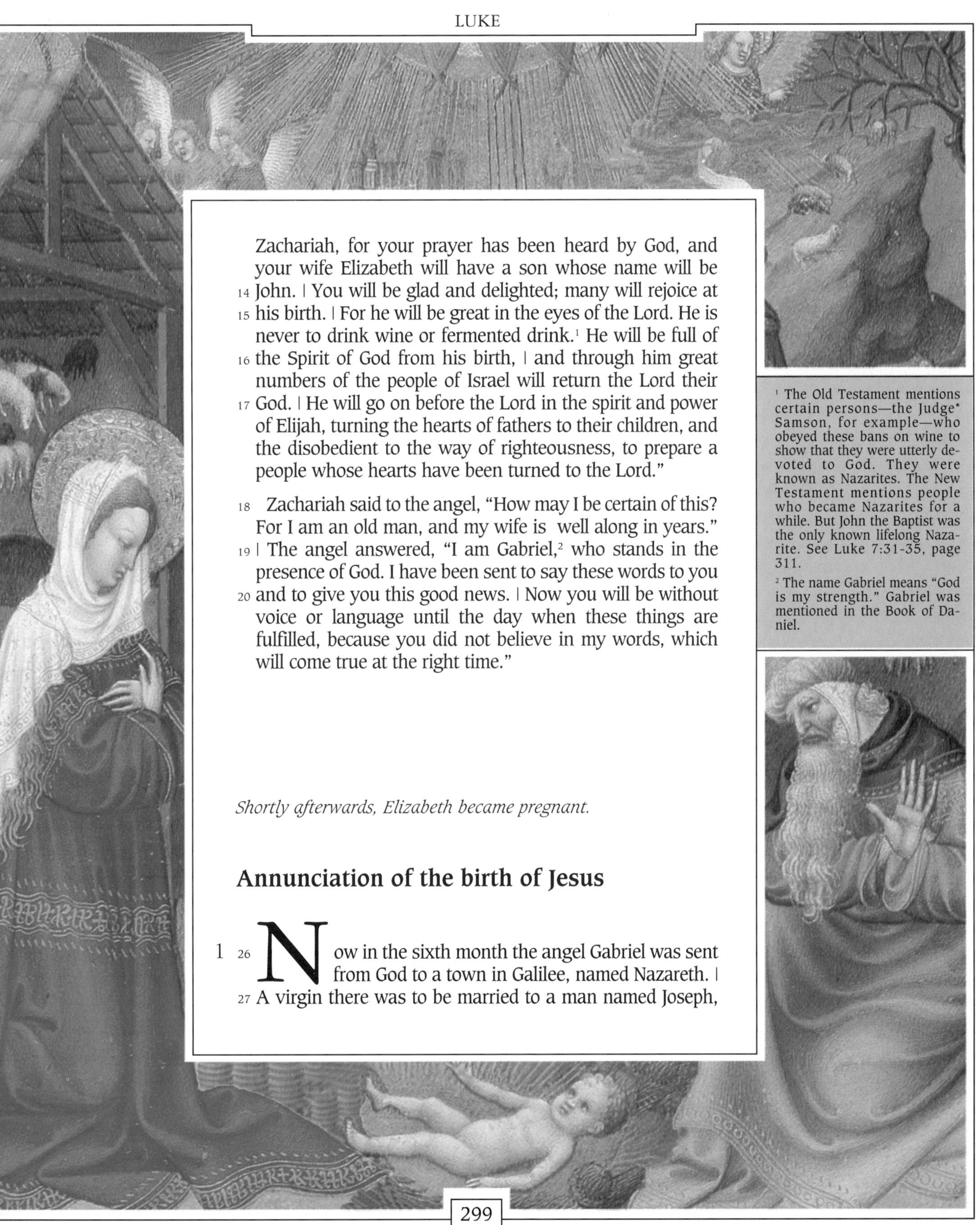

Zachariah, for your prayer has been heard by God, and
your wife Elizabeth will have a son whose name will be
14 John. | You will be glad and delighted; many will rejoice at
15 his birth. | For he will be great in the eyes of the Lord. He is
never to drink wine or fermented drink.[1] He will be full of
16 the Spirit of God from his birth, | and through him great
numbers of the people of Israel will return the Lord their
17 God. | He will go on before the Lord in the spirit and power
of Elijah, turning the hearts of fathers to their children, and
the disobedient to the way of righteousness, to prepare a
people whose hearts have been turned to the Lord."

18 Zachariah said to the angel, "How may I be certain of this?
For I am an old man, and my wife is well along in years."
19 | The angel answered, "I am Gabriel,[2] who stands in the
presence of God. I have been sent to say these words to you
20 and to give you this good news. | Now you will be without
voice or language until the day when these things are
fulfilled, because you did not believe in my words, which
will come true at the right time."

[1] The Old Testament mentions certain persons—the Judge* Samson, for example—who obeyed these bans on wine to show that they were utterly devoted to God. They were known as Nazarites. The New Testament mentions people who became Nazarites for a while. But John the Baptist was the only known lifelong Nazarite. See Luke 7:31-35, page 311.

[2] The name Gabriel means "God is my strength." Gabriel was mentioned in the Book of Daniel.

Shortly afterwards, Elizabeth became pregnant.

Annunciation of the birth of Jesus

1 26 Now in the sixth month the angel Gabriel was sent
from God to a town in Galilee, named Nazareth. |
27 A virgin there was to be married to a man named Joseph,

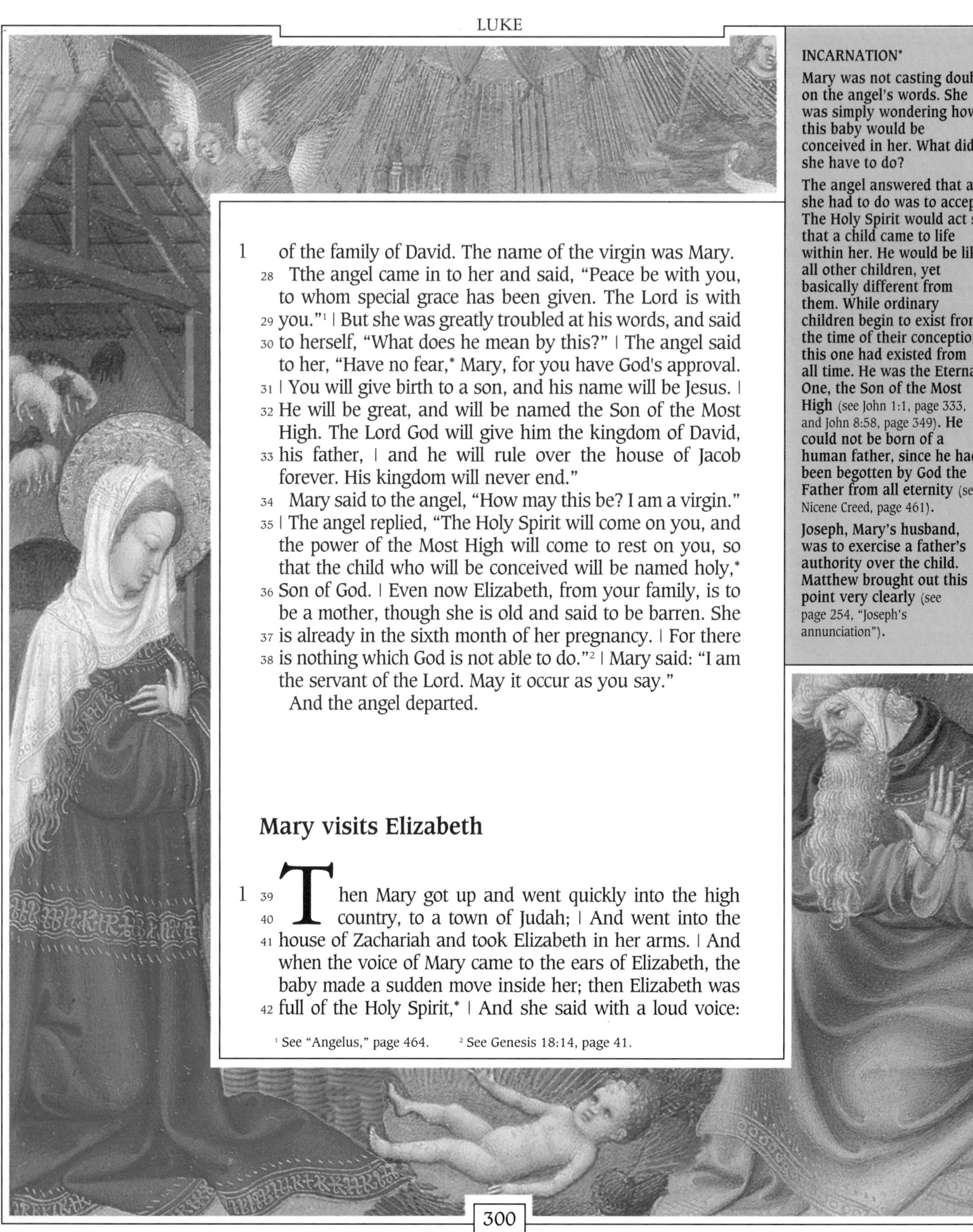

1 of the family of David. The name of the virgin was Mary.
28 Tthe angel came in to her and said, "Peace be with you,
to whom special grace has been given. The Lord is with
29 you."[1] | But she was greatly troubled at his words, and said
30 to herself, "What does he mean by this?" | The angel said
to her, "Have no fear,* Mary, for you have God's approval.
31 | You will give birth to a son, and his name will be Jesus. |
32 He will be great, and will be named the Son of the Most
High. The Lord God will give him the kingdom of David,
33 his father, | and he will rule over the house of Jacob
forever. His kingdom will never end."
34 Mary said to the angel, "How may this be? I am a virgin."
35 | The angel replied, "The Holy Spirit will come on you, and
the power of the Most High will come to rest on you, so
that the child who will be conceived will be named holy,*
36 Son of God. | Even now Elizabeth, from your family, is to
be a mother, though she is old and said to be barren. She
37 is already in the sixth month of her pregnancy. | For there
38 is nothing which God is not able to do."[2] | Mary said: "I am
the servant of the Lord. May it occur as you say."
And the angel departed.

Mary visits Elizabeth

1 39 Then Mary got up and went quickly into the high
40 country, to a town of Judah; | And went into the
41 house of Zachariah and took Elizabeth in her arms. | And
when the voice of Mary came to the ears of Elizabeth, the
baby made a sudden move inside her; then Elizabeth was
42 full of the Holy Spirit,* | And she said with a loud voice:

[1] See "Angelus," page 464. [2] See Genesis 18:14, page 41.

INCARNATION*

Mary was not casting doub on the angel's words. She was simply wondering how this baby would be conceived in her. What did she have to do?

The angel answered that a she had to do was to accep The Holy Spirit would act s that a child came to life within her. He would be lik all other children, yet basically different from them. While ordinary children begin to exist from the time of their conception this one had existed from all time. He was the Eterna One, the Son of the Most High (see John 1:1, page 333, and John 8:58, page 349). **He could not be born of a human father, since he had been begotten by God the Father from all eternity** (see Nicene Creed, page 461).

Joseph, Mary's husband, was to exercise a father's authority over the child. Matthew brought out this point very clearly (see page 254, "Joseph's annunciation").

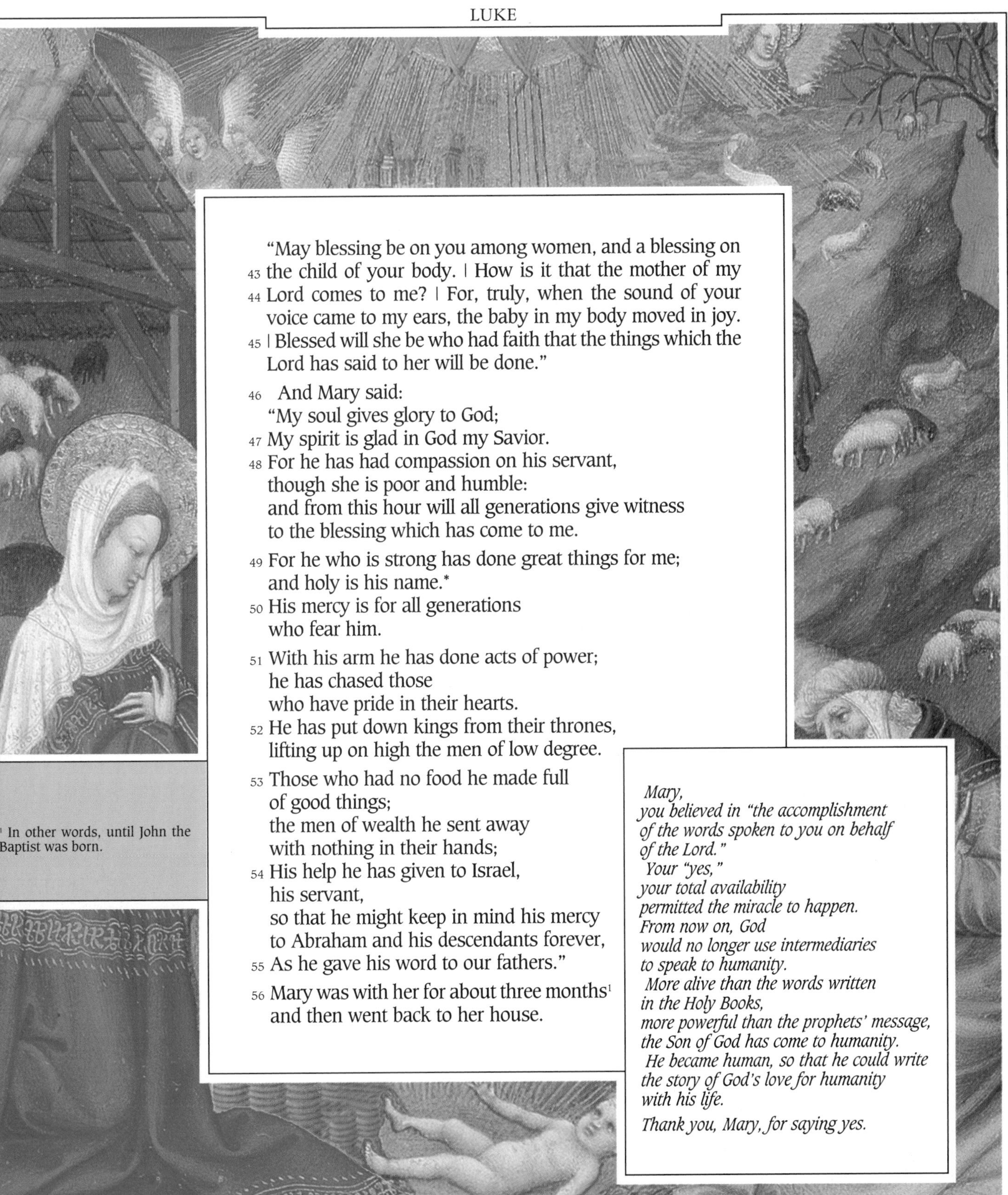

"May blessing be on you among women, and a blessing on
43 the child of your body. | How is it that the mother of my
44 Lord comes to me? | For, truly, when the sound of your
voice came to my ears, the baby in my body moved in joy.
45 | Blessed will she be who had faith that the things which the
Lord has said to her will be done."

46 And Mary said:
"My soul gives glory to God;
47 My spirit is glad in God my Savior.
48 For he has had compassion on his servant,
though she is poor and humble:
and from this hour will all generations give witness
to the blessing which has come to me.

49 For he who is strong has done great things for me;
and holy is his name.*
50 His mercy is for all generations
who fear him.

51 With his arm he has done acts of power;
he has chased those
who have pride in their hearts.
52 He has put down kings from their thrones,
lifting up on high the men of low degree.

53 Those who had no food he made full
of good things;
the men of wealth he sent away
with nothing in their hands;
54 His help he has given to Israel,
his servant,
so that he might keep in mind his mercy
to Abraham and his descendants forever,
55 As he gave his word to our fathers."

56 Mary was with her for about three months[1]
and then went back to her house.

Mary,
you believed in "the accomplishment
of the words spoken to you on behalf
of the Lord."
Your "yes,"
your total availability
permitted the miracle to happen.
From now on, God
would no longer use intermediaries
to speak to humanity.
More alive than the words written
in the Holy Books,
more powerful than the prophets' message,
the Son of God has come to humanity.
He became human, so that he could write
the story of God's love for humanity
with his life.

Thank you, Mary, for saying yes.

[1] In other words, until John the Baptist was born.

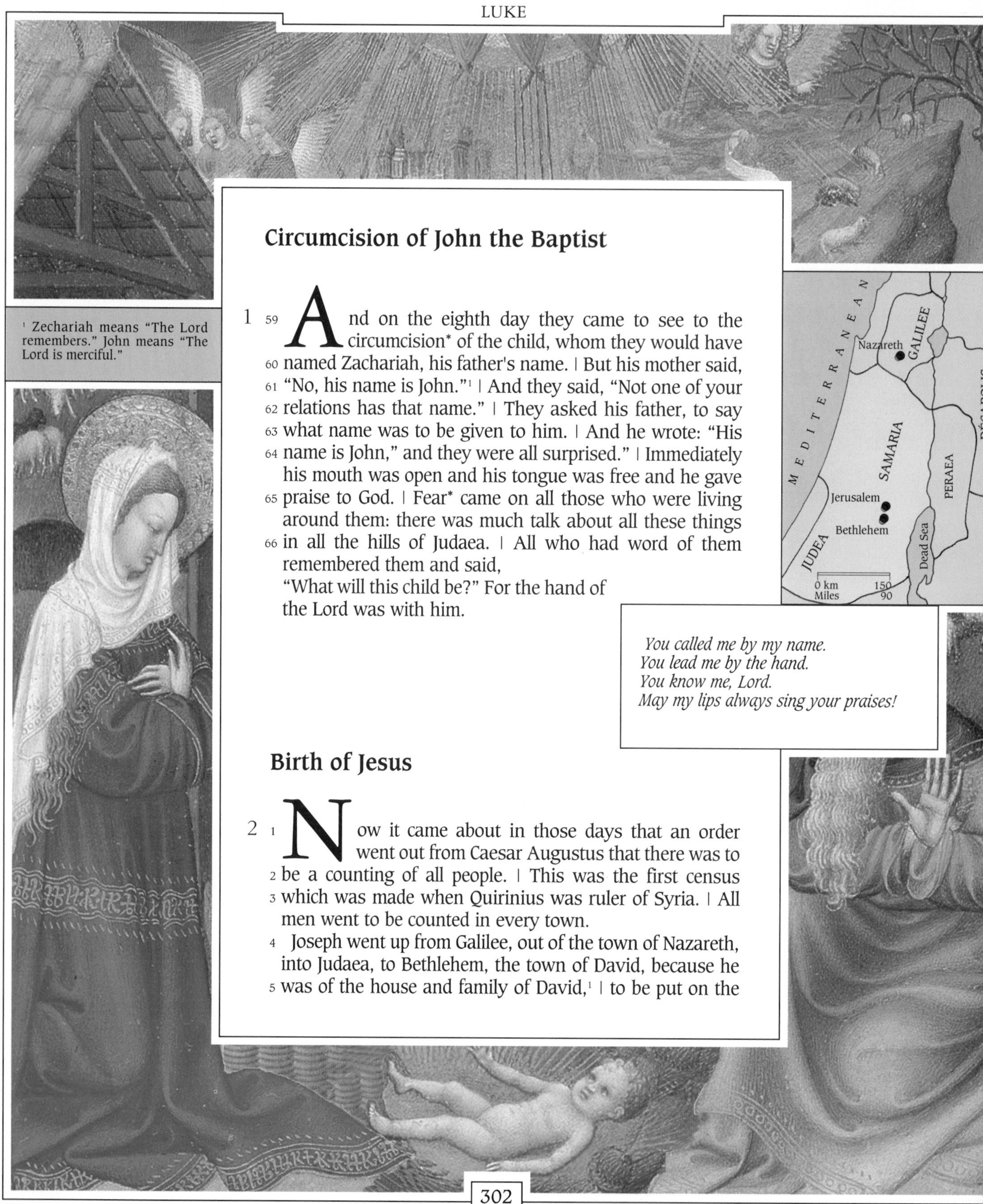

Circumcision of John the Baptist

1 59 And on the eighth day they came to see to the
circumcision* of the child, whom they would have
60 named Zachariah, his father's name. | But his mother said,
61 "No, his name is John."[1] | And they said, "Not one of your
62 relations has that name." | They asked his father, to say
63 what name was to be given to him. | And he wrote: "His
64 name is John," and they were all surprised." | Immediately
his mouth was open and his tongue was free and he gave
65 praise to God. | Fear* came on all those who were living
around them: there was much talk about all these things
66 in all the hills of Judaea. | All who had word of them
remembered them and said,
"What will this child be?" For the hand of
the Lord was with him.

[1] Zechariah means "The Lord remembers." John means "The Lord is merciful."

You called me by my name.
You lead me by the hand.
You know me, Lord.
May my lips always sing your praises!

Birth of Jesus

2 1 Now it came about in those days that an order
went out from Caesar Augustus that there was to
2 be a counting of all people. | This was the first census
3 which was made when Quirinius was ruler of Syria. | All
men went to be counted in every town.
4 Joseph went up from Galilee, out of the town of Nazareth,
into Judaea, to Bethlehem, the town of David, because he
5 was of the house and family of David,[1] | to be put on the

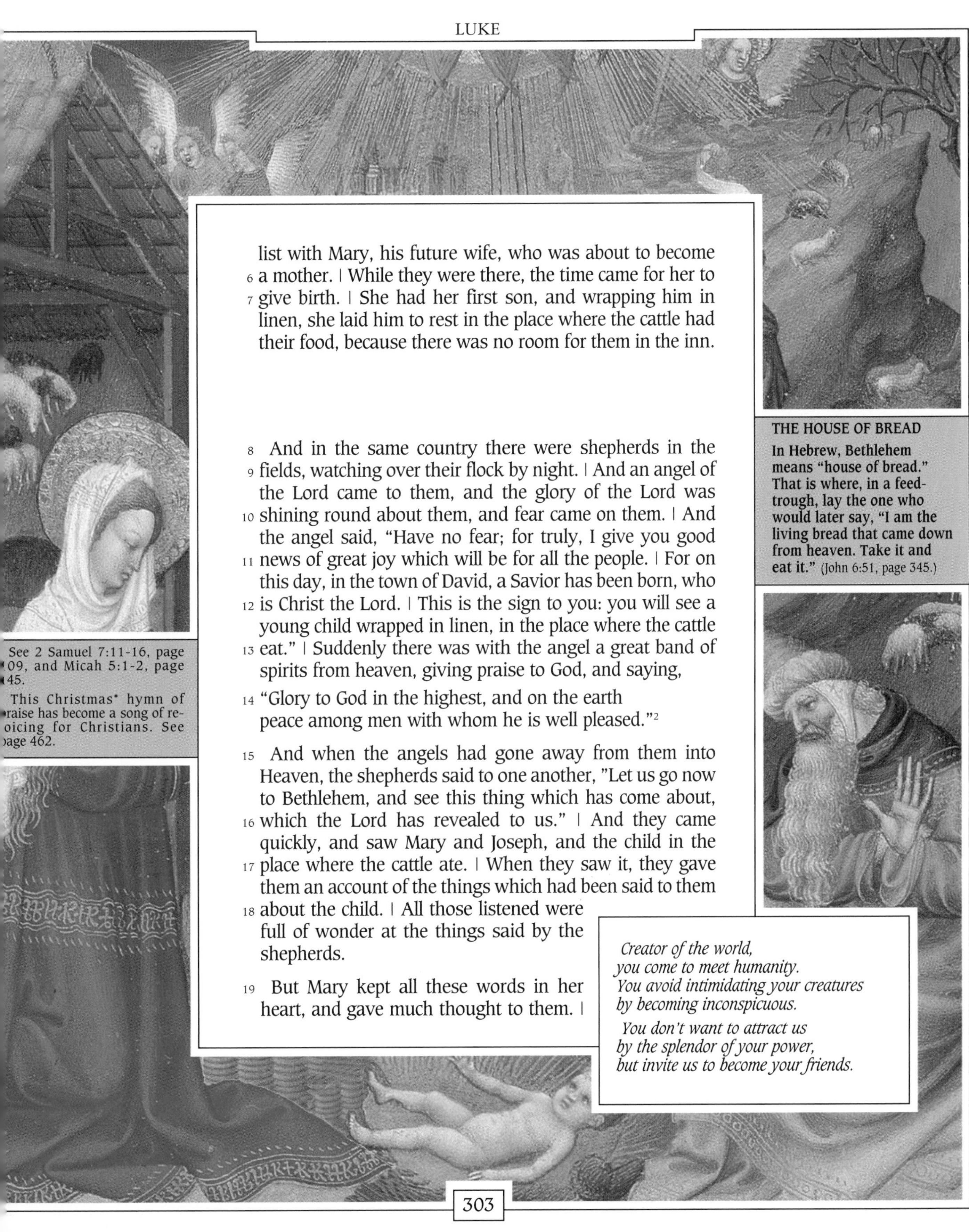

list with Mary, his future wife, who was about to become
6 a mother. | While they were there, the time came for her to
7 give birth. | She had her first son, and wrapping him in
linen, she laid him to rest in the place where the cattle had
their food, because there was no room for them in the inn.

8 And in the same country there were shepherds in the
9 fields, watching over their flock by night. | And an angel of
the Lord came to them, and the glory of the Lord was
10 shining round about them, and fear came on them. | And
the angel said, "Have no fear; for truly, I give you good
11 news of great joy which will be for all the people. | For on
this day, in the town of David, a Savior has been born, who
12 is Christ the Lord. | This is the sign to you: you will see a
young child wrapped in linen, in the place where the cattle
13 eat." | Suddenly there was with the angel a great band of
spirits from heaven, giving praise to God, and saying,

14 "Glory to God in the highest, and on the earth
peace among men with whom he is well pleased."[2]

15 And when the angels had gone away from them into
Heaven, the shepherds said to one another, "Let us go now
to Bethlehem, and see this thing which has come about,
16 which the Lord has revealed to us." | And they came
quickly, and saw Mary and Joseph, and the child in the
17 place where the cattle ate. | When they saw it, they gave
them an account of the things which had been said to them
18 about the child. | All those listened were
full of wonder at the things said by the
shepherds.

19 But Mary kept all these words in her
heart, and gave much thought to them. |

THE HOUSE OF BREAD

In Hebrew, Bethlehem means "house of bread." That is where, in a feed-trough, lay the one who would later say, "I am the living bread that came down from heaven. Take it and eat it." (John 6:51, page 345.)

See 2 Samuel 7:11-16, page 09, and Micah 5:1-2, page 45.

This Christmas* hymn of raise has become a song of re-oicing for Christians. See age 462.

Creator of the world,
you come to meet humanity.
You avoid intimidating your creatures
by becoming inconspicuous.

You don't want to attract us
by the splendor of your power,
but invite us to become your friends.

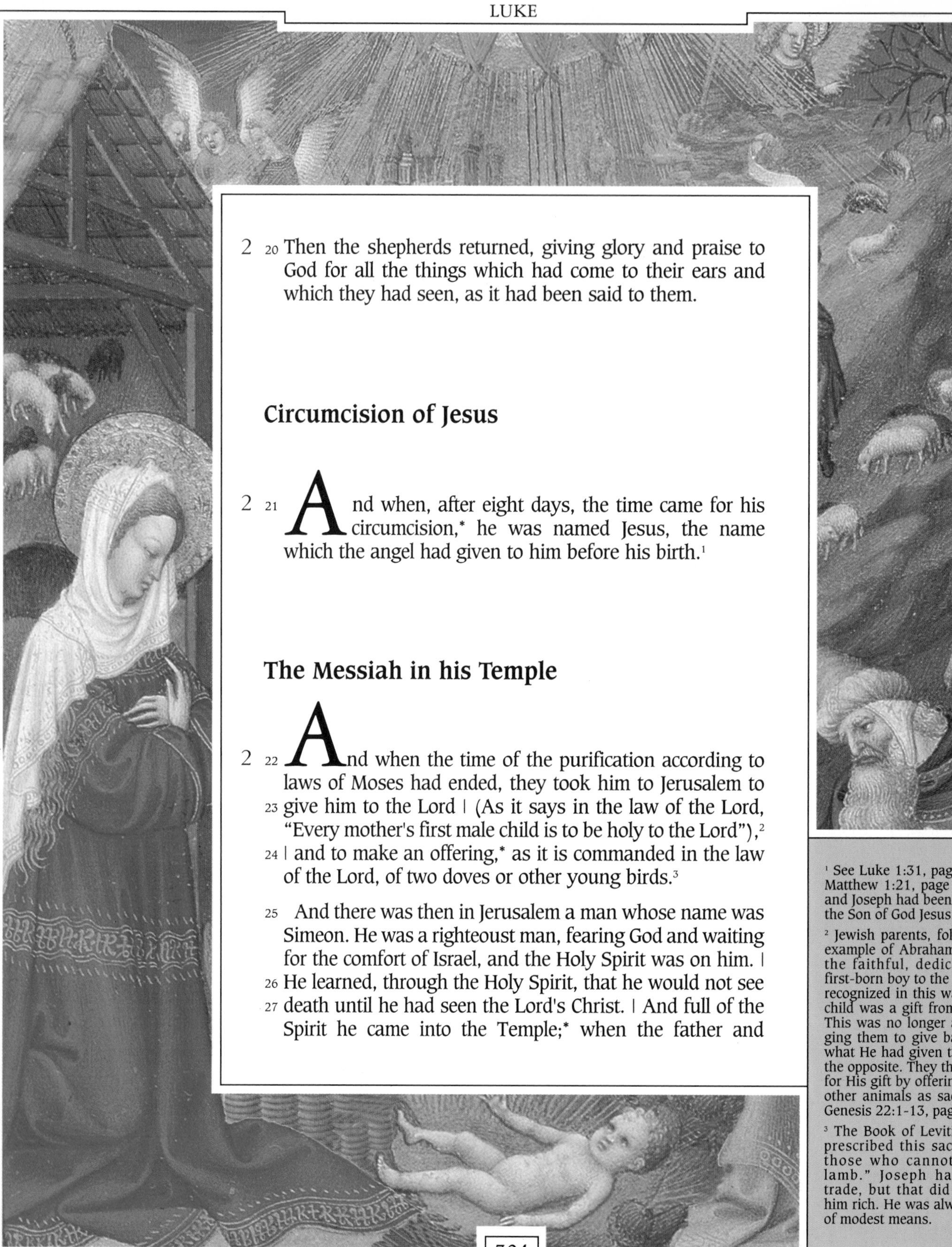

2 20 Then the shepherds returned, giving glory and praise to
God for all the things which had come to their ears and
which they had seen, as it had been said to them.

Circumcision of Jesus

2 21 And when, after eight days, the time came for his
circumcision,* he was named Jesus, the name
which the angel had given to him before his birth.[1]

The Messiah in his Temple

2 22 And when the time of the purification according to
laws of Moses had ended, they took him to Jerusalem to
23 give him to the Lord | (As it says in the law of the Lord,
"Every mother's first male child is to be holy to the Lord"),[2]
24 | and to make an offering,* as it is commanded in the law
of the Lord, of two doves or other young birds.[3]

25 And there was then in Jerusalem a man whose name was
Simeon. He was a righteoust man, fearing God and waiting
for the comfort of Israel, and the Holy Spirit was on him. |
26 He learned, through the Holy Spirit, that he would not see
27 death until he had seen the Lord's Christ. | And full of the
Spirit he came into the Temple;* when the father and

[1] See Luke 1:31, page 300, an Matthew 1:21, page 255. Mar and Joseph had been told to ca the Son of God Jesus.

[2] Jewish parents, following th example of Abraham, father c the faithful, dedicated thei first-born boy to the Lord. The recognized in this way that th child was a gift from the Lorc This was no longer a test obli ging them to give back to Go what He had given them. Quit the opposite. They thanked Go for His gift by offering a ram c other animals as sacrifice. Se Genesis 22:1-13, page 46.

[3] The Book of Leviticus* (5:7 prescribed this sacrifice "fc those who cannot afford lamb." Joseph had a goo trade, but that did not mak him rich. He was always a ma of modest means.

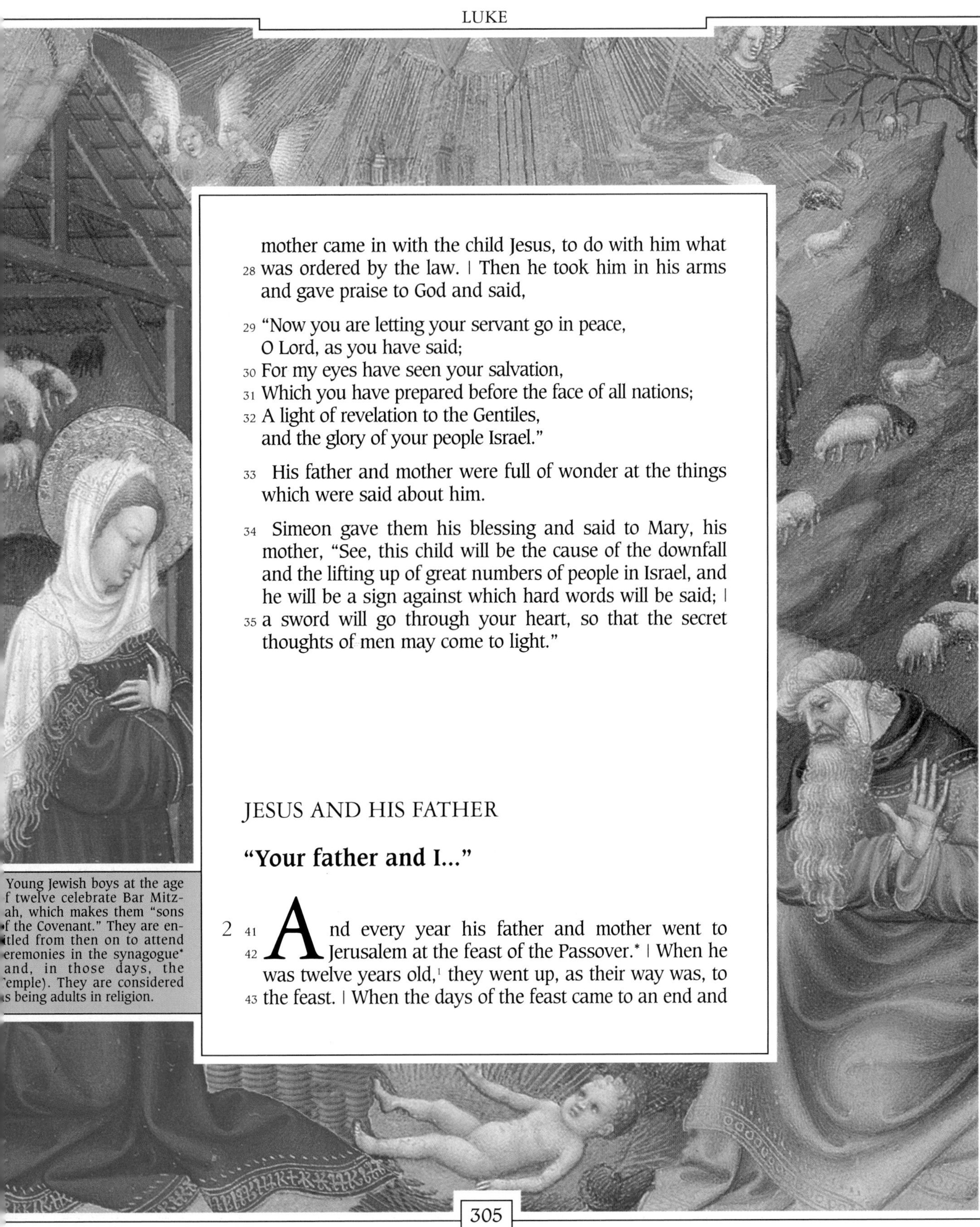

Young Jewish boys at the age of twelve celebrate Bar Mitzvah, which makes them "sons of the Covenant." They are entitled from then on to attend ceremonies in the synagogue* and, in those days, the Temple). They are considered as being adults in religion.

mother came in with the child Jesus, to do with him what
28 was ordered by the law. | Then he took him in his arms
and gave praise to God and said,

29 "Now you are letting your servant go in peace,
O Lord, as you have said;
30 For my eyes have seen your salvation,
31 Which you have prepared before the face of all nations;
32 A light of revelation to the Gentiles,
and the glory of your people Israel."

33 His father and mother were full of wonder at the things
which were said about him.

34 Simeon gave them his blessing and said to Mary, his
mother, "See, this child will be the cause of the downfall
and the lifting up of great numbers of people in Israel, and
he will be a sign against which hard words will be said; |
35 a sword will go through your heart, so that the secret
thoughts of men may come to light."

JESUS AND HIS FATHER

"Your father and I..."

2 41 And every year his father and mother went to
42 Jerusalem at the feast of the Passover.* | When he
was twelve years old,[1] they went up, as their way was, to
43 the feast. | When the days of the feast came to an end and

"THEY FOUND HIM IN THE TEMPLE"

Some Bible scholars call this episode "Jesus instructs the experts in the Law." But a close reading of the text shows that Jesus mainly listened, asked questions and answered when spoken to. Those present admired his intelligence but in no way acted as pupils before a teacher.

The ones who really learned something were Mary and Joseph. Jesus tried to tell them of the deep bond uniting him with his Father. They did not understand, since the life of God surpasses human understanding. Mary kept in her memory everything she did not understand immediately, trusting that the Holy Spirit would enlighten her.

The Holy Spirit is the inner teacher who will guide us to all truth (John 16:13, page 360).

2 they were going back, the boy Jesus was still in Jerusalem,
44 but they had no knowledge of it. | Believing that he was
with some of their number, they went a day's journey. Yet
after looking for him among their relations and friends, |
45 seeing that he was not there, they went back to Jerusalem,
to search for him.

46 After three days they found him in the Temple, seated
among the teachers,* listening to their words and putting
47 questions to them. | All who heard were full of wonder at
48 his knowledge and the answers which he gave. | And
when they saw him they were surprised, and his mother
said to him, "Son, why have you done this to us? Your
49 father and I have been looking for you with sorrow." | He
said to them, "Why were you looking for me? Was it not
clear to you that my right place was in my Father's house?"
50 | His words seemed strange to them.

51 He went down with them to Nazareth where he did as he
was ordered. His mother kept all these words privately in
52 her heart. | Jesus was increasing in wisdom and in age, and
in grace before God and men.

Jesus in history

3 1 Now in the fifteenth year of the rule of Tiberius*
Caesar, Pontius Pilate* being ruler of Judaea, and
Herod being king of Galilee,* his brother Philip king of the
country of Ituraea and Trachonitis, and Lysanias king of
2 Abilene, | when Annas* and Caiaphas* were high priests,[1]
the word of the Lord came to John, the son of Zacharias, in
the desert.

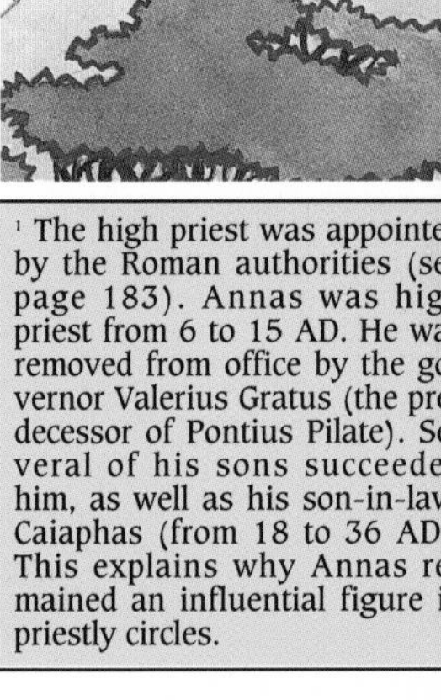

[1] The high priest was appointe by the Roman authorities (se page 183). Annas was hig priest from 6 to 15 AD. He wa removed from office by the go vernor Valerius Gratus (the pre decessor of Pontius Pilate). Se veral of his sons succeede him, as well as his son-in-law Caiaphas (from 18 to 36 AD This explains why Annas re mained an influential figure i priestly circles.

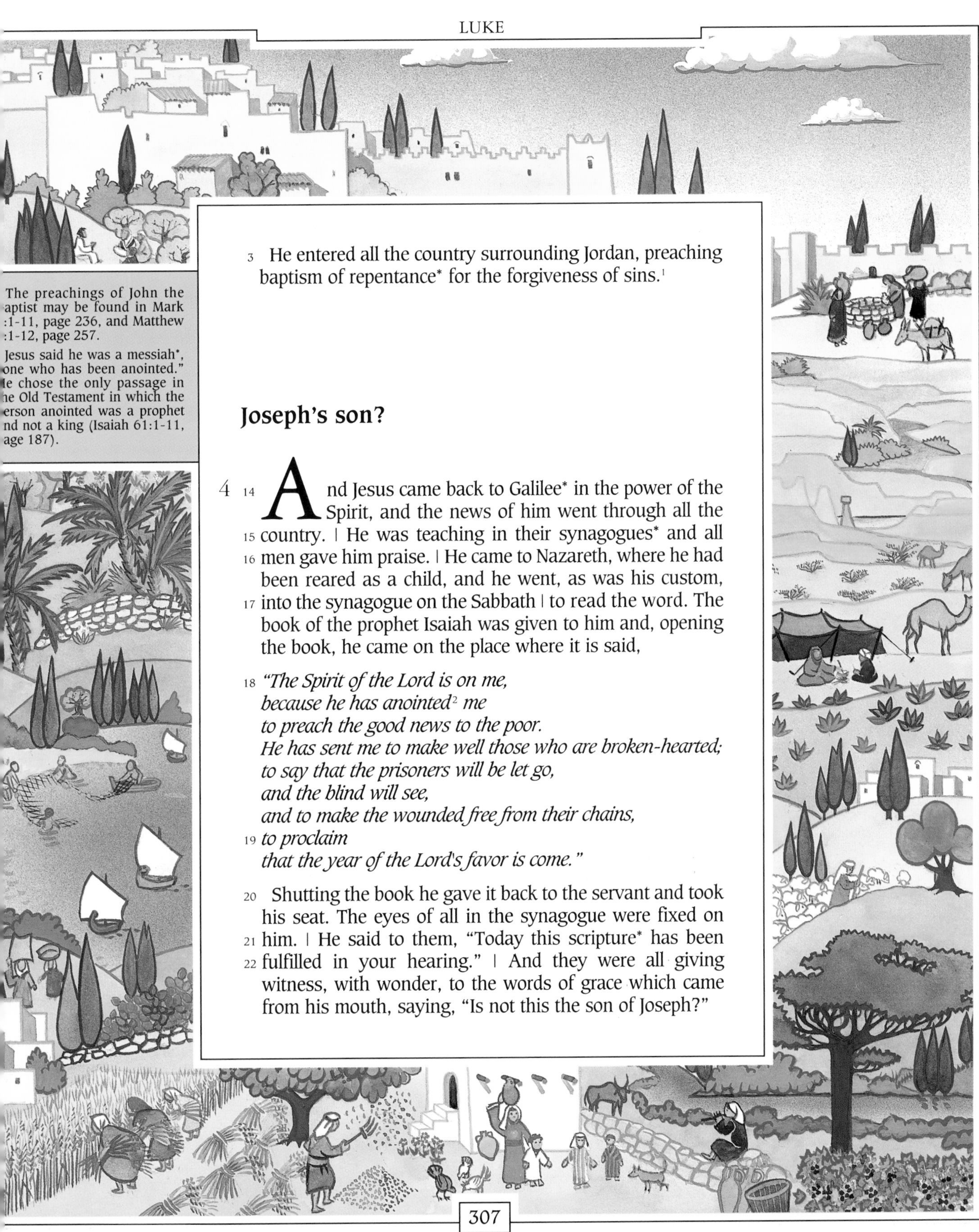

3 He entered all the country surrounding Jordan, preaching
baptism of repentance* for the forgiveness of sins.[1]

The preachings of John the
aptist may be found in Mark
:1-11, page 236, and Matthew
:1-12, page 257.

Jesus said he was a messiah*,
one who has been anointed."
le chose the only passage in
ne Old Testament in which the
erson anointed was a prophet
nd not a king (Isaiah 61:1-11,
age 187).

Joseph's son?

4 14 And Jesus came back to Galilee* in the power of the
Spirit, and the news of him went through all the
15 country. | He was teaching in their synagogues* and all
16 men gave him praise. | He came to Nazareth, where he had
been reared as a child, and he went, as was his custom,
17 into the synagogue on the Sabbath | to read the word. The
book of the prophet Isaiah was given to him and, opening
the book, he came on the place where it is said,

18 *"The Spirit of the Lord is on me,*
because he has anointed[2] *me*
to preach the good news to the poor.
He has sent me to make well those who are broken-hearted;
to say that the prisoners will be let go,
and the blind will see,
and to make the wounded free from their chains,
19 *to proclaim*
that the year of the Lord's favor is come."

20 Shutting the book he gave it back to the servant and took
his seat. The eyes of all in the synagogue were fixed on
21 him. | He said to them, "Today this scripture* has been
22 fulfilled in your hearing." | And they were all giving
witness, with wonder, to the words of grace which came
from his mouth, saying, "Is not this the son of Joseph?"

4 23 He replied, "Without doubt you will say to me, 'Let the
doctor make himself well: the things which to our
knowledge were done at Capernaum, do them here in your
24 country.'" | He said to them, "Truly I say to you, no
25 prophet is honored in his country. | Truly I say to you,
there were a number of widows in Israel in the days of
Elijah, when the heaven was shut up for three years and
26 six months and there was no food in the land. | But Elijah
was not sent to one of them, but only to Zarephath, in the
27 land of Sidon, to a woman who was a widow. | And there
were a number of lepers in Israel in the time of Elisha the
prophet, and not one of them was made clean, but only
Naaman the Syrian."[2]

28 All who were in the synagogue were very angry when
29 these things were said to them. | They got
up and took him out of the town to the
edge of the mountain on which their
town was, so that they might send him
30 down to his death. | But he walked right
through them and went on his way.

Lord, we want to follow you
in your love for all humanity.
Transform us into bearers of light,
into peacemakers,
into joyful witnesses of the Good News.

If we come across difficulties,
open a passage for us
so that we can continue
to courageously walk in your way.

JESUS AND THE APOSTLES

Jesus master fisherman

5 1 Now it came about that while the people crowded
to be near him, and to have knowledge of the
word of God, he was by a wide stretch of water named
2 Gennesaret. | He saw two boats by the edge of the water,
but the fishermen had left them and were washing their
3 nets. | And he got into one of the boats, the property of

[1] 1 Kings 17:17-24, page 122. [2] 2 Kings 5:1-17, page 126.

ꟷISHERS OF MEN"

ımon Peter and the others ılly understood this ‹pression. They were to aul men out of the waves, ymbol of the forces of evil ee pages 241-242).

sus used other images to escribe the mission of the postles — harvesters, grape atherers. For the time eing, he did not use the nage of the shepherd. God ad told Ezekiel that, in iew of the incompetence nd greed of the shepherds f Israel, He Himself would ad His flock (Ezekiel 34:1-16, ıge 163). **This was why, to egin with, Jesus reserved ıe title of shepherd for imself** (John 10:11, page 352). **nce he had taught what a ıepherd pleasing to God ıould be, he called upon ıs apostles to be shepherds ke himself** (John 21:15-19, ıge 394). **From then on, the tle of shepherd replaced ıe others, including that of shers of men.**

Simon, and made a request to him to go a little way out
from the land. And being seated he preached to the people
from the boat.
4 When his talk was ended, he said to Simon, "Go out into
5 deep water, and drop your nets for fish." | Simon,
answering, said, "Master, we were working all night and
we caught nothing, but at your word I will cast the nets." |
6 And when they had done this, they got such a great
number of fish that it seemed as if their nets would be
7 broken. | They signaled to their friends in the other boat to
come to their help. They came, and the two boats were so
full that they were sinking.
8 But Simon, when he saw it, went down at the knees of
Jesus and said, "Go away from me, O Lord, for I am a
9 sinner." | For he was full of wonder and so were all those
who were with him, at the number of fish which they had
10 taken. | So were James and John, the sons of Zebedee, who
were working with Simon. Jesus said to Simon, "Have no
fear. From this time forward you will be a fisher of men."[1]
11 | And when they had got their boats to the land, they gave
up everything and followed him.

Jesus at prayer

6 12 And it came about in those days that he went out to
the mountain for prayer, where he stayed all night
13 in prayer to God. | The day came and, turning to his
disciples, he made a selection from among them of twelve,*
14 to whom he gave the name of Apostles:[2] | Simon, to whom
he gave the name of Peter, and Andrew, his brother, and
15 James and John and Philip and Bartholomew | And Matthew
and Thomas and James, the son of Alphaeus, and Simon,
16 who was named the Zealot, | And Judas, the son of James,[3]
and Judas Iscariot, he who betrayed him.

[1] See page 277, note 1.

[2] See the corresponding episode in Mark 3:13-19, page 239. It is worth noting how Luke stressed the prayer of Jesus before he chose his apostles.

[3] Judas, son of James, may be identified with Thaddeus (Mark 3:19, page 239, and Matthew 10:3).

MIRACLES* BY JESUS

The centurion's slave

7 1 After he had finished speaking to all the
2 people, he went into Capernaum. | A certain centurion
had a servant who was very dear to him,[1] and who was ill
3 and near death. | When news of Jesus came to his ears, he
sent to him rulers of the Jews,[2] requesting that he would
4 come and make his servant well. | They, when they came
5 to Jesus, made their request warmly, saying, | "It is right
for you to do this for him, because he is a friend to our
nation, and himself has built a synagogue* for us."

6 So Jesus went with them. When he was not far from the
house, the man sent friends to him, saying, "Lord, do not
give yourself trouble, for I am not important enough for
7 you to come into my house.[3] | I had the feeling that I was
not even good enough to come to you, but say the word
8 only, and my servant will be well. | For I, myself, am a man
under authority, having men under me; and I say to this
one, 'Go', and he goes; and to another, 'Come', and he
comes; and to my servant, 'Do this', and he does it."

9 When these things were said to Jesus, he was surprised,
and, turning to the mass of people coming after him, said,
"I have not seen such great faith,* in all
10 of Israel." | And when those who were
sent came back to the house they saw
that the servant was healed.

[1] See how Matthew related the same event (Matthew 8:5-13, page 267).

[2] These elders* (word used in the Greek text) were synagogue officials.

[3] See meditation, page 267.

THE FAITH OF A HEATHEN

"Blessed are those who have not seen and yet have believe (John 20:29, page 389). Out o deference, the soldier in the occupying army did not try to meet Jesus. He realized that a Jew entering a heathen's hom could attract criticism (see Ac 11:2-3, page 416). Jesus had enough trouble as it was. He sent the message, "Don't expose yourself to more criticism on my account. Say but the word..."

Jesus and the Roman, althoug they never physically met, we in perfect harmony.

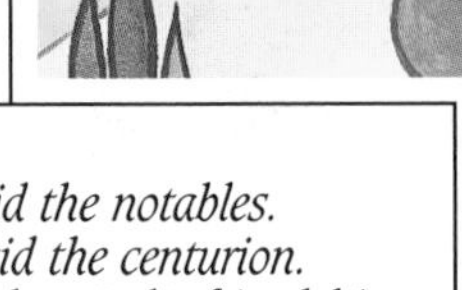

"He deserves it." said the notables.
"I'm not worthy." said the centurion.
He knows very well that God's friendship
cannot be obtained by being worthy.
Friendship cannot be on demand.
It is received as a gift.

Lord, I want to be poor
in spirit like the centurion,
so that I can welcome you as a friend.

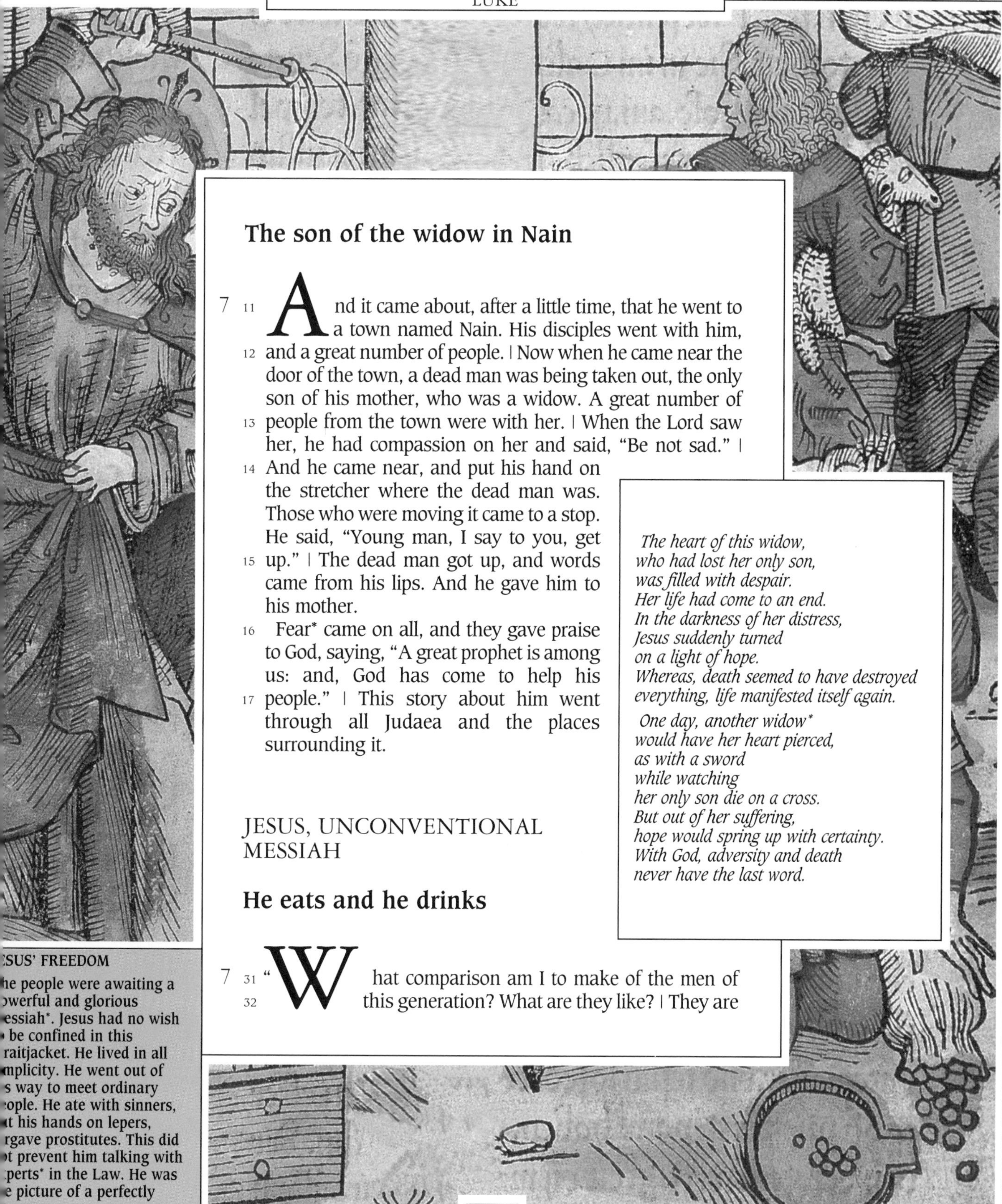

The son of the widow in Nain

7 11 And it came about, after a little time, that he went to
a town named Nain. His disciples went with him,
12 and a great number of people. | Now when he came near the
door of the town, a dead man was being taken out, the only
son of his mother, who was a widow. A great number of
13 people from the town were with her. | When the Lord saw
her, he had compassion on her and said, "Be not sad." |
14 And he came near, and put his hand on
the stretcher where the dead man was.
Those who were moving it came to a stop.
He said, "Young man, I say to you, get
15 up." | The dead man got up, and words
came from his lips. And he gave him to
his mother.
16 Fear* came on all, and they gave praise
to God, saying, "A great prophet is among
us: and, God has come to help his
17 people." | This story about him went
through all Judaea and the places
surrounding it.

The heart of this widow,
who had lost her only son,
was filled with despair.
Her life had come to an end.
In the darkness of her distress,
Jesus suddenly turned
on a light of hope.
Whereas, death seemed to have destroyed
everything, life manifested itself again.
*One day, another widow**
would have her heart pierced,
as with a sword
while watching
her only son die on a cross.
But out of her suffering,
hope would spring up with certainty.
With God, adversity and death
never have the last word.

JESUS, UNCONVENTIONAL MESSIAH

He eats and he drinks

7 31 "What comparison am I to make of the men of
32 this generation? What are they like? | They are

:SUS' FREEDOM

he people were awaiting a
ɔwerful and glorious
essiah*. Jesus had no wish
• be confined in this
raitjacket. He lived in all
mplicity. He went out of
s way to meet ordinary
ople. He ate with sinners,
it his hands on lepers,
rgave prostitutes. This did
ɔt prevent him talking with
perts* in the Law. He was
e picture of a perfectly
ee man.

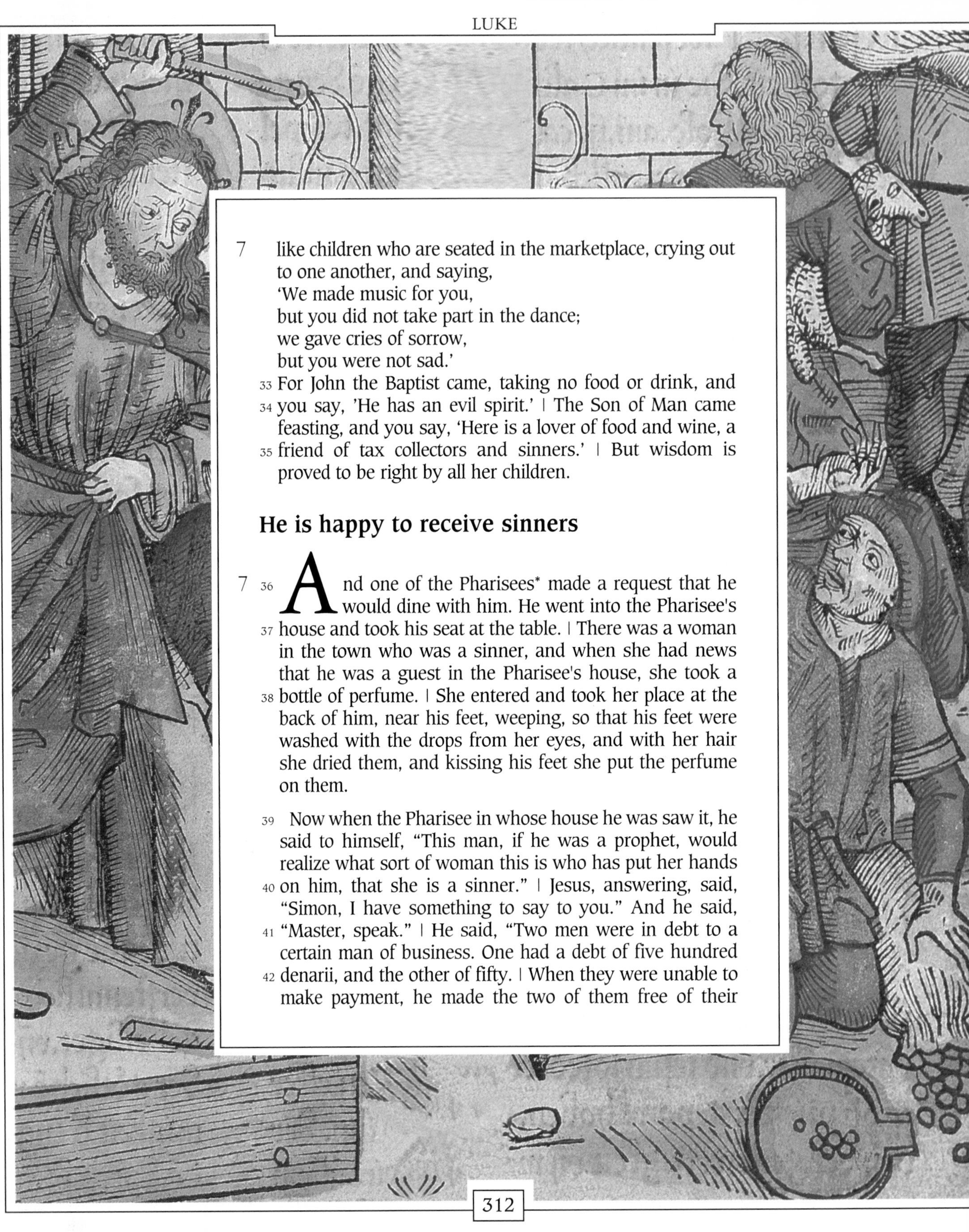

7 like children who are seated in the marketplace, crying out
to one another, and saying,
'We made music for you,
but you did not take part in the dance;
we gave cries of sorrow,
but you were not sad.'
33 For John the Baptist came, taking no food or drink, and
34 you say, 'He has an evil spirit.' | The Son of Man came
feasting, and you say, 'Here is a lover of food and wine, a
35 friend of tax collectors and sinners.' | But wisdom is
proved to be right by all her children.

He is happy to receive sinners

7 36 And one of the Pharisees* made a request that he
would dine with him. He went into the Pharisee's
37 house and took his seat at the table. | There was a woman
in the town who was a sinner, and when she had news
that he was a guest in the Pharisee's house, she took a
38 bottle of perfume. | She entered and took her place at the
back of him, near his feet, weeping, so that his feet were
washed with the drops from her eyes, and with her hair
she dried them, and kissing his feet she put the perfume
on them.

39 Now when the Pharisee in whose house he was saw it, he
said to himself, "This man, if he was a prophet, would
realize what sort of woman this is who has put her hands
40 on him, that she is a sinner." | Jesus, answering, said,
"Simon, I have something to say to you." And he said,
41 "Master, speak." | He said, "Two men were in debt to a
certain man of business. One had a debt of five hundred
42 denarii, and the other of fifty. | When they were unable to
make payment, he made the two of them free of their

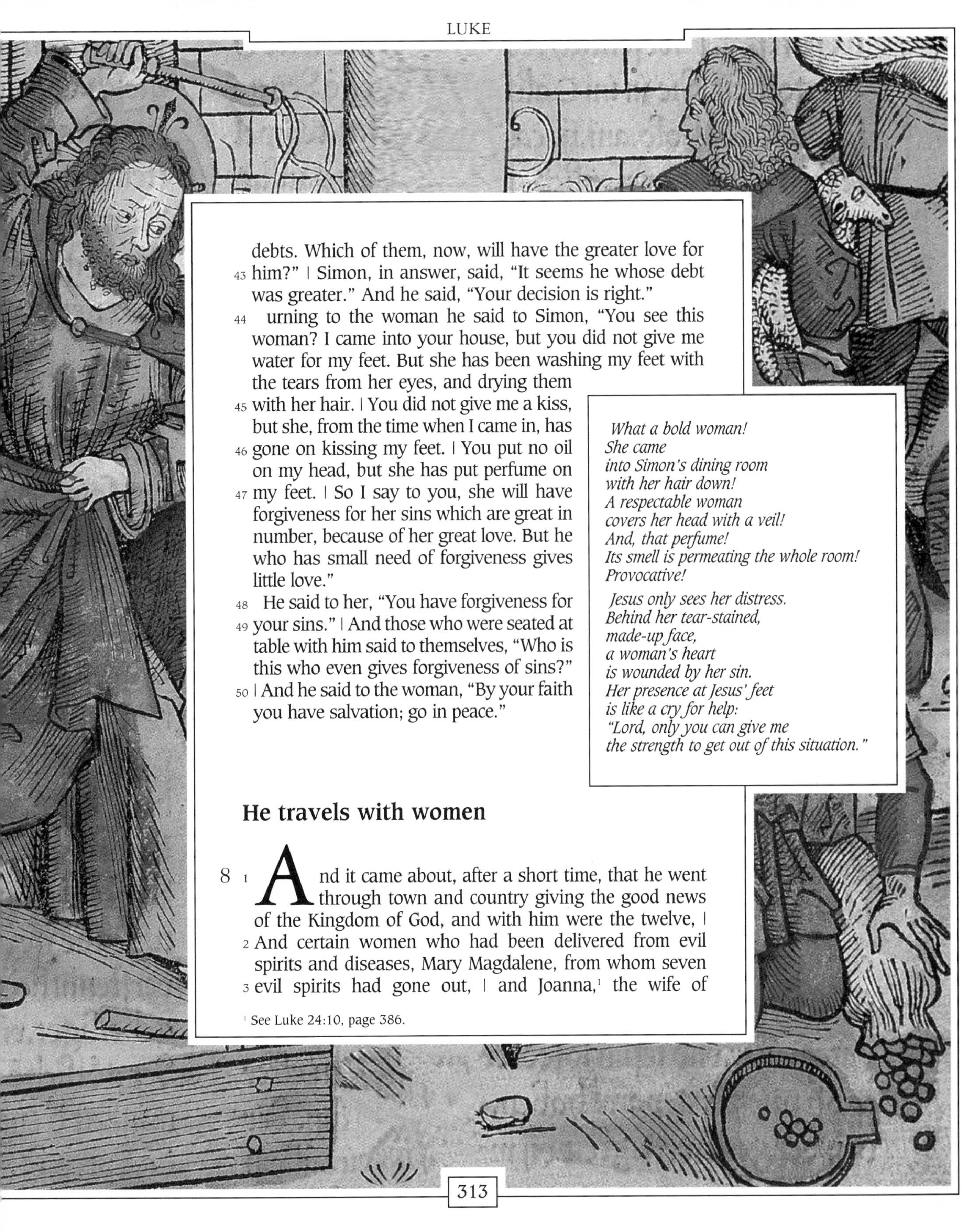

debts. Which of them, now, will have the greater love for
43 him?" | Simon, in answer, said, "It seems he whose debt
was greater." And he said, "Your decision is right."
44 urning to the woman he said to Simon, "You see this
woman? I came into your house, but you did not give me
water for my feet. But she has been washing my feet with
the tears from her eyes, and drying them
45 with her hair. | You did not give me a kiss,
but she, from the time when I came in, has
46 gone on kissing my feet. | You put no oil
on my head, but she has put perfume on
47 my feet. | So I say to you, she will have
forgiveness for her sins which are great in
number, because of her great love. But he
who has small need of forgiveness gives
little love."
48 He said to her, "You have forgiveness for
49 your sins." | And those who were seated at
table with him said to themselves, "Who is
this who even gives forgiveness of sins?"
50 | And he said to the woman, "By your faith
you have salvation; go in peace."

What a bold woman!
She came
into Simon's dining room
with her hair down!
A respectable woman
covers her head with a veil!
And, that perfume!
Its smell is permeating the whole room!
Provocative!

Jesus only sees her distress.
Behind her tear-stained,
made-up face,
a woman's heart
is wounded by her sin.
Her presence at Jesus' feet
is like a cry for help:
"Lord, only you can give me
the strength to get out of this situation."

He travels with women

8 1 And it came about, after a short time, that he went
through town and country giving the good news
of the Kingdom of God, and with him were the twelve, |
2 And certain women who had been delivered from evil
spirits and diseases, Mary Magdalene, from whom seven
3 evil spirits had gone out, | and Joanna,[1] the wife of

[1] See Luke 24:10, page 386.

8 Chuza, Herod's chief house-servant, and
Susanna and a number of others, who
gave from their wealth what he needed.

Who are you women,
leaving everything to follow Jesus,
like the Twelve?
Mary Magdalene,
a disciple all the way to Calvary,
you were the first one to recognize
the voice of the Resurrected
One calling your name.

Joanna, you, along with Mary,
were part of the joyous messengers
of the Resurrection.

And you, Susan,
we only know your name,
but you represent
all the anonymous women
who have ventured
outside of their homes
to invent the church.

He sets faith above the Law

8 41 Then there came a man named
Jairus, who was a ruler in the
synagogue. He bowed down at the feet
of Jesus, desiring him to come to his
42 house, | for he had an only daughter, about twelve years
old, who was near death. But while he was on his way, the
people were pushing to be near him.
43 A woman, who had had a flow of blood[1] for twelve years,[2]
and had given all her money to doctors, and not one of
44 them was able to make her well, | came after him and put
her hand on the edge of his robe. Immediately the flowing
45 of her blood was stopped. | Jesus said, "Who was touching
me?" And when they all said, "It is not I," Peter and those
who were with him said, "Master, the people are pushing
46 round you on every side." | But Jesus said, "Someone was
touching me, for I had the feeling that power had gone out
47 from me." | When the woman saw that she was not able to
keep it secret, she came, shaking with fear, and falling
down before him she made clear before all the people the
reason for her touching him, and how she was made well
48 immediately. | He said to her, "Daughter, your faith has
made you well; go in peace."
49 While he was still talking, someone came from the house
of the ruler of the synagogue, saying, "Your daughter is
50 dead. Do not go on troubling the Master." | But Jesus at
these words said to him, "Have no fear, only have faith,

[1] In those days, persons with bleeding were considered unclean, and anyone they touched became unclean. The woman should not have touched Jesus. She touched him anyway, because she believed in him. Jesus commended her. Her faith had made her free.

[2] Twelve, the figure mentioned in connection with both the daughter and the woman, was the number associated with the tribes of Israel. Luke was possibly suggesting to his readers that Jesus had come to give new life to Israel by proposing another Covenant.

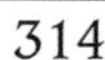

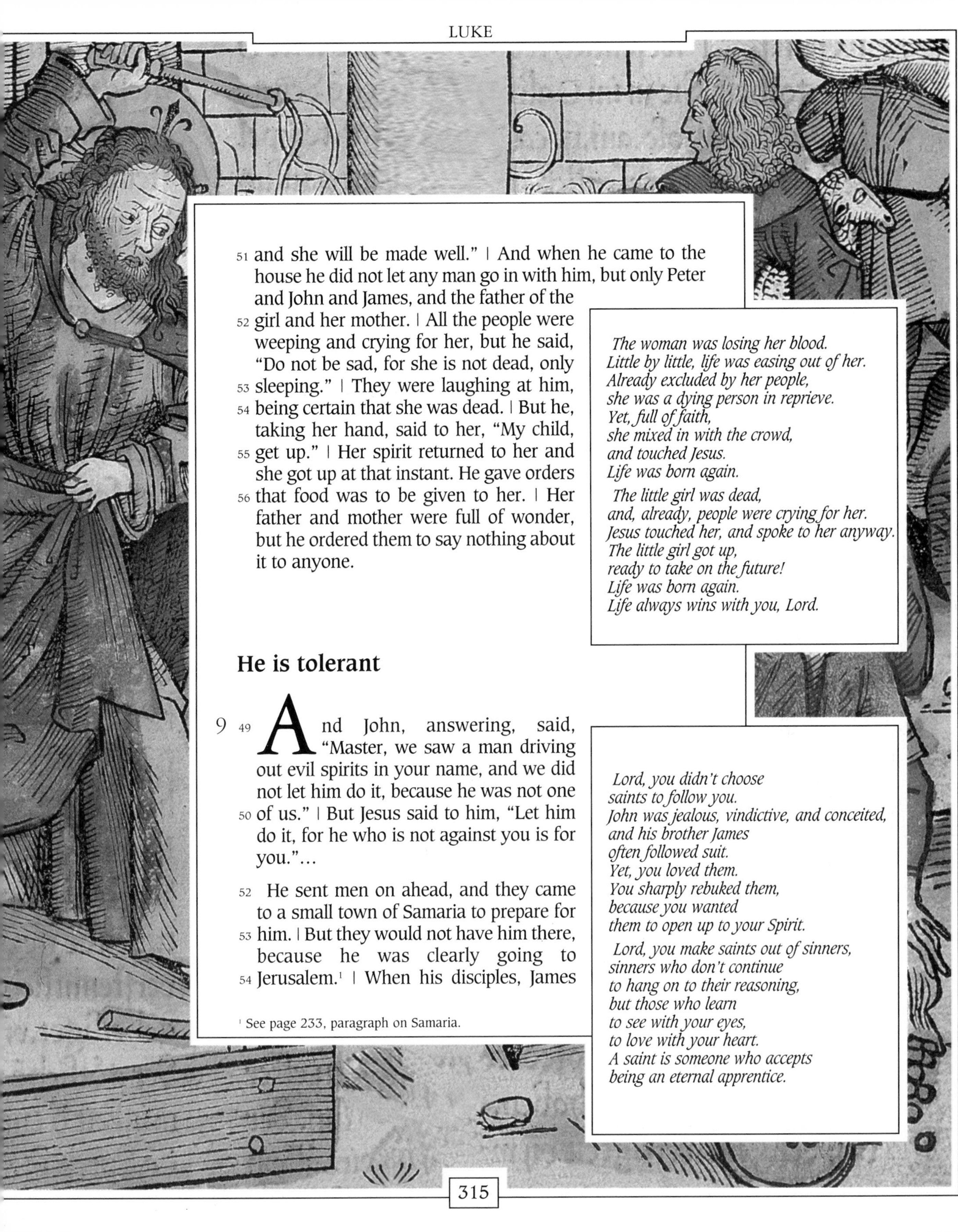

51 and she will be made well." | And when he came to the
house he did not let any man go in with him, but only Peter
and John and James, and the father of the
52 girl and her mother. | All the people were
weeping and crying for her, but he said,
"Do not be sad, for she is not dead, only
53 sleeping." | They were laughing at him,
54 being certain that she was dead. | But he,
taking her hand, said to her, "My child,
55 get up." | Her spirit returned to her and
she got up at that instant. He gave orders
56 that food was to be given to her. | Her
father and mother were full of wonder,
but he ordered them to say nothing about
it to anyone.

The woman was losing her blood.
Little by little, life was easing out of her.
Already excluded by her people,
she was a dying person in reprieve.
Yet, full of faith,
she mixed in with the crowd,
and touched Jesus.
Life was born again.

The little girl was dead,
and, already, people were crying for her.
Jesus touched her, and spoke to her anyway.
The little girl got up,
ready to take on the future!
Life was born again.
Life always wins with you, Lord.

He is tolerant

9 49 And John, answering, said,
"Master, we saw a man driving
out evil spirits in your name, and we did
not let him do it, because he was not one
50 of us." | But Jesus said to him, "Let him
do it, for he who is not against you is for
you."...

52 He sent men on ahead, and they came
to a small town of Samaria to prepare for
53 him. | But they would not have him there,
because he was clearly going to
54 Jerusalem.[1] | When his disciples, James

[1] See page 233, paragraph on Samaria.

Lord, you didn't choose
saints to follow you.
John was jealous, vindictive, and conceited,
and his brother James
often followed suit.
Yet, you loved them.
You sharply rebuked them,
because you wanted
them to open up to your Spirit.

Lord, you make saints out of sinners,
sinners who don't continue
to hang on to their reasoning,
but those who learn
to see with your eyes,
to love with your heart.
A saint is someone who accepts
being an eternal apprentice.

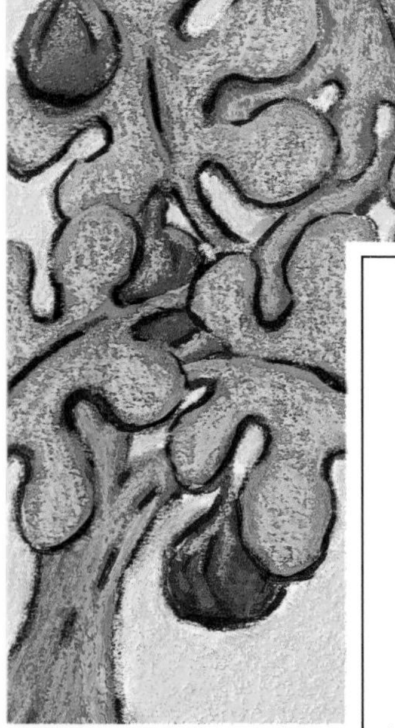

and John, saw this, they said, "Lord, may we send fire
55 from heaven and put an end to them?"[1] | But turning round
56 he rebuked them, | and they went to another small town.

He is revealed to little children

After sending the Twelve on mission,[2] Jesus chose seventy-two other disciples whom he sent in pairs to the villages where he intended to go. Luke was the only Evangelist to mention the mission of the seventy-two.

10 17 And the seventy came back with joy, saying, "Lord,
even the evil spirits are under our power in your
18 name." | He said, "I was watching for Satan, falling from
19 heaven like a star. | See, I have given you power to put
your feet on snakes and evil beasts, and over all the
strength of him who is against you. Nothing will harm
20 you. | Do not be glad, however, because you have power
over spirits, but because your names are recorded in
heaven."
21 In that same hour he was full of joy in the Holy Spirit and
said, "I give praise to you, O Father, Lord of heaven and
earth, because you have kept these things secret from the
wise and the men of learning, and have revealed them to
little children. For so, O Father, it was pleasing in your
22 eyes. | All things have been given to me by my Father, and
no one has knowledge* of the Son, but only the Father:
and of the Father, but only the Son, and he to whom the
23 Son will reveal it." | Turning to the disciples, he said
privately, "Blessed are the eyes which see the things you
24 see: | For I say to you that numbers of prophets and kings
have had a desire to see the things which you see, and
have not seen them, and to have knowledge of the things
which have come to your ears, and they had it not."

[1] This makes us understand why Jesus nicknamed the two brothers "Boanerges," which meant "sons of thunder." See Mark 3:17, page 239.

[2] See Matthew 10:5-33, page 269.

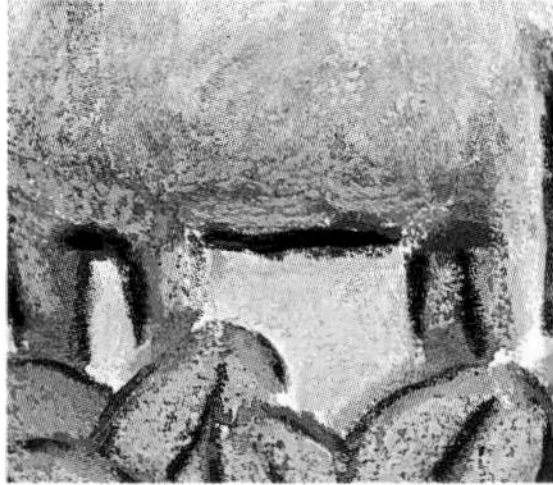

TRINITY

Moved by the Holy Spirit, the Son rejoices in knowing the Father to a degree unattainable by human reason.

This trinity of love is not turned inwards on its own bliss. Its greatest desire is for humans to become God's children along with the Son.

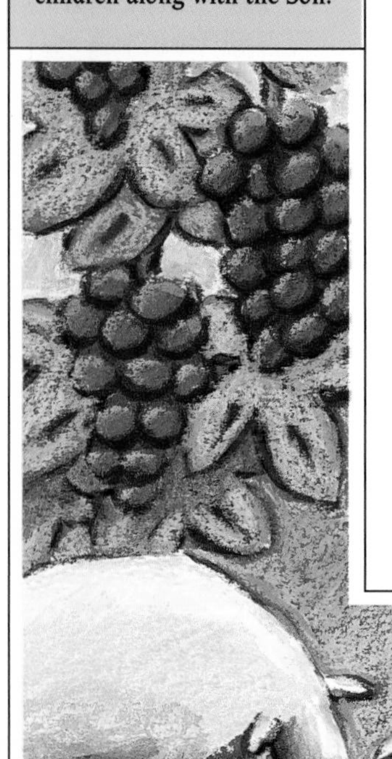

THE LIMITS OF HUMAN WISDOM

"The wise and the learned" mentioned by Jesus were those who chose to rely only on their own intelligence and more or less openly refused to let themselves be enlightened by the only real sage (see page 198).

They confused learning and knowledge. They had learned something about God but did not know Him. How, for example, could the carpenter from Nazareth be the Son of God, since God was supposed to be almighty?

Their learning prevented them from marveling at God as He actually revealed Himself.

Little children, on the other hand, are delighted to discover the plenitude of a love which, to reach everybody, stands on the lowest rung.

Paul, who with much pain gave up his human wisdom to receive the wisdom of God, eloquently described the conflict between the two (1 Corinthians 1:18-25, page 433).

LIVING IN CHARITY

Loving one's neighbor

10 25 And a certain teacher of the law got up and put him
to the test, saying, "Master, what have I to do so
26 that I may have eternal life?" | And he said to him, "What
27 does the law say, in your reading of it?" | And he,
answering, said, "Have love for the Lord your God with all
your heart and with all your soul and with all your strength
and with all your mind; and for your neighbor as for
28 yourself."[1] | And he said, "You have given the right answer:
do this and you will have life."[2]
29 But he, desiring to be right, said to Jesus, "And who is my
30 neighbor?" | And Jesus, answering him, said, "A certain
man was going down from Jerusalem to Jericho, and he fell
into the hands of thieves, who took his clothing and gave
him cruel blows, and when they went away, he was half
31 dead.[3] | And by chance a certain priest* was going down that
way. When he saw him, he crossed over to the other side. |
32 And in the same way, a Levite,* when he came to the place
33 and saw him, crossed over to the other side. | But a certain
man of Samaria,* journeying that way, came where he was,
and when he saw him, he was moved with compassion for
34 him, | He put clean linen around his wounds, with oil and
wine; he put him on his beast and took him to a house and
35 took care of him. | The day after he took two pennies and
gave them to the owner of the house and said, 'Take care of
him; if this money is not enough, when I come again I will
36 give you whatever more is needed.' | Which of these three
men, in your opinion, was neighbor to the man who fell into
37 the hands of thieves?" | He said, "The one who had mercy
on him." And Jesus said, "Go and do the same."

BEING A NEIGHBOR TO EVERYONE

The expert in the Law was asking what types of persons could be defined as his neighbor. Jesus replied that a neighbor was anyone in need of help, however different that person might be. No laws, customs or prejudices must be allowed to stand in the way. Energy and possessions had to be engaged without any thought of return.

[1] ...ee Deuteronomy 6:5, page 84, ...d Leviticus 19:18, page 73.

[2] ...ompare with Mark 12:28-34, ...ge 252.

[3] ...esus laid emphasis on the ...alf-dead" condition of the ...n left on the road by the rob...s. The priest and the Levite, ...en they saw him, wondered ...ether he was dead or alive. ...e Law forbade anyone, and ...ecially a priest, to touch a ...ose. The first two passers-by ...refore avoided going near the ...unded man for fear of brea...g the Law if he happened to ...dead. The message of Jesus ...s that blind obedience to the ...w can lead to breaking the ...damental commandment of ...rity.

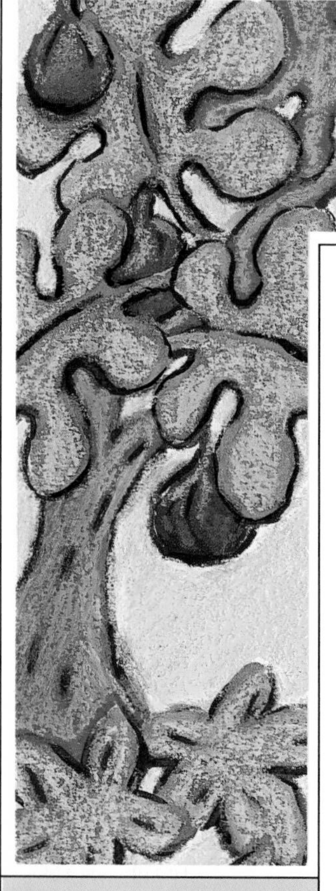

Martha, you worry and bustle about.
You think you know what needs
to be done to make Jesus feel welcome.
You think:
"Mary is wasting her time
listening to the Lord.
She has better things to do!"

Martha, have you forgotten
the first commandment?
"Hear, O Israel,
the Lord our God,
the Lord is one."

Mary remembered.
Since the Son of God
is in her house,
she is taking time to listen to him.

And Jesus says
that there is no better way
to welcome him.

Loving Jesus

10 38 Now, while they were on their
way, he came to a certain town.
A woman named Martha took him into
39 her house. | She had a sister, Mary, who
took her seat at the Lord's feet and paid
40 attention to his words. | But Martha had
her hands full of the work of the house,
and she came to him and said, "Lord, is
it nothing to you that my sister has let
me do all the work? Tell her that she is
41 to give me some help." | But the Lord,
answering, said to her, "Martha, Martha, you are full of
42 care and troubled about so many things. | Little is needed,
or even one thing only. Mary has taken that good part,
which will not be taken away from her."

[1] Once more Luke lets us discover Jesus at prayer. See Luke 6:12, page 309.

[2] Compare with Matthew 6:9-13, page 264.

Welcoming the Holy Spirit

11 1 And it came about that he was in prayer[1] in a certain
place, and when he finsihed, one of his disciples
said to him, Lord, will you teach us about prayer, as John
2 did to his disciples? | Jesus replied, "When you say your
prayers, say,[2]
'Father, may your name be kept holy
and your kingdom come.
3 Give us every day bread for our needs.
4 May we have forgiveness for our sins,
as we make free all those
who are in debt to us.
And lead us not into temptation.'"

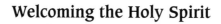

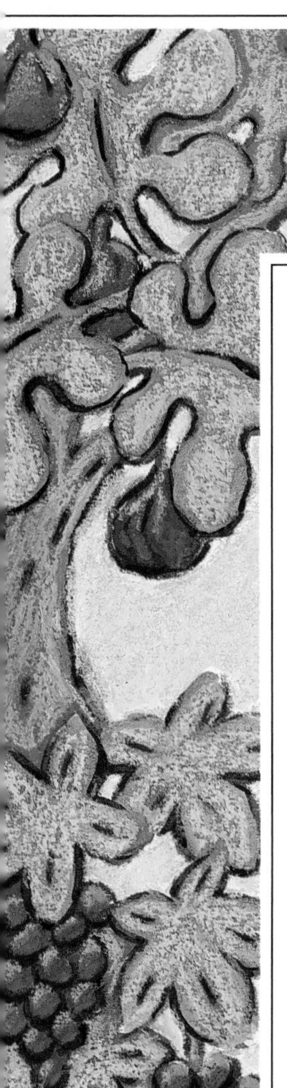

5 He said to them, "Which of you, having a friend, would
go to him in the middle of the night and say to him,
6 'Friend, let me have three cakes of bread, | because a friend
of mine has come to me on a journey, and I have nothing
7 to put before him;' | And he, from inside the house, would
say in answer, 'Do not be a trouble to me; the door is now
shut, and my children are with me in bed. It is not possible
8 for me to get up and give to you.'[1] | I say to you, Though
he will not get up and give to him, because he is his friend,
still, if he continues asking, he will get up and give him as
much as he needs.
9 I say to you, ask, and you will have answers; seek, and
10 you w!ill find; knock, the door will be open to you. | For to
everyone who asks, it will be given; and he who is
searching will find; and to him who knocks, the door will
11 be open. | And which of you, being a father, will give a
stone to his son, who makes request for bread? Or for a
12 fish, will give him a snake? | Or for an egg, will give him a
13 scorpion? | If, then, you who are evil[2] are able to give good
things to your children, how much more will your Father
in heaven give the Holy Spirit to those who ask?"

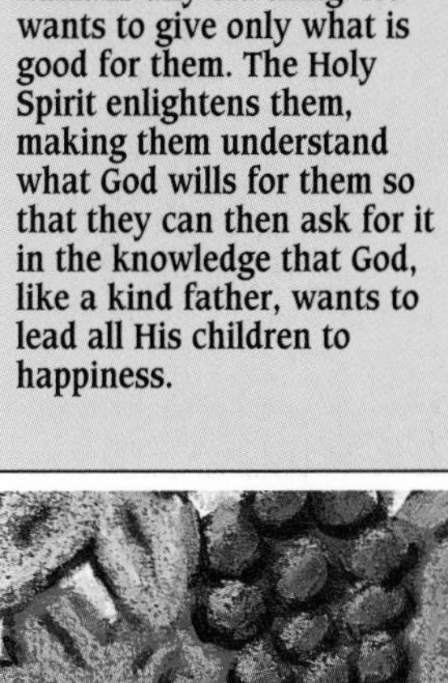

THE HOLY SPIRIT

The first of God's gifts to believers is the Holy Spirit. He does not want to give humans any old thing. He wants to give only what is good for them. The Holy Spirit enlightens them, making them understand what God wills for them so that they can then ask for it in the knowledge that God, like a kind father, wants to lead all His children to happiness.

SOME OF GOD'S QUALITIES

Patience

13 6 And he told this parable[3] to them:
"A certain man had a fig tree in his garden, and he
7 came to get fruit from it, and there was no fruit. | And he
said to the gardener, 'See, for three years I have been
looking for fruit from this tree, and I have not had any. Let
8 it be cut down; why is it taking up space?' | He said, 'Lord,

The houses those days were nall, often consisting of only e room. At night, mats or attresses were spread on the ound. During the day, they ere gathered into a corner. hen everyone was sleeping, it as not easy to open the door.

esus had just spoken of a fa- er's kindness towards his ildren. He was not contradic- ng himself when he called em "evil." He was merely re- arking that humans, however od, are still marked by sin mpared with God. Why not agine that he spoke these ords smilingly? "You know u aren't perfect, yet you do od things. So you can ima- ne how much greater is the odness of your heavenly Fa- er!"

Compare this parable with the tion recounted by Matthew in :18-22, page 288.

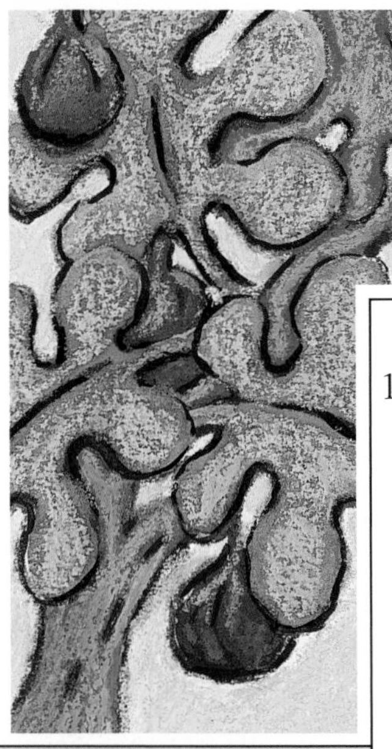

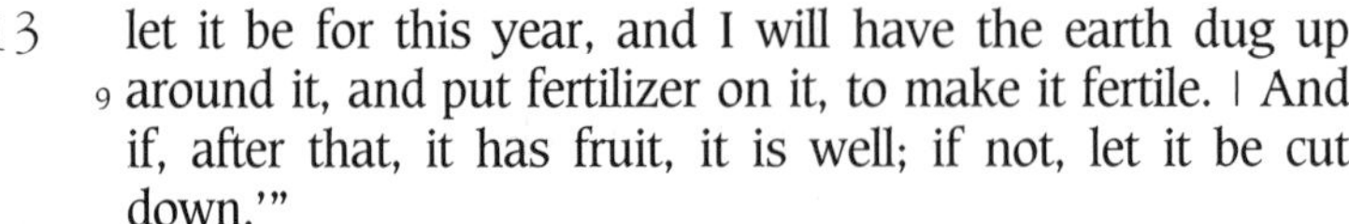

13 let it be for this year, and I will have the earth dug up
9 around it, and put fertilizer on it, to make it fertile. | And
if, after that, it has fruit, it is well; if not, let it be cut
down.'"

Mercifulness*

15 1 Now all the tax collectors* and sinners came near
2 to listen to him. | And the Pharisees* and scribes
were angry, saying, "This man gives approval to sinners,
and eats with them."

The shepherd with a hundred sheep

3-4 And he told a parable to them, saying, | "What man of
you, having a hundred sheep, if one of them gets loose and
goes away, will not let the ninety-nine be in the desert by
themselves, and go after the lost one, till he sees where it
5 is? | And when he has got it again, he takes it in his arms
6 with joy. | And when he gets back to his house, he sends
for his neighbors and friends, saying to them, 'Be glad
7 with me, for I have found my sheep which was lost.' | I say
to you that even so there will be more joy in heaven when
one sinner repents from his wrongdoing, than for ninety-
nine good men, who have no need of a change of heart."

The woman with the ten silver coins

8 "Or what woman, having ten bits of silver, if one bit
falls from her hands, will not get a light, and go
through her house, searching carefully until she sees it? |
9 And when she has it again, she gets her friends and

"THIS MAN WELCOMES SINNERS"

Luke continued with his surprising portrait of Jesus — a man who let himself be touched by a sinful woman (Luke 7:36-50, page 312)**, who was accused of gluttony and drunkenness** (Luke 7:34-35, page 312)**. Decidedly, he kept bad company, hardly befitting a respectable, devout person. To those who were scandalized, he told parables about mercy:**

- **The parable of the shepherd with a hundred sheep** (verses 3 to 7)
- **The parable of the woman with the ten silver coins** (verses 8 to 10)
- **The parable of the father who had two sons** (verses 11 to 32).

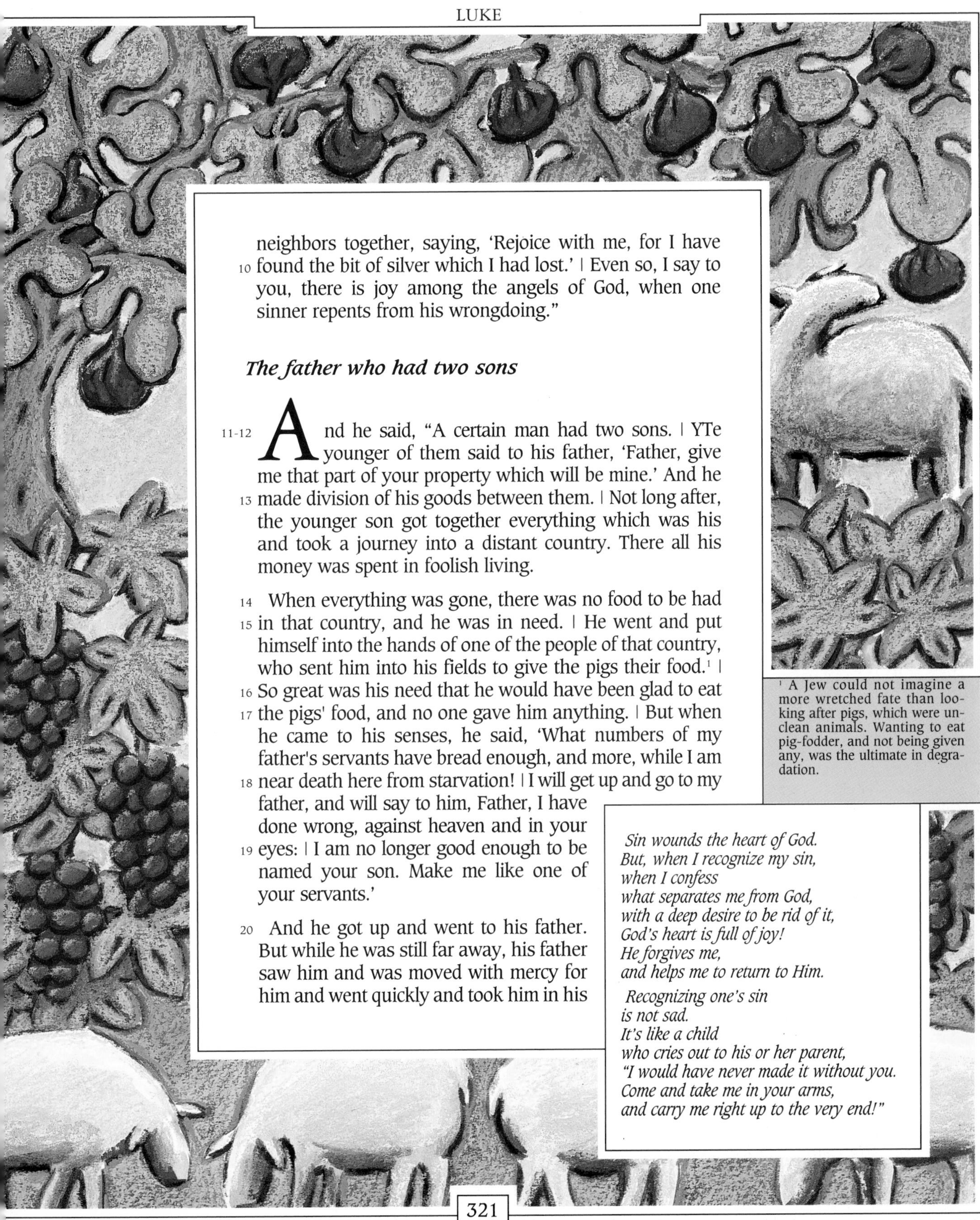

neighbors together, saying, 'Rejoice with me, for I have
10 found the bit of silver which I had lost.' | Even so, I say to
you, there is joy among the angels of God, when one
sinner repents from his wrongdoing."

The father who had two sons

11-12 And he said, "A certain man had two sons. | YTe
younger of them said to his father, 'Father, give
me that part of your property which will be mine.' And he
13 made division of his goods between them. | Not long after,
the younger son got together everything which was his
and took a journey into a distant country. There all his
money was spent in foolish living.

14 When everything was gone, there was no food to be had
15 in that country, and he was in need. | He went and put
himself into the hands of one of the people of that country,
who sent him into his fields to give the pigs their food.[1] |
16 So great was his need that he would have been glad to eat
17 the pigs' food, and no one gave him anything. | But when
he came to his senses, he said, 'What numbers of my
father's servants have bread enough, and more, while I am
18 near death here from starvation! | I will get up and go to my
father, and will say to him, Father, I have
done wrong, against heaven and in your
19 eyes: | I am no longer good enough to be
named your son. Make me like one of
your servants.'

20 And he got up and went to his father.
But while he was still far away, his father
saw him and was moved with mercy for
him and went quickly and took him in his

[1] A Jew could not imagine a more wretched fate than looking after pigs, which were unclean animals. Wanting to eat pig-fodder, and not being given any, was the ultimate in degradation.

Sin wounds the heart of God.
But, when I recognize my sin,
when I confess
what separates me from God,
with a deep desire to be rid of it,
God's heart is full of joy!
He forgives me,
and helps me to return to Him.

Recognizing one's sin
is not sad.
It's like a child
who cries out to his or her parent,
"I would have never made it without you.
Come and take me in your arms,
and carry me right up to the very end!"

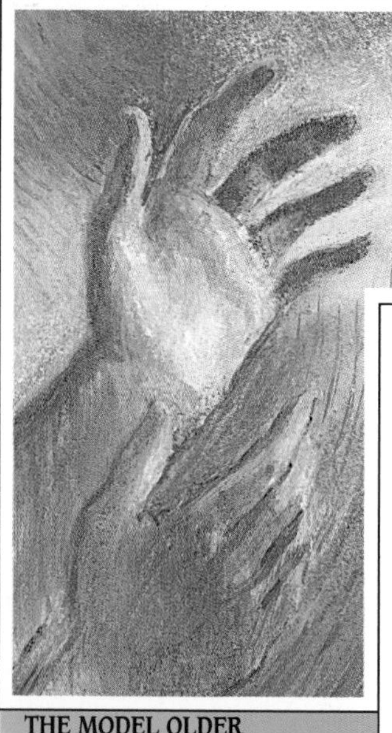

15 21 arms and gave him a kiss. | His son said to him, 'Father, I
have done wrong, against heaven and in your eyes: I am no
22 longer good enough to be named your son.' | But the father
said to his servants, 'Get out the first robe quickly, and put
it on him, and put a ring on his hand and shoes on his feet.
23 | Get the fat young ox and kill it, and let us have a feast, and
24 rejoice. | For my son, who was dead, is living again; he had
gone away from me, and has come back.' They were full of
joy.

25 Now the older son was in the field. When
he came near the house, the sounds of
26 music and dancing came to his ears. | And
he sent for one of the servants,
questioning him about what it might be. |
27 He said to him, 'Your brother has come;
and your father has had the young ox put
to death because he has returned safely.' |
28 But he was angry and would not go in. His
father came out and asked him to come in.
29 | But he replied, 'See, all these years I have
been your servant, doing your orders in
everything, yet you never gave me even a
young goat so that I might have a feast
30 with my friends. | But when your son
returned, who has been wasting your
property with bad women, you put to
31 death the fat young ox for him.' | He said
to him, 'Son, you are with me at all times,
32 and all I have is yours. | But it was right to
be glad and to have a feast, for your
brother, who was dead, is living again. He
had gone away and has come back.'"

THE MODEL OLDER BROTHER

The older brother was near-perfect, yet he did not love his father, or at least not enough. He thought his father was too soft with the younger brother and not very generous with himself, the faultless older son.

He was rather like the Scribes and Pharisees who criticized Jesus for hanging out with sinners. They were offended and jealous. They thought they were not being treated as they deserved. Jesus, they felt, should show them a bit more esteem, on account of their rectitude and virtue.

Jesus was unimpressed by this smug certainty of being righteous and virtuous. It was often a screen for looking down on others and acting mighty. A disciple's real virtue was to share in the mercifulness* of the Father.

A man had two grown sons.
It had been a long time
since he had had two children
who had thrown themselves
into his arms shouting "Abba".

The elder, hardworking, honest,
and a bit inflexible,
was always in the fields.

The younger one wanted to live his own life,
so he left home.
But, he realized
that he couldn't live
separated from his father.
Rediscovering his childlike heart,
he returned,
and threw himself
in his father's arms,
who gave him suitable clothes
and bread from his table.

The elder son, being sensible and honest,
remained frozen in his attitude.
He refused to accept his father's foolishness,
certain that he was right.
Not wanting to
"become like a child again,"
he could only stay
at the door of his father's house.

THE FRAUDULENT
MANAGER

You cannot doze off when istening to Jesus! His eachings always come as a olt. A teacher of religion night be expected to use virtuous characters as examples. Here Jesus tells the story of a dishonest and unlikable fellow, but one who is clever in his dealings. If the disciples* could put as much intelligence to work in serving the gospel, all would be perfect.

1 Along the same lines, Jesus, in Matthew 10:16, page 270, advised his disciples to be "as shrewd as snakes."

THE VIRTUES OF A DISCIPLE

Shrewdness

16 1 And another time he said to the disciples, "There
was a certain man of great wealth who had a
servant. It was said to him that this servant was wasting his
2 goods. | He sent for him and said, 'What is this which is said
about you? Give me an account of all you have done, for you
3 will no longer be the manager of my property.' | The servant
said to himself, 'What am I to do now that my lord takes
away my position? I have not enough strength for working
in the fields, and I would be shamed if I begged from people
4 in the streets. | I have come to a decision what to do, so that
when I am put out of my position they will take me into their
houses.'
5 Sending for every one who was in debt to his lord he said
to the first, 'What is the amount of your debt to my lord?'
6 | He said, 'A hundred measures of oil.' And he said, 'Take
7 your account immediately and put down fifty.' | Then he
said to another, 'What is the amount of your debt?' And he
said, 'A hundred measures of grain.' He said to him, 'Take
8 your account and put down eighty.' | His lord was pleased
with the false servant, because he had been wise; for the
sons of this world are wiser in relation to their generation
than the sons of light.[1]
9 I say to you, make friends for yourselves through the
wealth of this life, so that when it comes to an end, you
may be taken into the eternal resting places.
10 He who is faithful in a little, is faithful in much; he who
11 is deceitful in small things, is deceitful in great. | If, then,
you have not been faithful in your use of the wealth of this
life, who will trust you with true wealth?...

TRUE RICHES

Luke was very careful to quote Jesus' warnings on the subject of money. Jesus asked some of his disciples to sell everything they possessed (Luke 18:18-30, page 328).

Freely accepted poverty shows that true wealth is not material. To love God, to love one's neighbor, to receive the Word of God and to live one's life, that is what makes a person rich. This is why Jesus invited those of his disciples who held on to their property and money to use them in a tangible gesture of their love for their neighbors. They were asked to love not in words but in deeds — by sharing what they had, by providing work. Money was a servant that had its uses. Money as a master was always hateful.

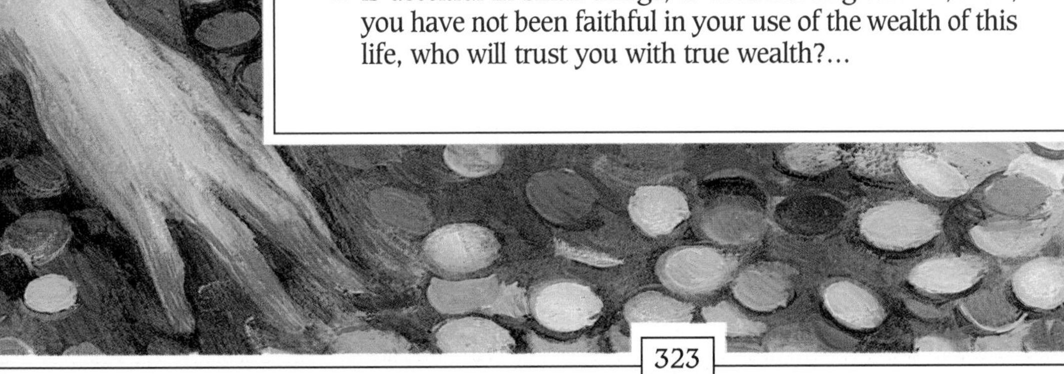

16 13 No man may be a servant to two masters, for he will hate
one and love the other. Or he will obey the one and have
no respect for the other. You may not be servants of God
and of wealth."

Noticing the poor

16 19 "Now there was a certain man of great wealth,
who was dressed in fine clothing of purple and
20 delicate linen, and was shining and glad every day. | A
certain poor man, named Lazarus, was stretched out at his
21 door, full of wounds, | desiring the scraps of food which
came from the table of the wealthy man. Even the dogs
came and licked his wounds.
22 And in time the poor man died, and angels took him to
Abraham's breast. The man of wealth came to his end, and
23 was buried. | In hell,[1] being in great pain, lifting up his eyes
he saw Abraham, far away, and Lazarus on his breast. |
24 And he gave a cry and said, 'Father Abraham, have mercy
on me and send Lazarus, so that he may put the end of his
finger in water and put it on my tongue, for I am cruelly
25 burning in this flame.' | But Abraham said, 'Remember, my
son, that when you were living, you had your good things,
while Lazarus had evil things: but now, he is comforted and
26 you are in pain. | In addition, there is a deep division fixed
between us and you, so that those who might go from here
to you are not able to do so, and no one may come from you
to us.'
27 He said, 'Father, it is my request that you will send him to
28 my father's house, | for I have five brothers. Let him give
them an account of these things, so that they may not come
29 to this place of pain.' | But Abraham said, 'They have Moses

[1] Jesus geared his language to the mentality of his listeners. He described the abode of the dead, sheol*, in terms that were common to the thinking of the time. While awaiting resurrection, the dead were divided into two groups. The righteous were assembled around Abraham in a sort of oasis, while the sinners were parched with thirst in a burning desert. Not all these sinners were obstinate in their rejection of God. Was not the rich man on the path to conversion?

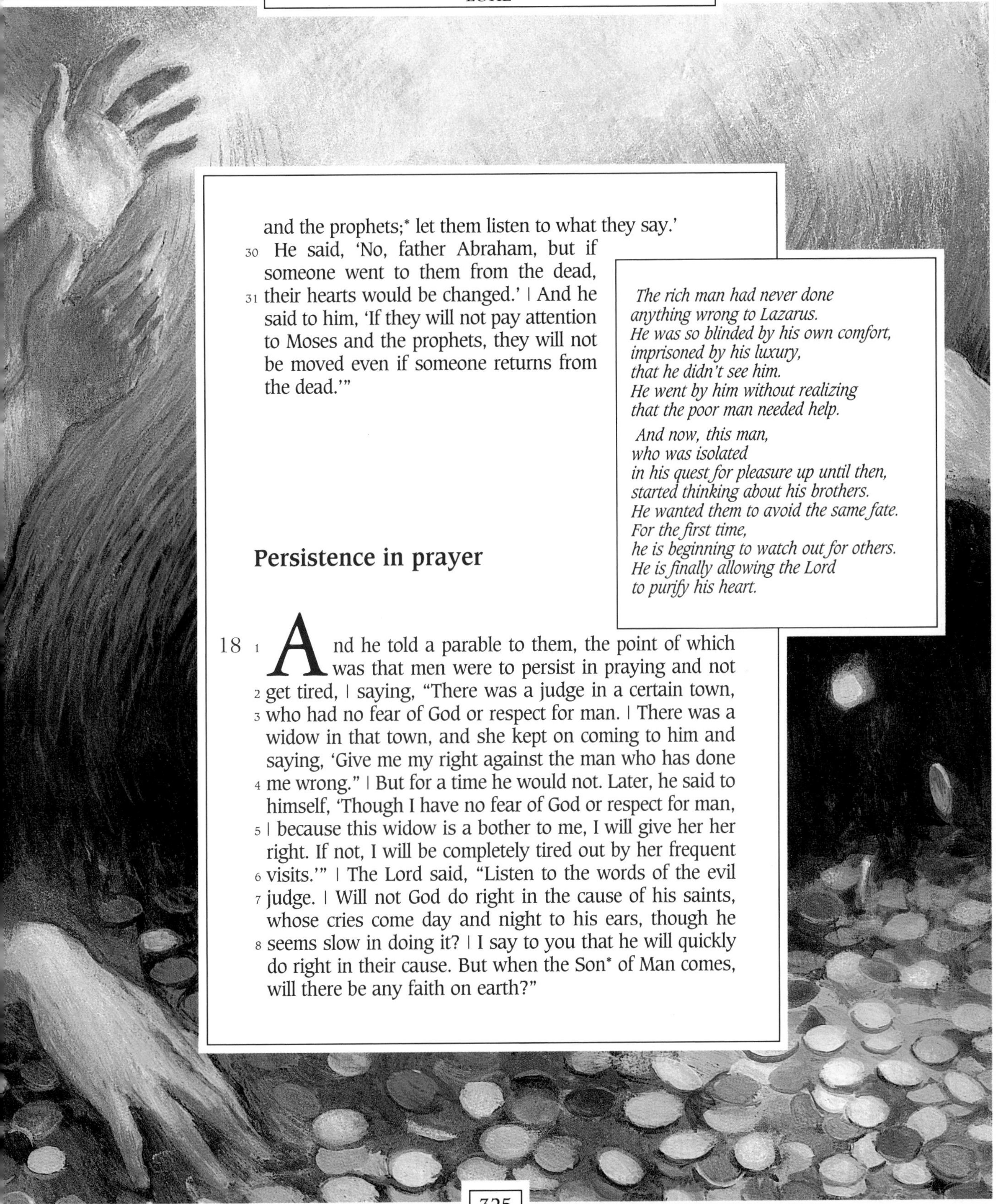

and the prophets;* let them listen to what they say.'
30 He said, 'No, father Abraham, but if
someone went to them from the dead,
31 their hearts would be changed.' | And he
said to him, 'If they will not pay attention
to Moses and the prophets, they will not
be moved even if someone returns from
the dead.'"

*The rich man had never done
anything wrong to Lazarus.
He was so blinded by his own comfort,
imprisoned by his luxury,
that he didn't see him.
He went by him without realizing
that the poor man needed help.*

*And now, this man,
who was isolated
in his quest for pleasure up until then,
started thinking about his brothers.
He wanted them to avoid the same fate.
For the first time,
he is beginning to watch out for others.
He is finally allowing the Lord
to purify his heart.*

Persistence in prayer

18 1 And he told a parable to them, the point of which
was that men were to persist in praying and not
2 get tired, | saying, "There was a judge in a certain town,
3 who had no fear of God or respect for man. | There was a
widow in that town, and she kept on coming to him and
saying, 'Give me my right against the man who has done
4 me wrong." | But for a time he would not. Later, he said to
himself, 'Though I have no fear of God or respect for man,
5 | because this widow is a bother to me, I will give her her
right. If not, I will be completely tired out by her frequent
6 visits.'" | The Lord said, "Listen to the words of the evil
7 judge. | Will not God do right in the cause of his saints,
whose cries come day and night to his ears, though he
8 seems slow in doing it? | I say to you that he will quickly
do right in their cause. But when the Son* of Man comes,
will there be any faith on earth?"

THE PARABLES OF JESUS

1. The murderous vineyard workers (Mark 12:1-12, page 250).

2. The good Samaritan (Luke 10:30-37, page 317).

3. The sower (Matthew 13:1-23, page 274).

4. The lost sheep (Luke 15:3-7, page 320).

5. The house built on rock and the house built on sand (Matthew 7:24-27, page 266).

6. "You know how to interpret the appearance of the sky, but you cannot interpret the signs of the times" (see Matthew 16:2-3).

7. The net (Matthew 13:47-50, page 277).

8. The barren fig-tree (Luke 13:6-9, page 319).

9. Solomon in all his glory was not dressed like one of these lilies of the field (see Luke 12:27).

10. The treasure found and reburied (Matthew 13:44, page 277).

11. "If anyone is thirsty, let him come to me" (John 7:37-39, page 346).

12. The sheep lifted out of a hole on the Sabbath (Matthew 12:11-12, page 272).

13. The guests who refuse to attend the wedding feast are replaced by people off the streets (Matthew 22:1-10, page 288).

14. The wise maiden keeps oil for her lamp, the foolish one has none left (Matthew 25:1-13, page 291).

15. *The wedding guests cannot mourn while the bridegroom is with them (Matthew 9:15, page 268).*

16. *Do not take the place of honor (see Luke 14:7-11).*

17. *The kingdom of heaven is like a king who prepared a wedding feast (Matthew 22:2, page 288).*

18. *"We played the flute for you and you did not dance" (Luke 7:32, page 312).*

19. *The workers of the eleventh hour (Matthew 20:1-15, page 286).*

20. *"Why do you look at the speck of sawdust in your brother's eye and pay no attention to the plank in your own eye?" (Luke 6:41-42).*

21. *The narrow gate (Matthew 7:13-14, page 265).*

22. *The yeast in the dough (Matthew 13:33, page 276).*

23. *Two women will be grinding grain together; one will be taken, the other left (see Luke 17-35).*

24. *You know how to give good gifts to your children (Luke 11:11-13, page 319).*

25. *New wine will burst the old wineskins (Matthew 9:17, page 269).*

26. *The vine branches that bear no fruit are cut off (John 15:1-8, page 358).*

27. *The lamp on the lamp-stand (Matthew 5:15, page 261).*

28. *The tiny seed grows into a large tree (Matthew 13:31-32, page 276).*

29. *The lost silver coin (Luke 15:8-10, page 320).*

30. *The father who had two sons (Luke 15:11-32, page 321).*

ONE-SIDED PRAYER

The Pharisee did not really pray. He did not listen to God (see Luke 10:39, page 318)**. He listened only to himself and took it for granted that God agreed. The Pharisee was a virtuous man, but his virtuousness went to his head. He felt he was a superior being, and expected God to recognize this and congratulate him for it. His God was a dispenser of rewards, not a partner in building a life, nor a friend on whom to lean.**

Humility

18 9 And he told this parable to some people who were
certain that they were good, and had a low opinion
10 of others: | "Two men went up to the Temple for prayer; one
11 a Pharisee,* and the other a tax collector.* | The Pharisee,
positioning himself to pray, said to himself: 'God, I give you
praise because I am not like other men,
who take more than they deserve, who are
sinners, who are unfaithful to their wives,
12 or even like this tax collector. | Twice in the
week I fast; I give a tenth of all I have.' |
13 The tax collector, on the other hand,
staying at a distance, and not lifting up
even his eyes to Heaven, grieved, saying,
14 'God, have mercy on me, a sinner.' | I say
to you, this man went back to his house
with God's approval, and not the other, for
everyone who exalts himself will be
humbled and whoever humbles himself
will be exalted."[1]

"Have pity on me, a sinner."

I love you, Lord,
and I want to follow you closer.
But, I always
let myself be trapped
by my jealousy and vanity.
All of my beautiful resolutions melt away!
But, I am before you once again,
Lord, filled with confidence.
I need your forgiveness.
Inspire me with resolutions
that I can keep!
I cannot be righteous without you.
Justify me!

[1] This sentence is also in Matthew 23:12, page 291. The same idea may be found in the hymn of Mary (Luke 1:52, page 301).

JESUS SEES THE HEART,
NOT OUTWARD APPEARANCES

A man trapped in his possessions

18 18 And a certain ruler questioned him, saying,
"Good Master, what must I do so that I may have
19 eternal life?" | Jesus said to him, "Why do you say that I
20 am good? No one is good, but only God. | You have

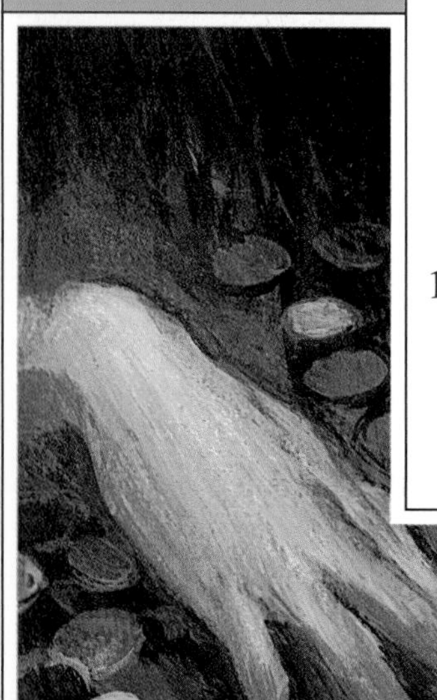

THE MONEYED MAN

This man really talked like a magnate. He had more than he needed in this life, and wanted to inherit eternal life as well. Jesus replied in the same terms. He asked him to make a choice. The riches he had stood in the way of his acquiring the treasure stored up for him by God. Was he ready to surrender what he could see and touch for something immaterial?

The man could not bring himself to do it. Despite his fine words, he had too little faith*. He preferred to keep what he had. His heart was not free. His master was money. Unless he threw off this master, he could not become a disciple* of Jesus.

knowledge of what the law says: *Do not be unfaithful to*
your wife. Do not murder. Do not steal, Do not lie. Give
21 *honor to your father and mother.*"[1] | And he said, "All
these things I have done from the time when I was a boy."
22 | Jesus, hearing it, said to him, "One thing you still have
need of. Sell your possessions, and give them to the poor,
23 as you will have wealth in heaven. Then follow me." | But
at these words he became very sad, for he had great
wealth.
24 And Jesus, looking at him, said, "How hard it is for the
25 wealthy to enter the Kingdom of God! | It is simpler for a
camel to go through the eye of a needle, than for a man
who has much money to enter the Kingdom of God." |
26 Those who were present said, "Then who may have
27 salvation?"[2] | But he said, "Things which are not possible
with man are possible with God."
28 Peter said, "Look, we have given up what is ours to
29 follow you." | He said to them, "Truly I say to you, there is
no man who has given up house or wife or brothers or
father or mother or children, because of the Kingdom of
30 God, | who will not get much more in this time, and in the
world to come, eternal life."

[1] A free paraphrase of some of the Ten Commandments (see Exodus, 20:12-17, page 71).

[2] Jesus' audience still held some antiquated ideas, despite the hammering these ideas had taken in the Book of Job (see pages 194 to 197). They thought that wealth was a sign of God's blessing. They were astonished to hear Jesus teach that it was a barrier between people and God (see page 323).

Zacchaeus, the tree-climbing official

19 1 And he entered Jericho, and when he was going
2 through it, | a man, named Zacchaeus, who was
3 the chief tax collector, and a man of wealth, | made an
attempt to see Jesus. He was not able to do so, because of

19 4 the people, for he was a small man. | He went quickly in
front of them and climbed into a tree to see him, for he was
5 going that way. | When Jesus came to the
place, looking up, he said to him,
"Zacchaeus, be quick and come down,
for I am coming to your house today." |
6 So he came down quickly, and took him
into his house, rejoicing.
7 When they saw it, they were all angry,
saying, "He has gone into the house of a
8 sinner." | And Zacchaeus, waiting before
him, said to the Lord, "See, Lord, half of
my possessions I give to the poor, and if
I have taken anything from anyone
wrongly, I give him back four times as
9 much." | Jesus said to him, "Today
salvation has come to this house, for
10 even he is a son of Abraham. | For the
Son of Man came for those who are lost
from the way, and to be their Savior."

Zacchaeus, your coffers are full,
but you are unhappy.
Couldn't the prophet from Nazareth
help you find
what you are missing?

You, the chief tax collector,
climbed up a tree,
like a child, to see him.
If he inspires confidence in you,
perhaps, you will go and question
him at night,
like Nicodemus.

But, he saw you first.
He suggested going to your house.
Now, you understand
what you are lacking:
his friendship.

The poor woman's amazing generosity

21 1 And looking up, he saw the wealthy men putting
2 their offerings* in the Temple treasury.[1] | And he
3 saw a certain poor widow putting in two small coins. | He
said, "Truly I say to you, this poor widow has given more
4 than all of them. | Tthey gave out of their wealth, having
more than enough for themselves: but she, even out of her
need, has put in all that she has."

[1] The funds placed in the box went towards the upkeep of the Temple and Herod the Great's extension works.

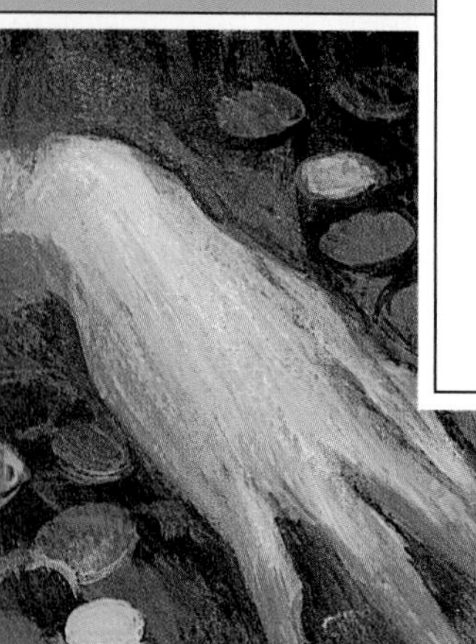

The Gospel of Luke continues with the accounts of the Passion and Resurrection of Jesus, page 363.

IV THE GOSPEL ACCORDING TO JOHN

Who was John?

Early Christian writers, such as Irenaeus of Lyons and Cyrillus of Alexandria, attributed the fourth Gospel to the apostle John and his disciples, living in Ephesus at the end of the 1st century AD.

The general opinion is that the author is the one who identified himself as "the disciple Jesus loved."[1] This self-effacing,[2] contemplative disciple was rather different from the John "son of thunder"[3] described in the other Gospels. Modern scholars surmise that the author of the fourth Gospel could be another disciple, also named John. He was probably of Judean, not Galilean, origin and familiar with the priestly community, since he knew the high priest.[4]

What is certain is that John, traditionally known as the "theologian," was the Evangelist who best explained the incarnation of the son of God. According to John, Jesus strongly asserted his divinity by using the expression "I AM" — the transcription of the name of God revealed to Moses[5] — on several occasions. Jesus had been made man to wrest humankind from the power of the "prince of this world."[6] Jesus proved his love for his Father by suffering crucifixion. All who believed in him would be reborn to eternal life over which death* would have no more power.*

Because of the keenness of his vision, John is symbolically represented by an eagle.[7]

[1] See page 387.

[2] In verse 20:5, for example, John reached the tomb first but stepped aside to let Peter go ahead of him. See page 387.

[3] See Mark 10:35-40, page 248, and Luke 9:49-56, page 315.

[4] John 18:15, page 371.

[5] See Exodus 3:14, page 58, John 8:58, page 349, and John 18:5-8, page 371.

[6] Title given by John to Satan.*

[7] See page 502, "Symbols of the Four Evangelists".

For whom did John write his Gospel?

John was writing for the Christians in Ephesus and neighboring congregations. These communities were torn by two disputes:

- One between the disciples of John the Baptist and the disciples of Jesus. The former held that their master was greater than Jesus. Had not John baptized Jesus? For some, this was proof that John had authority over Jesus.

Matthew and Luke had already made reference to this dispute.[1] *John wrote in no uncertain terms that John the Baptist paid homage to Jesus.*[2]

- There was another conflict between Jewish converts to Christianity and Jewish leaders. From 80-90 AD, Jews who acknowledged Jesus as the Messiah promised in the Scriptures were barred from the synagogues.[3]

There is evidence in the Gospel according to John of contacts with the Samaritans and the Essenes.**

[1] See Matthew 3:15, page 258, and "Gospel of the Childhood," page 298.

[2] See John 1:15, page 334.

[3] See John 9:22, page 350.

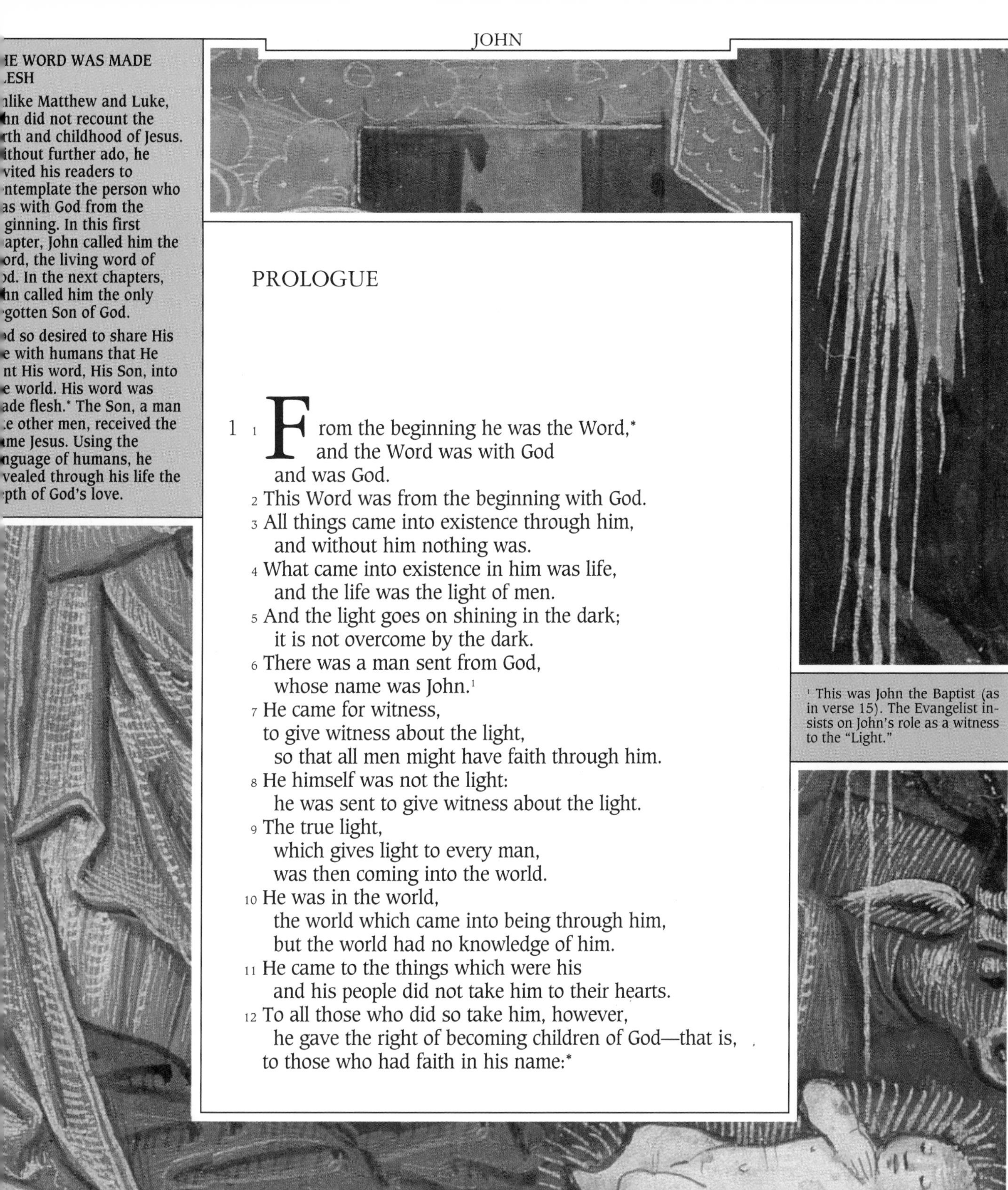

IE WORD WAS MADE
.ESH

ılike Matthew and Luke, hn did not recount the rth and childhood of Jesus. ithout further ado, he vited his readers to ntemplate the person who as with God from the ginning. In this first apter, John called him the ord, the living word of od. In the next chapters, hn called him the only gotten Son of God.

d so desired to share His e with humans that He nt His word, His Son, into e world. His word was ade flesh.* The Son, a man e other men, received the me Jesus. Using the nguage of humans, he vealed through his life the pth of God's love.

PROLOGUE

1 1 From the beginning he was the Word,*
and the Word was with God
and was God.
2 This Word was from the beginning with God.
3 All things came into existence through him,
and without him nothing was.
4 What came into existence in him was life,
and the life was the light of men.
5 And the light goes on shining in the dark;
it is not overcome by the dark.
6 There was a man sent from God,
whose name was John.[1]
7 He came for witness,
to give witness about the light,
so that all men might have faith through him.
8 He himself was not the light:
he was sent to give witness about the light.
9 The true light,
which gives light to every man,
was then coming into the world.
10 He was in the world,
the world which came into being through him,
but the world had no knowledge of him.
11 He came to the things which were his
and his people did not take him to their hearts.
12 To all those who did so take him, however,
he gave the right of becoming children of God—that is,
to those who had faith in his name:*

[1] This was John the Baptist (as in verse 15). The Evangelist insists on John's role as a witness to the "Light."

1 13 Whose birth was from God[1]
and not from blood,
or from an impulse
of the flesh and man's desire.
14 And so the Word became flesh
and took a place[2] among us for a time;
we saw his glory—
such glory as is given to an only son
by his father—
saw it to be true and full of grace.
15 John gave witness about him, crying, "This is he of whom
I said, 'He who is coming after me is greater than me
because he was in existence before me.'"[3]...

18 No man has seen God at any time; the only Son, who is at
the Father's side, has made him known.[4]*

Jesus, only you know the Father.
You have always been with Him.
You guide us to Him.
You show us His love.
You help us to know Him
not only with our minds,
but with all of the love that is in our hearts.

THE ONE SPOKEN OF IN THE SCRIPTURES

Jesus, Jacob's ladder

John revealed to his readers that Jesus stayed for some time in the company of John the Baptist. He met his first disciples among the prophet's followers. At the behest of John the Baptist himself, Andrew and the other unnamed disciple left their master to follow Jesus.

1 35 The day after, John was there again with two of his
36 disciples. | Looking at Jesus while he was walking
37 he said, "See, there is the Lamb* of God!" | Hearing what
38 he said, the two disciples followed Jesus. | And Jesus,
turning round, saw them coming after him and said to

[1] The apostle Peter, in his second Epistle, wrote plainly that God wishes to us "to participate in the divine nature" (2 Peter 1:4).

[2] John used a Greek verb whose exact meaning was "pitched his tent" among us. He implied that the tent* in the desert and even the Temple* in Jerusalem no longer enabled us to meet with God. Jesus was the true presence of God among mankind (see John 2:19-21, page 337).

[3] See Mark 1:7, page 236. "He who comes after me" described the disciple* who follows behind his teacher. For a while, Jesus gave the impression of being a follower of John the Baptist. In reality, he was much greater than John the Baptist because he was there "before" him.

[4] See Luke 10:22, page 316.

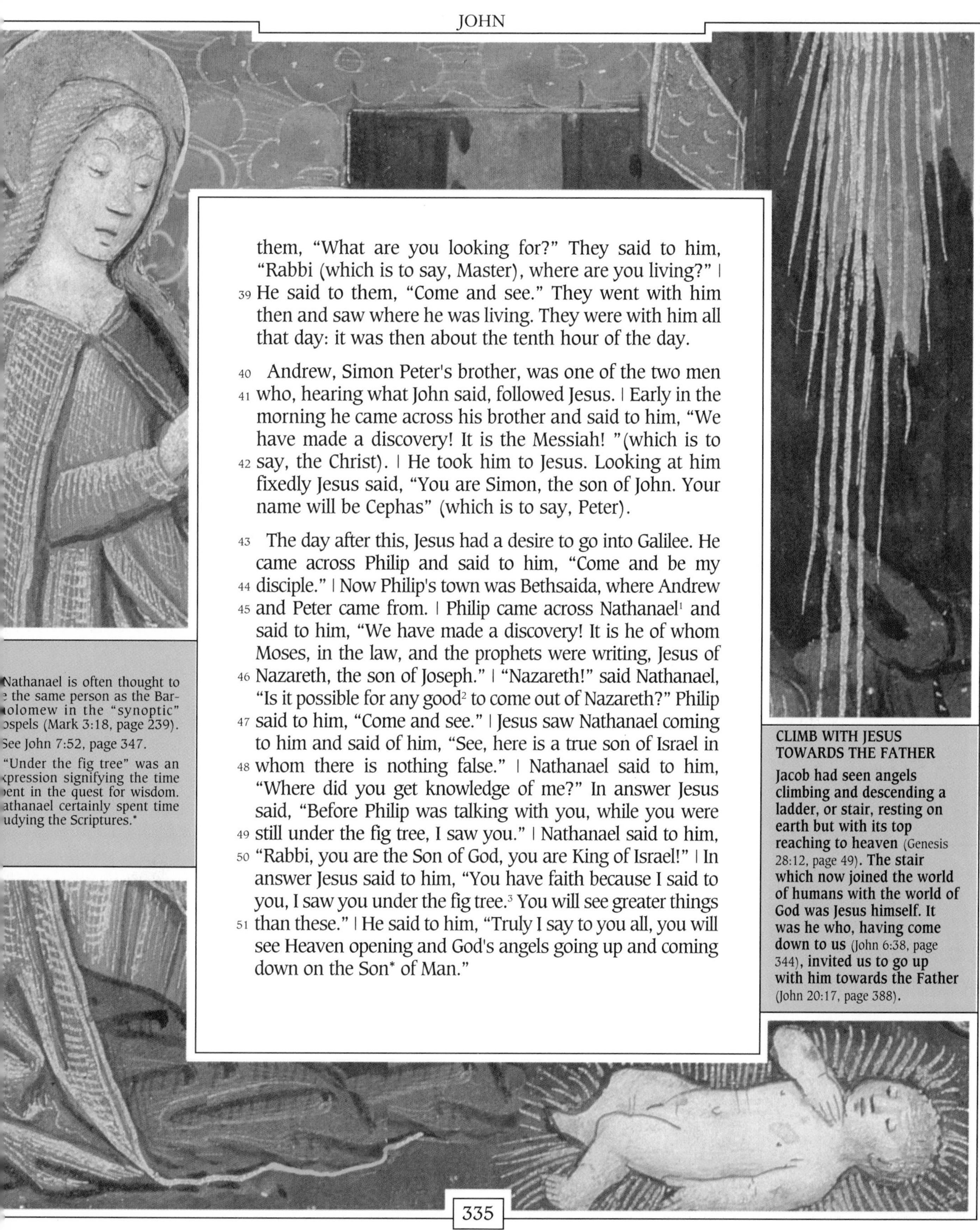

them, "What are you looking for?" They said to him,
"Rabbi (which is to say, Master), where are you living?" |
39 He said to them, "Come and see." They went with him
then and saw where he was living. They were with him all
that day: it was then about the tenth hour of the day.

40 Andrew, Simon Peter's brother, was one of the two men
41 who, hearing what John said, followed Jesus. | Early in the
morning he came across his brother and said to him, "We
have made a discovery! It is the Messiah! "(which is to
42 say, the Christ). | He took him to Jesus. Looking at him
fixedly Jesus said, "You are Simon, the son of John. Your
name will be Cephas" (which is to say, Peter).

43 The day after this, Jesus had a desire to go into Galilee. He
came across Philip and said to him, "Come and be my
44 disciple." | Now Philip's town was Bethsaida, where Andrew
45 and Peter came from. | Philip came across Nathanael[1] and
said to him, "We have made a discovery! It is he of whom
Moses, in the law, and the prophets were writing, Jesus of
46 Nazareth, the son of Joseph." | "Nazareth!" said Nathanael,
"Is it possible for any good[2] to come out of Nazareth?" Philip
47 said to him, "Come and see." | Jesus saw Nathanael coming
to him and said of him, "See, here is a true son of Israel in
48 whom there is nothing false." | Nathanael said to him,
"Where did you get knowledge of me?" In answer Jesus
said, "Before Philip was talking with you, while you were
49 still under the fig tree, I saw you." | Nathanael said to him,
50 "Rabbi, you are the Son of God, you are King of Israel!" | In
answer Jesus said to him, "You have faith because I said to
you, I saw you under the fig tree.[3] You will see greater things
51 than these." | He said to him, "Truly I say to you all, you will
see Heaven opening and God's angels going up and coming
down on the Son* of Man."

Nathanael is often thought to
e the same person as the Bar-
olomew in the "synoptic"
ospels (Mark 3:18, page 239).

See John 7:52, page 347.

"Under the fig tree" was an
xpression signifying the time
ent in the quest for wisdom.
athanael certainly spent time
udying the Scriptures.*

CLIMB WITH JESUS TOWARDS THE FATHER

Jacob had seen angels climbing and descending a ladder, or stair, resting on earth but with its top reaching to heaven (Genesis 28:12, page 49). **The stair which now joined the world of humans with the world of God was Jesus himself. It was he who, having come down to us** (John 6:38, page 344), **invited us to go up with him towards the Father** (John 20:17, page 388).

GOD'S NUPTIALS

The prophet Hosea had said that God loved His people as a husband loves his wife (Hosea 2:16-22, page 132). Jesus, by supplying the wine for the wedding in Cana, was showing that he was the God-Husband. As verse 10 makes clear, it was the bridegroom's job to provide the wine for a wedding. Jesus supplied a large quantity of very fine wine. It was a sign that his Covenant with mankind would supply them with an abundance of joy. But this sign remained confidential and known to a few intimates only.

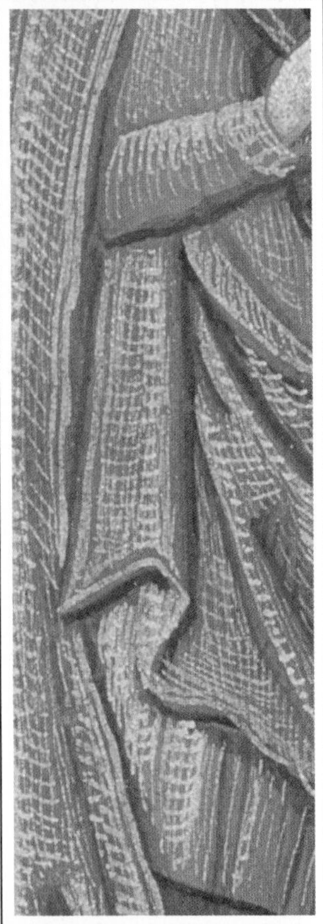

Jesus, bridegroom

2 1 On the third day two people were going to be
married at Cana in Galilee. The mother of Jesus
2 was there, | and Jesus with his disciples came as guests.
3 When they ran out of wine, the mother of Jesus said to
4 him, "They have no wine." | Jesus said to her, "Woman,
5 this is not your business. My time[1] is still to come." | His
mother said to the servants, "Whatever he says to you, do
6 it." | Now six stone pots, each holding twenty to thirty
gallons of water, were placed there for ceremonial
7 washing,[2] as is the custom of the Jews. | Jesus said to the
servants, "Make the pots full of water." And they made
8 them full to the top. | Then he said to them, "Now take
some, and give it to the master of the feast." So they took
9 it to him. | After tasting the water which had now become
wine, the master of the feast (having no idea where it
came from, though it was clear to the servants who took
10 the water out) sent for the bridegroom, | saying, "Every
man first serves his best wine and when all have had
enough he puts out what is not so good, but you have
kept the good wine till now."
11 This, the first of his signs,* Jesus did at Cana in Galilee
and let his glory* be seen openly. His disciples put their
12 faith in him. | After this he went down to Capernaum, with
his mother, his brothers, and his disciples, and they were
there not more than two or three days.

Jesus, a new Temple

2 13 The time of the Passover* of the Jews was near and
14 Jesus went up to Jerusalem. | There in the Temple*
he saw men trading in oxen and sheep and doves, and he

THE HOUR WAS NOT YET COME

The hour for loudly making known God's "betrothal" wit[h] His people had not yet come. The people were unready. Th[ey] were not yet pure enough to live fully in a Covenant with God. They observed all sorts [of] purification rituals but knew that they could not achieve self-purification. Jesus, by changing the water in the ceremonial washing jars into wine, gave a presage of how [he] would purify the people. The wine in Cana was a foretaste [of] the wine of the last supper, about which he would say, "This is my blood, shed for th[e] remission of sins." The wedding with God could be celebrated after Jesus, by loving to the point of dying o[n] the cross, had washed his people of all their impurities. That was the hour for which he had come (see John 12:23, page 357).

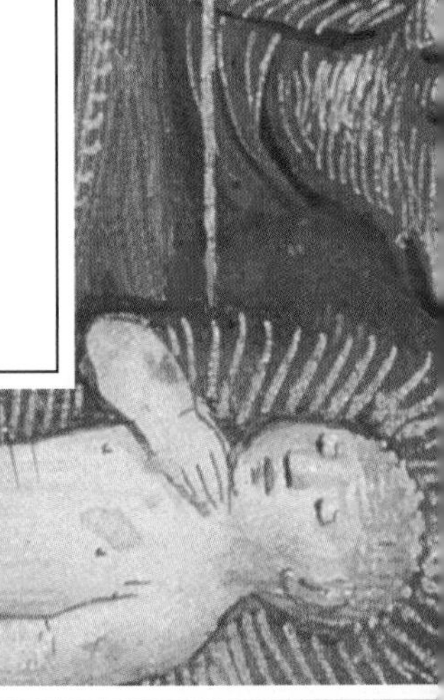

[1] This verse forms a close parallel with the account of Jesus' death, which John called his "hour" (John 12:23, page 357). A second element was the presence of the mother of Jesus, whom he addressed in the same way as "Woman" (John 19:26, page 379).

[2] The jars were used in purification rites.* See Ezekiel 36:25, page 165, and Mark 7:1-4, page 244. See also "pure."*

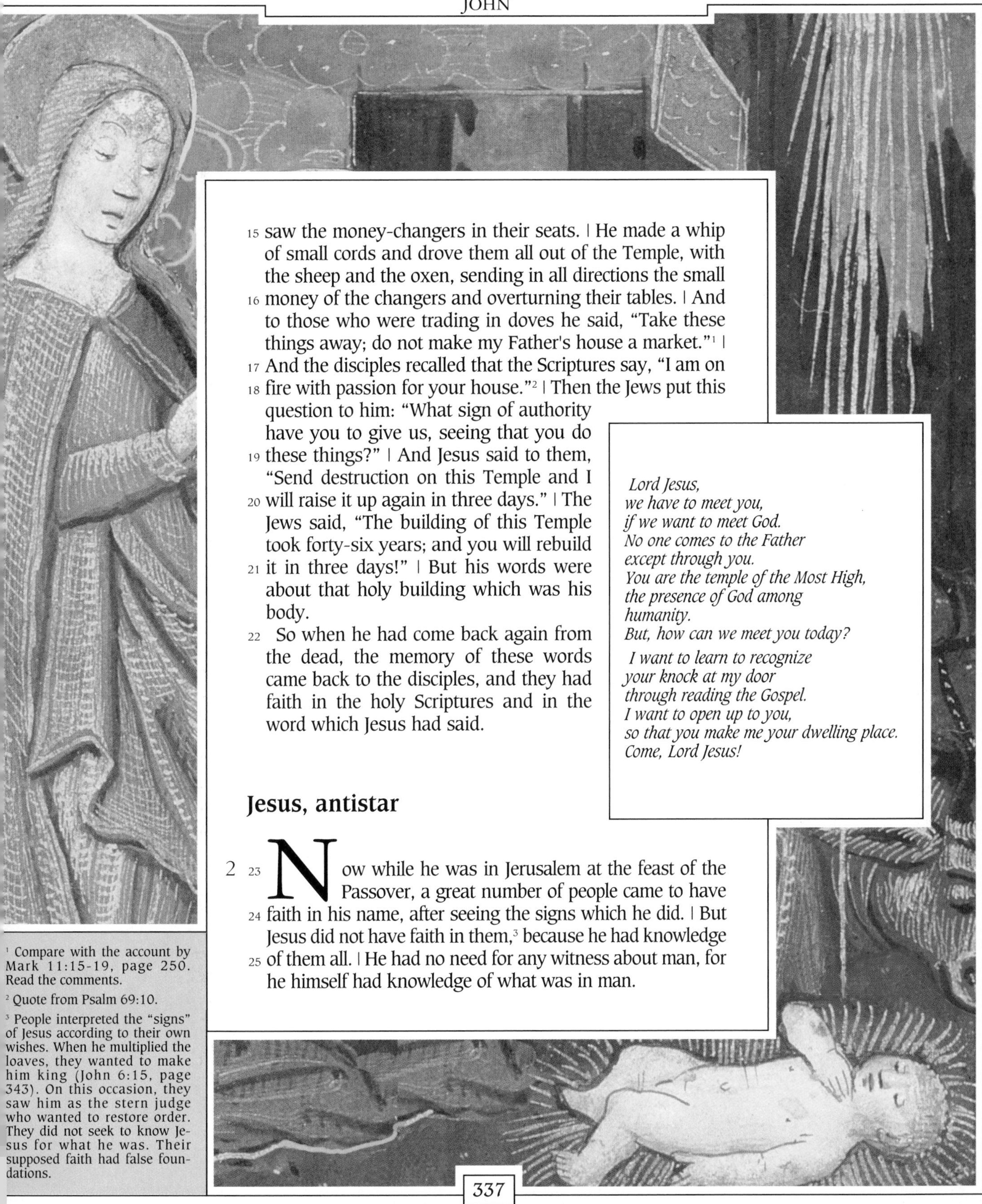

15 saw the money-changers in their seats. | He made a whip
of small cords and drove them all out of the Temple, with
the sheep and the oxen, sending in all directions the small
16 money of the changers and overturning their tables. | And
to those who were trading in doves he said, "Take these
things away; do not make my Father's house a market."[1] |
17 And the disciples recalled that the Scriptures say, "I am on
18 fire with passion for your house."[2] | Then the Jews put this
question to him: "What sign of authority
have you to give us, seeing that you do
19 these things?" | And Jesus said to them,
"Send destruction on this Temple and I
20 will raise it up again in three days." | The
Jews said, "The building of this Temple
took forty-six years; and you will rebuild
21 it in three days!" | But his words were
about that holy building which was his
body.
22 So when he had come back again from
the dead, the memory of these words
came back to the disciples, and they had
faith in the holy Scriptures and in the
word which Jesus had said.

Lord Jesus,
we have to meet you,
if we want to meet God.
No one comes to the Father
except through you.
You are the temple of the Most High,
the presence of God among
humanity.
But, how can we meet you today?

I want to learn to recognize
your knock at my door
through reading the Gospel.
I want to open up to you,
so that you make me your dwelling place.
Come, Lord Jesus!

Jesus, antistar

2 23 Now while he was in Jerusalem at the feast of the
Passover, a great number of people came to have
24 faith in his name, after seeing the signs which he did. | But
Jesus did not have faith in them,[3] because he had knowledge
25 of them all. | He had no need for any witness about man, for
he himself had knowledge of what was in man.

[1] Compare with the account by Mark 11:15-19, page 250. Read the comments.

[2] Quote from Psalm 69:10.

[3] People interpreted the "signs" of Jesus according to their own wishes. When he multiplied the loaves, they wanted to make him king (John 6:15, page 343). On this occasion, they saw him as the stern judge who wanted to restore order. They did not seek to know Jesus for what he was. Their supposed faith had false foundations.

TO BE BORN AGAIN FROM WATER AND THE SPIRIT

Jesus, only son with a child's heart

3 1 Now there was among the Pharisees a man named
Nicodemus, who was one of the rulers of the Jews.
2 | He visited Jesus at night[1] and said to him, "Rabbi,[2] we are
certain that you have come from God as a teacher, because
no man would be able to do these signs* which you do if God
3 was not with him." | Jesus said to him, "Truly, I say to you,
unless a man be born again he is not able to see the
4 Kingdom of God." | Nicodemus said to him, "How is it
possible for a man to be given birth when he is old?"...

5 Jesus replied, "Truly, I say to you, if a man's birth is not
from water as well as the Spirit, it is not possible for him to
6 enter the Kingdom of God. | That which has birth from the
flesh is flesh, and that which has birth from the Spirit is
7 spirit. | Do not be surprised that I say to you, 'It is necessary
8 for you to have a second birth.' | The wind goes where its
pleasure takes it, and the sound of it comes to your ears, but
you are unable to say where it comes from and where it
goes: so it is with everyone whose birth is from the Spirit....

14 As the snake* was lifted up by Moses in the desert,[3] even
15 so it is necessary for the Son of Man to be lifted up: | So that
whoever has faith may have in him eternal life.

16 For God had such love for the world that he gave his only
Son, so that whoever has faith in him may not never die but
17 have eternal life. | God did not send his Son into the world
to judge the world; he sent him so that the world might have
18 salvation through him. | The man who has faith in him is not
judged,* but he who has no faith in him has been judged
already, because he has no faith in the name of the only Son

[1] Nicodemus was still afraid of his movements being observed (see verses 19-21) but, gradually, he conquered his fear (John 7:50-52, page 347). On the day of the crucifixion, he would show his love for Jesus in broad daylight (John 19:39, page 384).

[2] A Hebrew term of respect, meaning "Teacher."

[3] The Book of Numbers* (21:4-9) told of the people being attacked by snakes in the desert. Moses had a pole put up with a bronze serpent on it. The lives of those who had been bitten were saved if they looked up at the bronze snake.

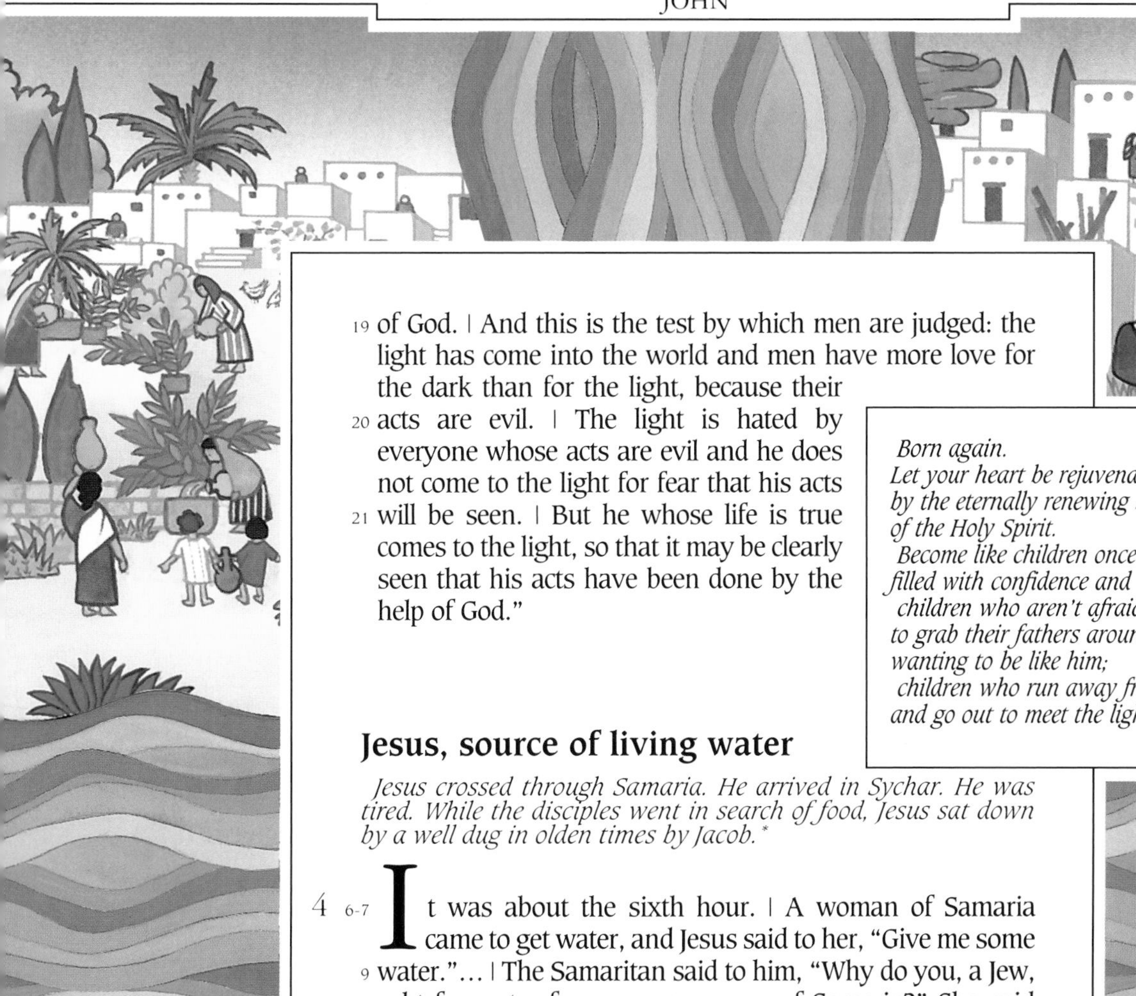

19 of God. | And this is the test by which men are judged: the
light has come into the world and men have more love for
the dark than for the light, because their
20 acts are evil. | The light is hated by
everyone whose acts are evil and he does
not come to the light for fear that his acts
21 will be seen. | But he whose life is true
comes to the light, so that it may be clearly
seen that his acts have been done by the
help of God."

Born again.
Let your heart be rejuvenated
by the eternally renewing breath
of the Holy Spirit.
Become like children once again,
filled with confidence and receptiveness:
children who aren't afraid
to grab their fathers around the neck,
wanting to be like him;
children who run away from the night,
and go out to meet the light!

Jesus, source of living water

*Jesus crossed through Samaria. He arrived in Sychar. He was tired. While the disciples went in search of food, Jesus sat down by a well dug in olden times by Jacob.**

4 6-7 It was about the sixth hour. | A woman of Samaria
came to get water, and Jesus said to her, "Give me some
9 water."... | The Samaritan said to him, "Why do you, a Jew,
askt for water from me, a woman of Samaria?" She said
this because Jews have nothing to do with the people of
10 Samaria. | In answer Jesus said, "If you had knowledge of
what God gives freely and who it is who says to you, 'Give
me water,' you would pray to him, and he would give you
11 living water."[1] | The woman said to him, "Sir, you have no
jar and the fountain is deep. From where will you get the
12 living water? | Are you greater than our father Jacob who
gave us the fountain and took the water of it himself, with
13 his children and his cattle?" | Jesus said to her, "Everyone
14 who takes this water will be thirsty again. | But whoever
takes the water I give him will never be thirsty again. The
water I give him will become in him a fountain of eternal

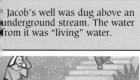

* Jacob's well was dug above an underground stream. The water from it was "living" water.

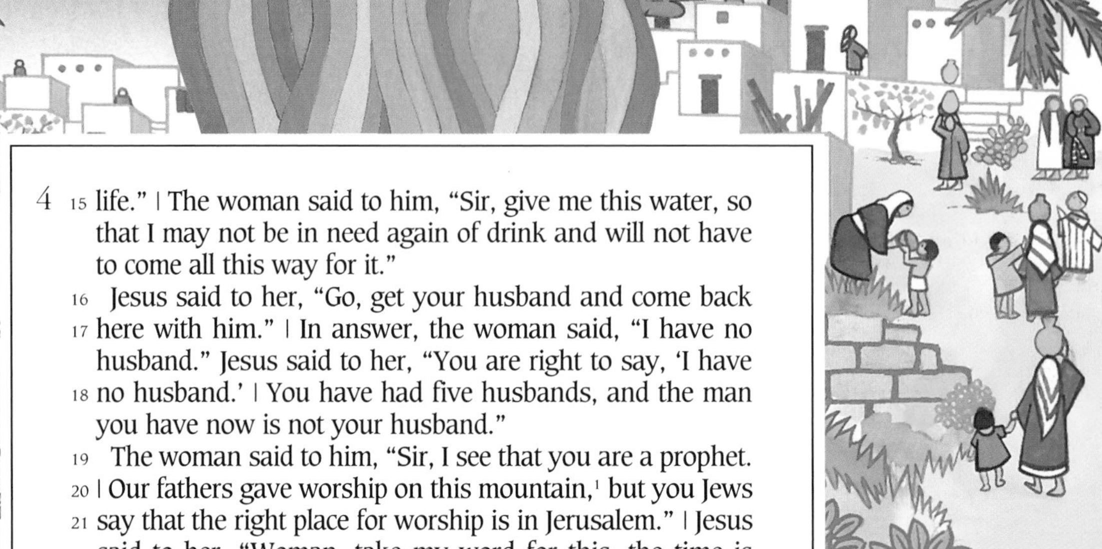

4 15 life." | The woman said to him, "Sir, give me this water, so
that I may not be in need again of drink and will not have
to come all this way for it."
16 Jesus said to her, "Go, get your husband and come back
17 here with him." | In answer, the woman said, "I have no
husband." Jesus said to her, "You are right to say, 'I have
18 no husband.' | You have had five husbands, and the man
you have now is not your husband."
19 The woman said to him, "Sir, I see that you are a prophet.
20 | Our fathers gave worship on this mountain,[1] but you Jews
21 say that the right place for worship is in Jerusalem." | Jesus
said to her, "Woman, take my word for this; the time is
coming when you will not worship the Father on this
23 mountain or in Jerusalem.... | But the time is coming, and
is already here, when the true worshippers will worship the
Father in the true way of the spirit, for
these are the worshippers desired by the
24 Father. | God is Spirit: then let his
worshippers worship him in the true way
25 of the Spirit." | The woman said to him, "I
am certain that the Messiah,* who is
named Christ, is coming. When he comes
26 he will reveal all things to us." | Jesus said
to her, "I, who speaks to you, am he."
27 At that point the disciples came back,
and they were surprised to see him
28 talking to a woman.... | Then the woman
put down her water jar and went into the
29 town, saying to the people, | "Come and
see a man who told me everything I ever
30 did! Is it possible that this is the Christ?" | So they left the
town to see him.

[1] This was Mount Garizim which overlooked the well. The Samaritans had built a temple on the mountain.

Lord, the first person to whom you revealed that you were the Messiah was that morally questionable Samaritan foreigner.
A dropout.
Apparently,
nothing justified such a choice.
But with great skill,
she made others want to meet you.
She stayed in the background,
so that others could drink
from the living waters of your Word.

Thank you, Lord, for trusting those we would never think of.

OKING FOR LOST SHEEP

us, like a shepherd (see
e 15:3-7, page 320, and John
1-18, page 352), **was
ays willing to go after
sheep in the oddest
ces.**

**e pool of Bethesda was in
likelihood a shrine of
gan origin. Sick people
nt there to be cured by its
gic powers. The first
son to jump in when its
ter started to churn was
utedly healed.**

**us did not mind going
n there to be a source of
.**

sus warned this man not to
on practicing idolatry. By
dening the heart, it led to
death* — separation from
living God.

Jesus, lord of the Sabbath

5 1 After these things there was a feast of the Jews, and
2 Jesus went to Jerusalem. | Now in Jerusalem near the
sheep market there is a public bath which in Hebrew is named
3 Bethzatha. It has five doorways. | In these doorways there were
a great number of people with different diseases: some unable
5 to see, some paralyzed, some with wasted bodies. | One man
6 was there who had been ill for thirty-eight years. | When Jesus
saw him there on the floor it was clear to him that he had been
now a long time in that condition, so he said to the man, "Is it
7 your desire to get well?" | The ill man said in answer, "Sir, I
have nobody to put me into the bath when the water is
moving. While I am on the way down some other person gets
8 in before me." | Jesus said to him, "Get up, take your bed and
9 go." | And the man became well that instant, and took up his
bed and walked. Now that day was the Sabbath.
10 So the Jews said to the man who had been healed, "It is the
Sabbath.* It is against the law for you to take up your bed." |
11 He said to them, "But he who made me well, said to me, 'Take
12 up your bed and go.'" | Then they put to him the question:
13 "Who is the man who said to you, Take it up and go?" | Now
he who had been made well had no knowledge who it was,
Jesus having gone away because of the number of people who
were in that place.
14 After a time Jesus came across him in the
Temple and said to him, "See, you are well
and strong. Do no more sin for fear a worse
15 thing comes to you."[1] | The man went away
and said to the Jews that it was Jesus who
16 had made him well. | And for this reason the
Jews were turned against Jesus, because he
was doing these things on the Sabbath.

*Lord, this sick person
had lost all confidence in you.
Thirty-eight years of suffering
and solitude is a long time!
You seemed to have forgotten him!
So, looking for healing,
he took paths that led away from you.
You found him again.
You put him back on his feet again.
You showed him
that there is no greater suffering
and solitude
than being cut off from you.
This is the meaning of sin.*

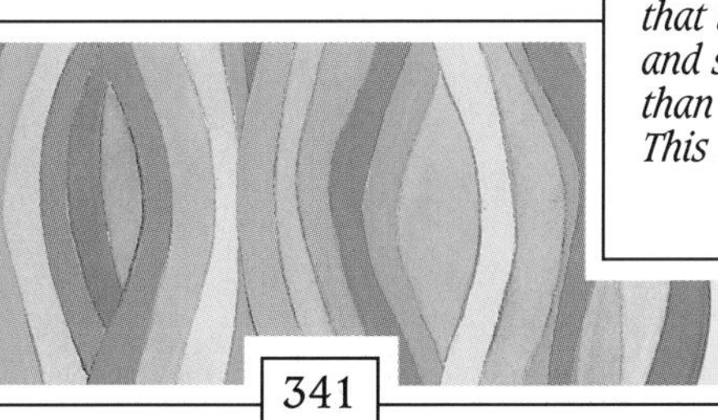

TRUE WITNESS

Jesus on many occasions criticized people who used religious behavior and words for the purpose of showing off (see Matthew 6:1-6, page 263, and 7:21-23, page 266). **They were only interested in their own glory.* The true believer seeks to glorify God** (Matthew 5:16, page 261). **The true witness* adopts a self-effacing attitude, leaving pride of place to the person she or he is trying to make known.**

EATING THE NEW MANNA

Jesus, prefigured by Moses

5 39 "You search the holy Scriptures, in the belief that
through them you receive eternal life. It is those
40 Scriptures which give witness about me. | And still you
have no desire to come to me so that you may have life.
41-42 I do not take honor from men, | but I know that you have
43 no love for God[1] in your hearts. | I have come in my Father's
name, and your hearts are not open to me. If another comes
with no other authority but himself, you will give him your
44 approval. | How is it possible for you to have faith while you
take honor one from another and have no
desire for the honor which comes from the
only God?
45 Put out of your minds the thought that I
will say things against you to the Father.
The one who says things against you is
46 Moses, on whom you put your hopes. | If
you had belief in Moses you would have
belief in me, for his writings are about me.
47 | If you have no belief in his writings, how
will you believe my words?"

Lord, you know very well
that we don't need "stars,"
or people who talk about themselves.
We need witnesses,
people who talk about you,
who give you all the room;
people who continually
dig in the Scriptures
to find out what to proclaim about you
through their words
and way of living.
Give us witnesses!
Make us your witnesses, Lord!

Jesus, bread of life

The whole of John, chapter 6, is devoted to the multiplication of the loaves[2] and what followed.

6 14 And when the people saw the sign which he had
done, they said, "Truly, this is the prophet who is

[1] See John 2:24, page 337. [2] See Matthew 14:13-21, page 278.

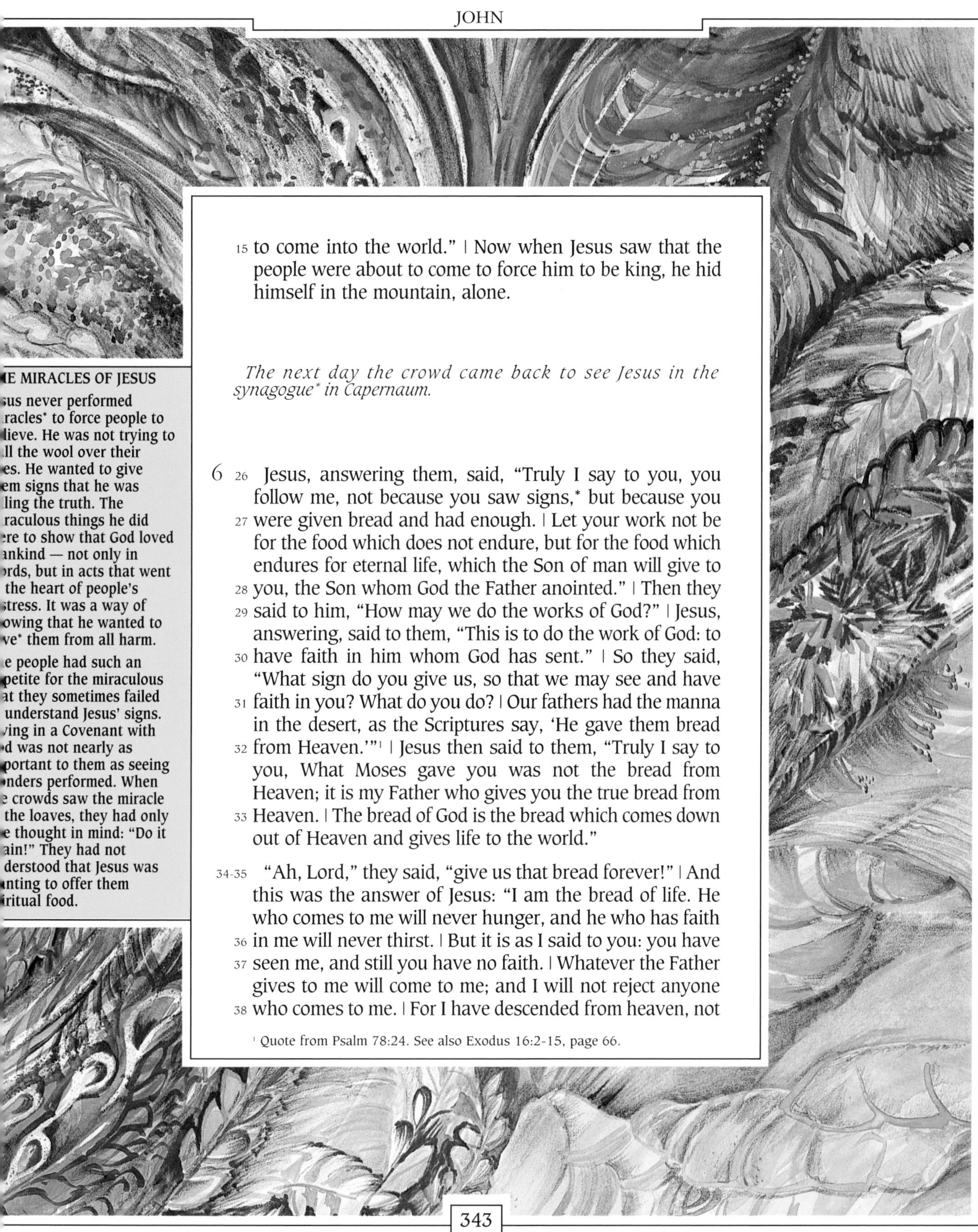

15 to come into the world." | Now when Jesus saw that the
people were about to come to force him to be king, he hid
himself in the mountain, alone.

The next day the crowd came back to see Jesus in the synagogue in Capernaum.*

6 26 Jesus, answering them, said, "Truly I say to you, you
follow me, not because you saw signs,* but because you
27 were given bread and had enough. | Let your work not be
for the food which does not endure, but for the food which
endures for eternal life, which the Son of man will give to
28 you, the Son whom God the Father anointed." | Then they
29 said to him, "How may we do the works of God?" | Jesus,
answering, said to them, "This is to do the work of God: to
30 have faith in him whom God has sent." | So they said,
"What sign do you give us, so that we may see and have
31 faith in you? What do you do? | Our fathers had the manna
in the desert, as the Scriptures say, 'He gave them bread
32 from Heaven.'"[1] | Jesus then said to them, "Truly I say to
you, What Moses gave you was not the bread from
Heaven; it is my Father who gives you the true bread from
33 Heaven. | The bread of God is the bread which comes down
out of Heaven and gives life to the world."

34-35 "Ah, Lord," they said, "give us that bread forever!" | And
this was the answer of Jesus: "I am the bread of life. He
who comes to me will never hunger, and he who has faith
36 in me will never thirst. | But it is as I said to you: you have
37 seen me, and still you have no faith. | Whatever the Father
gives to me will come to me; and I will not reject anyone
38 who comes to me. | For I have descended from heaven, not

[1] Quote from Psalm 78:24. See also Exodus 16:2-15, page 66.

IE MIRACLES OF JESUS

ɜus never performed
racles* to force people to
lieve. He was not trying to
ll the wool over their
es. He wanted to give
em signs that he was
ling the truth. The
raculous things he did
ere to show that God loved
ankind — not only in
ords, but in acts that went
the heart of people's
stress. It was a way of
owing that he wanted to
ve* them from all harm.

e people had such an
petite for the miraculous
at they sometimes failed
understand Jesus' signs.
ving in a Covenant with
d was not nearly as
portant to them as seeing
onders performed. When
e crowds saw the miracle
the loaves, they had only
e thought in mind: "Do it
ain!" They had not
derstood that Jesus was
anting to offer them
iritual food.

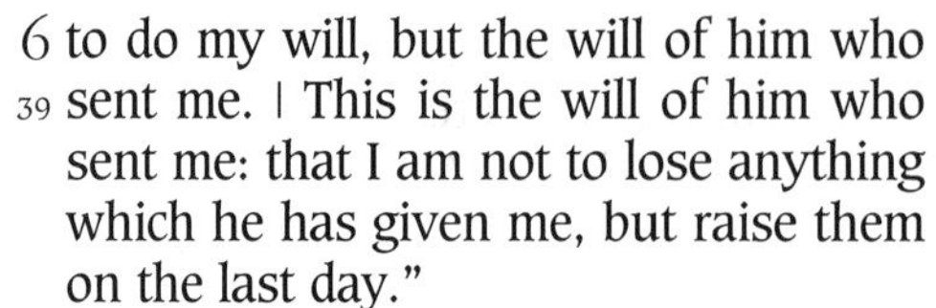

6 to do my will, but the will of him who
39 sent me. | This is the will of him who
sent me: that I am not to lose anything
which he has given me, but raise them
on the last day."

Lord, you make the new life which
was given to me on the day of my baptism,
grow within by giving me the bread of life.
You are this bread.
Your life transfigures mine, putting it
in harmony with all of my Christian
brothers and sisters.

We agree to let your life
show through ours, Lord!
Together, as a body,
we will be a sign of your presence
in the midst of humanity.

Jesus, true manna come down from heaven

6 41 Now the Jews said bitter things about Jesus
because of his words, "I am the bread which came
42 down from Heaven." | And they said, "Is not this Jesus, the
son of Joseph, whose father and mother we have seen?
How is it then that he now says, I have come down from
43 heaven?" | Jesus said, "Do not say things against me to
44 each other. | No man is able to come to me if the Father who
sent me does not give him the desire to come, and I will
45 raise him from the dead on the last day. | The Scriptures of
the prophets say, 'And they will all have teaching from
God.'[1] Everyone whose ears have been open to the teaching
46 of the Father comes to me. | Not that anyone has ever seen
the Father; only he who is from God, he has seen the
47 Father.[2] | Truly I say to you, he who has faith in me has
48-49 eternal life. | I am the bread of life. | Your fathers took the
50 manna in the desert—and they are dead.* | The bread which
comes from Heaven is such bread that a man may eat it for
food and never die.

[1] See Jeremiah 31:34, page 157. [2] See Luke 10:22, page 316.

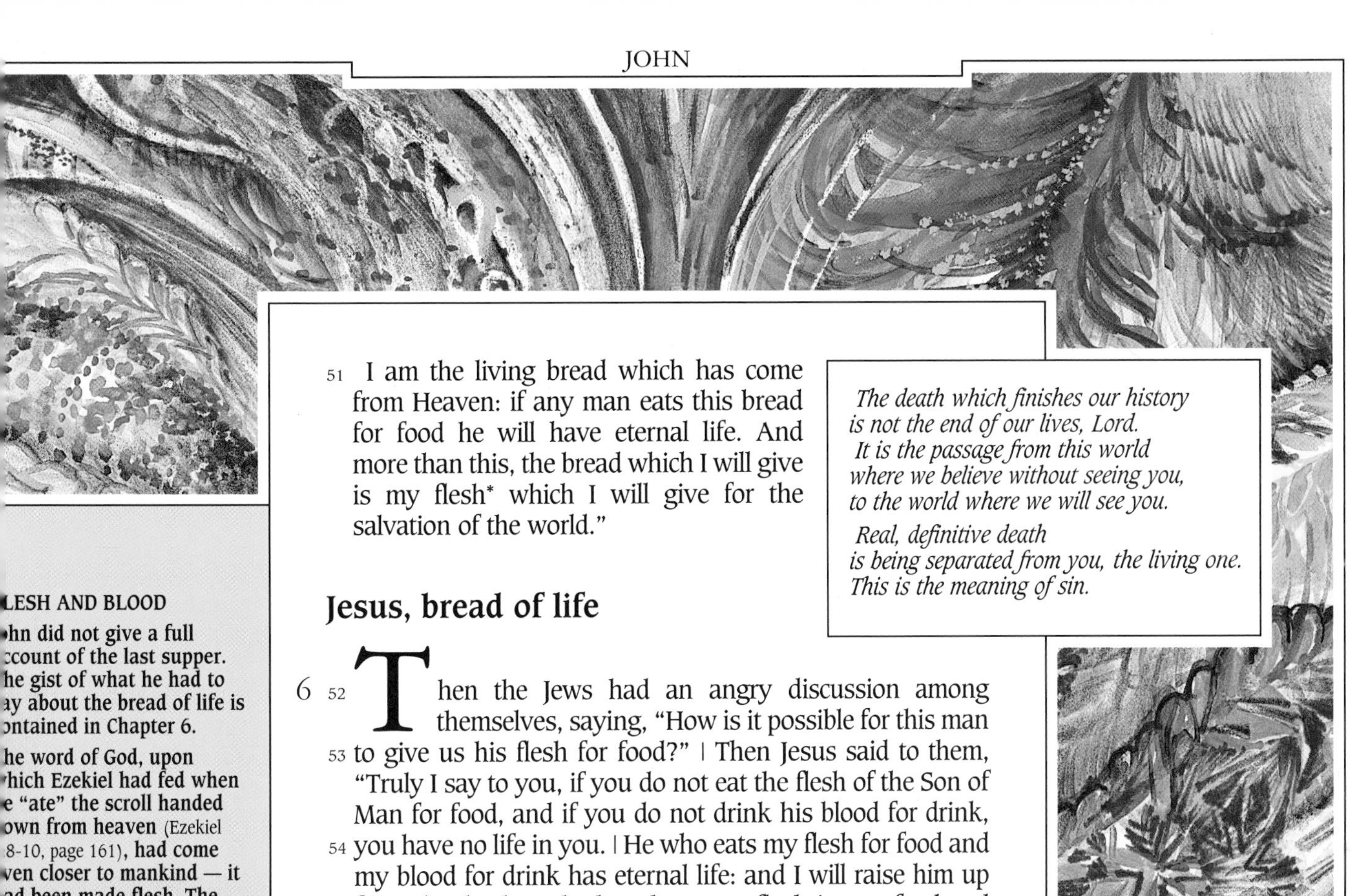

51 I am the living bread which has come
from Heaven: if any man eats this bread
for food he will have eternal life. And
more than this, the bread which I will give
is my flesh* which I will give for the
salvation of the world."

The death which finishes our history
is not the end of our lives, Lord.
It is the passage from this world
where we believe without seeing you,
to the world where we will see you.
Real, definitive death
is being separated from you, the living one.
This is the meaning of sin.

Jesus, bread of life

6 52 Then the Jews had an angry discussion among
themselves, saying, "How is it possible for this man
53 to give us his flesh for food?" | Then Jesus said to them,
"Truly I say to you, if you do not eat the flesh of the Son of
Man for food, and if you do not drink his blood for drink,
54 you have no life in you. | He who eats my flesh for food and
my blood for drink has eternal life: and I will raise him up
55 from the dead on the last day. | My flesh is true food and
56 my blood is true drink. | He who eats my flesh for food and
57 my blood for drink is in me and I in him. | As the living
Father has sent me, and I have life because of the Father,
even so he who takes me for his food will have life because
58 of me. | This is the bread which has come down from
Heaven. It is not like the food which your fathers had. They
ate the manna, and are dead, but he who eats this bread for
food will have eternal life."

Jesus, word of life

6 66 Because of what he said, a number of the disciples
67 went back and would no longer follow him. | So
Jesus said to the twelve,* "Have you a desire to leave?" |
68 Then Simon Peter answered: "Lord, to whom are we to

LESH AND BLOOD

hn did not give a full ccount of the last supper. he gist of what he had to ay about the bread of life is ontained in Chapter 6.

he word of God, upon hich Ezekiel had fed when e "ate" the scroll handed own from heaven (Ezekiel 8-10, page 161), **had come ven closer to mankind — it ad been made flesh. The isciples, in eating the bread hich Jesus gave them, were ed by his love, the love that ad led him to become man nd give up his life so as to ave* them.**

sus would go even further y inviting people to drink is blood. To Jews, this was n extremely violent image, ince they abstained from rinking the blood of nimals. (This illustrated their ncern not to take into their stems the life of other creatures. od alone was the master of life. e Acts 15:28-29, page 422.) **sus was telling his isciples that they could bsorb his life, and make it ow in their veins, so to peak. The blood of the ovenant had become more an just a symbol of the nion between God and umans** (see Exodus 24:8, page 4). **It was God's signature. e gave His blood to show ow important His Covenant ith humans was to Him.**

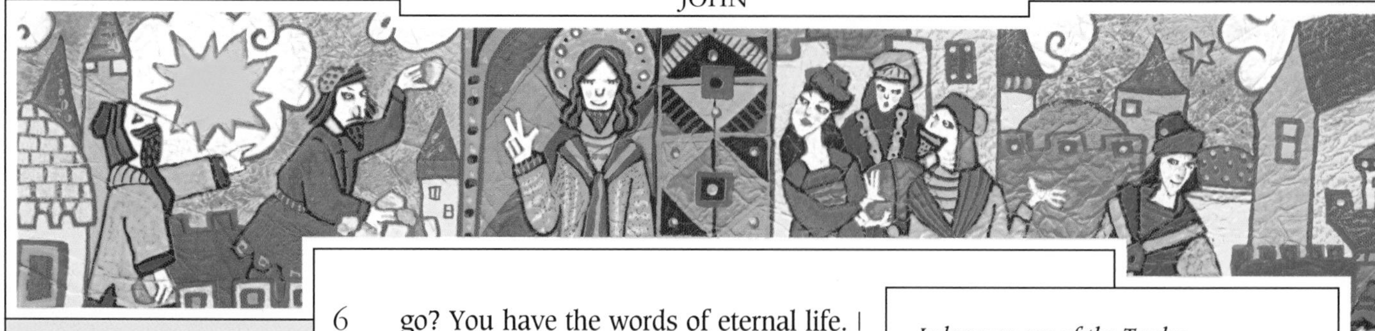

6 go? You have the words of eternal life. |
69 We have faith and are certain that you
are the Holy One of God."
70 Then Jesus said, "Did I not make a
selection of you, the twelve, and one of
71 you is a son of the Evil One?"[1] | He was
talking of Judas, the son of Simon
Iscariot. It was he who was to betray
Jesus—one of the twelve.

Judas was one of the Twelve.
You called him to be with you.
Yet, little by little,
he turned against you.
How was this possible?
He must have dreamed
so much about what you should say,
and what you should do,
that he was incapable of listening to you;
incapable of tasting the newness
of your Word.
Perhaps even when you spoke, all he
heard were strange and difficult words.
What about me, Lord?
Do I really listen to you?
Do I use all the possible means
of knowing you as you really are?

THE DIVINITY OF JESUS

Jesus and the Holy Spirit

7 37 On the last day, the great day of the feast,[2] Jesus
got up and said in a loud voice, "If any man is
38 thirsty let him come to me and I will give him drink. | He
who has faith in me, 'out of his body,' as the Scriptures
39 have said, 'will come rivers of living water.'[3] | This he said
of the Spirit* which would be given to those who had faith
in him: the Spirit had not been given then, because the
glory[4] of Jesus was still to come.
40 When these words came to their ears, some of the people
41 said, "This is certainly the prophet." | Others said, "This is
the Christ." But others said, "Not so; will the Christ come
42 from Galilee? | Do not the Scriptures say that the Christ
comes of the descendants of David and from Bethlehem,
43 the town where David was?"[5] | So there was a division
44 among the people because of him. | And some of them had
a desire to take him; but no man put hands on him.

[1] Judas was called a devil; Peter had been called Satan in Matthew 16:23, page 282.

[2] The Feast of Tabernacles, or booths, commemorated the period of wandering in the desert during the exodus.* Each family built a "booth" in which it took its meals and prayed. The feast lasted a week. See Nehemiah 8:1, page 176.

[3] Close variants of this phrase may be found in Isaiah, Ezekiel and Zechariah. See John 19:34, page 381. Blood and water flowed from the spear wound in Jesus' side.

[4] John wrote of Jesus communicating the Holy Spirit to his apostles when he first appeared in his risen form (John 20:22, page 389).

[5] The birth of the Messiah in Bethlehem was foretold by the prophet Micah (Micah 5:1, page 145).

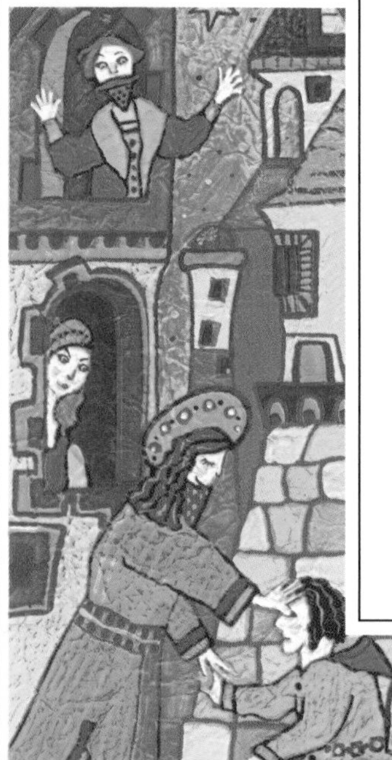

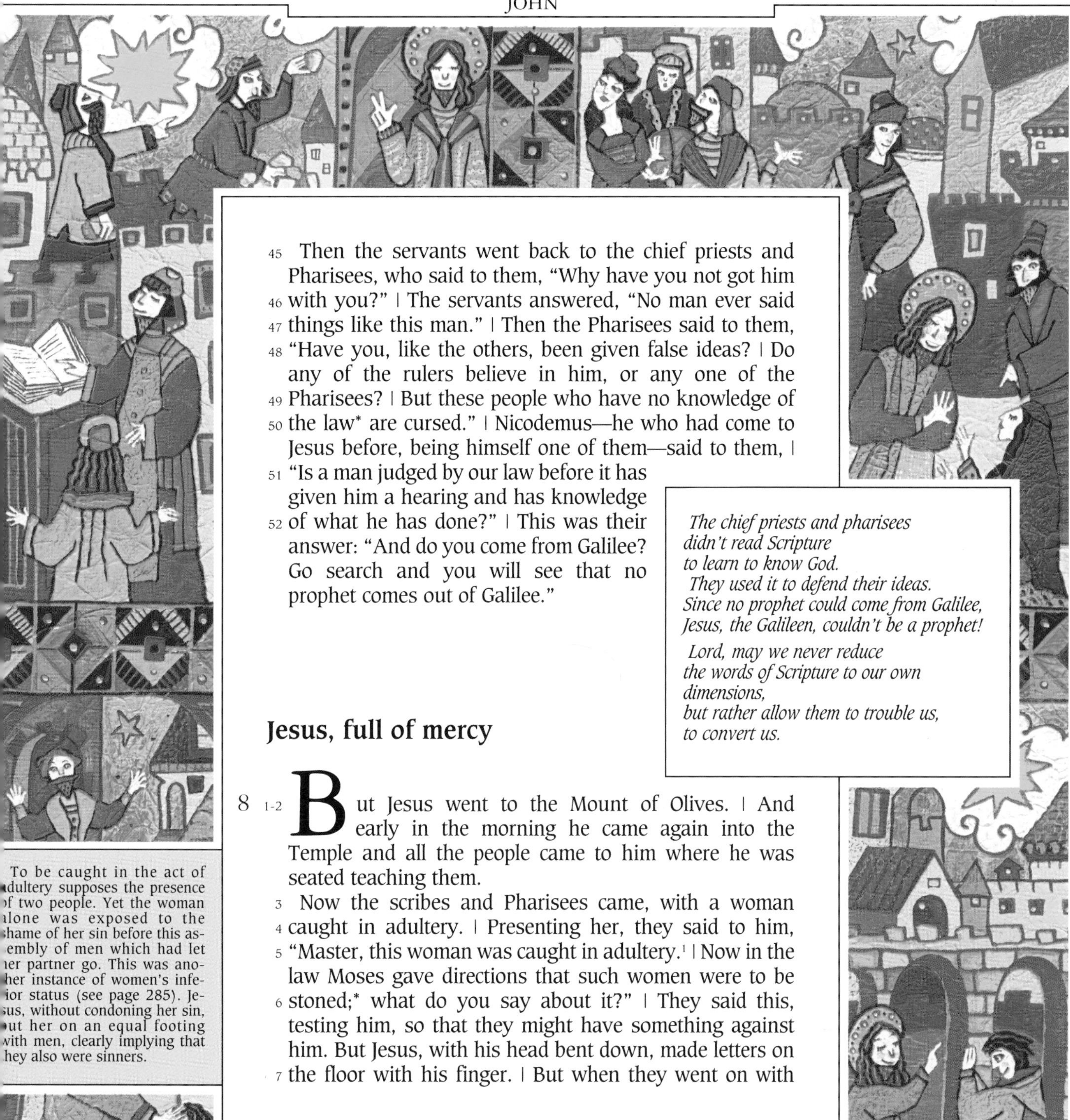

45 Then the servants went back to the chief priests and
Pharisees, who said to them, "Why have you not got him
46 with you?" | The servants answered, "No man ever said
47 things like this man." | Then the Pharisees said to them,
48 "Have you, like the others, been given false ideas? | Do
any of the rulers believe in him, or any one of the
49 Pharisees? | But these people who have no knowledge of
50 the law* are cursed." | Nicodemus—he who had come to
Jesus before, being himself one of them—said to them, |
51 "Is a man judged by our law before it has
given him a hearing and has knowledge
52 of what he has done?" | This was their
answer: "And do you come from Galilee?
Go search and you will see that no
prophet comes out of Galilee."

The chief priests and pharisees
didn't read Scripture
to learn to know God.
They used it to defend their ideas.
Since no prophet could come from Galilee,
Jesus, the Galileen, couldn't be a prophet!
Lord, may we never reduce
the words of Scripture to our own
dimensions,
but rather allow them to trouble us,
to convert us.

Jesus, full of mercy

8 1-2 But Jesus went to the Mount of Olives. | And
early in the morning he came again into the
Temple and all the people came to him where he was
seated teaching them.
3 Now the scribes and Pharisees came, with a woman
4 caught in adultery. | Presenting her, they said to him,
5 "Master, this woman was caught in adultery.[1] | Now in the
law Moses gave directions that such women were to be
6 stoned;* what do you say about it?" | They said this,
testing him, so that they might have something against
him. But Jesus, with his head bent down, made letters on
7 the floor with his finger. | But when they went on with

To be caught in the act of adultery supposes the presence of two people. Yet the woman alone was exposed to the shame of her sin before this assembly of men which had let her partner go. This was another instance of women's inferior status (see page 285). Jesus, without condoning her sin, put her on an equal footing with men, clearly implying that they also were sinners.

8 their questions, he got up and said to them, "Let him
among you who is without sin be the first to throw a stone
8 at her." | And again, with bent head, he wrote letters on
the floor.
9 And when they heard his words, they
went out one by one, starting with the
oldest even to the last, because they
were conscious of what was in their
hearts. Jesus was there by himself with
10 the woman before him. | Then he got up,
and seeing nobody but the woman, he
said to her, "Where are the men who
said things against you? Did no one
11 judge against you?" | And she said, "No
man, Lord." And Jesus said, "And I do
not judge you. Go, and never sin again."

Your name, profession
and family were of little importance.
For the pharisees,
your identity was confused with
your sin. You were just an adulteress!
Jesus refused to stick you with this label.
He invited your accusers
to take a look at themselves.
They willingly, but grudgingly recognized
that they were sinners as well.
You were not any more contemptible
than they were!
Much more than that,
with Jesus' forgiveness, you have regained
your dignity as God's daughter.

Jesus, I AM

8 51 "Truly I say to you, if a man obeys my word he will
52 never see death."* | The Jews said to him, "Now
we are certain that you are possessed by an evil spirit.
Abraham is dead, and the prophets are dead. You say, if
53 a man obeys my word he will never see death. | Are you
greater than our father Abraham, who is dead and the
54 prophets are dead? Who do you say that you are?" | Jesus
said in answer, "If I take glory for myself, my glory* is
nothing: it is my Father who gives me glory, of whom you
55 say that he is your God. | You have no knowledge of him,
but I have knowledge of him. If I said I have no knowledge
of him I would be talking falsely like you, but I have full
56 knowledge of him, and I obey his word. | Your father

Abraham was full of joy at the hope of
seeing my day: he saw it and was glad."
57 Then the Jews said to him, "You are
not fifty years old; have you seen
58 Abraham?" | Jesus said to them, "Truly I
say to you, before Abraham came into
59 being, I am."[1] | So they took up stones to
throw at him, but Jesus got secretly out
of their way and left the Temple.

[1] "I AM" was the Old Testament name of God (Exodus 3:14, page 58).

Lord, you are, and always have been.
Everything that exists comes alive in you.
Only you can truly
say, "I am."
And yet, you wanted to share
our mortal condition.

You came, in person, to explain to us,
that from the beginning of time,
God decided not only to give us life,
but to also associate us with His.

You invite us to enter
into the communion of love
which unites you to the Father in the Spirit.
With you, Lord,
I become your child forever.

Jesus, light of the world

9 1 And when he went on his way, he saw a man blind
2 from birth. | And his disciples put a question to
him, saying, "Rabbi,* was it because of this man's sin, or
the sin of his father and mother, that he has been blind
3 from birth?" | Jesus said in answer, "It was not because of
his sin, or because of his father's or mother's; it was so
4 that the works of God might be seen clearly in him. | While
it is day we have to do the works of him who sent me. The
5 night comes when no work may be done. | As long as I am
6 in the world, I am the light of the world." | Having said
these words, he put soil, mixed with saliva from his
7 mouth, on the man's eyes, | and said to him, "Go and
make yourself clean in the bath of Siloam" (which means
sent). So he went away and, after washing, came back
able to see.
8 Then the neighbors and others who had seen him before
in the street, with his hand out for money, said, "Is not
this the man who begged from people?"...
10 So they said to him, "How then were your eyes made
11 open?" | His answer was: "The man who is named Jesus

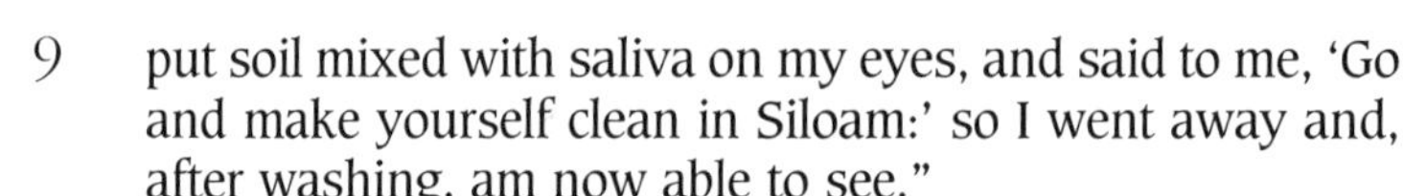

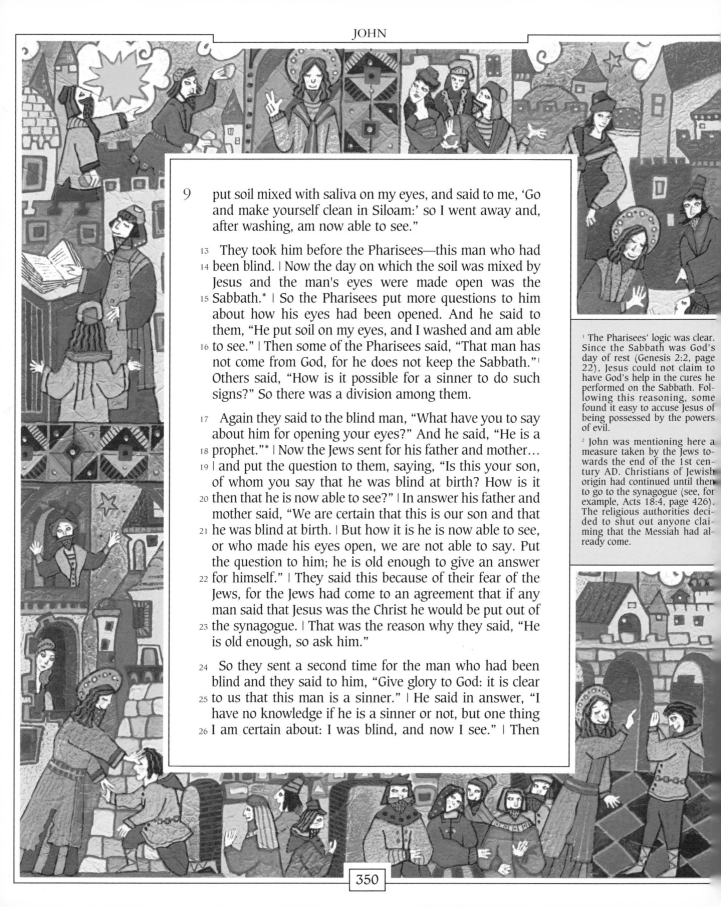

9 put soil mixed with saliva on my eyes, and said to me, 'Go
and make yourself clean in Siloam:' so I went away and,
after washing, am now able to see."

13 They took him before the Pharisees—this man who had
14 been blind. | Now the day on which the soil was mixed by
Jesus and the man's eyes were made open was the
15 Sabbath.* | So the Pharisees put more questions to him
about how his eyes had been opened. And he said to
them, "He put soil on my eyes, and I washed and am able
16 to see." | Then some of the Pharisees said, "That man has
not come from God, for he does not keep the Sabbath."[1]
Others said, "How is it possible for a sinner to do such
signs?" So there was a division among them.

17 Again they said to the blind man, "What have you to say
about him for opening your eyes?" And he said, "He is a
18 prophet."* | Now the Jews sent for his father and mother...
19 | and put the question to them, saying, "Is this your son,
of whom you say that he was blind at birth? How is it
20 then that he is now able to see?" | In answer his father and
mother said, "We are certain that this is our son and that
21 he was blind at birth. | But how it is he is now able to see,
or who made his eyes open, we are not able to say. Put
the question to him; he is old enough to give an answer
22 for himself." | They said this because of their fear of the
Jews, for the Jews had come to an agreement that if any
man said that Jesus was the Christ he would be put out of
23 the synagogue. | That was the reason why they said, "He
is old enough, so ask him."

24 So they sent a second time for the man who had been
blind and they said to him, "Give glory to God: it is clear
25 to us that this man is a sinner." | He said in answer, "I
have no knowledge if he is a sinner or not, but one thing
26 I am certain about: I was blind, and now I see." | Then

[1] The Pharisees' logic was clear. Since the Sabbath was God's day of rest (Genesis 2:2, page 22), Jesus could not claim to have God's help in the cures he performed on the Sabbath. Following this reasoning, some found it easy to accuse Jesus of being possessed by the powers of evil.

[2] John was mentioning here a measure taken by the Jews towards the end of the 1st century AD. Christians of Jewish origin had continued until then to go to the synagogue (see, for example, Acts 18:4, page 426). The religious authorities decided to shut out anyone claiming that the Messiah had already come.

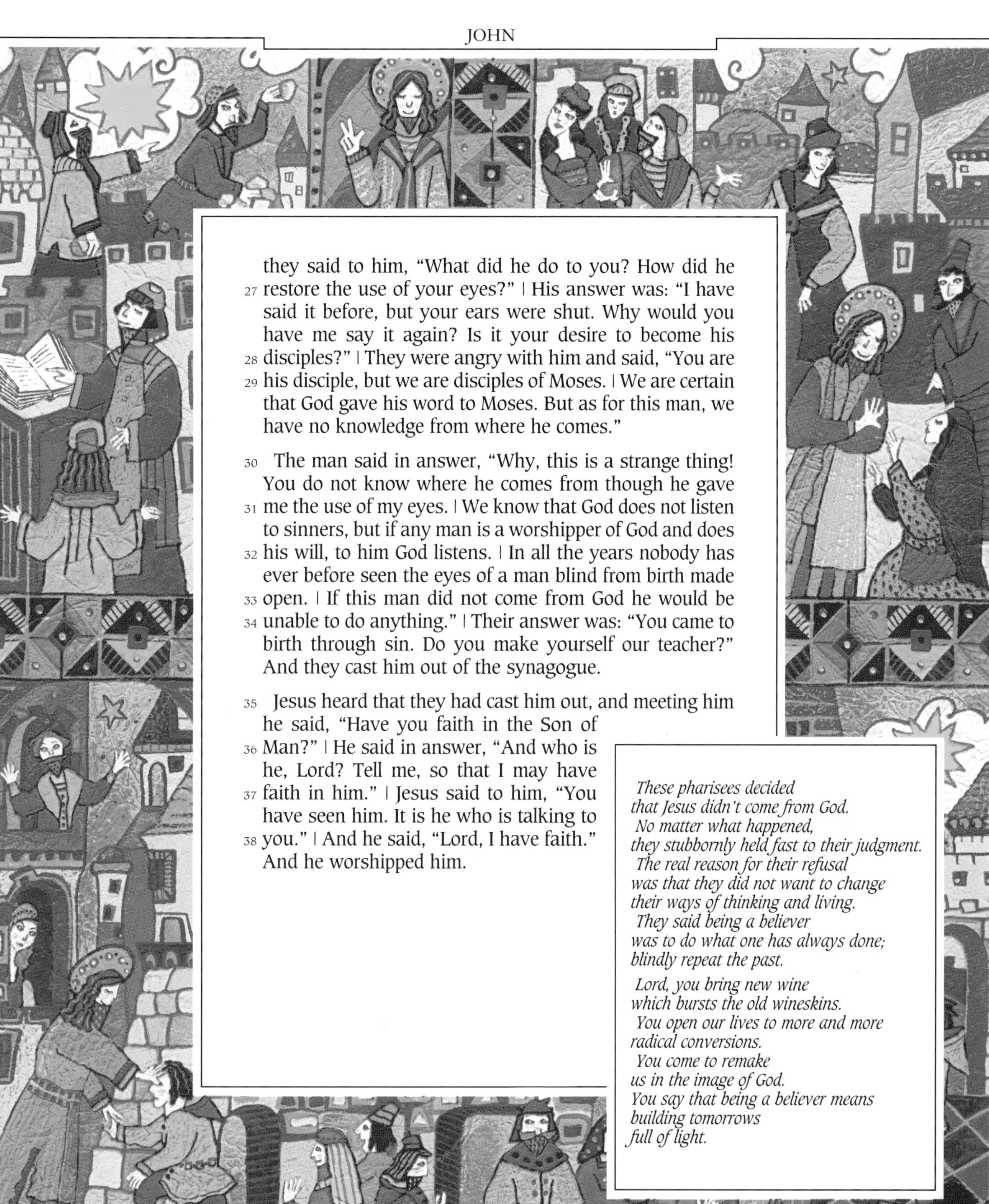

they said to him, "What did he do to you? How did he
27 restore the use of your eyes?" | His answer was: "I have
said it before, but your ears were shut. Why would you
have me say it again? Is it your desire to become his
28 disciples?" | They were angry with him and said, "You are
29 his disciple, but we are disciples of Moses. | We are certain
that God gave his word to Moses. But as for this man, we
have no knowledge from where he comes."

30 The man said in answer, "Why, this is a strange thing!
You do not know where he comes from though he gave
31 me the use of my eyes. | We know that God does not listen
to sinners, but if any man is a worshipper of God and does
32 his will, to him God listens. | In all the years nobody has
ever before seen the eyes of a man blind from birth made
33 open. | If this man did not come from God he would be
34 unable to do anything." | Their answer was: "You came to
birth through sin. Do you make yourself our teacher?"
And they cast him out of the synagogue.

35 Jesus heard that they had cast him out, and meeting him
he said, "Have you faith in the Son of
36 Man?" | He said in answer, "And who is
he, Lord? Tell me, so that I may have
37 faith in him." | Jesus said to him, "You
have seen him. It is he who is talking to
38 you." | And he said, "Lord, I have faith."
And he worshipped him.

These pharisees decided
that Jesus didn't come from God.
No matter what happened,
they stubbornly held fast to their judgment.
The real reason for their refusal
was that they did not want to change
their ways of thinking and living.
They said being a believer
was to do what one has always done;
blindly repeat the past.

Lord, you bring new wine
which bursts the old wineskins.
You open our lives to more and more
radical conversions.
You come to remake
us in the image of God.
You say that being a believer means
building tomorrows
full of light.

GOD TAKES PERSONAL CARE OF HIS PEOPLE

Ezekiel had prophesied that God, weary of the laziness and greed of priests and kings, would himself come to take care of His people as a good shepherd takes care of his flock (Ezekiel 34:1-16, page 163).

Jesus coolly claimed to be this good shepherd, in contrast to the uncaring hired hands.

Jesus, good shepherd

10 7 So Jesus said again, "Truly I say to you, I am the gate
8 for the sheep. | All who came before me are thieves
9 and outlaws, but the sheep did not listen to them. | I am
the gate: if any man goes in through me he will have
salvation, and will go in and go out, and will get food. |
10 The thief comes only to take the sheep and to put them to
death. He comes for their destruction. I have come so that
they may have life and have it in greater measure.

11 I am the good shepherd.* The good shepherd gives his
12 life for the sheep. | He who is a hireling,[1] and not the
shepherd who owns the sheep, sees the wolf coming and
flees away from the sheep. The wolf comes down on them
13 and sends them in all directions, | because he is a servant
14 he has no interest in the sheep. | I am the good sheperd; I
15 know my sheep, and they know me. | Even as the Father
has knowledge of me and I of the Father;[2] and I am giving
16 my life for the sheep. | I have other sheep which are not of
this field. I will be their guide in the same way, and they
will listen to my voice, so there will be one flock and one
17 shepherd. | For this reason am I loved by the Father,
18 because I give up my life so that I may take it again. | No
one takes it away from me; I give it up of myself. I have
power to give it up, and I have power to take it again.
These orders I have from my Father."

19 There was a division again among the Jews because of
20 these words. | And a number of them said, "He has an evil
spirit and is out of his mind. Why do you listen to him?"
21 | Others said, "These are not the words of one who has an
evil spirit. Is it possible for an evil spirit to make blind
people see?"

[1] Hired hands received a wage but a very miserable one. They were often accused of paying themselves in kind from the flock, and of being indifferent to the animals' wellbeing.

[2] See Luke 10:22, page 316.

Lord, whenever you give,
it's never with regret:
Hundreds of liters of wine at Cana,
Overflowing baskets
at the feeding of the five thousand.
You don't ration the gift of your life for us.
You offer it in abundance.

You want us to love like you do,
to be merciful like the Father.
You want us to be responsible, free, joyous;
like you.

Jesus, one with the Father

10 22 Then came the feast of the
opening of the Temple[1] in
23 Jerusalem. It was winter, | and Jesus was
24 walking in the Temple, in Solomon's Colonnade. | Then
the Jews gathered around him, saying, "How long are you
going to keep us in doubt? If you are the Christ, say so
25 clearly." | Jesus said in answer, "I have said it and you
have no belief: the works which I do in my Father's name,
26 these give witness about me. | But you have no belief
27 because you are not my sheep. | My sheep listen to my
28 voice, and I know them, and they follow me. | I give them
eternal life; they will never be destroyed, and no one will
29 ever steal them out of my hand. | That which my Father
has given to me has more value than all. No one is able to
30 steal anything out of the Father's hand. | I and my Father
are one."
31
32 Then the Jews took up stones again to throw at him. |
Jesus said to them in answer, "I have let you see a number
of good works from the Father. For which of those works
33 are you stoning* me?" | This was their answer: "We are
not stoning you for a good work but for evil words,
because being a man you make yourself God."

[1] See 1 Maccabees 4:36-59, page 179.

GOD-TRINITY*

"I and The Father are one." In making this claim, Jesus was inviting his listeners to deepen their knowledge* of God:

- **God was made man in the person of Jesus.**
- **God was not "the eternal lonely one of the universe." In the one God, Father and Son lived in loving communion. This communion operated through the Holy Spirit. God was a family. God was love** (1 John 4:8, page 448).
- **God wished to share this three-person love with mankind created in His likeness. Humans had been made to participate in the life of the Trinity.**

[1] See Luke 10:38-42, page 318. Martha, in the Gospels of both John and Luke, was a take-charge woman, full of practical good sense. She served the meal (John 12:2, page 356). In John's account, she remained calm. She listened, like her sister, and received the wonderful confidence of Jesus, "I am the resurrection."

Jesus, resurrection

11 1 Now a certain man named Lazarus was ill; he was
of Bethany, the town of Mary and her sister
3 Martha.[1]... | So the sisters sent to him, saying, "Lord, your
dear friend is ill."...

17 Now when Jesus came, he discovered that Lazarus had
18 been buried four days before. | Now Bethany was near to
19 Jerusalem, about two miles away. | A number of Jews had
come to Martha and Mary to comfort them about their
20 brother. | When Martha had the news that Jesus was on
the way, she went out to him, but Mary did not go from
21 the house. | Then Martha said to Jesus, "Lord, if you had
22 been here my brother would not be dead. | But I am certain
that, even now, whatever request you make to God, God
23 will give it to you." | Jesus said to her, "Your brother will
24 come to life again." | Martha said to him, "I am certain that
he will come to life again when all come back from the
25 dead on the last day." | Jesus said to her, "I am the
resurrection and the life. He who has faith in me will have
26 life even if he is dead. | No one who is living and has faith
27 in me will ever see death. Is this your faith?" | She said to
him, "Yes, Lord. My faith is that you are the Christ, the
Son of God, who was to come into the world."

28 And having said this, she went away and said secretly to
her sister Mary, "The Master is here and has sent for
29 you." | And Mary, hearing this, got up quickly and went
to him....
32 When Mary came to where Jesus was and saw him, she
bowed down at his feet, saying, "Lord, if you had been
33 here my brother would not be dead." | And when Jesus
saw her weeping, and saw the Jews weeping who came
34 with her, his spirit was moved and he was troubled. | He

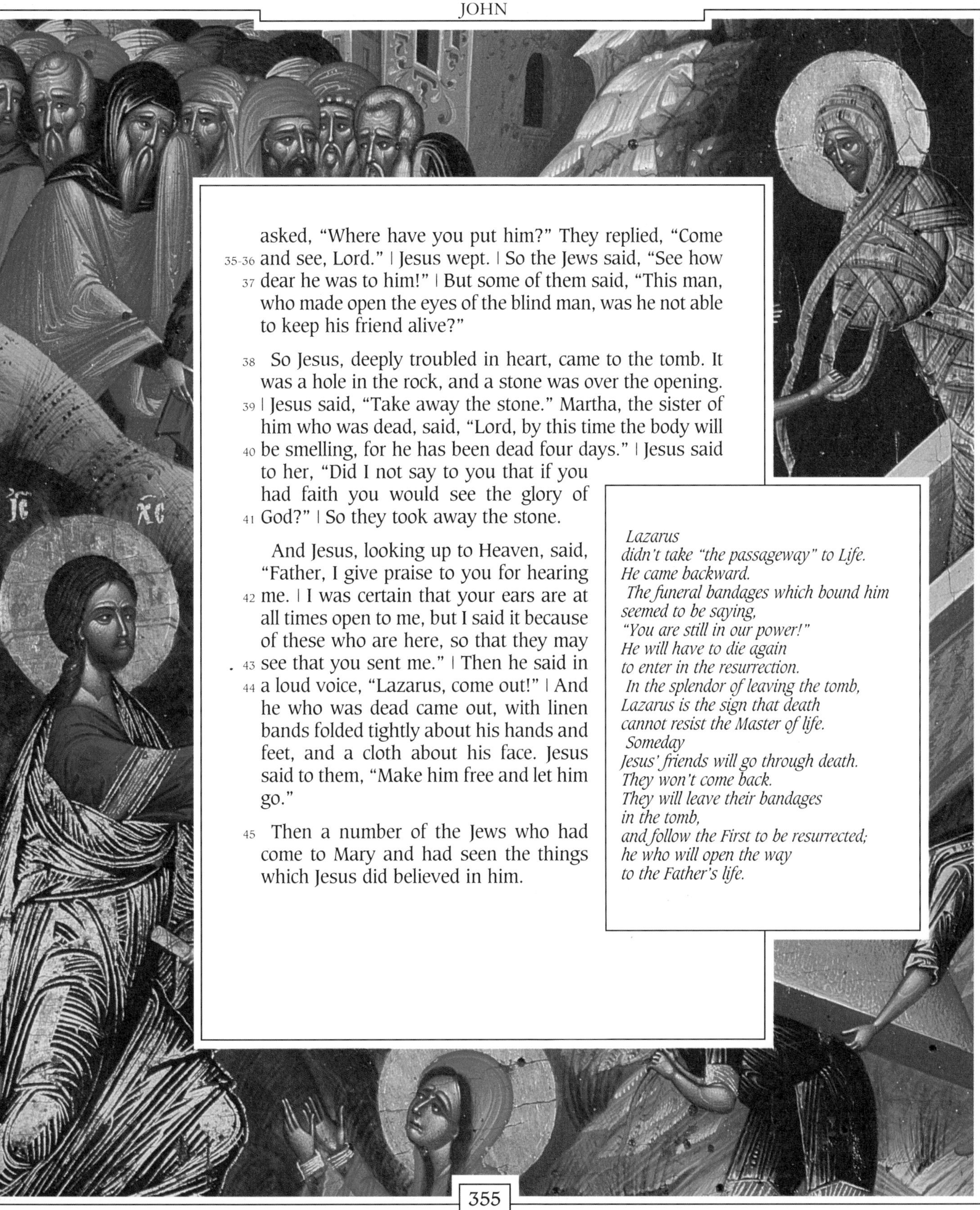

asked, "Where have you put him?" They replied, "Come
35-36 and see, Lord." | Jesus wept. | So the Jews said, "See how
37 dear he was to him!" | But some of them said, "This man,
who made open the eyes of the blind man, was he not able
to keep his friend alive?"

38 So Jesus, deeply troubled in heart, came to the tomb. It
was a hole in the rock, and a stone was over the opening.
39 | Jesus said, "Take away the stone." Martha, the sister of
him who was dead, said, "Lord, by this time the body will
40 be smelling, for he has been dead four days." | Jesus said
to her, "Did I not say to you that if you
had faith you would see the glory of
41 God?" | So they took away the stone.

And Jesus, looking up to Heaven, said,
"Father, I give praise to you for hearing
42 me. | I was certain that your ears are at
all times open to me, but I said it because
of these who are here, so that they may
43 see that you sent me." | Then he said in
44 a loud voice, "Lazarus, come out!" | And
he who was dead came out, with linen
bands folded tightly about his hands and
feet, and a cloth about his face. Jesus
said to them, "Make him free and let him
go."

45 Then a number of the Jews who had
come to Mary and had seen the things
which Jesus did believed in him.

Lazarus
didn't take "the passageway" to Life.
He came backward.
The funeral bandages which bound him
seemed to be saying,
"You are still in our power!"
He will have to die again
to enter in the resurrection.
In the splendor of leaving the tomb,
Lazarus is the sign that death
cannot resist the Master of life.
Someday
Jesus' friends will go through death.
They won't come back.
They will leave their bandages
in the tomb,
and follow the First to be resurrected;
he who will open the way
to the Father's life.

"THAT ONE MAN DIE"

Caiaphas followed a human line of reasoning. A few years earlier, preachers like Jesus had drawn crowds around them. The Romans had found this dangerous, and had committed massacres (see Acts of the Apostles 5:36-38, page 407). **Get rid of Jesus to save the people! In thinking this way, Caiaphas unwittingly interpreted the deeper meaning of Jesus' death. Jesus indeed perished to save the people from death,* but from the true death, that of sin. See "suffering."***

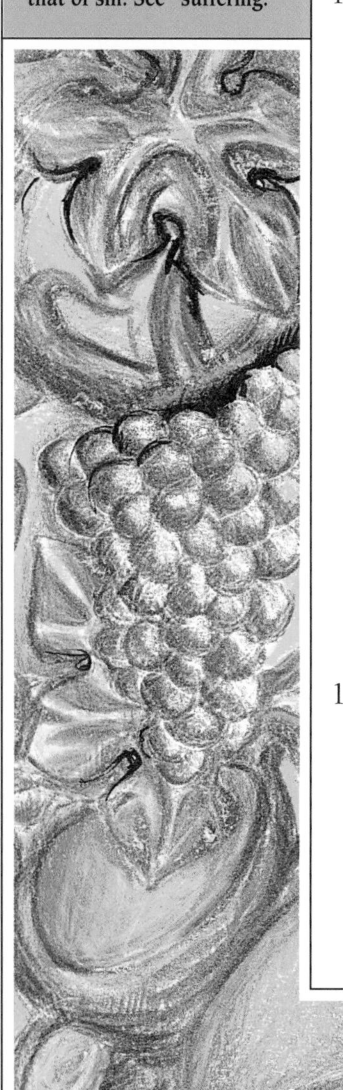

REFUSED BY HIS OWN

Jesus, salvation for mankind

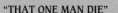

11 47 Then the high priests and the Pharisees called a
meeting of the Sanhedrin[1] and said, "What are we
48 doing? This man is doing a number of signs.* | If we let
him go on in this way, everybody will believe in him and
the Romans will come and take away our place and our
49 nation." | But one of them, Caiaphas,* who was high priest
that year, said to them, "You have no knowledge of
50 anything. | You do not see that it is in your interest for one
man to be put to death for the people, so that all the nation
51 may not come to destruction." | He did not say this of
himself, but being the high priest that year he said, as a
prophet,* that Jesus would be put to death for the nation.
52 | And not for that nation only, but for the purpose of
uniting in one body the people of God all over the world.
53 From that day they plotted to put him to death.

[1] In John's Gospel, the trial and death sentence against Jesus pronounced by the Sanhedrin* (grand council) occurred some days before he was arrested. The synoptic Gospels place them after the arrest.

Jesus, genuinely poor

12 1 Then, six days before the Passover, Jesus came to
Bethany where Lazarus was, whom Jesus had
2 raised from the dead. | So they made him a meal there,
and he was served by Martha, and Lazarus was among
those who were seated with him at table.
3 Then Mary, taking a pound of perfumed oil of great
value, spread it on the feet of Jesus, drying with her hair.
4 The house was filled with the smell of the perfume.[1] | But

Mary only wanted to thank you,
Lord, but like Caiaphas,
she unknowingly prophesied.
She announced your approaching burial.

But during this feast before
Lazarus, who was radiantly alive,
her announcement was scented
with hope.

You, who obtained Lazarus' release
from death from the Father, cannot
remain prisoner in the tomb.

one of his disciples, Judas Iscariot (who
5 was to betray him), said, | "Why was
this perfume not traded for three
hundred pence,[2] and the money given to
6 the poor?" | (He said this, not because he
cared about the poor, but because he
was a thief, and, having the money bag,
7 took for himself what was put into it.) | Then Jesus said,
"Let her be. Let her keep what she has for the day of my
8 death. | The poor you will always have with you, but me
you have not forever."

Jesus, grain of wheat fallen to the ground

12 20 Now there were some Greeks among the people
21 who had come up to worship at the feast. | They
came to Philip,* who was of Bethsaida in Galilee, and
made a request, saying, "Sir, we have a desire to see
22 Jesus." | Philip went and gave word of it to Andrew;* and
23 Andrew went with Philip to Jesus.[3] | And Jesus said to
them in answer, "The hour of the glory of the Son* of Man
24 has come.[4] | Truly I say to you, If a seed of grain does not
go into the earth and die, it is still just a seed; but through
25 its death it gives much fruit. | He who is
in love with life will have it taken from
him; he who has no care for his life in
this world will keep it for ever and ever.
26 | If any man is my servant, let him come
after me. Where I am, there will my
servant be. If any man becomes my
servant, my Father will give him
honor."

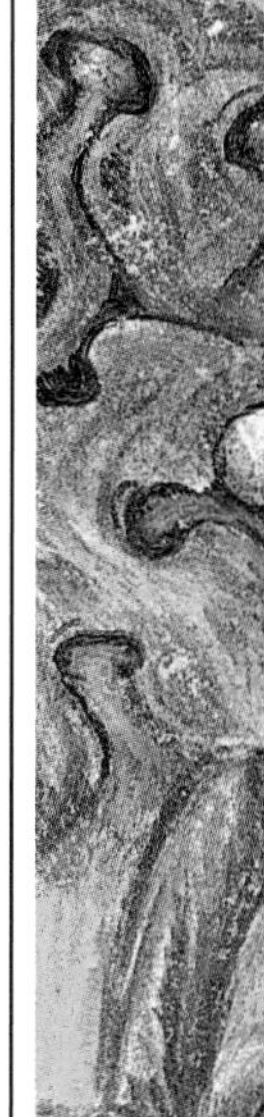

You don't ask us to despise
our lives, Lord.
You remind us that our years are not limited
to the ones following our birth
until death.
After death, we are called
to enter into the fullness of Your life.

If, out of blind love for the present life,
we act as if there
is nothing afterward,
we are really losers,
because we have lost you, Lord!

uke (Luke 7:36-50, page 2) attributed this act to a nful woman in a very different context.

This was the amount of money earned for a year of work. day's labor was paid for by e silver coin (see Matthew :2, page 286).

The twelve Apostles, who re Greek names, acted as intermediaries between Jesus and ese Greeks come to Jerusalem o worship." The expression plied that they were heaens who were believers at art. Since they refused Jesh ritual and laws (circumcion, food rules, etc.), they re not recognized as members of God's people (see page 3).

he hour which had not come Cana (John 2:4, page 346) d now arrived. To be glorid was to be crucified, to endure human ingratitude and respond to it by an outpouring of ve going as far as forgiveness. The glory* of God was t to impose Himself on humans but to love them even within their refusal.

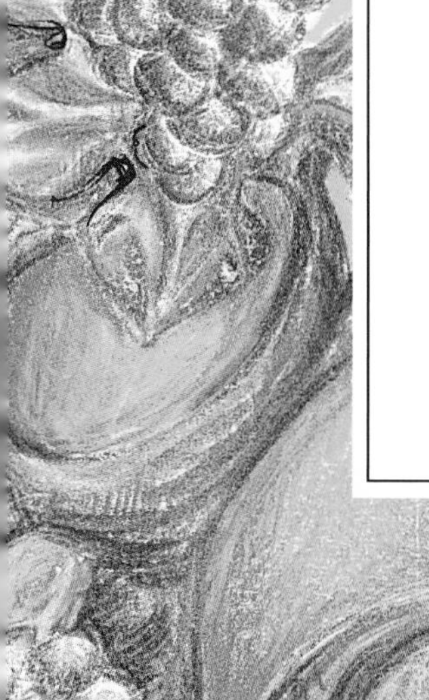

ORDER OF CHAPTERS 13 TO 17

John, in part of Chapter 13 of his Gospel, made mention of the last supper,* Jesus' last meal. He continued with a long homily by Jesus, four chapters long (Chapters 14 to 17), in which Jesus talked to his disciples about the separation to come. They would not see him again, but he would not abandon them. He would send them a protector, the Holy Spirit.

Excerpts from Chapter 13 are quoted in Part V, along with the other accounts of the passion and resurrection (pages 363 to 395).

The most characteristic passages from the homily after the last supper are set out here.

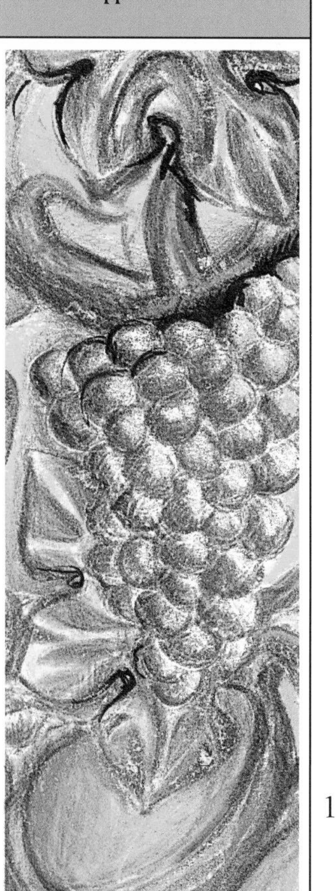

THE FINAL SERMON OF JESUS

Jesus, the way, the truth and the life

14 2 "In my Father's house are many rooms. If it was not
so, would I have said that I am going to prepare a
3 place for you? | And if I go and prepare a place for you, I
will come back again and will take you to be with me, so
4 that you may be where I am. | And you all know where I
am going, and of the way to it."
5 Thomas said, "Lord, we do not know where you are
6 going. How may we know the way?" | Jesus said to him,
"I am the true and living way: no one comes to the Father
7 but by me. | If you had known me, you
would have known my Father. You
know him now and have seen him."
8 Philip said to him, "Lord, let us see the
Father, and we have need of nothing
9 more." | Jesus said to him, "Philip, have
I been with you all this time, and still you
do not know me? He who has seen me
has seen the Father. Why do you say, let
10 us see the Father? | Have you not faith
that I am in the Father and the Father is
in me? The words which I say to you, I
say not from myself: but the Father who
is in me all the time does his works."

Humanity has always sought to know God.

But many have lost their way in the search.

They projected human failings onto God.
They depicted him as a tyrant.

Jesus, you make God's true face known to us.

When I listen to you, I am amazed, because I discover that God only knows how to love.

Jesus, the true vine

15 1-2 "I am the true vine and my Father is the gardener.[1] | He
removes every branch in me which has no fruit, and

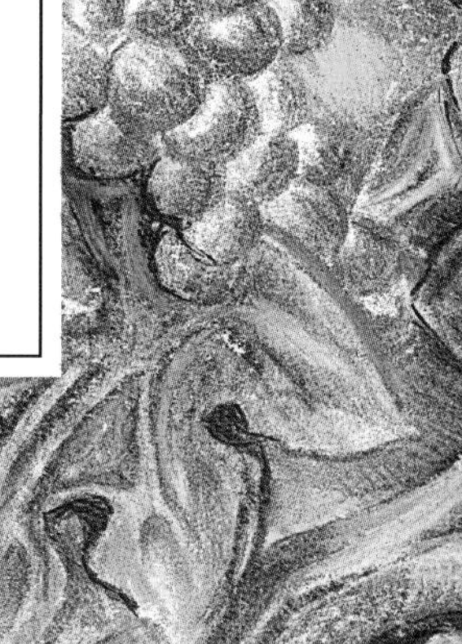

[1] See pages 135-136, and meditation.

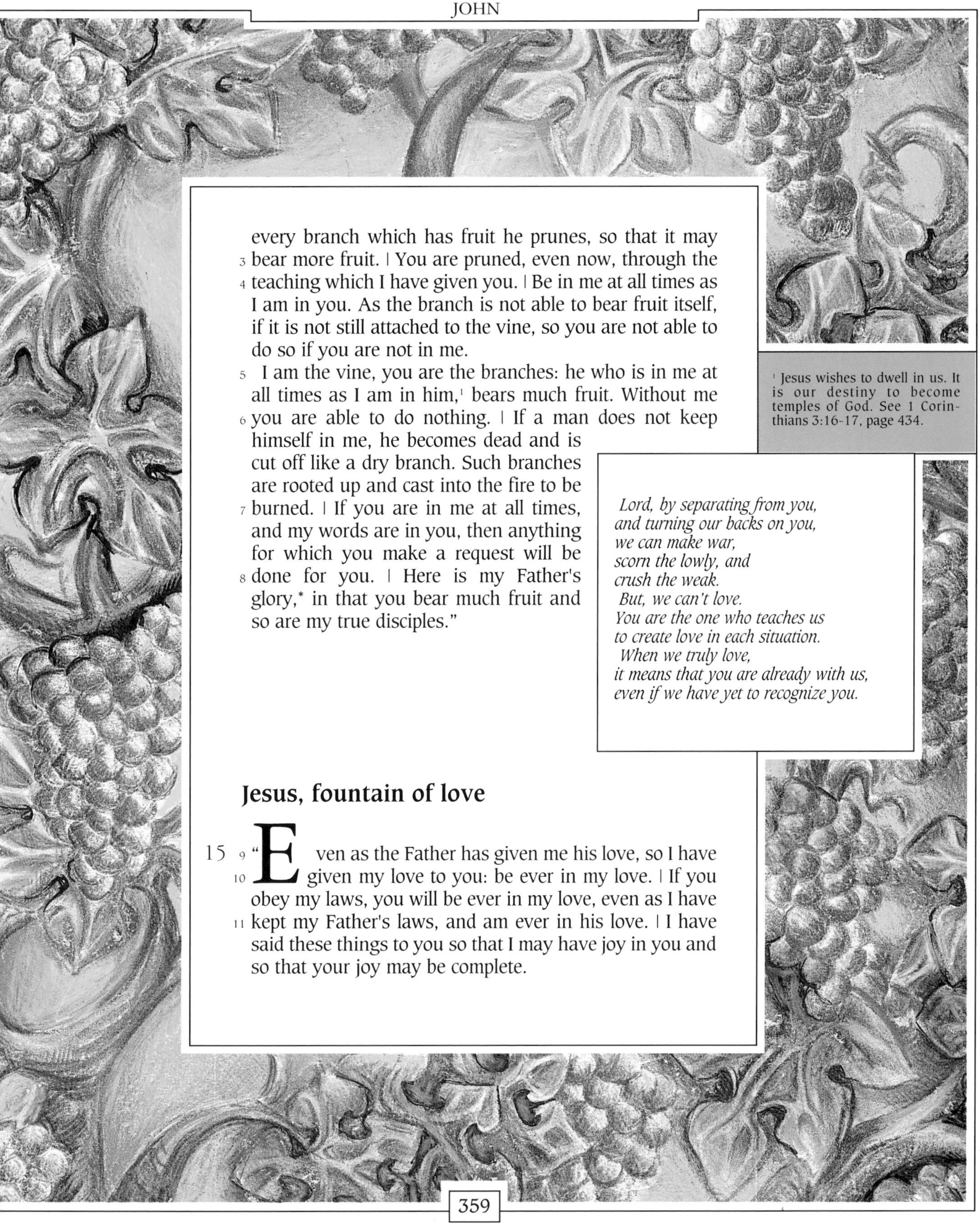

every branch which has fruit he prunes, so that it may
3 bear more fruit. | You are pruned, even now, through the
4 teaching which I have given you. | Be in me at all times as
I am in you. As the branch is not able to bear fruit itself,
if it is not still attached to the vine, so you are not able to
do so if you are not in me.
5 I am the vine, you are the branches: he who is in me at
all times as I am in him,[1] bears much fruit. Without me
6 you are able to do nothing. | If a man does not keep
himself in me, he becomes dead and is
cut off like a dry branch. Such branches
are rooted up and cast into the fire to be
7 burned. | If you are in me at all times,
and my words are in you, then anything
for which you make a request will be
8 done for you. | Here is my Father's
glory,* in that you bear much fruit and
so are my true disciples."

[1] Jesus wishes to dwell in us. It is our destiny to become temples of God. See 1 Corinthians 3:16-17, page 434.

Lord, by separating from you,
and turning our backs on you,
we can make war,
scorn the lowly, and
crush the weak.
But, we can't love.
You are the one who teaches us
to create love in each situation.
When we truly love,
it means that you are already with us,
even if we have yet to recognize you.

Jesus, fountain of love

15 9 "Even as the Father has given me his love, so I have
10 given my love to you: be ever in my love. | If you
obey my laws, you will be ever in my love, even as I have
11 kept my Father's laws, and am ever in his love. | I have
said these things to you so that I may have joy in you and
so that your joy may be complete.

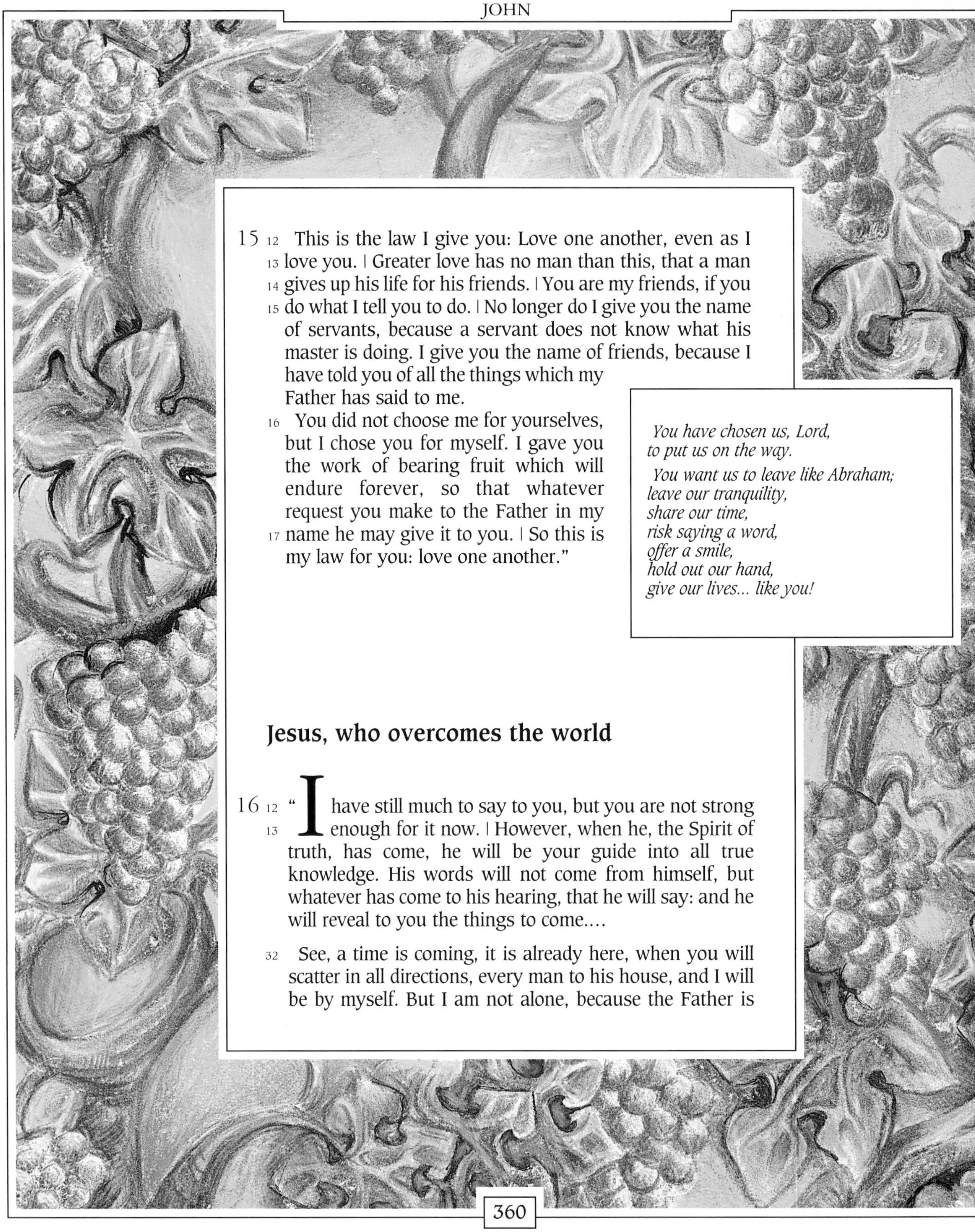

15 12 This is the law I give you: Love one another, even as I
13 love you. | Greater love has no man than this, that a man
14 gives up his life for his friends. | You are my friends, if you
15 do what I tell you to do. | No longer do I give you the name
of servants, because a servant does not know what his
master is doing. I give you the name of friends, because I
have told you of all the things which my
Father has said to me.
16 You did not choose me for yourselves,
but I chose you for myself. I gave you
the work of bearing fruit which will
endure forever, so that whatever
request you make to the Father in my
17 name he may give it to you. | So this is
my law for you: love one another."

You have chosen us, Lord,
to put us on the way.

You want us to leave like Abraham;
leave our tranquility,
share our time,
risk saying a word,
offer a smile,
hold out our hand,
give our lives... like you!

Jesus, who overcomes the world

16 12 "I have still much to say to you, but you are not strong
13 enough for it now. | However, when he, the Spirit of
truth, has come, he will be your guide into all true
knowledge. His words will not come from himself, but
whatever has come to his hearing, that he will say: and he
will reveal to you the things to come....

32 See, a time is coming, it is already here, when you will
scatter in all directions, every man to his house, and I will
be by myself. But I am not alone, because the Father is

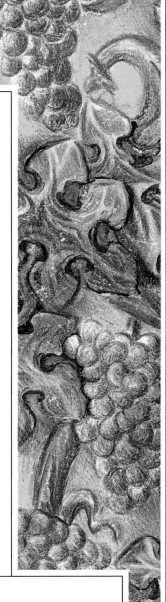

[JE]SUS PRAYS FOR A [U]NITED RELIGION

[T]he homily after the last [S]upper concluded with a [p]rayer for the disciples, [n]amely all who followed [Je]sus and all who would [ac]cept the witness of the [T]welve Apostles throughout [th]e ages by becoming [b]elievers. The prayer was [b]asically a prayer for unity.

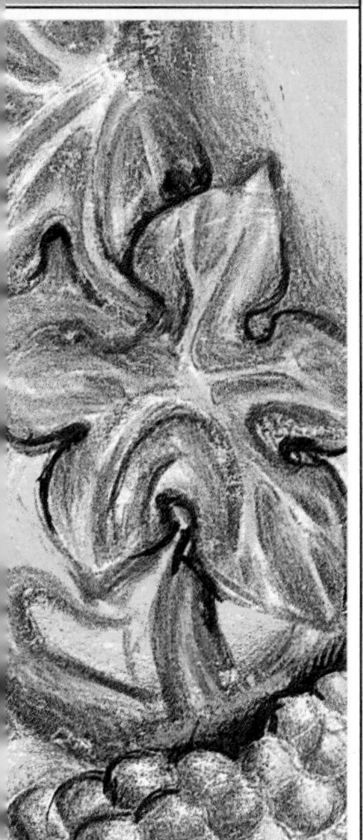

[1] In the language of John, the [te]rm "world" had several mea[ni]ngs which could be added to[g]ether. The world was, first, all [th]e people whom God loved [(s]ee John 3:16, page 338). It [w]as also the people who refu[se]d God (see John 17:14-15, at [ri]ght), since they were under [th]e sway of the "prince of this [w]orld," or Satan.*

[2] Yet another mention of the [h]our. See John 2:4, page 336, [an]d 12:23, page 357.

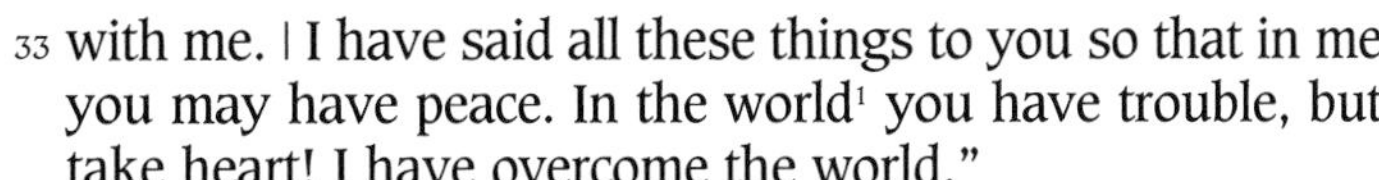

33 with me. | I have said all these things to you so that in me
you may have peace. In the world[1] you have trouble, but
take heart! I have overcome the world."

Jesus and his disciples

17 1 Lifting his eyes to Heaven, Jesus said, "Father, the
2 time has now come;[2] give glory to your Son.... | He
will give eternal life to all those whom you have given to
3 him. | This is eternal life: to know* you, the only true God,
6 and of him whom you have sent, even Jesus Christ. | I
have given knowledge of your name to the men whom
you gave me out of the worl. Yours they were, and you
7 gave them to me, and they have obeyed your words. | Now
it is clear to them that whatever you have given to me
8 comes from you. | Because I have given them the words
which you gave to me. They have accepted them, and
know with certainty that I came from you, having faith
9-11 that you sent me. | My prayer is for them... | Holy Father,
keep them in your name which you have given to me, so
12 that they may be one even as we are one. | While I was
with them I kept them safe in your name which you have
13 given to me.... | And now I come to you. These things I
say in the world so that they may have my joy complete
14 in them. | I have given your word to them, and they are
hated by the world, because they are not
of the world, even as I am not of the
15 world. | My prayer is not that you will
take them out of the world, but that you
will keep them from the Evil One."

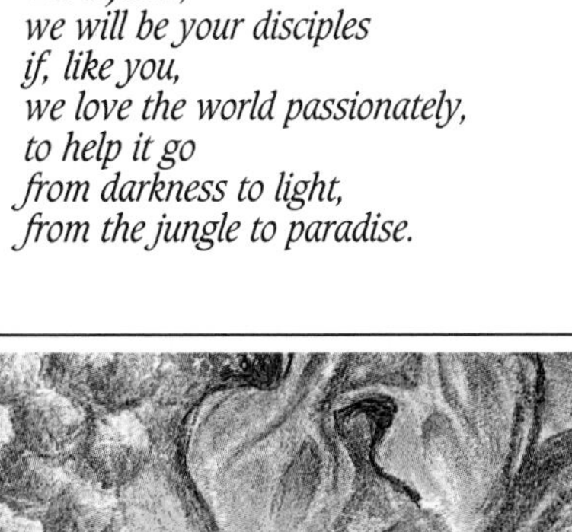

Lord Jesus,
we will be your disciples
if, like you,
we love the world passionately,
to help it go
from darkness to light,
from the jungle to paradise.

Jesus and his future disciples

17 20 "My prayer is not for them only, but for all who
21 will have faith in me through their word. | May
they all be one! Even as you, Father, are in me and I am
in you, so let them be in us, so that all men may come to
22 have faith that you sent me. | And the glory which you
have given to me I have given to them, so that they may
23 be one even as we are one. | I in them, and you in me, so
that they may be made completely one, and so that it may
become clear to all men that you have sent me and that
they are loved by you as I am loved by you.

24 Father, it is my desire that these whom
you have given to me may be by my side
where I am, so that they may see my glory
which you have given to me, because you
had love for me before the world came
25 into being. | Father of righteousness, I
have known you, though the world has
not. To these it is clear that you sent me. |
26 I have given to them knowledge of your
name,* and will give it, so that the love
which you have for me may be in them
and I in them."

Catholics, Orthodox,
Protestants, Anglicans—
Throughout the ages, Christians
have divided to their heart's content,
quarrelled, fought, and despised.
The marks can still be seen.
But, today,
we are living in great times, Lord,
where your desire for unity
has touched many hearts.
Make us peacemakers in your church.
Open up our fraternal curiosity
about our brothers' and sisters' differences.
Keep us from uniformity,
so that our hearts will rejoice
in the thousands of colors that your Gospel
radiates through different cultures
and continents.

Excerpts from the Gospel of John telling of Jesus' Passion and Resurrection are given in pages 363 to 395.

V
THE ACCOUNTS OF THE PASSION AND RESURRECTION

The disciple Paul summed up the original Christian teaching: "What I received I passed on to you... that Christ died for our sins... that he was buried, that he was raised on the third day... and that he appeared to Peter, and then to the Twelve."[1]

The apostles had much to overcome before they could proclaim such a message. To a people expecting a triumphant liberator as Messiah, * *the idea of a Messiah who had been crucified was shocking.*[2] *To add that he had risen was to invite disbelief.*

The apostles could well understand the doubts of their listeners since they had experienced the same doubts themselves. They had been scandalized * *by the death of Jesus and had needed a great deal of convincing before believing in his Resurrection.*

Thanks to the Holy Spirit, they had come to understand that the death on the cross was a supreme sign of love — the proof that when God loves, He loves totally. He loves humanity even when humanity rejects Him

All these ideas about the Passion were probably set down in writing quite quickly, so as to provide preachers with written background material. The Evangelists drew plentifully on these early texts. Each one wrote his account of the Passion and added notes bearing witness to the Resurrection. Each Evangelist's account should be read in full. The choice in this book has been to gather together extracts from the four Gospels. This for two main reasons:
- "Treasures of the Bible" presents only excerpts from the Scriptures. * *It would have been difficult to quote a passage on the Passion in the section on Mark and then other passages in the sections on Matthew, Luke and John. The effect would have been to dim the importance of these passages. Grouping them together is a way of showing that they are the core of the Gospel.*
- When they are read together, it is easier to notice their differences and see the points that each Evangelist wanted to stress in his teaching.

[1] 1 Corinthians 15, 3-5, page 438.

[2] See 1 Corinthians 1:23, page 433.

Different approaches

The accounts by Mark, Matthew and Luke are very similar — "synoptic" — based on eight episodes: the last supper, Gethsemane, the Jewish trial, the audience with Pilate, the crucifixion, the burial, the discovery of the empty tomb and the apparitions of the risen Christ. Each Evangelist adds his personal touch — individual traditions and memories, or the concerns of a particular set of readers.

John, although close to the other three, introduced two important differences:

• The last supper was not a Passover meal since, in John's version, Jesus was put to death on the eve of the Passover.

*• Jesus did not appear before the Sanhedrin.**

These discrepancies, which scholars make efforts to explain, served as a foundation for several important points of teaching:

*• According to John, Jesus died at the moment when the sacrifice of the lambs was beginning in the Temple. Families would eat the meat of these lambs during the Passover meal. John was implying that Jesus was the new Passover lamb.**

The synoptic Gospels taught the same thing, but differently. They told how Jesus shared the Passover meal with his apostles before being arrested. Yet the Passover lamb did not appear in these accounts. Jesus replaced the serving of the lamb's meat with the sharing of his own flesh and blood. He was indeed the new Passover lamb.

• John taught that the Sadducees were primarily responsible for Jesus' execution. They did not want him condemned, like the ancient prophets, for religious motives. They wanted him to be regarded as a dangerous agitator, a threat to law and order. So they had him sentenced by Pilate. The Sanhedrin did not come into the picture.* (SEE PAGE 371, "DEVIOUS MINDS.")

The synoptic Gospels stressed another aspect of the same events. They showed that if Jesus died on a cross like a bandit it was in the first place because the religious authorities refused to recognize him as a messenger of God. The three synoptic Evangelists exemplify this refusal by their account of the trial of Jesus before the Sanhedrin.

I HAVE EAGERLY)ESIRED TO EAT THIS 'ASSOVER WITH YOU"

ohn did not describe the reparations for the last upper. Matthew refers to hem but in general. Mark nd Luke mention the recautions taken by Jesus or not being disturbed by hose trying to arrest him.

esus needed to spend this ime with the apostles. ince he was about to be hysically separated from hem, he wanted to leave hem a sign that he would emain with them.

THE LAST SUPPER

Preparations

MARK
14 12 And on the first day of the Feast of Unleavened
Bread, when the Passover lamb is killed, his
disciples said to him, "Where are we to go and prepare for
13 you to eat the Passover meal?" | He sent two of his
disciples, and said to them, "Go into the town, and there
will come to you a man with a jar of water. Follow him, |
14 and wherever he goes in, say to the owner of the house,
the Master says, 'Where is my guest room, where I may eat
15 the Passover with my disciples?' | And he will lead you
himself to a great room with a table and seats. There
16 prepare for us." | And the disciples left and entered the
town, and saw that it was as he had said. They prepared
the Passover.[1]

[1] In the three synoptic Gospels, Jesus and the apostles were clearly celebrating the Passover meal (see Exodus 12:1-14 and comments, pages 63-64). The eating of the Passover lamb was glossed over. What was essential was the sharing of the bread of life and the blood of the Covenant. Jesus presented himself as the new Passover lamb who delivered us from the slavery of sin to freedom as children of God. John depicted Jesus as the new lamb in recounting his death (John 19:31-37, page 381).

Last appeal to Judas to repent

MARK
14 17 And when it was evening he came with the twelve.*
18 | And while they were seated eating food, Jesus
said, "Truly I say to you, one of you will betray me, one
19 who is eating with me." | They were sad, and said to him
20 one by one, "Is it I?" | And he said to them, "It is one of
the twelve, one who is putting his bread with me into the
21 same plate. | The Son of Man goes, even as the Scriptures
say of him.[2] but cursed is that man through whom the Son
of Man is betrayed! It would have been well for that man
if he had never been born."

Jesus perhaps had in mind 'salm 41, in which a sick person complained of being deserted by even the close friend vith whom he had shared his read. More surely, he was reerring to the "Songs of a Serant" (pages 168 to 172). The stonishing thing was that he ccepted the setbacks and sufferings of the Servant while alling himself the Son* of Aan. This title was usually associated with glory and victory see page 205). Jesus was proably saying that he would attain the glory of the Son of Aan only after adopting the umility of the Servant.

BETRAYAL

Mark, Matthew and Luke had earlier told how Judas had decided to deliver Jesus to the high priests. He sealed a bargain with them against the promise of reward: exactly thirty silver coins, according to Matthew. The fact that one of the Twelve could bring himself to do this was troubling for the Evangelists (see John 6:71, page 346) and is still the subject of conjecture by today's scholars. See "Judas."

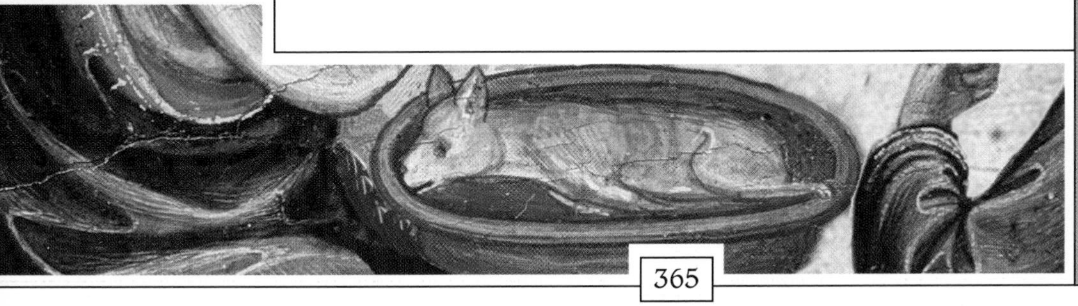

The account of the last supper appears in the three synoptic Gospels and in 1 Corinthians 11:23-26, page 434. (See also John 6:52-58, page 345.)

EXTRA WORDS

Luke's account contained two extra words compared with Mark's. Jesus instituted the new Covenant promised by Jeremiah and Ezekiel.

He asked for "remembrance" of this meal. Not just memory, but commemoration (see page 64, note 2).

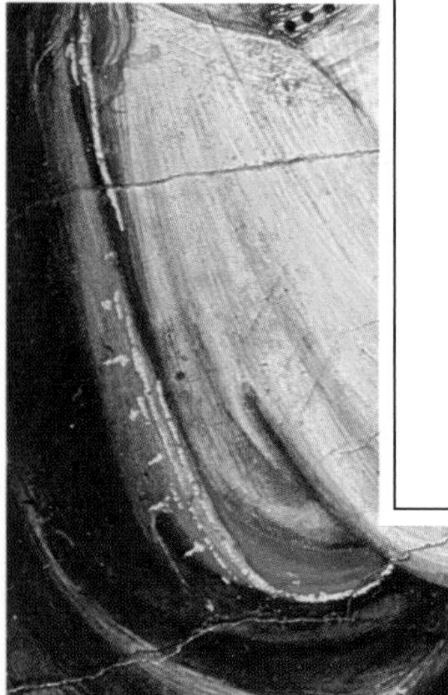

Institution of the new Covenant

MARK
14 22 And while they were eating, he took bread,
and after blessing it, he gave the broken bread to
23 them, saying, "Take it, this is my body." | And he took a
cup, and when he had given praise, he gave it to them, and
24 they all had a drink from it. | He said to them, "This is my
25 blood of the Covenant,[1] which is given for men. | Truly I
say to you, I will take no more of the fruit of the vine till
the day when I take it new in the Kingdom of God."

LUKE
22 14 And when the time had come, he took his seat, and
15 the Apostles with him. | He said, "I have had a
great desire to keep this Passover with you before I come
16 to my death. | For I say to you, I will not take it till it is
17 fulfilled in the kingdom of God." | He took a cup and,
having given praise, he said, "Divide this among
18 yourselves, | for I say to you, I will not
take of the fruit of the vine till the
Kingdom of God has come."
19 And he took bread and, having given
praise, he gave it to them when it had
been broken, saying, "This is my body,
which is given for you: do this in
20 memory of me." | And in the same way,
after the meal, he took the cup, saying,
"This cup is the new Covenant,[2] made
with my blood which is given for you."

[1] See Exodus 24:8, page 74.

[2] See Jeremiah 31:31-34, pag 157, and Ezekiel 36:25-28 page 165.

The apostles ate the bread
which was broken for them.
They drank the cup which was offered.
But they didn't understand.

The cross had to be put up
at Jerusalem's doors,
exposing to everyone's eyes,
the Body which was given,
and the Blood which was shed,
before anyone even began to understand.
Eating the bread and drinking the wine
of the New Covenant
means being united with Jesus,
who gave his life on the cross.

Communion
is receiving Jesus,
whose love is unending.
It is allowing our hearts
to burn with this boundless love.

All four evangelists recounted Peter's bluster that he would follow Jesus even to death. Luke was the only one to give Jesus' prayer for Peter.

Peter's denial foretold

LUKE
22 31 "Simon, Simon, Satan has made a request to have
you, so that he may put you to the test as grain is
32 tested: | But I have prayed for you, that your faith may not
go from you; When you have truned back, make your
brothers[1] strong."
33 And he said to him, "Lord, I am ready to go with you to
34 prison and to death." | And he said, "I say to you, Peter,
before the cock's second cry today, you will say three times
that you have no knowledge of me."

MATT
26 31 Then said Jesus to them, "All of you will abandon
me this night, for it is said in the Scriptures, *I will
put to death the shepherd, and the sheep of the flock will*
32 *be put to flight.*[2] | But after I am come back from the dead,
33 I will go before you into Galilee." | But Peter answered,
"Though all may abandon you, I will never be turned
34 away." | Jesus said to him, "Truly I say to you that this
night, before the hour of the cock's cry, you will say three
35 times that you have no knowledge of me." | Peter says to
him, "Even if I am put to death with you, I will not betray
you." So said all the disciples.

[1] This was a clear illustration of why Simon had been nicknamed Peter (Rock). He would be the one upon whom the others could lean to strengthen their faith.

[2] This was a prophecy made by Zechariah (Zechariah 13:7).

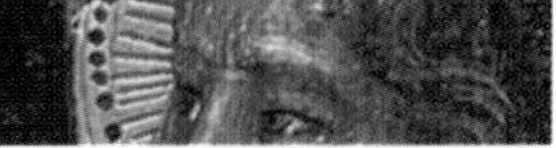

"YOU WILL ALL FALL AWAY ON ACCOUNT OF ME"

Jesus knew that the manner of his arrest and execution would deeply shock his disciples. How could they accept the liberator, the emissary of God, being nailed to the infamous wood of a cross? All those who were prepared to die with him in a fight for freedom would scatter in dismay.

Washing the feet

JOHN
13 1 Now before the feast of the Passover, it was clear
to Jesus that the time had come for him to leave
this world to be with the Father. Having once had love for
those in the world who were his, his love for them
2 remained to the end. | So while a meal was going on, the

SERVANT

John did not relate the sharing of the bread and wine at the last supper. He had written everything he had to say on the subject in his Chapter 6 (see pages 342 to 346)**. What he did describe was the washing of the feet, a symbolic act in which Jesus, the master, became servant. He kneeled as a servant even before those who would betray, disown and abandon him. In doing so, he showed that his love was absolute. No human failing could deter it.**

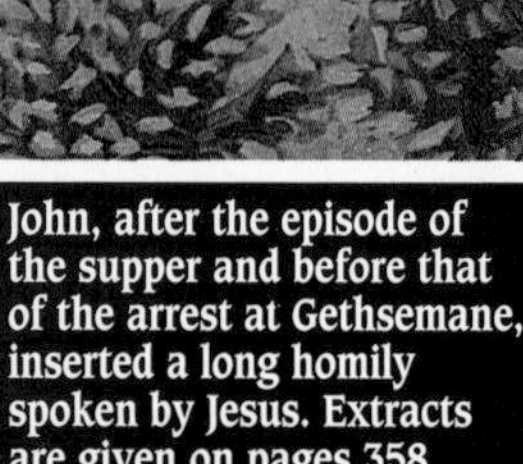

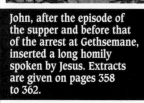

John, after the episode of the supper and before that of the arrest at Gethsemane, inserted a long homily spoken by Jesus. Extracts are given on pages 358 to 362.

Evil One[1] having now put it into the heart of Judas Iscariot,
3 Simon's son, to betray him, | Jesus, being conscious that
the Father had put everything into his hands, and that he
4 came from God and was going to God, | got up from table,
put off his robe and took a cloth and wrapped it around
5 him. | Then he put water into a basin and washed the feet
of the disciples, drying them with the cloth which was
around him.
6 So he came to Simon Peter. Peter said, "Lord, are my feet
7 to be washed by you?" | And Jesus, answering, said to
him, "What I do is not clear to you now, but it will be clear
8 to you in time to come." | Peter said, "I will never let my
feet be washed by you, never." Jesus said in answer, "If I
9 do not make you clean you have no part with me." | Simon
Peter said to him, "Lord, not my feet only, but my hands
10 and my head." | Jesus said to him, "He who is bathed has
need only to have his feet washed and then he is clean all
11 over. You, my disciples, are clean, but not all of you." | (He
knew who was to betray him, that is why he said, "You are
not all clean.")
12 Then, after washing their feet and
putting on his robe again, he took his
seat and said to them, "Do you see what
13 I have done to you? | You give me the
name of Master and Lord, and you are
14 right. That is what I am. | If then I, the
Lord and the Master, have made your
feet clean, it is right for you to make one
15 another's feet clean. | I have given you an
example, so that you may do what I have
done to you."

"When you have just taken a bath,
you are pure!"
The apostles were immersed
in the presence of Jesus.
They lived with him and shared his meals.
They travelled the same paths.
They listened to his word.
And even if this bathing had yet to produce
all of its effects on them,
it had already begun to purify them.

But, not all of them!
Judas was there.
On the outside, he looked like the others.
But within his obscure development
of freedom,
he refused to let himself be converted,
to be transfigured
by the presence of Jesus.

[1] John often used the phrase "prince of this world" as a title for the devil.

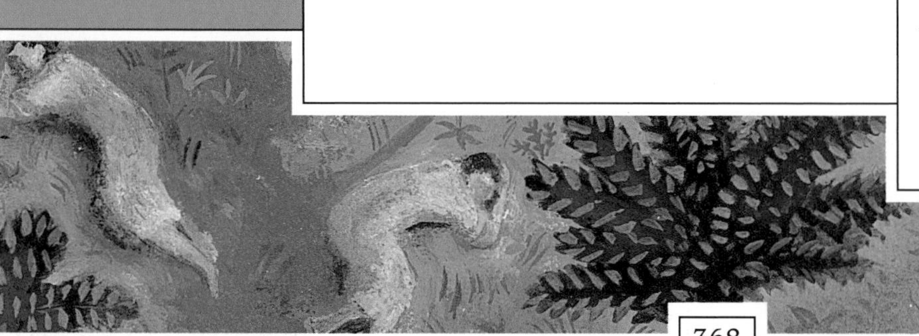

LONELINESS

Jesus went with his disciples into a garden called Gethsemane, which means "oil press," at the foot of the Mount of Olives. The synoptic Gospels recounted, with slight differences of detail, the loneliness of Jesus and his feelings of dejection and anguish.

The difference between "what I will" and "what You will" was not fundamental. Jesus in fact willed what his Father willed. Apprehension and dread made him try to imagine other ways out. But he knew they were not realistic alternatives.

GETHSEMANE

The last temptation of Jesus

MARK
14 32 And they came to a place which was named
Gethsemane where he said to his disciples, "Be
33 seated here while I say a prayer." | He took with him Peter
and James and John, and grief and great trouble filled him
34 him. | He said to them, "My soul is very sad, even to death:
35 stay here a little time, and keep watch." | And he went
forward a little, and falling down on the earth, asking that,
36 if possible, the hour might go from him. | And he said,
"Abba,* Father, all things are possible to you. Take away
this cup from me. But even so let not my will, but yours, be
37 done."[1] | He returned and saw them sleeping, and said to
Peter, "Simon, are you sleeping? were you not able to keep
38 watch one hour? | Keep watch with prayer, so that you may
not be put to the test. The spirit truly is willing, but the flesh*
39 is feeble." | And again he went away, and said a prayer,
40 using the same words. | Again he returned and saw them
sleeping, because their eyes were very tired, and they had
41 nothing to say in answer. | He came the third time, and said
to them, "Go on sleeping now and take your rest. it is
enough; the hour has come. The Son of man is delivered into
42 the hands of evil men. | Get up, let us be going. He who
betrays me is near."

LUKE
22 44 And his soul greatly troubled, the force of his
prayer became stronger, and great drops, like
blood, came from him, falling to the ground.

DARKNESS

During the last supper, Jesus had told the apostles that he would shed his blood for the many. He would impart to them his ability to love "to the very end." In the darkness at Gethsemane, he was tempted not to go to the very end. Why should he have to be crucified? Had he not already shown mankind the grandeur of God's love? Could he not leave it at that? "Do you not think that I can call upon my Father, and he will at once put at my disposal twelve legions of angels?" (See Matthew 26:53, page 370.)

Jesus struggled against this temptation, so hard that he sweated drops of blood. The only certainty left to him was his trust in his Father. So, like a child, he let himself be led, despite his feelings of repugnance. "Abba, not what I will, but what You will."

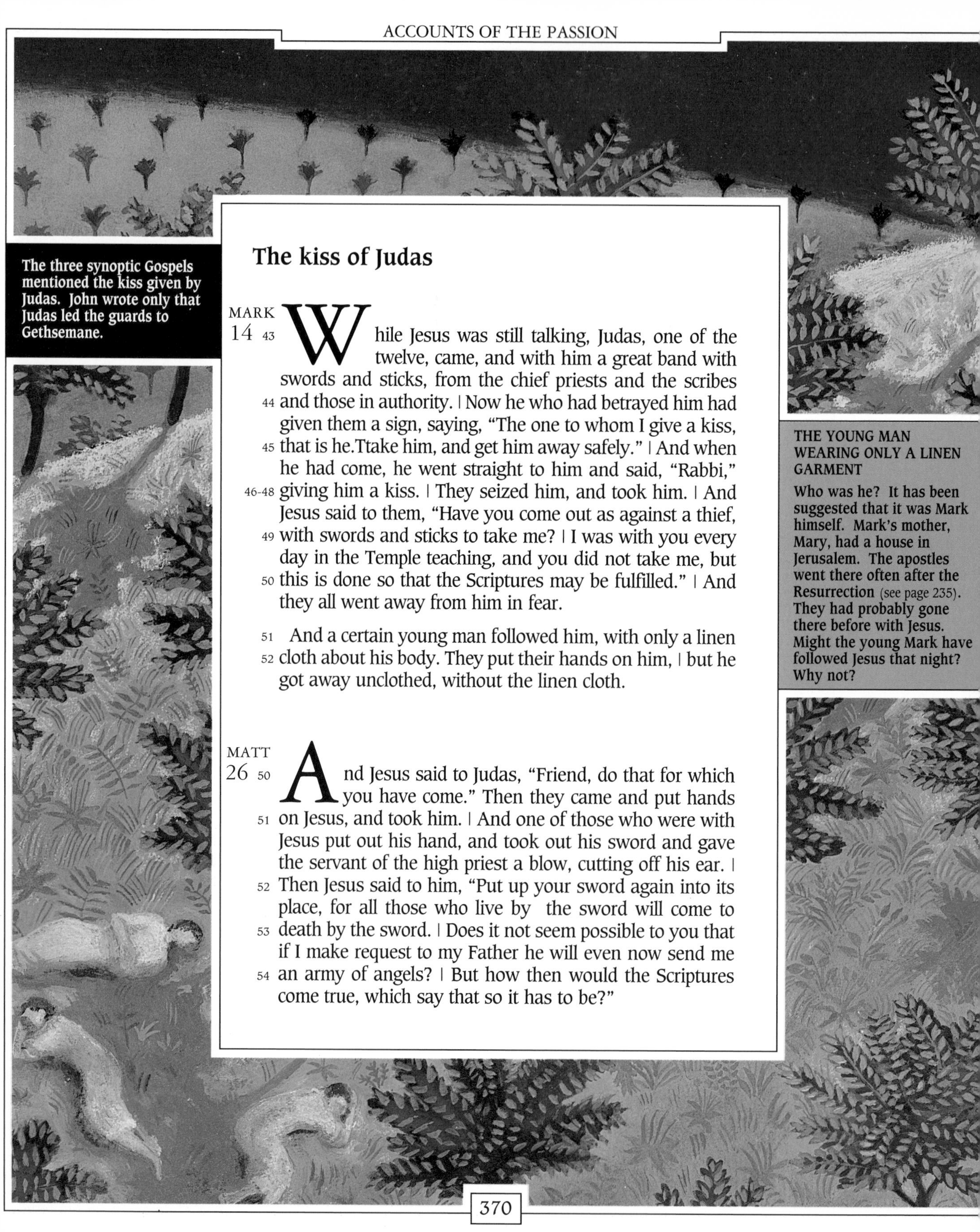

The three synoptic Gospels mentioned the kiss given by Judas. John wrote only that Judas led the guards to Gethsemane.

The kiss of Judas

MARK
14 43 While Jesus was still talking, Judas, one of the
twelve, came, and with him a great band with
swords and sticks, from the chief priests and the scribes
44 and those in authority. | Now he who had betrayed him had
given them a sign, saying, "The one to whom I give a kiss,
45 that is he.Ttake him, and get him away safely." | And when
he had come, he went straight to him and said, "Rabbi,"
46-48 giving him a kiss. | They seized him, and took him. | And
Jesus said to them, "Have you come out as against a thief,
49 with swords and sticks to take me? | I was with you every
day in the Temple teaching, and you did not take me, but
50 this is done so that the Scriptures may be fulfilled." | And
they all went away from him in fear.

51 And a certain young man followed him, with only a linen
52 cloth about his body. They put their hands on him, | but he
got away unclothed, without the linen cloth.

MATT
26 50 And Jesus said to Judas, "Friend, do that for which
you have come." Then they came and put hands
51 on Jesus, and took him. | And one of those who were with
Jesus put out his hand, and took out his sword and gave
the servant of the high priest a blow, cutting off his ear. |
52 Then Jesus said to him, "Put up your sword again into its
place, for all those who live by the sword will come to
53 death by the sword. | Does it not seem possible to you that
if I make request to my Father he will even now send me
54 an army of angels? | But how then would the Scriptures
come true, which say that so it has to be?"

THE YOUNG MAN WEARING ONLY A LINEN GARMENT

Who was he? It has been suggested that it was Mark himself. Mark's mother, Mary, had a house in Jerusalem. The apostles went there often after the Resurrection (see page 235). They had probably gone there before with Jesus. Might the young Mark have followed Jesus that night? Why not?

REE WILL

ohn laid great stress on sus' liberty in the face of is enemies. His mere resence lays them low. He ould easily have escaped. ut he chose to go through the end, to show that his ve was unswerving, gardless of how people sponded to it. He chose eely to go through with his assion.

EVIOUS MINDS

 John's Gospel, there was o meeting of the anhedrin* to try Jesus. It ad already reached its erdict (John 11:47-53, page 56). The priests not only anted Jesus to die; they lso wanted his death to be assed over in silence. They id not want any protests bout his being unjustly ondemned, as many rophets had been. They rranged for Jesus to be ied by the Roman governor s a dangerous rabble-ouser. That way he would e crucified. It would be an bvious sign to all that God ad abandoned him. There as a passage in euteronomy that anyone ung on the wood of a tree as under God's curse euteronomy 21:22-23).

JOHN 18 4 Then Jesus, having knowledge of everything which
was coming on him, went forward and said to them,
5 "Who are you looking for?" | Their answer was, "Jesus the
Nazarene." Jesus said, "I am he."[1] And Judas, who betrayed
6 him, was there at their side. | When he said to them, "I am
he," they went back, falling to the ground.

7 So again he put the question to them, "Who are you
8 looking for?" And they said, "Jesus the Nazarene." | Jesus
answered, "I have said that I am he. if you are looking for
me, let these men go away."...

10 Then Simon Peter, who had a sword, took it out and gave
the high priest's servant a blow, cutting off his right ear.
11 The servant's name was Malchus. | Then Jesus said to
Peter, "Put back your sword. Am I not to take the cup
which my Father has given to me?"

THE JEWISH TRIAL

Peter's denial

JOHN 18 12 Then the band and the chief captain and the police
13 took Jesus and put cords around him. | They took
him first to Annas, because Annas was the father-in-law
of Caiaphas who was the high priest that year.[2]...

15 And Simon Peter followed Jesus with another disciple.
Now that disciple was a friend of the high priest and he
16 went in with Jesus into the house of the high priest. | But
Peter was kept outside at the door. Then this other disciple,
who was a friend of the high priest, came out and had a

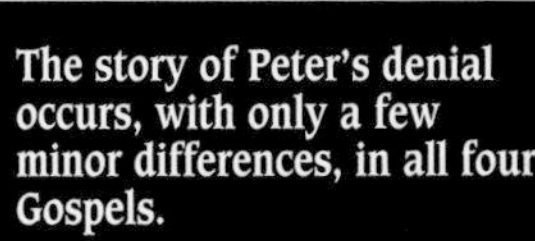

The story of Peter's denial occurs, with only a few minor differences, in all four Gospels.

[1] The expression in the Greek text used by Jesus could be rendered as "I AM." See John 8:58, page 349.

[2] Annas* simply wanted to see who Jesus was. He then sent him to his son-in-law, Caiaphas, to await daybreak. Jesus was taken from Caiaphas' house to the court of the Roman governor.

Peter, why do you claim that
you don't know Jesus?
Are you afraid of being arrested
or imprisoned?
Yet, you were sincerely ready
to give your life for him.
You courageously attacked
the troop of guards at Gethsemane.
But Jesus ordered you
to put your sword back in your sheath,
and the Messiah let himself be arrested.

word with the girl who kept the door,
17 and took Peter in. | Then the girl who
was the doorkeeper said to Peter, "Are
you not one of this man's disciples? He
answered, "I am not."

LUKE
22 58 And after a little time, another saw him and said,
"You are one of them." He said, "Man, I am not."
59 And after about an hour, another man
said, decisively, "Certainly this man was
60 with him, for he is a Galilaean." | And
Peter said, "Man, I have no knowledge
of these things of which you are
talking." And immediately, while he
was saying these words, a cock crowed.
61 And the Lord, turning, gave Peter a
look. Tthe words of the Lord came to
Peter's mind, how he had said, "This
night, before the hour of the cock's cry,
62 you will betray me three times." | And
he went out, weeping bitterly.

Peter, you can't understand anymore.
How can Jesus fulfill his mission
now that he is arrested,
bound, and powerless?
You are overcome by doubt, or perhaps anger.
"How could I have put my trust
in man like that?
I don't know him..."
You are scandalized.
But, Jesus is watching you.
Your scandal, anger, and doubts
are all carried away; swept away
by the only certainty that counts—
that you are loved,
no matter what your sin is.

Blasphemy!

MATT
26 59 Now the chief priests and all the Sanhedrin[1] were
looking for false witness against Jesus, so that
60 they might put him to death. | They were not able to get it,
61 though a number of false witnesses came. | But later there
came two who said, "This man said, I am able to give the

[1] The Sanhedrin, also known as the Grand Council.

WILY PRIESTS

The synoptic Gospels insisted on the fact that Jesus was sentenced to death because the leaders of the people refused to acknowledge him as the representative of God. They even accused him of blasphemy, speaking irreverently of God.

After the religious verdict, the priests went to great pains— as John well noted — to have Jesus crucified by the Roman authorities. Once Jesus was publicly exposed at the gates of Jerusalem hanging on a cross like a hoodlum, he would be just another "poor guy," worth a shrug of pity perhaps, but not a person you could put your faith in.

The ruse of the priests very nearly succeeded (see the reactions of the disciples in Emmaus, Luke 24:20-21, page 390).

Temple of God to destruction, and to build it up again in
62 three days." | And the high priest got up and said to him,
"Have you no answer? What is it that they say against
63 you?" | But Jesus said not a word. And the high priest said
to him, "I put you on oath, by the living God, that you will
64 say to us if you are the Christ, the Son of God." | Jesus said
to him, "You say so: but I say to you, From now you will
see the Son of Man seated at the right hand of power, and
coming on the clouds of heaven."[1] |
65 Then the high priest, violently parting
his robes,[2] said, "He has spoken
blasphemy.* What more need have we
of witnesses? For now his blasphemy
66 have come to your ears. | What is your
opinion?" They said, "It is right for him
to be put to death."
67 Then they put shame on him, and were
68 cruel to him, beating him, saying, | "Be
a prophet, O Christ, and say who gave
you a blow!"

The Word made flesh is accused
of blaspheming the Word of God,
and of speaking ill of God!
At no point
did those learned people, whose hearts
were as dry as parchment, ever question
their capacity to listen.
They were so sure of the truth.
In the name of the mute god
they had made for themselves,
they refused to hear the God
who was speaking to them.

[1] See Daniel 7:13, page 205. Jesus changed one detail of the vision in the Book of Daniel describing the Son of Man. By calling himself the Son of Man, not standing, but sitting at the right hand of the Mighty One, Jesus was claiming equality with God. For this he was accused of blasphemy.

[2] Tearing one's clothes was a gesture of outrage or grief. See 2 Kings 5:7, page 126.

Matthew reported that Judas was stricken with remorse on learning that Jesus had been condemned. He threw the thirty silver coins that he had been paid for betraying Jesus into the Temple, and hanged himself.

THE ROMAN TRIAL

Jesus and Pilate

JOHN
18 28 So they took Jesus from the house of Caiaphas to the
Praetorium. It was early. They themselves did not go

All four Evangelists described the hearing with Pilate. They agreed on the same main points — the questioning on Jesus' kingship, the freeing of Barabbas, the flogging of Jesus and the crucifixion demanded by the crowd.

Matthew was the only one to tell of Pilate washing his hands and saying, "I am innocent of this man's blood."

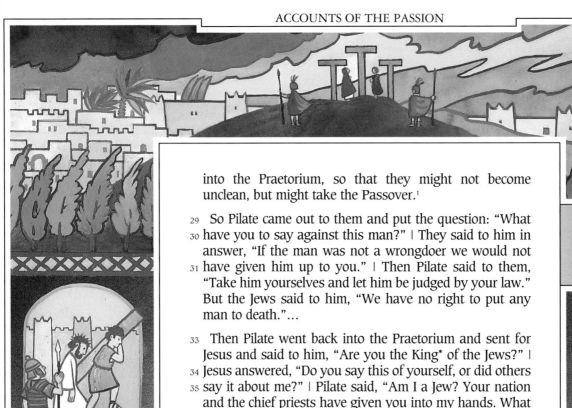

into the Praetorium, so that they might not become
unclean, but might take the Passover.[1]

29 So Pilate came out to them and put the question: "What
30 have you to say against this man?" | They said to him in
answer, "If the man was not a wrongdoer we would not
31 have given him up to you." | Then Pilate said to them,
"Take him yourselves and let him be judged by your law."
But the Jews said to him, "We have no right to put any
man to death."...

33 Then Pilate went back into the Praetorium and sent for
Jesus and said to him, "Are you the King* of the Jews?" |
34 Jesus answered, "Do you say this of yourself, or did others
35 say it about me?" | Pilate said, "Am I a Jew? Your nation
and the chief priests have given you into my hands. What
36 have you done?" | Jesus said in answer, "My Kingdom is
not of this world. If my Kingdom was of this world, my
disciples would have made a good fight to keep me out of
37 the hands of the Jews, but my Kingdom is not here." | Then
Pilate said to him, "Are you then a king?" Jesus answered,
"You say that I am a king. For this purpose was I given
birth, and for this purpose I came into the world, that I
might give witness to what is true.* Every lover of the truth
38 hears my voice." | Pilate said to him, "True? What is true?"
Having said this he went out again to the Jews and said to
them, "I see no wrong in him.

39 But every year you make a request to me to let a prisoner
go free at the Passover. Is it your desire that I let the King
40 of the Jews go free?" | Then again they gave a loud cry,
"Not this man, but Barabbas." Now Barabbas was an
outlaw.

[1] Going into a heathen's house was an impure act. See Acts of the Apostles 11:3, page 416. See also the sensitivity shown by the Roman centurion in Luke 7:1-10, page 310.

POSSESSED BY THE TRUTH

Pilate did not listen to Jesus carefully enough. If he had, he would have been astonished. People often claim to possess the truth. Jesus was talking of those who are possessed by the truth. He, Jesus, was the truth. "I am the way and the truth..." (John 14:6, page 358).

No disciple of Jesus can possess the truth. Who could claim to possess the Son of God? A disciple lets the truth dwell in her or him and accepts being changed by it.

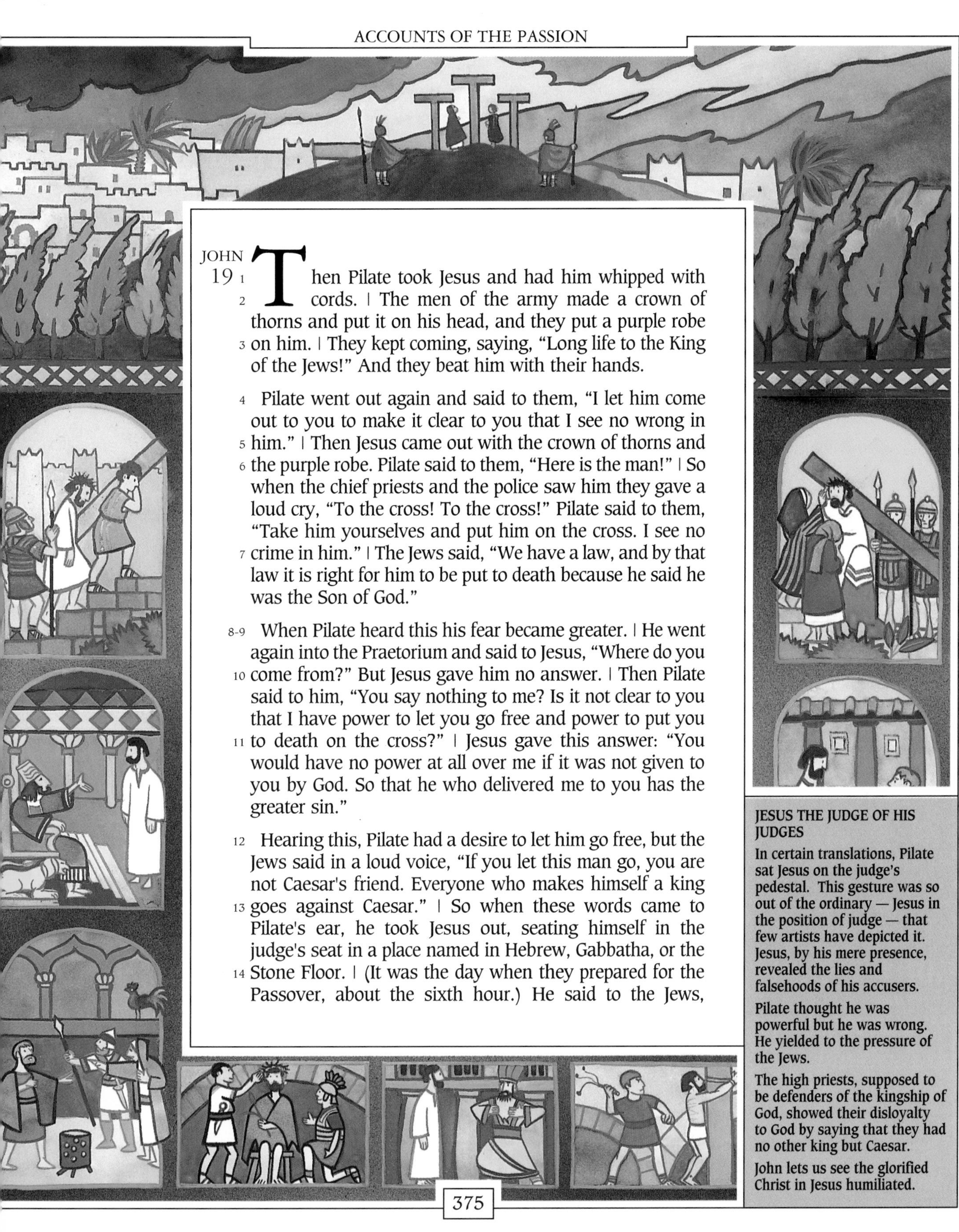

JOHN
19 1 Then Pilate took Jesus and had him whipped with
2 cords. | The men of the army made a crown of
thorns and put it on his head, and they put a purple robe
3 on him. | They kept coming, saying, "Long life to the King
of the Jews!" And they beat him with their hands.

4 Pilate went out again and said to them, "I let him come
out to you to make it clear to you that I see no wrong in
5 him." | Then Jesus came out with the crown of thorns and
6 the purple robe. Pilate said to them, "Here is the man!" | So
when the chief priests and the police saw him they gave a
loud cry, "To the cross! To the cross!" Pilate said to them,
"Take him yourselves and put him on the cross. I see no
7 crime in him." | The Jews said, "We have a law, and by that
law it is right for him to be put to death because he said he
was the Son of God."

8-9 When Pilate heard this his fear became greater. | He went
again into the Praetorium and said to Jesus, "Where do you
10 come from?" But Jesus gave him no answer. | Then Pilate
said to him, "You say nothing to me? Is it not clear to you
that I have power to let you go free and power to put you
11 to death on the cross?" | Jesus gave this answer: "You
would have no power at all over me if it was not given to
you by God. So that he who delivered me to you has the
greater sin."

12 Hearing this, Pilate had a desire to let him go free, but the
Jews said in a loud voice, "If you let this man go, you are
not Caesar's friend. Everyone who makes himself a king
13 goes against Caesar." | So when these words came to
Pilate's ear, he took Jesus out, seating himself in the
judge's seat in a place named in Hebrew, Gabbatha, or the
14 Stone Floor. | (It was the day when they prepared for the
Passover, about the sixth hour.) He said to the Jews,

JESUS THE JUDGE OF HIS JUDGES

In certain translations, Pilate sat Jesus on the judge's pedestal. This gesture was so out of the ordinary — Jesus in the position of judge — that few artists have depicted it. Jesus, by his mere presence, revealed the lies and falsehoods of his accusers.

Pilate thought he was powerful but he was wrong. He yielded to the pressure of the Jews.

The high priests, supposed to be defenders of the kingship of God, showed their disloyalty to God by saying that they had no other king but Caesar.

John lets us see the glorified Christ in Jesus humiliated.

15 "There is your King!" | Then they gave a loud cry, "Away
with him! Away with him! To the cross!" Pilate said to
them, "Am I to put your king to death on the cross?" The
16 chief priests answered, "We have no king but Caesar." | So
then he delivered him to them to be put to death on the
cross. They took Jesus away;

Jesus and Herod Antipas

Luke was the only Evangelist to relate Jesus' hearing before Herod. This was the same Herod Antipas who had had John the Baptist beheaded (see Mark 6:17-29, page 243).

LUKE
23 6 But at these words Pilate said, "Is the man a
7 Galilaean?" | And when he saw that he was under
the authority of Herod, he sent him to Herod, who was in
8 Jerusalem himself at that time. | Now when Herod saw Jesus
he was very glad, having for a long time had a desire to see
him. He had had accounts of him, and was hoping to see
9 some wonders done by him. | He put a great number of
10 questions to him, but he said nothing. | And the chief priests
and the scribes were there, vehemently making statements
11 against him. | Herod, with the men of his army, ridiculed him
and mocked him, and dressing him in shining robes, he sent
12 him back to Pilate. | That day Herod and Pilate became
friends with one another, for before they had been against
one another.

GOLGOTHA

On the way: Simon from Cyrene

The three synoptic* Gospels told of Simon carrying the cross.

John, always careful to stress the power of Jesus, wrote "carrying his own cross."

MARK
15 20 And they took him out to put him to death on the
21 cross.[1] | They made one, Simon of Cyrene, the
father of Alexander and Rufus, who was going by, coming

[1] A Roman cross was usuall[y] made up of two parts. One wa[s] an upright post left in th[e] ground at the execution sit[e]. The other was a horizonta[l] beam called the patibulum. [It] was this piece that the prisone[r] carried from jail to the place o[f] execution. Since Jesus had n[o] strength left, a passer-by wa[s] ordered to carry the beam fo[r] him (Matthew 5:41, page 262).

He didn't volunteer.
He was requisitioned.
He was forced to carry Jesus' cross.
But if Mark remembered his name,
as well as the names of his two sons,
it is, without any doubt,
because this forced meeting
changed Simon's life forever.
He recognized that this condemned person,
crushed under that instrument of torture,
was the one carrying
the sins of the world.
What began as forced labor,
finished as thanksgiving.

from the country, go with them, so that
22 he might take his cross. | And they took
him to the place named Golgotha, which
means Dead Man's Head.

Women on the way

LUKE
23 27 And a great band of people followed him, and
28 women mourning and weeping for him. | But
Jesus, turning to them, said, "Daughters of Jerusalem, let
not your weeping be for me, but for yourselves and for
29 your children. | For the days are coming in which they will
say, 'Blessed are those who have had no children, whose
bodies have never given birth, whose breasts have never
30 given milk.' | They will say to the mountains, 'Come down
31 on us, and to the hills, be a cover over us.' | For if they do
these things when the tree is green,[1] what will they do
when it is dry?"

Luke was the only Evangelist to report the women who wept.

On the cross

JOHN
19 19 And Pilate put on the cross a statement in writing.
The words were: "Jesus the Nazarene, the King of
20 the Jews."[2] | The words were seen by a number of the Jews,
for the place where Jesus was put to death on the cross was
near the town, and the writing was in Hebrew, Latin and
21 Greek. | Then the chief priests of the Jews said to Pilate,
"Do not write 'The King of the Jews', but, 'He said, I am the
King of the Jews.'"

22 Pilate answered, "What I have written will not be
changed."

The notice at the top of the cross was mentioned by all four Evangelists.

[1] Jesus was the green tree, the vinestock full of sap which gives new life to the vine stems (see John 15:1-8, page 358).

[2] In Latin, this was written "Iesus Nazarenus Rex Iudeorum." The notice with the initials INRI may often be seen in paintings and statues of the crucifixion.

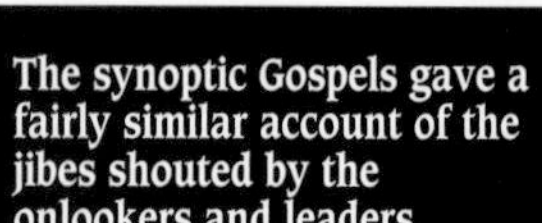

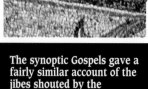

The synoptic Gospels gave a fairly similar account of the jibes shouted by the onlookers and leaders.

Insults

MARK
15 29 And those who went by mocked him, shaking
their heads, saying, "Ha! You who can destroy
30 the Temple, and build it up again in three days, | save
31 yourself from death, and descend from the cross." | In the
same way the chief priests, laughing at him among
themselves with the scribes,* said, "A savior of others, yet
32 he cannot save himself. | Let the Christ, the King of Israel,
come down now from the cross, so that we may see and
believe." Those who were hung on crosses with him said
evil things against him.

Two criminals

All four Evangelists wrote that Jesus was crucified along with two criminals. Luke was the only one to relate their conversation with Jesus.

LUKE
23 33 And when they came to the place which is named
Golgotha,* they nailed him on the
cross, along with the criminals, one on
the right side, and the other on the left. |
34 Jesus said, "Father, forgive them, for they
do not know what they are doing." Then
they divided his clothing among them by
casting lots.

39 One of the criminals on the cross bitterly
said to him, "Are you not the Christ?
40 Save yourself and us from this." | But the
other, protesting, said, "Have you no fear
of God? For you have a part in the same
41 punishment. | And rightly so, for we are
given what we deserve, but this man has
42 done nothing wrong." | He said, "Jesus,

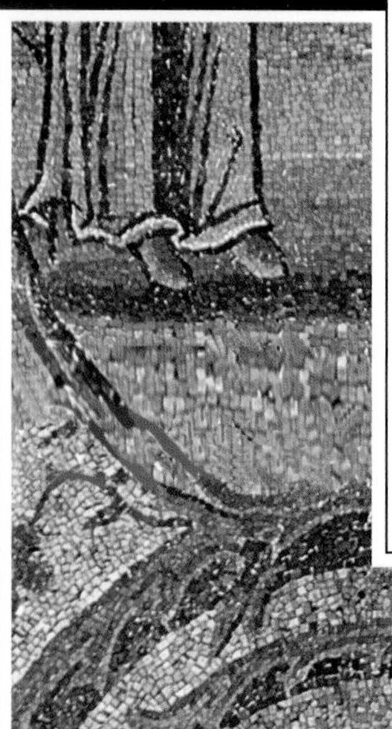

This condemned person
with a heavy past,
had retained a bit of innocence
in a corner of his heart.
He was able to recognize
in the disfigured face
of the one crucified beside him,
the one who could save him;
not from an immediate death,
but from beyond death.
"Remember me..."

Jesus took one of those whom he was
so frequently criticized for being with,
home to his Father.
There is no blaming,
no mistrust in his Father's house.
All of those with him are welcomed
as children.

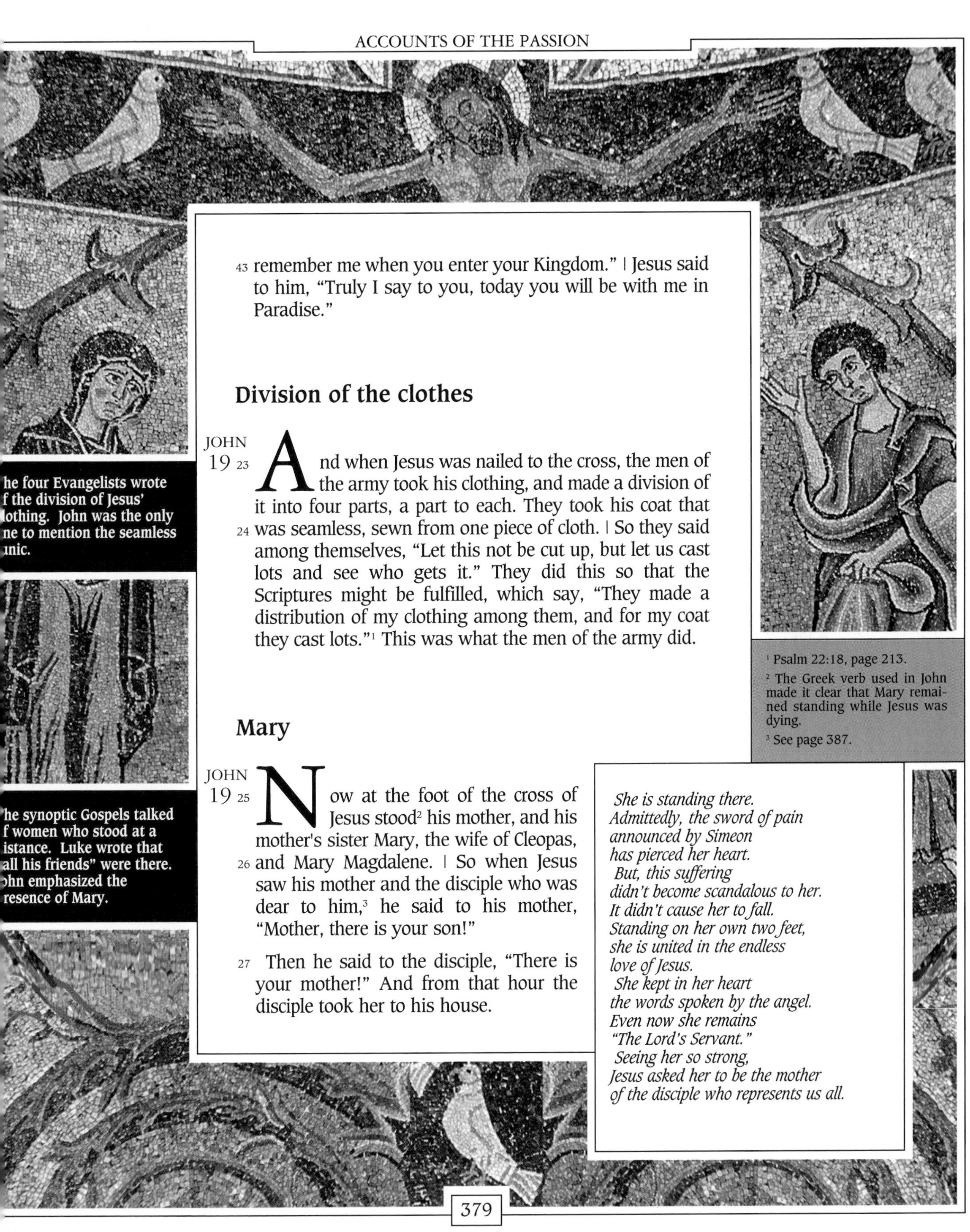

43 remember me when you enter your Kingdom." | Jesus said
to him, "Truly I say to you, today you will be with me in
Paradise."

Division of the clothes

JOHN
19 23 And when Jesus was nailed to the cross, the men of
the army took his clothing, and made a division of
it into four parts, a part to each. They took his coat that
24 was seamless, sewn from one piece of cloth. | So they said
among themselves, "Let this not be cut up, but let us cast
lots and see who gets it." They did this so that the
Scriptures might be fulfilled, which say, "They made a
distribution of my clothing among them, and for my coat
they cast lots."[1] This was what the men of the army did.

he four Evangelists wrote f the division of Jesus' lothing. John was the only ne to mention the seamless unic.

Mary

JOHN
19 25 Now at the foot of the cross of
Jesus stood[2] his mother, and his
mother's sister Mary, the wife of Cleopas,
26 and Mary Magdalene. | So when Jesus
saw his mother and the disciple who was
dear to him,[3] he said to his mother,
"Mother, there is your son!"

27 Then he said to the disciple, "There is
your mother!" And from that hour the
disciple took her to his house.

he synoptic Gospels talked f women who stood at a istance. Luke wrote that all his friends" were there. ohn emphasized the resence of Mary.

She is standing there.
Admittedly, the sword of pain
announced by Simeon
has pierced her heart.
But, this suffering
didn't become scandalous to her.
It didn't cause her to fall.
Standing on her own two feet,
she is united in the endless
love of Jesus.
She kept in her heart
the words spoken by the angel.
Even now she remains
"The Lord's Servant."
Seeing her so strong,
Jesus asked her to be the mother
of the disciple who represents us all.

[1] Psalm 22:18, page 213.

[2] The Greek verb used in John made it clear that Mary remained standing while Jesus was dying.

[3] See page 387.

The death of Jesus

LUKE
23 44 And it was now about the sixth hour. All the
45 land was dark till the ninth hour. | The light of the
sun went out, and the curtain in the Temple was parted in
46 two. | Jesus gave a loud cry, saying, "Father, into your
hands I give my spirit."[1] When he had said this, he gave
up his spirit.

47 And when the centurion saw what was done, he praised
God, saying, "Without doubt this was a righteous man." |
48 All the people who had come together to see it, when they
saw the things which were done, went back again beating
their breasts in grief.

Mark's account was nearly the same as Matthew's. Mark did not mention, as Matthew alone did, an earthquake or the dead coming back to life.

MATT
27 45 Now from the sixth hour it was dark over all the
46 land till the ninth hour. | About the ninth hour
Jesus gave a loud cry, saying, "*Eli, Eli, lama sabachthani*?"
that is, "My God, my God, why have you forsaken me
47 me?"[2] | Some of those who were near by, hearing it, said,
48 "This man is crying to Elijah." | And immediately one of
them went quickly, taking a sponge, and soaked it full of
bitter wine. Then he put it on a rod and gave him drink. |
49 The others said, "Let him be. Let us see if Elijah will come
50 to his help." | And Jesus gave another loud cry, and gave
up his spirit.

51 The curtain of the Temple was parted in two from end to
end. There was an earthquake, and the rocks were broken.
52 | The tombs opened and the bodies of many sleeping holy
53 people came to life. | Leaving their tombs, after Jesus was
resurrected, they went into the holy town and were seen by

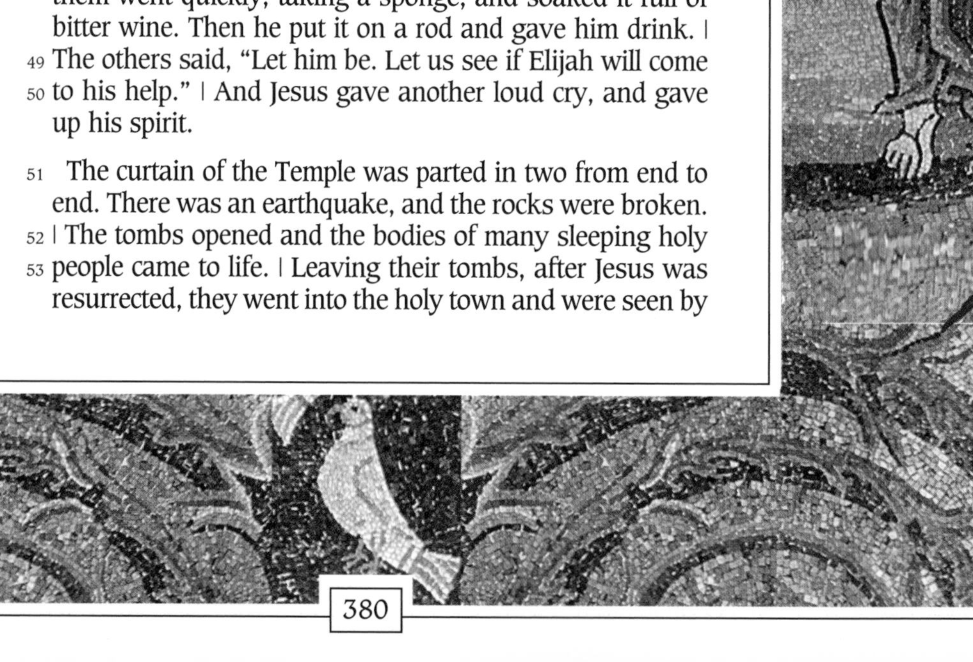

[1] From Psalm 31:6.

[2] In Aramaic, Jesus spoke the opening words of Psalm 22 (see page 212). Among the people standing around the cross were Romans and probably diaspora* pilgrims come for the Passover feast. They understood neither Hebrew nor Aramaic, whence their error. They thought Jesus was calling to Elijah.

Psalm 22 expressed the distress of a believer in pain. The sufferer was sure that God, despite His silence, heard his prayer and would save him.

54 a number of people. | Now the centurion and those who
were with him watching Jesus, when they saw the
earthquake and the things which were done, were in great
fearsaying, "Truly this was a Son of God."

BEYOND DEATH

Matthew seemed impatient to talk of Resurrection. He had hardly noted Jesus' last cry before going on to say that Jesus would not remain in death's power.

He would rise again, but not alone. He would carry the whole of humanity with him.

Sheol,* the abode of the dead imagined by people in the past, was an outdated idea. Jesus, in the darkness of the tomb, had thrown open the shining door of the Resurrection,* inviting us all to "go through." Death was no longer separation from God.

The pierced heart

JOHN
19 31 Now it was the day of preparing for the
Passover, and so that the bodies might not be on
the cross on the Sabbath* (because the day of that Sabbath
was a great day), the Jews asked Pilate that their legs[1]
32 might be broken, and that they might be taken away. | So
the men of the army came, and the legs of the first were
broken and then of the other who was put to death on the
33 cross with Jesus. | But when they came to Jesus, they saw
that he was dead by this time, and so his legs were not
34 broken. | One of the men made a wound in his side with a
35 spear, and immediately there flowed blood and water. | He
who saw it has given witness (and his witness is true; he
is certain that what he says is true) so that you may
36 believe. | These things came about so that the Scriptures
might be fulfilled,

"No bone of his body will be broken."[2]

37 And again another verse says,

"They will see him who was wounded by their spears."[3]

. NEW PASSOVER

n the Temple on the eve of he Passover, lambs were acrificed and taken away y each family for the 'assover meal, a ommemoration of the eparture from Egypt.

t the same hour, Jesus died n the cross without any of is bones being broken.

ohn, in drawing this arallel, was implying that he rites* of the Jewish 'assover were obsolete. The ew lamb sent by God elivered us from the lavery of sin and offered us reedom as the children of od.

Vith what flowed from his eart — the water of aptism and the blood of the ast supper, the gifts of his ove — he makes us pure.

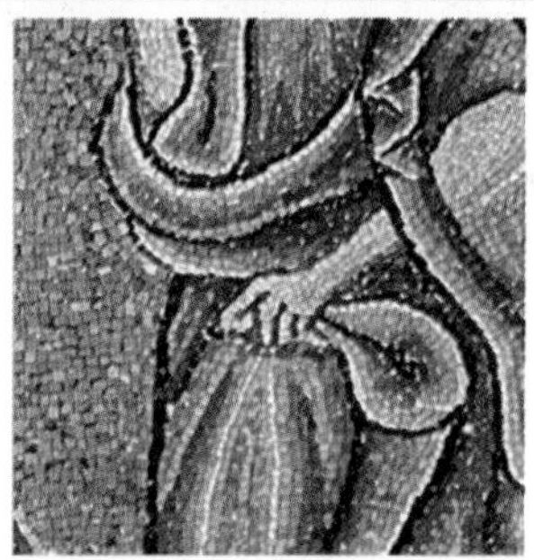

[1] The person crucified was nailed in such a way as to be supported in three places, by the two wrists and the feet, usually joined together. The body sagged and the lungs filled with air. To breathe out, the victim had to lift himself by pressing down on the nail through his feet and pulling on his arms. To shorten the agony, the victim had his legs broken. Unable to bear down on his feet, he died more quickly.

[2] From Exodus 12:46, referring to the Passover lamb.

[3] See Zechariah 12:10, page 193.

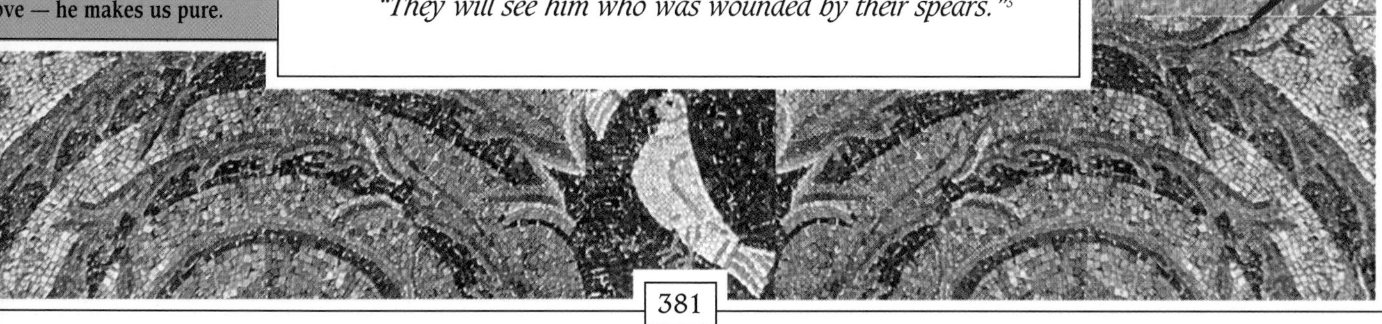

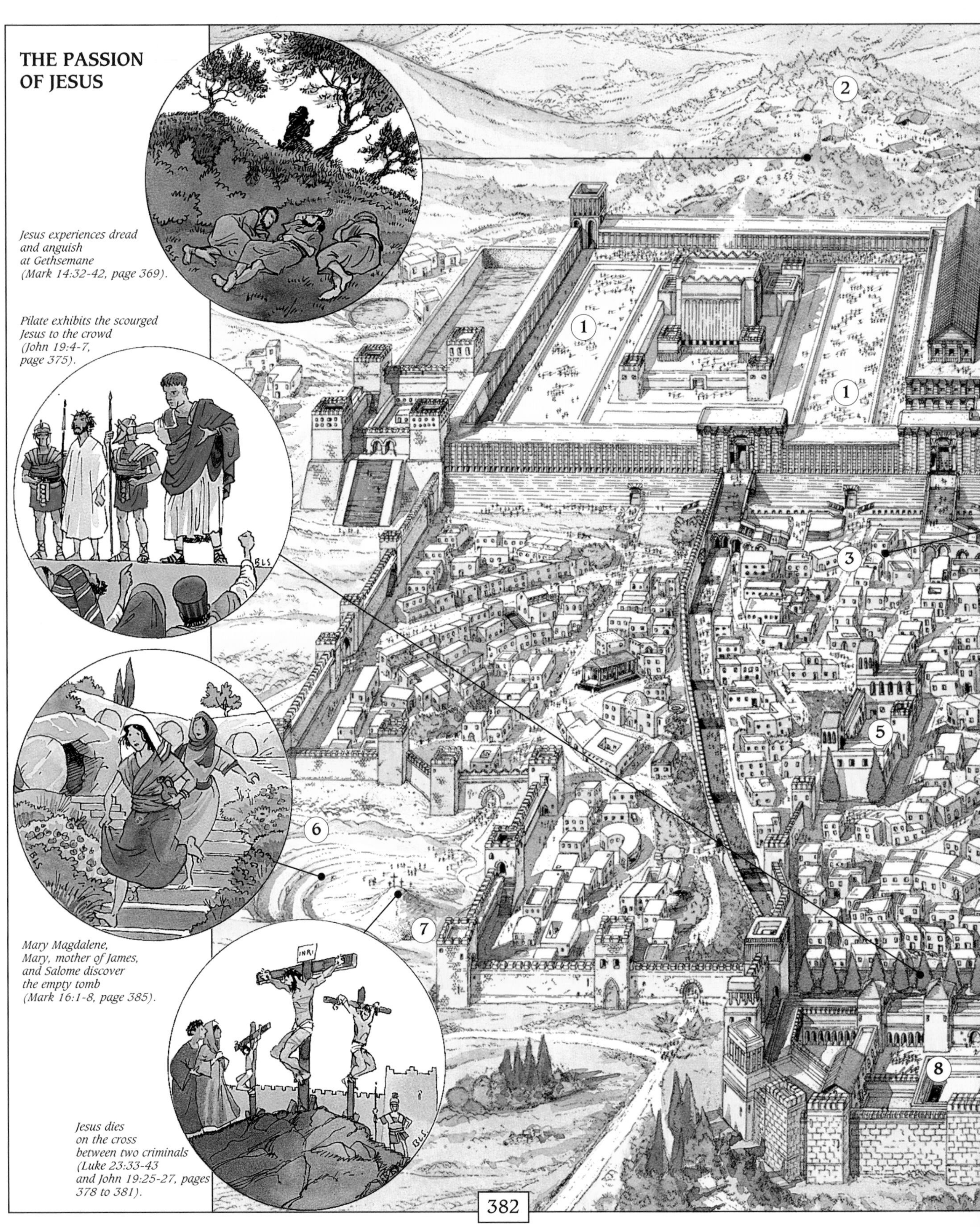

Jesus experiences dread and anguish at Gethsemane (Mark 14:32-42, page 369).

Pilate exhibits the scourged Jesus to the crowd (John 19:4-7, page 375).

Mary Magdalene, Mary, mother of James, and Salome discover the empty tomb (Mark 16:1-8, page 385).

Jesus dies on the cross between two criminals (Luke 23:33-43 and John 19:25-27, pages 378 to 381).

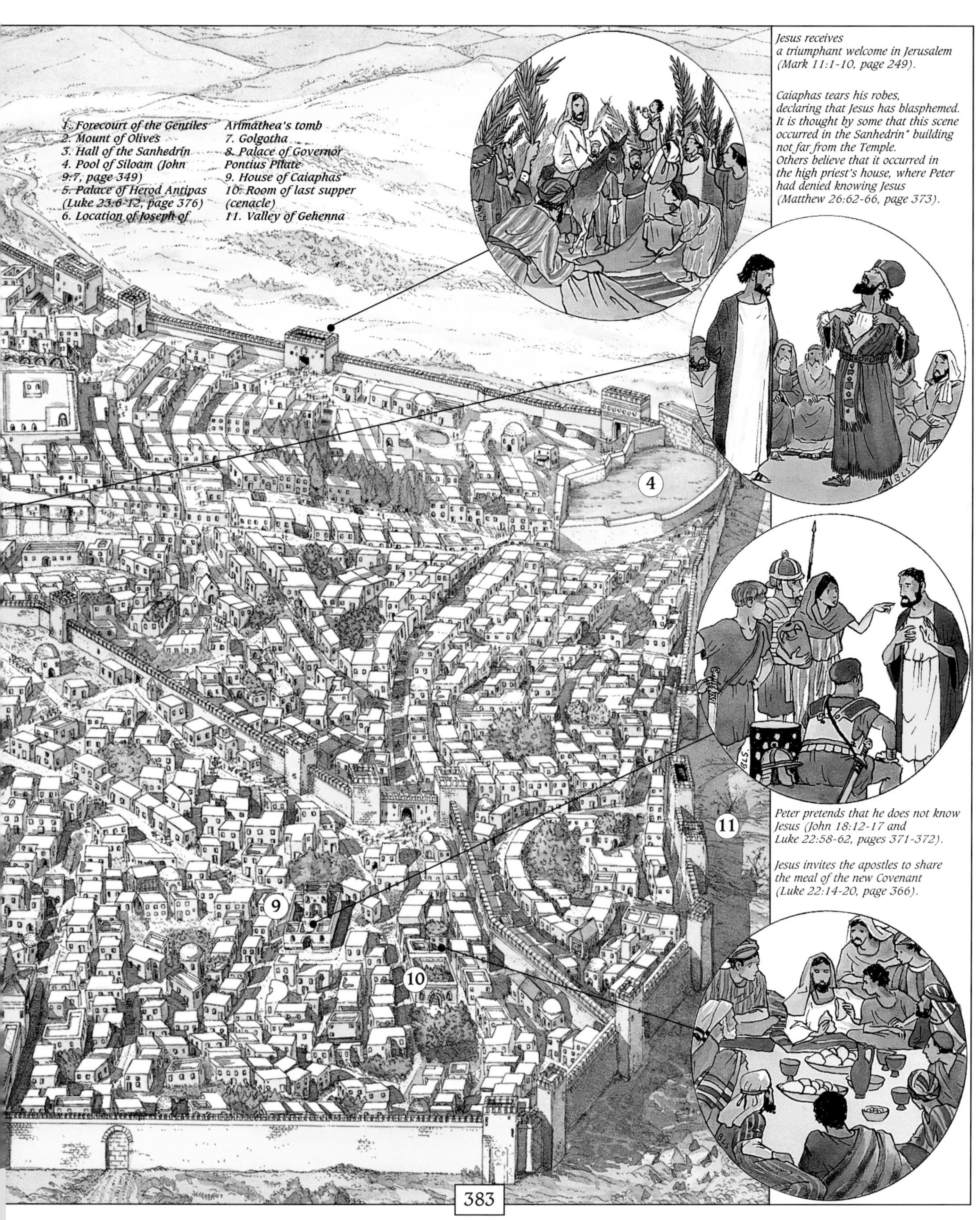

Jesus receives a triumphant welcome in Jerusalem (Mark 11:1-10, page 249).

Caiaphas tears his robes, declaring that Jesus has blasphemed. It is thought by some that this scene occurred in the Sanhedrin building not far from the Temple. Others believe that it occurred in the high priest's house, where Peter had denied knowing Jesus (Matthew 26:62-66, page 373).*

Peter pretends that he does not know Jesus (John 18:12-17 and Luke 22:58-62, pages 371-372).

Jesus invites the apostles to share the meal of the new Covenant (Luke 22:14-20, page 366).

The act of Joseph of Arimathea, named as a member of the Sanhedrin* by Mark and Luke, was reported by the four Evangelists. John was the only one to speak of Nicodemus being present.

The tomb

JOHN
19 38 After these things, Joseph of Arimathaea, who was
secretly a disciple of Jesus, out of fear of the Jews,
made a request to Pilate to let him take away the body of
Jesus. Pilate said he might do so. So he went and took
away his body.

39 Nicodemus came (he who had first come to Jesus by
night) with a roll of myrrh* and aloes mixed, about a
40 hundred pounds. | Then they took the body of Jesus,
folding linen about it with the spices, as is the custom of
the Jews when they bury the dead.

41 Now there was a garden near the cross, and in the garden
42 a new tomb in which no man had ever been buried. | So
they put Jesus there, because it was the Jews' day of
preparing for the Passover, and the place was near.

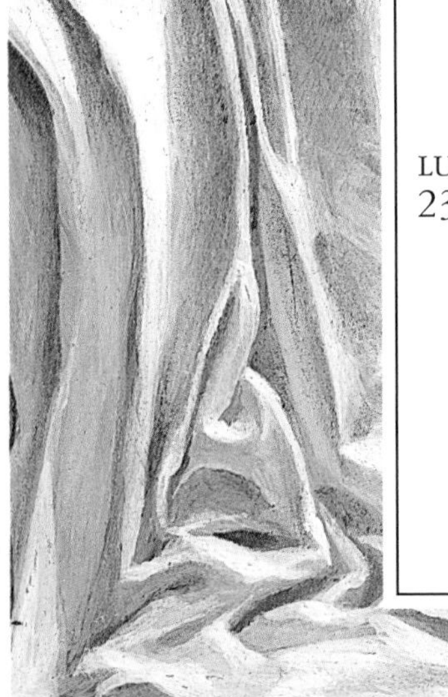

LUKE
23 55 And the women who had come
with him from Galilee went
after him and saw the place and how his
56 body had been put to rest. | They went
back and prepared spices and perfumes,
then on the Sabbath they rested,
obeying the law.

Joseph, a secret disciple,
and Nicodemus, a night visitor,
resemble each other.
Whereas those disciples,
who had been seen in the daylight
parading alongside a successful Jesus,
ran away,
these two timid,
discreet men showed up in broad daylight.
From a human point of view,
nothing more could be expected of Jesus,
and yet,
they went before the authorities
to simply tell them:
"We loved this man that you crushed,
humiliated and degraded."

EETING THE RISEN HRIST

he Evangelists drew on the ame sources in writing eir account of Jesus' esurrection, and in articular the women's iscovery of the empty mb. But each one used ese sources with nsiderable freedom. Their m was to help Christians recognize the presence of e risen Christ in their daily ves. Jesus could no longer e recognized with the five nses — he could no longer e seen or heard. He could e met only through faith.*

he accounts of Jesus' pparitions did not try to ve exact descriptions of e risen Christ. They were tended to strengthen the hristians' faith. He who ad died on the cross was uly present here and now.

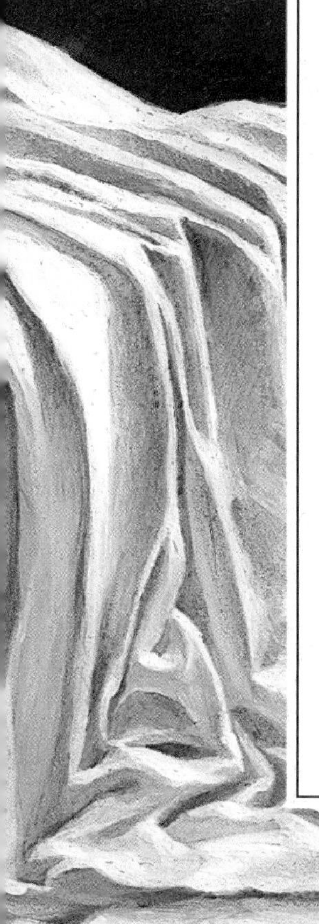

THE EMPTY TOMB

The women at the tomb

MARK
16 1 And when the Sabbath was past, Mary Magdalene
and Mary, the mother of James, and Salome, got
spices, so that they might come and put them on him.

2 Very early after dawn on the first day of the week, they
came at dawn to the place where the body had been put. |
3 They were saying among themselves, "Who will roll away
the stone from the door for us?"

4 Looking up, they saw that the stone was rolled back, and
5 it was of great size. | When they went in, they saw a young
man seated on the right side, dressed in a white robe. They
6 were full of wonder. | He said to them,

"Do not be troubled. You are looking for Jesus, the
Nazarene, who has been put to death on the cross. He has
risen from the dead. He is not here in the place where they
7 put him! | But go, say to his disciples and to Peter, 'He goes
ahead you into Galilee. There you will see him, as he said
to you.'"

8 They ran from the place, because fear and great wonder
had come on them. They said nothing to anyone, because
they were afraid...

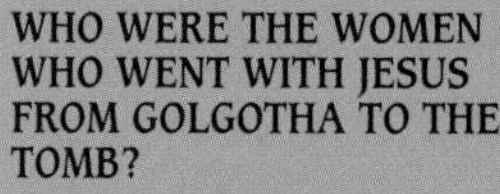

WHO WERE THE WOMEN WHO WENT WITH JESUS FROM GOLGOTHA TO THE TOMB?

The names given by the Evangelists did not completely match.

John was the only one to mention Mary, the mother of Jesus. All four, on the other hand, spoke of Mary* Magdalene.

Mark mentioned Salome, who was probably the "wife of Zebedee" spoken of by Matthew, and mother of the apostles John and James. Luke mentioned Joanna, the wife of Cuza.

Others named were Mary, wife of Clopas, in John; and Mary, mother of James, in Matthew, Mark and Luke. Some scholars consider that they were the same person. The James in question was no doubt the "brother of the Lord" referred to elsewhere.

THE THIRD DAY

None of the disciples, whether woman or man, thought in seeing the empty tomb, "It is the third day after his death and he has risen as he said he would." Mostly they thought that the body had been stolen.

The "third day" was not an exact date. It was rather the day chosen by God to resurrect the dead in general (see Hosea 6:2, page 133). **This resurrection on "the third day" would coincide with the end of time.**

Nobody at the tomb of Jesus thought that "the third day" had arrived, since there was no sign of the end of time.

Once the disciples became convinced that Jesus had risen, they viewed his Resurrection as the start of the general resurrection (this is the explanation of Matthew 27:51-54, page 380). **Paul imagined at one stage that he would still be alive for the general resurrection. Little by little, the early Christians came to realize that God would allow time to continue, so that they could carry out their mission of announcing the gospel to all nations** (see 2 Peter 3:8-10, page 447).

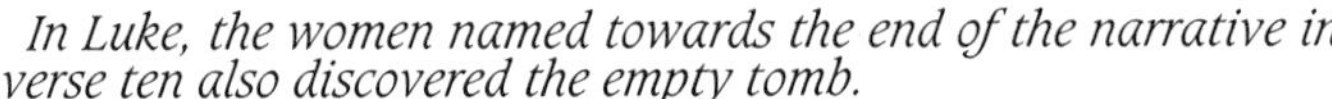

In Luke, the women named towards the end of the narrative in verse ten also discovered the empty tomb.

LUKE 24

4 And while they were wondering about it, they saw
5 two men in shining clothing by them. | While their
faces were bowed to the ground in fear, these said to them,

6 "Why are you looking for the living among the dead? | He
is not here, he has returned to life. Remember what he said
to you when he was still in Galilee, saying,

7 'The Son of man will be given up into the hands of evil-
doers, and be put to death on the cross, and on the third
day he will come back to life.'"

8 And his words returned to their minds.

9 They left that place and gave an account of all these
10 things to the eleven disciples and all the others. | They were
Mary Magdalene, and Joanna,[1] and Mary, the mother of
James, and the other women with them
11 said these things to the Apostles. | But
these words seemed foolish to them, and
they did not believe them.

12 But Peter went to the tomb where the
body had been put, and looking in, he
saw nothing but the linen cloths. He went
to his house full of wonder at what had
taken place.[2]

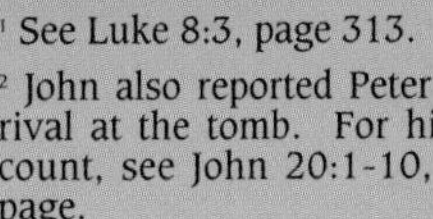

[1] See Luke 8:3, page 313.

[2] John also reported Peter
rival at the tomb. For hi
count, see John 20:1-10,
page.

Lord,
when I only speak about you in the past,
when I say, "Jesus was good.
Jesus healed the sick," etc.
I'm looking for you among the dead!

But, you are alive!
I find traces of your presence
in the present among the living.
Your smile can be found in the look
of someone who forgives.
Your radiance can be seen
in a missionary's enthusiasm.
You give your life in the battle
of one confronting injustice.

You are alive, Lord,
and you give us life so that we can shout
out everywhere that death
has been defeated.
We are alive forever in you!
From this very day, you are teaching us
to find our source of life in you, in love,
as Resurrected people!

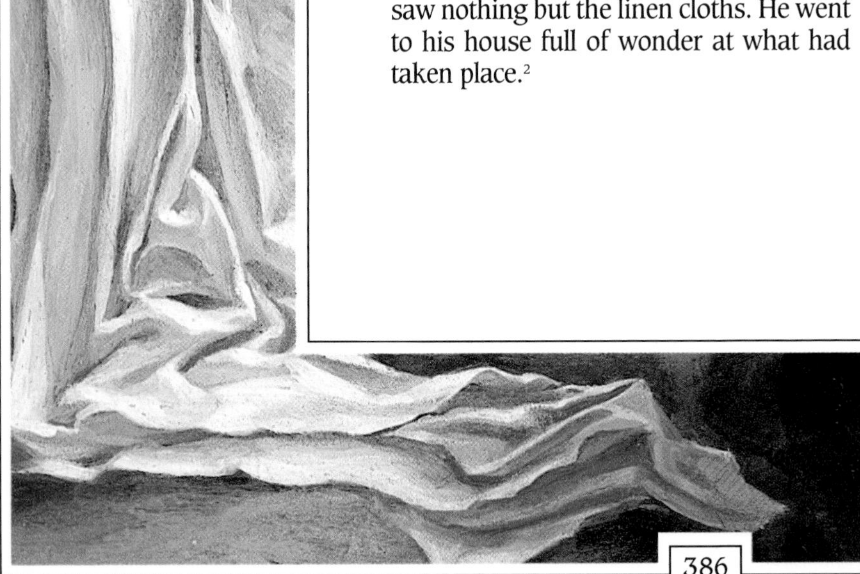

The empty shroud

JOHN
20 1 Now on the first day of the week,[1] very early, while
it was still dark, Mary Magdalene came to the
tomb and saw that the stone had been rolled away from it.
2 | Then she ran to Simon Peter, and to the other disciple
who was loved by Jesus, saying to them,

"They have taken away the Lord from the tomb and we do not know where they have put him."

3-4 So Peter and the other disciple went to the tomb. | They
went running together, and the other disciple got in front
5 of Peter, coming first to the hole in the rock. | Looking in,
he saw the linen bands on the ground, but he did not go
6 in. | Then Simon Peter followed him and went into the
7 tomb. He saw the linen bands on the ground, | and the
cloth, which had been around his head, not with the linen
bands but rolled up in a place by itself.

8 Then the other disciple who came there first went in. He
9 saw and belief came to him. | For at that time they had no
knowledge that the Scriptures* said that he would have to
rise from the dead.

10 Then the disciples left for their houses.

[1] See page 391, "Sunday."

THE DISCIPLE WHOM JESUS LOVED

This mysterious disciple, who seemed to be the Gospel's author, came into the story for the third time here as "the one Jesus loved." The first time, he had been beside Jesus at the last meal (John 13:23). **The second time, he had been at the foot of the cross** (John 19:26, page 379). **This time he was the first one to believe in the Resurrection. He noticed that the funeral wrappings, which had clung to Lazarus when he came out of the grave** (see page 355), **were here lying in the tomb. He realized that Jesus had gone beyond death, that he had risen. There is even a fourth mention of this disciple** (John 21:7, page 393). **He would be the first to recognize the presence of the risen Christ. The four passages amount to a description of the ideal disciple. The true disciple is the one who speaks with Jesus in the intimacy of the heart, the one who follows Jesus through trials and difficulties, the one who believes that Jesus is victorious over death and the one who is able to recognize Jesus' presence in everyday things.**

The "one whom Jesus loved" teaches us how to be a disciple ready to respond to Jesus' love.

APPARITIONS OF THE RISEN JESUS

Mary Magdelene and the "gardener"

JOHN
20 11 But Mary was still there outside the tomb,
weeping. While she was weeping and looking into
12 the tomb, | she saw two angels* in white seated where the
body of Jesus had been, one at the head and the other at
13 the feet. | They said to her, "Woman, why are you
weeping?" She said to them, "Because they have taken
away my Lord, and I have no knowledge where they have
put him."

14 Tthen looking around, she saw Jesus there, but had no
15 idea that it was Jesus. | Jesus said to her, "Woman, why are
you weeping? Who are you looking for?" She, thinking he
was the gardener, said to him, "Sir, if you have removed
him from here, tell me where you have put him and I will
take him away."

16 Jesus said to her, "Mary!" Turning, she
said to him in Hebrew,[1] *"Rabboni!"*
17 (which means "Master"). | Jesus said to
her, "Do not put your hand on me, for I
have not yet returned to the Father. But
go to my brothers and say to them, I am
returning to my Father and your Father,
to my God and your God."

18 Mary Magdalene took the news to the
disciples,* saying that she had seen the
Lord and that he had said these things to
her.

From now on, Mary,
you will no longer meet your Lord
through outward signs, but by faith.
A new way of knowing Him,
that he has placed in you
as a gift.
Faith tells you that the Lord is there,
even when darkness doesn't let
the least amount of light filter in;
even when your heart is dried up,
and when you feel desperately alone,
faith tells you so loudly
that the Lord is holding your hand,
that you can walk in confidence.
Your heart will be at peace.

[1] "Rabboni" was the same as the Hebrew "Rabbi."

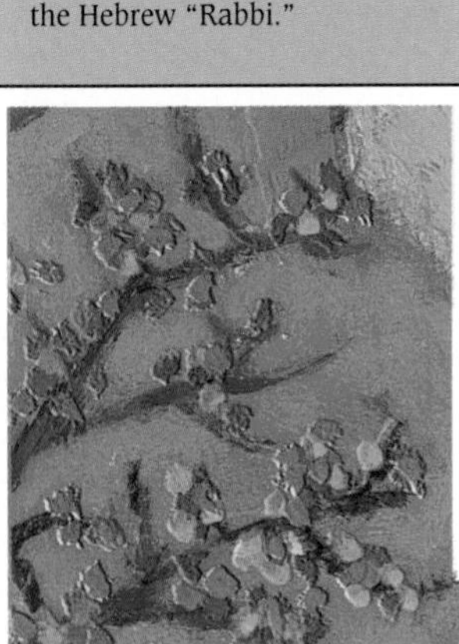

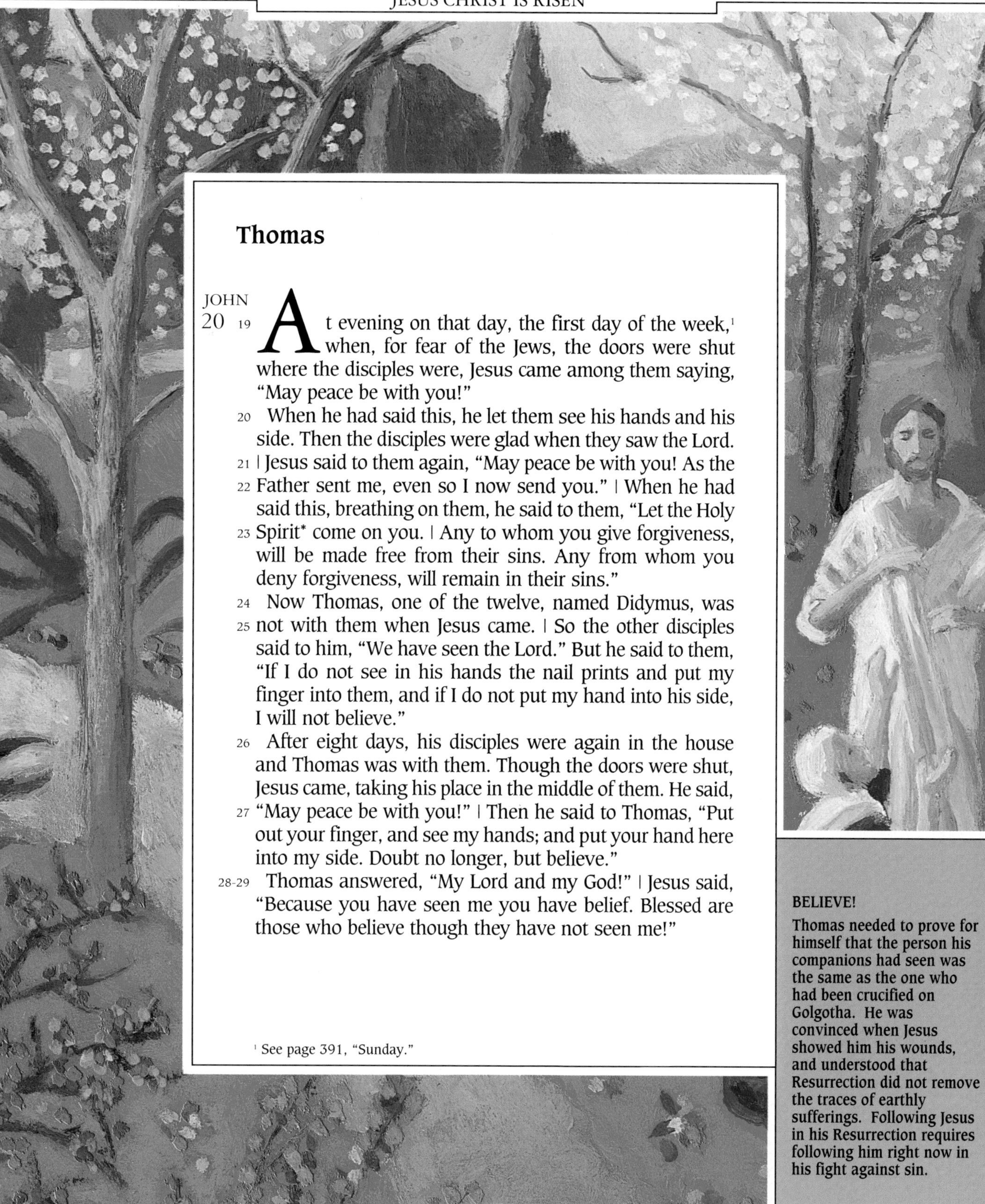

Thomas

JOHN
20 19 At evening on that day, the first day of the week,[1]
when, for fear of the Jews, the doors were shut
where the disciples were, Jesus came among them saying,
"May peace be with you!"
20 When he had said this, he let them see his hands and his
side. Then the disciples were glad when they saw the Lord.
21 | Jesus said to them again, "May peace be with you! As the
22 Father sent me, even so I now send you." | When he had
said this, breathing on them, he said to them, "Let the Holy
23 Spirit* come on you. | Any to whom you give forgiveness,
will be made free from their sins. Any from whom you
deny forgiveness, will remain in their sins."
24 Now Thomas, one of the twelve, named Didymus, was
25 not with them when Jesus came. | So the other disciples
said to him, "We have seen the Lord." But he said to them,
"If I do not see in his hands the nail prints and put my
finger into them, and if I do not put my hand into his side,
I will not believe."
26 After eight days, his disciples were again in the house
and Thomas was with them. Though the doors were shut,
Jesus came, taking his place in the middle of them. He said,
27 "May peace be with you!" | Then he said to Thomas, "Put
out your finger, and see my hands; and put your hand here
into my side. Doubt no longer, but believe."
28-29 Thomas answered, "My Lord and my God!" | Jesus said,
"Because you have seen me you have belief. Blessed are
those who believe though they have not seen me!"

[1] See page 391, "Sunday."

BELIEVE!

Thomas needed to prove for himself that the person his companions had seen was the same as the one who had been crucified on Golgotha. He was convinced when Jesus showed him his wounds, and understood that Resurrection did not remove the traces of earthly sufferings. Following Jesus in his Resurrection requires following him right now in his fight against sin.

The disciples in Emmaus

LUKE
24 13 And then, two of them, on that very day, were going
to a little town named Emmaus, which was about
14 seven miles from Jerusalem. | They were discussing all
those things which had taken place.

15 While they were talking together, Jesus himself came
16 near and walked with them. | But their eyes were not open
17 that they might recognize him. | He said to them, "What
are you talking about together while you walk?"

18 Then stopping, and looking sadly at him, one of them,
named Cleopas, said to him, "Are you the only man living
in Jerusalem who has not had news of the things which
19 have taken place there?" | He said to them, "What things?"
And they said, "The things to do with Jesus of Nazareth,
who was a prophet, great in his acts and his words, before
20 God and all the people. | Tthe chief priests and our rulers
21 had him put to death on the cross, | but we were hoping
that he would be the Savior of Israel. In addition to all this
he has now let three days go by from the time when these
22 things took place. | Certain women among us have said
amazing things, for they went early to the place where his
23 body had been put, | but it was not there. Then they came
saying that they had seen a vision of angels who said that
24 he was living. | Some of those who were with us went to
the place, and saw that it was as the women had said, but
him they did not see."

25 He said, "O foolish men! How slow you are to believe to
26 what the prophets have said. | Was it not necessary for the
Christ to go through these things, and to come into his
27 glory?" | He revealed to them all the things in the

[1] His wife was probably at the foot of the cross (John 19:25, page 379).

[2] Luke was aware of the apostles' visit to the tomb, as related in John 20:1-10, page 387.

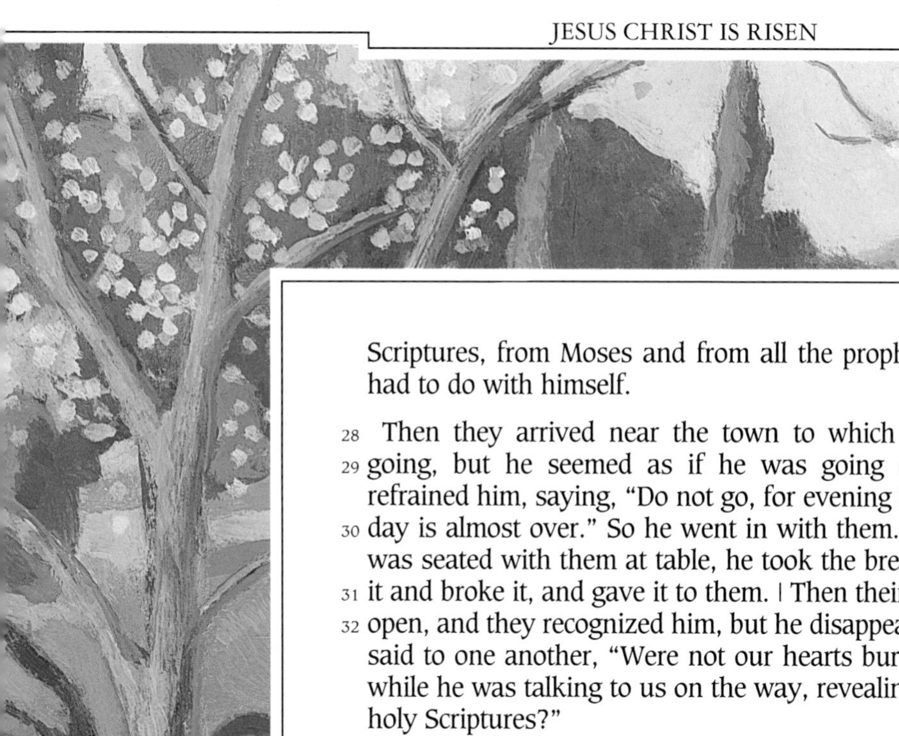

SUNDAY*

Luke apparently situated all the apparitions of the risen Christ, including the ascension,* on the same day. It was a way of giving prominence to the first day of the week, which Christians in many countries call "the Lord's day." Every Sunday, Christians gather together to give thanks. They are happy in the knowledge that the risen Jesus is still with them, even though they cannot physically see him.

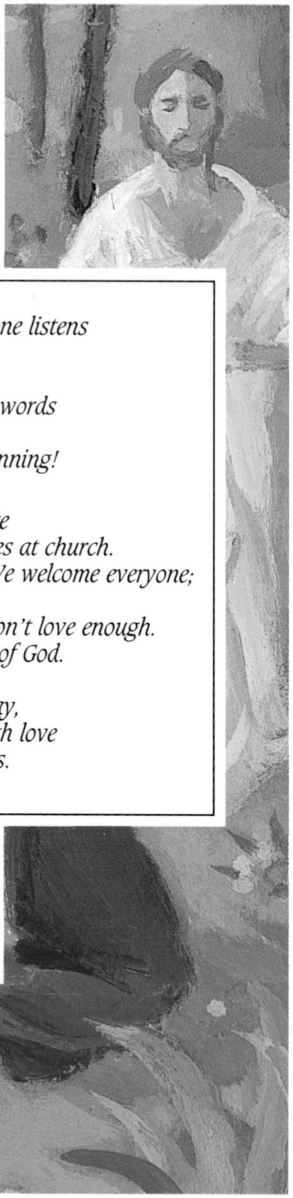

Scriptures, from Moses and from all the prophets, which had to do with himself.

28 Then they arrived near the town to which they were
29 going, but he seemed as if he was going on. | They
refrained him, saying, "Do not go, for evening is near, the
30 day is almost over." So he went in with them. | When he
was seated with them at table, he took the bread, blessed
31 it and broke it, and gave it to them. | Then their eyes were
32 open, and they recognized him, but he disappeared. | They
said to one another, "Were not our hearts burning in us[1]
while he was talking to us on the way, revealing to us the
holy Scriptures?"

33 That very hour they got up and went back to Jerusalem,
where the eleven and the others had
34 gathered. | They said to them, "The Lord
has truly come back to life again, and
35 Simon has seen him." | They recounted
the things which had taken place on the
way, and how, when he gave them
bread,[2] they had recognized him.

A stranger to whom one listens
and welcomes:
"Stay with us.."...
A book whose written words
set on fire...
Shared bread... A beginning!

Today,
we relive the experience
of the Emmaus disciples at church.
We meet each other. We welcome everyone;
those we love,
and those whom we don't love enough.
We listen to the Word of God.
We share bread,
and then go on our way,
our hearts burning with love
for the Lord and others.

1 Jeremiah had received the word of the Lord inside himself like a fire raging out of control (Jeremiah 20:9, page 154).

2 The "breaking of bread" or "dividing of bread" were expressions used by the early Christians to name their religious service.

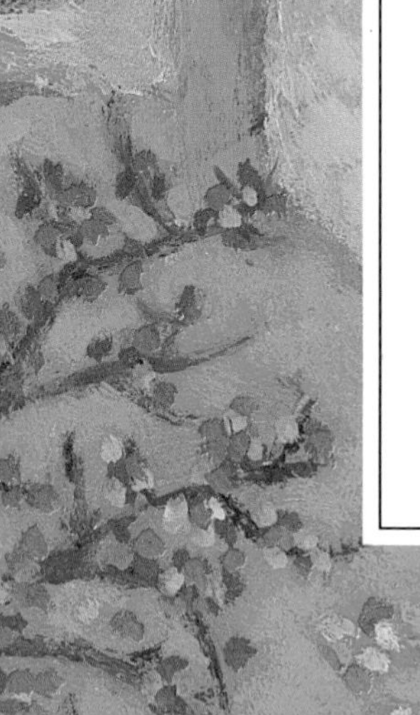

The Twelve

LUKE
24 36 And while they were saying these things, he himself
was among them. He said to them, "Peace be with
37 you!" | But they were full of fear, thinking that they were
38 seeing a spirit.[1] | He said to them, "Why are you troubled,
39 and why are your hearts full of doubt? | See my hands and
my feet? It is I myself. Put your hands on me and make
certain, for a spirit has no flesh and bones as you see that
40 I have." | When he had said this, he let them see his hands
41 and his feet. | But because, for joy and wonder, they were
still in doubt, he said to them, "Have you any food here?"

42-43 Tthey gave him a bit of cooked fish. | Before their eyes he
ate a meal.

44 He said to them, "These are the words which I said to you
when I was still with you, how it was necessary for all the
things which are in the Scriptures of Moses and the
prophets and in the Psalms about me, to be fulfilled." |
45 Then he made the holy Scriptures understandable to their
46 minds. | He said, "So it is in the Scriptures that the Christ
would undergo death, and return to life on the third day,[2]
47 | and that preaching about repentance and forgiveness of
sins is to be done first in Jerusalem and to all nations in his
48-49 name. | You are witnesses of these things. | Now I will send
to you what my father has planned to give you, but do not
leave the town until the power from Heaven comes to
you."
50 And he took them out until they were near Bethany.
51 Lifting up his hands, he gave them a blessing, | and while
52 he was doing so, he was taken up into Heaven. | They gave
53 worshipped, returning to Jerusalem with great joy. | They
were continually in the Temple, praising God.

[1] Luke wanted to show his Greek readers that the Resurrection of Jesus had nothing to do with superstitious beliefs — often frightening — in ghosts or spirits of the dead. Jesus lived. He had come back not to harry his friends but to enlighten them and fill them with joy.

[2] See page 386, "The third day."

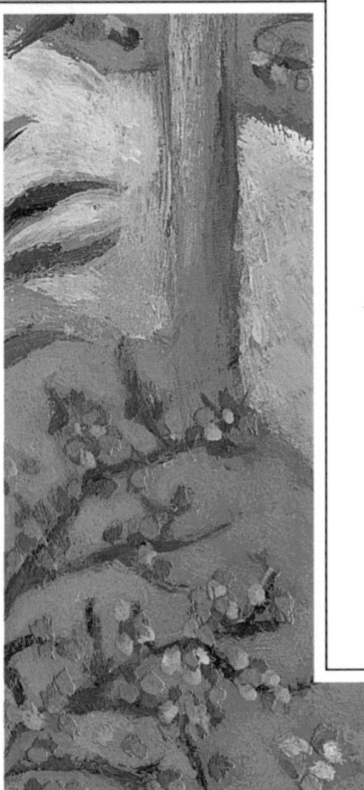

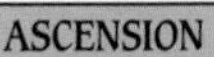

ASCENSION

Luke, with the image of Jesus lifted into heaven, was teaching that the risen Jesus remained supremely close to God — "sitting at the right hand of...th Father" as the Apostles' Creed (page 460) puts it. Resurrection and ascension were two sides o the same reality. The risen Jesu having left human history, was united with the eternity of God. Yet the Evangelists separated th ascension from the Resurrection by the "period" of the apparitions. The ascension thu seemed to mark the end of the apparition period. This presentation tended to make th resurrection and the ascension look like two different realities. Luke avoided this danger in his Gospel by not specifying the length of the apparition period. In the Acts of the Apostles, he wrote that the ascension took place forty days after Easter (as in the Christian calendar). But i his Gospel, it occurred in the same time-frame as the Resurrection (see page 391, "SUNDAY").

Simon, do you love me?

JOHN
21 1 After these things Jesus revealed himself again to
the disciples* at the Sea of Tiberias. It came about
2 in this way. | Simon Peter, Thomas named Didymus,
Nathanael[1] of Cana in Galilee, the sons of Zebedee, and
3 two others of his disciples were all together. | Simon Peter
said to them, "I am going fishing." They said to him, "We
will come with you." They got into the boat, but that night
they caught no fish.

4 Now very early in the morning Jesus was there by the
shore (though the disciples were not conscious that it was
5 Jesus). | So he said to them, "Children, have you taken any
6 fish?" They answered, "No." | He said to them, "Let down
the net on the right side of the boat and you will get some."
So they put it in the water, unable to pull it up again
7 because of the great number of fish. | So the disciple who
was dear to Jesus[2] said to Peter, "It is the Lord!"* Hearing
that it was the Lord, Peter put his coat around him
(because he was not clothed) and went into the sea.

8 The other disciples stepped into the little boat (they were
not far from land, only about one hundred yards) pulling
the net full of fish.

9 When they got to land, they saw a fire
of coals there, with fish cooking on it,
10 and bread. | Jesus said to them, "Get
some of the fish which you have now
11 taken." | So Peter went to the boat and
came back pulling the net to land, full of
great fish, a hundred and fifty-three.
Despite their number the net was not

THE APPARITION BY THE LAKE

John, in a final chapter added to his Gospel, which had seemed to end with Chapter 20, related an apparition of Jesus in Galilee. This narrative was probably used apart from the others to give instruction on the presence of the risen Jesus in the early church, on the forgiveness of sins and the on the role of the apostles.

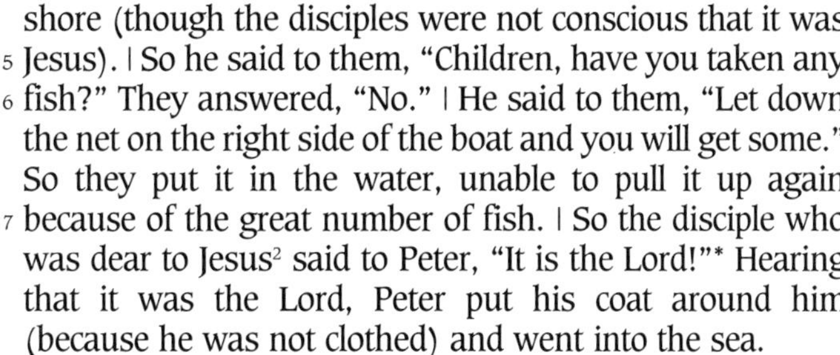

[1] See "Bartholomew."*

[2] See page 387.

When Peter recognized the Lord's presence,
he quickly realized that he was naked,
like Adam in the garden.
Peter believed himself to be much stronger
than the others.
"Even if the others abandon you,
I will never abandon you."
Today, he realized how
poor and naked he was.
But, unlike Adam,
he did not hide.
He came forth and revealed himself to Jesus.

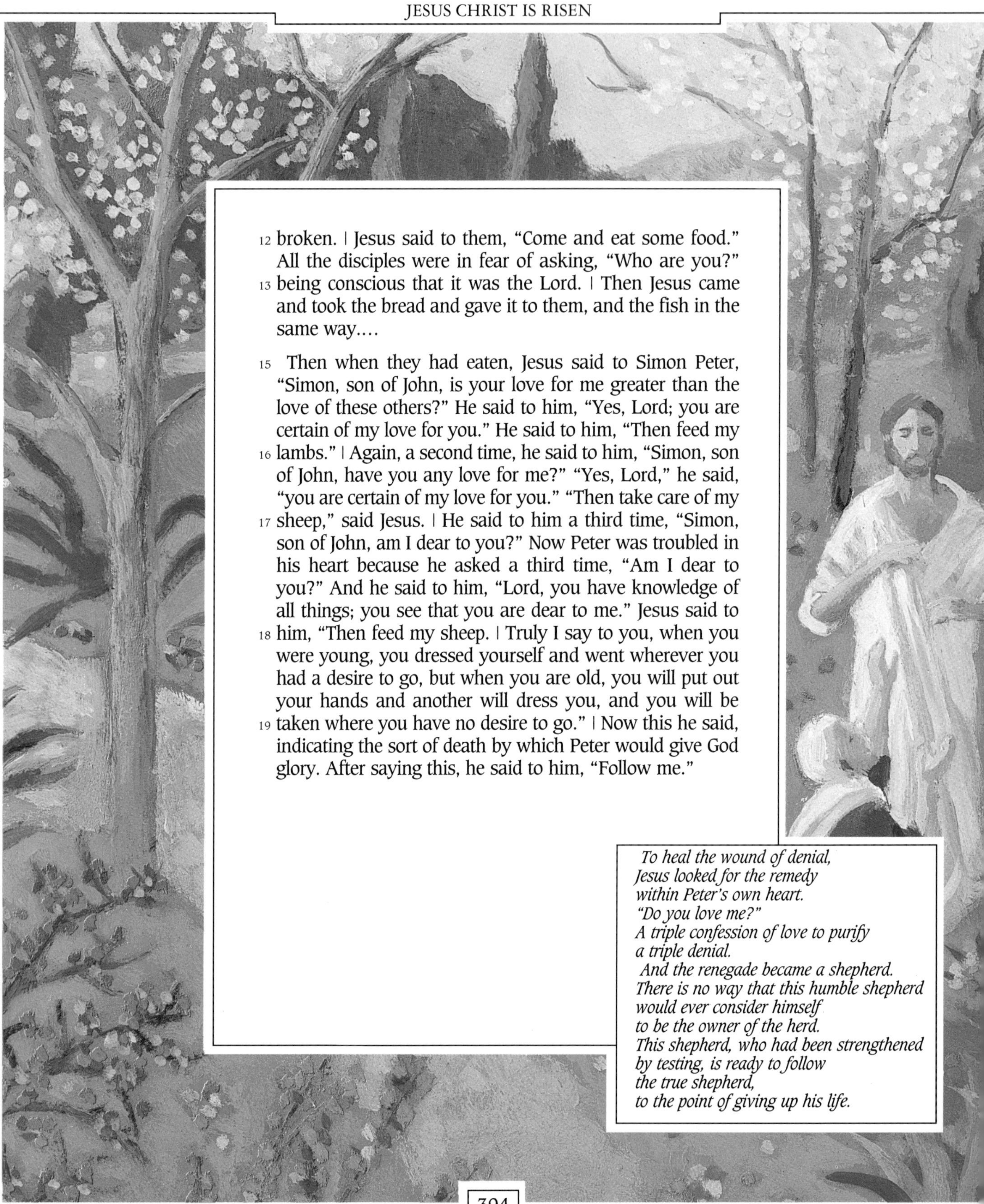

12 broken. | Jesus said to them, "Come and eat some food."
All the disciples were in fear of asking, "Who are you?"
13 being conscious that it was the Lord. | Then Jesus came
and took the bread and gave it to them, and the fish in the
same way....

15 Then when they had eaten, Jesus said to Simon Peter,
"Simon, son of John, is your love for me greater than the
love of these others?" He said to him, "Yes, Lord; you are
certain of my love for you." He said to him, "Then feed my
16 lambs." | Again, a second time, he said to him, "Simon, son
of John, have you any love for me?" "Yes, Lord," he said,
"you are certain of my love for you." "Then take care of my
17 sheep," said Jesus. | He said to him a third time, "Simon,
son of John, am I dear to you?" Now Peter was troubled in
his heart because he asked a third time, "Am I dear to
you?" And he said to him, "Lord, you have knowledge of
all things; you see that you are dear to me." Jesus said to
18 him, "Then feed my sheep. | Truly I say to you, when you
were young, you dressed yourself and went wherever you
had a desire to go, but when you are old, you will put out
your hands and another will dress you, and you will be
19 taken where you have no desire to go." | Now this he said,
indicating the sort of death by which Peter would give God
glory. After saying this, he said to him, "Follow me."

To heal the wound of denial,
Jesus looked for the remedy
within Peter's own heart.
"Do you love me?"
A triple confession of love to purify
a triple denial.
And the renegade became a shepherd.
There is no way that this humble shepherd
would ever consider himself
to be the owner of the herd.
This shepherd, who had been strengthened
by testing, is ready to follow
the true shepherd,
to the point of giving up his life.

...of all nations

MATT
28 16 But the eleven disciples went into Galilee, to the
mountain where Jesus had given them orders to
17 go. | And when they saw him they worshipped him. Some
18 were in doubt. | Jesus came to them and said, "All authority
19 has been given to me in Heaven and on earth. | Go then,
and make disciples of all the nations,* baptising them in
the name of the Father and of the Son and of the Holy
20 Spirit, | teaching them to obey everything which I have
commanded you. Surely, I am with you always, even to the
end of time."

UNIVERSALITY

Matthew concluded his Gospel — which was intended for Jews converted to Christianity — with this quite new commandment, "...make disciples of all nations."

Until then, all the disciples of the Lord had been Jews. How should believers from the "nations," in other words the heathen peoples, be treated?

Should they be invited to become Jews by submitting to circumcision* and the other Jewish laws? This was the most crucial and critical question then facing the Christian communities (see page 415).

It was Paul who provided the answer. The true disciple was the one who inwardly believed, regardless of his origins.

The apostles, by baptizing all who had faith in Jesus, gave rise to a religion which gradually drifted away from the Jewish people.

PART FIVE

THE FIRST CHRISTIANS

During the first years after the Resurrection of Jesus, his disciples kept their close ties with Judaism. They formed a new school of thought alongside the Pharisees, Sadducees and Essenes.*[1] *These different groups had trouble living together. There were many disputes, especially as regards the acceptance of heathens.*

The Jews of the diaspora had spread word of the Bible among the heathens they came across. Some of these heathens had fully embraced Judaism and been circumcised. Others were less committed. They took part in prayer meetings or went on pilgrimages to Jerusalem, but they were unwilling to join the Jewish world completely and to cut themselves off from their familiar universe.*[2] *Many of these uncircumcised believers, when they heard of the Gospel, asked to be received into the Christian community. After a period of hesitation, the apostles decided to accept them without requiring them to obey Jewish laws.*

From then on, the Christian communities brought together Jewish Christians (Judeo-Christians) and Christians converted from heathenism. Community life entailed the eating of meals in common by Jews and non-Jews. The Jewish religious authorities took a serious view of this commingling.[3] *Near the end of the 1st century AD, Judeo-Christians were barred from entering synagogues.* This exclusion made them very unhappy, especially as they did not feel at home among the growing numbers of heathen converts.*

The Christians of heathen origin were for their part unfamiliar with Judaism. They considered it to be outdated.

A number of New Testament writings describe the beginnings of Christianity:

[1] See page 233, "A people spiritually divided".

[2] See page 233, the paragraph on the Jews of the diaspora.

[3] It was forbidden for Jews to eat with heathens. See Acts 11:3, page 416.

[4] These letters are usually called "epistles".

I
THE ACTS OF THE APOSTLES

The Book of the Acts of the Apostles compiled by Luke was, like his Gospel, addressed to Theophilus.[1] *Luke told how the Holy Spirit moved the apostles to leave Jerusalem and bear witness to the risen Jesus in not only Judea and Samaria but "to the ends of the earth".*

Peter is the focus of the first part of the book. He led the earliest community of Jesus' disciples, in Jerusalem. In 36 or 37 AD, after the persecution during which Stephen was stoned to death, Peter went on missionary tours of Samaria and the Mediterranean coast. He baptized an uncircumcised Roman centurion, so marking a first step in the acceptance of heathens.

In the second part of the book, Luke recounts the missionary work of Paul. Paul began as an opponent of the Gospel, but was converted and became the "apostle" of the non-Jews. Luke's book ends with Paul's arrival in Rome.

[1] See page 297, "For whom did Luke write his Gospel?"

JERUSALEM

The ascension

*The risen Jesus appeared during forty days to his apostles.**

1 4 And when they were all together, with him, Jesus
gave them orders not to go away from Jerusalem,
but to keep there, waiting till the word of the Father was
put into effect, of which, he said, "I have given you
5 knowledge: | For the baptism of John was with water, but
you will have baptism with the Holy Spirit, after a little
6 time." | So, when they were together, they said to him,
"Lord, will you at this time give back the kingdom to
7 Israel?" | And he said to them, "It is not for you to have
knowledge of the time and the order of events which the
8 Father has kept in his control. | But you will have power,
when the Holy Spirit has come on you;
and you will be my witnesses in
Jerusalem and all Judaea and Samaria,
and to the ends of the earth."

9 And when he had said these things,
while they were looking, he was taken
up, and went from their view into a
10 cloud.[1]* | And while they were looking up
to heaven with great attention, two men
11 came to them, in white clothing, | And
said, "O men of Galilee, why are you
looking up into heaven? This Jesus, who
was taken from you into heaven, will
come again, in the same way as you saw
him go into heaven."

[1] The cloud confirmed the divinity of Jesus who "ascended" to retake his place close to his Father. See page 373.

For the people of the past,
heaven was a mysterious
and inaccessible place.
It evoked the "world of God."
"To go to heaven"
was another way of saying
"living with God."

Today, heaven has become
a place to explore like any other.
Unbelievers
have come back saying:
"I didn't meet God."

Their hearts, like ours so often,
are blinded.
God is not some sort of distant individual
sitting on a cloud!
He comes to meet us
in the faces of others.
When we know how to welcome Him,
He makes us his dwelling;
a corner of heaven's radiance
in the midst of our darkness.

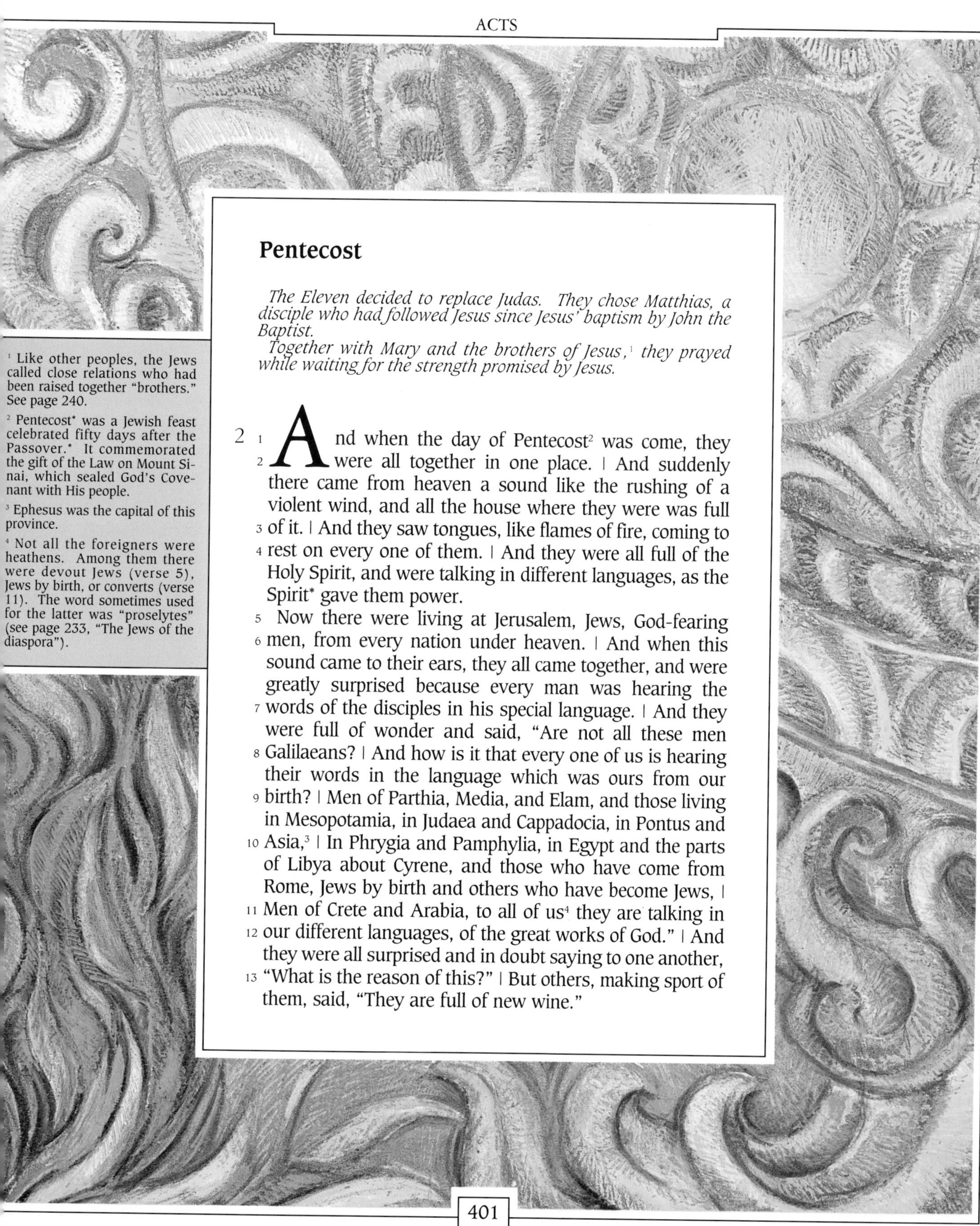

Pentecost

The Eleven decided to replace Judas. They chose Matthias, a disciple who had followed Jesus since Jesus' baptism by John the Baptist.

Together with Mary and the brothers of Jesus,[1] they prayed while waiting for the strength promised by Jesus.

2 1 And when the day of Pentecost[2] was come, they
2 were all together in one place. | And suddenly
there came from heaven a sound like the rushing of a
violent wind, and all the house where they were was full
3 of it. | And they saw tongues, like flames of fire, coming to
4 rest on every one of them. | And they were all full of the
Holy Spirit, and were talking in different languages, as the
Spirit* gave them power.
5 Now there were living at Jerusalem, Jews, God-fearing
6 men, from every nation under heaven. | And when this
sound came to their ears, they all came together, and were
greatly surprised because every man was hearing the
7 words of the disciples in his special language. | And they
were full of wonder and said, "Are not all these men
8 Galilaeans? | And how is it that every one of us is hearing
their words in the language which was ours from our
9 birth? | Men of Parthia, Media, and Elam, and those living
in Mesopotamia, in Judaea and Cappadocia, in Pontus and
10 Asia,[3] | In Phrygia and Pamphylia, in Egypt and the parts
of Libya about Cyrene, and those who have come from
Rome, Jews by birth and others who have become Jews, |
11 Men of Crete and Arabia, to all of us[4] they are talking in
12 our different languages, of the great works of God." | And
they were all surprised and in doubt saying to one another,
13 "What is the reason of this?" | But others, making sport of
them, said, "They are full of new wine."

[1] Like other peoples, the Jews called close relations who had been raised together "brothers." See page 240.

[2] Pentecost* was a Jewish feast celebrated fifty days after the Passover.* It commemorated the gift of the Law on Mount Sinai, which sealed God's Covenant with His people.

[3] Ephesus was the capital of this province.

[4] Not all the foreigners were heathens. Among them there were devout Jews (verse 5), Jews by birth, or converts (verse 11). The word sometimes used for the latter was "proselytes" (see page 233, "The Jews of the diaspora").

*A gust of wind
opened closed doors,
and pushed the timid
into the middle of a crowd.
Tongues of fire
burned them with the desire
to share their joy.
Foreigners understood
the Good News in their own language!*

*Lord, your church radiated
youth and energy.
Your disciples were so happy
that some disgruntled people
thought they had drunk too much.*

*Give us your Spirit,
and we will be witnesses,
filled with joy!*

Conversions

2 14 But Peter, getting up, with the
eleven, said in a loud voice, "O
men of Judaea, and all you who are living
in Jerusalem, take note of this and give
ear to my words.
15 For these men are not overcome with
wine, as it seems to you, for it is only the
third hour of the day;...

22 Men of Israel, give ear to these words: Jesus of Nazareth,
a man who had the approval of God, as was made clear to
you by the great works and signs* and wonders which God
did by him among you, as you yourselves have
23 knowledge, | Him, when he was given up, by the decision
and knowledge of God, you put to death on the cross, by
24 the hands of evil men: | But God gave him back to life,
having made him free from the pains of death because it
was not possible for him to be overcome by it....

33 And so, being lifted up to the right hand of God, and
having the Father's word that the Holy Spirit would come,
he has sent this thing, which now you see and have
knowledge of....
36 For this reason, let all Israel be certain that this Jesus,
whom you put to death on the cross, God has made Lord*
37 and Christ." | Now when these words came to their ears
their hearts were troubled, and they said to Peter and the
38 other Apostles, "Brothers, what are we to do?" | And Peter
said, "Let your hearts be changed, every one of you, and
have baptism in the name of Jesus Christ, for the
forgiveness of your sins; and you will have the Holy Spirit*
given to you."

A NEW BAPTISM

The apostles, to celebrate the admission of new members into the community, revived the rite of baptism, which they had seen performed by John the Baptist. The ceremony was the same — an immersion in water to obtain the forgiveness of sins — but its meaning had changed:

- **To be plunged into water was a sign of death. The evil desires swirling in our hearts had to be drowned, as God had drowned wickedness in the waters of the flood** (Genesis* 6:13-17, page 27).
- **To be lifted from the water was a sign of resurrection. The person baptized received the life of the risen Jesus, was united with him. Jesus dwelt in that person. The Holy Spirit which had — like the dove in the flood — hovered over Jesus when he was baptized came and reinvigorated the newly baptized person.** See Matthew 3:16-17, page 258.

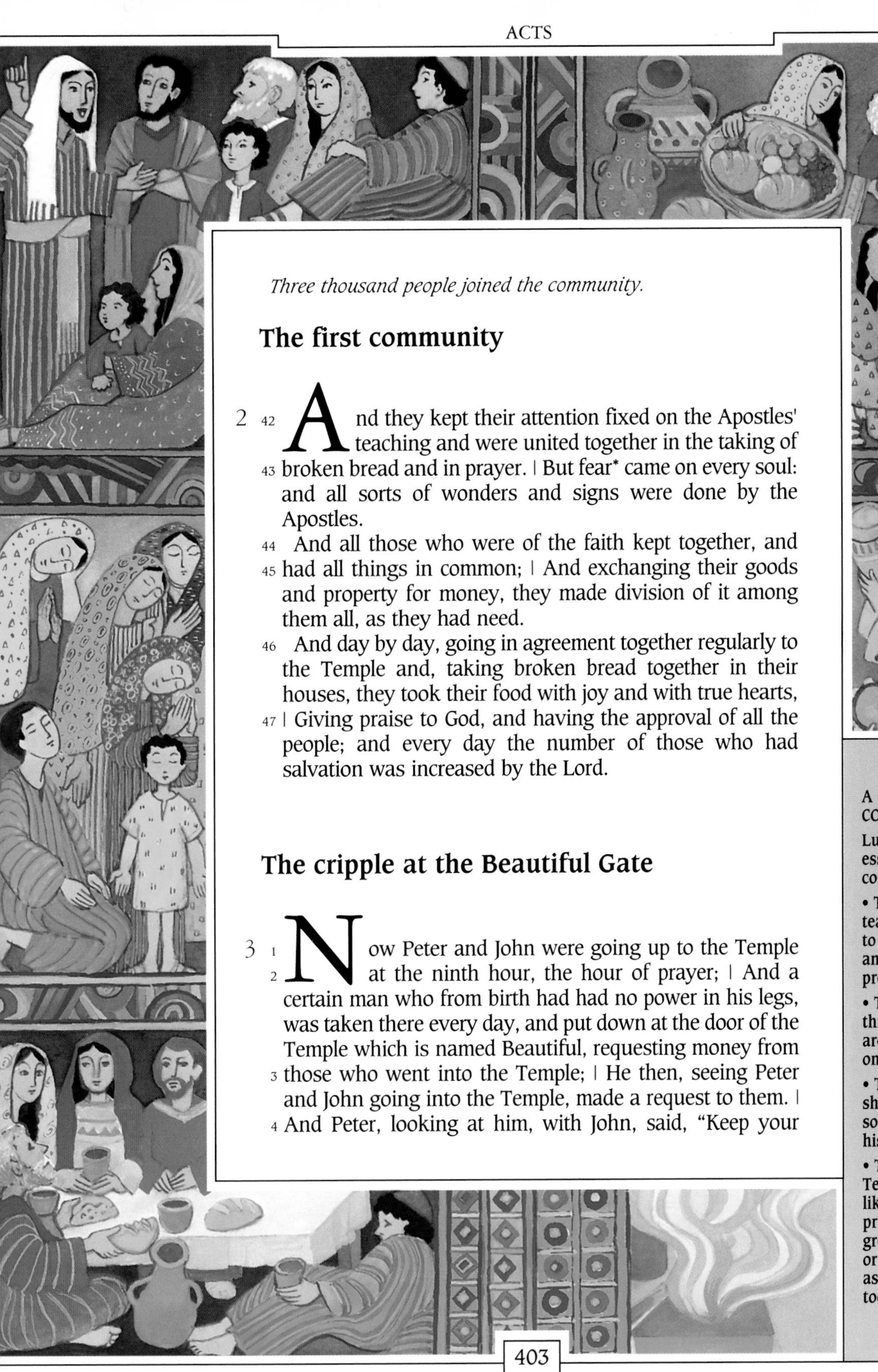

Three thousand people joined the community.

The first community

2 42 And they kept their attention fixed on the Apostles'
teaching and were united together in the taking of
43 broken bread and in prayer. | But fear* came on every soul:
and all sorts of wonders and signs were done by the
Apostles.
44 And all those who were of the faith kept together, and
45 had all things in common; | And exchanging their goods
and property for money, they made division of it among
them all, as they had need.
46 And day by day, going in agreement together regularly to
the Temple and, taking broken bread together in their
houses, they took their food with joy and with true hearts,
47 | Giving praise to God, and having the approval of all the
people; and every day the number of those who had
salvation was increased by the Lord.

The cripple at the Beautiful Gate

3 1 Now Peter and John were going up to the Temple
2 at the ninth hour, the hour of prayer; | And a
certain man who from birth had had no power in his legs,
was taken there every day, and put down at the door of the
Temple which is named Beautiful, requesting money from
3 those who went into the Temple; | He then, seeing Peter
and John going into the Temple, made a request to them. |
4 And Peter, looking at him, with John, said, "Keep your

A GOOD CHRISTIAN COMMUNITY

Luke listed the four essentials of a Christian community:

- To be faithful to the teaching of the apostles, i.e. to take life from the Gospel and give welcome to the presence of the risen Jesus.
- To live in fellowship. "By this all men will know you are my disciples, if you love one another" (John 13:35).
- To "break bread," i.e. to share the Lord's meal and so partake in the power of his love (see page 391, note 2).
- To attend prayers in the Temple or the synagogue like the first disciples, or to pray regularly in small groups such as the family, or again on major occasions as Christians still pray today.

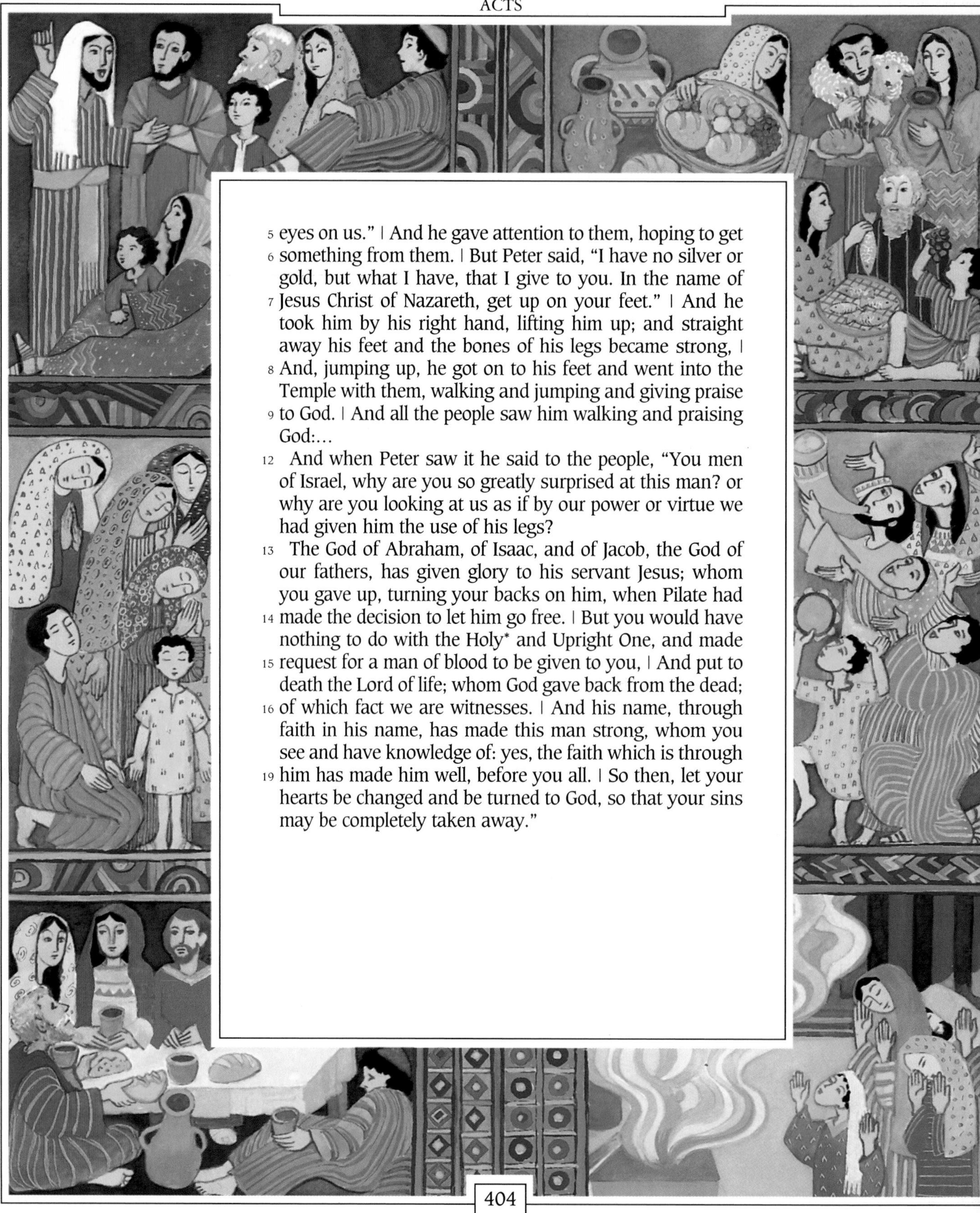

5 eyes on us." | And he gave attention to them, hoping to get
6 something from them. | But Peter said, "I have no silver or
gold, but what I have, that I give to you. In the name of
7 Jesus Christ of Nazareth, get up on your feet." | And he
took him by his right hand, lifting him up; and straight
away his feet and the bones of his legs became strong, |
8 And, jumping up, he got on to his feet and went into the
Temple with them, walking and jumping and giving praise
9 to God. | And all the people saw him walking and praising
God:...

12 And when Peter saw it he said to the people, "You men
of Israel, why are you so greatly surprised at this man? or
why are you looking at us as if by our power or virtue we
had given him the use of his legs?

13 The God of Abraham, of Isaac, and of Jacob, the God of
our fathers, has given glory to his servant Jesus; whom
you gave up, turning your backs on him, when Pilate had
14 made the decision to let him go free. | But you would have
nothing to do with the Holy* and Upright One, and made
15 request for a man of blood to be given to you, | And put to
death the Lord of life; whom God gave back from the dead;
16 of which fact we are witnesses. | And his name, through
faith in his name, has made this man strong, whom you
see and have knowledge of: yes, the faith which is through
19 him has made him well, before you all. | So then, let your
hearts be changed and be turned to God, so that your sins
may be completely taken away."

"We cannot help speaking about what we have seen"

The high priests had Peter and John arrested. They were accused before the Sanhedrin of causing disturbance within the Temple.*

4 8 Then Peter, being full of the Holy Spirit, said to
them, "O you rulers of the people and men of
9 authority, | If we are questioned today about a good work
done to a man who was ill, as to how he has been made
10 well, | Take note, all of you, and all the people of Israel, that
in the name of Jesus Christ of Nazareth, whom you put to
death on the cross, whom God gave back from the dead,
even through him is this man now before you completely
11 well. | 'He is the stone which you builders had no use for,
but which has been made the chief stone of the building.'[1]
12 | And in no other is there salvation: for there is no other
name under heaven, given among men, through which we
may have salvation."
13 Now when they saw that Peter and John were without
fear, though they were men of no education or learning,
they were greatly surprised; and they took note of them
14 that they had been with Jesus. | And, seeing that the man
who had been made well was there with them, they were
15 not able to say anything against it. | But when they had
given them orders to go out of the Sanhedrin, they had a
16 discussion among themselves, | Saying, "What are we to
do with these men? for certainly it is clear that a most
important sign has been done by them,...
17 But so that it may not go farther among the people, let us
put them in fear of punishment if they say anything in
future in this name."

[1] Psalm 118:22. Peter altered the words to name the members of the Sanhedrin as the builders who rejected the capstone. "You builders," he said to them.

4 18 And they sent for them, and gave them orders not to
make statements or give teaching in the name of Jesus. |
19 But Peter and John in answer said to them, "It is for you to
say if it is right in the eyes of God to give attention to you
20 more than to God: | For it is not possible for us to keep from
saying what we have seen and have knowledge of."

The members of the Sanhedrin were unsure of what to do. They feared the people's reaction. They released the apostles after issuing them a warning.

SHARING

The fellowship mentioned in Acts 2:42, page 403, was more than just a fine-sounding idea. The disciples put it into practice by sharing their possessions.

For Luke, it was an example of the proper use of money, a subject which had received much emphasis in his Gospel (see page 323).

One in heart and mind

4 32 And all those who were of the faith were one in
heart and soul: and not one of them said that any
of the things which he had was his property only; but they
had all things in common.

34 And no one among them was in need; for everyone who
had land or houses, exchanging them for money, took the
35 price of them, | And put it at the feet of the Apostles for
distribution to everyone as he had need.[1]

36 And Joseph, who was given by the Apostles the name of
Barnabas* (the sense of which is, Son of comfort), a
37 Levite* and a man of Cyprus by birth, | Having a field, got
money for it and put the money at the feet of the Apostles.

[1] Widows were particularly cared for. See Acts 6:1, page 408.

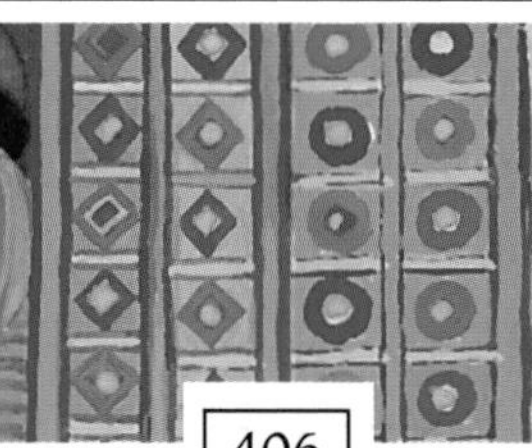

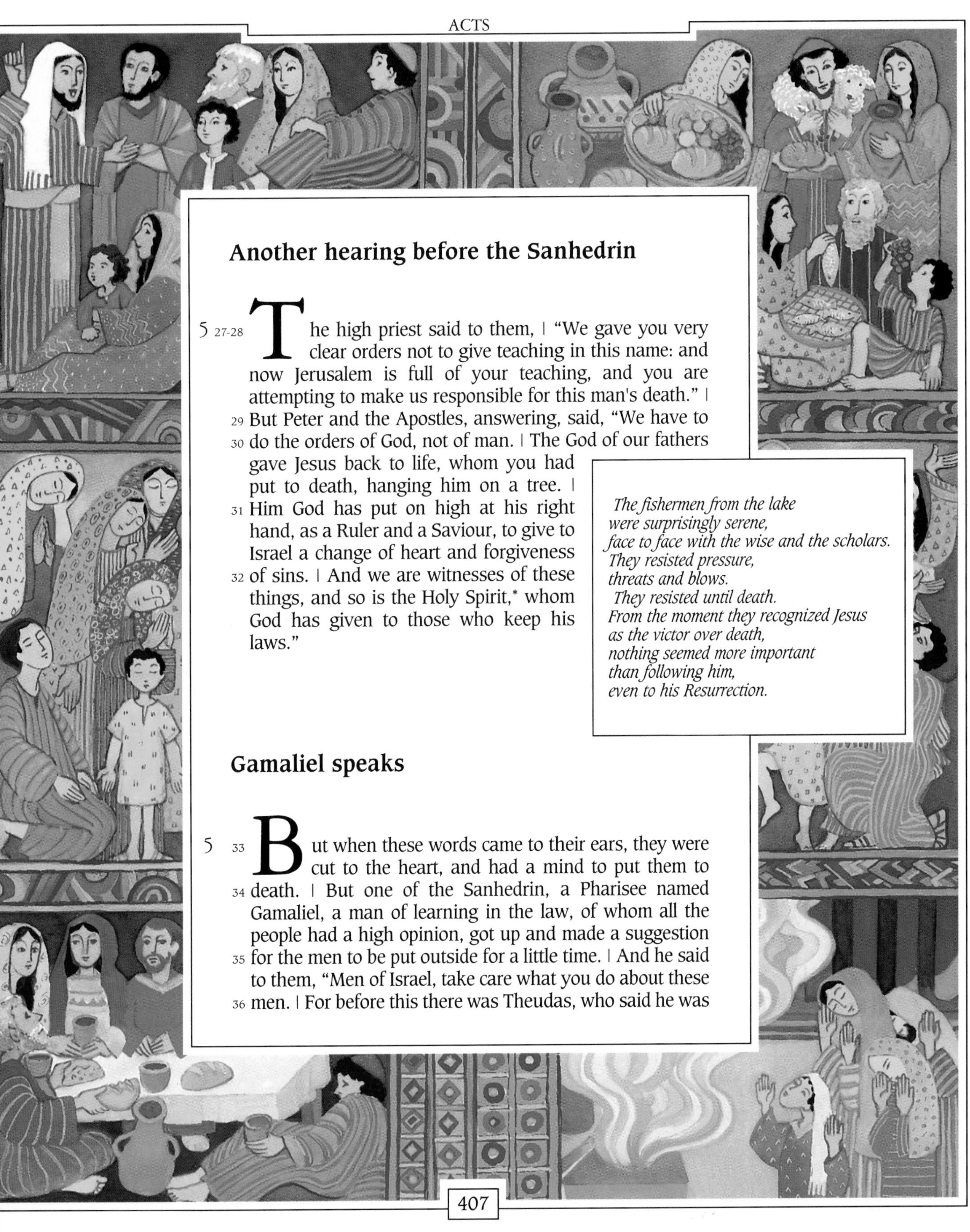

Another hearing before the Sanhedrin

5 27-28 The high priest said to them, | "We gave you very
clear orders not to give teaching in this name: and
now Jerusalem is full of your teaching, and you are
attempting to make us responsible for this man's death." |
29 But Peter and the Apostles, answering, said, "We have to
30 do the orders of God, not of man. | The God of our fathers
gave Jesus back to life, whom you had
put to death, hanging him on a tree. |
31 Him God has put on high at his right
hand, as a Ruler and a Saviour, to give to
Israel a change of heart and forgiveness
32 of sins. | And we are witnesses of these
things, and so is the Holy Spirit,* whom
God has given to those who keep his
laws."

The fishermen from the lake
were surprisingly serene,
face to face with the wise and the scholars.
They resisted pressure,
threats and blows.
They resisted until death.
From the moment they recognized Jesus
as the victor over death,
nothing seemed more important
than following him,
even to his Resurrection.

Gamaliel speaks

5 33 But when these words came to their ears, they were
cut to the heart, and had a mind to put them to
34 death. | But one of the Sanhedrin, a Pharisee named
Gamaliel, a man of learning in the law, of whom all the
people had a high opinion, got up and made a suggestion
35 for the men to be put outside for a little time. | And he said
to them, "Men of Israel, take care what you do about these
36 men. | For before this there was Theudas, who said he was

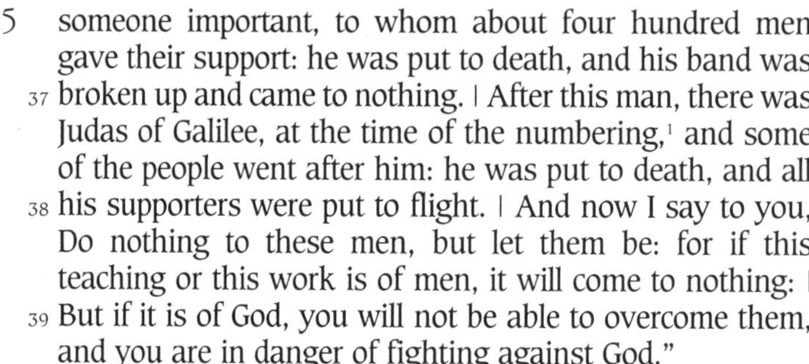

"DELIVERERS?"

Gamaliel was the grandson of Hillel, a renowned expert in the Law (see page 285). He was the teacher of Saul, who would become the disciple Paul. His references to Theudas and Judas the Galilean are confirmed by the Jewish historian, Flavius Josephus* (although Josephus placed Judas the Galilean much earlier than Theudas). The fairly frequent emergence of these "deliverers" stung the Romans into carrying out bloody purges. This had partly explained the priests' apprehensions regarding Jesus (John 11:47-50, page 356).

5 someone important, to whom about four hundred men
gave their support: he was put to death, and his band was
37 broken up and came to nothing. | After this man, there was
Judas of Galilee, at the time of the numbering,[1] and some
of the people went after him: he was put to death, and all
38 his supporters were put to flight. | And now I say to you,
Do nothing to these men, but let them be: for if this
teaching or this work is of men, it will come to nothing: |
39 But if it is of God, you will not be able to overcome them,
and you are in danger of fighting against God."

40 And he seemed to them to be right: and they sent for the
Apostles, and, after having them whipped and giving them
orders to give no teaching in the name of Jesus, they let
41 them go. | So they went away from the Sanhedrin, happy
42 to undergo shame for the Name. | And every day, in the
Temple and privately, they went on teaching and
preaching Jesus as the Christ.*

How to settle disputes

6 1 Now in those days, when the number of the
disciples was increasing, protests were made by
the Greek Jews against the Hebrews, because their widows
were not taken care of in the distribution of food every day.
2 | And the Apostles sent for all the disciples and said, "It is
not right for us to give up preaching the word of God in
3 order to make distribution of food. | Take then from among
you seven men of good name, full of the Spirit and of

THE SEVEN

The disciples' community was a mixture of Hebrew speakers and Greek speakers. The latter, sometimes called "Hellenists," were Jews whose families had lived abroad. Having returned to Jerusalem for various reasons, they had trouble in being accepted since they spoke little Hebrew or Aramaic. Their widows were ignored because they could not communicate at all, and were left out when aid was being distributed.

The apostles chose seven men among the Hellenists and made them responsible for seeing that aid was shared out fairly. As the future would show, their task went further than that. They were also preachers. Their familiarity with Greek language and culture gave them an advantage in dealing with the diaspora* Jews and the heathens. Their number, seven and not twelve, suggested the nations (see page 280). These seven would help the budding religion, still confined to Jerusalem, to spread to the "four corners of the earth."

[1] Flavius Josephus gave the census in 6 AD as the date of Judas the Galilean's insurgency. It was not the census that Luke reported as coinciding with the birth of Jesus. The Romans used the uprising of Judas as a pretext for placing Judea under direct rule. They accused Herod's son, Archelaus, of laxity and replaced him with a Roman governor.

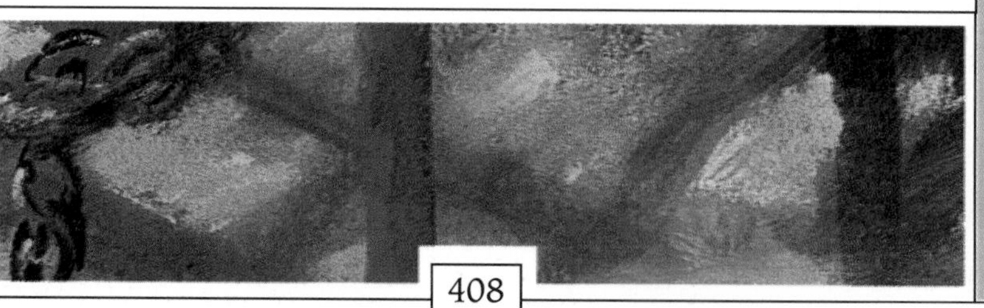

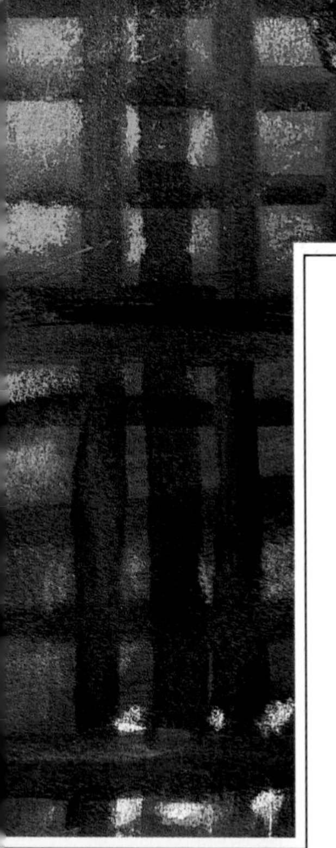

wisdom, to whom we may give control of this business. |
4 Then we will give all our time to prayer and the teaching of
5 the word." | And this saying was pleasing to all of them:
and they made selection of Stephen, a man full of faith and
of the Holy Spirit, and Philip and Prochorus and Nicanor
and Timon and Parmenas and Nicolas of Antioch, who had
6 become a Jew: | These they took to the Apostles, who, after
prayer, put their hands on them.
7 And the word of God was increasing in power; and the
number of the disciples in Jerusalem became very great,
and a great number of priests were in agreement with the
faith.

TONED TO DEATH

amaliel's appeal for oderation was not heeded or long. The preaching of tephen and his Hellenist ompanions, more transigent than that of the welve, met with enraged pposition. Stephen ownplayed the role of the emple, as Jeremiah (Jeremiah 1-11, page 150) **and articularly Jesus** (John 2:19, ıge 337, and John 4:20-24, page 40) **had done before him. He eclared that God did not ve in man-made houses.** tephen based his argument on 2 amuel 7:5-7, page 108. See also hn 4:21-23, page 340.)

ws from Cilicia and Asia .e. Ephesus) had Stephen rought before the anhedrin* and condemned death by stoning.

mong the Jews from Cilicia as Saul of Tarsus, a pupil f Gamaliel. Turning a deaf ar to his teacher's counsels, aul embarked on a fierce ersecution of Stephen's ompanions.

PERSECUTION

Stephen

6 8 And Stephen, full of grace and power, did great
9 wonders and signs* among the people. | But some
of those who were of the Synagogue named that of the
Libertines, and some of the men of Cyrene and of
Alexandria and those from Cilicia and Asia, had
10 arguments with Stephen. | But they were not able to get the
better of him, for his words were full of wisdom and of the
Spirit.
11 Then they got men to say, "He has said evil against
12 Moses and against God, in our hearing." | And the people,
with the rulers and the scribes, were moved against him,
13 and they came and took him before the Sanhedrin,* | And

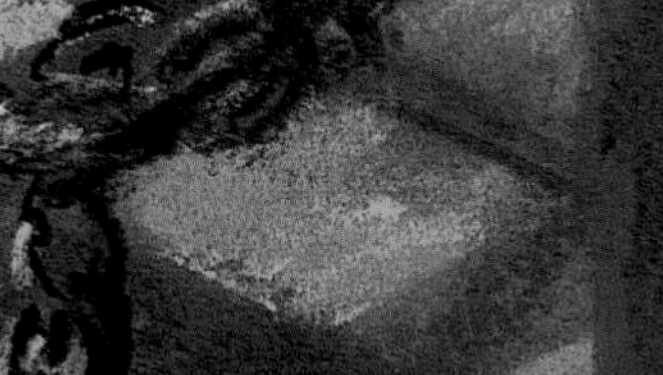

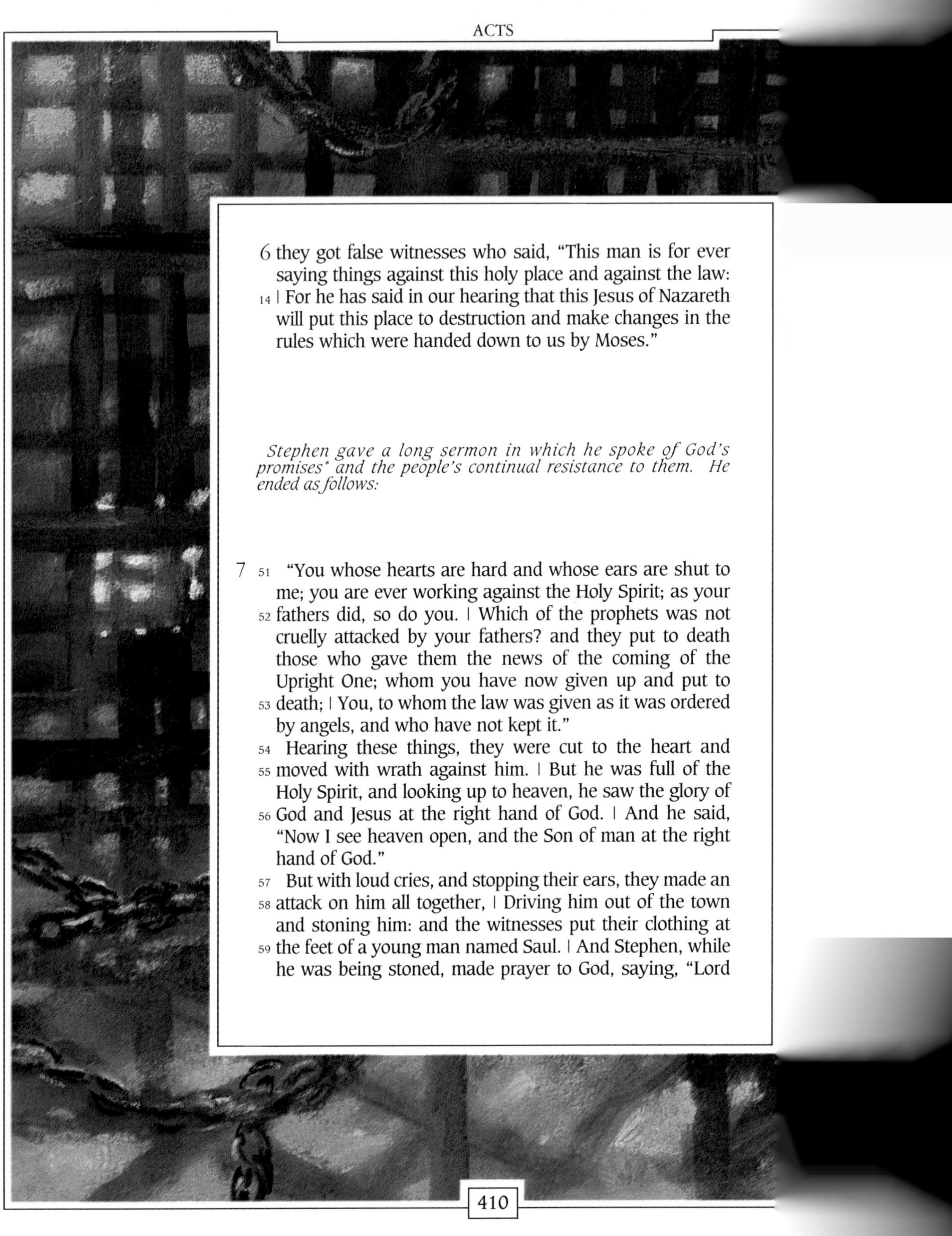

6 they got false witnesses who said, “This man is for ever
saying things against this holy place and against the law:
14 | For he has said in our hearing that this Jesus of Nazareth
will put this place to destruction and make changes in the
rules which were handed down to us by Moses.”

Stephen gave a long sermon in which he spoke of God's promises and the people's continual resistance to them. He ended as follows:*

7 51 “You whose hearts are hard and whose ears are shut to
me; you are ever working against the Holy Spirit; as your
52 fathers did, so do you. | Which of the prophets was not
cruelly attacked by your fathers? and they put to death
those who gave them the news of the coming of the
Upright One; whom you have now given up and put to
53 death; | You, to whom the law was given as it was ordered
by angels, and who have not kept it.”
54 Hearing these things, they were cut to the heart and
55 moved with wrath against him. | But he was full of the
Holy Spirit, and looking up to heaven, he saw the glory of
56 God and Jesus at the right hand of God. | And he said,
“Now I see heaven open, and the Son of man at the right
hand of God.”
57 But with loud cries, and stopping their ears, they made an
58 attack on him all together, | Driving him out of the town
and stoning him: and the witnesses put their clothing at
59 the feet of a young man named Saul. | And Stephen, while
he was being stoned, made prayer to God, saying, “Lord

THE INNER CONFLICT OF SAUL

Luke described the death of Stephen in much the same terms as the death of Jesus. Saul resembled the Roman centurion by the cross. Luke probably meant to suggest that Saul, like the centurion, was disturbed by the scene. Saul was impressed by Stephen's dignity and bravery. But he was not convinced, far from it. He was persuaded that Stephen was wrong and that anybody who thought like him had to be silenced. He refused to let himself be "goaded" by the Lord (Acts 26:14, page 413)**. He would wage a long fight before yielding at last to conversion.***

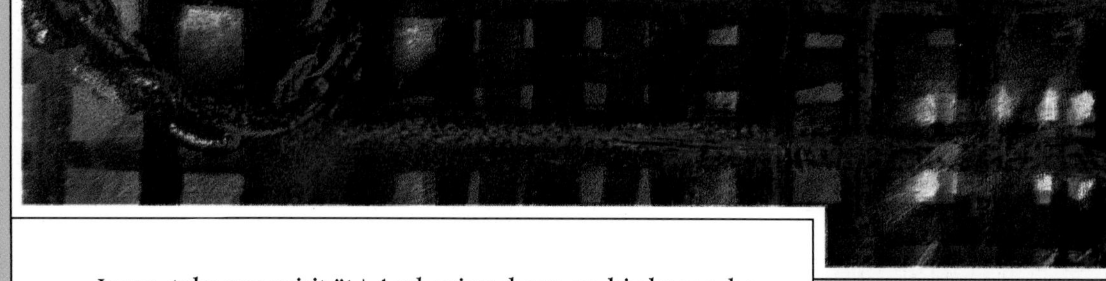

60 Jesus, take my spirit."[1] | And going down on his knees, he
said in a loud voice, "Lord, do not make them responsible
for this sin."[2] And when he had said this, he went to his
rest.

8 1 And Saul gave approval to his death.

Philip and the Ethiopian

The killing of Stephen was followed by a wave of arrests directed more especially against the Hellenists. The Hellenists, remembering the words of Jesus,[3] slipped out of Jerusalem and went to other towns where they bravely preached the Gospel. Philip, one of the seven, after evangelizing Samaria, baptized a "worshipper of God."[4]

8 26 But an angel of the Lord said to Philip, "Get up, and
go to the south, to the road which goes from
27 Jerusalem to Gaza, through the waste land." | And he went
and there was a man of Ethiopia, a servant of great
authority under Candace, queen of the Ethiopians, and
controller of all her property, who had come up to
28 Jerusalem for worship; | He was going back, seated in his
carriage, and was reading the book of the prophet Isaiah. |
29 And the Spirit said to Philip, "Go near, and get on his
carriage."
30 And Philip, running up to him, saw that he was reading
Isaiah the prophet, and said to him, "Is the sense of what
31 you are reading clear to you?" | And he said, "How is that

[1] See Luke 23:46, page 380.

[2] See Luke 23:34, page 378.

[3] See Matthew 10:23, page 270.

[4] This was the usual term for the heathens who, while believing in the God of Israel, preferred not to observe Jewish law (see page 233, "The Jews of the diaspora"). Philip was therefore baptizing a heathen, the first recorded case in the New Testament. This incident seemed to have been overlooked, since the first baptism of a heathen was attributed to Peter (Acts 10:25-48, page 415, and Acts 15:7-9, page 421). Paul was given credit for making the practice general (see page 420, "From law to faith").

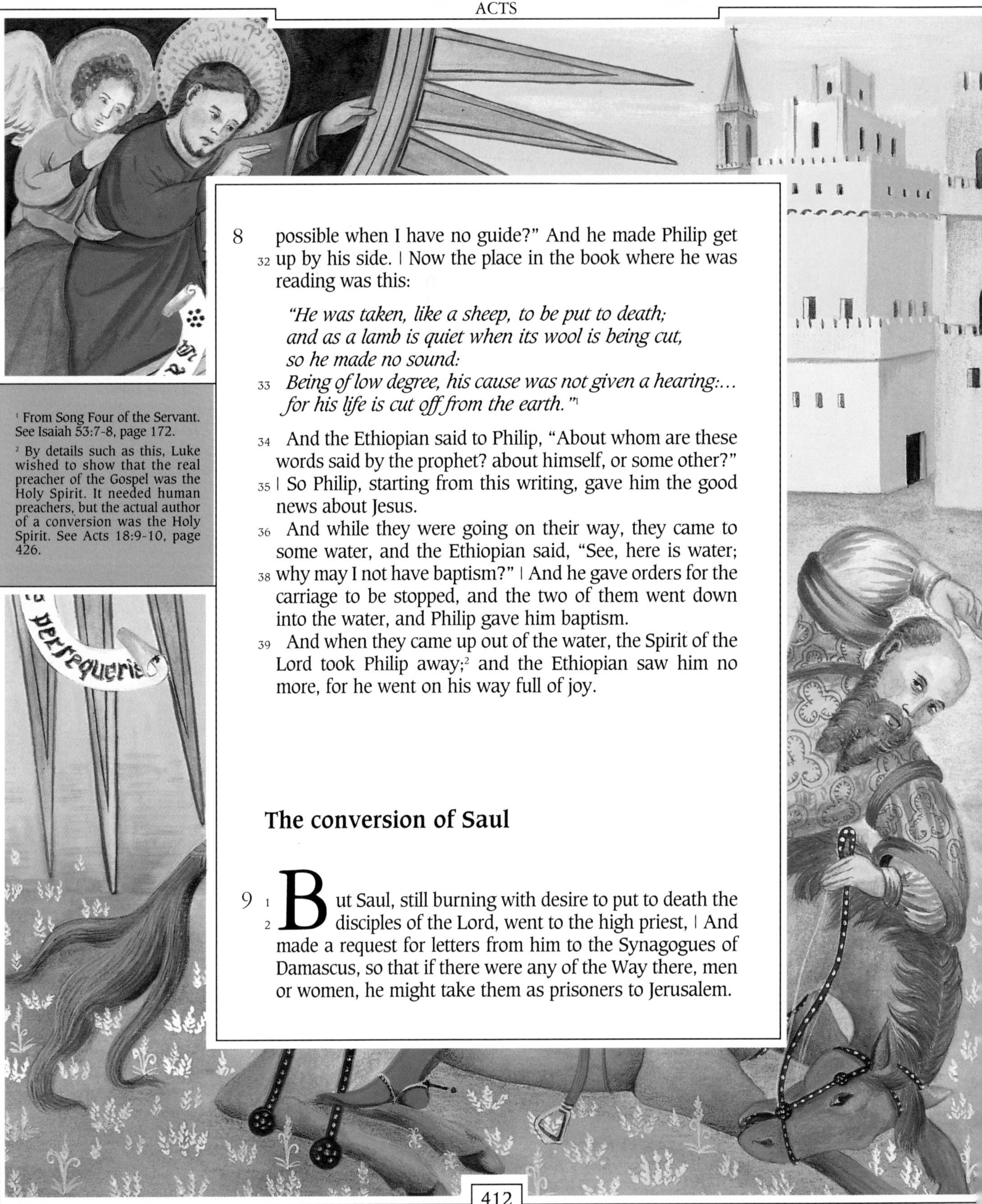

8 possible when I have no guide?" And he made Philip get
32 up by his side. | Now the place in the book where he was
reading was this:

"He was taken, like a sheep, to be put to death;
and as a lamb is quiet when its wool is being cut,
so he made no sound:
33 *Being of low degree, his cause was not given a hearing:...*
for his life is cut off from the earth."[1]

34 And the Ethiopian said to Philip, "About whom are these
words said by the prophet? about himself, or some other?"
35 | So Philip, starting from this writing, gave him the good
news about Jesus.
36 And while they were going on their way, they came to
some water, and the Ethiopian said, "See, here is water;
38 why may I not have baptism?" | And he gave orders for the
carriage to be stopped, and the two of them went down
into the water, and Philip gave him baptism.
39 And when they came up out of the water, the Spirit of the
Lord took Philip away;[2] and the Ethiopian saw him no
more, for he went on his way full of joy.

The conversion of Saul

9 1 But Saul, still burning with desire to put to death the
2 disciples of the Lord, went to the high priest, | And
made a request for letters from him to the Synagogues of
Damascus, so that if there were any of the Way there, men
or women, he might take them as prisoners to Jerusalem.

[1] From Song Four of the Servant. See Isaiah 53:7-8, page 172.

[2] By details such as this, Luke wished to show that the real preacher of the Gospel was the Holy Spirit. It needed human preachers, but the actual author of a conversion was the Holy Spirit. See Acts 18:9-10, page 426.

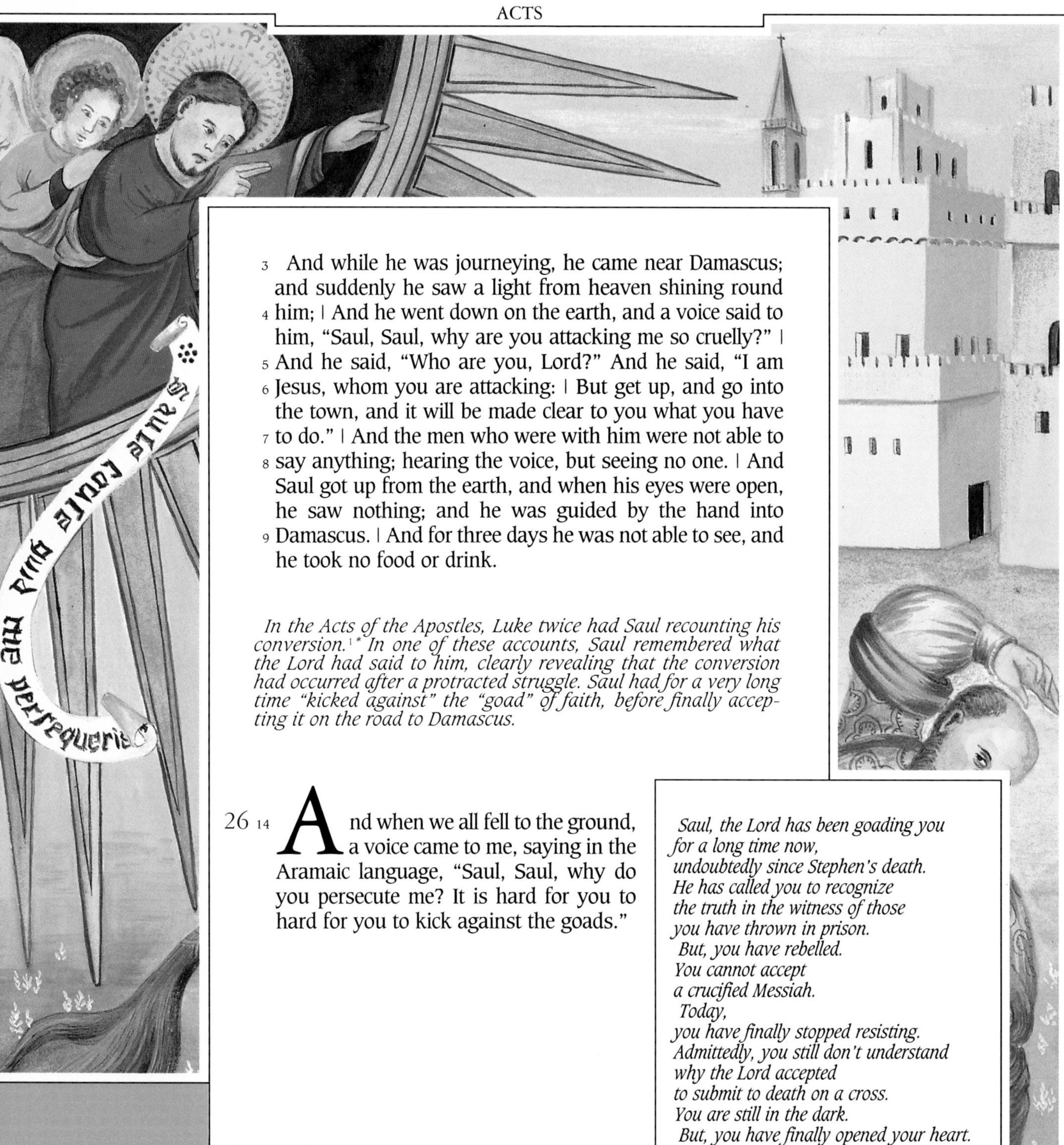

3 And while he was journeying, he came near Damascus;
and suddenly he saw a light from heaven shining round
4 him; | And he went down on the earth, and a voice said to
him, "Saul, Saul, why are you attacking me so cruelly?" |
5 And he said, "Who are you, Lord?" And he said, "I am
6 Jesus, whom you are attacking: | But get up, and go into
the town, and it will be made clear to you what you have
7 to do." | And the men who were with him were not able to
8 say anything; hearing the voice, but seeing no one. | And
Saul got up from the earth, and when his eyes were open,
he saw nothing; and he was guided by the hand into
9 Damascus. | And for three days he was not able to see, and
he took no food or drink.

In the Acts of the Apostles, Luke twice had Saul recounting his conversion.[1] In one of these accounts, Saul remembered what the Lord had said to him, clearly revealing that the conversion had occurred after a protracted struggle. Saul had for a very long time "kicked against" the "goad" of faith, before finally accepting it on the road to Damascus.*

26 14 And when we all fell to the ground, a voice came to me, saying in the Aramaic language, "Saul, Saul, why do you persecute me? It is hard for you to hard for you to kick against the goads."

Saul, the Lord has been goading you
for a long time now,
undoubtedly since Stephen's death.
He has called you to recognize
the truth in the witness of those
you have thrown in prison.
But, you have rebelled.
You cannot accept
a crucified Messiah.
Today,
you have finally stopped resisting.
Admittedly, you still don't understand
why the Lord accepted
to submit to death on a cross.
You are still in the dark.
But, you have finally opened your heart.
You have given up your ideas,
so as to allow yourself to be taught
by the Lord.

See how Paul wrote of his onversion in the Letter to the hilippians 3:5-14, page 441.

In Aramaic, the name of Saul f Tarsus was pronounced the ame as the name of King Saul.

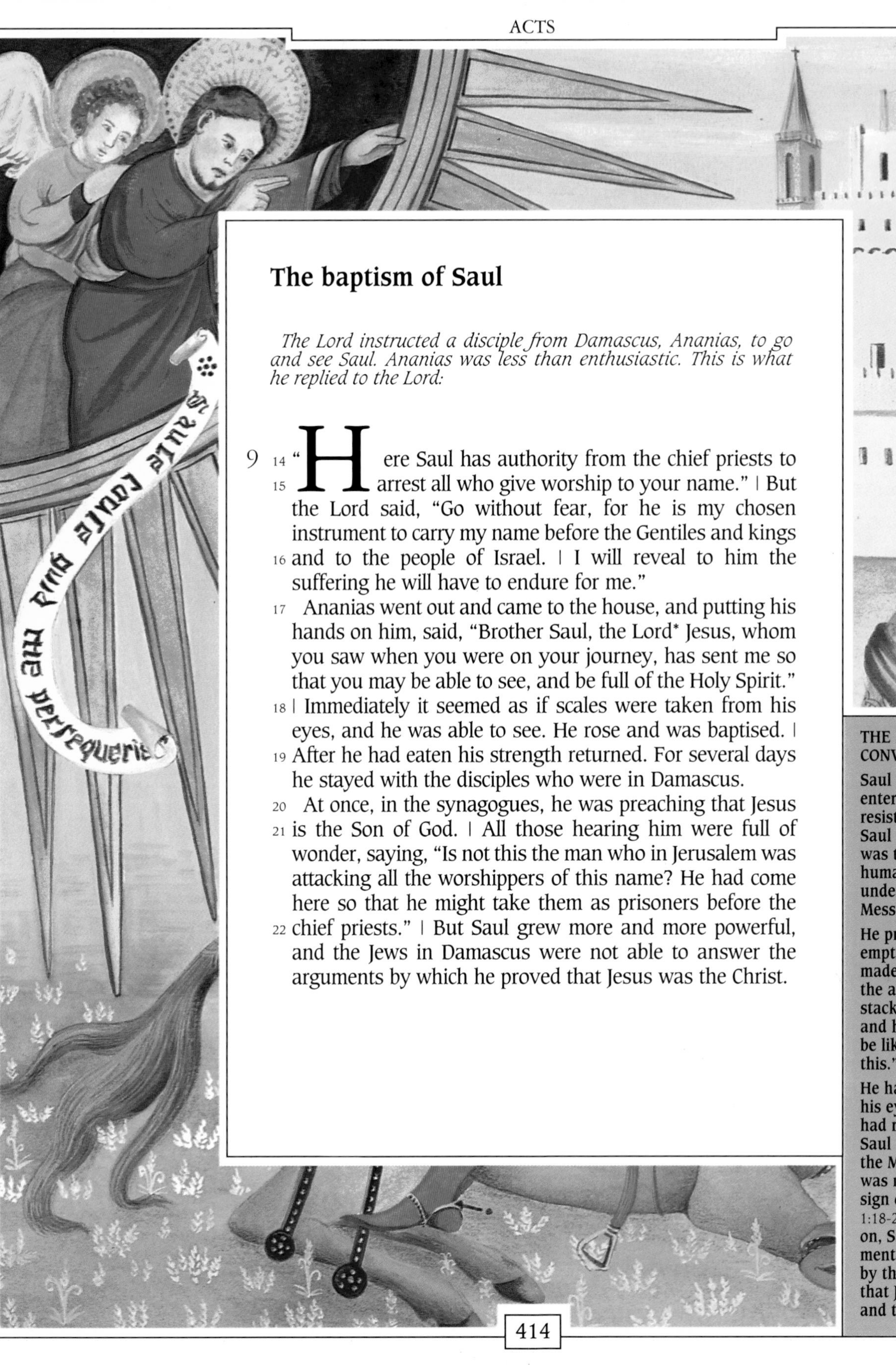

The baptism of Saul

The Lord instructed a disciple from Damascus, Ananias, to go and see Saul. Ananias was less than enthusiastic. This is what he replied to the Lord:

9 14 "Here Saul has authority from the chief priests to
15 arrest all who give worship to your name." | But
the Lord said, "Go without fear, for he is my chosen
instrument to carry my name before the Gentiles and kings
16 and to the people of Israel. | I will reveal to him the
suffering he will have to endure for me."
17 Ananias went out and came to the house, and putting his
hands on him, said, "Brother Saul, the Lord* Jesus, whom
you saw when you were on your journey, has sent me so
that you may be able to see, and be full of the Holy Spirit."
18 | Immediately it seemed as if scales were taken from his
eyes, and he was able to see. He rose and was baptised. |
19 After he had eaten his strength returned. For several days
he stayed with the disciples who were in Damascus.
20 At once, in the synagogues, he was preaching that Jesus
21 is the Son of God. | All those hearing him were full of
wonder, saying, "Is not this the man who in Jerusalem was
attacking all the worshippers of this name? He had come
here so that he might take them as prisoners before the
22 chief priests." | But Saul grew more and more powerful,
and the Jews in Damascus were not able to answer the
arguments by which he proved that Jesus was the Christ.

THE FRUITS OF CONVERSION

Saul was blind upon entering Damascus. After resisting for a long time, Saul now believed that Jesu was the Messiah. But his human brain could not understand why this Messiah had been crucified.

He prayed and fasted. He emptied his mind of ready-made ideas. He threw out the arguments that he had stacked up between the Lor and himself like: "God can't be like that, or He can't do this."

He had been baptized and his eyes could see. The Lo had revealed himself to him Saul now understood that the Messiah's crucifixion was not a disgrace but a sign of love (1 Corinthians 1:18-25, page 433). **From ther on, Saul would use all his mental energies, enlightene by the Holy Spirit, to show that Jesus was the Messiah and the Son of God.**

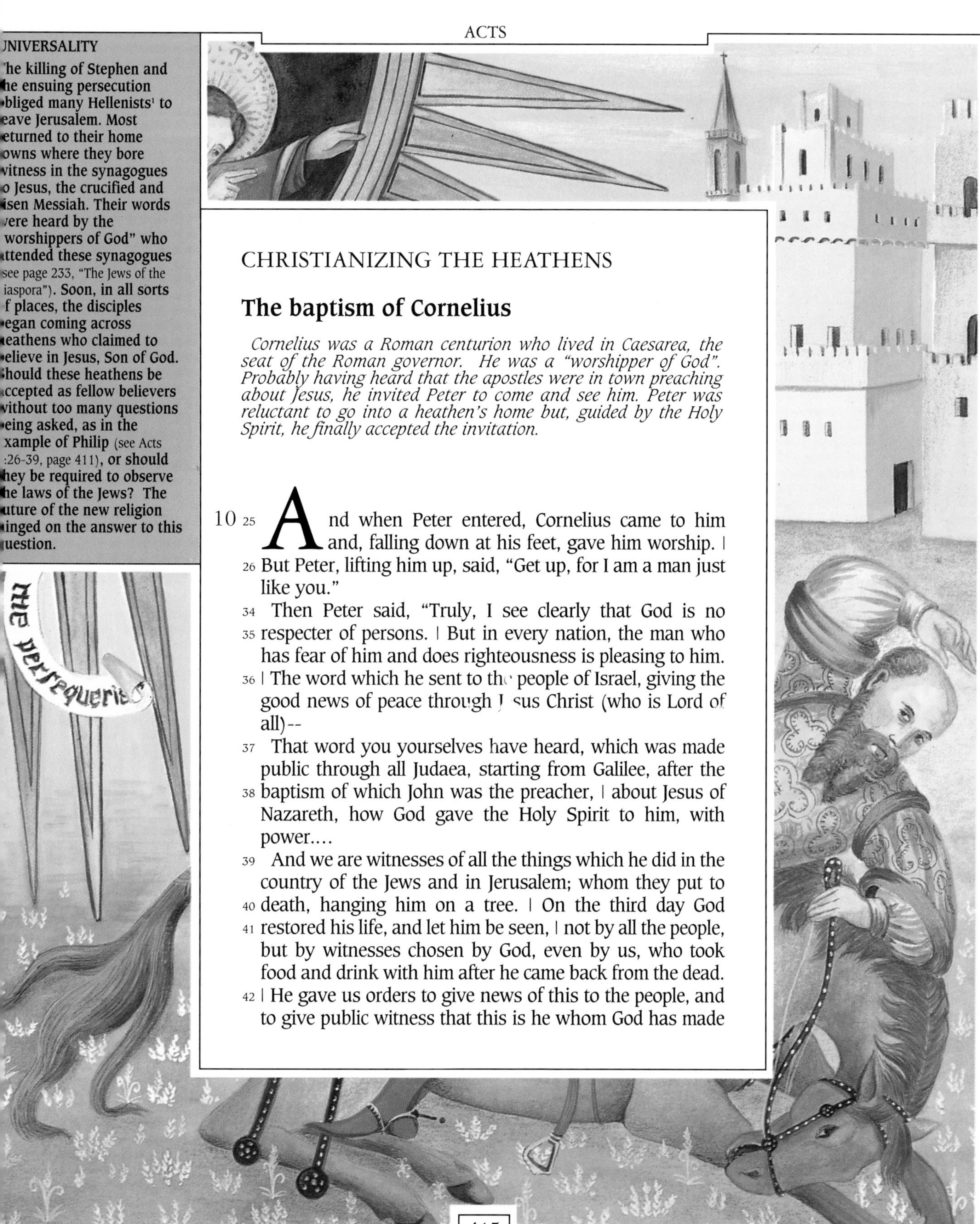

JNIVERSALITY

'he killing of Stephen and
he ensuing persecution
bliged many Hellenists[1] to
eave Jerusalem. Most
eturned to their home
owns where they bore
vitness in the synagogues
o Jesus, the crucified and
isen Messiah. Their words
vere heard by the
worshippers of God" who
ttended these synagogues
see page 233, "The Jews of the
iaspora"). Soon, in all sorts
f places, the disciples
egan coming across
eathens who claimed to
elieve in Jesus, Son of God.
hould these heathens be
ccepted as fellow believers
vithout too many questions
eing asked, as in the
xample of Philip (see Acts
:26-39, page 411), or should
hey be required to observe
he laws of the Jews? The
uture of the new religion
inged on the answer to this
uestion.

CHRISTIANIZING THE HEATHENS

The baptism of Cornelius

Cornelius was a Roman centurion who lived in Caesarea, the seat of the Roman governor. He was a "worshipper of God". Probably having heard that the apostles were in town preaching about Jesus, he invited Peter to come and see him. Peter was reluctant to go into a heathen's home but, guided by the Holy Spirit, he finally accepted the invitation.

10 25 And when Peter entered, Cornelius came to him
and, falling down at his feet, gave him worship. |
26 But Peter, lifting him up, said, "Get up, for I am a man just
like you."
34 Then Peter said, "Truly, I see clearly that God is no
35 respecter of persons. | But in every nation, the man who
has fear of him and does righteousness is pleasing to him.
36 | The word which he sent to the people of Israel, giving the
good news of peace through Jesus Christ (who is Lord of
all)--
37 That word you yourselves have heard, which was made
public through all Judaea, starting from Galilee, after the
38 baptism of which John was the preacher, | about Jesus of
Nazareth, how God gave the Holy Spirit to him, with
power....
39 And we are witnesses of all the things which he did in the
country of the Jews and in Jerusalem; whom they put to
40 death, hanging him on a tree. | On the third day God
41 restored his life, and let him be seen, | not by all the people,
but by witnesses chosen by God, even by us, who took
food and drink with him after he came back from the dead.
42 | He gave us orders to give news of this to the people, and
to give public witness that this is he whom God has made

10 43 judge of the living and the dead. | To him all the prophets
give witness, that through his name everyone who has
faith in him will have forgiveness of sins."
44 While Peter was saying these words, the Holy Spirit came
45 on all those who were hearing the word. | And the Jews of
the faith, who had come with Peter, were full of wonder,
46 because the Holy Spirit was given to the Gentiles. | They
were talking in tongues, and giving glory to God. Then
47 Peter said, | "Will any man say that these may not have
baptism who have been given the Holy
48 Spirit as we have?" | Thus, he gave
orders for them to be baptised in the
name of Jesus Christ. Then they stayed
him with them for several days.

The Holy Spirit was becoming impatient,
seeing clearly that Peter did not
dare to fully welcome
Cornelius, under the pretext
that he did not belong
to the "people of the Covenant."
The Holy Spirit was revealed
in a bubbling newness,
so that Peter would renounce
his old reasoning.
He was convinced.
The Spirit of God truly blows
where It wills!

Community reactions in Jerusalem

11 2 When Peter entered Jerusalem, those who obeyed
the rule of circumcision had an argument with him, |
3 saying, "You visited with uncircumcised men and ate food
4 with them."[1] | But Peter gave them an account of it all
precisely as it happened, saying, ...

Peter told in particular how he had observed the Holy Spirit at work among the heathens.

[1] The weight of tradition* is one of the hardest things of all to budge. To understand the Jew's repugnance at going into heathen homes, see page 310 and John 18:28, page 373.

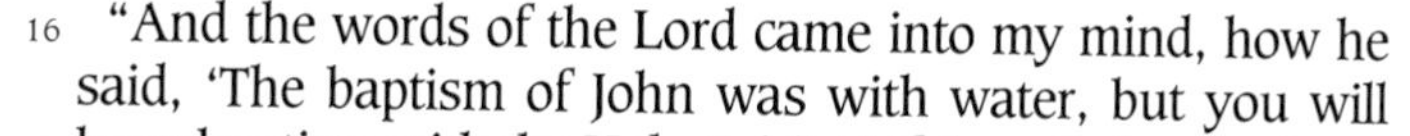

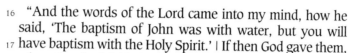

16 "And the words of the Lord came into my mind, how he
said, 'The baptism of John was with water, but you will
17 have baptism with the Holy Spirit.' | If then God gave them,
when they had faith in the Lord Jesus Christ, the same as
he gave to us, who was I to go against God?"
18 And hearing these things they said nothing more, but
gave glory to God, saying, "Then to the Gentiles* as to us
has God given a change of heart, so that they may have
life."

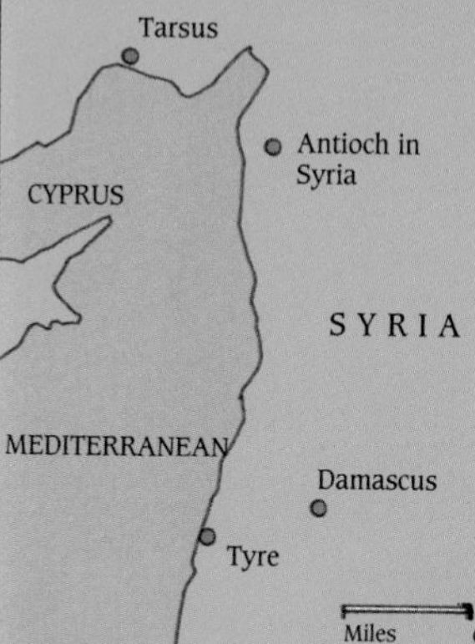

Christians in Antioch

Saul, after being forced to leave Damascus, traveled to Jerusalem, where he met Barnabas. He then returned to his home town, Tarsus, about a hundred kilometers from Antioch.

11 19 Then those who had been scattered by the
trouble concerning Stephen, went as far as
20 Phoenicia and Cyprus, preaching to the Jews only. | But
some of them, men of Cyprus and Cyrene, when they came
to Antioch, gave the good news about the Lord Jesus to the
21 Greeks. | The power of the Lord was with them, and a great
number had faith and were turned to the Lord.
22 News of them reached the church at Jerusalem: and they
23 sent Barnabas[2] as far as Antioch,[3] | who, when he came
and saw the grace of God, was glad. He explained to them
the need of staying near the Lord with all the strength of
24 their hearts. | Because he was a good man and full of the
Holy Spirit and of faith, a great number were joined to the
25 Lord. | Then he went on to Tarsus, looking for Sau.; |
26 When he found him, he took him to Antioch. And they
were with the church there for a year, teaching the people;

[2] See Acts 4:36, page 406.

[3] Antioch on the Orontes, also known as Antioch in Syria, was the former capital of Antiochus IV (see page 178, "The Greek occupation"). At the time, it ranked as the third most important city in the Roman Empire.

11 and the disciples were first given the name of "Christians" in Antioch.[1]

Martyrdom of James and freeing of Peter

12 1 Now, about that time, Herod[2] the king arrested
2 some of the Christians. | He put James, the
3 brother of John, to death with the sword.[3] | When he saw
that this was pleasing to the Jews he took Peter as well.
This was at the time of the Feast of Unleavened Bread.

4 His purpose being to bring him out for a public trial after
5 the Passover. | So Peter was kept in prison, but the church
prayed earnestly to God for him.

Peter was miraculously set free

12 And when this dawned on him, he went to the house of
Mary, the mother of John named Mark, where a number of
13 them had gathered for prayer. | He knocked on the door,
14 and a young girl, named Rhoda, answered. | Hearing the
voice of Peter, in her joy she went running, without
15 opening the door, to say that Peter was outside. | They said
to her, "You are out of your mind." But she insisted,
decisively, that it was so. They said, "It is his angel." |
16 Peter continued knocking on the door, and when it was

[1] The preaching of the disciples focused on the Messiah* (translated into Greek as "Christos"). They proclaimed that he had come, whereas the other Jews continued to wait. The followers of the "Christ" became known as Christians.

[2] Herod Agrippa I was the grandson of Herod* the Great and of Mariamm the Hasmonean.* He was therefore Jewish on his grandmother's side. From 41 to 44 AD (the year of his death), he was recognized as king of Judea and Samaria by the Roman emperor.

[3] James, son of Zebedee and one of the three apostles to witness the transfiguration, died in 43 or 44 AD.

THE MINISTRY OF PETER CONTINUES

It was the week of Easter. Peter, although condemned to death and guarded by soldiers, was freed. After his escape, a woman recognized him, but the disciples thought she was crazy. They thought she had simply seen an angel or a spirit. Peter asked that the good news of his liberation be spread, then he left...

When Luke wrote the book of Acts, Peter was already dead. Through recalling this story of Peter's liberation from prison modeled after the Resurrection of Jesus, Luke wanted to emphasize that something from Peter was still alive in the Church: his ministry of unity–a ministry that should continue in the same spirit in which Peter practiced it.

open they saw him, and they were amazed.
17 But he signaled to them with his hand to be quiet, and
recounted how the Lord had freed him from prison. He
said, "Give the news to James[1] and the brothers." Then he
left.

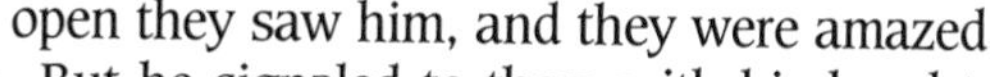

Barnabas and Saul sent on mission

The Christians in Antioch were not a closed community. They were eager for all people to receive the treasure of the Gospel as they had done.

13 2 And while they were worshiping the Lord and
fasting, the Holy Spirit said, "Let Barnabas and
Saul be given to me for the special work for which they
3 have been chosen by me." | Then, after fasting[2] and
praying they placed their hands on them, and sent them
away.

4 So, being sent out by the Holy Spirit, they went down to
5 Seleucia. From there they went by ship to Cyprus. | And at
Salamis they were preaching the word of God in the
synagogues of the Jews. John was with them, helping
them.

From Salamis the small band left for Paphos, where they converted the proconsul Sergius Paulus to the gospel. The voyage continued...

13 Then Paul and those who were with him went by ship
from Paphos to Perga in Pamphylia. There John left them
and returned to Jerusalem.

[1] This was James,* the brother of the Lord.

[2] See page 268, "To hunger after the word of God."

[3] John (also called Mark), son of Mary of Jerusalem (Acts 12:12, facing page), was the cousin of Barnabas (Colossians 4:10). He was also Mark the future Evangelist (see page 235).

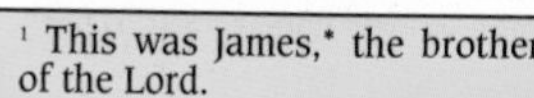

LAYING ON* OF HANDS

The person laying on hands passes on a gift she or he has received. The Christian leaders in Antioch had been called by the Holy Spirit to depart on mission. They delegated the call to Barnabas and Saul. Paul would later use the same gesture to consecrate* the organizers of newly-founded communities.

PAUL, GROUP LEADER

Verse 13 signaled a turning-point in the missionary journey. Until then, Barnabas had always been given first mention as leader of the group. Henceforward, he was replaced as leader by Saul, who had dropped his Jewish name and adopted the Roman name Paul. In doing so, he showed that from then on he would devote his ministry* primarily to the heathens. The humility of Barnabas in stepping down to allow Paul to achieve his full stature as a leader was possibly not to the liking of John, who quit the expedition.

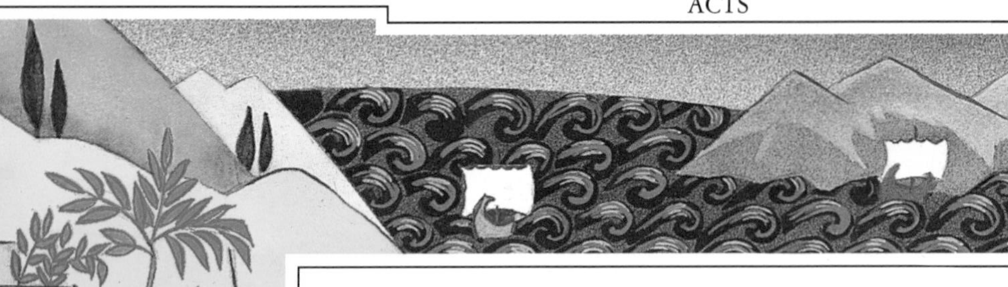

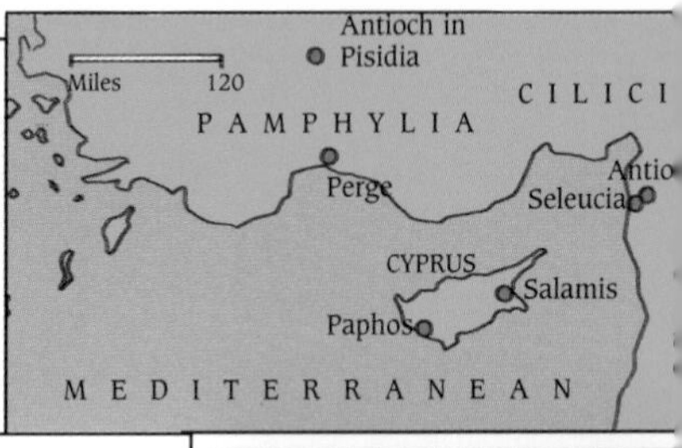

The new religion reaches out to the heathens

13 14 Paul and Barnabas, going through from Perga, came
to Antioch in Pisidia;[1] they entered the synagogue
on the Sabbath* and were seated.
15 After the reading of the Law and the Prophets, the rulers
of the synagogue sent to them, saying, "Brothers, if you
16 have a word of comfort for the people, speak." | And Paul,
getting up and motioning with his hand, said, "Men of
Israel, and you who have the fear of God,[2] listen....

Paul preached that all the promises in the Old Testament were fulfilled in Jesus. He concluded by saying:*

32 And wetell you the good news: what God promised our
33 fathers, | he has fulfilled for our children, by raising up
Jesus;...

38 And so, let it be clear to you, my brothers, that through this
39 man forgiveness of sins is offered to you: | and through him
everyone who has faith is justified from everything from
43 which the Law of Moses was not able to justify you." | Now
when the meeting was ended, a number of the Jews and of
the God-fearing Gentiles[3] who had become Jews, followed
Paul and Barnabas. who urged them about how important it
was to continue in the grace of God.

44 On the following Sabbath, almost all the town came
45 together to listen to the word of God. | But when the Jews
saw such a great number of people, they were envious and
46 said evil words against Paul's preaching. | Then Paul and

FROM LAW TO FAITH

In verse 38, Paul summed up his own spiritual experience. Observing the Law of Moses had not made him righteous since, in the name of that law, he had persecuted the Christians. Only when he had accepted the gift of faith* did he experience the joy of being loved by God and being saved (see Philippians 3:8-9, page 441).

Having made this discovery, Paul had no problem accepting as Christians people who did not observe the law of Moses but who had true faith in Jesus.

[1] Antioch in Pisidia, not to be confused with Antioch in Syria, was a town near the middle of present-day Turkey. Some of its ruins are still to be seen near the village of Yalvaç.

[2] The community of Antioch in Pisidia was made up of Jews by birth, converted Jews (see verse 43) and "worshippers of God," i.e. heathens in search of faith. See page 233.

[3] These converts to Judaism were sometimes known as "proselytes."*

Barnabas without fear said, "It was necessary for the word
of God to be given to you first, but because you will have
nothing to do with it, and have no desire for eternal life, it
47 will now be offered to the Gentiles. | For so the Lord has
given us orders, saying, *'I have given you for a light to the
Gentiles so that you may be for salvation to the ends of the
earth.'"*[1]

48 The Gentiles, hearing this, were glad and gave glory to
the word of God.

[1] Quoted from Isaiah 49:6. See a very similar verse in Isaiah 42:6, page 168.

[2] Peter was alluding to the baptism of Cornelius. See Acts 10:25-48, page 415.

The new religion confirms its acceptance of heathens

Paul and Barnabas report back on the conversions of heathens during their missionary travels.*

15 4 And when they came to Jerusalem, they had a
meeting with the Church, the Apostles and the
elders, and they gave an account of all the things which
5 God had done through them. | But some of the Pharisees,
who were fellow believers, said, "It is necessary for them
to have circumcision* and to obey the Law of Moses." |
6 And the Apostles and the elders met together to discuss
the question.

7 After much discussion, Peter got up and said to them,
"My brothers, you have have heard that long ago it was
God's will that by my mouth the good news might be given
8 to the Gentiles so that they might have faith.[2] | And God,
the searcher of hearts, was a witness to them, giving them
9 the Holy Spirit even as he did to us, | making no distinction
between them and us, but cleansing their hearts by faith. |
10 Why then are you testing God, by putting on the neck of

HE "COUNCIL OF :RUSALEM"

he name "Council of rusalem" is sometimes iven to the gathering of postles and elders* which, fter long debate, decided to dmit uncircumcised males the church. Scholars omparing this chapter of e Acts with details given the Letters of Paul believe at, in it, Luke grouped gether decisions taken at ifferent times and in ifferent circumstances. The nportant thing to nderstand is that the first wish-born Christians, nlightened by the Holy pirit, decided to admit ncircumcised believers in sus as fellow believers.

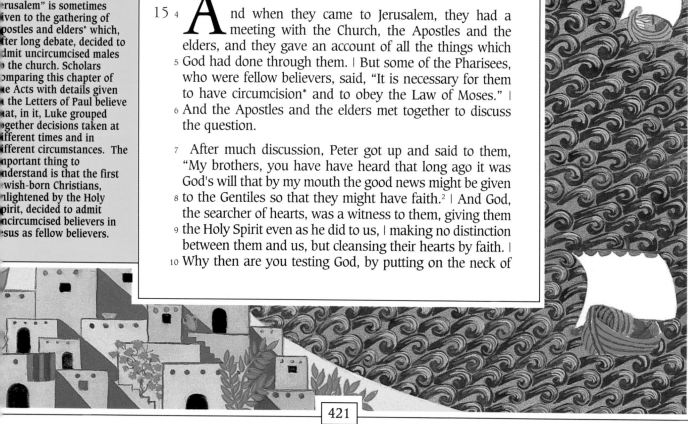

15 the disciples a yoke so heavy that not even our fathers or
11 we were strong enough for it?[1] | We have faith that we will
get salvation through the grace* of the Lord Jesus in the
same way as they."

12 All the people were quiet while Barnabas and Paul gave
an account of the signs and wonders which God had done
13 among the Gentiles by them. | When they had come to an
end, James,[2] answering, said, "My brothers, listen to m.

19 For this reason my decision is that we should not make it
difficult for those who from among the Gentiles are turned
20 to God. | Instead, we should tell them to abstain from
offerings to false gods, from sexual immorality, and from
the meat of animals strangled to death, and from blood."

The assembly therefore wrote a letter to the Christians in Antioch and neighboring communities which read as follows:

23 "The Apostles and the elders, to the brothers who are of
the Gentiles in Antioch and Syria and Cilicia, may joy be
with you:...

28 For it seemed good to the Holy Spirit and to us, to burden
29 you with nothing more than these necessary things: | To
abstain from food sacrificed to idols,[3] from blood,[4] from the
meat of strangled animals, and from sexual immorality. if
you abstain from these, you will do well. May you be
happy."

MAKING JEWS AND HEATHENS LIVE IN FELLOWSHIP

Of the "abstinences" demanded of the communities in Syria and Cilicia — which many others did not observe — only the last one was essential to Christian morals. The other three were in the nature of compromises asked of Christians of heathen origin so as not to shock the sensibilities of their Jewish-born fellow believers. They enabled all to gather around the same table and share in the Lord's meal.

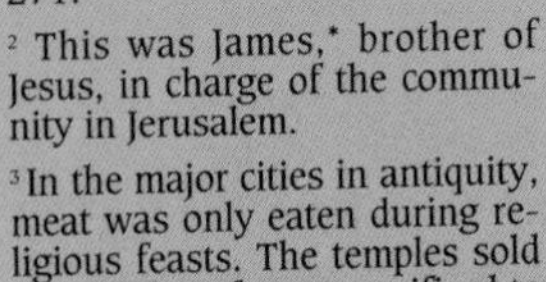

[1] See Matthew 11:28-30, page 271.

[2] This was James,* brother of Jesus, in charge of the community in Jerusalem.

[3] In the major cities in antiquity, meat was only eaten during religious feasts. The temples sold the surplus of meat sacrificed to idols.

[4] It was believed at that time that blood was the source of life. Man could give birth to life; he could also take it away (which was forbidden). But he could not create it: God alone is the creator of life. To show that they recognized that all life was a gift from God, the Jews meticulously avoided ingesting blood.

AUL AND HIS HELPERS

aul continued his issionary journeys around e Mediterranean. He was elped by many ompanions: Silas (or ylvanus), Titus,* Timothy* nd others.

each community, Paul put lders* in charge. It was a ay of giving everybody a ense of responsibility. The hurch was a body which eeded the energies of all.

aul has trailed a reputation or bring a misogynist down e centuries. A closer look hows that he placed trust women. He gave the title f deacon* ("servant" in our ersion) to Phoebe of enchrea, for example omans 16:1, page 432). He ad full confidence in riscilla (Acts 18:2, page 426), nd Lydia had an important ole to play in Philippi.

ee the extracts from the tter Paul wrote to Lydia nd the Christians in hilippi, pages 440 and 441.

he author of the Book, tradi-onally considered to be Luke, as recounting personal expe-ences. He wrote as one di-ctly involved in the events at he related. See page 297.

ydia was not Jewish. She was "worshipper of God." In those ys, the trade in purple cloth as very lucrative.

EXPANDING THE CHURCH

Lydia of Philippi

16 11 So, from Troas we[1] went straight by ship to
12 Samothrace and the day after to Neapolis. | From
there we went to Philippi, which is the most important
town of Macedonia and a Roman colony. We were there for
13 some days. | On the Sabbath* we went outside the town,
by the river, where we decided to pray. Seated, we talked
14 with the women who had gathered. | A woman named
Lydia, a trader in purple cloth of the town of Thyatira, and
a God-fearing woman,[2] listened to us. The Lord opened her
heart to pay attention to the things which Paul was saying.
15 | When she and her family were baptised, she made a
request to us, saying, "If it seems to you that I am true to
the Lord, come into my house and be my guests." And she
persuaded us.

Lydia, your material success
has not made you close your heart.
You come to listen to the Jewish preachers
on the Sabbath
by the river banks.
One day, one of them
will speak of Jesus:
God, wearing a human face;
God, rejected;
God, resurrected.
The doors of your house
are wide open for Paul,
so that you can show how
much you have opened your life
to the one who has sent him to you.

THE TRAVELS OF PAUL

1. Saul encounters Jesus on the road to Damascus (Acts 9:1-9, page 412).

2. Barnabas goes to find Saul in Tarsus and brings him back with him to Antioch (Acts 11:25-26, page 417).

3. Barnabas and Saul evangelize Cyprus and convert Sergius Paulus (see page 419).

4. First group baptisms in Antioch in Pisidia (Acts 13:14-48, page 420).

5. Paul is stoned in Lystra.

6. In Philippi, Paul and Silas are invited to the home of Lydia who has just been baptized (Acts 16:11-15, page 423).

7. In Corinth, Paul is taken to court before Gallio, the brother of Seneca. The case is dismissed.

8. In Ephesus, Paul sends his followers to evangelize the nearby towns.

9. Paul is arrested on the forecourt of the Temple during the feast of Pentecost in 58 AD.

10. Paul is placed in custody by the Roman governor in Caesarea from 58 to 60 AD.

11. Paul, taken to Rome to be tried by the emperor, is shipwrecked in Malta (see page 427).

12. Paul is beheaded on the Via Ostia in Rome, probably in 67 AD.

ADVENTURERS OF THE GOSPEL

Paul had many helpers in Corinth: Titius Justus, Crispus, Gaius, Erastus the city treasurer, etc. (See Romans 16, page 432.) **The most prominent of them all were Priscilla and Aquila, a couple of "adventurers of the Gospel," who founded communities in Corinth, Ephesus and Rome.**

Many people

18 1 After this, he left Athens, and went to Corinth.[1] |
2 There he met a Jew named Aquila, a native of
Pontus, who not long before had come from Italy with his
wife Priscilla,[2] because Claudius had ordered that all Jews
3 were to leave Rome. Paul went to see them. | Because he
was a tentmaker as they were, he lived with them, and
4 they did their work together. | Every Sabbath he reasoned
in the synagogue, converting Jews and Greeks to the faith.

5 When Silas and Timothy* came down from Macedonia,[3]
Paul was exclusively preaching, witnessing to the Jews
6 that the Christ was Jesus. | When they opposed him, and
said evil words, he said, shaking his clothing, "Your blood
be on your heads, I am clean. From now I will go to the
7 Gentiles." | Moving from there, he stayed at the house of a
man named Titus Justus, a God-fearing man, whose house
8 was very near the synagogue. | Crispus, the ruler of the
synagogue, with all his family, had faith in the Lord; and
a great number of the people of Corinth, hearing the word,
had faith and were baptised.

9 Tthe Lord said to Paul in the night, in a vision, "Have no
10 fear and go on preaching, | for I am with you, and no one
will attack or harm you. because I have a number of people
in this town."

11 He was there for a year and six months.

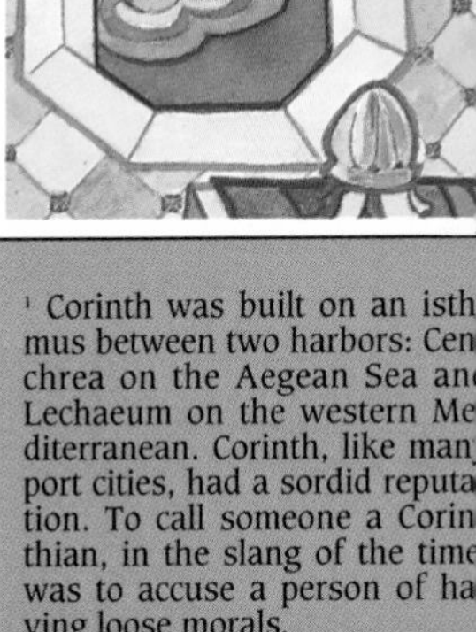

[1] Corinth was built on an isth
mus between two harbors: Cen
chrea on the Aegean Sea an
Lechaeum on the western Me
diterranean. Corinth, like man
port cities, had a sordid reputa
tion. To call someone a Corin
thian, in the slang of the time
was to accuse a person of ha
ving loose morals.

[2] Paul was a very affectionat
friend of Priscilla and Aquila
In his letter to the Romans (Ro
mans 16:3, page 432), he cal
led Priscilla by her nicknam
Prisca. Priscilla and Aquila fo
lowed Paul to Ephesus, wher
they remained. There they me
Apollos. After instructing him
they sent Apollos to Corinth t
strengthen the Christian com
munity, since he was a gifte
preacher. When Paul wrote hi
letter to the Romans in 57-5
AD, Priscilla and Aquila had re
turned to Rome. Their house i
Rome was a gathering place fo
a small "church"* of believer
(see Romans 16:5).

[3] Two of Paul's main helpers
Silas and Timothy, had staye
behind on mission in differen
towns in Macedonia previousl
visited by Paul. After puttin
the communities there on
stronger footing, they rejoine
Paul and continued their mis
sion together.

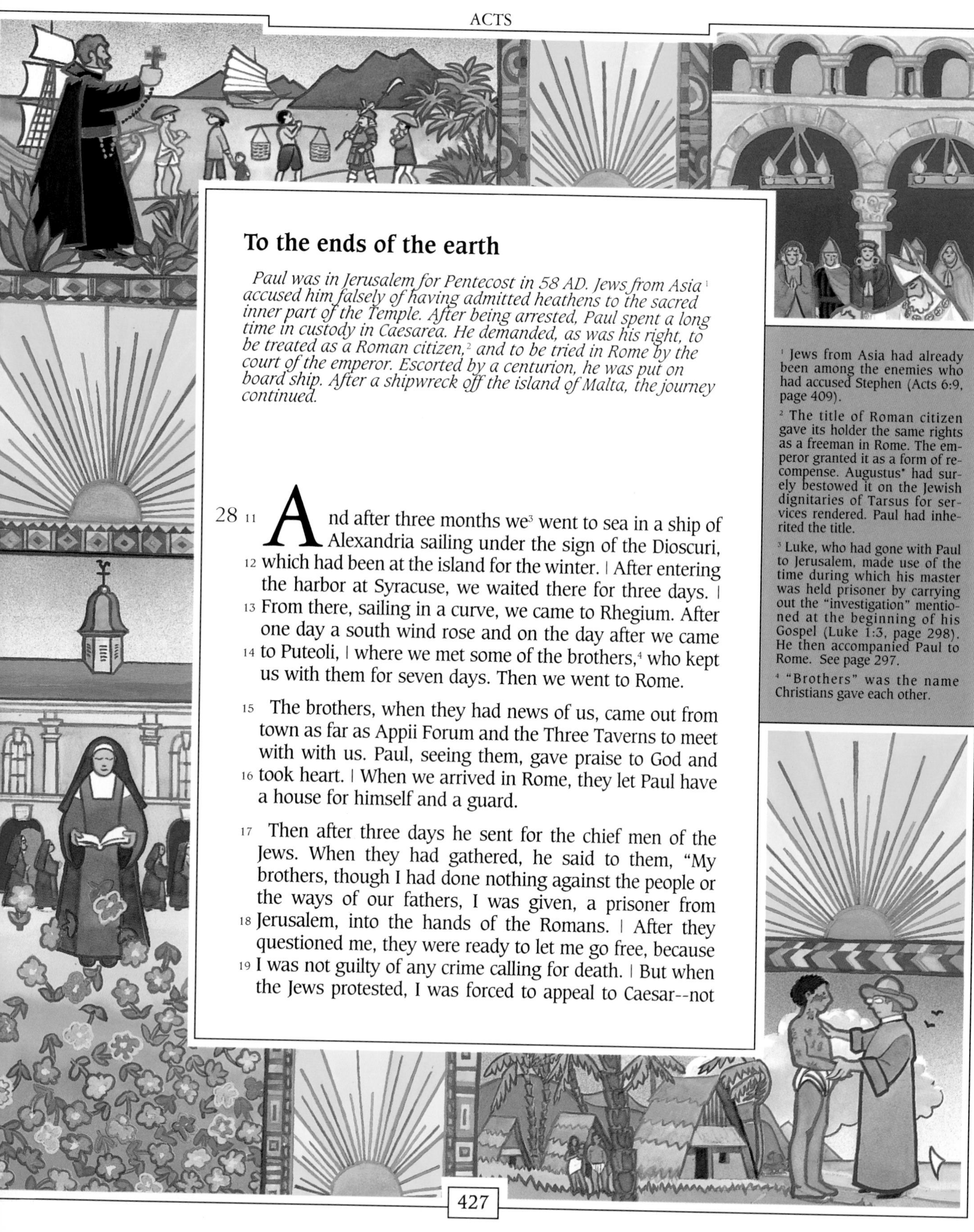

To the ends of the earth

Paul was in Jerusalem for Pentecost in 58 AD. Jews from Asia[1] accused him falsely of having admitted heathens to the sacred inner part of the Temple. After being arrested, Paul spent a long time in custody in Caesarea. He demanded, as was his right, to be treated as a Roman citizen,[2] and to be tried in Rome by the court of the emperor. Escorted by a centurion, he was put on board ship. After a shipwreck off the island of Malta, the journey continued.

28 11 And after three months we[3] went to sea in a ship of
Alexandria sailing under the sign of the Dioscuri,
12 which had been at the island for the winter. | After entering
the harbor at Syracuse, we waited there for three days. |
13 From there, sailing in a curve, we came to Rhegium. After
one day a south wind rose and on the day after we came
14 to Puteoli, | where we met some of the brothers,[4] who kept
us with them for seven days. Then we went to Rome.

15 The brothers, when they had news of us, came out from
town as far as Appii Forum and the Three Taverns to meet
with with us. Paul, seeing them, gave praise to God and
16 took heart. | When we arrived in Rome, they let Paul have
a house for himself and a guard.

17 Then after three days he sent for the chief men of the
Jews. When they had gathered, he said to them, "My
brothers, though I had done nothing against the people or
the ways of our fathers, I was given, a prisoner from
18 Jerusalem, into the hands of the Romans. | After they
questioned me, they were ready to let me go free, because
19 I was not guilty of any crime calling for death. | But when
the Jews protested, I was forced to appeal to Caesar--not

[1] Jews from Asia had already been among the enemies who had accused Stephen (Acts 6:9, page 409).

[2] The title of Roman citizen gave its holder the same rights as a freeman in Rome. The emperor granted it as a form of recompense. Augustus* had surely bestowed it on the Jewish dignitaries of Tarsus for services rendered. Paul had inherited the title.

[3] Luke, who had gone with Paul to Jerusalem, made use of the time during which his master was held prisoner by carrying out the "investigation" mentioned at the beginning of his Gospel (Luke 1:3, page 298). He then accompanied Paul to Rome. See page 297.

[4] "Brothers" was the name Christians gave each other.

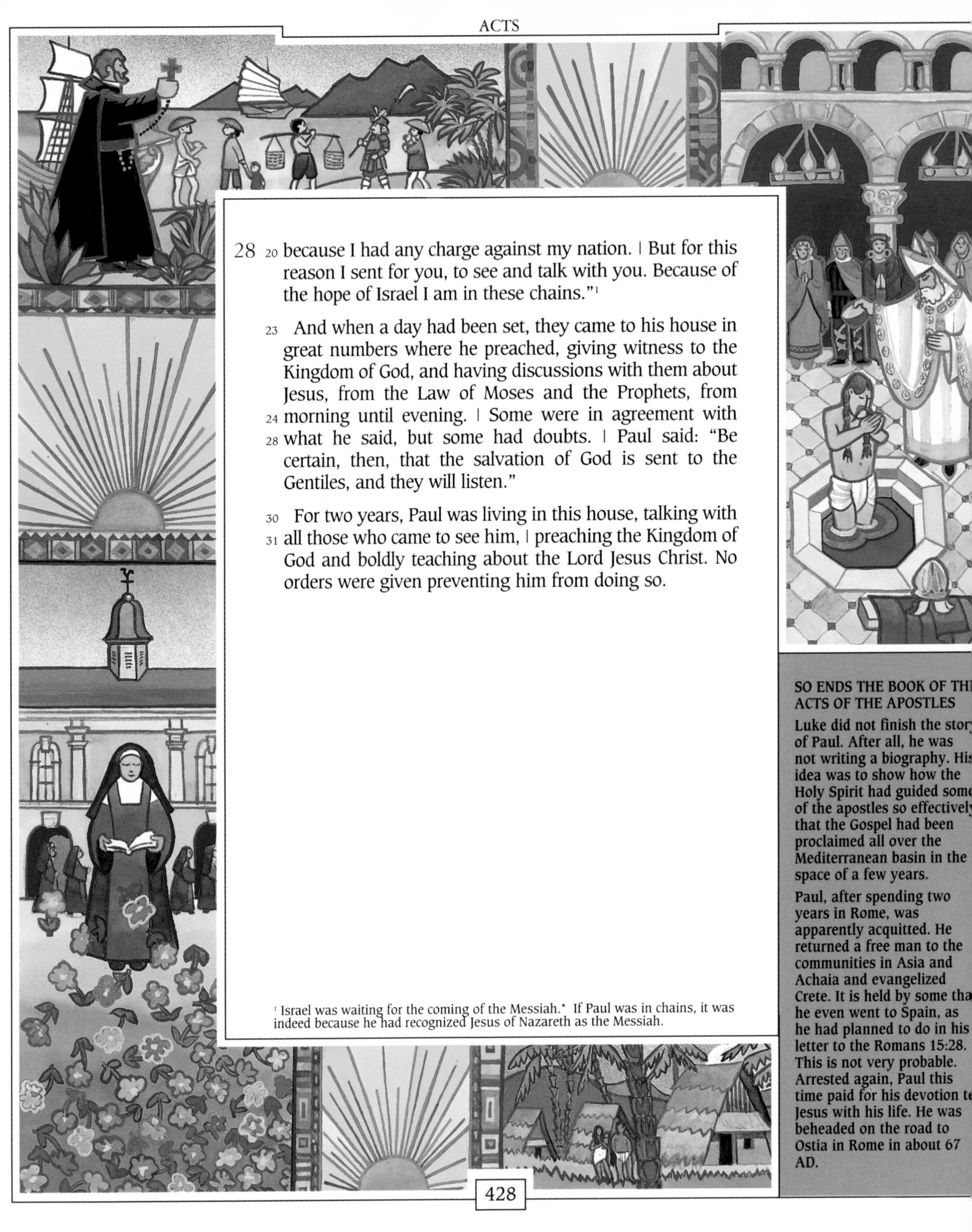

28 20 because I had any charge against my nation. | But for this
reason I sent for you, to see and talk with you. Because of
the hope of Israel I am in these chains."[1]

23 And when a day had been set, they came to his house in
great numbers where he preached, giving witness to the
Kingdom of God, and having discussions with them about
Jesus, from the Law of Moses and the Prophets, from
24 morning until evening. | Some were in agreement with
28 what he said, but some had doubts. | Paul said: "Be
certain, then, that the salvation of God is sent to the
Gentiles, and they will listen."

30 For two years, Paul was living in this house, talking with
31 all those who came to see him, | preaching the Kingdom of
God and boldly teaching about the Lord Jesus Christ. No
orders were given preventing him from doing so.

[1] Israel was waiting for the coming of the Messiah.* If Paul was in chains, it was indeed because he had recognized Jesus of Nazareth as the Messiah.

SO ENDS THE BOOK OF TH[E] ACTS OF THE APOSTLES

Luke did not finish the stor[y] of Paul. After all, he was not writing a biography. Hi[s] idea was to show how the Holy Spirit had guided som[e] of the apostles so effectivel[y] that the Gospel had been proclaimed all over the Mediterranean basin in the space of a few years.

Paul, after spending two years in Rome, was apparently acquitted. He returned a free man to the communities in Asia and Achaia and evangelized Crete. It is held by some tha[t] he even went to Spain, as he had planned to do in his letter to the Romans 15:28. This is not very probable. Arrested again, Paul this time paid for his devotion t[o] Jesus with his life. He was beheaded on the road to Ostia in Rome in about 67 AD.

II
THE EPISTLES

The New Testament contains twenty-one letters, or epistles, arranged in two groups. Authorship of fourteen of them is attributed to Paul. The seven others, by different authors, are collected under the name of "general" epistles.*

The Epistles of Paul

Paul was the first New Testament writer. He started writing his letters in 51 AD, before the composition of the Gospels had begun.

Paul was a prolific writer. Thirteen letters attributed to him survived. The fourteenth letter in the group has always been considered as the work of one of his disciples, perhaps Apollos.[1] Of the thirteen others, some were very likely reworked by disciples. They are of very different kinds. In some of them, Paul sets down his doctrine, especially on the relation between Law and faith.* The letter to the Romans is a perfect example of one of these doctrinal letters. In other letters, Paul addresses very specific problems concerning a far-flung community.*

The "general" Epistles

This very old designation was intended to show that these letters, unlike the epistles of Paul, were not written to a particular person or community. They were intended for several communities at once. Their scope, in other words, was more universal, more "general."

The "general" epistles are made up of a letter by James, two attributed to Peter, three by John and a note by Jude.**

[1] See page 426, note 2, and 1 Corinthians 1:12, page 432.

LETTER TO THE ROMANS

Paul had found it very hard to believe in a crucified[1] Messiah. He finally understood that the cross was the instrument by which God showed mankind the depth of His love. The Son of God crucified, mocked and reviled spoke only words of forgiveness. Could there be any greater proof of love?

[1] See meditation page 413 and 1 Corinthians 1:23, page 433.

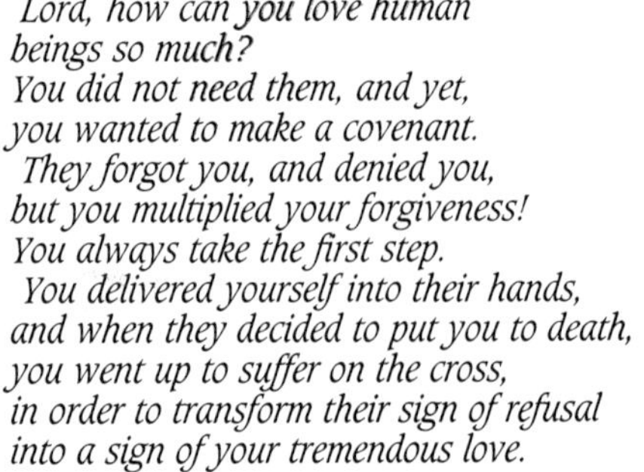

Lord, how can you love human beings so much?
You did not need them, and yet, you wanted to make a covenant.
They forgot you, and denied you, but you multiplied your forgiveness!
You always take the first step.
You delivered yourself into their hands, and when they decided to put you to death, you went up to suffer on the cross, in order to transform their sign of refusal into a sign of your tremendous love.

THE EPISTLES OF PAUL

Proof that God loves us

5 5 And hope does not disappoint, because our
hearts are full of the love of God through the Holy
6 Spirit* which is given to us. | For when we were still
without strength, at the right time Christ gave his life for
7 sinners. | Now it is hard for anyone to give his life even for
a righteous man, yet for a good man someone would more
8 easily give his life. | But God has revealed his love for us,
in that, when we were still sinners, Christ gave his life for
9 us. | All the more, if we now have righteousness* by his
blood, we will be saved through him from the wrath* of
10 God. | For if, when we were enemies of God, the death of
his Son reconciled us with him, much more, now that we
are his friends, will we have salvation through his life.

BEARING GOOD FRUIT

Paul knew better than anyone that people, left to themselves, cannot bear good fruit. Before his meeting with the risen Jesus (see page 412)**, he had oppressed the Christian communities. The only way to do good was to accept the guidance of the Holy Spirit.**

Slaves of sin

7 21 So I see a law that, though I want to do good, evil*
22 is present in me. | In my heart I take pleasure in the
23 Laws of God, | but I see another law in my body, fighting
the law of my mind, making me the slave of sin which is
24 in my flesh. | How unhappy am I!

To escape from this unhappy condition, we must accept the action of the Holy Spirit in our hearts.

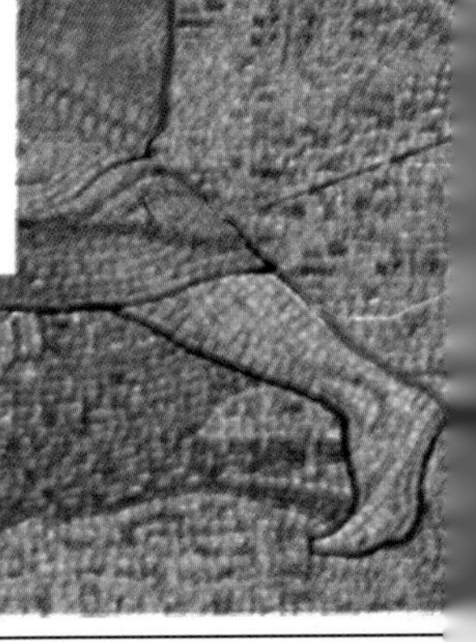

Freed by the Spirit

8 14 All those who are guided by the Spirit* of God
15 are sons of God. | For you did not get the spirit of
servants only to return to fear, but the spirit of sons was
given to you so that you might cry, "Abba,* Father."

16 The Spirit testifies with our spirit that we are children of
17 God: | if we are children, we are heirs in the things of God
and Christ. If we share his pain, so shall we share his
glory.*

Real sacrifice

12 1 For this reason I ask you,
brothers, by the mercies of God,
that you will give your bodies as a living
sacrifice, holy, pleasing to God, which is
2 your spiritual act of worship.* | Let not
your behavior conform to this world,
but be changed and renewed in your
mind, so that through experience, you
will know the good, pleasing and perfect
will of God.

True sacrifice is neither suffering,
nor making a temporary effort!
It's putting all of life,
the sorrows and the joys,
the failures and the successes,
the deepest desires,
the most twisted and the most generous.
Lord, it's putting everything
under your watchful care!

Here am I, just as I am.
Purify me so that I can do your will.

THE CHURCHES AS BODY* OF CHRIST

Paul wrote the letter to the Romans in Corinth in about 57-58 AD. It ended with this list of names, which gives a good idea of the duties assumed by Christians so as to form a living body (see page 435).

Paul's helpmates

16 1 It is my desire to say a good word about Phoebe,
a servant[1] of the church in Cenchreae:[2]

3 Give my love to Priscilla and Aquila, fellow-workers of
4 mine in Christ Jesus. | They risked their necks for my life,
thus I and all the churches of the Gentiles are indebted to
5 them. | Say a kind word to the church which is in their
house.[3] Give my love to my dear Epaenetus, who is the first
convert of Asia to Christ.

6 Give my love to Mary, who worked very hard for you. |
7 Give my love to Andronicus and Junia, my relations, who
were in prison with me, who are noted among the
13 Apostles,* and who were in Christ before me. | Give my
love to Rufus,[4] one of the Lord's chosen, and to his mother
16 and mine. | Greet one another with a holy kiss. All the
22 churches of Christ send their love to you. | I, Tertius, who
have done the writing of this letter, send love in the Lord.
23 | Gaius, with whom I am living, whose house is open to all
the church, sends his love, so does Erastus, the the city's
director of public works,[5] and Quartus, the brother.

Foolishness or wisdom of God?

1 COR
1 11 I have been told by the household of Chloe, that there are
12 divisions among you, my brothers. | Some of you say, "I
am of Paul; "others say, "I am of Apollos;"[1] others say, "I

CORINTH, AN UNRULY COMMUNITY

The Christians in Corinth had trouble binding together. They were divided among themselves. Paul, in answer to the questions put to him, returned over and over again in this letter to the central issue of Christian living: unity.

[1] See page 423, "Paul and hi helpers."

[2] Cenchrea was one of Corinth' two harbors. See page 42(note 1.

[3] See page 426, note 2.

[4] Some scholars think this Ru fus might be the one mentione by Mark in his Gospel, whic was also intended for th Christians in Rome (Mar 15:21, page 376). If so, h would be the son of Simon c Cyrene.

[5] In Corinth, archeologists hav discovered an inscription bea ring the name of Erastus. Du ring his term as director of pu blic works, he paid for paving square near the theatre out c his own pocket.

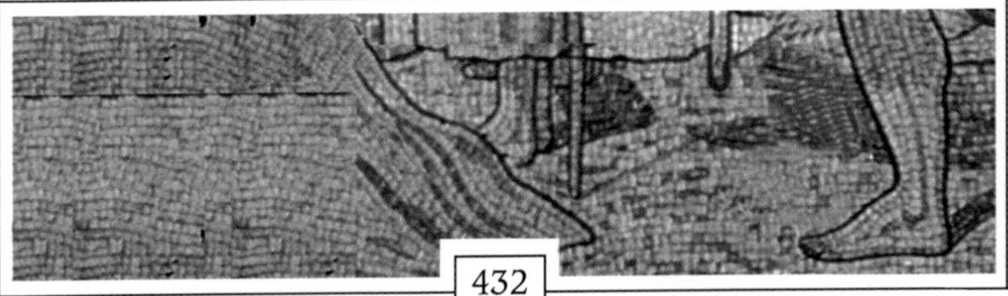

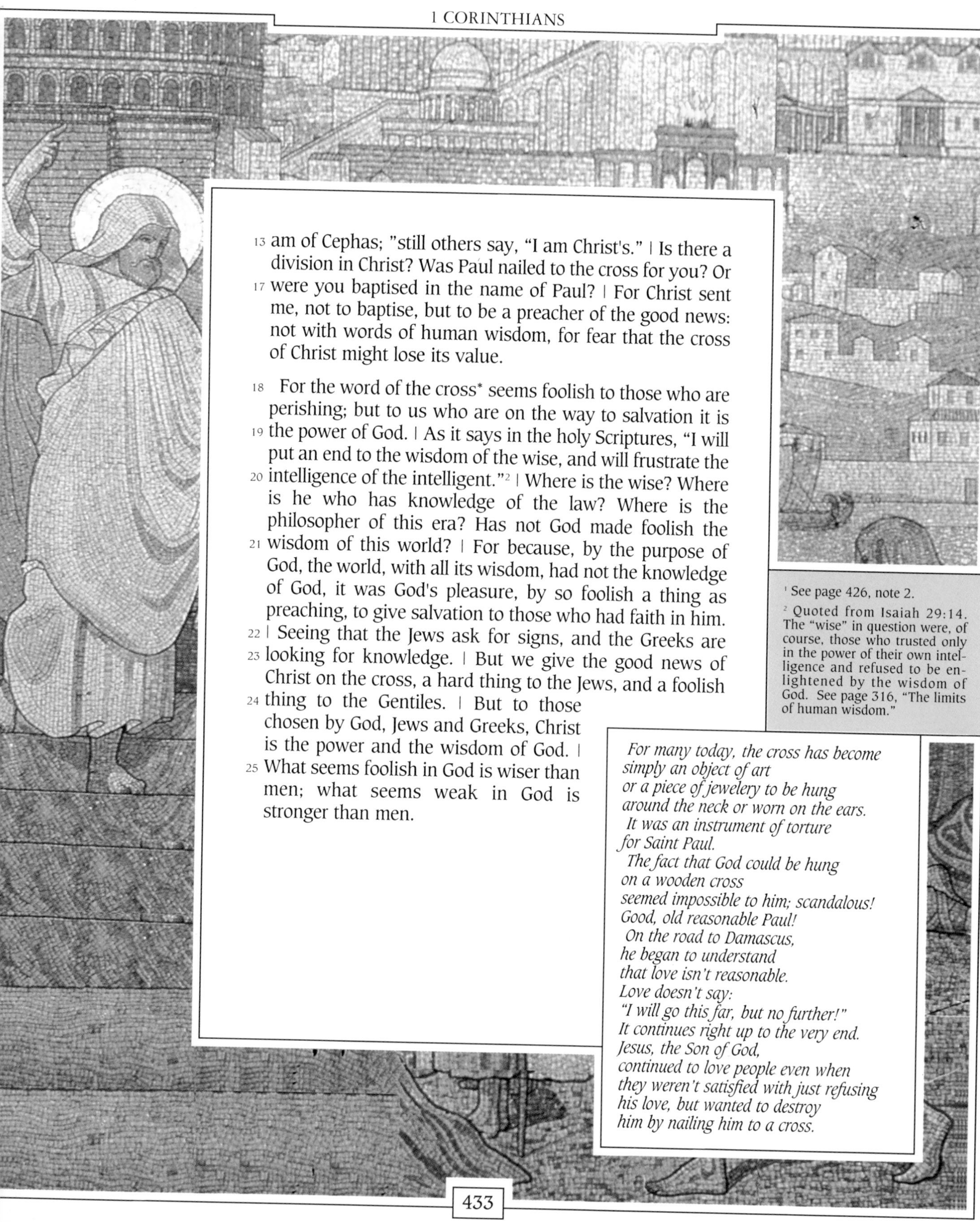

13 am of Cephas; "still others say, "I am Christ's." | Is there a
division in Christ? Was Paul nailed to the cross for you? Or
17 were you baptised in the name of Paul? | For Christ sent
me, not to baptise, but to be a preacher of the good news:
not with words of human wisdom, for fear that the cross
of Christ might lose its value.

18 For the word of the cross* seems foolish to those who are
perishing; but to us who are on the way to salvation it is
19 the power of God. | As it says in the holy Scriptures, "I will
put an end to the wisdom of the wise, and will frustrate the
20 intelligence of the intelligent."[2] | Where is the wise? Where
is he who has knowledge of the law? Where is the
philosopher of this era? Has not God made foolish the
21 wisdom of this world? | For because, by the purpose of
God, the world, with all its wisdom, had not the knowledge
of God, it was God's pleasure, by so foolish a thing as
preaching, to give salvation to those who had faith in him.
22 | Seeing that the Jews ask for signs, and the Greeks are
23 looking for knowledge. | But we give the good news of
Christ on the cross, a hard thing to the Jews, and a foolish
24 thing to the Gentiles. | But to those
chosen by God, Jews and Greeks, Christ
is the power and the wisdom of God. |
25 What seems foolish in God is wiser than
men; what seems weak in God is
stronger than men.

[1] See page 426, note 2.

[2] Quoted from Isaiah 29:14. The "wise" in question were, of course, those who trusted only in the power of their own intelligence and refused to be enlightened by the wisdom of God. See page 316, "The limits of human wisdom."

For many today, the cross has become simply an object of art or a piece of jewelery to be hung around the neck or worn on the ears.
It was an instrument of torture for Saint Paul.
The fact that God could be hung on a wooden cross seemed impossible to him; scandalous! Good, old reasonable Paul!
On the road to Damascus, he began to understand that love isn't reasonable.
Love doesn't say:
"I will go this far, but no further!"
It continues right up to the very end.
Jesus, the Son of God, continued to love people even when they weren't satisfied with just refusing his love, but wanted to destroy him by nailing him to a cross.

WELCOMING GOD IN OURSELVES

God did not want to live in man-made houses (see 2 Samuel 7:5-7, page 108). **He sent His son, God made man, to be the true place of meeting between God and humanity** (John 2:19-21, page 337). **The Son revealed that God wants to live in our hearts. He is at the door and is knocking to enter. If anyone hears his voice and opens, he will come in** (see Revelation 3:20, page 450).

We are asked to empty ourselves of enough of our self to leave room for God in the only temple where He wants to live.

You are God's temple

3 16 Do you not see that you are God's temple, and
17 that the Spirit of God lives in you? | If anyone
makes the temple of God unclean, God will destroy him, for
the temple of God is holy, and you are his temple.

How to approach the Lord's Supper

11 17 But in these orders, there is one thing about
which I am not pleased: it is that when you come
18 together you do more harm than good. | First of all, I have
learned that when you gather in the church, there are
divisions among you. I take the statement to be true in
19 part. | For divisions are necessary among you, in order that
those who have God's approval may be clearly seen among
you.

20 But now, when you come together, it is not possible to
21 take the Lord's Supper: | for when you eat your food,
everyone eats in the presence of the other. Some have not
22 enough food, and others get drunk. | What? Have you not
houses in which to eat? Have you no respect for the church
of God, putting the poor to shame? What am I to say to
you? Am I to give you praise? Certainly not.

23 For it was revealed to me from the Lord,[1] as I reveal it to
you, that the Lord Jesus, on the night when Judas betrayed
24 him, took bread, | and when it had been broken with

[1] Paul here gave the earliest account of the communion rite. See Mark 14:22-25 and Luke 22:14-20, page 366.

THE LORD'S MEAL

The Lord's meal was the institution that united the people of God. Each person, by communicating in the body* of Christ found the strength to be one with the others.

In Corinth, however, the Lord's meal had become a source of widening differences. At that time, the last supper of Jesus was commemorated around a full meal. The Corinthian Christians probably gathered in the homes of their wealthiest members, where banquet halls could hold the whole community. Gaius or Erastus (Romans 16:23, page 432) **were no doubt among those who received the congregation in their houses. Each guest brought her or his own food. The poor and the slaves arrived last with only a humble meal. The more affluent had already started eating and drinking, sometimes to excess. Paul vigorously condemned this practice.**

People soon stopped "breaking bread" in the course of an ordinary meal and began using only a token quantity of bread and wine.

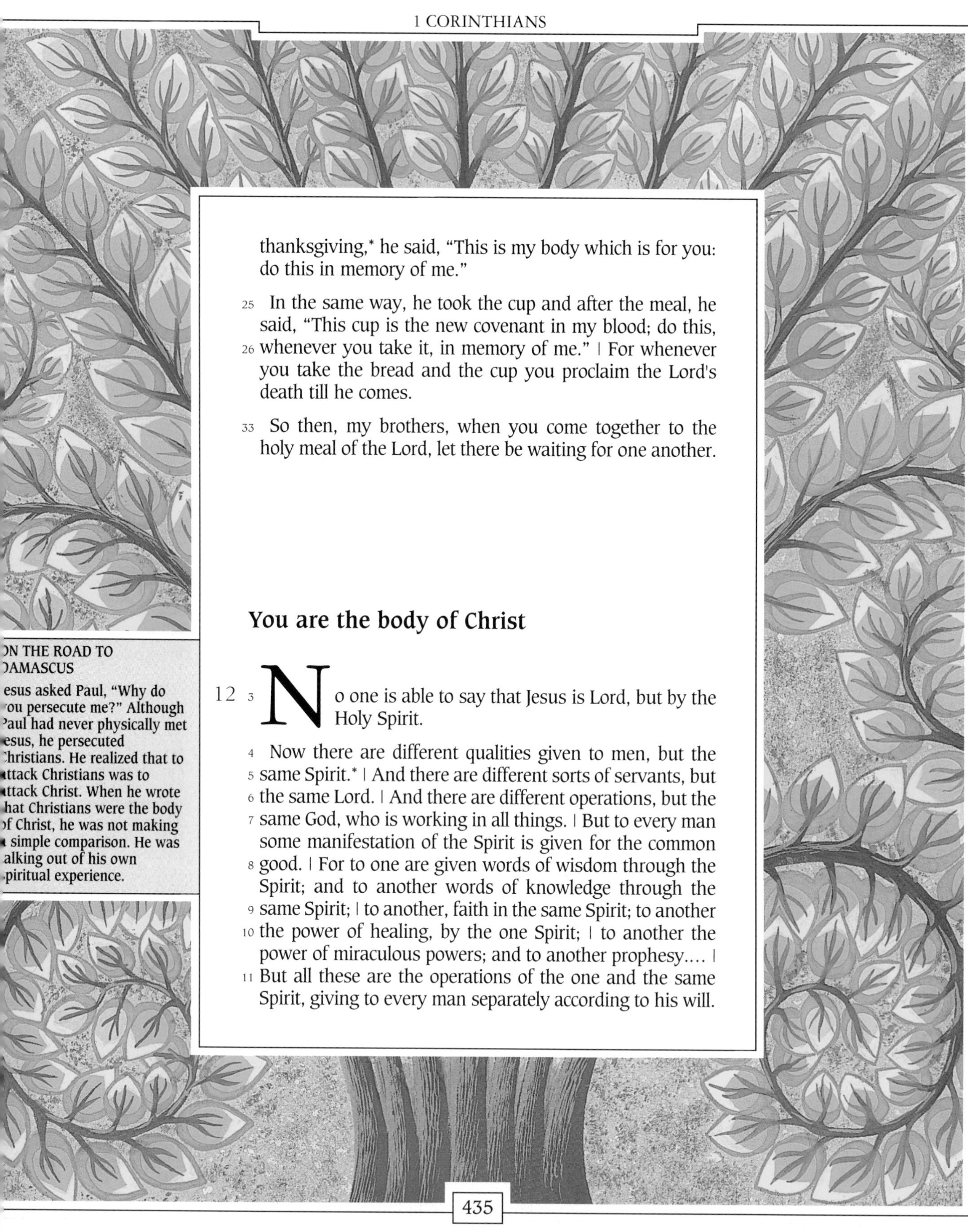

thanksgiving,* he said, "This is my body which is for you:
do this in memory of me."

25 In the same way, he took the cup and after the meal, he
said, "This cup is the new covenant in my blood; do this,
26 whenever you take it, in memory of me." | For whenever
you take the bread and the cup you proclaim the Lord's
death till he comes.

33 So then, my brothers, when you come together to the
holy meal of the Lord, let there be waiting for one another.

You are the body of Christ

12 3 No one is able to say that Jesus is Lord, but by the
Holy Spirit.

4 Now there are different qualities given to men, but the
5 same Spirit.* | And there are different sorts of servants, but
6 the same Lord. | And there are different operations, but the
7 same God, who is working in all things. | But to every man
some manifestation of the Spirit is given for the common
8 good. | For to one are given words of wisdom through the
Spirit; and to another words of knowledge through the
9 same Spirit; | to another, faith in the same Spirit; to another
10 the power of healing, by the one Spirit; | to another the
power of miraculous powers; and to another prophesy.... |
11 But all these are the operations of the one and the same
Spirit, giving to every man separately according to his will.

ON THE ROAD TO DAMASCUS

Jesus asked Paul, "Why do you persecute me?" Although Paul had never physically met Jesus, he persecuted Christians. He realized that to attack Christians was to attack Christ. When he wrote that Christians were the body of Christ, he was not making a simple comparison. He was talking out of his own spiritual experience.

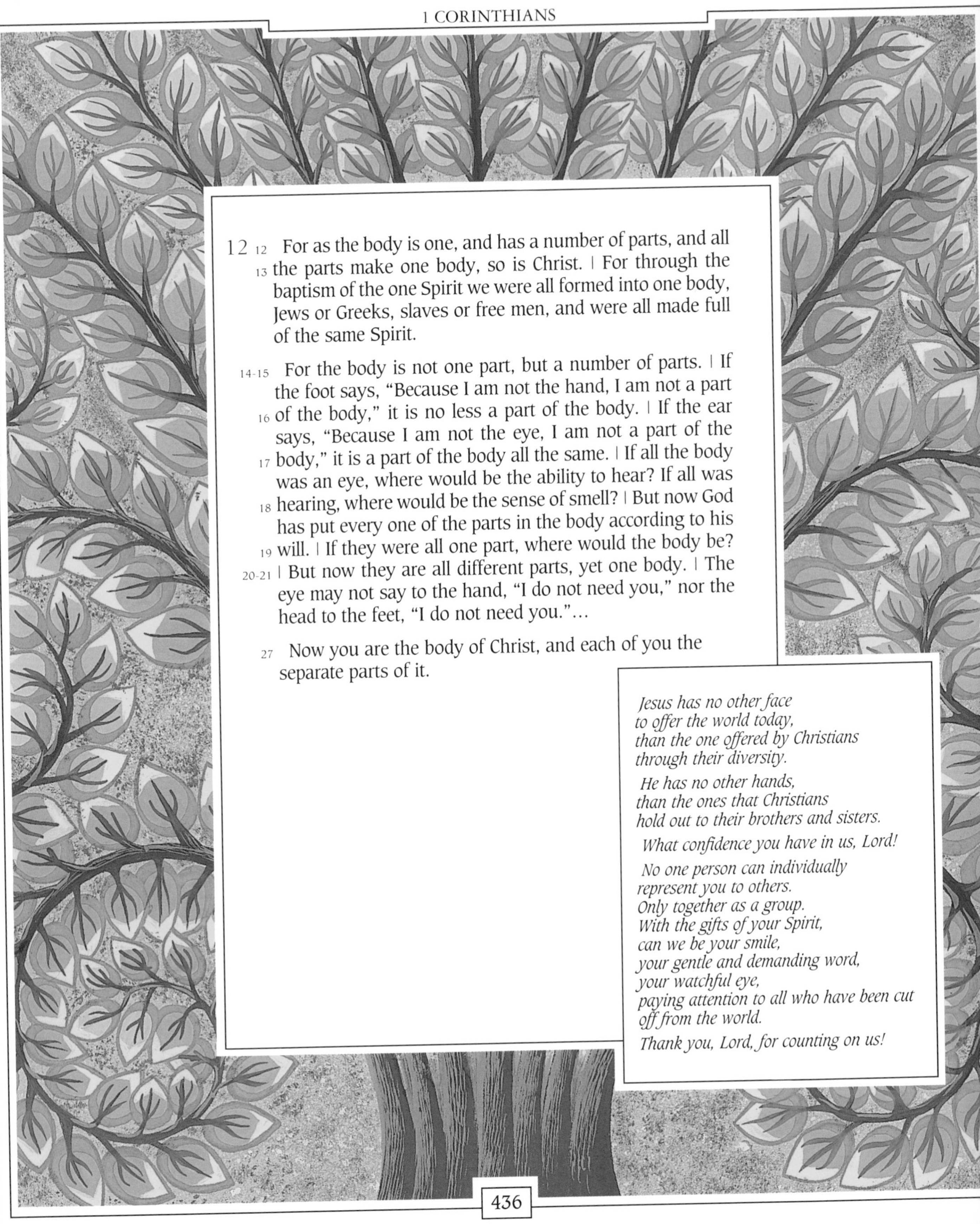

12 12 For as the body is one, and has a number of parts, and all
13 the parts make one body, so is Christ. | For through the
baptism of the one Spirit we were all formed into one body,
Jews or Greeks, slaves or free men, and were all made full
of the same Spirit.

14-15 For the body is not one part, but a number of parts. | If
the foot says, "Because I am not the hand, I am not a part
16 of the body," it is no less a part of the body. | If the ear
says, "Because I am not the eye, I am not a part of the
17 body," it is a part of the body all the same. | If all the body
was an eye, where would be the ability to hear? If all was
18 hearing, where would be the sense of smell? | But now God
has put every one of the parts in the body according to his
19 will. | If they were all one part, where would the body be?
20-21 | But now they are all different parts, yet one body. | The
eye may not say to the hand, "I do not need you," nor the
head to the feet, "I do not need you."...

27 Now you are the body of Christ, and each of you the
separate parts of it.

Jesus has no other face
to offer the world today,
than the one offered by Christians
through their diversity.

He has no other hands,
than the ones that Christians
hold out to their brothers and sisters.

What confidence you have in us, Lord!

No one person can individually
represent you to others.
Only together as a group.
With the gifts of your Spirit,
can we be your smile,
your gentle and demanding word,
your watchful eye,
paying attention to all who have been cut
off from the world.

Thank you, Lord, for counting on us!

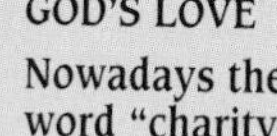

GOD'S LOVE

Nowadays the beautiful word "charity" has acquired a meaning close to almsgiving — charity is giving money to the poor. But charity used to be the love of God which transfigured and purified human love. Christians were filled with charity when they let the Holy Spirit remodel their inner being. It made them capable of loving with the same sensitivity and perseverance as Jesus.

A hymn to charity

12 31 But earnestly desire the more important
things given by the Spirit. And now I am pointing
out to you an even better way.

13 1 If I make use of the tongues of men and of angels, and
have not love, I am like sounding brass, or a clanging bell.
2 | If I have a prophet's power, and have knowledge of all
secret things, and if I have enough faith to move
3 mountains, but have not love, I am nothing. | If I give all
my goods to the poor, and if I give my body to be burned,
but have not love, it is of no profit to me.

4 Love is patient; love is kind; love is kind; love does not
5 brag; love has no pride. | Love's ways are always fair, it is
not self-centered; it is not quick to anger, it keeps no record
6 of evil. | It takes no pleasure in wrongdoing, but has joy in
7 what is true. | Love endures all things, believes all things,
8 hopes all things. | Though the prophet's word may come to
an end, tongues come to nothing, and knowledge have no
9 more value, love has no end. | For we know in part, and
10 we prophesy only part of what is true, | but when that
which is perfect comes, then that which
12 is imperfect will disappear. | Then my
knowledge will be complete, even as
God's knowledge of me.

Lord, you are love,
and you have placed in each one of us
a reflection of your image.
We can't be happy
just focusing on ourselves.
We can have all the success
in the world, and
receive armloads of compliments,
but these will never be enough
to satisfy the desires
that you put in our heart.
Allowing you to teach us
to love is the only way that we will finally
find meaning in our live,
forever, because love never dies.

KERYGMA*

Paul here outlined the substance of early Christian teaching. It consisted mainly in proclaiming the death and Resurrection of Christ.* The preacher took pains to demonstrate that the scandal-provoking death of Christ had in fact been foretold by the Scriptures. The Resurrection, vouched for by witnesses, showed that the death of Jesus was not a fiasco but the supreme sign of God's wisdom. What humans might regard as foolishness (see page 432) was the proof of God's unconditional love for humanity (see page 430).

The Christian credo

15 1 Now I am going to remind you, my brothers,
what the good news was which I gave to you. |
2 By it you have salvation; that is to say, the form in which
it was given to you, if it is fixed in your minds, and if your
faith in it is not in vain.

3 For I gave to you first of all what was handed down to me,
how Christ underwent death for our sins,
as it says in the Scriptures.
4 He was put in the tomb,
and on the third day he rose from the dead,
as it says in the Scriptures.
5 He was seen by Cephas, then by the twelve;*
6 Then by more than five hundred brothers at the same time,
7 most of whom are still living, but some are sleeping. | Then
8 he was seen by James, then by all the Apostles.* | And last
of all, he was seen by me, as to one who was abnormally
born.

9 I am the least of the Apostles, having no right to be
named an Apostle, because of my persecution of the
10 church of God. | But by the grace of God, I am what I am.
His grace* which was given to me has not been for
nothing, for I did more work than all of them, though not
I, but the grace of God which was with me.

11 If then it is I who am the preacher, or they, this is what
we preach, and this is what you believed.

[1] See page 386, "The third day."

WHO HAD SEEN THE RISEN CHRIST?

Paul differentiated three groups of people privileged by apparitions of the risen Jesus. First, the Twelve and their leader, Peter. Second, the "brothers," i.e. Christians of all sorts. Third, the "apostles" under the leadership of James, "brother of Jesus," who had not been one of the Twelve.

"APOSTLES"

Paul used this term to name eveeyone who had been called to spread the gospel (see, for example, Romans 16:7, page 432), whereas Luke usually reserved it for the Twelve.

This text shows that the New Testament authors did not always give the same meaning to words.

THE RESURRECTION WILL NOT CHANGE WHO WE ARE

We shall rise as human beings, that is, with a body. Paul suggested to the Corinthians that they should not try too much to imagine this risen body. Enveloped by the power of the divine life, we shall be transfigured while remaining ourselves. During our lifetime, our bodies change a lot. Yet we can recognize ourselves in photos taken when we were babies and in photos that show the changes in us afterwards. When risen, we shall be different again, while feeling wonderfully at home with ourselves.

The resurrection

15 35 But someone will say, “How do the dead come back?
and with what sort of body do they come?” |
36 Foolish man, it is necessary for the seed which you put into
the earth to die in order that it may come to life again. |
37 When you put it into the earth, you do not put in the body
which it will be, but only the seed, of grain or some other
42 sort of plant. | So is it with the resurrection from the dead.
43 It is planted in death; it comes again in life. | It is planted
in shame; it comes again in glory. Though weak when it is
44 planted, it returns in power. | It is planted as a natural
body; it comes again as a body of the spirit. If there is a
natural body, there is equally a body of the spirit.

Paul rounded out his explanation by referring to the first man, Adam, and Jesus, whom he called the second man. On earth we exist in the likeness of Adam, but we shall be refashioned in the likeness of Jesus.*

47 The first man is from the earth, and of the earth: the
48 second man is from heaven. | Those who are of the earth
are like the man who was from the earth. Those who are
49 of heaven are like the one from heaven. | In the same way
as we have taken on us the image of the man from the
earth, so we will take on us the image of the one from
heaven.

LETTER TO THE PHILIPPIANS

Paul wrote to the Christians of Philippi (see page 423) **on the astounding depth of God's love. God never forced Himself on people. On the contrary, He acted as their servant.**

The mystery of Christ

2 1 If then there is any comfort in Christ, any help given by
love, any uniting of hearts in the Spirit, any loving
2 mercies and pity, | make my joy complete by being of the
same mind, having the same love, being in harmony and
3 of one mind. | Do nothing through envy or through pride,
4 but with humility, treat others better than yourself, | not
looking after your own interests, but also the interests of
others.

5 Let this attitude be in you which was in Christ Jesus:

6 To whom, though himself in the form of God, did not
7 consider equality with God something to seize. | Instead,
he made himself as nothing, taking the form of a servant,
being made like men.

8 Being found in the form of a man, he took the lowest
place, and let himself be put to death, even the death of the
cross.*

9 For this reason God has put him in the
highest place and has given to him the
name* which is greater than every
10 name, | so that at the name of Jesus
every knee may bow, of those in heaven
and those on earth and those in the
11 underworld,[1] | and that every tongue
may confess that "Jesus Christ is Lord,"
to the glory of God the Father.

Adam wanted to be God's equal,
but he didn't know God.
He wanted to be all powerful,
so that he could dominate others!
He transmitted this desire, the source of
so much unhappiness, to his descendants.

Jesus came to reveal God's face
in order to heal humanity.
Far from dominating, he served!
The Almighty
is all powerful love.

In being victorious over evil,
Jesus brings the old Adam and all
humanity into his Resurrection.
He gives them much more
than they had ever coveted.
He has made them heirs with him
of his Father's kingdom.

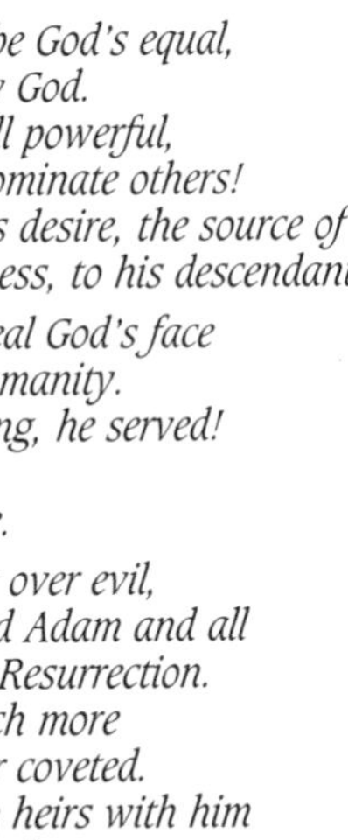

[1] Heaven, earth and the abyss represented the universe and everything in it (see double-page spread, pp.32-33). Heaven was the realm of God and His angels. Earth was the home of human beings. The abyss, or sheol,* was where the dead descended. But now, everywhere, Jesus was recognized as Lord,* that is, as God.

INNER CHANGE

Luke related the conversion of Paul on the road to Damascus (Acts 9:3-9, page 413) as a tangible, visible event. His readers could be forgiven for being struck by the external details — the fall, the blinding, the "scales" on the eyes. When Paul himself dealt with the subject, he spoke only of the inner change that come over him when he met the risen Christ.

Paul's conversion

3 5 Being given circumcision* on the eighth day, of the
people of Israel, of the tribe of Benjamin, a Hebrew
6 of Hebrews;[1] in relation to the law, a Pharisee:[2] | Out of
hatred, I was cruel to the church. I obeyed all the
7 righteousness of the Law to the last detail, | but those
8 things which were profit to me, I gave up for Christ. | Yes
truly, and I am ready to give up all things for the
knowledge* of Christ Jesus my Lord, which is more than all
for whom I have lost all things. To me they are less than
9 nothing, so that I may have Christ as my reward, | and be
seen in him, not having my righteousness* which is of the
Law, but that which is through faith in Christ, the
10 righteousness which is of God by faith, | that I may have
knowledge of him, and of the power of his resurrection,
11 and share his pains, becoming like him in his death. | If in
12 any way I may have the reward of life from the dead. | Not
that I have already obtained all this, or been made perfect;
I go on in the hope that I may take hold of that for which I
13 was made the servant of Christ Jesus. | Brothers, it is clear
to me that I have not yet taken hold, but one thing I do,
forgetting that which past, and pushing
on to the things which are set before me.
14 | I push ahead to the goal, the reward for
which God has called me to Heaven in
Christ Jesus.

[1] Paul, although born in the diaspora,* came from a family which had not stopped speaking the tongue of its ancestors. Paul knew Hebrew. He had studied the sacred texts in Hebrew under Gamaliel in Jerusalem.

Paul resisted a long time
before recognizing
in the crucified Jesus, the one sent by God.
His reasoning created an obstacle!
But ever since the living
Christ has taken hold of him,
nothing has become more important
than knowing him.

Lord, may the desire and joy
of knowing you, never die in me.
May my life be a race
to be "with you."
I am not afraid of running out of breath,
because you fill me with your Spirit!

FIRST LETTER TO TIMOTHY

Timothy was one of Paul's main helpers. They had met during his first missionary journey with Barnabas. Paul wrote to him around 65 AD. Timothy was in Ephesus, capital of the province of Asia. Among other things, Paul reminded him that God desired the salvation of all mankind.

The salvation of all people

2 1 My desire is, first of all, that you will make
requests, prayers, intercessions* and
2 thanksgiving* for all men; | for kings and all those in
authority; so that we may have a calm and quiet life in fear
3 of God and serious behavior. | This is good and pleasing in
4 the eyes of God our Savior, | whose desire is that all men
may have salvation and come to the knowledge of what is
true.

5 For there is one God and one
peacemaker between God and men, the
6 man[1] Christ Jesus, | who gave himself as
a ransom for all, testimony of which
7 was to be given at the right time. | For
this I became a preacher and an Apostle*
(what I say is true, not false,) and a
teacher of the Gentiles in the true faith.

8 It is my desire, then, that in every place
men may devote themselves to prayer,
lifting up holy hands, without wrath or
argument.

[1] Jesus was truly human like ourselves (see "Incarnation"*) but was also Son* of God (see meditation page 168). Man and God, he was the perfect mediator between humanity and his father.

PRAYER FOR ALL

Paul's recommendation that Timothy should intercede for all mankind was the beginning of a prayer for all. Every Sunday, Christians ask God to make their hearts as all-embracing as His.

For peace in the entire world, for the prosperity of God's holy church, and for the unity of all peoples, we pray, O, Lord.
Lord, have mercy.

For this holy place, and for those who enter in faith, piety and the fear of God, we pray, O, Lord.
Lord, have mercy.

For our pope and bishop, for the priests an decons serving in Christ for all the clergy and people, we pray, O, Lord.
Lord, have mercy.

For our leaders and their advisors, we pray, O, Lord.
Lord, have mercy.

For clean air, the abundance of the fruits of the earth, and a time of peace, we pray, O, Lord.
Lord, have mercy.

For those who travel by road, sea and air, for the sick, for those who suffer, for the prisoners, for the salvation of all, we pray, O, Lord.
Lord, have mercy.

(An extract of the liturgy of Saint John of Chrysostome.)

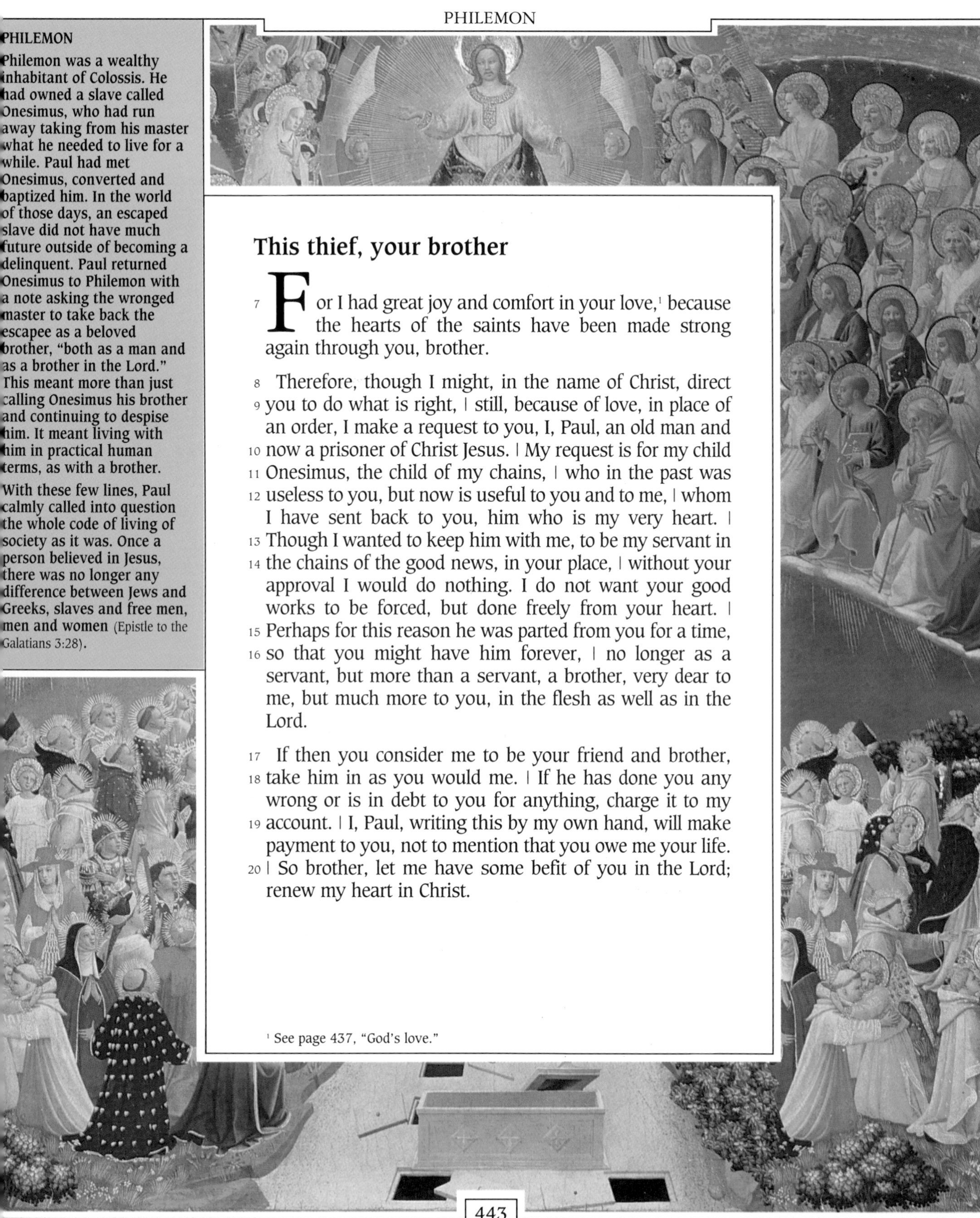

PHILEMON

Philemon was a wealthy inhabitant of Colossis. He had owned a slave called Onesimus, who had run away taking from his master what he needed to live for a while. Paul had met Onesimus, converted and baptized him. In the world of those days, an escaped slave did not have much future outside of becoming a delinquent. Paul returned Onesimus to Philemon with a note asking the wronged master to take back the escapee as a beloved brother, "both as a man and as a brother in the Lord." This meant more than just calling Onesimus his brother and continuing to despise him. It meant living with him in practical human terms, as with a brother.

With these few lines, Paul calmly called into question the whole code of living of society as it was. Once a person believed in Jesus, there was no longer any difference between Jews and Greeks, slaves and free men, men and women (Epistle to the Galatians 3:28).

This thief, your brother

7 For I had great joy and comfort in your love,[1] because
the hearts of the saints have been made strong
again through you, brother.

8 Therefore, though I might, in the name of Christ, direct
9 you to do what is right, | still, because of love, in place of
an order, I make a request to you, I, Paul, an old man and
10 now a prisoner of Christ Jesus. | My request is for my child
11 Onesimus, the child of my chains, | who in the past was
12 useless to you, but now is useful to you and to me, | whom
I have sent back to you, him who is my very heart. |
13 Though I wanted to keep him with me, to be my servant in
14 the chains of the good news, in your place, | without your
approval I would do nothing. I do not want your good
works to be forced, but done freely from your heart. |
15 Perhaps for this reason he was parted from you for a time,
16 so that you might have him forever, | no longer as a
servant, but more than a servant, a brother, very dear to
me, but much more to you, in the flesh as well as in the
Lord.

17 If then you consider me to be your friend and brother,
18 take him in as you would me. | If he has done you any
wrong or is in debt to you for anything, charge it to my
19 account. | I, Paul, writing this by my own hand, will make
payment to you, not to mention that you owe me your life.
20 | So brother, let me have some befit of you in the Lord;
renew my heart in Christ.

[1] See page 437, "God's love."

THE EPISTLE OF JAMES

In no uncertain terms, James denounced the human tendency to judge by appearances, to admire those who have fine clothes and suspect those who look poor. Did a community behaving like that deserve to be called Christian?

THE "GENERAL" EPISTLES

False values

2 1 My brothers, if you have the faith of our Lord
2 Jesus Christ of glory, do not show favoritsm. | If
a man enters your synagogue in fine clothing and with a
gold ring, and a poor man comes in with dirty clothing, |
3 and you honor the man in fair clothings saying, "Come
take this good place;"[1] yet you say to the poor man, "Take
4 up your position there, or be seated at my feet," | is there
not discrimination among you? Have you not become
judges with evil thoughts?

5 Listen, my dear brothers. Are not those who are poor in
the things of this world chosen by God to have faith* as
their wealth, and the kingdom* for their heritage which he
6 has said he will give to those who love him?[2] | But you
have put the poor man to shame. Are not the men of
wealth exploiting you? Do they not dragging before their
7 judges? | Do they not say evil of the holy name which was
8 given to you? | But if you keep the greatest Law of all, as
it is given in the holy Scriptures, "Love your neighbor as
9 yourself,"[3] you are doing right | But if you discriminate,
you do evil, and are judged as lawbreakers by the law.

If the Church accepts
the world's prejudices,
if she wants to be "like the others,"
what kind of flavor will it give to the world?

Because the Church is the Body of Christ,
she has to be the voice of those
without a voice;
a refuge for those shipwrecked in life;
a place of freedom, justice and peace;
a place where all can find
reasons to hope!

[1] Compare with what Jesus had to say in Matthew 23:5-7, page 290.

[2] See Romans 8:17, page 431.

[3] See Leviticus 19:18, page 73, and Mark 12:31, page 252.

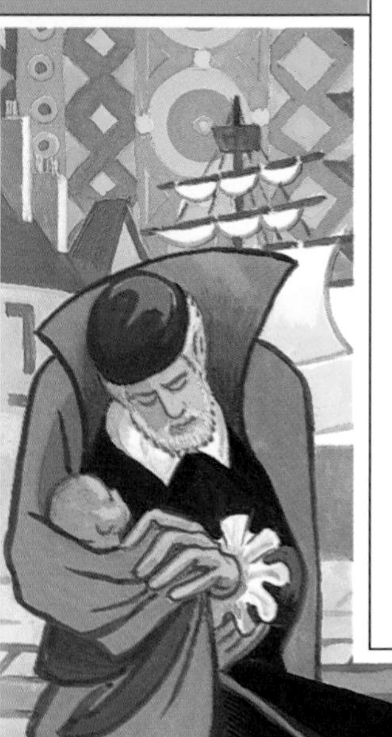

RAYER FOR THE SICK

his passage from James is
ead by Catholics when their
acrament* for the seriously
l is administered. The rite
epeats some of the many
estures of compassion
hown by Jesus towards the
ck. The touching with oil
hows that the Lord gives
he sufferer strength to fight
gainst despondency and
oubt. Sickness is, like any
ainful experience, an
ccasion for trial and
emptation. It is not
nusual to hear things like,
What have I done to God
or Him to inflict this sort of
uffering on me?"

he rite saves and uplifts
he ailing person by
evealing that, despite
eeming powerlessness, she
r he can be of great
omfort to fellow Christians
y joining with Jesus
uffering on the cross.

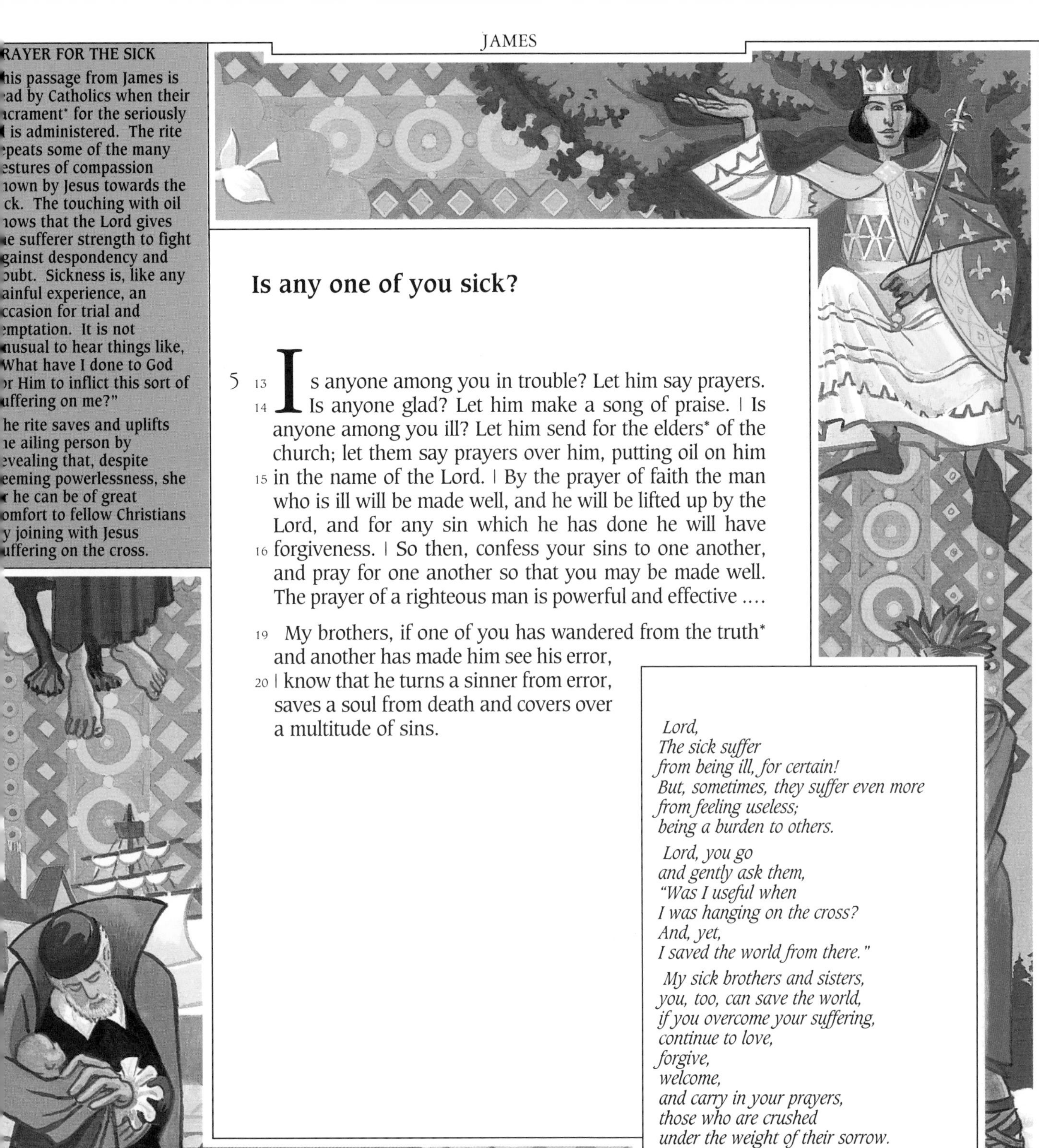

Is any one of you sick?

5 13 Is anyone among you in trouble? Let him say prayers.
14 Is anyone glad? Let him make a song of praise. | Is
anyone among you ill? Let him send for the elders* of the
church; let them say prayers over him, putting oil on him
15 in the name of the Lord. | By the prayer of faith the man
who is ill will be made well, and he will be lifted up by the
Lord, and for any sin which he has done he will have
16 forgiveness. | So then, confess your sins to one another,
and pray for one another so that you may be made well.
The prayer of a righteous man is powerful and effective ....

19 My brothers, if one of you has wandered from the truth*
and another has made him see his error,
20 | know that he turns a sinner from error,
saves a soul from death and covers over
a multitude of sins.

Lord,
The sick suffer
from being ill, for certain!
But, sometimes, they suffer even more
from feeling useless;
being a burden to others.

Lord, you go
and gently ask them,
"Was I useful when
I was hanging on the cross?
And, yet,
I saved the world from there."

My sick brothers and sisters,
you, too, can save the world,
if you overcome your suffering,
continue to love,
forgive,
welcome,
and carry in your prayers,
those who are crushed
under the weight of their sorrow.

Give the reason for the hope that you have

3 15 But give honor to Christ in your hearts as your
Lord. Be ready at any time when you are
questioned about the hope* which is in you, to account for
16 the fear of the Lord. Do so without pride, | being conscious
that you have done no wrong, so that those who say evil
things about your righteous way of life as Christians may
17 be shamed. | If it is God's purpose for you to suffer, it is
better to do so for doing good than for doing evil.

18 Because Christ once suffered for sins, the righteous one
taking the place of sinners, so that through him we might
come back to God; being put to death in the flesh, but
19 given life in the Spirit; | by whom he went to the spirits in
20 prison, preaching to those | who, in the days of Noah,
disobeyed God's orders, but God in his mercy refrained
from giving punishment, while Noah got ready the ark, in
which a small number, eight persons, got salvation
21 through water. | And baptism, of which this is an image,
now gives you salvation, not by washing clean the flesh,
but by making you free from the sense of sin before God,
22 through the resurrection of Jesus Christ. | He has entered
heaven, and is at the right hand of God, angels and
authorities and powers having been put under his rule.

THE FIRST EPISTLE OF PETER

The context was one of persecution. The author of the first letter of Peter exhorted Christians to bear witness to the hope that inspired them (see Matthew 10:18-20, page 270). **Even if this witness resulted in their being tried and condemned to death, the author reminded them that Christians, through baptism, shared in the life of the risen Christ. Their persecutors were powerless to extinguish that life** (see Matthew 10:28, page 270).

The Greek word "martyr" meant "witness." The first Christians were well aware of the risks they took in "professing" their faith in Jesus Christ. But they felt that those risks were less serious than separating themselves from Jesus.

HE DESCENDED INTO HELL

The mercifulness* of Jesus was not reserved for those who lived after him. It was also given to those who came before (see verse 19, left).

To express this certainty, the early Christians said that he descended into "hell," sheol (see Apostles' Creed, page 460). **In their icons showing the Resurrection, they represented Jesus in glory rising from sheol along with all the people who had lived before him. Icons of this kind are still venerated in Eastern churches. In them, the powerful gesture of Jesus may be seen as he takes Adam* and Eve* by the wrists and leads them up with him.** (One such icon is reproduced on page 531.)

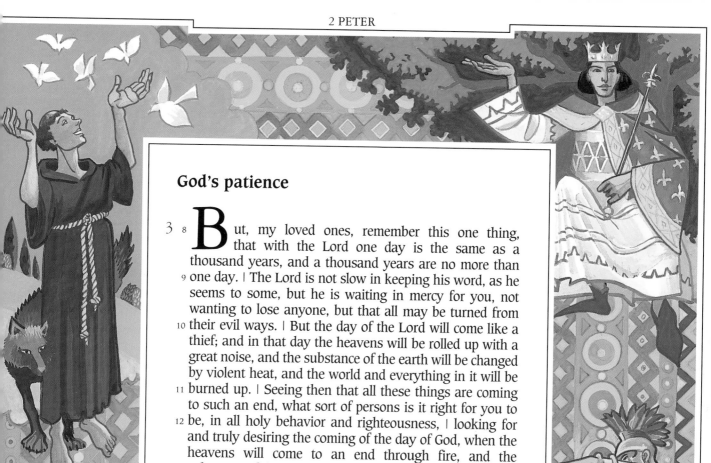

God's patience

3 8 But, my loved ones, remember this one thing,
that with the Lord one day is the same as a
thousand years, and a thousand years are no more than
9 one day. | The Lord is not slow in keeping his word, as he
seems to some, but he is waiting in mercy for you, not
wanting to lose anyone, but that all may be turned from
10 their evil ways. | But the day of the Lord will come like a
thief; and in that day the heavens will be rolled up with a
great noise, and the substance of the earth will be changed
by violent heat, and the world and everything in it will be
11 burned up. | Seeing then that all these things are coming
to such an end, what sort of persons is it right for you to
12 be, in all holy behavior and righteousness, | looking for
and truly desiring the coming of the day of God, when the
heavens will come to an end through fire, and the
substance of the earth will be changed by the great heat?...

14 For this reason, my loved ones, as you are looking for
these things, take great care that when he comes you may
be in peace before him, free from sin and every evil thing.
15 | And be certain that the long waiting of the Lord is for
salvation; even as our brother Paul has said in his letters
17 to you, from the wisdom which was given to him. | For this
reason, my loved ones, having
knowledge of these things before they
take place, take care that you are not
turned away by the error of lawless
men, so falling from your true faith. |
18 But be increased in grace* and in the
knowledge* of our Lord and Savior
Jesus Christ.

Time...
What do I do with my time?
I don't have time.
It's taking a long time!
(or It's taking forever!)
You have to take time.
So many expressions show that we don't take "time" seriously.

Each second is a gift from you, Lord,
an occasion to know you better,
and to make you known.
Lord, help me to not waste my time!

FIRST EPISTLE OF JOHN

John, in his first letter, shared with his readers his spiritual experience of loving one's neighbor. He had understood that there were not two commandments — love God and love your neighbor. There was only one. You could not love God if you did not love other people. More to the point, all real love of your fellow person brought you closer to God and, in a sense, made you God's ally.

The person who loves knows God

3 15 Anyone who hates his brother is a murderer,
and you may be certain that no murderer has
eternal life in him.
16 In this we see what love is, because he gave his life for
us; and it is right for us to give our lives for the brothers.
17 But if a man has great wealth, and sees that his brother
is in need, and keeps his heart closed to his brother, how
is it possible for the love of God to be in him?
18 My little children, do not let our love be in word and in
tongue, but let it be in action and in truth....

4 7 My loved ones, let us love one another, because love is of
God, and everyone who has love is a child of God and
knows God.
8 He who has no love does not know God, because God is
love....
18 There is no fear[1] in love: true love has no room for fear,
because where fear is, there is pain. He who is not free
from fear is not perfect in love.
19 We love, because he first loved us.
If a man says, "I love God," and hates
20 his brother, his words are false: for how
is the man who has no love for his
brother whom he has seen, able to have
love for God whom he has not seen?

[1] John was talking of ordinary fear, not the "fear"* of God which was a gift of the Holy Spirit.

I can make wonderful
speeches about God,
but if I don't love my neighbor
or the foreigner who crosses my path;
if I use others,
without ever serving them;
then the words in my speech
about God are meaningless.
I don't know God.

If I start listening to others,
if I rejoice in their differences,
if I share;
even if I don't talk about God,
I already know Him in the depths
of my being.

III
THE REVELATION OF JOHN

The Book of Revelation, also known as The Apocalypse, is the last book in the Bible. It was written by the apostle John in the middle of a period of heavy persecution. The apostle had been banished to the island of Patmos by the emperor Domitian,[1] who demanded to be worshipped as a god. Many Christians were tortured and put to death.*

To bolster the morale of the "churches" under his care, John adopted the style of the old apocalypses.[2]* By means of symbol-laden images, he revealed the hidden sense of the harsh reality which Christians were enduring. The world of injustice and cruelty would pass away. The only abiding reality was the Kingdom of God. John asked his readers to turn their gaze towards the sacrificed lamb. This was the symbol of Jesus. The lamb was surrounded by terrifying beasts. They were the symbol of the forces of persecution. The lamb, in spite of his apparent defenselessness, and in spite of his death, rose as conqueror and ushered into his kingdom* all who had remained faithful to him.*

[1] Domitian was the brother of Titus*, whom he succeeded as emperor from 81 to 96 AD. The persecution of Christians occurred in the closing years of his reign.

[2] See page 204.

THE SEVEN CHURCHES

The Book of Revelation begins with a series of seven letters addressed to the Christian communities in Asia. John did not invent what was in these letters. In the tradition of the great Old Testament prophets,* he transmitted a message from the Lord. The real author of the letters was Jesus. The churches in Ephesus, Smyrna (modern Izmir), Pergamum, Thyatira (the home town of Lydia, see page 423), Sardis, Philadelphia and Laodicea received advice geared to each one's situation.

The figure seven was not chosen at random. The seven churches represented all the Christian communities. In the seven letters, all Christians everywhere were urged to remain vigilant.

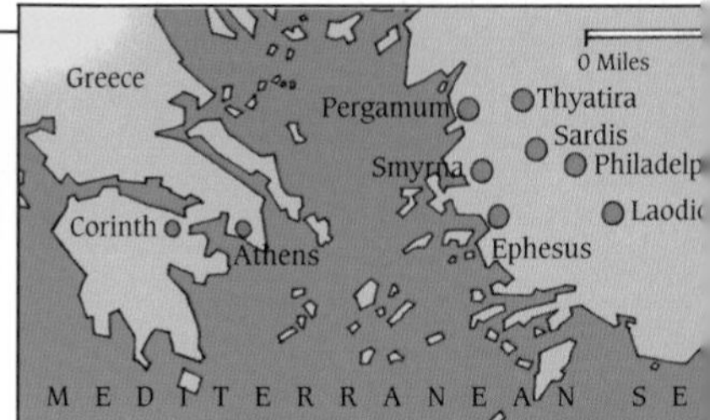

Letter to the church in Laodicea

3 14 And to the angel[1] of the church
in Laodicea[2] write:
These things give the true and certain witness,
the head of God's new order.
15 I know of your deeds,
that you are not cold or warm:
it would be better if you were cold or warm.
16 So because you are not one thing or the other,
I will have no more to do with you.
17 For you say, "I have wealth,
and have amassed goods and land,
and have need of nothing."
You are not conscious
of your sad and unhappy condition,
that you are poor and blind and without clothing.
18 If you are wise
you will buy from me gold refined by fire,
so that you may have true wealth,
and white robes to wear,
so that your shame[3] may not be seen,
and oil for your eyes, so that you may see.
19 To all those who are dear to me,
I rebuke and discipline:
then with all your heart repent from your evil ways.
20 See, I am waiting at the door
and knocking.
If any man hears
he will open the door,
I will come in to him,
and will dine with him and he with me.

[1] Each letter was addressed to an angel. The word angel had a special meaning in this context. It signified the "spirit" of the Christian community.

[2] Laodicea was a town famous for its hot springs, its cloth and its remedies for eye ailments. Its inhabitants lived a comfortable existence.

[3] Nakedness was associated with the state of sin. See Genesis 3:7, page 24, and John 21:7, page 393. The white clothes were a sign of adoption by God. See next page, note 3.

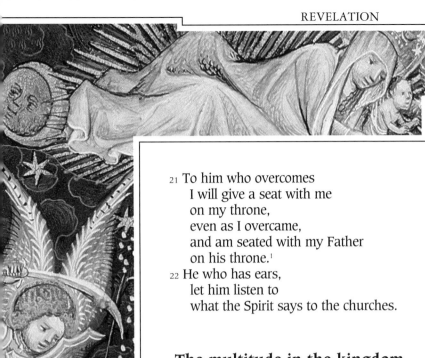

The community at Laodicea,
occupied by its comfort and riches,
used to an easy life,
asleep in its mediocrity,
no longer heard the Lord
knocking at their door.
They no longer responded to
the Lord's desire to live in the hearts
of his faithful.
Wake up!
He's knocking at our doors, today.

21 To him who overcomes
I will give a seat with me
on my throne,
even as I overcame,
and am seated with my Father
on his throne.[1]
22 He who has ears,
let him listen to
what the Spirit says to the churches.

ALL SAINTS
John, in a vision filled with light and joy, described the arrival of the myriads of believers, especially those who had suffered martyrdom,* before God.

The multitude in the kingdom

7 2 And I saw another angel coming up from the east,
having the seal of the living God:
and he said with a great voice to the four angels,
to whom it was given to harm the earth
and the sea,
3 "Do no harm the earth, or the sea, or the trees,
till we have put a seal
on the servants of our God."
4 And there came to my ears the number of those
who had the seal on their brows, a hundred
and forty-four thousand, who were sealed
out of every tribe* of the people of Israel.
9 After these things I saw a great army of people
too many to count,
out of every nation and of all tribes and peoples
and languages,[2]
taking their places before the throne and before
the Lamb,
dressed in white[3] robes,
and with branches in their hands,

[1] See Matthew 26:64, page 373.

[2] John showed the fidelity of God who opened His kingdom* first to the representatives of the people of Israel, then to the multitudes from all the nations.

[3] White was the color of God (see Mark 9:3, page 246). The fact of wearing a white garment was a sign of being adopted by God through baptism or martyrdom (Revelation 7:14).

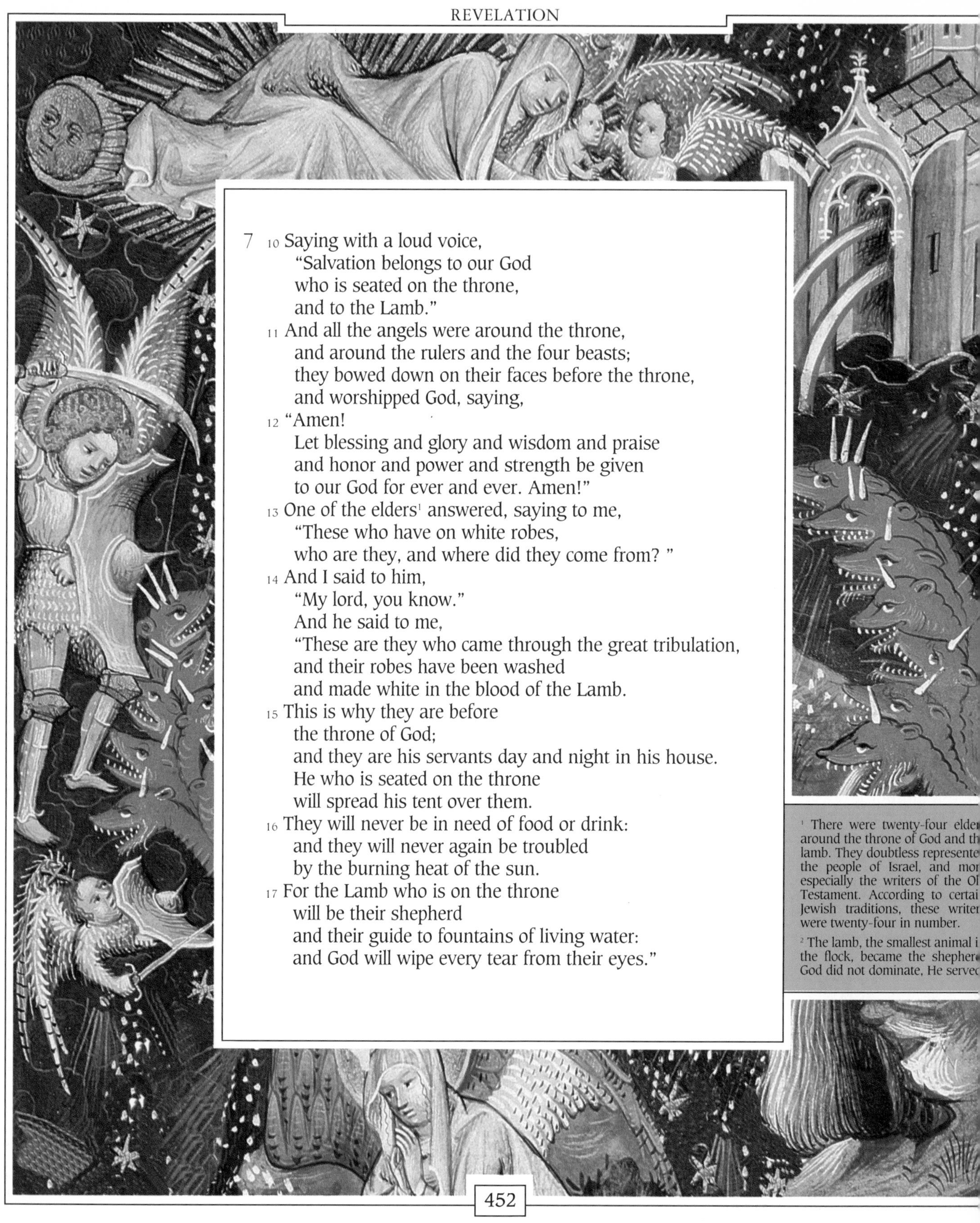

7 10 Saying with a loud voice,
"Salvation belongs to our God
who is seated on the throne,
and to the Lamb."
11 And all the angels were around the throne,
and around the rulers and the four beasts;
they bowed down on their faces before the throne,
and worshipped God, saying,
12 "Amen!
Let blessing and glory and wisdom and praise
and honor and power and strength be given
to our God for ever and ever. Amen!"
13 One of the elders[1] answered, saying to me,
"These who have on white robes,
who are they, and where did they come from? "
14 And I said to him,
"My lord, you know."
And he said to me,
"These are they who came through the great tribulation,
and their robes have been washed
and made white in the blood of the Lamb.
15 This is why they are before
the throne of God;
and they are his servants day and night in his house.
He who is seated on the throne
will spread his tent over them.
16 They will never be in need of food or drink:
and they will never again be troubled
by the burning heat of the sun.
17 For the Lamb who is on the throne
will be their shepherd
and their guide to fountains of living water:
and God will wipe every tear from their eyes."

[1] There were twenty-four elde around the throne of God and th lamb. They doubtless represente the people of Israel, and mor especially the writers of the Ol Testament. According to certai Jewish traditions, these writer were twenty-four in number.

[2] The lamb, the smallest animal i the flock, became the shepher God did not dominate, He serve

E VICTORY OF JESUS

e prophesy in Genesis
4-15 (page 25) had come
e. The offspring of the
man, Jesus, crushed the
ad of the dragon, which
s the ancient serpent
led the devil, or Satan.

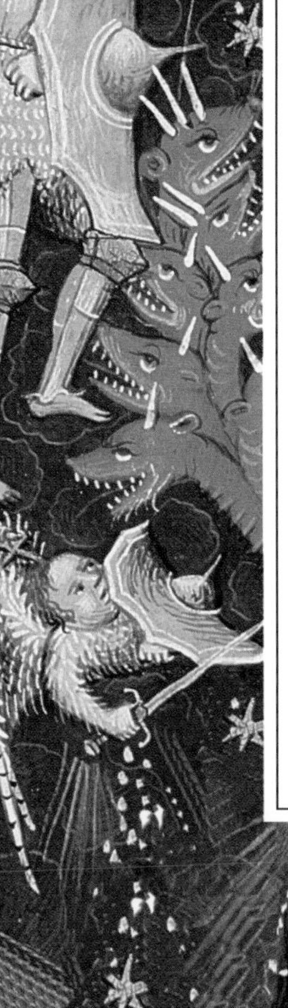

The woman and the serpent

12 1 And a great sign was seen in heaven:
A woman clothed with the sun,
and with the moon under her feet,
and on her head a crown of twelve stars.
2 And she was with child; she gave a cry,
in the pains of childbirth.
3 And there was seen another sign in heaven:
a great red dragon,
having seven heads and ten horns,[1]
and on his heads seven crowns.
4 And his tail was pulling a third part of the stars
of heaven down to the earth,
and the dragon took his place before the woman
who was about to give birth,
so that when the birth had taken place
he might kill her child.
5 She gave birth to a son, a male child,
who was to have rule over all the nations
with a rod of iron.[2]
Her child was taken up to God and to his throne.
6 And the woman fled to the desert,
where she had a place prepared by God.
7 There was war in heaven:
Michael and his angels went out to fight
the dragon.[3]
The dragon and his angels fought back.
8 They were defeated,
and there was no more place for them in heaven.
9 The great dragon was hurled down--
the old snake,* who is named the Evil One and Satan,*

[1] These attributes (seven heads with crowns, ten horns, etc.) were evidence of the power of this dragon which John, in his Gospel, called the "prince of this world." See also 4:8-9, page 259. Yet despite its power it would be conquered by the offspring of the woman, who was Jesus. The only weapon of Jesus was the strength of his love.

[2] The child of the woman was the Messiah,* described with details from Psalm 2 (page 209). The woman thus represented both the people of Israel which had produced the Messiah and Mary whom John in his Gospel had addressed several times as "Woman" (see John 2:4, page 336, and John 19:26, page 379). The "woman" suggested also the Church, which was at that time going through the desert of persecution.

[3] See Daniel 12:1, page 205.

12 by whom all the earth is turned from the right way--
was hurled down to the earth,
and his angels[1] were hurled down with him.
10 A great voice in heaven came to my ears,
saying,
"Now salvation has come,
and the power, and the kingdom
of our God,
and the authority of his Christ,
because he who says evil against
our brothers
before our God day and night
is hurled down.
11 And they overcame him through
the blood of the Lamb
and the word of their testimony.
Loving not their lives
they freely gave themselves up
to death.
12 Be glad then, O heavens,
and you who are in them.

The devil tried to turn people away from God by using lies and insinuations. "What good is it to love a God who allows people to struggle with so much suffering?"

Jesus revealed to us that God has not lost interest in people who suffer. Jesus has become one of them. He showed on the cross, that even when one is overcome with suffering, one can become radiant with love for others by leaning on God.

The new world

21 1 And I saw a new heaven and a new earth:
for the first heaven and the first earth were gone,
and there was no more sea.[2]
2 I saw the Holy City, the new Jerusalem,
coming down out of heaven from God,
like a bride beautifully dressed for her husband.[3]
3 And there came to my ears a great voice
out of the throne, saying,

[1] They were demons.

[2] John did not pretend to give an exact description of the coming world; it was more symbolic. The sea totally disappeared because it was considered the dwelling place of Evil. See pages 241 ans 242.

[3] John returns to the wedding theme of God with his people. See principally Hosea 2:16-22, page 132 and John 2:1-12, page 336.

"See, the Tent of God is with men,
and he will live with them,
and they will be his people,
and God himself will be with them,
and be their God.
4 He will put an end to all their weeping;
there will be no more death, or sorrow, or crying,
or pain; for the old order has come to an end."
5 And he who is seated on the throne said,
"See, I make all things new."
He said,
"Write it in the book:
for these words are certain and true."
6 He said to me,
"It is done. I am the First and the Last,
the start and the end.
I will freely give of the fountain of the water of life[1]
to him who is in need.
7 He who overcomes will have
these things for his heritage;
I will be his God,
and he will be my son."...

22 2 In the middle of its street,
on each side of the river
stood the tree of life,
having twelve sorts of fruits,
giving its fruit every month;
and the leaves of the tree give life
to the nations.

[1] See John 4:14, page 339, and John 7:37-38, page 346.

In the beginning,
humanity lived in God's garden.
But, the people left to build a city,
and forgot God.

God does not forget the people.
God, tirelessly, invites them to come back.
And so, they will not be disoriented
or feel like foreigners,
God will build a city in His garden,
like humanity's,
but purified, and more attractive.

In the middle of the square in the city,
there is a tree.
It is the tree from the first garden,
the one humanity turned away from.
It is the tree of life
whose fruit is always replenished—
so much does God desire to share His life
with all of those who will live in His city.

SVSTVS
TIMOTEVS

PART SIX

CHRISTIAN PRAYERS AND CREEDS

The early Christians had at their disposition a treasure-house of prayers in the Old Testament book of Psalms.[1] They sang them with Jesus when they gathered together for temple celebrations and feasts.[2] Jesus also used them during his time of personal prayer with the Father.[3]

Jesus wanted his disciples to enter so deeply into prayer that it would become a genuine dialogue of trust between a child and his "Abba." Thus, he taught them the Lord's Prayer.[4]*

The Psalms and the Lord's Prayer were, for the first Christians, the referential texts which nourished both their personal and communal prayer.

Very soon, however, they wanted to enrich their heritage with new prayers:

• They needed statements of the Christian faith to recite together particularly at baptisms, as well as during the more ceremonial communions. Thus, after a time of intense reflection and even conflict, creeds were gradually developed into the declarations that we know today. Today, Catholics, Protestants, and Orthodox alike profess their faith in the same manner in the Nicene Creed.[5]

• The liturgy was also a time for developing song, worship or intercession that was specifically Christian. Throughout the centuries, the Sanctus, the doxologies, and the Gloria sung at Sunday masses and worship services in the western world are beautiful examples of hymns of prayers of the Church.[6]

• Throughout the centuries, Catholic Church devotions have given an important place to Mary, the mother of Jesus. They believe that the Gospel asks all followers of Christ to "invite her into their homes."[7] "Hail Mary, Full of Grace", whose formulation was concretized in the 16th century, is one of the most widely-used prayers in the western Catholic Church. It is often used in the rosary or the Angelus.[8]

• For personal prayer, some Christians in the Catholic Church use prayer formulas which they know by heart, such as the "I confess to God", or the acts of contrition, of faith, hope and charity.[9]

1 Pages 208-228.

2 See, for example, John 7:37, page 346 or 10:22, page 353.

3 Luke 23:46, Matthew 27:46, page 380.

4 Page 459.

5 Page 461.

6 Pages 462-463.

7 See John 19:27, page 379.

8 Pages 464-465.

9 Pages 466-468.

The Lord's Prayer

Our Father, who art in heaven,
hallowed be your name,
your kingdom come,
your will be done
on earth as it is in heaven.
Give us this day our daily bread.
Forgive us our trespasses,
as we forgive those who trespass against us.
Lead us not into temptation,
but deliver us from evil.
For yours is the kingdom, and the power
and the glory.
For ever and ever!

Amen.

The Apostles' Creed

I believe in God, the Father Almighty,
Creator of heaven and earth.
And in Jesus Christ, his only son, our Lord,
who was conceived by the Holy Spirit,
born of the Virgin Mary,
suffered under Pontius Pilate,
was crucified, died and was buried.
He descended into hell.
On the third day, he arose again from the dead.
He ascended into heaven,
is seated at the right hand of God, the Father Almighty.
From thence, he shall come to judge the living and the dead.
I believe in the Holy Spirit, the holy catholic* Church,
the communion of saints,
the forgiveness of sins,
the resurrection of the body,
and life everlasting.
Amen.

* The word catholic means universal.

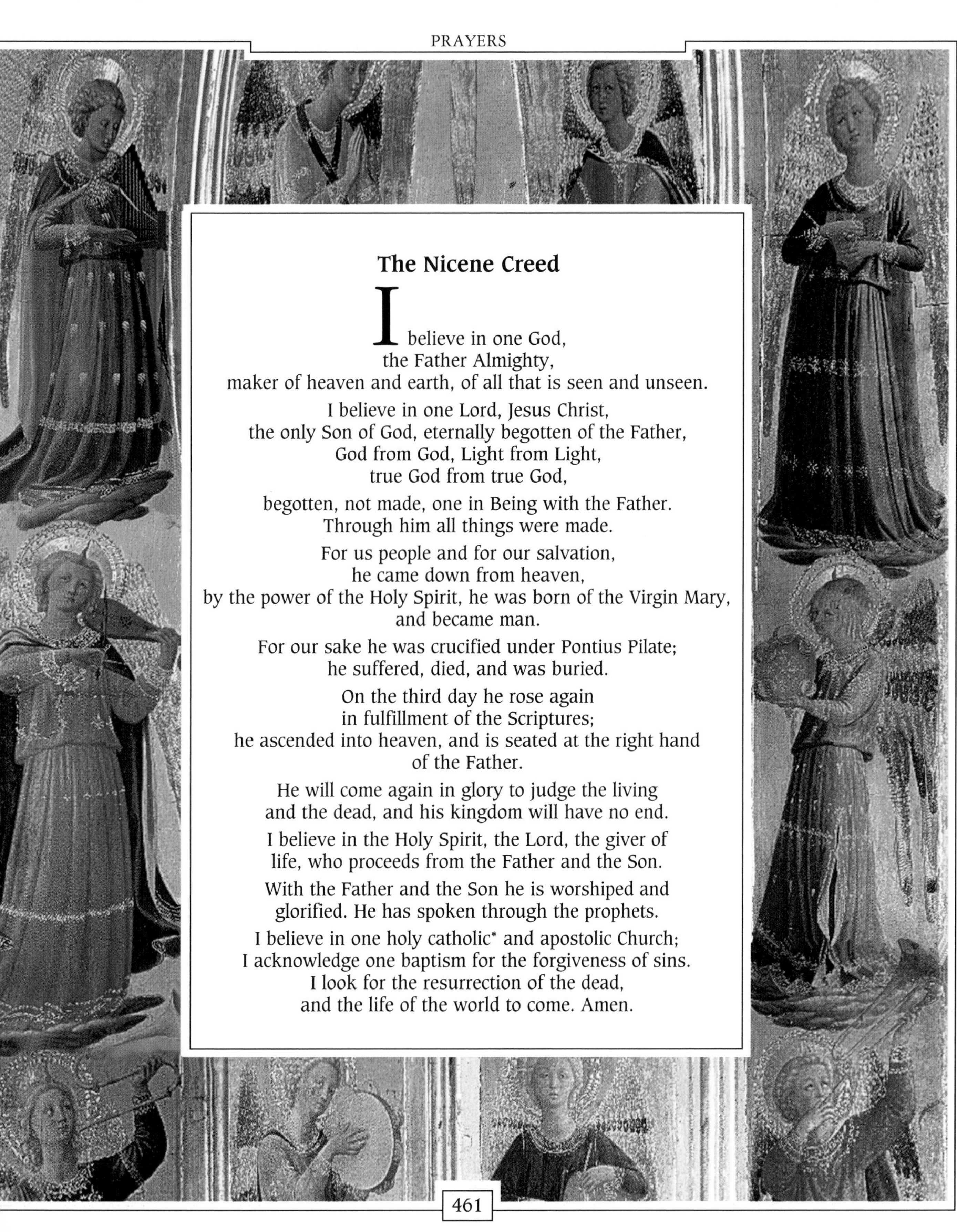

The Nicene Creed

I believe in one God,
the Father Almighty,
maker of heaven and earth, of all that is seen and unseen.

I believe in one Lord, Jesus Christ,
the only Son of God, eternally begotten of the Father,
God from God, Light from Light,
true God from true God,

begotten, not made, one in Being with the Father.
Through him all things were made.

For us people and for our salvation,
he came down from heaven,
by the power of the Holy Spirit, he was born of the Virgin Mary,
and became man.

For our sake he was crucified under Pontius Pilate;
he suffered, died, and was buried.

On the third day he rose again
in fulfillment of the Scriptures;
he ascended into heaven, and is seated at the right hand
of the Father.

He will come again in glory to judge the living
and the dead, and his kingdom will have no end.

I believe in the Holy Spirit, the Lord, the giver of
life, who proceeds from the Father and the Son.

With the Father and the Son he is worshiped and
glorified. He has spoken through the prophets.

I believe in one holy catholic* and apostolic Church;
I acknowledge one baptism for the forgiveness of sins.
I look for the resurrection of the dead,
and the life of the world to come. Amen.

The Gloria

Glory to God in the highest,
and peace to his people on earth.

We praise you, we bless you, we adore you.

We worship you, we give you thanks
for your glory.

Lord God, heavenly King, almighty God and Father,
Lord Jesus Christ, only Son of the Father,
Lord God, Lamb of God,
you who take away the sin of the world: have mercy on us;
you who take away the sin of the world: receive our prayer,
you, who are seated at the right hand of the Father:
have pity on us.

For you alone are Holy,
you alone are Lord,
you alone are the Most High, Jesus Christ,
with the Holy Spirit,
in the glory of God the Father.

Amen.

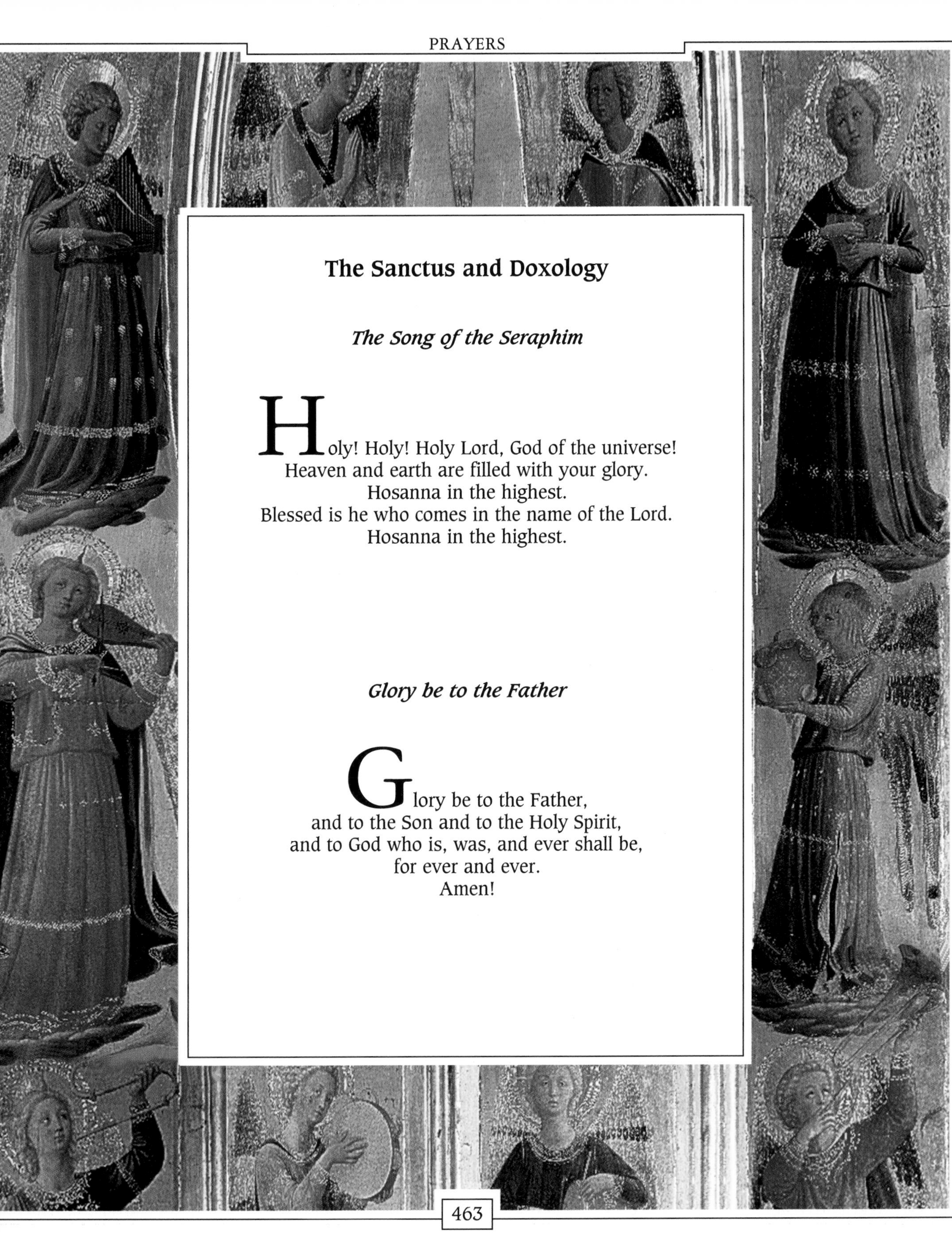

The Sanctus and Doxology

The Song of the Seraphim

Holy! Holy! Holy Lord, God of the universe!
Heaven and earth are filled with your glory.
Hosanna in the highest.
Blessed is he who comes in the name of the Lord.
Hosanna in the highest.

Glory be to the Father

Glory be to the Father,
and to the Son and to the Holy Spirit,
and to God who is, was, and ever shall be,
for ever and ever.
Amen!

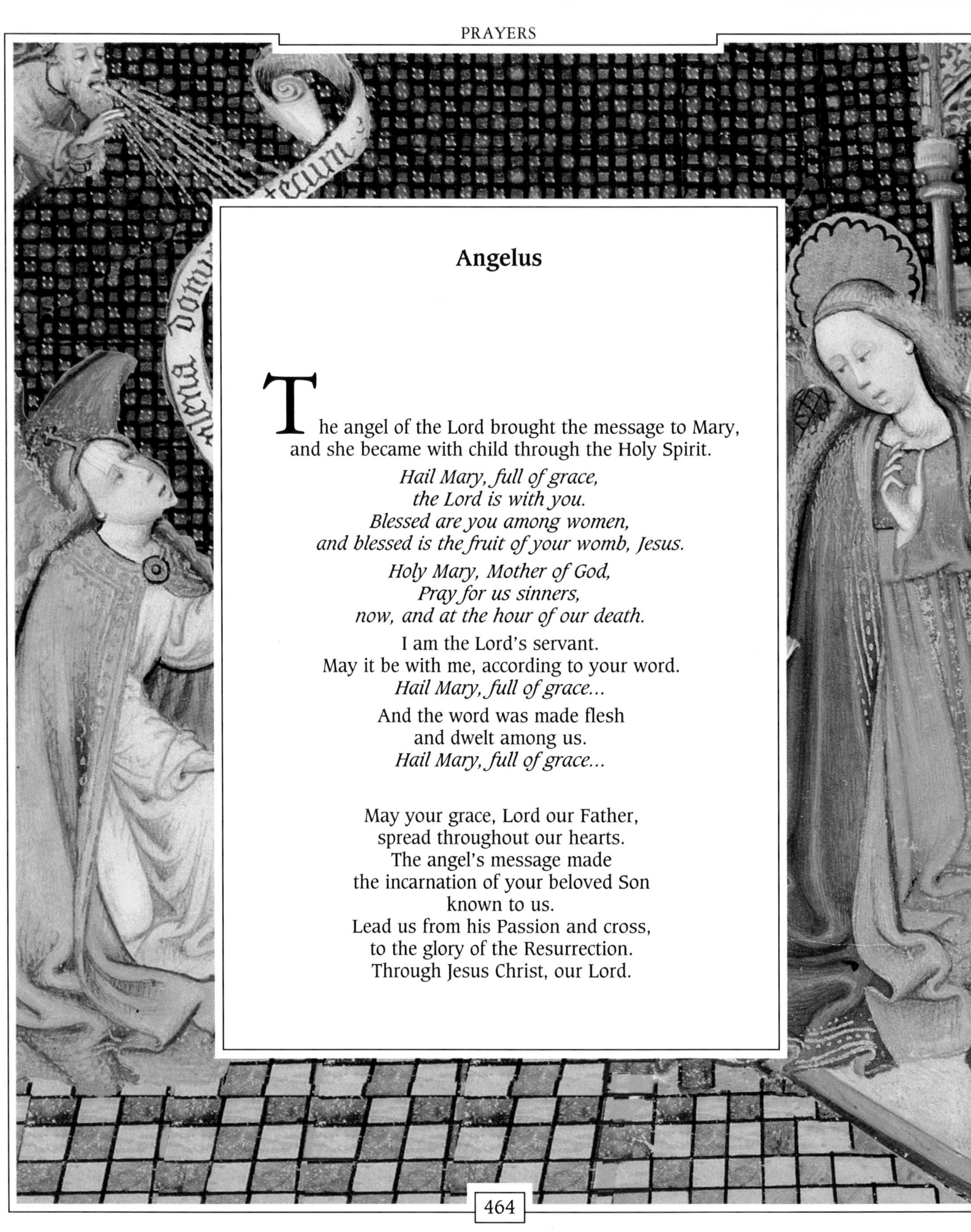

Angelus

The angel of the Lord brought the message to Mary,
and she became with child through the Holy Spirit.

Hail Mary, full of grace,
the Lord is with you.
Blessed are you among women,
and blessed is the fruit of your womb, Jesus.

Holy Mary, Mother of God,
Pray for us sinners,
now, and at the hour of our death.

I am the Lord's servant.
May it be with me, according to your word.
Hail Mary, full of grace...

And the word was made flesh
and dwelt among us.
Hail Mary, full of grace...

May your grace, Lord our Father,
spread throughout our hearts.
The angel's message made
the incarnation of your beloved Son
known to us.
Lead us from his Passion and cross,
to the glory of the Resurrection.
Through Jesus Christ, our Lord.

GLORY

JOY

THE ANNUNCIATION (Luke 1:26-38)

THE VISITATION (Luke 1:39-56)

THE NATIVITY (Luke 2:1-20)

THE PRESENTATION IN THE TEMPLE (Luke 2:22-35)

THE DIVINE SONSHIP (Luke 2:41-52)

THE AGONY IN THE GARDEN (Mark 14:32-42)

THE SCOURGING (John 19:1)

THE CROWNING WITH THORNS (John 19:2)

THE CARRYING OF THE CROSS (Mark 15:21-22)

THE CRUCIFIXION (Luke 23:33-34)

THE RESURRECTION (John 20:1-10)

THE ASCENSION (Acts 1:9-11)

PENTECOST (Acts 2:1-11)

THE ASSUMPTION

THE CROWNING OF MARY

Rejoice Mary,
full of grace!
The Lord is with you.
You are blessed among women,
and Jesus, your child, is blessed.
Holy Mary, Mother of God,
pray for us sinners,
now
and at the hour of our death.
Amen!

SORROW

I confess to God
(Penitential Rite)

I confess to almighty God, and to you,
my brothers and sisters,
that I have sinned in thought and word,
in what I have done,
and in what I have failed to do,
and I ask Mary, ever virgin,
all the angels and saints,
and you my brothers and sisters,
to pray for me to the Lord our God.
Amen!

An Act of Contrition

Father, God of tenderness and mercy,
I have sinned against you and my brothers and sisters.
I am not worthy to be called your child.
But with you, there is forgiveness.
Accept my repentance.
May your Spirit give me the strength
to live according to your love,
by imitating the One who died for our sins,
your son, Jesus Christ,
today, and for ever and ever.
Amen!

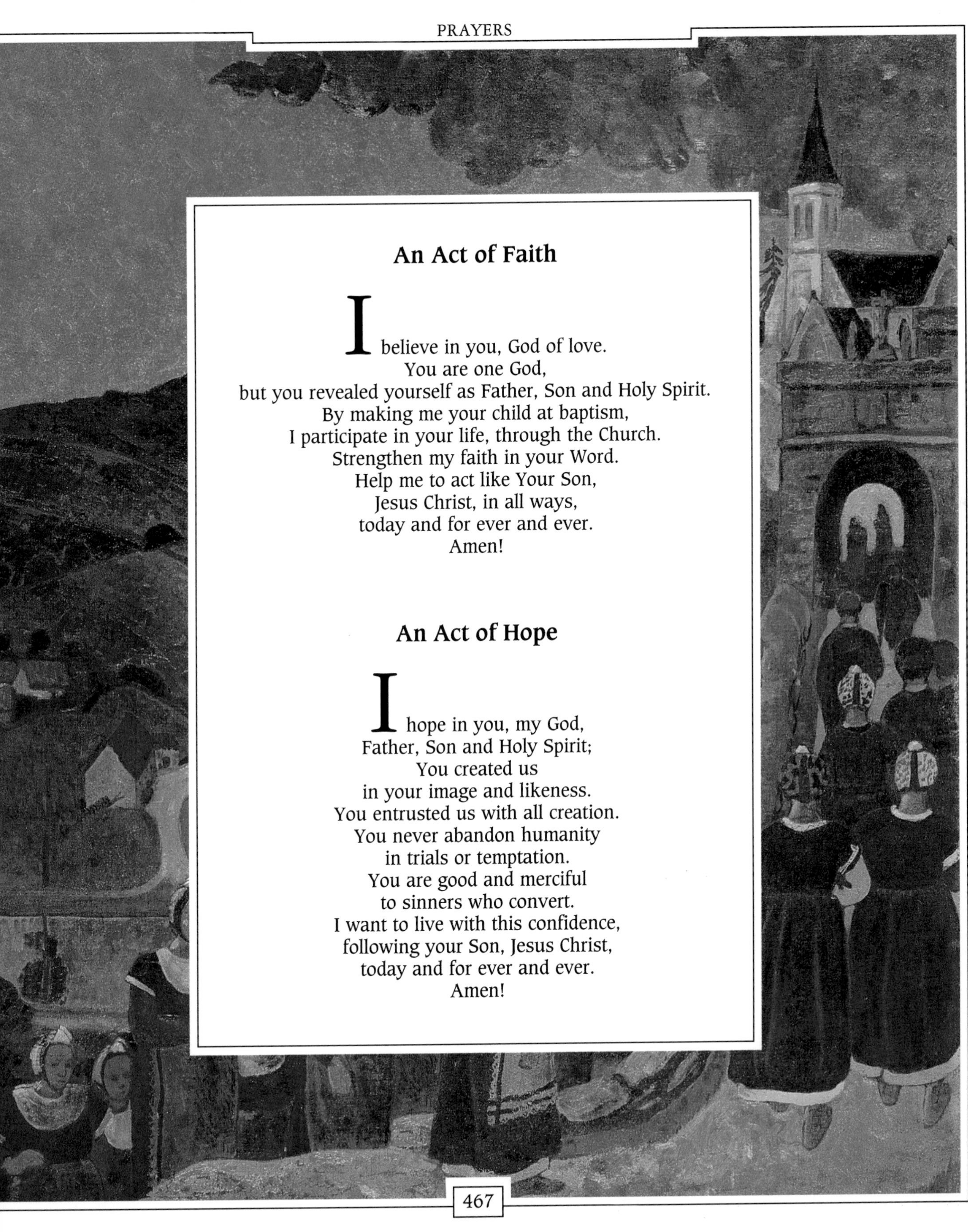

An Act of Faith

I believe in you, God of love.
You are one God,
but you revealed yourself as Father, Son and Holy Spirit.
By making me your child at baptism,
I participate in your life, through the Church.
Strengthen my faith in your Word.
Help me to act like Your Son,
Jesus Christ, in all ways,
today and for ever and ever.
Amen!

An Act of Hope

I hope in you, my God,
Father, Son and Holy Spirit;
You created us
in your image and likeness.
You entrusted us with all creation.
You never abandon humanity
in trials or temptation.
You are good and merciful
to sinners who convert.
I want to live with this confidence,
following your Son, Jesus Christ,
today and for ever and ever.
Amen!

An Act of Love

I love you, my God,
Father, Son
and Holy Spirit,
source of all love.
I love you with my whole heart,
more than anything else.
I love my neighbor as myself
for the love of you.
I want to live in this love,
following your Son, Jesus Christ,
today and for ever and ever.
Amen!

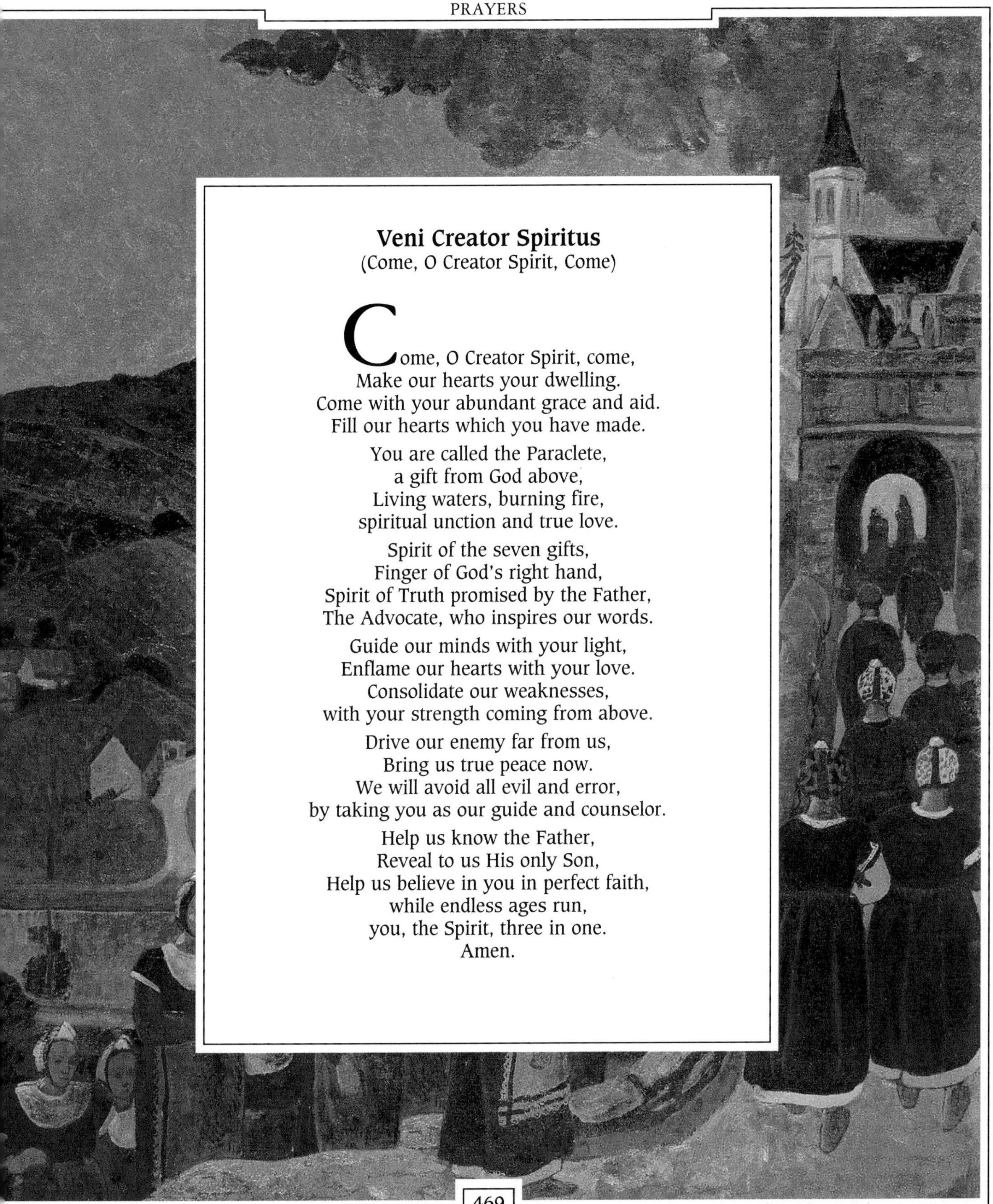

Veni Creator Spiritus

(Come, O Creator Spirit, Come)

Come, O Creator Spirit, come,
Make our hearts your dwelling.
Come with your abundant grace and aid.
Fill our hearts which you have made.

You are called the Paraclete,
a gift from God above,
Living waters, burning fire,
spiritual unction and true love.

Spirit of the seven gifts,
Finger of God's right hand,
Spirit of Truth promised by the Father,
The Advocate, who inspires our words.

Guide our minds with your light,
Enflame our hearts with your love.
Consolidate our weaknesses,
with your strength coming from above.

Drive our enemy far from us,
Bring us true peace now.
We will avoid all evil and error,
by taking you as our guide and counselor.

Help us know the Father,
Reveal to us His only Son,
Help us believe in you in perfect faith,
while endless ages run,
you, the Spirit, three in one.
Amen.

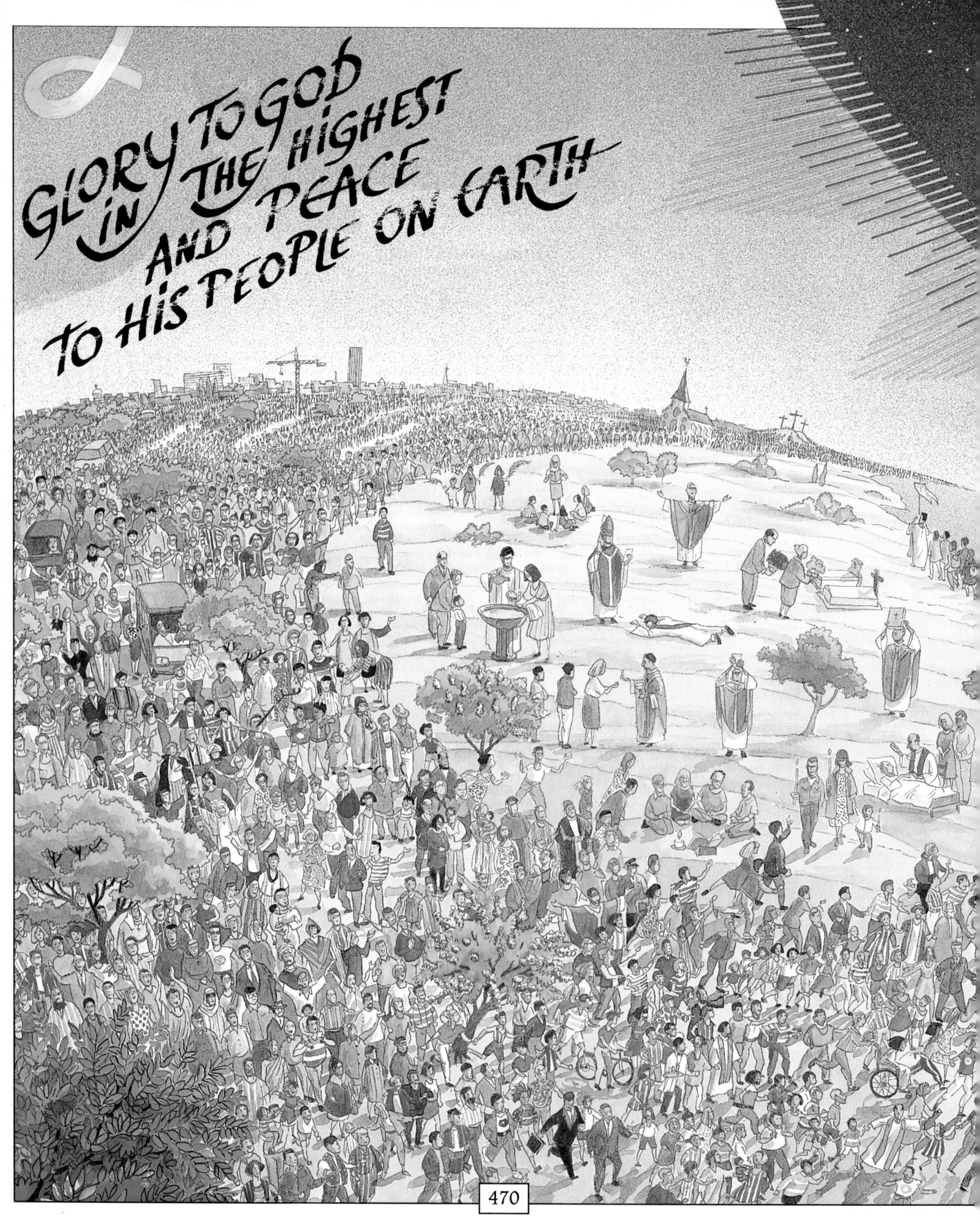
GLORY TO GOD
IN THE HIGHEST
AND PEACE
TO HIS PEOPLE ON EARTH

With their great company
and all the angels,
we praise your glory
as we cry out
with one voice:
Holy, holy,
holy Lord...
B. LE SOURD

BONO
BILE
FECIT
OPUS

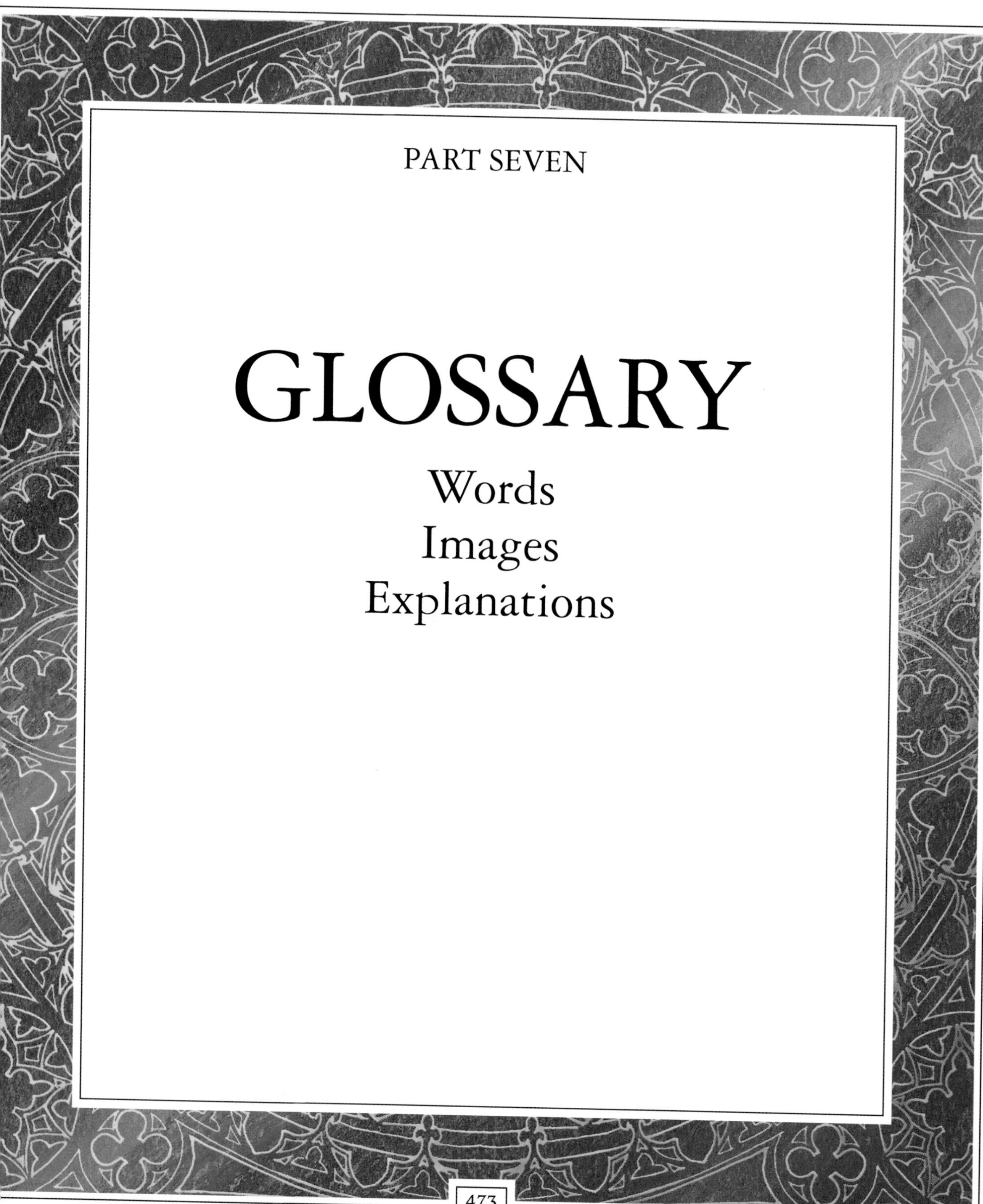

PART SEVEN

GLOSSARY

Words
Images
Explanations

Aaron

Aaron was the older brother of Moses* in whom he placed great trust. Because of Aaron's superior eloquence he often acted as Moses' spokesman (Exodus 4:14-16, page 59). Despite Aaron's disobedience in the incident of the golden calf (Exodus 32:21-24, page 75), he was anointed as high priest and his sons as priests to minister in the wilderness tabernacle. Furthermore, from that point on in history, the Jewish priests* would always be chosen from Aaron's descendents of the tribe of Levi. Aaron died before reaching the Promised Land.

Abba

Derived from an Aramaic word meaning "daddy." Children today use it as an affectionate term for their fathers. Jesus used it in the same manner to address God when he prayed, thus indicating the necessity and desirability of approaching God with the heart attitude of a child (Mark 14:36, page 369).

"Count the stars if you can..." (Genesis 15:5, page 39).

Abraham

Ancestor of the people of Israel. Accounts of his life, initially passed on by word of mouth, are found in Genesis, the first book of the Bible. Abram, which was his original name before God changed it, left Ur in Mesopotamia (known today as Iran) with his father Terah. He first settled in Haran (nowadays Turkey), then set off for the land of Canaan* with his wife Sarai and his nephew Lot* (Genesis 12:1-4, page 36 and illustration, pages 44-45). He was a traveler and a nomad. God chose him to be the founding father of his chosen people, thereby promising him that he would be the father of a multitude of descendents. With that covenant, God then renamed him Abraham and his wife, Sarah* (Genesis 17:5-15, page 39), and promised them a son, whom they would name Isaac,* a sign of God's covenant. Abraham died at a very old age and was buried in Hebron. His name appears seventy-five times in the New Testament.

THROUGH YOU WILL BE BLESSED ALL THE PEOPLES ON EARTH

From the very beginning of their relationship, God promised Abraham: *"All the peoples on earth - all the nations - will be blessed through you."* (Genesis 12:3, page 36). The authors of the Bible recount how this promise was fulfilled. By tracing Abraham's lineage, they show how all the ensuing tribes of the Hebrews are related to him. God's blessing on Abraham extended to all the families descended from him, directly or indirectly. Ishmael, the son of Hagar (see page 39), became the father of a great people and Isaac, the son of Sarah, the ancestor of the Hebrews. Abraham's lineage continued to extend itself after the death of his first wife, Sarah. The Bible recounts that he remarried, and with this last wife, Keturah, had six sons. In the New Testament, John* the Baptist refuted a common teaching of the day that kinship with Abraham was sufficient for acceptance into Godís Kingdom; John taught that personal repentance was required (Matthew 3:9, page 257). Paul the apostle also proclaimed that the true descendants of Abraham are all those who, like Abraham, have faith* in God. Today Jews, Christians and Muslims call Abraham "father of the believers in the one and only God."

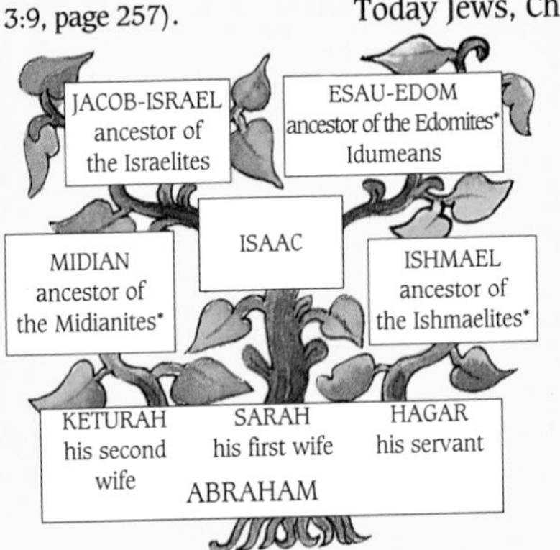

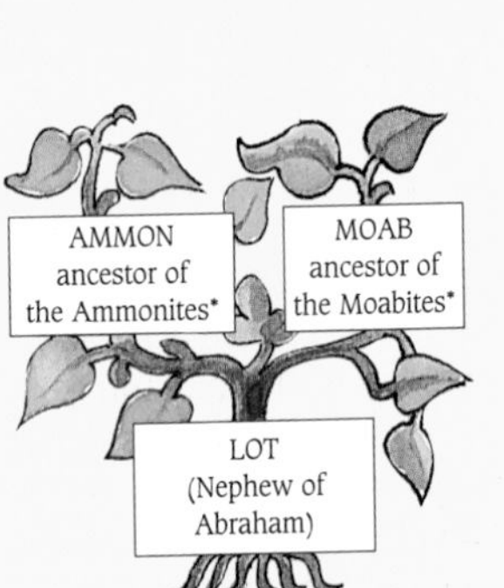

Adam

The name Adam, in addition to being a proper name, has the Hebrew meaning "mankind." The author of the third chapter of Genesis, in naming the first man Adam, drew on the Hebrew word adamah, "ground." The creature modeled from the adamah was an adam, "he who is drawn from the ground." Thus, the word became the name Adam for the first man. According to Paul the apostle, Jesus is the new Adam, the true model of man. This model is in complete keeping with God's conception of man whom He said is "his image" (Colossians 1:15).

Creation of Adam.
Engraved wood, Nuremberg, 1493. God models Adam out of a lump of clay similar to a potter's (see Jeremiah 19:1-4, page 153)

Advent

Word translated from *adventus* in Latin signaling the arrival of someone important. Christians speak of the triple advent (coming) of Jesus. HE HAS COME: He was born in Bethlehem two thousand years ago, lived as a man, and died on a cross.* HE COMES: The risen Christ is with Christians always, as He promised (Matthew 28:20, page 395). Christians recognize His presence in their lives through His Holy Spirit, Scripture, the sacraments, and events in the world. HE WILL RETURN: Christians await his final return at the end of time. Then Christ will gather together all believers in Him to establish his Kingdom.* Christians celebrate Advent as a liturgical period of four weeks before Christmas. It is a time spent celebrating the three advents of Jesus and renewing desire for Christ's final return: "Come Lord Jesus." (Revelation 22:20).

Advent crown with the four candles evoking the four Sundays.

Alleluia or Hallelujah

Hebrew word meaning "Praise the Lord! Acclaim him!" The word is often found in Christian songs and hymns or spoken in prayer as a way of expressing praise.

All Saints' Day

Celebrated on the first of November in the Catholic Church, it is a day honoring all saints, known and unknown. A day of thanksgiving to God for the testimony* of all those who, now dead, led lives faithful to God.

*SEE ILLUSTRATION, PAGES 470-471.

SEE DEATH,* RESURRECTION* AND HOLY.*

Alpha and Omega

Alpha is the first letter of the Greek alphabet and omega is the last. Christians call Jesus the Alpha, because he is the origin of all things. They also call him the Omega, because he will return at the end of time in order to open his Eternal Kingdom to those who have believed in Him (Revelation 21:6, page 455). In the Catholic church these two letters are always inscribed on the paschal candle. See illustration, pages 470-471.

Altar

Table on which sacrifices were offered to God. Altars were first made of a single rock or built with stones but later a very large altar, measuring 30-feet long and wide and 15-feet high, was built in the Temple of Jerusalem. The wood required for burning the offerings was put on the top.
In the Catholic and certain Protestant churches and their liturgies, the Communion table is called the altar because Christians believe that Jesus substituted for all the Old Testament sacrifices by offering his own life to God through love for all men. This altar is situated in the choir (chancel) of the church and in front of it, following Jesus' leading, believers offer their lives to God. Many churches, however, feel reluctant to call the Lord's Table an altar because of their symbolic understanding of the Lord's Supper.

Amalekite

Tribe descended from Amalek, grandson of Esau* (Genesis 36:12). Joshua initiated a victorious battle against the Amalekites in Rephidim (Exodus 17:8-13, page 68). See box, page 474.

Amen

Hebrew word that can be translated "It is true" or "I believe it." Jesus often said

ALTARS

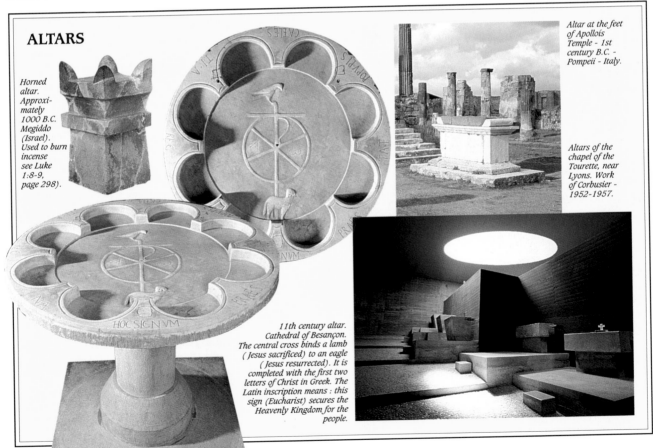

Horned altar. Approximately 1000 B.C. Megiddo (Israel). Used to burn incense see Luke 1:8-9, page 298).

Altar at the feet of Apollo's Temple - 1st century B.C. - Pompeii - Italy.

Altars of the chapel of the Tourette, near Lyons. Work of Corbusier - 1952-1957.

11th century altar. Cathedral of Besançon. The central cross binds a lamb (Jesus sacrificed) to an eagle (Jesus resurrected). It is completed with the first two letters of Christ in Greek. The Latin inscription means : this sign (Eucharist) secures the Heavenly Kingdom for the people.

"Amen, I tell you." His word is true. He is the truth.* In the book of Revelation,* it is written that Jesus is the Amen, the faithful and true witness (Revelation 3:14, page 450).

Ammonite

People descended from Ammon, son of Lot,* settled on the land of what is known today as Jordan (see chart, page 474). Uriah* the Hittite died while besieging Rabbah (known today as Amman), major city of the Ammonites (2 Samuel 11:1-17, page 109).

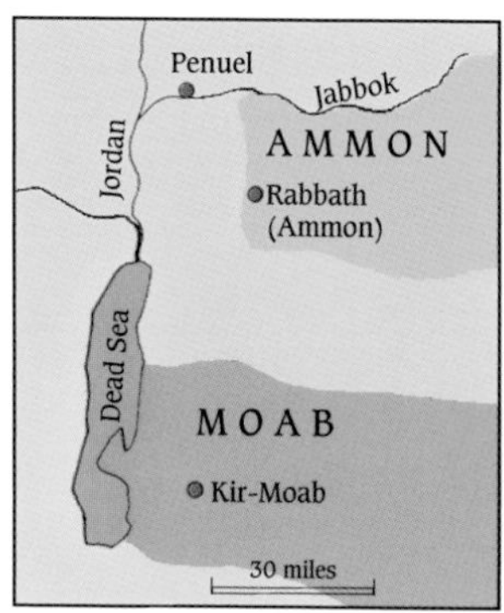

Amos

A Shepherd, he was perhaps in charge of the herds of the king or of the Temple of Jerusalem.* God called on him to be a prophet.* He had a superior eloquence, and denounced the rich in his exhortations, saying that they wallowed in luxury and oppressed the poor (Amos 6:1-7, page 129). He prophesied between 760 and 750 B.C. SEE ILLUSTRATION, PAGES 146-147.

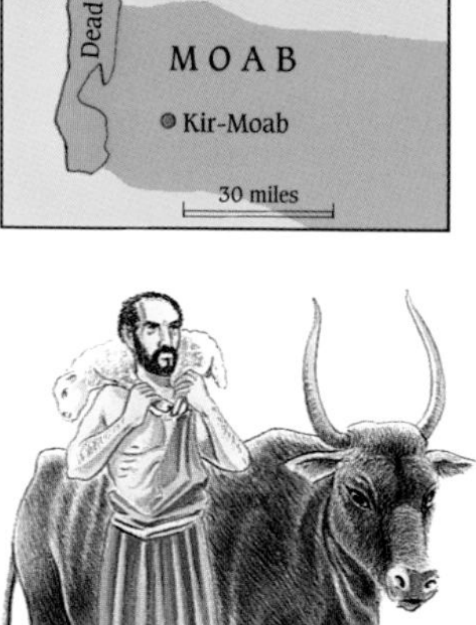

"The Lord took me from tending the flock" (Amos 7:15, page 131).

Andrew

His name, Greek in origin, means "the virile." Born in Bethsaida, he was Simon Peter's* brother, and like him, a fisherman on the Sea of Galilee. John the Baptist introduced him to Jesus, who, in turn, invited him to become one of the twelve* disciples. Andrew introduced Greek believers to Jesus (John 12:21-22, page 357). According to accounts of his ministry, he evangelized Greece and was put to death in Patras on an X-shaped cross.

Angel

From a Greek word meaning "messenger." Some early accounts in the Bible refer to the angel of the Lord who is thought to be a reference to God himself communicating directly with mankind (Exodus 3:2, page 56). More often, however, when the Bible speaks of angels, they are spiritual, living beings who are messengers of God. Their tasks vary greatly, but their overarching mission is to be a liaison between God and humans (Genesis 28:12, page 49). Their presence indicates that God is present, at work in the world for the salvation of all mankind. For example, in Nazareth, it is the angel Gabriel who announces to Mary that the Lord is with her and that she is going to have a son. Some angels have names. Michael means "Who is like God?" Gabriel means "strength of God," and Raphael means "God heals." See CHERUBIM* and SERAPH.*

***Angel playing music.** Melozzo da Forlì - 15th century - Vatican. Angels praising God in Luke 2:13, page 303, have often inspired representations of angels singing or playing music. Being messengers, they often have wings.*

Anger

Sometimes the Bible describes God as being angry and jealous. This can be disturbing, since anger and jealousy are typically considered character flaws when they occur in a person. Indeed, using human language to describe God is at times more than a challenge; it can be impossible. The depth of God's character and the quality of love He offers is vast, far beyond what is experienced in human relationships. Consequently, there are times in the Bible that the words used to describe His behavior and character provide simply an adequate and sufficient beginning of an understanding of the heavenly Creator. Afterall, it was God who chose the written word as one of the primary ways of communicating about Himself; we can trust that He deemed human language up to the task.

Thus, the term anger as applied to God can have multiple dimensions. Sometimes when the Bible speaks of God's anger it is to underscore the fact that, on other occasions, His mercy* is not a sign of weakness or permissiveness. God loves all humans. He says that we have but to ask Him, in the name of Jesus, and He forgives our sin.* On the other hand, He does not force anyone to respond to His call. From beginning to end, the Bible is one long story of humans rejecting or reconciling with God; when He is rejected, God is described as grieved, as One who cries out. God's anger at times can be understood as that: a vigorous call for conversion* (see pages 30 and 192).

Animal

The Bible often speaks of animals, and indeed, their presence is significant. Either animals symbolize the evil in the human heart, or they are the symbol of harmony with the Creator. In Genesis, animals were considered to be man's property; Adam was the one to name them (Genesis 2:19, page 23). They were put under the dominion of mankind, and therefore dependent upon their masters. Thus, according to the prophet Isaiah, when man ceases to revolt against

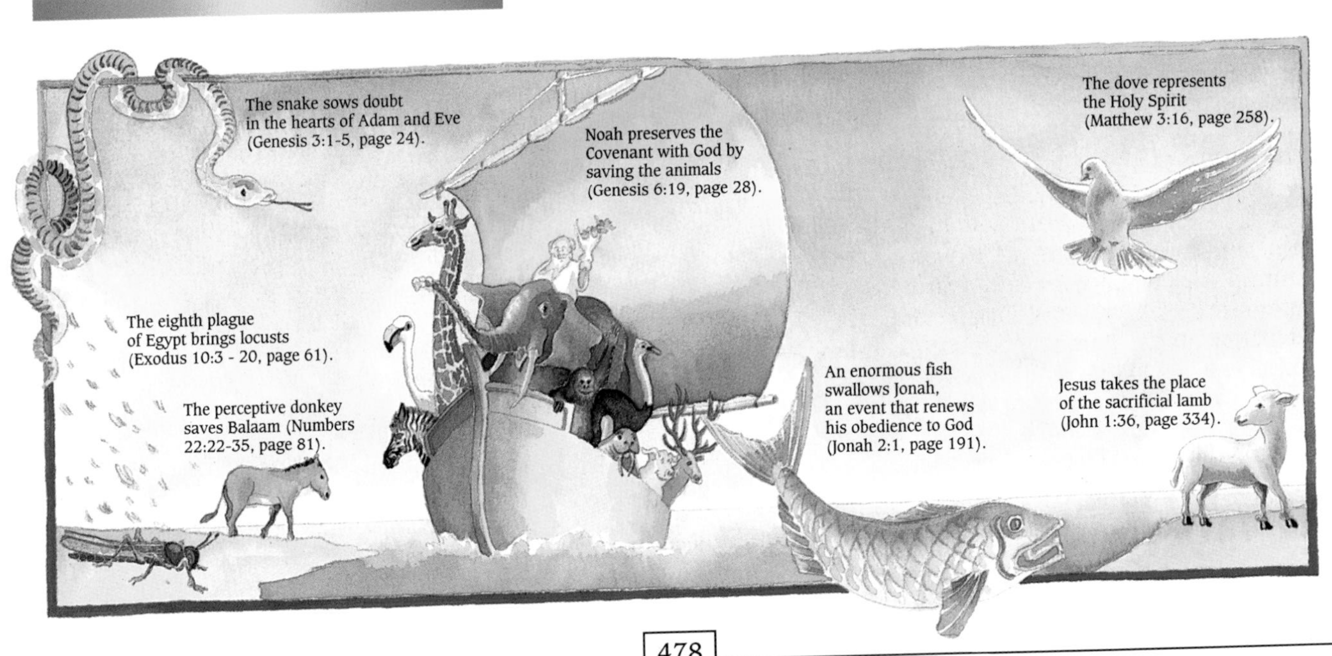
The snake sows doubt in the hearts of Adam and Eve (Genesis 3:1-5, page 24).
Noah preserves the Covenant with God by saving the animals (Genesis 6:19, page 28).
The dove represents the Holy Spirit (Matthew 3:16, page 258).
The eighth plague of Egypt brings locusts (Exodus 10:3 - 20, page 61).
The perceptive donkey saves Balaam (Numbers 22:22-35, page 81).
An enormous fish swallows Jonah, an event that renews his obedience to God (Jonah 2:1, page 191).
Jesus takes the place of the sacrificial lamb (John 1:36, page 334).

God, animals will no longer be fearsome and dangerous (Isaiah 11:6-9, page 141).
In other passages, animals serve as role models for obeying the will of God; we are invited to follow their example. For example, Isaiah compared the ox and donkey who know the master who feeds them, to people who do not recognize the blessings of God (Isaiah 1:3). Today, a donkey and an ox are often included in the nativity scenes some Christians recreate at Christmas in memory of Isaiah's words.

Anna

The name Anna means "grace." Those mentioned in the Bible:

-**Anna**, an 84-year-old woman who lived in the temple of Jerusalem, serving God day and night through prayer and fasting. Along with Simeon, she welcomed Jesus the first time he entered the Temple. Being a prophetess,* her heart recognized him as the Son of God (Luke 2:36-38).

-**Anna**, Mary's mother. We have no information in the Bible about Jesus's grandparents, but according to tradition, they were called Anna and Joachim.

-**Annas** the high priest. Annas was the high priest when Jesus was young; he was highly influential. He was the father-in-law of Caiaphas.* It was Annas who asked to see Jesus immediately after his arrest (John 18:13, page 371).

Annunciation

SEE MARY AND ANGEL.

Anna with Mary and Jesus

Apocalyptic Books

Apocalypse is from a Greek word meaning "revelation."
From 2nd century B.C. on, many books were written which are called apocalyptic. They are filled with extraordinary images, sometimes difficult to understand. According to the authors of these books, the world is in a lamentable condition because mankind allows itself to be dominated by Satan. However, the authors portend that God will re-establish his reign at the end of time, after an extraordinary war against the forces of Evil.* There will then be a final judgement* by God who will separate His followers from the nonbelievers. The followers of God will live with Him throughout eternity.
There are apocalyptic passages in the Old Testament in the book of Daniel (see pages 204-205).
The apocalyptic message of John in his book called Revelation in the New Testament, is in accordance with the phophecies in Daniel, but he insists that, despite present and future difficulties and persecution, the abundant life Christ offers us is already available in him. It is the only true life which is eternal.

Apocrypha

From a Greek word meaning "hidden." It is a technical term concerning the relationship of certain books to the Old Testament. All church denominations do not regard the Apocrypha in the same manner:
- For most denominations outside the Catholic Church, the Apocrypha books, such as the Deuterocanonical* books which the Catholics include in the Old Testament, are not approved for public reading during the worship service; these denominations do not consider the origin of the Apocrypha books divinely inspired by God. They are nevertheless, by some denominations, valued for private study and edification.

- For Catholics, the Apocrypha are books falsely attributed to prophets or apostles. They often contain errors. For example, the Gospel of Thomas probably written in the second century, refers to Jesus only as a sage who was also a teacher. Thomas records only the words of Jesus, and none of the events of his life, including the Passion. Another example is found in the Gospel of James. It invents such wonderful details of Jesus's childhood that the reader might wonder what happened to God's desire to become a man. Despite these problems, however, there might be information recorded in these books which can be enlightening from an historical perspective. Certain traditions from the first Christian communities may be recorded in the Apocrypha, as well as other details which simply help historians get a better understanding of the words and events presented in the four Gospels of the New Testament.

Apostasy

The condition of one who publicly denounces his faith* after having claimed to be a believer.

Apostle

Derived from the Greek verb meaning "to send."

In the book of Acts, the title of apostle first of all refers to the original twelve* Jesus chose to be with him (Mark 3:14, page 239). Their mission was to inform all men that the crucified Jesus of Nazareth had risen from the dead. Today, in the Catholic Church, when the bishops are called "successors of the apostles," this is referring to the Twelve and their mission.

In the Bible other people were also called apostles: Jesus (Hebrews 3:1), Andronicus and Junias, Roman Christians (Romans 16:7, page 432), Barnabas (Acts 14:14) and of course Paul, chosen by Christ to be the apostle of the gentiles. See "Who Has Seen the Resurrected Jesus?" page 438.

Aramaean

People from Syria and Mesopotamia. Abraham was called a "wandering Aramaean" (Deuteronomy 26:5). The Aramaic language became the common language in the entire Middle East. Some books of the Bible (such as Ezra and Daniel) were written partly in Aramaic. Jesus himself spoke this language. He calls his father Abba* (Mark 14:36, page 369). On the cross he recites the beginning of Psalm 22 in Aramaic (Matthew 27:46, page 380). Today some of the Christians in Turkey, Iraq or Iran still speak Aramaic and recite the Lord's Prayer in the language Jesus taught his disciples.

The apostles with Mary. Woodcarving - Munich. On Mary's left and right, Peter and John. Far right, James the Elder is recognizable by the shell of his hat.

The Ark introduced in the Temple.
" The Very Rich Hours of the Duke of Berry" - 15th century. Very whimsical vision of the Ark, represented as a 15th century church.

King Josiah celebrates Passover.
16th century manuscript. The sacrifice of the Lamb before the Ark is not portrayed realistically.

David before the Ark.
Germany - 19th century. Notice the two cherubims worshiping God. The Tablets of the written Law are visible, inlaid in the Ark.

Crossing the Jordan with the Ark.
Illustration in the Book of Joshua. Mozarabic Bible -10th century - Leon (Spain).

The Ark made of acacia wood, gold-plated inside and out. It is 3.75 ft long, 2.25 ft wide and 2.25 ft high.

Ark of the Testimony or Ark of the Covenant

Chest made in the times of Moses* to contain the Ten Commandments* which had been engraved on stone tablets.

- The Ark was kept under the tabernacle* (Exodus 40:16-21, page 78). Later, King David had it carried to Jerusalem (2 Samuel 6:12-19, page 107) to show that the twelve tribes were united by their obedience to God's Laws (Psalm 122, page 221).

- His son Solomon then built a magnificent Temple.* The Ark was hidden from the people and placed in the Most Holy Place where only the high priest was permitted to visit it on the day of Atonement.*

In 587 B.C., when Jerusalem was captured by Nebuchadnezzar (page 157), the Ark of the Testimony and the Tablets of the written Law were destroyed. The prophet Jeremiah announced that henceforth God would write His Law on the hearts of believers (Jeremiah 31:31-33, page 157). Some, however, could not accept the idea that the Ark was definitively

lost, and consequently people began claiming that Jeremiah had hid it in a cave of mount Nebo. There is something of this legend in 2 Maccabbees 2:1-12.

See illustration, pages 114-115.

Ascension

Chrisitan feast celebrated forty days after Easter commemorating the day that the resurrected Jesus was taken to be with God his Father in Heaven (Acts 1:4-11, page 400).

Since his Ascension, Jesus is no longer visible in the flesh, but he promises that Christians can experience his presence through faith (John 20:29, page 389). Jesus said: "For where two or three come together in my name, there am I with them." (Matthew 18:20, page 283. See also the illustration, pages 470-471.)

In his gospel, Luke mentioned the Ascension of Jesus as if he dated it to the same evening of His resurrection. He wanted to assert that once risen, Jesus could not return to the same physical life he was living before His death. He had already entered eternal life (see Ascension, page 392). But, in the Book of Acts, Luke emphasized another aspect of the ascension, more faithful to chronology. He indicated that Jesus appeared to his apostles throughout the forty days following Easter. Forty in the Bible often signifies a time of preparation, thus Luke asserted that Jesus took the time to prepare the apostles for their mission as witnesses of the Resurrection. Throughout these forty days of preparation, Jesus solidified their belief in his Resurrection (see pages 388 to 395).

Assumption

SEE MARY.*

Atonement

The word "atonement" is one of the few theological terms with primarily Anglo-Saxon roots. It means "a making at one," and signifies the process of gathering back into the fold those who are estranged. In the Old Testament, the word comes from the Hebrew word group, kpr, today written Kippur, meaning expiation. The Jews of the Old Testament observed the Day of Atonement, just as today's Jews do, on what is called Yom Kippur. For a ten-day period which begins with Rosh Hashanah—the Jewish New Year —they practice the "Ten Days of Penitence." This ten-day period spent in prayer and fasting culminates in the most solemn day of the year, Yom Kippur, the final day of atonement for their sins. In ancient times, the high priest chased into the desert a goat that supposedly bore all the sins of Israel. Sacrifices were also offered for the forgiveness* of sins (see 2 Maccabees 12:43-46,

Ascension. *Jean Fouquet - 15th century - Etienne Chevalieris Book of Hours - Museum of Chantilly. Fouquet illustrates the main elements cited in the book of Acts: cloud, angels addressing the apostles. He adds the presence of Mary and another woman, probably Mary Magdalene.*

page 182). They hoped that in doing so they would regain God's favor, and that He would forgive them all their infidelities.
Atonement was sometimes defined as suffering* necessary to obtain God's forgiveness, but this is a false notion. God has never bartered nor will ever barter His forgiveness for our suffering. His forgiveness is a grace* offered to us free of charge. Knowing how to accept his forgiveness is the essence of atonement.
SEE ATONEMENT COVER AND GRACE.

Atonement Cover (Mercy Seat)

Gold plate covering the lid of the Ark* of the Covenant. On the day of atonement,* it was the place where God was believed to be favorably disposed to forgiving His people.

Bust of Augustus.
British Museum - London.

Augustus

Additional name of Roman Emperor Caesar Octavian, adoptive son of Julius Caesar. It means "the venerable." Jesus was born under his reign (Luke 2:1, page 302).

Baal

The Hebrew noun means "master" or "possessor." It is sometimes used to name all the false gods (Hoseah 2:19, page 132). In the Old Testament, Baal was used as a proper name by the Canaanites for Hadad, the powerful storm-god. He was considered to be sovereign over nature.
When settling in the land of Canaan, the Hebrews, under the rule of Ahab, began to worship Baal, god of the farmers, instead of or in addition to worshiping YHVH* or God. They believed that YHVH was just a god of nomadic shepherds and not necessarily the

***Baal** wears a horned helmet.*
See page 122, note 2.

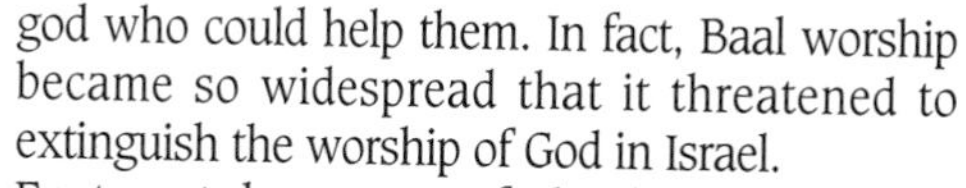

god who could help them. In fact, Baal worship became so widespread that it threatened to extinguish the worship of God in Israel.
Fortunately, some of the leaders of the Canaanites remained faithful to their Covenant with YHVH. One of these faithful leaders, Obadiah, took great risks to preserve the lives of many of YHVH's prophets during Ahab's reign. He was especially instrumental in helping the prophet Elijah who confronted and overthrew Baal's prophets in the celebrated contest on Mount Carmel. During that confrontation, he declared that YHVH was the only God. Later, fleeing for his life, Elijah would experience the tender mercy of YHVH in the gentleness of a breeze (see page 125).
SEE BEELZEBUB.

Baptism

Ancient cross-shaped Baptistery.
Crete.

The word baptism comes from a Greek verb meaning "to immerse."
The Bible alludes to several baptisms:
- In the Old Testament, the prophet Elisha invited the commander of the Syrian army, Naaman, to be immersed into the waters of the Jordan in order to be cleansed from the leper (2 Kings 5:10-14, page 127).
- According to the New Testament, John the Baptist preached "a baptism of repentance for the forgiveness of sins." It was a baptism with water in the Jordan river. Its aim was to prepare the coming of the One who would baptize with the Spirit.*

B

Baptistery covered in mosaics.
6th century - Bardo Museum - Tunis. Notice the Greek letters alpha and omega reproduced several times; we see also the first two Greek letters of the word Christ.

- The baptism of Jesus by John the Baptist is the model of the Christian baptism. It proclaims that, as God does with Jesus, God acknowledges us as His children: "This is my Son, whom I love."

Baptism is linked, in one way or another, to the gift of the Holy Spirit who, like the dove of the flood, speaks of a new creation (Matthew 3:16, page 258). Some think that John compares baptism to a new birth (John 3:3-8, page 338). For the apostle Paul, it is an immersion into death with Christ in order that, just as Christ was raised from the dead, we too, may live a new life (Romans 6:2-11).

Baptism is the first sacrament but Christians are divided as to its "efficiency." There are those for whom one becomes a Christian and a member of the Body of Christ through baptism. For others, baptism has a symbolic meaning which is linked to a prior spiritual experience.

In the first Christian churches, it was primarily adults who were baptized, either alone (Acts 8:36-38, page 412) or with all their families (Acts 10:44-48, page 416). Today, in certain churches, parents are invited to have their children baptized during the months following their births as a sign of the love of God which always comes first. Other churches baptize only young or adult believers who confess a personal experience of conversion to God.

SEE PURE.

Bartholomew's martyrdom.
Anonymous sculpture - Valladolid (Spain).

Barnabas

He was a Levite* whose real name was Joseph. His nickname means "son of encouragement" (Acts 4:36, page 406). He was known for his deep compassion and insight, was universally respected as a faithful follower of Christ. It was Barnabas who reconciled Saul, persecutor of Christians who became the great apostle Paul, to the apostles by convincing them of his sincerity and conversion (see page 419). In an episode involving his young cousin John, later called Mark, we see the extent of Barnabas' fidelity in his relationships. During an evangelical mission, Mark deserted the effort. Some time later, Paul and Barnabas prepared for a second journey, on which Barnabas wanted to include Mark. Paul was opposed but Barnabas stood firm, resulting in the two men parting company. Barnabas sailed for Cyprus with Mark by his side. Mark developed a powerful ministry as an evangelist, and was eventually affirmed by Paul himself. Barnabas is said to have died a martyr on his native island of Cyprus.

Bartholomew

He is one of the Twelve.* We find his name on each list of the twelve disciples, but he is otherwise not mentioned in the New Testament. He is generally acknowledged to be Phillip's friend, Nathanael, although complete certainty of this is not attainable. If he was one and the same person, his whole name would be Nathanael (God has given) *Bar Talmai* (son of Talmai). Tradition has it that he was a highly effective missionary in Persia, Armenia and Mesopotamia. He is believed to have been skinned alive.

Bathsheba

Wife of Uriah* the Hittite,* mother of Solomon. She was seduced by David while her husband

B

was at war (2 Samuel 11:1-17, page 109). The Gospel of Matthew alludes to her in the genealogy of Jesus (Matthew 1:6, page 254).

Beatitudes

Derived from the Latin word meaning "blessed" and "happy." Jesus began his famous Sermon on the Mount with what is referred to as the Beatitudes (Matthew 5:1-12, page 260). They are not to be viewed as a list of rules, but rather as truisms about those who live godly lives. We learn in the Beatitudes that despite persecution and difficulties, those who know that they are sons and daughters of God and thereby members of His Kingdom,* experience great joy. There are additional, similar truisms found throughout the Gospels (Matthew 16:17, page 281; Luke 1:45, page 301; Luke 10:23, page 316 ; John 20:29, page 389). The joy spoken of in the Beatitudes is a timeless gift from God, but it will be fully enjoyed in His Kingdom.

Beelzebub

In the Gospels, this word refers to the prince of demons* (Mark 3:22, page 240). It is a modification of the Hebrew expression Baal Zebub (Baal the Prince, or literally, god of the flies), which evolved into the name Beelzebub who is also called Satan.

Ben-Sira, Joshua

In Hebrew Ben means "son" just as Bar does in Aramaic. Joshua ben-Sira was a scribe* in Jerusalem. In approximately 190 B.C., he wrote a book of counsel in Hebrew called the Wisdom of ben-Sira. His goal was to convince his readers to embrace Jewish traditions which at that time were threatened to be replaced by Greek ones (see page 178). Some time later, his book was translated into Greek, retitled

Satan tempts Jesus.

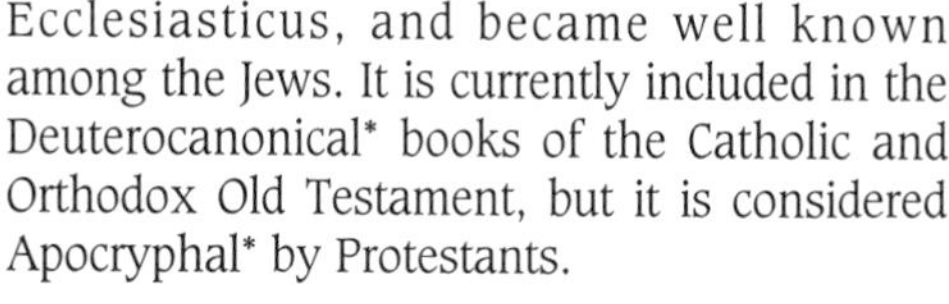

Ecclesiasticus, and became well known among the Jews. It is currently included in the Deuterocanonical* books of the Catholic and Orthodox Old Testament, but it is considered Apocryphal* by Protestants.

Bible

All the texts composing the Old and New Testament,* considered canonical* by the Christian Church.
The word Bible is derived from the name of the ancient Phoenician port of Byblus, whose name was based on the Greek diminutive biblos. Biblos means any kind of document written on papyrus. Since Byblus, the port, was a trading center for papyrus, the Greeks gave papyrus the name of the city where they bought it.
Christians consider the Bible to be the authoritative Word of God, written by human believers under the divine inspiration of the Holy Spirit.
SEE CANON.

Blasphemy

From a Greek word meaning "words that offend." Blasphemy is an insult towards God.

Blessing

To bless means "to bestow good." The New Testament sense of the word denotes both the bestowal of material and spiritual good, although God does not assure material success for everyone. What is assured is that when God bestows good, the results will always be fruitful in the way most needed for the particular situation or person. For Christians, the greatest blessing is to know God personally and to live in Covenant* with Him. (Deuteronomy* 30:15-20, page 85). It is to experience the certainty of being loved today and forever.

- We read also in the Bible that Christians are called on to bless God. This means that the Christian acknowledges God as the source of his or her entire life.

- Since the 3rd century, some Christians have practiced the ritual of blessing objects. This ritual is still performed by Catholics today. They do this not in an attempt to infuse an object with a magical power. Rather, by seeing the blessed object every day, they are thereby reminded to give thanks to God (see THANKSGIVING) and recall His greatness on a regular basis.

Body of Christ

This phrase has three different uses in the New Testament:

-The apostle Paul described a group of believers as "one body in Christ" and "body" in reference to a local church or the universal Church. Paul grasped this truth on the road to Damascus when the risen Christ asked him: "Why do you persecute me?" (Acts 9:4, page 413). Until that moment, he had been a greatly feared persecutor of Christians. Although Paul had never before met Jesus, he immediately understood that to harm Christians was to harm Jesus. He grasped that Christians were the Body of Christ, physical witnesses of the Good News of Jesus for all to see and follow (1 Corinthians 12:3-27, page 435).

-The human body of Jesus Christ. The reality of Christ's body is central to Christian doctrine: Jesus, who was God made man, physically lived among mankind for thirty-three years.

-The bread at the Last Supper over which Jesus spoke the words "This is my body." The words have been interpreted differently by Christians throughout history as "This symbolizes my sacrifice" and also "This is myself."

SEE CHURCH.

The ceremonial robe of the High Priest is described in detail in the book of Exodus. A pectoral (breastpiece) with twelve different gems for the twelve tribes of Israel was attached to the front of the robe.

Breaking of the Bread

SEE LAST SUPPER AND EUCHARIST.

Burnt Offering

SEE HOLOCAUST.

Caiaphas

Name meaning "the sage" given to Joseph, high priest from 18 to 36 A.D. Caiaphas was the son-in-law of Annas.* According to the apostle John, Caiaphas bore great responsibility for the death of Jesus (John 11:49-51, page 356). After Jesus was arrested he was presented to Caiaphas who sent him directly to Pilate to be condemned to death (John 18:28, page 373).

Canaan

Son of Ham, grandson of Noah. Canaan is the ancestor of both the Canaanites and the

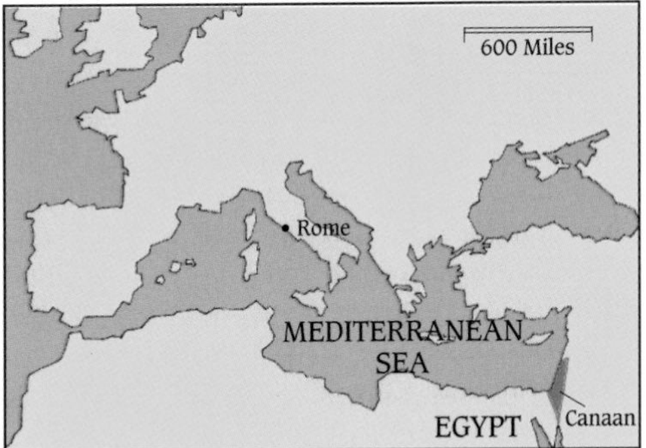

C

Egyptians. The territory of land called Canaan was promised by God to Abraham and his descendants. Canaan later became known as Israel, then Palestine.*

Canon, canonical

The term "Canon" comes from the Greek word meaning "a rule" or "a standard." The word has been used by Christians since the 4th century to denote the authoritative list of books belonging to the Old or New Testament of the Bible* to be used in public worship.

-Concerning the Old Testament: There has been a long history of theological controversy about the books which should be included in the Old Testament, and indeed, its Canon has not been easy to determine. Originally, in the synagogue,* the Jewish people read the Law (the Torah), the Psalms, writings of various prophets and other books. There was no official list. The texts which were read were written on separate scrolls and were not collected in a single book.

Then, in 70 A.D., the fall of Jerusalem brought about dramatic changes in the relationship between the Jews and the early Christians. The Jewish authorities established a definitive list of the books recognized as God's Word. This list was called the Canon of Jamnia, so named after the city where it had been established, and was comprised exclusively of books written in Hebrew.

The Christians abided by this list, but added to it a second one comprised of books generally written in Greek. After a period of disagreement about the contents of this second list, an historic division in the Christian Church occured at the Reformation in 1517. The church of Rome maintained that both lists should be included in the Old Testament. The first list, the Canon of Jamnia, was considered canonical. The second, considered deuterocanonical, today by the Catholic Church and a part of the Orthodox Church include the two books of Maccabees (pages 178 to 183), the Wisdom of Joshua ben-Sira (in Greek, Ecclesiasticus) (pages 199 to 201), the Wisdom of Solomon (pages 202 to 203), Judith, Tobit, the book of Baruch, and certain chapters of Daniel and Esther. The Protestant Church accepted only the first list as Canon, and do not print the Deuterocanonical books (apocrypha*) in their Bibles.

- Concerning the New Testament, things were much easier. From the beginning, all Christians acknowledged the four Gospels and the letters of Paul as inspired by God. There has been some discussions about Revelation, the epistle of James or one or another New Testament books, but since the 4th century, the Canon has been definitively fixed throughout the entire Christian Church as the twenty-seven books known today as the New Testament.

SEE ILLUSTRATION, PAGES 10-11.

Captivity

SEE EXILE.

The Pharisee and the publican
(Luke 18:9-14 page 328), image in a catechism. 1930.

Catechism

From a Greek verb meaning "instruction," basis for the Latin derivative meaning "religious instruction." In the early days of the Christian Church, the role of catechism was to clarify for newly converted Christians the kerygma,* the fundamental Gospel message of the apostles. Today, the word catechism refers to oral instruction about the fundamentals of Christianity using the Old and New Testament of the Bible (Luke 1:1-4, page 298).

Catholic

From a Greek word meaning "universal." The Apostle's Creed (page 460) and the Nicene Creed (page 461) define the Church founded by Jesus Christ using the adjective catholic, thereby meaning destined for all nations (Matthew 28:19, page 395).

C

Historical events led to calling the Christians acknowledging the Pope's authority Catholics, thus distinguishing them from other Christians.

Charity

In the Bible, the word refers to the love of God for mankind and of the love people can give to one another. God offers to supply His charity (His love) inside the human heart to enable people to love each other as Jesus does (1 Corinthians 12:31-13:8, page 437).
(SEE "THE LOVE OF GOD," PAGE 437.)

Cherubim

Plural for cherub and represented in the Old Testament as heavenly, symbolic beings. The Hebrews regarded cherubims as guardians of the sacred, such as the Tree of Life in Eden (Genesis 3:24, page 25). The Old Testament does not describe their appearance clearly, apart from being generally represented as winged creatures with hands and feet. The Hebrews imagined them as Assyrian spirits or genies, half men, half animals. When the Hebrews returned from Exile,* their faith having deepened, the visual representation of cherubim changed. They became angels* responsible for celebrating the glory of God rather than communicating with men.
Much later in history, a cherub is represented in Baroque paintings as the head of a child propelled by two wings.
SEE ARK OF THE COVENANT.

Child

Jesus asked his disciples* to be like children before God. He said that
children are capable of placing complete trust in their "Abba"*; they know that if they ask God for a fish, He will not give them a snake instead (Luke 11:10-13, page 319).

The Holy Face.
Icon - School of Rostov - 13th century.

Unfortunately, this child-like capacity to trust God often disappears. Jesus taught that the adult is more confident in his reasoning than in God's. His parable* of the lost son provided a good illustration of this tendency in human nature (Luke 15:11-32, page 321).
The self-confident older son opposed his father, but the younger brother retrieved the trusting heart of a child and returned to him. Through this parable, Jesus was making a larger point: To enter the Kingdom of God, we must adopt the heart of a child, a heart capable of having complete trust in the Father (Mark 10:13-16, page 247).

Christ

From a Greek word meaning "the anointed one," corresponds to the Hebrew word masiah–messiah. Christ and messiah have the same meaning. Although Jesus never denied being the Christ, the Messiah, he more often referred to himself using the Aramaic title the "Son of Man." He did this expressly: first, to dissociate himself from the popular definition of the role of an earthly king or messiah. Second, he wanted to present his own unique concept of messiah, one that described a king of future authority and vindication, not one of present political power (see MESSIAH).
On the other hand, after Jesus' resurrection, the apostles used the name Christ very often to speak of the risen Jesus (Acts 2:36, page 402). When they said that Jesus was Christ, they proclaimed that he who was crowned with thorns and nailed on a cross was risen. They announced that he was and is the King of Israel, although not as the former ancient messiahs* or christs of Israel were kings, but as the King of Lords, one and the same person who Isaiah had seen in his Temple (Isaiah 6:1-8, page 137).

In other books of the New Testament, the word Christ is very often used as a name added to Jesus: "and every tongue confess

that Jesus Christ is Lord" (Philippians 2:11, page 440). Hence, the title Christians* for all disciples of Jesus.

Christians

The apostle Luke places the first use of this name given to the disciples of Jesus Christ* in Antioch around the year 43 A.D. (Acts 11:26, page 418).

Christmas

Contraction of the Latin *dies natalis* "day of birth."

Christians began celebrating the birth of Jesus in the 3rd century. The Gospels do not give the exact date of his birth, so the Christians of Rome chose the 25th of December, the date when the days began to lengthen. They regarded this as a fitting symbol of Jesus being the "light for revelation to the Gentiles" (Luke 2: 32, page 305 and John 9:5, page 349): light is victorious over darkness. Thus, the Son of

God made man, will bring new joy to those who are walking in darkness. (Isaiah 9:1-6, page 140; see also A Star Rises, page 83).

SEE COMING, ADVENT, ANIMAL, HEROD THE GREAT.

Church

Since the 3rd century, the English word church (written with a lower-case c) is derived from the Greek word meaning "the Lord's house" and refers to a building; in the New Testament however, the word in Greek means a local congregation of Christians and never a building. Because of this, some Christian denominations today prefer to call their building a temple. In the New Testament, as well as today, the word can refer to the universal Church (the whole of all congregations) and to a local congregation (see symbols of faith, pages 460-461). Former local congregations referred to in the New Testament include the churches of Corinth, Rome, and Laodicea.

The Gospel of Matthew uses the word just just twice (Matthew 16:18, page 281), but the book of Acts, the Epistles,* and Revelation often speak of the Church as Jesus' chosen congregation. The Church of the New Testament, as begun by the Twelve,* was not entirely new: it inherited Israel's mission to bear witness for God throughout all nations.* Paul compared the New Testament Church to a branch grafted on the trunk of Israel. Because God is faithful to His Covenant with the people of Israel, He will love them forever. Today, after centuries of divisions often arising from theological differences of opinion, there are various denominations comprising the universal Christian Church.

The Church, in its entirety, is meant to be, among other things, a source of renewal and edification for Christians, as each member of the Body of Christ* ministers according to his or her gifts. The Church is also a continual witness for Christ, charged by him to "go into all the world and preach the good news" (Mark 16:15).

SEE BODY OF CHRIST AND PAGES 470-471.

C

Circumcision

Circumcision is a surgical procedure that partially or completely cuts off the foreskin of the male penis.
God chose this mark, visible on the human body, to symbolize His Covenant* with Abraham and his descendants. Thus every man and boy of the house of Abraham from that point on were to be circumcised (Genesis 17:10, page 40).
Jesus was circumcised eight days after his birth, just as John the Baptist was, in accordance with the Law (Luke 1:59 and 2:21, pages 302 and 304). The first disciples* of Jesus, being Jewish, were also circumcised. After Pentecost, Gentiles began converting to Christianity. Circumcision, on the other hand, was often poorly viewed in the Gentile community, and the Jerusalem Church accepted the first Gentile converts on an equal basis with Jewish converts without the necessity of being circumcised. However, some of the Christian Jews, the ultra-Judaic party, demanded circumcision for all converts, Gentiles included. After much discussion, the disciples and elders decided not to impose this obligation on new Christians. They proclaimed that one becomes a Christian through faith* in the risen Jesus, not through circumcision (Acts 15:4 - 20 , page 421).

Cloud

In the Bible, the cloud is an element of the sky and a symbolic residence of God (see meditation page 400). In the Old Testament, when a cloud descended towards men, it was a sign of the Lord's "visit." It signaled His presence even though He was not visible (see Exodus 34:5, page 76).
In the Gospel, the cloud is mentioned at the moment of the Transfiguration (Mark 9:7, page 247) and the Ascension (Acts 1:9, page 400), thus signifying the divinity of Jesus. When Jesus appeared before the Sanhedrin,* he used the cloud to reveal his divinity by saying: "You will see the Son of Man... coming on the clouds of heaven" (Matthew 26:64, page 373).

The creative hand of God emerging from the cloud.

Coming

SEE ADVENT.

Commandment

The book of Exodus refers to the "ten commandments" whose Hebrew meaning is "ten words." The Ten Commandments were given to teach people how to lead a life with God at the center (Exodus 20:1-17, page 71).
In the New Testament, Jesus revealed that all the Commandments of the first Covenant were summarized in the two Commandments of love: to love God and to love one's neighbor (Mark 12:28-34, page 252).
The apostle John expressed the essence of Jesus' message in the celebrated verse: "Love one another as I have loved you." (John 15:12, page 360). John was not suggesting that we place loving our neighbors above loving God; he suggested that by loving our neighbor, we are demonstrating our love for God (see John's First Epistle, page 448).

In the 1950s-1960s, Hollywood movies were frequently based on Bible stories. Here, Charlton Heston as Moses in Cecil B. de Mille's "The Ten Commandments" (1955).

Communion

We read in the Book of Acts that the disciples* of Jesus devoted themselves to fellowship, that is to say, to live in brotherly communion (Acts 2:42, page 403). In fact, in John's Gospel, he tells us that it is impossible to be a disciple of Jesus without seeking this common-union among brothers. Fraternal love is one of the great Commandments* Jesus gave (John 15:12, page 360). Part of that brotherly communion was and is celebrated in what is sometimes referred to during a worship service as communion, or the breaking of bread. It is a re-enactment of the Last Supper that Christ had with his apostles. Because Jesus considered each person a temple of his presence (1 Corinthians 3:16, page 434), he taught that Christians assembled together are his Body.* The breaking of bread, or communion, also serves as a witness for Christ for everyone to see. Some Christians believe that the bread eaten during communion is literally the embodiment of the presence of Christ; others consider the bread a symbolic reminder of his sacrifice.

Compassion

SEE MERCY.

Confirmation

SEE PENTECOST.

Consecrate

From a Latin derivative meaning "to set aside as sacred," specifically to dedicate a person or an object to God. When God gave Moses the Ten Words (Commandments) of Life, He reminded him that He had consecrated or set aside the seventh day for rest. Thus, He commanded Moses to consecrate the seventh day, the Sabbath, to God (Exodus 20:11, page 71).

Paul's conversion.
A. Berruguete (1490-1561). Valladolid (Spain). The sculptor represented Paul surrounded by Heavenly light (Acts 9:3, page 413) just before he fell to the ground, hearing the voice of Jesus.

Conversion

Derived from the Hebrew word meaning "turn" or "return." In the Bible, conversion involves an act that signals a change in direction, a change of heart, a transformation. There are different types of conversion:
- The conversion of the nonbeliever, changing from nonbelief in the existence of God to belief in Him as a result of an encounter with the living God.
- The conversion of a religious person or one who adheres to the form of religion but has no personal relationship with God through Christ, changing from a false or inaccurate understanding of God to knowledge* of God as He really is. An example of this is Saul* of Tarsus, the zealous religious scholar who became the zealous Christian Paul* the Apostle after his encounter with the risen Christ on the road to Damascus (Philippians 3:5-14, p.441).
- The day-to-day conversion of the Christian, evolving into a disciple who accepts God's counsel through praying and reading the Bible. The Bible teaches that this evolution in character is brought about by the Holy Spirit who reveals, among other things, attitudes to be corrected and judgments to be discarded. Consequently, the Holy Spirit is in the continual role of forming the Christian into the likeness of Christ.

Covenant

It has always been God's desire to establish a covenant, or alliance, with mankind; His desire for a covenant is in evidence from the first to the last page of the Bible. For example, in the account of the Creation* in the book of Genesis,* we are told that God created man in His own image to establish a relationship with him (Genesis 1:26-27, page 21). Later, we learn that He re-established a Covenant with mankind through Noah (Genesis 9:8-15, page 30) before choosing Abraham* to make a

C

covenant with all his descendants (Genesis 17:3 - 20, page 39).
We read in the book of Exodus* that Moses asked the people of God, at last liberated from Egyptian slavery, to live according to God's Covenant with them. The Lord committed Himself personally to them by saying: "I will be your God and you will be my People." The people then promised to follow the commandments of the Law* which explained how to live in accordance with God's Covenant (see Exodus 24:3-8, page 74).
Later, the prophets* reminded the people of their Covenant with their faithful God. The prophets frequently compared the Covenant to marriage, saying that God's love for His people was like a husband's love for his wife. Unfortunately, God's people were often unfaithful and turned away from God, with great misery resulting. Then in the book of Jeremiah, we read that the prophets Jeremiah and Ezekiel announced that God would make a new Covenant (Jeremiah 31:31-34, page 157 and Ezekiel 36:25-28, page 165). This Covenant would be fulfilled by Jesus. Today, during the celebration of the Lord's Supper, Christians often repeat the words of Christ*: *" This is my blood, the blood of the new and eternal Covenant, which is poured out for many."* (See page 366).

On the Sinai, Joshua close to him, Moses receives God's Tablets of the written Law. Bible of the 9th century, Perugia. In a sign of respect, Moses's hands are covered with his coat. Moses is sometimes portrayed receiving the tablets with bare hands (see illustrated frame, pages 71-79).

Creator, Creation

Calling God the Creator means that He has always been at the origin of all things, and will be forever. God never stops creating. The writing style of the authors of the Bible varies greatly in describing the Creation. Notice, for example, the stylistic variation among the authors of Genesis 1 and 2 (pages 20 23), Job 38:8-18 (page 196), Psalm 8 (page 211). None of these documents claimed to be scientific explanations or descriptions; they simply described the world as it was in those days (see illustration, page 32-33), without trying to explain how it was created.

On the other hand, the Bible seeks to reveal why God is Creator: God creates in order to form an alliance (to make a Covenant*) with each person. When God, the Eternal,* establishes a Covenant, it is forever; our physical death does not break the alliance He forms with us. This means that when we die, faith in God, the Creator, promises eternal life in His presence with the hope or future resurrection. (2 Maccabees 7:22-29, page 181).

Creeds

In the first centuries of the Church, Christians wrote fixed formulas which summarized their faith. They confessed outloud these brief statements of faith, called creeds, during public celebrations, particularly at baptisms (see pages 460-461).
The Latin word credo means "I believe," which are the first two words of the Apostles' and Nicene Creed. The creeds of faith were carefully composed so that all Christians, when proclaiming them, recognize that they share the same faith.
Today Catholics, Protestants, and Orthodox accept the Nicene Creed (page 461).

Ecumenical Council of Nicea (325) *presided over by emperor Constantin, surrounded by predominately oriental bishops. At his feet, Arius, whose doctrine was banned. Byzantine fresco - Monastery of the Meteors - Greece.*

Cross

The torture on the cross has Persian origins. It was widespread among all of antiquity as the most cruel and degrading of deaths., and was practised in different ways. The Roman philosopher, Seneca, who lived during the first century A.D., described the horror: "I see crosses before my eyes, not all of the same type, but changing according to the master who had them made: some hang their victims head down, others impale them, others spread their arms on gallows." Sadduceans* went to great length to have Jesus crucified. The Bible states that hanging a man on a tree signifies a curse of God (Deuteronomy 21:22-23). Thus, by publicly displaying Jesus hung on the tree of the cross, the Sadduceans had hoped to demonstrate that he was not sent by God (see "Tortuous Hearts," page 371). Jesus accepted this gruesome torture to demonstrate the opposite: the depth of God's love for mankind.
SEE SCANDAL AND REVELATION.

Sacramentary of Gellone. Manuscript, 8th century.

Odilon Redon.
Christ on the Cross (about 1910), Paris - Orsay Museum.

Painted wooden cross.
South American artisan.

Curse

Generally defined, it is the contrary of a blessing*; to curse is to speak evil* against someone or something.
Early in their history, the Hebrew* people believed that God's curse wished them harm. Soon, however, the prophets revealed that God loved them like a "father with a mother's heart" (Hosea 11:1-9, page 134). God's curse, in the biblical sense of the word, was His denunciation of sin. It was misunderstood by a disobedient people. For the rebel of the law, it was perceived as an attempt to harm him. For the faithful, God's denunciation of their sin was rightly understood as an implementation of His Covenant. It was perceived as an act of love and the promise of life, because it revealed evil. Evil was exposed enabled the faithful to turn away from its deadly consequences (Deuteronomy 30:15 - 20, page 85).
SEE FORGIVE.

David

Born in Bethlehem, in the tribe of Judah,* David was Jesse's youngest son. Shepherd and musician, he was anointed by Samuel, a sign that God had chosen him to be the second king of Israel (1 Samuel 16:10-13, page 100). After the death of Saul, David's father-in-law, he officially assumed the throne as king of the twelve tribes of Israel (from about 1010 to 970 B.C.). He conquered Jerusalem and claimed it as as his capital (see page 106), and had the Ark* of the Covenant installed there.
David had several wives, and his sons fought over his succession. One of his sons, Absolom, tried in vain to take over his father's throne while he was still alive. (see pages 111 to 113) in the end, David appointed Solomon, the second son of his wife Bathsheba, to succeed him.
It was through the lineage of David that Jesus was born. The prophet Nathan had prophesied that through David, God's promise of a messiah would be carried out: "I will raise up your offspring to succeed you, who will come from your own body, and I will establish his kingdom." (2 Samuel 7:12, page 109). Consequently, the prophet Isaiah later prophesied that "a small branch will come out of Jesse's stump," a messiah* after the Lord's heart (page 141). The birth of Jesus, the Messiah, was the fulfillment of this prophecy (Luke 1:32-33, page 300).
David is credited as the author of the book of Psalms.* His name appears fifty times in the New Testament.
See illustration, pages 114-115.
SEE MESSIAH.

David, the musician.
Santiago de Compostella Cathedral (Spain) 12th century. Amos asserted that David invented musical instruments (Amos 6:5, page 129). The sculptor may have remembered this.

Deacon

From the Greek word diakonos meaning "minister," "servant." In the first Christian communities, the appellations deacon, presbyter (priest), episcope (bishop), do not correspond to the specific functions as they do today in some Christian churches. In the New Testament, the word deacon itself carries no trace of a technical meaning relating to specialized functions, although they appeared to be an officially recognized group in the Church who acted as servants of the elders. Today, some Christian churches appoint a staff of deacons modeled after the account of the seven men chosen to serve the Grecian Jews (Acts 6:1-7, page 408), although the texts do not directly name them as deacons. Appointed to help the widows by the laying on* of hands, those seven men also preached the Word of God, and baptized.
Other churches today define the role of a deacon according to Paul's teaching in his letter to the Romans. He acknowledged the role of deacon as a special gift, parallel with other gifts such as prophecy and government, to be exercised by those who have it. He cited Phoebe as an example of someone specially gifted as a deaconess. (Romans 16:1, page 432).
SEE STEPHEN.

Death

In the Bible, the word "death" has two meanings.
- Physical death that a believer in Christ will experience in order to be resurrected and live in the Kingdom* of God. This death is not to be feared (Matthew 10:28, page 270, and John 11:25, page 354).
- Spiritual death, that occurs by refusing to make a Covenant with God, who is the source of life. Jesus taught that spiritual death is to be feared above all things (Matthew 10:28, page 270). Man can avoid this, however, because Jesus promised that "whoever lives and believes in me will never die" (John 11:26, page 354).

Decalogue

From the Greek *deka logoï* : "the ten words." It refers to the Ten Words of Life (the Ten Commandments) given by God to Moses (Exodus 20:1-17, page 71).
SEE COMMANDMENT.

Demon

Third Temptation of Christ.
Matthew 4:8-10, page 259.
"The Very Rich Hours of the Duke of Berry" - 15th century.
Chantilly Museum.

This word is often used in the plural. The demons are Satan's* acolytes, spiritual beings hostile to God and humans. Often presented as angels who have turned their backs on God and who try to lead people into Evil.*
SEE DEVIL, POSSESSED AND THE COMMENTS ON PAGE 241.

Deuterocanonical

SEE CANONICAL.

Deuteronomy

Name given to the fifth book of the Bible, meaning "the second law." It is most likely the book that King Josiah and his secretary, Shafane, found in the Temple in 622, and on which they based their massive religious reformation (see page 148). Deuteronomy summarizes many parts of the books of Exodus* and Numbers,* but with a more approachable tone of voice. It encouraged the people of Israel to live faithfully in Covenant* with God (30:10-20, page 84), and to love God "with all your heart and with all your soul and with all your strength" (6:4-5, page 84).

Devil

From the Greek diabolos meaning "divider," "slanderer." The word "Devil" is used in the Greek translation of the Bible (see page 203) to refer to the one called Satan,* "the adversary," in the Hebrew translation. The Devil or Satan is considered the prince of demons.* Both words are used in the Gospels of the New Testament.
SEE BEELZEBUB, EVIL.

"Tell these stones to become bread"
(Matthew 4:3, page 259). Church of Saint-Pierre-de-Chauvigny - 12th century. The sculptor recalls that according to the Bible, the Devil is a fallen angel, therefore he is shown with wings.

Diaspora

Greek word meaning "a scattering," "dispersion." Can refer to the Jews scattered in the non-Jewish world after the Babylonian captivity or the places in which they lived.
Most Jews of the Diaspora spoke Greek and had forgotten Hebrew. When they came to Jerusalem on a pilgrimage, they were called Hellenists. The Jews of the Diaspora were the ones present at the Pentecost event (Acts 2:5-11, page 401).
During Jesus' lifetime, there were approximately one million Jews in the Parthian empire (Babylon); one million in Egypt, with two hundred thousand in Alexandria where the Bible had been translated into Greek (see page 203); between two and three million in the rest of the Roman Empire; and two million in the land of Israel.
See pages 232-233.

Disciple

From Latin meaning "pupil," corresponding to the Greek word meaning "to learn," thus one who follows a master to receive his teaching. "To follow Jesus" or "to become his disciple" have the same meaning.

Dove

Only bird to be offered as a sacrifice* in the Temple (Luke 2:24, page 304, and Mark 11:15, page 250).

Dove *representing the Holy Spirit.*

E

Two biblical accounts spotlight the dove. In the account of the great flood of Noah, the dove flew over the floodwaters which had destroyed the world condemned as sinful by God. The dove then returned to Noah with a freshly plucked olive leaf, a sign that God had created a new world (Genesis 8:8-12, page 29). In the account of the baptism of Jesus, the Spirit of God is represented by a similar dove. The dove signified the inauguration by the Holy Spirit of Jesus' ministry, and as well symbolized the baptism of the Holy Spirit that would give new and eternal life to any person who would follow Christ. Followers of Christ would become Sons of God (Matthew 3:13-17, page 258).

The baptism of Christ.
Daphni mosaic (Greece).
11th century.

Easter

SEE PASSOVER.

Edomites

Descendants of Edom, nicknamed Esau, Isaac's son and Jacob's brother; Edom was known for his red hair. The Edomites first settled in the south of current Jordan, then, driven by historic events, finally established themselves in the area of Hebron.

During Greek occupation, they readily submitted to Antiochus Epiphanes's authority (see page 178). Abandoning Qos, their national god, for Zeus, the Edomites adopted Greek customs and were called Idumeans. The most famous Idumean in the Bible is Herod* the Great.

Elijah in the desert.
16th century icon - Russia.
Elijah fed by a raven.
Illustration of an event
that took place before he went to
Zarephath (see page 122).

Elders

In the Jewish culture, elders were heads of the family, sages, who ran a Diaspora* village or a Diaspora community. They were the synagogue* officials.

We read in the New Testament* that Paul* the apostle instituted elders when founding churches. Their mission was to take care of the community, and to preside over the communion meal and the "breaking of bread" in memory of Jesus (1 Corinthians 11:24, page 434).

In Greek the word elder is Presbuteros, which is the origin of the word "priest" and "presbyterian" in English.

Elijah

Prophet in the 9th century B.C., successfully defended the followers of the Lord against those of Baal* (see pages 122/124). In a celebrated passage in the Old Testament, he encountered God in the gentleness of a light breeze (1 Kings 19:1-13, page 125).

The Bible teaches that Elijah never experienced a physical death; he was borne up bodily on a chariot of fire to rejoin God. This account foreshadowed the bodily Resurrection of Christ and served to build faith in the reality of resurrection*: if God could save Elijah from death, would He not do the same for His faithful followers?

In the Old Testament,* Elijah and Moses* shared a great desire to see God with their eyes. In an extraordinary account, God does indeed appear to them on a mountain (1 Kings 19:9-13, page 125). In the Gospels of the New Testament, Elijah and Moses appear at the time of the Transfiguration (Mark 9:2-8, page 246). Their presence confirmed that Jesus is the Son of God.

See illustration, pages 188-189.

Ephraim

Son of Joseph and grandson of Jacob-Israel; he becomes, with his brother Manasseh, father of one of the twelve tribes of Israel (see page 52, note 1).

At the time of the division of God's people into two kingdoms, the tribe of Ephraim played a significant role in the history of Israel.* Their role thus privileged them in certain ways; the name Ephraim was often used to refer to the entire Northern Kingdom (Hoseah 6:4, page 133).

See TRIBE and the map, page 511.

Epiphany

From a Greek word meaning "appearance" or "heavenly manifestation."
-Since he considered himself as a manifestation of Zeus, the Greek King Antiochus IV was nicknamed Antiochus Epiphanes (see page 178).
- Christians celebrate the manifestation of God's Son to the world under the name Epiphany. This liturgical celebration was first held in the 4th century in the East, and refered to the three events in the life of Jesus:
1. The visit of the Magi* (Matthew 2:1-12, page 255).

"Having been warned in a dream not to go back to Herod, the Magi returned to their country by another route." (Matthew 2:12, page 256). an Autun capital - 12th century.

2. The baptism of Jesus by John the Baptist during which the Holy Spirit appeared and God the Father designated Jesus as his beloved son (Matthew 3:16-17, page 258).
3. The first sign Jesus performed at Cana in Galilee to demonstrate his divinity (John 2:1-12, page 336).
Today, in the occidental Christian Church, Epiphany is celebrated January sixth or the closest Sunday to this date.

Epistle

From the Greek word meaning "letter" or "message." The New Testament* contains twenty-one epistles or letters written by the apostles. Thirteen are attributed to Paul; the epistle to the Hebrews is generally attributed to the work of one of his collaborators (see page 429). The remaining seven epistles were called by the early Church the "Catholic" or "Universal" epistles because they did not address a specific Christian congregation as Paul's letters did. This group includes James* (see page 444), Jude,* first and second Peter (see pages 446 to 447), and all three letters of John (see page 448). Their impact was intended to be more universal in nature (see catholic).

Paul dictating his letter to the Romans to his stenographer, Tertius (Romans 16:22, page 432).

Esau

Jacob's* brother and ancestor of the Edomites*; in Hebrew his name means "the hairy."

Essenes

A Jewish religious community which was formed around 150 B.C.; according to the most reliable sources they lived near a type of monastery at Qumran on the shores of the Dead Sea. The Essenes did not associate with other Jews, nor did they go to the Temple. Instead, they followed an internally prescribed set of rituals, one of which was a daily bath of purification.* They spent long hours copying the books of the Bible and writings of their own onto parchment. No further accounts have been found about the Essenes after 70 A.D., but we do know that before they dispersed, they stored their parchments into clay jars

Piece of manuscript. *1st century B.C.. Excerpts of Psalms 31, 25 and 33, found in a cave near Qumran.*

sealed with lids and hid them in nearby caves. Historians have yet to fully understood why. In 1947, a young Bedouin shepherd discovered a few scrolls. The ensuing excavations undertaken from 1949 to 1956 uncovered six hundred scrolls scattered in eleven caves. They were written in Hebrew or in Aramaic (see ARAMAEAN); approximately a fourth of them were biblical texts, and the rest were Essene writings. They became known as the Dead Sea Scrolls.
See illustration, pages 10-11.

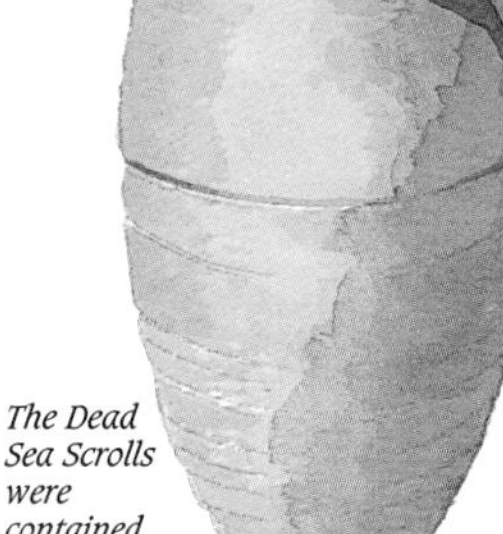

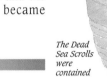

The Dead Sea Scrolls were contained in similar jars.

Eternal

Of the various names for God in Hebrew, one is El Olam which means the Everlasting God (Genesis 21:33). El Olam is eternal: He has always existed, He will exist forever, He is the origin of all things. He revealed this to Moses by disclosing another of His names, Yahweh, which means "I Am the One who Is" (Exodus 3:14, page 58). Jesus called himself by the same name, but in a shorter form meaning "I Am" (John 8:58, page 349).
The eternity of God is revealed in everything He is and everything He does. For example, we read in the Bible that God is forever faithful (Hoseah 2:21-22, page 132, and Psalm 100:5, page 218). His love is forever invincible (Isaiah 9:6, page 140). And as the source of Eternal Life, He will resuscitate* all His followers since death is no obstacle to His omnipotent love.
God's love for an individual continues forever. Consequently, when Christians worship God, they are thanking Him for His eternal presence in their lives, for His acts of love past, present, and future.
SEE ALPHA AND OMEGA.

Eternal Life

SEE ETERNAL AND RESURRECTION.

The risen Christ.
Sculpture by a contemporary artist. Audience room Paul VI - Vatican.

Eucharist

Derived from the Greek *eucharistia* meaning thanksgiving*; used by Anglicans and Catholics. This word in the Bible is not used to refer to the meal of the New Covenant instituted by Jesus. That meal was called the Lord's Supper (1 Corinthians 11:20, page 434), or "the breaking of bread" (Acts 2:42, page 403), but the Eucharist entered into the Catholic and Anglican Church vocabulary to mean the same thing.
During this meal, the death and Resurrection of Jesus were and still are commemorated (Luke 22:19, page 366). For the Christian today, it is an opportunity to give the greatest of thanks for the gift of eternal life. Through Jesus, with him and in him, Christians throughout the ages give glory to the Father, in the oneness of the Holy Spirit. They thank him for having sent His son, the Savior of the World (John 3:17, page 338), who gives himself completely to those who believe in him (John 10:52-58, page 345). For Catholics, "celebrate the Eucharist" has the same meaning as "celebrate mass." The word eucharist is sometimes used to refer to the hosts consecrated by the priest during mass. It is also called eucharistic bread; eucharistic reserve refers to the hosts laid in the Tabernacle.* These expressions emphasize the fact that through the communion* of his body, as represented by the Eucharist, Jesus wants to help each Christian lead a life which is, in itself, glorifying to God and a daily offering of thanksgiving and praise.
SEE MEMORIAL.

Eve

Name in Hebrew meaning "the living," given to the first woman in the account of the Creation (Genesis 3:20, page 25).

E

Evil

Evil is anything that leads a person away from God. The Bible teaches that God is separate from all evil and is in no way responsible for it. He permits it in the universe, yet He overrules it and uses it toward His own righteous purposes.
The Bible sometimes refers to evil as the cunning and the wicked. It bears many different names such as the Devil,* Satan,* the Snake,* the Dragon, the Adversary, the Enemy, the Prince of Darkness, and the Tempter. The celebrated story of Job in the Old Testament provides a rich, classic example of a man who successfully struggled against the temptation of evil (see pages 194-197). In the New Testament, Jesus was definitively victorious over the forces of evil. On the cross, despite his unimaginable suffering, his heart was filled with love for all of mankind and for his Father (see Luke 23:33-43, page 378). Among other things, his Resurrection demonstrates to believers of all time that love is stronger than evil. The cross provides conclusive proof that any believer in Christ can be victorious over evil by depending on him. Earlier in his ministry, Jesus demonstrated this when he invited Peter to walk on the sea (Matthew 14:22-33, page 278).

Exile

Period of sixty years in the 6th century B.C. during which the Jewish were deported from the Promised Land* of Israel.
Beginning in 598 B.C., Nebuchadnezzar sent part of Jerusalem's inhabitants into captivity in Babylon. He did this again in 587 B.C., the year of the Temple's destruction, and yet again in 582 B.C. After a period of great spiritual destitution (Psalm 137, page 225), the exiled Jews, with the help of the prophets including Ezekiel and the "third Isaiah" (see pages 160-172), experienced a deepening of their faith. They discovered that God is faithful, even in a foreign land, and that His presence among them was not dependent upon the existence of a temple. The Jews* understood that a genuine relationship with God did not lie in the rituals they performed, such as the sacrifice of animals, but that it lay in the readiness of the heart to receive God's love (Psalm 51:18-19, page 216). The Exile ended in 538 B.C. Cyrus, king of Persia and conqueror of Babylon, allowed the exiled Jews to return to their land of origin (see page 173).
Interestingly enough, some of the Jews did not return. They had learned to live their faith outside their land,* thus felt no urgency to return. This marked the beginning of their dispersion in many lands, known as the Diaspora.*
SEE REVELATION AND PAGES 146-147.

GOD ALSO SPEAKS ON FOREIGN SOIL

The Hebrews,* like all the neighboring tribes, often made a very strong connection between God and their land. Their God was the God of the country of Israel. This explained why Naaman took with him some soil from Israel to enable him to pray to the Lord in Syria (2 Kings 5:17, page 127). To their surprise, God revealed Himself profoundly on foreign soil, and, indeed, it was outside their native Israel that the faith of the Jewish people deepened:
- the Covenant between God and His people was made on Mount Sinai (Exodus 3:1-12, page 56 and 19:1-6, page 69);
- Elijah discovered the gentleness of God on this same mountain (1 Kings 19:8-13, page 125);
- the Exile* was a time of intense revelation. The scribes* wrote many pages of the Bible. God's people realized that an authentic relationship with the Father was rooted in being fed by his Word, not by going to the Temple*;
- Jesus himself left Israel. He visited Decapolis (Mark 4:35, page 241) and the land of Tyre and Sidon (Matthew 15:21, page 279). He announced the founding of his Church in Caesarea Philippi (Matthew 16:13, page 281). SEE LAND.

Exodus

Name of the second book of the Bible. When we specify the Exodus, we are referring to the forty years the Jewish people spent in the desert after their escape from Egypt.
The Bible teaches that God deemed forty years a necessary allotment of time to transform His people. They had been

recalcitrant, rebellious slaves and yet during their forty years in the desert, they became an organized, obedient people living in Covenant* with God. The Exodus ended in approximately 1250 B.C. when the tribes* settled in the land of Canaan.*

SEE COMMANDMENT AND DECALOGUE.
See illustration, pages 86-87.

Ezekiel

Priest of Jerusalem, exiled* to Babylon in 598 B.C. Five years later he received his call as prophet. At one point, he became mute, signifying that God had had enough of speaking through him to a people who would not listen. He regained his voice the following day at the announcement of Jerusalem's destruction in 587 B.C. His message was then filled with hope.* He prophesied that God's people would not disappear, that God would raise them from the graves (Ezekiel 37:1-14, page 165), then return them to the land of Israel. There the people would live a new Covenant* with God.

See illustration, pages 188-189.

"The hand of the Lord was upon me..."
(Ezekiel 37:1, page 165). Fresco of the synagogue in Doura Europos (current Syria) - 3rd century A.D. Damascus Museum. The painter shows the beginning of the vision of the dry bones.

Ezra

Jewish priest born in Babylon during the Exile.* His name means "God is help." He arrived in Jerusalem in 458 B.C., charged with the task of enforcing the uniform observance of the Jewish law. This reformation led to the contested expulsion of foreign spouses (Ezra 10:1-3, page 175). Ezra conducted the feast of the renewal of the Covenant* (Nehemiah 8:1-12, page 176).

Faith

The word faith in the Old Testament is often expressed by the words "believe," "trust," or "hope"; in the New Testament, the word faith itself is used abundantly. According to its biblical meaning, faith is the attitude that allows an individual to have complete trust in Christ, and Christ alone for one's salvation. Although faith requires accepting certain facts, it is not merely accepting these facts as true: faith is trusting the Person Christ. Indeed, the Bible teaches that it is a gift of God that only those with the heart attitude of a child* are able to receive. The gift of faith enables the heart to believe that God is alive, and convinces it to live in harmony with Him. Thus, faith enable the Christian to follow the One they know* through the signs of His presence, without ever seeing Him (John 20:29, page 389). In the book of Exodus, Moses used a provocative image to clarify this faith in an invisible God who nonetheless makes His presence known. He wrote that, for now, we are able to see only God's back (Exodus 33:18-23, page 76). After we die and enter into Eternal Life, we will be permitted to see His face. Until the Christian is united with God in Eternal Life, faith must battle against false images of God. Paul wrote that it is through the guidance of the Holy Spirit that we recognize the true God and call Him "Abba" (Romans 8:15, page 431). Through the presence of the Holy Spirit in our hearts, we can, with unshakeable faith, proclaim "Jesus is Lord" (1 Corinthians 12:3, page 435).

Father

SEE ABBA.

Fear of the Lord

There are numerous words to denote fear in the Bible. One of the most common, however, is the Hebrew form meaning "reverence." In this meaning, to fear the Lord is considered a gift of the Holy Spirit (Isaiah 11:2, page 141), as our fear (reverence) indicates that we are indeed experiencing His presence.

Although the word fear is not employed, the account of the burning bush is a perfect example of fear of the Lord (Exodus 3:1-12, page 56). In a state of reverent fear, Moses removed his sandals and hid his face. He realized that we are not to use God, we are to serve Him. Yet despite his state of reverence, he was still able to speak with God and, in fact, they had a discussion. Thus we can glean that the fear he experienced was not at all of the petrifying variety.

The fear of the Lord is not fright since it leads to knowing* He who Is love. The Bible teaches that love casts out fear (1 John 4:18, page 448). Only a false conception of God, one conceiving Him to be full of harshness, could lead to fright and panic.

M. Civitali (1436-1501) - Angel in worship - Lucca (Italy). Angels who continually see the face of the Father in heaven (Matthew 18:10, page 283), live in perpetual adoration.

Flesh

In the Bible, the Greek and the Hebrew word most often does not intend to mean the body, but the whole man, with all his abilities, but also with the sense that the flesh is fragile and mortal. For example:

- When John wrote in his Gospel: "and the Word became flesh," he meant that the Son of God became human and thus mortal (John 1:14, page 334).
- When Jesus told Peter: "this was not revealed to you by man..." Jesus is indicating that Peter had received his insight about Jesus being the Christ through divine revelation and not through human influences, as they had not been sufficient to understand his genuine identity (Matthew 16:17, page 281).
- When Jesus instructed the disciples to eat his flesh and drink his blood (John 6:53, page 345), he meant that just as one eats and drinks in order to maintain a physical existence on earth, so it is necessary to appropriate Christ to have Eternal Life.

***Detail from painting by** Van der Weyden- (around 1435-40), **depicting Mary,** the mother of Jesus. Flanders. Saint-Petersbourg Hermitage Museum.*

Foreign women

In some Bible accounts, we read of a suspiciousness and distrust of foreign women (Ezra 9:7-10:3, page 174). In others, they are revered, and presented as outstanding examples of faith in God. Among the most famous are Tamar, Rahab, and Ruth. In his Gospel, Matthew includes Rahab in the genealogy of Jesus (see page 254).

Tamar was a Canaanite. She married the eldest son of Judah, one of the ancestors of the twelve tribes.* Although she was a widow with no children, she never gave up hope to provide descendants for her tribe. In the end, her hope was fulfilled (Genesis 38). **Rahab** was a harlot who lived in Jericho. She took a great risk in hiding two Hebrew scouts (spies) from her people who wanted to kill them. By marrying one of the spies, she became an ancestor of David.

Ruth was a Moabitess who lived in the time of the Judges. She married a Hebrew from the tribe of Judah. After her husband's death, she decided to follow her mother-in-law to Bethlehem. She was a model of loyalty, simplicity, and faithfulness in God. She was remarried to Boaz and became David's great-grandmother.

Forgive

For-giving, means to give beyond, to give completely and freely. In biblical terms, to forgive means not only to renounce the punishment of an offense, but forgiveness also offers reconciliation to the offender (see RECONCILE). The word does not indicate that the offense is forgotten; it says, "I love you nonetheless." God alone is capable of such a gift (Luke 23:34, page 378). He offers mankind His forgiveness. The forgiveness of God cannot be bought through massive sacrifices,* rather, it is a gift to be received. And, in the heart of those who receive God's forgiveness, a new and greater ability to love is born. Thus

Peter, forgiven for his public denial of knowing Jesus, truly became the rock on which the faith of the Church could be built (John 21:15-18, page 394).

All those who receive God's forgiveness become, in turn, capable of forgiving others (Matthew 18:21-35, page 283).

Galilee

Name of the region north of Palestine, the Promised Land,* where Jesus spent his boyhood and early ministry (see map opposite). Forming the western coast of the the Sea of Galilee (also called the Sea of Tiberias or Sea of Chinnereth), Galilee possessed a fertile, lush soil and a pleasant climate making Galilee an historically popular crossroads of many cultures. In fact, the Jews of Jerusalem distrusted the Jews of Galilee because of their frequent contact with the Gentiles afforded by Galilee's location. Galilee's reputation among the Jerusalem Jews was such that conventional wisdom believed that no prophet could come out of Galilee (John 7:52, page 347). Only rebels, such as the Zealots,* or Judas the Galilean, could be produced by such a region (Acts 5:37, page 408).

The Galilean accent was easy to recognize, thus they were readily identified by that alone. (Luke 22:59, page 372).

The Gospels mention the prince of Galilee, Herod* Antipas, in many occasions.

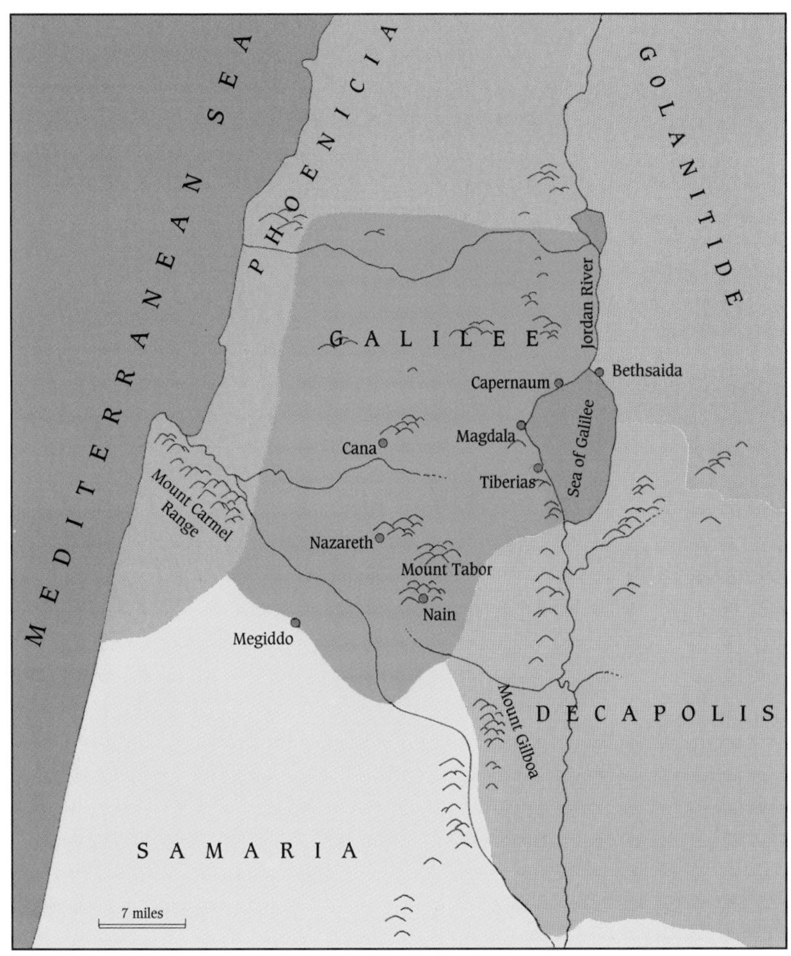

Garden

In Greek, garden is *paradeisos*, "paradise." For an oriental, and especially for a desert nomad, a well irrigated garden symbolized rest and well-being—paradise.

The book of Genesis offers another aspect of a garden's paradise in his description of the garden of Eden (Genesis 2:8-9, page 22). Eden is not only an image of God-created fertility, it is a symbol of the happiness God offers mankind: to live joyfully by His side in peace and complete harmony. It is sin that excludes mankind from this paradise; it is the love of God that invites them to come back.

Over the centuries, Christian artists have variously represented this paradise that will open its gate to the righteous after the day of Judgement.* Oriental artists depict a garden, surrounded by walls, like the New Jerusalem described in the book of Revelation (Revelation 21:2, page 454). They depict the first Christians to enter as Mary, the mother of Jesus, and the crucified thief to whom Jesus had promised:

"Today you will be with me in paradise" (Luke 23:43, page 379). Western artists seem to neglect the link between paradise and a garden. Living with God is depicted as being in Heaven with Him. Thus paradise is often portrayed as an ethereal place in the sky filled with angels on luminous clouds.

The joy of God's followers, meeting in the garden of paradise. Giovanni di Paolo - 15th century - Sienna.

Gehenna

Also called the valley of Ben Hinnom, Gehenna was a valley south of Jerusalem where children were sacrificed by fire in pagan rites. In the 7th century B.C., King Josiah forbade these sacrificial rites and turned

Typical representation of hell "where the damned are boiled" (François Villon). Catalonian Romanesque painting - 11th - 12th century - Barcelona.

the valley into a dump for burning city garbage. (Jeremiah 19:1-6, page 153). In the New Testament, Jesus used Gehenna as an image to describe the state of those refusing to live with God. He exhorted them, saying that their hearts burned with loathsome, shameful desires including murder, jealousy, and the love of money, all of which would lead to death.*

SEE HELL AND PAGES 382-383.

Genesis

From the Greek word genesis which means "origin," title of the first book of the Bible. The Hebrew word for genesis means "in the beginning" and is used as the first word of the entire book (Genesis 1:1, page 20). The Book of Genesis is the first book of a larger work called the Pentateuch.* The Pentateuch includes the first five books of the Old Testament: Genesis, Exodus, Leviticus, Numbers and Deuteronomy.

Genesis presents the history of the beginning of the world, man, sin, civilization, the nations, and Israel. It also includes the real life history of individual people, including such historic Israelite ancestors as Abraham, Isaac, and Jacob.

SEE ILLUSTRATION, PAGES 32-33 AND 44-45.

Gentile

French word from the Latin gentes, meaning "of the same race" or, depending on the context and time period, "foreigner" or "heathen." Originally it was a general term for "nations"; later gentiles were referred to as simply nation members, indicating that they were non-Jews, and thus were not considered part of God's chosen people.

In the Diaspora,* some gentiles were inspired by the Jewish religion.

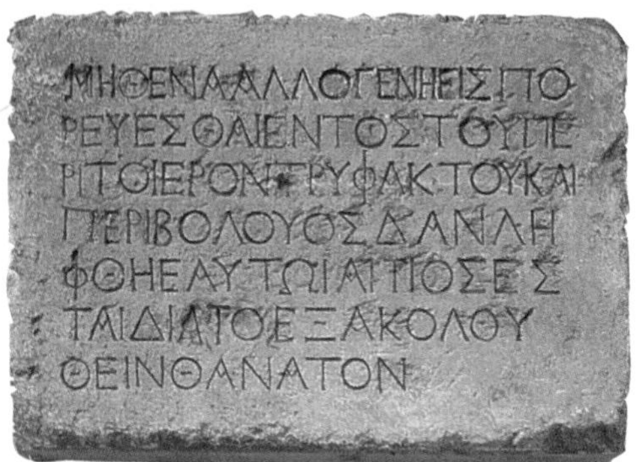

Greek inscription *(17 - 4 B.C.) Istanbul Museum (Turkey). Such inscriptions were placed at the border of the outer court of the Gentiles. They forbade non-Jews, punishable by death, to enter the Jewish square.*

They occasionally visited the Temple of Jerusalem, restricted to the terraces outside referred to as the outer court of the Gentiles (see page 233).

By the time of Christ, after centuries of struggling to keep themselves separate from the Gentiles, many Jews used the word pejoratively for non-Jews.

Paul is called the "apostle of the Gentiles."

SEE PAGAN AND TEMPLE.

Glory

Represents the Hebrew word denoting "worthiness." In today's vernacular, a person's glory is rooted in his merits which assure a good reputation. In the Old Testament, we read that the glory of Israel was not its material assets, but God (Jeremiah 2:11), a theme repeated throughout the Bible and applied to all believers. A common concept of glory in the Bible also referred to the revelation of God's presence to mankind, sometimes with physical signs.

At times, when the authors of the Bible talk about God's followers glorifying Him, they are referring to their recognition of His goodness and mercy (see the Gloria, page 462).

Jesus taught that when his disciples* are grafted to him like branches to a vine, they bear much fruit, and thus give glory to the Lord (John 15:8, page 359). In turn, others will also glorify the Lord upon seeing the fruit produced by the faithful disciple (Matthew 5:16, page 261).

See illustration, pages 470-471.

Golgotha

The place where Jesus was crucified (Mark 15:22, page 377). In Aramaic, Golgotha means "skull." The Romans referred to the site as calvarius, "calvary." It was a large rock situated outside Jerusalem's walls. Golgatha lay in an old quarry where graves had been dug. Today, Golgatha can be viewed in the Holy Sepulcher Church in Jerusalem.

See illustration, pages 382-383.

During the period of the Kings a quarry was opened west of the Temple. The stone-cutters left behind poor quality rock.

At the beginning of our era, the abandonned quarry became a burial ground or sepulture.

The site was made into a garden. The rock called a "skull," was used as a gallows.

Gospel

From the Greek word *evangelion* meaning "good news," found more than 75 times in the New Testament. It is the name given to the four books written by Matthew, Mark, Luke and John (see pages 230-231). because these four books announce the Gospel: the good news that God in Jesus Christ has fulfilled His promises to Israel, and that a way of salvation has been opened to all.
Mark began his book with this proclamation: "The beginning of the gospel (*evangelion*) about Jesus Christ, the Son of God." (Mark 1:1, page 236). Luke explained that the birth of Jesus is good news for all the people (Luke 2:10, page 303). In Matthew, Jesus announced the good news of the Kingdom in his preaching (Matthew 9:35, page 269). John did not use the word gospel, but wrote that Jesus came to fill his disciples with joy (John 15:11, page 359). The word gospel is used outside the four Gospels. For example, Paul wrote that he had been sent by the Christ to proclaim the gospel (1 Corinthians 1:17, page 433 and 15:1, page 438).

THE SYMBOLS OF THE FOUR EVANGELISTS

While reading the prophetic books of Revelation and Ezekiel (1:4-10, page 160), the early Christians were impressed by the image of the four living creatures carrying God's chariot. The first resembled a lion; the second, a young bull; the third had a human face; and the fourth resembled a flying eagle. The connection between these living creatures and the four Evangelists was a subject of great discussion. Eventually, Christians agreed with Jerome's interpretation made in the 5th century.

Mark is the lion, a desert animal, because he began his Gospel with John the Baptist's preaching in the desert.

John is represented by the eagle because of the eloquent stature of his prologue (John 1:1-18, page 333).

The bull, a sacrificial animal, symbolises Luke's discussion in the first chapter about the Temple.

Matthew began his book by listing the ancestors of Jesus, and is thus assigned the symbol of a man.

Grace

All that we receive from God is grace: life, His Covenant,* His Son, His Word, the Church... Grace cannot be bought or earned by any human merit. It is a free gift of God who takes care of his children and leads them as a shepherd, enabling them to pray: "Surely goodness and love will follow me" (Psalm 23:6, page 214).

Guilt Offering

SEE ATONEMENT.

Hasmoneans

Name of the dynasty founded by the descendants of the Maccabees.* They claimed to be the heir of an ancestor called Hasmon. At the end of the second century B. C., they called themselves "kings of the Jews." In the year 40 B.C., the Romans removed the Hasmoneans from power. They gave the throne of Jerusalem to an Idumean, Herod,*who had married a Hasmonean, Mariamme. Herod killed nearly all the Hasmoneans to remain in power, but from 41 to 44 A.D., one of his descendants, the grandson of Mariamme the Hasmonean, became king. He was Herod* Agrippa I, the king who had James the apostle beheaded (Acts 12:1-2, page 418).

H

Heathen

SEE PAGAN.

Hebrew

Comes from the word *ieber* meaning "one from across." The Hebrew was therefore, in the beginning, considered "he who comes from the other side" or "the foreigner." Undoubtedly, this was what the Egyptians and the Philistines* called the descendants of Abraham. After a period of time, they were no longer called the Hebrews, rather, they were referred to as the sons of Israel or the Jewish.* Their language, however, was still called Hebrew. Most of the texts of the Old Testament* are written in Hebrew.

After the Exile,* the Jews spoke other languages: Aramaic* in the Holy Land and Greek in the Diaspora.* Hebrew then became the language of the religious scholars who studied the Bible. The family of the apostle Paul spoke Hebrew (Philippians 3:5, page 441).

Alleluia in Hebrew.

Hell

This word, as it is occurs in the New Testament reads as Gehenna, a name derived from a Hebrew word for the Hinnom valley near Jerusalem. In this valley, children had been sacrificed by fire during pagan rites. In later Jewish texts, Gehenna came to mean the place of punishment for sinners, depicted as one of continual fire. The word hell itself, in the singular, is not found in the Bible. It is not to be mistaken for Sheol,* "underworld," the dwelling of the dead.

Today, when we use the word hell, it typically corresponds to the images Jesus provided, such as the "Gehenna* of fire" (Matthew 5:22, page 261).

Throughout the Bible, we see that God respects the individual's free will to reject Him and seek happiness through self-focus. But He firmly warns that life apart from Him is death for the soul.* Jesus taught often that life in Eternity apart from the Father would be spent in Hell, the most redoubtable of fates. (Matthew 10:28, page 270).

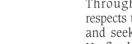

Portrayal of King Herod the Great.

Herod

Name of several kings of one family. With the political support of the Romans, they reigned over the Jewish people from 37 B.C. until A.D. 100.

THE MONK'S DIFFICULT TASK IN ESTABLISHING THE CHRISTIAN CALENDAR

The Gospels clearly state that Jesus was born under the reign of King Herod the Great (Matthew 2:1, page 255; Luke 1:5, page 298). But history books teach just as clearly that Herod died in 4 B.C.! How to account for this discrepancy? The explanation can be found in the work of the monk, Denys the Small. In the 6th century, he was put in charge of establishing a Christian calendar, beginning with the year of Christ's birth. In calculating his dates, Denys did not take into account the date of Herod's death. Thus, historians today estimate that he made an error of four to six years regarding Jesus' birth. He was actually born a few years before the date we consider the beginning of the Christian era.

H

Herod the Great. Of Idumean* descent, he was crowned king by the Roman Senate in 37 B.C. Herod advanced the emperor's cultural projects by undertaking lavish building projects. His greatest project was the reconstruction of the Jerusalem Temple, making it more beautiful. Unfortunately, he also erected temples to idols to win favor with the Roman emperor. He lived a heathen lifestyle, marrying then repudiating ten women with whom he had fifteen sons. He was ruthless about maintaining the throne. He had his opponents murdered, and even some of his children. He died in Jericho in 4 B.C.

Herod Antipas. Son of Herod the Great. When his father died, he became governor of Galilee. He divorced his first wife to marry Herodias, the wife of one of his brothers. When John the Baptist criticized him for this marriage, he had him arrested and executed (Mark 6:17-29, page 243). He was in Jerusalem at the time of the trial and death of Jesus (Luke 23:6-12, page 376). He hoped the Romans would crown him as king, but in 39 A.D., he was exiled to Gaul.

Herod Agrippa I. Grandson of Herod the Great and brother-in-law to Herod Antipas. He was descended from the Hasmoneans* through Mariamm, one of Herod the Great's wives. He was brought up in Rome and became a friend of the Romans, especially of emperor Caligula. He was appointed king of several provinces, and then became king of Judea and Samaria in 41 A.D. He had James the apostle, son of Zebedee, beheaded, and Peter imprisoned (Acts 12:1-5, page 418). He died in 44 A.D.

Herodians

Supporters of the Herod* dynasty (see page 234).

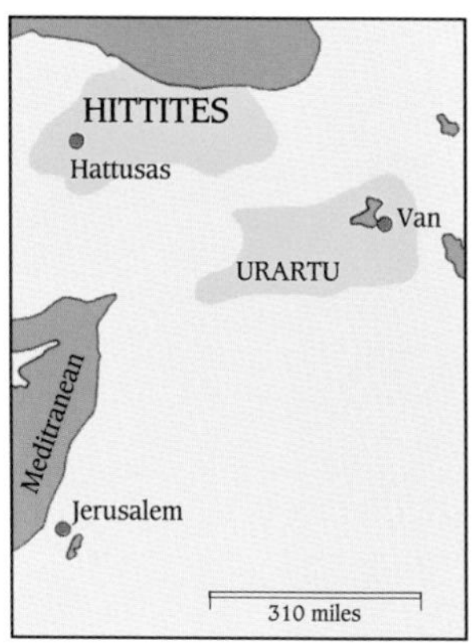

Territory of the Hittites

Hittites

Hittites came from Central Anatolia (current Turkey). At one point they annexed the kingdom of Urartu to their territory (see page 29, note 1).

The Bible mentions Uriah,* a Hittite with an Urartu name. Uriah* the Hittite undoubtedly came from this high mountain region where it was once believed Noah's Ark stopped, but in fact, God made a Covenant with all of mankind (Genesis 9:8-15, page 30). The name of Uriah, mentioned in the genealogy of Jesus (Matthew 1:6, page 254), shows that God had not forgotten His universal Covenant.

Holocaust

Sacrifice* offered to God. The animals offered in holocaust were totally consumed by the sacrificial fire. It was an act of worship,* an homage to God that declared: "You are the Master of everything. All we have comes from you. We want to use everything that you give us to give you glory.*"

The holocaust of animals was practiced in the Temple* of Jerusalem until 70 A.D. For a long time, the Hebrews debated imitating their neighbors by offering the Lord human holocausts (Micah 6:6-8, p. 145). The question was resolved for most people through the account of Abraham and his son Isaac; It was understood that God was not interested in this kind of sacrifice (Genesis 22:1-13. p. 46).

Nevertheless, human sacrifice was occasionally practiced, often offered to alien gods, until the time of the prophet Jeremiah (Jeremiah 19:4-6, p.153).

The word "holocaust" is incorrectly used to refer to the genocide of the Jews by the Nazis during World War II. By burning Jewish bodies in the crematorium, the Nazis were not making a sacrifice to God; these acts of murder showed only contempt for God. The genocide of the Jews is more correctly called the Shoah, which means "destruction."

H

Holy

God alone is holy (Isaiah 6:3, page 137 and the Gloria, page 462).
To speak of God's holiness is to evoke all his qualities: tenderness, mercy,* kindness, to name just a few. It is to recall that He administers these qualities in a way unique to His Being alone.
By extension, all things belonging to God are called holy, such as the Holy Land (Exodus 3:5, page 57), the Holy History,* and the Holy People.

On the other hand, God is not interested in a slave-owner relationship with his followers, rather, He wants them to be like Him. "Be holy because I am holy," said the Lord (Leviticus 19:2, page 72).

Jesus was a model of holiness for his disciples. He invited them to imitate him: "Love each other as I have loved you" (John 15:12, page 360). To them and to all believers, he imparts his Holy Spirit* who forms the heart into one that hungers and thirsts for justice.* In the Catholic and Orthodox Church, Christians who have been witnesses of faith* and charity* throughout their lives are called "saints." They serve as examples for the other Christians (see Revelation 7:2-17, page 451).
SEE ALL SAINTS DAY.

The wind blows wherever it pleases (John 3:8).

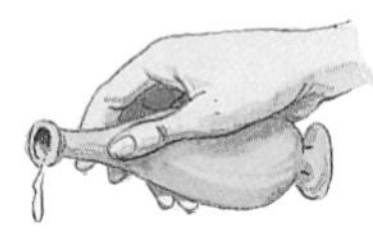

The Spirit of the Lord came upon David (1 Samuel 16:13).

Holy History

When the history of the people of Israel is referred to as "holy history," it does not imply a sacred superiority of the people over others. Like the history of every people, theirs is filled with wars, murders, slaughters, injustices, and idolatries The event that is unique to the Jewish people, however, is that, amidst the tumult recounted in the Old Testament, the Lord Himself, the Holy,* intervened and revealed Himself. Then, in the New Testament, we read that He entered physically among them as His Son Jesus, thereby becoming a member of His people. Thus, it is the presence of God and not the actions of the people that make their history holy.

Holy Spirit

The Bible typically uses images to describe the the Holy Spirit.
- The Hebrew word for spirit has various meanings, best viewed as parts of a puzzle; once assembled, they create a portrait of the Holy Spirit. The most prominent meanings of the word are "divine power," "wind," and "breath." For example, on one occasion the Holy Spirit, the breath of God was a breath of life (Genesis 2:7, page 22).
- The action of the Holy Spirit was also symbolized by the unction of oil, or anointing, a ritual performed in the Old and New Testament. The penetration of the oil as it was applied to the skin was an outward sign that the Holy Spirit was penetrating the heart of his chosen. Among other things, the anointing of oil symbolized a divinely appropriated ability to discern God's will (1 Samuel 16:13, page 100 and Isaiah 11:2, page 141). It was the presence of the Holy Spirit that empowered the messiahs* and the prophets.*
We are told in the New Testament that it was through the Holy Spirit that the Son of God took "flesh from the Virgin Mary" (Luke 1:35,

page 300). And it was the Holy Spirit that enabled Elizabeth to recognize the yet-to-be born Jesus as the Son of God, filling her with joy (Luke 1:41-44, page 300).
Jesus was inhabited by the Spirit of God, the Spirit of truth and might. He literally blew this divine force into all his disciples, thus changing them from timid apostles into bold witnesses whose evangelizing and teaching would begin gathering from all corners of the world God's chosen followers (Acts 2:1-13).
The early Christians were quick to understand that the Spirit of God was not simply an inner strength: it was "of God." In 381 A.D., the council of Constantinople formalized the theological doctrine of the Church. Their doctrine, one which is still upheld by today's Christian Church, clearly stated that Christians believe in the triune nature of God, also called the Trinity: one God comprised of three persons—the Father, the Son and the Holy Spirit—who abide communally, bound by love (see page 461).
SEE DOVE AND TRINITY.

Like tongues of fire... (Acts 2:3).

Streams of living water... (John 7:37-39).

Hope

Hope in the biblical sense of the word is possible only through belief in the Living God. It is the complete certainty that Evil* cannot win out, because Jesus definitively overcame Evil through his death and Resurrection. The word "expect" and "hope" do not mean the same thing and are not to be confused. Expectation is limited to earthly horizons, whereas biblical hope is rooted in the horizon of eternal life, a life that supersedes human failure and death. For the Christian, human failure is a temporary state of affairs; physical death opens the door to a new life. Biblical hope is not attainable by relying on willpower. It is a gift that the Christian must ask for from God.

Hosanna

From two Hebrew words which mean, in this order, "save," "we beseech thee." The crowd who had heralded Jesus' arrival in Jerusalem, had called out: "Hosanna, blessed is he who comes in the name of the Lord." (Mark 11:9, page 249).
This same acclamation is sung in the hymn "Holy, Holy, Holy be the Lord" (see page 463).
Hosea
The only prophet* and writer who came from the northern kingdom of Israel. (see page 132).
Hosea began his long ministry* around 750 B.C. He witnesses the decline of the northern kingdom, which had grown increasingly more enslaved by the Assyrians.
Hosea had a difficult marriage. Although his wife, Gomer, was unfaithful, he sought after her and was considered a fool for it. (Hosea 9:7). Through this painful experience, he discovered that God loved his people like a faithful husband would. Israel resembled an unfaithful wife, forgetting her Covenant* with the Lord to pursue other gods. Nevertheless the Lord would not reject the unfaithful wife. On the contrary, He longed for her return and her conversion.*
See illustration, pages 188-189.

Idol

From the Greek eidolon meaning "image," "representation." Idols are created by turning objects, persons or ideas into divinities. When the word is used in the Bible, the definition specifies "trivial being" and "powerless being." The second Commandment* that the Lord gave Moses states: "You shall have no other gods before me" (Exodus 20:3, page 71), followed by a detailed restriction in verse four against making and worshipping representations of God. The Bible teaches that He is infinitely greater than any idol, and in no way can He be contained within the limits of a material object.

I

Idolatry

The worship of other gods.
SEE IDOL.

Idumean

SEE EDOMITES.

Immanuel

Immanuel means "God with us," used only twice (possibly three times) in the Old Testament and once in the New Testament. When this word is used for the first time, it announces the birth of a child (Isaiah 7:14, page 139). This birth was the sign that God had not forgotten His people. He was present ("is with him") in hardship. The second time that this same word Immanuel is used, it is again for a birth (Matthew 1:23, page 255). Here the child, Jesus, truly is "God with us," the Son of God made man for his mission on earth.

Incarnation

From the Latin word caro meaning flesh.* Incarnation is the endowment of a human body. The Bible regards the body, or flesh, as a theologically significant symbol of the life God created for humans. God created a life which required flesh, a physical organ, to sustain it. In the same manner, God created flesh for Himself in the person of Jesus. When Christians refer to the mystery* of the Incarnation, they are referring to the fact that in Jesus, God became flesh, that He was made human like us (John 1:14, page 334, and see page 300).

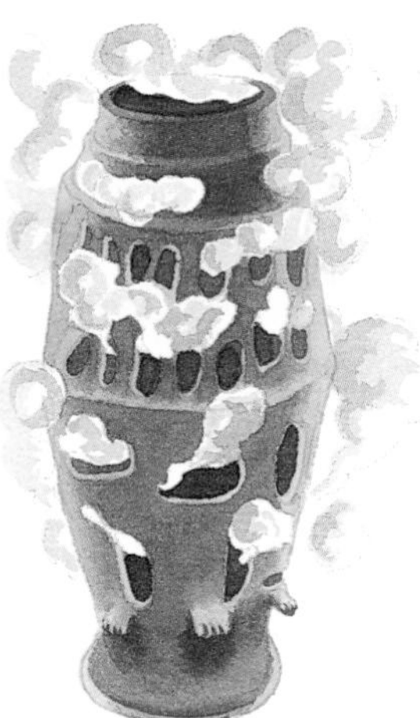

Clay Censer
from the Canaanan era.
Seeds of incense were placed inside it on burning coal.

Our Lady of Pity or Pieta.
Labesserette - Cantal (France).
Polychrome stone,
end of 15th century.

Incense

Gum from Bosweilla trees, found in Arabia and Africa. The word refers both to the gum and to the strong, pleasant odor it produces while burning. The incense used in Israel mainly came from the southern Arabian kingdom of Sheba (Isaiah 60:6, page 186). It was an expensive but common offering in Old Testament ritual, a symbolic way of acknowledging deity. In the New Testament account, we see that it was burned on the Temple's altar of perfumes (Luke 1:9-11, page 298). It is also used throughout the Bible as a symbol for prayer. Incense (in the form of frankincense) was one of the gifts the Magi presented to the infant Jesus, an act that has been interpreted as symbolizing the infant's priestly station (Matthew 2:11, page 256).

Inspiration

Christians and the Jewish claim that the prophets* and the authors of the Bible were inspired by God to write and speak in His name. This means that their hearts were guided by God's Holy Spirit, a guidance that enlightened their intelligence and enabled them to present the truth of and about God. It was the presence of the Holy Spirit who provided the initiative, the stimulus and the enlightenment.

This does not mean that the prophets and authors were merely stenographers for God; it is presumed that the Holy Spirit did not dictate the exact words to be written or spoken. A person is never a machine in God's eyes, rather, God respects individual expression. Thus, the prophets announced God's messages filtered through their own sensitivity, culture, and within the innate limits of their own mental capacity. Therefore, the edification by prophets such as Isaiah, Jeremiah and John the Baptist, had a double authorship: the primary author, God, and man, the secondary author, sensitized by God's Holy Spirit.

I

Intercession

The act of pleading on someone's behalf. In the Old Testament, Abraham interceded in favor of the inhabitants of Sodom (Genesis 18:16-33, page 42).

The prayer of intercession is not meant to soften God's heart, nor to inform Him of another person's problem. God is never without mercy and He, the Father, knows what His children need before they ask Him (Matthew 6:8, page 263). Specifically, intercessory prayer puts the praying Christian in communion* with the merciful God and with the person suffering. By sincerely praying—interceding—on the person's behalf, the Christian can experience a deepening of his commitment to the person.

Jesus is the model intercessor. Throughout his ministry on earth, he did not rank himself above those for whom he interceded. He was with and among them. (Matthew 3:13-15, page 258).

Isaac

Son of Abraham* and Sarah.* His name means "God laughs." He is the son of the Covenant* God made to Abraham that He would infinitely multiply his descendants, God's chosen people (for details, see pages 39-40).
SEE ISHMAEL.

Isaiah

Hebrew name meaning "Yahweh is salvation," son of Amoz. Isaiah lived in Jerusalem. He may have been one of the king's counselors. He began prophesying in 740 B.C. and fulfilled his mission during the reigns of Uzziah, Jotham, and Hezekiah (see page 136).

According to a Jewish tradition, he may have died a martyr (after 685 B.C.) during the reign of Manasseh, although there is little sound historical evidence for it. The story recounts that Isaiah was hidden in a tree trunk when the king ordered to saw him in half with the tree.

Isaiah's prophecies were gathered and written on scrolls by his disciples. Prophecies of other prophets, whose names are today unknown, were added to his (see page 143). In the New Testament, there are sixty cross-references to the book of Isaiah. His name is quoted twenty-two times.

See illustration, pages 188-189.

"I want men everywhere to lift up holy hands in prayer..." (1 Timothy 2:8, page 442). Paul, in the same letter, specified the need for intercessory prayer for all men. Funeral mosaic of the 5th century. Sfax Museum (Tunisia).

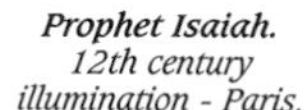

Prophet Isaiah. *12th century illumination - Paris.*

Ishmael

Son of Abraham by Hagar, the Egyptian handmaid of his wife Sarah (page 39). Ishmael was not the son of the Promise*; that son was Isaac.* Nonetheless, Ishmael was blessed by the Lord who promised him twelve princes and ultimately a great nation. The Bible presents him as the ancestor of the Arab tribes.

The Koran, the Muslims' sacred book, considers him to be Abraham's most important son. During their religious celebration Aïd-el-Kébir, Muslims commemorate the near-sacrifice of Ishmael, similar to the one of Abrahams' near-sacrifice of Isaac (Genesis 22:1-13, pages 46-47).

Israel

Hebrew name meaning "contender with God." Israel is the name given to two people: First, to Jacob, grandson of Abraham, after his night of wrestling at Penuel. His supernatural antagonist gave him this name saying that he had "striven with God and with men and [had] prevailed." (Genesis 32:29-30, page 50). The name Israel is also given to the nation which traced its ancestry back to the twelve sons of Jacob. The twelve sons of Jacob are also referred to as Israel, the people of Israel,

J

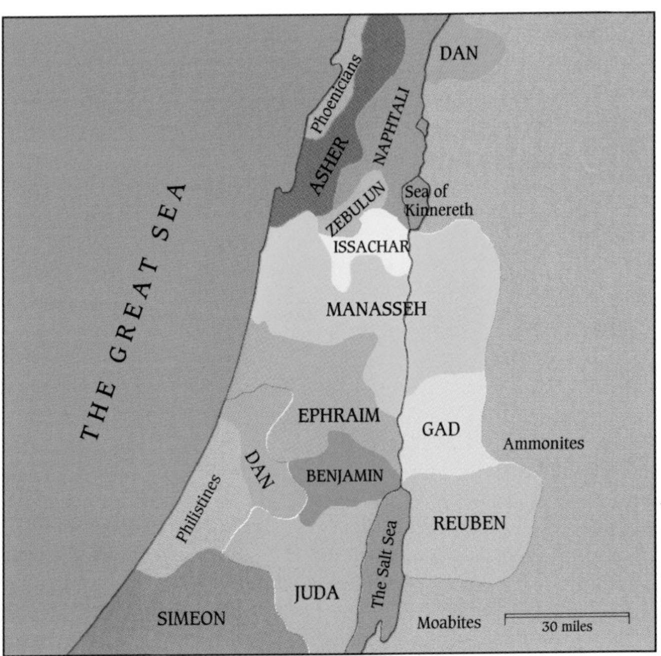

The tribe of Dan migrated from the South, near Philistia, to the North. The twelve tribes are indicated by colored sections on the map.

the twelve tribes of Israel, and/or the Israelites. Today, Israel is best known as the land where these twelve tribes had settled.

In approximately 931 B.C., after the division of the people of Israel into two different kingdoms (page 121), the prophets willingly named the northern kingdom Israel, which was comprised of ten tribes. Ephraim,* the name of one of these tribes, was also used to refer to the kingdom of Israel.

Jacob

Name meaning "heel-catcher" or "supplanter" because he was born clutching the heel of his elder twin Esau.* Jacob is considered the father of Israel, the chosen people of God. Almost a fourth of the book of Genesis is devoted to his biography. Jacob was the son of Isaac* and Rebekah (Rebecca). God renamed him Israel* after his victory at Penuel. Polygamy was permitted during his time, thus he had two wives, Leah and Rachel. He had thirteen children: twelve boys and a girl, named Dinah. With Rachel, his preferred wife, Jacob had only two sons, Joseph and Benjamin. Leah, whom he neglected, is considered the real mother of the people of God because she gave birth to Reuben, Simeon, Levi,* Judah,* Issachar and Zebulun, all ancestors of the main tribes of Israel (see pages 51-52).

SEE ILLUSTRATION, PAGES 44-45.

***James,** son of Zebedee, or James the Elder, dressed as a pilgrim of Compostela. Notice his staff, his gourd, and the shell on his hat.*

James

This name has the same meaning as Jacob.* In the New Testament, the three James most often mentioned are:

James, the son of Zebedee, a Galilean fisherman who was called with his brother John to be one of the Twelve.* He was also referred to in the New Testament as James the Elder to distinguish him from another of the twelve apostles, James, the son of Alphaeus. Jesus nicknamed the two brothers "sons of thunder" because they once wanted fire from heaven to burn a Samaritan village which had rejected Jesus during his travels. He greatly loved Jesus, but in his humanness, he was one of those who fell asleep during Jesus' agony at Gethsemane (Mark 14:33, page 369). James was one of the privileged witnesses of the Transfiguration (Mark 9:2, page 246). He died beheaded, on the order of Herod Agrippa I, in 43 or 44 A.D. (Acts 12:2, page 418).

Tradition claims that he evangelized Spain and that his body was buried in Compostela. In the Middle Ages, pilgrims from all over Europe created the "roads to Compostela," lined with churches, hospitals and monasteries. The Spanish named him guardian of the "recovery" when they ousted the Arabs occupying Spain. He was given the dubious title of Matamore, "killer of Moors." Today's European pilgrims have relinquished this title which they consider in opposition to the spirit of brotherhood insisted upon in the Gospel.

James, the son of Alphaeus. One of the Twelve* (Mark 3:18, page 239). He had a brother, Joses. Very little is known about him. He has often been mistaken for James, the brother of the Lord.

James, the brother of Jesus. He is not one of the Twelve.* Before the Resurrection, he did not accept the authority of his half-brother, Jesus (Mark 3:21, page 240). The risen Jesus appeared to him (1 Corinthians 15:7, page 438) and soon he became a leader of the first Jewish-Christian church of Jerusalem (Acts 12:17, page 419). Catholics think that he was the cousin of Jeus, who was brought up with the Lord. For many Protestants, Mary had had other children after the birth of Jesus. Flavius Josephus,* a celebrated historian, and Clement of Alexandria, reported his death in 62 AD. They recorded that James was stoned before being beaten to death with a rod by a dyer. This is why in paintings he was often shown with a rod. An epistle* of the New Testament is attributed to him (see pages 444-445). Some identify him as John the Younger.

Santiago de Compostela Cathedral (Spain). 18th century baroque façade.

Jeremiah

From the Hebrew name *Yirmeyah* meaning "Yahweh exalts." Jeremiah was born in Anathoth (Jeremiah 1:1, page 149). He belonged to the tribe of Levi,* but his ancestors had been denied any function in the Temple* under King Solomon. He started his mission as a prophet in 627 B.C. He witnessed the first captivity in Babylon of the Hebrew people, in 598 B.C.. He was present at the destruction of Jerusalem and the Temple, and at the disappearance of the Ark* of the Covenant in 587 B.C. His ministry spanned forty years. Jeremiah's personality is the most clearly portrayed of any of the Old Testament prophets. He was a man of extreme contrasts, often emotional and high-strung. At the beginning of his ministry,* Jeremiah was a disconsolate prophet. At times he wondered if God hadn't given up on His people and His Covenant* with them. But by the end of his life, he had a complete change of mind and became a luminous preacher of hope.* He announced that God would make a New Covenant, and would lead His people back to their land. He concluded that since the Tablets of the Law* disappeared with the Ark of the Covenant, God would write His laws on the hearts of His believers which they would obey in love (Jeremiah 31:31-34, page 157). His prophesy was at last fulfilled in the coming of Christ.

Thus, throughout his entire life as a persecuted righteous man, tormented in his spirit by the people's infidelity to God, he prophesied the new relationship that Jesus would establish with his people. (Matthew 16:14, page 281). Jeremiah died in Egypt.

See illustration, pages 188-189.

Prophet Jeremiah.
Mosaic - 13th century. San Marco Basilica - Venice.

Jerusalem

City chosen by David as capital of his kingdom (page 106). It is situated on a plateau, at an altitude of approximately 2,300 feet, and is defined by valleys (Kidron Valley, Gehenna* Valley, etc.) and mountain peaks such as the Mount of Olives (2 Samuel 15:30, page 112; see also page 369). David had the Ark* of the Covenant brought to Jerusalem, around which the tribes of Israel gathered to renew their commitment to unity (Psalm 122, page 221).

J

Jerusalem - In the foreground, the dome of the mosques, on the terrace of the ancient temple. Left and above the golden dome, we can almost see the dome and the romanesque steeple of the Holy Sepulchre.

Solomon* had the Temple* built there (page 118). Jesus died crucified at the gates of the city probably on Friday, the 7th of April in 30 A.D., which was the day before being resurrected on the day known as Easter (see illustration, pages 382 -383).
Today, the Jews and the Muslims consider Jerusalem a holy city. The Muslims call it al-Quds (the Sanctuary), and built the mosquem Al Aqsa, to commemorate a vision of Mohammed. For Christians, there is no "holy city," but over the years, millions have visited and been deeply moved by the biblical and historical resonance of the city. (Revelation 21:1 - 22:2, page 454).

Jesse

SEE DAVID.

Jew

SEE JUDAH.

Jewish Religious Feasts

Joyful feasts: *Pessah* "Passover"; *Shavuoth* "Pentecost" (see Acts 2:1, page 401); and *Succoth* "Feast of the Tabernacles" (see John 7:37, page 436 with note 2). **Feasts of Penitence**: *Rosh*

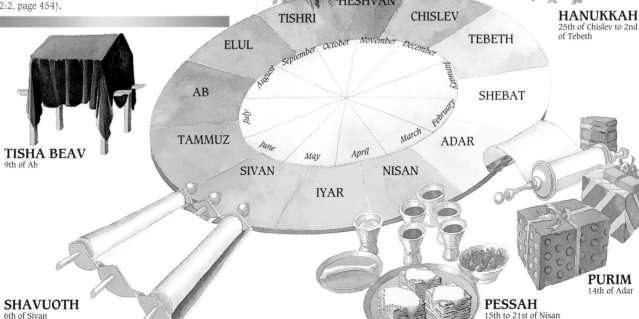

ROSH HASHANAH
1st of Tishri

YOM KIPPUR
10th of Tishri

SUCCOTH
1st to 21st of Tishri

HANUKKAH
25th of Chislev to 2nd of Tebeth

HESHVAN
TISHRI
CHISLEV
ELUL
TEBETH
AB
SHEBAT
TAMMUZ
ADAR
SIVAN
NISAN
IYAR
September
October
November
December
January
August
February
July
March
June
May
April

TISHA BEAV
9th of Ab

PURIM
14th of Adar

SHAVUOTH
6th of Sivan

PESSAH
15th to 21st of Nisan

Hashanah "New Year" (or Trumpets); and *Yom Kippur* (see Atonement*).
Minor feasts: *Hanukkah* "Dedication to the Temple" (see page 180, note 2, and John 10:22, page 353); and *Purim* (see in the Book of Esther).
A new feast: *Tisha Beav*, which commemorates, among other things, the destruction of the Temple.

John

From the Hebrew name *Yohanan* meaning "Yahweh is gracious."
John the Baptist. Son of Zechariah,* a priest in the Temple of Jerusalem, and Elizabeth, a descendant of Aaron* and of Mary's family. His birth was announced by the angel Gabriel (Luke 1:15-20, page 298). He grew up in the wilderness of Judaea where he received his prophetic call.
John preached the imminent arrival of the Messiah* (Matthew 3:1-12, page 257). He entreated the crowds to be prepared for it by receiving the baptism of repentance. Thus his nickname: John the Baptist (see also pages 188-189). It was John the Baptist who baptized Jesus.
When John publicly denounced the marriage of Herod* Antipas to Herodias, Herod has him arrested and then beheaded in his cell (Mark 6:17-29, page 243).
John the evangelist. Author of the fourth Gospel (see page 331). John died in Ephesus. A huge basilica, today in ruins, was erected on his grave.
John Mark. Called Mark the evangelist (see page 235). He is considered the first bishop of Alexandria in Egypt. When the city fell into the hands of the Muslims, Mark's relics were taken to Venice where "Mark's lion" was adopted as its insignia.

John the evangelist
with his symbol, the eagle.

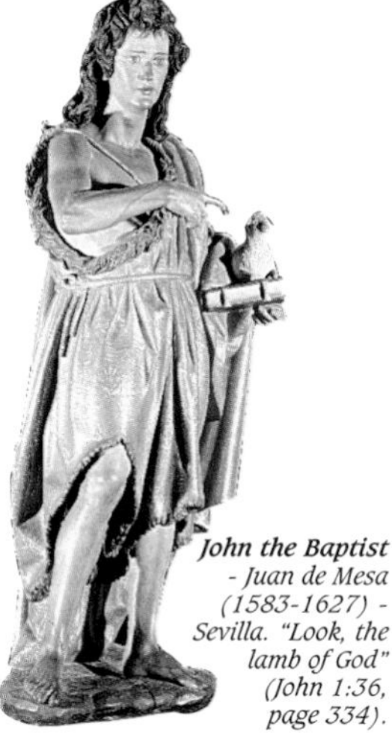

John the Baptist
- Juan de Mesa (1583-1627) - Sevilla. "Look, the lamb of God" (John 1:36, page 334).

Joseph

A Hebrew name meaning "May God add (sons)." Prominent Josephs in the Bible include:

Joseph, son of Jacob. First child of Rachel and eleventh son of Jacob-Israel. His jealous brothers sold him to some Ishmaelites (Genesis 37:3-28, page 51). In Egypt he became a slave, but soon gained the favor of Pharaoh, who appointed him as his minister. His two children, Ephraim and Manasseh, are adopted by Jacob-Israel. They replaced Joseph as the ancestors of the twelve tribes of Israel (page 52, note 1).
Joseph, the carpenter. From the tribe of Judah.* God asked him to be the protector of Jesus, His Son, born of Mary (Matthew 1:18-25, page 254). He was a carpenter. Thus Joseph acted as a father towards Jesus.
It is almost certain that Joseph was not alive during the ministry of Jesus.
Joseph of Arimathea. Member of the Sanhedrin* who had not voted the death of Jesus, and a secret disciple; the moment Jesus died, Joseph publicly asked Pilate for permission to remove his body. Joseph was rich, so he provided fine linens to wrap the body before laying it in his own tomb (John 19:38-42, page 384).
Josephus (Flavius). He is not mentioned in the Bible, but he was an important Jewish historian. Josephus was born in 37 or 38 A.D.

Joseph escapes to Egypt with Jesus and Mary.
15th century manuscript - Saint Geneviève Library - Paris.

in the tribe of Levi. Having become a Roman citizen, he adopted the name of his patron's family, Flavius. He wrote several books to introduce the history of the Jews to the Romans. In one of them, The Antiquities of the Jews, he mentioned John* the Baptist, Jesus and James,* the brother of Jesus.

Josephus, Flavius

SEE JOSEPH.

Joshua

From the Hebrew name *Yehoshua* meaning "the Lord saves" (see page 68, note 3). Joshua was a servant of Moses. He fought the Amalekites in Rephidim (Exodus 17:8-13, page 68). He was with Moses on Mount Sinai when he was given the Tablets of the Law (Exodus 32:15-17, page 75). Because of his faithfulness, he entered the Promised Land. He oversaw the division of the country among the twelve tribes of Israel. All the tribes of Israel assembled at Shechem attributed the solemn renewal of the Covenent* to him (Joshua 24:1-25, page 94).

Judah/ Judas

From the Hebrew name *Yehudah* meaning "praised." Son of Jacob* and Leah, Judah is the ancestor of the tribe of Judah, one of the twelve tribes of Israel.

The tribe of Judah had a great destiny. God promised David, one of its members, that the Messiah* would be chosen from among his offspring (2 Samuel 7:12, page 109). After separating from the northern tribes, the land of Judah constituted nearly the totality of the kingdom of Jerusalem. It was called Judaea, and its inhabitants, Judaeans. When the kingdom of Samaria ceases to exist, the Judaeans become the main representatives of God's people.

In English, the word "Judean" gradually evolved into "Jew."

Judas Maccabee. Third son of Mattathias. His father chose him as his successor to lead the military resistance against the Greeks (see page 179). His nickname Maccabee* gradually came to mean his entire family.

Judas Iscariot. One of the Twelve.* He betrayed Jesus by leading the guards of the Temple to Gethsemane, where they arrested him.

According to John the evangelist, Judas betrayed Jesus for the money (see page 365, and also John 12:4-8, page 357). Over the centuries, there has been much speculation about other motivations. One binding reality is that Judas lives on as a portrait of an uncommitted follower of Christ who was by his side, but not of the same spirit. He may have awaited a political Messiah who would fight the Romans and was disappointed by Jesus' nonviolence.

Kiss of Judas. *Fra Angelico (1400 - 1455). San Marco convent - Florence. The dark halo of Judas contrasts with the golden halos of Jesus and Peter. Peter cuts off Malchus's ear (John 18:10, page 371).*

Judaism

The "Juda" in Judaism refers to the tribe of Judah.* Since the Exile* it has been used to refer to the religion of the people with whom God made His original Covenant.

The Judaeans had once been taken into exile to Babylon by Nebuchadnezzar. These

JK

Judaeans discovered that experiencing the presence of God was not dependent on going to the Temple,* but to an open heart to the Word of God through prayer. From that discovery on, they began routinely gathering in the synagogue* to listen to the reading of the sacred texts.
This new way of living in covenant with God, inaugurated by the Judeans, is called Judaism.
SEE DIASPORA.

Silver candelabra used in celebrating Hanukah (see page 180 not 2).

Jude

In the New Testament two people bear this name.
Jude, one of the twelve apostles, also called Thaddeus (Luke 6:16, page 309).
Jude, brother of Jesus* and James, he wrote the epistle* in the New Testament bearing his name.

Judge

Judicial arbiters of one or several tribes* of Israel; the seventh book of the Bible which recounts the accomplishments of the main judges and the history of Israel from Joshua's death to the rise of Samuel. The main judges were Gideon, Jephthah, Samson and a woman, Deborah. The last judge is Samuel. He appoints Saul first king of the People of Israel (see page 93). These judges were more than judicial arbiters. They were endowed with God's Holy Spirit to deliver and preserve the nation of Israel. For example, after settling into the Promised Land, the judges were instrumental in helping the tribes settle their conflicts with other peoples (see page 92).

Judgment

SEE LAST JUDGEMENT.*

Kerygma

From the Greek word *kerygma* that means "preaching," "proclamation." The kerygma is the primary gospel* message about Jesus Christ, sometimes called the the Good News. The gospel proclamation serves to convert nonbelievers through the teaching of Jesus's death and resurrection, signs of his love for all mankind, and of the eternal life he promises. The First Epistle to the Corinthians includes a good example of the kerygma of the apostles (1 Corinthians 15:1-8, page 438).

Peter preaching.
P. Serra - 14th century - Bilbao (Spain).

King

God is the true King of Israel (Isaiah 6:1-8, page 137). Over the centuries, He has chosen kings and entrusted them with the mission* of helping His people know its one and only King, and to serve Him.
SEE MESSIAH AND PROPHET.
See illustration, pages 114-115.

KL

Kingdom of God

To live in the Kingdom of God is to live fully with God (Matthew 25:34, page 295). The Kingdom of God cannot be earned by valiant or sacrificial acts. It is to be received as a gift of God (see page 274). The Kingdom is opened immediately to the person who accepts God's forgiveness through Christ; once inside, living in the Kingdom means putting the Word of God into practice, respecting others, sharing with them, forgiving them as he has been forgiven. The person who receives the Kingdom today will enter it in its fullness after his passage from death to eternal life.
The apostle Matthew used the expression "Kingdom of Heavens" when he addressed the Jews who, out of respect, avoided pronouncing the Name of God.

Know

In the Bible, the Greek derivative of the verb implies understanding and comprehension. It is important not to confuse "to know" as it is meant in the Bible with "to know about." For example, we can know many things about a neighbor without truly knowing him. According to God's teaching, to know Him is not first to know things about Him. It means to meet Him through faith* in His existence and through living with Him. Knowing God means listening to Him by reading what He teaches us in the Bible and talking with Him in prayer. It means, through the inspiration of the Holy Spirit, seeking a loving response to all the events and circumstances of our lives (Matthew 7:21-23, page 266).
The apostle Paul vividly explains this notion of knowing God in his letter to the Philippians (3:5-11, page 441). He told the Philippians that he had known many things about God throughout his life, yet he hadn't truly known Him until he met Him on the road to Damascus. Since that encounter, Paul wrote that nothing mattered more to him than knowing Jesus Christ.

Lamb of God

In the Bible, the Lamb of God refers to Jesus. John, in his Gospel, refers to Jesus as the Lamb of God to indicate that Jesus came to replace all the sacrifices* offered for forgiveness during the time of the Old Covenant*: Jesus is our Passover lamb in Exodus 12:1-14, page 63, and John 19:31-37, page 381.
Jesus is also the Servant* of the Lord, led like a lamb to slaughter (Isaiah 53:7, page 172). He sacrificed his life to physically demonstrate God's forgiveness of sin and the greatness of His love for all mankind.
SEE SUFFERING.*

Land

God promised Abraham to give his descendants the land of Canaan* (Genesis 12:7, page 36). Hence, the Hebrew expression the "Promised Land." It refered to the sacred land of the Lord where they believed He abided in the Temple of Jerusalem.
This belief they had, however, that God was only present in the territory of Israel was challenged during their Exile.* The Jews* discovered that God, in fact, was also present in Babylon. They had encountered Him through listening to His Word.
After this experience, the Jews were convinced that they could live in the presence of God outside the boundaries of the Promised Land. Thus many of them did not return to Israel when they were given the opportunity. By staying in Babylon or settling in the Mediterranean basin, they created the Diaspora* (SEE "GOD ALSO SPEAKS ON FOREIGN GROUNDS," PAGE 503).

L

Last Judgment

In the book of Revelation, John describes his vision of the end of the age. After seeing a catastrophic series of world events, John saw the physical return of Christ who stops the carnage of the war of wars and establishes his Kingdom on earth, the New Jerusalem. Before Jesus does this however, John specifies a final Judgment, often referred to as the Last Judgment. God will separate His followers, whose names are written in the Book of Life, from the nonbelievers.

During his ministry, Jesus confirmed a final judgment, but added that a person's heart relation to God is evidenced by his treatment of others, thus our daily behavior ports a judgment long before the Last Judgment (Matthew 25:31-46, page 295). In his Gospel, John reiterated what Jesus taught, writing that there is no judgment for those who believe in Christ (John 3:18, page 338). From that moment on, life with God begins, a life that will continue into eternity.

SEE JUSTICE.

Law

The Hebrew word *tôrâ* is used in some cases in the Old Testament for law in general (see page 18). In the majority of cases it is used for commandments from a person of higher authority to a lower one.

- The Torah is, first of all, the first five books of the Bible.

They contain the rules which God's people were to follow in order to live in Covenant* with God. These rules were not just commandments,* they were living guidance. The people, in turn, made discoveries through the events of their lives, thus learning to distinguish which behaviors and attitudes were in keeping with the heart of the

Commandments, and which ones deviated. Consequently, in the Torah, we read moving, edifying, real-life stories of success and of failure, all lived out by people trying to live in covenant with God. Each story contains object lessons for anyone seeking to grow in faith.
- Sometimes the Torah refers to the entire Old Testament,* since all its books teach how to live in harmony with God.

JESUS AND THE LAW

The New Testament reveals that Jesus did not come to abolish the Law of the first Covenant but to fulfill it (Matthew 5:17, page 261). He put this first Law into practice by retrieving and emphasizing its essence: love. As a result, he abolished certain religious traditions that had been established in the past because of man's hardened heart (Matthew 19:8, page 285. See Stoning*). Instead, Jesus' teaching penetrated to the heart of the Law, which he said was embodied in a single commandment: Love the Lord and love your neighbor (Luke 10:25-28, page 317). He even specified that the commandment to love goes as far as laying down your life for others (John 15:12-14, page 360).
The apostle Paul added that abiding by the Law did not make man righteous* before God. Man only become righteous before God through faith in his Son, not by performing righteous works. Furthermore, the Law had not only emphasized the need for righteous works in order to gain a righteous status, but it had not provided the strength to accomplish them. Paul taught that the strength comes from the Holy Spirit living inside all those who open their hearts to faith* in God. Filled with this strength, the believer can continue growing into the likeness of Christ (Philippians 3:5-14, page 441).

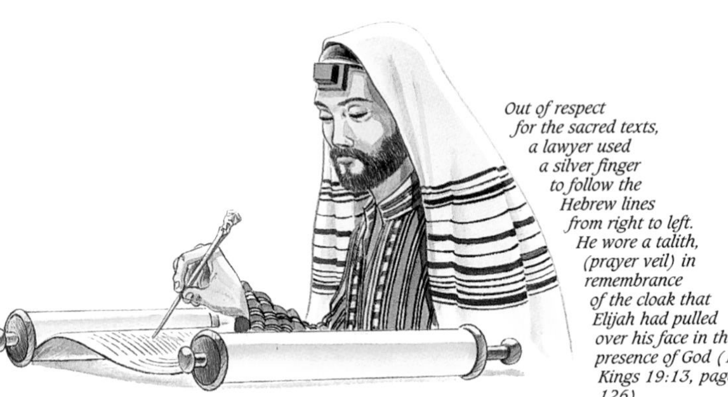

Out of respect for the sacred texts, a lawyer used a silver finger to follow the Hebrew lines from right to left. He wore a talith, (prayer veil) in remembrance of the cloak that Elijah had pulled over his face in the presence of God (1 Kings 19:13, page 126).

Laying on of Hands

Ancient rite used to pass on a gift of God, a blessing,* or a call.
The Elders of Antioch lay hands on Paul and Barnabas as a formal sign of appointment to their mission for God. (Acts 13:3, page 419). Sometimes the laying on of hands was related to healing (Mark 5:23) or to the impartation of the Holy Spirit* (Acts 8:17, 9:17, 19:6). The laying on of hands is still practiced today among many Christians.
See illustration pages 470-471.

Lazarus

From the Hebrew word *Eléazar* meaning "God has helped." Two of the most notable Lazaruses in the New Testament include: Lazarus, a beggar, and the focus of a parable of Jesus (Luke 16:19-31, page 324).
Lazarus, of Bethany. Brother of Martha* and Mary* of Bethany, a beloved friend of Jesus. Jesus cried when he learned of his death. When Jesus arrived at his tomb, he called Lazarus back to life (John 11:1-45, page 354). One legend claims that Lazarus died a martyr in Cyprus, where he was a bishop. According to another, he was the first bishop of Marseilles or Autun, in France. The Christians in the Middle Ages named Lazarus guardian of the lepers, because they mistook him for

Resurrection of Lazarus. *12th century Byzantine manuscript. Lazarus is wrapped in mortuary strips of cloth. An assistant holds his nose which recalls Mary's comment in the scriptural account: "He smells already."*

the Lazarus of the parable, suffering from skin disease. For this reason, the leper-houses were called lazarets.

Lent

SEE PASSOVER.

Levi

Third son of Jacob and Leah, at the origin of one of the twelve tribes of Israel. Moses,* Aaron,* Jeremiah,* Ezekiel,* the Maccabees,* Zechariah,* Elizabeth, John the Baptist,* Caiaphas* and Barnabas,* all came from the tribe of Levi.

Unlike the other eleven tribes, the tribe of Levi had no land. This was because, following Aaron and his son, the members of the tribe were consecrated to perform the worship ceremony. Thus, they resided in every city of Israel. As priests or levites,* they installed themselves in the Temple of Jerusalem when it was their turn to perform the service (Luke 1:8, page 298).

Matthew the evangelist is called Levi twice in the New Testament.

SEE MATTHEW.

Levite *playing the cithara.*

Levite

Name of those belonging the tribe of Levi, who had less important duties than the priests in the Temple* of Jerusalem. They were divided into two groups. Singers and musicians formed the upper class; the others were guardians, in the service of the Temple. They did all the cleaning, except for the priest's square, which could only be cleaned by them alone. They maintained order in the Temple by making sure, for example, that women did not enter the square of men. It is the guardians who tried to seize Jesus the day of the Feast of Tabernacles (John 7:45-52, page 347) before arresting him in Gethsemane (Mark 14:43-50, page 370).

Leviticus

Name of the third book of the Bible. This book gives detailed information about sacrifices* and the role of the priests.*

Liturgy

The Greek word *leiturgia* is used in the Bible for the service performed by priests* and levites* in the Temple.

Today, the word liturgy designates the fixed form of public worship and prayer used in certain Churches, especially during the celebration of the Lord's Supper, the Eucharist. Other Churches are much more in favor of spontaneous prayers during their worship services.

See illustration, pages 470-471.

Lord

In Greek the word *Kurios*, "LORD," is used to translate YHVH,* the Name of God.
The resurrection of Jesus enabled the apostles

to fully recognize his divinity. From that point on, they gave him the title of Lord (Acts 2:36, page 402). They named "Day of the Lord" the first day of the week, day of the Resurrection.

Lord's Supper (The)

It was during his last evening meal with his disciples that the Lord instituted what is called the Lord's Supper or the Breaking of the Bread by most Protestants, or the Eucharist* by Anglicans and Catholics.
See illustration, pages 382-383.

Lot

Nephew of Abraham (Genesis 12:4-5, page 36), and according to the Bible, the father of Moab* and Edom.*
Lot was rescued first by Abraham, then by two angels from the wicked environment of Sodom where Lot himself fell prey to temptation. Jesus taught about Lot's return from Sodom, as did Peter. The first Christian Church celebrated Lot's hospitality and purity (see PURE) of heart while he lived among sinful Sodom.
See illustration, pages 44-45.

Luke

Gentile physician, author of the Gospel bearing his name and of the Acts of the Apostles (see page 297); close friend and companion of the apostle Paul, but not an eyewitness of the life of Jesus. Though a physician by profession, he was primarily an evangelist. He accompanied Paul in missionary work. Luke was a well-educated man, a gifted writer and a consummate historian who regarded himself as a servant of the Word.

Maccabee

Surname of the Jewish hero Judas,* main leader of the Jewish rebellion against the Greeks in 2nd century B.C. (see page 179). Maccabee means "hammerer." His name may have referred to the strength with which he opposed the Greeks. Later, the name of Maccabee was extended to his entire family.

Lot and his daughters.
Albert Dürer (around 1505). National Gallery of Art - Washington D.C.. In the background, Sodom burns.

M

Magi

In the past, the Magi were a class of "wise men" or astrologers who interpreted dreams and messages of the gods. Later, Christian traditions regarded the Magi as kings. In the New Testament, the term also included all who practiced magic arts. The Magi were frequently consulted before any decision was made. They were asked for their blessings, or sometimes for their curses* against the enemies (see page 81-83).
The most celebrated Magi in the Bible are those mentioned at the beginning of Matthew's Gospel (2:1-12, page 255). By some, they were regarded as foreigners with strange practices who had come to worship* the newborn King of the Jews.
Matthew was deliberate when he reported the presence of the Magi in his account of Jesus' birth. The Magi represented the fact that Jesus had come for all men, including Gentiles. Matthew used the wisdom of the Magi as a vigorous wake-up call to the Jews: if Gentiles as foreign as the Magi had recognized the manifestation of God in the birth of Jesus, why couldn't the Jews? Matthew reasoned that they, the Jews, God's covenant people, had been privileged to centuries of prophesies about the arrival of the Messiah.
In the 9th century occidental world, some Magi were regarded as kings and descendants of the three sons of Noah: Melchior, descended from Ham, ancestor of the Africans; Balthasar, descended from Shem, ancestor of the Asians; Caspar, descended from Japheth, ancestor of the Europeans.

The Magi. *6th century mosaic. Sant' Apollinare il Nuovo. Ravenna. The Magi are not yet likened to kings (see page 186). They represent the three ages of man: the old man first, followed by the young and the adult.*

12th century stained-glass window. Saint-Denis basilica. The Magi have become kings, but they do not yet represent all the continents.

Mark

Also called John Mark; the author of one of the four Gospels, close friend of the apostle Peter.
SEE JOHN MARK AND PAGE 235.

The lion of Mark *presenting the Gospel, source of Peace. V. Carpaccio (1455-1525) - Venice.*

Martha

Sister of Lazarus* and Mary* of Bethany. According to Luke's account, she was a productive, generous woman, who was gently admonished by Jesus for spending too much time and energy on the meal. (Luke 10:38-42). Martha was equally loved by Jesus; he simply pointed out to her that she was worried about the wrong thing. On the other hand, he pointed out that her sister Mary had chosen what was better. Martha encountered Jesus again, at Lazarus's death. She readily received Jesus' astonishing revelation: "I am the resurrection and the life." (John 11:17-27, page 354).

Martyr

From the Greek word *marturos* meaning "witness," those who willingly suffer and die rather than renounce their faith. The history of the Christian Church is replete with examples demonstrating that those who bear witness to their faith by proclaiming the Word of God are seldom welcomed (Luke 4:24-30, page 308; Matthew 5:12, page 260). Over the centuries, countless Christians have been persecuted and put to death. Jesus asked his disciples* not to fear the death of the body but to persevere with their testimonies until the end (Matthew 10:16-33, page 270). Stephen (Acts 7:51-60, page 410), James (Acts 12:1-2, page 418), Peter (John 21:18-19, page 394), Paul, Barnabas and many others followed his command. They bore witness to their faith* despite being menaced, persecuted and, in the end, killed (Acts 5:28-32, page 407). They were veritable martyrs, willing to lay down their lives for their faith in Christ.

Mary

Miriam in Hebrew; the name appears in Greek in the New Testament as Maria or Mariam.
Mary, mother of Jesus. She must have been from the tribe of Levi, being a cousin of Elizabeth who was descended from Aaron (Luke 1:5, page 298). Mary lived in Nazareth. She was pledged to be married to Joseph, a carpenter, who was a descendant of David, from the tribe of Judah. At the Annunciation, she accepted to become the mother of the Messiah* (Luke 1:26-38, page 299). She gave birth to a son in Bethlehem and gave him the name Jesus.

The references to Mary in the Gospels are few and relatively uninformative. She is always associated with Jesus. Her presence near him was very discreet while he was experiencing popularity. But when he endured opposition and death, she was there, boldly standing near the cross as an expression of her motherly love and faith (John 19:25-27, page 379).

Miriam, sister of Moses and Aaron. Called a prophetess. She led the women in music, dancing and singing praise to celebrate the crossing of the Red Sea during the Exodus. She died at Kadesh (Numbers 20:1, page 80).

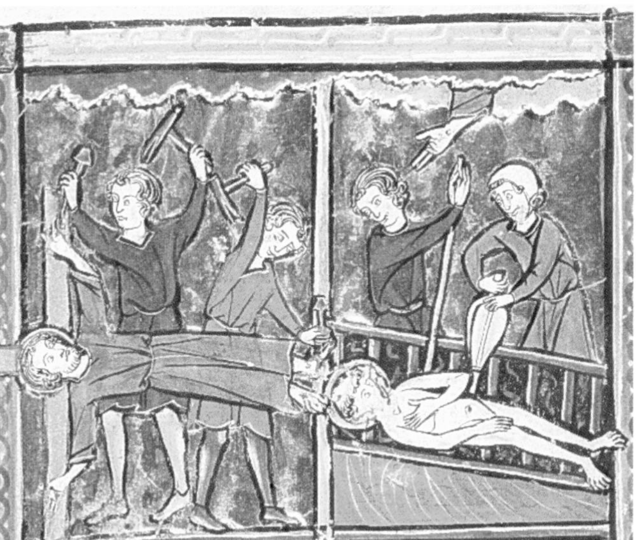

***Martyrdoms of Peter** (crucified head down) and **Lawrence** (burned at the stake). Book of Hours - approximatley 1250 - Carpentras.*

MARY AND CHRISTIANS

- All Christians believe that Mary became the mother of Jesus as a virgin (see the Nicene Creed, page 461). For most Protestants, she gave birth to other children after the virginal birth of Jesus.

- On the eighth of December, Catholics celebrate the Immaculate Conception of Mary, which was defined by Pope Pius IX in 1854. According to this belief, from the time of her conception Mary was never an accessory to sin.

- It was in 1950 that Pope Pius XII officially proclaimed what many had believed for centuries: the Assumption of Mary. Mary was raised up after her death and entered the Kingdom of God. She will live in the presence of God for eternity. The Assumption is celebrated on the fifteenth of August.

- Regarding Mary's death (referred to by the Orthodox as "dormition"), there are two traditions. One proposes that Mary died and rose from the dead in Jerusalem. Her tomb would be situated in the Kidron Valley. The other contends that Mary left Jerusalem for Ephesus with the apostle John and died there. One can visit the ruins of a house where she might have lived.

- The Annunciation is celebrated on the twenty-fifth of March, and Mary's birth on the eighth of September.

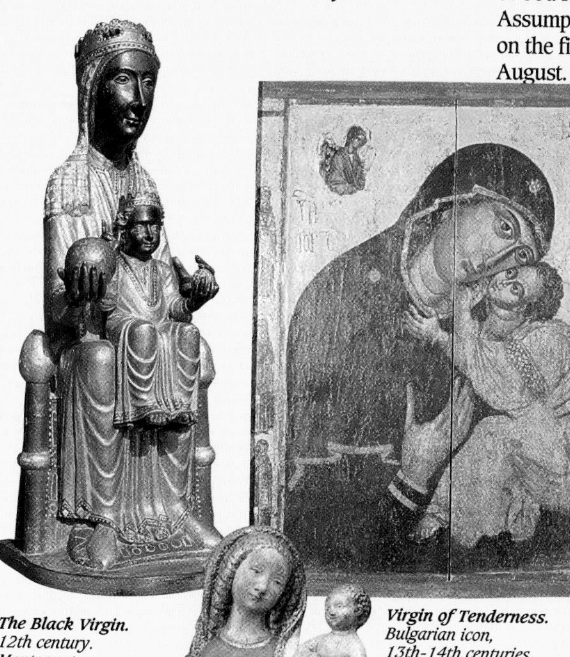

The Black Virgin. *12th century. Montserrat Monastery (Spain).*

Virgin of Tenderness. *Bulgarian icon, 13th-14th centuries, Sofia.*

The Immaculate Conception. *Contemporary painting by a monk.*

Virgin and child. *Ivory, 13th century. Louvre Museum, Paris.*

Our Lady of the Honest Valley. *Cantal, France. Gold and polychromatic stone, about 1500.*

Mary with Joseph. *Contemporary wood sculpture, Barret-Laprade.*

Crowned Virgin Mother. *Stained-glass of Bourges (1220-1225).*

M

"Mary! - Rabbi!" John 20:16, page 388).

Mary of Bethany. Sister of Martha* and Lazarus.* Remembered for giving her full attention to listening to Jesus (Luke 10:38-42, page 318). She is considered a model for all Christians: a believer is concretely enabled to do God's will by knowing how to listen to and absorb the Word of God.

Mary Magdalene. Jesus expelled seven demons from her (Luke 8:2, page 313). That he expelled seven indicated how deeply imprisoned she was by sin; for the Jews, seven was the number of fullness or completeness. She was the first one to see Jesus risen, and was immediate in telling the apostles (John 20:11-18, page 388). For this reason, the first Christians called her "the apostle of the apostles."

She has often been identified as "the sinful woman" who poured perfume on Jesus' feet (Luke 7:36-50, page 312). Many mistake her for Mary of Bethany who did the same thing (John 12:3-8, page 356).

Matthew

Apostle of Jesus and author of the first of the four Gospels in the New Testament (see page 253). Tradition suggests that he was stabbed to death in the back with a sword while celebrating the Last Supper. His body has been venerated in Salerno, Italy, since the 10th century.

Matthew.
Mass book - end of 10th century. Athens.

Memorial

See page 64, note 2.

Mercenary

One who works strictly for the money. In the Bible, the mercenary is depicted as a bad shepherd, one who shows no concern for the sheep in his charge. When he doesn't receive much money, he does not hesitate to steal wool and meat from his flock.

Jesus used the image of the bad shepherd, such as those mentioned by Ezekiel (34:1-16, page 163). He accused the officials of the people of being mercenaries, because they spurned those entrusted to them by God. They were not ready to give their lives to save their flock (John 7:47-49, page 347, and 11:47-53, page 356).

Mercy

The word "mercy," of Latin origin, translates a Hebrew word describing the love of a mother for the child to whom she has given birth. The Lord's mercy is the all encompassing love with which He surrounds mankind. Without ever growing weary of rejection, He forgives and helps them return to life as children of God. Hoseah describes beautifully God's maternal love for His people (see Hoseah 11:1-9, page 134).

Messiah

From the Hebrew word *masiah* meaning "the anointed one." In Greek it is Chrestos meaning "Christ".* In the past, certain leaders of the people–messiahs–were anointed with oil. In a special ceremony, they received what was called the unction of oil, a ritual that consisted of pouring oil on the head to confirming their authority as a king, prophet, or priest. As a messiah in one of the following leadership roles, however, they were not regarded as the Messiah to come, the Christ, about whom there were many prophesies.

The king as a messiah. Among the people of Israel, one became king by being anointed with oil. Oil was the symbol of the Spirit* of the Lord. Thus, the anointing of oil was a figurative act to represent the Holy Spirit's penetration of the heart of the anointed, making it supple to accomplish God's will (1 Samuel 16:3, p. 100). The anointed king was chosen to lead the people on the path to the Covenant. This ministry* was so important that God considered the anointed king as his own son* (Psalm 2:7, p. 209).

Unction of David by Samuel.
Ingeburge of Denmark's Psalter made in France around 1210. Museum of Chantilly.

The prophet as a messiah. Prophets were not anointed with oil; instead, the Holy Spirit literally penetrated their hearts (Isaiah 61:1, p. 187). They were often persecuted as they denounced sin in a disobedient people and urged them to be converted. They also announced that God would send a "Messiah according to his heart" to renew the Covenant.*

The priest as a messiah. During the initiation ceremony, the high priest* was anointed with oil. Apparently this practice assumed a particular importance after the return from Exile.* Herod* abolished it because he wanted to be the only one to appoint and dismiss the high priests (see p. 183).

The Messiah. Jesus was the Messiah, the Christ announced by the prophets throughout the Old Testament. Jesus was very cautious about using this title because he knew that the people had been waiting for a powerful king. But Jesus wasn't interested in fulfilling his mission as a worldly king. He was a messiah in a manner reminiscent of the prophets. (Luke 4:16-21, p. 307).

Micah

Prophet* and writer who lived in 8th century B.C. A book in the Old Testament bears his name. He was from peasant origin, and throughout his life defended the poor, crying out for social justice. He heralded a messiah that would bring peace (Micah 5:1-4, page 145). He was a contemporary of Hosea and Isaiah.

Midianites

Consisted of five families, desert-dwellers, known for riding, trading and using camels in warfare. They are related to Abraham through their ancestor Midian, son of Abraham's concubine, Keturah (see page 474).

Moses married a Midianite, Zipporah, Jethro's daughter. Jethro was well known for his great wisdom (see page 56). However, later in history, during the time of the judges,* the Midianites attacked Israel who were rescued by Gideon and his small band (Isaiah 9:3, page 140).

Ministry

From the Latin word ministerium meaning "service."

When God entrusts a responsibility to someone, it is always a "ministry," that is to say a responsibility in the service of his people and all others. Thus, kings* and prophets,* as part of their ministry, were called upon to help their people know God.

Jesus, Son of God, called himself a servant (John 13:1-5, page 367 and Philippians 2:5-8, page 440).

The New Testament mentioned several specific ministries, among others, which existed in the early Christian Church: deacon,* apostle,* elder,* and doctor.*

Acts 6:2-6, page 408, Romans 16:1-23, page 432, and 1 Corinthians 12:7-11, page 435).

Miracle

From the Latin word *miraculum,* meaning "strange thing," "wonder," "marvel."
To understand what a miracle was in in the Gospels, consider first that Jesus had always refused to perform wonders to surprise or impress people (Matthew 4:5-7, page 259). He was interested in providing signs.* The miracles which Jesus performed signaled something more profound at work: they served to help the people understand something not visible to the human eye. For example, Jesus healed a paralytic in front of many witnesses. The most important result was not his healing; rather, through it, Jesus invited sinners to trust him. He also demonstrated through signs that he could reconcile them with God by forgiving their sins* (Mark 2:1-12, page 238).
The miracles of Jesus were the signs that his word was the truth.
See illustration, pages 292-293.

The recovery of the paralytic in Capernaum.
Mosaic - 6th century - Sant' Apollinare il Nuovo, Ravenna.
The artist accurately depicted Mark's account, 2:10-11, page 238.

Mission

To entrust a mission to someone means to send that person out to accomplish a specific task. The Bible is filled with people sent by God on a mission.
God sent His prophets* off with the mission of calling His people to be converted* (Jeremiah 1:1-10, page 149). Jesus sent his apostles off to proclaim the Gospel and to baptize (Matthew 28:16-20, page 395).
The Church has as its missions to go into all parts of the world, announcing to all men that they are loved by God. (Acts 13:2-48, page 419).

Moabite

Tribe whose ancestor was Moab, descended from Lot* (see family tree, page 474).
The Moabites had settled in the territory of current Jordan, east of the Dead Sea. They were under David's authority, but they later regained their independence. Archeologists found a stele (an upright stone slab) dating back to 9th century B.C., on which King Mesha had recounted the problems he had experienced with the kings of Israel. To ensure his victory, he had offered his son in sacrifice to the national god, Chemosh.
The most famous Moabite in the Bible is Ruth, King David's great-grandmother.
SEE FOREIGN WOMEN.

Moses

From the tribe of Levi, brother of Miriam (see Mary*) and Aaron.* Moses was the great leader, prophet and lawgiver who, in answer to God's call, led the Hebrews out of Egypt, where they were enslaved. He then led them to Mount Sinai to make a Covenant with God. Throughout this arduous journey, he was a faithful, long-suffering leader for a stiff-necked people whose hearts were hardened to God. Just before reaching the Promised Land, Moses disobeyed God's orders in a moment of doubt. Thus, although God forgave him, He did not permit Moses to enter the Promised Land (Numbers 20:1-12, page 80). He died in the land of Moab* on Mount Nebo, across from Jericho. (Deuteronomy 34:1-10, page 89). See illustration, pages 86-87.

N

THE HORNS OF MOSES

Moses was so close to God that his face was transformed whenever he encountered Him. It radiated joy and majesty (Exodus 34:29-35, page 77). To describe this fact, the Hebrew text used a verb drawn from the word "horn." For the peoples of the Middle East, horns were a sign of strength, power, and beauty. Jerome, in the Latin version of the Bible, translated word for word : "the face of Moses had horns..." Western artists based their depiction of Moses with a horned face on this translation.

Moses.
Michelangelo (1475-1564).
Church of Saint Peter in Chains (San Pietro in Vincoli) - Rome.

Myrrh

Aromatic gum resin producing perfumes once used to embalm the dead. The Magi offered myrrh at the birth of Jesus (Matthew 2:11, page 256). Nicodemus offered myrrh at Jesus' death (John 19:39, page 384).

Mystery

The Greek meaning of the word is "anything hidden or secret." In the Gospels, mystery refers to the secret plan of God that was accomplished in the person of His son, Jesus Christ. God's secret plan was salvation: to send his Son, Jesus, who opened God's Kingdom to all those who believed in the Son. But all that concerns God is mysterious: everything cannot by understood by men. The Gospel is "the revelation of a mystery hidden for long ages past, but now revealed and made known" (Romans 16:25-26).

The Christian's knowledge (see KNOW) of this mystery deepens day by day. It deepens by meditating on God's Word in the Bible, through teaching received in the Church, and living out Jesus' commandment to love as he loves. The Catholics and the Orthodox also believe that the participation in the sacraments* enables the Christian to enter into the mystery of God more perfectly each day.

Growing in the knowledge of God is a process that never ends for the Christian. God's infinite greatness and the depth of His love is a continual source of awe and wonder. Thus, believers are, indeed, eternal "seekers of God" who justifiably pray: "I want to know you better, Lord. Show me your face."

Illustration:

Book of Hours of François de Guise - 14th century - Chantilly Museum. Jesus changes the name of Simon to Peter. Curiously, Peter wears a tiara, similar to a 14th century Pope.

Name

To have a name is to exist. In antiquity, to call someone by his name meant that you had a good relationship with him. It sometimes even indicated you had a certain power over him.

The names of men. In ancient times, names were not just labels to distinguish people. They told something about the one bearing it. A name might indicate the land of origin, as in Uriah's name (see HITTITES); a childhood event as in the name of Moses (Exodus 2:10, page 55); a parental wish for Jacob.* A man could receive a new name when he was entrusted with a mission,* or when his specific character qualities were widely acknowledged: Abram became Abraham (Genesis 17:5, page 39), Simon became Peter (Matthew 16:18, page 281), Joseph was called Barnabas (Acts 4:36, page 406).

The names of God. When Moses asked God his name, God replied: "I Am." Then He gave as an equivalent, the name written with four consonants YHVH* (Exodus 3:13-20, page 58). The Jews did not pronounce this name of God, because did not want to exert any power over Him by using it. Instead they said "the Lord," or simply "The Name" (1 Kings 5:17-19, page 118).

Jesus asked his disciples to pray by saying, "Hallowed be your Name." In John's Gospel, Jesus introduced himself with God's name: "I Am" (John 8:58, page 349).

Paul the apostle wrote that the risen Jesus received the Name that is above every name. He was saying that the Resurrection enabled the disciple to recognize that Jesus was indeed called the name of God, that he was of divine nature. (Philippians 2:5-11, page 440).

Nathanael

SEE BARTHOLOMEW.

Nation

SEE GENTILE.

Nehemiah

From the Hebrew word *Nehemyah* meaning "The Lord comforts" (see page 175, note 2). Nehemiah was a Jew working in the service of the king of Persia. He was informed of the difficulties the Jews encountered in returning from exile.* He obtained official authorization to go to Jerusalem between 445 and 433 B.C. As the appointed governor of Judah, he rebuilt the walls of Jerusalem and fought social injustice (Nehemiah 5:1-12, page 175). He came back to Jerusalem for a second mission in 424 B.C.

A book of the Bible bears his name.

Neighbor

In the first books of the Bible, the "neighbor" is defined as a compatriot, someone from the same people. (Leviticus 19:16-18, page 73). But gradually, over time, the Jews discovered that loving one's neighbor went beyond all boundaries. Jesus taught in the Gospels that a neighbor is anyone who needs help (Luke 10:29-37, page 317).

Nicodemus

Greek name meaning "victorious people." In the Gospel, Nicodemus was a Pharisee* and a ruler of the Jewish people. He secretly visited Jesus at night and became his friend (John 3:1-8, page 338 and 7:50-52, page 347). During Jesus' crucifixion, he publicly presented himself as his disciple (John 19:39, page 384).

Nicodemus brought a mixture of myrrh and aloes..." (John 19:39); On the right, the carrier of perfume. Van der Weyden - Flanders. Deposition (around 1435). Prado Museum - Madrid.

Numbers

The name of the fourth book of the Bible. Numbers begins with the account of the census of the tribes of Israel, thus it was given the title of "Numbers" in the Greek bible. There are also accounts of the desert plight of the people of Israel, the incident of Moses's "doubt" (Numbers 20:1-12, page 80), and of Balaam's intervention (pages 81-83).

Offering

SEE SACRIFICE.

Oracle

Jonah proclaiming the oracle against Niniveh. *Conversion of the king and the entire population. Book of Hours of the Constable of Montmorency - 16th century. Chantilly Museum.*

In the Bible, oracles were important declarations of the prophets* made in the name of God. Very often they were vigorous calls to be converted.* They served as a reminder that God was faithful to His Covenant, and they invited men to reject Evil* and to live with God.
The following phrases at the end of a preaching, "Oracle of the Lord," "Declares the Lord" or "The mouth of the Lord of the universe has spoken," meant that the message had truly come from God. The prophet had not invented the message on his own. (Jeremiah 19:6, page 153).
SEE INSPIRATION.

Pagan

Derived from the Latin word *paganus* meaning "peasant," pagan refered to people, neither Jewish nor Christian, who still practiced the worship of idols.* Pagan, which was used only in a few expressions, was nearly a synonym of "gentile".*

Palestine

The country where Jesus lived was named Palestine (country of the Philistines) only around 135 A.D.
While Jesus lived there, Palestine was the coastal plain surrounding Gaza and Ashkelon, where the Philistines* had formerly lived. In 135 A.D., emperor Hadrian, exasperated by Jewish rebellions, led a pitiless repression of them. His goal was to remove them from their land, and furthermore, to erase every trace of their prior existence. He changed the names of places as if the Jews had never lived there, thus the name of Palestine was given to the whole territory. The "country of the Jews" became the "country of the Philistines," as if David had never killed Goliath!
Therefore it is not accurate to say that Jesus lived in Palestine. This is, in fact, a poor anachronism.

Parable

Short, simple story to explain something more complex.
Jesus spoke in parables to explain the Kingdom of God, and to help people welcome it in their hearts. In other cases, his parables often warned against sinful attitudes: for example, the young girls who were not vigilant in their faith (Matthew 25:1-13, page 291); the older son who had a self-righteous attitude (Luke 15:11-32, page 321). Jesus taught that a sincere listener in need of changing his attitudes would recognize himself in one of the characters. While quietly listening, one could more easily and privately search one's heart than by being publicly accused of sin (see illustration, pages 326-327).

P

Paradise

SEE GARDEN.

Passion

Account of the arrest, the judgment, the crucifixion and the death of Jesus (see pages 365-384 and the illustration, pages 382-383).

Passover

From the Hebrew word *pessah* referring to the "passage".

Passover
The Jewish Feast of Passover is the memorial* of the day when God freed the Jewish people from Egyptian slavery (Exodus 12:1-14, page 63). It was also a pilgrimage: those who were able, ascended to the Temple* of Jerusalem. It was also called the "Feast of Unleavened Bread." During the week of Passover, only unleavened bread was served in memory of the bread hastily baked by the Jews escaping Egypt. Passover lasted seven days. The first night the entire family shared the Passover supper. The account of the exodus was read while eating the paschal lamb which was sacrificed* that afternoon in the Temple. Today's Jews celebrate Passover almost like their ancestors did, with the exception of sacrificing a lamb. Since the day the Temple was destroyed in 70 A.D., lambs were no longer sacrificed.

Easter
Easter is the most important celebration for Christians. Preparations can begin forty days in advance, beginning with Lent when many renew their faith through fasting, more assiduous prayer and sharing with the poor. At Easter, Christians celebrate three things at the same time:
- the memorial of the Jewish Passover;
- the memorial of the Passover Supper of Jesus;
- and their hope in the Resurrection*

Resurrection. *Mosaic - 11th century - Greece. Jesus returns from hell after having destroyed its doors. He takes the whole of humankind, symbolized by Adam and Eve, along with him in his victory over death.*

With the Jews, their ancestors in faith,* they celebrate God freeing men from bondage. With Jesus, whose death and Resurrection occurred during the Jewish Passover, they celebrate God who saves from the death of sin. All believers in Jesus then celebrate the eternal life made possible by the Lord. Because of his death and Resurrection, every person can pass from death* to eternal life with God.

Marking of the doors with the blood of the sacrificed lambs. Ancient rite of protection still practiced by the shepherds. Here, in Taiyiba (Israel).

Pastor

SEE SHEPHERD.

Patriarch

Name referring to the person at the origin of a family or a people.
There were three Patriarches of the people of Israel: Abraham, Isaac and Jacob. This word is sometimes used to refer to the sons of Jacob, ancestors of the twelve tribes of Israel.
See the illustration, pages 44-45.

P

Paul

SEE SAUL.
See illustration, pages 424-425.

Penitence

SEE REPENTANCE.

Pentateuch

Greek name given to the first five books of the Bible which are called by the Jewish by their Hebrew name *Torah*. The Greeks called them *pentateuchos biblos*, meaning "the book composed of five scrolls." The Pentateuch is composed of the books of Genesis,* Exodus,* Leviticus,* Numbers* and Deuteronomy.*

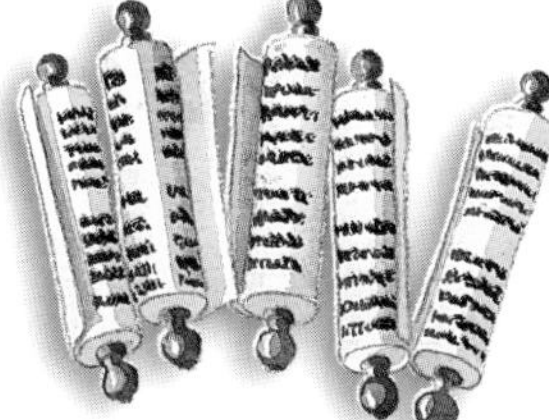

Pentecost

Important celebration for the Jews and the Christians.

In Judaism, Pentecost is known by its Hebrew name *Shavuoth*, "Festival of Weeks." It is celebrated fifty days after Passover,* hence the origin of the Greek word Pentecost which means "fifty." It is a one-day pilgrimage, during which the gift of the Law* given on Mount Sinai is celebrated.

For Christians, Pentecost celebrates the day when the Holy Spirit descended to fill the Twelve with its power (Acts 2:1-13, page 401). It wrote the Law of the New Covenant* on their hearts. It put an end to the division of the different peoples (Genesis 11:9, page 31). People who spoke different languages were able to understand each other and to live in brotherly communion, because they were filled with the same Spirit.

The Spirit affirmed and strengthened the Twelve's faith.* It gave them the courage to be bold witnesses* for Christ. In the Catholic Church, the sacrament of confirmation is offered to renew this affirmation and strengthening.

Persecution

SEE MARTYR.

Peter

SEE SIMON.

Painters habitually represented the Holy Spirit as a dove, but in the texts, the dove only appeared when Jesus was baptized. At Pentecost, the Holy Spirit descended as a strong wind and tongues of fire.

P

Pharisee

A Jew who was very attached to the Torah* and to the meticulous respect of the Lord's commandments* (see page 233).

The New Testament speaks harshly of the Pharisees, except for a few, including Nicodemus* and Gamaliel (Acts 5:33-40, page 407). The Pharisees themselves wrote texts in which they criticized their own faults, particularly their tendency to believe that they were superior to other people.

The gravest problem of the Pharisees was that they knew so much about God that it prevented them from truly knowing* Jesus. They were scandalized* by his poverty and his freedom. Saul* of Tarsus explained the difficulty he had in giving up his Phariseen mentality in order to believe in Jesus (Philippians 3:5-14, page 441).

Philip

Greek name meaning "lover of horses."

Philip, one of the Twelve. He came from Bethsheda, like Peter* and Andrew.* He led Nathanael to Jesus (John 1:43-48, page 335). With Andrew, he was a mediator between Jesus and the Greek worshippers of God (John 12:20 - 22, page 357). He once asked Jesus to show them the Father, to which Jesus replied: "Anyone who has seen me has seen the Father" (John 14:8-9, page 358). Philip evangelized regions west of Anatolia (current Turkey). He died a martyr with two of his daughters in Hierapolis, under the reign of Domitian (81-96 A.D.).

Philip, one of the Seven. He was among the seven men chosen by the apostles to oversee the equal division of assistance given to the poor (Acts 6:5, page 409). He baptized an Ethiopian (Acts 8:26-39, page 411). He had four daughters who helped him in his ministry. He lived in Caesarea, capital of Roman Judea and home of the governor. According to tradition, he died a martyr in Tralles, near Ephesus, around the year 80.

MEDITERRANEAN SEA
Ekron
Ashdod
Ashkelon
Gath
Gaza
PHILISTINES
20 miles

The five major Philistine cities.

Philip baptizes the Ethiopian.
Théodore Chasseriau (1819-1856).
St. Roch Church - Paris.

Philistines

People who came from Greece or Anatolia (current Turkey). They were among the "peoples of the sea" who tried to invade Egypt, under the reign of Ramses III (around 1175 B.C.). Repelled by the Egyptians, they disembarked in Canaan,* the southern part of the Mediterranean coast. At the same time, the tribes of Israel arrived near the Jordan. In their desire to expand their territory, these two peoples constantly fought against each other. Some of their wars have since become famous, such as the confrontation of David and Goliath (1 Samuel 17:32-49, page 100), and the death of Saul and Jonathan (page 105). The Philistines submitted to King David, but beginning with the reign of King Solomon, they had put themselves under Egyptian protection. Consequently, they once again clashed with the Hebrews. They survived several occupations: Assyrian, Babylonian and Persian. In the 4th century B.C. they adopted the Greek culture (see page 178), and from that time on, were no longer referred to as a distinct people.

SEE PALESTINE.

Philistines, *prisoners of the Egyptians. Bas-relief (around 1200 B.C.). Notice their curious helmets topped by feathers, or perhaps horsehair.*

P

Phylactery

Greek word used to refer to the Jewish teffilin which were small black leather boxes, containing four paragraphs of the Torah* (Exodus 13:1-10 and 13:11-16; Deuteronomy 6:4-9 and 11:13-21). The Jews tied them with straps of leather to their foreheads and to their left arms, near the heart (see page 84). The teffilin on the forehead reminded the Jew that his mind must be guided according to the Torah, by justice and love. The one on the arm reminded him that all his actions must be done in the service of God.

Prayer near the western wall of the Temple of Jerusalem, formerly called the Wailing Wall.

Pilate

Nickname of Pontius, procurator of Judea, from 26 to 36 A.D. Pontius Pilate lived in Caesarea, a magnificent pagan* city built by Herod* the Great, on the shores of the Mediterranean Sea. He traveled to Jerusalem during the pilgrimages, so that he could better survey the crowds.
Flavius Josephus,* the historian, recounted that he was a very harsh and violent man who routinely ordered summary executions of the people. In the year 36, he was asked to account for his behavior before the Roman emperor. Some claim that he committed suicide, others that he was executed.
See illustration, pages 382-383.

*On this stone found in Caesarea, the first line mentions emperor Tiberius. On the second line, "**..ntius Pilatus**" means ".. nce Pilate." On the third line "**....ctus Judae**" corresponds to "police of Judea."*

Possessed

In Jesus' day, it was commonly believed that a person who behaved sinfully was possessed, meaning inhabited by evil spirits.
Occasionally, the physically ill were also called possessed. It was believed that evil spirits caused illnesses, that they attempted to separate the sick person from God through doubt in God's goodness. Jesus delivered the possessed who became violent in his presence. (Mark 5:1 - 20, page 242). He healed the sick, thus demonstrating that he was victorious over Evil,* and stronger than Satan* and his demons.

Poverty

For a long time, the Jews believed that poverty was the sign of a curse* and that wealth was the sign of a blessing.*
Jesus took a very different position by denouncing the dangers of wealth. He said that wealth blinded man. Wealth led man to believe that he was self-sufficient, that he needed no one else. Furthermore, wealth could lead to veritable bondage: man would no longer use money, but would instead keep it and worship it. Jesus reminded his listeners that no one could serve two masters: God and money (Luke 16:1-13, page 323). Jesus praised those who shared their possessions, despite having few, and he praised those who chose to be poor (Luke 21:1-4, page 330; Matthew 5:3, page 260). Poverty frees man; it permits an open heart to meeting God.
Jesus' teaching shocked those who still believed that the rich were blessed by God (Luke 18:24-30, page 329).
The early Christians knew how to live in this kind of poverty. They willingly shared all that they had (Acts 4:32-35, page 406).
On the other hand, poverty is not to be confused with destitution. which is the lack of life's bare essentials such as food, a home, clothes, and work. This is misery.

P

Praise

SEE GLORY.

Prayer

A prayer is a dialogue with God. It starts with listening (Deuteronomy 6:4, page 84) and continues with thanksgiving,* praise and intercession.* See "The prayer of the People of God," pages 207-227, and "Christian Prayers and symbols of faith," pages 457-471.
See illustration, pages 470-471.

Priest

The priests. The Old Testament priests had mainly a sacrificial office. They made sure that the sacrifices offered in the Temple of Jerusalem were all perfect for God. They eliminated animals, incense, flour or any other offering of bad quality.
The high priest. The high priest was in charge of the Temple and presided over the Sanhedrin.* His function assumed an even greater importance after the return from Exile.* At that time, there was no longer a king and the high priest became the only religious leader of the people of Israel.
SEE ELDER AND MESSIAH.

Profane

A Latin word meaning "to take out of the temple." To profane someone or something is to divest it of its religious or sacred nature. To profane a sanctuary or sacred object is to ridicule it and to use it against God.
To profane the name of the Lord is to use it without respect, without fear,* in blasphemies,* or in black magic incantations.

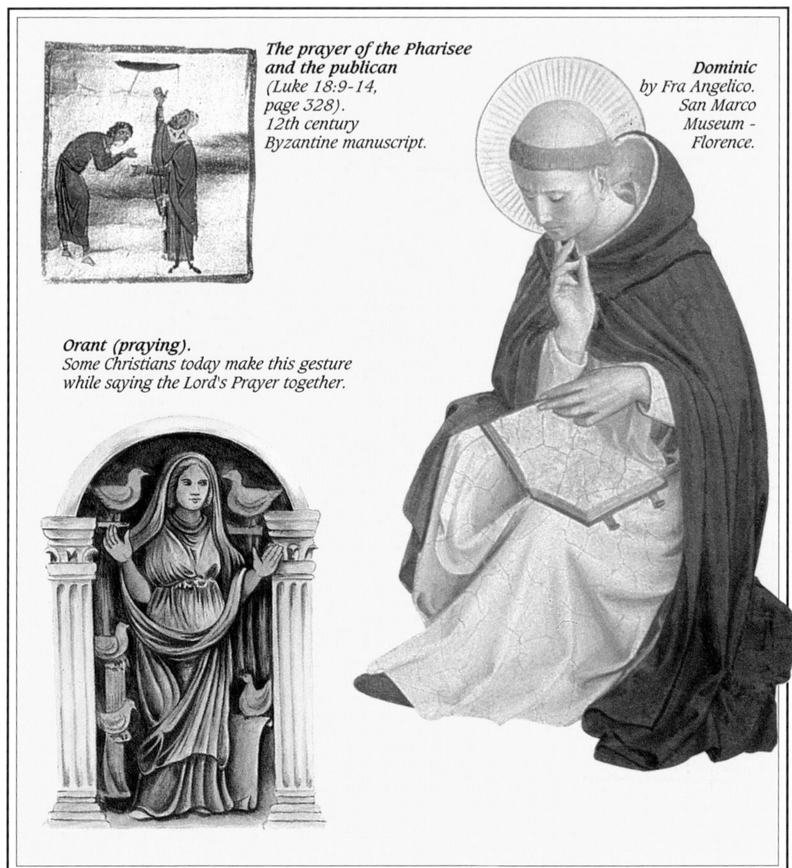

The prayer of the Pharisee and the publican *(Luke 18:9-14, page 328). 12th century Byzantine manuscript.*

Dominic *by Fra Angelico. San Marco Museum - Florence.*

Orant (praying). *Some Christians today make this gesture while saying the Lord's Prayer together.*

Promise

The Bible is replete with God's promises, addressed to His people. God promised to give His people all they needed to live in keeping with His Covenant. He promised a guide, a messiah* one after His own heart (2 Samuel 7:11-16, page 109). He promised a New Covenant (Jeremiah 31:31-34, page 157). These promises were fulfilled with the arrival of Jesus. But Jesus also brought a new promise from God: those believing in Him would all become sons of God (John 1:12-13, page 333).
SEE PROPHET.

Prophet

Someone speaking in the name of God.

In the Old Testament, the prophet was not just a soothsayer who predicted the future. He transmitted a message from God through forceful speech and, at times, surprising behaviors. For example, Jeremiah strapped a yoke to his shoulders to foretell the domination of Babylon (Jeremiah 28:2- 11, page 155). The prophet very often intervened when other leaders of the people, particularly the king, neglected their roles. Thus God chose Isaiah to be his messenger instead of King Jotham who was incapable of fulfilling his mission (Isaiah 6:1-8, page 137). It was the same case for the prophet Jeremiah (1:1-10, page 149).

Prophet Jeremiah. *Church of Moissac (Tarn et Garonne - France) 12th century.*

The prophet did not seek to be popular. He wasted no time heaping false praise on a disobedient people, congratulating them when they rebelled against their covenant with God. On the contrary! He was an agitator. He shone a light on behaviors and events which many would have preferred left in the dark. In short, he unveiled the sins* of the people. He unceasingly called men to be converted.

Prophet-writer. Prophet whose oracles* were collected, most often by his disciples,* in a book bearing his name. In the Bible, we find generally four "major" prophet-writers: Isaiah, Jeremiah, Ezekiel and Daniel, and twelve "minor" prophet-writers : Amos, Hosea, Micah, Zephaniah, Nahum, Habakkuk, Obadiah, Haggai, Zechariah, Joel, Jonah and Malachi. The adjective major and minor refer to the length of the book rather than to the importance of the message.

In the New Testament, John the Baptist is presented as a prophet (Luke 3:2, page 306). Jesus, powerful in word and in action, is recognized as a prophet (Luke 7:16, page 311), (Luke 24:19-21, page 390). Referring to himself, he once said: "No prophet is accepted in his home town" (Luke 4:24, page 308). He was a messiah* reminiscent of the prophets.
In the Church,* some receive a particular gift to be prophets (1 Corinthians 12:10, page 435). All Christians act as prophets when they testify to the Word of God.

Prophet Elijah, *borne up on a chariot of fire to rejoin God, leaves his coat to Elisha, his disciple. 16th century manuscript. Valenciennes (France).*

The four prophets of the Portal of Glory. *Santiago de Compostela - 12th century. Moses (holding the Tablets of the Law), Isaiah, Daniel (smiling) and Jeremiah.*

PR

Proselytism

In the past, it was the invitation to non-Jews by a religious teacher to embrace the Jewish faith. Those who answered the invitation were called "proselytes" (see page 233).
In the Christian Church, announcing the Gospel to the pagans was referred to with words such as "testimony"* or "missionary action" or "evangelization".
Today, the word proselytism has become derogatory. Cults are said to proselytize because of the impression that one is not free to say no.

Psalm

From the Greek word *psalmos*, meaning "song accompanied by the cithara." The psalm is a prayer in the style of a poem, accompanied by music.
It was a prayer to praise or implore God, to exclaim joyfully or to cry out in anguish, to confide in God a disappointment or to ask for His mercy. Every aspect, every thought, every feeling of a person's life can become a prayer if he or she tells God about it (see page 208).

Publican

SEE TAX COLLECTOR.

Pure

Something not mixed with any other substance nor alloy. In the Bible, a pure heart is a heart entirely given to God, a heart that does not serve two masters (Luke 16:13, page 324). A pure heart does not take pleasure in the darkness of "secret gardens" which God cannot enter. "Blessed are the pure in heart, for they will see God" (Matthew 5:8, page 260).

David is considered to be the first composer of psalms (see page 105).

Jesus teaching, surrounded by the apostles. Romane painting - Catalonia - 11th or 12th century.

The Bible teaches that men cannot purify themselves; only the Lord can and will purify them. He promises to give them new and faithful hearts (Ezekiel 36:25-28, page 165). Baptism* is the outward act testifying that a Christian has chosen to follow Christ, thus accepting the purification Christ offers. With Jesus, the baptized Christian dies to sin and its solicitation. He has been reborn as a son of God.

Rabbi

Hebrew word meaning "master." In the official Judaism, the title of "rabbin" was reserved for the scribes* and the lawyers,* because they had studied the Torah* and Jewish traditions for a long time. Today, this word has evolved into "rabbi."

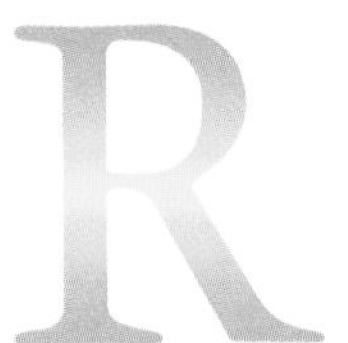

The disciples used it to refer to Jesus, because he was a master to them, a guide, a model. Nicodemus,* an important man among the Pharisees, also called Jesus "Rabbi" (John 3:2, page 338).
Jesus asked his disciples not to call themselves rabbi, because they were, in the first place, brothers. Enlightened by the Holy Spirit, they were to help each other live as sons of the Father and disciples of Jesus. (Matthew 23:8 -12, page 290).

Reconciliation

There is reconciliation when two opponents forgive each other and renew their friendship. Christians are called upon to be reconciled:

With God
It is always God's will to renew His Covenant with a sinner. With praise and thanksgiving* a sinner must receive God's offer of forgiveness, and allow himself to be reconciled with God (Romans 5:10, page 430).

Reconciliation of the lost son and his father
(Luke 15:11-32, page 321). Pompeo Batoni (1773). Vienna - Austria.

With others
Christians must always forgive, as they themselves have been forgiven (Matthew 18:21-35, page 283).
For Catholics, reconciliation with God and with others is achieved through a sacrament. This sacrament is sometimes called "confession" because man is invited to confess (to admit) his sins before the merciful Lord.
This is also called "penitence"* to emphasize the fact that the sinner can only ask for forgiveness if he enters a process of conversion.* But its most resonant title is "sacrament of reconciliation" as it underscores God's joy when he welcomes a sinner who has returned (Luke 15:7 and 10, pages 320 and 321). For the Protestants, the Church cannot intervene "sacramentally" in the process between God and man. Its duty is to preach the reconciliation Gospel of the forgiveness of our sins.

Remission of sins

The word "remission" comes from the verb "remit" which means "forgive." God alone has the power to remit–to forgive–sins. (Mark 2:1-12, page 238).
SEE FORGIVE AND RECONCILIATION.

Repentance

From the Latin paenitere, "to repent." It is a process followed by one who regrets having offended God. In the book of Jonah, the king of Niniveh covered himself with sackcloth and sat in ashes to demonstrate his desire for conversion (Jonah 3:6, page 191). In the Catholic Church, penitence is expressed through acts such as the confession of sins, fasting or other deeds of humility.
SEE ATONEMENT AND RECONCILIATION.

Resurrection

The passage from death to life.

DEATH AND RESURRECTION IN THE BIBLE

The Jews needed a long time to understand what happens after death. At the beginning of their history, the Hebrews believed that the dead departed for another world where they were in contact with God. Clairvoyants and necromancers even claimed they could contact and speak with the dead. They were questioned about the future and were almost considered as deities. King Saul condemned the necromancers because their practices diverted people from their search for God.

When the necromancers disappeared, representations of the beyond became very sinister. The dead were portrayed as shadows with no memory. They lived in the darkness of sheol* where there was no contact with God. It was believed that man could only know God while he was alive. After death, his relationship with God ended.

Some believers gradually rejected this vision of death. The hope of a real life after death began to grow, rooted in an increasingly more profound knowledge of God's qualities.

Eventually they embraced the fact that God is powerful: He can create beings, and He is able to recreate the dead who, in life, had served him.

They also understood that God is faithful: He could not abandon His followers in sheol, especially if death had come prematurely

Thus, faith in life after death spread among the people, but not to everyone. In Jesus' day, the Sadduceans* still had not believed in resurrection (Mark 12:18, page 251).

Representations of life after death.
In the past, it was believed that God would give another life after a period of sleeping or waiting in sheol. This afterlife was very similar to normal life. Hence the word "resurrection" was used, which meant "restore." God would restore his followers from physical death. The image Ezekiel used to describe the resurrection of the people after the Exile,* became the image of the resurrection of the dead at the end of time (Ezekiel 37:1-14, page 165).

Holy women at the tomb, *easter morning. Maurice Denis (1894). Saint Germain-en-Laye, France. Jesus and Mary Magdalene are seen in the background*

The day of resurrection: "the third day."
The prophet Hosea had predicted: "After two days, he will revive us; on the third day, he will restore us." (Hosea 6:2, page 133.) The "third day" became the typical reference to the day when the dead were restored.
When Jesus said he would rise on the "third day," the disciples had believed that he would rise later, with all the dead (see page 386).

What Jesus taught.
Jesus taught that there were not two lives, the one before and the one after. The moment we accept him in our hearts, we have received the life of the Son of God. This life will be perfected after death (Philippians 3:10-14, page 441). Death is therefore a "passage" (Passover*). There is no more waiting or sleeping; sheol has disappeared. "Today, you will be in paradise with me," Jesus said to one of those crucified with him (Luke 23:43, page 379).

Jesus emphasized the changes that believers will experience with the resurrection: they will be the same but far more spiritual, "like angels in the sky" (Mark 12:25, page 252).

His disciples barely recognized the risen Jesus (see pages 388, 390). The apostle Paul compared the mortal body to a seed planted in the earth and the risen body to the flower grown from it (1 Corinthians 15:35-44, page 439). SEE LORD.

Revelation

This word refers to all things God discloses to make Himself or His purpose known. It is the unveiling of something hidden. Over the course of history, God has chosen a people to be His witness among the nations.* He has sent prophets,* and then His own Son.
The pinnacle of God's revelations was Jesus crucified. Paul wrote that the cross was a folly revealing how far the love of God goes: even if people reject Him, the Lord still loves them (1 Corinthians 1:22-25, page 433). The Son of God crucified, scorned and ridiculed, still receives and forgives (Luke 23:27- 48, pages 377-380).
Revelation, also the title of the last book of the Bible, recounts John's vision of the end of time.
SEE APOCALYPTIC BOOKS AND WORD.

John describes his visions. *Notice the four living creatures and the martyrs under the altar in the sky. Dutch manuscript - National Library - Paris.*

Righteous

The Bible teaches that God alone is righteous because He always accomplishes what He sets out to do. He always fulfills His promises.* God wants to share everything with mankind. But in order for us to enter into a relationship with the righteous God, He needed to give us a new moral standing–a righteousness like His own. Jesus' death on the cross provided that, thus demonstrating God's love for all sinners: Jesus suffered in our place the judgment for our sin, thereby making us righteous, justified, in the eyes of God, and morally suitable to be at one with Him. "We have now been justified by his blood" (Romans 5:9, page 430).
A righteous person is one who allows God to justify him. Once justified, he begins reconciling with God's will for his life, thus becoming more able to answer "yes" to His calls.

Righteousness

A righteous* God must be, by definition, just. The justice of God does not consist solely of punishment, however, based on a heartless, rote sorting of the good and the evil. Understood on a deeper level, the goal of God's justice is to make a person righteous like Him. Thus, the drive behind God's justice is His infinite mercy and tenderness.
SEE LAST JUDGEMENT.

Rite

From the Latin *ritus* meaning "usage," "custom." In the religious realm, rites are codified gestures made during a ceremony. They are recognizable by all the members of the assembly. One example is the laying on of hands.
In a wider sense, the word rites alludes to all gestures and words of a ceremony, for instance the rites of baptism, burial rites, and so forth. The Catholic Church has special books called "Rituals" which explain its rites.
See illustration, pages 470-471.

Sabbath

Seventh day of the week (Genesis 2:2-3, page 22). Day of rest in honor of the Lord (Exodus 20:8-11, page 71).
Rabbis recounted that God conceived the week by "marrying" the first six days, two by two. The seventh day, the Sabbath (a feminine word in Hebrew) stood alone, so God gave it to Israel as a fiancée. Thus every Sabbath served as a reminder to the people that they lived a Covenant of love with the Lord.
The celebration of the Sabbath began Friday evening at sunset (John 19:42, page 384). Every home held a family liturgy during which the mother lit two candles to commemorate the two commandments to obey throughout the Sabbath: "Remember" and "Put into practice." The evening often continued with the study of biblical texts.
To reinforce the fact that the Sabbath was a holy day, the Essenes* and the Pharisees* greatly multiplied the number of activities that were forbidden on that day (Matthew 12:1-14,

S

page 272 and John 5:10, page 341). Jesus had not at all agreed, saying: "The Sabbath was made for man, not man for the Sabbath" (Mark 2:27). Thus, the Sabbath was created to help man grow in his knowledge and love of God, and not to bind him to a list of rules which prevented him from living.

Sacrament

SEE SIGN.

Sacrifice

Sacrifice of Abraham. *Indo-Iranian miniature - 18th century.* *The near-sacrifice of Isaac by Abraham plays a major role in the Muslim religion. It is evoked every year during the pilgrimage to the Mecca.*

Old Testament sacrifices showed how God expiated our sins through substitution. At the same time, by offering the firstborn of their livestock and the first fruits of their crops men confessed that they owed everything to God.

Prophets stressed that the sacrifices value did not lie in the rite itself but depended on the person's attitude (Amos 5:21-24, page 128, and Hosea 6:6, page 133).

Jesus invites his disciples to understand that their daily life, with its joys and sorrows, its accomplishments and failures, should become a love offering to God. This is the sacrifice pleasing to Him.

Jesus set the example. His life was wholly offered to his Father and his human fellows, and his death is a perfect sacrifice which substitutes for all the Old Testament Temple offerings. Christians commemorate his sacrifice during the Lord's Supper and find in him the strength to offer their lives as living sacrifices to God (Romans 12:1-2, page 431).

SEE HOLOCAUST.

Sadducees

A group of people composed of the families of the high priests and other important families of Jerusalem, living during the 2nd century B.C. (see page 233). Their name came from Zadok, whom Solomon* had chosen a few centuries earlier to be responsible for the Temple.

The Sadducees were the primary architects behind the death of Jesus: It was the Sadduccee, Caiaphas,* who had decided that Jesus had to be put to death (John 1:49-52, page 356). The Sadduccees paid Judas and sent the Temple guardians to arrest Jesus (Mark 14:43, page 370). Then they pressured Pilate to have him crucified (John 19:15, page 376).

Samaritans

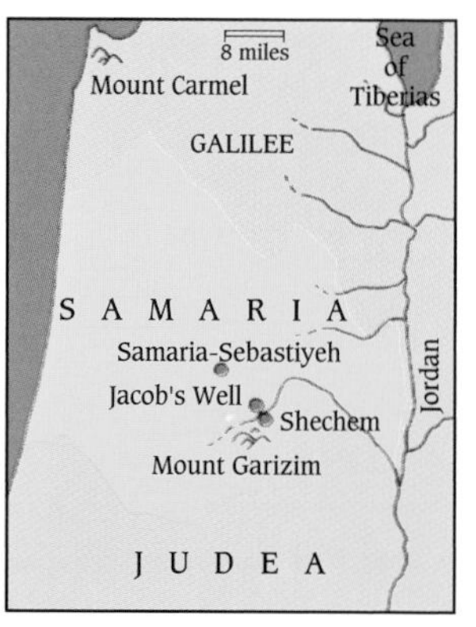

Inhabitants of Samaria.

After the conquest of Samaria in 721 B.C., the Assyrians deported many Israelites and replaced them with foreign populations. This was the origin of the people still known today as the Samaritans (see page 134). The Samaritans adopted the Law of Moses, nevertheless the Jews barred them from the Temple of Jerusalem. The Samaritans responded by building their own temple on mount Garizim. Unfortunately, a Hasmonean* king destroyed it, and it was never rebuilt. Nonetheless, the Samaritans never stopped their worship celebration at the top of mount Garizim (John 4:20, page 340).

In Jesus' day, the Jews and the Samaritans did not intermingle (John 4:9). The Samaritans were

S

The Samaritan Woman. *In the distance, the apostles are returning from the city where they bought food. Jesus reveals to the woman: "I am the Messiah" (John 4:7-30, page 339). Philippe de Champaigne (1602-1674). Caen Museum.*

not hospitable to the Galilean pilgrims on their way to Jerusalem (Luke 9:52-56, page 315). Despite this, Jesus spoke benevolently of them (Luke 10:33-36, page 317). He revealed to a Samaritan woman that he was the Messiah.* After his Resurrection, he sent his apostles to evangelize Samaria (Acts 1:8, page 400).
Today, Samaritans gather every year on Mount Garizim to celebrate Passover,* nearly as their ancestors did in Jesus' day, sacrificing the paschal lamb.

Samuel

Name meaning "He who is of God." His mother, Hannah, was sterile. She prayed to the Lord for many years to have a child. God brought her Samuel, and soon after his birth, she entrusted him and his education to Eli, the priest in charge of the temple of Silo. Samuel served in the Ark* of the Covenant (see page 96).
Samuel chose Saul* to be the first king* of Israel (1 Samuel 8:11-22, page 97). Then he anointed David (1 Samuel 16:1-13, page 99).
See illustration, pages 114-115.

Sanhedrin

From the Greek word *sunedrion*, meaning "Council."
Nehemiah,* in 5th century B.C., created a Council of 71 members, to assist him with his duties as governor. His idea was drawn from the Council assembled by Moses (Numbers 11:16, page 79).
From the time of Herod* the Great's rule, the Sanhedrin only judged religious matters. Occasionally, they pronounced death by stoning,* as in Stephen's trial (Acts 6:12-58, page 409).

Three groups were represented in the Sanhedrin:

- Elders, the majority of whom were Sadducees*
- High priests*; the high priest on duty served as president
- Scribes* or lawyers,* the majority of whom were Pharisees*

Sarah

Wife of Abraham* (see pages 36-47). God promised her a child, yet she remained barren until she was in her nineties when she gave birth to Isaac.* After her death, Abraham purchased the cave of Machpelah in Hebron to bury her. Today in its place stands the imposing tomb of the patriarchs built by Herod* the Great.
See illustration, pages 44-45.

The site of Sarah's tomb in Hebron.

S

Satan

Hebrew word meaning "accuser," "adversary"; corresponds to the Greek word meaning "Devil."
- Satan is seldom cited in the Old Testament. In the book of Job, he is an angel of the heavenly court, acting as a public accuser. Through numerous trials, he tests Job's loyalty to God.
- The apocryphal* or pseudepigraphic books dating to the 2nd and 1st centuries B.C. often mention Satan. He is presented as the leader of a group of angels opposed to God, who strive to lead men into disobeying God.
- The Gospels resume this portrait of Satan, or the Devil,* leader of the evil angels (Matthew 25:41, page 296), bent on destroying God's plans.
At the beginning of Jesus' ministry,* Satan tried to lead Jesus into temptation during their desert confrontation (Matthew 4:1-11, page 259). This confrontation was a microcosm of the battle Jesus fought until the end of his life. Throughout his ministry, Jesus never once sinned; he consistently turned away from any temptation that could have prevented him from doing his Father's will. This explains why Jesus called Peter "Satan" when Peter refused to believe in Jesus' imminent death; Peter's attitude of denial tempted the easy way out, which Jesus knew was not God's plan (Matthew 16:23, page 282). Judas was also called a devil (John 6:70, page 346).

Saul

A Hebrew word meaning "asked of God."

King Saul. From the tribe of Benjamin. He was chosen by Samuel* to be the first king of the twelve tribes of Israel (from 1030 to approximately 1010 B.C.). Saul was a mighty warrior who, with his valiant son, Jonathan, led the battles against the Philistines* and the Amalekites.* During his reign, he was exhorted by Samuel for his disobedience to the terms of his appointment to king. Samuel prophesied to him that he would be dethroned. Consequently Saul contended with David,* his son-in-law, whom he regarded as a competitor. He died with Jonathan in a battle against the Philistines (see pages 98 to 105 and pages 114-115).

Saul listening to David playing the harp. *See page 103.* *Rembrandt (1630)*

***Paul** preaching in a synagogue. Mosaic. End of the 12th century. Monreale (Italy).*

Saul of Tarsus. From the tribe of Benjamin. He was born in Tarsus, in the Diaspora,* and inherited the title of "Roman citizen" (see page 427, note 2). He was educated in Jewish law by the renowned scribe, Gamaliel, in Jerusalem (Acts 5:34-39, page 407).
After having persecuted the Church, he was converted* on the road to Damascus (Acts 9:1-9, page 412). He became the Apostle of the gentiles.* He died a martyr in Rome on the road to Ostia, in the year 67.
The epistles* he wrote to the communities which he had evangelized. are found in the New Testament* (see page 429).
See illustration, pages 424-425.

Savior

God revealed Himself as a Savior to the people of Israel. He freed the People from slavery in Egypt, then saved them from extermination, and Exile* (Jeremiah 50:4 - 20, page 159). Jesus, whose name

S

means "the Lord saves," came "to save men from sin" (Matthew 1:21, page 255). It is God's stated will that all of mankind be saved (1 Timothy 2:4, page 442). It is His will that they abide with him and be united in Christ in his Kingdom.*
SEE DEATH AND FORGIVE.

Scandal

Originally, a trap set to cause one's enemy to stumble. In the Bible, it is scandal that stumbles faith. Jesus told his disciples that he would be for them a scandal, a reason for them to fall away in their faith! (Matthew 26:31, page 367). And, in fact, his dishonoring death on a cross* did indeed scandalize them; it created a temporary stumbling block to their faith that plunged them into a state of utter confusion and doubt. Why? Because they reasoned that the Messiah* should not die in such a degrading way (see 1 Corinthians 1:23, page 433).

Devout - Christ of Perpignan - 14th century. Very realistic representation of the suffering that scandalized the disciples

Scribe

SEE TEACHERS OF THE LAW.

Scripture

In the Gospels of the New Testament, the biblical texts of the Old Testament are sometimes called Scripture or Scriptures. The resurrected Jesus used this word when he appeared to two disciples on the road to Emmaus, saying "in the whole Scripture what was said concerning himself." They didn't recognize him though, nor did they understand what he meant. Later, as Jesus broke bread with them, he opened their minds to recognize who he was and so that they could understand the Scriptures (Luke 24:27 and 45, pages 391-392). Today, Christians refer to the entire Bible* as Scripture or the Scriptures, in the plural.

Angels celebrating the celestial liturgy. One of them wears a cope, another wears (perhaps) a diaconal stole.

Sea

Hebrews were afraid of the sea. Their fear was rooted in the ancient Semitic belief that the sea was the realm of Leviathan, the powerful sea dragon (see illustration, pages 32-33). On the other hand, for Israel, the sea had been created by their Lord and thus under His command.

In Jesus' time, some people continued to believe that demons* lived in the sea. This is why he sent evil spirits back into it (Mark 5:1 - 20, page 242). When Jesus pacified the storm and walked on the sea, he demonstrated his victory over Satan* (Mark 4:35-41, page 241 and Matthew 14:25-33, page 279).
In the new world that God is preparing, the sea disappears because Satan will be defeated (Revelation 21:1, page 454).

Semites

Descendants of Shem, older son of Noah (Genesis 6:10, page 27). The Jews and the Arabs, descendants of Abraham,* are Semites. However, the word anti-semitism refers uniquely to prejudice against the Jews. Christians vigorously denounce anti-semitism: to scorn the Jews is to scorn Jesus, the prophets and the apostles.

Seraphim

Name meaning "to burn." They are angels,* mentioned only in the early vision of Isaiah. Like the cherubim,* they led divine worship, celebrating the glory of God and proclaiming His holiness* (Isaiah 6:2-7, page 137).

S

Jesus, the servant, washes Peter's feet *(John 13:1-15). Peter's gestures correspond to what he says to Jesus: "Not only the feet, but also the hands and the head." Byzantine painting - 14th century - Salonika (Greece).*

Servant

One of the Bible's most surprising revelations* is its presentation of God as a servant.
Some of the people in the Old Testament* wholeheartedly sought to become good servants of God. Indeed, the prophets* were models of this quest.

But Jesus revealed two new things:

- God Himself is a servant of man. Jesus, the Son of God, had not come to dominate but to serve and to give his life as a ransom for many (Mark 10:35-45, page 248).

- God is not looking for servants. He wants sons, friends (John 15:15, page 360) who, like him, with him, will be servants of others. As servants, his friends thus reveal the extent of God's love for those served (John 13:1-15, page 367).

Sheol

Hebrew word referring to the dwelling place of the dead, sometimes translated as "hell." Sheol was envisioned as a subterranean abode: one descended to Sheol (see illustration, pages 32-33). The most ancient of texts presented it as a place of sleep and oblivion (Job 3:13-17, page 194). But faith in ressurection helped believers to understand that Sheol was only a kind of waiting place divided between the just who were with Abraham, and the wicked (Luke 16:22-31, page 324).

According to the Apostolic Creed, Jesus descended to Hell (1 Peter 3:19, page 446). Some think that at his Resurrection he took all the just who had preceded him with him to Heaven. Death is thus no more a place of sleep! (Luke 23:43, page 379).

The Good Shepherd. *Ivory sculpture, 3rd century. Louvre Museum. "I have found my lost sheep." (Luke 15:6, page 320)*

Shepherd

Often used in the Bible, this word can be literal or metaphorical, but both signify one who guides and cares for others. In the Old Testament, God Himself is referred to as the Shepherd of Israel.
David, who was a literal shepherd in his youth, later became king and served as the shepherd of his people. It was a daunting task; David found himself severely criticized by the prophet Nathan for failing his flock (page 110).
The descendants of David fared worse. Consequently we read that the prophet Ezekiel announced that God would no longer endure shepherds mistreating His flock, His people (see page 163), and would personally intervene to shepherd them. Indeed, we see Ezekiel's prophecy fulfilled in the New Testament; God intervened as the person of Jesus Christ. It was Christ's mission to be Shepherd, willing to lay down his life for his sheep (John 10:11, page 352).
Jesus asks Peter and the Twelve* with him to imitate him and become the shepherds of the flock he leaves in their care (John 21:15-17, page 394).
Today, in some churches, the bishop is vested with the mission to care for Christians as shepherds. In the Catholic Church, the hooked staff, called a crosier, carried by the bishop symbolizes the staff carried by a literal shepherd. His ministry, which includes teaching and counseling, is called a pastoral in the diocese. In Protestant churches, shepherding is considered a role of the pastor.

S

Shroud

Cloths in which the dead were wrapped. Joseph* of Arimathea and Nicodemus* wrapped the body of Jesus in a fine linen shroud after removing him from the cross (John 19:40, page 384).

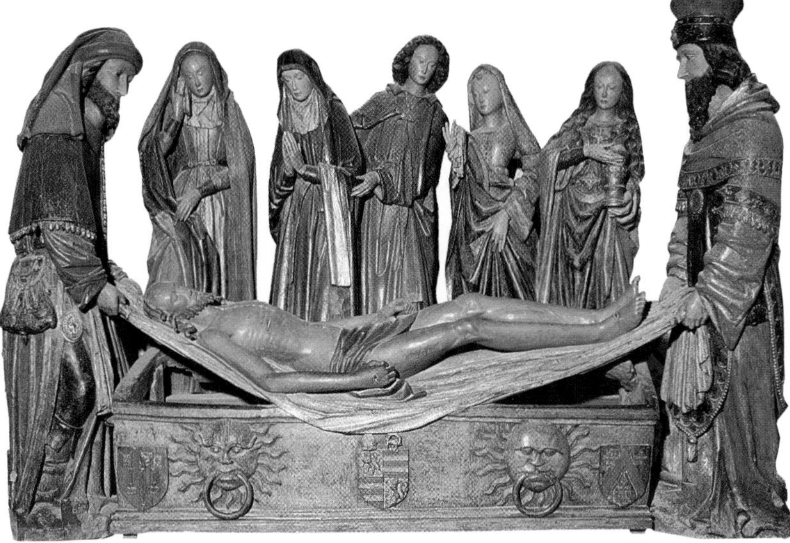

Entombment.
Church of Moissac (Tarn-et-Garonne - France) 15th century. When "the disciple whom Jesus loved" saw the shroud "lying there," he believed in the resurrection.

Sign

Everyone every day makes many signs with his hands, his eyes, his body. For example, hands can wave, offer gifts, or make fists; eyes can wink, cry or widen in disbelief. Human relationships are based upon signs. This is why God gave men signs of His Covenant: the rainbow (Genesis 9:13, page 30), His Name (Exodus 3:13-15, page 58), the cloud (Exodus 34:5, page 76). Prophets performed signs to fortify their words (Jeremiah 19:1-11, page 153). Jesus, too, performed many signs to proclaim his Father's love. He was baptized, touched the leprous, ate with tax collectors, healed the lame. His whole life, his death and his Resurrection are signs of God's victory over death.
Today God gives signs of His love through the sacraments. They are seven in number according to the Catholic Church and two for the Protestants.
See illustration, pages 470-471.

Simon

Later version of Hebrew name Simeon, meaning "the Lord has heard." There were numerous Simons or Simeons mentioned in the Bible. Of the more significant:

Simeon, the patriarch. Second son of Jacob and Leah. One of the ancestors of the twelve tribes of Israel (see page 51).

Simon, son of Jonas (or John), the first one among the Twelve. From Bethsheda, brother of Andrew.* He was a fisherman who lived with his mother-in-law in Capernaum. Jesus gave him the Aramaic name Kepha, Peter, meaning "rock." He entrusted him with the task of watching over his Christian brothers and strengthening them in faith* (Matthew 16:18, page 281, and Luke 22:31-32, page 367).

Scandalized* by the arrest of Jesus, Peter denied him three times (John 18:12-17, page 371).

Simon Peter crucified head down.
Luca della Robbia (1400-1482) - Terracotta. Bargello Museum - Florence.

But in a triple confession of love to Jesus' question, he was forgiven his former denials (John 21:15-19, page 394).

After the Pentecost,* he became the leader of the Christian community of Jerusalem. Later, he left this responsibility to James,* the brother of the Lord, for a mission.* He baptized centurion Cornelius in Caesarea. He visited Antioch and Rome. Tradition suggests that he died a martyr in the Roman games in 67 A.D. (see John 21:18-19, page 394).

Simon the Zealot, one of the Twelve, also called Simon the Canaanite. Little is known about him. His nickname suggests that he adhered to the Zealot party, but it is debatable whether he was a Zealot in the political or religious sense. According to some, he evangelized Armenia, with Judas the son of James, and died a martyr sawn in half.

Simeon, the old man in the Temple (see Luke 2:25-35, page 304).

Simeon welcomes the infant Jesus when he is presented in the Temple.
Mosaic - 13th century. Santa Maria in Trastevere - Rome.

Sin

Refusal to live with God.
This refusal can be total: to renounce God, to reject Him definitively. Or it can be limited: to be unfaithful to His Covenant,* to forget Him, to disobey Him.
Sin can be aimed directly at God: not wanting anything to do with him, prefering other gods such as money or power. Or sin can be an indirect refusal of God: not taking His Commandments* seriously, not loving others, deciding alone about what is good and what is evil.
According to the Bible, sin is the source of genuine death,* because man has been created to be in relationship with God and others. When he refuses this relationship, he destroys himself, and thereby chooses death (Deuteronomy 30:15-20, page 85).

The Tempter.
Strasbourg. Approximately 1280-1285.
The sculptor portrayed Satan as a seducer.
He holds the fruit of the garden (Genesis 3:1-5, page 24) and wears the crown of the "prince of this world."

Snake

The snake, representation of the Devil. The snake in the Garden of Eden (Genesis 3:1-5, page 24; see illustration, pages 32-33) is likened to the Devil* in the books of Wisdom and Revelation (12:9, page 453).
In what seems paradoxical, Jesus commanded his disciples to be as shrewd as snakes (Matthew 10:16, page 270). By this, he was warning them against being gullible fools. Why allocate shrewdness just to the Devil? But Jesus drew the necessary distinction: he commanded his disciples to develop a facility in doing good, not Evil* (Luke 16:8, page 323).
The bronze snake. The image that God commanded Moses to put up on a pole, a standard, in the desert. It protected the people from an invasion of poisonous snakes (see illustration, pages 86-87). Later it became an obstacle to Israel's faith, because it was worshipped as an idol.* King Hezekiah, a contemporary of Isaiah,* had it destroyed.
The apostle John refers to the bronze snake in his Gospel (John 3:14, page 338). He regarded the raising of the snake on its pole as a prophetic symbol of the elevation of Jesus on "the standard of the cross."

S

Solomon

Son of David* and Bathsheba.* He reigned from 970 to 931 B.C. He built the first Temple* of Jerusalem (see page 118). He is remembered for his great wisdom,* but the end of his life serves as a cautionary tale against the temptation of idolatry.*
See illustration, pages 114-115.

The judgement of Solomon.
Nicolas Poussin (1594-1665) - Louvre Museum. Solomon is very young here, his wisdom being a gift of God and not the result of his experience (page 116). But Poussin erred: The woman begging for mercy should be holding the dead child, and not the contrary (carefully read page 117).

Son

In the Gospels, Jesus is occasionally called "Son." God called him Son at his baptism and the Transfiguration, saying: "You are my Son whom I love." (Mark 1:11, page 236 and 9:7, page 247). In Luke's Gospel account, he records Jesus' words: "No one knows who the Father is except the Son" (Luke 10:22, page 316). In the parable of the vineyard, Jesus said that he was the son (Mark 12:6-8, page 250). John the evangelist often talks about Jesus as the "Son" or the "unique Son." Through this name, divinely appropriated for Jesus, the Gospels reveal the completely unique relationship uniting him and the Father.
SEE ABBA AND CHRIST.

Son of God

In Judaic world before Jesus was born, the title Son of God referred to the Messiah* (Psalm 2:7, page 209), and in a broader sense, to righteous men (Wisdom 2:13, page 202). It meant that God was like a father to man, His most beloved creation. Although Jesus resisted using this title, others around him were no doubt calling him that; it is clear in the Gospel accounts that the Jewish authorities caught wind of the claim and suspected that Jesus himself was claiming to be the Messiah. After his Resurrection, when it became gradually obvious to more and more people that Jesus had truly come from God, the title of Son of God gained a new meaning : As Son of God, he was "begotten by the Father," and "having the same nature." (see Nicene Creed, page 461).

Son of Man

On specific occasions Jesus referred to himself by this title. Although the title seem to suggest otherwise, it does not refer solely to the humanness of Jesus. In Daniel's visions (see page 205), the Son of Man had heavenly origins; Daniel saw him on clouds.* Jesus even described himself as sitting at the right hand of the Mighty One, the Father (Matthew 26:64, page 373).

By calling himself the Son of Man, Jesus revealed an aspect of his divinity.
SEE CHRIST.

S

Soul

In the Bible, the word "soul" has a variety of meanings. Hebrews* and Greeks had different definitions of the soul. The Hebrews believed the soul is life. Therefore, to give up one's soul is to die, and to save one's soul is to live. So, for the Hebrews, the soul referred to the entire person, and the expression "my soul blesses the Lord" means "I bless the Lord." On the other hand, the Greeks believed the soul is simply part of the person, that the soul is immortal and rejoins God after death (Wisdom of Solomon 2:22, page 202, and Matthew 10:28, page 270). Christianity draws on the Greek understanding of the soul, but rejects their belief that a person is divided into two distinct parts: the body which the Greeks judged as bad, and the soul which they considered good. Christianity believes in the unity of the human person. The soul is believed to be immortal, a seed that promises a Christian's physical and spiritual resurrection.*

Angel presenting a soul.
R. Guariento - 14th century - Padua. The soul rejoining God is represented as a child, since entering eternal life is often compared to birth.

Spirit

SEE HOLY SPIRIT.

Stephen

The first of the seven men asked by the apostles after the resurrection of Christ to take care of the widows (Acts 6:1-7, page 408). Christian hurch tradition considered him the first deacon.* He also performed miracles and preached. When Stephen was brought before the Sanhedrin (Jewish supreme court of law) on false charges of blasphemy, he boldly criticized the Jewish people by recounting their rebellious history of killing the prophets, then exhorted them for continuing in the tradition of their ancestors by killing the Messiah (Acts 7:52, page 410). He was immediately sentenced to stoning* at the instigation of Cilician and Asian Jews. Saul of Tarsus, who would become the apostle Paul,* was among the Cilicians; he was also present at Stephen's terrible death, during which Stephen prayed for his persecutors to be forgiven (Acts 7:58-8:1, page 410). Stephen's death undoubtedly played an important role in Paul's conversion.

Stoning

To kill by throwing stones. The Jewish law prescribed stoning for the crimes of idolatry,* blasphemy and adultery. But Jesus gave a new, categorical teaching on this subject: "If anyone of you is without sin, let him be the first to throw a stone" (John 8:1-11, page 347). According to Jesus, the Law* existed as a bridge toward a greater love, not towards death.

Jesus himself was threatened with stoning because he was accused of blasphemy (John 8:59, page 349 and 10:31-33, page 353). Stephen (Acts 7:57-60, page 410) and James,* the brother of the Lord, were both killed by stoning. Paul was stoned in the city of Lystra, but survived his wounds (see the big illustrated plate, pages 424 -425).

Stoning of Stephen.
S. Camaldolese (1381-1426) Miniature - Florence. Stephen is dressed as a 14th century deacon. Above him, Paul points an accusing finger, but his spirit is uneasy. His spiritual combat begins, one that will end with his conversion.

Suffering

Suffering and sin. For centuries, suffering was regarded as a punishment of God. A sick person was a sinner* punished by God. Some even believed that God punished the offspring of sinners. Thus, the death of David and Bathsheba's was believed to be the punishment of his parents' sin (2 Samuel 12:14, page 111).

Rites* were invented to avoid such a punishment. People went to the Temple of Jerusalem to offer sacrifices* of atonement.* Some believed that the graver their sin, the greater the sacrifice offered to God needed to be (Micah 6:6-7, page 145). The prophet sometimes called the "second Isaiah" (see page 167) spoke beyond man's invention of sacrificial atonement. He foretold of a Servant of God that would willingly be punished in the place of the sinners. This Servant would offer his life in a definitive sacrifice of atonement so that the punishment would never fall on sinners. Through his sacrifice, he would prevent men from despairing or rebelling against God.

Still other prophets claimed that God forgave freely (Jeremiah 50:20, page 159; Ezekiel 36:20-28, page 164). They claimed that God did not require the suffering or death of the sinner to grant His forgiveness. And God certainly did not require the suffering of the innocent.

The Suffering of Jesus. Jesus revealed that suffering is not a punishment of God. His own suffering came from the men who rejected him and crucified him on a cross. Nonetheless, Jesus accepted this death and transformed it into an extraordinary act of love. He abided by his own words, "Greater love has no one than this, that he lay down his life for his friends." (John 15:13, page 360). Jesus thus fulfilled the "second Isaiah's" prophecy of a Servant of God. He gave his life to pronounce the gravity of man's sin and the magnitude of God's love. Men seek to reject God and God forgives, because man's rejection does not discourage God's love. Salvation is a free gift from Him.

The Passion.
(1932) Georges Rouault. National Museum of Modern Art - Paris.

Sunday

SEE LORD.

Synagogue

Jewish building of assembly for prayer and instruction.

- In the past, the Jewish gathered to study the Torah* in the synagogue on Saturday, Monday and Thursday. Children received religious instruction. Boys of twelve or thirteen, if sufficiently competent with the Scriptures, gave their first public reading in the synagogue in a ceremony called the Bar Mitzvah. Through this ceremony the boys became true "sons of the Covenant" (see page 305, note 1). This ceremony is still practiced today among the Jewish.

- Each day, there were three times of prayer in the synagogue: at dawn, at sunset and at sunrise. These times corresponded exactly to those once devoted to sacrifices in the Temple.

- The responsibility of the synagogue was entrusted to a group of Elders* (Luke 7:3 and note 2, page 310).

Safed Synagogue (Israel). In the middle, the bema, from where the Holy Scriptures are read. To the left, the sacred ark containing the scrolls of the Bible is open.

Synoptic

From the Greek word *sunoptikos* meaning "in a single glance," refers to the first three books of the New Testament–the Gospels of Matthew, Mark and Luke. They present a great deal of similar material about the life of Christ. They are sometimes printed on three parallel columns which permits a comparison of their contents "in a single glance." (see page 232).

Tabernacle

From the Latin word *tabernaculum,* "tent." (See Tent of Meeting* for explanation.) Name used today by Catholics for the armoire in which the hosts consecrated during mass are kept.
SEE EUCHARIST.

Tax Collector

Employee in charge of collecting taxes. The Romans had created a system of taxes on the goods passing from one Roman province to another. They entrusted the collection of these taxes to certain citizens, the publicans. The Jews did not like the publicans because they collaborated with the pagans.
Two publicans are very well known: Matthew (or Levi), who had a customs office in Capernaum (Matthew 9:9, page 268), and Zacchaeus, chief of the publicans of Jericho (Luke 19:1 - 2, page 329).

Teachers of the Law

Teachers of the law (also called scribes) were experts in the study of the Torah--the Law of Moses. Originally, they were royal officials who served as accountants as well as authors of the king's memoirs.
Under King Solomon, they began documenting the religious tradition of the tribes of Israel, thus creating the framework of the first five books of the Bible (see illustration, pages 10-11).
After the Babylonian Exile,* the scribes became experts in the study of the law of Moses, and they received the title of rabbi.* Highly respected schools were established where scribes taught the law. Jesus had never studied in a scribe's school, consequently their distrust of him is not surprising.
SEE RABBI AND MINISTRY.

Temple of Jerusalem

The Bible mentions the temple of Silo (page 96) and the temple of Bethel (pages 128-130). The Temple of Jerusalem was the most important temple of the Lord. When the Jews returned from Exile,* all the other temples had disappeared except the Temple of Jerusalem. It was the only remaining Jewish place of worship.

The first Temple of Jerusalem was built by Solomon around 960 B.C (1 Kings 5:16-8:43, page 118. See also pages 114-115). The Ark* of the Covenant was kept there, in the inner sanctuary called the "Most Holy Place". Nebuchadnezzar, king of Babylon, destroyed the Temple and the Ark of the Covenant in 587 B.C. (see page 157).

Coin (around 135 A.D.) showing the front of the Temple.

The Temple was rebuilt after the Exile, between 520 and 515 B.C. It was much smaller. In 167 B.C., the Greek king Antiochus Epiphane profaned* the Temple by offering sacrifices to the god Zeus in it. The Maccabees* purified it in 164 B.C., which was the origin of the Feast of Dedication, also called Hanukkah (1 Maccabees 4:36-59, page 179). In 20 B.C., Herod the Great began a reconstruction project (see pages 382-383) that continued for nearly forty years, until about 62 A.D. The Temple was definitively destroyed on August 28th in 70 A.D. by the emperor Titus.*
All Jews, in all lands, paid an annual tax for the maintenance of the temple. Inside the temple, only the former currency fabricated during the reign of the Hasmoneans* could be used (see page 250).

1. Outer court of the Gentiles. Non-Jews were forbidden to go beyond it (see page 507).

2. Outer court of the women. They could climb the fifteen steps that led to the door of Nicanor, and from there, see the sacrifices and the front of the sanctuary.

3. Door of Nicanor.

4. Outer court of the men.

5. Outer court of the priests.

6. Altar of holocausts. A fire burned there night and day.

7. Basin for the priests' purification before the sacrifices.

8. Vestibule of the sanctuary.

9. Holy Place that only priests could enter. Beyond the curtain, the Most Holy Place.

The esplanade of the Temple measured 480 meters by 300. It was divided into several areas: the outer court of Gentiles,* the outer court of the women, the outer court of the men and the outer court of the priests.

The altar* of sacrifices* and the entrance to the sanctuary were in the outer court of the priests. The sanctuary had a vestibule. It led to a large hall of worship, the Holy Place. The seven-branched gold candelabra, called a menorah, was found there. There was also a table and an altar.

Every day several loafs of bread for the Lord were placed on this table (Matthew 12:4, page 272). Perfumes were burned twice a day on the altar (Luke 1:9, page 298). The "Holy of Holies" was at the back of this hall, behind a double curtain. A plain stone replaced the Ark of the Covenant from the time of its disappearance. The high priest* placed an active incense burner on it once a year, on the day of Atonement.*

T

Temptation

Inner desire that leads to sin.* Jesus warned his followers to be vigilant and pray so as not to fall into temptations (Mark 14:38, page 369). He taught that the believer is to pray to the Father not to be led into temptation (Matthew 6:13, page 264).

The Bible teaches that the Devil* is most often at the origin of temptation (Genesis 3:1-7, page 24, and Matthew 4:1-11, page 259), which explains why he is called "the Tempter" (Matthew 4:3, page 259). But temptation can come from someone else, sometimes even from a friend. Peter had tempted Jesus to choose the easy way out, which had not been the will of God (Matthew 16:22-23, page 282).

Tent of Meeting

Tent erected in the desert to shelter the Ark* of the Covenant in the times of Moses (Exodus 40:16-21, page 78) before the Tabernacle was built. It was called the "tent of meeting" because Moses entered it to meet God. It was later used as a model for the temple* built by Solomon.

In his Gospel, John writes that the Son of God "made his dwelling among us" (John 1:14, page 334). He thus teaches that God is no longer to be encountered in the old tents nor in the temple. Rather, God is encountered through Jesus. He is the presence of God among men (John 3:19-21, page 339).

Testament

In the Bible, the word testament has almost the same meaning as covenant.* The Old and the New Testament recount the story of God's one great desire: to live in covenant, in alliance, with men (see pages 7-15).

Thaddeus

SEE JUDE, ONE OF THE TWELVE.

Thanksgiving

To "render grace" or give thanks to God for His Covenant,* and for offering His love freely and abundantly to all mankind. The Greek word for thanksgiving is *eucharistia* (see EUCHARIST).

Thomas

One of the Twelve.* He asked Jesus which path to take to follow him (John 14:5, page 358). He demanded and received visual and tactual proof of Jesus' Resurrection (John 20:24-29, page 389).

According to tradition, Thomas evangelized India. He is greatly revered in some churches on the coast of Malabar. Near the city of Madras, a cross bearing a 7th century inscription marks the place of his martyrdom.

Thomas and the resurrected Jesus. *Bas-relief - Romanesque cloister of Santo Domingo de Silos (Spain).*

T

Tiberius

Adopted son of emperor Augustus, he was the emperor of Rome from 14 to 37 A.D. Herod Antipas built and named the city of Tiberias after him. Jesus carried out his ministry under his reign (Luke 3:1, page 306).

Silver coin with the portrait of Tiberius.

Timothy

Greek name meaning "honoring God." Timothy came from Lystra. His father was a Greek and his mother a Jewess. Paul addressed two epistles* to Timothy who was one of his best known disciples (see page 442). Paul, along with other Elders, laid hands on him, thus confirming Timothy as his collaborator in his ministry as an apostle.* Timothy traveled with Paul to all the major cities of the Mediterranean basin. At the time of Paul's final imprisonment, Timothy was responsible for the Christian community in Ephesus. He died from stoning.*

Timothy holding the palm of martyrdom. *Stained-glass window - 12th century - Neuwiller Abbey (Alsace - France).*

Titus (Emperor)

A Roman general whose name is not found in the Bible, but whose role in the history of Jerusalem was significant. He arrived in Galilee in 67 A.D. with his father, Vespasian, to end a massive Jewish rebellion. Vespasian became emperor in 69 A.D. Titus continued the war, conquering Jerusalem and destroying the Temple.* Titus succeeded his father as emperor of Rome from 79 to 81 A.D.

Titus (Paul's disciple)

According to the Bible, he is the first Gentile to have an important ministry* in the Church. He succeeded in organizing the Christian communities on the island of Crete. Afterwards, he left for Dalmatia. According to some accounts he evangelized Spain; according to others, he returned to Crete where he served as bishop until old age.

Paul speaking to Titus, *shown wearing a bishop's robe. Miniature - 15th century - Saint Geneviève Library - Paris.*

T

Torah

SEE LAW.

Tradition

Teaching or custom passed on from generation to generation. This "heritage from the past" may affect all areas of life: the way people dress, eat, pray, marry, build houses, and so forth.

- Any respect of tradition which consists only in reproducing the past hinders people from adapting themselves to concrete life situations. Jesus reproached the Pharisees for having let go of the commands of God and holding on to the traditions of men (Mark 7:8, page 245). They were simply applying predetermined rules without taking into account specific events and people.

- A tradition is beneficial when it takes the past into account in order to help people live better in the present. Traditions of the Church should enable Christians to live their faith in fraternal love regarding every situation.

Tribe

An ensemble of families living in the same territory, descended from the same ancestor. The people of Israel was formed by the union of the twelve* tribes claiming to be descended from the twelve sons of Jacob*-Israel (see pages 51-52, and the map, page 511). After the reign of Saul,* approximately 1010 B.C., the tribes divided, then reformed under King David's authority (see "King of the Twelve Tribes," page 106). After Solomon's death (931 B.C.), the tribes definitively separated. Thus were formed two kingdoms who were often enemies. In the north, the kingdom of Israel, composed of the ten northern tribes; in the south, the smaller kingdom of Judah (see page 121).

Trinity

A word derived from the number three. The word itself does not appear in the Bible, but it is part of Christian language and has a distinctive place in the formal theology of the Church. The concept of the trinity makes three affirmations: That there is but one God; that the Father, the Son and the Holy Spirit is each God; and that the Father, the Son and Spirit is each a distinct Person.

Trinity.
Father and Son with an identical face, wrapped in the same coat, both holding the globe of the world, saved by the cross. The Holy Spirit is represented by the dove.

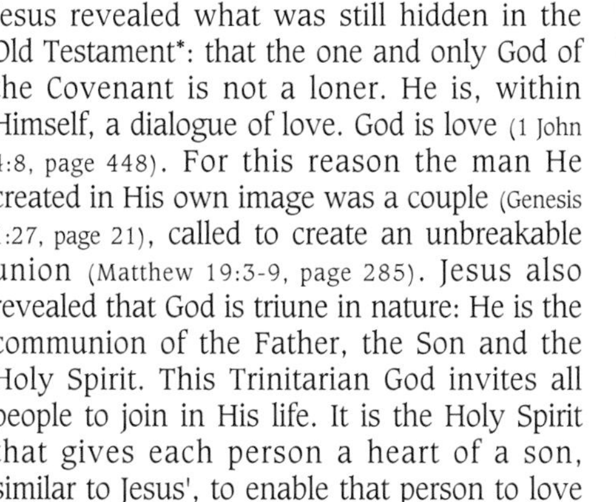

Jesus revealed what was still hidden in the Old Testament*: that the one and only God of the Covenant is not a loner. He is, within Himself, a dialogue of love. God is love (1 John 4:8, page 448). For this reason the man He created in His own image was a couple (Genesis 1:27, page 21), called to create an unbreakable union (Matthew 19:3-9, page 285). Jesus also revealed that God is triune in nature: He is the communion of the Father, the Son and the Holy Spirit. This Trinitarian God invites all people to join in His life. It is the Holy Spirit that gives each person a heart of a son, similar to Jesus', to enable that person to love the Father (Romans 8:14-17, page 431).
SEE BAPTISM.

Trinity.
Father and Son with their faces joined. A dove for the Holy Spirit.

Truth

In the Bible, truth is not an abstract reality, it is a person. Jesus is Truth (John 14:6, page 358). Thus, the Christian is not someone who owns truth and then imposes it on others. He is a seeker of truth, driven by his desire to know* the Lord Jesus better (Philippians 3:10-14, page 441). This is a witness of the truth in the biblical sense.

Twelve

The number twelve has great significance throughout the entire Bible. It was the number of Patriarches* at the origin of God's people, Jacob's twelve sons, and it was the number purposefully used by Jesus to choose a select few men among his many followers "to be with him" during his earthly ministry (Mark 3:14, page 239).
These men were called the twelve disciples,* the twelve apostles, or simply the Twelve. Their number signified that Jesus came to renew the Covenant of God with His people, as predicted by the prophets. There are instances in the New Testament where others outside the Twelve are given the title, such as Paul, Barnabas,* and Silas. But the Twelve Jesus called all shared the same, distinct qualifications: disciples of Jesus from the time of his baptism to his Ascension; versed in his entire ministry; and witnesses of the Resurrection.
During the initial phase of his ministry, Jesus was uniquely focused on the people of Israel (Matthew 10:5-6, page 269). He wanted to re-establish his people as a witness to all nations* of the love of God. But confronted with rejection by part of the Jews, Jesus announced that he would thereby establish a new people by reaching out to the Gentiles

The Last Supper.
Armenian manuscript from the 13th century Erevan (Armenia). The table is decorated with a traditional Armenian cross. The Twelve are painted wearing halos, even Judas., although it is more a decoration than a symbol of saintliness.

(Matthew 8:11-12, page 267). This new community built up very slowly however; the first Christian Church was still only comprised of Jews. Consequently, it was presided over by the twelve Jewish apostles, Matthias having replaced Judas.
The evolution from an exclusively Jewish-Christian Church to one that included Gentiles

began after the apostle James's death (Acts 12:1-3, page 418). James was the first of the twelve to be martyred, and no one replaced him. The symbol twelve was no longer necessary, since the people of God had symbolically crossed the borders of Israel by becoming the Church*: Jews and Gentiles united by their faith in the risen Christ.
Christ's Church is founded eternally on the Twelve. The Twelve remain a reminder that the faith of Christians throughout time is rooted in the faith of the Jewish people.
SEE APOSTLE AND SHEPERD.

Unction

SEE HOLY SPIRIT, MESSIAH, KING.

Uriah the Hittite

A foreigner and member of King David's elite guard. David committed adultery with Uriah's wife, Bathsheba, while Uriah was away at battle, courageously serving in the king's army. He died at war (2 Samuel 11:1-17, page 109).
In the genealogy of Jesus, Matthew wrote that David "was the father of Solomon whose mother had been Uriah's wife" (Matthew 1:6, page 254), thus stressing the fact that Jesus had come to bring salvation to all men of every race and culture.
SEE BATHSHEBA AND HITTITES.

Hittite couple.
8th or 7th century B.C.
Maras Museum
(Turkey).

God call Abraham!

Virgin

Man or woman who has never had sexual intercourse. In the Greek translation of the Old Testament, it is prophesied that the mother of the Messiah* would be a virgin (see AND NOW THE YOUNG WOMAN..., page 138). This prophecy was fulfilled through Mary, the mother of Jesus (Luke 1:26-34, page 299). In the Catholic Church, Mary is called the "Virgin Mary" or the "Holy Virgin."

Vocation or Calling

From the Latin word vocare meaning "to call." A vocation is a call from God that a person is invited to answer. In the Old Testament, God unceasingly called Abraham to be the father of a great people, and Moses to guide his people throughout the Covenant with God (Exodus 3:4, page 57). God called men to be prophets* (Isaiah 6:1-8, page 137; Jeremiah 1:1-10, page 149; Ezekiel 2:2 - 3:4, page 161). In the New Testament, Jesus called men to be apostles* (Luke 6:12-16, page 309).
All people are called to belong to the family of God (Revelation 3:20, page 450). Each one answers this call in his own way: one through matrimony, another through celibacy, some through service to the secular community, still others will use their gifts to announce the Gospel. Christians are called to many different vocations, but they are all members of the same Body* (1 Corinthians 12:3-27, page 435).

Wisdom

In biblical terms, wisdom is an intensely practical and religious way of thinking which stems from the fear* of the Lord; it is the specific orientation of several books of the Bible (see page 194). Wisdom in the most complete sense is owned by God alone, although God grants it to His followers as a

gift. For example, Solomon* was granted wisdom in order to accomplish his official duties. He has been credited with several works, in particular the book of Proverbs (see page 198).

Witness

SEE MARTYR.

Word

Word used solely in the first chapter of the Gospel of John (see page 333). It refers to the Son of God. John taught that God cannot content Himself with speaking to men through intermediaries, the prophets.* He wanted to speak to them Himself, directly. For this reason the Word became flesh,* the Son of God was made man: Jesus. Jesus' entire life, all that he said and did, was a message of love from God to men.

Traditionally, angels formed the heavenly court that glorified God in worship.

Worship

The vocabulary of this word is vast in the Bible, but the term essentially meant service, and in the Hebrew sense of the word, an act of service required a servant's physical demonstration of respect, awe and adoration. In today's Christian vernacular, the word signifies the acknowledgement of the greatness of God, the Heavenly Father to whom Christians turn with hearts full of admiration and love. According to the Bible, Christians are to worship God and God alone (Exodus 20:3-7, page 71). Although there are numerous ways of physically worshiping God, such as in song or prayer, the act of worship does not necessarily require words; one may simply assume a mental attitude of wonder in the presence of God's love and greatness. What is essential for Christians in the act of worship is to maintain an open heart toward God, responding to Him personally as He makes His presence known.

SEE FEAR AND TRINITY.

Worship Service or Ceremony

Public gathering of a church with the goal of praising God, giving Him thanks, and praying together. The worship service is typically organized by church leaders in a specified locale at regularly designated times throughout the year. The prophet Amos denounced the religious people of his day who celebrated religious festivals and ceremonies without changing anything in their way of living and thinking (Amos 5:21-24, page 128).

See illustration, pages 470-471.

Wrath

SEE ANGER.

YHVH (or YHWH)

Transcription in the Latin alphabet of the four Hebraic consonants of the Name* of God revealed to Moses (Exodus 3:13-15, page 58). Out of respect, the Jews did not pronounce this name. Instead they read *Adonai*, which means "the Lord."*

Christians sometimes say "Yahweh," but most often they use the word"Lord" to transcribe these four consonants, called a tetragram. The pronunciation "Jehovah" comes from an error in reading that spread during the 19th century.

Z

Zealots

A political and religious party opposed to the Roman occupation (see page 234).
In Jesus' day, the word "zealot" was seldom used. But many Jews, particularly from Galilee, vehemently demanded the liberation of Israel. Inspired by the uprising of the Maccabees,* they were ready to used violent means against the Romans.
Simon* the Zealot, one of the Twelve, was probably a member of the Zealot party, but it is not certain if he was a Zealot in the political or religious sense.

Zechariah

From the Hebrew word *Zakaryah* meaning "the Lord remembers."
Zechariah, the prophet. The book of Zechariah contains the oracles* of two prophets. The first one, announced after the Jews returned from Exile,* encouraged them to rebuild the Temple of Jerusalem. The second one, which was announced shortly after, prophesied the coming of a humble, persecuted messiah (see page 193 and pages 188-189).
Zechariah, father of John the Baptist. (See Luke 1:5 - 20, page 298).

Zion the Holy.
Dome of the Rock (called the Mosque of Omar) to the right. To the left, the dome (opened) of the Holy Sepulcher. 15th century illumination in a guide used by the pilgrims titled "Directional Advice for the Overseas Passage".

Zechariah
writes the name of John and regains his speech (Luke 1:59-66, page 302). 15th century miniature.
Saint Geneviève Library, Paris.

Zion

Originally, it was the Canaanite name for the citadel of Jerusalem (2 Samuel 5:7, page 106). This name was also applied to the "mount of the Temple," next to the citadel (see Psalm 137:1, page 225). In the years to follow, Zion was used to refer to the entire city. To speak of Zion or Jerusalem was the same thing. The "Daughter of Zion" is a personification of the city of Jerusalem (Zechariah 9:9, page 193).
See illustration, pages 114-115.

INDEX TO THE THEMES OF THE OLD TESTAMENT

INDEX TO THE THEMES OF THE FOUR GOSPELS

THE PEOPLE JESUS ENCOUNTERED

THEMES DEVELOPED IN THE BOXED INFORMATION

(situated in the illustrated frames)

GOD

Generalities

Qualities of the Father

Titles and qualities of the Son

The Holy Spirit

THE PEOPLE OF GOD

God calls all men

The Church

What pleases God

Faith

Hope

Charity

MAN

At the center of the world...

...sinner...

...called to conversion...

...to become a friend of God...

...forever.

INDEX TO THE TWO-PAGE ILLLUSTRATIONS

INDEX TO THE PRAYERS

PSALMS

PRAYERS IN THE BIBLICAL TEXTS

LITURGICAL PRAYERS

INDEX TO THE BIBLICAL PLACES

COMMENTS ON THE ILLUSTRATED FRAMES

When we adopted the idea of using illustrated frames for the pages of this book, we decided not to illustrate the Word of God in the more traditional sense, but rather to create a visual environment making His Word, the source of life, more accessible.

These frames have been created by contemporary artists or have been illustrated with Christian art produced over the centuries.

Thus the reader will discover that these texts have inspired and still inspire artists of all ages, temperaments, eras and cultures.

Here now, for your contemplation, are some brief, elucidating commentaries about the illustrated frames.

THE ROSE WINDOW
Régine Le Sourd, 1994. (pages 3-18 and throughout the book)

This motif, which adorns most cathedrals, marks all the pages structuring this book: the introduction, outline, titles of the various sections, and so forth.

THE CREATION
Régine Le Sourd, 1994. (pages 19-25)

The abundant gifts of God: minerals and colors, flowers and fruit, insects and animals, an infinite variety of shapes... everything incites admiration and contemplation. But the earth God created awaits man.

THE COVENANT
Laurent Parienty, 1994. (pages 26-31)

Dove, rainbow, olive branches, remind us that God is a God of peace. In a beautiful, peaceful world, He desires to satisfy man with the richness of nature. Is not the the olive tree a sign of abundance?

THE CREATION OF THE WORLD
Medieval miniature. National Library. © Edimedia (page 34)

With concentric circles, the artist depicts the firmament with stars and birds of the sky; the earth separated from the waters; the garden where God will place man, created in His image (see pages 32-33).

ABRAHAM THE NOMAD
Sophiek, 1994. After a mosaic of Ur. (pages 35-39)

With courage, and placing his trust in God, a man sets off with his family. He has answered the call of God, which commanded him: "Leave your country!" To find God, we must let go of our habits. God reveals Himself to those who prove their desire to find Him and know Him.

THE PROMISE OF GOD
Régine Le Sourd, 1996. (pages 40-47)

The artist depicts the climactic moments of Abraham's life. From God's promise of descendants as numerous as the stars in the sky, to the near-sacrifice of Isaac, through the three visitors' announcemnt of his son's birth by Sarah.

JACOB'S DREAM
Provençal School. Petit Palais Museum. Avignon. © Ken Takase/Artephot. (pages 48-52)

This painting beautifully portrays the contrast between earth-bound man, and the angel rising in the sky. The Son of God will come to abolish this difference by sharing man's condition, and thus opening the door of access to his Father (see John 1:35-51, page 334).

EGYPT
Sophiek, 1994. (pages 53-63)

The splendors of Egypt have long fascinated Israel. In the desert, the People of God longed for Egyptian food (see page 66). After the time of Solomon, Israelite royalties modeled themselves after Egyptian ones. (see the illustrated frame on pages 120-127). In the time of Jeremiah, their longing for Egypt became suicidal (see THE END OF THE KINGDOM OF JERUSALEM, page 157). In this frame, we see a beetle, Horus the falcon, the flail and the scepter, the Nile, a war helmet... The confrontation between the shepherd (left) and the Pharaoh (right) illustrates the choice that Israel was forced to make between the false security of Egypt and the adventure with God in the desert.

THE SINAI
Laurent Parienty, 1994. (pages 64-70)

To scale a high mountain is to discover fresh perspectives and new light; atop a mountain, a different way of seeing is made possible. For this reason, the ancients considered the mountain to be the best place for the revelations of God.

MOSES RECEIVES

Before the people, high on a mountain,

THE TABLETS OF THE LAW
Psalter of Ingeburge. 13th century. Chantilly Museum. © Giraudon. (pages 71-78)

Moses opens himself to the gift of God. He fully embraces the Tablets of the Law, prepared to follow the path opened before him by the Words of God, Words of Life, Words of Covenant.

THE PEOPLE OF GOD IN THE DESERT
Laurent Parienty, 1994. (pages 79-89)

The people of God walk in the desert--children, women, strong men, the elderly... They cannot see who leads in front. In fact, it is God, whom Moses had seen only from behind (see Exodus 33:20-23, page 76). The walk is arduous. Doubt enters the hearts of some... Some turn toward God... Everyone needs each other.

THE ARK OF THE COVENANT
Medieval Hebraic manuscript. © British Library: Bridgeman Giraudon. (page 90)

Two seraphim watch over the Ark. In the foreground, a table with the consecrated bread (see Matthew 12:3-4, page 272).

SAUL, SAMUEL AND DAVID
Isabelle Carrier, 1994. (pages 93-100)

The People demand a powerful king who wields a victorious sword. Concurrently, in the name of God, Samuel anoints a shepherd with the unction of oil. As king, David will prove a worthy guide for the People in the way of the Covenant. The harp serves as a reminder that David was a musician, and that he is the author of the book of Psalms.

DAVID AND GOLIATH
Isabelle Carrier, 1994. (pages 101-105)

The Philistines, a sea-faring people, wearing feathered helmets, confront the Hebrews, desert nomads, who fight using mules and horses. David, armed with his simple faith in God, the liberator, confronts Goliath.

JERUSALEM
Mosaic of Madaba. 6th century. © G. Dagli Orti. (pages 106-109)

Jerusalem, the city conquered by David, becomes the assembly place of the tribes (see Psalm 122, page 221). Centuries later, Christians will gather in Jerusalem to pray at Jesus's tomb. The mosaic of Madaba bespeaks this Christian interest, still alive nowadays.

DAVID'S SIN
Beham, German hunting table (1534). Louvre Museum. c Lauros - Giraudon (pages 110-113)

David's life is filled with incredible adventures, the most celebrated being a love story. David willfully sends Uriah, the husband of beautiful Bathsheba, to be killed at war, so that he may have Bathsheba for himself. God convicts David of his sin through the prophet Nathan. David's repentance is as celebrated as his sin.

THE JUDGEMENT OF SOLOMON
Nicolas Poussin, 1649. © Louvre: Edimedia (pages 116 - 119)

See the comment on this painting in the glossary, page 544.

SOLOMON AND BAAL
Sophiek, 1994. (pages 120 - 127)

Solomon, the sage (left), builder of palaces and of the Temple (above), was not vigilant enough against idolatry. At the end of his reign, false gods such as Baal, portrayed here with a horned helmet, are worshipped with praise and offerings. After the division of Judah and Israel, the Lord himself will be represented by a young bull (see page 122, in particular, note 2).

THE THOUGHTLESS RICH
Laurent Corvaisier, 1994. (pages 128 -131)

While the poor suffer grim nights of exclusion, the rich, unaware, wallow in pleasure, entertained by music from their newly invented instruments (Amos 6:4-6, page 129).

STEADFAST LOVE
Monique Bruant, 1994. After Matisse. (pages 132-134)

It is through the love between humans--conjugal, fatherly, motherly--that the prophet Hosea discovers the love of God for man. God is like a faithful husband to his People. He nurtures them with tenderness and guides them like a father with a maternal heart.

THE SERAPHIM IN ISAIAH'S VISION
Romanesque fresco of Catalonia. © Giraudon. (pages 135-137)

Many eyes cover the six wings of the seraphim because the painter accurately portrays the prophet Ezekiel's description: "Their entire bodies, their back, their hands and their wings were full of eyes" (Ezekiel 10:12). It is an image that expresses the fact that nothing escapes God's notice, such as the suffering of his People.

ISAIAH DANCING
Catherine Chion, 1994. After a 12th century sculpture, church of Souillac. (pages 138-143)

Isaiah is carried away in joyful dance to celebrates the holiness of God. All of Creation--the waters, earth and sky--share his joy.

MICAH, PROPHET OF PEACE
Bruno Le Sourd, 1994. (pages 144 -145)

Peace will dwell in the hearts of men when they become able to share the fruits of their harvest. They will sit under fig trees (see page 335, note 3), singing the Lord's praises to the sound of harps.

THE VASE RESHAPED AND BROKEN
Valérie Loiseau, 1994. (pages 148 -153)

The illustration unfolds its story across each double-page spread. On the left, the well-shaped vase, skillfully molded by the potter's hands (Jeremiah 18:1-10, page 152). On the right, the broken vase, foretelling the misfortunes of the people who obstinately refuses to be molded by God (Jeremiah 19:1-11, page 153).

BABYLON'S YOKE
Sophiek, 1994. (pages 154-156)

The Assyrian Empire, which destroyed Samaria, was conquered by the king of Babylon. The Jews assume that the conqueror of this cruel and rapacious Empire must be even more brutal. They imagine its domination based on what they know of Assyria. Thus the predominating Assyrian palette in the drawings of this frame. Those exiled to Babylon will discover that their conqueror is not so terrfying!

FRESH HOPE
Valérie Loiseau, 1994. (pages 157-159)

Hard times fade away. The sun of God shines on a new earth and humanity. The rainbow, sign of the Covenant, appears (see frame, pages 26-31). The weapons of war are removed. Birds fly toward the sun.

THE FOUR LIVING CREATURES
Catherine Chion, 1994. (pages 160-163)

In the Bible, Ezekiel is the first person to describe the four living creatures. These creatures are mentioned again in the Revelation of John, before being revealed as the symbols of the four evangelists, Matthew, Marc, Luke, and John (see lexicon page 502).

THE DRIED BONES
After an engraving of Gustave Doré, 1832-1883. © Museum of Decorative Arts :Charmet. (pages 164-165)

Ezekiel stands in the middle of the Valley of Dry Bones. He sees bones transforming into a living army through the impetus of the Spirit of the Lord. This vision foretells the resurrection of the people of Israel after their hardships in Exile. Later, it will be used to represent the resurrection of the dead. Believers will understand that God cannot leave his friends as prisoners of death. He calls them to share eternal life with Him.

THE SERVANT
Laurent Parienty, 1994. (pages 166-172)

The unknown prophet, called "the second Isaiah", has the extraordinary premonition of a humble Savior who will not reign as a powerful worldly king. He will save man by suffering in his place. The crown of thorns and the stigmata on his hands portend Jesus who will come to definitively define and fulfill these prophesies.

PERSIAN OCCUPATION
Sophiek, 1994. (pages 173-177)

Some of the people return to Jerusalem, but they lives under Persian domination. The power and refined culture of Cyrus and his successors are represented by motifs from actual sculptures of Persepolis and Susa.

GREEK OCCUPATION
Laurent Parienty, 1994. (pages 178-180)

The Greeks have succeeded the Persians. Antiochus Epiphane wants to force the worship of Greek gods onto all his subjects. Some Jews fight this imposition. Armed, risking their lives, they fight to have their faith in the one true God respected.

MARTYRS OF ISRAEL
Laurent Parienty, 1994. (pages 181-183)

Many Jews lose their lives fighting the Greeks. Some are killed on the battlefields, while others die as martyrs in torture chambers where the Greeks pressure them unsuccessfully to renounce God.

JERUSALEM, LIGHT OF THE NATIONS
Laurent Parienty, 1994. (pages 184 -187)

In Jerusalem, modestly rebuilt and under Persian occupation, the third Isaiah announces that the nations will flock to the city. They will come seeking knowledge of the true God. Thus Jerusalem will be radiant with wealth and glory. Jesus will temper this triumphal appetite by denouncing the danger of wealth (see frame, pages 322-330).

THE STORY OF JONAH
Isabelle Carrier, 1994. (pages 190 -192)

This frame depicts the different episodes of the life of Jonah: the finger of God pointing the prophet toward Niniveh; the storm; the enormous fish; his preaching to the Ninivites; the repentant king of Niniveh in sackcloth, sitting in ashes; and Jonah under the castor oil plant.

THE HUMBLE MESSIAH
Isabelle Carrier, 1994. (page 193)

Astonishing contrast, sign of tragedy to come! Above and to the left, bathed in light, the people exult the peaceful messiah. Below and to the right, in darkness and mourning, the people grieve the pierced Messiah.

THE STORY OF JOB
Régine and Bruno Le Sourd, 1994. Based on ancient illuminations (pages 194-197)

In a beautiful decorative frame, two medallions. One showing God with his angels, authorizing Satan to test Job's faith. In the other, Job, ill, on his manure heap. His wife feeds him with tongs while his three friends look on.

WISDOM
Monique Bruant, 1994. Based on stained-glass windows and Gothic sculptures. (pages 198-203)

The sage meditates on daily life. He reflects on how to serve God in his work, his free time, his neighborhood relationships, his family.... Meditating on the Proverbs and the other books of Wisdom, the believer allows the wisdom of God to enlighten all aspects of his life. The illustrator recaptures eighteen scenes of life in the Middle Ages, as they are depicted in the stained-glass windows of French cathedrals.

DANIEL'S VISIONS
Daniela Foltynova, 1994. (pages 204-205)

The apocalyptic visions present a very pessimistic vision of the world; plagues and wars will devastate the earth, but after a great battle, God will reign with justice and in glory.

GOD'S MESSENGERS
Fra Angelico, 15th century, San Marco Museum, Florence. © Orsi Battaglini:Giraudon. (page 206)

Around the central circle in which the Apostles and evangelists appear, the painter portrays the main caracters of the Old Testament. The prophet-writers hold a streamer similar to the scrolls bearing their names in the Bible. From the right Ezekiel, Jeremiah, Micah, Jonah, Joel, Malachi, then, at the top, Daniel holding the Tablets of the Law, Moses surrounded by David and Solomon. Isaac and Ezra are also shown.

PSALMS
Bruno Le Sourd, 1994 - 1996. (pages 208-221)

Several frames are used to tell the story with a change in color. The Psalms are the prayers of a people in which each person adds his voice for harmonic unity. The artist depicts instruments mentioned often in the book of Psalms: drum and tambourine, chofar (ram horn), horn, various flutes, harp, cymbals, lute...

THE SONG OF THE EXILED
Régine Le Sourd, 1996. (pages 222-227)

The entire story of the Exile is depicted in this frame; leaving the burning Jerusalem, the long and desolate walk to Babylon, and the joyous return, filled with singing and dancing.

DAVID THE MUSICIAN
Psalter of Saint Augustin, 12th century. © Lausat:Explorer. (page 228)

David suronded by scribes, musicians, and dancers.

AT CAPERNAUM
Régine Le Sourd, 1996. (pages 235-239)

The artist vibrantly depicts daily life of a small city in the time of Jesus. At

Capernaum, where Mark puts the first acts of Jesus, life was certainly like this.

THE SEA OF GALILEE

Laurent Parienty, 1994. (pages 240-245)

The artist portrays Jesus praying early in the morning. His ministry begins on the shores of the sea of Tiberias (Mark 1:35, page 237). Facing this vast expanse of water, Jesus draws from his Father the strength to fight sin, hatred, evil, injustice... So often, sin does not present an ugly face. Like the lake, it can seem attractive, seductive in its beauty. But when the careless are tempted by its superficial charm, unexpected storms can threaten to drown them. Jesus commanded the sea, thus demonstrating his power over the forces of Evil.

THE TRANSFIGURATION

Bruno Le Sourd, 1996. (pages 246 -249)

Using enamels, the artist portrays Jesus in white, "his clothes were as white as snow", surrounded by the prophets Moses and Elijah. Below to the right, the apostles Andrew, James and John discover the true face of Jesus, illuminated by the light of God.

WHO IS THIS MAN?

Psalter of Ingeburge, 13th century. Chantilly Museum. © Giraudon. (pages 250-252)

The Gospel of Mark is uniquely devoted to answering this question. The account of the Transfiguration, which is central to his Gospel, affirms that Jesus is the Son of God. In the illustratin, Jesus is flanked by Moses and Elijah who, by their presence, attest to his Sonship. With an affirming gesture of his hand, the apostle Peter, Mark's teacher, testifies to the same fact: Jesus is the Son of God.

THE MAGIS

Nathalie Guillonnet, 1994. (pages 253-259)

Under a sky brilliant with stars which evokes both the star of Balaam and the multitude of Abraham's descendants (Genesis 15:5-6, page 39), the magis are walking towards the place where the "king of the Jews" is born. The nature of their gifts show that the child of Bethlehem is the awaited Messiah (see comment and note 2, page 256). The angel in worship signifies that the child is also the Son of God.

TO DO THE FATHER'S WILL

Laurent Parienty, 1994. (pages 260- 265)

The entire sermon on the mount is an invitation to receive faith into your life, resulting in willing hands to put this faith into action. "Not everyone who says to me, Lord, Lord, will enter the kingdom of heaven, but only he who does the will of my Father" (Matthew 7:21-23, page 266). The gestures of the hands evoke mercy, the refusal of violence and revenge, reconciliation, prayer, tenderness, gift-giving, and sharing: "do not let your left hand know what your right hand is doing." (Matthew 6:3)

THE HARVEST

Régine Le Sourd, 1996. (pages 266-271)

The theme of work as it relates to the harvest is evoked in this frame. Just as a seed is planted in the earth, so the Word of God penetrates the heart of man and produces a bountiful harvest, true nourishment. This harvest also refers to multitude of believers in whom God's Word has produced fruit.

THE NET

Isabelle Carrier, 1994. (pages 272-277)

See page 277, note 1.

THE LOAVES OF BREAD AND FISH

Sophie Dressler, 1994. (pages 278-284)

Jesus invites men to sit at the table of his supper. There he breaks the bread of his Word and the bread of his Body. The fish, which was barely mentioned in the stories of Jesus' miraculous multiplication of it, rapidly became a symbol for the first Christian communities. Indeed, in Greek, fish is IXTHUS. Each letter is the first letter of the words of the sentence: *Iesous Xrestos Theou Uios Soter*, which means: "Jesus Christ Son of God Savior."

JESUS TEACHING

13th century Book of Hours. Mazarine Library. © Charmet. (pages 285-289)

The Gospel of Matthew is the Gospel of the teachings of Jesus: the Sermon on the Mount, the teaching about the mission, his teaching in parables... Jesus embodies the role of a true teacher. He presents himself as the only master (Matthew 23:10, page 290). He is concerned about correctly training his apostles so that they can teach the multitudes (Matthew 13:36, page 275).

THE YOUNG WOMEN WITH THEIR LAMPS

Monique Bruant, 1996. (pages 290-296)

The flame of the lamps feed on oil, and like them, faith feeds on the Word of God, on taking part in the eucharist and on faithfulness in prayer. Thus the light of faith illuminates life.

THE NATIVITY

Very Rich Hours of the Duke of Berry, 1416. Chantilly Museum. © Giraudon. (pages 297-305)

The angels sing the glory of God. The shepherds are filled with wonder. And Mary retains all these events, meditating on them in her heart.

THE LAND OF JESUS

Bruno Le Sourd, 1994. (pages 306-310)

The artist depicts Jerusalem, the desert, the Jordan, the verdant Galilee and its sea... Women gather near the well, as in Sichar. Nomads cook outside their tents. A shepherd leads his flock. Children listen to the flute on the village square... Below, to the left, a delightful harvest scene. The lake fishermen are also there, and in the hills, those assembled for a teaching in the shade of the fig and olive trees.

THE DISCONCERTING MESSIAH

Wohlgemut, wood engraving, 1491. Nuremberg. © Charmet. (pages 311 to 315) :

Jesus was not the image of a judgmental God. On the contrary, he seemed so tolerant and accepting of sinners that he disconcerted many of his contemporaries. On the other hand, Jesus is uncompromising in his exposure of sin. In the Gospel of Luke, he vigorously denounces the dangers of wealth. Hence the violence of his reaction to the merchants in the Temple.

PARABLES

Isabelle Carrier, 1994. (pages 316-321)

Fig tree, vine and sheep immediately bring to mind the parables found on these pages. The fig tree, planted in the vine, does not give fruit; the docile sheep wait for the shepherd gone in search of the lost lamb... But, on a deeper level, the fig tree evokes the hearing of the Word of God (see page 335, note 3), the vine evokes the last supper of Jesus, and the sheep the People of God...

MONEY
Laurent Parienty, 1994. (pages 322-330)

It is essential to know how to use money for the good of others, like Zacchaeus; or how to free oneself entirely from it, as Peter did, leaving everything behind him to follow Jesus. Otherwise, we become slaves of money, like the rich man (Luke 18:18-30), and no longer able to serve God.

THE WORD WAS MADE FLESH
D.R. (pages 331-337)

The artist attempts to illustrate the mystery of the Incarnation (see INCARNATION, page 300) by linking the heavens, and a enormous, brilliant ray of light, to this tiny child of man, depicted in all his frailty.

THE SAMARITAN WOMAN
Régine Le Sourd, 1996. (pages 338-341)

In the land of Jesus, water is rare and precious. It is vital to the life of plants, animals and men. The women carry it carefully in big jars. Wells are places of meeting and trade. It is near a well that Jesus meets a woman of Samaria whom he promises water that gives eternal life.

WATER AND WHEAT
Daniela Foltynova, 1994. (pages 342-345)

Jesus brings to all of humanity "the flowing waters of eternal life" and the "true bread descended from heaven, that gives life to the world"...

THE DIVINITY OF JESUS
Stéphany Devaux, 1996. (pages 346-351)

In these pages of the Gospel of John, the divinity of Jesus is revealed trough his acts and words. He renews the dignity of the adulterous woman, and opens the eyes of the man born blind. Jesus incurs the wrath of some: who does this Jesus think he is?

JESUS, SOURCE OF LIFE
Icon of Albania, 16th century. © Bulloz. (pages 352-355)

In answer to Mary's prayer, Jesus recalls Lazarus from his tomb. Servants remove the stone and some Jews from Jerusalem witness the miracle: Lazarus rises from his tomb, still bound in burial gauze. (see meditation, page 355).

THE VINE
Valérie Loiseau, 1994. (pages 356-362)

"I am the vine... The one who resides in me bears much fruit." Beyond the meaning in this final teaching of Jesus, the symbol of the vine also refers to the blood of the Covenant.

THE LAST SUPPER
Mariotto di Nardo. 15th century. Museum of Fine Art, Nantes. c Giraudon. (pages 363-367)

The overlapping golden halos represent the fraternity between the Twelve and Jesus. However the last halo, in the right-hand corner, is dark. It is the halo of Judas who pretends with a kiss to be in fraternal union with Jesus, but whose heart remains closed to his calls.

GETHSEMANE
Laurent Parienty, 1994. (pages 368-371)

In a frame destined to contrast a tranquil late-night ambiance with the profound distress of Jesus, we see the Son of God illuminated in the lunar light. He is alone, far from his sleeping disciples. He is already marked with the red of the Passion.

THE PASSION
Régine Le Sourd, 1996. (pages 372-377)

Following the pattern of a cross, the trial of Jesus and his sentence are depicted, the whole dominated by the calvary. Starting from the first illustration above and left: Simon of Cyrene carries the cross, Jesus before Herod, Peter's denial, the coronation with thorns, Jesus before the high priest, the flogging, Jesus before the people of Jerusalem, Jesus before Pilate, Jesus carrying his cross.

THE CRUCIFIXION
Mosaic, 12th century. Saint Clement Church, Rome. © G. Dagli Orti. (pages 378 -381)

The cross, like a vine stock, extends its branches over the entire world. Doves stand ready to carry the message of peace to all men: "God does not want to destroy this sinful humanity. He loves all men, despite their rejection. He offers them his forgiveness."

THE TOMB
Laurent Parienty, 1994. (pages 384-387)

The shroud has been left behind. There is only silence and mourning. But the light of Easter pierces the darkness of "the place where a dead man had been laid to rest". The Christ has risen. He opens the passage to Life.

THE EASTER GARDEN
Laurent Parienty, 1994. (pages 388-395)

The dried trees of winter quiver with life on this spring morning. The risen Jesus illuminates the mourning of Mary Magdalene. She tries to grab hold of him, but from now on, she will only embrace him through faith.

THE MYSTICAL LAMB
Carolingian manuscript. Library of Valenciennes. © G. Dagli Orti. (page 396)

The Lamb is surrounded by the four living creatures, symbols of the evangelists. (See glossary, page 502).

SUN AND FIRE
Valérie Loiseau, 1994. (pages 399-401)

The sun of the resurrection and the fire of Pentecost suggest the intense apostolic dynamism of the first Christian communities: "It is impossible for us not to tell what we have seen and heard."

THE FIRST COMMUNITY
Monique Bruant, 1996. (pages 402-407)

In just a few images, the artist portrays community life of the first believers, breaking of bread, prayer, listening to the Word, sharing possessions.

PRISONS
Laurent Parienty, 1994. (pages 408-411)

Jewish prison, Roman prisons or other... Christians who announce the Gospel disturb and always will. Consider the martyrs throughout the centuries and about Jesus who identified himself with the prisoner (Matthew 25:36, page 295).

PAUL'S CONVERSION
Valérie Stetten, 1996, based on a 15th century German work. (pages 412-415)

Even if the text of the Acts of the apostles does not describe Paul falling down from his horse, it is the way the artist chose to depict the deeply moving, staggering encounter that changes Paul, enemy of the Christians, into a burning apostle of the christ.

THE GOSPEL THAT RISKS THE SEA
Régine Le Sourd, 1994. (pages 416 -421)

Caesarea... Antioch of Syria... Paul travels still further on the shores of the Mediterranean sea, called Mare Nostrum by the Romans. Cyprus... Malta... Sicily... Rome... The Good News arrives in the ports, spreading throughout the country... The breath of the Spirit blows throughout the world.

THE MISSION
Monique Bruant, 1996. (pages 422 to 428)

Remi baptizing Clovis, Francis-Xavier announcing the Gospel to Japan, Theresa of Lisieux praying for the missions, father Damian curing the leprous, all these saints have continued the work of Paul and the first Christian communities and have spread the Gospel to the far ends of the earth.

WITNESS OF THE GOSPEL
Mosaic of Lameire (1905-1910). Basilica of Fourvière, Lyons.
© Hubert:Explorer (pages 429-433)

Through this depiction of bishop Pothin's arrival in Lyons, France, one imagines Paul addressing the Corinthians, the Athenians or the inhabitants of Philippi. The apostle was bursting to share the Good News that changed his life.

THE TREE
Régine Le Sourd, 1994. (pages 434 to 437)

Like many before him, Paul compares Israel to a tree (Romans 11:16-24). Christians are like branches grafted to this tree. Every leaf receives life from the sap drawn up from the roots. Together, the leaves form a dynamic and living whole which, in turn, recalls the image of the body (see 1 Corinthians 12:12-27).

IN THE GLORY OF GOD
Fra Angelico, 15th century. The day of judgment, c Giraudon. (pages 438-443)

The risen Christ, raised in the glory of God, calls men to him. He is the head of the Church, which is his body.

TO LIVE AS A CHRISTIAN
Bruno Le Sourd, 1996 (pages 444-448)

Martin of Tours, Francis of Assisi, Louis IX, king of France, Vincent of Paul, all these saints took the Gospel seriously. Troughout their whole life, they announced the love of God, charity, share, justice, and the concern for the poor and the ill.

KEEPING A CLEAR CONSCIENCE
Stained glass of Saint Lubin, Chartres, France, 13th century. © C. Bibollet/TOP. (pages 444-448)

This stained glass illustrates very well the words "keeping a clear conscience in Christ" (1 Peter 3:16): in studies, meditation, work, free-time . . . everything is under Christ's watchful gaze. All situations, actions, choices and activities in life become roads that lead to Christ.

THE WOMAN AND THE DRAGON
Dutch Apocalypse, © National Library: Artephot. (pages 449-455)

In the heavens, Woman, wrapped in sun, the moon under her feet, brings a son into the world. To her right, the Temple of God. Below, waiting for the birth of the child, the dragon with seven heads hurls a third of the stars to earth. Left, archangel Michael and his angels fight the dragon. Defeated, he wants vengeance against Woman who receives the wings of an eagle to escape his attack.

JESUS CROWNS SIXTUS AND TIMOTHY
Paleo-christian engraved glass, Vatican. © A. Held:Artephot. (page 456)

Sixtus, who died in 125 A.D., is considered to be the fourth successor of Peter, in Rome. For Timothy, see page 554, and for the coronation, see note 2, page 465.

ANGELIC MUSICIANS
Fra Angelico, 15th century. Tabernacle of Linaioli, Florence. San Marco museum. © Orsi Battaglini:Giraudon. (pages 457-463)

Angels are models of prayer. They continually view the face of the Father in heaven (Matthew 18:10, page 283). The prayer of man to the Father tends to be listening and thanksgiving... By portraying an orchestra of angels, Fra Angelico makes the point that beyond personal prayer, Christians gather for communal prayer. Like an orchestra, each member is indispensable to creating a harmony.

HAIL, MARY, FULL OF GRACE
D.R. (pages 464-465)

Mary is on her knees. She meditates on the Word of God in a book found outside the frame. She turns toward the angel, appearing surprised. The angel holds a banner on which these words are written: "Hail, Mary, full of grace, the Lord is with you..." Above it, the Father blows his breath, his Spirit: "He who will be born will be called Son of the Almighty."

YOU ASK ME TO PARTICIPATE IN YOUR LIFE, IN CHRISTIAN COMMUNITY
Pardon of Châteauneuf, 1896. Sérusier. Museum of Quimper. © Bulloz. (pages 466-469)

To live as Christians is to live as a united people ... an energetic people, standing tall, united in brotherly love, deriving joy from being a witness for Christ in all aspects of life.

BENEDICT PRAYING
Romanesque mosaic. © Belzeaux: Rapho:Gallimard. (page 472)

Benedict, born approximately 408 A.D. in Nursia, near Perugia in Italy, died in 547 at Mount Cassin. He established the rules of western monasticism. The Benedictines spread throughout Europe, contributing significantly to its evangelization.

SUMMARY

THE OLD TESTAMENT

THE NEW TESTAMENT

GLOSSARY ILLUSTRATORS

Bruno Le Sourd
Cyrille de Nanteuil
Laurent Parienty
Valérie Stetten
Joëlle d'Abbadie
Monique Bruant
Jean-Yves Decottignies
Cartes: Cyrille de Nanteuil

TWO-PAGE ILLUSTRATIONS

Bruno Le Sourd : pages 10-11, 114-115, 188-189, 292-293,
326-327, 470-471
Bruno et Régine Le Sourd: pages 32-33
Bruno Le Sourd et Julien Grycan : pages 382-383
Claire Cormier: pages 44-45, 86-87, 424-425
Valérie Stetten: pages 146-147

COVER

Bruno Le Sourd.
Monique Bruant

GLOSSARY PHOTO CREDITS

Abbaye d'En Calcat: 525c
© Archipress/Salmon: 476
© Artephot/B.N.: 541 - © Artephot/Held : 503a - 511a - 521 - 537a - 544a - 546a - © Artephot/Babey : 537a -
© Artephot/Brumaire: 480 - © Artephot/Cercle d'Art : 488 - 496b - © Artephot/d'Heilly: 497a - 512 - © Artephot/Fabbri : 547b - © Artephot/Faillet: 545a - © Artephot/Mandel : 517a -
© Artephot/Nimatallah: 477a - 483a - 501a - 539 - 548a
© Artephot/Oronoz: 503b - 515a - 517b - 525a - 530 - 538 - 556b - © Artephot/Percheron : 500 - 536a - 543b - 558b -
© Artephot/Salou: 547a - © Artephot/Ken Takase : 496 - 532a - © Artephot/Trela: 526 - © Artephot/Varga : 555c
Bruno Le Sourd: 493c
© Bulloz: 529a - 534a - © Bulloz/ADAGP - Paris, 1994 : 551
© Cautral/P. Nicaud: 525c - © Cautral/Gayral : 510b
© Charmet: 481c - 515b - 560b
© Charmet/Bibliothèque Mazarine: 475
© Charmet/Bibliothèque Nationale: 542
© Ciric/Paolo Cocco: 498
© CNMHS/SPADEM: 476b - 476c
© Collection Christophe L.: 490
© Dagli Orti: 492 - 495a - 523a - 537b
© Edimedia: 484a - 484b - 491 - 522 - 549 - 557b - 560a -
© Edimedia/Bibliothèque Nationale: 511b
© Explorer/Willi Peter: 525d
© Giraudon: 481d - 493b - 501b - 523c - 524 - 527 - 528a - 528b - 529b - 531 - 534b - 543a - 544b - 548b - © Giraudon/Alinari: 476b - 550a
© Giraudon/Musée de Chantilly: 481a - 494 - © Giraudon/Orsi Battaglini: 550a - 516 - 536b - © Lauros/Giraudon/SPADEM 1994: 540 - © Lauros/Giraudon : 482a - 513ac - 519 - 523b - 525b - 537c - © Magnum/Lessing : 504
© Tournus: 476a - 483b - 487 - 493a - 497b - 513b - 514 - 525f - 525g - 532b - 552 - 554 - 555a - 558a
© D.R.: 480a - 481b - 485 - 492 - 495 - 545b - 556 - 557a

I.S.B.N. : 0-7651-9186-5
Photogravure : Argé +